W9-APH-087

Developmental Psychology
Childhood and Adolescence
Fourth Edition

David R. Shaffer is a professor of psychology, chair of the Social Psychology program, and past chair of the Life-Span Developmental Psychology program at the University of Georgia, where he has taught courses in human development to graduate and undergraduate students for the past 20 years. His many research articles have concerned such topics as altruism, attitudes and persuasion, moral development, sex roles and social behavior, self-disclosure, and social psychology and the law. He has also served as associate editor for the *Journal of Personality and Social Psychology, Personality and Social Psychology Bulletin,* and *Journal of Personality.* In 1990 Dr. Shaffer received the Josiah Meigs award for Excellence in Instruction, the University of Georgia's highest instructional honor.

Developmental Psychology
Childhood and Adolescence
Fourth Edition

David R. Shaffer
University of Georgia

Brooks/Cole Publishing Company

I(T)P™ An International Thomson Publishing Company

Pacific Grove • Albany • Bonn • Boston • Cincinnati • Detroit • London • Madrid • Melbourne
Mexico City • New York • Paris • San Francisco • Singapore • Tokyo • Toronto • Washington

Sponsoring Editor: *Jim Brace-Thompson*
Marketing Team: *Jean Thompson and Gay Meixel*
Editorial Assistants: *Jodi Hermans and Patsy Vienneau*
Production Coordinator: *Fiorella Ljunggren*
Production: *GTS Graphics, Inc.*
Manuscript Editor: *Sheila Pulver*
Permissions Editor: *Richard Lange, GTS Graphics, Inc.*
Interior Design: *Jamie Sue Brooks*
Interior Illustration: *Cyndie C. H. Wooley and GTS Graphics, Inc.*
Cartoons: *Ryan Cooper and Wayne Clark*

Photo Research: *Ann Beurskens*
Cover Design: *Vernon T. Boes*
Cover Photo: *Arthur Tilley, FPG International*
Print Buyer: *Vena M. Dyer*
Typesetting: *GTS Graphics, Inc.*
Color Separations: *GTS Graphics, Inc.*
Cover Printing: *Phoenix Color Corporation, Inc.*
Printing and Binding: *Quebecor Printing, Hawkins*
(Credits continue on p. C1)

COPYRIGHT © 1996, 1993, 1989, 1985 by Brooks/Cole Publishing Company
A division of International Thomson Publishing Inc.
I(T)P The ITP logo is a trademark under license.

For more information contact:

BROOKS/COLE PUBLISHING COMPANY
511 Forest Lodge Road
Pacific Grove, CA 93950
USA

International Thomson Editores
Campos Eliseos 385, Piso 7
Col. Polanco
11560 México D. F. México

International Thomson Publishing Europe
Berkshire House 168–173
High Holborn
London WC1V 7AA
England

International Thomson Publishing GmbH
Königswinterer Strasse 418
53227 Bonn
Germany

Thomas Nelson Australia
102 Dodds Street
South Melbourne, 3205
Victoria, Australia

International Thomson Publishing Asia
221 Henderson Road
#05–10 Henderson Building
Singapore 0315

Nelson Canada
1120 Birchmount Road
Scarborough, Ontario
Canada M1K 5G4

International Thomson Publishing Japan
Hirakawacho Kyowa Building, 3F
2-2-1 Hirakawacho
Chiyoda-ku, Tokyo 102
Japan

All rights reserved. No part of this work may be reproduced, stored in a retrieval system, or transcribed, in any form
or by any means—electronic, mechanical, photocopying, recording, or otherwise—without the prior written permission
of the publisher, Brooks/Cole Publishing Company, Pacific Grove, California 93950.

Printed in the United States of America.

10 9 8 7 6 5 4 3 2

Library of Congress Cataloging-in-Publication Data

Shaffer, David R. (David Reed), [date]
    Developmental psychology: childhood and adolescence / David R.
Shaffer.—4th ed.
        p.   cm.
    Includes bibliographical references and index.
    ISBN 0-534-26436-0
    1. Child psychology. 2. Adolescent psychology. 3. Developmental
psychology. I. Title
BF721.S4688 1996
155.4–dc20   95-17908
                      CIP

Brief Contents

Contents

PART III LANGUAGE, LEARNING, AND COGNITIVE DEVELOPMENT 200

PART IV SOCIAL AND PERSONALITY DEVELOPMENT 418

Preface

My purpose in writing this book has been to produce a current and comprehensive overview of child and adolescent development that reflects the best theories, research, and practical advice that developmentalists have to offer. Throughout my many years of teaching, I had longed for a substantive developmental text that is also interesting, accurate, up to date, and written in clear, concise language that an introductory student can easily understand. At this level, a good text should talk *to* rather than *at* its readers, anticipating their interests, questions, and concerns and treating them as active participants in the learning process. In the field of human development, a good text should also stress the processes that underlie developmental change, so that students come away from the course with a firm understanding of the causes and complexities of development. Last but not least, a good text is a relevant text—one that shows how the theory and research that students are asked to digest can be applied to a number of real-life settings. The present volume represents my attempt to accomplish all of these objectives.

I take applications very seriously, and I have striven to show how information gleaned from theory and basic research has helped us to understand and, in many cases, to solve a variety of real-world problems. For example, the laws of genetics are discussed in terms of their broad implications for human development and their contributions to the treatment and prevention of hereditary disorders. I have shown how basic research on physical/neurological growth, learning, and perceptual processes has furthered our understanding of personality development, while also suggesting a number of very useful strategies for accomplishing the objectives of preschool curricula, treating phobic reactions, promoting the development of social skills, and reducing racial and ethnic prejudice. Many helpful hints for teachers are presented and analyzed as we examine the course and content of children's intellectual development. Theory and research on parent/infant attachment are discussed in terms of their relevance to emotional development as well as their implications for the structuring of orphanages, nursery schools, and day-care centers. Many other contemporary issues and practices such as home birthing, maternal employment, mainstreaming, compensatory education, after-school care, single parenting, stepparenting, child abuse, and the importance of establishing close friendships are examined from both a theoretical and a practical perspective. In summary, I have tried to write a book that is both rigorous and applied; one that challenges students to think about the fascinating process of human development, to share in the excitement of our young and dynamic discipline, and to acquire a knowledge of developmental principles that will serve them well in their roles as parents, teachers, nurses, day-care workers, pediatricians, psychologists, or in any other capacity by which they may one day influence the lives of developing persons.

Philosophy

Certain philosophical views are inherent in any systematic treatment of a field as broad as human development. My philosophy can be summarized as follows:

I believe in theoretical eclecticism. There are many theories that have contributed to what we know about developing persons, and this theoretical diversity is a strength rather than a weakness. Although some theories may do a better job than others of explaining particular aspects of development, we will see—time and time again—that *different theories emphasize different developmental phenomena* and that knowledge of many theories is necessary to explain the course and complexities of human development. So this book will not attempt to convince its readers that any one theoretical viewpoint is "best." The psychoanalytic, behavioristic, cognitive-developmental, ecological, sociocultural, information-processing, ethological, and behavioral genetic viewpoints (as well as several less-encompassing theories that address selected aspects of development) are all treated with respect.

The best information about human development comes from systematic research. To teach this course effectively, I believe that one must convince students of the value of theory and systematic research. Although there are many ways to achieve these objectives, I have chosen to contrast the modern developmental sciences with their "prescientific" origins and then to discuss and illustrate the many methodological approaches that researchers use to test their theories and answer important questions about developing children and adolescents. I've taken care to explain why there is no one "best method" for studying development, and I've repeatedly stressed that our most reliable findings are those that can be replicated using a variety of methods.

I favor a strong "process" orientation. A major complaint with many developmental texts (including some best-sellers) is that they describe human development without explaining why it occurs. In recent years, investigators have become increasingly concerned about identifying and understanding developmental processes—the biological and environmental factors that cause us to change—and this book clearly reflects this emphasis. My own process orientation is based on the belief that students are more likely to remember what develops and when if they know and understand the reasons *why* these developments take place.

I favor a strong "contextual" orientation. One of the more important lessons that developmentalists have learned is that children and adolescents live in historical eras and sociocultural contexts that affect each and every aspect of their development. I have chosen to highlight these contextual influences in the following ways. First, cross-cultural comparisons are discussed throughout the text. Not only do students enjoy learning about the development of people in other cultures and ethnically diverse subcultures, but cross-cultural research also helps them to see how human beings can be so much alike and, at the same time, so different from one another. In addition, the impacts of such immediate contextual influences as our families, neighborhoods, schools, and peer groups are considered (1) throughout the first 14 chapters as we discuss each aspect of human development, and (2) again in the final two chapters as important topics in their own right.

Human development is a holistic process. Although individual researchers may concentrate on particular topics such as physical development, cognitive development, or the development of moral reasoning, development is not piecemeal but *holistic:* Human beings are at once physical, cognitive, social, and emotional creatures, and each of these components of "self" depends, in part, on the changes that are taking place in other areas of development. This holistic perspective is a central theme in the modern developmental sciences—and one that is emphasized throughout the text.

A developmental text should be a resource book for students—one that reflects current knowledge. I have chosen to cite nearly 1000 recent studies and reviews (many of which were published since the third edition) to ensure that my coverage (and any outside readings that students may undertake) will represent our current understanding of a topic or topics. However, I have tried to avoid the tendency, common in textbooks, to ignore older research simply because it is older. In fact, many of the "classics" of our discipline are prominently displayed throughout the text to illustrate important breakthroughs and to show how our knowledge about developing persons gradually builds on these earlier findings and insights.

Organization

There are two traditional ways of presenting human development. In the *chronological*, or "ages and stages," approach, the coverage begins at conception and proceeds through the life span, using ages or chronological periods as the organizing principle. By contrast, the *topical* approach is organized around areas of development and follows each from its origins to its most mature forms. Both types of presentations have their advantages and disadvantages. On the one hand, a chronological focus highlights the holistic character of development but may obscure the links between early and later events within each developmental domain. On the other hand, a topical approach highlights developmental sequences and processes but at the risk of failing to convey that development is a holistic enterprise.

I've chosen to organize this book topically to focus intently on developmental processes and to provide the student with an uninterrupted view of the sequences of change that children and adolescents experience within each developmental domain. In my opinion, this topical approach best allows the reader to appreciate the flow of development—the systematic, and often truly dramatic, transformations that take place over the course of childhood and adolescence, as well as the developmental continuities that make each individual a reflection of his or her past self. At the same time, I consider it essential to paint a holistic portrait of the developing person. To accomplish this objective, I've stressed the fundamental interplay among biological, cognitive, social, and cultural influences in my coverage of *each and every aspect of development*. So even though this text is topically organized, students will not lose sight of the whole person and the holistic character of human development.

Content

Because the first three editions of this text were well received by both students and professors, I made every effort to retain in this new edition the major qualities that people have said they like. One such characteristic is the book's division into five major parts, each of which is introduced by a brief opener. Part I presents an orientation to the discipline and the tools of this trade, including a thorough discussion and illustration of research methodologies (Chapter 1) and a succinct review of psychoanalytic, behavioristic, ecological, cognitive-developmental, and evolutionary theories of development (Chapter 2). An important feature of this coverage is my analysis of the contributions and the limitations of each research method and each of the major developmental theories.

Parts II through V focus on major themes, processes, products, and contexts of development: biological foundations and physical development (Part II); language, learning, and cognitive development (Part III); social and personality development (Part IV); and the ecology of human development (Part V).

New to This Edition

This fourth edition contains many important changes in the treatment of theoretical, empirical, and practical issues. At the most general level, these changes include: (1) much more attention throughout to cultural/subcultural/historical influences, with a special emphasis on the impacts of economic deprivation on child development; (2) an even stronger focus on the intricate interplays among biological and environmental forces in shaping development; (3) clearer illustrations that developmental outcomes depend crucially on the "goodness of fit" between people and their socializing environments; (4) greater emphasis on the importance of peer relations (and on the interplays between families and peers as socializing agents); and (5) expanded coverage of adolescent development. The empirical literature has been extensively updated, with the result that nearly 40 percent of the references date from 1990 through early 1995, when this book went into production.

Each chapter has been thoroughly revised to add the new topics that reflect recent trends in our discipline and to condense or otherwise reorganize other material to make way for these additions. Here is a sampling of these changes:

- Chapter 1 now concludes with a section ("On Becoming a Wise Consumer of Developmental Research") that illustrates the practical benefits of acquiring methodological knowledge. Many new research illustrations also appear.
- To complement the "grand theories" of human development, Wilson's socio-biological perspective and brief introductions to the neo-Freudian, sociocultural, information-processing, and ecological viewpoints have been added to Chapter 2.
- Breakthroughs in understanding and treatment of genetic diseases now appear in Chapter 3, which also includes a stronger critique of inferences drawn from behavioral genetics research.
- Chapter 4 contains new evidence on the teratogenic effects of cocaine and other illicit drugs, on the development of preterm and low-birth-weight infants, and on biological and social contributors to postpartum depression.
- Sociocultural influences on physical growth and development are now high-lighted in Chapter 5, which also includes the latest evidence for the new "actions systems" perspective on the growth of motor skills, as well as a new section on the cognitive and social implications of early motor development.
- Exciting new discoveries about the perceptual capabilities of very young infants now appear in Chapter 6, which has been reorganized to better illus-trate how sociocultural factors influence perceptual competencies and how maturation and experience interact to influence perceptual development.
- Coverage of Lev Vygotsky's sociocultural theory of cognitive development has been greatly expanded in Chapter 7. Emphasis is placed on the *sociocultural* premises of this theory, which are then used as an interpretive framework for other aspects of development in subsequent chapters.
- Coverage of the development of learning in Chapter 8 has been streamlined to permit a more detailed examination of such topics as infantile amnesia, attention deficits, the growth of memory and problem solving, and sociocul-tural influences on information-processing skills.
- A new section on Gardner's theory of multiple intelligences and expanded coverage of the impacts of economic disadvantage on intellectual performance are highlights of Chapter 9. The latest research on home-based compensatory education is also included.
- Chapter 10 has been reorganized to better showcase the provocative theoreti-cal controversies that surround language development. New research on the growth of vocabulary during middle childhood, on the processing constraints young children use to infer word meanings, and on the dramatic successes of bilingual educational programs has also been added.
- Chapter 11 has been extensively updated to reflect recent knowledge about the development and regulation of emotions. New treatment of attachments from a "working models" perspective better illustrates how secure and inse-cure attachments can have meaningful implications for later development. Helpful hints for reducing toddlers' separation anxieties are also incorporated.
- New sections on the development of self-regulation and self-control, on chil-dren's theory of mind, and on the growth of academic self-concept appear in Chapter 12. Discussions of familial and cultural/historical contributors to

self-esteem and personal identity have been greatly expanded and now include research on the issues minority youths must resolve when forging an ethnic identity.

- New research on gender differences as self-fulfilling prophecies, on gender segregation in childhood, on interventions to reduce gender-role stereotyping, and on the development of sexual orientation are among the major additions to Chapter 13.
- Chapter 14 now focuses much more intently on the cultural and familial roots of childhood aggression and their implications for the growth of delinquency and antisocial conduct. New psychoanalytic perspectives on moral development have been added, and Kohlberg's theory now receives more critical scrutiny, including the addition of cross-cultural work that questions the "universality" of moral growth. A comparison of the processes by which parents and peers influence moral reasoning is another important addition.
- Expanded coverage of the extended-family context, sociocultural influences on infant care, sibling influences, and the development of only children appears in Chapter 15. Major influences (for example, parenting practices and part-time employment) that foster (or inhibit) an adolescent's quest for autonomy are important additions, as is the revised coverage of maltreated children, which has been rewritten to highlight the potential long-term implications of neglect and abuse (including sexual abuse).
- Coverage of schooling effects in Chapter 16 has been thoroughly updated and reorganized to emphasize how academic and extracurricular outcomes (including ethnic variations in academic performance) depend very heavily on the "goodness of fit" between children and their learning environments. In addition, much more emphasis is now placed on the importance of peer relations, the role(s) that friends play in child and adolescent development, and the contributions that parents make to a child's or an adolescent's peer sociability/acceptance.

Writing Style

My goal has been to write a book that speaks directly to its readers and treats them as active participants in an ongoing discussion. I have tried to be relatively informal and down-to-earth in my writing style and to rely heavily on questions, thought problems, and a number of other exercises to stimulate students' interest and involvement. Most of the chapters were "pretested" on my own students, who red-penciled whatever wasn't clear to them and suggested several of the concrete examples, analogies, and occasional anecdotes that I've used when introducing and explaining complex ideas. So, with the valuable assistance of my student-critics, I have attempted to prepare a manuscript that is substantive and challenging but that reads more like a story than like an encyclopedia.

Special Features

The pedagogical features of the text have been greatly expanded in this fourth edition. Among the more important features that are included to make the book more interesting and the material easier to learn are the following:

- **New full-color design.** An attractive new full-color design brightens the book immensely and makes photographs, drawings, and other illustrations come alive.
- **Outlines and chapter summaries.** An outline and brief introductory section at the beginning of each chapter provide the student with a preview of what will be covered. Each chapter concludes with a succinct summary that allows the student to quickly review the chapter's major themes.

- **Subheadings.** Subheadings are employed very frequently to keep the material well organized and to divide the coverage into manageable bites.
- **Vocabulary/key terms.** More than 700 key terms appear in boldface type to alert the student that these are important concepts to learn.
- **Running glossary, key-term lists, and comprehensive end-of-the-book glossary.** A running glossary provides on-the-spot definitions of boldfaced key terms as they appear in the text. These marginal glossary terms are presented against a colored background to command attention. At the end of each chapter is a list of key terms that appeared in the narrative, as well as the page number on which each term is defined. A complete glossary of key terms for the entire text appears at the end of the book.
- **Boxes.** Each chapter contains two to five boxes that call attention to important ideas, issues, or applications. The aim of these boxes is to permit a closer or more personal examination of selected topics while stimulating the reader to think about the questions, controversies, practices, and policies under scrutiny. Many of the boxes center around interesting theoretical or empirical controversies (Why do we not remember our infant years? Do socioeconomic differences between races explain race differences in IQ?), whereas others concentrate on practical concerns (how to prevent birth defects), applications (improving children's social skills; easing the pain of separation), and policy issues (should preschoolers attend school?). Twenty-four boxes are new to this edition, and the majority of the holdovers have been thoroughly updated or revised. All of the boxes are carefully woven into the chapter narrative and were selected to reinforce central themes in the text.
- **Illustrations.** Photographs, tables, and figures are used extensively. Although these features are designed, in part, to provide visual relief and to maintain student interest, they are not merely decorations. All visual aids, including the occasional cartoons, were selected to illustrate important principles and concepts and thereby enhance the educational goals of the text.
- **Concept checks.** Another feature new to this edition is the inclusion of "concept checks"—brief exercises to help students *actively* assess their understanding of what they have read and their mastery of important ideas. Some of the concept checks are quite challenging; but students find them engaging, and they report that such exercises are more useful checks on comprehension than "brief summary" sections (which are perceived as too brief and too general to be of much use). Three sets of concept checks appear in each chapter, and the answers to these exercises can be found in the Appendix at the back of the book.

Supplementary Aids

Instructor's Manual

For the instructor, the Instructor's Manual (written by Marcia Z. Lippman of Western Washington University; Deborah J. McClendon-Magnuson; and Barbara E. Collamer of Western Washington University) contains chapter outlines, summaries and objectives, key terms, suggestions for class lectures/discussions/demonstrations, transparency masters to accompany these materials, and lists of particularly effective media materials. Also available are 75 **acetate transparencies** and **videotape** options.

Testing File and Test-Item Bank

A testing file (updated by Nancy P. Clark) is available to all instructors who adopt the text. The test file for each chapter consists of a variety of multiple-choice items and essay questions (both conceptual and applied), as well as answers for *all* test items. Many conceptual types of multiple-choice questions have been added in this edition. The test bank contains over 1200 items and comes in both printed and computerized formats (DOS, Windows, and Macintosh).

Study Guide and Activities

A very thorough study guide (written by Marcia Z. Lippman of Western Washington University; Deborah J. McClendon-Magnuson; and Barbara E. Collamer of Western Washington University) is also available to help students master the information in the text. The study materials for each chapter include a detailed summary that highlights important principles and concepts, a study checklist, vocabulary fill-ins so that students can build their own glossary, and study questions designed to help the student process the material. In addition, the study guide contains class activities and projects (some with children) designed to help reinforce and/or promote learning through concrete activities. The applications in several of these activities help students relate personally to the material presented. This study guide should be a particularly helpful learning aid for students, and I urge the instructor to take a close look at it.

Acknowledgments

As is always the case with projects as large as this one, there are many, many individuals whose assistance was invaluable in the planning and production of this volume. The quality of any textbook in human development depends to a large extent on the quality of the prepublication reviews from developmentalists around the world. Many colleagues (including a couple dozen or so interested and unpaid volunteers) have influenced this book by contributing detailed and constructive criticisms, as well as useful suggestions, references, and a whole lot of encouragement. Each of those experts has helped to make the final product a better one, and I thank them all.

The reviewers of the first edition were Martin Banks, University of California, Berkeley; Don Baucum, Birmingham-Southern College; Jay Belsky, Pennsylvania State University; Keith Berg, University of Florida; Marvin Berkowitz, Marquette University; Dana Birnbaum, University of Maine at Orono; Kathryn Black, Purdue University; Robert Bohlander, Wilkes College; Cathryn Booth, University of Washington; Yvonne Brackbill, University of Florida; Cheryl Bradley, Central Virginia Community College; John Condry, Cornell University; David Crowell, University of Hawaii; Connie Hamm Duncanson, Northern Michigan University; Mary Ellen Durrett, University of Texas at Austin; Beverly Eubank, Lansing Community College; Beverly Fagot, University of Oregon; Larry Fenson, San Diego State University; Harold Goldsmith, University of Oregon; Charles Halverson, University of Georgia; Lillian Hix, Houston Community College; Patricia Leonhard, University of Illinois at Champaign-Urbana; Frank Laycock, Oberlin College; Mark Lepper, Stanford University; John Ludeman, Stephens College; Phillip J. Mohan, University of Idaho; Robert Plomin, Pennsylvania State University; Judith Powell, University of Wyoming; Daniel Richards, Houston Community College; Peter Scharf, University of Seattle; and Rob Woodson, University of Texas.

The reviewers of the second edition were Kathryn Black, Purdue University; Thomas J. Brendt, Purdue University; Mary Courage, Memorial University of Newfoundland; Donald N. Cousins, Rhode Island College; Mark L. Howe, Memorial University of Newfoundland; Gerald L. Larson, Kent State University; David Liberman, University of Houston; Sharon Nelson-Le Gall, University of Pittsburgh; Richard Newman, University of California at Riverside; Scott Paris, University of Michigan; Thomas S. Parish, Kansas State University; Frederick M. Schwantes, Northern Illinois University; Renuka R. Sethi, California State University, Bakersfield; Faye B. Steuer, College of Charleston; Donald Tyrell, Franklin and Marshall College; and Joachim K. Wohlwill, Pennsylvania State University.

The reviewers of the third edition were David K. Carson, University of Wyoming; Marcia Z. Lippman, Western Washington University; Philip J. Mohan, University of Idaho; Gary Novak, California State University, Stanislaus; Elizabeth Rider, Elizabethtown College; James O. Rust, Middle Tennessee State University; Mark Shatz, Ohio University; and Linda K. Swindell, University of Mississippi.

The reviewers of this edition were M. Kay Alderman, University of Akron; Peggy A. DeCooke, Purchase College, State University of New York; David Dodd, University of Utah; Beverly Fagot, University of Oregon; Rebecca Glover, University of Arkansas; Paul A. Miller, Arizona State University West; Amy Needham, Duke University; Spencer Thompson, University of Texas of the Permian Basin; and Albert Yonas, University of Minnesota–Twin Cities.

I am also heavily indebted to Carol K. Sigelman of The George Washington University, a most talented writer with whom I have collaborated on another Brooks/Cole project (*Life-Span Human Development*, 1st and 2nd editions), which has significantly influenced this book. About once every four to six weeks, Carol provided me with new references and many, many useful suggestions for supplementing or clarifying my presentation. It is clearly an understatement to say that Dr. Sigelman has had a meaningful and salutary effect on every section of this book, for she is directly or indirectly responsible for many of its positive qualities. Thank you, Carol, for your invaluable support and assistance.

Special thanks go to Pat Harbin and Robin Moore, two word-processing wizards, who turned my rough drafts into presentable, error-free manuscripts, and to Sylvia Stogden, who often saved my hide by packaging bundles in record time to meet the stern requirements of my FedEx masters. I can't conceive of trying to produce a volume of this sort without the many valuable contributions of these wonderful associates.

Many other people have contributed their professionalism and skills to the production of the fourth edition of this text. I am especially grateful to my friend Fiorella Ljunggren, Production Services Manager at Brooks/Cole, for her dedication to my books over the past 18 years; to Jamie Sue Brooks, the book designer, for listening carefully to my design requests and then creating a product that exceeded my expectations; to Vernon T. Boes, Brooks/Cole's art director, for creating once again a stunning cover for the book; to Sheila Pulver, the manuscript editor, for her attention to detail in copy-editing; to Margaret Pinette and Richard Lange of GTS Graphics for carrying out the production of this book with skill and efficiency; and to Ann Beurskens, the photo researcher, for her diligence and patience in finding images to illustrate my points.

Last, but not least, I owe especially important debts of gratitude to my past and present sponsoring editors. C. Deborah Laughton conceived this project many years ago and was always there throughout the first and most of the second edition, answering questions, solving problems, and finding ways to get more work out of me than I believed was possible. Vicki Knight came on board for the third edition, and her dedication to the project would make one think that she had conceived it herself. Finally, Jim Brace-Thompson has skillfully shepherded me through the fourth edition and is responsible for many of the improvements in the book's design and content. Though different in their styles, these individuals are all splendid editors who have taught me a great deal about the publication of effective educational materials. I am indeed fortunate to have had access to their knowledge and counsel over the years, and I wish to thank them sincerely for their many, many efforts on my behalf.

David R. Shaffer

Developmental Psychology
Childhood and Adolescence
Fourth Edition

Part I

An Overview of Human Development

This is a book about children and adolescents—a description and explanation of their behaviors, thoughts, perceptions, emotions, and abilities. At the same time, this is a book about human development—the study of how individuals develop and change over the course of their lives.

Part I consists of two chapters designed to orient you to the field of human development. Chapter 1 sets the stage. We will first discuss the meaning of development and see just how recent this concept really is. After considering how the scientific community gradually became interested in child development, we will focus on the methods and strategies that researchers have used to detect and explain developmental change.

Perhaps the most useful tools that developmental researchers have at their disposal are the many theories that have been proposed to account for human development. In Chapter 2 we will take a closer look at the role of theory in the developmental sciences as we examine several of the more influential theories of child and adolescent development.

Taken together, these opening chapters provide an orientation and some important background for the material presented throughout the text. They will help you understand what the developmental sciences are and how researchers go about answering questions they may have about developing children and adolescents.

Introduction

1

I would like to begin this book with a question: Why did you choose to enroll in a course on human development? For many students majoring in psychology, home economics, elementary education, or nursing, the class is required and there is no way around it. Expectant parents may take the course in order to learn more about babies as they prepare for parenthood. Occasionally, students will elect the course because they are seeking to answer specific questions about their own behavior or that of a friend or a family member. For example, a college roommate of mine, who happened to be a fisheries major, studied child development, hoping to discover why he and his identical twin often seemed to be thinking the same things in similar situations.

Whatever your reasons for taking this course, at one time or another you have probably been curious about one or more aspects of human development. For example:

- Have you ever wondered what the world looks like to newborn infants? Do you suppose they can make any sense of their new surroundings?
- When do you think infants will first recognize their mothers? their fathers? themselves (in a mirror)?
- Why do many 1-year-olds seem so attached to their mothers and rather wary of strangers?
- Foreign languages are difficult to follow if we merely listen to foreigners converse. Yet infants and toddlers pay close attention to conversations and will acquire their native language without any formal instruction. How is this possible? Is language learning easier for children than for adults? Is it tougher for a child in a bilingual home?
- Why do many young children think that things that move, like the sun and clouds, are alive?
- Why are some people friendly and outgoing while others are shy and reserved? Does the character of family life determine one's personality? If so, then why are children from the same family often so different from one another?
- What are the effects on children of losing a parent (due to death or divorce) or gaining a stepparent?
- What roles do close friends play in a child's (or an adolescent's) development?

These are just a few of the issues that students say they wish to learn more about in electing a course in human development. As one perceptive sophomore recently remarked, I want to know why all of us turn out so much alike and, at the same time, so different from one another. As we will see, her interest is shared by all developmental researchers.

 WHAT IS DEVELOPMENT?

Simply stated, **development** refers to systematic changes in the individual that occur between the moment of conception (when the father's sperm penetrates the mother's ovum, creating a new organism) and death. The word *systematic* implies that developmental changes are somehow orderly or patterned, so that temporary mood swings and other transitory changes in our appearances, thoughts, and behaviors are therefore excluded.

If development represents the systematic changes an individual experiences from "womb to tomb," the science of development is the study of these changes. Actually, we might well speak of the *sciences* of development, for this area of study is truly a multidisciplinary enterprise. **Developmental psychology,** the largest of these disciplines, is concerned with identifying and explaining the changes that individuals undergo during the life span. And yet, many biologists, sociologists, anthropologists, educators, physicians, home economists, and even historians share this interest and

development: the process by which organisms grow and change over the course of their lives.

developmental psychology: branch of psychology devoted to the study of how individuals change over time and the factors that produce these changes.

have contributed in important ways to our understanding of both human and animal development. Because the science of development is multidisciplinary, we use the term *developmentalist* to refer to any scholar—regardless of discipline—who seeks to understand the developmental process.

What Causes Us to Develop?

To grasp the meaning of development more fully, we must understand two important processes that underlie developmental change. One of these processes, **maturation**, refers to the biological unfolding of the individual according to a plan contained in the *genes*—the hereditary material passed from parents to their child at conception. Just as seeds systematically unfold to become mature plants, assuming that they receive adequate moisture and nourishment from the environment, human beings "unfold" within the womb. The human maturational program also calls for us to walk and to utter our first meaningful words at about 1 year of age, to reach sexual maturity at about age 11 to 14, and even to age and to die on roughly similar schedules. Since the brain undergoes many maturational changes, maturation is partly responsible for psychological changes such as our increasing ability to concentrate, to solve problems, and to understand what another person may be thinking or feeling. So one reason that we humans are so similar in so many important respects is that our common "species heredity," or maturational blueprints, guide all of us through many of the same developmental changes at about the same points in our lives.

A second critical developmental process is **learning**—the process through which our *experiences* produce relatively permanent changes in our feelings, thoughts, and behaviors. Let's consider a very simple example. Although a certain degree of physical maturation is necessary before a grade-school child can become reasonably proficient at dribbling a basketball, careful instruction and many, many hours of practice are essential if this youngster is ever to approximate the ball-handling skills of such wizards of the hardwoods as the Harlem Globetrotters. Most of our abilities and habits do not simply unfold as part of nature's grand plan; we often learn to feel, think, and behave in new ways from our observations of and interactions with parents, teachers, and other important people in our lives, and we are affected by the events that we experience. Stated another way, we change in response to our *environments*—particularly in response to the actions and reactions of the people around us. Of course, most developmental changes are the product of *both* maturation and learning. And as we will see throughout this book, some of the more lively debates about human development are arguments about which of these processes contributes most to particular developmental changes.

What Goals Do Developmentalists Pursue?

Just what objectives have developmentalists set for themselves? Three major goals stand out: to describe, to explain, and to optimize development (Baltes, Reese, & Lipsitt, 1980). In pursuing the goal of *description*, human developmentalists carefully observe the behavior of people of different ages, seeking to specify how human beings change over time. Though there are typical pathways of development that virtually all people follow, researchers have discovered that no two persons are exactly alike. Even when raised in the same home, children will often display very different interests, values, abilities, and patterns of social behavior. Thus, to describe development adequately, one must necessarily focus both on typical patterns of change (or **normative development**) and on individual variations (or **idiographic development**), seeking to identify the important ways that developing humans resemble and differ from each other as they proceed through life.

Adequate description provides us with the "facts" about development, but it is only the starting point. Ultimately, developmentalists seek to explain the changes they

Despite the common assumption that superstars are natural athletes, the "special" skills they display require an enormous amount of practice. Indeed, Michael Jordan, the world's best basketball player, struggled just to become a "promising" professional baseball player.

maturation: developmental changes in the body or behavior that result from the aging process rather than from learning, injury, illness, or some other life experience.

learning: a relatively permanent change in behavior (or behavioral potential) that results from one's experiences or practice.

normative development: developmental changes that characterize most or all members of a species; typical patterns of development.

idiographic development: individual variations in the rate, extent, or direction of development.

have observed and cataloged. In pursuing this goal of *explanation*, researchers hope to determine *why* humans develop as they typically do and *why* some individuals turn out differently than others. Stated another way, explanation centers both on normative changes *within* individuals and variations in development *between* individuals. As we will see throughout the text, it is often easier to describe development than to establish conclusively (explain) why it occurs.

Finally, many researchers and practitioners hope to "optimize" development by applying what they have learned in attempts to help human beings develop in positive directions. This is clearly a practical side to the study of human development, a focus that has led to such breakthroughs as:

- Ways of promoting strong affectional ties between fussy, unresponsive infants and their disillusioned parents.
- Ways of assisting children with learning difficulties to achieve more success at school.
- Ways of helping socially unskilled children and adolescents to prevent the emotional difficulties that could result from having no close friends and being rejected by peers.

Of course, such *optimization* goals often cannot be achieved until researchers have adequately described normal and abnormal pathways of development and have explained why these developments take place.

Some Basic Observations about the Character of Development

Now that we have defined development and talked very briefly about the goals that developmentalists pursue, let's consider some of the conclusions they have drawn about the character of human development.

Human Development Is a Continual and Cumulative Process

In his famous poem *Paradise Lost*, John Milton wrote: "Childhood shows the man as morning shows the day." This interesting analogy can be interpreted in at least two ways. It could be translated to mean that the events of childhood have little or no real impact on one's adult life, just as a sunny summer morning often fails to forecast an impending afternoon thundershower. Yet most people do not interpret Milton's statement that way. Most take it to mean that the events of childhood play a very meaningful role in forecasting the future. Human developmentalists clearly favor this latter interpretation.

Although no one can specify precisely what adulthood holds in store from even the most meticulous examination of a person's childhood, developmentalists have learned that the first 12 years are an extremely important part of the life span—one that sets the stage for adolescence and adulthood. And yet, how we perform on that stage will also depend on the experiences we have later as adolescents and adults. Obviously, you are not the same person you were at age 10 or even at age 15. You have probably grown somewhat (either up or out), acquired new academic skills, and developed very different interests and aspirations from those you had as a fifth-grader or a high school sophomore. And the path of such developmental change stretches ever onward, through middle age and beyond, culminating in the final change that occurs when we die. In sum, human development is best described as a *continual* and cumulative process. The only thing that is constant is change, and the changes that occur at each major phase of life can have important implications for the future.

Table 1-1 presents a chronological overview of the life span as developmentalists see it. Our focus in this text is on development during the first five periods of life—the epochs known as childhood and adolescence. By examining how children develop from the moment they are conceived until they reach young adulthood, we will each learn more about ourselves and the determinants of our behavior. Our survey will also provide some insight as to why no two children are ever exactly alike, even when

Table 1-1   A Chronological Overview of Human Development

Period of life	Approximate age range
1. Prenatal period	Conception to birth
2. Infancy	First two years of life
3. Preschool period	2 to 6 years of age (some prefer to describe children who have begun to walk and are age 1 to 3 as "toddlers")
4. Middle childhood	6 to 12 or so years of age (until the onset of puberty)
5. Adolescence	12 or so to 20 years of age (many developmentalists define the end of adolescence as the point at which the individual begins to work and is reasonably independent of parental sanctions)
6. Young adulthood	20 to 40 years of age
7. Middle age	40 to 65 years of age
8. Old age	65 years of age and older

Note: The age ranges listed here are approximate and may not apply to any particular individual. For example, a few 10-year-olds have experienced puberty and are properly classified as adolescents. Some teenagers are fully self-supporting, with children of their own, and are best classified as young adults.

raised together in the same home. I'll not promise that you will find answers to every important question you may have about developing children and adolescents. The study of human development is still a relatively young discipline with many unresolved issues. But as we proceed, it should become quite clear that developmentalists of the past half century have provided an enormous amount of very practical information about the younger set that can help us to become better educators, better child/adolescent practicioners, and better-informed parents.

Human Development Is a Holistic Process

It was once fashionable to divide developmentalists into three camps: (1) those who studied *physical growth* and development, including bodily changes and the sequencing of motor skills, (2) those who studied *cognitive* aspects of development, including perception, language, learning, and thinking, and (3) those who concentrated on *psychosocial* aspects of development, including emotions, personality, and the growth of interpersonal relationships. Today, we know that this classification is somewhat misleading, for researchers who work in any of these areas have found that changes in one aspect of development have important implications for other aspects. Let's consider an example.

What determines a person's popularity with peers? If you were to say that social skills are important, you would be right. Social skills such as warmth, friendliness, and willingness to cooperate are characteristics that popular children typically display. Yet there is much more to popularity than meets the eye. We now have some indication that the age at which a child reaches puberty, an important milestone in physical development, has a very real effect on social life. For example, boys who reach puberty early enjoy better relations with their peers than boys who reach puberty later. Let's also note that bright children who do well in school tend to be more popular with their peers than children of average intelligence or below who perform somewhat less admirably in the classroom.

We see, then, that one's "popularity" depends not only on the growth of social skills but also on various aspects of both cognitive and physical development. As this example illustrates, development is not piecemeal but **holistic;** human beings are

holistic perspective: a unified view of the developmental process that emphasizes the important interrelationships among the physical, mental, social, and emotional aspects of human development.

physical, cognitive, and social creatures, and each of these components of "self" depends, in part, on changes that are taking place in other areas of development. This holistic perspective is perhaps the dominant theme of human development today—and the theme around which our book is organized.

There Is Much Plasticity in Human Development

Plasticity refers to a capacity for change in response to positive or negative life experiences. Although we have described development as a continual and cumulative process and noted that past events often have implications for the future, developmentalists have known for some time that the course of development can change abruptly if important aspects of one's life change. For example, somber babies living in barren, understaffed orphanages often become quite cheerful and affectionate when placed in socially stimulating adoptive homes (Rutter, 1981). Highly aggressive children who are intensely disliked by peers often improve their social status after learning and practicing the social skills that popular children display (Mize & Ladd, 1990; Shure, 1989). It is indeed fortunate that human development is so plastic, for children who get off to what appear to be horrible starts can often be helped to overcome their deficiencies.

Development Is Shaped by Its Historical/Cultural Context

No single portrait of development is accurate for all cultures, social classes, or racial and ethnic groups. Each culture (and subculture) transmits a particular pattern of beliefs, values, customs, and skills to its younger generations, and the content of this cultural socialization will have a strong influence on the attributes and competencies that individuals come to display. Development is also influenced by societal changes in our own time, including historical events such as wars, technological breakthroughs such as the development of home computers, and social movements such as women's liberation. Each generation develops in its own way, and each generation changes the world for generations that follow. So we should not automatically assume that developmental sequences observed in samples of North American or European children (the most heavily studied populations) are optimal, or even that they characterize persons developing in other eras or cultural settings (Laboratory for Comparative Human Cognition, 1983). Only by adopting a cultural/historical perspective can we fully appreciate the richness and diversity of human development.

A Brief Overview of the Text

To this point we have learned that human development is a complex, multifaceted process—a process that is cumulative, holistic, plastic, and heavily influenced by the era and the cultural setting in which it occurs. How did developmentalists make these important discoveries? What methods do they use to chart developmental sequences? How do they decide what to study and why it may be important to look at these phenomena?

The aim of this book is to answer each of these questions by introducing you to the methods, theories, findings, and practical accomplishments of the modern developmental sciences. Part I sets the stage. In the remainder of this first chapter, we will see how the scientific community gradually became interested in developing children and then devised a number of strategies for detecting and explaining developmental change. In Chapter 2, we take a closer look at the role of theory in developmental psychology as we examine four major theories of human development and see that the assumptions theorists make largely determine the phenomena they choose to study.

The rest of the text is organized around broad areas of study and research. Human beings are biological creatures, and our emphasis in Part II is on physical changes and the biological bases of development. Among the more remarkable developments

plasticity: capacity for change; a developmental state that has the potential to be shaped by experience.

of childhood and adolescence are the changes that occur in perceiving, thinking, reasoning, and remembering. These cognitive, or intellectual, developments are examined in detail in Part III. Of course, humans are also social animals, and our focus in Part IV shifts to social and personality development. And in Part V, we will concentrate on important contextual influences as we consider how families, schools, new technologies, and the society of one's peers affect the development of children and adolescents.

One more point: we will be emphasizing research and its application in this text because most of what we know about developmental processes comes from the results of empirical research. Today, there are many excellent procedures for studying human development—techniques that we will soon discuss in some detail. But before we do, it is necessary to take a brief look at the history of developmental psychology in order to understand and appreciate why this field has become an empirical science.

 ## HUMAN DEVELOPMENT IN HISTORICAL PERSPECTIVE

Contemporary Western societies can be described as "child-centered": people often regard births as "blessed events," spend large amounts of money to care for, protect, and educate their young, and do not require children to shoulder the full responsibilities of citizenship until attaining the legal age of 14–21 (depending on the society), when they have presumably gained the wisdom and skills to "pull their own weight." Yet, childhood and adolescence were not always regarded as the very special and sensitive periods that we know them to be today. To understand how developmentalists think about and approach the study of children, it is necessary to see how the concept of childhood "developed" over time. And you may be surprised at just how recent our modern viewpoint really is. Of course, only after people came to view childhood as a very special period did they begin to study children and the developmental process.

Childhood in Premodern Times

In the early days of recorded history, children had few if any rights, and their lives were not always valued by their elders. Archeological research, for example, has shown that the ancient Carthaginians often killed children as religious sacrifices and embedded them in the walls of buildings to "strengthen" these structures (Bjorklund & Bjorklund, 1992). Until the fourth century A.D., Roman parents were legally entitled to kill their deformed, illegitimate, or otherwise unwanted infants. After this active infanticide was outlawed, unwanted babies were often left to die in the wilderness or were sold as servants or as objects for sexual exploitation upon reaching middle childhood (deMause, 1974).

Even "wanted" children were often treated rather harshly by today's standards. For example, male children in the city-state of Sparta in ancient Greece were exposed to a strict regimen designed to train them for the grim task of serving a military state. As infants, they took cold-water baths to "toughen" them. At age 7, when children in our society today are entering second grade, Spartan boys were taken from their homes and housed in public barracks, where they were often beaten or forced to go without food for days at a time, to instill in them the discipline they would need to become able warriors (deMause, 1974; Despert, 1965).

Not all early societies treated their children as harshly as the citizens of Carthage, Rome, and Sparta. Yet, for several centuries after the birth of Christ, children were viewed as family "possessions" who had no rights (Hart, 1991) and whom parents were free to exploit as they saw fit. In fact, it wasn't until the 12th century A.D. in

Although medieval children dressed like their elders and often worked alongside them, it is doubtful that they were considered miniature adults.

Christian Europe that secular legislation equated infanticide with murder (deMause, 1974)!

Currently, there is some debate about what childhood was like during the medieval era. Historian Philippe Aries (1962) has analyzed documents and paintings from medieval Europe and concluded that European societies had *no* concept of childhood as we know it before 1600. Medieval children were not coddled or indulged to the extent that today's children are. They were often dressed in down-sized versions of adult clothing and were depicted in artwork as working alongside adults (usually close relatives) in the shop or the field or as drinking and carousing with adults at parties. Medieval law exempted *infants* from criminal culpability for their harm doing, but generally made no distinctions between childhood and adult offenses (Borstelmann, 1983; Kean, 1937).

But were medieval children really considered to be miniature adults? Probably not. More recent and extensive examinations of medieval history reveal that childhood was generally recognized as a distinct phase of life and that children were thought to have certain needs above and beyond those of adults (see Borstelmann, 1983; Kroll, 1977). Clearly, the experiences of children were different during medieval times than they are today: Emotional bonds between parents and their young may not have been as strong then as now, and medieval children routinely performed economic functions within the family that closely resemble "career" activities by today's standards. But it is almost certainly an overstatement to conclude that medieval societies had absolutely no concept of childhood and merely treated their young as miniature adults.

Origins of Modern-Day Views on Childhood

During the 17th and 18th centuries, attitudes toward children and child rearing began to change. Religious leaders of that era stressed that children were innocent and helpless souls who should be shielded from the wild and wanton behavior of adults. One method of accomplishing this objective was to send young people to school. Although the primary purpose of schooling was to provide a proper moral and religious education, it was now recognized that important subsidiary skills such as read-

BOX 1-1

On the "Invention" of Adolescence

Although modern-day concepts of childhood date to the 1700s, formal recognition of *adolescence* as a distinct phase of life came even later—during the early years of this century (Hall, 1904). Ironically, the spread of industry in Western societies is probably the event most responsible for the "invention" of adolescence. As immigrants poured into industrialized nations and took jobs that had formerly been filled by children and teenagers, young people became economic liabilities rather than assets (or, as one person put it, "economically worthless but emotionally priceless" (Zelizer, cited in Remley, 1988). Moreover, the increasingly complex technology of industrial operations placed a premium on obtaining an educated labor force. So the late 19th century was a period when laws were passed to restrict child labor and make schooling compulsory (Kett, 1977). Suddenly teens were spending much of their time surrounded by agemates and separated from adults. And as they hung out with friends and developed their own colorful "peer cultures," teenagers came to be viewed as a distinct class of individuals—those who had clearly emerged from the innocence of childhood but who were not yet ready to assume adult responsibilities (Hall, 1904).

After World War II, the adolescent experience broadened as increasing numbers of high school graduates postponed marriages and careers to pursue college (and postgraduate) educations. Today, it is not at all unusual for young people to delay their entry into the workaday adult world until their mid to late 20s (Hartung & Sweeney, 1991; Vobejda, 1991). And we might add that society condones this "extended adolescence" by requiring workers to obtain increasingly specialized training to pursue their chosen careers (Elder, Liker, & Cross, 1984).

Interestingly, many of the world's cultures have no concept of adolescence as a distinct phase of life. The St. Lawrence Eskimos, for example, simply distinguish boys from men (or girls from women), following the tradition of many preliterate societies that passage to adulthood occurs at puberty (Keith, 1985). And yet, other cultures' depictions of the life span are much more intricate than our own. The Arasha of East Africa, for example, have at least *six* meaningful age strata for males: youths, junior warriors, senior warriors, junior elders, senior elders, and retired elders.

In some cultures, passage to adulthood occurs at puberty, and adolescents are expected to assume adult responsibilities.

The fact that age does not have the same meaning in all eras or cultures reflects a basic truth that we have already touched on and will emphasize repeatedly throughout this book: The course of human development in one historical or cultural context is apt to differ, and to differ substantially, from that observed in other eras and cultural settings. Aside from our biological link to the human race, we are largely products of the times and places in which we live!

ing and writing must be taught in order to transform the innocents into "servants and workers" who would provide society "with a good labor force" (Aries, 1962, p. 10; see also Box 1-1). Although children were still considered family possessions, parents were now discouraged from abusing their sons and daughters and were urged to treat them with more warmth and affection (Aries, 1962; Despert, 1965).

Early Philosophical Perspectives on Childhood

Why did attitudes toward children change so drastically in the 17th and 18th centuries? Although the historical record is not altogether clear on this point, it is likely that the thinking of influential social philosophers contributed in a meaningful way

Innate purity

Original sin

to the new perspective on children and child care. Lively speculation about human nature led these philosophers to consider carefully each of the following issues:

1. Are children inherently good or inherently bad?
2. Are children driven by inborn motives and instincts; or, rather, are they products of their environments?
3. Are children actively involved in shaping their characters; or are they passive creatures molded by parents, teachers, and other agents of society?

Debates about these philosophical questions produced quite different perspectives on children and child rearing, ranging from Thomas Hobbes's (1651/1904) doctrine of **original sin,** which held that children are inherently selfish egoists who must be controlled by society, to Jean Jacques Rousseau's (1762/1955) doctrine of **innate purity**—the notion that children are born with an intuitive sense of right and wrong that is often misdirected by society. These two viewpoints clearly differ in their implications for child rearing. Proponents of original sin argued that parents must actively restrain their egoistic offspring, while the innate purists viewed children as "noble savages" who should be given more freedom to follow their inherently positive inclinations.

Another influential view on children and child rearing was suggested by John Locke (1690/1913), who believed that the mind of an infant is a **tabula rasa,** or "blank slate," and that children have *no* inborn tendencies. In other words, children are neither inherently good nor inherently bad, and how they turn out will depend entirely on their worldly experiences. Like Hobbes, Locke argued in favor of disciplined child rearing to ensure that children develop good habits and acquire few, if any, unacceptable ones.

These philosophers also differed on the question of children's participation in their own development. Hobbes maintained that children must learn to rechannel their naturally selfish interests into socially acceptable outlets; in this sense, they are passive subjects to be molded by the more powerful elements of society—namely, parents. Locke, too, believed that the child's role is passive, since the mind of an infant is a blank slate on which experience writes its lessons. But a strikingly different view was proposed by Rousseau, who believed that children are actively involved in shaping their intellects and personalities. In Rousseau's words, the child is not a "passive recipient of the tutor's instruction" but a "busy, testing, motivated explorer. The active searching child, setting his own problems, stands in marked contrast to the receptive one . . . on whom society fixes its stamp" (quoted in Kessen, 1965, p. 75).

Clearly, these philosophers had some interesting ideas about children and how they should be raised. But how could anyone decide whether their views were correct? Unfortunately, the philosophers collected no objective data to back their contentions, and the few observations they did make were limited and unsystematic. Can you anticipate the next step in the evolution of developmental psychology?

Children as Subjects: The Baby Biographies

The first glimmering of a systematic study of children can be traced to the late 19th century. This was a period in which investigators from a variety of academic backgrounds began to observe the development of their own children and to publish these data in works known as **baby biographies.**

Perhaps the most influential of the baby biographers was Charles Darwin, who made daily records of the early development of his son (Darwin, 1877; and see Charlesworth, 1992). Darwin's curiosity about child development stemmed from his earlier theory of evolution. Quite simply, he believed that young, untrained infants share many characteristics with their nonhuman ancestors, and he advanced the (now discredited) idea that the development of the individual child will retrace the entire

original sin: the idea that children are inherently negative creatures who must be taught to rechannel their selfish interests into socially acceptable outlets.

innate purity: the idea that infants are born with an intuitive sense of right and wrong that is often misdirected by the demands and restrictions of society.

tabula rasa: the idea that the mind of an infant is a "blank slate" and that all knowledge, abilities, behaviors, and motives are acquired through experience.

baby biography: a detailed record of an infant's growth and development over a period of time.

evolutionary history of the species, thereby illustrating the "descent of man." So Darwin and many of his contemporaries viewed the baby biography as a means of answering questions about our evolutionary past.

Baby biographies left much to be desired as works of science. Different baby biographers emphasized very different aspects of their children's behavior, so that different baby biographies were difficult to compare. Then, too, parents are not entirely objective about their own children, and baby biographers like Charles Darwin may also have let their assumptions about the nature of development bias their observations so that they "found" what they were looking for. Finally, each baby biography was based on a single child—and often the child of a distinguished individual, at that. Conclusions based on a single case may not hold true for other children.

Despite these shortcomings, baby biographies were a step in the right direction. The fact that eminent scientists such as Charles Darwin were now writing about developing children implied that human development was a topic worthy of scientific scrutiny.

Emergence of a Psychology of Childhood (and Adolescence)

Introductory textbooks in virtually all academic areas typically credit someone as the "founder" of the discipline. In developmental psychology, there were several influential pioneers who might merit consideration for this honor. Still, the person who is most often cited as the founder of developmental psychology is G. Stanley Hall.

Well aware of the shortcomings of baby biographies, Hall set out in the late 19th century to collect more objective data on larger samples. Specifically, he was interested in the character of children's thinking, and he developed what is now a very familiar research tool—the **questionnaire**—to explore "the contents of children's minds" (Hall, 1891). By asking children questions about a large number of topics, Hall discovered that children's understanding of the world grows rapidly during childhood and that the "logic" of young children is not very logical at all. Hall later wrote an influential book titled *Adolescence* (1904) that was the first work to call attention to adolescence as a unique phase of the life span. Here, then, were the first large-scale scientific investigations of developing youth, and it is on this basis that G. Stanley Hall merits consideration as the founder of developmental psychology (White, 1992).

At about the time Hall was using questionnaires to study children's minds, a young European neurologist was trying a different method of probing the mind and revealing its contents. The neurologist's approach was very fruitful, providing information that led him to propose a theory that revolutionized thinking about children and childhood. The neurologist was Sigmund Freud. His ideas came to be known as *psychoanalytic theory.*

In many areas of science, new theories are often revisions or modifications of old theories. But in Freud's day, there were few "old" theories of human behavior to modify. Freud was truly a pioneer, formulating his psychoanalytic theory from the thousands of notes and observations he made while treating patients for various kinds of emotional disturbances.

Ever the astute observer, Freud noticed that patients often described very similar experiences or events that had been noteworthy to them while they were growing up. He inferred that there must be important milestones in human development that all people share. As he continued to observe his patients and listen to accounts of their lives, Freud concluded that each milestone in the life history of a patient was meaningfully related to earlier events. He then recognized that he had the data—the pieces of the puzzle—from which to construct a comprehensive theory of human development.

Freud's highly creative and unorthodox theorizing soon attracted a lot of attention. Shortly after the publication of Freud's earliest theoretical monographs, the *International Journal of Psychoanalysis* was founded, and other researchers began to report their tests of Freud's thinking. By the mid-1930s much of Freud's work had

American psychologist G. Stanley Hall (1846–1924) is recognized as one of the founders of developmental psychology.

questionnaire: a research instrument that asks the persons being studied to respond to a number of written questions.

been translated into other languages, and the impact of psychoanalytic theory was felt around the world. Over the years, Freud's theory proved to be quite *heuristic*, meaning that it continued to generate new research and to prompt other researchers to revise and extend Freud's thinking. Clearly, the field of developmental psychology was thriving by the time Freud died in 1939.

Freud's work—and other scientists' reactions to it—aptly illustrates the role theories play in the scientific study of human development. Although the word *theory* is an imposing term, theories are something that everybody has. If I were to ask you why males and females appear to be so very different as adults when they seem so very similar as infants, you would undoubtedly have something to say on the issue. In answering, you would be stating or at least reflecting your own underlying theory of sex differences. So a **theory** is really nothing more than a set of concepts and propositions that allows the theorist to describe and explain some aspect of experience. In the field of psychology, theories help us to describe various patterns of behavior and to explain why those behaviors occur.

Good theories have another important feature: the ability to predict future events. These theoretical predictions, or **hypotheses,** are then tested by collecting additional data. The information we obtain when testing hypotheses not only provides some clues about the theory's ability to explain new observations but may also lead to new theoretical insights that extend our knowledge even further.

Today, there are many theories that have contributed to our understanding of child and adolescent development, and in Chapter 2 we will examine several of the more influential of these viewpoints. Although it is quite natural for people reading about these theories to pick a favorite, the scientist uses a rather stringent principle to evaluate theories: He or she will formulate hypotheses and conduct research to see whether the theory can adequately predict and explain new observations. Thus, there is no room for subjective bias when evaluating a theory. Theories in developmental psychology are only as good as their ability to predict and explain important aspects of human development.

In the next section of this chapter, we will focus on the "tools of the trade"—that is, the research methods that developmentalists use to test their theories and gain a better understanding of the child's world.

▶ RESEARCH METHODS IN DEVELOPMENTAL PSYCHOLOGY

When detectives are assigned cases to solve, they first gather the facts, formulate hunches, and then sift through the clues or collect additional information until one of their hunches proves correct. Unraveling the mysteries of development is in many ways a similar endeavor. Investigators must carefully observe their subjects, study the information they collect, and use these data to draw conclusions about the ways people develop.

Our focus in this section is on the methods that researchers use to gather information about developing children and adolescents. Our first task is to understand why developmentalists consider it absolutely essential to collect all these facts. We will then discuss the advantages and disadvantages of five basic fact-finding strategies: interviews and questionnaires, case studies, clinical methodologies, naturalistic observation, and structured observation. Finally, we will consider the ways developmentalists might design their research to detect and explain age-related changes in children's feelings, thoughts, abilities, and behaviors.

The Scientific Method

Modern developmental psychology is appropriately labeled a scientific enterprise because those who study developing organisms have adopted a value system we call the **scientific method** that guides their attempts at understanding. There is nothing

theory: a set of concepts and propositions designed to organize, describe, and explain an existing set of observations.

hypothesis: a theoretical prediction about some aspect of experience.

scientific method: an attitude or value about the pursuit of knowledge that dictates that investigators must be objective and must allow their data to decide the merits of their theorizing.

mysterious about the scientific method. It is really more of an *attitude* or *value* than a method; the attitude dictates that, above all, investigators must be *objective* and must allow their observations (or data) to decide the merits of their thinking.

In earlier eras, when social philosophers such as Hobbes, Locke, and Rousseau were presenting their views on children and child rearing, their largely unsubstantiated claims were often interpreted as fact. It was as if people assumed that great minds always had great insights. Very few individuals questioned the word of these well-known scholars because the scientific method was not yet a widely accepted criterion for evaluating wisdom or knowledge.

The intent here is not to criticize the early social philosophers. In fact, today's developmentalists (and children) are deeply indebted to them for helping to modify the ways in which society thought about and treated its young. However, so-called great minds may produce miserable ideas on occasion, and if poorly conceived notions have implications for the way human beings are to be treated, it behooves us to discover these erroneous assumptions before they harm anyone. The scientific method, then, is a value that helps to protect the scientific community and society at large against flawed reasoning. The protection comes from the practice of evaluating the merits of various theoretical pronouncements against the objective record, rather than simply relying on the academic, political, or social credibility of the theorist. Of course, this means that the theorist whose ideas are being evaluated must be equally objective and, thus, willing to discard pet notions when there is evidence that they have outlived their usefulness.

Gathering Data: Basic Fact-Finding Strategies

No matter what aspect of development we hope to study—be it the perceptual capabilities of newborn infants, the growth of friendships among grade-school children, or the origins of drug use among adolescents—we must find ways to measure what interests us. Today, researchers are fortunate in having many tried-and-true procedures to measure behavior and to test their hypotheses about human development. But regardless of the technique one employs, scientifically useful measures must always display two important qualities: **reliability** and **validity.**

A measure is *reliable* if it yields consistent information over time and across observers. Suppose that you go into a classroom and record the number of times each child behaves aggressively toward others, but your research assistant, using the same scheme to observe the same children, does not agree with your measurements. Or you measure each child's aggressiveness one week but come up with very different aggressiveness scores while applying the same measure to the same children a week later. Clearly, your observational measure of aggression is unreliable because it yields highly inconsistent information. To be reliable and thus useful for scientific purposes, your measure would have to produce comparable estimates of children's aggression from independent observers (*interrater reliability*), and yield similar scores for individual children from one testing to another shortly thereafter (*temporal stability*).

A measure is *valid* if it measures what it is supposed to measure. Perhaps you can see how an instrument must be reliable and measure consistently before it can possibly be valid. Yet reliability, by itself, does not guarantee validity. For example, a highly reliable observational scheme that is intended as a measure of children's aggression may provide grossly overinflated estimates of aggressive behavior if the investigator simply classifies all acts of physical force as examples of aggression. What the researcher has failed to recognize is that many such high-intensity antics may simply represent enjoyable forms of rough-and-tumble play without harmful or aggressive intent. Clearly, researchers must demonstrate that they are measuring the attribute they say they are measuring before we can have much faith in the data they collect or the conclusions they reach.

With the importance of establishing the reliability and validity of measures in mind, let us consider some of the different ways in which aspects of human development might be measured.

reliability: the extent to which a measuring instrument yields consistent results, both over time and across observers.

validity: the extent to which a measuring instrument accurately reflects what the researchers intended to measure.

Self-Report Methodologies

Four common procedures that developmentalists use to gather information and test hypotheses are interviews, questionnaires (including psychological tests), the clinical method, and case studies. Although these approaches are similar in that each asks subjects to answer questions posed by the investigator, they differ in the extent to which the investigator treats individual participants alike.

Interviews and questionnaires. Researchers who opt for the interview or the questionnaire techniques will ask the child (or the child's parents) a series of questions pertaining to one or more aspects of development. Collecting data via a questionnaire (and most psychological tests) simply involves putting questions on paper and asking participants to respond to them in writing, whereas interviews require participants to respond orally to the investigator's queries. If the procedure is a **structured interview** or **structured questionnaire,** all who participate in the study are asked the same questions in the same order. The purpose of this standardized or structured format is to treat all participants alike so that their responses can be compared.

One interesting application of the interview technique is a project in which kindergarten, second-grade, and fourth-grade children responded to 24 questions designed to assess their knowledge of social stereotypes about males and females (Williams, Bennett, & Best, 1975). Each question related to a different short story in which the central character was described by either stereotypically masculine adjectives (for example, *aggressive, forceful, tough*) or stereotypically feminine adjectives (for example, *emotional, excitable*). The child's task was to indicate whether the character in each story was male or female. Williams and his associates found that even kindergarteners could usually tell whether the stories referred to boys or girls. In other words, these 5-year-olds were quite knowledgeable about gender stereotypes, although children's thinking became much more stereotyped between kindergarten and the second grade. One implication of these results is that stereotyping of the sexes must begin very early if kindergartners are already thinking along stereotyped lines.

Interviews and questionnaires have some very real shortcomings. First, neither approach can be used with very young children who cannot read or comprehend speech very well. Investigators must also hope that the answers they receive are honest and accurate and are not merely attempts by respondents to present themselves in a favorable or socially desirable light. Might not many adolescents, for example, be reluctant to admit that they regularly masturbate or that they sniff glue or enjoy the challenge of shoplifting? Clearly, inaccurate or untruthful responses will lead to erroneous conclusions. Finally, investigators must be careful to ensure that participants of different ages interpret questions in the same way; otherwise, the age trends observed in one's study may reflect differences in children's ability to comprehend and communicate rather than real underlying changes in their feelings, thoughts, or behaviors.

Despite these potential shortcomings, structured interviews and questionnaires can be excellent methods of obtaining large amounts of useful information in a short period of time. Both approaches are particularly useful when the investigator guarantees that the participants' responses will be confidential and/or challenges participants to display exactly what they know about an issue, for the socially desirable response to such guarantees and challenges is likely to be a truthful or accurate answer. In the gender-stereotyping study, for example, the young participants probably considered each question a personal challenge or a puzzle to be solved and were thus motivated to answer accurately and to display exactly what they knew about males and females. Under the circumstances, then, the structured interview was an excellent method of assessing children's perceptions of the sexes.

The case study. Yet another method of researching human development is the **case study.** An investigator who uses this method prepares detailed descriptions of one or

structured interview or structured questionnaire: a technique in which all participants are asked the same questions in precisely the same order so that the responses of different participants can be compared.

case study: a research method in which the investigator gathers extensive information about the life of an individual and then tests developmental hypotheses by analyzing the events of the person's life history.

more individuals and then attempts to draw conclusions by analyzing these "cases." In preparing an individualized record, or "case," the researcher will typically include many items of information about the individual, such as his or her family background, socioeconomic status, level of education, work history, health record, self-descriptions of significant life events, and performance on psychological tests. Much of the information included in any case history comes from interviews with the individual, although the questions asked are typically not standardized and may vary considerably from case to case.

The baby biographies of the 19th and early 20th centuries are examples of case studies, each of which was based on a single subject. But perhaps the best known of the case-study researchers was Sigmund Freud, who formulated his psychoanalytic theory from the life histories of his patients.

Although Freud was a strong proponent of the case study and used it to great advantage, there are three major drawbacks to this approach. First, the validity of an investigator's conclusions will obviously depend on the accuracy of information received. Unfortunately, the potential for inaccuracy is vast in a method in which older subjects try to recall the causes and consequences of important events that happened years ago in childhood. Second, the data on any two (or more) individuals may not be directly comparable if the investigator has asked each participant different questions rather than posing a standard set of questions to all. Finally, the case study may lack *generalizability*; that is, conclusions drawn from the experiences of the particular individuals who were studied may not apply to most people. In fact, one recurring criticism of Freud's psychoanalytic theory is that it was formulated from the experiences and recollections of *emotionally disturbed* patients who were hardly typical of the general population. So, the case study can serve as a rich source of ideas about human development. However, its limitations are many, and any conclusions drawn from case studies should be verified through the use of other research techniques.

The clinical method. The **clinical method** is a very close relative of the interview technique. The investigator is usually interested in testing a hypothesis by presenting the research participant with a task or stimulus of some sort and then inviting a response. When the participant has responded, the investigator will typically ask a second question or introduce a new task in the hope of clarifying the participant's original answer. Although subjects are often asked the same questions initially, each participant's answer determines what he or she is asked next. Thus, the clinical method is not standardized; it considers each subject to be unique.

Jean Piaget, a famous Swiss psychologist, relied extensively on the clinical method to study children's moral reasoning and intellectual development. The data from Piaget's research are largely protocol records of his interactions with individual children. Here is a small sample from Piaget's work (1932/1965, p. 140) on the development of moral reasoning that shows that this young child thinks about lying in a very different way than adults do:

> Do you know what a lie is? — *It's when you say what isn't true.* — Is 2+2=5 a lie? — *Yes, it's a lie.* — Why? — *Because it isn't right.* — Did the boy who said 2+2=5 know it wasn't right or did he make a mistake? — *He made a mistake.* — Then if he made a mistake, did he tell a lie or not? — *Yes, he told a lie.*

We need only examine the richness of Piaget's thinking (as we will in Chapters 2 and 7) to see that the clinical method can provide a wealth of information about developing children. However, the clinical approach is a controversial method that presents some thorny interpretive problems. We have already noted the difficulties in comparing cases or protocols generated by a procedure that treats each participant differently. Furthermore, the nonstandardized treatment of participants raises the

clinical method: a type of interview in which a participant's response to each successive question (or problem) determines what the investigator will ask next.

Investigator using the clinical method. All participants are asked the same questions at first, but each participant's answers to these initial questions determine what the researcher will ask next.

possibility that the examiner's preexisting theoretical biases may affect the questions asked and the interpretations provided. Since conclusions drawn from the clinical method depend, in part, on the investigator's *subjective* interpretations, it is always desirable to verify these insights using other research techniques.

Observational Methodologies

Often, researchers prefer to observe people's behavior directly rather than asking them questions about it. One method that many developmentalists favor is **naturalistic observation**—observing people in their common, everyday (that is, natural) surroundings. To observe children, this usually means going into homes, schools, or public parks and playgrounds and carefully recording what happens. Rarely does the investigator try to record every event that occurs; he or she is usually testing a specific hypothesis about one type of behavior, such as cooperation or aggression, and focuses exclusively on acts of this kind. One strength of naturalistic observation is the ease with which it can be applied to infants and toddlers, who often cannot be studied through methods that demand verbal skills. But perhaps the greatest advantage of the observational technique is that it is the only method that can tell us how people actually behave in everyday life (Willems & Alexander, 1982).

However, naturalistic observation also has its limitations. First, some behaviors occur so infrequently (for example, heroic rescues) or are so socially undesirable (for example, overt sex play or thievery) that they are unlikely to be witnessed by a strange observer in the natural environment. Second, many events are usually happening at the same time in the natural setting, and any (or some combination) of them may affect people's behavior. This makes it difficult to pinpoint the causes of participants' actions or of any developmental trends in behavior. Finally, the mere presence of an observer can sometimes make people behave differently than they otherwise would. Children may "ham it up" when they have an audience, whereas parents may be on their best behavior, showing a strong reluctance, for example, to spank a misbehaving child. For these reasons, observational researchers often attempt to minimize their influence by (1) videotaping their participants from a concealed location or (2) spending time in the setting before collecting their "real" data so that the individuals they are observing will grow accustomed to their presence and behave more naturally.

Recently, Mary Haskett and Janet Kistner (1991) conducted an excellent piece of naturalistic observation to look for differences in the social behaviors of physically abused and nonabused preschool children. The investigators first defined examples

naturalistic observation: a method in which the scientist tests hypotheses by observing people as they engage in everyday activities in their natural habitats (for example, at home, at school, or on the playground).

of the behaviors they wished to record—both *desirable* behaviors such as appropriate social initiations and positive play and *undesirable* behaviors such as aggression and negative verbalizations. They then monitored 14 abused and 14 nonabused preschool children as they mingled with peers in a play area of a day-care facility. Each child was observed during three 10-minute play sessions on three different days. To minimize their influence on the play activities, observers stood outside the play area while making their observations.

The results were disturbing. Compared with nonabused children, those who had been abused initiated fewer social interactions and were somewhat socially withdrawn. And when they did interact with playmates, the abused youngsters displayed many more aggressive acts and other negative behaviors than did their nonabused companions. Indeed, nonabused children often blatantly ignored the positive social initiations of an abused child, as if they did not want to get involved with him or her.

In sum, Haskett and Kistner's observational study shows that abused children are unattractive playmates who are likely to be disliked and even rejected by peers. But, as is almost always the case in naturalistic observational research, it is difficult to pinpoint the exact cause of these findings. Did the negative behaviors of abused children cause their peers to reject them? Or did peer rejection cause the abused children to display negative behaviors? Either possibility can account for Haskett and Kistner's results.

How might observational researchers study unusual or undesirable behaviors that they are unlikely to observe in the natural environment? They can do so by conducting **structured observations** in the laboratory. In a structured observational study, each participant is exposed to a setting that might evoke the behavior in question and is then surreptitiously observed (via a hidden camera or through a one-way mirror) to see if he or she performs the behavior. For example, Leon Kuczynski (1983) got children to promise to help him with a boring task and then left them alone to work at it in a room where attractive toys were present. This procedure enabled Kuczynski to determine whether youngsters would break a promise to work (a socially undesirable act) when they thought there was no one present to observe their transgression.

Aside from being a most feasible way of studying behaviors that occur infrequently or are not openly displayed in the natural environment, structured observations also ensure that every participant in the sample is exposed to the *same* eliciting stimuli and has an *equal opportunity* to perform the target behavior—circumstances that are not always true in the natural setting. Of course, the major disadvantage of structured observations is that participants may not always respond to a contrived laboratory setting as they would in everyday life.

Children's tendency to perform for an observer is one of the problems that researchers must overcome when using the method of naturalistic observation.

Concept Check 1-1 ⌄ Matching Research Methods to Research Questions

Check your understanding of the uses and strengths of various research methods by figuring out which method is best suited for investigating each of the following questions. Choose from the following methods: (a) structured interview, (b) case study, (c) naturalistic observation, (d) structured observation. Answers appear in the Appendix in the back of the book.

_____ 1. Will young elementary school children break a solemn promise to watch a sick puppy when no one is around to detect their transgression?

_____ 2. Do 6-year-olds know any negative stereotypes about minority group members?

_____ 3. Have adults who now suffer from clinical depression shared similar childhood experiences?

_____ 4. Are the aggressive actions that boy playmates display toward one another different from those that occur in girls' play groups?

Table 1-2 provides a brief review of the data-gathering schemes that we have examined thus far. In the sections that follow, we will consider the issue of how investigators design their research to test hypotheses and detect developmental changes.

structured observation: an observational method in which the investigator cues the behavior of interest and observes participants' responses in a laboratory.

Table 1-2 Strengths and Limitations of Some General Methods of Collecting Scientific Data

Method	Strengths	Limitations
Interviews and questionnaires	Relatively quick way to gather much information: standardized format allows the investigator to make direct comparisons among data provided by different participants.	Data collected may be inaccurate, may be less than completely honest, or may reflect variations in respondents' verbal skills and ability to understand the questions.
Case studies	Very broad method that considers many sources of data in drawing inferences and conclusions about individual participants.	Kind of data collected often differs from case to case and may be inaccurate or less than honest; conclusions drawn from individual cases are subjective and may not apply to other people.
Clinical methods	Flexible methodology that treats subjects as unique individuals; freedom to probe can be an aid in ensuring that the participant understands the meaning of the questions one asks.	Conclusions drawn may be unreliable in that participants are not all treated alike; flexible probes depend, in part, on the investigator's subjective interpretations of the participant's responses; can be used only with highly verbal participants.
Naturalistic observation	Allows study of behavior as it actually occurs in the real world.	Possibly subject to observer bias; observed behaviors may be influenced by observer's presence; unusual or undesirable behaviors are unlikely to be observed during the periods when observations are made.
Structured observation	Offers a standardized environment that provides every child an opportunity to perform target behavior; excellent way to observe infrequent or socially undesirable acts.	Observations may not always represent the ways children behave in the natural environment.

Detecting Relationships: Correlational and Experimental Designs

Once researchers have decided what they want to study, they must then devise a research plan, or design, that permits them to identify relationships among events and behaviors and to specify the causes of these relationships. Here we consider the two general research designs that investigators might employ: correlational and experimental.

The Correlational Design

In a **correlational design,** the investigator gathers information to determine whether two or more variables of interest are meaningfully related. If the researcher is testing a specific hypothesis (rather than conducting preliminary exploratory research), he or she will check to see whether these variables are related as the hypothesis specifies that they should be. No attempts are made to structure or to manipulate the participants' environment in any way. Instead, correlational researchers take people as they find them—already "manipulated" by natural life experiences—and try to determine whether variations in people's life experiences are associated with differences in their behaviors or patterns of development.

To illustrate the correlational approach to hypothesis testing, we will work with a simple theory specifying that youngsters learn a lot from watching television and are apt to imitate the actions of the characters they observe. One hypothesis we might derive from this theory is that the more often children observe TV characters who display violent and aggressive acts, the more inclined they will be to behave aggressively toward their own playmates. After selecting a sample of children to study, our next step in testing our hypothesis is to measure the two variables that we think are related. To assess children's exposure to violent themes on television, we might use

correlational design: a type of research design that indicates the strength of associations among variables; although correlated variables are systematically related, these relationships are not necessarily causal.

the interview or naturalistic observational methods to determine what each child watches, and then count the number of aggressive acts that occur in this programming. To measure the frequency of the children's own aggressive behavior toward peers, we could observe our sample on a playground and record how often each child behaves in a hostile, aggressive manner toward playmates. Having now gathered the data, it is time to evaluate our hypothesis.

The presence (or absence) of a relationship between variables can be determined by subjecting the data to a statistical procedure that yields a **correlation coefficient.** A correlation coefficient (symbolized by an r) provides a numerical estimate of the strength and the direction of the relationship between two variables. It can range in value from $+1.00$ to -1.00. The absolute value of r (disregarding its sign) tells us the *strength* of the relationship. An r of .00 indicates that the two variables are unrelated, whereas an r with an absolute value larger than .50 indicates a moderate to strong relationship. The sign of the correlation coefficient indicates the *direction* of the relationship. If the sign is positive, this means that, as the variable increases, the other variable also increases. For example, height and weight are positively correlated: As people grow taller, they (usually) get heavier. Negative correlations, however, indicate inverse relationships; as one variable increases, the other *decreases*. Among middle-aged men, exercise and heart disease are negatively correlated: Men who exercise more often are less likely to develop heart disease.

Now let's return to our hypothesized positive relationship between televised violence and children's aggressive behavior. A number of investigators have conducted correlational studies similar to the one we have designed, and the results (reviewed in Liebert & Sprafkin, 1988) suggest a moderate positive correlation (between $+.30$ and $+.50$) between the two variables of interest: Children who watch a lot of violent television programming are more likely to approve of violence and to behave more aggressively toward playmates than are other youngsters who watch little violent programming (see Figure 1-1 for a visual display).

Do these correlational studies firmly establish that exposure to violent TV programming *causes* children to become more aggressively inclined? *No, they do not!* Although we have detected a relationship between exposure to televised violence and children's aggressive behavior, the causal direction of the relationship is not at all clear. An equally plausible alternative explanation is that relatively aggressive children are the more inclined to prefer violent programming. Another possibility is that the association between TV viewing and aggressive behavior is actually caused by a third variable that we have not measured. For example, perhaps parents who fight a lot at home (an unmeasured variable) cause their children to become more aggressive *and*

correlation coefficient: a numerical index, ranging from -1.00 to $+1.00$, of the strength and direction of the relationship between two variables.

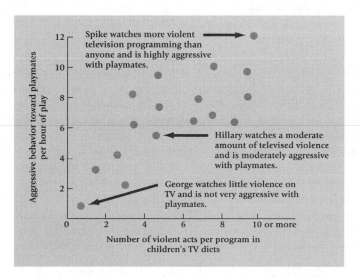

Figure 1-1
Plot of a hypothetical positive correlation between the amount of violence that children see on television and the number of aggressive responses they display. Each dot represents a specific child who views a particular level of televised violence (shown on the horizontal axis) and commits a particular number of aggressive acts (shown on the vertical axis). Although the correlation is less than perfect, we see that the more acts of violence a child watches on TV, the more inclined he or she is to behave aggressively toward peers.

to favor violent TV programming. If this were true, the latter two variables may be correlated, even though their relationship to each other is not one of cause and effect.

In sum, the correlational design is a versatile approach that can detect systematic relationships between any two or more variables that we might be interested in and are capable of measuring. However, its major limitation is that *it cannot unambiguously indicate that one thing causes another.* How, then, might a researcher establish the underlying causes of various behaviors or other aspects of human development? By conducting experiments.

The Experimental Design

In contrast to correlational studies, **experimental designs** permit a precise assessment of the cause-and-effect relationship that may exist between two variables. Let's return to the issue of whether viewing violent television programming *causes* children to become more aggressively inclined. In conducting a laboratory experiment to test this (or any) hypothesis, we would bring participants to the lab, expose them to different treatments, and record as data their responses to these treatments. The different treatments to which we expose our participants represent the **independent variable** of our experiment. To test the hypothesis that we have proposed, our independent variable (or treatments) would be the type of television program that we show to our participants. Half of our children might view a program in which one or more characters behave in a violent or otherwise aggressive manner toward others, whereas the other half would watch a program that contains little, if any, violence.

Children's reactions to the television shows would become the data, or **dependent variable,** in our experiment. Since our hypothesis centers on children's aggression, we would want to measure (as our dependent variable) how aggressively children behave after watching each type of television show. A dependent variable is called "dependent" because its value presumably "depends" on the independent variable. In the present case, we are hypothesizing that future aggression (our dependent variable) will be greater for children who watch violent programs (one level of the independent variable) than for those who watch nonviolent programs (the second level of the independent variable). If we are careful experimenters and exercise precise control over *all* other factors that may affect children's aggression, then the pattern of results that we have anticipated will allow us to draw a strong conclusion: Watching violent television programs *causes* children to behave more aggressively.

An experiment similar to the one we have proposed was actually conducted (Liebert & Baron, 1972). Half of the 5- to 9-year-olds in this study watched a violent 3½-minute clip from *The Untouchables* that contained two fistfights, two shootings, and a stabbing. The remaining children watched 3½ minutes of a nonviolent but exciting track meet. So the *independent variable* was the type of program watched. Then each child was taken into another room and seated before a panel that had wires leading into an adjoining room. On the panel was a green button labeled HELP, a red button labeled HURT, and a white light between the buttons. The experimenter then noted that a child in the adjoining room would soon be playing a handle-turning game that would illuminate the white light. The subject was told that by pushing the buttons when the light was lit, he or she could either help the other child by making the handle easy to turn or *hurt* the child by making the handle become very hot. When it was clear that the subject understood the instructions, the experimenter left the room, and the light came on 20 times over the next several minutes. So each subject had 20 opportunities to help or hurt another child. The total amount of time that each subject spent pushing the hurt button served as a measure of his or her aggression—the *dependent variable* in this study.

The results were clear: Despite the availability of an alternative, helping response, *both boys and girls were much more likely to press the HURT button (that is, behave aggressively) if they had watched the violent television program.* However, children in the two experimental conditions did not differ in their willingness to push the HELP button.

experimental design: a research design in which the investigator introduces some change in the participant's environment and then measures the effect of that change on the participant's behavior.

independent variable: the aspect of the environment that an experimenter modifies or manipulates in order to measure its impact on behavior.

dependent variable: the aspect of behavior that is measured in an experiment and assumed to be under the control of the independent variable.

So it appears that a mere 3½ minute exposure to televised violence can *cause* children to behave more aggressively toward a peer, even though the aggressive acts they witnessed on television bore no resemblance to those they committed themselves.

When students discuss this experiment in class, someone invariably challenges this interpretation of the results. For example, one student recently proposed an alternative explanation that "maybe the kids who watched the violent film were naturally more aggressive than those who saw the track meet." In other words, he was suggesting that a **confounding variable**—children's preexisting levels of aggression—had determined their willingness to hurt a peer and that the independent variable (type of television program) had had no effect at all! Could he have been correct? How do we know that the children in the two experimental conditions really didn't differ in some important way (such as their preexisting aggressive inclinations) that may have affected their willingness to hurt a peer?

This question brings us to the crucial issue of **experimental control.** In order to conclude that the independent variable is causally related to the dependent variable, the experimenter must ensure that all other confounding variables that could affect the dependent variable are *controlled*, that is, equivalent in each experimental condition. One way to equalize these extraneous factors is to do what Liebert and Baron (1972) did: randomly assign children to their experimental treatments. The concept of *randomization,* or **random assignment,** means that each research participant has an equal probability of being exposed to each experimental treatment or condition. Assignment of individual participants to a particular treatment is accomplished by an unbiased procedure such as the flip of a coin. If the assignment is truly random, there is only a very slim chance that participants in the two (or more) experimental conditions will differ in any characteristic that might affect their performance on the dependent variable. All these confounding variables will have been randomly distributed within each condition and equalized across the different conditions. Because Liebert and Baron randomly assigned subjects to experimental conditions, they could be reasonably certain that children who watched the violent TV program were not naturally more aggressive than those who watched the nonviolent TV program. So it was reasonable for them to conclude that the former group of children was more aggressive *because* they had watched a TV program in which violence and aggression were central.

A possible limitation of laboratory experiments. Critics of laboratory experimentation have argued that the tightly controlled laboratory environment is often very contrived and artificial and that children are likely to behave very differently in these surroundings than they would in a natural setting. Urie Bronfenbrenner (1977) has charged that a heavy reliance on laboratory experiments has made developmental psychology "the science of the strange behavior of children in strange situations with strange adults" (p. 19). Similarly, Robert McCall (1977) notes that experiments tell us what *can* cause a developmental change but do not necessarily pinpoint the factors that *actually do* cause such changes in natural settings. Consequently, it is quite possible that conclusions drawn from laboratory experiments will not always apply to the real world. In Box 1-2, we consider a step that experimentalists can take to counter this criticism and assess the **ecological validity** of their laboratory findings.

The Natural (or Quasi-) Experiment

There are many issues to which an experimental design either cannot be applied or should not be used, for ethical reasons. Suppose, for example, that we wish to study the effects of social deprivation in infancy on children's intellectual development. Clearly we cannot ask one group of parents to lock their infants in an attic for two years so that we can collect the data we need. It is simply unethical to subject children to any experimental treatment that would adversely affect their physical or psychological well-being.

confounding variable: some factor other than the independent variable which, if not controlled by the experimenter, could explain any differences across treatment conditions in participants' performance on the dependent variable.

experimental control: steps taken by an experimenter to ensure that all extraneous factors that could influence the dependent variable are roughly equivalent in each experimental condition; these precautions must be taken before an experimenter can be reasonably certain that observed changes in the dependent variable were caused by the manipulation of the independent variable.

random assignment: a control technique in which participants are assigned to experimental conditions through an unbiased procedure so that the members of the groups are not systematically different from one another.

ecological validity: state of affairs in which the findings of one's research are an accurate representation of processes that occur in the natural environment.

BOX 1-2

Assessing Causal Relationships in the Real World: The Field Experiment

*H*ow can we be more certain that a conclusion drawn from a laboratory experiment also applies in the real world? One way is to seek converging evidence for that conclusion by conducting a similar experiment *in a natural setting*—that is, a **field experiment**. This approach combines all the advantages of naturalistic observation with the more rigorous control that experimentation allows. In addition, subjects are typically not apprehensive about participating in a "strange" experiment because all the activities they undertake are everyday activities. Indeed, they may not even be aware that they are being observed or participating in an experiment.

Let's consider a field experiment (Leyens et al., 1975) that sought to test the hypothesis that heavy exposure to media violence can cause viewers to become more aggressive. The subjects were Belgian delinquents who lived together in cottages at a minimum-security institution for adolescent boys. Before the experiment began, the experimenters observed each boy in their research sample to measure his characteristic level of aggression. These initial assessments served as a *baseline* against which future increases in aggression could be measured. The baseline observations suggested that the institution's four cottages could be divided into two subgroups consisting of two cottages populated by relatively aggressive inmates and two cottages populated by less aggressive peers. Then the experiment began. For a period of one week, *violent* movies (such as *Bonnie and Clyde* and *The Dirty Dozen*) were shown each evening to one of the two cottages in each subgroup, and *neutral* films (such as *Daddy's Fiancée* and *La Belle Américaine*) were shown to the other cottages. Instances of physical and verbal aggression among residents of each cottage were recorded twice daily (at lunchtime and in the evenings after the movie) during the movie week and once daily (at lunchtime) during a posttreatment week.

The most striking result of this field experiment was the significant increase in *physical* aggression that occurred in the evenings among residents of both cottages assigned to the violent-film condition. Since the violent movies contained a large number of physically aggressive incidents, it appears that they evoked similar responses from the boys who watched them. But as shown in the figure, violent movies prompted larger increases in aggression among boys who were already relatively high in aggression. Furthermore, exposure to the violent movies caused the highly aggressive boys to become more *verbally aggressive* as well—an effect that these boys continued to display through the movie week *and* the posttreatment week.

Clearly, the results of the Belgian field experiment are consistent with Liebert and Baron's (1972) laboratory study in suggesting that exposure to media violence does indeed instigate aggressive behavior. Yet it also qualifies the laboratory findings by implying that the instigating effects of media violence *in the natural environment* are likely to be stronger and more enduring for the more aggressive members of the audience (and see Friedrich & Stein, 1973 for similar results with nursery school children).

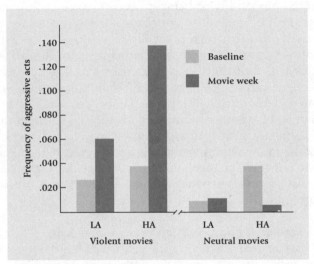

Mean physical aggression scores in the evening for highly aggressive (HA) and less aggressive (LA) boys under baseline conditions and after watching violent or neutral movies. Adapted from Leyens, Parke, Camino, & Berkowitz, 1975.

However, we might be able to accomplish our research objectives through a **natural (or quasi-) experiment** in which we observe the consequences of a natural event that subjects have experienced. So if we were able to locate a group of children who had been raised in impoverished institutions with very limited contact with caregivers over the first two years, we could compare their intellectual development with that of children raised at home with their families. This comparison would provide valuable information about the likely impact of early social deprivation on children's intellectual development. (Indeed, precisely this kind of natural experiment is described in detail in Chapter 11.) The "independent variable" in a natural experiment is the "event" that subjects experience (in our example, the social deprivation experienced by institutionalized infants). The "dependent variable" is whatever outcome measure one chooses to study (in our example, intellectual development).

field experiment: an experiment that takes place in a naturalistic setting such as the home, the school, or a playground.

natural (or quasi-) experiment: a study in which the investigator measures the impact of some naturally occurring event that is assumed to affect people's lives.

Let's note, however, that researchers conducting natural experiments do not control the independent variable, nor do they randomly assign participants to experimental conditions; instead, they merely observe and record the apparent outcomes of a natural happening or event. And in the absence of tight experimental control, it is often hard to determine precisely what factor is responsible for any group differences that are found. Suppose, for example, that our socially deprived institutionalized children showed a poorer pattern of intellectual outcomes than did children raised at home. Is the *social deprivation* that institutionalized children experienced the factor that accounts for this difference? Or is it that institutionalized children differed in other ways from family-reared children (for example, were more sickly as infants, were more poorly nourished, or simply had less intellectual potential) that might explain their poorer outcomes? Without randomly assigning participants to treatments and controlling other factors that may vary across treatments (for example, nutrition received), we simply *cannot* be certain that *social deprivation* is the factor responsible for the poor intellectual outcomes that institutionalized children display.

Despite its inability to make precise statements about cause and effect, the natural experiment is useful nonetheless. Why? Because it can tell us whether a natural event could *possibly* have influenced those who experienced it and, thus, can provide some meaningful clues about cause and effect.

Concept Check 1-2 ∨ Detecting Relationships

Check your understanding of the meaning of various relationships that developmentalists might detect as described in items 1 and 2. Answers appear in the Appendix.

1. Jo Brown finds that the better children feel about themselves (that is, the higher their *self-esteem* as reported in an interview), the higher their grades at school. Check any *acceptable* conclusions based on these data.

    _____ a. Low grades cause low self-esteem.

    _____ b. Self-esteem and grades earned are positively correlated.

    _____ c. Having high self-esteem causes children to earn good grades.

    _____ d. Youngsters with low self-esteem tend to earn poorer grades than those with high self-esteem.

    _____ e. Self-esteem and grades earned are negatively correlated.

2. Ike Chang assigns ten boys to a condition in which they receive positive feedback about their academic abilities, a manipulation that increases their self-esteem. Ten girls in the same class receive no such feedback. Chang then finds that the ten boys earn higher grades over the course of the next year than the ten girls do. He might conclude that:

    _____ a. Increases in self-esteem cause children to earn higher grades.

    _____ b. Increases in self-esteem cause boys, but not girls, to earn higher grades.

    _____ c. Children who are inclined to show improvements in their grades are most susceptible to manipulations designed to increase their self-esteem.

    _____ d. None of the above; Chang's experiment has failed to control for confounding variables (name one if you choose this answer).

Designs to Measure Developmental Change

Developmentalists are not merely interested in examining people's progress at one particular phase of life; instead, they hope to determine how people's feelings, thoughts, abilities, and behaviors *develop* or *change* over time. How might we design research to chart these developmental trends? Let's briefly consider three approaches: the cross-sectional design, the longitudinal design, and the sequential design.

The Cross-Sectional Design

In a **cross-sectional design,** people who *differ in age* are studied at *the same point in time.* By comparing the responses of participants in the different age groups, investigators can often identify age-related changes in whatever aspect of development they happen to be studying.

An experiment by Brian Coates and Willard Hartup (1969) is an excellent example of a cross-sectional comparison. Coates and Hartup were interested in determining why preschool children are less proficient than first- or second-graders at learning new responses displayed by an adult model. Their hypothesis was that younger children do not spontaneously *describe* what they are observing, whereas older children will produce verbal descriptions of the modeled sequence. When asked to perform the actions they have witnessed, the preschoolers are at a distinct disadvantage because they have no verbal "learning aids" that would help them to recall the model's behavior.

To test these hypotheses, Coates and Hartup designed an interesting cross-sectional experiment. Children from two age groups (4- to 5-year-olds and 7- to 8-year-olds) watched a short film in which an adult model displayed 20 novel responses, such as throwing a beanbag between his legs, lassoing an inflatable toy with a Hula Hoop, and so on. Some of the children from each age group were instructed to describe the model's actions, and they did so as they watched the film (induced-verbalization condition). Other children were not required to describe the model's actions as they observed them (passive-observation condition). When the show ended, each child was taken to a room that contained the same toys seen in the film and was asked to demonstrate what the model had done with these toys.

Three interesting findings emerged from this experiment (the data appear in Figure 1-2). First, the 4- to 5-year-olds who were *not* told to describe what they had seen (that is, the passive observers) reproduced *fewer* of the model's responses than the 4- to 5-year-olds who described the model's behavior (the induced verbalizers) or the 7- to 8-year-olds in either experimental condition. This finding suggests that 4- to 5-year-old children may not produce the verbal descriptions that would help them to learn unless they are explicitly instructed to do so. Second, the performance of younger and older children in the induced-verbalization condition was comparable. So younger children can learn just as much as older children by observing a social model *if the younger children are told to describe what they are seeing.* Finally, 7- to 8-year-olds in the passive-observation condition reproduced about the same number of behaviors as 7- to 8-year-olds in the induced-verbalization condition. This finding suggests that instructions to describe the model's actions had little effect on 7- to 8-year-olds, who will apparently describe what they have seen even when not told to do so. Taken together, the results imply that 4- to 5-year-olds may often learn less from social models because they, unlike older children, do not spontaneously produce the verbal descriptions that would help them to remember what they have observed.

An important advantage of the cross-sectional design is that the investigator can collect data from children of different ages over a short time. For example, Coates and Hartup did not have to wait three years for their 4- to 5-year-olds to become 7- to 8-year-olds in order to test their developmental hypotheses. They merely sampled from two age groups and tested both samples simultaneously. Yet there are two important limitations of cross-sectional research.

Cohort effects. Notice that in cross-sectional research, participants at each age level are *different* people. That is, they come from different cohorts, where a *cohort* is defined as a group of people of the same age who are exposed to similar cultural environments and historical events as they are growing up. The fact that cross-sectional comparisons always involve different cohorts can create a thorny interpretive problem, for any age differences that are found in the study may not always

cross-sectional design: a research design in which subjects from different age groups are studied at the same point in time.

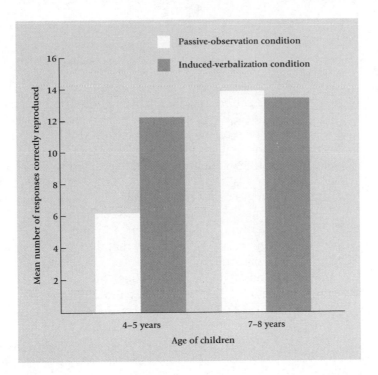

Figure 1-2
Children's ability to reproduce the behavior of a social model as a function of age and verbalization instructions.
Adapted from Coates & Hartup, 1969.

be due to age or development but, rather, may reflect other cultural or historical factors that distinguish members of different cohorts. Stated another way, cross-sectional comparisons *confound age and cohort effects.*

An example should clarify the issue. For years, cross-sectional research had consistently indicated that young adults score slightly higher on intelligence tests than do middle-aged adults, who, in turn, score much higher than the elderly. But does intelligence decline with age, as these findings would seem to indicate? Not necessarily! More recent research (Schaie, 1965; 1986) revealed that individuals' intelligence test scores remain relatively stable over the years and that the earlier studies were really measuring something quite different: age differences in education. The older adults in the cross-sectional studies had had less schooling and, therefore, scored lower on intelligence tests than did the middle-aged and young adult samples. Their test scores had not declined but, rather, had always been lower than those of the younger adults with whom they were compared. So the earlier cross-sectional research had discovered a **cohort effect,** not a true developmental change.

Despite this important limitation, the cross-sectional comparison is still the design used most often by developmentalists. Why? Because it has the great advantage of being quick and easy; we can go out this year, sample individuals of different ages, and be done with it. Moreover, this design is likely to yield valid conclusions when there is little reason to believe that the cohorts being studied have had widely different experiences while growing up. So if we compared 4- to 5-year-olds with 7- to 8-year-olds, as Coates and Hartup did, we might feel reasonably confident that history or the prevailing culture had not changed in any major way in the three years that separate these two cohorts. It is mainly in studies that attempt to make inferences about development over a span of many years that cohort effects are a serious problem.

Data on individual development. There is a second noteworthy limitation of the cross-sectional design: It tells us nothing about the development of *individuals* because each person is observed *at only one point in time.* So cross-sectional comparisons cannot provide answers to questions such as "When will *my* child become more independent?" or "Will aggressive 2-year-olds become aggressive 5-year-olds?" To address

cohort effect: age-related difference among cohorts that is attributable to cultural/historical differences in cohorts' growing-up experiences rather than to true developmental change.

issues like these, investigators often turn to a second kind of developmental comparison, the longitudinal design.

The Longitudinal Design

In a **longitudinal design**, the same participants are observed repeatedly over a period of time. The time period may be relatively brief—six months to a year—or it may be very long, spanning a lifetime. The researchers may be studying one particular aspect of development, such as intelligence, or many. By repeatedly testing the same participants, investigators can assess the *stability* of various attributes for each person in the sample. They can also identify normative developmental trends and processes by looking for commonalities, such as the point(s) at which most children undergo various changes and the experiences, if any, that children seem to share prior to reaching these milestones. Finally, tracking several participants over time will help investigators to understand *individual* (or idiographic) *differences* in development, particularly if they are able to establish that different kinds of earlier experiences lead to very different outcomes.

One of the most famous longitudinal projects in the history of developmental psychology began in 1929 at the Fels Research Institute in Yellow Springs, Ohio (Kagan & Moss, 1962). Imagine that you had been a new parent in 1929 and had responded to an ad requesting that you bring your newborn infant to the Fels Institute. The purpose of your visit: so that you and your child might participate together in an exciting new research project. When you arrive, a member of the Fels staff explains that this project is an ambitious one that will teach us a great deal about the child's world and the ways children develop. As he describes the project further, you suddenly realize that he is asking you to submit to at least one interview a year and to have your child weighed, measured, tested, and observed, both at home and at school, *for the next 18 years!* Would you volunteer? Many mothers did, for the Fels researchers began their longitudinal study with a total of 89 children, 45 males and 44 females.

Can you imagine the work involved in analyzing all this information? Indeed, the data were analyzed, and they allowed members of the research team to draw important conclusions about the long-term stability or instability of behaviors such as aggression, achievement, and sociability. The investigators were also able to make inferences about the effects of various methods of parenting on the child's later perceptions, aspirations, and behavior. Clearly, the Fels project was a monumental undertaking—one that we will refer to again as we continue our journey through the child's world.

Although we have portrayed the longitudinal design in a very favorable manner, the procedure has several potential drawbacks as well. For example, longitudinal projects can be very *costly* (imagine the bill for 18 years of research in the Fels study) and *time consuming.* The latter point is more important than it may first appear, for the focus of theory and research in developmental psychology is constantly changing, and longitudinal questions that seem very exciting at the beginning of a long-term project may seem rather trivial by the time the project ends. As longitudinal researchers, we may also have a problem with *subject loss;* children may move away, get sick, or become bored with repeated testing, and they occasionally have parents who, for one reason or another, will not allow them to continue in the study. The result is a smaller and potentially **nonrepresentative sample** that not only provides less information about the developmental issues in question but also may limit the conclusions of the study to those healthy children who do not move away and who remain cooperative over the long run.

There is another shortcoming of very-long-term longitudinal studies that students often see right away—the **cross-generational problem**. Children in a longitudinal project are typically drawn from one cohort and are likely to have very different kinds of growing-up experiences than youngsters from other eras. Consider, for example, how the times have changed since the 1930s and 1940s, when the Fels children were

longitudinal design: a research design in which one group of subjects is studied repeatedly over a period of months or years.

nonrepresentative sample: a subgroup that differs in important ways from the larger group (or population) to which it belongs.

cross-generational problem: the fact that long-term changes in the environment may limit conclusions of a longitudinal project to that generation of children who were growing up while the study was in progress.

Leisure activities of the 1930s (left) and the 1990s (right). As these photos illustrate, the kinds of experiences that children growing up in the 1930s had were very different from those of today's youth. Many believe that cross-generational changes in the environment may limit the results of a longitudinal study to the youngsters who were growing up while the research was in progress.

growing up. In this age of dual-career families, more youngsters are attending day-care centers and nursery schools than ever before. Modern families are smaller than those of years past, meaning that children now have fewer brothers and sisters. Families also move more frequently than they did in the 1930s and 1940s, so that many children from the modern era are exposed to a wider variety of people and places than was typical in years gone by. And no matter where they may be living, today's youngsters grow up in front of television sets and computers, influences that were not available to the Fels children. So children of the 1930s and 1940s lived in a very different world, and we cannot be certain that these youngsters developed in precisely the same way as today's children do. Stated another way, cross-generational changes in the environment may limit the conclusions of a longitudinal project to those children who were growing up while the study was in progress.

We have seen that the cross-sectional and the longitudinal designs each have distinct advantages and disadvantages. Might it be possible to combine the best features of both approaches? A third kind of developmental comparison—the sequential design—tries to do just that.

The Sequential Design

Suppose that we hoped to optimize social development by creating a training program to reduce racial prejudice among 6- to 10-year-olds. Before administering our program on a large scale, we would surely want to try it out on a smaller number of children to see whether it really works. However, there are a number of additional questions that others may have about our program, such as "When can children first understand it?"; "At what age will children respond most favorably to the training?"; and "Do any immediate reductions in prejudice produced by our program persist over time?" To address all these issues in our research, we will need a design that measures *both* the short-term and the long-term effects of our program on children of *different ages*.

Clearly, the cross-sectional comparison, which tests participants at only one point in time, cannot tell us anything about the long-term effects of our program. The longitudinal method can tell us about long-term effects. But since all the participants would be exposed to the program at the same age (say, age 6), a longitudinal study

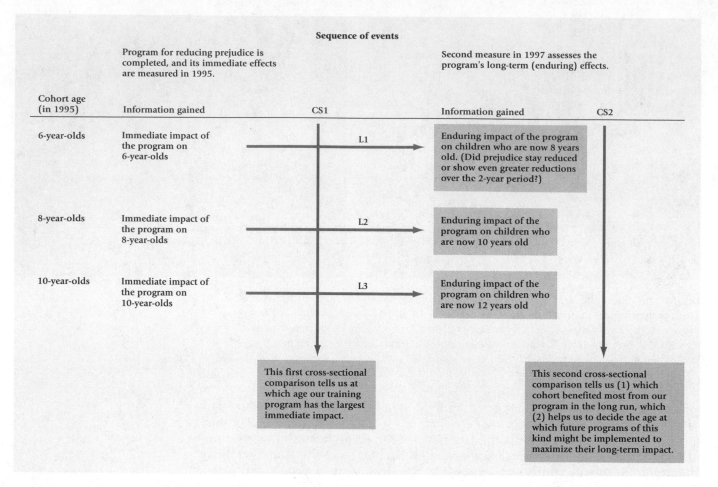

Figure 1-3
Illustration of a simple sequential design and a summary of the information gained
from such a procedure.

would not tell us whether this training would be any more (or less) effective if it were first administered when children were older.

The only approach that allows us to answer all our questions is a **sequential design** (Schaie, 1965; 1986). Sequential designs combine the best features of the cross-sectional and the longitudinal approaches by selecting participants of different ages and then studying each of these cohorts over time. For purposes of our proposed research, we might begin by administering our training program to groups of 6-, 8-, and 10-year-olds. Of course, we would want to randomly assign other 6-, 8-, and 10-year-olds to control groups that are not exposed to the training program. The children who were "trained" would then be observed and compared with their agemates in the control group to determine (1) whether the program was immediately effective at reducing racial prejudice, and if so, (2) the age at which the program had its largest *immediate* impact. This is the information we would obtain had we conducted a standard cross-sectional experiment (see the comparison labeled CS1 in Figure 1-3).

However, our choice of the sequential design allows us to measure the enduring effects of our program by simply retesting our samples of 6-, 8-, and 10-year-olds two years later (see comparisons labeled L1, L2, and L3 in Figure 1-3). This design has several advantages over the standard longitudinal design. The first is a *time saving:* in only two years, we have learned about the long-term effects of the program on those children who are still between the target ages of 6 and 10. A standard longitudinal

sequential design: a research design in which subjects from different age groups are studied repeatedly over a period of months or years.

comparison would require four years to provide similar information. Second, the sequential design actually yields *more information* about long-term effects than the longitudinal approach does. If we had chosen the longitudinal design, we would have data on the long-term effects of a program administered *only* to 6-year-olds. However, the sequential approach allows us to determine whether the program has *comparable* long-term effects when administered to 6-, 8-, and 10-year-olds (see comparison labeled CS2 in Figure 1-3). Clearly, this combination of the cross-sectional and longitudinal designs is a rather versatile alternative to either of those approaches.

We have now discussed a variety of research designs, each of which has definite strengths and weaknesses. To help you review and compare these designs, Table 1-3 provides a brief description of each, along with its major advantages and disadvantages.

Other Research Strategies: Comparative and Cross-Cultural Designs

There are two additional research strategies on which developmentalists often rely: comparative research and cross-cultural comparisons.

Comparative Research

Might we learn anything about human development by studying and attempting to explain the development of various animal species? Developmentalists who conduct **comparative research** certainly think so. Theorists from the ethological tradition (a theoretical approach we will discuss in Chapter 2), for example, study animal behavior in search of the evolutionary underpinnings of similar human behaviors (Hinde, 1989). Other developmentalists have raised animals (for example, chimpanzees) in humanlike cultural envirnments, seeking to clarify the role that culture may play in the development of human and animal potentials (see, for example, Tomasello, Savage-Rumbaugh, & Kruger, 1993). Finally, the comparative approach permits researchers to conduct tightly controlled tests of hypotheses in studies that would be prohibited with humans for ethical reasons. For example, a researcher who suspects that early social deprivation has adverse developmental consequences cannot isolate human infants for research purposes. But he or she can test the hypothesis by subjecting infant monkeys to varying degrees of social deprivation and observing the effects of these treatments. In sum, the comparative approach is a valuable research strategy that has helped both human and animal researchers find answers for important developmental questions.

Cross-Cultural Comparisons

Developmentalists are often hesitant to publish a new finding or conclusion until they have studied enough people to determine that their "discovery" is reliable. However, their conclusions are frequently based on subjects living at one point in time within one particular culture or subculture, and it is difficult to know whether these conclusions will apply to future generations or even to children currently growing up in other societies or subcultures (Lerner, 1991). Today, the generalizability of findings across samples and settings has become an important issue, for many theorists have implied that there are "universals" in human development—events and outcomes that all children share as they progress from infancy to adulthood.

Cross-cultural studies are those in which participants from different cultural or subcultural backgrounds are observed, tested, and compared on one or more aspects of development. Studies of this kind serve many purposes. For example, they allow the investigator to determine whether conclusions drawn about the development of children from one social context (such as middle-class, white youngsters in the United States) also characterize children growing up in other societies or even those from different ethnic or socioeconomic backgrounds within the same society (for

comparative research: an approach whereby investigators compare behavior and/or development across species.

BOX 1-3
A Cross-Cultural Comparison of Gender Roles

One of the greatest values of cross-cultural comparisons is that they can tell us whether a developmental phenomenon is or is not universal. Consider the roles that males and females play in our society. In our culture, playing the masculine role has traditionally required traits such as independence, assertiveness, and dominance. By contrast, females are expected to be more nurturant and sensitive to other people. Are these masculine and feminine roles universal? Could biological differences between the sexes lead inevitably to sex differences in behavior?

Some years ago, anthropologist Margaret Mead (1935) compared the gender roles adopted by people in three tribal societies on the island of New Guinea, and her observations are certainly thought provoking. In the Arapesh tribe, both men and women were taught to play what we would regard as a feminine role: They were cooperative, nonaggressive, and sensitive to the needs of others. By contrast, both men and women of the Mundugumor tribe were brought up to be aggressive and emotionally unresponsive to other people—a masculine pattern of behavior by Western standards. Finally, the Tchambuli displayed a pattern of gender-role development that was the direct opposite of the Western pattern: Males were passive, emotionally dependent, and socially sensitive, whereas females were dominant, independent, and assertive!

Mead's cross-cultural comparison suggests that cultural learning may have far more to do with the characteristic behavior patterns of men and women than biological differences do. So we very much need cross-cultural comparisons such as Mead's. Without them, we might easily make the mistake of assuming that whatever holds true in our society holds true everywhere; with their help, we can begin to understand the contributions of biology and environment to human development.

The roles assumed by men and women may vary dramatically from culture to culture.

example, American children of Hispanic ancestry or those from economically disadvantaged homes). So the **cross-cultural comparison** guards against the overgeneralization of research findings and, indeed, is the only way to determine whether there are truly "universals" in human development.

However, many investigators who favor the cross-cultural approach are looking for *differences* rather than similarities. They recognize that human beings develop in societies that have very different ideas about issues such as the proper times and procedures for disciplining children, the activities that are most appropriate for boys and for girls, the time at which childhood ends and adulthood begins, the treatment of the aged, and countless other aspects of life. They have also learned that people from various cultures differ in the ways they perceive the world, express their emotions, think, and solve problems. So apart from its focus on universals in development, the cross-cultural approach also illustrates that human development is heavily influenced by the cultural context in which it occurs (see Box 1-3 for a dramatic illustration of cultural influences on gender roles).

Isn't it remarkable how many methods and designs that developmentalists have at their disposal? This diversity of available procedures is a definite strength because findings gained through one procedure can then be checked and perhaps confirmed through other procedures. Indeed, providing such *converging evidence* serves a most important function by demonstrating that the discovery one has made is truly a "discovery" and not merely an artifact of the method or the design used to collect the original data. So there is no "best method" for studying children and adolescents; each of the approaches we have considered has contributed substantially to our understanding of human development.

cross-cultural comparison: a study that compares the behavior and/or development of people from different cultural or subcultural backgrounds.

Table 1-3   An Overview of Commonly Used Research Designs

Design	Procedure	Strengths	Limitations
General designs			
Correlational	Gathers information about two or more variables without researcher intervention.	Estimates the strength and direction of relationships among variables in the natural environment.	Does not permit determination of cause-and-effect relationships among variables.
Laboratory experiment	Manipulates some aspect of subjects' environment (independent variable) and measures its impact on subjects' behavior (dependent variable).	Permits determination of cause-and-effect relationships among variables.	Data obtained in artificial laboratory environment may lack generalizability to the real world.
Field experiment	Manipulates independent variable and measures its impact on the dependent variable in a natural setting.	Permits determination of cause-and-effect relationships and generalizability of findings to the real world.	Experimental treatments may be less potent and harder to control when presented in the natural environment.
Natural (quasi-) experiment	Gathers information about the behavior of people who experience a real-world (natural) manipulation of their environment.	Permits a study of the impact of natural events that would be difficult or impossible to simulate in an experiment; provides strong clues about cause-and-effect relationships.	Lack of precise control over natural events or the participants exposed to them prevents the investigator from establishing definitive cause-and-effect relationships.
Developmental designs			
Cross-sectional	Observes people of different ages (or cohorts) at one point in time.	Demonstrates age differences and hints at developmental trends; relatively inexpensive; takes little time to conduct.	Age trends may reflect extraneous differences among cohorts rather than true developmental change; provides no data on the development of individuals because each participant is observed at only one point in time.
Longitudinal	Observes people of one cohort repeatedly over time.	Provides data on the development of individuals; can reveal links between early experiences and later outcomes; indicates how individuals are alike and how they are different in the ways they change over time.	Relatively time consuming and expensive; subject loss may yield nonrepresentative sample that limits the generalizability of one's conclusions; cross-generational changes may limit one's conclusions to the cohort that was studied.
Sequential	Combines the cross-sectional and the longitudinal approaches by observing different cohorts repeatedly over time.	Discriminates true developmental trends from cohort effects; indicates whether developmental changes experienced by one cohort are similar to those experienced by other cohorts; often less costly and time consuming than the longitudinal approach.	More costly and time consuming than cross-sectional research; despite being the strongest design, may still leave questions about whether a developmental change is generalizable beyond the cohorts that were studied.

Concept Check 1-3 ∨ Selecting a Design

Check your understanding of the uses and strengths of various developmental designs by selecting a design that seems most appropriate for each of the following research questions. Choose from the following designs: (a) cross-sectional, (b) longitudinal, (c) sequential, (d) cross-cultural. Answers appear in the Appendix.

_____ 1. A researcher wants to quickly assess whether 4-, 6-, and 8-year-olds differ in their willingness to donate part of their allowance to children less fortunate than themselves.

_____ 2. A researcher who has money for a 6-week summer preschool education program wants to know whether the program will have greater long-term benefits for 2-year-olds than for 3- or 4-year-olds.

_____ 3. A developmentalist hopes to determine whether all children go through the same stages of intellectual development between infancy and adolescence.

_____ 4. A specialist in early childhood education hopes to learn whether especially bright 2-year-olds are likely to remain smarter than most peers by the time they are 6 years old.

ETHICAL CONSIDERATIONS IN DEVELOPMENTAL RESEARCH

When designing and conducting research with humans, researchers may face thorny issues centering on **research ethics**—the standards of conduct that investigators are ethically bound to honor in order to protect their research participants from physical or psychological harm. Some ethical issues are easily resolved: One simply does *not* conduct experiments that will almost certainly cause physical or psychological damage—experiments in which participants are physically abused, starved, isolated for long periods, and the like. However, most ethical issues are far more subtle. Here are some of the dilemmas that developmentalists may have to resolve during their careers as researchers:

- Can I expose children to temptations that virtually guarantee that they will violate certain prohibitions?
- Can I ask children or adolescents about the ways that their parents punish them, or is this line of questioning an invasion of the family's privacy?
- Am I ever justified in deceiving children, either by misinforming them about the purpose of my study or by telling them something untrue about themselves (for example, "You did poorly on this test")?
- Can I observe my participants in the natural setting without informing them that they are the subjects of a scientific investigation?
- Is it acceptable to tell children that their classmates think that an obviously incorrect answer is "correct" to see whether participants will conform to the judgments of their peers?
- Am I justified in using verbal disapproval as part of my research procedure?

Before reading further, you may wish to think about these issues and formulate your own opinions. Then read Table 1-4 and reconsider each of your viewpoints.

Have any of your opinions changed? It would not be terribly surprising if they hadn't. As you can see, the guidelines in Table 1-4 are very general; they do not explicitly permit or prohibit specific operations or practices such as those described in the dilemmas. In fact, any of the dilemmas outlined above can be resolved in ways that permit an investigator to use the procedures in question and still remain well within current ethical guidelines. For example, it is generally considered permissible to observe young children in natural settings (for example, at school or in a park) without informing them that they are being studied if the investigator has previously obtained the *informed consent* (see Table 1-4) of the adults responsible for the children's care and safety in these settings. Ethical guidelines are just that: guidelines. The

research ethics: standards of conduct that investigators are ethically bound to honor in order to protect their research participants from physical or psychological harm.

Table 1-4   Major Rights of Children and Responsibilities of Investigators Involved in Psychological Research

Ethical considerations are especially complex when children participate in psychological research. Children are more vulnerable than adolescents and adults to physical and psychological harm. Moreover, young children may not always fully understand what they are committing themselves to when they agree to participate in a study. In order to protect children who participate in psychological research and to clarify the responsibilities of researchers who work with children, the American Psychological Association (1982) and the Society for Research in Child Development (1990) have endorsed special ethical guidelines, the more important of which are as follows:

*Protection from harm**

The investigator may use no research operation that may harm the child either physically or psychologically. Psychological harm, to be sure, is difficult to define; nevertheless, its definition remains the responsibility of the investigator. When the investigator is in doubt about the possible harmful effects of the research operations, he or she should seek consultation from others. When harm seems possible, he or she is obligated to find other means of obtaining the information or abandon the research.

Informed consent

The informed consent of parents as well as others who act in the child's behalf—teachers, superintendents of institutions—should be obtained, preferably in writing. Informed consent requires that the parent or other responsible adult be told all features of the research that may affect his or her willingness to allow the child to participate. Moreover, federal guidelines in the United States specify that all children 7 years of age and older have the right to have explained to them, in understandable language, all aspects of the research that could affect their willingness to participate. Child participants (and adults responsible for them) always have the right to discontinue participation in research at any time. (This provision is a tricky one, however: Even if they are told that they can stop participating in a study at any time, young children may not really grasp how to go about doing so or may not really believe that they can stop without incurring a penalty of some kind [Abramovitch et al., 1991]).

Confidentiality

Researchers must keep in confidence all information obtained from research participants. Children have the right to concealment of their identity on all data collected and reported, either in writing or informally. (Exception: some states have laws that prohibit an investigator from withholding the names of suspected victims of child abuse.)

Deception/debriefing/knowledge of results

Although children have the right to know the purposes of a study in advance, a particular project may necessitate concealment of information or deception. Whenever concealment or deception is thought to be essential to the conduct of research, the investigator must satisfy a committee of peers that this judgment is correct. If deception or concealment is used, participants must later be *debriefed*—that is, told, in language they can understand, the true purpose of the study and why it was necessary to deceive them. Children also have the right to be informed, in language they can understand, of the results of the research in which they have participated.

---

*Ross Thompson (1990) has recently published an excellent essay on this topic—one that I would recommend to anyone who conducts (or plans to conduct) research with children.

ultimate responsibility for treating children fairly and protecting them from harm falls squarely on the shoulders of the investigator.

How, then, do investigators decide whether to use a procedure that some may consider questionable on ethical grounds? They generally weigh the advantages and

Ethical considerations may force an investigator to abandon procedures that cause harm or pose unforeseen risks to research participants.

disadvantages of the research by carefully calculating its possible *benefits* (to humanity or to the participants) and comparing them against the potential *risks* that participants may face. If the potential benefits greatly outweigh the potential risks, and if there are no other less-risky procedures that could be used to produce these same benefits, the investigator will generally proceed. However, there are safeguards against overzealous researchers who underestimate the riskiness of their procedures. In the United States, for example, universities, research foundations, and government agencies that fund research with children have set up "human-subjects review committees" to provide second (and sometimes third) opinions on the ethical ramifications of all proposed research. The function of these review committees is to reconsider the potential risks and benefits of the proposed research and, more important, to help ensure that all possible steps are taken to protect the welfare of those who may choose to participate in the project.

Of course, final approval of one's procedures by a review committee does not absolve an investigator of the need to reevaluate the benefits and costs of his or her projects, even while the research is in progress (Thompson, 1990). Suppose, for example, that a researcher studying children's aggression in a playground setting came to the conclusion that her subjects had (1) discovered her own fascination with aggressive behavior and (2) begun to beat on one another in order to attract her attention. At that point, the risks to participants would have escalated far beyond the researcher's initial estimates, and she would have been ethically bound (in my opinion) to stop the research immediately.

In the final analysis, guidelines and review committees do not guarantee that research participants will be treated responsibly; only investigators can do that, by constantly reevaluating the consequences of their operations and by modifying or abandoning any procedure that may compromise the welfare or the dignity of those who have volunteered to participate.

▶ POSTSCRIPT: ON BECOMING A WISE CONSUMER OF DEVELOPMENTAL RESEARCH

At this point, you may be wondering "Why do I need to know so much about the methods that developmentalists use to conduct research?" This is a reasonable question given that the vast majority who take this course will pursue other careers and will never conduct a scientific study of developing children or adolescents. So why not simply present the research findings and skip the methodological details?

My answer is straightforward: Although survey courses such as this one are designed to provide a solid overview of theory and research in the discipline to which they pertain, they should also strive (in my opinion, at least) to help you evaluate the relevant information you may encounter in the years ahead. And you will encounter such information; even if you don't read academic journals in your role as a teacher, school administrator, nurse, probation officer, social worker, or other professional who works with developing persons, then certainly you will be exposed to such information through the popular media—television, newspapers, magazines, and the like. How can you know whether that seemingly dramatic and important new finding you've just read or heard about should be taken seriously?

This is an important issue, for new information about human development is often chronicled in the popular media several months or even years before the data on which the media reports are based finally make their appearance in professional journals (if they ever do). Professional journals are slow. Scientists' oral convention presentations, which are often the sources of popular media reports, must first be written, submitted for publication, and examined by other expert reviewers (who often suggest necessary revisions that are made, rereviewed, and often revised again) before a decision is made to publish the research in an academic journal. This professional publication process may take anywhere from one and a half to four years! Moreoever, less than 30% of the papers that developmentalists submit are judged sufficiently worthy of publication by the most rigorous and reputable journals in our discipline. So many media reports of "dramatic" new findings are based on research that other scientists don't view as very dramatic (or even worthy of publication) after all.

Even if a media report is based on a published article, coverage of the research and its conclusions is often misleading. For example, one recent network story reported on a published article, saying that there was clear evidence that "alcoholism is inherited." As we will see in Chapter 3, this is a far more dramatic conclusion than the authors actually drew. Another metropolitan newspaper report summarized a recent article from the prestigious journal *Developmental Psychology* with the headline "Day care harmful for children." What was never made clear in the newspaper article was the researcher's (Howes, 1990) conclusion that *very-low-quality* day care may be harmful to the social and intellectual development of *some* preschool children but that most youngsters receiving good day care suffer no adverse effects. (The issue of day care and its effects on developing children is explored in depth in Chapter 11.) One major cause of such inaccuracies and overstatements is the fact that many reporters writing about the developmental sciences are not trained science writers and simply lack the background to summarize the findings of developmental research properly.

I don't mean to imply that you can never trust what you read; rather, I'd caution you to be skeptical and to evaluate media (and journal) reports, using the methodological information presented in this chapter. You might start by asking: How were the data gathered, and how was the study designed? Were appropriate conclusions drawn, given the limitations of the method of data collection and the design (correlational vs. experimental; cross-sectional vs. longitudinal) that the investigators used? Were there proper control groups? Have the results of the study been reviewed by other experts in the field and published in a reputable academic journal? And please don't assume that published articles are beyond criticism. Many theses and dissertations in the developmental sciences are based on problems and shortcomings that students have identified in previously published research, and professors in courses such as this one will occasionally assign readings to give students opportunities to critique published research. So take the time to read and evaluate published reports that seem especially relevant to your profession or to your role as a parent. Not only will you have a better understanding of the research and its conclusions, but any lingering questions and doubts you may have can often be addressed through a letter (or a phone call) to the author of the article.

In sum, one must become a knowledgeable consumer in order to get the most out of what the field of human development has to offer. Our discussion of research methodology was undertaken with these objectives in mind, and a solid understanding of these methodological lessons should help you to evaluate properly the research you will encounter, not only throughout this text but in many, many other sources in the years to come.

◢ SUMMARY

Developmental psychology is the largest of several disciplines that study *development*—that is, the systematic changes in the individual that occur between conception and death and that reflect the influence of biological maturation and learning. Developmentalists are particularly concerned with *describing* significant changes in physical growth, mental abilities, emotional expression, and social behavior, with *explaining* why these changes occur, and with intervening to *optimize* such development whenever possible. Although we will focus mainly on the developments of childhood and adolescence in this book, it is important to recognize that human development is a continual and cumulative process that occurs throughout life—a process that is *holistic*, highly *plastic*, and heavily influenced by the historical and cultural contexts in which it occurs.

Children who lived in medieval times (and earlier) were often treated rather harshly by their elders and were afforded few of the rights, privileges, and protections of today's youth. The viewpoints of important social philosophers of the 17th and 18th centuries contributed to a more humane outlook on children and child rearing, and shortly thereafter, people began to observe their sons and daughters and to report their findings in baby biographies. The scientific study of children did not emerge until nearly 1900 as G. Stanley Hall, in the United States, and Sigmund Freud, in Europe, began to collect data and formulate theories about human growth and development. Soon other investigators were conducting research to evaluate and extend these theories, and the study of developmental psychology began to thrive.

Developmental psychology today is a truly objective science. Gone forever are the days when the merits of a theory depended on the social or academic prestige of the theorist. Today, a developmentalist, guided by the scientific method, determines the adequacy of a theory by deriving hypotheses and conducting research to see whether the theory can predict and explain the new observations that he or she has made. There is no room for subjective bias in evaluating ideas; theories of human development are only as good as their ability to account for the important aspects of children's growth and development.

For research to be meaningful, the data that investigators collect must be *reliable* and *valid*. A research method is reliable if it produces consistent, replicable results. The method is valid if it measures precisely what it claims to measure. The most common methods of collecting data on developing children and adolescents include self-report measures such as interviews, questionnaires, case studies, and clinical procedures, and direct behavioral observations that are made either in the natural environment or in structured laboratory settings.

Two general research designs—correlational and experimental—permit researchers to identify relationships among variables that interest them. Although *correlational* studies estimate the strength and the direction of relationships among variables, they cannot specify whether variables are causally related. The *experimental design*, however, does point to cause-and-effect relationships; the experimenter manipulates one (or more) independent variables, controls all other extraneous variables that might affect participants' performance, and then observes the *effect(s)* of the manipulation(s) on one or more dependent variables. Experiments may be performed in the laboratory, or alternatively, in the natural environment, thereby increasing the generalizability of the results. The impact of real-world events that researchers cannot manipulate or control can be studied in natural (quasi-) experiments. However, lack of control over natural events prevents the quasi-experimenter from drawing definitive conclusions about cause and effect.

Cross-sectional, longitudinal, and sequential designs are employed to detect developmental change. The *cross-sectional design*, which compares different age groups at a single point in time, is easy to conduct; but it cannot tell us how individuals develop, and its results may be misleading if the age trends that one observes are actually due to cohort effects rather than to true developmental change. The *longitudinal design* detects developmental change by repeatedly examining the same participants as they grow older. Though it provides information on the development of individuals, the longitudinal design is costly, time consuming, and subject to problems such as cross-generational changes in environments and participant loss (resulting in nonrepresentative samples). The *sequential design*, a combination of the cross-sectional and longitudinal approaches, offers the investigator the best features of both strategies.

Developmentalists often rely on two other research strategies. *Comparative research* is undertaken to identify similarities and differences in the development of animals and humans. *Cross-cultural studies*, in which participants from different cultures and subcultures are compared on one or more aspects of development, are becoming increasingly important. Only by comparing people from many cultures can we identify "universal" patterns of development and, at the same time, demonstrate that other aspects of development are heavily influenced by the social context in which it occurs.

Research conducted with children raises some unique ethical considerations. No matter how important the knowledge that might be gained, care must be taken not to harm children, to gain their informed consent (and/or that of their parents), to keep in confidence the information they provide, and to explain carefully any deception that may have been necessary to collect the data. The knowledge gained from research with children should benefit us all, but it is the responsibility of investigators to guarantee that this knowledge does not come at the expense of the participants who so generously provide it.

Key Terms

baby biography [12]	development [4]	longitudinal design [28]	reliability [15]
case study [16]	developmental psychology [4]	maturation [5]	research ethics [34]
clinical method [17]		natural (or quasi-) experiment [24]	scientific method [14]
cohort effect [27]	ecological validity [23]		sequential design [30]
comparative research [31]	experimental control [23]	naturalistic observation [18]	structured interview or structured questionnaire [16]
confounding variable [23]	experimental design [22]	nonrepresentative sample [28]	
correlation coefficient [21]	field experiment [24]		structured observation [19]
correlational design [20]	holistic perspective [7]	normative development [5]	
cross-cultural comparison [32]	hypothesis [14]	original sin [12]	tabula rasa [12]
	idiographic development [5]	plasticity [8]	theory [14]
cross-generational problem [28]	independent variable [22]	questionnaire [13]	validity [15]
cross-sectional design [26]	innate purity [12]	random assignment [23]	
dependent variable [22]	learning [5]		

2 Theories of Human Development

In our introductory chapter, we talked only briefly about theories, portraying them as sets of concepts and propositions that describe and explain certain aspects of our experience. We also noted that everyone is a "theorist," for each of us has definite points of view reflecting what we believe to be true about many issues, observations, and events. How important are theories to today's developmentalists? They are so important that many contemporary researchers cannot conceive of how knowledge might be advanced without them. In fact, when developmentalists describe themselves to other developmentalists, they are most likely to mention (1) their primary area of interest (for example, emotional development in infancy) and (2) the theoretical perspectives that guide their research. So a developmentalist's professional identity may depend, in part, on the theories he or she favors.

That's only true in theory, not in practice!

—*Anonymous*

There is nothing as practical as a good theory.

—*Kurt Lewin*

▶ THE NATURE OF SCIENTIFIC THEORIES

A *scientific* theory is a public pronouncement that indicates what a scientist believes to be true about his or her specific area of investigation (Kaplan, 1983). And the beauty of scientific theories is that they help us to organize our thinking about a broad range of observations and events. Imagine what life might be like for a researcher who plugs away at collecting data and cataloging fact after fact without organizing this information around a set of concepts and propositions. Chances are that this person would eventually be swamped by seemingly unconnected facts, thus qualifying as a trivia expert who lacks a "big picture." So theories are of critical importance to developmental psychology (or any other scientific discipline), for each of them provides us with a "lens" through which we might interpret any number of specific observations about developing individuals.

What are the characteristics of a good theory? Ideally, it should be concise, or **parsimonious,** and yet be able to explain a broad range of phenomena. A theory with few principles that accounts for a large number of empirical observations is much more useful than a second theory that requires many more principles and assumptions to explain the same number (or a lesser number) of observations. In addition, good theories are **falsifiable**—that is, capable of making explicit predictions about future events so that the theory can be supported or disconfirmed. And, as implied by the falsifiability criterion, good theories do not limit themselves to that which is already known. Instead, they are **heuristic,** meaning that they build on existing knowledge by continuing to generate testable hypotheses that, if confirmed by future research, will lead to a much richer understanding of the phenomena under investigation (see Figure 2-1).

Clearly, a theory that simply "explains" a set of observations without making any new predictions is neither falsifiable nor heuristic and is of limited scientific value. And even if a theory is parsimonious, falsifiable, and sufficiently heuristic to formulate some hypothesis, it may still be inaccurate, or *invalid*, and may have to be discarded altogether if its predictions are consistently disconfirmed. So it may seem at times that some theoretical pronouncements *are* true only in theory, not in practice. However, there is clearly another side to this issue. Couldn't we argue that even "bad" theories that are later disconfirmed have served a useful purpose by stimulating the new knowledge that led to their ultimate demise? We might also note that good theories survive because they continue to generate new knowledge, much of which may have practical implications that truly benefit humanity. In this sense, there is nothing quite so practical as a *good* theory.

In this chapter, we will examine the basic premises of four broad theoretical perspectives that have each had a major impact on the science of human development: the *psychoanalytic* viewpoint, the *learning* viewpoint, the *cognitive-developmental* viewpoint, and the *evolutionary* viewpoint. Occasionally labeled the "big four" by contemporary writers, these theories could be characterized as the conceptual bedrock of developmental psychology. However, there are several other recent viewpoints that

parsimony: a criterion for evaluating the scientific merit of theories; a parsimonious theory is one that uses relatively few explanatory principles to explain a broad set of observations.

falsifiability: a criterion for evaluating the scientific merit of theories. A theory is falsifiable when it is capable of generating predictions that could be disconfirmed.

heuristic value: a criterion for evaluating the scientific merit of theories. An heuristic theory is one that continues to stimulate new research and new discoveries.

Figure 2-1
The role of theory in scientific investigation.

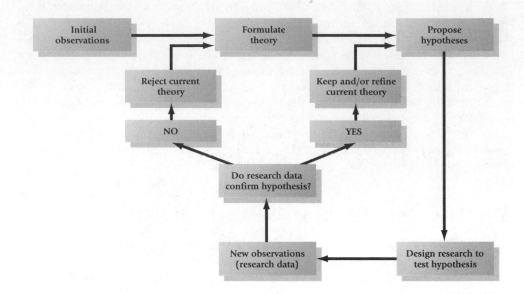

have emerged as extensions of, complements to, or (as some would argue) replacements for the four "grand theories," and we will be considering the strengths and weaknesses of these alternative approaches at various junctures throughout the text. For example, exciting new theories of **behavioral genetics** are introduced in Chapter 3, where we concentrate on hereditary influences on human development. And *information-processing* theory, an important new look at children's intellectual growth with roots in computer science, learning theory, and cognitive-developmental theory, is a central focus of Chapter 8 on intellectual development.

As we will see in the pages that follow, different theories emphasize different areas or aspects of development. In addition, each theory makes different assumptions about human nature and the causes of development. So before reviewing the content of our four "grand theories," it may be helpful to consider some of the more basic issues on which they differ.

 ## QUESTIONS AND CONTROVERSIES ABOUT HUMAN DEVELOPMENT

What are developing humans like? How does development come about? What courses does it follow? Let us look at five major issues on which developmental theories often disagree.

Assumptions about Human Nature

In Chapter 1, we learned that influential social philosophers of the 17th and 18th centuries portrayed children as inherently bad (doctrine of *original sin*), as inherently good (doctrine of *innate purity*), or as neither bad nor good (doctrine of *tabula rasa*). Each of these ideas remains with us today in one or more contemporary theories of human development. Although one may search a theory in vain for explicit statements about human nature, the theorist will typically emphasize either the positive or negative aspects of children's character or perhaps will note that positivity or negativity of character depends on the child's experiences. These assumptions about human nature are important, for they influence the content of each developmental theory, particularly what the theory has to say about child rearing.

behavioral genetics: the scientific study of how one's hereditary endowment interacts with environmental influences to determine such attributes as intelligence, temperament, and personality.

The Nature/Nurture Issue

Is human development primarily the result of nature (biological forces) or nurture (environmental forces)? Perhaps no theoretical controversy has been any more heated than this **nature/nurture issue.** Here are two opposing viewpoints:

> Heredity and not environment is the chief maker of man.... Nearly all of the misery and nearly all of the happiness in the world are due not to environment.... The differences among men are due to differences in germ cells with which they were born [Wiggam, 1923, p. 42].
>
> Give me a dozen healthy infants, well formed, and my own specified world to bring them up in and I'll guarantee to take any one at random and train him to become any type of specialist I might select—doctor, lawyer, artist, merchant, chief, and yes, even beggar-man and thief, regardless of his talents, penchants, tendencies, abilities, vocations, and race of his ancestors. There is no such thing as an inheritance of capacity, talent, temperament, mental constitution, and behavioral characteristics [Watson, 1925, p. 82].

Of course, there is a middle ground, one that is endorsed by most contemporary developmentalists who believe that the relative contributions of nature and nurture depend on the aspect of development in question. However, developmentalists stress that all complex human attributes such as intelligence, temperament, and personality are the end products of a long and involved interplay between biological predispositions and environmental forces (see, for example, Plomin, 1990). Their advice to us, then, is to think less about nature *versus* nurture and more about how these two sets of influences combine or *interact* to produce developmental change.

The Activity/Passivity Issue

Another topic of theoretical debate is the **activity/passivity issue.** Are children curious, active creatures who largely determine how agents of society treat them? Or are they passive souls on whom society fixes its stamp? Consider the implications of these opposing viewpoints. If it could be shown that children are extremely malleable—literally at the mercy of those who raise them—then perhaps individuals who turned out to be less than productive would be justified in suing their overseers for malfeasance. Indeed, one troubled young man in the United States used this logic to bring a malfeasance suit against his parents. Perhaps you can anticipate the defense that the parents' lawyer offered. Counsel argued that the parents had tried many strategies in an attempt to raise their child right but that he responded favorably to none of them. The implication is that this young man played an *active* role in determining how his parents treated him and is largely responsible for creating the climate in which he was raised.

Which of these perspectives do you consider the more reasonable? Think about it, for very soon you will have an opportunity to state your views on this and other topics of theoretical debate.

The Continuity/Discontinuity Issue

Think for a moment about developmental change. Do you think that the changes that we experience occur very gradually? Or would you say that these changes are rather abrupt?

On one side of this **continuity/discontinuity issue** are continuity theorists who view human development as an additive process that occurs gradually and continuously, without sudden changes. They might represent the course of developmental change with a smooth growth curve like the one in Figure 2-2(a). By contrast, discontinuity theorists describe the road to maturity as a series of abrupt changes, each of

nature/nurture issue: the debate within developmental psychology over the relative importance of biological predispositions (nature) and environmental influences (nurture) as determinants of human development.

activity/passivity issue: a debate among developmental theorists about whether children are active contributors to their own development or, rather, passive recipients of environmental influence.

continuity/discontinuity issue: a debate among theorists about whether developmental changes are quantitative and continuous, or, rather, are qualitative and discontinuous (i.e., stagelike).

Figure 2-2
The course of development as described by continuity and discontinuity (stage) theorists.
Based on Berk, 1994. Data from Shaffer, 1977.

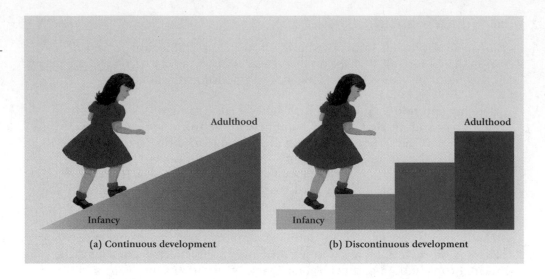

which elevates the child to a new and presumably more advanced level of functioning. These levels, or "stages," are represented by the steps of the discontinuous growth curve in Figure 2-2(b).

A second aspect of the continuity/discontinuity issue centers on whether developmental changes are quantitative or qualitative in nature. Quantitative changes are changes in *degree*. For example, children grow a little taller and run a little faster with each passing year; and they acquire more and more knowledge about the world around them. By contrast, qualitative changes are changes in *kind*, changes that make the individual fundamentally different in some way than he or she was before. The transformation of a tadpole into a frog is a qualitative change. Similarly, we might regard the infant who lacks language as qualitatively different from a preschooler who speaks well, or the adolescent who is sexually mature as fundamentally different from a classmate who has yet to reach puberty. Continuity theorists generally think that developmental changes are basically quantitative in nature, whereas discontinuity theorists tend to portray development as a sequence of qualitative changes.

Interestingly, different societies may take different positions on the continuity/discontinuity issue. Some Pacific and Far Eastern cultures, for example, have words for infant qualities that are never used to describe adults, and adult terms such as *intelligent* or *angry* are never used to characterize infants (Kagan, 1991). People in these cultures view personality development as discontinuous, and infants are regarded as so fundamentally different from adults that they cannot be judged on the same personality dimensions. By contrast, North Americans and northern Europeans are more inclined to assume that personality development is a continuous process and to search for the seeds of adult personality in babies' temperaments.

In sum, continuity theorists hold that developmental changes are gradual and quantitative, whereas discontinuity theorists view these changes as abrupt and qualitative. Indeed, discontinuity theorists are the ones who propose that we progress through **developmental stages,** each of which is a distinct phase of life characterized by a particular set of abilities, emotions, motives, or behaviors that form a coherent pattern. Presumably, each of these stages is qualitatively different than the stage that proceeds or follows it. By contrast, continuity theorists view development as an additive process that occurs continuously and is not at all stagelike.

The Universality/Particularity Issue

Finally, theorists often disagree about whether the most noteworthy aspects of development are *universal* (that is, normative outcomes that everyone is said to display) or *particularistic* (trends or outcomes that vary from person to person). Stage theorists typically believe that their developmental sequences apply to all normal people

developmental stage: a distinct phase within a larger sequence of development; a period characterized by a particular set of abilities, motives, behaviors, or emotions that occur together and form a coherent pattern.

in all cultures and are therefore universal. For example, all normal humans begin to use language at 11–14 months of age, experience cognitive changes that prepare them for school at age 5–7 years, reach sexual maturity during the preteen or teenage period, and show some signs of aging (for example, wrinkles, a decline in certain sensory abilities) by midlife. From this perspective, then, the most important aspects of development are the universal patterns that all humans display.

However, other theorists believe that a singular focus on developmental universals is woefully incomplete. Why? Because it ignores all the factors that conspire to make each of us unique. Paths of development followed in one culture may be very different from those followed in another culture. And within any culture, developmental outcomes may vary across different subcultural or ethnic groups, from family to family, and from individual to individual. So the message of these "particularistic" theorists is that human development can (and does) proceed in many directions and is much less universal than stage theorists would have us believe.

Concept Check 2-1 ⌄ Understanding Controversies about Human Development

Check your understanding of four conceptual controversies about the nature of human development by matching the statements below with one of the following controversies: (a) nature vs. nurture, (b) activity vs. passivity, (c) continuity vs. discontinuity, (d) universal vs. particularistic development. The answers appear in the Appendix at the back of the book.

_____ 1. Infants the world over show the same sequence of cognitive developments, although some infants progress through this sequence much faster than others.

_____ 2. Approximately 50% of the variability in the scores that people make on IQ tests are attributable to the genes they have inherited.

_____ 3. The "American dream" holds that anyone who chooses to can rise above his or her origins to achieve a position of power and influence in society.

_____ 4. Children grow an average of 1–2 in. per year until puberty, when they may display a sudden spurt of 6–10 in. in height in a single year.

These, then, are the major developmental controversies that different theories resolve in different ways. Perhaps you may wish to clarify your own stand on the issues by completing the brief questionnaire in Box 2-1. At the end of the chapter, Box 2-5 indicates how the major developmental theorists might answer these same questions so that you can compare their assumptions about human development with your own.

Now let's begin our survey of the theories, starting with Freud's psychoanalytic approach.

 THE PSYCHOANALYTIC VIEWPOINT

It is difficult to think of a theorist who has had a greater impact on Western thought than Sigmund Freud, the Viennese physician who lived from 1856 to 1939. This revolutionary thinker challenged prevailing notions about human nature by proposing that we are driven by motives and conflicts of which we are largely unaware and that our personalities are shaped by our earliest life experiences. In this section of the chapter, we will first consider Freud's fascinating *psychoanalytic* perspective on human development and then compare Freud's theory with that of his best-known follower, Erik Erikson.

Freud's Psychoanalytic Theory

Central to Freud's psychoanalytic theory is the notion that human beings have powerful biological urges that must be satisfied. What kind of urges? Undesirable ones! Freud (1923/1974) viewed the newborn as a "seething cauldron"—an inherently selfish

BOX 2-1
How Do You Stand on Major Developmental Issues?

1. Children are
   a. creatures whose basically negative or selfish impulses must be controlled.
   b. neither inherently good nor inherently bad.
   c. creatures who are born with many positive and few negative tendencies.
2. Biological influences (heredity, maturational forces) and environmental influences (culture, parenting styles, learning experiences) are thought to contribute to development. Overall,
   a. biological factors contribute more than environmental factors.
   b. biological and environmental factors are equally important.
   c. environmental factors contribute more than biological factors.
3. People are basically
   a. active beings who play a major role in determining their own abilities and traits.
   b. passive beings whose characteristics are molded either by social influences (parents and other significant people, outside events) or by biological factors beyond their control.
4. Development proceeds
   a. through stages, so that the individual changes rather

abruptly into a quite different kind of person than he or she was in an earlier stage.
   b. continuously—in small increments without abrupt changes or distinct stages.
5. Traits such as aggressiveness or dependency
   a. emerge in childhood and remain largely stable over the years.
   b. first appear in childhood but often disappear or give way to quite different traits at some later time.
6. When we compare the development of different individuals, we see
   a. mainly similarities; children and adults develop along universal paths and experience similar changes at similar ages.
   b. mainly differences; different people often undergo different sequences of change and have widely different timetables of development.

			Question			
	1	2	3	4	5	6
Your pattern of answers:	___	___	___	___	___	___

creature who is relentlessly "driven" by two kinds of **instincts** that he called **Eros** and **Thanatos.** Eros, or the *life instinct,* promotes survival by directing life-sustaining activities such as breathing, eating, sex, and the fulfillment of all other bodily needs. By contrast, Thanatos—the *death instinct*—was viewed as destructive forces present in all human beings that are expressed through such behaviors as arson, fistfights, sadistic aggression, murder, and even masochism (harm directed against the self).

Freud also stressed that people are often unaware that these biological instincts are the driving force behind their behaviors. A teenage girl, for example, may not realize that her devotion to the Jane Fonda workout is a way of channeling her strong sexual or aggressive urges along a socially desirable path. As Freud developed his psychoanalytic therapy, he came to rely on such methods as hypnosis, free association (a spontaneous blurting out of one's thoughts), and dream analysis because they gave some indication of patients' **unconscious motives.** Dreams, for example, were assumed to reveal our true desires, unhindered by social prohibitions that tend to suppress these motives when we are awake. By analyzing patients' unconscious motives and the events that caused these motives to become suppressed, Freud concluded that human development is a conflictual process: As biological creatures, we have basic needs that *must* be served; yet society dictates that many of these urges are undesirable and *must* be restrained or controlled. According to Freud, these biosocial conflicts emerge at several points during childhood and play a major role in shaping one's conduct and character.

Three Components of Personality: Id, Ego, and Superego

Freud (1933) claimed that each individual has a fixed amount of *psychic* (or mental) *energy* that can be used to gratify the instincts. As a child develops, this psychic energy

instinct: an inborn biological force that motivates a particular response or class of responses.

Eros: Freud's name for instincts such as respiration, hunger, and sex that help the individual (and the species) to survive.

Thanatos: Freud's name for inborn, self-destructive instincts that were believed to characterize all human beings.

unconscious motives: Freud's term for feelings, experiences, and conflicts that influence a person's thinking and behavior, but lie outside the person's awareness.

is eventually divided among three components of personality: the id, the ego, and the superego.

The id: Legislator of the personality. At birth, the personality is all **id.** The sole function of the id is to serve the instincts by seeking objects that will satisfy them.

Have you ever heard a hungry baby cry until someone comes to feed him? A Freudian would say that the baby's cries and agitated limb movements are energized by the hunger instinct. Presumably, the id directs these actions as a means of attracting the mother or another adult and thereby producing the object (food or, literally, the mother's breast) that reduces hunger.

According to Freud, the id is very impulsive and will seek immediate gratification for instinctual needs. This impulsive thinking (also called "primary-process thinking") is rather unrealistic, however, for the id will invest psychic energy in any object that seems as if it will gratify the instincts, regardless of whether it can. If we had never progressed beyond this earliest type of thinking, we might gleefully ingest wax fruit to satisfy hunger, reach for an empty pop bottle when thirsty, or direct our sexual energies at racy magazines and inflatable love dolls. Perhaps you can see the problem: We would have a difficult time satisfying our needs by relying on our irrational ids. Freud believed that these very difficulties lead to the development of the second component of personality: the ego.

The psychoanalytic theory of Sigmund Freud (1856–1939) changed our thinking about developing children.

The ego: Executive of the personality. According to Freud (1933), the **ego** emerges when psychic energy is diverted from the id to energize important cognitive processes such as perception, learning, and logical reasoning. The goal of the rational ego is to find realistic ways of gratifying the instincts. At the same time, the ego must invest some of its psychic energy to block the id's irrational impulses.

Freud stressed that the ego is both servant and master to the id. It masters the id by delaying gratification until needs can be realistically met. But the ego continually serves the id by weighing alternative courses of action and selecting a plan that will best satisfy the id's basic needs.

The superego: Judicial branch of the personality. The third component of the Freudian personality is the **superego**—the person's internalized moral standards. The superego develops from the ego and strives for *perfection* rather than for pleasure or reality (Freud, 1933). It gradually takes shape as 3- to 6-year-olds *internalize* (take on as their own) the moral values and standards of their parents. Once the superego emerges, children do not need an adult to tell them that they have been good or bad; they are now aware of their own transgressions and will feel guilty or ashamed of their unethical conduct. So the superego is truly an internal censor. It insists that the ego find socially acceptable outlets for the id's undesirable impulses.

Obviously, these three components of personality do not see eye-to-eye and conflict is inevitable. In the mature, healthy personality, a dynamic balance operates: The id communicates basic needs, the ego restrains the impulsive id long enough to find realistic methods of satisfying these needs, and the superego decides whether the ego's problem-solving strategies are morally acceptable. The ego is clearly "in the middle"; it must serve two harsh masters by striking a balance between the opposing demands of the id and the superego, all the while accommodating to the realities of the external world.

According to Freud (1940/1964), psychological problems often arise when the fixed amount of psychic energy that a person has is unequally distributed among the id, ego, and superego. For example, the sociopath who routinely lies and cheats to achieve his aims may have a very strong id, a normal ego, and a very weak superego, having never learned to respect the rights of others. By contrast, a woman who is paralyzed by anxiety at the thought of having sex with her steady may be dominated by an overly strong superego. By using clinical methods to analyze the balances (and imbalances) among the three components of personality, Freud believed that he

id: psychoanalytic term for the inborn component of the personality that is driven by the instincts.

ego: psychoanalytic term for the rational component of the personality.

superego: psychoanalytic term for the component of the personality that consists of one's internalized moral standards.

could explain many individual differences in development and the origins of many psychological disorders.

Stages of Psychosexual Development

Freud viewed the sex instinct as the most important of the life instincts because he often discovered that the mental disturbances of his patients revolved around childhood sexual conflicts that they had **repressed**—that is, forced out of conscious awareness. Sex in childhood! Certainly, the notion of childhood sexuality was among the more controversial of Freud's ideas. Yet, his use of the term *sex* refers to much more than a need to copulate. Many simple bodily functions that most of us would consider rather asexual were viewed by Freud as "erotic" activities.

Although the sex instinct is presumably inborn, Freud (1940/1964) felt that its character changes over time, as dictated by biological maturation. As the sex instinct matures, its energy, or **libido,** gradually shifts from one part of the body to another, and the child enters a new stage of *psychosexual* development. Freud called these stages "psychosexual" to underscore his view that the maturation of the sex instinct leaves distinct imprints on the developing psyche (that is, the mind, or personality).

The oral stage (birth to 1 year). Freud was struck by the fact that infants spend much of the first year spitting, chewing, sucking, and biting on objects, and he concluded that the sex instinct seeks pleasure through the mouth during this **oral stage.** Feeding was thought to be a particularly rich source of oral gratification, and Freud proposed that the child's later psychological development could be very much affected by the mother's feeding practices. For example, an infant girl who was weaned too early could feel deprived of "oral gratification" and might as a woman crave close contact and be overdependent on her husband. Note the implication here: Freud is saying that *early experiences can have a long-term effect on personality development.* In Box 2-2, we will see why Freud believed that early traumas and conflicts are likely to surface in the adult personality.

The anal stage (1 to 3 years). As the sphincter muscles mature in the second year of life, infants acquire the ability to withhold or expel fecal material at will. Not only does voluntary defecation become the primary method of gratifying the sex instinct during this **anal stage,** but infants must endure the demands of toilet training. For the first time, outside agents are regularly interfering with instinctual impulses by insisting that the child inhibit urges to defecate (or urinate) until she reaches a designated locale. Freud believed that the emotional climate parents create while toilet training could leave lasting imprints on the personality. For example, he claimed that children who are harshly punished for their "accidents" are apt to become anxious, inhibited adults who may be messy or wasteful.

The phallic stage (3 to 6 years). We now come to an aspect of Freudian theory that has proved to be very controversial. Freud's view was that 3- to 4-year-old children have matured to the point that their genitals become an interesting and sensitive area of the body. Libido presumably flows to this area as children derive pleasure by fondling their genitals. What is so controversial? According to Freud, all children at this age develop a strong incestuous desire for the parent of the other sex. He called this period the **phallic stage** because he believed that the phallus (penis) assumes a critically important role in the psychosexual development of both boys and girls.

Let's examine this stage for boys. According to Freud, 3- to 4-year-old boys develop an intense sexual longing for their mothers. At the same time, they become jealous: If they could have their way, they would destroy their chief rivals for maternal affection, their fathers. Freud called this state of affairs the **Oedipus complex** after the legendary Oedipus, king of Thebes, who unwittingly killed his father and married his mother.

repression: a type of motivated forgetting in which anxiety-provoking thoughts and conflicts are forced out of conscious awareness.

libido: Freud's term for the biological energy of the sex instinct.

oral stage: Freud's first stage of psychosexual development (from birth to 1 year), in which children gratify the sex instinct by stimulating the mouth, lips, teeth, and gums.

anal stage: Freud's second stage of psychosexual development (from 1 to 3 years of age), in which anal activities such as defecation become the primary methods of gratifying the sex instinct.

phallic stage: Freud's third stage of psychosexual development (from 3 to 6 years of age), in which children gratify the sex instinct by fondling their genitals and developing an incestuous desire for the parent of the other sex.

Oedipus complex: Freud's term for the conflict that 3- to 6-year-old boys experience when they develop an incestuous desire for their mothers and, at the same time, a jealous and hostile rivalry with their fathers.

BOX 2-2

Early Experience, Defense Mechanisms, and the Adult Personality

At each psychosexual stage, the id's impulses and social demands inevitably come into conflict. Even a young infant's seemingly harmless tendency to explore objects with his mouth is likely to put him at odds with his mother, thereby making him anxious, if his explorations frequently center on objects that mother considers inappropriate, such as her lipstick, cigarette butts, or bugs that he has cornered. How do children cope with the conflicts and anxieties that they experience?

Freud (1940/1964) described several mechanisms that children may use to defend themselves (literally, their egos) against the anxieties or uncertainties of growing up. One such defense mechanism—**sublimation**—occurs when the ego finds socially acceptable outlets for unacceptable motives. Freud believed that frequent use of sublimation could have long-term effects on the personality. For example, a teenage girl who habitually sublimates her sexual urges by taking cold showers may become a "cleanliness nut" as an adult.

Another important ego defense mechanism is **fixation,** or arrested development. According to Freud, the child who experiences severe conflicts at any particular stage of development may be reluctant to move or incapable of moving to the next stage, where the uncertainties are even greater. The child may then fixate at the earlier stage, and further development will be arrested or at least impaired. Freud be-

lieved that some people become fixated at the level of primary-process thinking and consequently remain "dreamers" or "unrealistic optimists" throughout their lives. Others fixate on particular behaviors. An example is the chronic thumbsucker whose oral fixation may be expressed later in life in substitute activities such as chain-smoking, incessant talking, or oral sex.

A person who experiences too much anxiety or too many conflicts at any stage of development may retreat to an earlier, less traumatic stage. Such developmental reversals are examples of an ego-defense mechanism that Freud called **regression.** For example, a 4-year-old who is made insecure by the arrival of a new baby in the house may revert to infantile acts, such as temper tantrums or requesting juice from a baby bottle, to attract her share of parental attention. Even well-adjusted adults may regress from time to time in order to forget problems or reduce anxiety. For example, masturbation is one earlier mode of sexual functioning that a person may undertake to reduce sexual conflicts or frustrations. Dreaming is a regressive activity that enables a person to resolve conflicts and obtain pleasure through the magic of wishful thinking.

In sum, Freud insists that the past lives on. He claims that early childhood experiences and conflicts may haunt us in later life and influence our adult interests, behaviors, and personalities.

Now, preschool boys are not as powerful as King Oedipus, and they face certain defeat in their quest to win the sexual favors of their mothers. In fact, Freud suggests that a jealous young son will have many conflicts with his paternal rival and will eventually fear that his father might castrate him for this rivalrous conduct. When this *castration anxiety* becomes sufficiently intense, the boy (if development is normal) will then resolve his Oedipus complex. How? In two ways. First, he will repress his incestuous desires for the mother and partake in no more rivalrous conduct, thereby lessening the chances of castration. And through the process of **identification,** he will seek to emulate his father, incorporating all of the father's attitudes, attributes, and behaviors. Freud believed that there are two important outcomes of a boy's identification with his father: He will learn his masculine sex role, and he will develop a superego by internalizing his father's moral standards.

What about preschool girls? Freud admitted that he was less sure about them. Once a 4-year-old girl discovers that she lacks a penis, she is believed to blame her mother for this "castrated" condition. She transfers her affection from her mother to her father, envies her father for possessing a penis, and hopes that he will share with her the valued organ that she lacks. (Freud assumed that her real underlying motive is to bear her father's child, especially a male child, to compensate for her lack of a penis.) This is the heart of the girl's **Electra complex.**

But how is the girl's conflict resolved? Boys fear castration, and that fear motivates them to identify with their fathers, but what do girls fear? After all, they supposedly believe that they have already been castrated. Freud (1924/1961) assumed that the Electra complex may simply fade away as the girl faces reality and recognizes the impossibility of possessing her father. The next best thing for her may be to identify with her mother, who *does* possess her father.

sublimation: a defense mechanism by which the ego finds socially acceptable outlets for the id's undesirable impulses.

fixation: arrested development at a particular psychosexual stage; often occurs as a means of coping with existing conflicts and preventing movement to the next stage, where stress may be even greater.

regression: a defense mechanism whereby the ego copes with stress and conflict by producing behaviors that are more characteristic of an earlier stage of development.

identification: Freud's term for the child's tendency to emulate another person, usually the same-sex parent.

Electra complex: female version of the Oedipus complex, in which a 3- to 6-year-old girl was believed to envy her father for possessing a penis and to seek him as a sex object in the hope of sharing the organ that she lacks.

According to Freud, a transfer of affection from mother to father occurs in little girls between ages 3 and 5.

Although the inner conflicts of the phallic period may be more emotionally intense for a boy than for a girl, the similarities between the sexes are also clear. Children of each sex value the male phallus: Girls hope to gain one, and boys hope to keep theirs. Moreover, both boys and girls perceive the parent of the same sex as their major rival for the affection of the other parent. And finally, both boys and girls are believed to resolve their conflicts by identifying with the same-sex parent, thereby taking on a "masculine" or "feminine" role and developing a superego.

The latency period (ages 6 to 12). During the **latency period,** or the elementary school years, the sexual conflicts of the phallic stage have been repressed, and libidinal energy is channeled into socially acceptable activities such as schoolwork and vigorous play. The ego and the superego continue to grow stronger, Freud claimed, as the child gains new problem-solving abilities at school and internalizes additional societal values. But this lull in childhood sexuality will end abruptly with the coming of puberty.

The genital stage (age 12 onward). With the onset of puberty comes the **genital stage,** which is characterized by maturation of the reproductive system, an upsurge of sex hormones, and, according to Freud, a reactivation of the genital zone as an area of sensual pleasure. The underlying goal of the sex instinct now becomes biological reproduction through sexual intercourse. However, adolescents face conflicts in learning how to manage these new sexual urges in socially acceptable ways. Throughout adolescence and young adulthood, libido is invested in activities—forming friendships, preparing for a career, courting, and marriage—that prepare the individual to eventually satisfy the mature sex instinct by having children. Here, in the genital stage, is where Freud believed that people remain for the rest of their lives.

Contributions and Criticisms of Freud's Theory

How plausible do you think Freud's ideas are? Do you think that we are all relentlessly driven by sexual and aggressive instincts? Could we really have experienced Oedipus or Electra complexes and simply repressed these traumatic events? Or did Freud get carried away with sex? Could the sexual conflicts that he thought were so important merely have been reflections of the sexually repressive Victorian era in which he and his patients lived?

Few contemporary developmentalists accept all of Freud's theory. For example, there is not much evidence that the oral and anal conflicts of childhood predict one's later personality. Nor is there reason to believe that most children experience Oedipus and Electra complexes. To experience these conflicts, 3- to 6-year-old children would have to recognize the anatomical differences between the sexes, and there is little evidence that they do. In fact, Alan Katcher (1955) found that the majority of 4- to 5-year-olds are inept at assembling a doll so that its genitals match other parts of its body. Even 6-year-olds often made mistakes such as attaching a lower torso containing a penis to an upper body with breasts. Clearly, these "oedipal-aged" children were confused or ignorant about sex differences in genital anatomy (see also Bem, 1989), and it seems highly unlikely that they could be experiencing any castration anxiety or penis envy.

But we cannot reject all of Freud's ideas simply because some of them may seem a bit outlandish. Indeed, contemporary scholars (see, for example, Emde, 1992) have carefully reexamined Freud's work and concluded that there are several reasons why Sigmund Freud will always remain an important figure in the history of the behavioral sciences. Perhaps Freud's greatest contribution was his concept of unconscious motivation. When psychology came into being in the mid-19th century, investigators were concerned with understanding isolated aspects of *conscious* experience, such as sensory processes and perceptual illusions. It was Freud who first noted that these scientists were studying the tip of an iceberg when he proclaimed that the vast major-

latency period: Freud's fourth stage of psychosexual development (age 6 to puberty), in which sexual desires are repressed and the child's available libido is channeled into socially acceptable outlets such as schoolwork or vigorous play.

genital stage: Freud's final stage of psychosexual development (from puberty onward), in which the underlying aim of the sex instinct is biological reproduction.

ity of psychic experience lay below the level of conscious awareness. Freud also deserves considerable credit for focusing attention on the importance of early experience for later development. Debates continue about exactly how critical early experiences are, but few developmentalists today doubt that some early experiences *can* have lasting effects. Finally, we are indebted to Freud for studying the emotional side of human development—the loves, fears, anxieties, and other powerful emotions that play important roles in our lives, as well as the defense mechanisms that we use to cope with emotional conflicts. Unfortunately, these aspects of life have often been overlooked by developmentalists who have tended to concentrate on observable behaviors or rational thought processes.

In sum, Freud was truly a great pioneer who dared to navigate murky, uncharted waters that his predecessors had not even thought to explore. In the process, he changed our views of humankind.

Erikson's Theory of Psychosocial Development

Erik Erikson (1902–1994) emphasized the sociocultural determinants of personality in his theory of psychosocial development.

As Freud became widely read, he attracted many followers. However, Freud's pupils did not always agree with the master, and eventually they began to modify some of Freud's ideas and became important theorists in their own right. Among the best known of these *neo-Freudian* scholars is Erik Erikson.

Comparing Freud with Erikson

Erikson (1963, 1982) accepted many of Freud's ideas. He agreed that people are born with a number of basic instincts and that the personality consists of an id, ego, and superego. He also assumed that development occurs in stages and that the child must successfully resolve some crisis or conflict at each stage in order to be prepared for the crises that will emerge later in life.

However, Erikson is truly a revisionist, for his theory differs from Freud's in several important respects. First, Erikson (1963) stressed that children are *active, adaptive* explorers who seek to control their environment rather than passive creatures who are slaves to their biological urges and are molded by their parents. He has also been labeled an "ego psychologist" because he believed that one must first understand the *realities* of the social world (an ego function) in order to adapt successfully and show a normal pattern of personal growth. So, unlike Freud, who felt that the most interesting aspects of behavior stemmed from conflicts between the id and the superego, Erikson assumed that human beings are basically rational creatures whose thoughts, feelings, and actions are largely controlled by the ego.

Yet another crucial difference between Erikson and Freud is that Erikson placed much less emphasis on sexual urges and much more emphasis on social influences than Freud did. Clearly, Erikson's thinking was shaped by his own varied experiences. He was born in Denmark, raised in Germany, and spent much of his adolescence traveling throughout Europe. After receiving his professional training, Erikson came to the United States, where he studied college students, combat soldiers, civil rights workers in the South, and American Indians. Having observed many similarities and differences in development across these diverse social groups, it is hardly surprising that Erikson emphasized *social* and *cultural* aspects of development in his own theory. In sum, Erikson's approach is truly a new theory of *psychosocial* development, rather than a restatement of Freud's psychosexual viewpoint.

Eight Life Crises

Erikson believed that human beings face eight major crises, or conflicts, during the course of their lives. Each conflict has its own time for emerging, as dictated by both biological maturation and the social demands that developing people experience at particular points in life. Table 2-1 briefly describes each of Erikson's eight crises (or psychosocial stages) and lists the Freudian psychosexual stage to which it

Table 2-1   Erikson's and Freud's Stages of Development

Approximate age	Erikson's stage or "psychosocial" crisis	Erikson's viewpoint: significant events and social influences	Corresponding Freudian stage
Birth to 1 year	**Basic trust versus mistrust**	Infants must learn to trust others to care for their basic needs. If caregivers are rejecting or inconsistent in their care, the infant may view the world as a dangerous place filled with untrustworthy or unreliable people. The mother or primary caregiver is the key social agent.	**Oral**
1 to 3 years	**Autonomy versus shame and doubt**	Children must learn to be "autonomous"—to feed and dress themselves, to look after their own hygiene, and so on. Failure to achieve this independence may force the child to doubt his or her own abilities and feel shameful. Parents are the key social agents.	**Anal**
3 to 6 years	**Initiative versus guilt**	Children attempt to act grown up and will try to accept responsibilities that are beyond their capacity to handle. They sometimes undertake goals or activities that conflict with those of parents and other family members, and these conflicts may make them feel guilty. Successful resolution of this crisis requires a balance: The child must retain a sense of initiative and yet learn not to impinge on the rights, privileges, or goals of others. The family is the key social agent.	**Phallic**
6 to 12 years	**Industry versus inferiority**	Children must master important social and academic skills. This is a period when the child compares him- or herself with peers. If sufficiently industrious, children will acquire the social and academic skills to feel self-assured. Failure to acquire these important attributes leads to feelings of inferiority. Significant social agents are teachers and peers.	**Latency**
12 to 20 years	**Identity versus role confusion**	This is the crossroad between childhood and maturity. The adolescent grapples with the question "Who am I?" Adolescents must establish basic social and occupational identities, or they will remain confused about the roles they should play as adults. The key social agent is the society of peers.	**Early genital (adolescence)**
20 to 40 years (young adulthood)	**Intimacy versus isolation**	The primary task at this stage is to form strong friendships and to achieve a sense of love and companionship (or a shared identity) with another person. Feelings of loneliness or isolation are likely to result from an inability to form friendships or an intimate relationship. Key social agents are lovers, spouses, and close friends (of both sexes).	**Genital**
40 to 65 years (middle adulthood)	**Generativity versus stagnation**	At this stage, adults face the tasks of becoming productive in their work and raising their families or otherwise looking after the needs of young people. These standards of "generativity" are defined by one's culture. Those who are unable or unwilling to assume these responsibilities will become stagnant and/or self-centered. Significant social agents are the spouse, children, and cultural norms.	**Genital**
Old age	**Ego integrity versus despair**	The older adult will look back at life, viewing it as either a meaningful, productive, and happy experience or a major disappointment full of unfulfilled promises and unrealized goals. One's life experiences, particularly social experiences, will determine the outcome of this final life crisis.	**Genital**

corresponds. Note that Erikson's developmental stages do not end at adolescence or young adulthood as Freud's do. Erikson believed that the problems of adolescents and young adults are very different from those faced by parents who are raising children or by the aged who might be grappling with the specter of retirement, a sense of uselessness, and death. Most contemporary developmentalists would definitely agree.

An analysis of the first psychosocial stage—**basic trust versus mistrust**—should help to illustrate Erikson's thinking. Recall that Freud emphasized the infant's oral activities during the first year of life, and he believed that a mother's feeding practices could have a lasting impact on her child's personality. Erikson agreed. However, he went on to argue that what is most important to an infant's later development is not merely the caregiver's feeding practices but, rather, her *overall reponsiveness* to the infant and his needs. To develop a basic sense of trust, infants must be able to count on their primary caregivers to provide food, to relieve discomfort, to come when beckoned, to smile when smiled upon, and to display warmth and affection. And should close companions often neglect, reject, or respond inconsistently to an infant, the child will learn a very simple lesson: Other people are not to be trusted.

The development of trust provides the basis for healthy coping with the second major life crisis, the conflict of **autonomy versus shame and doubt.** Infants who have learned to trust other people are apt to feel sufficiently confident to communicate their wishes and assert their wills. During the "terrible twos" phase, for example, toddlers may loudly proclaim their desire for autonomy by resisting toilet training and by favoring three words to all others: "no," "me," and "mine." However, a toddler who *mistrusts* others may lack the self-confidence to be assertive as a 2-year-old. As a result, he may fail to become autonomous and could experience shame and doubt. A year or two later, this shameful, self-doubting youngster may have difficulty concocting and pursuing "bold plans" during the preschool crisis of **initiative versus guilt,** and may instead be too inhibited to scale the highest rung of the jungle gym or to give Nintendo a try. So Erikson proposes that a successful resolution of each life crisis prepares the individual for the next psychosocial conflict. By contrast, the person who fails to resolve one or more of life's social conflicts is almost certain to encounter problems in the future.

Contributions and Criticisms of Erikson's Theory

Many people prefer Erikson's theory to Freud's because they simply refuse to believe that human beings are dominated by sexual instincts. An analyst like Erikson, who stresses our rational, adaptive nature, is so much easier to accept. In addition, Erikson emphasizes many of the social conflicts and personal dilemmas that people may remember, are currently experiencing, can easily anticipate, or can see affecting people they know.

Erikson does seem to have captured many of the central issues of life in his eight psychosocial stages. Indeed, we will see just how stimulating his ideas have been as we discuss such topics as the emotional development of infants in Chapter 11, the growth of the self-concept in childhood and the identity crisis facing adolescents in Chapter 12, and the influence of friends and playmates on social development in Chapter 16 (see also Sigelman & Shaffer, 1995, for a discussion of Erikson's contributions to the field of adult development). On the other hand, Erikson's theory can be criticized for being vague about the *causes* of development. What kinds of experiences must people have to cope with and successfully resolve various psychosocial conflicts? How exactly does the outcome of one psychosocial stage influence personality at a later stage? Unfortunately, Erikson is not very explicit about these important issues. So his theory is really a *descriptive* overview of human social and emotional development that does not adequately *explain* how or why this development takes place.

basic trust versus mistrust: the first of Erikson's eight psychosocial stages, in which infants must learn to trust their closest companions or else run the risk of mistrusting other people later in life.

autonomy versus shame and doubt: the second of Erikson's psychosocial stages, in which toddlers either assert their wills and attend to their own basic needs or else become passive, dependent, and lacking in self-confidence.

initiative versus guilt: the third of Erikson's psychosocial stages, in which preschool children either develop goals and strive to achieve them or feel guilty when their ambitions are thwarted by others.

Psychoanalytic Theory Today

Freud and Erikson are only two of many psychoanalysts who have had (or are having) a meaningful influence on the study of human development (Tyson & Tyson, 1990). For example, Karen Horney (1967) challenged Freud's ideas about sex differences in development and is now widely credited as a founder of the discipline we know today as the psychology of women. Alfred Adler (1929/1964), a contemporary of Freud's, was among the first to suggest that *siblings* (and sibling rivalries) are important contributors to social and personality development—a proposition we will explore in detail in Chapter 15. And American psychoanalyst Harry Stack Sullivan (1953) wrote extensively about how close, same-sex friendships during middle childhood set the stage for intimate love relationships later in life (see Chapter 16 for a discussion of this and other contributions that friends may make to social and personality development). Although their theories differ in focus, all these *neo-Freudians* place more emphasis than Freud did on *social* influences on development—and much less emphasis on the role of sexual instincts.

But despite the important contributions that Freud and the neo-Freudians have made, many contemporary developmentalists have largely rejected the psychoanalytic perspective. Why? The main reason is that its propositions are very difficult to either falsify or confirm. Suppose, for example, that we wanted to test the basic Freudian hypothesis that the "healthy" personality is one in which psychic energy is evenly distributed among the id, ego, and superego. How could we do it? There are objective tests that we could use to select "mentally healthy" subjects, but we have no instrument that measures psychic energy or the relative strengths of the id, ego, and superego. The point is that many psychoanalytic hypotheses are untestable by any method other than the interview or a clinical approach, and, unfortunately, these techniques are time consuming, expensive, and among the least objective of all methods used to study human development.

Of course, the main reason that so many developmentalists have abandoned the psychoanalytic perspective is that other theories seem more compelling. One theory favored by many is the learning approach, to which we now turn.

 ## THE LEARNING VIEWPOINT

Earlier, we encountered a developmentalist who claimed that he could take a dozen healthy infants and train them to be whatever he chose—doctor, lawyer, beggar, and so on—regardless of their backgrounds or ancestry. What a bold statement! It implies that nurture is everything and that nature, or hereditary endowment, counts for nothing. This claim was made by John B. Watson, a strong proponent of the importance of learning in human development and the father of a school of thought in psychology that came to be known as **behaviorism** (see Horowitz, 1992).

Watson's Behaviorism

A basic premise of Watson's (1913) behaviorism is that conclusions about human development should be based on observations of overt behavior rather than on speculations about unconscious motives or cognitive processes that are unobservable. Moreover, Watson believed that well-*learned* associations between external stimuli and observable responses (called **habits**) are the building blocks of human development. Like John Locke, Watson viewed the infant as a *tabula rasa* to be written on by experience. Children have no inborn tendencies; how they turn out will depend entirely on the environment in which they grow up and the ways in which their parents and other significant people in their lives treat them. According to a behavioral perspective, then, it is a mistake to assume that children progress through a series of distinct stages, dictated by biological maturation, as Freud (and others) have argued. Instead,

John B. Watson (1878–1958) was the father of behaviorism and the first social-learning theorist.

behaviorism: a school of thinking in psychology that holds that conclusions about human development should be based on controlled observations of overt behavior rather than on speculation about unconscious motives or other unobservable phenomena; the philosophical underpinning for the early theories of learning.

habits: well-learned associations between various stimuli and responses that represent the stable aspects of one's personality.

development is viewed as a continuous process of behavioral change that is shaped by the person's unique environment and may differ dramatically from person to person.

To prove just how malleable children are, Watson set out to demonstrate that infantile fears and other emotional reactions are acquired rather than inborn. In one demonstration, for example, Watson and Rosalie Raynor (1920) presented a gentle white rat to a 9-month-old named Albert. Albert's initial reactions were positive ones; he crawled toward the rat and played with it as he had previously with a dog and a rabbit. Then, two months later, came an attempt to instill a fear response. Every time Albert reached for the white rat, Watson would slip behind him and bang a steel rod with a hammer. Did little Albert eventually associate the white rat with the loud noise and come to fear his furry playmate? Indeed he did, thus illustrating that fears are easily learned.

Watson's belief that children are shaped by their environments carried a stern message for parents: that it was they who were largely responsible for what their child would become. Watson (1928) cautioned parents that they should begin to train their child at birth and to cut back on the coddling and babying if they hoped to instill good habits. Treat them, he said,

> . . . as though they were young adults. . . . Let your behavior always be objective and kindly firm. Never hug and kiss them, never let them sit on your lap. . . . Shake hands with them in the morning. Give them a pat on the head if they have made an extraordinarily good job of a difficult task. . . . In a week's time, you will find how easy it is to be perfectly objective . . . [yet] kindly. You will be utterly ashamed at the mawkish, sentimental way you have been handling [your child] (pp. 81–82).

Since Watson's day, several theories have been proposed to explain how we learn from our social experiences and form the habits that Watson viewed as "bricks in the edifice of human development." Perhaps the one theorist who has done more than anyone to advance the behaviorist approach pioneered by Watson was B. F. Skinner of Harvard University.

Skinner's Operant-Learning Theory (Radical Behaviorism)

Through his research with animals, Skinner (1953) recognized a very important form of learning that he believed to be the basis for most of the habits that organisms form. Quite simply, Skinner proposed that both animals and humans will repeat responses that lead to favorable outcomes and will suppress responses that produce unpleasant or unfavorable outcomes. Thus, a rat that presses a bar and receives a tasty food pellet is apt to perform that response again. In the language of Skinner's theory, the freely emitted bar-pressing response is called an *operant*, and the food pellet that strengthens this response (by making it more probable in the future) is called a **reinforcer.** Similarly, a girl may form a long-term habit of showing compassion toward distressed playmates if her parents consistently reinforce her kindly behavior with praise, or a teenage boy may become more studious should such conduct "pay off" in higher grades. **Punishers,** on the other hand, are consequences that suppress a response and decrease the likelihood that it will occur in the future. If the rat who had been reinforced for bar pressing were suddenly given a painful shock each time it pressed the bar, the bar-pressing habit would begin to disappear. Similarly, a teenage girl who is grounded every time she stays out beyond her curfew should become more concerned about being home on time.

Like Watson, then, Skinner believed that the habits that each of us develop result from our unique learning experiences. One boy's aggressive behavior may be reinforced over time because his playmates "give in" to (reinforce) his forceful tactics. Another boy may become relatively nonaggressive because his peers actively suppress

reinforcer: any consequence of an act that increases the probability that the act will recur.

punisher: any consequence of an act that suppresses that act and/or decreases the probability that it will recur.

B. F. Skinner (1904–1990) proposed a learning theory that emphasized the role of external stimuli in controlling human behavior.

(punish) aggressive conduct by fighting back. The two may develop in entirely different directions based on their different histories of reinforcement and punishment. According to Skinner, there is no need to speak of an "aggressive stage" in child development or of an "aggressive instinct" within human beings. Instead, he claimed that the majority of habits that children acquire—the very responses that comprise a "personality" and make us unique—are freely emitted operants that have been shaped by their consequences. So Skinner proposed that the directions in which we develop depend very critically on *external* stimuli (reinforcers and punishers) rather than on internal forces such as instincts, drives, or biological maturation.

In Chapter 8, we will take a closer look at the process of **operant learning** and see that it can provide explanations for many aspects of human development. Today's developmentalists have come to appreciate that human behavior can take many forms and that habits can emerge and disappear over a lifetime depending on whether they have positive or negative consequences (Gewirtz & Pelaez-Nogueras, 1992). Yet many learning theorists believe that Skinner placed far too much emphasis on operant behaviors shaped by *external* stimuli (reinforcers and punishers) while ignoring important *cognitive* contributors to social learning. One such critic is Albert Bandura, who has proposed a social-cognitive theory of human development that is widely respected today.

Bandura's Cognitive Social-Learning Theory

Are we on firm ground in trying to explain human social learning on the basis of research with animals? Bandura (1977, 1986, 1989) doesn't think so. He does agree with Skinner that operant conditioning is an important type of learning, particularly for animals. However, Bandura stresses that humans are *cognitive* beings—active information processors—who, unlike animals, are likely to think about the relationships between their behavior and its consequences, and are often more affected by what they *believe* will happen than by the events they actually experience. Consider your own plight as a student. Your education is costly and time consuming and may impose many demands that you find less than satisfying. Yet, you tolerate the costs and unpleasantries because you can probably *anticipate* greater rewards once you obtain your degree. Your behavior is not shaped by its immediate consequences; if it were, few students would ever make it through the trials and turmoils of college. Instead, you persist as a student because you have *thought about* the long-term benefits of obtaining an education and have decided that they outweigh the short-term costs you must endure.

Nowhere is Bandura's cognitive emphasis clearer than in his decision to highlight **observational learning** as a central developmental process. Observational learning is simply learning that results from observing the behavior of other people (called models). A 2-year-old may learn how to approach and pet the family dog simply by noting how his older sister does it. An 8-year-old may acquire a very negative attitude toward a minority group (as well as derogatory labels for these people) after hearing her parents talk about this group in a disparaging way. Observational learning simply could not occur unless cognitive processes were at work. We must *attend* carefully to the model's behavior, actively digest, or *encode,* what we observe, and then *store* this information in memory if we are to imitate what we have observed at a later date. Indeed, we will see in Chapter 8 that children need not even be reinforced in order to learn this way.

Why does Bandura stress observational learning in his social-learning theory? Simply because this active, cognitive form of learning permits young children to quickly acquire literally thousands of new responses in a variety of settings where their "models" are simply pursuing their own interests and are not trying to teach them anything. In fact, many of the behaviors children attend to, remember, and imitate are actions that models display but would like to discourage—practices such as swearing, smoking, or eating between meals. Bandura's point is that children are continually

operant learning: a form of learning in which freely emitted acts (or operants) become either more or less probable, depending on the consequences that they produce.

observational learning: learning that results from observing the behavior of others.

learning both desirable and undesirable responses by "keeping their eyes (and ears) open," and he is not at all surprised that human development proceeds so very rapidly along so many different paths.

Social Learning as Reciprocal Determinism

Compared with psychoanalytic theory, learning theories may seem rather bleak and barren. Nowhere does one find lists of habits or traits that describe the healthy or the abnormal personality. There are no "stages" in learning theory. Presumably, development proceeds in small steps without sudden changes, and this gradual learning process occurs over the entire life span. In addition, early versions of learning theory were largely tributes to Watson's doctrine of **environmental determinism:** Young, unknowing children were viewed as passive recipients of environmental influence; they would become whatever parents, teachers, and other agents of society groomed them to be. In fact, B. F. Skinner, the famous "radical behaviorist" of recent times, took a position that many students find difficult to accept: Not only are we products of our experiences, but we have little say in determining the character of those experiences. In other words, Skinner (1971) is arguing that "free will," or the concept of conscious choice, is merely an illusion.

Now contrast Skinner's position with that of Bandura (1986; 1989), who has repeatedly emphasized that children are *active*, thinking beings who contribute in many ways to their own development. Observational learning, for example, requires the observer to actively attend to, encode, and retain the behaviors displayed by social models. And children are often free to choose the models to whom they will attend; hence, they have some say about what they will learn from others.

Recently, Bandura (1986) has proposed the concept of **reciprocal determinism** to describe his view that human development reflects an interaction among an "active" person (P), the person's behavior (B), and the environment (E) (see Figure 2-3). Unlike Watson and Skinner, who maintained that the environment (E) shaped the child and her behavior, Bandura and others (most notably Richard Bell, 1979) propose that links among persons, behaviors, and environments are *bidirectional*. Thus, a child might influence his environment by virtue of his own conduct. Consider an example.

Suppose that a 4-year-old discovers that he can gain control over desirable toys by assaulting his playmates. In this case, control over the desired toy is a pleasant outcome that reinforces the child's aggressive behavior. But note that the reinforcer here is produced by the child himself, through his aggressive actions. Not only has bullying behavior been reinforced (by obtaining the toy), but *the character of the play environment has changed.* Playmates who were victimized may become more inclined to "cave in" to the bully, which, in turn, can make him more likely to victimize these patsies in the future (Patterson, Littman, & Bricker, 1967).

Albert Bandura (1925–   ) has emphasized the cognitive aspects of learning in his social-learning theory.

environmental determinism: the notion that children are passive creatures who are molded by their environments.

reciprocal determinism: the notion that the flow of influence between children and their environments is a two-way street; the environment may affect the child, but the child's behavior also influences the environment.

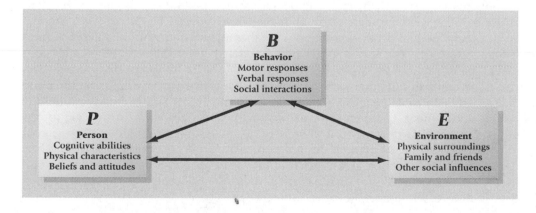

Figure 2-3
Bandura's model of reciprocal determinism.
Adapted from Bandura, 1978.

In sum, cognitive learning theorists believe that human development is best described as a continuous *reciprocal interaction* between children and their environments. The situation or "environment" that a child experiences surely affects her, but her behavior is thought to affect the environment as well. The implication is that children are actively involved in shaping the very environments that will influence their growth and development.

Contributions and Criticisms of Learning Theories

Developmentalists have benefited from the learning viewpoint in many ways. One very positive feature of this approach (indeed, Watson's most enduring legacy; see Horowitz, 1992) is that learning theorists stress *objectivity* in all phases of their work. Their units of analysis are objective behavioral responses, rather than subjective phenomena that are difficult to observe or measure. They carefully define their concepts, test hypotheses, and conduct tightly controlled experiments to provide objective evidence for the suspected causes of developmental change. The success of their approach has encouraged researchers from all theoretical backgrounds to become more objective when studying developing children.

Perhaps the major contribution of the learning viewpoint is the wealth of information it has provided about developing children and adolescents. By observing how their subjects react to various environmental influences, learning theorists have begun to understand how and why children form emotional attachments, adopt sex roles, make friends, become interested in doing well at school, learn to abide by moral rules, and so on. As we will see throughout the text, behavioral learning theories and Bandura's cognitive-social learning theory have contributed immensely to our understanding of many aspects of human development (see also Gewirtz & Pelaez-Nogueras, 1992; Grusec, 1992).

Finally, the learning theorist's emphasis on overt behavior and its immediate causes has produced a number of important clinical insights and practical applications. For example, many problem behaviors can now be quickly eliminated by various behavior modification techniques in which the therapist (1) identifies the reinforcers that sustain undesirable habits and eliminates them while (2) reinforcing alternative behaviors that are more desirable. Thus, distressing antics such as bullying or name-calling can often be eliminated in a matter of weeks, rather than the months (or years) that a psychoanalyst might take probing the child's unconscious, searching for a conflict that may underlie these hostilities.

In spite of its strengths, however, many view the learning approach as a grossly oversimplified account of human development. One group of critics can agree with the behaviorists that development depends very heavily on the contexts in which it occurs. However, they argue that the "environment" that so powerfully influences development is really a series of social systems that interact with each other (and with the individual) in complex ways that are impossible to simulate in a laboratory. In Box 2-3, we will briefly examine this **ecological systems model** and see why its proponents say that only by studying people in their natural settings are we likely to understand how environments truly influence development.

Another clue that behavioral theories are incomplete stems from analyses of individual differences. The learning viewpoint is that people follow different developmental paths because no two persons grow up in exactly the same environment. Yet critics are quick to note that each person comes into the world with something else that provides an equally plausible explanation for his or her "individuality": a unique genetic endowment. Children also mature at different rates, a factor that (1) affects how other people will respond to them (for an interesting example, see the material in Chapter 5 on rate of maturation and popularity) and (2) determines what a person is capable of learning at any given point in life. So learning theorists may have oversimplified the issue of individual differences in development by downplaying the contribution of important biological influences.

ecological systems model: Bronfenbrenner's view emphasizing that the developing person is embedded in a series of environmental systems that interact with one another and with the person to influence development.

BOX 2-3

A New Look at "Environment": The Ecological Perspective

What is this entity we call *environment?* Traditional views offered by Watson and Skinner depict environment as any and all external forces that shape the individual's development. Though modern learning theorists (for example, Bandura, 1986) have backed away from this extremely mechanistic view by acknowledging that environments both influence and *are influenced by* individuals, they continue to provide only vague descriptions of the environmental contexts in which development takes place.

Perhaps the most detailed analysis of environmental influences that has appeared to date is Urie Bronfenbrenner's (1979; 1989) ecological systems model of human development. Bronfenbrenner begins with the assumption that *natural* environments are the major source of influence on developing children—a source often overlooked (or simply ignored) by researchers who choose to study development in the highly artificial context of the laboratory. Bronfen-

brenner (1979) goes on to define "environment" (or the natural ecology) as "a set of nested structures, each inside the next, like a set of Russian dolls" (p. 22). In other words, the developing child is said to be embedded in several environmental systems, ranging from immediate settings such as the family to more remote contexts such as the broader culture (see figure). Each of these systems is thought to interact with the others and with the individual to influence development in complex ways. Let's take a closer look.

Bronfenbrenner's innermost environmental structure, or **microsystem,** consists of the immediate contexts that individuals actually experience. For most young infants, the microsystem may be limited to the family. Yet, this structure eventually becomes much more complex as children mature and are exposed to day care, preschool classes, youth

(continued)

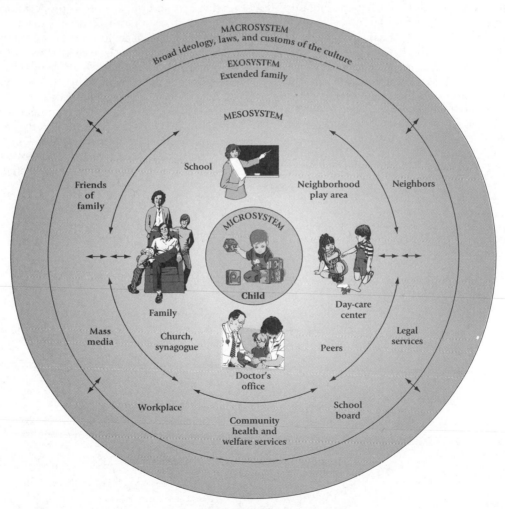

Bronfenbrenner's ecological model of the environment as a series of nested structures. The microsystem refers to relations between the child and the immediate environment, the mesosystem to connections among the child's immediate settings, the exosystem to social settings that affect but do not contain the child, and the macrosystem to the overarching ideology of the culture. Based on Bronfenbrenner, 1979.

BOX 2-3 (continued)

A New Look at "Environment": The Ecological Perspective

groups, and neighborhood play areas. Not only are children apt to be influenced by the people present in their microsystems, but they influence those people as well. For example, an extremely irritable or difficult infant can alienate her parents or even create friction between them that may be sufficient to damage their marital relationship. Microsystems are truly dynamic systems in which each person influences and is influenced by the other persons present.

The next environmental layer, or **mesosystem,** refers to the links or interrelationships among microsystems. Bronfenbrenner believes that children's development is likely to be optimized by strong, supportive links between microsystems. For example, toddlers who have established secure emotional ties to their parents may be well prepared to approach and cooperate with other children upon entering day care. A child's ability to master arithmetic in elementary school may depend not only on the instruction his teacher provides, but also on the extent to which such scholastic activities are valued and encouraged at home.

Bronfenbrenner's third environmental layer, or **exosystem,** consists of settings that children never experience directly but which may still affect their development. For example, children's emotional relationships at home can be influenced considerably by whether or not their parents enjoy their work. Similarly, children's experiences in school may also be affected by their exosystem—by a social integration plan adopted by the school board, or by a plant closing in their community that results in a decline in the school's revenue.

Finally, Bronfenbrenner stresses that development always takes place in a **macrosystem**—that is, a cultural or subcultural context in which microsystems, mesosystems, and exosystems are imbedded. The macrosystem is really a broad, overarching ideology that dictates (among other things) how children should be treated, what they should be taught, and the goals for which they should strive. Of course, these values differ from culture to culture (and across subcultures) and can greatly influence the kinds of experiences children have in their homes, neighborhoods, schools, and all other contexts that affect them, directly or indirectly. To cite one example, the incidence of child abuse in families (a microsystem experience) is much lower in those cultures (or macrosystems) that discourage physical punishment of children and advocate nonviolent ways of resolving interpersonal conflict (Belsky, 1980; Levinson, 1989).

Although we have barely touched on the ecological perspective here and will explore its propositions throughout the text, perhaps you can already see that it provides a much richer description of environment (and environmental influences) than anything offered by learning theorists. Each of us functions in particular microsystems that are linked by a mesosystem and embedded in the larger contexts of an exosystem and a macrosystem. It makes little sense to an ecological theorist to try to study environmental influences in contrived laboratory contexts. Instead, they argue that only by observing transactions between developing persons and their ever-changing *natural* settings will we ever understand how individuals influence and are influenced by their environments.

Concept Check 2-2 ⌄ Understanding the Positions of Four Major Theorists: Freud, Erikson, Skinner, and Bandura

Check your understanding of the implications of some of the major theories reviewed in this chapter by indicating who is likely to have made each statement quoted below. Choose from the following: (a) Sigmund Freud, (b) Erik Erikson, (c) B. F. Skinner, (d) Albert Bandura. The answers appear in the Appendix.

_____ 1. "Growing is . . . differentiation during a sequence of critical periods. In personality growth, it is a task of the ego and of the social processes together [so that] at all times a human being is an ego and a member of society."

_____ 2. "Cognition has causal influence on behavior. A theory that denies that thoughts can regulate actions does not lend itself . . . to the explanation of complex human behavior."

_____ 3. "In the traditional view, a person is free. . . . He can therefore be held responsible for what he does and justly punished if he offends. That view must be reexamined when a scientific analysis reveals unsuspected controlling relations between behavior and environment."

_____ 4. "The task of making conscious the most hidden recesses of the mind is one which . . . is quite possible to accomplish."

One final point: Despite the popularity of recent cognitively oriented learning theories that stress the child's active role in the developmental process, some critics maintain that *no* learning theorist pays enough attention to the *cognitive* determinants of development. Proponents of this third, or "cognitive-developmental," viewpoint believe that the child's mental abilities undergo a series of qualitative changes (or stages) that behaviorists completely ignore. Further, they argue that a child's impressions of and reactions to the environment depend largely on his or her level of **cognitive development.** Let's now turn to this viewpoint and see what it has to offer.

In his cognitive-developmental theory, Swiss scholar Jean Piaget (1896–1980) focused on the growth of children's knowledge and reasoning skills.

 ## THE COGNITIVE-DEVELOPMENTAL VIEWPOINT

No theorist has contributed more to our understanding of children's thinking than Jean Piaget (1896–1980), a Swiss scholar who began to study intellectual development during the 1920s. Piaget was truly a remarkable individual. At age 10, he published his first scientific article about the behavior of a rare albino sparrow. This early interest in the ways that animals adapt to their environments eventually led him to pursue a doctorate degree in zoology, which he completed in 1918. Piaget's secondary interest was *epistemology* (the branch of philosophy concerned with the origins of knowledge), and he hoped to be able to integrate his two interests. Thinking that psychology was the answer, Piaget journeyed to Paris, where he accepted a position at the Alfred Binet laboratories, working on the first standardized intelligence test. His experiences in this position had a profound influence on his career.

In the testing approach to the study of mental ability, an estimate is made of the person's intelligence based on the number and kinds of questions that he or she answers correctly. However, Piaget soon found that he was more interested in children's *incorrect* answers than their correct ones. He first noticed that children of about the same age were producing the same kinds of wrong answers. But why? As he proceeded to question children about their misconceptions, using the clinical method that he had learned earlier while working in a psychiatric clinic, he began to realize that young children are not simply less intelligent than older children; their thought processes are completely different. Piaget then set up his own laboratory and spent 60 years charting the course of intellectual growth and attempting to determine how children progress from one mode (or stage) of thinking to another.

Piaget's View of Intelligence and Intellectual Growth

Influenced by his background in biology, Piaget (1950) defined intelligence as a basic life process that helps an organism to *adapt* to its environment. By adapting, Piaget means that the organism is able to cope with the demands of its immediate situation. For example, the hungry infant who grasps a bottle and brings it to her mouth is behaving adaptively, as is the adolescent who successfully interprets a road map while traveling or changes a tire should the need arise. As children mature, they acquire ever more complex "cognitive structures" that aid them in adapting to their environments.

A cognitive structure—or what Piaget called a **scheme**—is an organized pattern of thought or action that is used to cope with or explain some aspect of experience. For example, many 3-year-olds will insist that the sun is alive because it comes up in the morning and goes down at night. According to Piaget, these children are operating on the basis of a simple cognitive scheme: the idea that things that move are alive. The earliest *schemes*, formed in infancy, are motor habits, such as reaching, grasping, and lifting, that prove to be adaptive indeed. For example, a curious infant who combines the responses of extending an arm (reaching) and grasping with the hand is suddenly capable of satisfying her curiosity by exploring almost any interesting object that is no more than an arm's length away. Simple as these behavioral schemes may be, they permit infants to operate toys, to turn dials, to open cabinets, and to otherwise master their environments. Later in childhood, cognitive schemes will take the

microsystem: the immediate settings (including role relationships and activities) that the person actually encounters; the innermost of Bronfenbrenner's environmental layers or contexts.

mesosystem: the interconnections among an individual's immediate settings or microsystems. The second of Bronfenbrenner's environmental layers or contexts.

exosystem: social system that children and adolescents do not directly experience but that may nonetheless influence their development; the third of Bronfenbrenner's environmental layers or contexts.

macrosystem: the larger cultural or subcultural context in which development occurs; Bronfenbrenner's outermost environmental layer or context.

cognitive development: age-related changes that occur in mental activities such as attending, perceiving, learning, thinking, and remembering.

scheme: an organized pattern of thought or action that a child develops to make sense of some aspect of his or her experience; Piaget sometimes uses the term *cognitive structures* as a synonym for schemes.

Piaget believed that children are naturally curious explorers who are constantly trying to make sense of their surroundings.

assimilation: Piaget's term for the process by which children interpret new experiences by incorporating them into their existing schemes.

disequilibriums: imbalances or contradictions between one's thought processes and environmental events. By contrast, *equilibrium* refers to a balanced, harmonious relationship between one's cognitive structures and the environment.

accommodation: Piaget's term for the process by which children modify their existing schemes in order to incorporate or adapt to new experiences.

invariant developmental sequence: a series of developments that occur in one particular order because each development in the sequence is a prerequisite for the next.

form of "actions of the head" (for example, mental addition or subtraction) that allow children to manipulate information and think logically about the issues and problems they encounter in everyday life. At any age, children rely on their current cognitive structures to understand the world around them. And because cognitive structures take different forms at different ages, younger and older children may often interpret and respond to the same objects and events in very different ways.

How do children develop more complex schemes and increase their understanding of the world? Piaget claimed that infants have no inborn knowledge or ideas about reality, as some philosophers have claimed. Nor are children simply handed information or taught how to think by adults. Instead, they *actively construct* new understandings of the world based on their own experiences. How? By being the curious and active explorers that they are. Children watch what goes on around them; they experiment with objects they encounter; they make connections or associations between events; and they are puzzled when their current understandings (or schemes) fail to explain what they have experienced.

To illustrate, let's return for a moment to the 3-year-old who believes that the sun is alive. Surely this idea is not something the child learned from an adult; it was apparently constructed by the child on the basis of her own worldly experiences. After all, many things that move *are* alive. So long as the child clings to this understanding, she may regard any new moving object as alive; that is, new experiences will be interpreted in terms of her current cognitive structures, a process Piaget called **assimilation.** Eventually, however, this child will encounter moving objects that almost certainly couldn't be alive, such as a paper airplane that was nothing more than a sheet of newsprint before dad built it, or a windup toy that invariably stops moving unless she winds it again. Now here are contradictions (or what Piaget termed **disequilibriums**) between the child's understanding and the facts to be understood. It becomes clear to the child that her "objects-that-move-are-alive" scheme needs to be revised. So she will be prompted by these disconfirming experiences to **accommodate**—that is, to alter her existing schemes so that they provide a better explanation of the distinction between animate and inanimate objects (perhaps by concluding that only things that move under their own power are alive).

So it goes through life; Piaget believed that we are continually relying on the complementary processes of assimilation and accommodation to adapt to our environments. Initially, we attempt to understand new experiences or to solve problems using our current cognitive schemes (assimilation). But we will often find that our existing schemes are inadequate for these tasks, which then prompts us to revise them (through accommodation) so that they provide a better "fit" with reality (Piaget, 1952). Biological maturation also plays an important role: As the brain and nervous system mature, children become capable of increasingly complex cognitive activities that help them to construct better understandings of what they have experienced (Piaget, 1970b). Eventually, curious, active children, who are always forming new schemes and reorganizing this knowledge, will have progressed far enough to be thinking about old issues in entirely new ways; that is, they pass from one stage of cognitive development to the next, higher stage.

Four Stages of Cognitive Development

Piaget proposed four major periods (or stages) of cognitive development: the *sensorimotor* stage (birth to age 2), the *preoperational* stage (ages 2 to 7), the *concrete-operational* stage (ages 7 to 11 or 12), and the *formal-operational* stage (ages 11 to 12 and beyond). These stages form what Piaget called an **invariant developmental sequence:** That is, all children progress through the stages in exactly the order in which they are listed. There is no skipping of stages because each successive stage builds on the previous stage and represents a more complex way of thinking.

Table 2-2 describes the key features of Piaget's four cognitive stages. Each of these periods of intellectual growth will be discussed in much greater detail when we return to the topic of cognitive development in Chapter 7.

Table 2-2 Piaget's Stages of Cognitive Development

Approximate age	Stage	Primary schemes or methods of representing experience	Major developments
Birth to 2 years	Sensorimotor	Infants use sensory and motor capabilities to explore and gain a basic understanding of the environment. At birth, they have only innate reflexes with which to engage the world. By the end of the sensorimotor period, they are capable of complex sensorimotor coordinations.	Infants acquire a primitive sense of "self" and "others," learn that objects continue to exist when they are out of sight (object permanence), and begin to internalize behavioral schemes to produce images or mental schemes.
2 to 7 years	Preoperational	Children use symbolism (images and language) to represent and understand various aspects of the environment. They respond to objects and events according to the way things appear to be. Thought is egocentric, meaning that children think everyone sees the world in much the same way that they do.	Children become imaginative in their play activities. They gradually begin to recognize that other people may not always perceive the world as they do.
7 to 11 years	Concrete operations	Children acquire and use cognitive operations (mental activities that are components of logical thought).	Children are no longer fooled by appearances. By relying on cognitive operations, they understand the basic properties of and relations among objects and events in the everyday world. They are becoming much more proficient at inferring motives by observing others' behavior and the circumstances in which it occurs.
11 years and beyond	Formal operations	Adolescents' cognitive operations are reorganized in a way that permits them to operate on operations (think about thinking). Thought is now systematic and abstract.	No longer is logical thinking limited to the concrete or the observable. Adolescents enjoy pondering hypothetical issues and, as a result, may become rather idealistic. They are capable of systematic, deductive reasoning that permits them to consider many possible solutions to a problem and to pick the correct answer.

Contributions and Criticisms of Piaget's Viewpoint

Like Freud and Watson, Piaget was an innovative renegade. He was unpopular with psychometricians because he claimed that their intelligence tests only measure what children know and tell us nothing about the most important aspect of intellect: how children think. In addition, Piaget dared to study an unobservable, mentalistic concept, "cognition," that had fallen from favor among psychologists from the behaviorist tradition. So in the beginning, Piaget and his closest associates stood alone, receiving little, if any, encouragement from other members of the psychological community.

Clearly, times have changed. Not only did Piaget's early theorizing interest researchers in children's thinking and hasten the development of what we know today as "cognitive psychology," but his early work linking moral development to cognitive development (see Chapter 14 for an extended discussion) spawned a whole new area of developmental research: the study of **social cognition.** Recent social-cognitive theorists such as Lawrence Kohlberg and Robert Selman have found that the same mind that gradually constructs increasingly sophisticated understandings of the physical world also comes, with age, to form more complex ideas about sex differences,

social cognition: the study of children's thinking about the thoughts, motives, intentions, and behaviors of themselves and other people.

moral values, the significance of human emotions, the meaning and obligations of friendship, and countless other aspects of social life. The development of social cognition is a primary focus of Chapter 12, and the links between one's social-cognitive abilities and various aspects of social and personality development are discussed throughout the text.

Finally, Piaget was the first major developmental theorist to stress that children are active, adaptive creatures whose thought processes are very different from those of adults. Educators soon recognized the implications of this line of reasoning for their own field as they began to treat children less like little adults and more like curious explorers who should be given educational experiences that are carefully tailored to their levels of understanding. For example, many preschool teachers now introduce the difficult concept of number by presenting young children with different numbers of objects to stack, color, or arrange. Presumably, new concepts like number are best taught by a method in which active children can apply their existing schemes and make the critical "discoveries" for themselves.

Although Piaget's pioneering efforts have left a deep and lasting imprint on our thinking about human development (see Beilin, 1992), many of his ideas have been challenged. Russian developmentalist Lev Vygotsky (1934/1962), for example, claimed that cognitive development is neither as sequentially invariant (universal) nor as stagelike as Piaget had thought. In his own *sociocultural theory*, Vygotsky focused on how *culture*—the beliefs, values, customs, and skills of a social group—is transmitted from generation to generation. Rather than depicting children as independent explorers who make critical discoveries on their own, Vygotsky viewed cognitive growth as a *socially mediated activity*—one in which children gradually acquire new ways of thinking and behaving though cooperative dialogues with more knowledgeable members of society. Vygotsky also rejected the notion that all children progress through the same stages of cognitive growth. Why? Because the new skills that children master through their interactions with more competent associates are often specific to their culture rather than universal cognitive structures. So from Vygotsky's perspective (which we will explore more carefully in Chapter 7), Piaget largely ignored important social and cultural influences on human development.

Other theorists, disenchanted with behaviorism and with problems they saw in Piaget's theory, have turned to fields such as adult cognitive psychology and computer science in the hope of better understanding the nature and changing character of children's thinking. Their *information-processing* theory depicts the human mind as a system through which information flows (Klahr, 1992). Using the computer as an analogy, information-processing theorists view cognitive development as the changes that occur in the mind's *hardware* (that is, the brain and central nervous system) and *software* (mental processes such as attention, perception, memory, and problem-solving strategies). Unlike Piaget, many information processing theorists insist that intellectual growth is not at all stagelike; instead, they argue that the mental programs we use to gather, store, retrieve, and operate on information to solve problems develop gradually and continuously over the course of childhood and adolescence. So cognitive development from an information-processing perspective involves *quantitative*, rather than qualitative, change. And as we will see in Chapter 8, this exciting "new look" at cognitive growth has not only addressed issues on which Piaget's theory was rather vague, but has proved useful in a very practical sense by illustrating why children may have difficulties with their reading, math, or science lessons and by suggesting ways to improve their performances.

Finally, psychoanalysts have faulted Piaget for largely ignoring the influence of motivation and emotion on human thought processes, whereas other critics (particularly learning theorists) believe that Piaget, a zoologist by training, was simply too preoccupied with basic biological processes and overemphasized their role in human development. This is an interesting critique because others might argue that Piaget paid insufficient attention to biological factors. Who would make such a claim? Proponents of the *evolutionary* viewpoint.

▶ THE EVOLUTIONARY VIEWPOINT

Behaviorist John Watson may have taken the extreme environmental stand that he did partly because other prominent theorists of his era, most notably Arnold Gesell (1880–1961), took an equally extreme but opposing position that human development is largely a matter of biological maturation. Gesell's (1933) view was that children, like plants, simply "bloomed," following a pattern and timetable laid out in their genes; how parents raised their young was thought to be of little importance.

Although today's developmentalists have largely rejected Gesell's radical claims, the notion that biological influences play a significant role in human development is alive and well in **ethology**—the scientific study of the evolutionary bases of behavior and development. Although the origins of this discipline can be traced to Charles Darwin, ethology arose from the work of Konrad Lorenz and Niko Tinbergen, two European zoologists whose animal research highlighted some important links between evolutionary processes and adaptive behaviors. Other biologists (for example, E. O. Wilson, 1975) have proposed a related model, called **sociobiology**, that seeks to determine the evolutionary bases for human *social* behaviors. Here, we will briefly examine each of these perspectives and their implications for human development.

Assumptions of Classical Ethology

The most basic assumption ethologists make is that members of all animal species are born with a number of "biologically programmed" behaviors that (1) are products of evolution and (2) are adaptive in that they contribute to survival. Many species of birds, for example, seem to come biologically prepared to engage in such instinctual behaviors as following their mothers (a response called **imprinting** that helps to protect the young from predators and to ensure that they find food), building nests, and singing. These biologically programmed characteristics are thought to have evolved as a result of the Darwinian process of **natural selection**; that is, over the course of evolution, birds with genes responsible for these adaptive behaviors were more likely to survive and to pass their genes on to offspring than were birds lacking these adaptive characteristics. Over many, many generations, then, the genes underlying the most adaptive behaviors would become widespread in the species, characterizing nearly all individuals.

So ethologists focus on inborn or instinctual responses that (1) are shared by members of a species and (2) may steer individuals along similar developmental paths. Where might one search for these adaptive behaviors and study their developmental implications? Ethologists have always preferred to study their subjects in the natural environment. Why? Simply because they believe that the inborn behaviors that shape human (or animal) development are most easily identified and understood if observed in the natural settings where they evolved and have proven to be adaptive (Hinde, 1983; 1989).

Ethology and Human Development

Instinctual responses that seem to promote survival are relatively easy to spot in animals. But do humans really display such behaviors? And if they do, how might these preprogrammed responses influence their development?

Human ethologists such as John Bowlby (1969; 1973) not only believe that children display a wide variety of preprogrammed behaviors, they also contend that each of these responses promotes a particular kind of experience that will help the individual to survive and develop normally. For example, the cry of a human infant is thought to be a biologically programmed "distress signal" that brings caregivers running. Not only are infants said to be biologically programmed to convey their

ethology: the study of the bio-evolutionary bases of behavior and development.

sociobiology: a branch of biology that focuses on the evolutionary origins of social motives and behaviors.

imprinting: an innate or instinctual form of learning in which the young of certain species will follow and become attached to moving objects (usually their mothers).

natural selection: an evolutionary process, proposed by Charles Darwin, stating that individuals with characteristics that promote adaptation to the environment will survive, reproduce, and pass these adaptive characteristics to offspring; those lacking these adaptive characteristics will eventually die out.

The cry is a distress signal that attracts the attention of caregivers.

distress with loud, lusty cries, but ethologists also believe that caregivers are biologically predisposed to respond to such signals. So the adaptive significance of an infant's crying is to ensure that (1) the infant's basic needs (for example, hunger, thirst, safety) will be met and (2) the infant will have sufficient contact with other human beings to form primary social and emotional attachments (Bowlby, 1973).

Although ethologists are especially critical of learning theorists for largely ignoring the biological bases of human development, they are well aware that development could not progress very far without learning. For example, the cry of an infant may be an innate signal that promotes the human contact from which emotional attachments emerge. However, these emotional attachments do not simply "happen" automatically. The infant must first *learn* to discriminate familiar faces from those of strangers before he will show any evidence of being emotionally attached to a regular companion. Presumably, the adaptive significance of this discriminatory learning goes back to that period in evolutionary history when humans traveled in nomadic tribes and lived outdoors. In those days, it was crucial that an infant become attached to familiar companions and wary of strangers, for failure to cry in response to a strange face might make the infant "easy pickings" for a predatory animal.

Now consider the opposite side of the coin. Some caregivers who suffer from various life stresses of their own (for example, prolonged illnesses, depression, an unhappy marriage) may be routinely inattentive or neglectful, so that the infant's cries rarely promote any contact with them. Such an infant will probably not form strong emotional attachments to her caregivers and could remain rather shy and emotionally unresponsive to other people for years to come (Ainsworth, 1979; 1989). What this infant has learned from her early experiences is that her closest companions are unreliable and are not to be trusted. Consequently, she may become ambivalent or wary around her caregivers and may later assume that other regular associates, such as teachers and peers, are equally untrustworthy individuals who should be avoided whenever possible.

How important are an individual's early experiences? Like Freud, ethologists believe that they are *very* important. In fact, they have argued that there may be "critical periods" for the development of many attributes. A **critical period** is a part of the life cycle during which the developing organism is particularly sensitive or responsive to specific environmental influences; outside this period, the same events or influences are thought to have little if any lasting effects. To illustrate, some ethologists believe that the first three years of life are a critical period for the development of social and emotional responsiveness in human beings. Presumably, we are most uniquely susceptible to forming close emotional ties during the first three years, and should we have little or no opportunity to do so during this period, we would find it difficult to make close friends or to enter into intimate emotional relationships with other people later in life. Clearly, this is a most interesting and provocative claim about the emotional lives of human beings—one that we will examine carefully when we take up the topic of early social and emotional development in Chapter 11.

In sum, ethologists clearly acknowledge that we are largely a product of our experiences. Yet they are quick to remind us that we are inherently biological creatures whose inborn characteristics affect the kinds of learning experiences we are likely to have.

The Sociobiological Perspective

Ethologists are not the only ones who are interested in the evolutionary bases of development. Sociobiologist E. O. Wilson (1975) and his followers have attempted to explain how evolutionary processes might contribute to the development of broad *social* motives and *social* behaviors that are adaptive and promote survival.

Sociobiologists make different assumptions about the workings of evolution than ethologists do. Recall the ethological notion that adaptive behaviors are those that ensure survival of the *individual*. Wilson and the sociobiologists disagree with this premise, arguing instead that adaptive behaviors are those that ensure the survival of the individual's *genes*. This may seem like a subtle distinction, but it has a very important implication: According to sociobiologists, a behavior can be adaptive (and, hence, become more common over generations through natural selection) if it ensures that our genes survive. It is not necessary that the behavior ensure that *we* (as individuals) survive.

Sociobiologists cite **altruism**—a genuine concern for the welfare of others and a willingness to act on that concern—as a prime example of a social motive (or behavioral predisposition) that illustrates their viewpoint. Consider a father who risks his life reentering his burning house in an attempt to save his twins trapped in an upstairs bedroom. This selfless behavior on the father's part is hard for an ethologist to explain: Taking such a risk does not promote the *father's* survival. Sociobiologists, however, would explain the father's behavior by noting that the children he saves (1) *carry his genes* and (2) have many more reproductive years ahead of them than he does. Thus, the father's altruism is *adaptive* from a sociobiological point of view. By rescuing his children, the father has ensured the survival of *his genes* (or, more literally, those who carry his genes), even if he should perish.

Although sociobiologists view genes as self-serving entities that seek to ensure their own survival, Wilson notes that human beings share many genes with each other. Consequently, the gene-preservation process often occurs at the cultural or societal level. Cultural prescriptions against incest, robbery, and murder, for example, may be outcomes of an evolutionary process that favored individuals whose social behaviors were advantageous to all members of the group (thus promoting the survival of everyone's genes). Indeed, Box 2-4 describes how altruism might have evolved at the

critical period: a (typically) brief period in the development of an organism when it is particularly sensitive to certain environmental influences; outside this period, the same influences will have little, if any, effect.

altruism: a concern for the welfare of others that is expressed through such prosocial acts as sharing, cooperating, and helping.

BOX 2-4

Is Altruism Part of Human Nature?

Darwin's notion of "survival of the fittest" seems to argue against altruism as an inborn motive. Many have interpreted Darwin's idea to mean that powerful, self-serving individuals who place their own needs ahead of others' are the ones who are most likely to survive. If this were so, evolution would favor the development of selfishness and egoism—not altruism—as basic components of human nature.

Martin Hoffman (1981) has challenged this point of view, listing several reasons why the concept of "survival of the fittest" actually implies altruism. His arguments hinge on the assumption that human beings are more likely to receive protection from natural enemies, satisfy all their basic needs, and successfully reproduce if they live together in cooperative social units. If this assumption is correct, cooperative, altruistic individuals would be the ones who are most likely to survive long enough to pass along their "altruistic genes" to their offspring; individualists who "go it alone" would probably succumb to famine, predators, or some other natural disaster that they could not cope with by themselves. So, over thousands of generations, natural selection would favor the development of innate social motives such as altruism. Presumably, the tremendous survival value of being "social" makes altruism, cooperation, and other social motives much more plausible as components of human nature than competition, selfishness, and the like.

It is obviously absurd to argue that infants routinely help

other people. However, Hoffman believes that even new-born babies are capable of recognizing and experiencing the emotion of others. This ability, known as **empathy,** is thought to be an important contributor to altruism, for a person must recognize that others are distressed in some way before he or she is likely to help. So Hoffman is suggesting that at least one aspect of altruism—empathy—is present at birth.

Hoffman's claim is based on an experiment (Sagi & Hoffman, 1976) in which infants less than 36 hours old listened to (1) another infant's cries, (2) an equally loud computer simulation of a crying infant, or (3) no sounds at all (silence). The infants who heard a real infant crying soon began to cry themselves, to display physical signs of agitation such as kicking, and to grimace. Infants exposed to the simulated cry or to silence cried much less and seemed not to be very discomforted. (A second study by Martin & Clark, 1982, has confirmed these observations.)

Hoffman argues that there is something quite distinctive about the human cry. His contention is that infants listen to and experience the distress of another crying infant and become distressed themselves. Of course, this finding does not conclusively demonstrate that humans are altruistic by nature. But it does imply that the capacity for empathy may be present at birth and thus may serve as a biological basis for the eventual development of altruistic behavior.

group, or societal, level and offers some evidence that there may be a biological basis for certain aspects of altruism.

Contributions and Criticisms of the Evolutionary Viewpoint

If this text had been written 25 years ago, it would not have included a section on evolutionary theories. Although ethology came into its own in the 1960s, the early ethologists studied animal behavior. Only within the past 20 years have ethologists made a serious attempt to specify evolutionary contributors to human development. Moreover, sociobiology was not even recognized as a scientific discipline until 1975, the year that Wilson published his now-classic volume *Sociobiology: The New Synthesis.* So the evolutionary theories are very new and have not yet succeeded in providing us with satisfactory explanations for all aspects of human development. Nevertheless, they have already contributed to our discipline by reminding us that every child is a biological creature who comes equipped with a number of adaptive, genetically programmed characteristics that will influence other people's reactions to the child and, thus, the course that development is likely to take. In addition, the ethologists have made a major methodological contribution by showing us the value of (1) studying human development in normal, everyday settings and (2) comparing human development to that of other species.

By way of criticism, evolutionary approaches are like psychoanalytic theory in that they are very hard to test. How does one prove that various motives, mannerisms, and behaviors are inborn, are adaptive, or are products of evolutionary history?

empathy: the ability to experience the same emotions that someone else is experiencing.

Such claims are often difficult to confirm. Ethological theory has also been criticized as a *retrospective*, or "post hoc" explanation of development. One can easily apply evolutionary concepts to explain what has already happened, but can the theory predict what is likely to happen in the future? Many developmentalists believe that it cannot.

Finally, proponents of other viewpoints (most notably, learning theory) have argued that, even if there is a biological basis for certain human motives or behaviors, these biological predispositions will soon become so modified by learning that it may not be helpful to spend much time wondering about their prior evolutionary significance. Even strong, genetically influenced attributes can easily be modified by experience. Consider, for example, that young mallard ducklings clearly prefer their mothers' vocal calls to those of other birds (for example, chickens)—a behavior that ethologists say is innate and adaptive as a product of mallard evolution. Yet Gilbert Gottlieb (1991a) has shown that duckling embryos that were prevented from vocalizing and exposed to chicken calls before hatching come to prefer the call of a chicken to that of a mallard mother! In this case, the ducklings' *prenatal experiences* overrode a genetic predisposition. Of course, human beings have a much greater capacity for learning than ducklings do, thus leading many critics to argue that cultural learning experiences quickly overshadow innate evolutionary mechanisms in shaping human conduct and character.

Despite these criticisms, the evolutionary perspective remains a valuable addition to the field of developmental psychology. Not only has it provided a healthy balance to the heavy environmental emphasis of learning theories by identifying important biological contributions to human development, but it has also reinforced Bronfenbrenner's ecological view that there is much to be learned about the process of development by studying children and adolescents in their everyday environments.

Concept Check 2-3 ⌄ Understanding Criticisms of Four Major Theoretical Perspectives

Check your understanding of some of the criticisms that have been made of four major theoretical perspectives by noting to which theory each criticism best applies. Choose from the following options: (a) psychoanalytic theory, (b) learning theory, (c) Piaget's cognitive-developmental theory, (d) the evolutionary viewpoint. The answers appear in the Appendix.

_____ 1. A stage model that has been criticized for ignoring motivational influences as well as the social and cultural determinants of development.

_____ 2. Oversimplified explanation that is said to pay insufficient attention to the cognitive contributors to development and to biological bases for individual differences in development.

_____ 3. A "retrospective" explanation of development that is said to have limited predictive power.

_____ 4. A stage model that focuses on conflicts and processes that are very difficult to measure objectively.

 THEORIES AND WORLD VIEWS

We have now completed our survey of the "grand theories" of human development. How might we compare them? One way is to group the theories into even grander categories, for each is grounded in a broader *world view*, or set of philosophical assumptions. By examining the fundamental suppositions that underlie different theories, we can better appreciate just how deeply some of their disagreements run.

Most developmental theories rest on either of two broad world views (Overton, 1984). The first, or **mechanistic model**, likens human beings to machines by viewing

mechanistic model: view of children as passive entities whose developmental paths are primarily determined by external (environmental) influences. Represented by learning theorists.

them as (1) a collection of parts (behaviors) that can be decomposed, much as machines can be taken apart piece by piece, (2) passive, changing mostly in response to outside influences (much as machines depend on external energy sources to operate), and (3) changing gradually or continuously as their parts (specific behavior patterns) are added or subtracted. By contrast, the **organismic model** compares humans to plants and other living organisms by viewing them as (1) whole beings who cannot be understood as a simple collection of parts, (2) active in the developmental process, changing under the guidance of internal forces (such as instincts or maturation), and (3) evolving through distinct (discontinuous) stages as they progress through life.

Which theorists have adopted which model? Clearly, learning theorists such as Watson and Skinner favor the mechanistic world view, for they see human beings as passively shaped by environmental stimuli and they analyze human behavior response by response. Bandura's social learning theory is primarily mechanistic; yet it does reflect the important organismic assumption that human beings are active creatures who both influence and are influenced by their environments. By contrast, psychoanalytic theorists such as Freud and Erikson and cognitive developmentalists from the Piagetian tradition all base their theories primarily on the organismic model: Given some nourishment from their surroundings, human beings will progress through discontinuous steps or stages as directed by forces lying within themselves, much as seeds evolve into blooming roses.

Another broad world view, the **contextual model**, has recently evolved and become the perspective that many developmentalists favor (Dixon & Lerner, 1992). The contextual model views development as the product of a dynamic interplay between person and environment. People are assumed to be active in the developmental process (as in the organismic model), *and* the environment is active as well (as in the mechanistic model). Development may have both universal aspects *and* aspects particular to certain cultures, times, or individuals. The potential exists for both qualitative and quantitative change, and development may proceed along many different paths depending on the intricate interplay between internal forces (nature) and external influences (environment).

Although none of the theories we've reviewed provides a pure example of the contextual world view, two come reasonably close. Ethological theorists adopt a biological perspective, claiming that humans are born genetically equipped for certain behaviors that promote adaptive developmental outcomes. But as we've noted, ethologists know full well that biological predispositions, by themselves, do not guarantee healthy development and that a child's outcomes depend very critically on the environment he experiences. By contrast, Bronfenbrenner's ecological theory that we discussed in Box 2-3 emphasized the "nurture" side of the nature-nurture issue. It describes a series of environmental systems, ranging from the home to the wider society, that influence the developing person. Yet Bronfenbrenner is keenly aware that active individuals influence their environments, just as environments influence individuals. Today, then, biologically oriented and environmentally oriented theorists can agree: Nature and nurture are *both* critical in the developmental process.

Box 2-5 describes the philosophical assumptions underlying each of the theories that we have reviewed. As you compare your own viewpoints with those of the theorists, you should be able to determine your "world view" on human nature and the character of human development.

In case you are wondering, we don't expect you to choose one of these theories as a favorite and to reject the others. Indeed, because different theories emphasize different aspects of development, one may be more relevant to a particular issue or to a particular age group than another. Today, many developmentalists are theoretical **eclectics**, individuals who rely on many theories, recognizing that none of the grand theories can explain all aspects of development and that each has had something important to contribute to our understanding. Indeed, our approach for the remainder of this book is eclectic, borrowing from many theories to integrate their

organismic model: view of children as active entities whose developmental paths are primarily determined by forces from within themselves. Represented by psychoanalytic and cognitive-developmental theorists.

contextual model: view of children as active entities whose developmental paths represent a continuous, dynamic interplay between internal forces (nature) and external influences (nurture). Represented (loosely) by ethologists and ecological systems theorists.

eclectics: those who borrow from many theories in their attempts to explain human development.

BOX 2-5
Match Wits with the Theorists

You were asked in Box 2-1 (prior to reading about each of the theoretical perspectives that we have now reviewed) to indicate your positions on six basic developmental issues—the very issues that the theorists often debate. If you copy your answers below, you can compare your stands with those of the major developmental theorists. With whom do you seem to agree the most?

	Question					
	1	2	3	4	5	6
Your pattern of answers:	___	___	___	___	___	___
Freud's psychoanalytic theory:	a	a	b	a	a	a

Freud believed that (1) the child's urges are basically selfish and aggressive; (2) biological forces push the child through the psychosexual stages (although parents influence the outcome of each stage); (3) children are passively influenced by forces (that is, instincts, child-rearing practices) that are largely beyond their control; (4) development is stagelike; (5) traits established in childhood often carry over into adulthood; and (6) psychosexual stages are universal.

| Erikson's psychosocial theory: | c | b | a | a | a | a |

Erikson assumed that (1) we are born with basically good qualities; (2) biological forces push the individual toward each life crisis and social forces largely determine the outcomes of these crises; (3) children are active participants in determining developmental outcomes; (4) development is stagelike; (5) there is carryover from early life to later life (although Erikson was more optimistic than Freud about the possibilities for overcoming early problems); and (6) psychosocial stages are universal.

| Learning theory: Skinner's version | b | c | b | b | b | b |

Skinner maintained that (1) children are inherently neither good nor bad; (2) nurture is more important than nature; (3) people are passively shaped by environmental forces; (4) development is gradual and not at all stagelike; (5) early behavior may change dramatically if the environment changes; and (6) development can proceed in many directions, depending on life experiences.

| Learning theory: Bandura's version | b | c | a | b | b | b |

Bandura argues that (1) children are inherently neither good nor bad; (2) nurture is more important than nature; (3) people influence their environments and are thus active in their own development; (4) development is continuous rather than stagelike; (5) traits and habits are unlikely to be stable if the environment changes; and (6) development can proceed in many directions, depending on life experiences.

| Piaget's cognitive-developmental theory: | c | b | a | a | a | a |

Piaget suggested that (1) we are born with predominantly positive tendencies such as curiosity; (2) both nature and nurture are important; (3) we are active in our own development as we "construct" more sophisticated understandings of ourselves, our worlds, and our niches in those worlds; (4) development is stagelike; (5) each new stage incorporates the elements of previous stages, implying a connectedness between earlier and later developments; and (6) stages of development are universal.

| The ethological perspective: | c | a | a | b | a | a |

The ethologists propose that (1) children are born with predominantly positive (adaptive) characteristics, (2) nature is more important than nurture (although unusual experiences can override biological predispositions); (3) children are active participants in determining developmental outcomes; (4) development is a continuous process (ethologists frequently discuss phases of growth and development, but these phases are often not qualitatively distinct from one another); (5) traits and attributes tend to be stable over the years; and (6) biological forces steer children along similar developmental paths (although ethologists allow for greater variation in the course of development than do many of the stage theorists).

---

contributions into a unified, holistic portrait of the developing person. Yet, we will also continue to explore theoretical controversies, for these squabbles often produce some of the most exciting breakthroughs in the field. So please join us now in examining not just the specific "facts" about human development, but also the broader theoretical insights that have generated these facts and that give them a larger meaning.

SUMMARY

A theory is a set of concepts and propositions that help to describe and explain observations that one has made. Theories are particularly useful if they are concise (parsimonious) and yet applicable to a wide range of phenomena. Good theories are also *precise*, that is, capable of making *falsifiable* predictions that can be evaluated in later research.

Theories of human development differ with respect to their stands on five basic issues: (1) Are human beings inherently good or bad? (2) Is development primarily determined by nature or nurture? (3) Are humans actively or passively involved in their development? (4) Is development a quantitative and continuous process, or does it proceed in a discontinuous fashion through a series of qualitatively distinct stages? (5) Are the most important developments universal or particularistic?

The psychoanalytic perspective originated from the work of Sigmund Freud, who depicted children as "seething cauldrons" driven by inborn erotic and destructive instincts of which they are largely unaware. At birth, the child's personality consists only of these instinctual forces (called the *id*). However, id forces are gradually diverted into a system of rational thought, the *ego*, and an irrational but ethical component of personality, the *superego*. The child is thought to pass through five psychosexual stages—oral, anal, phallic, latency, and genital—that unfold as the sex instinct matures. Each stage is characterized by *conflicts* that may create the need for ego defense mechanisms and can have lasting effects on the developing personality.

Erik Erikson has revised and extended Freud's theory by concentrating less on the sex instinct and more on important sociocultural determinants of human development. According to Erikson, people progress through a series of eight *psychosocial* conflicts, beginning with *trust versus mistrust* in infancy and concluding with *integrity versus despair* in old age. Each conflict must be resolved in favor of the positive trait (trust, for example) if development is to be healthy.

The learning viewpoint originated with John B. Watson, who argued that infants are *tabulae rasae* who change (develop) as a result of their learning experiences. Development was viewed as a continuous process that could proceed in many different directions, depending on the kinds of environments to which a person is exposed. B. F. Skinner, who extended Watson's theory, claimed that development reflects the operant conditioning of children who are *passively* shaped by their experiences. By contrast, Albert Bandura's social-learning theory viewed children as *active* information processors who learn by observation and who have a hand in creating the environments that influence their growth and development. Bronfenbrenner's ecological systems model provides the most complex view of environmental influence, describing a series of interacting environmental systems that influence (and are influenced by) developing persons.

The cognitive-developmental viewpoint of Jean Piaget stresses that children are active explorers who have an intrinsic need to adapt to their environments. Piaget described the course of intellectual development as an invariant sequence of four stages: sensorimotor, preoperational, concrete-operational, and formal-operational. According to Piaget, the child's stage of cognitive development determines how he will interpret various events and, thus, what the child will learn from his experiences. The implication is that cognitive abilities play a central role in many aspects of development.

The evolutionary viewpoint is that humans are born with a number of adaptive responses that evolved over the course of human history and serve to channel development along particular paths. Ethologists recognize that human beings are influenced by their experiences (learning). However, they remind us that we are biological creatures whose innate characteristics affect the kind of learning experiences that we are likely to have.

Theories can be grouped into families based on the "world views" that underlie them. As developmentalists have come to appreciate the incredible complexity of human development, more of them are favoring a *contextual* world view over the *mechanistic* model that guides learning theories or the *organismic* model that underlies stage theories. In addition, most contemporary developmentalists are theoretically *eclectic*, recognizing that no single theory offers a totally adequate account of human development and that each contributes in important ways to our understanding of developing persons.

Key Terms

accommodation [62]

activity/passivity issue [43]

altruism [67]

anal stage [48]

assimilation [62]

autonomy versus shame and doubt [53]

basic trust versus mistrust [53]

behavioral genetics [42]

behaviorism [54]

cognitive development [61]

contextual model [70]

continuity/discontinuity issue [43]

critical period [67]

developmental stage [44]

disequilibriums [62]

eclectics [70]

ecological systems model [58]

ego [47]

Electra complex [49]

empathy [68]

environmental determinism [57]

Eros [46]

ethology [65]

exosystem [61]

falsifiability [41]

fixation [49]

genital stage [50]

habits [54]

heuristic value [41]

id [47]

identification [49]

imprinting [65]

initiative versus guilt [53]

instinct [46]

invariant developmental sequence [62]

latency period [50]

libido [48]

macrosystem [61]

mechanistic model [69]

mesosystem [61]

microsystem [61]

natural selection [65]

nature/nurture issue [43]

observational learning [56]

Oedipus complex [48]

operant learning [56]

oral stage [48]

organismic model [70]

parsimony [41]

phallic stage [48]

punisher [55]

reciprocal determinism [57]

regression [49]

reinforcer [55]

repression [48]

scheme [61]

social cognition [63]

sociobiology [65]

sublimation [49]

superego [47]

Thanatos [46]

unconscious motives [46]

Part II

Biological Foundations of Development

Human beings are biological creatures, and our emphasis in Part II is on the biological bases of development. In Chapter 3 we will discuss the concept of heredity and see that hereditary processes contribute in important ways to our physical, social, and intellectual development. We will also learn how our knowledge of genetic transmission has helped to promote healthy development by allowing us to prevent or minimize the effects of many hereditary abnormalities.

Our focus in Chapter 4 shifts to the remarkable developments that take place during the prenatal period—the nine months between conception and birth during which a single cell evolves into a recognizable human being. Although prenatal development unfolds in an orderly sequence and follows a distinct biological timetable, we will see that the 266 days before birth are truly a sensitive period in which a variety of environmental influences can interfere with nature's grand plan and produce any number of harmful consequences.

Psychological development depends to a large extent on physical development: our size, shape, strength, sensory capabilities, and muscle coordination clearly affect how we feel, think, and act. Chapter 5 describes the characteristics and capabilities of newborns and then traces their physical development from infancy through adolescence as they grow, acquire important motor skills, and become more and more like adults, both in appearance and in physical prowess.

Although in this section we concentrate on aspects of development that are heavily influenced by our biological heritage, each of the areas we will consider is subject to a variety of social and environmental influences. Thus the three chapters in Part II also illustrate how the forces of nature and nurture combine (or interact) to determine developmental outcomes.

Hereditary Influences on Development

3

an you remember when you were first introduced to the concept of heredity? Consider the experience of one first-grader at a parent-teacher conference. The teacher asked the boy whether he knew in which country his ancestors had lived before coming to the United States. He proudly proclaimed "the Old West" because he was "half cowboy and half black." Everyone present had a good laugh and then tried to convince the boy that he couldn't be of African-American ancestry because his parents were not, that he could only become what mom and dad already were. Evidently, the "constraints" of heredity did not go over too well. The child became rather distressed and asked "You mean I can't be a fireman?"

In this chapter, we will consider human development from a hereditarian's perspective, seeking to determine how one's **genotype** (the **genes** that he or she inherits) comes to be expressed as a **phenotype** (one's observable or measurable characteristics). We will first explore how hereditary information is transmitted from parents to their offspring and why the workings of heredity conspire to make us unique individuals. We will then review the evidence for hereditary contributions to such important psychological attributes as intelligence, personality, and even our inclinations toward displaying mentally healthy (or unhealthy) patterns of behavior. Indeed, this evidence implies that many (and some would say all) of our most noteworthy phenotypic characteristics are influenced by the genes passed to us by our parents. And yet, the most important message we might take from this chapter is that genes, by themselves, determine very little and that the expression "hereditary constraint" is something of a misnomer. As we will see, most complex human attributes are the result of a long and involved interplay between the forces of nature (heredity) and nurture (environment) (Plomin, 1990).

PRINCIPLES OF HEREDITARY TRANSMISSION

To understand the workings of heredity, we must start at **conception,** the moment when a woman's ovum is fertilized by a man's sperm. Once we have established what is inherited at conception, we can examine the mechanisms by which genes influence the characteristics we display.

Conception

About once every 28 days, midway between menstrual periods, human females **ovulate:** An ovum or egg cell ripens, leaves the ovary, and enters the fallopian tube. The vast majority of these ovulations are rather uneventful: The ripened ovum simply disintegrates when it reaches the uterus, and it leaves the body about seven to ten days later as part of the woman's menstrual flow.

Suppose, however, that a woman has sexual intercourse with a fertile male a few days before or after ovulation. When the male ejaculates, his seminal fluid may contain half again as many sperm cells (300–450 million) as there are people in the United States. These tiny, tadpolelike sperm immediately begin to swim in all directions. Perhaps as many as 5,000–20,000 of them will survive the long journey from the vagina to the fallopian tubes, where one may meet and penetrate the shell of a ripened ovum that is beginning its descent from the ovary (see Figure 3-1). This is *conception:* the beginning of a long developmental process.

The very first development that occurs is protective: When a sperm cell penetrates the lining of the ovum, a biochemical reaction repels other sperm, thus preventing them from repeating the fertilization process. Within a few hours, the sperm cell begins to disintegrate, releasing its genetic material. The ovum also releases its genetic material, and a new cell nucleus forms around the hereditary information provided by the father's sperm and the mother's ovum. This new cell, called a **zygote,** is only 1/20th the size of the head of a pin. Yet this tiny cell contains the code, or bio-

genotype: the genetic endowment that an individual inherits.

genes: hereditary blueprints for development that are transmitted unchanged from generation to generation.

phenotype: the ways in which a person's genotype is expressed in observable or measurable characteristics.

conception: the moment of fertilization, when a sperm penetrates an ovum, forming a zygote.

ovulation: the process in which a female gamete (ovum) matures in one of the ovaries and is released into the fallopian tube.

zygote: a single cell formed at conception from the union of a sperm and an ovum.

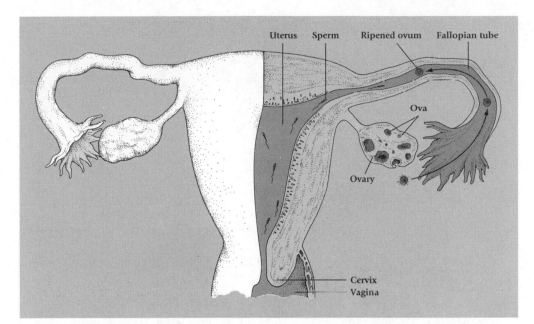

Figure 3-1
The anatomy of conception. Conception occurs in the fallopian tube as a sperm penetrates a ripened ovum that is descending from the ovary to the uterus.

Labels in figure: Uterus, Sperm, Ripened ovum, Fallopian tube, Ova, Ovary, Cervix, Vagina

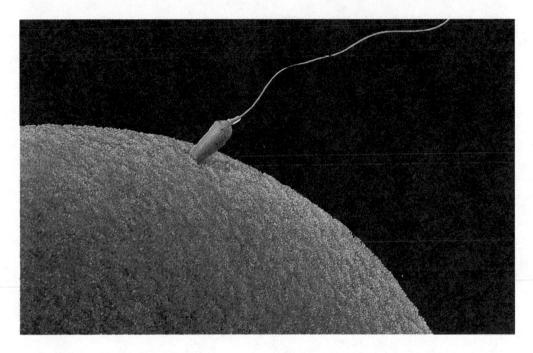

Development begins at conception, when one tiny sperm intersects and unites with a relatively large egg in the fallopian tube.

chemical recipe, for the zygote's development from a single cell into a recognizable human being.

What genetic material is present in a human zygote? The new cell nucleus contains 46 elongated, threadlike bodies, called **chromosomes,** each of which consists of thousands of chemical segments, or *genes*—the basic units of heredity. With one exception that we will soon discuss, chromosomes come in matching pairs. Each member of a pair corresponds to the other in size, shape, and the hereditary functions it serves. One member of each chromosome pair came from the mother's ovum and the other from the father's sperm cell. Thus, each parent contributes 23 chromosomes to each offspring.

The genes on each chromosome also function as pairs, the two members of each gene pair being located at the same sites on their corresponding chromosomes. Genes

chromosome: a threadlike structure made up of genes; in humans, there are 46 chromosomes in the nucleus of each body cell.

Figure 3-2
Mitosis: the way that cells reproduce themselves.

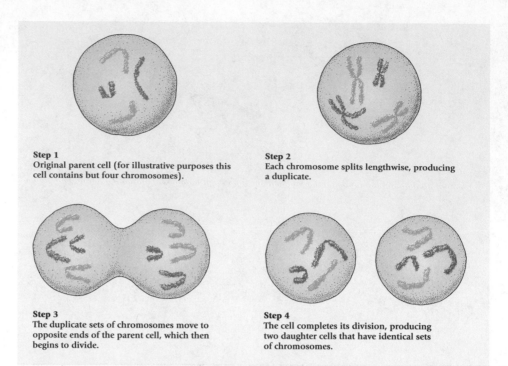

Step 1
Original parent cell (for illustrative purposes this cell contains but four chromosomes).

Step 2
Each chromosome splits lengthwise, producing a duplicate.

Step 3
The duplicate sets of chromosomes move to opposite ends of the parent cell, which then begins to divide.

Step 4
The cell completes its division, producing two daughter cells that have identical sets of chromosomes.

are actually stretches of **deoxyribonucleic acid,** or **DNA,** a complex, "double-helix" molecule that resembles a twisted ladder and provides the chemical "code" for development. A unique feature of DNA is that it can duplicate itself. The rungs of the ladder split in the middle, opening somewhat like a zipper. Then each remaining half of the molecule guides the replication of its missing parts. This special ability of DNA to replicate itself is what makes it possible for a one-celled zygote to develop into a marvelously complex human being.

Growth of the Zygote and Production of Body Cells

As the zygote moves through the fallopian tube toward its prenatal home in the uterus, it begins to reproduce itself through the process of **mitosis.** At first, the zygote divides into two cells, but the two soon become four, four become eight, eight become sixteen, and so on. Just before each division, the cell duplicates its 46 chromosomes, and these duplicate sets move in opposite directions. The division of the cell then proceeds, resulting in two "daughter" cells, each of which has the identical 23 pairs of chromosomes (46 in all) and thus the same genetic code as the original parent cell. This remarkable process is illustrated in Figure 3-2.

By the time a child is born, he or she consists of billions of cells, each of which has been created through mitosis. Indeed, all the *somatic* (body) cells that make up our muscles, bones, organs, and other bodily structures are products of mitosis. Mitosis continues throughout life, creating new cells that enable us to grow and replacing old ones that are damaged. With each division, the hereditary blueprint is duplicated, so that every new cell contains an exact copy of the 46 chromosomes that we inherited at conception.

Germ Cells and Hereditary Transmission

We have learned that sperm and egg combine to form a zygote that has 46 chromosomes (23 from each parent). But if cells normally contain 46 chromosomes apiece, why doesn't a person start life with 92 chromosomes, 46 coming from the father's sperm cell and 46 from the mother's ovum?

deoxyribonucleic acid (DNA): long, double-stranded molecules that make up chromosomes.

mitosis: the process in which a cell duplicates its chromosomes and then divides into two genetically identical daughter cells.

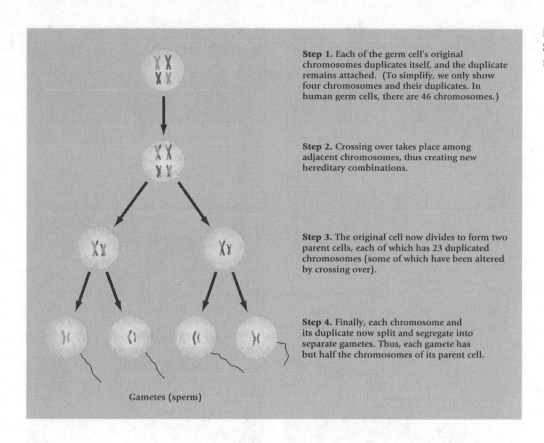

Step 1. Each of the germ cell's original chromosomes duplicates itself, and the duplicate remains attached. (To simplify, we only show four chromosomes and their duplicates. In human germ cells, there are 46 chromosomes.)

Step 2. Crossing over takes place among adjacent chromosomes, thus creating new hereditary combinations.

Step 3. The original cell now divides to form two parent cells, each of which has 23 duplicated chromosomes (some of which have been altered by crossing over).

Step 4. Finally, each chromosome and its duplicate now split and segregate into separate gametes. Thus, each gamete has but half the chromosomes of its parent cell.

Gametes (sperm)

Figure 3-3
Simplified diagram of the meiosis of a male germ cell.

The answer is relatively simple. In addition to body cells, human beings have *germ* cells that serve one particular hereditary function: to produce *gametes* (sperm in males and ova in females). When male germ cells in the testes and female germ cells in the ovaries produce sperm and ova, they do so through a process called **meiosis** that is illustrated in Figure 3-3. The germ cell first duplicates its 46 chromosomes. Then an event called **crossing over** often takes place: Adjacent chromosomes cross and break at one or more points along their length, exchanging segments of genetic material, much the same as if you were to exchange a couple of fingers with a friend after a handshake. Notice, then, that this transfer of genes during crossing over creates new and unique hereditary combinations. Next, pairs of duplicated chromosomes (some of which have been altered by crossing over) segregate into two parent cells that each contain 46 chromosomes. Finally, the parent cells divide so that each of their daughter cells (or gametes) contains 23 single, or *unpaired*, chromosomes. At conception, then, a sperm with 23 chromosomes unites with an ovum with 23 chromosomes, producing a zygote with a full complement of 46 chromosomes.

Genetic Uniqueness and Relatedness

Full brothers and sisters have the same mother and father and have inherited 23 chromosomes from each of these parents. In view of their common heritage, why is it that children from the same family sometimes barely resemble each other?

Again, the answer is relatively simple. When a pair of chromosomes segregates during meiosis, it is a matter of chance which of the two chromosomes will end up in a particular parent cell. And because each chromosome pair segregates independently of all other pairs, according to the principle of **independent assortment,** there are many different combinations of chromosomes that could result from the meiosis of a single germ cell. Since human germ cells contain 23 chromosome pairs, each of which is segregating independently of the others, the laws of probability tell us

meiosis: the process in which a germ cell divides, producing gametes (sperm or ova) that each contain half of the parent cell's original complement of chromosomes; in humans, the products of meiosis contain 23 chromosomes.

crossing over: a process in which genetic material is exchanged between pairs of chromosomes.

independent assortment: the principle stating that each pair of chromosomes segregates independently of all other chromosome pairs during meiosis.

Figure 3-4
Identical, or monozygotic, twins (left) develop from a single zygote. Because they have inherited identical sets of genes, they will look alike, be of the same sex, and share all other inherited characteristics. Fraternal, or dizygotic, twins (right) develop from separate zygotes and have no more genes in common than siblings born at different times. Consequently, they may not look alike (as we see in this photo) and may not even be the same sex.

monozygotic (or identical) twins: twins that result when a single zygote divides into two separate but identical cells that each develop independently. As a result, each member of a monozygotic twin pair has inherited exactly the same set of genes.

dizygotic (or fraternal) twins: twins that result when a mother releases two ova at roughly the same time and each is fertilized by a different sperm, producing two zygotes that are genetically different.

that each parent can produce 2^{23}—more than 8 million—different genetic combinations in their sperm or ova. If a father can produce 8 million combinations of 23 chromosomes and a mother can produce 8 million, any couple could theoretically have 64 *trillion* babies without producing two children who inherited precisely the same set of genes! In fact, the odds of exact genetic replication in two siblings are even smaller than 1 in 64 trillion. Why? Because the crossing-over process, which occurs during the earlier phases of meiosis, actually alters the genetic composition of chromosomes and thereby increases the number of possible variations in an individual's gametes far beyond the 8 million that could occur if chromosomes segregated cleanly, without exchanging genetic information.

Of course, brothers and sisters will resemble one another to some extent because their genes are drawn from a gene pool provided by the same two parents. Each brother or sister inherits half of each parent's genes, although two siblings never inherit the same half, owing to the random process by which parental chromosomes (and genes) segregate into the sperm and ovum that combine to produce each offspring. Thus, each individual is genetically unique. The one exception to this rule is **monozygotic** (or **identical**) **twinning,** which occurs when a single zygote splits into two identical cells that develop independently. Identical twins occur in approximately 1 of every 250 births (Plomin, 1990); and because they are genetically identical, monozygotic twins should show very similar developmental progress if the genes that people inherit have much effect on human development.

More common, however (occurring in approximately 1 of every 125 births), are **dizygotic,** or **fraternal, twins**—pairs that result when a mother releases *two* ova at approximately the same time and each is fertilized by a *different* sperm. So even though fraternal twins are born together, they have no more genes in common than any other pair of siblings. As illustrated in Figure 3-4, fraternal twins often differ considerably in appearance. Indeed, they need not even be the same sex.

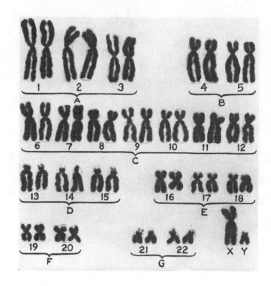
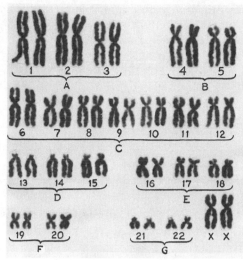

Figure 3-5
These karotypes of a male (left) and a female (right) have been arranged so that the chromosomes could be displayed in pairs. Note that the 23rd pair of chromosomes for the male consists of one elongated X chromosome and a Y chromosome that is noticeably smaller, whereas the 23rd pair for the female consists of two X chromosomes.

Determination of Sex

A hereditary basis for sex differences becomes quite clear if we examine the chromosomes of normal men and women. These chromosomal portraits, or **karyotypes,** reveal that, of the 23 pairs of chromosomes that individuals inherit, 22 (called *autosomes*) are similar in males and females. Sex is determined by the 23rd pair. For the normal male, the 23rd pair consists of one elongated body known as an **X chromosome** and a short, stubby companion called a **Y chromosome.** In the female, both these sex chromosomes are Xs (see Figure 3-5). Located on the Y chromosome is a single "sex gene" that triggers male sexual development (Milunsky, 1992; Sinclair et al., 1990). So, the presence of a Y chromosome in one's hereditary blueprint makes one a genetic male, while the absence of a Y chromosome defines a genetic female.

Pity the many thousands of women who, throughout history, have been belittled, tortured, divorced, or even beheaded for failing to bear their husbands a male heir! Since the father is the only parent who can provide the offspring with a Y chromosome, it is he who determines a child's gender. When the sex chromosomes segregate into gametes during meiosis, half of the sperm of a genetic (XY) male will contain an X chromosome and half will contain a Y chromosome. By contrast, the ova produced by a genetic (XX) female will normally contain a single X chromosome. Thus, the determination of gender is straightforward: If an ovum is fertilized by a sperm bearing a Y chromosome, the product is an XY zygote, which will become a male. But if a sperm carrying an X chromosome reaches the ovum first, the result is an XX zygote, or a female.

So far, so good: We have a genetically unique boy or girl who has inherited about 500,000 genes in all on his or her 46 chromosomes. Now an important question: How do genes regulate development and influence a person's phenotypic characteristics?

Translation of the Genetic Code

What do genes do? At the most basic, biochemical level, they call for the production of enzymes and other proteins that are necessary for the formation and functioning of new cells. Genes, for example, regulate the production of a pigment called melanin in the iris of the eye. People with brown eyes have genes that call for much of this pigment, whereas people with lighter (blue or green) eyes have genes that call for less pigmentation. Genes also guide cell differentiation, thus insuring that some cells become the brain and central nervous system, whereas others become the circulatory system, bones, skin, and so on. However, no one completely understands the remarkable process that transforms a single-celled zygote into a remarkably complex, living, breathing human being.

karyotype: a chromosomal portrait created by staining chromosomes and then photographing them under a high-power microscope.

X chromosome: the longer of the two sex chromosomes; normal females have two X chromosomes, whereas normal males have but one.

Y chromosome: the shorter of the two sex chromosomes; normal males have one Y chromosome, whereas females have none.

Apparently, some genes are responsible for *regulating* the pace and timing of development. Current thinking is that specific gene pairs with specific developmental blueprints are "turned on" or "turned off" by regulatory genes at different points in the life span (Scarr & Kidd, 1983). Regulatory genes, for example, might "turn on" other genes responsible for the growth spurt we experience as adolescents and then shut these growth genes down in adulthood.

Finally, an important point: *Environmental factors clearly influence how messages coded in the genes are carried out* (Gottlieb, 1991b). Consider, for example, that a child who inherits genes for tall stature may or may not be tall as an adult. Should he experience very poor nutrition for a prolonged period early in life, he could end up being only average or even below average in height, despite having the genetic potential for exceptional stature. So environmental influences combine with genetic influences to determine how a genotype is translated into a particular phenotype—the way one looks, feels, thinks, and behaves.

Another way to approach the riddle of how genes influence development is to consider the major patterns of genetic inheritance: the ways in which parents' genes are expressed in their children's phenotypes.

Patterns of Genetic Expression

There are three main patterns of genetic expression: single gene-pair inheritance, sex-linked inheritance, and polygenic (or multiple gene) inheritance.

Single Gene-Pair Inheritance

Through **single gene-pair inheritance,** some human characteristics are influenced by only one pair of genes (called **alleles**): one from the mother, one from the father. Although he knew nothing of genes, a 19th-century monk named Gregor Mendel contributed greatly to our knowledge of single gene-pair inheritance by cross-breeding different strains of peas and observing the outcomes. His major discovery was a predictable pattern to the way in which two alternative characteristics (for example, smooth seeds or wrinkled seeds, green pods or yellow pods) would appear in the offspring of cross-breedings. He called some characteristics (for example, smooth seeds) "dominant" because they appeared more often in later generations than did their opposite traits, which he called "recessive" traits. Among peas and among humans, an offspring's phenotype often is not simply a "blend" of the characteristics of mother and father. Instead, one of the parental genes often dominates the other, and the child will resemble the parent who contributed the dominant gene.

To illustrate the principles of Mendelian heredity, consider the fact that about three-fourths of us have the ability to see distant objects clearly (that is, normal vision), whereas the remaining one-fourth of us cannot and are myopic (nearsighted). It happens that the gene associated with normal vision is a **dominant allele.** A weaker gene calling for nearsightedness is said to be a **recessive allele.** So a person who inherits one allele for normal vision and one allele for myopia would display a phenotype of normal vision because the "normal vision" gene overpowers (that is, dominates) the nearsightedness gene.

Since a normal vision allele dominates a nearsightedness allele, we represent the normal vision gene with a capital N and the nearsightedness gene with a lower-case n. Perhaps you can see (no pun intended) that there are three possible genotypes for this visual characteristic: (1) two normal vision alleles (NN), (2) two nearsightedness alleles (nn), and (3) one of each (Nn). People whose genotype for an attribute consists of two genes of the same kind are said to be **homozygous** for that attribute. Thus, an NN individual is homozygous for normal vision and will pass only genes for normal vision to his or her offspring. An nn individual is homozygous nearsighted (the only way that one can actually be nearsighted is to inherit two of these recessive alleles) and will pass nearsightedness genes to his or her offspring. Finally, an Nn individual is said to be **heterozygous** for this visual trait because he or she

single gene-pair inheritance: genetic process through which a characteristic is influenced by only one pair of genes, one from the father and one from the mother.

alleles: alternative forms of a gene that is coded for a particular trait.

dominant allele: a relatively powerful gene that is expressed phenotypically and masks the effect of a less powerful gene.

recessive allele: a less powerful gene that is not expressed phenotypically when paired with a dominant allele.

homozygous: having inherited two alleles for an attribute that are identical in their effects.

heterozygous: having inherited two alleles for an attribute that have different effects.

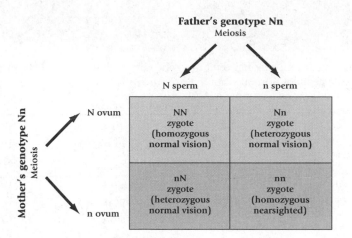

has inherited alternative forms of the allele. As we have seen, this individual will have normal vision, because the N allele is dominant. And what kind of allele will the heterozygous person pass along to offspring? Either a normal vision gene or a nearsightedness gene! Even though a heterozygous person has normal vision, exactly half the gametes produced by this individual will carry a gene for normal vision, and half will carry a gene for nearsightedness.

Can two individuals with normal vision ever produce a nearsighted child? The answer is yes, as long as each parent is heterozygous for normal vision (that is, Nn) and is thus a "carrier" of the recessive allele for nearsightedness. In Figure 3-6, the genotype of a heterozygous normal vision father appears at the head of the columns, and that of a heterozygous normal vision mother appears at the left of the rows. When the germ cells of each parent undergo meiosis, the resulting gametes will each contain only one allele for this visual trait: either a normal vision allele or a nearsightedness allele. What kind of vision will the children have? The various possibilities appear in the four quadrants of the chart. If a sperm bearing a normal vision (N) allele unites with an ovum carrying a normal vision (N) allele, the result is an NN, or a child that is homozygous for normal vision. If a sperm bearing an N gene fertilizes an ovum carrying an n gene, or if an n sperm fertilizes an N ovum, the result is a heterozygous child with normal vision. Finally, if both sperm and ovum carry an n gene, the child will be nearsighted. Since each of these four combinations is equally likely in any given mating, the odds are 1 in 4 that a child of two Nn parents will be nearsighted.

The normal vision/nearsightedness trait is but one of several human attributes determined by a single gene pair in which one particular allele dominates another. Box 3-1 lists a number of other common dominant and recessive characteristics that people can inherit.

Incomplete dominance. Alternative forms of a gene do not always follow the simple dominant/recessive pattern described by Gregor Mendel. For example, some "dominant" alleles fail to mask all the effects of a "recessive" gene; that is, theirs is an **incomplete dominance.** A child who inherits heterozygous alleles of this type will have a phenotype that represents a "blending" of the two genes, although the stronger (or incompletely dominant) gene plays the major role in determining the child's phenotype.

The *sickle-cell* trait is a noteworthy example of incomplete dominance in human heredity. About 9% of all African Americans (and a relatively few whites) are heterozygous for this attribute, carrying a recessive "sickle-cell" allele (Schulman & Black,

incomplete dominance: condition in which a stronger allele fails to mask all the effects of a weaker allele; a phenotype results that is similar but not identical to the effect of the stronger gene.

BOX 3-1

Examples of Dominant and Recessive Traits in Human Heredity

Our discussion of dominant and recessive genes has centered on two particular alleles: a gene for normal vision and a gene for nearsightedness. Listed here are a number of other dominant and recessive characteristics in human heredity (Burns & Bottino, 1989; McKusick, 1989). A quick glance through the list reveals that most of the undesirable or maladaptive attributes are recessive. For this, we can be thankful; otherwise, genetically linked diseases and defects might cripple or eventually decimate the species.

One important genetic disease produced by a *dominant* gene is Huntington's disease, a condition that causes a gradual deterioration of the nervous system, leading to a progressive decline in one's physical and mental abilities and ultimately to death. Although some victims of Huntington's disease die in young adulthood, normally the disease appears much later, usually after age 40. Fortunately, the dominant allele that is responsible for this lethal condition is very rare.

Recently, geneticists have learned that *Alzheimer's disease*—a deterioration of the nervous system involving loss of mental and motor control—is greatly affected by a dominant gene (or genes) on one particular chromosome (Hardie, 1994; Kay, 1989). However, it cannot be said that this gene (or genes) is the sole cause of Alzheimer's disease because there are several pairs of identical twins who share the gene(s) without sharing the disease (Plomin, 1990). Might certain environmental experiences (that identical twins may not share) be necessary to trigger the disease in those who are genetically predisposed? This is a likely possibility, but one that can only be evaluated through future research.

Dominant traits	Recessive traits
Dark hair	Blond hair
Full head of hair	Pattern baldness
Curly hair	Straight hair
Facial dimples	No dimples
Farsightedness	Normal vision
Normal vision	Color blindness*
Roman nose	Straight nose
Extra digits	Five digits
Pigmented skin	Albinism
Type A blood	Type O blood
Type B blood	Type O blood
Normal blood clotting	Hemophilia*
Normal hearing	Congenital deafness
Normal blood cells	Sickle-cell anemia*
Huntington's disease	Normal brain and body maturation
Normal physiology	Cystic fibrosis*
Normal physiology	Phenylketonuria*
Normal physiology	Tay-Sachs disease*

*This condition is discussed elsewhere in the chapter.

1993). The presence of this one recessive gene causes a substantial percentage of the person's red blood cells to assume an unusual crescent, or sickle, shape (see Figure 3-7). Sickled cells can be a problem because they tend to cluster together, distributing less oxygen throughout the circulatory system. Yet overt symptoms of circulatory distress, such as painful swelling of the joints and fatigue, are rarely experienced by these sickle-cell "carriers," unless they experience oxygen deprivation as they might at high altitudes, after heavy physical exertion, or while under anesthesia (Burns & Bottino, 1989).

The consequences are much more severe for those individuals who inherit two recessive sickle-cell genes. They will develop a severe blood disorder, called **sickle-cell anemia,** that causes massive sickling of red blood cells and inefficient distribution of oxygen at all times. Indeed, many who suffer from this painful disease will die from heart and/or kidney failure during childhood, and they are particularly vulnerable to pneumonia and other respiratory diseases (Schulman & Black, 1993). By contrast, heterozygous individuals, who carry but one sickle-cell gene, are more phenotypically similar to the person who inherits two "normal" genes; their blood cells sickle to some extent, but they remain unaffected by this condition for the most part.

We see, then, that the "dominant" allele that produces normal red blood cells does not completely suppress the effects of a sickle-cell allele. If the dominance were complete, those who inherited a single sickle-cell gene would not produce any sickled red blood cells.

sickle-cell anemia: a genetic blood disease that causes red blood cells to assume an unusual sickled shape and to become inefficient at distributing oxygen.

Codominance. In yet other cases of single gene-pair hereditary, two genes influence a trait but neither dominates the other. This is called **codominance** because the phenotype of the heterozygous individual represents an exact compromise between the two genes that he or she has inherited.

The genes for the human blood types A and B are equally expressive. Each dominates the gene for blood type O, but neither of the two alleles dominates the other. A heterozygous person who inherits an allele for blood type A and one for blood type B has equal proportions of A antigens and B antigens in his or her blood. If you have inherited the blood type known as AB, you illustrate this principle of genetic codominance.

Sex-Linked Inheritance

Some traits are called **sex-linked characteristics** because they are determined by genes located on the sex chromosomes. In fact, the vast majority of these sex-linked attributes are produced by recessive genes that are found only on X chromosomes. Who do you suppose is more likely to inherit these recessive X-linked traits: males or females?

The answer is males, a point we can easily illustrate with a common sex-linked characteristic: *red/green color blindness.* Many people cannot distinguish red from green, an inability caused by a recessive gene that appears only on X chromosomes. Now recall that a normal (XY) male has but one X chromosome—the one he inherited from his mother. If this X chromosome carries a recessive gene for color blindness, the male will be color blind. Why? Because there is no corresponding gene on his Y chromosome that might counteract the effect of this "color-blind" allele. By contrast, a genetic female who inherits but one gene for color blindness will not be color blind, for the "color-normal" gene on her second X chromosome will dominate the color-blind gene, enabling her to distinguish red from green (see Figure 3-8). Thus, a female cannot be color blind unless *both* of her X chromosomes contain a recessive gene for color blindness.

So immediately we have reason to suspect that more males than females will be color blind. Indeed, roughly 8 males in 100 cannot distinguish red from green. This finding suggests that the ratio of "color-blind" to "color-normal" genes in the gene pool is approximately 1:12. Since the odds are only 1 in 12 that any single X chromosome will contain a gene for color blindness, the likelihood that a female will

Figure 3-7
Normal (round) and "sickled" (elongated) red blood cells from a person with sickle-cell anemia.

codominance: condition in which two heterozygous but equally powerful alleles produce a phenotype in which both genes are fully and equally expressed.

sex-linked characteristic: an attribute determined by a gene that appears on only one of the two types of sex chromosomes, usually the X chromosome.

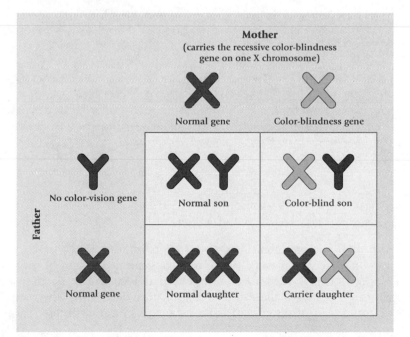

Mother
(carries the recessive color-blindness gene on one X chromosome)

Normal gene — Color-blindness gene

Father

No color-vision gene — Normal son — Color-blind son

Normal gene — Normal daughter — Carrier daughter

Figure 3-8
Sex-linked inheritance of red/green color blindness. In the example here, the mother can distinguish reds from greens but is a carrier because one of her X chromosomes contains a color-blind allele. Notice that her sons have a 50% chance of inheriting the color-blind allele and being color blind, whereas none of her daughters would display the trait. A girl can be color blind only if her father is *and* her mother is at least a carrier of the color-blindness gene.

inherit two of these genes (and be color blind) is 1/12 × 1/12, or only 1 in 144 (Burns & Bottino, 1989).

There are many sex-linked characteristics other than color blindness, and most of them are disabling. These include hemophilia (a disease in which the blood does not clot), diabetes, two kinds of muscular dystrophy, degeneration of the optic nerve, and certain forms of deafness and night blindness (Schulman & Black, 1993). Because these disorders are determined by recessive genes on X chromosomes, males are much more likely than females to suffer their harmful effects.

Polygenic Inheritance

To this point, we have considered only those traits that are influenced by a single pair of alleles. However, most important human characteristics are influenced by multiple pairs of alleles and are called **polygenic traits.** Examples of polygenic traits include height, weight, intelligence, skin color, temperamental attributes, susceptibility to cancer, and a host of others (Plomin, 1990). Imagine that height influenced by three pairs of genes, and that the alleles AA, BB, and CC would tend to produce giants, whereas the genotype aa, bb, and cc would tend to produce dwarfs. Without going into the mathematics, there are 27 distinct genotypes that could result if we calculated all possible children that one couple of average height (each with an Aa Bb Cc genotype, for example) could produce. Gene combinations that call for average height would be more likely than combinations calling for very tall or very short stature. When a trait is influenced by multiple genes, we would therefore expect many phenotypes to appear in the population, and we would expect many people to be near the average and few to be extreme. This is exactly the way height and most other measurable human traits are distributed in large populations.

To date, nobody knows exactly how many pairs of alleles influence physical stature (height), intelligence, or other polygenic traits. All we can say is that unknown numbers of genes, interacting with environmental influences, create a wide range of individual differences in most important human attributes.

Concept Check 3-1 ⌄ Understanding Principles of Hereditary Transmission

Check your understanding of the principles of hereditary transmission by answering each of the following questions. Answers appear in the Appendix at the back of the book.

1. You are a monozygotic (identical) twin. The odds that you and your twin are the same sex (that is, two boys or two girls) are

   a. 100%   b. 50%   c. impossible to calculate

2. Most people can curl their tongues—a trait that is determined by a dominant gene. Your father can curl his tongue, but neither your mother nor your sister can. The odds that you can curl your tongue are

   a. 100%   b. 75%   c. 50%   d. 25%

3. Knowing what you know about your parents' tongue-curling abilities (from item 2 above), if you can curl your tongue, your own genotype for tongue curling is

   a. homozygous   b. heterozygous   c. impossible to determine

4. If both *biological* parents cannot curl their tongues, then the odds that their child will be *unable* to curl his (her) tongue are

   a. 100%   b. 50%   c. 0%

---

polygenic trait: a characteristic that is influenced by the action of many genes rather than a single pair.

congenital defect: a problem that is present (though not necessarily apparent) at birth; such defects may stem from genetic and prenatal influences or from complications of the birth process.

Huntington's disease: a genetic disease caused by a dominant allele that typically appears later in life and causes the nervous system to degenerate (see Box 3-1).

 CHROMOSOMAL AND GENETIC ABNORMALITIES

Although the vast majority of newborn infants are pronounced healthy at birth, approximately 7 of every 100 have a congenital problem of some kind (Schulman & Black, 1993). By definition, **congenital defects** are those that are present at birth, although many of these afflictions are not detectable when the child is born. For example, **Huntington's disease** is a congenital problem because the gene that produces this disease is present from the moment of conception. But as we learned in Box 3-1, the gradual deterioration of the nervous system associated with this condition is not apparent at birth and will not ordinarily appear until much later—usually after age 40.

In Chapter 4, we will consider a variety of congenital defects that are likely to result from abnormalities in the birth process or from harmful conditions to which children are exposed while developing within the womb. Here, we will look only at those problems that are caused by abnormal genes and chromosomes.

Chromosomal Abnormalities

When a germ cell divides during meiosis, the distribution of its 46 chromosomes into sperm or ova is sometimes uneven. In other words, one of the resulting gametes may have too many chromosomes, while the other has too few. The vast majority of these chromosomal abnormalities are *lethal*, meaning that a zygote formed from the union of an abnormal and a normal gamete will fail to develop or will be spontaneously aborted. However, some chromosomal aberrations are not lethal, as illustrated by the finding that approximately 1 child in 200 is born with either one chromosome too many or one too few (Plomin, 1986).

Abnormalities of the Sex Chromosomes

Many chromosomal abnormalities involve the 23rd pair: the sex chromosomes. Occasionally, males are born with an extra X or Y chromosome, producing the genotype XXY or XYY, and females will often survive if they inherit a single X chromosome (XO) or even three (XXX), four (XXXX), or five (XXXXX) X chromosomes. Each of these conditions has somewhat different implications for the child's development, as we will see in examining four of the more common sex chromosome abnormalities in Table 3-1.

In addition to the abnormalities described in the table, about 1 individual in 1000 has an X chromosome that is brittle in places and may even have separated into two or more pieces—a condition known as the **fragile-X syndrome** (Jenkins, Shapiro, & Brown, 1992). This condition is second only to Down syndrome (which we will soon discuss) as a genetic cause of mental retardation, and recent research suggests that it may contribute to some cases of *infantile autism*, a serious emotional disorder of early childhood characterized by extreme self-involvement, repetitive self-stimulating behaviors, and delayed (or absent) language and social skills (Jenkins et al., 1992). About 75 percent of fragile-X males show some degree of mental retardation (ranging from mild to severe), whereas the clear majority of females with a fragile-X chromosome are either intellectually normal or display only mild learning disabilities (Schulman & Black, 1993). Recently, investigators have located the gene responsible for this chromosomal abnormality—a *recessive* gene on the X chromosome. So the fragile-X syndrome is apparently yet another example of a sex-linked disorder that, like all other X-linked recessive traits, will appear more often in males than in females.

Autosomal Abnormalities

Several hereditary abnormalities are attributable to the *autosomes*—that is, the 22 pairs of chromosomes that are similar in males and females. The most common type of autosomal abnormality occurs when an abnormal sperm or ovum carrying an extra autosome combines with a normal gamete to form a zygote that has 47 chromosomes (2 sex chromosomes and 45 autosomes). In these cases, the extra chromosome appears along with one of the 22 pairs of autosomes to yield three chromosomes of that type, or a *trisomy*.

By far the most frequent of all autosomal abnormalities (occurring once in every 600 births) is **Down syndrome**, or *trisomy 21*, a condition in which the child has

fragile-X syndrome: a sex chromosome abnormality in which individuals have a compressed or broken X chromosome; affected individuals (particularly males) may show mild to severe mental retardation.

Down syndrome: a chromosomal abnormality (also known as trisomy 21) caused by the presence of an extra 21st chromosome; people with this syndrome have a distinct physical appearance and are moderately to severely retarded.

Table 3-1   Four Common Sex Chromosome Abnormalities

Name/genotype(s)	Incidence	Developmental implications
Female abnormalities		
Turner's syndrome; XO	1 in 3000 female births	*Appearance:* Phenotypically female but small in stature with stubby fingers and toes, a webbed neck, a broad chest, and small, under-developed breasts. Normal sexual development lacking at puberty, although Turner females can assume a more "womanly" appearance by taking the female hormone estrogen. *Fertility:* Sterile. *Intellectual characteristics:* Normal in verbal intelligence but frequently score below average on tests of spatial abilities such as puzzle assembly or the mental rotation of figures (see Downey et al., 1991).
Poly-X or "superfemale" syndrome; XXX, XXXX, or XXXXX	1 in 1000 female births	*Appearance:* Phenotypically female and normal in appearance. *Fertility:* Fertile; produce children with the usual number of sex chromosomes. *Intellectual characteristics:* Score somewhat below average in intelligence, with their greatest deficits on tests of verbal reasoning. Intellectual deficits are detectable as early as age 2 and are reflected by delays in reaching developmental milestones such as walking and talking. Developmental delays and intellectual deficits become more pronounced with an increase in the number of extra X chromosomes they have inherited (Robinson et al., 1992).
Male abnormalities		
Klinefelter's syndrome; XXY or XXXY	1 in 500 male births	*Appearance:* Phenotypically male, with the emergence of some female secondary sex characteristics (enlargement of the hips and breasts) at puberty. Significantly taller than normal (XY) males. In the past, Klinefelter males from Eastern-bloc countries may have competed as females in athletic events, leading to the current practice of administering sex tests to all female Olympic athletes. *Fertility:* Have underdeveloped testes and are sterile. *Intellectual characteristics:* About 20%–30% of Klinefelter males are deficient in verbal intelligence, and their deficiencies become more pronounced with an increase in the number of extra X chromosomes they have inherited (Burns & Bottino, 1989; Robinson et al., 1992).
Supermale syndrome; XYY, XYYY, or XYYYY	1 in 1000 male births	*Appearance:* Phenotypic males who are significantly taller than normal (XY) males, have large teeth, and who often develop severe acne during adolescence. *Fertility:* Typically fertile, although many of these men have abnormally low sperm counts. *Intellectual characteristics:* Although once thought to be subnormal intellectually and prone to violence and aggression, later research has proved both these assumptions wrong (Burns & Bottino, 1989). IQs of supermales span the full range of those observed in normal (XY) males. Moreover, careful studies of large numbers of XYYs indicate that these boys and men are no more violent or aggressive than normal males, and are sometimes shy and retiring.

inherited an extra 21st chromosome. Children with Down syndrome are mentally retarded, with IQs that average 50 (the average IQ among normal children is 100). They may also have congenital eye, ear, and heart defects and are usually characterized by a number of distinctive physical features, including a sloping forehead, a protruding tongue, short stubby limbs, a slightly flattened nose, and a distinctive fold to the eyelids that gives their eyes an Oriental appearance (see Figure 3-9). In years gone by, people often called these children "mongoloid idiots" and believed that they were largely incapable of learning. This was an unfortunate assumption, for recent research indicates that these so-called idiots reach many of the same developmental milestones as normal children, but at a slower pace (Kopp, 1983; Thompson, Cicchetti, Lamb, & Malkin, 1985). Furthermore, most of these youngsters do learn to care for their basic needs, and some have even learned to read and write (Gibson & Harris, 1988; Kopp, 1983). Their developmental progress appears to be best when parents and other regular companions are persistent in their attempts to stimulate them while providing ample emotional support (Mundy, Sigman, Kasari, & Yirmiya, 1988; Thompson et al., 1985). However, they will often spend much of their adult life in an institution because their developmental handicaps usually prevent them from becoming economically self-sufficient.

Figure 3-9
Children with Down syndrome can lead happy lives if they receive affection and encouragement from their companions.

Causes of Chromosomal Abnormality

Perhaps the most basic cause of chromosomal abnormalities is *uneven segregation of chromosomes* into daughter cells during meiosis. Sometimes, for example, the meiosis of a female germ cell produces one ovum containing two X chromosomes and a second ovum with no X chromosome. Such an imbalance permits several interesting possibilities. If the first (XX) ovum is fertilized by a sperm bearing an X chromosome, the result is a poly-X (XXX) female. However, if a sperm bearing a Y chromosome reaches that ovum first, the zygote will become a Klinefelter male (XXY). And if the ovum containing no X chromosome is fertilized by an X-bearing sperm, the child will be an XO female who has Turner's syndrome. Of course, some of these abnormalities can also result from the uneven meiosis of a male germ cell.

The probability that a child will inherit Down syndrome, Klinefelter's syndrome, or the poly-X syndrome increases dramatically if the mother is over 35 (Verp, Simpson, & Ober, 1993). Table 3-2 illustrates the relationship of Down syndrome to the age of the mother. Note that mothers who have already given birth to a child with

Table 3-2   Risk of Down Syndrome and Other Chromosomal Abnormalities as a Function of Mother's Age

| | Probability that child will have Down syndrome | | Probability of |
Age of mother	At any pregnancy	After birth of a child with Down syndrome	any chromosomal abnormality at birth
<29	<1 in 1000	1 in 100	1 in 450
30–34	1 in 700	1 in 100	1 in 350
35–39	1 in 220	1 in 100	1 in 150
40–44	1 in 65	1 in 25	1 in 40
45–49	1 in 25	1 in 15	1 in 12

Sources: Adapted from Pueschel & Goldstein, 1983, and from Verp, Simpson, & Ober, 1993.

Down syndrome are much more likely to have another child with Down syndrome, should they give birth again, than are other women of the same age.

Why is the older woman at higher risk for bearing a child with chromosome abnormalities? Consider the **"aging-ova" hypothesis.** Ova are formed only once, during prenatal development. So, a 45-year-old woman's ova are more than 45 years old and may simply degenerate and become abnormal as she nears the end of her reproductive years. Of course, an alternative explanation is that older women may have had more opportunities to become exposed to environmental hazards such as radiation, drugs, chemicals, and viruses that could damage their ova.

Interestingly, there is some support for both hypotheses—evidence that also indicates that we should not blame mothers for all chromosomal abnormalities. For example, even though most cases of Down syndrome can be traced to mothers' abnormal ova, about one-fourth of these children receive their extra 21st chromosome from their fathers rather than their mothers (Magenis et al., 1977). The risk of chromosomal abnormalities is also greater if a father has been exposed to such environmental hazards as repeated abdominal X rays (radiation) that can damage his chromosomes (Strigini et al., 1990). And it now appears that the majority of girls with Turner's syndrome (see Table 3-1) originate from a normal (X) ovum that has been fertilized by an abnormal *sperm* that contains neither an X nor a Y chromosome (Burns & Bottino, 1989). Only the XYY (or supermale) syndrome is always attributable to one parent—in this case, the father—because mothers have no Y chromosomes to transmit to their offspring.

Genetic Abnormalities

Parents who are themselves healthy are often amazed to learn that a child of theirs could have a hereditary defect. Their surprise is certainly understandable, for most genetic problems are recessive traits that few, if any, close relatives have had. In addition, these problems simply will not appear unless both parents carry the harmful allele *and* the child inherits this particular gene from each parent. The exceptions to this rule are sex-linked defects that a male child will display if the recessive alleles for these traits appear on the X chromosome he inherits from his mother (recall that, because a boy has only one X chromosome, he has no corresponding gene that might counteract the effect of an X-linked recessive allele).

Earlier in the chapter, we discussed two recessive hereditary defects, one that is sex linked (color blindness) and one that is not (sickle-cell anemia). Table 3-3 describes a number of additional crippling or fatal diseases that are attributable to a single pair of recessive alleles.

Genetic abnormalities may also result from **mutations,** that is, changes in the chemical structure of one or more genes that have the effect of producing a new phenotype. Many mutations occur spontaneously and are harmful or even fatal (see discussion of hemophilia in Table 3-3). Mutations can also be induced by environmental hazards such as toxic industrial waste, radiation, agricultural chemicals that enter the food supply, and possibly even some of the additives and preservatives in processed foods (Burns & Bottino, 1989).

Might mutations ever be beneficial? Evolutionary theorists think so. Presumably, any mutation that is induced by stressors present in the natural environment may provide an "adaptive" advantage to those who inherit the mutant genes, thus enabling these individuals to survive. The sickle-cell gene, for example, is a mutation that originated in Africa, Central America, and other tropical areas where malaria is widespread. Heterozygous children who inherit a single sickle-cell allele are well adapted to these environments because the mutant gene makes them more resistant to malarial infection and thus more likely to survive. Of course, the mutant sickle-cell gene is not advantageous (and can be harmful) in environments where malaria is not a problem.

aging-ova hypothesis: the hypothesis that an older mother is more likely to have children with chromosomal abnormalities because her ova are degenerating as she nears the end of her reproductive years.

mutation: a change in the chemical structure or arrangement of one or more genes that has the effect of producing a new phenotype.

Table 3-3 Brief Description of Some Major Recessive Hereditary Defects

Defect	Description
Cystic fibrosis	A fatal disease that occurs in about 1 in 1000 births. The child lacks an enzyme that prevents mucus from obstructing the lungs and digestive tract. Many who inherit this condition die in childhood or adolescence, although advances in treatment have enabled some victims to live until their mid-30s. Over 10 million Americans are carriers who can transmit the gene for cystic fibrosis to their offspring.
Muscular dystrophy (MD)	There are more than ten forms of this genetic disease, which attacks the muscles. As the disease progresses, the individual often begins to show slurred speech, becomes unable to walk, and may gradually lose most or all motor capabilities. Occasionally, MD causes death. Two forms, Duchenne's and Becker's muscular dystrophies, are sex linked. About 1 in 3500 males will develop Duchenne's disease; more than 100,000 Americans have inherited some form of MD.
Phenylketonuria (PKU)	The child lacks an enzyme necessary to digest foods (including milk) that contain the amino acid phenylalanine. If this condition is not detected and the child placed on a diet of milk substitutes, phenylpyruvic acid will accumulate in the body and attack the developing nervous system. Long-term affects of untreated PKU are hyperactivity and severe mental retardation. PKU occurs in 1 of every 10,000 Caucasian births; it is much less frequent among those of African and Asian ancestry.
Tay-Sachs disease	A degenerative disease of the nervous system that will kill its victims, usually by their third birthday. Primarily affects Jewish children of Eastern European ancestry. Approximately 1 in 30 American Jews is a carrier.
Hemophilia	A sex-linked condition sometimes called "bleeder's disease." The child lacks a substance that causes the blood to clot and could bleed to death if scraped, bruised, or cut. Hemophilia was well known among the royal families of Europe and can be traced to Queen Victoria of England. Since no hemophilia is known in Victoria's ancestry, it appears that the recessive gene for hemophilia may have been a mutation that Queen Victoria then passed on to her offspring.* Although quite rare in females, hemophilia may occur as often as once in every 1000 male births.
Diabetes	An inherited condition in which the individual is unable to metabolize sugar properly because the body does not produce enough insulin. Two of the many forms of this disease are sex linked. If untreated, diabetes is usually fatal. However, the disease can be controlled by taking insulin and restricting one's diet. Diabetes usually appears later in adulthood, although as many as 1 child in 2500 is diabetic.

*Of course, this does not mean that everyone who has hemophilia is related to Queen Victoria. A mutation, such as that producing the recessive allele for hemophilia, may occur spontaneously at any time. In at least 30% of cases of hemophilia, there is no family history of the disease. These new cases probably arise from spontaneous mutations.

Source: From Ayala & Kiger, 1984, and Lin, Verp, & Sabbagha, 1993.

Applications: *Genetic Counseling and Treatment of Hereditary Disorders*

Now try to imagine that one of your relatives has a recessive genetic disorder such as sickle-cell anemia and you suspect you might be a carrier. You then meet and marry a person who also believes he or she might be a carrier of this same defect. Assuming that both of you want to have children, should you now decide against it? Can you tell whether your child will be abnormal before birth? Is all hope lost should you produce a child who has a hereditary disease? These are issues that you and your spouse would probably wish to explore with a genetic counselor.

Genetic counseling is a service that helps prospective parents to assess the likelihood that their children will be free of hereditary defects. Persons serving as genetic counselors are trained in genetics, the interpretation of family histories, and counseling procedures. They may be geneticists, medical researchers, or practitioners, such as a pediatrician. Although any couple who hopes to have children might wish to talk with a genetic counselor about the hereditary risks their children may face, genetic counseling is particularly helpful for couples who have relatives with hereditary disorders or for parents who have already borne an abnormal child.

Establishing the Likelihood of a Defect

Once a genetic counselor has established that the parents' concerns are truly hereditary in origin, he or she may obtain a complete family history from each prospective parent that includes information about the diseases and causes of death of siblings, parents, and other blood relatives; the ethnicity and countries of origin of blood relatives who were immigrants; intermarriages that may have occurred in the past between close relatives (such as cousins); and previous problems in the childbearing process, such as miscarriages or stillbirths. For some defects (certain types of **muscular dystrophy**, for example), family histories are the only basis for determining whether a couple's children might be affected. Should a client's family history reveal several cases of a disorder, there is a good possibility that he or she carries the recessive gene for this hereditary defect. Yet, the likelihood that the client's children would inherit the disorder may still be very small unless the same disorder has also occurred among the *spouse's* blood relatives.

Fortunately, several recessive genes that produce hereditary defects can be detected by simple laboratory tests. For example, blood tests can determine whether a prospective parent carries the recessive allele for Tay-Sachs disease, sickle-cell anemia, hemophilia, phenylketonuria, or the fragile-X syndrome (Edwards, 1993). In addition, many chromosomal abnormalities can be detected by taking a small sample of each parent's skin and preparing karyotypes. Finally, a client whose own mother or father was a victim of *Huntington's disease*—the dreaded condition caused by a *dominant* allele that leads to gradual deterioration of the nervous system in middle age—can now be tested to determine the likelihood of passing this gene (and hence, the disease) to children (the odds are 1 in 2, or 50%, if one's parent is affected). Before this test became available, children of a Huntington's disease victim had to wonder for much of their lives whether they had inherited the gene for this terrible disorder and would fall prey to it themselves. The slightest signs of clumsiness, mood swings, or personality changes might arouse fear that the disease had struck (Bishop & Waldholz, 1990). Many sons and daughters of Huntington's victims, not knowing their own status, were afraid to have children, fearing that their offspring would be affected. Now that the test is available, not all individuals at risk choose to take it; for some, the prospect of learning that they will definitely experience an incurable genetic disease is simply too frightening. But many who take the test do feel better knowing one way or another what the future holds (Wiggins et al., 1992).

Now let's consider how genetic counseling might work for adults who are not aware (as sons and daughters of Huntington's victims are) that they are at risk of transmitting harmful genetic disorders to their offspring. One married couple whom

genetic counseling: a service designed to inform prospective parents about genetic diseases and to help them determine the likelihood that they would transmit such disorders to their children.

muscular dystrophy: a genetic disease that attacks the muscles and results in a gradual loss of motor capabilities (see Table 3-3).

I know recently requested genetic counseling and learned that they were both carriers for **Tay-Sachs disease,** a condition that normally kills an affected child within the first three years of life (see Table 3-3). The genetic counselor explained to this couple that there was 1 chance in 4 that any child they conceived would inherit a recessive allele from each of them and have Tay-Sachs disease. However, there was also 1 chance in 4 that the child would inherit the dominant gene from each parent, and there were 2 chances in 4 that the child would be just like its parents—phenotypically normal but a carrier of the recessive Tay-Sachs allele. After receiving this information, the young woman expressed strong reservations about having children, feeling that the odds were just too high to risk having a baby with a fatal disease.

At this point, the counselor informed the couple that, before they made a firm decision against having children, they ought to be aware of procedures that can detect many genetic abnormalities, including Tay-Sachs disease, early in the pregnancy. He told them that these screening procedures cannot reverse any abnormalities that are found, but they allow expectant parents to decide whether to terminate a pregnancy rather than give birth to a defective child.

Prenatal Detection of Hereditary Abnormalities

The most common method of detecting abnormalities during the prenatal period is **amniocentesis.** A large, hollow needle is inserted into the abdomen of a pregnant woman in order to withdraw a sample of the amniotic fluid that surrounds the fetus. Fetal cells in this fluid can then be tested to determine the sex of the fetus and the presence of chromosomal abnormalities such as Down syndrome. In addition, more than 100 genetic disorders—including Tay-Sachs disease, cystic fibrosis, Duchenne's muscular dystrophy, sickle-cell anemia, and hemophilia—can now be diagnosed by analyzing fetal cells in amniotic fluid (Pergament & Fine, 1993). Although amniocentesis is considered a very safe procedure, it can trigger a miscarriage in a very small percentage of cases. In fact, the risk of miscarriage (though very small) is thought to be greater than the risk of a birth defect if the mother is under age 35 (Elias & Simpson, 1992).

A major disadvantage of amniocentesis is that it is not easily performed before the 14th to 16th week of pregnancy, when amniotic fluid becomes sufficiently plentiful to withdraw for analysis. Since the results of the tests will not come back for another two weeks, parents have little time to consider a second-trimester abortion if the fetus has a serious defect and abortion is their choice. But there is a newer technique that looks promising as an alternative to amniocentesis. This procedure, called **chorionic villus sampling (CVS)** collects tissue for the same tests as amniocentesis does and can be performed during the 8th or 9th week of pregnancy (Pergament & Fine, 1993). As shown in Figure 3-10, there are two approaches to CVS. A catheter inserted through the mother's vagina and cervix or a needle through her abdomen penetrates a membrane called the *chorion* that surrounds the fetus. Fetal cells are then extracted and tested for hereditary abnormalities, with the results typically available within 24 hours. So CVS often allows parents to know whether their fetus bears a suspected abnormality very early on, leaving them more time to consider carefully the pros and cons of continuing the pregnancy in the event that the fetus is abnormal. But despite its advantages, CVS is currently recommended only to parents at high risk of conceiving an abnormal child, for it entails a slightly greater chance of miscarriage than does amniocentesis, and its use has, in rare instances, been linked to birth defects (Seabrook, 1994).

Another prenatal diagnostic technique is **ultrasound** (sonar), a method of scanning the womb with sound waves. Ultrasound provides the attending physician with an outline of the fetus in much the same way that sonar reveals outlines of the fish beneath a fishing boat. It is a very safe procedure that is particularly useful for detecting multiple pregnancies and gross physical defects. It is also used to guide practitioners as they perform amniocentesis and CVS (see Figure 3-10).

Tay-Sachs disease: a genetic disease that attacks the nervous system, causing it to degenerate (see Table 3-3).

amniocentesis: a method of extracting amniotic fluid from a pregnant woman so that fetal body cells within the fluid can be tested for chromosomal abnormalities and other genetic defects.

chorionic villus sampling (CVS): an alternative to amniocentesis in which fetal cells are extracted from the chorion for prenatal tests. CVS can be performed earlier in pregnancy than is possible through amniocentesis.

ultrasound: method of detecting gross physical abnormalities by scanning the womb with sound waves, thereby producing a visual outline of the fetus.

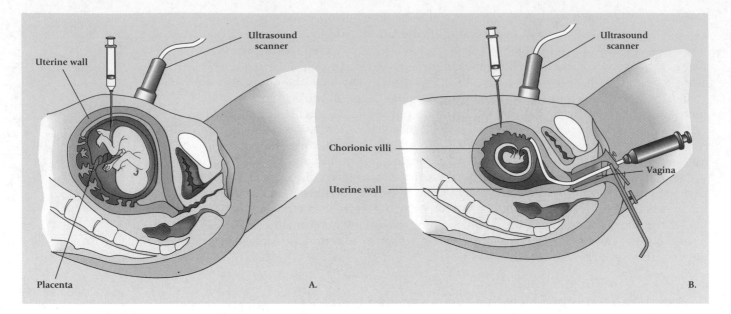

Uterine wall
Ultrasound scanner
Chorionic villi
Ultrasound scanner
Vagina
Uterine wall
Placenta
A.
B.

Figure 3-10

Amniocentesis and chorionic villus sampling. (A) In amniocentesis, a needle is inserted through the abdominal wall into the uterus. Fluid is withdrawn and fetal cells are cultured, a process that takes about three weeks. (B) Chorionic villus sampling can be performed much earlier in pregnancy, and results are available within 24 hours. Two approaches to obtaining a sample of chorionic villi are shown here: inserting a thin tube through the vagina into the uterus or a needle through the abdominal wall. In either of these methods, ultrasound is used for guidance.

Adapted from Moore, 1993.

phenylketonuria (PKU): a genetic disease in which the child is unable to metabolize phenylalanine; if left untreated, it soon causes hyperactivity and mental retardation (see Table 3-3).

Treating Hereditary Disorders

Prenatal detection of a hereditary disorder leaves many couples in a quandary, particularly if their religious background or personal beliefs argue against abortion. If the disease in question is invariably fatal, like Tay-Sachs, the couple must decide either to violate their moral principles and terminate the pregnancy or to have a baby who will appear normal and healthy but will show a rapid decline in all of his or her functions and die young.

Might this quandary someday become a thing of the past? Very possibly. Only 35 years ago, medical science could do little for children with another degenerative disease of the nervous system: **phenylketonuria,** or **PKU.** Like Tay-Sachs disease, PKU is a metabolic disorder. Affected children lack a critical enzyme that would allow them to metabolize phenylalanine, a component of many foods, including milk. As phenylalanine accumulates in the body, it is converted to a harmful substance, phenylpyruvic acid, that attacks the nervous system. In years gone by, the majority of children who inherited this disorder soon became hyperactive and severely retarded.

The major breakthroughs came in the mid-1950s when scientists developed a diet low in phenylalanine, and in 1961, when they developed a simple blood test that could determine within a few days after birth if a child had PKU. Newborn infants are now routinely screened for PKU, and affected children are immediately placed on the low-phenylalanine diet. The outcome of this therapeutic intervention is a happy one: Children who remain on the diet throughout middle childhood will suffer few, if any, of the harmful consequences of this formerly incurable disease. Outcomes are best when affected individuals remain on the special diet *for life*. This is particularly true of PKU women who hope to have children of their own, for if they are off the diet and their phenylalanine levels are high, they face great risk of miscarrying a pregnancy or of bearing a mentally deficient child (Verp, 1993).

Today, the potentially devastating effects of many hereditary abnormalities can be minimized or controlled. For example, new surgical techniques, performed *on fetuses in utero*, have made it possible to repair some genetically transmitted defects of the neural tube and urinary tract and to lessen the complications of many other genetic disorders by bone marrow transplantation (Golbus & Fries, 1993). Children who inherit either Turner's syndrome or Klinefelter's syndrome can be placed on hormone therapy to make them more normal in appearance. Diabetes can be controlled by a low-sugar diet and by periodic doses of insulin, which help the patient to metabolize sugar. And youngsters who have such blood disorders as hemophilia or sickle-cell anemia may now receive periodic transfusions to provide them with the clotting agents or the normal red blood cells they lack.

Finally, advances in the treatment of cystic fibrosis (CF) nicely illustrate the remarkable rate at which researchers are gaining knowledge they need to combat genetic diseases. Only ten years ago, about all that could be done for CF patients was to administer antibiotics to lessen the discomfort of their chronic lung obstructions and infections. But in 1989, researchers located the CF gene, and only one year later, two research teams succeeded at neutralizing the damaging effects of this gene in the laboratory (Denning et al., 1991; Seligman, 1990). Soon thereafter came the development and testing of a *gene replacement therapy* that involves inserting normal genes, carried by genetically engineered cold viruses, into the noses and lungs of patients with cystic fibrosis in the hopes that these imported genes can override the effects of the CF genes. And the earliest returns look extremely promising (Husted, 1993).

In sum, many abnormal children can lead approximately normal lives if their hereditary disorders are detected and treated before serious harm has been done. And inspired by recent successes in fetal medicine, genetic mapping, and gene replacement therapy, geneticists and medical practitioners are hopeful that many untreatable genetic defects will become treatable, or even curable, in the near future.

Meanwhile, scientists and society as a whole will have to grapple with thorny ethical issues that are arising from the rapid progress being made. Most fetal surgical procedures, for example, are still experimental and often induce miscarriages or other complications. Is it in the fetus's best interests to undergo an operation in utero that may end its life? Should a mother be held legally responsible if she refuses a fetal therapy that might prevent her from delivering a handicapped child? These are some of the issues that medical and legal practitioners are currently debating (Evans, Robertson, & Fletcher, 1993). Moreover, the reality of gene replacement therapies and even future *genetic splicing* techniques (in which a harmful gene is surgically replaced with a nonharmful one at the early embryonic stage, thus permanently correcting a genetic defect) brings us to the verge of a brave new world in which human beings will be capable of altering their own genotypes. How much such genetic engineering should be allowed? To what purposes should it be limited? These issues will be hotly debated in the years ahead.

 # HEREDITARY INFLUENCES ON BEHAVIOR

We have seen that genes play a major role in determining our physical appearance and many of our metabolic characteristics. But to what extent does heredity affect such characteristics as intelligence? Can a strong case be made for genetic contributions to personality, temperament, and mental health?

In recent years, investigators from the fields of genetics, zoology, population biology, and psychology have asked the question, "Are there certain abilities, traits, and patterns of behavior that depend very heavily on the particular combination of genes that an individual inherits, and if so, are these attributes likely to be modified by one's experiences?" Those who focus on these issues in their research are known as *behavioral geneticists.*

Before we take a closer look at the field of **behavioral genetics**, it is necessary to dispel a common myth. Although behavioral geneticists view development as the process through which one's *genotype* (the set of genes that one inherits) is expressed in one's *phenotype* (observable characteristics and behaviors), they are not strict hereditarians. They recognize, for example, that even physical characteristics such as height depend to some extent on environmental variables, such as the adequacy of one's diet (Plomin, 1990). They acknowledge that the long-term effects of inherited metabolic disorders such as PKU and diabetes also depend on one's environment—namely, the availability of personnel to detect and to treat these conditions. In other

behavioral genetics: the scientific study of how genotype interacts with environment to determine behavioral attributes such as intelligence, temperament, and personality.

words, the behavioral geneticists are well aware that even attributes that have a strong hereditary component are often modified in important ways by environmental influences.

How, then, do behavioral geneticists differ from ethologists, who are also interested in the biological bases of development? The answer is relatively simple. Ethologists study inherited attributes that characterize *all* members of a species and thus conspire to make them *alike* (that is, attributes that contribute to *common* developmental outcomes). By contrast, behavioral geneticists focus on the biological bases for *variation* among members of a species. They are concerned with determining how the unique combination of genes that each of us inherits might be implicated in making us *different* from one another. Let's now consider the methods they use to perform this task.

Methods of Studying Hereditary Influences

There are two major strategies that behavioral geneticists use to assess hereditary contributions to behavior: *selective breeding* and *family studies*. Each of these approaches attempts to specify the **heritability** of various attributes, that is, the amount of variation in a trait or a class of behavior that is attributable to hereditary factors.

Selective Breeding

Members of any species, particularly human beings, differ considerably in their basic abilities, peculiarities, and patterns of behavior. Could these individual differences be hereditary? Do they simply reflect the fact that no two individuals (except identical twins) inherit the same pattern of genes?

Many investigators have tried to answer this question by seeing whether they could selectively breed particular attributes in animals. A famous example of a selective breeding experiment is R. C. Tryon's (1940) attempt to show that maze-learning ability is a heritable attribute in rats. Tryon started by testing a large number of rats for ability to run a complex maze. Rats that made few errors were labeled "maze-bright"; those that made many errors were termed "maze-dull." Then, across several successive generations, Tryon mated the brightest of the maze-bright rats together, while also inbreeding the dullest of the maze-dull group. This was a well-controlled experiment in that Tryon occasionally took offspring from each group and had them raised by mothers from the other group. This *cross-fostering* procedure helps to ensure that any difference in maze-learning ability between the offspring of the two strains is due to selective breeding (heredity), rather than the type of early stimulation that the young animals received from their mother figure (environment).

Figure 3-11 shows the results of Tryon's selective breeding experiment. Note that across generations the differences in maze-running performance between the maze-bright and the maze-dull groups became increasingly apparent. By the 18th generation, the worst performer among the maze-bright group was better at running mazes than the best performer from the maze-dull group. Clearly, Tryon had shown that maze-learning ability in rats is influenced by hereditary factors. Other investigators have used the selective breeding technique to demonstrate clear genetic contributions to such attributes as activity level, emotionality, aggressiveness, and sex drive in rats, mice, and chickens (Plomin, DeFries, & McClearn, 1989).

Family Studies

Since it is obviously unethical to conduct selective breeding studies with humans, the field of human behavioral genetics relies on an alternative methodology known as the family study. In a typical family study, persons who live in the same household are compared to see how similar they are on one or more attributes. If the attribute in question is heritable, then the similarity between any two pairs of individuals who live in the same environment should increase as a function of their **kinship,** that is, the extent to which they have the same genes.

heritability: the amount of variability in a trait that is attributable to hereditary factors.

kinship: the extent to which two individuals have genes in common.

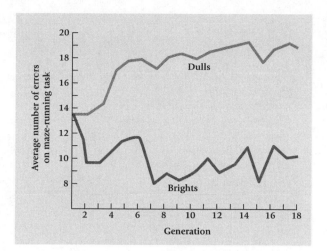

Figure 3-11
Maze-running performance by inbred maze-bright and maze-dull rats over 18 generations.
From Plomin, DeFries, & McClearn, 1989.

Two kinds of family (or kinship) studies are common today. The first is the **twin design,** or **twin study,** which asks the question "Are pairs of identical twins reared together more similar to each other on various attributes than pairs of fraternal twins reared together?" If genes affect the attribute(s) in question, then identical twins should be more similar, for they have 100% of their genes in common (kinship = 1.00) while fraternal twins share only 50% (kinship = .50). Extending this logic, we could also predict that fraternal twins should be more similar on a heritable attribute than either half-siblings (kinship = .25) or pairs of genetically unrelated children who live in the same household (kinship = .00).

The second common family study, the **adoption design,** focuses on adoptees who are genetically unrelated to other members of their adoptive families. A researcher searching for hereditary influences would ask "Are adopted children similar to their biological parents, whose *genes* they share (kinship = .50), or are they similar to their adoptive parents, whose *environment* they share?" If adoptees resemble their biological parents in intelligence or personality, even though these parents did not raise them, then genes must be influential in determining such attributes.

Family studies can also help us to estimate the extent to which various abilities and behaviors are influenced by the environment. To illustrate, consider a case in which two genetically unrelated adopted children are raised in the same home. Their degree of kinship with each other and with their adoptive parents is .00. Consequently, there is no reason to suspect that these children will resemble each other or their adoptive parents unless their common environment plays some part in determining their standing on the attribute in question. Another way that the effects of environment can be inferred is to compare identical twins raised in the same environment with identical twins raised in different environments. The kinship of all pairs of identical twins, reared together or apart, is 1.00. So if identical twins reared together are more alike on an attribute than identical twins reared apart, we can infer that the environment plays a role in determining that attribute.

Estimating the Contribution of Genes (and Environment)

Behavioral geneticists rely on some simple and some not-so-simple mathematical calculations to tell them (1) whether or not a trait is genetically influenced and (2) the degree to which heredity *and* environment can account for individual differences in that trait. When studying traits that a person either does or does not display (for example, a drug habit or clinical depression), researchers calculate and compare **concordance rates**—the percentages of pairs of people (for example, identical twins, fraternal twins, parents and their adoptive children) in which *both* members of the pair display the trait if one member has it. Suppose that you are interested in determining whether homosexuality in men is genetically influenced. You might locate gay

twin study: study in which sets of twins that differ in zygosity (kinship) are compared to determine the heritability of an attribute or attributes.

adoption design: study in which adoptees are compared with their biological relatives and their adoptive relatives to estimate the heritability of an attribute or attributes.

concordance rate: the percentage of cases in which a particular attribute is present for both members of a pair if it is present for one member.

Concept Check 3-2 ⌄ Understanding the Logic of Behavioral
Genetic Methods

Check your understanding of the methods that behavioral geneticists use to detect hereditary
influences on specific attributes by filling in the blanks in the statements below. The answers
appear in the Appendix.

1. The findings from *twin studies* suggest a hereditary influence on a trait if _____
   are more similar on that trait than _____ .

2. The findings from *adoption* studies suggest a hereditary influence on a trait if adoptees are
   more similar to their _____ parents on that trait than to their
   _____ parents.

3. The findings from family studies suggest that heredity does not influence a trait when
   _____ is not related to _____ .

4. One clue that the environment influences a trait is when pairs of individuals who live
   _____ are more similar on that trait than equally related pairs of individuals
   who _____ .

men who have twins, either identical or fraternal, and then track down their twin
siblings to determine whether they too are gay. In one such study (Bailey & Pillard,
1991), the concordance rate for identical twins was 52% (29 of the 56 co-twins of
gay men were also gay), whereas the concordance rate for fraternal twins was only
22% (12 of the 54 co-twins were also gay). This suggests that genotype does contribute to a man's sexual orientation. But because identical twins are not perfectly
concordant for sexual orientation, we can also conclude that their *experiences* (that is,
environmental influences) must also have influenced their sexual orientations. After
all, 48% of the identical twin pairs had *different* sexual orientations, despite their
identical genes.

When a trait can assume many values (for example, height, intelligence), behavioral geneticists calculate *correlation coefficients* (see Chapter 1) rather than concordance rates. In a behavioral genetics study of IQ scores, for example, a correlation
coefficient would indicate whether the IQ scores of twins are systematically related
to the IQ scores of their co-twins. Larger correlations indicate closer resemblances in
IQ, thus implying that, if one twin is bright, the other is bright too, and if one twin
is dull, the other is probably dull as well.

As we noted earlier, behavioral genetics studies can tell us about *both* genetic and
environmental influences on development. This point is easily illustrated by considering a review of a family study of intellectual performance (IQ) based on 113,942
pairs of children, adolescents, or adults, the results of which appear in Table 3-4. Here
we will focus on the twin correlations (identical and fraternal) to show how behavioral geneticists can estimate the contributions of three factors to individual differences in intellectual performance (IQ):

1. *Gene influences.* Genetic influences on IQ are clearly evident in Table 3-4;
   identical twins, reared together or apart, are consistently more similar
   in intellectual performance than fraternal twins are. Clearly, intellectual
   performance is influenced by heredity. But just how strong is the hereditary
   contribution?

   In recent years, behavioral geneticists have proposed a statistical technique to estimate the amount of variation in a characteristic that is attributable to hereditary factors. This index, called a **heritability coefficient,** is calculated as follows:

$$H = (r \text{ identical twins} - r \text{ fraternal twins}) \times 2$$

In words, the equation reads: Heritability of an attribute equals the correlation between identical twins minus the correlation between fraternal twins,
all multiplied by a factor of 2 (Plomin, 1990).

heritability coefficient: a numerical estimate, ranging from .00
to +1.00, of the amount of
variation in an attribute that is
due to hereditary factors.

Table 3-4 Average Correlation Coefficients for Intelligence-Test Scores from Family Studies Involving Persons at Four Levels of Kinship

Genetic relationship (kinship)	Reared together (in same home)	Reared apart (in different homes)
Unrelated siblings (kinship = .00)	+.34	−.01*
Adoptive parent/adoptive offspring (kinship = .00)	+.19	—
Half-siblings (kinship = .25)	+.31	—
Biological parent/child (kinship = .50)	+.42	+.22
Siblings (kinship = .50)	+.47	+.24
Twins		
Fraternal (kinship = .50)	+.60	+.52
Identical (kinship = 1.00)	+.86	+.72

*This is the correlation obtained from random pairings of unrelated people living apart.
Source: From Bouchard & McGue, 1981.

Now we can estimate the contribution that genes make to individual differences in intellectual performance. If we focus on sets of twins raised together in the same homes, our estimate becomes:

$$H = (.86 - .60) \times 2 = .52$$

The resulting heritability estimate for IQ is .52, which, on a scale ranging from 0 (not at all heritable) to 1.00 (totally heritable), is moderate at best. We might conclude that, within the populations from which our twins reared together came, IQ is influenced to a moderate extent by hereditary factors. However, it appears that much of the variability among people on this trait is attributable to nonhereditary factors—that is, to environmental influences and to errors we may have made in measuring the trait (no measure is perfect).

Interestingly, the data in Table 3-4 also allow us to estimate the contributions of *two* sources of environmental influence:

2. **Nonshared environmental influences (NSE).** These are experiences that are unique to the individual and are *not* shared by other members of the family and, thus, make family members *different* from each other (Rowe & Plomin, 1981; Rowe, 1993). Where is evidence of nonshared environmental influence in Table 3-4? Notice that identical twins raised together are not perfectly similar in IQ, even though they share 100% of their genes and the same family environment: A correlation of +.86, though substantial, is less than a perfect correlation of +1.00. *Differences* between identical twins raised together must necessarily be due to *differences* in their experiences. Perhaps they were treated differently by parents and friends, or perhaps one twin favors puzzles and other intellectual games more than the other twin does. Since the only factor that can make identical twins raised together any *different* from each other is experiences they do *not* share, we can estimate the influence of nonshared environmental influences by the following formula (Rowe & Plomin, 1981):

$$NSE = 1 - r \text{ (identical twins reared together)}$$

nonshared environmental influence (NSE): an environmental influence that people living together do not share and that makes these individuals different from one another.

Thus, the contribution of nonshared environmental influences to individual differences in IQ performance (that is, $1 - .86 = .14$) is small, but detectable nevertheless. As we will see, nonshared environmental influences make a bigger contribution to other attributes, most notably personality traits.

3. *Shared environmental influences (SE).* These are experiences that individuals living in the same home environment share and that conspire to make them *similar* to each other. As you can see in Table 3-4, both identical and fraternal twins (and, indeed, biological siblings and pairs of unrelated individuals) show a greater intellectual resemblance if they live together than if they live apart. One reason that growing up in the same home may increase children's degree of intellectual similarity is that parents model similar interests for *all* their children and tend to rely on similar strategies to foster their intellectual growth (cf. Hoffman, 1991; Lewin, Hops, Davis, & Dishion, 1993).

How do we estimate the contribution of shared environmental influence (SE) to a trait? One rough estimate can be made as follows:

$$SE = 1 - (H + NSE)$$

In words, the equation reads: Shared environmental influences on a trait equal 1 (the total variation for that trait) minus the variation attributable to genes (*H*) *and* nonshared environmental influences (NSE). Previously, we found that the heritability of IQ in our twins-reared-together sample was .52, and the contribution of nonshared environment was .14. Thus, the contribution of shared environmental influences to individual differences in IQ (that is, $SE = 1 - [.52 + .14] = .34$) is moderate and meaningful.

One final note: While heritability coefficients are useful for estimating whether genes make any meaningful contribution to various human attributes, these statistics are poorly understood and often misinterpreted. In Box 3-2, we will take a closer look at what heritability estimates do and *do not* tell us.

Hereditary Influences on Intellectual Performance

As we have just seen from data presented in Table 3-4, IQ is a moderately heritable attribute: Genes account for about half the total variation in people's IQ scores. But because the correlations presented in Table 3-4 are based on studies of children *and* adults, they do not tell us whether the contributions of genes and environment to individual differences in intellectual performance might change over time. Might genes be more important early in life but might differences in our home and school experiences increasingly account for the variations we show in intellectual performance as we get older? Sensible as this idea may sound, it seems to be wrong. As children mature, genes actually seem to contribute *more* (rather than less) to individual differences in their IQs (McCartney, Harris, & Bernieri, 1990).

Consider a longitudinal study of the intellectual development of twins reported by Ronald Wilson (1978; 1983). Wilson found that identical twins were no more similar than fraternal twins on tests of infant mental development during the first year of life. By age 18 months, however, genetic influences were already detectable. Not only did identical twins show a greater resemblance in test performance than fraternal twins did, but *changes* in test scores from one testing to the next also became more similar for identical twins than for fraternal twins. If one identical twin had a big spurt in mental development between 18 and 24 months of age, the other twin was likely to show a similar spurt at the same time. Thus, it seemed as if genes were now influencing both the *course* and the *extent* of infants' mental development.

shared environmental influence (SE): an environmental influence that people living together share and that makes these individuals similar to one another.

BOX 3-2

Some Common Misconceptions about Heritability Estimates

Heritability coefficients are controversial statistics that are poorly understood and frequently misapplied. One of the biggest misconceptions that people hold is the notion that heritability coefficients can tell us whether we have inherited a trait. *This idea is simply incorrect.* When we talk about the heritability of an attribute, we are referring to the extent to which *differences* among individuals on that attribute are related to differences in the genes that they have inherited (Plomin, 1990). To illustrate that *heritable* means something other than *inherited*, consider that everyone inherits two eyes. Agreed? Yet the heritability of eyes is .00, simply because everyone has two and there are no individual differences in "eyeness" (except for those attributable to environmental events such as accidents).

In interpreting heritability coefficients, it is important to recognize that these estimates apply only to populations and *never to individuals.* So if you studied the heights of many pairs of 5-year-old twins and estimated the heritability of height to be .70, you could infer that a major reason that 5-year-olds *differ* in height is that they have different genes. But since heritability estimates say nothing about individuals, it is clearly inappropriate to conclude from an *H* of .70 that 70% of Freddie Jones's height is inherited, while the remaining 30% reflects the contribution of environment.

Let's also note that heritability estimates refer only to the particular trait in question as displayed by members of a *particular population* under *particular environmental circumstances.* Indeed, heritability coefficients may differ substantially for different research populations raised in different environments. Suppose, for example, that we located a large number of identical and fraternal twin infants, each of whom was raised in an impoverished orphanage in which his or her crib was lined with sheets that prevented much visual or social contact with other infants or with adult caregivers. Previous research (which we will examine in Chapter

11) suggests that, if we measured how sociable these infants are, we would find that they vary somewhat in sociability, but that virtually all of them are much less sociable than babies raised at home—a finding that we could reasonably attribute to their socially depriving early environment. But because all these twins experienced *the same depriving environment,* the only reason that they might show any *differences* in sociability is due to differences in their genetic predispositions. The heritability coefficient for sociability would actually approach 1.0 in this population—a far cry from the *H*s of .25 to .40 found in studies of other infants raised at home with parents (Plomin, 1990).

Finally, people have assumed that clearly heritable traits cannot be modified by environmental influences. *This, too, is a false assumption!* In Chapter 11, we will see that the depressed sociability of institutionalized infants can be improved substantially by placing them in socially responsive adoptive homes. Similarly, in Chapter 9, we will see that children who score low on the heritable attribute of IQ can dramatically improve their intellectual and academic performances when exposed to intellectually stimulating home and school environments. To assume that *heritable* means *unchangeable* (as some critics of compensatory education have done) is to commit a potentially grievous error based on a common misconception about the meaning of heritability coefficients.

In sum, the term *heritable* is not a symptom for *inherited,* and heritability estimates, which may vary widely across populations and environments, can tell us nothing about the development of individuals. And though heritability estimates are useful for helping us to determine whether there is any hereditary basis for the *differences* people display on any attribute we might care to study, they say nothing about children's capacity for change and should not be used to make public policy decisions that could constrain children's development or adversely affect their welfare.

Figure 3-12 shows what happened as these twins continued to develop. Identical twins remained highly similar in their intellectual performance (average *r* = +.85) from age 3 through age 15. By contrast, fraternal twins were most similar intellectually at age 3 (*r* = +.79) and gradually became less similar over time. By age 15, they showed no greater intellectual resemblance (*r* = +.54) than pairs of nontwin siblings. Notice, then, that if we calculated heritability coefficients at each age shown in the figure, the heritability of IQ for these twin samples would actually increase from infancy to adolescence.

Adoption studies paint a similar picture. The IQs of adopted *children* are correlated with the intellectual performances of both their biological parents (suggesting a genetic influence) and their adoptive parents (indicating effects of shared family environment). By adolescence, the resemblance to biological parents is still apparent, but adoptees no longer resemble their adoptive parents intellectually (Scarr & Weinberg, 1978). What seems to be happening, both in the twin and the adoption

Figure 3-12
Changes in the correlations between the IQ scores of identical
and fraternal twins over
childhood.
Data from Wilson, 1983.

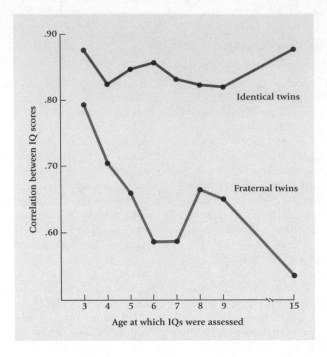

studies, is that the influence of shared environment on intellectual performance declines with age, whereas the influence of both genes and nonshared environment become increasingly stronger. Indeed, there is a very influential theory that accounts for these changing patterns of influence on IQ scores, and on temperament and personality as well. But before we examine this theory, let's review the evidence that suggests that our temperaments and personalities are influenced by the genes we have inherited.

Hereditary Contributions to Temperament and Personality

As parents well know, different babies have different "personalities." In trying to describe infant personality, researchers have focused on aspects of **temperament**—our tendencies to respond in predictable ways to environmental events that some believe to be the building blocks of personality (Goldsmith et al., 1987). Although different researchers do not always define or measure temperament in precisely the same way, most would agree that such attributes as *activity level* (the typical pace or vigor of our behavior), *irritability* or *emotionality* (how easily and intensely upset we become over negative events), *soothability* (how easy we are to calm after being upset), *fearfulness,* and *sociability* (receptiveness to social stimulation) are important components of temperament (Buss & Plomin, 1984; Rothbart, 1981; Goldsmith et al., 1987).

How Heritable Is Temperament?

To many, the very term *temperament* implies a biological foundation for individual differences in behavior—a foundation that is heritable and stable over time (Bates, 1987; Buss & Plomin, 1984). Selective breeding studies with various animal species reveal that temperamental characteristics such as activity, fearfulness, and sociability do have a strong hereditary component (Plomin et al., 1989). Could the same be true for human beings?

Behavior geneticists have tried to answer this question by comparing the temperamental similarities of pairs of identical and pairs of fraternal twins. At birth, it is difficult to detect the influence of genes on babies' temperaments. Twins are similar on such traits as irritability, but this is apparently due to environmental factors,

temperament: a person's characteristic modes of response to the environment, including such attributes as activity level, irritability, fearfulness, and sociability.

because identical twins are no more similar than fraternal twins are (Riese, 1990). Later in the first year and into the second year, the picture changes (Loehlin, 1992). Now identical twins are more alike on such temperamental dimensions as activity level, demands for attention, irritability, and sociability than fraternal twins are (Braungart et al., 1992; Emde et al., 1992; Wilson & Matheny, 1986). Although the heritability estimates for these attributes are moderate at best (averaging about .40), we can conclude that at least some components of temperament are influenced by the genes we have inherited.

Stability of temperament. Is early temperament stable over time? Is the "fearful" 8-month-old who is highly upset by a strange face likely to remain wary of strangers at 24 months and to shun new playmates as a 4-year-old? Longitudinal research indicates that several components of temperament—namely activity level, negative emotionality (fearfulness, irritability), and attention to novelty—are moderately stable through infancy, childhood, and even into the early adult years (Campos, Campos, & Barrett, 1989; Caspi, Elder, & Bem, 1987, 1988; Pedlow et al., 1993; Ruff et al., 1990). Behavioral geneticists point to such stability as evidence that many temperamental traits are clearly influenced by the genes we inherit (McGue, Bacon, & Lykken, 1993). However, not all individuals are so temperamentally stable.

Consider what Jerome Kagan and his associates found while conducting longitudinal studies of a temperamental attribute they called **behavioral inhibition**: the tendency to withdraw from unfamiliar people or situations (Kagan, 1989; Kagan, Reznick, & Snidman, 1988). Children identified as inhibited or uninhibited when first tested at age 21 months often remained relatively inhibited or uninhibited when retested at 4, $5^1/_2$, and $7^1/_2$ years of age. Not only were the inhibited children shy around peers and wary of strange adults, but they were also more cautious than uninhibited children about playing with novel toys that involved an element of risk (for example, a balance beam), and they often displayed intense physiological arousal (for example, high heart rates) in response to novel situations that barely fazed the uninhibited children. The physiological data in particular suggested to Kagan that behavioral inhibition is a reasonably stable temperamental trait that has deep biological roots, and a recent twin study clearly implies that inhibition is a heritable attribute (Robinson et al., 1992). Nevertheless, both Kagan and associates (1989) and a research team in Sweden (Kerr et al., 1994) found that it was only those children at the *extremes* of the continuum—the most highly inhibited and most highly uninhibited youngsters (particularly girls)—who displayed long-term stability; the other children's levels of inhibition fluctuated considerably over time. These latter findings imply that heritable aspects of temperament are often modified by environmental forces. Interestingly, a similar conclusion emerges from Alexander Thomas and Stella Chess's classic longitudinal research on children's temperamental profiles, to which we will now turn.

Temperamental profiles. In their earliest reports, Thomas and Chess (1977; Thomas, Chess, & Birch, 1970) found that certain components of infant temperament tend to cluster together, forming broader temperamental profiles. Indeed, the majority of infants in their sample could be placed into one of three categories according to the overall patterning of their temperamental qualities:

1. *Easy temperament.* Easygoing children are even-tempered, are typically in a positive mood, and are quite open and adaptable to new experiences. Their habits are regular and predictable.
2. *Difficult temperament.* Difficult children are active, irritable, and irregular in their habits. They often react very vigorously to changes in routine and are slow to adapt to new persons or situations.

behavioral inhibition: a temperamental characteristic reflecting one's tendency to withdraw from unfamiliar people or situations.

easy temperament: temperament such that the child quickly establishes regular routines in infancy, is generally good natured, and adapts easily to new routines.

difficult temperament: temperament in which the child is irregular in daily routines and adapts slowly to new experiences, often responding negatively and intensely.

3. *Slow-to-warm-up temperament.* These children are quite inactive and moody. They, too, are slow to adapt to new persons and situations, but, unlike the difficult child, they typically respond to novelty or to changes in routine with mild forms of passive resistance. For example, they may resist cuddling by directing their attention elsewhere rather than by crying or kicking.

Apparently, these broader temperamental patterns may persist over time and influence the child's adjustment to a variety of settings and situations later in life. For example, children with difficult temperaments are more likely than other children to have problems adjusting to school activities, and they are often irritable and aggressive in their interactions with siblings and peers (Lytton, 1990; Pettit & Bates, 1989; Thomas, Chess, & Korn, 1982). By contrast, children who are slow to warm up often show a different kind of adjustment problem, as their hesitancy to embrace new activities and challenges may cause them to be ignored or neglected by peers (Chess & Thomas, 1984).

Do these observations imply that early temperamental profiles are immutable and will largely determine the outcomes of our social and personality development? No, they do not! Thomas and Chess (1986; Chess & Thomas, 1984) find that early temperamental characteristics *sometimes do* and *sometimes do not* carry over into later life. In other words, temperament can change, and one factor that often determines whether it does change is the **"goodness of fit"** between the child's temperamental style and patterns of child rearing used by parents. Let's first consider a "good fit" between temperament and child rearing. Difficult infants who fuss a lot and have trouble adapting to new routines often become less cranky and more adaptable over the long run if parents remain calm, exercise restraint, and allow these children to respond to novelty at a more leisurely pace. Indeed, many difficult infants who experience such patient and sensitive caregiving are no longer classifiable as temperamentally difficult later in childhood or adolescence (Chess & Thomas, 1984). Yet it is not always easy for a parent to be patient and sensitive with a highly active, moody child who resists their bids for attention; in fact, many parents become irritable, impatient, demanding, and punitive with such children. Unfortunately, these attitudes and behaviors constitute a "poor fit" with a difficult child, who is apt to become all the more fussy and resistant in response to the parent's forceful and punitive tactics. And true to form, Chess and Thomas (1984) found that difficult infants were especially likely to remain difficult and to display behavior problems later in life if their parents had been impatient, demanding, and forceful with them.

In sum, many of the temperamental qualities that we display and that may affect our social and emotional adjustment later in life are clearly influenced by the genes we have inherited. However, early temperamental patterns can be altered, and the changes in temperament commonly observed over the course of childhood suggest that this aspect of personality is highly susceptible to environmental influence.

Hereditary Contributions to the Adult Personality

Although psychologists have generally assumed that the relatively stable habits and traits that make up our adult personalities are shaped by our environments, family studies reveal that many core dimensions of personality are genetically influenced (Loehlin, 1992). For example, **introversion/extroversion,** a trait that is widely believed to be an outgrowth of early sociability, shows about the same moderate level of heritability that IQ does (Martin & Jardine, 1986; Scarr et al., 1981). Another important attribute that may be influenced by heredity is **empathic concern.** A person who is high in empathy is a compassionate soul who recognizes the needs of others and is concerned about their welfare. In Box 2-4, we saw that newborn infants react to the distress of another infant by becoming distressed themselves—a finding that implies that the capacity for empathy may be innate. But are there any biological bases for *individual differences* in empathic concern?

slow-to-warm-up temperament: temperament in which the child is inactive and moody and displays mild passive resistance to new routines and experiences.

"goodness-of-fit" model: Thomas and Chess's notion that development is likely to be optimized when parents' child-rearing practices are adapted to (or are compatible with) the child's temperamental characteristics.

introversion/extroversion: the opposite poles of a personality dimension: Introverts are shy, anxious around others, and ready to withdraw from social situations; extroverts are highly sociable and enjoy being with others.

empathic concern: a measure of the extent to which an individual recognizes the needs of others and is concerned about their welfare.

Difficult infants are likely to retain their difficult temperaments if parents are impatient and forceful with them.

Indeed there are. As early as 14 to 20 months of age, identical twin infants are already more similar in their levels of concern for distressed companions than fraternal twin infants are (Zahn-Waxler, Robinson, & Emde, 1992). And by middle age, identical twins who have lived apart for several years since leaving home still resemble one another on measures of empathic concern ($r = +.41$), whereas fraternal twins do not ($r = +.05$), thus suggesting that this attribute is a reasonably heritable trait (Matthews et al., 1981). In fact, the authors of this adult twin study noted that "If empathic concern . . . leads to altruistic motivation, [our] study provides evidence for a genetic basis for individual differences in altruism" (p. 246).

To what extent are our personalities influenced by the genes we have inherited? We can get some idea by looking at personality resemblances among family members, as shown in Table 3-5. Note that identical twins are more similar to each other on this composite measure of personality than fraternal twins are. Were we to use the twin data to estimate the genetic contribution to personality, we might conclude that many personality traits are moderately heritable (i.e., $H = +.40$). Of course, one implication of a moderate heritability coefficient is that personality is heavily influenced by environmental factors.

What features of the environment contribute most heavily to the development of our personalities? Developmentalists have traditionally assumed that the home environment is especially important in this regard. Yet Table 3-5 reveals that genetically unrelated individuals who live in the same home barely resemble each other on the

Table 3-5 Personality Resemblances among Family Members at Three Levels of Kinship

	Kinship			
	1.00 (identical twins)	.50 (fraternal twins)	.50 (nontwin siblings)	.00 (unrelated children raised in the same household)
Personality attributes (average correlations across several personality traits)	.50	.30	.20	.07

Sources: From Loehlin, 1985, and Loehlin & Nichols, 1976.

composite personality measure ($r = .07$). Therefore, aspects of the home environment that all family members *share* must not contribute much to the development of personality. How, then, does environment affect personality?

According to behavioral geneticists David Rowe and Robert Plomin (1981; Rowe, 1993), the aspects of environment that contribute most heavily to personality are *nonshared environmental influences*—influences that make individuals *different* from each other. And there are many sources of "nonshared" experience in a typical home. Parents, for example, often treat sons differently than daughters, or first-born children differently than later borns. To the extent that siblings are not treated alike by parents, they will experience different environments, which will increase the likelihood that their personalities will differ in important ways. Interactions among siblings provide another source of "nonshared" environmental influence on the developing personality. For example, an older sibling who habitually dominates a younger one may become generally assertive and dominant as a result of these home experiences. But for the younger child, this home environment is a dominating environment that may foster the development of such personality traits as passivity, tolerance, and cooperation.

Measuring the effects of nonshared environments. How could we ever measure the impact of something as broad as nonshared environments? One strategy used by Denise Daniels and her associates (Daniels, 1986; Daniels & Plomin, 1985) is simply to ask pairs of adolescent siblings whether they have been treated differently by their parents and/or have experienced other important differences in their lives (for example, differences in their popularity with peers). She finds that siblings do report such differences and, more important, the greater the *differences* in parental treatment and other experiences that siblings report, the more dissimilar siblings are in their personalities.

Do siblings have different experiences because they have different genes? Stated another way, isn't it possible that a child's heritable attributes might influence how other people respond to her, so that a "difficult" youngster, for example, is apt to be treated very differently by parents and peers than a sibling with an easy temperament would be? Although genes do contribute to some extent to the different experiences reported by siblings (Baker & Daniels, 1990; Daniels, 1986; Plomin et al., 1994), there is ample reason to believe that our highly individualized, unique environments are not solely attributable to our having inherited different genes. How do we know this?

The most important clue comes from studies of identical twins. Since identical twins are perfectly matched from a genetic standpoint, any *differences* between them must necessarily reflect the contribution of environmental influences that they do *not* share. Clearly, these nonshared environmental influences cannot be attributed to the twins' different genes, because identical twins have identical genotypes! This is why the formula for estimating the contribution of nonshared environmental influences (that is, $1 - r$ [identical twins raised together]) makes sense, for the estimate that it provides is based on environmental influences that are *not* in any way mediated by genes.

With these facts in mind, let's return to Table 3-5. Here, we see that the average correlation for identical twins across many personality traits is only $+.50$, which implies that identical twins are alike in some respects and different in others. Applying the formula for estimating NSE ($1 - .50 = .50$) tells us that nonshared environmental influences are very important contributors to adult personality—at least as important as genes are (see also Loehlin, 1992).

In sum, the family environment does contribute importantly to personality, but not simply because it has a standard effect on all family members that makes them alike. True, there are some important areas of socialization for which parents do treat all their children alike and foster similarities among them (Hoffman, 1991). For example, parents often model and seek to encourage the same moral, religious, and political interests and values in all their children. For these and many other psychological characteristics, *shared environmental influences* are often as important as, and sometimes much more important than, genes are in creating likenesses between brothers and sisters (Hoffman, 1991; Plomin, 1990). But when it comes to the shaping of many other basic personality traits, it is the *nonshared* experiences people have—in concert with genetic influences—that contribute most to their phenotypes (Plomin, 1990; Rowe, 1993).

Concept Check 3-3 ⌵ Estimating Hereditary and Environmental Influences

A behavioral geneticist conducts a twin study to try to determine whether heredity contributes in any meaningful way to the personality trait of creativity. She finds that the correlation between identical twins on this attribute is +.61, whereas the correlation between fraternal twins is +.50 (data from Plomin, 1990). Check your answers in the Appendix.

_____ 1. The hereditary contribution to creativity is best described as:

    a. substantial   b. moderate   c. low

_____ 2. Do either shared environmental influences (SE) or nonshared environmental influences (NSE) contribute more than heredity does to individual differences in creativity?

    a. Both SE and NSE contribute more than heredity does.

    b. Only NSE contributes more than heredity does.

    c. Only SE contributes more than heredity does.

    d. Neither SE nor NSE contributes more than heredity does.

Hereditary Contributions to Behavior Disorders and Mental Illness

Is there a hereditary basis for mental illness? Might some among us be genetically predisposed to deviant or antisocial acts? Although these ideas seemed absurd 25 years ago, it now appears that the answer to both questions is a qualified yes.

Consider the evidence for **schizophrenia,** a serious mental illness, characterized by severe disturbances in logical thinking, emotional expression, and social behavior, which typically emerges in late adolescence or early adulthood. A survey of several twin studies of schizophrenia suggests an average concordance rate of .46 for identical twins but only .14 for fraternal twins (Gottesman & Shields, 1982). This is a strong indication that schizophrenia is genetically influenced. In addition, studies of adults who grew up in adoptive homes reveal that the incidence of schizophrenia (and other disorders) among these adoptees is more closely related to the incidence of schizophrenia among their *biological* relatives than among members of their adoptive families (Plomin, 1990).

In recent years, it has become quite clear that heredity also contributes to abnormal behaviors and conditions such as alcoholism, criminality, depression, hyperactivity, **manic-depressive** psychosis, and a number of **neurotic disorders** (Baker, Mack, Moffitt, & Mednick, 1989; Carey, 1992; Rowe, Rodgers, & Meseck-Bushey, 1992; Plomin, 1990). Now, it is possible that you have close relatives or ancestors who were diagnosed as alcoholic, neurotic, manic-depressive, or schizophrenic. Rest assured that this does *not* mean that you or your children will develop these problems. Only 10%–14% of children who have one schizophrenic parent ever develop any symptoms that might be labeled "schizophrenic" (Kessler, 1975). Even if you are an identical twin whose co-twin has a serious psychiatric disorder, the odds are only between 1 in 2 (for schizophrenia) and 1 in 10 (for most other disorders) that you would

schizophrenia: a serious form of mental illness characterized by disturbances in logical thinking, emotional expression, and interpersonal behavior.

manic-depression: a psychotic disorder characterized by extreme fluctuations in mood.

neurotic disorder: an irrational pattern of thinking or behavior that a person may use to contend with stress or to avoid anxiety.

ever experience anything that even approaches the problem that affects your twin.

Since identical twins are usually *discordant* (that is, not alike) with respect to mental illnesses and behavior disorders, it is obvious that environment must be a very important contributor to these conditions. In other words, people do not inherit behavioral disorders; instead, they inherit *predispositions* to develop certain illnesses or deviant patterns of behavior. And even when a child's family history suggests that such a genetic predisposition may exist, it usually takes a number of very stressful experiences (for example, rejecting parents, a failure or series of failures at school, or dissolution of the family due to divorce) to trigger the illness in question (see Plomin & Rende, 1991; Rutter, 1979). Clearly, these latter findings provide some basis for optimism, for it may be possible someday to prevent the onset of most heritable disorders should we (1) learn more about the environmental triggers that precipitate these disturbances while (2) striving to develop interventions or therapeutic techniques that will help "high-risk" individuals to maintain their emotional stability in the face of environmental stress.

▶ HEREDITY AND ENVIRONMENT AS DEVELOPMENTAL COCONSPIRATORS

Only 30 years ago, developmentalists were embroiled in the nature/nurture controversy: Was heredity or environment the primary determinant of human potential? Although this chapter has focused on biological influences, it should now be apparent that *both* heredity and environment contribute in important ways to developmental outcomes and that the often extreme positions taken by the hereditarians and environmentalists of yesteryear are grossly oversimplified. Today, most behavioral geneticists no longer think in terms of nature *versus* nurture; they concentrate instead on trying to determine how these two important influences might combine or interact to promote developmental change. Let's now see what they have to say about the interplay between genes and environments.

The Canalization Principle

Although both heredity and environment contribute to most human traits, our genes influence some attributes more than others. Some years ago, Conrad Waddington (1966) used the term **canalization** to refer to cases where genes operate so as to limit or restrict development to a small number of outcomes. One example of a highly canalized human attribute is babbling in infancy. All infants, even deaf ones, babble in pretty much the same way over the first 8–10 months of life. The environment has little, if any, effect on this highly canalized attribute, which simply unfolds according to the maturational program in our genes. By contrast, less canalized attributes such as intelligence, temperament, and personality can be deflected away from their genetic pathways in any of several directions by a variety of life experiences.

Interestingly, we now know that potent *environmental* influences can also limit, or canalize, development. In Chapter 2, for example, we discussed Gilbert Gottlieb's (1991a) intriguing finding that duckling embryos exposed to chicken calls before hatching come to prefer the calls of chickens to those of their own mothers. In this case, the ducklings' prenatal *experiences* (environment) overrode the presumably canalized genetic predisposition to favor the vocalization of their own species.

In sum, the canalization principle is a relatively simple idea and, yet, a very useful one that illustrates that: (1) there are multiple pathways along which an individual might develop, (2) nature and nurture combine to determine these pathways, and (3) either genes or enviroment may limit the extent to which the other factor can influence development. Irving Gottesman makes the same points about gene

canalization: genetic restriction of phenotype to a small number of developmental outcomes; a highly canalized attribute is one for which genes channel development along predetermined pathways, so that the environment has little effect on the phenotype that emerges.

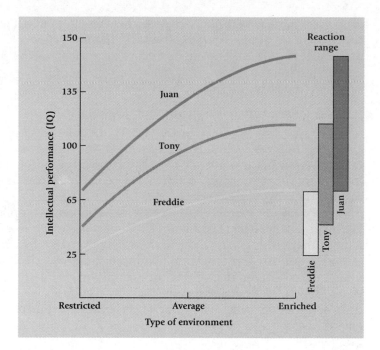

Figure 3-13
Hypothetical reaction ranges for
the intellectual performances of
three children in restricted, average, and intellectually enriching
environments.
Adapted from Gottesman, 1963.

influences in a slightly different way in his own theory of genotype/environment interactions.

The Range-of-Reaction Principle

According to Gottesman (1963), genes do not rigidly canalize behavior. Instead, an individual genotype establishes a range of possible responses that a person will show to different kinds of life experiences: the so-called **range of reaction.** In other words, Gottesman claims that genotype sets boundaries on the range of possible phenotypes that one might display to different environments. An important corollary is that, because people differ genetically, no two individuals should respond in precisely the same way to any particular environment.

The concept of reaction range, as applied to intellectual performance, is illustrated in Figure 3-13. Here we see the effects of varying degrees of environmental enrichment on the IQs of three children: Juan, who has high genetic potential for intellectual development, Tony, whose genetic endowment for intelligence is average, and Freddie, whose potential for intellectual growth is far below average. Notice that, under similar environmental conditions, Juan always outperforms the other two children. Juan also has the widest reaction range, in that his IQ might vary from well below average in a restricted environment to far above average in an enriched environment. By contrast, Freddie has a very limited reaction range; his potential for intellectual development is low, and, as a result, he shows smaller variation in IQ across environments than do the other two children.

In sum, the range-of-reaction principle is a clear statement about the interplay between heredity and environment. Presumably, one's genotype sets a range of possible outcomes for any particular attribute, and the environment largely influences where within that range the individual will fall.

Genotype/Environment Correlations

Up until now, we have talked as if heredity and environment were *independent* sources of influence that somehow combined to determine our observable characteristics, or phenotypes. This view is probably much too simplistic. In recent years, behavioral

range-of-reaction principle: the idea that genotype sets limits on the range of possible phenotypes that a person might display in response to different environments.

geneticists have argued that our genes may actually influence the kinds of environments that we are likely to experience (Plomin, DeFries, & Loehlin, 1977; Scarr & McCartney, 1983). And how might genes have such an effect? There are at least three ways.

Passive Genotype/Environment Correlations

According to Scarr and McCartney (1983), the kind of home environment that parents provide for their children is influenced, in part, by the parents' own genotypes. And since parents also provide their children with genes, it so happens that the rearing environments to which children are exposed are correlated with (and are likely to suit) their own genotypes.

The following example illustrates a developmental implication of these **passive genotype/environment correlations.**[1] Parents who are genetically predisposed to be athletic may create a very "athletic" home environment by encouraging their children to play vigorously and to take an interest in sporting activities. Besides being exposed to an "athletic environment," the children may have inherited their parents' "athletic" genes, which might make them particularly responsive to that environment. So children of athletic parents may come to enjoy athletic pursuits for *both* hereditary and environmental reasons, and the influences of heredity and environment are tightly intertwined.

Evocative Genotype/Environment Correlations

Earlier, we noted that the environmental influences that contribute most heavily to many aspects of personality are "nonshared" experiences that make individuals *different* from one another. Might the differences in environments that children experience be partly due to the fact that they have inherited different genes and thus may elicit different reactions from their companions?

Scarr and McCartney (1983) think so. Their notion of **evocative genotype/environment correlations** assumes that a child's heritable attributes will affect the behavior of others toward the child. For example, smiley, active babies may receive more attention and social stimulation than moody and passive ones. Teachers may respond more favorably to physically attractive students than to their less attractive classmates. Clearly, these *reactions* of other people to the child (and the child's heritable attributes) are environmental influences that play an important role in shaping that child's personality. So once again, we see an intermingling of hereditary and environmental influences: Heredity affects the character of the social environment in which the personality develops.

Active Genotype/Environment Correlations

Finally, Scarr and McCartney (1983) propose that the environments that children prefer and seek out will be those that are most compatible with their genetic predispositions. For example, a child with genes for sociability is likely to invite friends to the house, be an avid partygoer, and generally prefer activities that are socially stimulating. By contrast, the child with genes for shyness may actively avoid large social gatherings and choose instead to pursue activities such as coin collecting that can be done alone. So one implication of these **active genotype/environment correlations** is that people with different genotypes will *select* different "environmental niches" for themselves that may have a powerful effect on their future social, emotional, and intellectual development.

passive genotype/environment correlations: the notion that the rearing environments that biological parents provide are influenced by the parents' own genes, and hence are correlated with the child's own genotype.

evocative genotype/environment correlations: the notion that our heritable attributes will affect others' behavior toward us and thus will influence the social environment in which development takes place.

active genotype/environment correlations: the notion that our genotypes affect the types of environments that we prefer and will seek out.

---

[1]This kind of correlation between genes and environment is called *passive* because it is not the result of any deliberate action on the part of parents or children.

How Do Genotype/Environment Correlations Influence Development?

According to Scarr and McCartney (1983), the relative importance of active, passive, and evocative gene influences will change over the course of development. During the first few years, infants and toddlers are not free to roam the neighborhood, choosing friends and building environmental niches. Most of their time is spent at home in an environment that parents structure for them, so that passive genotype/environment correlations are particularly important early in life. But once children reach school age and venture away from home on a daily basis, they suddenly become much freer to pick their own interests, activities, friends, and hangouts. Thus, active, niche-building correlations should exert more and more influence on development as the child matures (see Figure 3-14). Finally, evocative genotype-environment correlations are always important; that is, a person's heritable attributes and patterns of behavior may influence the ways that other people react to him or her throughout life.

If Scarr and McCartney's theory has any merit, then virtually all siblings other than identical twins should become less similar over time as they emerge from the relatively similar rearing environments that parents impose during the early years and begin actively to select different environmental niches for themselves. Indeed, there is ample support for this assertion. Pairs of genetically unrelated adoptees who live in the same home do show some definite similarities in conduct and intellectual performance during early and middle childhood (Scarr & Weinberg, 1978). Since these adoptees share no genes with each other or with their adoptive parents, their resemblances must be attributable to their common rearing environments. Yet, by late adolescence, genetically unrelated siblings no longer resemble each other in intelligence, personality, or any other aspect of behavior, presumably because they have selected very different environmental niches which, in turn, have steered them along differing developmental paths (Scarr & McCartney, 1983; Scarr et al., 1981). Even fraternal twins, who have 50% of their genes in common, are much less alike as adolescents or adults than they were as children (McCartney et al., 1990; and recall the declining resemblance in fraternal twins' IQs over time as shown in Figure 3-10). Apparently, the genes that fraternal twins do *not* share cause these individuals to select different environmental niches, which, in turn, contribute to their declining resemblance over time.

By contrast, pairs of identical twins bear a close behavioral resemblance throughout childhood and adolescence. Why should this be? Scarr and McCartney suggest two reasons: (1) not only do identical twins elicit similar reactions from other people, but (2) their identical genotypes predispose them to prefer and to select very *similar* environments (that is, friends, interests, and activities), which then exert

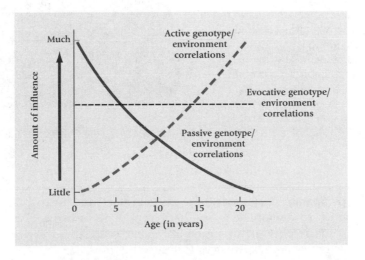

Figure 3-14
Relative influence of passive, evocative, and active (niche-picking) genotype/environment correlations as a function of age.

BOX 3-3

Similarities (and Differences) Between Identical Twins Reared Apart

Raised as a strict Catholic by his mother in Czechoslovakia, Oscar Stohr became involved in the Hitler Youth Movement and remained loyal to the German Nazis during World War II. In middle age, he is now a loyal union member, employed as a factory supervisor in Germany. Jack Yufe, a store owner in California, was raised by his Jewish father and came to loathe Nazis as he grew up in a Caribbean country halfway around the world. Today, Jack holds quite liberal attitudes, whereas Oscar is very traditional and conservative.

It turns out that these two men, who seem so very different, are part of a study of *separated identical twins* being conducted by Thomas Bouchard and his associates at the University of Minnesota (Bouchard et al., 1990; Farber, 1981). Oscar and Jack, like other twin pairs that Bouchard has examined, were separated as infants (when their parents divorced) and have lived apart from that point on. And, despite their very different outlooks on life, Oscar and Jack are like other separated twins in that they show some remarkable similarities. For example, both men excel at sports and have difficulty with math. They have similar mannerisms and temperaments, and both tend to be absentminded. And then there are the little things, such as their common tastes for spicy foods and sweet liqueurs, their habit of storing rubber bands on their wrists, and their preference for flushing the toilet before *and* after using it.

Bouchard and his colleagues have now studied more than 30 pairs of separated identical twins, finding that virtually all of them display some noteworthy similarities in their habits, mannerisms, and performances on various psychological tests. And yet the data also show that these twins tend to differ in several respects: One twin usually displays more self-assurance or is more outgoing or aggressive or has a different outlook on life than the other.

How can separated identical twins be so different and, at the same time, so similar to each other? The concept of *active gene influences* may help to explain the seemingly uncanny resemblances. When we learn that twins grow up in different environments, our tendency is to think of these settings as more dissimilar than they really are. In fact, identical twins raised apart are members of the same life cohort who are likely to be exposed to many of the same kinds of objects, activities, educational experiences, and historical events as they are growing up. So, if identical twins are genetically predisposed to select comparable aspects of the environment for special attention, and if their "different" environments provide them with reasonably similar sets of experiences from which to build their environmental niches, then these individuals might well be expected to

resemble each other in their habits, mannerisms, abilities, and interests.

Why, then, do separated identical twins often differ? According to Scarr and McCartney (1983), twins could be expected to differ on any attribute for which their rearing environments are so dissimilar as to prevent them from ever establishing comparable niches. For example, a pair of twins might be genetically predisposed to be outgoing and sociable. But if one of them grows up with her mother in New York City and the other with a reclusive father in the Alaskan bush, the former twin will have had ample opportunity to act on her biological predispositions by mixing with other people and becoming highly extroverted, whereas her sister, lacking these opportunities, might actually become rather shy and reserved in social contexts.

The fact that separated identical twins often differ in meaningful ways helps to illustrate an important point about genotype/environment interactions and their impact on development. The point is this: Although our genes may influence the kinds of life experiences that we are likely to have, they do not *determine* our environments. Indeed, the events and experiences that we actually encounter depend largely on what is available to us in the particular culture or subculture in which we are raised. Should some of the life experiences available to one person be radically discrepant from those of another, these two individuals will inevitably differ in important ways, regardless of the similarity of their genes or genetic predispositions.

Jack Yufe (left) and Oscar Stohr (right).

comparable influences on these twin pairs and virtually guarantee that they will continue to resemble one another. Even identical twins raised apart should be similar in some respects if their identical genes cause them to seek out and to prefer similar activities and experiences (see Box 3-3).

CONTRIBUTIONS AND CRITICISMS OF THE BEHAVIORAL GENETICS APPROACH

Human behavioral genetics is a relatively new discipline that is beginning to have a strong influence on the way scientists look at human development. We now know, for example, that many attributes previously thought to be shaped by environment are influenced, in part, by genes. As Scarr and McCartney put it, we are products of "cooperative efforts of the nature/nurture team, directed by the genetic quarterback" (1983, p. 433). In effect, genes may exert many of their influences on human development by influencing the experiences we have, which in turn influence our behavior. And one very important implication of this viewpoint is that many of the "environmental" influences on development that have previously been identified may reflect, in part, the workings of heredity (Plomin, 1990; Plomin et al., 1994).

Of course, not all developmentalists would agree that genetic endowment is the "quarterback" of the "nature/nurture team" (see Gottlieb, 1991b, and Wachs, 1992, for example). Moreover, my own students often object to Scarr and McCartney's theory after initially deriving the impression that genotypes *determine* environments. But this is not what the theory implies. What Scarr and McCartney are saying is that people with different genotypes are likely to evoke different responses from others and to select different environmental niches for themselves. But it is also true that the responses they evoke and the aspects of the environment that they select when building their "niches" will depend to no small extent on the particular individuals, settings, and circumstances that are available to them. The separated identical twins that we met in Box 3-3 clearly illustrate this point. Oscar and Jack are alike in many ways because their two rearing environments permitted them access to many of the same kinds of experiences (for example, sports, math classes, spicy foods, rubber bands), thereby enabling these two genetically identical individuals to develop similar habits, mannerisms, and interests. However, it was almost inevitable that Oscar and Jack would differ in their political ideologies because their sociopolitical environments were sufficiently *dissimilar* to prevent them from ever building the kinds of "niches" that would have made them social and political bedfellows.

In sum, genotypes and environments *interact* to produce developmental change and variations in developmental outcomes. True, genes exert some influence on those aspects of the environment that we are likely to experience. But the particular environments available to us also limit the possible phenotypes that are likely to emerge from a particular genotype (Gottlieb, 1991b). Perhaps Donald Hebb (1980) was not too far off when he said that behavior is determined 100% by heredity and 100% by the environment, for it seems that these two sets of influences are completely and inextricably intertwined.

Interesting as these new ideas may be, critics argue that the behavioral genetics approach is merely a descriptive overview of how development might proceed rather than a well-articulated *explanation* of development. One reason for this sentiment is that we know so little about how genes exert their effects. Genes are coded to manufacture proteins and enzymes, not to produce such attributes as intelligence or sociability. Although we now suspect that genes affect behavior *indirectly* by influencing the experiences we evoke from others or create for ourselves, we are still a long way from understanding how or why genes might impel us to prefer particular kinds of stimulation or to find certain activities especially satisfying. In addition, behavioral geneticists apply the term *environment* in a very global way, making few, if any, attempts to measure environmental influences directly or to specify *how* environments act on individuals to influence their behavior. Perhaps you can see the problem: The critics contend that one has not *explained* development by merely postulating that *unspecified* environmental forces influenced in *unknown* ways by our genes *somehow* shape our abilities, conduct, and character.

How exactly do environments impinge on individuals to influence their abilities, conduct, and character? What environmental influences, given when, are particularly noteworthy in this regard? These are questions that we will seek to answer throughout the remainder of this text. We begin in our next chapter by examining how environmental events that occur even before a child is born combine with nature's grand plan to influence the course of prenatal development and the characteristics of newborn infants.

SUMMARY

Development begins at conception, when a sperm cell from the father penetrates an ovum from the mother, forming a zygote. A normal zygote contains 46 chromosomes (23 from each parent), each of which consists of several thousand genes. Each zygote may have as many as 500,000 genes that provide the hereditary blueprint for the development of this single cell into a recognizable human being.

Human beings consist of two kinds of cells: (1) body cells, which make up our bodies and organs, and (2) germ cells, which produce gametes—sperm in males and ova in females. Our body cells each contain duplicates of the 46 chromosomes (23 pairs) that we inherited at conception. Germ cells, which also have 23 pairs of chromosomes, divide by a process called meiosis to produce gametes that each contain 23 single (unpaired) chromosomes. Since individual gametes contain but half of the parent's chromosomes, which segregate independently during meiosis, the genetic composition of each sperm or ovum will differ. Therefore, each child inherits a unique combination of genes. The one exception is identical twins, who are formed from a single zygote that divides to create two individuals with identical genes.

There are many ways in which one's genotype may affect phenotype—the way one looks, feels, thinks, or behaves. At least one phenotypic characteristic—gender—is determined by the 23rd pair of chromosomes (that is, the sex chromosomes). Normal females have inherited one relatively large sex chromosome (called an X chromosome) from each parent, whereas males have inherited an X chromosome and a smaller Y chromosome. An adult female (XX) can pass only X chromosomes to her offspring. However, an adult male (XY) can transmit either an X chromosome or a Y chromosome to his offspring. Thus, the father, not the mother, determines the sex of a child.

Some characteristics are determined by a single pair of genes, one of which is inherited from each parent. In dominant/recessive pairs, the individual will exhibit the phenotype of the dominant gene. If a gene pair is codominant or incompletely dominant, the individual will develop a phenotype in between those ordinarily produced by the dominant and the dominated (or recessive) genes. Sex-linked characteristics are caused by recessive genes that appear on only one of the two kinds of sex chromosomes (usually the X chromosome). Females must inherit two of these recessive genes (one on each X chromosome) in order to exhibit a sex-linked characteristic. However, males need only inherit one recessive gene to show the characteristic, because they have only one X chromosome. However, most complex human attributes such as intelligence and personality are polygenic, meaning that they are influenced by several pairs of genes rather than a single pair.

Occasionally, children inherit abnormal genes and chromosomes. In most cases of chromosome abnormalities, the child has inherited too few or too many sex chromosomes. In about 1 in 600 births, a child inherits an extra 21st chromosome. The resulting phenotype is known as Down syndrome, in which the child has a number of distinctive physical features and is mentally retarded.

There are also a number of genetic diseases that children may inherit from parents who themselves are not affected but who carry the abnormal genes. Genetic counseling can help people to calculate the odds that they might bear a child with a genetic disorder. Family histories and blood tests can often identify the carriers of many disorders caused by a single gene pair, and abnormalities in the fetus can be detected through amniocentesis, chorionic villus biopsy, and ultrasound. Harmful effects of several hereditary disorders can now be minimized by medical interventions. And because knowledge of human genetics is rapidly increasing, many more genetic defects are likely to become detectable and treatable in the near future.

Behavioral genetics is the study of how genes and environment contribute to individual variations in development. Although animals can be studied in selective breeding experiments, human behavioral geneticists must conduct family studies, estimating hereditary contributions to various attributes from the similarities and differences among family members who differ in kinship. These family studies reveal that the genes people inherit exert an important influence on their intellectual performances, temperaments, personality, and their tendencies to display abnormal patterns of behavior. However, family studies also show that the environment contributes in important ways to individual variations in development, and that all behavioral attributes of lasting developmental significance are products of a long and involved interplay between the forces of nature and nurture.

Several theories have been proposed to explain how heredity and environment might combine to produce developmental change. For example, the canalization principle implies that genes channel development along predetermined pathways that are sometimes difficult for the environment to alter. The range-of-reaction principle adds that for most traits, heredity sets a range of developmental potentials and the environment influences the extent of development. A more recent theory is that our genotypes influence the environments we are likely to experience—environments that then shape our conduct and character. So the current view is that heredity and environment *interact* to produce developmental change and that these two important influences are completely (and perhaps inseparably) intertwined.

Although behavioral genetics research has changed the way we look at human development, this approach has been criticized as a description rather than a true explanation of development.

Key Terms

active genotype/ environment correlations [112]

adoption design [99]

aging-ova hypothesis [92]

alleles [84]

amniocentesis [95]

behavioral genetics [97]

behavioral inhibition [105]

canalization [110]

chorionic villus sampling (CVS) [95]

chromosome [79]

codominance [87]

conception [78]

concordance rate [99]

congenital defect [88]

crossing over [81]

deoxyribonucleic acid (DNA) [80]

difficult temperament [105]

dizygotic (or fraternal) twins [82]

dominant allele [84]

Down syndrome [89]

easy temperament [105]

empathic concern [106]

evocative genotype/ environment correlations [112]

fragile-X syndrome [89]

genes [78]

genetic counseling [94]

genotype [78]

"goodness-of-fit" model [106]

heritability [98]

heritability coefficient [100]

heterozygous [84]

homozygous [84]

Huntington's disease [88]

incomplete dominance [85]

independent assortment [81]

introversion/ extroversion [106]

karyotype [83]

kinship [98]

manic-depression [109]

meiosis [81]

mitosis [80]

monozygotic (or identical) twins [82]

muscular dystrophy [94]

mutation [92]

neurotic disorder [109]

nonshared environmental influence (NSE) [101]

ovulation [78]

passive genotype/ environment correlations [112]

phenotype [78]

phenylketonuria (PKU) [96]

polygenic trait [88]

range-of-reaction principle [111]

recessive allele [84]

schizophrenia [109]

shared environmental influence (SE) [102]

sex-linked characteristic [87]

sickle-cell anemia [86]

single gene-pair inheritance [84]

slow-to-warm-up temperament [106]

Tay-Sachs disease [95]

temperament [104]

twin study [99]

ultrasound [95]

X chromosome [83]

Y chromosome [83]

zygote [78]

4 Prenatal Development and Birth

irst, answer the "true-or-false" questions at right. Now here is a "fill-in-the-blank" item that you may find a little easier: How old are you? It turns out that this apparently straightforward question means slightly different things to different people. Many Asian cultures date children from the moment of conception and consider them to be about 1 year old when they emerge from the womb. By contrast, we Westerners date ourselves from the moment of birth.

From a strict developmental perspective, the Asian method of reckoning age may be the more realistic. Not only do hundreds of remarkable developments occur before a child is born, but many of these events take place within eight short weeks of conception. As we trace the miraculous evolution of a one-celled zygote into a recognizable human being, it will become quite clear that human growth and development occur most rapidly during the *prenatal* period, months before birth.

When might environmental influences first occur? Once again, the answer is long before birth. **Prenatal development** does not take place in a vacuum; it occurs within the mother's uterus—an "environment" that differs from mother to mother and may well affect the product that emerges in the delivery room. We may be quite accustomed to thinking of the intrauterine environment as a safe, protective haven that enables an unborn child to take shape, grow, and become stronger in preparation for birth. This impression was created by influential scientists of the 18th century who described the womb as a kind of vacuum-packed mausoleum that "entombs" a fetus, protecting it from all external hazards (MacFarlane, 1977). Yet, we will see that the degree of safety or protection offered by the womb depends on a variety of factors, including the mother's age, health, and emotional state, the food she eats, the drugs she takes, and the chemicals or levels of radiation to which she is exposed.

In years gone by, many people believed that a fetus could be affected by just about any experience that the mother might have. For example, it was once assumed, even by some physicians, that women who failed to bear their husbands a male heir were "at fault" because they got insufficient exercise while pregnant. Presumably, maternal exercise caused an unborn child to move, thereby stimulating the development of fetal muscle and increasing the probability that the fetus would become a male! Other common beliefs included the notions that a pregnant woman who often listened to music would have a musical child and that mothers who were sexually active while pregnant would produce sexually precocious children. Today, we know that these ideas are unfounded, for only those maternal experiences that directly affect the intrauterine environment can influence an embryo or fetus. The reason will become clear as we look at the course of prenatal development and learn more about the interesting relationship between a mother and the unborn organism in her womb.

◢ FROM CONCEPTION TO BIRTH

In Chapter 3, we learned that development begins in the fallopian tube when a sperm penetrates the wall of a ripened ovum, forming a zygote. From the moment of conception, it takes approximately 266 days for this tiny, one-celled zygote to become a fetus of some 200 billion cells that is ready to be born.

Prenatal development is often divided into three major phases. The first phase, called the **germinal period,** (or the *period of the zygote*), lasts from conception until implantation, when the developing zygote becomes firmly attached to the wall of the uterus. The germinal period normally lasts about 8–14 days. The second phase of prenatal development, the **period of the embryo,** lasts from the beginning of the third week through the end of the eighth. This is the time when virtually all the major organs are formed and the heart begins to beat. The third phase, the **period of the fetus,** lasts from the ninth week of pregnancy until the child is born. During this phase, the major organ systems begin to function, and the developing organism grows rapidly.

TRUE OR FALSE?

1. Human beings develop most rapidly between birth and 2 years of age.

2. The mother's womb is a protective haven that shields an unborn child from external hazards such as pollution and disease.

3. The environment has its initial effect on human development at the moment a baby is born.

prenatal development: development that occurs between the moment of conception and the beginning of the birth process.

germinal period: first phase of prenatal development, lasting from conception until the developing organism becomes attached to the wall of the uterus (also called period of the zygote).

period of the embryo: second phase of prenatal development, lasting from the third through the eighth prenatal week, during which the major organs and anatomical structures take shape.

period of the fetus: third phase of prenatal development, lasting from the ninth prenatal week until birth; during this period, all major organ systems begin to function and the fetus grows rapidly.

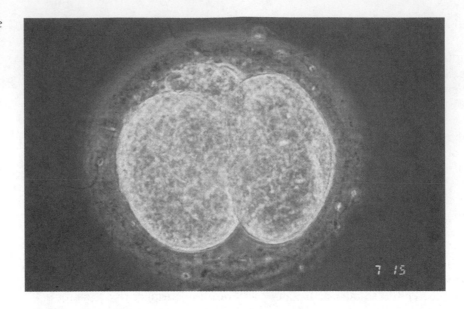

Within hours of conception, the fertilized ovum (zygote) divides, beginning a continuous process of cell differentiation.

The Germinal Period (or Period of the Zygote)

After conception, the fertilized ovum, or zygote, continues its journey down the fallopian tube toward the uterus. Within 24–36 hours, the zygote divides by mitosis into two cells. These two cells and all their daughter cells continue to divide at periodic intervals, forming a ball-like structure, or **blastocyst,** that will contain 60–80 cells within four days of conception. Cell differentiation has already begun. The inner layer of the blastocyst, called the **embryonic disk,** will become the **embryo.** The outer layer of cells, or **trophoblast,** will develop into tissues that protect and nourish the embryo.

As the blastocyst approaches the uterus 6–10 days after conception, small burrlike tendrils have emerged from the outer surface of the trophoblast. As nature would have it, the blastocyst reaches the uterus at the point in the woman's menstrual cycle when the uterine lining is engorged with small blood vessels that can provide nourishment to this primitive little creature. When the blastocyst contacts the uterine wall, its tendrils burrow inward, tapping into the woman's blood supply. This is **implantation.** Soon, cells from the uterus grow around the implanted blastocyst, providing a rudimentary protective covering. Within 8–14 days after conception, the site of implantation looks like a small, translucent blister on the lining of the uterus (see Figure 4-1). At this point, the germinal period comes to an end.

Implantation is a critical event in human development. Only about half of all fertilized ova are successfully implanted in the uterus (Roberts & Lowe, 1975), and perhaps as many as half of all implanted embryos are genetically abnormal (or burrow into a site incapable of sustaining them) and are soon miscarried (spontaneously aborted) (Simpson, 1993). So it appears that about one zygote in four will survive the initial phases of prenatal development.

The Period of the Embryo

The period of the embryo lasts from implantation through the eighth week of pregnancy, when all of the embryo's major organ systems will be present, at least in rudimentary form.

Development of Support Systems

During the second and third weeks after conception, four major support structures develop from the blastocyst's outer cell layer, or trophoblast. One membrane, the **amnion,** is a watertight sac that surrounds the embryo, filling with fluid that seeps

blastocyst: a hollow sphere of about 100–150 cells that results from the rapid division of the zygote as it moves through the fallopian tube.

embryonic disk: inner cluster of cells of the blastocyst, from which the embryo develops.

embryo: name given to the prenatal organism from the third through the eighth week after conception.

trophoblast: outer cells of the blastocyst, which develop into tissues that protect and nourish the embryo.

implantation: the burrowing of the blastocyst into the lining of the uterus.

amnion: a watertight membrane that develops from the trophoblast and surrounds the developing embryo, serving to regulate its temperature and to cushion it against injuries.

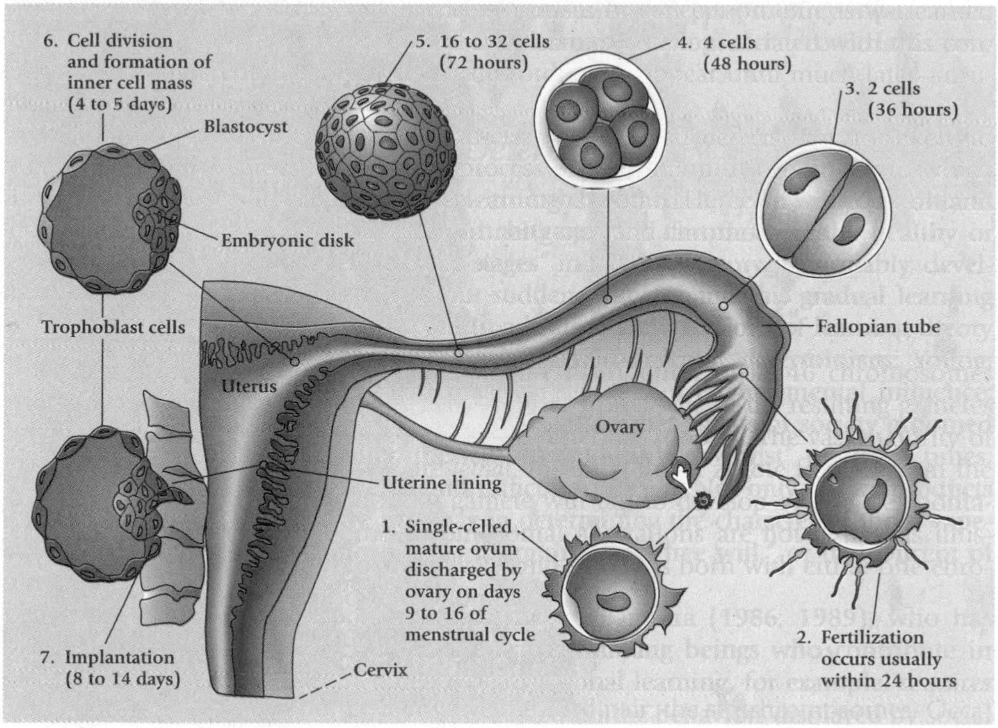

Figure 4-1
The germinal period.

6. Cell division and formation of inner cell mass (4 to 5 days)

Blastocyst

Embryonic disk

Trophoblast cells

Uterus

7. Implantation (8 to 14 days)

Cervix

5. 16 to 32 cells (72 hours)

4. 4 cells (48 hours)

3. 2 cells (36 hours)

Fallopian tube

Ovary

Uterine lining

1. Single-celled mature ovum discharged by ovary on days 9 to 16 of menstrual cycle

2. Fertilization occurs usually within 24 hours

in from the mother's tissues. The purpose of the amnion and its amniotic fluid is to cushion the developing organism against injuries, to regulate its temperature, and to provide a weightless environment that will make it easier for the unborn child to move. Floating beside the tiny, developing embryo is a balloon-shaped *yolk sac* that produces blood cells until the embryo is capable of producing its own. This yolk sac is attached to a third membrane, the **chorion**, which surrounds the amnion and eventually becomes the lining of the **placenta**—a multipurpose organ that we are about to discuss in detail. A fourth membrane, the *allantois*, forms the embryo's **umbilical cord**.

Purpose of the Placenta

Once the placenta develops, it is fed by blood vessels from the mother and the embryo, although the hairlike villi of the placenta act as a barrier that prevents these two bloodstreams from mixing. This placental barrier is semipermeable, meaning that it allows some substances to pass through but not others. Gases such as oxygen and carbon dioxide, salts, and various nutrients such as sugars, proteins, and fats are small enough to cross the placental barrier. However, blood cells are too large.

As maternal blood flows into the placenta, oxygen and nutrients pass through this semipermeable membrane into the embryo's bloodstream. The embryo is connected to the placenta by means of its lifeline, the umbilical cord, which carries oxygen and foodstuffs to the embryo and transports carbon dioxide and metabolic wastes from the embryo. These waste products then cross the placental barrier, enter the mother's bloodstream, and are eventually expelled from the mother's body along with her own metabolic wastes. Clearly, the placenta plays a crucial role in prenatal development, because this remarkable organ is the site of all metabolic transactions that sustain the embryo (see Figure 4-2).

Development of the Embryo

Once implantation has occurred, the embryonic disk rapidly differentiates into three distinct layers of cells (Sameroff, 1983). The outer layer, or *ectoderm*, will eventually become the child's skin, hair, nails, oil and sweat glands, and nervous system. The middle layer, or *mesoderm*, will form muscles, bones, connective tissue, and the circulatory

chorion: a membrane that develops from the trophoblast and becomes attached to the uterine tissues to gather nourishment for the embryo.

placenta: an organ, formed from the lining of the uterus and the chorion, that provides for respiration and nourishment of the unborn child and the elimination of its metabolic wastes.

umbilical cord: a soft tube containing blood vessels that connects the embryo to the placenta.

Figure 4-2
The embryo and its prenatal
environment.

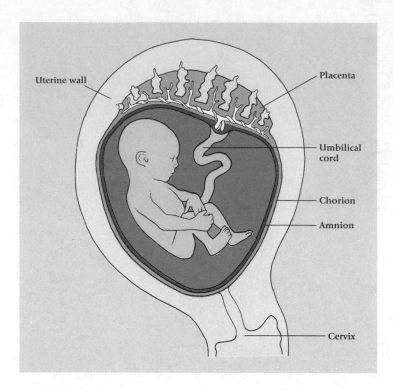

Uterine wall

Placenta

Umbilical
cord

Chorion

Amnion

Cervix

and excretory systems. From the inner layer, or *endoderm*, come the digestive tract, trachea, bronchi, lungs, and other vital organs such as the pancreas and liver.

Development proceeds at a breathtaking pace during the period of the embryo. In the third week after conception, a portion of the ectoderm folds into a **neural tube** that soon becomes the brain and spinal cord. By the end of the fourth week, the heart has not only formed but has already begun to beat. The eyes, ears, nose, and mouth are also taking shape, and buds that will become arms and legs suddenly appear. Thirty days after conception, the embryo is only about 1/4 of an inch long, but 10,000 times the size of the zygote from which it developed. At no time in the future will this organism ever grow as rapidly or change as much as it has during the first prenatal month.

During the second month, the body becomes much more human in appearance as it grows about 1/30th of an inch per day. A primitive tail appears (see Figure 4-3), but it is soon enclosed by protective tissue and becomes the tip of the backbone, the coccyx. By the middle of the fifth week, the eyes have corneas and lenses. By the seventh week, the ears are well formed and the embryo has a rudimentary skeleton. Limbs are now developing from the body outward; that is, the upper arms appear first, followed by the forearms, hands, and then fingers. The legs follow a similar pattern a few days later. The brain develops rapidly during the second month, and it directs the organism's first muscular contractions by the end of the embryonic period.

During the seventh and eighth prenatal weeks, the embryo's sexual development begins with the appearance of a genital ridge called the **indifferent gonad**. If the embryo is a male, a gene on its Y chromosome triggers a biochemical reaction that instructs the indifferent gonad to produce testes. If the embryo is a female, the indifferent gonad receives no such instructions and will produce ovaries. As the testes mature during the ninth and tenth prenatal weeks, they produce *testosterone*, the male sex hormone that stimulates the development of a male reproductive system. However, the female fetus will develop a female reproductive system even if its tiny ovaries are damaged or do not function. It appears, then, that nature's first choice is female and that "maleness" requires a "male" gene to (1) trigger the development of testes, which (2) must then function properly in order to produce other male sex organs.

neural tube: the primitive spinal cord that develops from the ectoderm and becomes the central nervous system.

indifferent gonad: undifferentiated tissue that produces testes in males and ovaries in females.

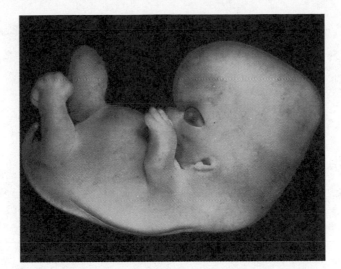

Figure 4-3
A human embryo at 40 days. The heart is now beating, and the limbs are rapidly forming. Note the primitive tail (soon to become the tip of the backbone) in the far left-hand portion of the photo.

Figure 4-4
A human embryo at 60 days. All the major organs have begun to form, and the embryo is now a fetus.

At 60 days after conception, the embryo is slightly more than an inch long and weighs less than one-quarter of an ounce. It appears human (see Figure 4-4), although its head is at least as long as the rest of its body. Apgar and Beck (1974, p. 57) offer the following description of the eight-week-old embryo:

> All of the structures which will be present when the baby is born in seven more months have already been formed, at least in beginning stages. . . . Medically, the unborn baby is no longer an embryo, but a fetus; not an it, but a he or she; not an indistinct cluster of cells, but an increasingly recognizable, unique human being in the making.

The Period of the Fetus

The last seven months of pregnancy, or the period of the **fetus**, is a period of rapid growth (see Figure 4-5) and refinement of all organ systems. Indeed, very noticeable changes are already apparent by the end of the third prenatal month. Bones are hardening, muscles are rapidly developing, and the fetus is now performing many interesting maneuvers in its watery environment—moving its arms, kicking its legs, making fists, twisting its body—although these activities are not yet detected by the

fetus: name given to the prenatal organism from the ninth week of pregnancy until birth.

Figure 4-5
Rate of body growth during the
fetal period. Increase in size is
especially dramatic from the 7th
to the 20th week.
Adapted from Moore & Persaud, 1993.

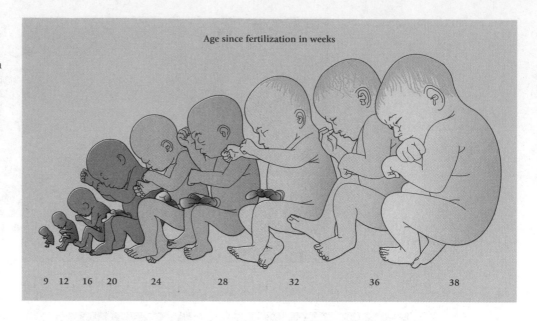

Age since fertilization in weeks

9 12 16 20 24 28 32 36 38

mother (Annis, 1978). Several organ systems are operational, allowing the fetus to swallow, to digest nutrients, and to urinate. Gender is readily apparent, and the fetal reproductive system already contains immature ova or sperm cells. All this detail is present after 12 weeks even though the fetus is a mere 3 inches long and still weighs less than an ounce.

The Second Trimester

Development continues at a rapid pace during the fourth, fifth, and sixth months of pregnancy—a period called the *second trimester*. At age 16 weeks, the fetus is 8–10 inches long and weighs about 6 ounces. Its motor activity may include refined actions such as thumbsucking, as well as kicks that may be strong enough to be felt by the mother. The fetal heartbeat can now be heard with a stethoscope, and the hardening skeleton can be detected by ultrasound. By the end of the fourth month, the fetus has assumed a distinctly human appearance, even though it stands absolutely no chance of surviving outside the womb.

During the fifth and sixth months, the nails begin to harden, the skin thickens, and eyebrows, eyelashes, and scalp hair suddenly appear. At 20 weeks, the sweat glands are functioning, and the fetal heartbeat is often strong enough to be heard by placing an ear on the mother's abdomen. The fetus is now about 12 inches long and weighs between 12 and 16 ounces. By the 25th week, the fetus's visual and auditory senses are apparently functional. We know this because preterm infants born only 25 weeks after conception will become alert at the sound of a loud bell and blink in response to a bright light (Allen & Capute, 1986). Six months after conception, the fetus is approximately 14–15 inches long and weighs about 2 pounds.

At some point between the 22nd and 28th weeks after conception, the fetal brain and respiratory system have matured to an extent that the fetus attains the **age of viability,** the point at which survival outside the uterus *may* be possible (Moore, 1989). In the spring of 1989, a young girl in Chicago made medical history by becoming the smallest baby ever to be born and live (Gehorsam & King, 1991). This hardy young lady weighed in at 9.9 ounces (280 grams) when she was delivered in her 27th prenatal week. Although she weighed only 12 pounds on her second birthday, this "littlest survivor" is healthy and is developing normally. (Other babies have been born earlier—as early as the 22nd week—and survived, but none of these infants weighed less than this girl.) Until this birth, only a handful of infants weighing less than 1 pound had ever survived. In fact, the majority of newborns who weigh less

age of viability: a point between the 24th and 28th prenatal weeks when a fetus may survive outside the uterus if excellent medical care is available.

By the end of the seventh month, the rapidly growing fetus is about 16 to 17 inches (40 cm) long and weighs about 4 pounds. Its odds of survival in the event of a premature birth are increasing each day.

than 2¼ pounds (1000 grams) do not survive, even with excellent medical care (Lin, 1989).

There is a very clear relationship between the birth weight of a child and the child's probability of surviving: The less a baby weighs at birth, the greater the likelihood that he or she will die during the birth process or soon thereafter (see Table 4-1). Each additional day that a fetus develops within the uterus increases the probability of survival in the outside world.

The Third Trimester

The seventh, eighth, and ninth months of pregnancy—the third trimester—is a "finishing" phase before birth. By the end of the seventh month, the fetus weighs about 4 pounds and is about 16–17 inches long. One month later, it has grown to 18 inches and put on another 1–2½ pounds. Much of this weight comes from a padding of fat, deposited just beneath the skin, that will later help to insulate the newborn child from changes in temperature. Not so visible is the rapid maturation of the brain's respiratory centers and the air sacs of the lungs—developments that underlie a baby's ability to breathe should he or she be born prematurely. By the time a fetus weighs

Table 4-1 Infant Mortality as a Function of Birth Weight

	Birth weight		Percentage of babies who die
	In grams	*In pounds*	
Very low birth weight	500– 749	1 lb, 9 oz or less	67
	750– 999	1 lb, 10 oz–2 lb, 3 oz	33
	1000–1249	2 lb, 4 oz–2 lb, 12 oz	16
Low birth weight	1249–1499	2 lb, 13 oz–3 lb, 4 oz	9
	1500–2500	3 lb, 5 oz–5 lb, 8 oz	6
Average birth weight	2500–3000	5 lb, 9 oz–6 lb, 9 oz	2
	3001–4500	6 lb, 10 oz–9 lb, 14 oz	1

Source: From Lin, 1989.

$3^{1}/_{2}$ to 4 pounds, odds of survival in the event of a premature birth are high (see Table 4-1), although it may still be necessary to provide oxygen to help the infant to breathe (Austin & Moawad, 1993). Yet, a fetus weighing at least 5 pounds at birth may not even require an incubator.

As the uterus expands during the third trimester, it assumes the shape of an inverted pear. By the middle of the ninth month, the fetus is so large that the most comfortable position within its restricted uterine environment is likely to be a head-down posture at the base of the uterus, with the limbs curled up in the so-called fetal position. At irregular intervals over the last month of pregnancy, the mother's uterus will contract and then relax. These contractions serve to tone the uterine muscle, dilate the cervix, and help position the head of the fetus into the gap between the pelvic bones through which it will soon be pushed. As the uterine contractions become stronger, more frequent, and regular, the prenatal period draws to a close. The mother is now in the first stage of labor, and within a matter of hours she will give birth.

Concept Check 4-1 ⌄ Understanding the Timing of Prenatal Milestones

For each of the following prenatal milestones, indicate the period (germinal, embryonic, or fetal) in which it occurs, the time span (in weeks or months) covered by this period of prenatal development, and the term used to refer to the developing organism during this period. The answers appear in the Appendix.

Event	Period	Time span	Name for organism
Implantation	_____	_____	_____
Age of viability	_____	_____	_____
First heartbeats	_____	_____	_____
Kicks first felt by mother	_____	_____	_____
Organs form	_____	_____	_____

▶ ENVIRONMENTAL INFLUENCES ON PRENATAL DEVELOPMENT

The pattern of prenatal development just described is an overview of what typically occurs between conception and birth. The vast majority of unborn children follow this "normal" pattern, and for that we can be thankful. Nevertheless, there are those who encounter environmental roadblocks during the prenatal period that may be sufficiently formidable to channel their development along an abnormal path. We will now consider a number of factors that can have adverse effects on an unborn child.

Maternal Characteristics

The Mother's Age

Are some ages safer than others for women to become pregnant and bear children? The answer is a qualified "yes." As shown in Figure 4-6, there is a relationship between a mother's age and the risk of death for her fetus or **neonate** (newborn). Compared with mothers in their 20s, those under age 15 face greater odds of bearing a stillborn fetus or a baby that fails to live. Younger mothers also experience more obstetrical complications and are more likely to die during childbirth than those in their 20s (Leppert, Namerow, & Barker, 1986; Planned Parenthood Federation of America, 1976). Why are younger mothers and their offspring at risk? Part of the problem is that some very young teens have not matured enough physically to sustain a fetus. But by far, the greater problem is that pregnant teens are often from low-income family backgrounds characterized by poor nutrition, high levels of stress, and little access to supervised prenatal care (Abma & Mott, 1991). Indeed, teenage moth-

neonate: a newborn infant from birth to approximately 1 month of age.

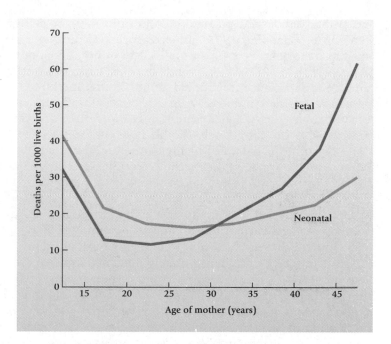

Figure 4-6
Relationship between mother's age and risk of death for the fetus or neonate.
From Kessner, 1973.

ers and their babies are usually *not* at risk when they receive good prenatal care and competent medical supervision during the birth process (Baker & Mednick, 1984; see also Seitz and Apfel, 1994a).

What risks do women face should they delay childbearing until after age 35? As Figure 4-6 indicates, there is an increased incidence of spontaneous abortion, due in part to the older woman's greater likelihood of conceiving children with chromosomal abnormalities (Verp, 1993; see Chapter 3). The risks of other complications during pregnancy and delivery are also greater for older women partly because they, like adolescents, are less likely than women in their 20s and early 30s to seek adequate prenatal care early in their pregnancies (Brown, 1988). Older women are also more likely than younger ones to have developed chronic health problems that could affect the outcomes of pregnancy. Even so, it is important to emphasize that the *vast majority* of older women—particularly those who are healthy and well-nourished and who receive adequate prenatal care—have normal pregnancies and healthy babies (Leroy, 1988).

The Mother's Emotional State

Although many women are happy to learn that they are pregnant, the fact remains that over half of all pregnancies are unplanned ("Half Our Pregnancies," 1983) and single women and those who are unhappily married are often bitter, depressed, or angry about their pregnancies (Browne & Dixon, 1978). In fact, it is quite normal for any woman to show some symptoms of anxiety and depression while she is pregnant (Kaplan, 1986). Do these emotional states and attitudes toward pregnancy have any effect on prenatal development? Can they affect the birth process? Indeed they can, in some cases at least.

Although there are no direct connections between a woman's nervous system and that of her fetus, a mother's emotional state can affect the outcome of her pregnancy. When a mother becomes emotionally aroused, her endocrine glands secrete powerful activating hormones, such as adrenalin, that may cross the placental barrier and enter the fetal bloodstream, where, at the very least, they can significantly increase the fetus's motor activity. Temporarily stressful episodes such as a fall, a frightening experience, or a disagreement with one's spouse will have few, if any, harmful consequences (Stott & Latchford, 1976). But if their emotional distress is *prolonged* and *severe*, expectant mothers are at risk for complications such as miscarriage, lengthy and painful labor, and premature or low-birth-weight deliveries (Katz et al., 1991; Sameroff & Chandler, 1975). Indeed, such outcomes are actually quite common when distressed mothers (1) are ambivalent or negative about their marriages or their pregnancies and (2) have no friends or other bases of social support to whom they can turn for assistance (McDonald, 1968; Stott & Latchford, 1976). Counseling may help these mothers immensely. In one study, the babies of stressed mothers who received counseling weighed significantly more at birth than did babies of stressed mothers who did not get help (Rothberg & Lits, 1991).

Once born, the babies of highly stressed mothers tend to be highly active, irritable, and quite irregular in their feeding, sleeping, and bowel habits (Sameroff & Chandler, 1975; Sontag, 1944). It has been argued that this "difficult" temperamental profile is genetically based or is caused by the activating hormones associated with the mother's heightened emotional state during pregnancy (Carey & McDevitt, 1980). However, later research points to another possibility. Tiffany Field and her associates (1985) found that mothers who were highly anxious, depressed, or resentful during the last trimester of pregnancy usually remained anxious or upset after their babies were born. And compared with a group of new mothers who had had happy pregnancies, the distressed mothers were more *punitive* and *controlling* in their approach to child rearing and had infants who were *fussier* and *more variable* in mood. Brian Vaughn and his associates (1987) have reported a similar link between maternal distress late in pregnancy and infant temperament six months after birth. Yet, the most intriguing finding in this second study was that the actual levels of activating hormones present in the intrauterine environment late in pregnancy did *not* predict infants' later temperamental characteristics. Although these findings are hardly definitive, they suggest that the negative temperamental qualities often observed among children of distressed mothers could be *socially* mediated. That is, mothers who have been anxious or resentful about their pregnancies may often retain some of these feelings after giving birth and then respond to their babies in ways that make these children irritable or "difficult" (Vaughn et al., 1987; see also Cohn, Campbell, Matias, & Hopkins, 1990; Field, Healy, Goldstein, & Guthertz, 1990).

The Mother's Diet (Nutrition)

Fifty years ago, doctors routinely advised expectant mothers to gain no more than two pounds a month while pregnant, the rationale being that a tiny fetus could easily extract the nutrients it needs, even if a mother gained very little weight. Today, most obstetricians would be very concerned if a patient of theirs gained too little weight, for they are now well aware of the many harmful complications that can result from inadequate prenatal nutrition. Women are currently advised to gain 3–4 pounds during the first three months of pregnancy and approximately a pound a week thereafter—a total increase of 25–30 pounds (Whitney & Hamilton, 1987).

Much of what we know about the role of nutrition in prenatal development comes from studies of expectant mothers who were severely malnourished. Severe malnutrition increases the risk of congenital defects, prolonged labor, stillbirth, and infant mortality during the first year. Apparently, the harmful consequences of prenatal malnutrition are greatest when the nutritional deficiency occurs later in pregnancy, especially during the last three months (see Box 4-1). Not only is this third trimester the period when an unborn child is gaining most of its eventual birth weight, but the fetus's brain cells are also growing rapidly and forming trillions of connections with other brain cells (Tanner, 1990). So perhaps we should not be surprised to learn that (1) mothers who are severely malnourished during the third trimester are likely to deliver rather small babies, or (2) autopsies of stillborn children reveal that infants born to malnourished mothers have brain cells that are fewer and smaller than those in infants whose mothers were adequately nourished (Lewin, 1975; Winick, 1976).

The long-term effects of prenatal malnutrition will depend to a large extent on the adequacy of the child's diet after birth. A malnourished infant who lives in an

BOX 4-1

Effects of Famine on Infant Mortality and Intellectual Development

*B*etween October 1944 and March 1945, a large area of western Holland was subjected to conditions of famine. During this period of World War II, many Dutch citizens were trying to support Allied forces, and the occupying German troops retaliated by closing the roads and the rail system, thereby restricting civilian transport. The embargo severely limited the availability of food and other essential supplies to most large cities, and shortage of food soon became serious. Rations dropped from over 2000 calories per person per day before the famine to 500–700 calories (with a severe reduction in protein) by the time conquering Allied troops lifted the blockade.

Some 30 years later, Zela Stein and her associates (Stein & Susser, 1976; Stein, Susser, Saenger, & Marolla, 1975) examined hospital birth and death records from this period to study the effects of famine on infant mortality. And because all Dutch males must take intelligence tests when they undergo compulsory military training at age 19, it was also possible to determine whether the surviving male children born during or shortly after the famine showed any long-term intellectual deficits as a result of their early malnutrition.

The short-term effects were clear. Stein et al. (1975) found that women who were malnourished during the *last three months* of their pregnancies were much more likely to have small, underweight babies than mothers who were malnourished during their first or second trimester. The effects of malnutrition on infant mortality were almost identical, as indicated in the accompanying table.

Stein and her colleagues then compared the later intellectual performance of military inductees from the famine area with that of their peers born in parts of Holland not affected by the famine. Once again, the results were clear

and somewhat surprising: Malnourished males from the famine area scored no lower on the test battery than well-nourished males from nonfamine areas.

Since it is well known that malnourished fetuses often have smaller brains and fewer brain cells (see text for details), why do you suppose that the malnourished males in this study showed no long-term cognitive deficits? Stein and her colleagues offer one possible explanation. They note that the mothers of these boys (and the boys themselves) were adequately nourished after the famine. Since the first two years of life is a period of rapid brain growth and development, it is certainly possible that adequate nutrition during this critical phase may compensate for any adverse effects of poor prenatal nutrition. In other words, if the fetally malnourished infant should survive, it appears that a good *postnatal* diet may help to prevent long-term deficits in neurological development and intellectual performance.

Condition	Infant mortality in first 12 months (deaths per 1000 births)
Child born before famine (mother not malnourished)	9
Mother malnourished— last 3 months of pregnancy	30
Mother malnourished— first 6 months	18
Mother malnourished— first 3 months	6
Child conceived and born after famine (mother not malnourished)	6

economically impoverished environment where nutrition *remains* inadequate is likely to show later deficits in physical growth as well as impairments in social, emotional, and intellectual development (Barrett, Radke-Yarrow, & Klein, 1982; Lozoff, 1989; Rose, 1994). Moreover, it appears that some of these long-term effects are linked to the infant's own behavior. Philip Zeskind and Craig Ramey (1981) have found that fetally malnourished infants are often unresponsive, apathetic babies who become rather irritable when aroused—qualities that may make them unpleasant to deal with. As a result, these children are likely to alienate their caregivers and fail to elicit the kinds of playful stimulation and emotional support that would promote their social and intellectual development. Fortunately, dietary supplements given to malnourished mothers during the last half of pregnancy or to their infants soon after birth tend to make these children more active and outgoing, thereby reducing the likelihood that early malnutrition will have harmful consequences that persist over time (Barrett et al., 1982; Joos, Pollitt, Mueller, & Albright, 1983; Pollitt et al., 1992). Dietary supplements are particularly effective when combined with stimulating day care for the infants (Zeskind & Ramey, 1981) and with programs that help their parents to become more sensitive and responsive caregivers (Super, Herrera, & Mora, 1990).

Teratogens

The term **teratogen** refers to any disease, drug, or other environmental agent that can harm a developing embryo or fetus by causing physical deformities, severely retarded growth, blindness, brain damage, and even death. The list of known and suspected teratogens has grown frighteningly large over the years, making many of today's parents quite concerned about the hazards their unborn children could face (Kelley-Buchanan, 1988; Verp, 1993). Before considering the effects of some of the major teratogens, let's emphasize that over 90% of babies are perfectly normal and that many of those born with defects have mild, temporary, or reversible problems (Baird et al., 1988; Heinonen, Slone, & Shapiro, 1977). Let's also lay out a few generalizations about the effects of teratogens that will aid us in interpreting the research that follows:

1. The effects of a teratogen on a body part or organ system are worst during the period when that structure is forming and growing most rapidly.
2. Not all embryos or fetuses are equally affected by a teratogen; susceptibility to harm is influenced by the unborn child's genetic makeup as well as by the mother's genetic makeup and the quality of the prenatal environment she provides.
3. The same defect can be caused by different teratogens.
4. A variety of defects can result from a single teratogen.
5. The longer the exposure to or the higher the "dose" of a teratogen, the more likely it is that serious harm will be done.

Let's look more closely at the first generalization, for it is very important. Each major organ system or body part has a **critical period** when it is most sensitive to teratogenic agents—namely, the time when the particular part of the body is evolving and taking shape. Recall that most organs and body parts are rapidly forming during the period of the embryo (weeks 3–8 of prenatal development). As we see in Figure 4-7, this is precisely the time—before a woman may even know that she is pregnant—that most organ systems are most vulnerable to damage. The most crucial period for gross physical defects of the head and central nervous system is the third through the fifth prenatal weeks. The heart is particularly vulnerable from the middle of the third through the middle of the sixth prenatal week; the most vulnerable period for many other organs and body parts is the second prenatal month. Is it any wonder, then, that the period of the embryo is often called the critical phase of pregnancy?

Once an organ or body part is fully formed, it becomes somewhat less susceptible to damage. However, as Figure 4-7 also illustrates, some organ systems (particularly the eyes, genitals, and nervous system) can be damaged throughout pregnancy. Several years ago, Olli Heinonen and his associates (Heinonen et al., 1977) concluded that many of the birth defects found among the 50,282 children in their sample were *anytime malformations*—problems that could have been caused by teratogens at any point during the nine-month prenatal period. So it seems that the entire prenatal epoch could be considered a **sensitive period** for human development!

Let's now consider some of the more common diseases, drugs, chemicals, and other environmental teratogens that can disrupt prenatal development and produce serious birth defects.

Maternal Diseases

Many disease agents are capable of crossing the placental barrier and doing much more damage to a developing embryo or fetus than to the mother herself. This makes sense when we remember that an unborn child has an immature immune system that cannot produce enough antibodies to effectively combat most disease agents.

Rubella. The medical community became aware of the teratogenic effect of diseases in 1941 when an Australian physician, McAllister Gregg, noticed that many mothers who had had **rubella (German measles)** early in pregnancy were delivering

teratogens: external agents such as viruses, drugs, chemicals, and radiation that can harm a developing embryo or fetus.

critical period: a (typically) brief period in the development of an organism when it is particularly susceptible to certain environmental influences; outside this period, the same influences will have little, if any, effect.

sensitive period: a period during which an organism is quite susceptible to certain environmental influences; outside this period, the same environmental influences must be much stronger to produce comparable effects on development (weaker form of the critical-period concept).

rubella (German measles): a disease that has little effect on a mother but may cause a number of serious birth defects in unborn children who are exposed in the first 3–4 months of pregnancy.

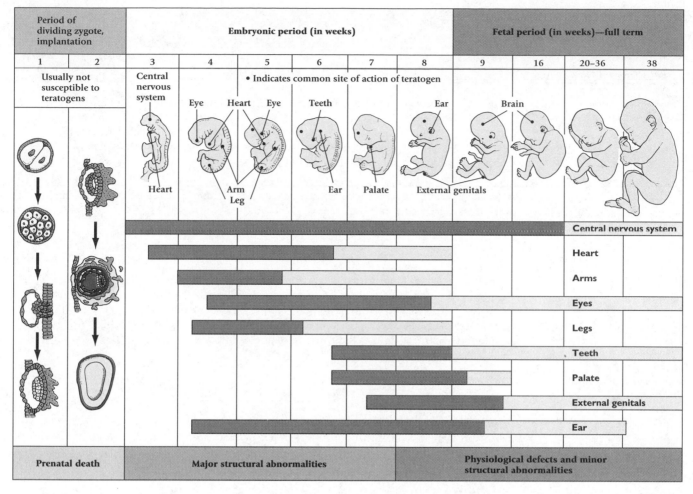

Period of dividing zygote, implantation		Embryonic period (in weeks)						Fetal period (in weeks)—full term			
1	2	3	4	5	6	7	8	9	16	20–36	38

Usually not susceptible to teratogens

Central nervous system

• Indicates common site of action of teratogen

Eye Heart Eye Teeth Ear Brain

Heart Arm Leg Ear Palate External genitals

Central nervous system
Heart
Arms
Eyes
Legs
Teeth
Palate
External genitals
Ear

Prenatal death	Major structural abnormalities	Physiological defects and minor structural abnormalities

babies who were congenitally blind. After Gregg alerted the medical community, doctors began to notice that pregnant rubella patients were regularly bearing children with a variety of defects, including blindness, deafness, cardiac abnormalities, and mental retardation. Rubella is most dangerous during the first trimester. Studies have shown that 60%–85% of babies whose mothers had rubella in the first eight weeks of pregnancy will have birth defects, compared with about 50% of those infected in the third month and 16% of those infected in weeks 13–20 (Kelley-Buchanan, 1988). This disease clearly illustrates the critical-period principle. The risk of eye and heart defects are greatest in the first eight weeks (when these organs are forming), whereas deafness is more common if the mother comes down with rubella in weeks 6–13. Today, doctors stress that no woman should try to conceive unless she has had rubella or has been immunized against it.

Other infectious diseases. Many diseases other than rubella are known teratogens (see Table 4-2 for several examples). One of the more common of these diseases, **syphilis,** is most harmful in the middle and later stages of pregnancy, since syphilitic spirochetes (the microscopic organisms that transmit the disease) cannot cross the placental barrier until the 18th prenatal week. This is fortunate in one sense, for the disease can be diagnosed with a blood test and treated with antibiotics long before it could harm the fetus. However, the mother who receives no treatment runs the risk of miscarrying or of giving birth to a child who has serious eye, ear, bone, or brain damage (Kelley-Buchanan, 1988; see also Table 4-2).

Two viruses in the herpes group, neither of which is curable, are known to be powerful teratogens. One is **cytomegalovirus (CMV),** a common intrauterine infection that can cause blindness, deafness, brain damage, and fetal death. In fact, CMV

Figure 4-7
The critical periods of prenatal development. Each organ or structure has a critical period when it is most sensitive to damage from teratogens. Dark band indicates the most sensitive periods. Light band indicates times that each organ or structure is somewhat less sensitive to teratogens, although damage may still occur.
Adapted from Moore & Persaud, 1989.

syphilis: a common venereal disease that may cross the placental barrier in the middle and later stages of pregnancy, causing miscarriage or serious birth defects.

cytomegalovirus (CMV): a virus in the herpes group that produces few, if any, symptoms in mothers but is the most common infectious cause of congenital deafness and mental retardation.

Table 4-2 Some Diseases That May Affect an Embryo, Fetus, or Newborn

Sexually transmitted diseases	Description and effects
Acquired immune deficiency syndrome (AIDS)	Although AIDS is listed as a sexually transmitted disease, many mothers who transmit it to their offspring have acquired it from transfusions of contaminated blood or from their use of contaminated syringes while taking drugs. Babies born with AIDS have deficient or nonoperative immune systems and thus little protection against any infectious disease. The vast majority of these AIDS babies will die early in life (see text).
Gonorrhea	Major hazard is that the gonococcus organism may attack the eyes of a child passing through an infected birth canal. Infections are treated with silver nitrate eyedrops immediately after birth. If left untreated, gonorrhea can blind the child within two days.
Herpes simplex (genital herpes)	See text.
Syphilis	Untreated syphilis may cause miscarriage or several serious birth defects (see text). Occasionally, babies of untreated mothers are born without showing any syphilitic symptoms. If this "latent" syphilis is not detected and treated, it will produce severe consequences 5–15 years later. The most common problems include blindness, deterioration of the central nervous system, and congestive heart failure. The vast majority of children who have long-term (tertiary) syphilis will die from its complications.

Other maternal conditions or diseases	Effects on the fetus or newborn
Chicken pox	Rarely produces fetal malformations but may lead to spontaneous abortion or premature delivery. A premature infant who has chicken pox is usually very weak and likely to die.
Cytomegalovirus	Produces no symptoms in adults but many produce microcephaly (small head), brain damage, and blindness in the embryo or fetus. May also induce miscarriages.
Diabetes	Diabetics face a greater risk than nondiabetics of delivering a stillborn fetus or a child who will die in the first few days after birth. Babies of diabetics may have any of a number of malformations. Also, these babies are often very large because they have accumulated a large amount of fat during the third trimester. Although a diabetic mother requires special care to prevent the death of her child, more than 85% of these children currently survive.
Hepatitis	A child born to a mother with hepatitis is likely to have this disease. The infection is thought to occur during the birth process when the fetus swallows infected maternal blood that may be present as the umbilical cord separates from the placenta.
Hypertension (chronic high blood pressure)	Increases the probability of miscarriages and infant death. The higher a woman's blood pressure, the greater the likelihood of prenatal complications.

genital herpes: a sexually transmitted disease that can infect infants at birth, causing blindness, brain damage, or even death.

cesarean delivery: surgical delivery of a baby through an incision made in the mother's abdomen and uterus (also called cesarean section).

acquired immune deficiency syndrome (AIDS): a viral disease that can be transmitted from a mother to her fetus or neonate and that results in a weakening of the body's immune system and, ultimately, death.

is now considered the most common infectious cause of congenital deafness and mental retardation. Fortunately, only 5%–10% of babies infected prenatally show any serious complications (Ismail, 1993). The virus that causes **genital herpes** (herpes simplex) can also cross the placental barrier, although most infections occur at birth as the newborn comes in contact with lesions on the mother's genitals (Hanshaw, Dudgeon, & Marshall, 1985). The consequences of a herpes infection can be severe: This incurable disease will kill about one-third of all infected neonates and cause such disabilities as blindness, brain damage, and other serious neurological disorders in another 25%–30% (Ismail, 1993). For these reasons, mothers with active herpes infections are now routinely advised to undergo a **cesarean delivery** (a surgical birth in which the baby is delivered through an incision in the mother's abdomen) to avoid infecting their babies.

The sexually transmitted disease of even greater concern today is **acquired immune deficiency syndrome (AIDS),** the fatal disease that is caused by the virus

Table 4-2 Some Diseases That May Affect an Embryo, Fetus, or Newborn *(continued)*

Other maternal conditions or diseases	Effects on the fetus or newborn
Influenza	The more powerful strains may induce neural tube defects and spontaneous abortion during the first trimester, although some researchers suspect that the high fever accompanying the flu (rather than the influenza virus) is the agent responsible for such effects.
Mumps	If contracted during the first trimester, this mild disease increases the risk of spontaneous abortion.
Rh disease	This results from an incompatibility between Rh-positive fetuses, who have a protein called Rh factor in their blood, and Rh-negative mothers, who lack this substance. During labor and delivery, when they are exposed to the fetus's Rh-positive blood, Rh-negative mothers produce Rh antibodies—substances that may cross the deteriorating placental barrier and attack the fetus's red blood cells, resulting in *erythroblastosis* (Rh disease). This complication can produce serious birth defects and even death. Firstborns are usually not affected because the Rh-negative mother has no Rh antibodies until giving birth to a first Rh-positive child. Fortunately, Rh disease can be controlled by administering *rhogam* after the delivery—a drug that prevents the mother from forming the Rh antibodies that could harm her next Rh-positive child.
Rubella	See text.
Toxemia (eclampsia)	Toxemia of pregnancy is a disorder of unknown origin that affects about 5% of pregnant women in the United States during the third trimester. Its mildest form, called *preeclampsia*, mainly affects the mother and includes symptoms such as high blood pressure, rapid weight gain, and protein in the urine. Untreated preeclampsia may worsen and become *eclampsia*, a condition that may cause maternal convulsions and coma. About half the unborn children and 10%–15% of affected mothers will die from eclampsia; surviving infants are likely to suffer brain damage.
Toxoplasmosis	About one-fourth of adults have had this mild disease, which produces symptoms similar to a common cold. The agent responsible is a parasite present in raw meat and cat feces. If a medical exam reveals that a woman has no antibodies against toxoplasmosis, she should avoid undercooked meat and locations where cat feces are likely to be present (for example, garden, pet's litter box) during her pregnancy. Toxoplasmosis is a powerful teratogen that can produce serious eye or brain damage and induce spontaneous abortions.
Urinary tract infection	Low-grade bacterial infection of the urinary tract will develop into serious kidney infections (acute pylonephritis) in about 20%–40% of pregnant women. Left untreated, these latter infections significantly increase the risk of premature delivery and infant death shortly before or after birth.

Sources: From Evans, Fletcher, Dixler, & Shulman, 1989; Kelley-Buchanan, 1988; and Lin, Verp, & Sabbagha, 1993.

HIV, which destroys the immune system and makes victims susceptible to rare, so-called "opportunistic" infections that eventually kill them. HIV-infected mothers can transmit the virus to their babies (1) prenatally, if the virus passes through the placenta; (2) during birth, when there may be an exchange of blood between mother and child as the umbilical cord separates from the placenta; or (3) after birth, if the virus is passed through the mother's milk during breast feeding (Task Force on Pediatric AIDS, 1989). Despite all these possibilities for infection, it appears that only around 25% of babies born to HIV-infected mothers are infected (Gabiano et al., 1992). Although these infants are living longer today than they did at the outset of the AIDS epidemic, thanks to the development of better treatments, they live only about three years on average (Jones et al., 1992). Mother-to-child transmission of HIV in the United States is especially common among inner-city minority women who take drugs intravenously or have sexual partners who do (Mitchell, 1989). These mothers are often poor, sick themselves, and unwilling or unable to care adequately for their sick children. Many experts believe that interventions aimed at modifying unsafe sexual practices and drug use may be about the only effective means to combat the AIDs epidemic, for it may be many years before a cure for this disease is found.

Drugs

People have long suspected that drugs taken by pregnant women could have any number of harmful effects on unborn children. Even Aristotle thought as much when he noted that many drunken mothers have feeble-minded babies (Abel, 1981). Today, we know that these suspicions were often correct and that even mild drugs that have few, if any, lasting effects on a mother may prove extremely hazardous to a developing embryo or fetus. Unfortunately, the medical community learned this lesson the hard way.

The thalidomide tragedy. In 1960, a West German drug company began to market a mild tranquilizer, sold over the counter, that was intended to alleviate the periodic nausea (morning sickness) that many women experience during the first trimester of pregnancy. Presumably, the drug was perfectly safe; in tests on pregnant rats, it had had no ill effects on mothers or offspring. The drug was **thalidomide.**

What came to pass quickly illustrated that drugs that appear harmless in tests with laboratory animals may turn out to be violent teratogens for human beings. Thousands of women who had used thalidomide during the first two months of pregnancy suddenly began to give birth to defective children. And the birth defects were horrible: Thalidomide babies often had badly deformed eyes, ears, noses, and hearts and a variety of lesser malformations, such as fusing of the fingers and toes. But perhaps the most striking of all birth defects produced by this powerful teratogen was **phocomelia**—a structural abnormality in which all or parts of the limbs are missing and the feet or hands may be attached directly to the torso like flippers.

Doctors soon discovered that the kinds of birth defects produced by thalidomide depended on when the drug was taken. Babies of mothers who had taken the drug on or around the 21st day after conception were likely to be born without ears. Those whose mothers had used thalidomide on the 25th through the 27th day of pregnancy often had grossly deformed arms or no arms at all. If the mother had taken the drug between the 28th and the 36th day, her child might have deformed legs or no legs. But if she had waited until the 40th day before using thalidomide, her baby was usually not affected (Apgar & Beck, 1974). Let's note, however, that most mothers who took thalidomide delivered babies with no apparent birth defects—a finding that illustrates the dramatic individual differences that unborn children display in response to teratogens.

Other common drugs. Despite the lessons learned from the thalidomide tragedy, about 60% of pregnant women take at least one prescription or over-the-counter drug during pregnancy (Schnoll, 1986). Unfortunately, some of the most commonly used drugs can produce birth defects. Heavy use of aspirin, for example, has been linked to fetal growth retardation, neonatal bleeding, poor motor control in infants, and even infant death (Barr et al., 1990, Kelley-Buchanan, 1988). Other studies have linked heavy caffeine consumption with such complications as miscarriage, low birth weight, and poor motor control in newborns.[1] Medications containing sex hormones (or their active biochemical ingredients) can also affect a developing embryo or fetus.

thalidomide: a mild tranquilizer that, taken early in pregnancy, can produce a variety of malformations of the limbs, eyes, ears, and heart.

phocomelia: a prenatal malformation in which all or parts of the limbs are missing.

---

[1]Let's note, however, that the teratogenic effects of caffeine have not been conclusively established. In fact, some researchers (see, for example, Verp, 1993) believe that the adverse reproductive outcomes associated with caffeine may well be attributable to other drugs that mothers have used—most notably alcohol and nicotine, which we will soon discuss.

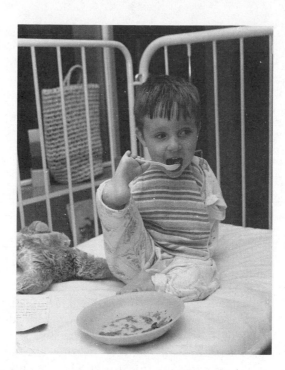

This boy has no arms or hands —two of the birth defects that may be produced by thalidomide.

For example, oral contraceptives contain female sex hormones, and if a woman takes the pill, not knowing that she is pregnant, her unborn child faces a slightly increased risk of heart defects and other minor malformations (Heinonen et al., 1977; Kelley-Buchanan, 1988).

One synthetic sex hormone that can have serious long-term effects is **diethylstilbestrol (DES)**—the active ingredient of a drug that was widely prescribed for the prevention of miscarriages between the mid-1940s and 1965. The drug seemed safe enough; newborns whose mothers had used DES appeared to be normal in every way. But in 1971, physicians clearly established that 17- to 21-year-old females whose mothers had used DES were at risk for developing abnormalities of the reproductive organs, including a rare form of cervical cancer. Clearly, the risk of cancer is not very great; fewer than 1 in 1000 DES daughters have developed the disease thus far (Brody, 1993). However, there are other complications, most notably adverse reproductive outcomes. For example, DES daughters who themselves become pregnant are more likely than nonexposed women to miscarry or to deliver prematurely. What about DES sons? Although there is no conclusive evidence that prenatal exposure to DES causes cancer in sons, a small number of men who were exposed to DES in utero have developed genital trait abnormalities, fertility problems, and disorders of the immune system (Brody, 1993).[2]

Clearly, the vast majority of women who use aspirin and caffeine, who become pregnant while on the pill, or who have taken DES deliver perfectly normal babies. Nevertheless, the fact that seemingly harmless drugs can produce congenital defects has convinced many mothers to restrict or eliminate their intake of all drugs during pregnancy.

Alcohol. Should a no-drug policy be extended to alcohol? Most contemporary researchers think so. In 1973, Kenneth Jones and his colleagues described a **fetal alcohol syndrome (FAS)** that affects many children of alcoholic mothers (Jones, Smith,

diethylstilbestrol (DES): a synthetic hormone, formerly prescribed to prevent miscarriage, that can produce cervical cancer in adolescent female offspring and genital-tract abnormalities (and sterility) in males.

fetal alcohol syndrome (FAS): a group of serious congenital problems commonly observed in the offspring of mothers who abuse alcohol during pregnancy.

[2]Because the eldest DES children are barely 50 years old, we do not yet know whether they will face increased risks of developing cancer or other life-threatening complications at a later age. Consequently, the U.S. Department of Health and Human Services now advises all DES children (sons and daughters) to make their exposures known to their doctors and to keep up with the latest medical information.

This girl's widely spaced eyes, flattened nose, and underdeveloped upper lip are three of the common physical symptoms of fetal alcohol syndrome.

Ulleland, & Streissguth, 1973). The most noticeable characteristics of fetal alcohol syndrome are defects such as microcephaly (small head) and malformations of the heart, limbs, joints, and face. FAS babies are likely to display excessive irritability, hyperactivity, seizures, and tremors. They are also smaller and lighter than normal, and their physical growth lags behind that of normal age-mates. Finally, the majority of FAS children score well below average in intelligence throughout childhood and adolescence, and many are mentally retarded (Abel, 1984; Streissguth et al., 1993).

How much drinking puts a baby at risk? The answer is a lot less than you might imagine. In keeping with the dosage principle of teratology, the symptoms of FAS are most severe when the "dose" of alcohol is highest, that is, when the mother is clearly an alcoholic. Yet, even moderate alcohol consumption or "social drinking" (1–3 ounces a day) can lead to a set of less serious problems, called **fetal alcohol effects (FAE)**, in some babies. Such effects include retarded physical growth and minor physical abnormalities, as well as such problems as poor motor skills, difficulty paying attention, and subnormal intellectual performance (Jacobson et al., 1993; Streissguth et al., 1993). Even a mother who drinks less than an ounce of alcohol a day is more likely than a nondrinker to have an infant whose mental development is slightly below average. And there is no well-defined critical period for fetal alcohol effects; drinking late in pregnancy can be just as risky as drinking soon after conception (Jacobson et al., 1993). In 1981, the U.S. Surgeon General concluded that *no amount* of alcohol consumption is entirely safe and has since advised pregnant women not to drink at all (Schardein, 1985).

Cigarette smoking. Twenty years ago, neither doctors nor pregnant women had any reason to suspect that cigarette smoking might affect an unborn child. Now we know otherwise. Although there is little evidence that smoking causes congenital malformations (Kelley-Buchanan, 1988; Verp, 1993), one review of more than 200 studies concluded that smoking clearly retards the rate of fetal growth and increases the risk of spontaneous abortion and neonatal death in otherwise normal infants (U.S. Department of Health, Education, and Welfare, 1979). Smoking impairs functioning of the placenta, especially the exchange of oxygen and nutrients to the fetus. And these events are clearly related: The more cigarettes mothers smoke per day, the greater their risk of spontaneous abortion or of delivering a low-birth-weight baby who may struggle to survive (Carson, 1993). Newborn infants of fathers who smoke are also likely to be smaller than normal. Why? Because a smoke-filled home environment turns mothers into "passive smokers," who inhale such substances as nicotine and carbon monoxide that can dampen fetal growth (Rubin et al., 1986).

Some researchers have reported that children of smokers show *long-term* deficits in physical growth and are more likely than children of nonsmokers to experience learning difficulties at school (see Naeye & Peters, 1984; U.S. Department of Health, Education, and Welfare, 1979). Yet it is possible that some factor common to women who smoke other than smoking itself is responsible for these long-term effects. For example, if women who smoke have poorer diets or drink more alcohol than nonsmokers, their dietary inadequacies or alcohol consumption could be responsible for long-term consequences that researchers may have erroneously attributed to smoking.

Monroe Lefkowitz (1981) has looked closely at the long-term effects of maternal smoking on 9–11-year-olds. This study was carefully controlled in that mothers who had smoked during pregnancy were comparable with those who did not smoke in age, education, income, and family size—factors known to affect physical growth and intellectual development. Data available on each child in the sample included measures of height, weight, reading ability, classroom achievements, IQ, popularity, and conduct at school. The findings were clear: 9 to 11 years after birth, the children of smokers were no smaller, no less intelligent, and no less achievement oriented, nor were they less well behaved or popular, than the children of nonsmokers. In another

fetal alcohol effects (FAE): a group of mild congenital problems that are sometimes observed in children of mothers who drink sparingly to moderately during pregnancy.

set of well-controlled studies that took mothers' alcohol consumption into account, Ann Streissguth and associates also found that maternal smoking during pregnancy had no lasting effects on children's motor skills or intellectual performances (Barr et al., 1990, Streissguth et al., 1989).

Despite the uncertainty that remains about *long-term* effects of maternal smoking on developing children, we do know that smoking during pregnancy can and often does retard fetal growth and increases the risk of spontaneous abortion and neonatal death (not to mention, of course, the harmful long-term effects that this habit could have on the mother herself). For these reasons, physicians today routinely advise pregnant women to stop smoking—if not forever, at least for the duration of their pregnancies.

Hallucinogens. In view of their popularity as recreational drugs, it is unfortunate that we do not know more about the possible teratogenic effects of marijuana, LSD, mescaline, and other psychoactive agents. *Heavy* use of marijuana by pregnant women has been linked to premature birth, low birth weights, and behavioral abnormalities in newborns, but it does not appear to have long-lasting effects on most children (Fried et al., 1992; Lester & Dreher, 1989; MacGregor & Chasnoff, 1993). Research on the teratogenic effects of LSD is inconclusive: Some studies have found that women who used LSD before or during pregnancy faced an increased risk of miscarriage, stillbirth, or having babies with a variety of congenital defects, including chromosomal abnormalities (see Schardein, 1985). However, it is difficult to tell whether LSD was responsible for these complications, because the LSD users in these studies were frequently sick, undernourished, or using other known or suspected teratogens (such as alcohol and narcotic agents).

Narcotics. Although addicting agents such as codeine, heroin, methadone, and morphine do not appear to produce gross structural abnormalities, women who use these drugs are more likely than nonusers to miscarry, deliver prematurely, or have stillborn infants (Schardein, 1985). Moreover, 70%–90% of the babies of heroin addicts become addicted in the womb, and about 50% of these children are undersized (Kelley-Buchanan, 1988). When deprived of the drug after birth, the addicted infant experiences withdrawal symptoms such as vomiting, dehydration, convulsions, extreme irritability, weak sucking, and high-pitched crying. Symptoms such as restlessness, tremors, and sleep disturbances may persist for as long as three to four months.

Methadone, the synthetic opiate often prescribed for addicts as an alternative for heroin, produces many of the same effects as heroin does (Kelley-Buchanan, 1988). Moreover, babies born addicted to this drug are somewhat more likely than nonaddicted infants to fall victim to *sudden infant death syndrome (SIDS)*, a complication in which infants simply stop breathing and die in their sleep.

Today, much concern centers on the risks associated with cocaine use and the characteristics of so-called "crack babies." As we will see in Box 4-2, there are ample reasons for such concern.

Table 4-3 catalogs a number of other drugs and their known or suspected effects on unborn children. What should we make of these findings? Assuming that our first priority is the welfare of unborn children, Virginia Apgar has perhaps summarized it best: "A woman who is pregnant, or who thinks she could possibly be pregnant, should not take any drugs whatsoever unless absolutely essential—and then only when prescribed by a physician who is aware of the pregnancy" (Apgar & Beck, 1974, p. 445).

Environmental Hazards

Radiation. Soon after the atomic blasts of 1945 in Japan, scientists became painfully aware of the teratogenic effects of radiation. Not one pregnant woman who was within one-half mile of these explosions gave birth to a live child. In addition,

BOX 4-2
Cocaine Babies

*U*se of cocaine as a recreational drug has increased dramatically with the introduction of the cheaper form of "crack cocaine," which can be smoked. In one study of low-income inner-city women, 18% were estimated to have used cocaine during pregnancy (Zuckerman et al., 1989), and it is currently estimated that as many as 375,000 American babies a year are exposed to cocaine in utero (Shearer, 1994). Because cocaine use constricts the blood vessels, it reduces the flow of oxygen to the fetus (Zuckerman et al., 1989) and increases fetal blood pressure, and cases have been reported in which unborn fetuses of cocaine-using mothers have died of strokes (MacGregor & Chasnoff, 1993). Cocaine also suppresses the mother's appetite, which can contribute to fetal malnutrition (Zuckerman, et al., 1989). So perhaps we should not be surprised to learn that mothers who regularly use cocaine, particularly crack cocaine, are at risk for miscarriage or premature delivery, and their babies (like babies addicted to other narcotic agents) tend to be smaller than normal, extremely irritable when aroused, and susceptible to serious respiratory problems, including SIDS (Hawley & Disney, 1992; Neuspiel & Hamel, 1991; Singer, Farkas, & Kliegman, 1992).

Barry Lester and his associates (1991) have identified two patterns of behavior common to cocaine babies. One pattern seems to reflect the toxic effects of cocaine itself on the developing nervous system; it is characterized by prolonged high-pitched crying and extremely irritable and excitable behavior. The second pattern is one of sluggish, unresponsive behavior with less crying—a pattern that characterizes many low-birth-weight babies and thus may be an indirect effect of cocaine exposure. Some cocaine babies show both patterns: They are lethargic most of the time but become extremely irritable when aroused. Both of these early temperamental profiles (or their combination) can interfere with the social and emotional bonding that normally occurs between infants and their caregivers. Indeed, one recent study has found that a majority of cocaine-exposed infants fail to establish secure emotional ties to primary caregivers (Rodning, Beckworth, & Howard, 1991). These poor emotional outcomes may stem from either the babies' unpleasant emotional demeanor or from the less-than-adequate stimulation and care that these babies may receive from their drug-using adult companions. Further research is needed to clarify this issue.

Cocaine babies also seem to derive less joy from learning than normal infants do, and they show much less concern (that is, less anger or sadness) when their attempts to achieve various objectives prove unsuccessful (Alessandri et al., 1993). Other preliminary studies suggest that cocaine babies at age 2 or 3 years display signs of hyperactivity, delayed motor development, and attention deficits of the kind that predict later problems at school (Chasnoff et al., 1992).

In sum, the available research not only implicates cocaine as a powerful teratogen, but also points to the need for *longitudinal* research to assess properly the impact of this drug (and other narcotic agents) on children's social, emotional, and intellectual development.

75% of the pregnant women who were within a mile and a quarter of the blasts had seriously handicapped children who soon died, and the infants who did survive were often mentally retarded (Apgar & Beck, 1974; Vorhees & Mollnow, 1987). Even clinical doses of radiation such as those used in some cancer treatments are capable of causing mutations, spontaneous abortions, and a variety of birth defects, especially if the mother is exposed during the first trimester.

Unfortunately, no one knows just how much radiation it takes to harm an embryo or a fetus. There is also the possibility that irradiated infants who appear normal at birth will be at risk for developing complications such as cancer later in life (Kelley-Buchanan, 1988). For these reasons, expectant mothers are routinely advised to avoid X rays, particularly those of the pelvis and abdomen, unless such treatment is absolutely necessary for their own survival.

Chemicals and pollutants. Pregnant women routinely come in contact with potentially toxic substances in their everyday environments, including organic dyes and coloring agents, food additives, artificial sweeteners, pesticides, and cosmetic products, some of which are known to have teratogenic effects in animals (Verp, 1993). Unfortunately, the risks associated with a large number of these common chemical additives and treatments remain to be determined.

Then there are the pollutants in the air we breathe and the water we drink. For example, pregnant women may be exposed to concentrations of lead, zinc, mercury, or antimony discharged into the air or water by industrial operations or present in

Table 4-3 **Partial List of Drugs and Treatments That Affect (or Are Thought to Affect) the Fetus or the Newborn**

Drug	Effect
Alcohol	Small head, facial abnormalities, heart defects, low birth weight, and mental retardation (see text).

Amphetamines
  Dextroamphetamine
  Methamphetamine
	Premature delivery, stillbirth, irritability, and poor feeding among newborns.

Antibiotics
  Streptomycin
  Terramycin
  Tetracycline
	Heavy use of streptomycin by mothers can produce hearing loss in fetuses. Terramycin and tetracycline may be associated with premature delivery, retarded skeletal growth, cataracts, and staining of the baby's teeth.

Aspirin	Used in large quantities, may cause neonatal bleeding and gastrointestinal discomfort. Also linked to low birth weight and to neonatal death in preliminary reports.
Barbiturates	All barbiturates cross the placental barrier. In clinical doses, they cause the fetus or newborn to be lethargic. In large doses, they may cause anoxia (oxygen starvation) or interfere with the baby's breathing. One such drug, Primidone, has been implicated in malformations of the heart, face, and limbs.

Hallucinogens
  LSD
  Marijuana
  Mescaline
	Suspected to cause chromosome damage, spontaneous abortion, and behavioral abnormalities among newborn infants (see text).

Lithium	Heart defects, lethargic behavior in newborns.

Narcotics
  Cocaine
  Codeine
  Heroin
  Methadone
  Morphine
	Addiction increases the risk of premature delivery. Moreover, the fetus is often addicted to the narcotic agent, which results in a number of complications. Heavy cocaine use can seriously elevate fetal blood pressure and even induce strokes (see text).

Sex hormones
  Androgens
  Progestogens
  Estrogens
  DES (diethylstilbestrol)
	Sex hormones contained in birth-control pills and drugs to prevent miscarriages can have a number of harmful effects, including heart malformations, cervical cancer (in female offspring), masculinization of the fetus, and other anomalies (see text).

Tranquilizers (other than thalidomide)
  Chlorpromazine
  Reserpine
  Valium
	May produce respiratory distress in newborns. Valium may also produce poor muscle tone and lethargy.

Tobacco	Cigarette smoking is known to retard fetal growth and to increase the risk of spontaneous abortion, stillbirth, and infant mortality (see text).
Vaccines	Immunization with live-virus vaccines should be avoided during pregnancy unless essential; many of these viruses (for example, mumps, measles, smallpox) are powerful teratogens.
Vitamins	Excessive amounts of vitamin A can cause cleft palate, heart malformation, and other serious birth defects. The popular antiacne drug Accutane, derived from vitamin A, is one of the most powerful of all known teratogens. Excessive doses of vitamins B_6, C, D, and K cause prenatal deformities in many animal species. Of these, only vitamin D (in large amounts) has been suspected of causing birth defects in humans.

Sources: From Anderson & Golbus, 1989; Kelley-Buchanan, 1988; and Verp, 1993.

paint and water pipes. These "heavy metals" are known to impair the physical health and mental abilities of adults and children and to have teratogenic effects (producing physical deformities and mental retardation) on developing embryos and fetuses (Anderson & Golbus, 1989). Polluting chemicals called *PCBs (polychlorinated biphenyls)*, now outlawed but once widely used in plastics and carbon paper, represent another hazard. Joseph Jacobson and his colleagues (1984) found that even low-level exposure to PCBs, resulting from mothers eating contaminated fish from Lake Michigan, was enough to make newborns smaller on average and less responsive and neurologically mature than babies whose mothers did not eat polluted fish. At age 4, these children showed deficits in short-term memory, and the extent of their deficits corresponded to the dose of PCBs they received prenatally (Jacobson, Jacobson, & Humphrey, 1990).

Even a father's exposure to environmental toxins can affect a couple's children. Studies of male doctors and dentists reveal that prolonged exposure to radiation, anesthetic gases, and other toxic substances can damage a father's chromosomes and increase the likelihood of genetic defects and/or spontaneous abortions by his wife (Gunderson & Sackett, 1982; Stone, 1992; Strigini et al., 1990). And even when expectant mothers do *not* drink alcohol or use drugs, they are much more likely to deliver a low-birth-weight baby if the father is a heavy drinker or drug user (Toner, 1991). Why? Possibly because certain substances (for example, cocaine and maybe even alcohol, PCBs, and other toxins) can apparently bind directly to live sperm and, thus, alter prenatal development from the moment of conception (Yazigi, Odem, & Polakoski, 1991). Taken together, these findings imply that (1) environmental toxins can affect the reproductive system of either parent so that (2) both mothers *and* fathers should limit their exposure to substances known to be teratogenic.

On the Prevention of Birth Defects

Reading a chapter such as this one can be frightening to anyone who hopes to have a child. It is easy to come away with the impression that "life before birth" is a veritable minefield: After all, so many hereditary accidents are possible, and even a genetically normal embryo or fetus may encounter a large number of potential hazards while developing within the womb.

But, clearly, there is another side to this story. Recall that the majority of genetically abnormal embryos do not develop to term. And it appears that the prenatal environment is not so hazardous when we note that more than 90% of newborn babies are perfectly normal and that many of the remaining 7%–10% have minor congenital problems that are only temporary or easily correctable (Heinonen et al., 1977). Although there *is* reason for concern, parents can significantly reduce the odds that their baby will be abnormal if they follow the simple recommendations in

Concept Check 4-2 ⌄ Understanding the Prenatal Environment

Check your understanding of environmental influences on prenatal development by filling in the blanks in each of the following statements. The answers appear in the Appendix.

1. Although *prenatal malnutrition* is always a risk factor, its harmful consequences for the unborn organism are greatest when the nutritional deficiency occurs during

   _____.

2. Although _____ is often described as the "critical period" of pregnancy, the fact that organ systems often remain susceptible to birth defects until birth suggests that the entire prenatal period is a _____ for human development.

3. Research reveals that diseases such as _____ and such drugs as _____ can be violent teratogens, even though they have few, if any, harmful effects on a mother.

4. Drinking, smoking, and drug-using *fathers* may contribute to a low-birth-weight baby, even if the mother uses none of these substances, because _____. (Can you list two possible reasons?)

BOX 4-3

How to Prevent Birth Defects: A Checklist for Prospective Parents

*I*n their excellent book *Is My Baby All Right?* (1974), Dr. Virginia Apgar and Joan Beck suggest several ways that prospective parents can significantly reduce the likelihood of bearing a defective child. As you read through the list, see whether you can recall why each recommendation makes good sense. In so doing, you will have reviewed much of the material on congenital defects presented in this chapter (as well as Chapter 3).

1. *If you think a close relative has a disorder that might be hereditary, you should take advantage of genetic counseling.* Do you remember what kinds of services a genetic counselor may offer or suggest? If not, you may wish to review "Applications: Genetic Counseling and the Treatment of Hereditary Disorders" in Chapter 3.
2. *The ideal age for a woman to have children is between 18 and 35.* What complications do older and younger mothers face?
3. *Every pregnant woman needs good prenatal care supervised by a medical practitioner who keeps current on medical research in the field of teratology and who will help her deliver her baby in a reputable, modern hospital.* We have not yet examined the birth process and its complications. When we review the pros and cons of "home births," we will see that not everyone agrees that a woman should always give birth in a hospital.
4. *No woman should become pregnant unless she is sure that she has either had rubella or been effectively immunized against it.* What defects can rubella cause? When during pregnancy is the disease particularly dangerous?
5. *From the very beginning of pregnancy, a woman should do everything possible to avoid exposure to contagious diseases.* Do you remember the teratogenic effect of congenital syphilis, gonorrhea, herpes, and other infectious agents?

If not, you may wish to review Table 4-2 and the section of this chapter entitled "Maternal Diseases."
6. *Pregnant women should avoid eating undercooked red meat or having contact with any cat (or cat feces) that may carry toxoplasmosis infection.* What are the possible consequences of toxoplasmosis for the mother? For her unborn child?
7. *A pregnant woman should not take any drugs unless absolutely essential—and then only when prescribed by a physician who is aware of the pregnancy.* Do you remember the effects of DES, alcohol, the hallucinogens, narcotics, and other commonly used substances? If not, you may wish to review Table 4-3 and the section of this chapter entitled "Drugs."
8. *Unless it is absolutely essential for her own well-being, a pregnant woman should avoid radiation treatments and X-ray examinations.* What are the possible consequences of such examinations or treatments for the unborn child? How did scientists become aware of the teratogenic effects of radiation?
9. *Cigarettes should not be smoked during pregnancy.* Why not? Does a mother's cigarette smoking during pregnancy have long-term effects on her children?
10. *A prospective mother who is Rh negative should make sure her physician takes the necessary steps to protect her unborn baby and all subsequent children from Rh disease.* How are subsequent children protected? Hint: see Table 4-2.
11. *A nourishing diet, rich in proteins and adequate in total calories, is essential during pregnancy.* What are the possible effects of maternal malnutrition on the developing child? Should a pregnant woman take large amounts of extra vitamins in order to ensure that her baby will be healthy?

Box 4-3. Failure to abide by one or more of the guidelines will not necessarily mean that your child will be defective. Nor will exact compliance guarantee that the child will be healthy; accidents do happen. Following these recommendations may seem rather tedious at times and perhaps unnecessary to parents who have already given birth to healthy children. However, Apgar and Beck (1974, p. 452) remind us that "Each pregnancy is different. Each unborn child has a unique genetic make-up. The prenatal environment a mother provides is never quite the same for another baby. Thus, we believe no amount of effort is too great to increase the chances that a baby will be born normal, healthy, and without a handicapping birth defect."

 ## BIRTH AND THE PERINATAL ENVIRONMENT

The **perinatal environment** is the environment surrounding birth; it includes influences such as drugs given to the mother during delivery, practices used in the delivery, and the social environment shortly after the baby is born. As we will see, this perinatal environment is an important one that can affect a baby's well-being and the course of her future development.

> **perinatal environment:** the environment surrounding birth, including influences such as childbirth medication, obstetrical practices, and the social stimulation that a baby may receive.

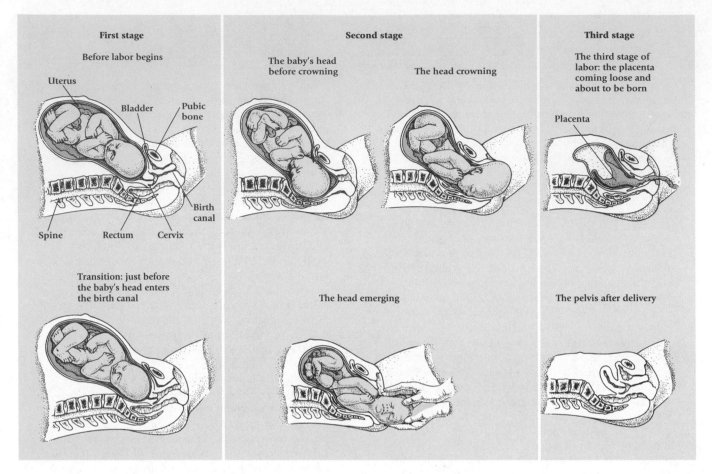

First stage

Before labor begins

Uterus

Bladder

Pubic bone

Birth canal

Spine   Rectum   Cervix

Transition: just before the baby's head enters the birth canal

Second stage

The baby's head before crowning

The head crowning

The head emerging

Third stage

The third stage of labor: the placenta coming loose and about to be born

Placenta

The pelvis after delivery

Figure 4-8
The three stages of childbirth.

The Birth Process

Childbirth is a three-stage process (see Figure 4-8). The **first stage of labor** begins as the mother experiences uterine contractions spaced at 10–15-minute intervals, and it ends when her cervix has fully dilated so that the fetus's head can pass through. This phase lasts an average of 8–14 hours for first-born children and 3–8 hours for later-borns. As labor proceeds, the uterus contracts more frequently, and the contractions become more intense. When the head of the fetus is positioned at the cervical opening, the second phase of labor is about to begin.

The **second stage of labor,** or *delivery*, begins as the fetus's head passes through the cervix into the vagina and ends when the baby emerges from the mother's body. This is the time when the mother may be told to bear down (push) with each contraction to assist her child through the birth canal. A quick delivery may take a half hour, whereas a long one may last more than an hour and a half.

The **third stage of labor,** or *afterbirth*, takes only 5–10 minutes as the uterus once again contracts and expels the placenta from the mother's body.

The Social Environment Surrounding Birth

It was not that long ago when giving birth could accurately be described as a necessary ordeal for a pregnant woman that offered little in the way of immediate rewards. After all, most hospitals barred fathers from delivery rooms and whisked babies away from their mothers and on to nurseries within minutes of a delivery. However, the times have changed—so much so that a birth today is much more likely to be a dramatic experience for the whole family. Let's briefly consider the birth experience from the mother's, the father's, and the baby's perspectives.

first stage of labor: the period of the birth process lasting from the first regular uterine contractions until the cervix is fully dilated.

second stage of labor: the period of the birth process during which the fetus moves through the vaginal canal and emerges from the mother's body (also called the delivery).

third stage of labor: expulsion of the placenta (afterbirth).

The Mother's Experience

It is now clear that psychological factors such as the mother's attitude toward her pregnancy, her knowledge about the birth process, and the support she receives from her partner and other people are important determinants of her birth experience. When the father or another supportive companion is present during labor and delivery, women experience less pain, use less medication, are less likely to have cesarean sections, and are likely to feel more positively about the whole birth process (Hodnett & Osborn, 1989; Kennell et al., 1991).

Preparing for birth. In many Western societies, expectant mothers (and their mates) are advised to prepare for their day in the delivery room by attending childbirth classes. This **prepared** (or **natural**) **childbirth** movement arose from the work of Grantly Dick-Read in England and Fernand Lamaze in France. These two obstetricians claimed that many women could give birth comfortably without medication if they had been taught to associate childbirth with pleasant feelings and to ready themselves for the process by learning exercises, breathing methods, and relaxation techniques that make childbirth easier (Dick-Read, 1933/1972; Lamaze, 1958). Over the past 30 years, increasing numbers of expectant parents have opted for prepared childbirth as scientists began to report that the pain-killing drugs often given during labor could have adverse effects on a baby.

Parents who decide on a prepared childbirth usually attend classes for 6–8 weeks before the delivery. Here, they will learn what to expect during labor and may even visit a delivery room and become familiar with procedures used there as part of their preparation. They are also given a prescribed set of exercises and relaxation techniques to master. Typically, the father (or another companion) becomes a coach who assists the mother to tone her muscles and perfect her breathing for the event that lies ahead. He is also encouraged to be there to help his partner with the delivery.

Apparently, such prenatal preparation does affect the mother's birth experience. Women who regularly attend childbirth classes are more relaxed during labor, experience less pain, use less medication, and have more positive attitudes toward themselves, their families, and the whole birth experience (Lindell, 1988; Wideman & Singer, 1984). Traditional childbirth classes are even more effective when supplemented with effective pain management techniques, such as hypnosis (Harmon, Hynan, & Tyre, 1990).

Special moments after birth. The first few moments after birth are often a joyous time in which a mother may come to thoroughly enjoy her baby, provided she is given the opportunity. Indeed, Marshall Klaus and John Kennell believe that the first 6–12 hours after birth are a *sensitive period* for the **emotional bonding** of a mother to her infant, a time when the mother is especially ready to respond to and develop a strong sense of affection for her baby (Kennell, Voos, & Klaus, 1979). In a study testing this hypothesis, Klaus and Kennell (1976) had half of a group of new mothers follow the then-traditional hospital routine: They saw their babies briefly after delivery, visited with them 6–12 hours later, and had half-hour feeding sessions every four hours thereafter for the remainder of a three-day hospital stay. By contrast, mothers in an "extended-contact" group were permitted five "extra" hours a day to cuddle their babies, including an hour of skin-to-skin contact that took place within three hours of birth.

In a follow-up one month later, mothers who had had early extended contact with their babies appeared to be more involved with them and held them closer during feeding sessions than did mothers who had followed the traditional hospital routine. A year later, the extended-contact mothers were still the more highly involved group of caregivers, and their 1-year-olds outperformed those in the traditional-routine group on tests of physical and mental development. Apparently, extended early contact in the hospital promoted early mother-infant bonding which, in turn, may have

prepared or natural childbirth: a delivery in which physical and psychological preparations for the birth are stressed and medical assistance is minimized.

emotional bonding: term used to describe the strong affectional ties that parents may feel toward their infant; some theorists believe that the strongest bonding occurs shortly after birth, during a sensitive period.

motivated mothers to continue to interact in highly stimulating ways with their babies. In response to this and other similar studies, many hospitals have altered their routines to allow the kinds of early contact that can promote emotional bonding.

Does this mean that mothers who have no early contact with their newborns will miss out on forming the strongest possible emotional ties to them? No, it does not! Later research has shown that early contact effects are nowhere near as large or long lasting as Klaus and Kennell presumed (Goldberg, 1983; Myers, 1987). Consider that most adoptive parents, who rarely have any early contact with their infants, develop strong emotional ties to their adoptees (Levy-Shiff, Goldschmidt, & Har-Even, 1991)—ties that are just as secure, on average, as those seen in nonadoptive homes (Singer et al., 1985). So even though early contact can be a very pleasant experience that can help a mother *begin* to form an emotional bond to her child, she need not fear that any problems will arise should birth complications prevent her from having this experience.

Postpartum depression. Unfortunately, there is a "downside" to the birth experience for some mothers, who may find themselves depressed, tearful, irritable, and even resentful of their babies shortly after birth. Milder forms of this condition, called the *maternity blues*, may characterize as many as one-half of all new mothers (Kraus & Redman, 1986). This mild depression, which usually passes within a matter of days, is probably linked to hormonal changes following childbirth and to the stresses associated with the new responsibilities of parenthood.

By contrast, slightly more than 10% of new mothers fail to bounce back quickly, experiencing instead a more serious depressive reaction called **postpartum depression** that can last for months. Most victims of postpartum depression have a history of depressive episodes and are experiencing other life stresses on top of those associated with becoming a new mother (O'Hara et al., 1991; Whiffen, 1992). Lack of social support—particularly a poor relationship with one's partner—dramatically increases the odds of postpartum depression (Field et al., 1985; Gotlib et al., 1991). Susan Campbell and her associates (1992) found that many of these depressed women often did not want their infants in the first place and perceived them as difficult babies. They also interacted less positively with their infants and in some cases seemed downright hostile toward them. Other studies suggest that, when a mother is depressed, withdrawn, and unresponsive, the attachment that develops between her and her infant is likely to be insecure, and infants may develop depressive symptoms and behavior problems of their own (Field et al., 1985; Murray, 1992; Radke-Yarrow et al., 1985). For their own sake and for the sake of their infants, then, mothers experiencing more than a mild case of the "maternity blues" should seek professional help in overcoming their depression.

The Father's Experience.

The birth process can also be a highly significant event in the life of a father, for he, like the mother, often displays a sense of **engrossment** with the baby—an intense fascination with and a strong desire to touch, hold, and caress this newest member of the family (Greenberg & Morris, 1974; Peterson, Mehl, & Liederman, 1979). One young father put it this way: "When I came up to see [my] wife . . . I go look at the kid and then I pick her up and put her down. . . . I keep going back to the kid. It's like a magnet. That's what I can't get over, the fact that I feel like that" (Greenberg & Morris, 1974, p. 524). Some studies find that fathers who have handled and helped care for their babies in the hospital later spend more time with them at home than other fathers who have not had these early interactions with their newborns (Greenberg & Morris, 1974). Other studies have failed to find these long-term effects on father-infant interactions but suggest that early contact with a newborn can make fathers feel closer to their wives and more a part of the family (Palkovitz, 1985). So a father who is present at birth may not only play an important supportive role for his partner, but is just as likely as the mother to enjoy close contact with their neonate.

postpartum depression: strong feelings of sadness, resentment, and despair that may appear shortly after childbirth and can linger for months.

engrossment: paternal analogue of maternal emotional bonding; term used to describe fathers' fascination with their neonates, including their desire to touch, hold, caress, and talk to the newborn baby.

The Baby's Experience

Is birth an unpleasant experience for a baby? French obstetrician Frederick Leboyer (1975) thinks so. After all, a perfectly contented fetus is being expelled from a soft, warm uterus, where all its needs are met, into a cold, bright world where, for the first time, it will experience chills, pain, hunger, and the startling rush of air into the lungs. Leboyer clearly objects to common obstetrical practices as striking the infant to stimulate breathing, hastily severing the umbilical cord, or weighing the baby on cold metal scales—procedures that he describes as the "torture of the innocents." Instead, he favors making birth much less traumatic through his method of **gentle birthing**.

In a gentle birth, the delivery room is quiet, and the lights are dimmed as the baby emerges. The infant is then placed on the mother's stomach and caressed until the umbilical cord stops pulsating and the child is breathing freely on her own. After the umbilical cord is severed, the baby is placed in a warm bath to simulate conditions experienced in the womb. Every attempt is made to eliminate all possible sources of discomfort and to make the child's first several minutes as pleasant as possible. Leboyer (1975) contends that babies who experience gentle births are happy little people who are likely to elicit highly positive, loving reactions from their parents and to experience favorable developmental outcomes.

The Leboyer method of gentle birthing is highly controversial. Many obstetricians fear that potentially harmful complications may pass undetected and remain untreated if neonates are examined in dimly lit rooms. In addition, there is no evidence that infants who experience gentle birthing are any more calm and blissful at birth or display any better developmental outcomes over the first year than babies who undergo standard obstetrical procedures (Maziade, Boudreault, Cote, & Thivierge, 1986; Nelson et al., 1980). Finally, there is little reason to believe that birth is especially traumatic for a baby. Aidan MacFarlane (1977) has carefully observed newborn babies and noted that most of them quiet down rapidly and begin to cope with their new surroundings soon after that first loud cry. Nevertheless, Leboyer and his followers have had an impact on obstetrical practices. Although newborn babies are rarely given warm baths in dim rooms, they are now routinely handed to their mothers for soothing and comforting soon after they are born.

Elated by the birth of twins, this father displays the fascination with his newborns known as engrossment.

Perinatal Hazards and Complications

Childbirth does not always proceed as smoothly as indicated in our earlier account of the "normal" delivery. A number of factors can complicate the process, and some of these complications can place infants at risk of experiencing adverse developmental outcomes.

Before we discuss the causes and consequences of various perinatal complications, let's briefly consider how the more serious of these problems are detected.

Perinatal Screening

In the first minute of life, a baby takes his or her first test. A nurse or a doctor checks the infant's physical condition by looking at five standard characteristics that are rated from 0 to 2, recorded on a chart, and totaled (see Table 4-4). A baby's score on this **Apgar test** (named for its developer, Dr. Virginia Apgar) can range from 0–10, higher scores indicating a better condition. Five minutes after birth, the Apgar procedure is repeated in order to check on the first observation and/or to measure improvements in the infant's physical state.

Infants who score 7 or higher on the second testing are not in any immediate danger: They have a steady heartbeat, well-developed reflexes, a pinkish tone to their skin, and are breathing freely. However, infants scoring 4 or lower are in trouble: Their heartbeats are sluggish or nonexistent, their muscles are limp, and their breathing is shallow and irregular, if they are breathing at all. These children often require immediate medical intervention in order to survive.

Now let's consider some of the major contributors to poor perinatal outcomes.

gentle birthing: Leboyer's method of childbirth, in which the neonate is comforted, massaged, shielded from unpleasant sensory stimulation, and bathed in warm water in an attempt to reduce any traumas associated with birth.

Apgar test: a quick assessment of the newborn's heart rate, respiration, color, muscle tone, and reflexes that is used to gauge perinatal stress and to determine whether a neonate requires immediate medical assistance.

Table 4-4 The Apgar Test

Characteristic	Score		
	0	*1*	*2*
Heart rate	Absent	Slow (fewer than 100 beats per minute)	Over 100 beats per minute
Respiratory effort	Absent	Slow or irregular	Good; baby is crying
Muscle tone	Flaccid, limp	Weak, some flexion	Strong, active motion
Color	Blue or pale	Body pink, extremities blue	Completely pink
Reflex irritability	No response	Frown, grimace, or weak cry	Vigorous cries, coughs, sneezes

Anoxia

Perhaps the greatest hazard during the birth process is **anoxia,** or oxygen starvation. In many cases of anoxia, the child's supply of oxygen is interrupted because the umbilical cord has become pinched or tangled during childbirth. However, anoxia may also occur after birth if sedatives given to the mother cross the placental barrier and interfere with the baby's breathing or if mucus ingested during childbirth becomes lodged in the baby's throat. The birth of an anoxic child is a medical emergency: If a baby's brain is deprived of oxygen for more than a few minutes, the infant may suffer serious brain damage and possibly even die. The areas of the brain most noticeably affected are those that control motor activity. Indeed, severe anoxia appears to be a major contributor to *cerebral palsy,* a motor disability in which the affected individual has difficulties controlling muscles of the arms, legs, or head (Vaughn, McKay, & Behrman, 1984).

Children suffering from mild anoxia are often irritable at birth and may score below average on tests of motor development and concept formation during the first three years of life (Sameroff & Chandler, 1975). However, these differences between mildly anoxic and normal children eventually lessen to the point that they are no longer apparent by age 7 (Corah et al., 1965). So even though *prolonged* oxygen deprivation can cause neurological damage and permanent disabilities, there is no compelling evidence that mild anoxia has any lasting effects on children's motor skills or intellectual development (Vaughn et al., 1984).

Abnormal Positioning of the Fetus

Nine times out of ten, a fetus is born head first. Some, however, are born feet or buttocks first—a condition known as a **breech birth.** The breech presentation is hazardous because the birth process takes longer, increasing the likelihood of anoxia and its complications. Although the vast majority of breech babies are perfectly normal and healthy at birth, about 1 infant in 500 delivered this way dies at birth or soon thereafter, and another 2%–4% experience serious cranial bleeding or some degree of cerebral palsy (Lin, 1993a). Many obstetricians choose to eliminate these complications by routinely delivering breech babies by cesarean section, and c-sections are clearly justified in 20%–30% of these cases. However, most breech babies are positioned in ways that allow the doctor to either turn them to a head-first position during the early stages of labor or to perform safe, uncomplicated breech deliveries through the vagina (Lin, 1993a).

This brings us to some potential hazards associated with delivery procedures themselves. In years gone by, many doctors believed that routine use of *obstetrical*

anoxia: a lack of sufficient oxygen to the brain; may result in neurological damage or death.

breech birth: a delivery in which the fetus emerges feet first or buttocks first rather than head first, as is usual.

forceps (an instrument resembling an oversized pair of salad tongs) was the best way to speed up the birth process and thereby avoid complications such as anoxia (see Figure 4-9). Unfortunately, application of forceps to the soft skull of a fetus can cause cranial bleeding and brain damage! Careful use of forceps may still be warranted, however, to deliver babies whose lives are in danger.

Cesarean sections have also become controversial. Clearly, this alternative to the normal vaginal delivery has saved the lives of many infants who were suffering from anoxia in utero or were positioned abnormally. Moreover, cesarean sections have become about as safe as vaginal deliveries and appear to create only minor respiratory problems for some newborns and no adverse effects on children's later personality or intellectual development (Entwisle & Alexander, 1987). So why the controversy? Largely because cesarean sections have become so common, now accounting for nearly one-fourth of all births in the United States (Van Tuinen & Wolfe, 1993). Critics contend that doctors rely far too heavily on this major abdominal surgery (from which mothers may take *months* to fully recover) simply because it is convenient and it protects the physician from malpractice suits that might otherwise result from complications in a vaginal delivery. Interestingly, the percentage of babies delivered by c-section peaked in 1988 and has been declining since then (Van Tuinen & Wolfe, 1993), due, in part, to research suggesting that many high-risk fetuses (for example, breech babies) can be safely delivered through the vagina (Lin, 1993a).

Effects of Obstetric Medication

In the United States, as many as 95% of mothers receive some kind of drug (and often several) while giving birth (Brackbill, 1979). These drugs may include analgesics and anesthetics to reduce pain, sedatives to relax the mother, and stimulants to induce or intensify uterine contractions. Obviously, these agents are administered in the hope of making the birth process easier for the mother. However, birth medications can have some undesirable consequences for an infant.

Yvonne Brackbill and her associates (1985) have summarized the results of 59 studies, finding that babies whose mothers received relatively large doses of obstetric medication were atypical in several respects: They smiled infrequently, were generally inattentive and irritable when aroused, and were difficult to feed or comfort during the first few weeks of life. Unfortunately, parents of a heavily medicated infant

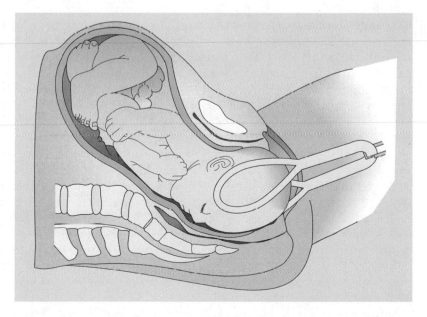

Figure 4-9
A forceps delivery. The pressure that must be applied to pull the infant from the birth canal involves risk of injury to the baby's head.

may find it difficult to become very involved with or emotionally attached to such a sluggish, inattentive, and irritable companion (Murray et al., 1981). Moreover, Brackbill et al. (1985) report that some babies of heavily medicated mothers continue to show some deficits in physical and mental development for at least one year after birth. The children most affected by obstetric medication are those whose mothers had inhaled general anesthetics such as nitrous oxide (which are rarely used in childbirth today); but even small doses of local anesthetics can affect the behavior of some newborns (Brackbill et al., 1985). Why? Probably because a dose of medication large enough to affect a 140-pound mother can pack quite a wallop for many 7-pound infants, who have immature circulatory and excretory systems that may take weeks to purge their bodies of these powerful drugs. As a result, heavily medicated babies get off to a very slow start, and they may take months (or longer) to catch up with their age-mates who were not so heavily medicated at birth.

So should mothers avoid obstetric medication at all costs? Probably not. Some women are at risk of birth complications because they are small, irregularly built, or delivering large babies. For these mothers, sedatives given in appropriate doses can actually *reduce* the chances of anoxia by depressing fetal metabolism, thereby prolonging the brain's tolerance for oxygen deprivation (Myers, 1980; Myers & Myers, 1979). It is also important to recognize that some medications are safer than others and that doctors today are more likely than those of the past to use less toxic drugs in smaller doses at the safest times (Finster, Pedersen, & Morishima, 1984). So taking obstetric medications today is not as risky as it once was. However, the potentially negative impact of these drugs on parent-infant interactions is an excellent reason for limiting their use.

Complications of Low Birth Weight

More than 90% of babies in the United States are born between the 37th and 42nd weeks of pregnancy and are considered "timely." The average full-term, or "timely," infant is 19–21 inches long and weighs about 3500 grams.

The remaining 7%–8% of babies weigh less than 2500 grams (5½ pounds) at birth (Austin & Moawad, 1993) and, until recently, were simply labeled "premature." Yet there are actually two kinds of low-birth-weight babies. Most are born more than three weeks before their due dates and are called **preterm infants.** Although small in size, the body weights of these babies are often appropriate for the amount of time that they spent in the womb. Other low-birth-weight babies, called **small for date,** have experienced slow growth as fetuses, and are seriously underweight, even when born close to their normal due dates. Although both kinds of low-birth-weight babies are vulnerable and may have to struggle to survive, small-for-date infants are at greater risk of displaying serious complications. For example, they are more likely to die during the first year or to show signs of brain damage. They are also more likely than preterm infants to remain small in stature throughout childhood, experience learning difficulties and behavior problems at school, and perform poorly on IQ tests (Lin, 1993b).

What are the causes of low birth weight? We have already seen that mothers who smoke and drink heavily, use drugs, are malnourished, or are in their teens are likely to deliver low-birth-weight babies. Indeed, low-income women from ethnic minority groups are particularly at risk, largely because their diets and the prenatal care they receive are often inadequate (Kopp & Kaler, 1989; Lin, 1993b). Moreover, some illnesses, such as preeclampsia (see Table 4-2), or any accident that impairs the functioning of the placenta can retard fetal growth and result in a baby who is preterm or small for date. Yet another frequent contributor to undersized babies is multiple births. Multiple fetuses generally gain much less weight than a singleton after the 29th week of pregnancy (Pridjian & Lin, 1993). And in addition to being small for date, triplets and quadruplets rarely develop to term in the uterus; in fact, they are often born 5–12 weeks early (Browne & Dixon, 1978).

preterm babies: infants born more than three weeks before their normal due dates.

small-for-date babies: infants whose birth weight is far below normal, even when born close to their normal due dates.

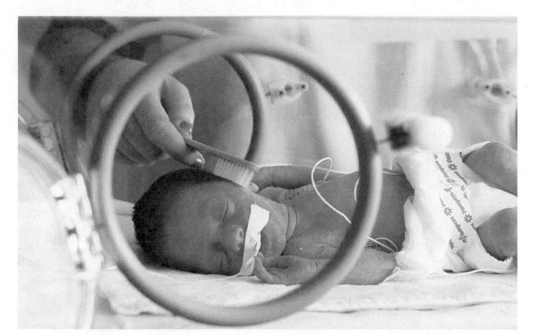

Figure 4-10
Isolettes do isolate. The holes in the apparatus allow parents and hospital staff to care for, talk to, and touch the baby, but close, tender cuddling is nearly impossible.

Short-term consequences of low birth weight. The most trying task for a low-birth-weight baby is simply surviving the first few days of life. Although more and more of these infants are surviving each year, better than 50% of those who weigh less than 1000 grams (2.2 pounds) die at birth or shortly thereafter, even in the best hospitals (Lin, 1989). Small-for-date babies are often malformed, undernourished, or genetically abnormal—factors that will obviously hinder them as they struggle to survive. Moreover, preterm infants are likely to experience a number of additional problems as a consequence of their general immaturity. Their most serious difficulty is breathing. A preterm infant often has very little *surfactin,* a substance that normally coats the lungs during the last three to four weeks of pregnancy to prevent them from collapsing. A deficiency of surfactin may result in **respiratory distress syndrome**—a serious respiratory ailment in which the affected child breathes very irregularly and may stop breathing altogether.

Preterm infants often spend their first few weeks of life in heated *isolettes* that maintain their body temperature and protect them from infection. Isolettes are aptly named because they do isolate: The infant is fed, cleaned, and changed through a hole in the device that is much too small to allow the visiting parents to cuddle and love their baby in the usual way (see Figure 4-10). But there are also other reasons that preterm infants may be difficult to love: They are likely to be tiny, wrinkled, and fragile in appearance, easily upset, and difficult to comfort—in short, a far cry from the smiling, animated creatures that appear in ads for baby products. Moreover, preterm infants can be very unpleasant companions. Compared with full-term infants, they are reluctant to initiate social interactions and frequently respond to a parent's bids for attention by looking away or otherwise resisting such overtures (Lester, Hoffman, & Brazelton, 1985; Malatesta et al., 1986). Mothers of preterm infants often remark that their babies are "hard to read," and they are apt to become rather frustrated as their persistent attempts to carry on a social dialogue are apparently rebuffed by an aloof, fussy, squirming little companion (Field, 1979; Lester et al., 1985). Moreover, preterm infants may also disappoint parents by the delays that they show throughout the first year in motor skills and intellectual development (Crnic et al., 1983; Rose, Feldman, McCarton, & Wolfson, 1988). And although the vast majority of these babies are never mistreated by their caregivers, they are more likely than full-term infants to become targets of child abuse (Starr, 1979). So it seems that the preterm child's early isolation, forlorn and fragile appearance, and irritable

respiratory distress syndrome: a serious condition in which a preterm infant breathes very irregularly and is at risk of dying (also called hyaline membrane disease).

and irregular behavior can impede the formation of positive emotional bonds with caregivers—occasionally to the point that the child elicits abusive rather than affectionate responses.

On optimizing the development of low-birth-weight infants. Only 10–15 years ago, hospitals permitted parents little, if any, early contact with low-birth-weight infants for fear of harming these fragile little creatures. Today, parents are encouraged to visit their child often in the hospital and to become actively involved during their visits by touching, caressing, and talking to their baby. The objective of these "early acquaintance" programs is to allow parents to get to know their child and to foster the development of affectionate emotional bonds between all parties involved. But there may be important additional benefits, for babies in intensive care often become less irritable and more responsive and show quicker neurological and mental development if they are periodically rocked, handled, or soothed by the sound of a mother's voice (Barnard & Bee, 1983; Scafidi et al., 1986, 1990; Schaefer, Hatcher, & Barglow, 1980).

Low-birth-weight babies can also benefit from programs that teach their parents how to provide them with sensitive and responsive care at home. In one study, a pediatric nurse visited periodically with mothers and taught them how to read and respond appropriately to the atypical behaviors of their preterm infants. Although the intervention lasted only 3 months, the low-birth-weight infants whose mothers participated had caught up intellectually with normal-birth-weight peers by the age of 4 (Achenbach et al., 1990). And when combined with stimulating day-care programs, parental interventions not only foster the cognitive growth of low-birth-weight children, but can reduce the likelihood of their displaying behavioral disorders as well (Brooks-Gunn et al., 1993; Spiker, Ferguson, & Brooks-Gunn, 1993).

Of course, not all low-birth-weight infants (or their parents) have opportunities to participate in successful interventions. What happens to them?

Long-term consequences of low birth weight. Before 1975, many researchers had reported that low-birth-weight infants were likely to experience more learning difficulties later in childhood, to score lower on IQ tests, and to suffer more emotional problems than normal-birth-weight infants (Caputo & Mandell, 1970; Drillien, 1969). Today, we know that these conclusions are badly overstated and that the long-term prognosis for low-birth-weight children depends largely on the environment in which they are raised. Most preterm or small-for-date infants who are raised in stable, supportive homes develop healthy emotional attachments to both their parents by 12–20 months of age (Easterbrooks, 1989; Goldberg, Perrotta, Minde, & Corter, 1986) and show little evidence of serious intellectual impairment or learning difficulties later in life (Kopp & Kaler, 1989; Cohen & Parmelee, 1983). However, low-birth-weight children from unstable or economically disadvantaged backgrounds are likely to remain smaller in stature than full-term children, experience more emotional problems, and show some long-term deficits in intellectual growth and academic achievement (Baker & Mednick, 1984; Kopp & Kaler, 1989).

Consider what Ronald Wilson (1985) found in his study of developing twins. Although twins are generally small for date and are often preterm, Wilson focused closely on twins who were especially small (weighing under 1750 grams, or less than 3¾ pounds). In Figure 4-11, we see that these preterm, low-birth-weight babies were indeed deficient in mental development throughout the first three years of life (a score of 100 on the tests reflects average intellectual performance). Yet, the figure also shows that low-birth-weight twins from middle-class (high-SES) homes eventually made up their intellectual deficits, scoring average (or slightly above) on the tests by age 6, whereas their counterparts from low-income (low-SES) backgrounds remained substantially below average in their intellectual performances. So the long-term prognosis for preterm and small-for-date children does seem to depend very critically on the *postnatal environment* in which they are raised (see also Bradley et al., 1994).

Concept Check 4-3 ⌄ Perinatal Influences on Development

Check your understanding of some potentially important perinatal influences on development by matching the perinatal events listed below with the following *possible* consequences: (a) cranial bleeding, (b) emotional bonding/engrossment, (c) respiratory distress syndrome, (d) sluggish, inattentive demeanor for months after birth, (e) cerebral palsy. The answers appear in the Appendix.

_____ 1. heavy exposure to obstetric medication

_____ 2. delivery by obstetrical forceps

_____ 3. preterm delivery

_____ 4. severe anoxia

_____ 5. close contact with responsive people

On Reproductive Risk and Infants' Capacity for Recovery

We have now discussed many examples of what can go wrong during the prenatal and perinatal periods, as well as some steps that expectant parents can take to try to prevent such results (see, for example, Box 4-3). Once they occur, some of these damaging effects are irreversible: A baby blinded by rubella, for example, will never regain its sight, and a child who develops cerebral palsy due to anoxia will have it for life. And yet, there are a lot of adults walking around today who turned out perfectly normal even though their mothers smoked, drank, or contracted harmful diseases while pregnant or received heavy doses of obstetric medication while in labor and childbirth. Why is this? One reason is simply that not all embryos, fetuses, and newborns who are exposed to teratogens are affected by them. But what about those who are affected? It is possible that many of these infants will eventually overcome their early handicaps later in life?

Indeed it is, and some of the findings we have already reviewed tell us so. For example, Monroe Lefkowitz's (1981) longitudinal study found that 9–11 years after birth, children whose mothers had smoked during pregnancy were not any smaller, any less healthy, any less intelligent, less achievement oriented, or less well adjusted than children of nonsmokers. Moreover, we've seen in Box 4-1 that, as young adults, Dutch males whose mothers had experienced famine during their pregnancies were no less intelligent, on average, than age-mates who had received adequate prenatal nutrition. And the literature we just reviewed on the long-term implications of low birth weight clearly indicates that many of these initially frail and seemingly pitiful creatures will eventually outgrow their early deficiencies.

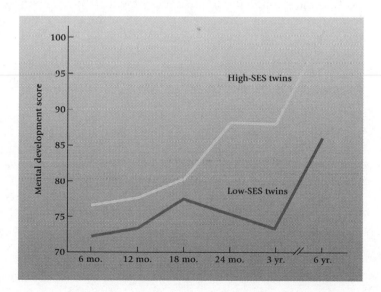

Figure 4-11
Age trends in intellectual development for low-birth-weight twins from middle-class (high-SES) and lower socioeconomic (low-SES) backgrounds.
Adapted from Wilson, 1985.

Might we, then, characterize human infants as resilient creatures who display a *strong* capacity for recovery? Arnold Sameroff and Michael Chandler (1975) certainly think so. In fact, Sameroff and Chandler believe that most babies who display prenatal and perinatal complications eventually recover and develop normally as long as they are not brain damaged and have a stable and supportive environment in which to grow.

A major longitudinal study by Emmy Werner and Ruth Smith (1982, 1992) provides strong support for Sameroff and Chandler's hypotheses. Werner and Smith followed up on all 670 babies born in 1955 on the Hawaiian island of Kauai. At birth, approximately 16% of these infants showed moderate to severe complications, another 31% showed mild complications, and 53% appeared normal and healthy. When the babies were reexamined at age 2 years, there was a clear relationship between severity of birth complications and developmental disorders: The more severe their neonatal complications, the more likely children were to be deficient in social and intellectual development. However, effects of the postnatal environment were already apparent. In homes that were rated high in emotional support and educational stimulation, children who had shown severe birth complications scored slightly below average on tests of social adjustment and intellectual development. But in homes that were low in emotional support and educational stimulation, the intellectual performance of children who had experienced equally severe perinatal complications was *far* below average (see also Bradley et al., 1994).

Werner and Smith then followed up on the children at ages 10 and 18, and again as young adults. What they found was striking. By age 10, perinatal complications no longer predicted children's intellectual performance, but certain characteristics of the children's home environments did. Children from unstimulating and unresponsive home environments continued to perform very poorly on intelligence tests, whereas their counterparts from stimulating and supportive homes showed no marked deficiencies in intellectual performance. Clearly, children who had suffered the most severe early complications were the ones who were least likely to overcome all their initial handicaps, even when raised in optimal home environments (see also Bendersky & Lewis, 1994). But in summarizing the results of this study, Werner and Smith noted that long-term problems related to the effects of poor environments outnumbered those attributable to perinatal stress by a ratio of 10 to 1.

What, then, are we to conclude about the long-term implications of reproductive risk? First, we do know that prenatal and perinatal complications can leave lasting scars, particularly if these insults are severe. Yet, the longitudinal data we have reviewed suggest ample reason for optimism should you ever give birth to a frail, irritable, unresponsive baby that is abnormal in its appearance or behavior. Given a supportive and stimulating home environment in which to grow and the unconditional love of at least one caregiver, a majority of these children will display a strong "self-righting" tendency and will eventually overcome their initial handicaps (Werner & Smith, 1992).

Ecological Considerations: Should You Have Your Baby at Home?

Today, women have more choices about how and where they will give birth than they did 20 years ago. Although nearly 99% of all babies in the United States are born in a hospital (U.S. Bureau of the Census, 1990), fewer and fewer mothers give birth flat on their backs, with their legs in stirrups, while heavily medicated. Interestingly, hospital birthing is a relatively recent practice: Before 1900, only 5% of U.S. babies were born in hospitals; and most infants in many third-world tribal cultures are still born at home, often with the mother in a vertical or squatting position, surrounded by family members or assisted by other women (Mead & Newton, 1967). Cultures clearly differ in their rituals surrounding birth. Some cultures, such as the Navaho of North America, play special music for women in labor; others, such as the Jararu of

Childbirth is treated as a natural event in many of the world's cultures. Women may give birth, in full view of others, wherever they may be at the moment.

South America, view childbirth as so much a part of daily life that a woman may give birth wherever she may be, in full view of everyone, including small children. And now that natural childbirth classes have become more popular in Western societies, many people favor a return to the days when birth was viewed as a natural family event rather than a medical crisis to be managed with high technology (Edwards & Waldorf, 1984).

Indeed, more and more couples are now opting for home deliveries, often with the aid of a certified nurse-midwife who is trained in nonsurgical obstetrics. Home birthing advocates believe that there are many good reasons for a woman to deliver at home (see Table 4-5 for a partial list), not the least of which is freedom from the potentially harmful interventions (for example, heavy medication, cesarean deliveries) that obstetric practitioners may favor. And it does seem that the relaxed atmosphere of the home setting can have a calming effect on many mothers, for women who deliver at home have shorter and less stressful labors and use far less obstetric medication, on average, than those who deliver in hospitals (Brackbill et al., 1985; Sagov & Brodsky, 1984). (Of course, an alternative interpretation is that mothers delivering at home may have better experiences because they have received better prenatal care and have prepared more diligently for childbirth; see Brackbill et al., 1985).

Are home births as safe as hospital deliveries? Those who favor home birthing have examined childbirth statistics from many countries and concluded that having a baby at home is at least as safe as having one in a hospital (Sagov & Brodsky, 1984; Schramm, Barnes, & Bakewell, 1987). Consider the data from Holland, where about half of all babies are born at home with the assistance of a nurse or midwife. In 1973, the mortality rates for Dutch infants were 16.3 per 1000 births for babies delivered in hospitals, but only 4.5 per 1000 for babies delivered at home (MacFarlane, 1977). In addition, 60% of mothers who gave birth in hospitals experienced some postpartum depression, compared with 16% for home births. Of course, the infant mortality rate in hospitals may be artificially high in Holland (or any other country) because all mothers who have already experienced (or are likely to experience) prenatal distress or birth complications are instructed to give birth in a hospital. Nevertheless, the low mortality rate for infants born at home suggests that the physical

Table 4-5 Most Frequently Cited Reasons for Delivering at Home by Couples Choosing This Alternative

1. To give birth in a relaxed environment where obstetric medication is not encouraged, where friends and relatives can give the laboring woman the support she desires, and where the birth experience can become as positive a personal/family psychological event as possible.

2. To be able to choose who will be present at the delivery and to avoid unfamiliar and nonsupportive attendants, nurses, aides, students, residents, and physicians.

3. To be attended by supportive *women* attendants—midwives or physicians—who will remain with the woman throughout her labor and birth.

4. To avoid invasive intervention (for example, routine cesarean section of breech infants).

5. To avoid separation of family members after birth, including father, mother, baby, and siblings.

risks of home deliveries are not great for *healthy* mothers who have received *excellent prenatal care.*

Obstetricians in the United States have resisted the home birth movement, partly because they fear birth complications and partly because home births threaten their monopoly as providers of birthing services (Edwards & Waldorf, 1984). In response to the criticisms of conventional delivery practices and the growing home birth movement, many hospitals have created birthing rooms, or **alternative birth centers,** that provide a homelike atmosphere but still make medical technology available (Klee, 1986). Other alternative birth centers have been developed independently of hospitals and place the task of delivery in the hands of certified nurse-midwives, typically registered nurses who have taken additional coursework in obstetrics. In either case, mates or other close companions, and often even the couple's children, can be present during labor, and healthy infants can remain in the same room with their mothers (rooming in) rather than spending their first days in the hospital nursery. So far, the evidence suggests that delivery in low-risk alternative birth centers is no more risky to mothers and their babies than delivery in a hospital and is less likely to involve interventions such as anesthesia and cesarean sections (Fullerton & Severino, 1992). Linnea Klee (1986) finds that mothers who choose alternative birth centers often want access to medical technologies "in case something goes wrong," whereas mothers who choose home delivery more often distrust the medical establishment. Clearly, a woman today whose pregnancy is going smoothly has considerable freedom to give birth as she chooses.

alternative birth center: a hospital birthing room or other facility that provides a homelike atmosphere for childbirth but still makes medical technology available.

SUMMARY

During the 266 days between conception and birth, the unborn child passes through three successive phases. Within the first 2 weeks, or germinal period, the single-celled zygote becomes a multicelled blastocyst that travels down the fallopian tube, implants itself in the uterine lining, and begins to grow. The inner layer of the blastocyst, or embryonic disk, becomes the embryo. The outer layer of cells, or trophoblast, develops into the amnion and placenta—tissues that protect and nourish the embryo.

The second phase of prenatal development lasts from the third through the eighth week of pregnancy and is called the period of the embryo. By the end of this phase, the unborn child is only about an inch long and weighs about 1/10th of an ounce.

However, it already bears some resemblance to a human being because most of its organs and body parts have formed and begun to function.

From the end of the eighth week until birth is the period of the fetus. As the fetus rapidly grows, the genitals appear, the muscles and bones develop, and all organ systems become integrated in preparation for birth. Between the 24th and 28th weeks, the brain and respiratory system mature to an extent that the fetus attains the age of viability—the point at which survival outside the uterus *may* be possible. At the beginning of the seventh month, the fetus weighs 2 pounds and is 14–15 inches long. By the end of the ninth month, the full-term fetus has grown to 19 or 20 inches and weighs about 7–7$\frac{1}{2}$ pounds.

Many environmental influences can complicate prenatal development and the birth process. Among these influences are characteristics of the mother such as age, emotional state, and quality of diet. If a mother is malnourished, particularly during the last three months of pregnancy, she runs an increased risk of having a stillborn infant or a premature baby who may fail to survive. In addition, the fetally mal nourished infant may be sluggish, irritable, and neurologically immature—liabilities that could contribute to long-term deficits in social and intellectual development.

Prenatal development may also be disrupted by teratogens—drugs, diseases, chemicals, and radiation—that can attack the developing embryo or fetus and produce serious birth defects. Teratogens are dangerous throughout pregnancy; however, many of these agents are especially troublesome during the first eight weeks, when the major organs and body parts are developing. Many diseases may produce birth defects; rubella, syphilis, herpes, and toxoplasmosis are particularly harmful. A large number of drugs, including thalidomide, alcohol, tobacco, hormones, narcotics, and even some antibiotics, are known to cause congenital malformations and complications at birth. In addition, radiation and chemical pollutants such as mercury, lead, and PCBs may have adverse effects on an unborn child.

Childbirth is a three-step process that begins when the uterus contracts and prepares to push the fetus through the cervical opening and ends a few minutes after birth of the baby, when the afterbirth is expelled from the body. Many women feel exhilarated after giving birth and can begin to form a strong emotional bond with their babies if they have early and extended contact with them in the hours after birth. Fathers, too, are often engrossed with their newborns, and the support of fathers, both as participants during prepared childbirth classes and as companions during labor and delivery, can make the childbirth experience easier for mothers. Some developmentalists believe that birth is a traumatic experience for newborns and suggest "gentle birthing" as a way of making the process less terrifying. Yet the evidence implies that birth is not an especially traumatic experience for most babies.

Although most births proceed normally, serious complications can occur. Anoxia, or oxygen starvation, is a major cause of cerebral palsy. The likelihood of anoxia is increased by complicated breech deliveries and overuse of obstetric medication.

Women who have inadequate diets and poor prenatal care are at risk of delivering low-birth-weight babies. *Small-for-date* babies, who are seriously underweight for their age, usually have more severe and longer lasting problems than do *preterm* infants, whose body weights are normal for the time spent in the uterus. Interventions to stimulate these infants and to teach their parents how to respond appropriately to these vulnerable creatures can help to normalize their developmental progress. Fortunately, the problems stemming from both prenatal and perinatal complications are often overcome in time, provided that the child is not brain damaged and has a stable and supportive postnatal environment in which to grow.

An increasing number of couples are choosing to forgo hospital deliveries and have their babies within the familiar surroundings of their own homes. However, many obstetricians are critical of the home birth movement, arguing that home deliveries may jeopardize the mother and her infant should complications arise. One compromise that many women are choosing is to give birth in *alternative birth centers* that provide a homelike atmosphere but still make medical technology available if needed.

Key Terms

acquired immune deficiency syndrome [132]

age of viability [124]

alternative birth center [154]

amnion [120]

anoxia [146]

Apgar test [145]

blastocyst [120]

breech birth [146]

cesarean delivery [132]

chorion [121]

critical period [130]

cytomegalovirus (CMV) [131]

diethylstibestrol (DES) [135]

embryo [120]

embryonic disk [120]

emotional bonding [143]

engrossment [144]

fetal alcohol effects (FAE) [136]

fetal alcohol syndrome (FAS) [135]

fetus [123]

first stage of labor [142]

genital herpes [132]

gentle birthing [145]

germinal period [119]

implantation [120]

indifferent gonad [122]

neonate [126]

neural tube [122]

perinatal environment [141]

period of the embryo [119]

period of the fetus [119]

phocomelia [134]

placenta [121]

postpartum depression [144]

prenatal development [119]

prepared (or natural) childbirth [143]

preterm babies [148]

respiratory distress syndrome [149]

rubella (German measles) [130]

second stage of labor [142]

sensitive period [130]

small-for-date babies [148]

syphilis [131]

teratogens [130]

thalidomide [134]

third stage of labor [142]

trophoblast [120]

umbilical cord [121]

The Physical Self: Development of the Brain, the Body, and Motor Skills

5

During the 266 days since conception, the fetus has grown from a single cell into a marvelously complex being. At birth, a newborn child, or *neonate*, is roughly 19–21 inches long, weighs 7 to 7½ pounds, and is quite well prepared to respond adaptively to its environment. This new individual—and the many physical changes that occur as its brain and body develop throughout infancy, childhood, and adolescence—is the subject of this chapter.

We will begin by considering the mannerisms and motor capabilities of newborn infants during the *neonatal* period—the first month of life. We will then concentrate on a most fascinating aspect of human development: the rapid transformation of a largely dependent and immobile little creature into a running, jumping bundle of energy who may eventually surpass the physical stature of his or her parents. Our initial focus will be on the development of the brain, the body, and the growth of motor skills throughout childhood. We then consider the events of puberty—both the dramatic physical changes that all adolescents experience and their psychological impact on the individual. Finally, we will close by discussing the many factors that influence physical growth and development throughout childhood and adolescence.

Having experienced most (if not all) of the changes covered in this chapter, students often assume that they know quite a bit about physical development. Yet, they often discover that there is much they *don't* know. To check your own knowledge, take a minute to decide whether the following statements are true or false:

1. A baby can learn to swim before he or she can walk.   T   F
2. Half the nerve cells in the average baby's brain die (and are not replaced) over the first few years of life.   T   F
3. Most children walk when they are ready, and no amount of encouragement will enable a 6-month-old to walk alone.   T   F
4. Hormones have little effect on human growth and development until puberty.   T   F
5. Emotional trauma can seriously impair the growth of young children, even those who are adequately nourished, healthy, and not physically abused.   T   F

Jot down your responses and we will see how you fared on this pretest as we discuss these issues in the chapter. (If you would like immediate feedback, the correct answers appear at the bottom of this page).

THE NEONATE

Although many parents might argue the point, newborn infants are not very attractive. Their passage through the narrow cervix and birth canal may leave them with flattened noses, misshapen foreheads, and an assortment of bumps and bruises. As the baby is held upside down and measured, parents are likely to see a wrinkled, red-skinned little creature all covered with sticky fluid. Although a neonate's appearance will change for the better over the next few weeks, it will be some time before he or she resembles the smiling, bouncing little imps who appear in baby-food commercials.

How might new parents be assured that their baby is all right? The Apgar procedure that we discussed in Chapter 4 is a quick method of detecting *severe* physical or neurological irregularities that require immediate attention, but it may miss less obvious complications. A second test, the **Brazelton Neonatal Behavioral Assessment Scale (NBAS)**, is a more subtle measure of a neonate's behavioral repertoire and neurological well-being (Brazelton, 1979). Typically administered a few days after birth, the NBAS assesses the strength of 20 inborn reflexes, as well as the infant's state and reactions to social stimuli. One important value of this test is its ability to identify

Brazelton Neonatal Behavioral Assessment Scale (NBAS): a test that assesses a neonate's neurological status and responsiveness to environmental stimuli.

Answers to pretest: 1. T; 2. T; 3. T; 4. F; 5. T

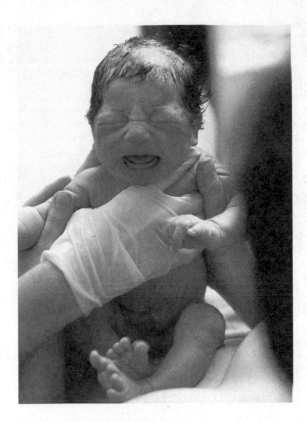

Immediately after birth, babies are not particularly attractive, but their appearance will improve over the first few weeks of life.

in the first few days of life those babies who are slow to react to a variety of everyday experiencies. If the infant is *extremely* unresponsive, the low NBAS score may indicate brain damage or other neurological dysfunction. If the baby is merely sluggish when responding to social stimuli, and if his responsiveness does not improve when retested several days later, it is possible that he will not receive enough playful attention in the months ahead to develop secure emotional ties to his caregivers. So a low NBAS score is an early indication that problems may arise. Fortunately, the NBAS can also be used to help parents of these socially unresponsive infants get off to a good start with their babies (see Box 5-1).

The Neonate's "Preparedness" for Life

In the past, newborns were thought to be fragile, helpless little organisms who were hardly ready for the cold, cruel world. Indeed, this view may have been adaptive in an era when medical practices and procedures were rather primitive and a substantial percentage of newborns did die. T. Berry Brazelton (1979, p. 35) notes that "many cultures in which the neonatal death rate is high still institutionalize such practices as not speaking of the newborn as a [human] baby . . . or of not naming him until he is 3 months old and more likely to survive."

Today, we know that neonates are much better prepared for life than many doctors, parents, and developmentalists had initially assumed. As we will see in our next three chapters, neonates are capable of taking in what is happening around them and successfully adapting to their environments. For example, all of the infant's major senses are functioning reasonably well at birth: Babies do indeed see and hear, and they respond to tastes, touches, and smells in predictable ways as well. Neonates are also capable of simple kinds of learning and often remember the particularly vivid experiences they have had.

Two other indications that newborns are "organized" creatures who are well prepared for life are their repertoire of inborn reflexes and their predictable patterns of daily activity.

BOX 5-1

On Optimizing Development: Using the NBAS to Train Parents

*B*abies who are extremely irritable or are unresponsive and apathetic can be very unpleasant companions who fail to elicit enough attention and comforting to foster the development of a warm, loving emotional bond with their parents. However, Berry Brazelton (1979) believes that many such adverse emotional outcomes can be prevented if parents of these "high-risk" neonates are shown how to stimulate and comfort their babies properly.

Earlier in Chapter 4, we noted that elaborate *long-term* interventions help parents of preterm infants to become more sensitive and responsive caregivers. A simpler method of teaching parents how to interact with their babies is to have them either watch or take part as the NBAS is administered to their child. The NBAS is well suited as a teaching device because it is designed to elicit many of the infant's most pleasing characteristics, such as smiling, vocalizing, and gazing. As the test proceeds, parents will see that their neonate can respond positively to other people, and they will also learn how to elicit these pleasant interactions.

NBAS training has proved to be an effective strategy indeed. Mothers of high-risk children who have observed the NBAS become more responsive in face-to-face interactions with their babies. In addition, their infants score higher on the NBAS one month later than do other high-risk infants whose mothers were not trained (Widmayer & Field, 1980).

Other research (see Myers, 1982; Worobey, 1985) indicates that NBAS training even has positive effects on the parents of healthy, responsive infants. In Barbara Myers's (1982) study, parents in a treatment group were taught to give the NBAS to their neonates, whereas parents in a

control group received no such training. When tested four weeks later, parents who had received the NBAS training were more knowledgeable about infant behavior, more confident in their caretaking abilities, and more satisfied with their infants than were control parents. In addition, fathers who had been trained were much more involved in caring for their infants at home than were the fathers who had received no training.

Although many hospitals provide brief instructions on how to diaper and bathe a baby, parents are seldom told anything about the neonate's basic behavioral abilities, such as whether newborns can see, hear, or carry on meaningful social dialogues with other people. NBAS training clearly illustrates what a new baby is capable of doing, and it appears to have a number of positive effects on both parents and their infants. This brief intervention does not always accomplish wonders (see Belsky, 1985), and even Dr. Brazelton concedes that more powerful and longer-term interventions may be necessary for mothers of low-birth-weight babies or for families experiencing a lot of stress (Worobey & Brazelton, 1986; see also Lyons-Ruth et al., 1990). Nevertheless, NBAS training appears to be a good way to help start parents and babies on the right foot. As Barbara Myers (1982) points out, "the treatment is relatively inexpensive, it only takes about an hour, and the parents reported enjoying it. This type of intervention needs to be tested [further] on other populations . . . for possible consideration as a routine portion of a hospital's postpartum care" (p. 470).

Infant Reflexes

One of the neonate's greatest strengths is a full set of useful reflexes. A **reflex** is an unlearned and automatic response to a stimulus, as when the eye automatically blinks in response to a puff of air. Table 5-1 lists some reflexes that can be readily observed in all healthy newborns. Some of these graceful and yet complex patterns of behavior are called **survival reflexes** because they have clear adaptive value. Examples include the breathing reflex, the eye-blink reflex (which protects the eyes against bright lights or foreign particles), and the sucking and swallowing reflexes, by which the infant ingests food. Also integral to feeding is the *rooting* reflex: An infant who is touched on the cheek will turn in that direction and search for something to suck.

Other so-called **primitive reflexes** are not nearly as useful; in fact, many are believed to be remnants of our evolutionary history that have outlived their purpose. The *Babinski reflex* is a good example. Why would it be adaptive for infants to fan their toes when the bottoms of their feet are stroked? We don't know. Other primitive reflexes may still have some adaptive value, at least in some cultures (Bowlby, 1969; Fentress & McLeod, 1986). The *swimming reflex*, for example, may help keep afloat an infant who is accidently immersed in the tribal watering hole. And the *grasping reflex* may help infants who are carried in slings or on their mothers' hips to hang on. Finally, other responses, such as the *stepping reflex*, may be forerunners of useful voluntary behaviors that develop later in infancy (Thelen, 1984).

reflex: an unlearned and automatic response to a stimulus or class of stimuli.

survival reflexes: inborn responses such as breathing, sucking, and swallowing that enable the newborn to adapt to the extrauterine environment.

primitive reflexes: reflexes controlled by subcortical areas of the brain that gradually disappear over the first year of life.

Table 5-1   Major Reflexes Present in Full-Term Neonates

Name	Response	Development and course	Significance
I. Survival reflexes			
Breathing reflex	Repetitive inhalation and expiration.	Permanent	Provides oxygen and expels carbon dioxide.
Eye-blink reflex	Closing or blinking the eyes.	Permanent	Protects the eyes from bright light or foreign objects.
Pupillary reflex	Constriction of pupils to bright light; dilation to dark or dimly lit surroundings.	Permanent	Protects against bright lights; adapts the visual system to low illumination.
Rooting reflex	Turning the head in the direction of a tactile (touch) stimulus to the cheek.	Disappears over the first few weeks of life and is replaced by voluntary head turning.	Orients child to the breast or bottle.
Sucking reflex	Sucking on objects placed (or taken) into the mouth.	Is gradually modified by experience over the first few months of life.	Allows child to take in nutrients.
Swallowing reflex	Swallowing	Is permanent but modified by experience.	Allows child to take in nutrients.
II. Primitive reflexes			
Babinski reflex	Fanning and then curling the toes when the bottom of the foot is stroked.	Usually disappears within the first 8 months–1 year of life.	Its presence at birth and disappearance in the first year are an indication of normal neurological development.
Palmar grasping reflex	Curling of the fingers around objects (such as a finger) that touch the baby's palm.	Disappears in first 3–4 months and is then replaced by a voluntary grasp.	Its presence at birth and later disappearance are an indication of normal neurological development.
Moro reflex	A loud noise or sudden change in the position of the baby's head will cause the baby to throw his or her arms outward, arch the back, and then bring the arms toward each other as if to hold onto something.	The arm movements and arching of the back disappear over the first 4–6 months; however, the child continues to react to unexpected noises or a loss of bodily support by showing a startle reflex (which does not disappear).	Its presence at birth and later disappearance (or evolution into the startle reflex) are indications of normal neurological development.
Swimming reflex	An infant immersed in water will display active movements of the arms and legs and involuntarily hold his or her breath (thus giving the body buoyancy); this swimming reflex will keep an infant afloat for some time, allowing easy rescue.	Disappears in the first 4–6 months.	Its presence at birth and later disappearance are an indication of normal neurological development; on a practical note, some swimming instructors have taught very young infants to adapt the swimming reflex into a primitive type of locomotion in the water (swimming), which is possible long before an infant is capable of walking.
Stepping reflex	Infants held upright so that their feet touch a flat surface will step as if to walk.	Disappears in the first 8 weeks unless the infant has regular opportunities to practice this response.	Its presence at birth and later disappearance are taken as an indication of normal neurological development.

Note: Preterm infants may show little or no evidence of primitive reflexes at birth, and their survival reflexes are likely to be irregular or immature. However, the missing primitive reflexes will typically appear soon after birth and will disappear a little later than they do among full-term infants.

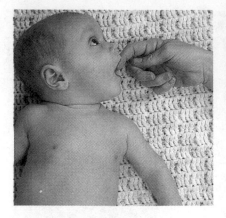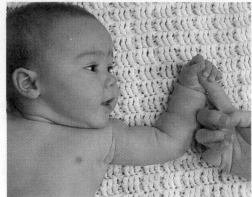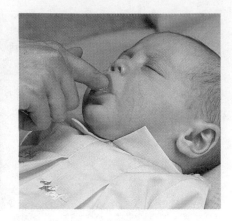

Three innate reflexes. The baby in the photograph at the left is displaying the *rooting reflex:* When an object touches the cheek, the infant will turn the head in the direction of the touch, searching for something to suck. In the center is an example of the *grasping reflex*—a curling of the fingers around objects that touch the palm. The infant in the photograph at the right illustrates the rhythmical sucking, or *sucking reflex,* that neonates display when objects are placed into their mouths.

Primitive reflexes normally disappear during the first few months of infancy. Why? Because they are controlled by the lower "subcortical" areas of the brain and are lost once the higher centers of the cerebral cortex mature and begin to guide voluntary behaviors. But even if many primitive reflexes are not very useful to infants, they are important diagnostic indicators to developmentalists. If these reflexes are *not* present at birth—or if they last too long in infancy—we know that something is wrong with a baby's nervous system.

In sum, a full complement of infant reflexes tells us that newborns are quite prepared to respond adaptively to a variety of life's challenges. And the timely disappearance of certain reflexes is one important sign that a baby's nervous system is developing normally.

Infant States

Newborns also display organized patterns of daily activity that are predictable and that foster healthy developmental outcomes. In a typical day (or night), a neonate will move in and out of six **infant states,** or levels of sleep and wakefulness, that are described in Table 5-2. During the first month, a baby may move rapidly from one state to another, as mothers will testify when their wide-awake babies suddenly nod off to sleep in the middle of a feeding. Neonates spend about 70% of their time (16–18 hours a day) sleeping and only 2–3 hours in the alert, inactive (attentive) state, when they are most receptive to external stimulation (Berg & Berg, 1987; Thoman, 1990). Sleep cycles are typically brief, lasting from 45 minutes to 2 hours. These frequent "naps" are separated by periods of drowsiness, alert or inalert activity, and crying, any of which may occur (as red-eyed parents well know) at all hours of the day and night.

The fact that neonates pass through a predictable pattern of states during a typical day suggests that their internal regulatory mechanisms are well organized. Yet, research on infant states also makes it clear that newborns show a great deal of individuality (Brown, 1964; Thoman & Whitney, 1989). For example, one newborn in one study was alert for only about 15 minutes a day, on average, whereas another was alert for more than 8 hours daily (Brown, 1964). Similarly, one infant cried about 17% of the time, but another spent 39% of its time crying. These differences among infants have some obvious implications for parents, who may find it far more pleasant to be with a bright-eyed baby who rarely cries than with one who is often fussy or inattentive (Colombo & Horowitz, 1987).

Developmental Changes in State

Sleep patterns. As infants develop, they spend less time sleeping and more time awake, alert, and attending to the environment. By age 4–6 weeks, babies are sleeping but 14–15 hours a day; and somewhere between 3 and 7 months of age, many infants reach a milestone that parents truly appreciate—they begin to sleep through

infant states: levels of sleep and wakefulness that young infants display.

Table 5-2 Infant States of Arousal

State	Description	Daily duration in newborn
Regular sleep	Baby is still with eyes closed and unmoving. Breathing is slow and regular.	8–9 hours
Irregular sleep	Baby's eyes are closed but can be observed to move under the closed eyelids (a phenomenon known as *rapid eye movements,* or *REMs*). Baby may jerk or grimace in response to stimulation. Breathing may be irregular.	8–9 hours
Drowsiness	Baby is falling asleep or waking up. Eyes open and close and have a glazed appearance when open. Breathing is regular but more rapid than in regular sleep.	1/2–3 hours
Alert inactivity	Baby's eyes are wide open and bright, exploring some aspect of the environment. Breathing is even, and the body is relatively inactive.	2–3 hours
Alert activity	Baby's eyes are open and breathing is irregular. May become fussy and display various bursts of diffuse motor activity.	1–3 hours
Crying	Intense crying that may be difficult to stop and that is accompanied by high levels of motor activity.	1–3 hours

Source: From Wolff, 1966.

the night and will require but two or three shorter naps during the day (Berg & Berg, 1987; Gesell et al., 1940).

At birth, babies spend approximately half their sleeping hours in **REM sleep,** a state of active, irregular sleep characterized by rapid eye movements (REMs) and brain-wave activity that is more typical of wakefulness than of regular (non-REM) sleep. However, the percentage of time spent in REM sleep declines steadily, leveling off by age 6 months at about 25%–30% of total sleep time.

Why do neonates spend so much time in REM sleep and why does it decline so dramatically early in life? Some developmentalists believe that REM sleep during the early months simply provides very young infants, who sleep so much, with abundant internal stimulation that allows their nervous sytems to mature (Roffwarg, Muzio, & Dement, 1966). Consistent with this **autostimulation theory** is the finding that babies who are given lots of interesting visual stimuli to explore while awake will spend less time in REM sleep than control infants who are denied these experiences (Boismier, 1977). Perhaps the reason that REM sleep declines sharply over the first six months is that the infant's brain is rapidly maturing, she is becoming more alert, and there is simply less need for the stimulation provided by REM activity.

Few babies have problems establishing regular sleep cycles unless their nervous system is abnormal in some way. Yet one of the major causes of infant mortality is a very perplexing sleep-related disorder called crib death, or **sudden infant death syndrome (SIDS),** that we will examine more closely in Box 5-2.

The course and functions of crying. The newborn's earliest cries are unlearned and involuntary responses to discomfort—distress signals by which babies make caregivers aware of their needs. Most of a neonate's early cries are provoked by such physical

REM sleep: a state of active or irregular sleep in which the eyes move rapidly beneath the eyelids and brain-wave activity is similar to the pattern displayed when awake.

autostimulation theory: a theory proposing that REM sleep in infancy is a form of self-stimulation that helps the central nervous system to develop.

sudden infant death syndrome (SIDS): the unexplained death of a sleeping infant who suddenly stops breathing (also called crib death).

BOX 5-2
Sudden Infant Death Syndrome (SIDS)

*E*very year in the United States, as many as 8000 seemingly healthy infants suddenly stop breathing and die in their sleep (Snow, 1989). In industrialized societies, this sudden infant death syndrome (SIDS) is the leading cause of infant mortality among 1- to 12-month-olds, accounting for more than one-third of all such deaths (Wilson & Neidich, 1991; and see figure below).

Unfortunately, the exact cause of SIDS is still unknown. We do know that low-birth-weight male babies (particularly African Americans and Native Americans) who had poor Apgar scores and had experienced respiratory distress as newborns are most susceptible (Public Health Service, 1986; Snow, 1989). We have also learned that mothers of SIDS victims are more likely to smoke or use narcotics and to have received poor prenatal care (MacGregor & Chasnoff, 1993), although most babies of such mothers do not fall prey to SIDS. SIDS is most likely to occur during the winter, among infants who are 2–4 months of age (see figure) and who have a respiratory infection, such as a cold. Some investigators think that a virus is responsible for these crib deaths; others have suggested causes as diverse as hypothermia (chilling), hyperthemia (overheating), and even allergic reactions to house mites (see Snow, 1989). Lewis Lipsitt (1979) believes that SIDS occurs most often at 2–4 months of age because this is the time when subcortical reflexes are diminishing in strength and voluntary cortical responses are not yet well established. Consequently, if mucus blocks the nasal passages, a 2–4-month-old may not struggle for a breath because his innate survival reflexes are waning and his learned, protective responses to discomfort are weak or nonexistent.

Without knowing its exact cause, SIDS is extremely difficult to prevent. What, if anything, can parents do to help prevent SIDS? They can watch for changes in the infant's respiratory effort and feeding activities, for 50%–75% of SIDS victims display serious breathing and digestive problems in the week before they die (Shannon et al., 1987). Should such symptoms appear, doctors may recommend installation of an *apnea monitor* in the home—a device that sounds an alarm to alert caregivers if the baby stops breathing for more than 20–30 seconds. However, even this intervention is controversial, as apnea monitors are not perfectly reliable and cannot guarantee that SIDS won't occur. Clearly, families that must cope with a crib death need information and ample support in their time of sorrow. And though it may not alleviate their grief or their feelings of helplessness, parents are often reassured to learn of the overwhelming odds (nearly 100%) against their having another baby who will suffer a similar fate (Chan, 1987).

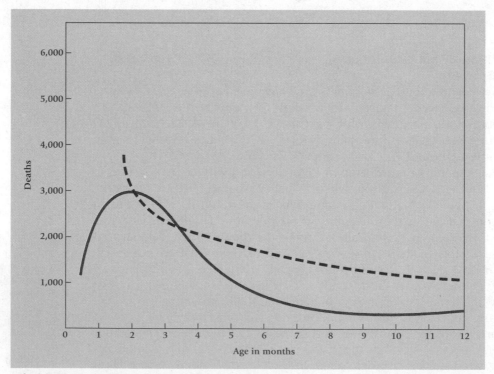

Infant deaths in the United States from SIDS (solid line) and from all other causes (broken line). SIDS occurs most often between 2 and 4 months of age and is the single biggest cause of infant death between the ages of 1 month and 1 year. Adapted from Naeye, 1980.

discomforts as hunger, pain, or symptoms of illness, although chills, loud noises, and even sudden changes in illumination (as when the light over a crib goes off) are often enough to make a young infant cry.

According to Peter Wolff (1969), healthy newborns produce at least three cries: (1) a "hunger" (or basic rhythmic) cry that starts with a whimper and becomes louder and more sustained, (2) a "mad" (or angry) cry that is also rhythmic but more intense, and (3) a "pain" cry that begins with a long shriek followed by seconds of silence (as the baby takes a deep breath) and then more vigorous crying. Wolff (1969) conducted an interesting experiment to see whether mothers could distinguish these three kinds of cries. While he was observing the neonates in their own rooms, Wolff played a tape recording of the infant crying and waited for the mothers to respond. And respond they did: At the sound of a pain cry, mothers immediately came running to see what was wrong with their babies. However, they responded much more slowly (if at all) to either "hungry" or "mad" cries.

Wolff's study seems to imply that different cries convey distinctly different messages. Not everyone agrees with this view. Whereas parents can *sometimes* distinguish the "pain" and the "anger" cries of their own babies, they cannot discriminate those of unfamiliar infants (Wiesenfeld, Malatesta, & DeLoach, 1981). Experience clearly plays a role in helping adults to diagnose the cause of an infant's cries, for parents are better than nonparents at this kind of problem solving, and mothers (who generally have more contact with infants) are better than fathers are (Holden, 1988). Moreover, Philip Zeskind and his associates (1985) find that adults perceive intense "hunger" cries as just as arousing and urgent as equally intense "pain" cries. So it is likely that crying conveys only one very general message—"Hey, I'm distressed"—and that the effectiveness of this signal at eliciting attention depends more on the *amount* of distress it implies than on the *kind* of distress that the baby is experiencing (Gustafson & Harris, 1990; Zeskind et al., 1992).

Will parents who are especially responsive to an infant's cries produce a spoiled baby who enslaves them with incessant demands for attention? Apparently not. According to Mary Ainsworth (Ainsworth, Bell, & Stayton, 1972), mothers who are relatively quick to respond to their infants' cries have babies who come to cry very little! The reason may be that caregivers who are sensitive to an infant's cries also tend to be responsive to other social signals, such as the smiles, babbles, and bright-eyed expressions that distressed infants are likely to emit once they quiet down. Thus, responsive companions are readily available to elicit and *reinforce* alternative modes of communication, which gradually replace crying as methods of attracting attention.

Finally, pediatricians and nurses are trained to listen carefully to the vocalizations of a newborn infant because congenital problems are sometimes detectable by the way an infant cries. Preterm babies, for example, and those who are malnourished or brain-damaged often emit shrill, nonrhythmic cries that are perceived as much more "sickly" and aversive than those of healthy full-term infants (Frodi et al., 1978; Zeskind, 1980). In fact, Barry Lester (1984) reports that it is even possible to discriminate preterm infants who will develop normally from those who are likely to experience later deficits in cognitive development by analyzing their crying in the first few days and weeks of life. So the infant cry is not only an important communicative signal for parents but is a meaningful diagnostic tool as well.

Methods of Soothing a Fussy Baby

Although babies can be delightful companions when alert and attentive, they may irritate the most patient of caregivers when they fuss, cry, and are difficult to pacify. Many people think that a crying baby is either hungry, wet, or in pain, and if the infant has not eaten in some time, feeding may be a very effective method of pacification. In fact, the presentation of a nipplelike pacifier, without food, is often sufficient to quiet a fussy baby—even one whose distress is caused by a painful experience such as an inoculation (Campos, 1989). Of course, the soothing effect of a pacifier may be short-lived if the baby really is hungry.

Other soothing techniques. When feeding or diaper changing doesn't work, rocking, humming, stroking, and other forms of continuous, rhythmic stimulation will often quiet restless babies. Swaddling (wrapping the infant snugly in a blanket) is also comforting because the wraps provide continuous tactile sensation all over the baby's body. Perhaps the infant's nervous system is programmed to respond to soft, rhythmic stimulation, for studies have repeatedly shown that rocking, swaddling, and continuous rhythmic sounds have the effect of decreasing a baby's muscular activity and lowering heart and respiratory rates (Brackbill, 1975; Campos, 1989).

One particularly effective method of soothing crying infants is simply to pick them up. Whereas soft, rhythmic stimulation may put babies to sleep, lifting is likely to have the opposite effect (Korner, 1972), causing them to become visually alert, particularly if their caregivers place them against their shoulders—an excellent vantage point for visual scanning. Anneliese Korner (1972) believes that parents who often soothe their infants by picking them up may be doing them a favor, for the visual exploration that this technique allows will help babies to learn more about their environment.

Individual and cultural differences in soothability. Just as infants differ in their sleeping patterns and daily rhythms, they also differ in their irritability and their ability to be soothed. Even in the first two days of life, some infants are easy to irritate and difficult to soothe, whereas others are rarely perturbed and will calm easily should they become overaroused (Birns, Blank, & Bridger, 1966). There are also cultural differences in infant soothability: Caucasian babies tend to be much more restless and difficult to calm than Chinese-American, Native American, or Japanese infants (Freedman, 1979; Nugent, Lester, & Brazelton, 1989). These differential reactions to stress and soothing are present at birth and may be genetically influenced. Yet it is also clear that child-rearing practices can affect a baby's demeanor. Many Asian and Native American mothers, for example, are often successful at improving the dispositions of even their most irritable babies by swaddling them, carrying them around (in slings or on their hips) as they do their chores, and being ready to nurse at the baby's first whimper (Nugent et al., 1989).

A baby who is not easily soothed can make a parent feel anxious, frustrated, or downright incompetent—reactions that may contribute to a poor parent-child relationship. For this reason, parents of difficult babies need to cast aside their preconceptions about the typical or "perfect" baby and learn how to adjust to the characteristics of their *own* child. Indeed, the NBAS training described in Box 5-1 was

Swaddling is an effective soothing technique that can improve the disposition of an irritable infant.

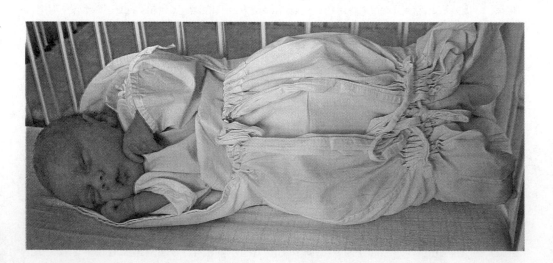

designed with just this objective in mind by (1) showing parents that even an irritable or unresponsive baby can react positively to them and (2) then teaching the parents how to elicit these favorable responses.

 # AN OVERVIEW OF MATURATION AND GROWTH

Adults are often amazed at how quickly children grow. Even tiny babies don't remain tiny for long; in the first few months of life, they gain nearly an ounce each day and an inch each month. Yet, the dramatic increases in height and weight that we can see are accompanied by a number of important *internal* developments in the muscles, bones, and central nervous system—changes that will largely determine the physical feats that children are capable of performing at different ages. In this section of the chapter, we will briefly chart the course of physical development from birth through adolescence and see that there is a clear relationship between those external aspects of growth that are so noticeable and the internal changes that are much harder to detect.

Changes in Height and Weight

Babies grow very rapidly during the first two years, often doubling their birth weight by 4–6 months of age and tripling it (to about 21–22 pounds) by the end of the first year. By age 2, infants are already half their eventual adult height and have quadrupled their birth weight, blossoming to 27–30 pounds. If children continued to grow at this rapid pace until age 18, they would stand about 12 feet, 3 inches and weigh several tons.

The child's growth is slow and steady from age 2 until puberty, averaging 2–3 inches in height and 6–7 pounds in weight each year. During middle childhood (ages 6–11), children may seem to grow very little; over an entire year, 2 inches and 6 pounds are hard to detect on a child who stands 4 to 4½ feet tall and weighs 60–80 pounds (Eichorn, 1979). However, physical growth and development are once again obvious at puberty, when adolescents enter a two- to three-year "growth spurt," during which they may post an annual gain of 10–15 pounds and 2–4 inches in height. After this initial growth spurt, there are typically small increases in height until full adult stature is attained in the mid to late teens (Tanner, 1990).

Changes in Body Proportions

To a casual observer, neonates may appear to be "all head"—and for good reason. The newborn's head is already 70% of its eventual adult size and constitutes one-quarter of the infant's total body length, the same fraction as the legs. If you asked your friends where you might find a creature whose head was as long as its legs, they might tell you to try science fiction.

As a child grows, body shape rapidly changes (see Figure 5-1). Development proceeds in a **cephalocaudal** (head downward) direction, and it is the trunk that grows fastest during the first year. At 1 year of age, a child's head accounts for only 20% of total body length. From the child's first birthday until the adolescent growth spurt, the legs grow rapidly, accounting for more than 60% of the increase in height (Eichorn, 1979). During adolescence, the trunk again becomes the fastest-growing segment of the body, although the legs are also growing rapidly at this time. When we reach our eventual adult stature, our legs will account for 50% of total height and our heads only 12%.

While children grow upward, they are also growing outward according to a **proximodistal** (center outward) pattern. During prenatal development, for example, the chest and internal organs form first, followed by the arms and legs, and then the

cephalocaudal development: a sequence of physical maturation and growth that proceeds from the head (cephalic region) to the tail (or caudal region).

proximodistal development: a sequence of physical maturation and growth that proceeds from the center of the body (the proximal region) to the extremities (distal regions).

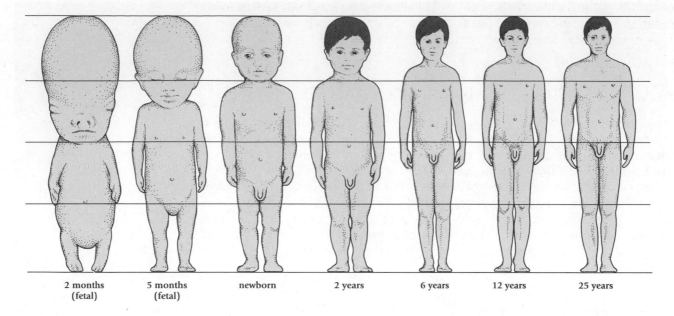

| 2 months (fetal) | 5 months (fetal) | newborn | 2 years | 6 years | 12 years | 25 years |

Figure 5-1
Proportions of the human body from the fetal period through adulthood. The head represents 50% of body length at 2 months after conception but only 12%–13% of adult stature. In contrast, the legs constitute about 12%–13% of the total length of a 2-month-old fetus but 50% of the height of a 25-year-old adult.

hands and feet. Throughout infancy and childhood, the arms and legs continue to grow faster than the hands and feet. However, this center-outward growth pattern reverses just before puberty, when the hands and feet begin to grow rapidly and become the first body parts to reach adult proportions, followed by the arms and legs and finally the trunk. One reason that teenagers often appear so clumsy or awkward is that their hands and feet (and later their arms and legs) may suddenly seem much too large for the rest of their bodies (Tanner, 1990).

Skeletal Development

The skeletal structures that form during the prenatal period are initially soft cartilage tissues that will gradually ossify (harden) into bony material. At birth, most of the infant's bones are soft, pliable, and difficult to break. One reason that neonates cannot sit up or balance themselves when pulled to a standing position is that their bones are too small and too flexible.

Fortunately for both a mother and her baby, the neonate's skull consists of several soft bones that can be compressed to allow the child to pass through the cervix and the birth canal. These skull bones are separated by six soft spots, or *fontanelles*, that are gradually filled in by minerals and will ossify to form a single skull bone by about age 2.

Other parts of the body—namely, the ankles and feet and the wrists and hands—develop *more* (rather than fewer) bones as the child matures. In Figure 5-2, we see that the wrist and hand bones of a 1-year-old infant are both fewer and less well integrated (interconnected) than the corresponding skeletal equipment of an adolescent.

One method of estimating a child's level of physical maturation is to X-ray the wrist and hand (as in Figure 5-2). The X ray shows the number of bones and the extent of their ossification, which is then interpretable as a **skeletal age.** Using this technique, researchers have found that females mature faster than males. At birth, girls are only 4–6 weeks ahead of boys in their level of skeletal maturity, but by age 12, the gender "maturation gap" has widened to two full years (Tanner, 1990).

Not all parts of the skeleton grow and harden at the same rate. The skull and the hands mature first, whereas the leg bones continue to develop until the mid to late teens. For all practical purposes, skeletal development is complete by age 18, although

skeletal age: a measure of physical maturation based on the child's level of skeletal development.

the width (or thickness) of the skull, leg bones, and hands will increase slightly throughout life (Tanner, 1990).

Muscular Development

Although one might think otherwise after listening to the claims of bodybuilders, neonates are born with all the muscle fibers they will ever have (Tanner, 1990). At birth, muscle tissue is 35% water, and it accounts for no more than 18%–24% of a baby's body weight (Marshall, 1977). However, muscle fibers soon begin to grow as the cellular fluid in muscle tissue is bolstered by the addition of protein and salts.

Muscular development proceeds in cephalocaudal and proximodistal directions, with muscles in the head and neck maturing before those in the trunk and limbs. Like many other aspects of physical development, the maturation of muscle tissue occurs very gradually over childhood and then accelerates during early adolescence. One consequence of this muscular growth spurt is that members of both sexes become noticeably stronger, although increases in both muscle mass and physical strength (as measured in tests of large-muscle activity) are more dramatic for males than for females (Malina, 1990). By the mid-20s, skeletal muscle accounts for 40% of the body weight of an average male, compared with 24% for the average female.

The skeletal and muscular development that occurs between infancy and young adulthood helps to explain the remarkable growth of motor skills that we see over this same period. The other necessary ingredient is a more fully developed brain.

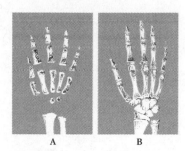

Figure 5-2
X rays showing the amount of skeletal development seen in (A) the hand of an average male infant at 12 months or an average female infant at 10 months and (B) the hand of an average 13-year-old male or an average $10^{1}/_{2}$-year-old female.

DEVELOPMENT OF THE BRAIN

The brain grows at an astounding rate early in life, increasing from 25% of its eventual adult weight at birth to 75% of adult weight by age 2. Indeed, the last three prenatal months and the first two years after birth have been termed the period of the **brain growth spurt** because more than half of one's adult brain weight is added at this time. Between the seventh prenatal month and a child's first birthday, the brain increases in weight by about 1.7 grams a day, or more than a milligram per minute.

However, an increase in brain weight is a rather gross index that tells us very little about how or when various parts of the brain mature and affect other aspects of development. Let's now take a closer look at the internal organization and development of the brain.

Neural Development and Plasticity

The human brain and nervous system consist of more than a trillion highly specialized cells that work together to transmit electrical and chemical signals across many trillions of **synapses,** or connective spaces between the cells. **Neurons** are the basic unit of the brain and nervous system—the cells that receive and transmit neural impulses. The brain alone may contain as many as 100–200 billion neurons, all of which have formed by the end of the second trimester of pregnancy—before the brain growth spurt even begins (Kolb & Fantie, 1989; Rakic, 1991)!

What, then, accounts for the brain growth spurt? One contributor is the development of a second type of nerve cell, called **glia,** which nourish the neurons and eventually encase them in insulating sheaths of a waxy substance called *myelin.* Glia are far more numerous than neurons are, and they continue to form throughout life (Tanner, 1990). In addition, neurons and glia will grow rapidly early in life as long as one's diet contains sufficient protein to sustain this growth. Finally, neurons are branching out to form new synapses, or connections, to other neurons.

One of the more interesting facts about the human nervous system is that the average infant has far more neurons and neural connections than you do. Indeed, as many as half the neurons produced early in life will also die early in life (Janowsky

brain growth spurt: the period between the seventh prenatal month and 2 years of age when more than half of the child's eventual brain weight is added.

synapse: the connective space (juncture) between one nerve cell (neuron) and another.

neurons: nerve cells that receive and transmit neural impulses.

glia: nerve cells that nourish neurons and encase them in insulating sheaths of myelin.

& Finlay, 1986). And the neurons that do survive are each forming hundreds of synapses, many of which will also disappear over the course of childhood (Goldman-Rakic et al., 1983). If we likened the developing brain to a house under construction, we might imagine a builder who merrily constructs many more rooms and hallways than he needs and then later goes back and knocks about half of them out!

What is happening here reflects the remarkable **plasticity** of the young infant's brain—the fact that its cells are highly responsive to the effects of experience. As William Greenough and his colleagues (1987) explain, the human brain has evolved so that it produces an excess of neurons and synapses in preparation for receiving any and all kinds of sensory and motor stimulation that a human being could conceivably experience (see also Rakic, 1991). Of course, no human being has this broad a range of experiences, so that much of one's neural circuitry remains unused. Presumably, then, the neurons and synapses that are most often activated will survive, whereas those that are not often used will eventually disappear. Note the implication then: The development of the brain early in life is not due entirely to the unfolding of a maturational program. It is the handiwork of both a biological program and early experience (Gandelman, 1992; Greenough et al., 1987).

How do we know that early experience plays such a dramatic role in the development of the brain and central nervous system? The first clue came from a program of research by Austin Riesen and his associates (Riesen, 1947; Riesen et al., 1951). Riesen's subjects were infant chimpanzees that were reared in the dark for periods ranging up to 16 months. His results were striking. Chimps raised in the dark experienced atrophy of the retina and the neurons that make up the optic nerve. This atrophy was reversible if the animal's visual deprivation did not exceed seven months but was irreversible, and often led to total blindness, if the deprivation lasted longer than one year. So neurons that are not properly stimulated will degenerate—a dramatic illustration of the "use it or lose it" principle.

If a lack of stimulation inhibits the development of the brain and nervous system, might we then foster such growth by exposing subjects to enriched environments that provide a variety of stimulation? This idea is not new by any means; in 1815, a practitioner by the name of Spurzheim claimed that "the organs of the brain increase by [mental] exercise." For more than 20 years now, Mark Rosenzweig and his associates have been evaluating the merits of this "mental exercise" hypothesis, using animals as subjects. And as we will see in Box 5-3, the results of this research clearly illustrate that both brain size and structure can be modified by experience.

Brain Differentiation and Growth

Not all parts of the brain develop at the same rate. At birth, the most highly developed areas are the *brain stem* and the *midbrain*, which control states of consciousness, inborn reflexes, and vital biological functions such as digestion, respiration, and elimination. Surrounding the midbrain are the *cerebrum* and *cerebral cortex*, the areas most directly implicated in voluntary bodily movements, perception, and higher intellectual activities such as learning, thinking, and production of language. The first areas of the cerebrum to mature are the *primary motor areas* (which control simple motor activities such as waving the arms), and the *primary sensory areas* (which control sensory processes such as vision, hearing, smelling, and tasting). Thus, human neonates are reflexive, "sensory-motor" beings because only the sensory and motor areas of the cortex are functioning well at birth. By 6 months of age, the primary motor areas of the cerebral cortex have developed to the point that they now direct most of the infant's physical activities. Inborn responses such as the palmar grasp and the Babinski reflex should have disappeared by now, thus indicating that the higher cortical centers are assuming proper control over the more primitive "subcortical" areas of the brain.

plasticity: capacity for change; a developmental state that has the potential to be shaped by experience.

BOX 5-3
Raising Rats in Enriched Environments: Effects on Brain Growth and Development

*E*nvironmental effects on the development of the brain are dramatically illustrated in a program of research by Mark Rosenzweig and his associates (Rosenzweig, 1966, 1984; Greenough, Black, & Wallace, 1987). In Rosenzweig's initial experiment, just-weaned rat pups were taken from their mothers and placed for the next 80 days in either an *enriched* or an *impoverished* environment. The enriched environment was truly enriched. Whereas standard laboratory conditions call for three rats to a cage with a continuous supply of food and water, animals raised in the enriched environment lived in groups of 10 to 12 in a large cage that contained not only food and water, but also a number of "toys"—ladders to climb, platforms and boxes to explore, exercise wheels, and so on. These toys were changed daily to ensure that the enriched animals did not become bored with their playthings. To further enrich their early experiences, the rats were given daily exploratory sessions in novel environments and practice at maze running. By contrast, "impoverished" animals were truly deprived. They lived by themselves in individual cages with solid walls that restricted their vision. Their cages contained no playthings and were placed in a quiet, dimly illuminated room. To control for genetic influences, each animal in the enriched condition had a littermate in the impoverished condition. Control groups were raised under standard laboratory conditions.

After 80 days, the rats were sacrificed and their brains were weighed, dissected, and chemically analyzed. The results were intriguing. Animals raised in the enriched environment had heavier cerebral cortexes (the "highest" brain center, which controls perception, learning, and memory) than those raised in the impoverished environment. This greater cortical development of the enriched animals was not attributable to their greater body weights, for in some of the experiments the enriched animals actually weighed less than their impoverished brethren. Furthermore, animals raised in enriched environments had larger neurons and a more extensive network of connections among neurons than did animals in the impoverished condition. Finally, there were biochemical differences in the neural tissues of the enriched and the impoverished animals, which suggested that the neural activity of the enriched animals was greater than that of their impoverished littermates.

Similar changes in brain size and structure have now been observed in adult rats exposed to enriched environments after having spent their early days in a standard laboratory setting (Greenough et al., 1987; Rosenzweig, 1984). Although it takes longer periods of enrichment to produce smaller effects in adult rats as compared to younger ones, the fact that fully mature animals show *any* enrichment effects is a clear demonstration that the brain retains some of its plasticity later in life.

Myelinization

As brain cells proliferate and grow, some of the glia begin to produce a waxy substance called *myelin*, which forms a sheath around individual neurons. This myelin sheath acts like an insulator to speed the transmission of neural impulses, thus allowing the brain to communicate more efficiently with different parts of the body.

Myelinization follows a definite chronological sequence that parallels the maturation of the nervous system. At birth or shortly thereafter, the pathways between the sense organs and the brain are reasonably well myelinated. As a result, the neonate's sensory equipment is in good working order. As neural pathways between the brain and the skeletal muscles myelinate (in a cephalocaudal and proximodistal pattern), the child becomes capable of increasingly complex motor activities such as lifting the head and chest, reaching with the arms and hands, rolling over, sitting, standing, and eventually walking and running. Although myelinization proceeds very rapidly over the first few years of life, some areas of the brain are not completely myelinated until the mid to late teens or early adulthood. For example, the *reticular formation*—a part of the brain that allows us to concentrate on a subject for lengthy periods—is not fully myelinated at puberty (Tanner, 1990). This may be one reason that the attention spans of infants, toddlers, and school-age children are much shorter than those of adolescents and adults.

How important is myelinization? The answer becomes obvious when we consider the plight of those with **multiple sclerosis**, a crippling disease that results when the myelin sheaths surrounding individual neurons begin to disintegrate. The cause of this incurable disease is unknown, and its symptoms vary depending on the part of the nervous system that deteriorates. As the condition worsens, the patient will first

myelinization: the process by which neurons are enclosed in waxy myelin sheaths that will facilitate the transmission of neural impulses.

multiple sclerosis: a crippling loss of muscular control that occurs when the myelin sheaths surrounding individual neurons begin to disintegrate.

lose muscular control over the affected area(s) and may eventually become paralyzed or even die. So without myelinization, life as we know it would be difficult if not impossible.

Cerebral Lateralization

The highest brain center, the **cerebrum,** consists of two halves (or *hemispheres*) connected by a band of fibers called the **corpus callosum.** Each of the hemispheres is covered by a **cerebral cortex**—an outer layer of gray matter that controls sensory and motor processes, perception, and intellectual functioning. Although identical in appearance, the left and the right cerebral hemispheres serve different functions and control different areas of the body. The left cerebral hemisphere controls the right side of the body, and, as illustrated in Figure 5-3, it contains centers for speech, hearing, verbal memory, decision making, and processing of language, to name a few. By contrast, the right cerebral hemisphere controls the left side of the body and contains centers for processing visual-spatial information, nonlinguistic sounds such as music, tactile (touch) sensations, and emotional expressions. Thus, the brain is a *lateralized* organ. **Cerebral lateralization** also involves a preference for using one hand or one side of the body more than the other. About 90% of adults rely on their right hands (or left hemispheres) to write, eat, and perform other motor functions, whereas these same activities are under the control of the right hemisphere among most people who are left-handed. However, the fact that the brain is a lateralized organ does not mean that each hemisphere is totally independent of the other, for the corpus callosum, which connects the hemispheres, plays an important role in integrating their respective functions.

When do the two cerebral hemispheres begin to "divide the work" and become lateralized? It was once thought that lateralization took place gradually throughout childhood and was not complete until adolescence (Lenneberg, 1967). Now, however, it is believed that brain lateralization may originate in the prenatal period and is clearly evident at birth (Kinsbourne, 1989). For example, it has been noted that about two-thirds of all fetuses end up positioned in the womb with their right ears facing outward, and it is believed that this gives them a right-ear advantage and illustrates the left hemisphere's specialization in language processing (Previc, 1991). From the first day of life, speech sounds stimulate more electrical activity in the left side of the cerebral cortex than in the right (Molfese, 1977). In addition, most newborns turn to the right rather than to the left when they lie on their backs, and these same babies later tend to reach for objects with their right hands (Michel, 1981; McCormick & Mauer, 1988). So it seems that the two cerebral hemispheres may be biologically programmed to assume different functions and have already begun to "divide the labor" by the time a baby is born (Kinsbourne, 1989; Witelson, 1987).

However, the brain is not completely specialized at birth; until puberty, children come to rely more and more on one particular hemisphere or the other to serve particular functions. Consider, for example, that even though left- or right-handedness is apparent early and is reasonably well-established by age 2, lateral preferences become stronger over time. In one experiment, preschoolers and adolescents were asked to pick up a crayon, kick a ball, look into a small, opaque bottle, and place their ears to a box to hear a sound. Only 32% of the preschoolers, but more than half of the adolescents, showed a consistent lateral preference by relying exclusively on one side of the body to perform all four tasks (Coren, Porac, & Duncan, 1981). Because the immature brain is not completely specialized, young children often show a remarkable ability to bounce back from traumatic brain injuries as neural circuits that might otherwise have been lost assume the functions of those that have died (Kolb & Fantie, 1989; Rakic, 1991). Although adults who suffer brain damage often regain a substantial portion of the functions they have lost, especially with the proper therapy, their recoveries are rarely as rapid or as complete as those of younger children (Kolb & Fantie, 1989). So the remarkable recuperative power of the human brain (that is, plasticity) is greatest early in life, before cerebral lateralization is complete.

cerebrum: the highest brain center; includes both hemispheres of the brain and the fibers that connect them.

corpus callosum: the bundle of neural fibers that connects the two hemispheres of the brain and transmits information from one hemisphere to the other.

cerebral cortex: the outer layer of the brain's cerebrum that is involved in voluntary body movements, perception, and higher intellectual functions such as learning, thinking, and speaking.

cerebral lateralization: the specialization of brain functions in the left and the right cerebral hemispheres.

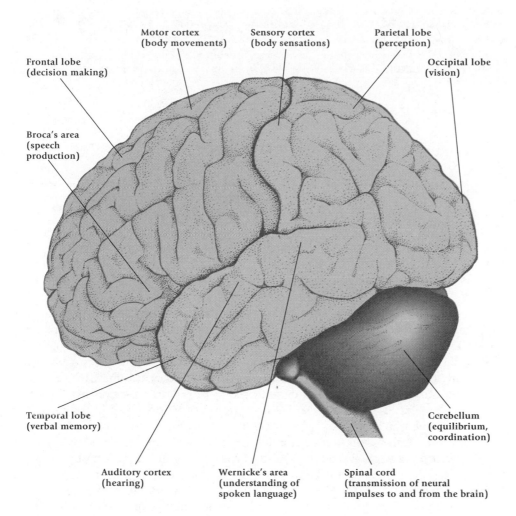

Motor cortex
(body movements)

Sensory cortex
(body sensations)

Parietal lobe
(perception)

Frontal lobe
(decision making)

Occipital lobe
(vision)

Broca's area
(speech
production)

Temporal lobe
(verbal memory)

Cerebellum
(equilibrium,
coordination)

Auditory cortex
(hearing)

Wernicke's area
(understanding of
spoken language)

Spinal cord
(transmission of neural
impulses to and from the brain)

Figure 5-3
Lateral view of the left cerebral cortex and some of the functions that it controls. Although the cerebellum and spinal cord are not part of the cerebral cortex, they serve important functions of their own.

What are the implications for children who fail to rely on one hemisphere or the other to perform specific functions? Leslie Tan (1985) finds that 4-year-olds who have not yet established a dominant hand are more likely than their left- or right-handed age-mates to be uncoordinated and delayed in their motor development. Other research has linked **dyslexia**—a serious impairment in one's ability to read that may affect as many as 5% of schoolchildren in the United States—to an abnormal pattern of cerebral lateralization for visual/spatial functions (Witelson, 1977). Although not everyone agrees that all forms of dyslexia have a neurological basis (see, for example, Scarborough, 1990), many dyslexics do show irregularities in cerebral lateralization that may well contribute to their reading difficulties (Wolff, Michel, Ovrut, & Drake, 1990).

 MOTOR DEVELOPMENT

One of the most dramatic developments of the first year of life is the remarkable progress that infants make in controlling their movements and perfecting motor skills. Literary figures are fond of describing newborns as "helpless babes"—a characterization that largely stems from the neonate's inability to move about on her

dyslexia: a general label used to describe the abnormal impairments that some seemingly normal individuals experience when learning to read.

Concept Check 5-1 ↘ The Developing Brain

Check your understanding of the developing brain and nervous system by matching each *development* listed below with an apparent consequence, or outcome, of that development. Select your answers from the following options: (a) decline in brain plasticity; (b) increases in attention span; (c) lateral preferences; (d) loss of inborn reflexes; (e) brain growth spurt. The answers appear in the Appendix.

_____ 1. Cerebral lateralization

_____ 2. Maturation of higher cortical centers

_____ 3. Proliferation of glia and neural synapses

_____ 4. Loss of neurons and synapses over the course of childhood

_____ 5. Myelinization

own. Oh, it is true that newborns are capable of such voluntary motor responses as turning their heads, flailing their arms, and kicking their legs; but they are clearly disadvantaged when compared with the young of many species, who can follow their mothers to food (and then feed themselves) very soon after birth.

Fortunately, babies do not remain immobile for long. By the end of the first month, the brain and neck muscles have matured enough to permit most infants to reach the first milestone in locomotor development: lifting their chins while lying flat on their stomachs. Soon thereafter, children lift their chests as well, reach for objects, roll over, and sit up if someone is there to support them. Investigators who have charted the motor development of human infants over the first two years find that locomotor skills evolve in a definite sequence, which appears in Table 5-3. Although the ages at which these skills first appear vary considerably from child to child, infants who are quick to proceed through this motor sequence are not necessarily any brighter or otherwise advantaged, compared with those whose rates of motor development are average or slightly below average. So even though the age norms in Table 5-3 are a useful standard for gauging an infant's progress as he or she begins to sit, stand, and take those first tentative steps, a child's rate of motor development really tells us very little about future developmental outcomes.

Basic Trends in Locomotor Development

The two fundamental "laws" that describe muscular development and myelinization also hold true for motor development during the first few years. Motor development proceeds in a cephalocaudal direction, with activities involving the head, neck, and upper extremities preceding those involving the legs and lower extremities. At the same time, development is proximodistal, with activities involving the trunk and shoulders appearing before those involving the hands and fingers.

How do we explain the sequencing and timing of early motor development? Let's briefly consider three possibilities: the *maturational viewpoint*, the *experiential* (or practice) *hypothesis*, and a newer *systems perspective* that views motor development as a product of a complex interaction between the child's biological predispositions and the experiences she has had (Thelen, 1989, 1995; Thelen et al., 1993).

The Maturational Viewpoint

The maturational viewpoint (Shirley, 1933) describes motor development as the unfolding of a genetically programmed sequence of events in which the nerves and muscles mature in a *downward* and *outward* direction. As a result, children gradually gain more control over the lower and peripheral parts of their bodies, displaying locomotor skills in the sequence shown in Table 5-3.

One clue that maturation plays a prominent role in motor development comes from cross-cultural research. Infants from around the world progress through the same *sequence* of locomotor milestones. Moreover, much of the early literature would

Table 5-3 Age Norms (in Months) for Important Locomotor Developments (Based on Anglo-American, Latino, and African-American Children in the United States)

Skill	Month when 50% of infants have mastered the skill	Month when 90% of infants have mastered the skill
Lifts head 90° while lying on stomach	2.2	3.2
Rolls over	2.8	4.7
Sits propped up	2.9	4.2
Sits without support	5.5	7.8
Stands holding on	5.8	10.0
Walks holding on	9.2	12.7
Stands alone momentarily	9.8	13.0
Stands well alone	11.5	13.9
Walks well	12.1	14.3
Walks up steps	17.0	22.0
Kicks ball forward	20.0	24.0

Source: Adapted from Frankenberg & Dodds, 1967.

lead one to believe that practice plays little, if any, part in the development of basic motor skills. Wayne and Marsena Dennis (1940), for example, found that Hopi Indian infants who had been swaddled and bound to cradleboards for the first 9–10 months of life were no slower to take their first unaided step than other Hopi infants whose parents had decided not to follow the tribal custom of tying them down. In addition, early studies in which one identical twin was allowed to practice motor skills (such as climbing stairs or stacking blocks) while the co-twin was denied these experiences suggested that practice had little effect on motor development: When finally allowed to perform, the unpracticed twin soon matched the skills of the co-twin who had had many opportunities to practice (Gesell & Thompson, 1929; McGraw, 1935). These findings seemed to imply that physical maturation is what underlies motor development and that practice merely allows a child to perfect those skills that maturation has made possible.

The Experiential or Practice Hypothesis

Although they would not deny that maturation is an important contributor to motor development, proponents of the experiential viewpoint believe that opportunities to practice motor skills are also important. Consider, for example, that the Hopi infants who spent their first 9 or 10 months on cradleboards had 3–4 months to move about and acquire motor skills before they finally began to walk. Even the "unpracticed" twins of the studies by McGraw (1935) and Gesell and Thompson (1929) were completely free to practice any number of other skills (such as grasping objects in their cribs, crawling, walking) that may have helped them to climb stairs or stack blocks when they were finally given an opportunity. Thus, the critics believe that practice is essential to motor development and that children might never learn to crawl, walk, run, jump, or throw if they are denied all opportunities to rehearse these basic skills. So what evidence is there that experience really matters?

Effects of lack of practice. Many years ago, Wayne Dennis (1960) studied two groups of institutionalized orphans in Iran who had spent most of their first two years lying flat on their backs in their cribs. These infants were never placed in a sitting position, were rarely played with, and were even fed in their cribs with their bottles propped on pillows. Was their motor development affected by these depriving early experiences? Indeed it was! None of the 1–2-year-olds could walk and less than half of them could even sit unaided. In fact, only 15% of the 3–4-year-olds could walk well alone! So Dennis concluded that maturation is *necessary but not sufficient* for the development of motor skills. In other words, infants who are physically capable of sitting, crawling, or walking will not be very proficient at these activities unless they have opportunities to practice them.

Cultural enrichment of motor experiences. Not only does a lack of practice inhibit motor development, but cross-cultural studies tell us that a variety of enriching experiences can accelerate the process. Brian Hopkins (1991), for example, has compared the motor development of white infants in England with that of black infants whose families had immigrated to England from Jamaica. As in several other comparisons of black and white infants, the black infants developed such important motor skills as sitting and walking at earlier ages (see also Super, 1981). Do these findings reflect genetic differences between blacks and whites? Probably not, because black babies were likely to acquire motor skills early only if their mothers had followed traditional Jamaican routines for handling infants and nurturing motor development. These routines include massaging infants, stretching their limbs, and holding them by the arms while gently shaking them up and down. Jamaican mothers expect early motor development, work to promote it, and achieve it.

Dovetailing nicely with the cross-cultural work are experiments conducted by Philip Zelazo and his associates (1972; 1993) with North American infants. Zelazo found that 2–8-week-old babies who were regularly held in an upright posture and encouraged to practice their *stepping reflex* showed a strengthening of this response (which usually disappears early in life; see Table 5-1). They also walked at an earlier age than did infants in a control group who did not receive this training.

Why might having one's limbs stretched or being held (or carried) in an upright posture hasten motor development? Esther Thelen's (1986; Thelen & Fisher, 1982)

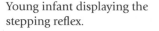

Young infant displaying the stepping reflex.

view is that babies who are often placed in an upright position will develop strength in the neck, trunk, and legs (an acceleration of muscular growth) which, in turn, will promote the early development of such motor skills as standing and walking. So it seems that both maturation and experience are important contributors to motor development. Maturation does place some limits on the age at which the child will first be capable of sitting, standing, and walking. Yet experiences such as upright posturing and various forms of practice may influence the age at which important physical capabilities are achieved and translated into action.

Motor Skills as Dynamic, Goal-Directed Systems

Until recently, developmentalists characterized infant motor skills as a series of preprogrammed actions or "structures" that will each appear when the time is right (as dictated by maturation and experience). Today, we know that each motor skill is not simply a preformed response that simply unfolds; instead, it is an intricate **action system** that gradually develops as an infant combines his existing capabilities into a new and more complex pattern of behavior.

Consider what Eugene Goldfield (1989) learned in studying infants' emerging ability to crawl. Goldfield found that 7–8-month-old infants began to crawl only after they (1) regularly turned and raised their heads toward interesting sights and sounds in the environment, (2) had developed a distinct hand/arm preference when reaching for such stimuli, and (3) had begun to thrust (kick) with the leg opposite to the outstretched arm. Apparently, visual orientation *motivates* the infant to approach interesting stimuli that she can't reach; reaching steers the body in the right direction; and kicking with the opposite leg propels the body forward. So far from being a preprogrammed skill that simply unfolds according to a grand maturational plan, crawling (and virtually all other motor skills) actually represents an intricate *reorganization* of *several existing capabilities* that is undertaken by a curious, active infant who has a particular *goal* in mind (see also Connolly & Dalgleish, 1989).

Why, then, do all infants proceed through the same sequence of locomotor milestones? Partly because of their human maturational programming, which sets the stage for various accomplishments, and partly because each successive motor skill must necessarily build on particular component activities that have developed earlier. How does experience fit in? According to the systems perspective, a real world of interesting objects and events provides infants with reasons to want to sit, walk, and crawl—that is, with *purposes* and *motives* that might be served by actually reorganizing their existing skills into new and more complex action systems. Of course, no two infants have exactly the same experiences, which may help to explain why each infant coordinates the component activities of an emerging motor skill in a slightly different way (see, for example, Thelen, 1995).

In sum, the development of motor skills is a whole lot more interesting and complex than earlier theories had assumed. Though maturation plays a very important role, the basic motor skills of the first two years emerge only after their component activities are practiced, perfected, and then combined into *totally novel patterns of action* by a curious, goal-driven infant whose purpose in so doing is to *achieve important objectives*.

Early Manipulatory Skills and Visual/Motor Coordination

The sequence of motor development described in Table 5-3 is concerned with skills that enable the child to sit, stand, and walk. Two other aspects of motor development also play important roles in the child's ability to adapt to the environment: manipulation of objects and visual/motor coordination.

An infant's ability to reach out and manipulate objects changes dramatically over the first year. Recall that newborns come equipped with a grasping reflex. They are also inclined to reach for things, although these primitive thrusts (or *prereaches*) are

action system: a more advanced motor skill that arises as the child combines and reorganizes existing skills.

The pincer grasp is a crucial motor milestone that underlies the development of many coordinated manual activities.

really little more than uncoordinated swipes at objects in the visual field. Prereaching is truly a hit-or-miss proposition (Bower, 1982). By 2 months of age, infants' reaching and grasping skills may even seem to deteriorate. The reflexive palmar grasp has disappeared, and prereaching occurs much less often (Bower, 1982). However, these apparent regressions are setting the stage for the appearance of *visually guided* reaching. Babies 3 months of age and older display this new competency as they extend their arms and make in-flight corrections, gradually improving in accuracy until they can reliably grasp their objectives (Hofsten, 1984; Thelen et al., 1993). Actually, there is some controversy about whether early reaching really is *visually* guided, for 3-month-old infants are just as successful at reaching for and grasping objects that they can only hear (in the dark) as they are at grabbing those that they can see (Clifton et al., 1993). Thus, early reaching may be guided as much (or more) by **proprioceptive information** from the arm muscles and joints as by visual cues per se.

Once an infant is able to reach inward across her body midline at about age 4 months, she will begin to grasp interesting objects with *both* hands, and her exploratory activities will forever change. Rather than merely batting or palming objects, she is now apt to hold them with one hand and finger them with the other (Rochat, 1989). Indeed, this fingering activity may be the primary method by which 4–6-month-olds gain information about objects, for their unimanual (one-handed) grasping skills are poorly developed: The reflexive palmar grasp has already disappeared by this age, and the **ulnar grasp** that replaces it (at about age 7 months) is itself a rather clumsy, clawlike grip that permits little tactile exploration of objects held this way.

During the latter half of the first year, fingering skills improve, and infants become much more proficient at tailoring all their exploratory activities to the properties of objects they are investigating (Palmer, 1989). Thus, wheeled toys are now apt to be scooted rather than banged, spongy objects are squeezed rather than scooted, and so on. The next major step in the growth of hand skills occurs near the end of the first year as infants use their thumbs and forefingers to lift and explore objects (Halverson, 1931). This **pincer grasp** transforms the child from a little fumbler into a skillful manipulator who may soon begin to corner crawling bugs and to turn knobs, dials, and rheostats, thereby discovering that he can use his newly acquired hand skills to produce any number of interesting results.

Throughout the second year, infants are becoming much more proficient with their hands. At 16 months of age, they can scribble with a crayon, and by the end of the second year, they can copy a simple horizontal or vertical line and even build towers of five or more blocks. What is happening is that the infant is gaining control over simple movements and then integrating these skills into increasingly complex, coordinated systems (Fentress & McLeod, 1986). Building a tower, for example, requires the child to first gain control over the thumb and the forefinger and then use the pincer grip as part of a larger action sequence that involves reaching for a block, grasping it, laying it squarely on top of another block, and then delicately releasing it. But despite their newly acquired ability to combine simple motor activities into increasingly complex sequences, 2- to 3-year-olds are not very good at catching and throwing a ball, cutting food with silverware, or drawing within the lines of their coloring books. These skills will emerge later in childhood as the muscles mature and children become more proficient at using visual information to help them coordinate their actions.

Psychological Implications of Early Motor Development

Life changes dramatically for both parents and infants once a baby is able to reach out and grasp interesting objects, especially after he can crawl or walk there himself to explore these treasures. Suddenly, parents may find they have to childproof their homes, or limit access to certain areas, or else run the risk of experiencing a

proprioceptive information: sensory information from the muscles, tendons, and joints that help one to locate the position of one's body (or body parts) in space.

ulnar grasp: an early manipulatory skill in which an infant grasps objects by pressing the fingers against the palm.

pincer grasp: a grasp in which the thumb is used in opposition to the fingers, enabling an infant to become more dexterous at lifting and fondling objects.

Life becomes more challenging for parents as infants perfect their motor skills.

seemingly endless string of disasters, including torn books, overturned vases, unraveled rolls of toilet paper, and irritable pets whose tails the little explorer has pulled. Nevertheless, many parents are thrilled by their infant's emerging motor skills, which not only provide clear evidence that development is proceeding normally, but also permit such pleasurable forms of social interaction as pat-a-cake, chase, and hide-and-seek.

Aside from the entertainment value it provides, a baby's increasing control over bodily movements has other important cognitive and social consequences as well. Mobile infants may feel much more bold, for example, about meeting people and seeking challenges if they know that they can retreat to their caregivers for comfort should they feel insecure (Ainsworth, 1979). Achieving various motor milestones may also foster perceptual development. For example, crawlers (as well as noncrawlers who are made mobile with the aid of special walkers) are better able to search for and find hidden objects than infants of the same age who are not mobile (Kermoian & Campos, 1988). And as we will see in Chapter 6, crawling and walking both contribute to an understanding of distance relationships and a healthy fear of heights (Adolph, Eppler, & Gibson, 1993; Campos, Bertenthal, & Kermoian, 1992). So once again, we see that human development is a *holistic* enterprise; changes in motor skills have clear implications for other aspects of development.

Beyond Infancy: Motor Development in Childhood

The term *toddler* aptly describes most 1–2-year-olds, who, like the notorious drunken sailor, often fall down or trip over stationary objects when they try to get somewhere in a hurry. But as children mature, their locomotor skills increase by "leaps and bounds." By age 3, children can walk or run in a straight line and leap off the floor with both feet, although they can clear only very small (8–10-inch) objects in a single bound and cannot easily turn or stop while running. Four-year-olds can skip, hop on one foot, catch a large ball with both hands, and run much farther and faster than they could one year earlier (Corbin, 1973). By age 5, children are becoming rather graceful: Like adults, they pump their arms when they run, and their balance has improved to the point that some of them can learn to ride a bicycle. With each passing year, school-age children can run a little faster, jump a little higher, and throw a

Top-heavy toddlers often lose their balance when they try to move very quickly.

ball a little further (Herkowitz, 1978; Keough & Sugden, 1985). Part of the reason that children are improving at these large-muscle activities is that they are growing larger and stronger. But they are also fine-tuning their motor skills. As shown in Figure 5-4, young children throw only with the arm, whereas adolescents are usually able to coordinate shoulder, arm, and leg movements to put their bodies behind their throws. So older children and adolescents can throw farther than younger children can, not solely because they are bigger and stronger, but because they also use more refined and efficient techniques of movement (Gallahue, 1989).

At the same time, eye/hand coordination and control of the small muscles are improving rapidly so that children can make more and more sophisticated use of their hands. Three-year-olds find it difficult to button their shirts, tie their shoes, or copy simple designs. By age 5, children can accomplish all of these feats and can even cut a straight line with scissors or copy letters and numbers with a crayon. By age 8 or 9, they can use household tools such as screwdrivers and have become skilled performers at games such as jacks and Tetris that require eye/hand coordination. Finally, older children display quicker **reaction times** than younger children do (Wilkinson & Allison, 1989)—a fact that helps to explain why they usually beat younger playmates at "action" games such as dodgeball or table tennis.

Boys and girls are nearly equal in physical abilities until puberty, when males gain on tests of large-muscle activities, whereas females level off or decline (Thomas & French, 1985; see Figure 5-5). These sex differences are, in part, attributable to biology: Adolescent males have more muscle and less fat than adolescent females and might be expected to outperform them on tests of physical strength (Tanner, 1990). Yet these biological developments do not account for all of the difference in large-muscle performance between boys and girls (Smoll & Schutz, 1990), nor do they adequately explain the *declining* performance of girls, who continue to grow taller, heavier, and presumably stronger between ages 12 and 17. Jacqueline Herkowitz (1978)

reaction time: a measure of the time it takes for a person to respond motorically to a test stimulus (for example, the time between seeing a flash and pressing a button).

Figure 5-4
As these initial tosses and mature throws illustrate, large-muscle activities become more refined and efficient with age (above).

Figure 5-5
Age and sex differences on two tests of large-muscle activity (below).
From Johnson & Buskirk, 1974.

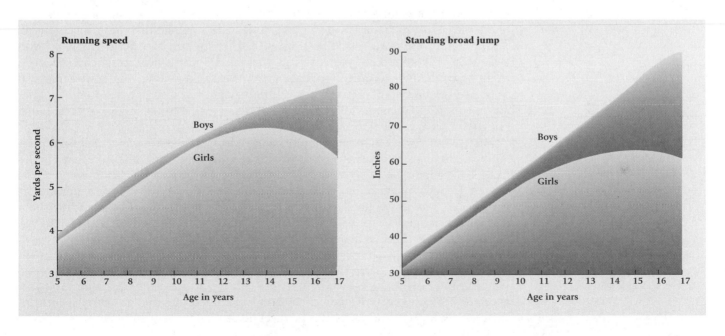

believes that the apparent physical decline of adolescent females is a product of sex-role socialization: With the widening of the hips and development of breasts, girls are often encouraged to become less tomboyish and more interested in traditionally feminine (and more sedentary) activities.

There is clearly an element of truth to Herkowitz's sex-typing hypothesis. Consider, for example, that female *athletes* show no apparent decline in physical performance over time; moreover, studies of world records in track, swimming, and cycling suggest that, as gender roles have changed in the past few decades, women have been improving their performances, and the male/female gap in physical performance has narrowed dramatically (Dyer, 1977; Whipp & Ward, 1992). The implications of these findings are clear: Adolescent girls would almost certainly continue to improve on tests of large-muscle activity if they chose to remain physically active.

▶ PUBERTY: THE PHYSICAL TRANSITION FROM CHILD TO ADULT

The onset of adolescence is heralded by two significant changes in physical development. First, children change dramatically in size and shape as they enter the **adolescent growth spurt.** They also reach **puberty** (from the Latin word *pubertas*, meaning "to grow hairy"), the point in life when an individual reaches sexual maturity and becomes capable of producing a child.

In this section of the chapter, we will first consider the physical changes that occur during the adolescent years as the child loses that "boyish" or "girlish" look and begins to resemble an adult. And in considering the physical events of adolescence from the perspective of the teenager who experiences them, we will discover that these dramatic biological upheavals play a major role in shaping a teenager's self-concept, which, in turn, may affect the ways he or she relates to other people later in life.

The Adolescent Growth Spurt

The term *growth spurt* describes the rapid acceleration in height and weight that marks the beginning of adolescence. Girls typically enter the growth spurt by age 10½, reach a peak growth rate by age 12, and return to a slower rate of growth by age 13–13½ (Tanner, 1981). Boys lag behind girls by two to three years. They typically begin their growth spurt by age 13, peak at age 14, and return to a more gradual rate of growth by age 16. Because girls mature much earlier than boys, it is not at all uncommon for females to be the tallest two or three students in a junior high school classroom.

In addition to growing taller and heavier, the body assumes an adultlike appearance during the adolescent growth spurt. Perhaps the most noticeable changes are a widening of the hips for girls and a broadening of the shoulders for boys. Facial features also assume adult proportions as the forehead protrudes, the nose and jaw become more prominent, and the lips enlarge. Gone forever is that soft-featured, innocent look that we associate with childhood.

The adolescent growth spurt is not as uniform as our overview might indicate. Body weight begins to increase first, followed four to six months later by a rapid increase in height (Tanner, 1990). The muscles are growing along with the rest of the body, although the period of greatest muscular development does not occur until a year after the maximum acceleration in height. And because this "muscle spurt" happens earlier for girls than for boys, there is a brief period when the average girl has as much or more muscle than most boys her age.

Sexual Maturation

Maturation of the reproductive system occurs at roughly the same time as the adolescent growth spurt and follows a predictable sequence for members of each sex.

adolescent growth spurt: the rapid increase in physical growth that marks the beginning of adolescence.

puberty: the point at which a person reaches sexual maturity and is physically capable of fathering or conceiving a child.

Sexual Development in Girls

For most girls, sexual maturation begins at about age 11 as fatty tissue accumulates around their nipples, forming small "breast buds." Usually pubic hair begins to appear a little later, although as many as one-third of all girls develop some pubic hair before the breasts begin to develop (Tanner, 1990).

As a girl enters her height spurt, the breasts grow rapidly and the sex organs begin to mature. Internally, the vagina becomes larger, and the walls of the uterus develop a powerful set of muscles that may one day be used to accommodate a fetus during pregnancy and to push it through the cervix and vagina during the birth process. Externally, the mons pubis (the soft tissue covering the pubic bone), the labia (the fleshy lips surrounding the vaginal opening), and the clitoris all increase in size and become more sensitive to tactile stimulation (Tanner, 1990).

At about age 12½–13, or fully two years after the onset of breast development, the average girl in Western societies reaches **menarche**—the time of her first menstruation. Through it is generally assumed that a girl becomes sexually mature at menarche, young girls often menstruate without ovulating and *may* remain functionally sterile for 12–18 months after menarche (Tanner, 1978). Within a year of menarche, female sexual development is nearly complete. The young woman's breasts and pubic hair will have fully developed and underarm hair appears.

Sexual Development in Boys

For boys, sexual maturation begins at about 11–12 with the initial enlargement of the testes. The growth of the testes is often accompanied or soon followed by the appearance of unpigmented pubic hair. By the time the penis is fully developed at age 14½–15, most boys will have reached puberty and are now capable of fathering a child. Spontaneous ejaculations of seminal fluid may occur even earlier; but just as girls often do not ovulate until some time after puberty, many boys do not produce any viable sperm for months after their first ejaculations (Tanner, 1978).

Somewhat later, boys begin to sprout facial hair, first at the corners of the upper lip and finally on the chin and jawline. Body hair also grows on the arms and legs, although that "hoped-for" matting of chest hair may not appear until the late teens or early twenties, if at all. Another hallmark of male sexual maturity is a lowering of the voice as the larynx grows and the vocal cords lengthen. In fact, many men may laugh (years later) about hearing their voices "crack" uncontrollably up and down between a squeaky soprano and a deep baritone, sometimes within a single sentence.

Individual Differences in Physical and Sexual Maturation

So far, we have been describing developmental norms, or the average ages when adolescent changes take place. But as Figure 5-6 indicates, there are great individual differences in the timing of physical and sexual maturation. An early-maturing girl who develops breast buds at age 8, starts her growth spurt at age 9½, and reaches menarche at age 10½ may nearly complete her growth and pubertal development before the late-developing girls in her class have even begun. Individual differences among boys are at least as great: Some boys reach sexual maturity by age 12½ and are as tall as they will ever be by age 13, whereas others begin growing later than that and do not reach puberty until their late teens. This perfectly normal biological variation may be observed in any junior high classroom, where one will find a wide assortment of bodies, ranging from those that are entirely childlike to those that are very adultlike.

Secular Trends: Are We Maturing Earlier?

Recently, the females in one family were surprised when a member of the younger generation began to menstruate shortly after her 12th birthday. The inevitable comparisons soon began, as the girl learned that neither of her great-grandmothers had

menarche: the first occurrence of menstruation.

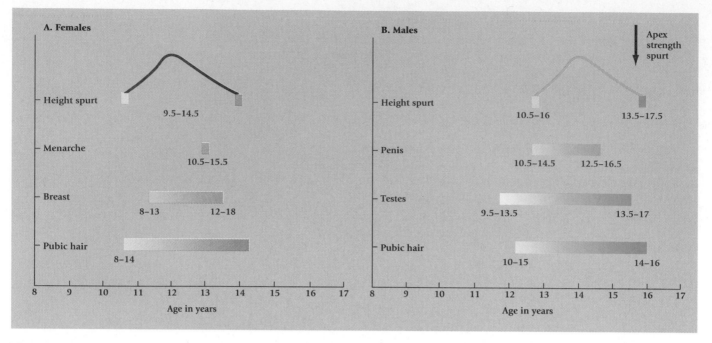

Figure 5-6
Sequence of events in the sexual maturation of females (A) and males (B). The numbers represent the variation among individuals in the ages at which each aspect of sexual maturation begins or ends. For example, we see that the growth of the penis may begin as early as age 10½ or as late as 14½.
From Tanner, 1990.

reached this milestone until age 15 and that her grandmother had been nearly 14 and her mother almost 13. At this point, the girl casually replied "Big deal! Lots of girls in my class have got their periods."

As it turns out, this young lady was simply "telling it like it is." In 1900, when her great-grandmother was born, the average age of first menstruation was 14–15. By 1950, most girls were reaching menarche between 13½ and 14, and today's norms have dropped even further, to age 12½ (Tanner, 1981). This **secular trend** toward earlier maturation started more than 100 years ago in the industrialized nations of the world, where it has recently leveled off, and it is now happening in the more prosperous nonindustrialized countries as well. In addition, people in industrialized nations have been growing taller and heavier over the past century.

What explains these secular trends? Better nutrition and advances in medical care seem to be most responsible (Tanner, 1990). Today's children are more likely than their parents or grandparents to reach their genetic potentials for maturation and growth because they are better fed and less likely to experience growth-retarding illnesses. Even within our own relatively affluent society, poorly nourished adolescents mature later than well-nourished ones do. Whereas overweight girls tend to mature early, many dancers, gymnasts, and other girls who engage regularly in strenuous physical activity may begin menstruating very late or stop menstruating after they have begun (Hopwood et al., 1990). Similarly, undernourished boys mature later and produce fewer viable sperm than their well-fed peers do (Frisch, 1983). Here, then, is a strong clue that nature and nurture *interact* to influence the timing of pubertal events.

Some Psychological Effects of Pubertal Development

What do adolescents think about the dramatic physical changes they are experiencing? In Western cultures, girls typically become quite concerned about their appearance and worry about how other people will respond to them (Greif & Ulman, 1982). In general, teenage girls hope to be perceived as attractive, and changes that are congruent with the "feminine ideal" are often welcomed. When breasts appear early in maturation, for example, many girls feel better about themselves and their abilities (Brooks-Gunn & Warren, 1988). Otherwise, adolescent females may be very concerned that they are growing too tall or too fat, and even well-proportioned teenage

secular trend: a trend in industrialized societies toward earlier maturation and greater body size now than in the past.

During early adolescence, girls are maturing more rapidly than boys.

girls often try to compensate for perceived physical inadequacies by slouching, wearing flats, or trying an endless number of fad diets. (For examples of what can happen if a girl becomes overly preoccupied with her weight, see Box 5-4).

Girls' reactions to menarche are mixed (Greif & Ulman, 1982). They are often a bit excited but may be somewhat confused as well, especially if they mature very early or have not been told what to expect (Brooks-Gunn, 1988). Few girls today are traumatized by menarche, but at the same time, few are overjoyed about becoming a woman (Ruble & Brooks-Gunn, 1982).

What about boys? Their body images are more positive than those of girls, and they are more likely to welcome their weight gain (Richards, Boxer, Petersen, & Albrecht, 1990). Teenage boys also hope to be tall, hairy, and handsome, and they may become preoccupied with the aspects of body image that center on physical and athletic prowess (Berscheid, Walster, & Bohrnstedt, 1973). Whereas menarche is a memorable event for girls, boys are often only dimly aware of the physical changes they are experiencing (Zani, 1991). When Alan Gaddis and Jeanne Brooks-Gunn (1985) interviewed a small sample of boys about their first ejaculation, they found that few boys told anyone. However, these boys seemed somewhat more positive about this sign of manhood and happier to be "grown up" than girls typically are about their first menstruation.

Changes in Parent-Child Relationships

Adolescents who are maturing physically and sexually not only begin to feel differently about themselves but they are viewed and treated differently by other people. Laurence Steinberg (1981, 1988) has examined changes in family relations. Around age 11 to 13, when pubertal changes are peaking, adolescents become more independent, less close to their parents, and more likely to experience conflicts with their parents, especially with their mothers (see also Hill, 1988). These conflicts are rarely severe; it's more often bickering about unmade beds, late hours, and loud music than arguments about core values, but it can be unpleasant nonetheless. Fortunately,

BOX 5-4
Two Serious Dieting Disorders of Adolescence

*T*hirty years ago, a young British model nicknamed "Twiggy" defined the height of fashion. As her name implied, Twiggy was very thin. And the attention she received from the popular media sent a none-too-subtle message to women around the Western world: skinny is beautiful, and it is a tragedy to be fat.

Unfortunately, some adolescents carry this maxim to a life-threatening extreme. **Anorexia nervosa** (or "nervous loss of appetite") is a potentially fatal eating disorder—one without any known organic cause—that may affect as many as 1 of every 200 adolescent girls (as compared with 1 in 2000 adolescent boys or adult females). Anorexics have a morbid fear of becoming obese and will do whatever they can to purge their bodies of fat. The typical anorexic is a quiet, obedient teenage girl from a middle-class or affluent family who suddenly begins to starve herself soon after experiencing the bodily changes associated with menarche. The process seems harmless at first as the young woman sets a modest goal and diets to the desired weight. But once she reaches her target, the anorexic simply continues to diet, eating less and less until she is little more than skin and bones. After she loses 20%–30% of her body weight, secondary sex characteristics (breasts and hips) may be scarcely noticeable, and menstruation often stops. And even though she may resemble a walking skeleton, the 60–70-pound anorexic will insist that she is well-nourished and will feel that she could stand to lose a few more pounds (Hsu, 1990).

Why do relatively few girls become anorexic, even though nearly all of them experience social pressure to be thin? Genetic factors may predispose some individuals to develop the disorder, for anorexia runs in families (Fisher & Brone, 1991). Yet eating disorders may rarely emerge unless a susceptible girl also experiences disturbed family relationships that trigger compulsive dieting. According to Salvador Minuchin and his associates (1978), most anorexics have trouble making decisions and forming a personal identity. Why? Because their parents tend to be firm, overprotective guardians who tolerate little dissent or negative emotionality. The result may be a young woman who can't seem to break free of her parents and who desperately hopes to establish some sense of control over her life, which she thinks she can do by dieting (Smolak & Levine, 1993).

Family therapy seems to be the most effective treatment for anorexia nervosa. Treatment may begin by hospitalizing the patient to tube-feed her (if her life is in danger) or to apply behavioral modification techniques (for example, rewarding her with praise and privileges for gaining weight)

to change her eating habits. Once the patient begins to eat, family therapy is initiated. The purpose of therapy is to persuade parents to exert less control over the adolescent's activities while convincing the anorexic that she can achieve autonomy and higher self-esteem through means other than self-starvation. Unfortunately, fewer than half of treated anorexics make a complete recovery (Zerbe, 1993), with the best prognosis for younger patients who have been ill less than three years (Russell et al., 1987). By contrast, only 25%–30% of *untreated* anorexics show any improvement, and as many as 5%–10% of them will end up committing suicide or starving themselves to death (Hsu, 1990).

Bulimia is another serious eating disorder that is much more common than anorexia. Bulimics are binge eaters who may consume several times their normal daily caloric intake in a single sitting and then purge themselves of this feast by vomiting or taking laxatives. Although anorexics are often bulimics, most who suffer from bulimia are of normal weight or slightly overweight. Like anorexics, bulimic individuals tend to have poor body images and are overly concerned about getting fat. However, bulimics differ from anorexics in that they are often extroverted and impulsive rather than quiet and reserved, and they are far more likely than anorexics to experience open conflict and a lack of affection in their homes (Smolak & Levine, 1993). Bulimia is most common among college-age populations, where as many as 5% of women (and less than 1% of men) regularly partake in this "binge/purge" syndrome (Hsu, 1990).

Like anorexia, bulimia can have any number of very serious side effects. Laxatives and diuretics used as purging agents can deplete the body of potassium and induce cardiac arrhythmia and heart attacks. Regular induction of vomiting can produce hernias, and bulimics have even drowned in their own vomit (Seabrook, 1987). Finally, binge eating is hardly a constructive approach to most problems, particularly for someone who is concerned about getting fat. So it is perhaps understandable that many bulimics are depressed and that some turn to suicide as a solution for their problems.

Treatment for bulimia includes individual psychotherapy, designed to help the patient understand the causes and control of binging, and antidepressant medication for those bulimics who show signs of clinical depression. Although most bulimics respond favorably to treatment (see Hsu, 1990, for a literature review), it has been estimated that the majority of affected individuals never recognize that they have a potentially serious problem and may continue to binge without ever seeking help.

Early-maturing males tend to be poised and confident in social settings and popular with their peers.

parent-child relationships become warmer again once the pubertal transition is completed (Hill, 1988; Paikoff & Brooks-Gunn, 1991).

Higher and more variable levels of sex hormones in early adolescence also heighten sexual motivation (Udry, 1990) and may help to explain increased conflict with parents and the increased moodiness and restlessness that many adolescents display (Buchanan, Eccles, & Becker, 1992). Overall, then, biological changes and changes in the social environment that accompany them *interact* to influence the way each individual experiences adolescence (Larson & Ham, 1993; Paikoff & Brooks-Gunn, 1991).

Does Timing of Puberty Matter?

Think back for a moment to your own adolescence—to that point when you first realized that you were rapidly becoming a man or a woman. Did this happen to you earlier than to your friends, or later? Do you think that the timing of these events could have influenced your personality or social life?

Timing of puberty does have some meaningful social implications, although its impact differs somewhat for males and females. Let's first consider the findings for boys and men.

Possible impacts on males. Longitudinal studies conducted by researchers at the University of California suggests that boys who mature early enjoy a number of social advantages over boys who mature late. One study followed the development of 16 early-maturing and 16 late-maturing male adolescents over a six-year period, and found late maturers to be more eager, anxious, and attention-seeking (and also rated less masculine and less physically attractive) than early maturers (Jones & Bayley, 1950). Moreover, early maturers tended to be poised and confident in social settings and were more likely to win athletic honors and election to student offices. Although this study was based on only 32 boys in California, other researchers have found that late-maturing males tend to feel somewhat socially inadequate and inferior (Duke et al., 1982; Livson & Peskin, 1980). Late-maturing boys also have lower educational aspirations than early maturers do, and they even score lower early in adolescence on school achievement tests (Dubas, Graber, & Petersen, 1991).

anorexia nervosa: a life-threatening eating disorder characterized by self-starvation and a compulsive fear of getting fat.

bulimia: a life-threatening eating disorder characterized by recurrent eating binges followed by such purging activities as heavy use of laxatives or vomiting.

Why is the early-maturing boy in such an advantageous position? One reason may be that his greater size and strength often make him a more capable athlete, which in turn is apt to bring social recognition from adults and peers (Simmons & Blyth, 1987). The early maturer's adultlike appearance may also prompt others to overestimate his competencies and to grant him privileges and responsibilities normally reserved for older individuals. Indeed, parents hold higher educational and achievement aspirations for early-maturing than for late-maturing sons (Duke et al., 1982), and they have fewer conflicts with early maturers about issues such as acceptable curfews and choice of friends (Savin-Williams & Small, 1986). Perhaps you can see how this generally positive, harmonious atmosphere might promote the poise or self-confidence that enables early maturers to become popular and to assume positions of leadership within the peer group. By contrast, if parents, teachers, and peers continue to treat a "boyish-looking" late maturer as if he were somehow less competent or less worthy of privileges or responsibility, it is easy to see how he could become unsure of himself and feel somewhat inferior.

Do these differences between early and late maturers persist into adulthood? In general, they fade over time. By 12th grade, for example, differences in academic performance between early and late maturers have already disappeared (Dubas et al., 1991). And there are some interesting twists in the plot. Jones (1965), for example, found that early-maturing boys from the University of California study were still somewhat more sociable, confident, and responsible in their 30s than their peers who had matured later in adolescence. So some of the advantages of early maturation carried over into adulthood. Yet these early maturers were also more rigid and conforming than the late maturers, who as men seemed more able to be playful and innovative and to cope with ambiguous situations. Possibly their need to struggle with the problems of being "late" helped late-maturing boys to be flexible and develop mental coping skills. By contrast, early-maturing boys may have been pushed into stereotyped adult roles before they really had much time to experiment.

Possible impacts on females. For girls, maturing early may be somewhat of a *disadvantage*. Although early breast development is associated with a favorable body image and increased *self-confidence* (Brooks-Gunn & Warren, 1988), several studies find that early-maturing girls are somewhat *less* outgoing and *less* popular than their prepubertal classmates (Aro & Taipale, 1987; Clausen, 1975; Faust, 1960) and are likely to report more symptoms of depression as well (Brooks-Gunn & Petersen, 1991). Intuitively, these findings make some sense. A girl who matures very early may look very different from female classmates, who may tease her, and from boys in the class, who will not mature for 3 to 4 years and are not yet all that enthused about the early maturer's more womanly attributes. As a result, early-maturing girls often seek older companions, who will often steer them away from academic pursuits and into less desirable activities such as smoking, drinking, drug use, and sex (Caspi et al., 1993; Stattin & Magnusson, 1990). However, the curses of early maturity (if any) appear to be short-lived for many girls, for these rapid developers are often admired later in junior high when the female peer group develops a strong interest in boy-girl relationships, and discovers that early-maturers tend to be popular with the guys (Faust, 1960). As young adults, women who matured early are no less well-adjusted than their late-maturing peers (Stattin & Magnusson, 1990); in fact, some evidence even suggests that they are more self-directed and better able to cope with challenges than late-developing women (Livson & Peskin, 1980).

Overall, then, both the advantages of maturing early and the disadvantages of maturing late are greater for males than for females. But even though late-maturing boys and early-maturing girls are more likely to find the adolescent period disruptive, the psychological differences between early and late maturers become smaller and more mixed in nature by adulthood. Finally, let us note that the differences between early and late maturers are not large and that many individuals will not necessarily mirror the patterns described above. As we will see in Chapters 12 and 16, many factors contribute to a person's self-image and social status, and timing of puberty is but one variable in this rather complex equation.

Concept Check 5-2 ⌵ Psychological Aspects of Physical and Motor Development

Check your understanding of some of the psychological aspects of physical and motor development by filling in the blanks in each of the statements below. The answers appear in the Appendix.

1. According to the "systems" model of motor development, an infant's tendency to _____ _____ is an important contributor to the emergence of such motor skills as reaching, crawling, and walking.

2. Infants may feel much bolder about meeting new people and seeking challenges *once they achieve* such motor milestones as _____ and can _____ _____ _____.

3. The events of puberty often result in an apparent *decline* in the strength of adolescent girls, owing largely to _____-_____ socialization. Boys are generally more _____ than girls about gaining weight, and some girls are so concerned about their weight that they may threaten their own lives by becoming _____ or _____ .

4. _____ with parents often increase as pubertal changes are peaking. Early maturation seems to be a social _____ for boys, a social _____ for girls—consequences which _____ over time.

 ## CAUSES AND CORRELATES OF PHYSICAL DEVELOPMENT

Although we have now charted the course of physical development from birth through adolescence, we've touched only briefly on the specific factors that influence growth. What *really* causes children to grow in the first place? And why do their bodies change so dramatically at adolescence, when growth accelerates? These thought questions normally provoke a lot of discussion in my own classes. Typically, someone will first offer a biological explanation, arguing that our genotypes and maturational timetables determine the rate and extent of physical growth, as well as the sequencing and timing of motor development. But invariably, other students point out that environmental factors such as nutrition or opportunities to practice motor skills may also influence physical development. By the end of the discussion, students usually conclude that physical growth and development represent a complex interplay between biological predispositions and environmental influences, with biology assuming the more dominant role. Now let's consider the data that have led many developmentalists to agree with this conclusion.

Biological Mechanisms

Clearly, biological factors play a major role in the growth process. Although children do not all grow at the same rate, we have seen that the *sequencing* of both physical maturation and motor development is reasonably consistent from child to child. Apparently, these regular maturational sequences that all humans share are species-specific attributes—products of our common genetic heritage.

Effects of Individual Genotypes

Aside from our common genetic ties to the human race, we have each inherited a unique combination of genes that will affect our physical growth and development. For example, family studies clearly indicate that stature is a heritable attribute: Identical twins are much more similar in stature than fraternal twins, whether the measurements are taken during the first year of life, at 4 years of age, or in early adulthood (Tanner, 1990; Wilson, 1976).

Rate of maturation is also heritable. James Tanner (1990) reports that female identical twins who live together reach menarche within 2–3 months of each other, whereas fraternal twin sisters are typically about 10 months apart. Tanner concludes that this genetic control of growth rate "operates throughout the whole process of growth, for skeletal maturity at all ages shows the same type of family correlations as menarche. The age of eruption of the teeth is similarly controlled [by one's genotype]" (p. 128).

Of course, knowing that genotype affects attributes such as stature and "rate of maturation" is only part of the story. The next logical question is "*How* does genotype influence growth?" To be honest, we are not completely certain, although it appears that our genes regulate the production of hormones, which, in turn, have a major effect on physical growth and development.

Hormonal Influences: The Endocrinology of Growth

Hormones begin to influence development long before a child is born. As we learned in Chapter 4, a male fetus assumes a malelike appearance because (1) a gene on his Y chromosome triggers the development of testes, which (2) secrete a male hormone (testosterone) that is necessary for the development of a male reproductive system. By the fourth prenatal month, the thyroid gland has formed and begins to produce **thyroxine,** a hormone that is essential if the brain and nervous system are to develop properly. Babies born with a thyroid deficiency soon become mentally handicapped if this condition goes undiagnosed and untreated (Tanner, 1990). Those who develop a thyroid deficiency later in childhood will not suffer brain damage, because their brain growth spurt is over. However, they will begin to grow very slowly, a finding that indicates that a certain level of thyroxine is necessary for normal growth and development.

Perhaps the most critical of the *endocrine* (hormone-secreting) glands is the **pituitary,** a "master gland" located at the base of the brain that triggers the release of hormones from all other endocrine glands. For example, the thyroid gland secretes thyroxine only if instructed to do so by a pituitary hormone called *thyroid-stimulating hormone,* or *TSH*. In addition to regulating the endocrine system, the pituitary produces a **growth hormone (GH)** that stimulates the rapid growth and development of body cells. Growth hormone is released in small amounts several times a day. When parents tell their children that lots of sleep helps one to grow big and strong, they are right: GH is normally secreted into the bloodstream about 60–90 minutes after a child falls asleep (Tanner, 1990). And GH is essential for *normal* growth and development. Children who lack this hormone do grow, and they are usually well proportioned as adults. However, they will stand only about 130 cm tall—a little over 4 feet (Tanner, 1990).

During infancy and childhood, physical growth seems to be regulated by thyroxine and the pituitary growth hormone. What, then, triggers the adolescent growth spurt and other pubertal changes?

Recent research (reviewed in Tanner, 1990) has clarified the endrocrinology of adolescence far beyond what we knew only a few years ago. Long before any noticeable physical changes occur, the hypothalamus (a part of the brain) instructs the pituitary to release *follicle stimulating hormone (FSH)* and *luteinizing hormone (LH)* which, in turn, cause a girl's ovaries to produce more **estrogen** and a boy's testes to produce more **testosterone.** Once estrogen in girls and testosterone in boys reach certain critical levels, the hypothalamus instructs the pituitary to secrete more growth hormone (GH). This increase in GH seems to be wholly responsible for the adolescent growth spurt in girls and is primarily responsible for the boys' growth spurt. As for sexual maturation, the female hormone estrogen is what triggers the growth of a girl's breasts, uterus, vagina, pubic and underarm hair, and the widening of her hips. In boys, testosterone is responsible for growth of the penis and prostate, voice changes,

thyroxine: a hormone produced by the thyroid gland, essential for normal growth of the brain and the body.

pituitary: a "master gland" located at the base of the brain that regulates the endocrine glands and produces growth hormone.

growth hormone (GH): the pituitary hormone that stimulates the rapid growth and development of body cells; primarily responsible for the adolescent growth spurt.

estrogen: female sex hormone, produced by the ovaries, that is responsible for female sexual maturation.

testosterone: male sex hormone, produced by the testes, that is responsible for male sexual maturation.

and the development of facial and body hair. And although GH may be the primary contributor to the male growth spurt, testosterone exerts its own independent effects on the growth of a boy's muscles, the broadening of his shoulders, and the extension of his backbone. So it seems that adolescent boys experience larger growth spurts than adolescent girls do simply because testosterone promotes muscular and bone growth in ways that estrogen does not.

It was once believed that androgen secreted by the adrenal glands was what triggered the female growth spurt and the development of a girl's pubic and body hair. However, recent research suggests that if adrenal androgens affect growth at all, they play only a secondary role to other hormones in promoting the development of muscles and bones (see Tanner, 1990).

What causes the pituitary to activate the endocrine glands, thereby precipitating the dramatic physical changes of adolescence? No one can say for sure. We know that skeletal maturity, which seems to be genetically controlled, is an excellent predictor of when menarche will occur (Tanner, 1990). Yet, any simple "genetic clock" theory that focuses on a singular precipitating influence is probably oversimplified, for the timing of breast growth, testicular development, and many other pubertal events is not closely synchronized with skeletal age (or with each other). So we have learned a great deal about *how* hormones affect human growth and development (see Table 5-4 for a brief review). However, the events responsible for the timing and regulation of these hormonal influences remain obscure.

Environmental Influences

Three kinds of environmental influence can have a profound effect on physical growth and development: nutrition, illnesses, and insensitive caregiving that produces emotional stress.

Nutrition

Diet is perhaps the most potent environmental influence on human growth and development. As you might expect, children who are inadequately nourished grow very slowly, if at all. The dramatic effect of malnutrition on physical development can

---

Table 5-4 **Hormonal Influences on Growth and Development**

Endocrine gland	Hormones produced	Effects on growth and development
Pituitary	Growth hormone (GH)	Regulates growth from birth through adolescence; triggers adolescent growth spurt.
	Activating hormones:	
	Thyroid-secreting hormone (TSH)	Instructs thyroid to secrete thyroxine.
	Follicle-stimulating hormone (FSH)	Instructs ovaries to produce estrogens.
	Luteinizing hormone (LH)	Instructs testes to produce testosterone.
Thyroid	Thyroxine	Affects growth and development of the brain and helps to regulate growth of the body during childhood.
Testes	Testosterone	Is responsible for development of the male reproductive system during the prenatal period; directs male sexual development during adolescence.
Ovaries	Estrogen	Directs female sexual development during adolescence.
Adrenal glands	Adrenal androgens	Play a supportive role in the development of muscle and bones.

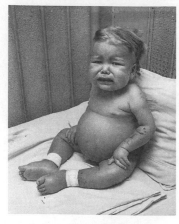

The lesions on this little boy's skin and his swollen stomach are symptoms of kwashiorkor. Without adequate protein in his diet, this child will be more susceptible to many diseases and may die from an illness that well-nourished children could easily overcome.

be seen by comparing the heights of children before and during wartime periods when food is scarce. In Figure 5-7, we see that the average heights of schoolchildren in Oslo, Norway increased between 1920 and 1940—the period between the two world wars. However, this secular trend was clearly reversed during World War II, when it was not always possible to satisfy children's nutritional needs.

Problems of undernutrition. If undernutrition is neither prolonged nor especially severe, children will usually recover from any growth deficits by growing much faster than normal once their diet becomes adequate. James Tanner (1990) views this **catch-up growth** as a basic principle of physical development. Presumably, children who have experienced short-term growth deficits because of malnutrition will grow very rapidly in order to regain (or catch up to) their genetically programmed growth trajectory.

However, prolonged undernutrition has a more serious impact, especially during the first five years of life. Brain growth may be seriously retarded, and the child may remain relatively small in stature (Barrett & Frank, 1987; Tanner, 1990). These findings make sense when we recall that the first five years is a period when the brain will normally gain about 65% of its eventual adult weight and the body will grow to nearly two-thirds of its adult height.

In many of the developing countries of Africa, Asia, and Latin American, as many as 85% of all children under age 5 experience one form of undernutrition or another (Barrett & Frank, 1987). When children are severely undernourished, they are likely to suffer from either of two nutritional diseases—**marasmus** and **kwashiorkor**—each of which has a slightly different cause. Marasmus affects babies who get insufficient protein and too few calories, as can easily occur if a mother is malnourished and does not have the resources to provide her child with a nutritious commercial substitute for mother's milk. A victim of marasmus becomes very frail and wrinkled in appearance as growth stops and the body tissues begin to waste away. Even if these children survive, they will remain small in stature and often suffer impaired social and intellectual development (Barrett & Frank, 1987).

Kwashiorkor affects children who get enough calories but little if any protein. As the disease progresses, the child's hair thins, the face, legs, and abdomen swell with water, and severe skin lesions may develop. In many poor countries of the world, about the only high-quality source of protein readily available to children is mother's milk. So breast-fed infants will not ordinarily suffer from marasmus unless their mothers are severely malnourished; however, they may develop kwashiorkor when they are weaned from the breast and thereby denied their primary source of protein.

In Western industrialized countries, the preschool children who experience protein/calorie deficiencies are rarely so malnourished as to develop marasmus or kwashiorkor. However, **vitamin and mineral deficiencies** affect large numbers of children in the United States, particularly African American and Latino children from lower socioeconomic backgrounds (Pollitt, 1994). Especially common among infants and toddlers are iron (and zinc) deficiencies that occur because rapid growth early in life requires more of these minerals than a young child's diet normally provides. Prolonged iron deficiency causes **iron-deficiency anemia,** which not only makes children irritable, inattentive, and listless, but also retards their growth rates and is associated with poor performances on tests of motor skills and intellectual development —deficiencies that will respond to treatment but are hard to completely overcome, even after the anemia is corrected by supplementing the child's diet (Lozoff, 1989). So iron deficiencies are a major health problem in the United States and around the world. Indeed, even mild cases later in childhood are associated with poor performances on school achievement tests (Pollitt, 1994), and children who experience prolonged vitamin/mineral deficiencies are also less resistant to a variety of illnesses that can affect intellectual performance and retard physical growth.

Although it is clear that severe malnutrition early in life can adversely affects physical growth and intellectual development, these deficits are not solely attributable

catch-up growth: a period of accelerated growth in which children who have experienced growth deficits grow very rapidly to "catch up" to the growth trajectory that they are genetically programmed to follow.

marasmus: a growth-retarding disease affecting infants who receive insufficient protein and too few calories.

kwashiorkor: a growth-retarding disease affecting children who receive enough calories but little, if any, protein.

vitamin and mineral deficiencies: a form of malnutrition in which the diet provides sufficient protein and calories but is lacking in one or more substances that promote normal growth.

iron-deficiency anemia: a listlessness caused by too little iron in the diet that makes children inattentive and may retard physical and intellectual development.

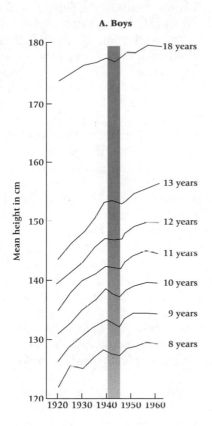

A. Boys

Mean height in cm

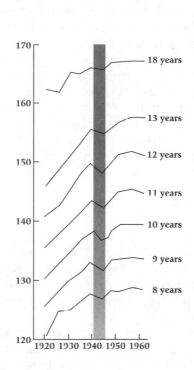

B. Girls

Figure 5-7
The effect of malnutrition on growth. These graphs show the average heights of Oslo school-children aged 8–18 between 1920 and 1960. Notice the trend toward increasing height (in all age groups) between 1920 and 1940, the period between the two world wars. This secular trend was dramatically reversed during World War II (the shaded section of the graphs), when nutrition was often inadequate.
From Tanner, 1990.

to biological insults. Recall from Chapter 4 that malnutrition can cause young children to be lethargic, inattentive, irritable, and intolerant of stressful situations—a behavioral profile that places them at risk of alienating their caregivers and thereby receiving little social or intellectual stimulation. This risk is increased if caregivers are also malnourished and are themselves lethargic, inattentive, and prone to become irritable. In other words, many of the long-term effects of undernutrition may stem, in part, from the unstimulating environments that malnourished children live in and have helped to create (Barrett & Frank, 1987; Valenzuela, 1990).

Nutritional supplements for malnourished children (and their parents) can make them more receptive to social/intellectual stimulation (and perhaps induce parents to provide it). Yet, the results of several recent intervention studies indicate that dietary supplements alone are not enough! Malnourished children are *least* likely to display long-term deficits in physical growth and social/intellectual development when (1) their diets are supplemented *and* (2) they receive more social and intellectual stimulation, either through high quality day-care (Zeskind & Ramey, 1981) or through a home visitation program that teaches caregivers about the importance of such stimulation while showing them how to provide it (Grantham-McGregor et al., 1994; Super, Herrera, & Mora, 1990).

Problems of overnutrition. Dietary excess (eating too much) is yet another form of poor nutrition that can have several long-term consequences. The most immediate effect is that the child may become **obese** and face added risk of diabetes, high blood pressure, and heart, liver, or kidney disease. Obese children may also find it difficult to make friends with age-mates, who are apt to tease them about their size and shape. Indeed, obese youngsters are often among the least popular students in grade school classrooms (Sigelman, Miller, & Whitworth, 1986; Staffieri, 1967).

obese: a medical term describing individuals who are at least 20% above the "ideal" weight for their height, age, and sex.

Is a plump baby likely to become an obese adolescent or adult? Probably not, for there is only a slight correlation between chubbiness in infancy and obesity later in life (Roche, 1981). However, obese 4- to 6-year-olds are much more likely than their thinner peers to be obese later in adolescence and adulthood. Heredity definitely contributes to these trends, for identical twins—even those raised apart—have very similar body weights, whereas the body weights of same-sex fraternal twins may differ dramatically (Stunkard et al., 1990). Moreover, sluggish activity levels (which may hinder one from burning calories) and even a preference for sweets are moderately heritable attributes (Mayer, 1975; Milstein, 1980). Yet, a genetic predisposition towards obesity does not guarantee that one will be obese. Highest levels of obesity are found among children who eat a high-fat diet and who do not get sufficient exercise to burn the calories they've consumed.

Bad eating habits that can lead to obesity are often established early in life (Birch, 1990). Some parents overfeed infants because they almost always infer that a fussy baby must be hungry. Other parents use food to reinforce desirable behaviors (for example, "clean your room and you can have some ice cream"); or they bribe their children to eat foods they do not want (for example, "No dessert until you eat your peas") (Klesges et al., 1986; Olvera-Ezzell, Power, & Cousins, 1990). Unfortunately, children may attach a special significance to eating that extends far beyond its role in reducing hunger if they are encouraged to view food as a reward or to think of eating as an activity that leads to positive outcomes. Moreover, use of high-fat desserts or snacks as a reward may convince young children that the healthier foods that they are being "bribed" to eat must really be yucky stuff after all (Birch, Marlin, & Rotter, 1984).

In addition to their poor eating habits, obese children are less active than normal-weight peers. Of course, their inactivity may both contribute to obesity (obese children burn fewer calories) and be a consequence of their overweight condition. One strong clue that activity restriction contributes to obesity is that the amount of time children spend in the sedentary activity of watching television is one of the best predictors of *future* obesity (Kolata, 1986). Television viewing may also promote poor eating habits. Not only do children tend to snack while watching TV, but the foods they see advertised are mostly high-calorie products containing lots of fat and sugar and few beneficial nutrients (Tinsley, 1992).

Crash diets for obese children are often counterproductive. Severe dietary restrictions can interfere with the development of the brain, muscles, and bones early in life, and older children on restrictive diets may feel mistreated, rejected, and more willing to partake in binge eating should the opportunity arise (Kolata, 1986). To date, the most effective treatments for childhood obesity have been behavioral approaches that involve obese youngsters *and* their parents. In one particularly effective program (Epstein et al., 1987; 1990), parents and their obese children were taught to revise their eating patterns and exercise habits, to monitor their own behavior carefully to ensure compliance with the regimen, and to encourage other family members to exercise more and to eat healthier foods. In addition, children entered into contracts with their parents whereby they could earn rewards for losing weight. As shown in Figure 5-8, obese children who received this intensive family therapy not only lost weight, but had kept it off when observed during a follow-up five years later. By contrast, obese youngsters who had participated in the same program without their parents were unable to maintain the weight loss they had initially displayed. Here, then, is a strong indication that childhood obesity is a *family* problem that is most likely to be overcome when family members *work together* to change a home environment that has permitted children to become obese.

Illnesses

Among children who are adequately nourished, common childhood illnesses such as measles, chicken pox, or even pneumonia have little if any effect on physical growth and development. Major illnesses that keep a child in bed for weeks may temporarily

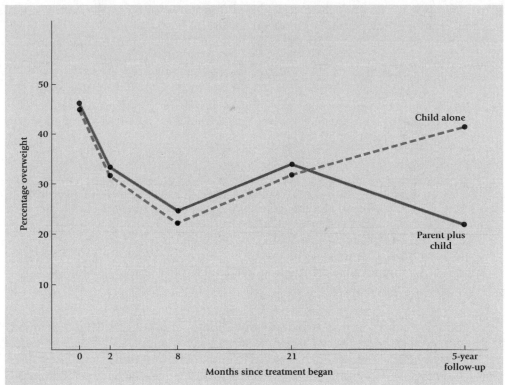

Figure 5-8
Average percentage of excess body weight for obese children who participated in a weight-loss program with and without a parent.
Adapted from Epstein, Wing, Koeske, & Valoski, 1987.

retard growth; but after recovering, the child will ordinarily experience a growth spurt (catch-up growth) that makes up for the progress lost while he or she was sick (Tanner, 1990).

Yet, diseases are likely to permanently depress the growth of children who are moderately to severely undernourished. A poor diet weakens the immune system, which means that childhood diseases will strike an undernourished child sooner and will have a more devastating impact (Tanner, 1990). Not only does malnutrition increase one's susceptibility to disease, but diseases contribute to malnutrition by suppressing a child's appetite and limiting the body's ability to absorb and utilize nutrients (Pollitt, 1994). In developing countries where gastrointestinal infections and upper respiratory illnesses are common, young school-age children who have been relatively disease-free are already 1–2 inches taller and 3–5 pounds heavier on average than their more "sickly" peers (Martorell, 1980; Roland, Cole, & Whitehead, 1977) and are outperforming their sickly classmates on a variety of cognitive tests as well (Pollitt, 1994).

Emotional Stress and Lack of Affection

Otherwise healthy children who experience too much stress and too little affection are likely to lag far behind their age-mates in physical growth and motor development. This **failure-to-thrive** syndrome may characterize as many as 6% of preschool children in the United States and up to 5% of all patients admitted to pediatric hospitals (Lozoff, 1989).

Perhaps the most intriguing research on the failure-to-thrive syndrome was reported by Lytt Gardner (1972), who studied otherwise healthy children who received adequate physical care but very little affection. One case involved twins—a boy and a girl—who grew normally for their first four months. Soon thereafter, the twins' father lost his job, their mother became pregnant with an unwanted baby, and the father then moved out of the house. Focusing her resentment on the boy twin,

failure to thrive: a condition in which seemingly healthy infants fail to grow normally and are much smaller than their age-mates.

deprivation dwarfism: Gardner's name for retardation in physical growth that is apparently triggered by emotional distress and/or a lack of love and attention.

the mother became emotionally detached and unresponsive to his bids for affection, although she did provide him with adequate nutrition and physical care. While his sister continued to grow normally, the boy twin at 13 months of age was about the size of an average 7-month-old infant. In other words, his growth was severely retarded, a condition that Gardner called **deprivation dwarfism.**

Gardner believes that deprivation dwarfism is directly related to the emotional deprivation that the child has experienced at home. He bases his conclusions on the behavior of many deprivation dwarfs who were hospitalized for observation and treatment. Here is a typical case:

> The 15-month-old child quickly responded to the attention she received from the hospital staff. She gained weight and made up for lost growth; her emotional state improved strikingly. Moreover, *these changes were . . . unrelated to any changes in food intake.* During her stay in the hospital, she received the same standard nutrient dosage she had received at home. It appears to have been the enrichment of her social environment, not of her diet, that was responsible for the normalization of her growth (Gardner, 1972, p. 17; italics added).

Gardner's deprivation dwarfs (and most children who fail to thrive) are infants and toddlers who have suffered *severe* emotional deprivation (see also Figure 5-9). Yet, there is evidence that older, school-age children who experience less severe emotional traumas may also grow more slowly than normal. In one study, for example, a group of orphans were given an enriched diet at the same time that they were placed under the care of a strict, emotionally unresponsive teacher. These children actually grew *at a slower rate* than a second group who remained on the standard orphanage fare (Widdowson, 1951). Apparently, the emotional distress that the first group of children experienced interfered with normal growth even though their diet had actually improved.

Why does emotional distress inhibit growth? Undernourishment may play a role in some cases, especially if children actively resist or avoid their unresponsive caregivers (Lozoff, 1989). But in other cases, growth failure is apparently not related to diet. Recall that Gardner's deprivation dwarfs who received attention in the hospital grew rapidly on the same diet on which they had "failed to thrive," and Widdowson's emotionally distressed orphans failed to thrive even though their diets had improved. Current thinking is that emotional traumas may cause a growth slowdown by inhibiting the production of pituitary growth hormone. Indeed, Gardner (1972) noted that deprivation dwarfs have abnormally low levels of growth hormone in their bloodstreams during periods of subnormal growth. But after these distressed young-

Figure 5-9
Three-year-old, treated for deprivation dwarfism 18 months earlier, actually lost weight on return to the care of a mother who appeared detached and unemotional in her relationship with the boy. His skeletal maturity on return to the hospital was at the level of a 15-month-old's; he was listless and lay on his back most of the time, his legs spraddled in a characteristic "frog" position. *From Gardner, 1972.*

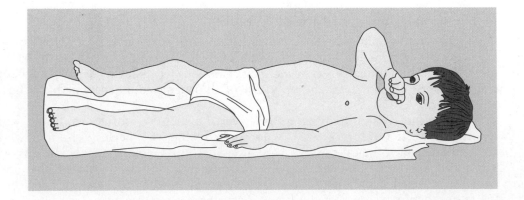

sters begin to receive attention, the secretion of growth hormone resumes, enabling them to grow rapidly and make up the lost ground. Yet, it is important to note that should a child's emotional distress continue for several years, he or she may remain smaller than normal and display long-term emotional problems and intellectual deficits as well (Brinich, Drotar, & Brinich, 1989; Lozoff, 1989).

The failure-to-thrive syndrome provides yet another indication that children require love and responsive caregiving if they are to develop normally. Fortunately, we are making some headway at identifying those parents whose children may be affected. Even before giving birth, women whose children will fail to thrive are more likely than other mothers to feel unloved by their parents, to reject their own mothers as a model, and to say that their own childhoods were unhappy; and within days of giving birth, they are already having more problems feeding and nurturing their babies than other mothers do (Altemeier et al., as cited in Lozoff, 1989). Like mothers of premature infants, these women need help and would almost certainly benefit (as would their infants) from structured interventions that teach them how to be sensitive, responsive companions.

Concept Check 5-3 ⌄ Understanding the Causes of Physical Development

Check your understanding of some of the causes of physical development by matching each of the consequences listed below with one of the following *causes* (or contributors) to that condition: (a) increase in GH production during adolescence; (b) severe malnutrition; (c) increase in testosterone/estrogen production during adolescence; (d) stress-induced inhibition of GH; (e) sedentary lifestyle. The answers appear in the Appendix:

_____ 1. Lethargic, inattentive, irritable demeanor

_____ 2. Adolescent growth spurt

_____ 3. Deprivation dwarfism

_____ 4. Obesity

_____ 5. Sexual maturation at puberty

◢ SUMMARY

Neonates are remarkably capable organisms who emerge from the womb prepared for life. They have functioning sense organs; they display some capacity for learning; and they come equipped with a repertoire of inborn reflexes (breathing, sucking, swallowing, and so on) that help them to adapt to their new surroundings. One of the first tests many babies take is the Brazelton Neonatal Behavioral Assessment Scale, an instrument designed to measure their reflexes, social responsiveness, and neurological well-being. This scale is particularly useful for identifying infants who may experience later emotional difficulties and for teaching parents how to stimulate their babies properly to prevent these problems.

The infant's state (that is, state of consciousness) changes many times during a typical day. Newborns spend nearly 70% of their time asleep—an adaptive state indeed, for rapid-eye-movement (REM) sleep provides stimulation necessary for development of the central nervous system. Over the first year, infants spend less time sleeping and more time alert and attending to the environment. Crying is the state by which infants communicate their distress. If a baby's cries are very shrill and non-rhythmic, he or she may be malnourished or brain-damaged. However, crying usually diminishes over the first year as caregivers learn to use any of several effective soothing techniques and as infants learn to use other methods of communicating with their caregivers.

The body is constantly changing between infancy and adulthood. Height and weight increase rapidly during the first two years. Growth then becomes more gradual until early adolescence, when there is a rapid "growth spurt." The shape of the body also changes because various body parts grow at different rates and different times. For example, the head and trunk grow rapidly during the prenatal period and infancy, the limbs are growing fastest in late childhood, and the trunk is once again the fastest-growing segment of the body during adolescence.

Skeletal and muscular development parallel the changes occurring in height and weight. The bones become longer and thicker, and they gradually harden, completing their growth and development by the late teens. Muscles increase in density and size, particularly during the growth spurt of early adolescence. Development of the skeletal, muscular, and nervous systems follows a cephalocaudal (head downward) and proximodistal (center outward) pattern: Structures in the upper and central regions of the body mature before those in the lower and peripheral regions.

The brain and nervous system develop very rapidly during the last three months of the prenatal period and the first two years of life, when neurons become organized into interconnected pathways and are encased in myelin—a waxy material that acts like an insulator to speed the transmission of neural impulses. Many neurons and synapses are formed, but only those that are often used are likely to survive. The brain has a great deal of plasticity—a characteristic that allows it to change in response to experience and to recover from many injuries. Although the brain may be organized from birth so that its two cerebral hemispheres serve different functions, children come to rely more and more on one particular hemisphere to serve specific functions.

Like the physical structures of the body, motor development proceeds in a cephalocaudal and proximodistal direction. As a result, motor skills evolve in a definite sequence, in which infants gain control over their heads, necks, and upper arms before they become proficient with their legs, feet, and hands. As the nervous system and muscles mature, children gradually acquire more control over their bodies. Yet, the increasingly complex motor skills that children display do not simply "unfold" according to a maturational timetable; each emerging skill represents a complex reorganization of several developing capabilities that is perfected through practice as a means of coping with environmental demands or achieving important objectives.

At about age 10½ for females, and age 13 for males, the adolescent growth spurt begins. Weight increases first, followed some 4–6 months later by a rapid increase in height. The muscles undergo a period of rapid growth about a year after the greatest growth in height.

Sexual maturation begins about the same time as the adolescent growth spurt and follows a predictable sequence for members of each sex. For females, the onset of breast and pubic-hair development is followed by a widening of the hips, enlarging of the uterus and vagina, menarche (first menstruation), and completion of breast and pubic-hair growth. For males, development of the testes and scrotum is followed by the emergence of pubic hair, the growth of the penis, the ability to ejaculate, the appearance of facial hair, and a lowering of the voice. Because of improved nutrition and health care, people in industrialized societies have been growing taller and heavier and are reaching sexual maturity earlier than was true in the past. Yet, there are wide individual variations in the timing of sexual maturation and growth. Early-maturing boys experience fewer psychological and social problems than late maturers. Among girls, the psychological correlates of early or late maturing are less apparent, although early-maturing girls seem to be less popular than prepubescent classmates in grade school but tend to become more popular and self-assured later in adolescence.

The course of physical development represents a complex interplay between biological and environmental influences. Individual genotypes set limits for stature, shape, and the tempo of growth. Growth is also heavily influenced by hormones released from the endocrine glands. Pituitary growth hormone and thyroxine regulate growth throughout childhood. At adolescence, the pituitary stimulates other endocrine glands to secrete their hormones, most notably estrogen from the ovaries, which triggers sexual development in girls, and testosterone from the testes, which instigates sexual development in boys.

Adequate nutrition is essential for normal growth and development, as is freedom from prolonged and serious illness. Undernutrition makes children more susceptible to the growth-retarding effects of disease; in turn, chronic diseases can interfere with nutrition. The growth disorder known as failure to thrive (deprivation dwarfism) illustrates that emotional traumas can inhibit growth and that sensitive, responsive caregiving is important for normal growth and development.

Key Terms

action system [177]

adolescent growth spurt [182]

anorexia nervosa [187]

autostimulation theory [163]

brain growth spurt [169]

Brazelton Neonatal Behavioral Assessment Scale (NBAS) [158]

bulimia [187]

catch-up growth [192]

cephalocaudal development [167]

cerebral cortex [172]

cerebral lateralization [172]

cerebrum [172]

corpus callosum [172]

deprivation dwarfism [197]

dyslexia [173]

estrogen [190]

failure to thrive [195]

glia [169]

growth hormone (GH) [190]

infant states [162]

iron-deficiency anemia [192]

kwashiorkor [192]

marasmus [192]

menarche [183]

multiple sclerosis [171]

myelinization [171]

neurons [169]

obese [193]

pincer grasp [178]

pituitary [190]

plasticity [170]

primitive reflexes [160]

proprioceptive information [178]

proximodistal development [167]

puberty [182]

reaction time [180]

reflex [160]

REM sleep [163]

secular trend [184]

skeletal age [168]

sudden infant death syndrome (SIDS) [163]

survival reflexes [160]

synapse [169]

testosterone [190]

thyroxine [190]

ulnar grasp [178]

vitamin and mineral deficiencies [192]

Part III

Language, Learning, and Cognitive Development

Some of the more remarkable developments of childhood and adolescence are the changes that occur in learning, interpreting, reasoning, remembering, and problem solving. These "cognitive," or intellectual, developments are examined in detail in Part III.

In Chapter 6 we will focus on the growth of perceptual skills and learn how children gradually become more proficient at interpreting the information they receive from their sensory receptors.

Chapters 7–9 concentrate on the topic of intellectual development. We begin in Chapter 7 with Jean Piaget's classic work on the growth of reasoning abilities throughout childhood and adolescence and with Lev Vygotsky's notions of how social influences shape cognitive development. In Chapter 8 we will consider a modern alternative to Piaget's theory that grew from the work of learning and information-processing theorists. In Chapter 9 we turn to the topic of intelligence testing and consider the many factors that contribute to individual differences in intellectual performance.

One characteristic that clearly distinguishes us humans from other species is our remarkable capacity for language. We conclude Part III with Chapter 10, where we will examine the growth of language and communication skills throughout childhood and adolescence.

As you proceed through this section, it will become obvious that all the various cognitive functions are interrelated. For example, infants and toddlers must first *perceive* the differences among various patterns of sound and then *remember* these distinctions before they can construct meaningful words and sentences. They must develop an *understanding* of concepts such as relative size and color before they can use words such as *tall* and *green* in the same ways that adults do. So the lines that are drawn between different cognitive operations are somewhat artificial, and we will see that changes in each cognitive process have important implications for all other aspects of cognitive functioning.

Perceptual Development

Imagine that you are a neonate, only 5–10 minutes old, who has just been sponged, swaddled, and handed to your mother. As your eyes meet hers, she smiles and says "Hi there, sweetie," as she moves her head closer and gently strokes your cheek. What would you make of all this sensory input? How would you interpret these experiences?

Developmentalists are careful to distinguish between sensation and perception. **Sensation** is the process by which sensory receptor neurons detect information and transmit it to the brain. Clearly, neonates "sense" the environment. They gaze at interesting sights, react to sounds, tastes, and odors, and, as countless mothers will verify, are likely to cry up a storm when poked by a misguided diaper pin. But do they "make sense" of these sensations? **Perception** is the interpretation of sensory input: recognizing what you see, understanding what is said to you, or knowing that the odor you've detected is fresh-baked bread. Are newborns capable of drawing any such inferences? Do they perceive the world, or merely sense it?

Perhaps we should start with a more basic question: Why should we concern ourselves with the development of sensation and perception? Perhaps because these processes are at the heart of human functioning. Virtually everything we do depends, in part, on our interpretations of sensory input—the things we experience. So the study of sensation and perception can provide some fundamental clues about how we gain knowledge of reality.

CONTROVERSIES ABOUT PERCEPTUAL DEVELOPMENT

Nature versus Nurture

Long before anyone began to conduct experiments on sensation and perception, philosophers were debating whether neonates could perceive. *Empiricists* such as John Locke (1690/1939) believed that infants were *tabula rasae* (blank slates) who must *learn* to interpret their sensations. William James (1890) agreed. James argued that the senses are integrated at birth, so that sights, sounds, and other sensory inputs combine to present the infant with a "blooming, buzzing confusion."

By contrast, *nativist* philosophers such as Rene Descartes (1638/1965) and Immanuel Kant (1781/1958) take the nature side of the nature/nuture issue, arguing that many basic perceptual abilities are innate. For example, they believed that we are born with an understanding of spatial relations. Presumably, infants do not need to learn that receding objects appear smaller or that approaching objects seem to increase in size; these were said to be adaptive perceptual understandings that have been built in to the human nervous system over the course of evolution.

Today's developmental theorists typically take less extreme stands on this nature/nurture issue. Although most would concede that babies see some order to the universe from day one, they recognize that the perceptual world of a human neonate is rather limited and that *both* maturational processes and experience contribute to the growth of perceptual awareness. Yet, even today, developmentalists grapple with nature/nurture issues (Bornstein, 1992), arguing about which perceptual abilities are innate and about the kinds of experiences that one must have for development to be normal.

Enrichment versus Differentiation

Now consider a second issue that philosophers have debated. Is the "coherent reality" that we experience through the senses simply "out there" to be detected; or rather, do we construct our own interpretations of that reality based on our experiences? This issue is hotly contested in two modern theories of perceptual development: enrichment theory and differentiation theory.

Both these theories argue that there is an objective reality out there to which we respond. However, **enrichment theory** (Piaget, 1954; 1960) claims that stimulation

sensation: detection of stimuli by the sensory receptors and transmission of this information to the brain.

perception: the process by which we categorize and interpret sensory input.

enrichment theory: a theory specifying that we must "add to" sensory stimulation by drawing on stored knowledge in order to perceive a meaningful world.

received by the sensory receptors is often fragmented or confusing. To interpret such ambiguous input, we must use our available cognitive schemes to add to or "enrich" it. You have heard radio contests where you call in to identify a song after hearing only a note or two. According to enrichment theory, contest winners can answer correctly because they draw on their memory of musical passages to add to what they have just heard and infer what the song must be. In sum, the enrichment position is that cognition "enriches" sensory experience. Our stored knowledge helps us impose meaning on the bits and pieces of sensory stimulation that we receive (see Figure 6-1).

By contrast, Eleanor Gibson's (1969; 1987; 1992) **differentiation theory** argues that sensory stimulation provides all we need to interpret our experiences properly. Our task as fledgling perceivers is simply to *detect* the differentiating information, or **distinctive features,** that would enable us to discriminate one form of experience from another. Consider that many 2-year-olds are apt to say "doggie" whenever they see a dog, a cat, or some other small, furry animal. They have not yet noticed the critical differences in sizes, shapes, behavior, or sounds that enable us to discriminate these creatures. Once this bit of perceptual learning is mastered, however, the child's continuing quest for differentiating information may soon enable him to discriminate long-nosed collies from either pug-faced boxers or spotted dalmations, while understanding that all these animals are properly labeled as dogs. Gibson's point is that the information needed to make these finer distinctions was always there, in the animals themselves, and that the child's perceptual capabilities blossom as he *detects* these distinctive features.

So which theory is correct? Maybe both of them are. The research we will review provides ample support for Gibson's view; children do get better at detecting information already contained in their sensory inputs. Yet, Piaget's view that existing knowledge provides a basis for enriching and interpreting our sensations is also well documented. So each position has some merit; enrichment activities and differentiation processes both contribute to the growth of perception.

Figure 6-1
Expectations affect perception. If told to name the *animal* in this drawing, you would likely see a rat with large ears and its tail circling in front of the body. Yet, if you saw the drawing amid other drawings of faces, you would likely perceive an elderly bald man with glasses (see him?). So, as Piaget and other enrichment theorists have argued, cognition does affect our interpretations of sensory stimulation.
Adapted from Reese, 1963.

 ## "MAKING SENSE" OF THE INFANT'S SENSORY (AND PERCEPTUAL) EXPERIENCES

As recently as the early 1900s, many medical texts claimed that human infants were functionally blind, deaf, and impervious to pain for several days after birth—that is, babies were described as hardly prepared to extract any "meaning" from the world around them. Today, we know otherwise. Why the change in views? It is not that babies have become any more capable or any smarter. Instead, researchers have gotten smarter, having developed some ingenious methods of persuading nonverbal infants to "tell us" what they can sense and perceive. Let's briefly discuss four such techniques.

The Preference Method

The **preference method** is a simple procedure in which at least two stimuli are presented simultaneously to see whether infants will attend more to one of them than to the other(s). This approach became popular during the early 1960s after Robert Fantz used it to determine whether very young infants could discriminate visual patterns (for example, faces, concentric circles, newsprint, and unpatterned disks). Babies were placed on their backs in a **looking chamber** (see Figure 6-2) and shown two or more stimuli. An observer located above the looking chamber then recorded the amount of time that the infant gazed at each of the visual patterns. If the infant looked longer at one target than the other, it was assumed that she preferred that pattern.

Fantz's early results were clear. Newborns could easily discriminate visual forms, and they preferred to look at patterned stimuli such as faces or concentric circles

differentiation theory: a theory specifying that perception involves detecting distinctive features or cues that are contained in the sensory stimulation we receive.

distinctive features: characteristics of a stimulus that remain constant; dimensions on which two or more objects differ and can be discriminated (sometimes called *invariances* or *invariant features*).

preference method: a method used to gain information about infants' perceptual abilities by presenting two (or more) stimuli and observing which stimulus the infant prefers.

looking chamber: an enclosed criblike apparatus used to study infants' visual preferences.

Figure 6-2
The looking chamber that Fantz
used to study infants' visual
preferences.

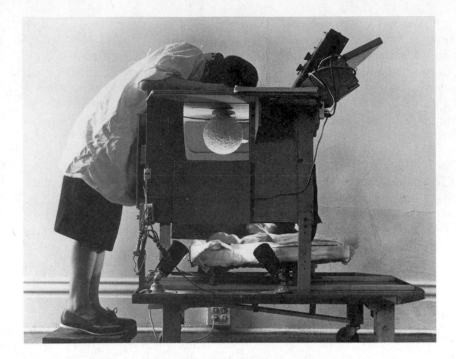

rather than at unpatterned disks. Apparently, the ability to detect and discriminate patterns is innate (Fantz, 1963).

The preference method has one major shortcoming. If an infant shows no preferences among the target stimuli, it is not clear whether she failed to discriminate them or simply found them equally interesting. Fortunately, each of the following methods can resolve this interpretive ambiguity.

The Habituation Method

Perhaps the most popular strategy for measuring infant sensory and perceptual capabilities is the habituation method. **Habituation** is the process whereby a repetitive stimulus becomes so familiar that responses initially associated with it (for example, head or eye movements, changes in respiration or heart rate) no longer occur. Thus, habituation is a simple form of learning. As the infant stops responding to the familiar stimulus, he is telling us that he recognizes it as "old hat"—something that he has experienced before (Tarquinio, Zelazo, & Weiss, 1990).

To test an infant's ability to discriminate two stimuli that differ in some way, the investigator first presents one of the stimuli until the infant stops attending or otherwise responding to it (habituates). Then the second stimulus is presented. If the infant discriminates this second stimulus from the first, he will indicate as much by attending closely to it, by showing a change in respiration or heart rate, or by otherwise altering his behavior. Should the infant fail to react, it is assumed that the differences between the two stimuli were too subtle for him to detect. Because babies habituate to so many different kinds of stimulation—sights, sounds, odors, tastes, and tactile experiences other than painful ones—the habituation paradigm is very useful for assessing their sensory and perceptual abilities.

Evoked Potentials

Yet another way of determining what infants can sense (or perceive) is to present them with a stimulus and record their brain waves. Electrodes are placed on the infant's scalp above those brain centers that process the kind of sensory information the investigator will be presenting. This means that responses to visual stimuli are recorded from the back of the head, at a site above the occipital lobe, whereas responses to sounds are recorded from the side of the head, above the temporal lobe.

habituation: a decrease in one's response to a stimulus that has become familiar through repetition.

If the infant detects (senses) the particular stimulus that we present, she will show a change in the patterning of her brain waves, or **evoked potential**, shortly after its presentation. Stimuli that are not detected will produce no changes in the brain's electrical activity. This "evoked potential" procedure can even tell us whether infants can discriminate various sights or sounds, for two stimuli that are sensed as "different" will produce different patterns of electrical activity.

High-Amplitude Sucking

Finally, most infants can exert enough control over their sucking behavior to tell us what they can sense and to give us some idea of their likes and dislikes. The **high-amplitude sucking method** provides infants with a special pacifier containing electrical circuitry that will enable them to exert some control over the sensory environment. After the researcher establishes an infant's baseline sucking rate, the procedure begins. Whenever the infant sucks faster or harder than she did during the baseline observations (high-amplitude sucking), she will trip the electrical circuit in the pacifier, thereby activating a slide projector or tape recorder that introduces some kind of sensory stimulation. Should the infant detect this stimulation and find it interesting, she can make it last by displaying bursts of high-amplitude sucking for as long as she may care to experience it. But once the infant's interest wanes and her sucking returns to the baseline level, the stimulation ceases. If the investigator now introduces a second stimulus that elicits a dramatic increase in high-amplitude sucking, he could conclude that the infant has discriminated the second stimulus from the first. This procedure can even be modified to let the infant tell us which of two stimuli she prefers. Suppose, for example, that we wanted to determine whether babies prefer marches to lullabies. We could adjust the pacifier's circuitry so that high-amplitude sucking activates one kind of music and low-amplitude (or no) sucking activates the other. By then noting what the baby does, we could draw some inferences about which of these musical compositions she prefers. Clearly, this high-amplitude sucking method is a clever and versatile technique!

Let's now see what these creative methods have taught us about babies' sensory and perceptual capabilities.

 ## INFANT SENSORY CAPABILITIES

How well do newborns "sense" their environments? Better, perhaps, than you might imagine. Let's begin our exploration of infants' sensory world by examining their visual capabilities.

Vision

Although most of us tend to think of vision as our most indispensible sense, vision may be the *least* mature of the newborn's sensory capabilities. Changes in brightness elicit a subcortical *pupillary reflex*, which indicates that the neonate is sensitive to brightness (Pratt, 1954). Babies can also detect movement in the visual field and are likely to track a visual stimulus with their eyes as long as the target moves slowly (Banks & Salapatek, 1983). Interestingly, newborn infants are more likely to track faces (or facelike stimuli) than other patterns (Goren, Sarty, & Wu, 1975; Johnson et al., 1991), although this preference for faces disappears within a month or two. Why do babies display it? Though no one can say for sure, one intriguing idea is that it represents an adaptive remnant of our evolutionary history—a *primitive reflex*, controlled by subcortical areas of the brain, that serves to orient babies to their caregivers and promote social interactions (Johnson et al., 1991).

Using the habituation method, researchers have found that neonates see the world in color, not in black and white as was once assumed. Although very young infants

evoked potential: a change in patterning of the brain waves that indicates that an individual detects (senses) a stimulus.

high-amplitude sucking method: a method of assessing infants' perceptual capabilities that capitalizes on the ability of infants to make interesting events last by varying the rate at which they suck on a special pacifier.

may have trouble telling blues from greens and reds from yellows, their color vision quickly improves. By 4–5 months of age, they not only recognize that an object's color doesn't change when the object grows brighter or dimmer (Dannemiller, 1989), but they are also dividing the color spectrum into the same basic categories—the reds, greens, blues, and yellows—that adults do (Bornstein, Kessen, & Weiskopf, 1976; Catherwood, Crassini, & Freiberg, 1989).

Despite these impressive capabilities, very young infants do not see all that well. Studies of **visual acuity** suggest that a neonate's distance vision is about 20/600, which means that she sees at 20 feet what an adult with excellent vision sees at 600 feet. Moreover, objects at any distance look rather blurry to a very young infant, who has trouble *accommodating*—that is, changing the shape of the lens of the eye to bring visual stimuli into focus. Given these limitations, it is perhaps not surprising that many patterns and forms are difficult for a very young infant to detect; she simply requires sharper **visual contrasts** to "see" them than adults do (Banks & Salapatek, 1983). However, vision improves very rapidly over the first few months: By age 6 months, babies' visual acuity is about 20/100 and they are accommodating well; by age 12 months, they see about as well as adults do (Aslin & Smith, 1988).

In sum, the young infant's visual system is not operating at peak efficiency, but it is certainly working. Even newborns can sense movement, colors, changes in brightness, and a variety of visual patterns—as long as these patterned stimuli are not too finely detailed and have a sufficient amount of light/dark contrast.

Hearing

Neonates hear fairly well. They are startled by loud noises and will turn away from them, but will turn in the direction of a softer sound as if searching for its source (Field et al., 1980). However, this early ability to localize sounds is very imprecise. In fact, it may be a reflex, for it disappears at age 2 months and then reappears at about 4 months of age—this time as a voluntary head-turning response that enables older infants to localize sounds much more quickly and accurately (Morrongiello, Fenwick, & Chance, 1990; Muir, 1985).

Using the evoked potential procedure, researchers have found that soft sounds that adults can hear must be made noticeably louder before a neonate detects them (Aslin, Pisoni, & Jusczyk, 1983). In the first few hours of life, infants may hear about as well as an adult with a head cold. Their insensitivity to softer sounds could be due, in part, to fluids that have seeped into the inner ear during the birth process. Despite this minor limitation, habituation studies indicate that neonates are capable of discriminating sounds that differ in loudness, duration, direction, and frequency (Bower, 1982). They hear rather well indeed.

Young infants are particularly responsive to the sounds of a human voice. Harriet Rheingold and Judith Adams (1980) found that caregivers speak often to newborn infants and appear to enjoy these "conversations." And what do adults find so interesting about a "conversation" with a nonverbal infant? Perhaps it is simply that infants will often stop crying, open their eyes, and begin to look around or to vocalize themselves when they are spoken to (Alegria & Noirot, 1978; Rosenthal, 1982). So a baby's general responsiveness to the speech of his companions is a characteristic that helps to elicit the attention and interpersonal contact that contribute in a positive way to his social, emotional, and intellectual development.

In sum, our most appropriate response to claims that babies can't hear is to "turn a deaf ear" to them. Newborns hear very well and are capable of discriminating a staggering number of auditory stimuli. Although a baby's auditory capabilities will improve over the first 4 to 6 months of life (Trehub et al., 1991), even neonates are remarkably well prepared for such significant achievements as (1) using voices to recognize and discriminate their companions and (2) breaking speech into smaller units—the building blocks of language. Stay tuned, for we will soon discuss these important developments.

visual acuity: a person's ability to see small objects and fine detail.

visual contrast: the amount of light/dark transition in a visual stimulus.

Taste and Smell

Infants are born with some very definite taste preferences. For example, they apparently come equipped with something of a sweet tooth, for babies suck faster and longer for sweet liquids than for bitter, sour, salty, or neutral (water) solutions (Crook, 1978). Different tastes also elicit different facial expressions from newborns. Sweets reduce crying and produce smiles and smacking of the lips, whereas sour substances cause infants to wrinkle their noses and purse their lips, and bitter solutions often elicit expressions of disgust—a downturning of the corners of the mouth, tongue protrusions, and even spitting (Blass & Ciaramitaro, 1994; Ganchrow, Steiner, & Daher, 1983; Rosenstein & Oster, 1988). Moreover, these facial expressions become more pronounced as solutions become sweeter, more sour, or more bitter, suggesting that newborns can discriminate different concentrations of a particular "taste."

Neonates are also capable of detecting a variety of odors, and they will react vigorously by turning away and displaying expressions of disgust in response to unpleasant smells such as vinegar, ammonia, or rotten eggs (Rieser, Yonas, & Wilkner, 1976; Steiner, 1979). Even more remarkable are data indicating that 1–2-week-old breastfed infants can already recognize their mother (and discriminate her from other women) by the smell of her breasts and underarms (Cernoch & Porter, 1985; Porter et al., 1992). Like it or not, each of us has a unique "olfactory signature"—a characteristic that babies use as an early means of "identifying" their closest companions.

Touch, Temperature, and Pain

Receptors in the skin are sensitive to touch, temperature, and pain. We learned in Chapter 5 that newborn infants reliably display a variety of *reflexes* if they are touched in the appropriate areas. Even while sleeping, neonates will habituate to stroking at one locale but respond again if the tactile stimulation shifts to a new spot—from the ear to the chin, for example (Kisilevsky & Muir, 1984). In fact, sensitivity to touch is apparent well before birth and may, along with the bodily sense that detects motion, be the first sense to develop (Field, 1990).

Later in the first year, infants are able to discriminate objects solely on the basis of touch. In one study (Streri & Pecheux, 1986), 5-month-olds habituated to a star-shaped plywood object that they had touched repeatedly but had never seen. When later given an opportunity to fondle this object or a new one with a different shape, the infants clearly preferred to explore the novel shape rather than the one they recognized by touch.

Newborns are also quite sensitive to warmth, cold, and changes in temperature. They will refuse to suck if the milk in their bottles is too hot, and they will try to maintain their body heat by becoming more active should the temperature of a room suddenly drop (Pratt, 1954).

Do babies experience much pain? Apparently so, for even 1-day-old infants cry lustily when pricked by a needle for a blood test (Fletcher, 1987). We also know something about infants' reactions to intense pain from studying male babies undergoing circumcision, an operation that takes place without anesthesia. While the actual surgery is in progress, infants emit high-pitched pain cries that are very similar to the wails of premature babies or those who are brain damaged (Porter, Porges, & Marshall, 1988). Moreover, plasma cortisol, a physiological indicator of stress, is significantly higher just after a circumcision than just before the surgery (Gunnar et al., 1985). Findings such as these challenge the medical wisdom of treating infants as if they are insensitive to pain. Indeed, babies are more likely to survive heart surgery if they receive deep anesthesia that keeps them unconscious for 24 hours after the operation than if they receive light anesthesia that provides less protection from the extremely painful aftereffects of the surgery (Anand & Hickey, 1992).

In sum, each of the major senses is functioning at birth (see Table 6-1 for a review) so that even neonates are well prepared to "sense" their environments. But do they interpret this input? Can they perceive?

Concept Check 6-1 ⌄ Understanding Infants' Sensory Capabilities

Check your understanding of infants' sensory capabilities and the methods used to obtain this information by filling in the blanks in each statement below. The answers appear in the Appendix.

1. An infant who has stopped responding to one visual stimulus has _____ to that stimulus. If he then begins to respond to a different visual stimulus, we can infer that he _____ the second stimulus from the first one.

2. Given a special pacifier, an infant associates fast sucking with a recording of Elvis Presley and slow (or no) sucking with "rap" music. The infant soon stops sucking and listens attentively to what he hears. We might infer that he or she _____.

3. One *social* consequence of the neonate's olfactory (smelling) capabilities is that he or she may use odors to _____.

4. _____ is the neonate's least well-developed sense. By age _____, however, the infant's capabilities in this sensory modality approximate those of an adult.

5. Although neonates detect and discriminate a variety of auditory stimuli, they are particularly responsive to _____ _____s.

▶ VISUAL PERCEPTION IN INFANCY

We have learned that newborn infants see well enough to detect and even discriminate patterns that are not too finely detailed. But what do they "see" when looking at these stimuli? If we show them a □, do they see a square, or must they learn to construct a square from an assortment of lines, angles, and edges? When do they interpret faces as meaningful social stimuli or begin to distinguish the faces of close companions from those of strangers? Can neonates perceive depth? Do they think that receding objects shrink, or do they know that these objects remain the same size

Table 6-1 The Newborn's Sensory Capabilities

Sense	Newborn capabilities
Vision	Least well-developed sense; accommodation and visual acuity limited; is sensitive to brightness; can discriminate some colors; tracks moving targets.
Hearing	Turns in direction of sounds; less sensitive than adult to soft sounds but can discriminate sounds that differ in such dimensions as loudness, direction, and frequency. Particularly responsive to speech.
Taste	Prefers sweet solutions; can discriminate sweet, salty, sour, and bitter tastes.
Smell	Detects a variety of odors; turns away from unpleasant ones. If breast-fed, can identify mother by the odor of her breast and underarm area.
Touch	Responsive to touch, temperature change, and pain.

and only look smaller when moved away? These are precisely the kinds of questions that have motivated curious investigators to find ways of persuading nonverbal infants to "tell" us what they see.

Perception of Patterns and Forms

Recall Robert Fantz's observations of infants in his looking chamber: babies only 2 days old could easily discriminate visual patterns. In fact, of all the targets that Fantz presented, including a drawing of a face, newsprint, a bull's-eye pattern, and unpatterned red, white, and yellow disks, the most-preferred stimulus was the face! Does this imply that neonates already interpret faces as a meaningful pattern? Might the nativists be correct in assuming that form *perception* is innate?

Early Pattern Perception (0–2 Months)

Other research implies that neonates' ability to "perceive" faces as a "meaningful" configuration is more illusory than real. When Fantz (1961) presented young infants with a face, a stimulus consisting of scrambled facial features, and a simpler stimulus that contained the same amount of light and dark shading as the facelike and scrambled face drawings, the infants were just as interested in the scrambled face as the normal one (see Figure 6-3). And even though newborn infants prefer to *track* a facelike drawing to a scrambled face (Johnson et al., 1991), this reflexlike preference merely tells us that they can discriminate one stimulus from the other, not that they *perceive* the face as a meaningful form. What, then, made the face and the scrambled face equally interesting to Fantz's young subjects?

Over the years, researchers have discovered several properties of visual stimuli that "turn babies on." For example, infants are attracted to *high-contrast* patterns with many definite boundaries between light and dark areas (Banks & Ginsburg, 1985). Very young infants also prefer to look at moderately complex patterns rather than simpler ones and at curvilinear rather than linear features (Olson & Sherman, 1983). Thus, faces and scrambled faces may have been equally interesting to Fantz's young subjects because these targets have the same amount of contrast, curvature, and complexity (and more of all these features than the black-and-white oval, which failed to command much attention). Finally, young infants are especially captivated by things that *move*. Even newborns will spend much more time looking at a rotating object than at a comparable one that is stationary (Slater et al., 1985).

Figure 6-3
Fantz's test of young infants' pattern preferences. Infants preferred to look at complex stimuli rather than at a simpler black-and-white oval. However, the infants did not prefer the facelike figure to the scrambled face.
Adapted from Fantz, 1961.

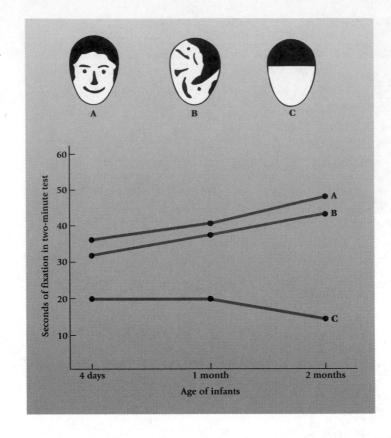

By analyzing the physical parameters of stimuli that babies do or do not prefer, we can estimate *what* they are seeing while scanning various targets. Figure 6-4, for example, suggests that very young infants see only a dark blob when looking at a *highly complex* checkerboard, probably because their immature eyes don't accommodate well enough to resolve the fine detail. By contrast, the infant sees a definite pattern when gazing at the *moderately complex* checkerboard (Banks & Salapatek, 1983). Martin Banks and his associates have summarized the looking preferences of very young infants quite succinctly: *Babies prefer to look at whatever they see well* (Banks & Ginsburg, 1985), and the things they see best are moderately complex, high-contrast targets, particularly those that capture their attention by moving. Indeed, Banks and other prominent infant watchers such as Marshall Haith (1980) characterize the very young infant as a *stimulus seeker* who is biologically programmed to scan the environment and to explore those visual stimuli that he can detect. This inborn tendency to scan and explore is thought to play a crucial role in perceptual development, for it keeps the baby's visual neurons firing, thereby promoting the development of the visual areas of the brain.

Do very young infants really *perceive* forms? If shown a triangle, do they see the △ that we do; or rather, do they detect only pieces of lines and maybe an angle (such as ∟)? Although the answers to these questions are by no means established, most researchers believe that 1–2-month-old infants detect few, *if any*, forms because they see so poorly and they scan visual stimuli in a very limited way (see Figure 6-5). So unless the form is very small, they are unlikely to see all of it, much less put all this information together to perceive a unified whole.

Later Form Perception (2 Months–1 Year)

Between 2 and 12 months of age, the infant's visual system is rapidly maturing. She now sees better and is capable of making increasingly complex visual discriminations. She is also organizing what she sees to perceive visual forms.

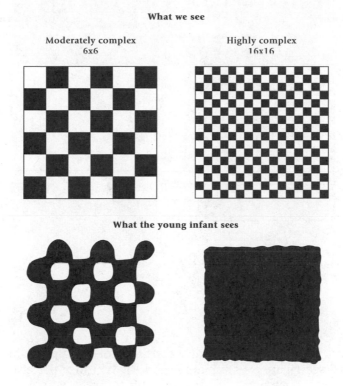

What we see

Moderately complex
6x6

Highly complex
16x16

What the young infant sees

Figure 6-4
What patterns look like to the young eye. By the time these two checkerboards are processed by eyes with poor vision, only the checkerboard on the left may have any pattern left to it. Poor vision in early infancy helps to explain a preference for moderately complex rather than highly complex stimuli.
Adapted from Banks & Salapatek, 1983.

Figure 6-5
By photographing eye movements, researchers can determine what babies are looking at when scanning a visual stimulus. Although very young infants rarely scan an entire form, 1-month-olds scan much less thoroughly than 2-month-olds do, concentrating most on specific outer edges or boundaries and least on internal features.
Adapted from Salapatek, 1975.

The most basic task in perceiving a form is to discriminate that object from its surrounding context (that is, other objects and the general "background"). How do you suppose an infant eventually recognizes that a bottle of milk in front of a centerpiece on the dining room table is not just a part of the centerpiece? What information does she use to perceive forms, and when does she begin to do so?

Philip Kellman and Elizabeth Spelke (1983; Kellman, Spelke, & Short, 1986) have been addressing these issues in some intriguing research with 4-month-olds. Infants

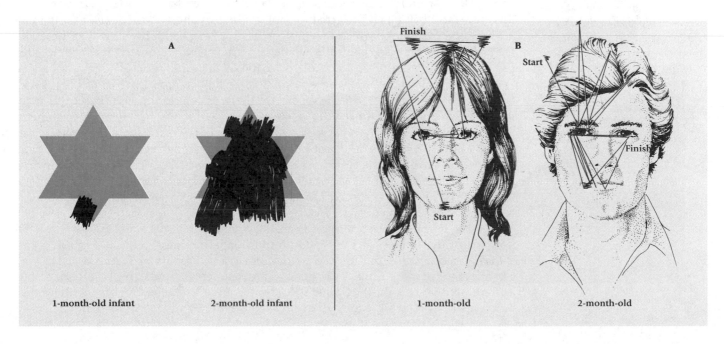

A

1-month-old infant

2-month-old infant

B

Finish

Start

1-month-old

Start

Finish

2-month-old

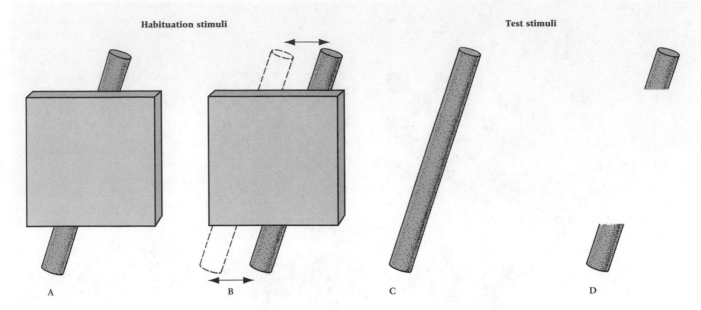

A   B   C   D

Figure 6-6

Perceiving objects as wholes. An infant is habituated to a rod partially hidden by the block in front of it. The rod is either stationary (A) or moving (B). When tested afterward, does the infant treat the whole rod (C) as "old hat"? We certainly would, for we could readily interpret cues that tell us that there is one long rod behind the block and would therefore regard the whole rod as familiar. But if the infant shows more interest in the whole rod (C) than in the two rod segments (D), he or she has apparently not been able to use available cues to perceive a whole rod. At 4 months of age, infants perceive a whole rod only if the rod moves as they are habituated to watching it.

Adapted from Kellman & Spelke, 1983.

are presented with a display consisting of a rod partly hidden by a block in front of it (see Figure 6-6, displays A and B). Will they perceive the rod as a whole object, even though part of it is not available for inspection, or, rather, will they act as though they had seen two short and separate rods?

To find out, Kellman and Spelke first presented 4-month-olds with either display A (stationary hidden rod) or display B (moving hidden rod) and allowed them to look at the display until they were no longer interested (habituation). Once they had habituated, the infants were shown displays C (a whole rod) and D (two rod segments), and their looking preferences were recorded. Infants who had habituated to the *stationary* hidden rod (display A) showed no distinct preference for displays C or D in the later test. In other words, they were apparently not able to use available cues—information such as the two identical rod tips oriented along the same line—to perceive a whole rod when part of the rod was hidden. By contrast, infants *did* apparently perceive the *moving* rod (display B) as "whole," for after habituating to this stimulus, they much preferred to look at the two short rods (display D) than at a whole rod (display C, which they now treated as "old hat"). It seems that these latter infants were inferring the rod's wholeness from its synchronized movement—the fact that its parts moved in the same direction at the same time.

How would 4-month-olds have responded if the two "rod tips" in display B had moved in *opposite* directions? They perceive them as *separate* objects, based on their independent motion (Hofsten & Spelke, 1985). So infants rely heavily on kinetic (motion) cues to identify objects as distinct forms. How soon they are able to use movement to perceive form is not known for sure, although research using Kellman and Spelke's procedure suggests that 3-month-olds can make such inferences (Spelke, Hofsten, & Kestenbaum, 1989) whereas newborn infants cannot. A newborn infant exposed to a partially screened moving rod sees two separate objects rather than a continuous form (Slater et al., 1990b).

Although synchronized motion is an important clue in determining what is or is not part of the same object, 3–4-month-old infants can also perceive form in some stationary scenes that capture their attention. Look carefully at Figure 6-7. Do you see a square in this display? So do 3–4-month-olds (Ghim, 1990)—a remarkable achievement indeed, for the boundary of this "square" is a *subjective contour* that must be constructed mentally rather than simply detected by the visual system.

Further strides in form perception occur later in the first year as infants begin to detect structural configurations from the barest of cues. By 9 months of age, infants exposed to the moving point-light displays shown in Figure 6-8 pay much more attention to display A than to displays B and C, as if they were interpreting this stimulus as a representation of the human form, just as adults do (Bertenthal et al., 1987). Twelve-month-old infants are even better at constructing form from limited information. After seeing a single point of light move so as to trace a complex shape such as a ▽, 12-month-olds (but not 8- or 10-month-olds) prefer to look at actual objects with *different* shapes. This preference for novelty on the part of the older infants indicates that they have perceived the form traced earlier by the light and now find it less interesting than other novel forms (Rose, 1988b; Skouteris, McKenzie, & Day, 1992).

Thus far, we have focused mainly on perception of abstract, inanimate forms—an ability that begins to emerge (clearly at least) by about 3 months of age. Let's now consider what we know about infants' perceptions of faces.

Face Perception

It could be argued that faces are among the more interesting visual stimuli that babies encounter in the natural environment. After all, faces have moving parts (lips, eyes), and that movement attracts attention. Faces are also rich in contrast, complexity, and curvature—features that we know will capture infants' attention. Finally, faces are readily available: A baby will be exposed to faces several times each day, whenever he or she is fed, soothed, bathed, or diapered. So there is reason to suspect that "faceness" may be one of the first forms that babies perceive and that infants may soon begin to discriminate the faces of familiar companions from those of strangers.

For the first 2 months, babies do not discriminate static drawings of faces from similar (scrambled face) representations, largely because they spend more time scanning high-contrast outer boundaries of visual stimuli rather than the internal features (eyes, mouth, and lips) that might define faces as meaningful (review Figure 6-5). By age 9–12 weeks, however, infants scan even more intensively and are becomimg much more interested in the internal features of a face than in its edges (Bronson, 1991; Haith, Bergman, & Moore, 1977). Does this increasing attention to internal detail mean that 3-month-olds are ready to perceive faces as a meaningful configuration? It seems that way. James Dannemiller and Ben Stephens (1988) have demonstrated that 3-month-olds (but not 6-week-olds) prefer normal faces to otherwise identical

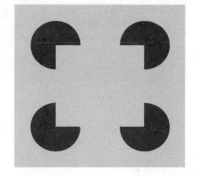

Figure 6-7

By 3 months of age, infants are perceiving subjective contours such as the "square" shown here.

Adapted from Bertenthal, Campos & Haith, 1980.

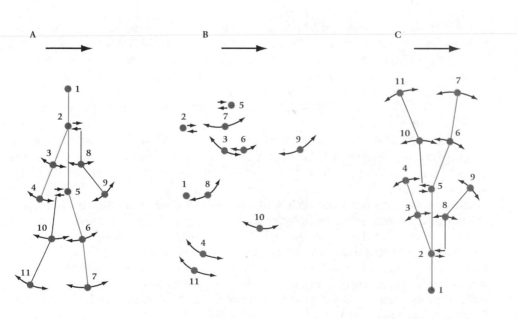

Figure 6-8

The three point-light displays used in Bertenthal's research.

From Bertenthal, Proffitt, & Cutting, 1984.

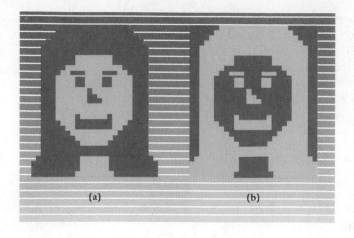

(a)   (b)

patterns in which areas that are normally dark on a face (eyes, mouth) were made light, and areas that are normally light (cheeks, forehead) were made dark (see Figure 6-9). Clearly, 3-month-olds know what real faces are supposed to look like. Equally remarkable are observations that 3-month-old infants are beginning to recognize photos of their mothers' faces and to prefer mom's photo to those of strangers. Moreover, 3-month-olds can discriminate the faces of two strangers, even when the strangers are thought to be quite similar in appearance by a panel of adult judges (Barrera & Maurer, 1981a; 1981b). Finally, 2–3-month-olds even prefer to look at faces that adults rate as attractive than at those that adults consider unattractive (Langlois et al., 1987). So somewhere between 9 and 12 weeks of age, infants seem to have formed a general scheme for the human face and a particular scheme for their mother's face. What's more, strangers do not all "look alike" and some faces are more appealing than others.

Let's note, however, that 3–4-month-olds may rarely discriminate one face from another unless they examine these stimuli for a long time. By contrast, 5–7-month-old infants can quickly discriminate their regular companions from strangers and may even recognize that a line drawing of a person's face and the person's photograph represent the same individual (Cohen, DeLoache, & Strauss, 1979; Nelson, 1987). In fact, 5–7-month-old infants are unlikely to "forget" a face, even if their exposure was brief (two or three minutes) and they do not see the face again for two weeks (Fagan, 1979).

Later in the first year, infants begin to *interpret* emotional expressions in their mother's face correctly and even to respond adaptively to this information. Although these latter abilities will be discussed later as social/emotional developments (see Chapter 11), they clearly illustrate that an infant's response to social interactions will depend, in part, on his ability to "read" faces.

Summing Up

Have you noticed that the development of face perception follows the same general course as the perception of other forms and patterns? Table 6-2 summarizes these achievements, pointing to three broad phases of development that infants display over the first year.

It should be clear from our review that neither "nature" nor "nurture" adequately explains how infants come to perceive forms, but that both of these influences are heavily involved. Newborns are biologically prepared to seek visual stimulation and to make visual discriminations. These visual *experiences* that a baby has then contribute to the development of the brain and its visual centers (maturation) which, in turn, help the infant to see more detail, to combine this information into organized wholes (forms), and to begin to interpret the forms he has detected. So the growth of form perception represents a fundamental interplay, or *interaction*, among the

Table 6-2 **Development of Form and Face Perception in the First Year**

Age/phase	General form perception	Face perception
Stimulus-seeking phase (0–2 months)	Incomplete scanning of visual stimuli with attention to boundaries or edges. Seeks visual input; prefers moderately complex stimuli with high visual contrast. Stimulus-seeking keeps visual neurons firing and contributes to maturation of vision centers of the brain.	No clear evidence of face perception.
Form-constructor phase (3–8 months)	Visual scanning of entire stimulus; combination of parts into an organized whole forms.	Prefers facelike stimulus to scrambled face. Perceives "faceness" and forms schemes for particular faces. Recognizes mother's face; prefers to look at some faces more than others.
Form-interpreter phase (9–12 months)	Infers meaningful form from limited information (for example, interpreting synchronous upright point-light display [see Figure 6-8] as a human form).	Correctly interprets others' simple emotional expressions; may use this information to regulate own behavior (see Chapter 11).

baby's innate endowment (a working, but immature, visual sense), maturational processes, and experience (or learning).

Let's see if this interactive model holds for spatial perception as well.

Perception of Three-Dimensional Space

Because we adults easily perceive depth and the third dimension, it is tempting to conclude that neonates can too. However, empiricists have argued that poor visual acuity and an inability to bring objects into sharp focus (that is, to accommodate) prevent the neonate from making accurate spatial inferences. In addition, infants younger than 4 months of age do not exhibit **stereopsis**—a convergence of the visual images of the two eyes to produce a singular, nonoverlapping image that has depth (Fox, Aslin, Shea, & Dumais, 1980). All these limitations may make it difficult for neonates to perceive depth and to locate objects in space.

However, nativists would argue that several cues to depth and distance are *monocular*—that is, detectable with only one eye. Movement of objects (such as the mother's head) toward and away from their faces may be one such cue that newborns can detect. And artists make good use of other **pictorial (or perspective) cues** to create the illusion of three-dimensionality on a two-dimensional surface. Examples are: *linear perspective* (making linear objects converge as they recede toward the horizon), *texture gradients* (showing more detail in nearby objects than in distant ones), *sizing cues* (drawing distant objects smaller than nearby ones), *interposition* (drawing a near figure to partly obscure one farther away), and *shading* (varying the lighting across an object's surface to create the impression of depth). If neonates can detect these monocular depth cues, then their world may be three-dimensional from the very beginning.

stereopsis: fusion of two flat images to produce a single image that has depth.

pictorial (perspective) cues: depth and distance cues, including linear perspective, texture gradients, sizing, interposition, and shading, that are monocular—that is, detectable with only one eye.

So when are infants capable of perceiving depth and making reasonably accurate inferences about size and spatial relations? Let's briefly consider four programs of research designed to answer these questions.

Early Use of Kinetic (Motion) Cues

As a moving object approaches, its retinal image becomes larger and larger and may expand to occupy the entire visual field (that is, it may loom) as it draws near the face. Do young infants react to **visual looming?** If so, we might infer that they perceive movement across the third dimension.

By 3 weeks of age, many infants will blink in response to looming objects, thus displaying a "defensive" reaction that becomes much stronger over the next 3 months (Nanez, 1987; Yonas, 1981). Do these findings mean that babies must learn to infer movement across the third dimension, as empiricists have claimed? Maybe so, but Albert Yonas (1981) is an *interactionist* who believes that early maturation of the visual system plays a major role in this learning. Consistent with his view is the finding that preterm infants, who are neurologically immature at birth, do not begin to blink at looming objects until several weeks after full-term infants do (Pettersen, Yonas, & Fisch, 1980). So it seems that a certain minimal amount of neural maturation may be necessary before infants interpret an object's approach as a cue for depth or distance.

By 4–5 months of age, infants are able to use other motion cues to make spatial inferences. They know, for example, that moving objects that eclipse other stimuli are "nearer" to them than the stimuli they conceal (Craton & Yonas, 1988). So, as was true of early form perception, very young infants rely heavily on kinetic (motion) cues to perceive depth and distance relations.

Development of Size Constancy

If a friend who stands 5 feet, 8 inches leaves your side and walks 20 feet away from you, the image of that person on your retina becomes much smaller. Yet you realize that your friend is still 5 feet, 8 inches and simply *looks* smaller because he or she is now farther away. This realization is an example of **size constancy**—the ability to infer that the dimensions of an object remain constant over a change in distance. Obviously, a person who displays size constancy has some understanding of spatial relations. Specifically, he or she recognizes that increases in distance can compensate for decreases in the size of a retinal image to preserve an object's absolute size.

When do babies first show any evidence of size constancy? Until very recently, researchers believed that this ability did not appear until 4–5 months of age, after infants had developed the binocular vision (stereopsis) that enables them to make accurate spatial inferences. But as Box 6-1 illustrates, even newborns know something about an object's real size.

Of course, the finding that neonates display some size constancy does not mean that this ability is fully developed. Apparently, binocular vision does promote the growth of size constancy, for the 4-month-olds who show greater evidence of this ability are those whose binocular capabilities are most mature (Aslin, 1987). Kinetic cues may also contribute; inferences about real size among 4½-month-olds are more likely to be accurate if the infants have watched an object approach and recede (Day & McKenzie, 1981). Size constancy steadily improves throughout the first year; however, this ability is not fully mature until 10–11 years of age (Day, 1987).

Use of Pictorial Cues

Albert Yonas and his associates have studied infants' reactions to monocular distance cues—the tricks that artists and photographers use to portray depth and distance on a two-dimensional surface. In the earliest of these studies (Yonas, Cleaves, & Pettersen, 1978), infants were exposed to a photograph of a bank of windows taken at a 45°

visual looming: the expansion of the image of an object to take up the entire visual field as it draws very close to the face.

size constancy: the tendency to perceive an object as the same size from different distances despite changes in the size of its retinal image.

BOX 6-1
Size Constancy in the Newborn

Alan Slater and his associates (1990a) designed a clever experiment to see whether newborn babies can perceive an object's real size across changes in distance. Each of their 2-day-old subjects was given ample opportunity to gaze at either a small (5.1-cm) cube or a large (10.2-cm) cube that was presented at six different distances (although none of the babies actually saw their cube move). The purpose of these six "familiarization" trials was to expose infants to changes in the size of the retinal image of the cube in the hope that this might direct their attention to the cube's *real* (unchanging) size.

After the six familiarization trials came the test for size constancy. Each infant now saw two cubes: the small one at a distance of 30.5 cm and the large one at 61 cm. At these distances, the two cubes cast retinal images of exactly the same size (see figure). How should a baby now respond if he perceives that the real size of the "familiar" cube was constant, despite changes in the size of its retinal image? He should quickly determine that whichever cube (large or small) that he had looked at before was still the "same old cube" and should now prefer to examine the novel cube.

This is precisely what 11 of Slater's 12 newborns did, spending more than 83% of their time gazing at whichever cube (large or small) they had not previously seen. So newborn infants were able to perceive the "real" size of the cube they had examined in the familiarization trials. In other words, they displayed clear evidence of size constancy in the first two days of life (see also Granrud, 1987).

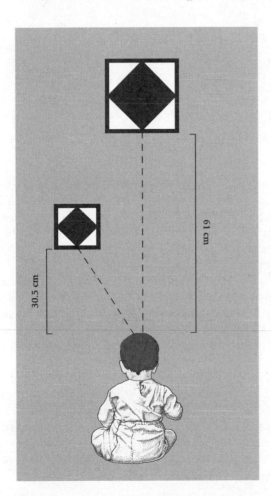

The test trial from the Slater, Mattock, & Brown (1990) experiment. As shown at the left, babies viewed a small cube at a distance of 30.5 cm and a cube twice as large at twice that distance, or 61 cm. At these distances, the two cubes cast the same-size retinal image. The illustration at the right shows what the baby saw on this "test trial."

Figure 6-10
This bank of windows is actually a large photograph taken at a 45° angle, and the two edges of this stimulus are in fact equidistant from an infant seated directly in front of it. If infants are influenced by pictorial cues to depth, they should perceive the right edge of the photo to be nearer to them and indicate as much by reaching out to touch this edge rather than the more "distant" edge to their left.

Adapted from Yonas, Cleaves, & Pettersen, 1978.

angle. As we see in Figure 6-10, the windows on the right appear (to us at least) to be much closer than those on the left. Which side of the large photograph would infants try to touch? If they perceive pictorial cues to distance, they might be fooled into thinking that the windows on the right are closer and might reach to the right. But if they are insensitive to pictorial cues, they should reach out with one hand about as often as they do with the other.

What Yonas found is that 7-month-olds reliably reached toward the windows that appear nearest, whereas 5-month-olds displayed no such reaching preferences. In later research, Yonas found that 7-month-olds are also sensitive to pictorial cues such as interposition (see Figure 6-11), relative size and shading cues, texture gradients, and linear perspective, whereas 5-month-olds are not (Yonas, Arterberry, & Granrud, 1987; Arterberry, Yonas, & Bensen, 1989).

In sum, infants become sensitive to different spatial cues at different ages. From a limited capacity for size constancy at birth, babies extract spatial information from kinetic cues between 1 and 3 months of age, binocular cues at 4 to 5 months, and monocular (pictorial) cues by age 6–7 months. Do these impressive accomplishments imply that a 6–7-month-old infant perceives depth and knows enough to avoid crawling off the edge of a sofa or a staircase? Let's see what researchers have learned from their attempts to answer these questions.

Development of Depth Perception

In the early 1960s, Eleanor Gibson and Richard Walk developed an apparatus they called the **visual cliff** to determine whether infants can perceive depth. The visual cliff (see Figure 6-12) consists of an elevated glass platform divided into two sections by a center board. On the "shallow" side, a checkerboard pattern is placed directly under the glass. On the "deep" side, the pattern is placed several feet below the glass, creating the illusion of a sharp dropoff, or a "visual cliff." The investigator tests an infant for depth perception by placing him on the center board and then asking the

visual cliff: an elevated platform that creates an illusion of depth, used to test the depth perception of infants.

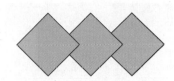

child's mother to try to coax the infant to cross both the "shallow" and the "deep" sides. Testing infants 6½ months of age and older, Gibson and Walk (1960) found that 90% of them would cross the shallow side, but fewer than 10% would cross the deep side. Apparently, most infants of crawling age clearly perceive depth and are afraid of dropoffs.

Might children who are too young to crawl also perceive depth? To find out, Joseph Campos and his associates (1970) recorded changes in infants' heart rates when they were lowered face down over the "shallow" and "deep" sides of the apparatus. Babies as young as 2 months of age showed a *decrease* in heart rate when over the deep side but no change in heart rate on the shallow side. Why a decrease in heart rate? When we are afraid, our hearts beat faster, not slower. A decrease in heart rate is a sign of interest. So 2-month-old infants *perceive a difference* between the deep and shallow sides, but they have not learned to *fear* dropoffs.

One reason that many 6–7-month-olds come to fear dropoffs is that they are more sensitive to kinetic, binocular, and monocular depth cues than younger infants are. Yet, this fear also depends very heavily on the experiences that older infants have had crawling about—and perhaps falling now and then. Joseph Campos and his associates (1992) found that infants who have crawled for a couple of weeks are much more afraid of dropoffs than are infants of the same age who are not yet crawling. In fact, precrawlers quickly develop a healthy fear of heights when given special walkers that allow them to move about on their own. So motor development provides experiences that change infants' interpretation of the meaning of depth.

Table 6-3 summarizes the infant's rapidly developing sensitivities to depth and spatial relations—a set of achievements that are best explained by an *interactive* model that stresses the contributions of maturation *and* learning (experience). Maturation of the visual sense enables infants to see better and to detect a greater variety of depth cues, while also contributing to the growth of motor skills. Yet learning is equally important: The first year is a time when curious infants are constantly making new and exciting discoveries about depth and distance relations as they become ever more skilled at reaching for and manipulating objects and at moving about to explore stairs, sloped surfaces, and other "visual cliffs" in the natural environment (Bertenthal, 1993; Bushnell & Boudreau, 1993).

Figure 6-11
If infants are sensitive to the pictorial cue of interposition, they should reliably reach for the "closest" area of a visual display (left side in this example). Seven-month-olds show this reaching preference, whereas 5-month-olds do not.
From Granrud & Yonas, 1984.

Figure 6-12
An infant at the edge of the visual cliff.

Table 6-3 Development of Spatial Perception in the First Year	
Age	*Perceptual sensitivities*
Newborn	Some evidence of size constancy.
3 weeks–4 months	Sensitivity to kinetic cues appears and improves; infant detects and reacts to looming objects; at age 2 months, infant perceives dropoffs (on a visual cliff).
4–6 months	Sensitivity to binocular cues appears and improves. Size constancy judgments become more reliable.
6–7 months (and beyond)	Sensitivity to pictorial cues appears; crawling infants develop a fear of heights.

 AUDITORY PERCEPTION IN INFANCY

Although we often think of humans as visual animals, babies less than 1 year old are actually more responsive to sounds than to sights (Lewkowicz, 1988). Not only do neonates pay careful attention to sounds, but it appears that they try to "make sense" of them as well—especially when what they hear is a human voice.

Perceiving Voices

Many people would undoubtedly chuckle if a mother were to claim that her week-old infant already recognizes her voice. Yet the mother might have the last laugh, for an experiment by Anthony DeCasper and William Fifer (1980) suggests that babies can recognize their mothers' voices during the first three days of life. Infants were given a special pacifier that recorded their sucking rate. Once their "baseline" sucking rates had been established, the procedure began. For half the infants, sucking faster than the baseline rate activated a recording of the mother's voice, and sucking slower than baseline produced a recording of a female stranger. Just the opposite was true for the remaining infants: Fast sucking produced the stranger's voice, and slow sucking activated a recording of the mother. DeCasper and Fifer found that their 1–3-day-old infants did whatever it took (that is, sucked faster or slower) in order to hear their own mothers. So they not only recognized the mother's voice but clearly preferred it to the voice of a female stranger.

More recently, DeCasper and Spence (1986; 1991) had mothers recite a passage (for example, portions of Dr. Seuss's *The Cat in the Hat*) many times during the last six weeks of their pregnancies. At birth, the infants were tested to see if they would suck more to hear the story they had heard before birth or a different story. Remarkably, they preferred the familiar story, whether it was read by their own mothers or another baby's mother. Somehow infants had learned and were able to recognize the distinctive sound patterns of the story they had heard in the womb. Of course, auditory learning before birth may also explain why newborns ordinarily prefer to hear their own mother's voice to that of another woman.

Perceiving the Components of Language

Not only do babies attend carefully to voices, but they are also able to discriminate basic speech sounds—called **phonemes**—very early in life. Peter Eimas (1975b, 1985) pioneered research in this area by demonstrating that infants 2 to 3 months old could distinguish consonant sounds that are very similar (for example, *ba* and *pa*). Indeed, infants less than 1 week old seem to be able to tell the difference between the vowels

phonemes: the basic units of sound that are used in a spoken language.

a and *i* (Clarkson & Berg, 1983) and even to segment words into discrete syllables (Bijeljac-Babic, Bertoncini, & Mehler, 1993). Just as babies divide the spectrum of light into basic color categories, they seem to divide the continuum of speech sounds into categories corresponding to the basic sound units of language (Kuhl, 1991). And they recognize a particular phoneme as the same sound even when it is spoken by different people (Marean, Werner, & Kuhl, 1992). These are impressive accomplishments.

Indeed, there are some phonemic discriminations that an infant can make better than an adult can (Werker & Tees, 1992). We begin life biologically prepared to learn any language that humans speak. But as we are exposed to a particular language, we normally become especially sensitive to the sound patterns that are important to that language and less sensitive to auditory distinctions that our language deems irrelevant. For example, infants easily discriminate the consonants *r* and *l* (Eimas, 1975a). So can you if your native language is English, French, Spanish, or German. However, Chinese and Japanese make no distinction between *r* and *l*, and adult native speakers of these languages cannot make this auditory discrimination as well as infants can (Miyawaki et al., 1975).

These findings illustrate two general principles of development that are very important. First, the growth of perceptual abilities, like so many other aspects of development, is not just a matter of adding new abilities; it is also a matter of *losing* unnecessary ones. Second, our *culture* largely determines which abilities are necessary or unnecessary. Language is a *cultural* tool, and the language we acquire influences our auditory perception. Richard Walk (1981; p. 61) aptly illustrates this point by concluding that "in some respects the Biblical story of the Tower of Babel is true—we have difficulty understanding each other's speech because to learn a new language is to change our auditory perception. We are . . . a foreigner in every language but our own."

The Sound of Music

Are babies musical creatures? Is listening to music an experience they enjoy? Apparently so. In one study that employed the high-amplitude sucking procedure, newborns either increased or decreased their rate of sucking on a pacifier when that strategy produced folk music, but they did whatever it took to *avoid* listening to nonrhythmic noise (see Figure 6-13). So it seems that babies really do like music and find noise aversive (Butterfield & Siperstein, 1972).

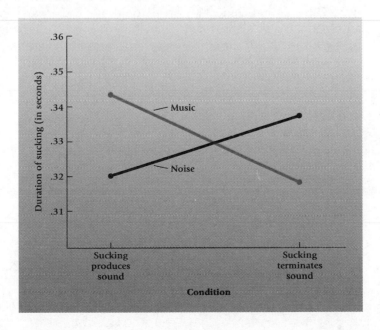

Figure 6-13
Duration of sucking by infants as a function of whether sucking produces music or noise. Clearly, newborns prefer music to noise.
From Butterfield & Siperstein, 1972.

By the age of 4–6 months, infants begin to "bounce" to music (Moog, 1976), and they are now becoming quite skilled at discriminating melodies and at recognizing the same tune despite changes in its pitch or tempo (Chang & Trehub, 1977; Trehub, 1985). They even perceive the structure of musical pieces, preferring to listen to Mozart appropriately segmented into natural musical phrases than to listen to the same Mozart piece stopped in the middle of a natural phrase (Krumhansl & Jusczyk, 1990). Although it is not yet clear whether young infants prefer Mozart to Muzak or Madonna, they are quite capable of perceiving those aspects of music that many of us find so enjoyable.

 ## INTERMODAL PERCEPTION

Suppose you are playing a game in which you are blindfolded and are trying to identify objects by touch. A friend places a small, perfectly spherical object in your hand. As you finger it, you determine that it is about 1½ inches in diameter, that it weighs a couple of ounces, and that it is very hard and covered with many small "dimples." You then say "aha" and conclude that the object is a _____.

A colleague who conducts this exercise in class reports that most students easily identify the object as a golf ball—even if they have never touched a golf ball in their lives. This is an example of **intermodal perception**—the ability to recognize by one sensory modality (in this case, touch) an object that is familiar through another (vision). As adults, we can make many inferences of this kind. When do babies first display these abilities?

Theories of Intermodal Perception

The timing of intermodal perception has been hotly debated over the years. On the one hand, *differentiation* theorists such as Thomas Bower (1982) and Eleanor Gibson (1969; 1992) believe that the senses are integrated at birth and that an interesting sight, sound, or touch sensation will cause infants to investigate further, using all their sensory modalities. Gibson (1969) adds that the "defining" features of many stimuli (shape, texture, and so on) are detectable by more than one modality. If she is correct, intermodal perception may be possible very early in life.

On the other hand, enrichment theorists such as Piaget (1954; 1960) believe that the senses are separate at birth and must mature independently before the infant will be able to compare and eventually integrate information from different sensory channels. Thus, an enrichment theorist would argue that very young infants who know an object only by sight would be unable to recognize it by touch (as in the dark) or to discriminate it from other objects on the basis of tactile cues alone.

Which theory is correct? Let's see if we can clarify the issue by examining the empirical record.

Are the Senses Integrated at Birth?

Suppose that you captured a baby's attention by floating a soap bubble in front of her face. Would she reach for it? If she did, how do you think she would react when the bubble pops at her slightest touch?

intermodal perception: the ability to use one sensory modality to identify a stimulus or pattern of stimuli that is already familiar through another modality.

virtual object: an intangible object (optical illusion), produced by a shadow caster, that appears to occupy a particular location in space.

Thomas Bower and his associates (Bower, Broughton, & Moore, 1970) exposed neonates to a situation similar to the soap-bubble scenario. The subjects were 8–31-day-old infants who could see an object well within reaching distance while they were wearing special goggles. Actually, this **virtual object** was an illusion created by a shadow caster. If the infant reached for it, his or her hand would feel nothing at all. Bower et al. found that the infants did reach for the virtual object and that they often became frustrated to tears when they failed to touch it. These results suggest that vision and touch are integrated: Infants expect to feel objects that they can see and reach, and an incongruity between vision and the tactile sense is discomforting.

According to differentiation theory, the senses are integrated at birth, and babies expect to touch and feel objects that they can see and reach. However, vision and touch are soon differentiated, so that this year-old infant might even enjoy making an object disappear at her slightest touch.

Other research on auditory-visual incongruities (Aronson & Rosenbloom, 1971) reveals that 1–2-month-olds often become distressed when they *see* their talking mothers behind a soundproof screen but *hear* mother's voice through a speaker off to the side. Their discomfort implies that vision and audition are integrated: A baby who sees his mother expects to hear her voice coming from the general direction of her mouth.

In sum, the differentiation theorists appear to be right on one score: The senses are apparently integrated very early in life. But even though young infants dislike sensory incongruities, their negative emotional reactions in no way establish that they are able to use one sense to recognize objects or experiences that are already familiar through another sense.

Development of Intermodal Perception

Although intermodal perception has never been observed in newborns, it seems that babies only 1 month old have the ability to recognize by sight at least some of the objects they have previously sucked. In one study, Eleanor Gibson and Arlene Walker (1984) allowed 1-month-old infants to suck either a rigid cylinder or a spongy, pliable one. Then the two objects were displayed visually to illustrate that the spongy cylinder would bend and the rigid one would not. The results were clear: Infants who had sucked on a spongy object preferred to look at the rigid cylinder, whereas those who had sucked on a rigid cylinder now gazed more at the pliable one. Apparently, these infants could "visualize" the object they had sucked and now considered it less interesting than the other stimulus, which was new to them.

Since 30-day-old infants have had ample experience sucking on both spongy objects (nipples) and rigid ones (their own thumbs), we cannot necessarily conclude that intermodal perception is innate. And before we get too carried away with the remarkable proficiencies of 1-month-olds, let's note that (1) oral-to-visual perception is the only cross-modal skill that has ever been observed in infants this young, and (2) this ability is weak, at best, in very young infants and will improve dramatically over the first year (Rose, Gottfried, & Bridger, 1981). Even the seemingly related ability to match tactile sensations (from grasping) with visual ones does not appear until 4–6 months of age (Rose et al., 1981; Streri & Spelke, 1988), largely because infants younger than this cannot grasp objects well (Bushnell & Boudreau, 1993).

Intermodal tranfer between vision and hearing emerges at about 4–5 months of age—precisely the time that infants begin to *voluntarily* turn their heads in the direction of sounds. By age 5 months, infants can even match visual and auditory cues for distance. So if they are listening to a sound track in which engine noise is becoming softer, they prefer to watch a film of a car moving away rather than one showing a vehicle approaching (Walker-Andrews & Lennon, 1985; see also Pickens, 1994). Clearly, 4–5-month-olds know what sights jibe with many sounds, and this auditory/visual matching continues to improve over the next several months.

Another Look at the Enrichment/Differentiation Controversy

So which theory—enrichment or differentiation—best explains the development of intermodal perception? The evidence we have reviewed tends to favor differentiation theory. Not only are very young infants often upset by sensory incongruities, just as differentiation theorists had expected, but the fact that 1-month-olds show *any* intermodal matching seems more consistent with the differentiation viewpoint (simultaneous detection of defining features by different modalities) than with the enrichment perspective (independent detection of defining features followed by a gradual integration of this information across modalities). And as we will see in Box 6-2, infants often need only brief exposures to *novel* stimuli in order to draw accurate intermodal inferences—a finding that is clearly consistent with differentiation theory.

Why, then, do intermodal judgments become more accurate over time? Probably because as each sense continues to develop, it becomes a more effective means of detecting the defining features of novel stimuli. But the fact that even young infants can match sensations across modalities is very significant, for this capacity helps them to organize and interpret a bewildering array of stimuli in the natural environment and keeps their world from becoming a "blooming, buzzing confusion." Indeed, infants who are especially skilled at integrating their sensory experiences will later tend to perform well on IQ tests, thus suggesting that intermodal perceptual ability is an early indicator of future intellectual performance (Rose et al., 1991).

Concept Check 6-2 ⌄ Infant Perceptual Development

Check your understanding of selected aspects of infant perceptual development by filling in the blanks in each statement below. The answers appear in the Appendix.

1. Neonates are biologically prepared to seek visual stimulation—*experiences* that contribute to the _____ of the brain's visual centers, which, in turn, enable the infant to see more detail and to perceive _____ _____.

2. Infants' early attention to _____ cues is thought to be important for the development of both _____ perception and _____ perception.

3. Although infants can perceive _____ cues by age 2 months, they are unlikely to _____ _____ before they begin to crawl.

4. An effect of _____ on auditory perception is aptly illustrated by the finding that infants are _____ than adults at discriminating sounds that are not used in the language of their culture.

5. Apparently, the senses are _____ at birth (or shortly thereafter), for very young infants often become _____ over sensory incongruities. This finding provides some support for the _____ theory of intermodal perception.

 INFANT PERCEPTION IN PERSPECTIVE

What remarkable perceptual competencies infants display! All their senses are functioning reasonably well at birth, and babies immediately put them to work, searching for stimuli to explore and identifying similarities and differences among these

BOX 6-2

Simultaneous Integration of Sights and Sounds in 3-Month-Olds

*R*ecently, Lorraine Bahrick (1988) found a way to test a central assumption of differentiation theory—namely, that young infants are able to integrate information *quickly* from different sensory channels to make accurate perceptual judgments. Bahrick worked with 3-month-olds because infants this young had shown *no* evidence of auditory/visual matches in previous laboratory research. During an initial familiarization session, each infant received brief (1-minute) exposures to each of the cylinders in the photograph. As each cylinder rotated, the infant heard tape-recorded impact sounds that were either *appropriate* or *inappropriate* for the sights they were witnessing. When viewing the cylinder full of marbles, for example, some infants heard the sounds of many objects striking the cylinder (sounds appropriate for sights), whereas others heard the sounds of one big object (sounds inappropriate for sights). In addition, these tape-recorded sounds were presented either in temporal synchrony or out of synchrony with the motions that infants observed.

After this brief familiarization period and a short rest, the test phase began. Infants were shown films, on a split screen, of one object and of several objects moving within their respective cylinders. However, the single sound track that infants heard was appropriate for only one of the two films (for example, impact sounds of several marbles in a cylinder). Did infants display accurate judgments by looking most at the test film for which the sights matched the sounds? Indeed they did, but only if their initial exposures to the cylinders (during the familiarization phase) had been accompanied by *appropriate* sounds played *in synchrony* with the movement of the objects. So naive 3-month-old infants, who do not ordinarily display auditory/visual matches, were able to link sights quickly with *synchronous* and *appropriate* sounds during a brief (1-minute) exposure in which they were induced to pay close attention to these sensory inputs. Apparently, differentiation theorists were correct: Integration of sensory information across modalities occurs almost simultaneously from the day infants are first able to detect such input in each sensory channel.

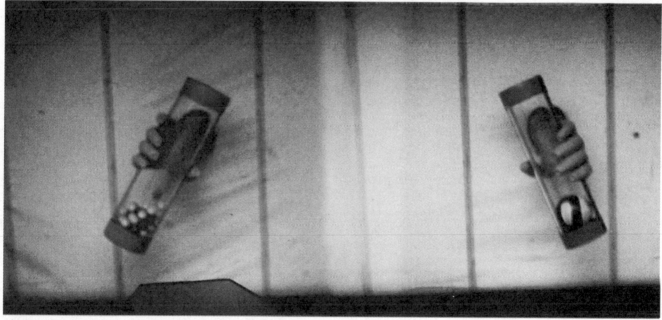

The visual stimuli observed by 3-month-olds in Bahrick's experiment.
From Bahrick, 1988.

sensory inputs. Within the first few months, infants become accomplished perceivers: They detect forms, react to depth and distance cues, recognize definite patterns in auditory inputs such as speech and music, and regularly combine information from the various sensory modalities (intermodal perception) to achieve a richer understanding of the natural environment. Not surprisingly, then, the most notable advances later in infancy reflect an increasing ability to *interpret* sensory experiences— recognizing, for example, that heights can be hazardous, that certain patterns of movement imply animation (recall 9-month-olds' reactions to Bertenthal's point-light displays in Figure 6-8), that dad's face implies security and good times, or (as we will see in Chapter 11) that mom's wary look suggests that "I should be cautious." We have concentrated heavily on the perceptual skills of infants because infancy is a period of rapid development when the most basic perceptual competencies emerge (Bornstein, 1992). Yet, we will find that there are other perceptual hurdles that children must overcome before they are capable of learning to read or are very proficient at such tasks as studying amid distractions or finding a well-camouflaged playmate during a game of hide-and-seek.

PERCEPTUAL LEARNING AND DEVELOPMENT IN CHILDHOOD

If most sensory and perceptual development is complete by the end of infancy, what then is left to accomplish? Perceptual development in childhood is largely a matter of the development of *attention*—that is, the ability to use one's senses planfully or strategically to gather information most pertinent to the tasks one faces.

Development of Attention

From birth, infants actively use their senses to explore the environment and even prefer some sensory stimuli to others (Gibson, 1987). Yet, the attention of young infants is "captured by" objects and events. One-month-olds, for example, do not deliberately choose to attend to a face; instead, faces attract their attention. Similarly, preschoolers who seem totally immersed in one activity can quickly lose interest and just as quickly get caught up in another activity. As children grow older, their attention spans increase, they become more selective in what they will attend to, and they are better able to formulate and carry out systematic plans for gathering information necessary to accomplish their goals.

Changes in Attention Span

Visit a nursery school and you will see that teachers are likely to switch classroom activities every 15–20 minutes. Why? Because young children have very short **attention spans;** they rarely concentrate on any single activity for very long. In one study of children's capacity for sustained attention (Yendovitskaya, 1971), subjects were asked to put strips of colored paper in appropriately colored boxes, and the time they devoted to this task was measured. Children aged $2^1/_2$–$3^1/_2$ worked at the task for an average of only 18 minutes and were easily distracted. By contrast, $5^1/_2$–6-year-olds were much more persistent, often working at the task for an hour or more. Even when doing things they like, such as playing with toys or watching TV, 2- and 3-year-olds often look away, move about, and direct their attention elsewhere, thus spending far less time on the activity at hand than older children do (Anderson et al., 1986; Ruff & Lawson, 1990).

The capacity for sustained attention continues to improve throughout childhood and early adolescence, and these improvements may be due, in part, to maturational changes in the central nervous system. For example, the **reticular formation,** an area of the brain responsible for the regulation of attention, is not fully **myelinated** until puberty. Perhaps this neurological development helps to explain why adolescents and young adults are suddenly able to spend hours on end cramming for upcoming exams or typing furiously to make morning deadlines on term papers.

Changes in Planfulness

As they grow older, children also become better able to plan and carry out systematic perceptual searches. We have already seen that 2–3-month-old infants are more likely than younger ones to explore a visual stimulus, both its edges and its interior. Nevertheless, a 3-month-old will scan only portions of a complex visual stimulus.

attention span: a person's capacity for sustaining attention to a particular stimulus or activity.

reticular formation: an area of the brain that serves to activate the organism and is thought to be important in regulating attention.

myelinization: the process by which neurons are encased in waxy myelin sheaths that facilitate transmission of neural impulses.

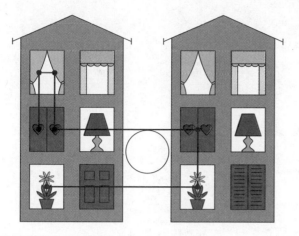
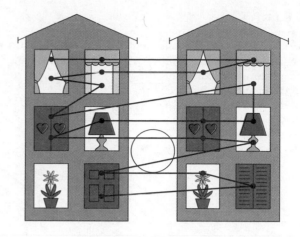

Five-year-old: "The same"   Eight-year-old: "Not the same"

Research conducted with Russian children reveals that visual scanning becomes considerably more detailed or "exhaustive" over the first six years of life (Zaporozhets, 1965). But the most revealing findings come from studies of how children conduct a visual search. Elain Vurpillot (1968) recorded the eye movements of 4–10-year-olds who were trying to decide whether two houses, each with several windows containing various objects, were identical or different. As shown in Figure 6-14, 4- and 5-year-olds were not very systematic or thorough: They searched only a few windows and often reached the wrong conclusion. By contrast, children older than 6½ were highly systematic. Their planned searches involved checking each window in one house with the corresponding window in the other house, pair by pair, until they arrived at a judgment (which was likely to be correct). Older children are also more likely than younger ones to have a systematic plan for searching the environment for objects that are lost (Wellman, 1985).

Changes in Selective Attention

With age, we develop **selective attention**—that is, we get better at concentrating on whatever it is that we are trying to attend to while ignoring irrelevant or distracting sensations. Consider what Eleanor Maccoby (1967) found when she placed kindergarten children and second-, third-, and sixth-graders in a situation similar to what we might experience at a noisy cocktail party, where it is often difficult to follow one conversation as other nearby conversations compete for our attention. The children in Maccoby's research first listened (on headphones) to different phrases spoken simultaneously by a male and a female and were later asked to identify what either the male or the female had said. On some occasions, the children knew in advance which voice they would be asked to recall. These "preparatory" trials were similar to the situation in which we are trying to listen to one speaker while ignoring other conversations around us. On the remaining trials, the children did not know in advance which voice they would be asked to recall. These "nonpreparatory" trials were in some ways similar to a party situation in which we are trying to monitor two conversations at the same time.

The results appear in Figure 6-15. As you can see, older children clearly outperformed younger children on both the preparatory and the nonpreparatory trials, indicating that selective attention improves with age. In addition, performance in all age groups was much better on the preparatory than on the nonpreparatory trials. Clearly, it is easier to understand what someone has said if we attend selectively to that person and do not try to monitor another voice (or conversation) at the same time.

To summarize, then, learning to control attention is an important aspect of perceptual development. With age, children become better able to (1) concentrate on a task for long periods; (2) search systematically for information that will help them

Figure 6-14
Are the houses in each pair exactly the same or different? Preschool children often guess incorrectly because they do not systematically compare all the pairs of windows as school-aged children do.
Based on Vurpillot, 1968.

selective attention: the focusing of attention on certain aspects of experience while ignoring irrelevant or distracting sensations.

Figure 6-15
Performance on a selective attention task as a function of age. Older children were more proficient than younger children at dividing their attention between two speakers (the nonpreparatory condition) and at concentrating on one speaker while ignoring the other (preparatory condition).
Adapted from Maccoby, 1967.

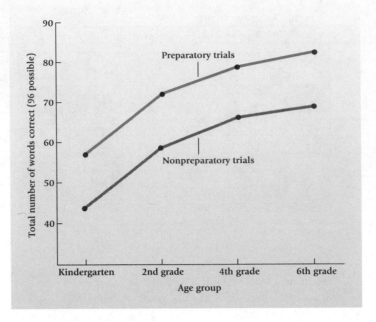

to accomplish goals; and once detected, (3) focus on this pertinent information while filtering out distractions.

Now let's consider the changes that occur in children's ability to perceive visual forms—changes that depend, in part, on the control of attention.

Development of Form Perception

Imagine that you are walking through a snow-covered forest when you notice what appears to be movement beside a bush on your left. You stop, stare, and lo and behold, you make out the shape of a white rabbit almost perfectly camouflaged against the sterile, white backdrop of a snowbank. Now suppose you had a 4-year-old child with you who had also seen the movement beside the bush. Do you think that he could have detected the camouflaged form as well as you did? If the child sees the form, could he easily identify it as a rabbit?

This perceptual task presents a young child with two basic challenges. First, he must be able to scan the area systematically and ignore such distractions as blowing snow or rustling limbs to have any chance of detecting a well-camouflaged form against a perceptually similar background. And even if he detects the form, he must then recognize that it is indeed a rabbit rather than a cat, a bird, or a squirrel. So how might young children fare when facing such tasks?

Unmasking Camouflaged Forms

Apparently, young children are not terribly proficient at unmasking visual forms, even when they know a hidden figure is present and they devote their attention to finding it. If you have read the children's section of your newspaper, you have undoubtedly seen "embedded figures" puzzles in which the task is to find hidden objects (for example, a spoon, a dog) in a distracting visual context. L. Ghent (1956) administered an **embedded figures test** to children of different ages (see Figure 6-16) and found that the ability to unmask hidden objects develops very slowly. For example, only 25% of Ghent's 8-year-olds were able to ignore the distracting background and find all the embedded figures in her relatively simple test.

Another method of testing children's ability to unmask visual forms is to present them with an incomplete figure and then gradually add information until they recognize the stimulus. Eugene Gollin (1960, 1962) showed 3–5-year-olds sketchy out-

embedded figures test: a measure of the ability to locate hidden objects in a distracting visual context.

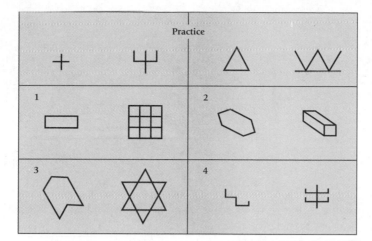

Figure 6-16
The embedded figures test used by Ghent to measure children's ability to unmask visual forms. On this test, the child's task is to find the figure at the left of each card within the more complex figure to the immediate right.
From Ghent, 1956.

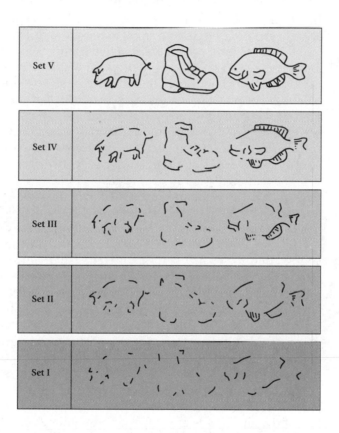

Figure 6-17
Sample stimulus figures that vary in completeness. Children are first shown figures from Set I, then Set II, and so on until they can identify the object.
Adapted from Gollin, 1962.

lines of common objects such as a pig, a shoe, and a fish (see Set I of Figure 6-17). If the child did not recognize the objects, more and more detail was added (Sets II–V) until he or she correctly identified them. Gollin found that many 3-year-olds reached Set IV before they could identify the objects, while 4-year-olds identified them at Set III, and 5-year-olds were often correct at Set II. A later study (Spitz & Borland, 1971) found that people become even more proficient at unmasking incomplete forms between kindergarten (age 5) and late adolescence.

What do these studies imply about a 4-year-old's ability to detect a camouflaged white rabbit? They seem to suggest that even an attentive 4-year-old may have difficulty seeing an all-white object "embedded" in a snowbank. And if the child caught a quick glimpse of the "figure" before it ran behind a bush, he might still be unable to identify it as a rabbit on the basis of such sketchy information.

Why do preschoolers require so much information in order to recognize common

Figure 6-18

Examples of figures used to test children's ability to detect the distinctive features of letterlike forms. Stimulus 1 is the standard. The child's task is to examine each of the comparison stimuli (stimuli 2–7) and pick out those that are the same as the standard.

Adapted from Gibson, Gibson, Pick, & Osser, 1962.

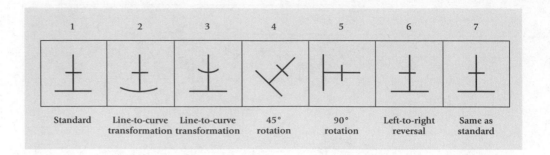

objects such as rabbits, pigs, or shoes? And just what characteristics of a visual display are likely to capture their attention? Eleanor Gibson's differentiation theory addresses these very issues.

Perceptual Learning in Childhood: Gibson's Differentiation Theory

According to Gibson (1969; 1987; 1992), **perceptual learning** occurs when we actively explore objects in our environment and detect their *distinctive (or invariant) features.* As we have noted, a distinctive feature is any cue that *differentiates* one stimulus from all others. A 3-year-old may initially confuse rabbits and cats, for both are furry animals of about the same size. However, the child will eventually discover that rabbits have long ears—a distinctive feature that differentiates them from cats, rats, squirrels, and all other small, furry animals. Gibson believes that the motivation for perceptual learning is inborn; from birth, humans are active information seekers who will search for order and stability (invariants) in the natural environment.

Of course, some invariants are easier to detect than others. Even a 4-year-old whose attentional strategies are relatively immature soon notices large distinctive features such as an elephant's trunk or a rabbit's long ears. However, a 4-year-old may not easily differentiate *b* from *d* because the distinctive feature that discriminates these letters (the direction of curvature) is subtle and not very meaningful to her.

Gibson and her colleagues have conducted an experiment to study the ability of young children to distinguish different letterlike forms (Gibson, Gibson, Pick, & Osser, 1962). Children aged 4 to 8 were shown a standard letterlike stimulus and several transformations of this "standard" form (examples appear in Figure 6-18). Their task was to pick out the stimuli that were identical to the standard. The 4- and 5-year-olds had difficulties with all the transformations; they often judged these stimuli to be identical to the standard. However, 6–8-year-olds were generally able to detect the "distinctive features" that differentiated the transformations from the "standard" stimulus.

Perhaps you can see the relevance of Gibson's work for elementary education—particularly reading education. Clearly, the ability to discriminate and categorize letters of the alphabet is a major perceptual milestone that is necessary before children can hope to decode words and become proficient readers (Gibson & Levin, 1975). Although preschool training in letter recognition (at home, at nursery school, and on educational television programs such as *Sesame Street*) helps children to recognize many letters and even a few words (such as their own names), preschoolers younger than 5–5½ continue to confuse letters such as *b, h,* and *d* or *m* and *w* that have similar perceptual characteristics (Chall, 1983). By contrast, Gibson's subjects began to detect and appreciate subtle differences in *unfamiliar* letterlike forms at precisely the time (age 6) that serious reading instruction began at school. As it turns out, learning to read is a very complex task—one that deserves a closer look. Box 6-3 describes several of the major perceptual hurdles that children must overcome to make sense of all those funny little squiggles on the printed page.

In sum, Gibson is a *differentiation* theorist. She believes that young children are constantly extracting new and more subtle information from the environment and thereby discovering the properties, patterns, and "distinctive features" that will enable

perceptual learning: changes in one's ability to extract information from sensory stimulation that occur as a result of experience.

BOX 6-3
How Do We Learn to Read?

One of the most challenging perceptual tasks that children in modern societies face is learning to read. How do they come to realize that the print on the page represents spoken words? How do they learn to translate print into spoken language?

Eleanor Gibson and Harry Levin (1975) have identified three phases in learning to read. First, children equate reading with storytelling: They may pick up a storybook and "read" very sensible sentences, most of which have no relation to the words on the page.

Next, children recognize that the squiggles on the printed page represent words. They may then try to match the spoken words of a familiar story to the symbols on the page, often incorrectly (Smith, 1977). Thus, a 3-year-old who knows that the title of her storybook is *Santa Is Coming to Town* might try to "read" the cover by touching each letter and uttering a word or syllable, as illustrated here. This kind of activity sets the stage for learning that each letter is related to a particular sound and that combinations of letters (and sounds) make up printed words (Crain-Thoreson & Dale, 1992).

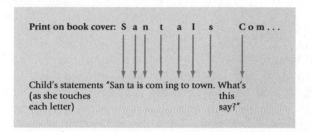

In the third and final phase of learning to read, children become quite skilled at decoding letters; they can "sound out" unfamiliar words by breaking them into individual sounds or syllables. Children gain solid mastery of the rules for translating letters into sounds by third or fourth grade (Morrison, 1984). However, the complexities of letter/sound correspondences in English can give even older readers problems: For example, the *c* in *circle* is pronounced very differently from the *c* in *cannery*, and the *gh* in *ghetto* does not sound a bit like the *gh* in *rough*.

In part, reading is an exercise in visual form perception. Readers must learn to recognize the distinctive features of letters, an ability that most youngsters begin to display by age 6 (see text). But reading is really a complex, *intermodal* task: To make sense of written words, children must not only differentiate among letters but must also learn which letters correspond to which sounds in spoken language. And detecting letter-sound correspondences seems to depend very heavily on *phonological awareness*—the realization that *spoken* words can be decomposed into basic sound units, or *phonemes*. Interestingly, the relationship between

phonological processing skills and reading-related knowledge is *bidirectional:* Early phonological processing skills permit children to become more knowledgeable about reading, which makes them better phonological processors, which contributes to further advances in reading-related knowledge (Wagner, Torgesen, & Rashotte, 1994).

Perceiving the distinctive features of letters and the correspondence between letters and sounds are tough tasks for preschool children.

What does all this suggest about teaching children to read? The merits of two broad approaches to reading instruction have been debated for years. The *"phonics"* or *"code-oriented"* approach teaches children to break words down into their component sounds—that is, it systematically teaches them letter/sound correspondence rules (Vellutino, 1991). By contrast, the *"whole-language"* approach emphasizes reading for meaning and teaches children to recognize whole words by sight or to figure out what they mean using clues in the surrounding context. This approach assumes that the "parts" of printed words (the letters) are not as meaningful as the whole words and that children can learn to read as effortlessly and naturally as they learn to understand speech.

Although children can learn to read by either form of instruction, research clearly indicates that, somehow or another, they must learn exactly what the phonics or code-oriented approach attempts to teach them if they are ever to read well (Adams, 1990; Hatcher, Hulme, & Ellis, 1994; Vellutino, 1991). However, many reading experts see advantages to both approaches and believe that children may learn best if they are taught letter/sound correspondences (phonics method) *and* are helped to find meaning and enjoyment in what they read (whole-language method) (Adams, 1990; Hatcher et al., 1994).

them to differentiate objects and events. As this differentiation continues, a child grows perceptually and becomes increasingly accurate at interpreting the broad array of stimuli that impinge on the sensory receptors.

 ## ENVIRONMENTAL INFLUENCES ON PERCEPTION

We have seen that newborn infants immediately sense their environments and display some amazing perceptual capabilities as well (for example, recognizing voices and perceiving the real size of objects that they have had lots of time to examine). But capable as neonates may be, the further development of all their basic perceptual skills depends, in part, on the *experiences* they have.

According to the *interactionist* model, one's experiences foster perceptual growth in at least two ways. First, environmental stimuli that are detected by the sensory receptors trigger neurological responses which, in turn, contribute to the maturation of the sensory areas of the brain and the neural pathways between the brain and the sensory receptors. In addition, the environment in which a child is raised largely determines the kinds of sensory input that her rapidly maturing neurological hardware will have to analyze and interpret.

Are there experiences that an individual *must* have in order to develop a normal repertoire of perceptual skills? Are the ways that we perceive the world at all influenced by the home and cultural settings in which we live? In this final section of the chapter, we will explore both of these issues and see that one's experiences are indeed important contributors to perceptual growth and development.

What Kinds of Early Experiences Are Important?

You have probably heard the expression "Use it or lose it," a cultural maxim implying that our basic abilities will deteriorate if we fail to exercise them. Students of perceptual development have tested this proposition by observing the progress of subjects (generally animals) that have been deprived of certain sensory or motor experiences. The logic underlying these "deprivation" experiments is straightforward. If subjects show a perceptual deficit of some kind after a period of sensory or motor deprivation, then the experiences that they did *not* have must be necessary for normal perceptual development.

Neurological Effects of Visual Deprivation

In Chapter 5, we briefly discussed Austin Riesen's classic research with visually deprived chimpanzees. Recall that chimps raised in the dark experienced atrophy (degeneration) of the optic nerve, which seriously restricted their vision. This atrophy was reversible if the animal spent no more than seven months in the dark but became permanent if the deprivation lasted much longer. And there is more. If dark-reared chimps were exposed to diffuse, *unpatterned* light for brief periods every day, damage to the optic nerve did *not* occur. Yet animals deprived of patterned stimulation later had difficulty discriminating forms such as circles and squares—a task that normal chimps can easily master (Riesen, 1965).

In short, the visual system requires stimulation, including *patterned* stimulation, early in life to develop normally—in humans as well as in chimpanzees. Some babies are born with cataracts that make them nearly blind. Once surgery restores their sight, they, like Riesen's chimps, have difficulty, at least initially, discriminating common forms such as spheres and cubes (Walk, 1981). Full and lasting recovery of perceptual abilities after a period of early visual deprivation is sometimes very difficult to achieve (Mitchell, 1988).

We even seem to require specific kinds of patterned stimulation for the visual areas of the brain to develop properly (Gandelman, 1992; Greenough, Black, & Wallace, 1987). Specific neural cells respond to either horizontal, vertical, or oblique (slanted) lines, for example. If a kitten is fitted with goggles that allow it to view only vertical stripes, it develops an abundance of "vertical" cells but loses some of the cells that would enable it to detect horizontal and oblique lines (Stryker et al., 1978). Similarly, humans who have severe **astigmatisms**—misshapen lenses that distort images—often have lasting difficulty seeing lines equally well in all orientations even after their vision is corrected (Mitchell et al., 1973).

This same message applies to the sense of hearing: Not only can auditory deprivation impair the development of the brain's auditory centers (Finitzo, Gunnarson & Clark, 1990), but hearing-impaired children who receive no special intervention before the age of 3 usually have lasting difficulties with speech and language skills (Associated Press, 1993). So maturation alone is not enough; *normal perceptual development also requires normal perceptual experience.*

Self-Produced Movement and Perception

Suppose that an infant were kept tied to a cradleboard (as is done in some cultures) so that she could see but could not move. Would this inability to reach for or to crawl toward interesting objects have an adverse effect on her visual perception?

An early study of kittens suggested that it might. Richard Held and Alan Hein (1963) raised kittens in the dark for 8–12 weeks before giving them access to a lighted environment for three hours a day. *Active* kittens moved about in the lighted environment while pulling the apparatus shown in Figure 6-19, whereas their *passive* partners merely rode in the cart and never moved about on their own. After several days of experience in the light, both groups of kittens were tested for fear of heights on the visual cliff. And the results were clear: Active kittens *always* avoided the deep side of the visual cliff, whereas passive kittens did not—at least not until they were given 48 hours of unrestrained access to a lighted environment. Held and Hein concluded that kittens (and possibly human infants) must move around on their own in an environment that contains visual cues before they are likely to develop any fear of heights.

However, Richard Walk (1981) suspected that young animals need not move about independently to perceive depth and distance relations as long as objects in the environment move, approaching and receding from the animal's own position. Walk tested his **motion hypothesis** by rearing kittens in the dark for seven weeks and then exposing them to different visual environments. He found that (1) kittens placed

astigmatism: a refractive defect of the lens of the eye that prevents the formation of clear, distinct images.

motion hypothesis: the notion that individuals must attend to objects that move in order to develop a normal repertoire of visual/spatial skills.

Figure 6-19
The experimental apparatus used by Held and Hein to study the effects of locomotion on visual perception. An active kitten (A) pulls its passive littermate (P). The two kittens have the same visual experiences, but only the active kitten is allowed to move about on its own.
Adapted from Held & Hein, 1963.

in restraining holders with no interesting movement to watch tended to doze off and showed no more depth perception than other kittens raised entirely in the dark, but that (2) kittens in restraining holders who had watched cars streak around a race-track, approaching and receding, had depth perception equal to that of "active" kittens who were free to move around in a lighted environment. So all that kittens needed to develop normal depth perception was passive exposure to *moving* objects that captured their attention.

Research with human infants. Is attention to moving objects sufficient to ensure normal visual perception in human infants? Possibly so, for thalidomide babies who are born without arms or legs come to perceive depth and distance relationships, even though their own bodily movements are severely restricted (Gouin-DeCarie, 1969). And yet, we have already seen that crawling infants who have had ample experiences moving on their own usually fear the deep side of a visual cliff, whereas precrawlers of the same age do not (Campos et al., 1992). Moreover, crawlers are better than precrawlers at remembering where hidden objects have been placed (Kermoian & Campos, 1988), possibly because crawlers (1) have learned that the visual environment changes when they move, and thus (2) have become more inclined to use some kind of *visual landmark* to help them define where they (and hidden objects) are located in relation to the larger spatial layout (Acredolo, 1978). So these latter observations seem to imply that self-produced movement is a strong contributor to the growth of visual perception.

How might we explain these seemingly inconsistent outcomes? A recent study by Dina Bai and Bennett Bertenthal (1992) provides some clues. Seven- to 8-month-old creepers and precreepers saw a toy placed into one of two different-colored containers on a table. Next, either the infant or the table was rotated 180° (see Figure 6-20), and the infant was allowed to search for the toy. The results were clear. When the infant was rotated, creepers were much better at finding the hidden toy than precreepers were, presumably because creepers were more inclined to use the color of the correct cup as a spatial landmark to tell them where to search after their own position in space had changed. But *when the table was rotated* (and the infant did not move), both creepers and precreepers tracked the movement *of the containers* and were equally proficient at finding the hidden toy. So human infants' knowledge of the location of objects in space depends very heavily on their visual tracking of moving objects *and* their use of spatial landmarks. While self-produced movement seems to promote tracking activities and landmark use (Horobin & Acredolo, 1986; Bai & Bertenthal, 1992), it is attention to motion-related visual cues (rather than self-produced movement per se) that contributes most directly to the development of spatial perception (see also Arterberry et al., 1989).

Taken together, these studies imply that our infant on the cradleboard will suffer no serious perceptual deficits as long as she is regularly exposed to moving objects that *capture her attention*. Of course, moving stimuli are very common in a typical home environment, which perhaps explains why children without arms and legs develop normal spatial abilities even though their motor activities are severely restricted.

Social and Cultural Influences

Do people who grow up in different societies and subcultures perceive the world in different ways? Certainly perceptual *preferences* differ from culture to culture. For example, there are cultures in which people are not at all revolted by the thought of eating rats and snakes, may think that hefty women with rounded physiques are more beautiful than the trim "Hollywood starlet" types, and are likely to favor a type of music that may or may not even appeal to us. So culture clearly provides standards for social perception—that is, for evaluating other people and their activities. But do our social backgrounds affect our perception of inanimate objects and the physical environment?

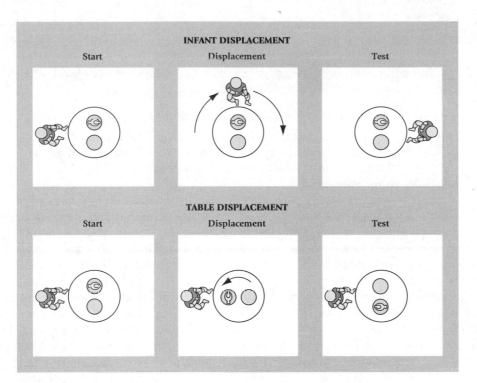

Figure 6-20
Test trials for the Bai and Bertenthal (1992) experiment. Infants were allowed to search for a hidden toy after they had moved (top row) or the table had rotated, causing the hidden object to move (bottom row).
Adapted from Bai & Bertenthal, 1992.

Perception of Physical Stimuli

People from different cultures rarely differ in such basic sensory capacities as the ability to discriminate degrees of brightness or loudness (Berry et al., 1992). However, their interpretations of sensory input can vary considerably, depending upon the experiences they have had. For example, we have already seen that infants eventually lose the ability to discriminate phonetic contrasts that are not important in their culture's language—a finding that indicates that auditory perception depends, in part, on one's linguistic environment. Michael Lynch and his associates (1990) found a similar effect for music perception. In Lynch's research, 6-month-old infants and American adults listened to seven-tone melodies in either the Western major/minor scale or the Javanese pelog scale, which sounds a bit strange to listeners from Western cultures. Inserted within the reported melodies was an occasional note that was "mistuned" and thus violated the musical scale. Remarkably, the 6-month-old infants often detected these mistuned notes, regardless of whether they violated a Western or a Javanese melody. Apparently, babies are born with the potential to perceive "musicality" and to discriminate good music from bad music in a variety of musical scales. By contrast, American adults were much less sensitive to bad notes in the unfamiliar Javanese musical system than to mistuned notes in their native Western scale, suggesting that their years of experience with the Western musical system had shaped their perceptions of music.

Important social and personal values may also color our perceptions. In an early study, Bruner and Goodman (1947) asked 10-year-olds to adjust a spot of light until they thought that it matched the size of a coin that had been presented in another part of the visual field. Children generally overestimated the sizes of all coins, and the overestimates were much greater for coins of high monetary value (dimes and quarters) than for coins of lesser value (pennies and nickels).

An interesting subcultural difference also emerged: Children from poorer homes overestimated the size of coins more than children from advantaged homes. Does this finding mean that the poorer children attached greater *value* to the coins or only that the poorer children were less *familiar* with the coins and their true sizes? Later research tends to support the value hypothesis: Poorer children are more likely than advantaged children to overestimate the size of a valuable object such as a dime, but the two groups produce comparable size estimates when judging an object without value, such as a metallic "slug" (Nelson & Lechelt, cited in Burtley, 1980). So it seems that our perception of an object's physical characteristics may depend, in part, on the extent to which we value that object.

Home Environments and Perceptual Styles

Does a child's home environment influence perceptual development? Herman Witkin (1967) thinks so. He claims that the techniques and strategies that parents use to raise their child affect the child's standing on a perceptual dimension known as **field dependence/independence.**

Field dependence and field independence represent two different perceptual styles. The *field-independent person* is able to process information and perceive objects and events without being distracted by background, or "contextual," factors. By contrast, the perceptions of a *field-dependent* person are likely to be influenced by irrelevant or distracting information. One measure of field dependence/independence is Witkin's "tilted room" test. Subjects are first placed in a special chair within a small room. Then the chair and the room are tilted in different directions, and the subject's task is to align the chair with the true gravitational upright. Persons classified as field dependent tend to concentrate on the visual context and to align the chair to the tilted environment, whereas those labeled as field independent are better able to ignore the distracting visual "field" and align themselves with the true upright position (even though the environment will still look tilted to them). Field independents are also better than field dependents at locating objects embedded in a distracting visual context. For example, a field-independent person will soon find the hidden "termite" in Figure 6-21, whereas the field-dependent person would have to search much longer.

What aspects of home life promote field-dependent and field-independent orientations? Witkin and his associates (Witkin, 1967; Witkin, Goodenough, & Oltman, 1979) believe that domineering parents who closely supervise their child's behavior and demand that the child conform to rigidly defined rules are likely to contribute to a field-dependent orientation. By contrast, parents who are less restrictive or domineering and generally willing to allow their children some individual initiative are probably fostering the development of a field-independent orientation.

Sex differences. Although there are vast individual differences within each sex, females tend to be more field dependent than males and this sex difference may be attributable to the ways that males and females are raised (Witkin & Goodenough, 1981). Specifically, parents are more likely to stress obedience for daughters and to restrict girls' initiative. And according to Witkin, this is precisely the pattern of child rearing that contributes to a field-dependent orientation.

Cross-cultural studies. Cross-cultural studies also support Witkin's child-rearing hypothesis. Anthropologists often classify nonindustrialized societies into two basic categories: (1) *farming and pastoral* societies, in which a large number of relatively immobile families live and work together tending flocks and raising crops, and (2) *hunter-gatherer* societies, in which small groups earn their livelihood by moving about in search of food. Parents in farming and pastoral societies stress the kinds of values that are necessary to maintain their way of life: Children are expected to be obedient and cooperative and to place the needs of the group ahead of their own personal goals. As expected, Witkin and Berry (1975) found that people from this kind of society were quite field *dependent.* Parents from hunter-gatherer societies also stress values that would help to maintain their way of life. But for the hunter-gatherer, who most often works alone, these values include assertiveness, independence, and self-reliance rather than cooperation and obedience. So Witkin and Berry (1975) were not surprised to find that children of hunter-gatherers were quite field *independent.*

field dependence/independence: a dimension of perceptual style—namely, the extent to which the surrounding context (the field) affects a person's perceptual judgments.

Figure 6-21
Find the termite (there is only one). (Answer appears at bottom of page.)

Perceptual style and personality. Finally, field-dependent individuals differ from field independents on dimensions other than perceptual style (McAdams, 1990). Field dependents, for example, are generally "people oriented": They tend to be more empathic, less aggressive, and better able to get along with others than field-independent individuals are. This is precisely the profile we might expect if the social environment has encouraged field dependents to become cooperative individuals who are sensitive to the needs and wishes of others. By contrast, field independents tend to be more tolerant of ambiguous situations, better able to function without explicit guidance or supervision, and more interested in individual accomplishments than field dependents are. Once again, these differences "make sense" if field independents have been encouraged to be independent and assertive and to pursue individual goals.

Concept Check 6-3 ⟍ Environmental Influences on Perception

Check your understanding of environmental influences on perception by matching each perceptual development listed below with one of the following experiences: (a) limited exposure to patterned visual stimuli; (b) attention to moving stimuli; (c) having relatively domineering parents; (d) living in a hunter-gatherer society; (e) learning a language. The answers appear in the Appendix.

_____ 1. Field-dependent orientation.

_____ 2. Insensitivity to certain phonetic contrasts.

_____ 3. Normal spatial perception.

_____ 4. Impaired form perception.

_____ 5. Field-independent orientation.

 POSTSCRIPT: WHAT IS
PERCEPTUAL DEVELOPMENT?

Now that we have considered the topic of perceptual development, here is a question for you to ponder: "What is perceptual development the development of?" Although there are many ways that one might choose to answer this question, perhaps we can agree that perceptual development is the growth of *interpretive* skills—a complex process that depends, in part, on the maturation of the sensory receptors, the kinds of sensory experiences that the child has available to analyze and interpret,

The termite is in the third drawing, nestled in the woman's hair.

the child's emerging motor skills, and the social context in which the child is raised. Although this chapter has focused on perceptual growth, we should remember that development is a *holistic* process and that a child's maturing perceptual abilities are likely to have a meaningful effect on many other aspects of development. Take intellectual development, for example. As we will see in Chapter 7, Jean Piaget argues that all the intellectual advances of the first two years spring from the infant's sensory and motor activities. How else, he asks, could infants ever come to understand the properties of objects without being able to see them, fondle them, and pop them into their mouths? How could infants ever use language without first perceiving meaningful regularities in the speech they hear? And when we recall Witkin's argument that children's perceptual styles have far-reaching implications for their developing personalities, we begin to see why so many developmentalists consider perceptual growth to be such an important topic. Simply stated, perception is central to everything; there is nothing we do (consciously, at least) that is not influenced by our interpretation of the world around us. So it is important to understand the growth of perceptual skills because *perception is truly at the heart of human development.*

SUMMARY

Sensation refers to the detection of sensory stimulation, whereas *perception* is the interpretation of what is sensed. Philosophers and developmentalists have debated whether basic perceptual skills are innate (the nativist position) or acquired (the empiricist position) and about whether perception involves *detection* of the distinctive aspects of different sensations (differentiation theory) or the cognitive *embellishment* of sensory input (enrichment theory). Today, most theorists have rejected extreme nativist or empiricist positions in favor of an *interactionist* viewpoint; and many would concede that both detection and embellishment of sensory information contribute to the growth of perceptual skills.

Researchers have devised several creative methods of persuading infants to tell us what they might be sensing or perceiving. Among the more useful of these approaches are the preference method, the habituation method, the method of evoked potentials, and the high-amplitude sucking method. Applying these methods, researchers have learned that the sensory equipment of young infants is in reasonably good working order. Neonates can see patterns and colors and can detect changes in brightness. Their visual acuity is poor by adult standards but improves rapidly over the first six months. Moreover, young infants can hear very well: Even newborns can discriminate sounds that differ in loudness, direction, duration, and frequency. The senses of taste and smell are also well developed at birth. Babies are born with definite taste preferences, favoring sweets over sour, bitter, or salty substances. They avoid unpleasant smells and soon come to recognize their mothers by odor alone if they are breast-fed. Newborns are also quite sensitive to touch, temperature, and pain.

Visual perception develops rapidly during the first year. For the first two months of life, babies are "stimulus seekers" who prefer to look at moderately complex, high-contrast targets, particularly those that move. Between 3 and 6 months of age, infants perceive forms and begin to recognize familiar faces. Although neonates display some size constancy, their spatial perception is immature. By the end of the first month, however, they are becoming more sensitive to kinetic cues and responding to looming objects. Their developing sensitivities to binocular cues (at 4-5 months) and pictorial cues (at 6–7 months), in conjunction with important motor developments and the experiences they provide, help to explain why older infants come to fear heights and to make more accurate judgments about size constancy and other spatial relations.

The neonate's auditory capabilities are truly remarkable. In the first three days of life, an infant can already recognize its mother's voice. Neonates are quite responsive to human speech, and they place the auditory components of language into roughly the same vowel and consonant categories that adults do. Finally, babies prefer music to unpatterned auditory stimulation, and they begin to "bounce" to music and to recognize changes in melody and tempo by 4–6 months of age.

Apparently, the senses are integrated at birth, for neonates will look in the direction of sound-producing sources, reach for objects they can see, and expect to see the source of sounds or to feel objects for which they are reaching. As soon as sensory information is readily detectable through two or more senses, infants are apt to display *intermodal perception*—the ability to recognize by one sensory modality an object or experience that is already familiar through another modality.

Several important perceptual changes take place between infancy and adolescence as attention develops. Specifically, children come to sustain attention for longer periods of time, to direct it more selectively, filtering out distracting information, and to plan and carry out more systematic perceptual searches. As children become more attentive, they begin to identify more of the distinctive features that differentiate objects and events. This "perceptual learning" is a continuing process that enables the child to become better and better at interpreting the broad array of stimuli that impinge on the sensory receptors.

The environment influences perceptual development in many ways. Deprivation experiments suggest that young animals (and presumably children) must be exposed to patterned visual stimuli that move and capture their attention if their visual perception is to develop normally. Moreover, our social/cultural environments may influence our auditory perception and our judgments about the physical characteristics of objects that we value. Finally, it appears that our cultural and family environments contribute to the development of broad perceptual "styles" (field dependence or field independence) that may have important implications for many other aspects of development.

Key Terms

astigmatism [235]	habituation [206]	perceptual learning [232]	virtual object [224]
attention span [228]	high-amplitude sucking method [207]	pictorial (perspective) cues [217]	visual acuity [208]
differentiation theory [205]			visual cliff [220]
distinctive features [205]	intermodal perception [224]	preference method [205]	visual contrast [208]
embedded figures test [230]	looking chamber [205]	reticular formation [228]	visual looming [218]
enrichment theory [204]	motion hypothesis [235]	selective attention [229]	
evoked potential [207]	myelinization [228]	sensation [204]	
field dependence/ independence [238]	perception [204]	size constancy [218]	
	phonemes [222]	stereopsis [217]	

7 Cognitive Development: Piaget's Theory and Vygotsky's Sociocultural Viewpoint

If you were asked to account for the reaction of the 9-year-old quoted in the margin, you might be tempted to conclude that he either lacks imagination or is being sarcastic. Actually, Billy's feelings about the assignment may be rather typical (see Box 7-4 on page 268), for 9-year-olds think differently than adults do, and they often find it ex-tremely difficult to reflect on hypothetical propositions that have no basis in reality.

Our next three chapters examine the growth of **cognition**—a term that developmentalists use to refer to the activity of knowing and the mental processes by which human beings acquire knowledge and use it to solve problems. The cognitive processes that help us to understand and adapt to the environment include such activities as attending, perceiving, learning, thinking, and remembering—in short, the unobservable events and undertakings that characterize the human mind (Flavell, Miller, & Miller, 1993).

The study of **cognitive development**—the changes that occur in children's mental skills and abilities over the course of their lives—is one of the more diverse and exciting topics in all of the developmental sciences. In this chapter, we begin our exploration of the developing mind, focusing first on the many important contributions of Swiss psychologist Jean Piaget, who charted what he (and others) believed to be a *universal* pattern of intellectual growth that unfolds during infancy, childhood, and adolescence. We will then compare and contrast Piaget's influential theory with Lev Vygotsky's *sociocultural* viewpoint—a theory that claims that much of cognitive growth is socially mediated and heavily influenced by one's culture and may be nowhere near as universal as Piaget and his followers had assumed (Wertsch & Tulviste, 1992).

Chapter 8 introduces a third influential perspective on the developing mind. First, we will examine how children *learn* (a basic cognitive process that affects many, many other aspects of development), and then we will consider the merits of contemporary *information-processing* perspectives on intellectual growth that arose, in part, from questions left unanswered by Piaget's earlier work. Our attention will then shift to the *psychometric*, or intelligence testing, approach in Chapter 9, where we will discuss the many factors that contribute to individual differences in children's intellectual performance.

> *Teacher (to a class of 9-year-olds):* For artwork today, I'd like each of you to draw me a picture of a person who has three eyes.
>
> *Billy:* How? Nobody has three eyes!

▶ PIAGET'S THEORY OF COGNITIVE DEVELOPMENT

In Chapter 2, we learned that Piaget was a zoologist with a background in *epistemology* (the branch of philosophy concerned with the origins of knowledge) who developed a strong interest in cognitive development while standardizing intelligence tests. This job required him to administer a large number of precisely worded questions to his young test takers in order to determine the age at which the majority of them could *correctly* answer each item. However, Piaget soon became interested in the children's *wrong* answers when he discovered that children of roughly the same age were making similar kinds of mistakes—errors that were typically quite different from the incorrect responses of younger or older children. Could these age-related differences in children's error patterns reflect developmental steps, or stages, in the process of intellectual growth? Piaget thought so, and he began to suspect that *how* children think is probably a much better indicator of their cognitive abilities than *what* they may know (Flavell, 1963).

Piaget began his studies by carefully observing his own three children as infants: how they explored new toys, solved simple problems that he arranged for them, and generally came to understand themselves and their world. Later, Piaget studied larger samples of children through what has become known as the **clinical method,** a flexible question-and-answer technique that he used to discover how children of different ages solved various problems and thought about everyday issues. From these naturalistic observations of his own children and his use of the clinical method to

cognition: the activity of knowing and the processes through which knowledge is acquired.

cognitive development: changes that occur in mental activities such as attending, perceiving, learning, thinking, and remembering.

clinical method: a type of interview in which a child's response to each successive question or problem determines what the investigator will ask next (see Chapter 1 for an extended discussion of this technique).

explore children's understanding of topics ranging from the rules of games to the laws of physics, Piaget formulated his *cognitive-developmental* theory of intellectual growth.

What Is Intelligence?

Piaget defined **intelligence** as a *basic life function* that helps the organism *to adapt to its environment*. We observe such adaptation as we watch a toddler figure how to turn on the TV, a school-aged child decide how to divide candies among friends, or an adolescent first struggle and then succeed at solving a tough geometry problem. Piaget adds that intelligence is "a form of *equilibrium* toward which all cognitive structures tend" (1950, p. 6). His point is simply that all intellectual activity is undertaken with one goal in mind: to produce a balanced, or harmonious, relationship between one's thought processes and the environment (such a balanced state of affairs is called **cognitive equilibrium**, and the process of achieving it is called *equilibration*). Piaget stressed that children are active and curious explorers who are constantly challenged by many novel stimuli and events that are not immediately understood. He believed that these imbalances (or cognitive disequilibria) between the child's modes of thinking and environmental events would prompt the child to make mental adjustments that would enable her to cope with puzzling new experiences and thereby restore cognitive equilibrium. So we see that Piaget's view of intelligence is an "interactionist" model, which implies that mismatches between one's internal mental schemes (existing knowledge) and the external environment stimulate cognitive activity and intellectual growth.

There is a very important assumption that underlies Piaget's view of intelligence: If children are to know something, they must construct that knowledge themselves. Indeed, Piaget described the child as a **constructivist**—an organism that acts on novel objects and events and thereby gains some understanding of their essential features. He added that the child's constructions of reality (that is, interpretations of objects and events) depend on the knowledge available to him at that point in time: The more immature the child's cognitive system, the more limited his interpretation of an environmental event. Consider the following example:

> A four-year-old child and his father are watching the setting sun. "Look Daddy. It's hiding behind the mountain. Why is it going away? Is it angry?" The father grasps the opportunity to explain to his son how the world works. "Well, Mark, the sun doesn't really feel things. And it doesn't really move. It's the earth that's moving. It turns on its axis so that the mountain moves in front of the sun . . ." The father goes on to other explanations of relative motion, interplanetary bodies and such. The boy . . . firmly and definitely responds, "But *we're* not moving. *It* is. Look, it's going down." (Cowan, 1978, p. 11)

This child is making an important assumption here that dominates his attempt at understanding—namely, that the way he sees things must correspond to the way they are. Obviously, it is the sun that is moving, ducking behind the mountain as if it were a live being who was expressing some feeling or serving a definite purpose by hiding. However, the father knows the characteristics that distinguish animate from inanimate objects (and a little about astronomy as well), so that he is able to construct a very different interpretation of the "reality" he and his son have witnessed.

Cognitive Schemes: The "Structure" of Intelligence

Piaget uses the term *schemes* to describe the models, or mental structures, that we create to represent, organize, and interpret our experiences. A **scheme** (sometimes called a *schema* in the singular, *schemata* in the plural) is a pattern of thought or action that

intelligence: in Piaget's theory, a basic life function that enables an organism to adapt to its environment.

cognitive equilibrium: Piaget's term for the state of affairs in which there is a balanced, or harmonious, relationship between one's thought processes and the environment.

constructivist: one who gains knowledge by acting or otherwise operating on objects and events to discover their properties.

scheme: an organized pattern of thought or action that one constructs to interpret some aspect of one's experience (also called cognitive structure).

Infants develop a broad range of behavioral schemes that they can use to explore and "understand" new objects and to solve simple problems.

is similar in some respects to what the layperson calls a strategy or a concept. Piaget (1952, 1977) has described three kinds of intellectual structures: behavioral (or sensorimotor) schemes, symbolic schemes, and operational schemes.

Behavioral (or Sensorimotor) Schemes

A **behavioral scheme** is an organized pattern of behavior that the child uses to represent and respond to an object or experience. These are the first intellectual structures to emerge, and for much of the first two years of life, an infant's knowledge of objects and events is limited to that which she can represent through overt actions. So for a 9-month-old infant, a ball is not conceptualized as a round toy that has a formal name; instead, a ball is simply an object that she and her companions can bounce and roll.

Symbolic Schemes

During the second year, children reach a point at which they can solve problems and think about objects and events without having acted on them. In other words, they are now capable of representing experiences mentally and using these mental symbols, or **symbolic schemes,** to satisfy their objectives. Consider the following observation of the antics of Jacqueline, Piaget's 16-month-old daughter:

> Jacqueline had a visit from a little boy (18 months of age) . . . who, in the course of the afternoon, got into a terrible temper. He screamed as he tried to get out of a playpen and pushed it backward, stamping his feet. Jacqueline stood watching him in amazement, never having witnessed such a scene before. The next day, she herself screamed in her playpen and tried to move, stamping her foot . . . several times in succession. (Piaget, 1951, p. 63)

behavioral schemes: organized patterns of behavior that are used to represent and respond to objects and experiences.

symbolic schemes: internal mental symbols (such as images or verbal codes) that one uses to represent aspects of experience.

Reversibility is an important cognitive operation that develops during middle childhood.

Clearly, Jacqueline was imitating the responses of her absent playmate, even though she had not performed those actions at the time they were modeled. It appears that she must have formed a mental representation, or image, of the boy's tantrum that preserved this scene and guided her later imitation.

Operational Schemes

According to Piaget, the thinking of children aged 7 and older is characterized by a third type of scheme, the operational structure. A **cognitive operation** is an internal mental activity that a person performs on his or her objects of thought to reach a logical conclusion. To illustrate, an 8-year-old who flattens a ball of playdough into a disk is not fooled into thinking that he now has more playdough as a result of spreading it out. Why? Because he can easily *reverse* this transformation in his head, thereby recognizing that the playdough would become the same ball if it were rolled up once again. By contrast, 5-year-olds, who cannot "operate" on their objects of thought, are constrained to make judgments largely on the basis of overt appearances. So were they to witness the ball-to-disk transformation, they would generally assume that the disk has more dough, since it now covers more area than the ball did. And even though they can imagine (with a little prompting) that the dough can be rolled up again, they do not yet recognize the logical consequences of doing so—that is, they continue to think that there is more dough in the disk.

According to Piaget, the most common cognitive operations are the mental activities implied by mathematical symbols such as $+$, $-$, $\times$, $\div$, $<$, and $>$. Notice that each of these mental operations is a *reversible* activity: Mental additions, for example, can quickly be undone by mental subtractions. Piaget believed that these fluid operational abilities permit grade school children and adolescents to construct rather elaborate intellectual schemes that will enable them to think logically and systematically—first about their actual experiences and eventually about abstract or hypothetical events.

cognitive operation: an internal mental activity that one performs on objects of thought.

How We Gain Knowledge: Piaget's Cognitive Processes

How do children construct and modify their intellectual schemes? Piaget believes that all schemes, all forms of understanding, are created through the workings of two inborn intellectual processes that he calls *organization* and *adaptation*.

Organization is the process by which children combine existing schemes into new and more complex intellectual structures. For example, a young infant who has "gazing," "reaching," and "grasping" reflexes will soon organize these initially unrelated schemes into a more complex structure—*visually directed reaching*—that enables her to reach out and discover the characteristics of many interesting objects in the environment. Although intellectual schemes may assume radically different forms at different phases of development, the process of organization is unchanging. Piaget believed that children are constantly organizing whatever schemes they have into more complex and adaptive structures.

The goal of organization is to promote **adaptation**—the process of adjusting to the demands of the environment. According to Piaget, adaptation occurs through two complementary activities: *assimilation* and *accommodation*.

Assimilation is the process by which the child tries to interpret new experiences in terms of her existing models of the world—the schemes that she already possesses. The young child who sees a horse for the first time will try to assimilate it into one of her existing schemes for four-legged animals and thus may think of this creature as a "doggie." In other words, she is trying to adapt to this novel stimulus by construing it as something familiar.

Yet, truly novel objects, events, and experiences may be difficult or impossible to interpret in terms of one's existing schemes. For example, our young child may soon notice that this big animal she is labeling a doggie has funny-looking feet and a most peculiar bark, and she may be inclined to seek a better understanding of the observations she has made. **Accommodation,** the complement of assimilation, is the process of modifying existing structures in order to account for new experiences. So the child who recognizes that a horse is not a dog may invent a name for this new creature or perhaps ask "What dat?" and adopt the label that her older companions use. In so doing, she has modified (accommodated) her scheme for four-legged animals to include a new category of experience—horses.

Although Piaget distinguishes assimilation from accommodation, he believes that these two processes work together to promote cognitive growth. They do not always occur together, as in the above example; but assimilations of experiences that do not quite "jibe" with existing schemes will eventually introduce cognitive conflict and prompt accommodations to those experiences. And the end result is adaptation, a state of equilibrium between one's cognitive structures and the environment.

Concept Check 7-1 ⌄ Understanding Piagetian Assumptions and Concepts

Check your understanding of some of Piaget's basic assumptions about cognitive development by indicating which of the following terms best describes each of the observations listed below. Choose from the following terms: (a) organization; (b) assimilation; (c) accommodation; (d) reversibility; (e) disequilibrium. The answers appear in the Appendix.

_____ 1. Thinking that objects fall when dropped, Jose is flabbergasted when a helium balloon rises, thus illustrating what Piaget calls _____.

_____ 2. Given a choice, Kai prefers a cookie that has dropped and broken over a whole one, saying that "Three little cookies are better than one big one." Kai lacks _____.

_____ 3. Jose's construction of an explanation for the fact that helium-filled balloons will rise involves the process of _____.

_____ 4. Ten-month-old Sammie lifts a pillow to grab a toy that his father has placed there. Sammie's coordination of his "lifting" and "grasping" schemes to achieve his goal is an example of _____.

_____ 5. Freda exclaims, "Oh, look at big kitty cat," upon seeing her first tiger at the circus. Freda's response illustrates _____.

organization: an inborn tendency to combine and integrate available schemes into coherent systems or bodies of knowledge.

adaptation: an inborn tendency to adjust to the demands of the environment.

assimilation: the process of interpreting new experiences by incorporating them into existing schemes.

accommodation: the process of modifying existing schemes in order to incorporate or adapt to new experiences.

Table 7-1   A Small Sample of Cognitive Growth from Piaget's Perspective

	Piagetian concept	Definition	Example
Start	Equilibrium	Harmony between one's schemes and one's experiences.	Toddler who has never seen anything fly but birds thinks that all flying objects are "birdies."
	Assimilation	Tries to adapt to new experience by interpreting it in terms of existing schemes.	Seeing an airplane in the sky prompts child to call the flying object a birdie.
	Accommodation	Modifies existing schemes to better account for puzzling new experience.	Toddler experiences conflict or disequilibrium upon noticing that the new birdie has no feathers and doesn't flap its wings. Concludes it is not a bird and invents a new name for it (or asks, "What dat?"). Successful accommodation restores equilibrium (for the moment, at least).
Finish	Organization	Rearranges existing schemes into new and more complex structures.	Forms hierarchical scheme consisting of a superordinate class (flying objects) and two subordinate classes (birdies and airplanes).

Note: As an exercise, you may wish to apply Piaget's concepts to chart the further elaborations of the child's schemes upon encountering a butterfly and a frisbee.

Table 7-1 provides one example of how cognitive growth might proceed from Piaget's point of view—a perspective that stresses that cognitive development is an *active* process in which children are regularly seeking and *assimilating* new experiences, *accommodating* their cognitive structures to these experiences, and *organizing* what they know into new and more complex schemes. So two inborn activities—adaptation and organization—make it possible for children to construct progressively greater understandings of the world in which they live.

 PIAGET'S STAGES OF COGNITIVE DEVELOPMENT

Piaget has identified four major periods of cognitive development: the *sensorimotor* stage (birth to 2 years), the *preoperational* stage (2 to 7 years), the stage of *concrete operations* (7 to 11 years), and the stage of *formal operations* (11 years and beyond). These stages of intellectual growth represent completely different levels of cognitive functioning and form what Piaget calls an **invariant developmental sequence**—that is, all children progress through the stages in precisely the same order, without ever skipping a stage. That the ordering of stages is the same for everyone (that is, universal) reflects Piaget's view that biological maturation plays an important role in determining how a child thinks. And aside from maturational constraints, Piaget argued that stages can never be skipped because each successive stage builds on the accomplishments of all previous stages.

invariant developmental sequence: a series of developments that occur in one particular order because each development in the sequence is a prerequisite for those appearing later.

Although Piaget believed that the *sequencing* of intellectual stages is fixed, or invariant, he recognized that there are tremendous individual differences in the ages at which children enter or emerge from any particular stage. In fact, his view was that cultural factors and other environmental influences may either accelerate or retard a child's *rate* of intellectual growth, and he considered the age norms that accompany his stages (and substages) as only rough approximations at best.

AN INFANT ACCOMMODATING HIS MOUTH TO THE SHAPE OF AN OBJECT

The Sensorimotor Stage (Birth–2 Years)

Piaget's **sensorimotor stage,** spanning the two years of infancy, is a period when infants are coordinating their *sensory* inputs and *motor* capabilities, forming behavioral schemes that permit them to "act on" and to "get to know" their environment. How much can they really understand by relying on overt actions to generate knowledge? More than you might imagine. During the first two years, infants evolve from *reflexive* creatures with very limited knowledge into planful problem solvers who have already learned a great deal about themselves, their close companions, and the objects and events in their everyday world. So dramatic is the infant's cognitive growth that Piaget divided the sensorimotor period into six substages (see Table 7-1) that describe the child's gradual transition from a *reflexive* to a *reflective* organism. Our review will focus on three important aspects of sensorimotor development: *problem-solving skills* (or means/ends activities), *imitative abilities,* and the growth of the *object concept.*

Development of Problem-Solving Skills

Piaget characterized the first month of life as a *stage of reflex activity*—a period when an infant's actions are pretty much confined to exercising innate reflexes, assimilating new objects into these reflexive schemes (for example, sucking on blankets and toys as well as on nipples), and accommodating their reflexes to these novel objects. Granted, this is not high intellect, but these primitive adaptations represent the beginning of cognitive growth.

Primary circular reactions (1–4 months). The first nonreflexive schemes emerge at 1–4 months of age as infants discover by chance that various responses that they can emit and control (for example, sucking their thumbs, making cooing sounds) are satisfying and, thus, worthy of repetition. These simple repetitive acts, called **primary circular reactions,** are always centered on the infant's own body. They are called *primary* because they are the first motor habits to appear and *circular* because the pleasure they bring stimulates their repetition.

Secondary circular reactions (4–8 months). Between 4 and 8 months of age, infants are discovering (again by chance) that they can make interesting things happen to objects outside of their own bodies, such as making a rubber duck quack by squeezing it. These new schemes, called **secondary circular reactions,** are also repeated for the pleasure they bring. According to Piaget, 4–8-month-olds' sudden interest in external objects indicates that they have learned the limits of their own bodies and have begun to differentiate themselves from the surrounding environment.

Is an infant who delights in such repetitive actions as swatting a brightly colored mobile or making a toy duck quack engaging in planful or *intentional* behavior? Piaget says no: The secondary circular reaction is not a fully intentional response, because the interesting result it produces was discovered by chance and was not a purposeful goal the first time the action was performed.

Coordination of secondary schemes (8–12 months). Truly planful responding first appears between 8 and 12 months of age as infants begin to coordinate two or more actions to achieve simple objectives. For example, if you were to place an attractive

sensorimotor stage: Piaget's first intellectual stage, from birth to 2 years, when infants are relying on behavioral schemes as a means of exploring and understanding the environment.

primary circular reaction: a pleasurable response, centered on the infant's own body, that is discovered by chance and performed over and over.

secondary circular reaction: a pleasurable response, centered on an external object, that is discovered by chance and performed over and over.

Blowing bubbles is an accommodation of the sucking reflex and one of the infant's earliest primary circular reactions.

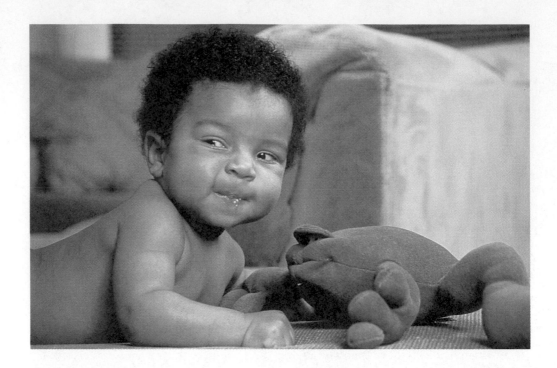

toy under a cushion, a 9-month-old might lift the cushion with one hand while using the other to grab the toy. In this case, the act of lifting the cushion is not a pleasurable response in itself; *nor is it emitted by chance*. Rather, it is part of a larger *intentional* scheme in which two initially unrelated responses—lifting and grasping—are coordinated as *a means to an end*. Piaget believed that these simple coordinations of secondary schemes represent the earliest form of true problem solving.

Tertiary circular reactions (12–18 months). Between 12 and 18 months of age, infants begin to experiment actively with objects and invent totally new methods of solving problems or reproducing interesting results. For example, an infant who had originally squeezed a rubber duck to make it quack may now decide to drop it, step on it, and crush it with a pillow to see whether these actions will have the same or different effects on the toy. Or she may learn from her explorations that flinging is more efficient than spitting as a means of getting food to stick to the wall. Although parents may be less than thrilled by this exciting new cognitive advance, these trial-and-error exploratory schemes, called **tertiary circular reactions,** reflect an infant's active *curiosity*—her strong motivation to learn about the way things work.

Symbolic problem solving (18–24 months). The crowning achievement of the sensorimotor stage occurs as infants begin to internalize their behavioral schemes to construct mental symbols, or images, that they can then use to guide future conduct. Now the infant can experiment *mentally* and may show a kind of "insight" as to how to solve a problem. Piaget's son Laurent nicely illustrated this symbolic problem solving, or **inner experimentation:**

tertiary circular reaction: an exploratory scheme in which the infant devises a new method of acting on objects to reproduce interesting results.

inner experimentation: the ability to solve simple problems on a mental, or symbolic, level without having to rely on trial-and-error experimentation.

> Laurent is seated before a table and I place a bread crust in front of him, out of reach. Also, to the right . . . I place a stick, about 25 cm. long. At first, Laurent tries to grasp the bread . . . and then he gives up . . . Laurent again looks at the bread, and without moving, looks very briefly at the stick, then suddenly grasps it and directs it toward the bread . . . [He then] draws the bread to him. (Piaget, 1952, p. 335)

Clearly, this is not trial-and-error experimentation. Instead, Laurent's problem solving occurred at an internal, symbolic level as he visualized the stick being used as an extension of his arm to obtain a distant object.

Development of Imitation

Piaget recognized the adaptive significance of imitation, and he was very interested in its development. His own observations led him to believe that infants are incapable of imitating *novel* responses displayed by a model until 8 to 12 months of age (the same age at which they show some evidence of intentionality in their behavior). Moreover, the imitative schemes of infants this young are rather imprecise. Were you to bend and straighten your finger, the infant might mimic you by opening and closing her entire hand (Piaget, 1951). Indeed, precise imitations of even the simplest responses may take days (or even weeks) of practice (Kaye & Marcus, 1981), and literally hundreds of demonstrations may be required before an 8–12-month-old will "catch on" and come to enjoy sensorimotor games such as pat-a-cake.

Voluntary imitation becomes much more precise at age 12 to 18 months, as we see in the following example:

> At [1 year and 16 days of age, Jacqueline] discovered her forehead. When I touched the middle of mine, she first rubbed her eye, then felt above it and touched her hair, after which she brought her hand down a little and finally put her finger on her forehead. (Piaget, 1951, p. 56)

According to Piaget, **deferred imitation**—the ability to reproduce the behavior of an *absent* model—first appears at 18 to 24 months of age. When discussing symbolic schemes, we noted an example of deferred imitation— Jacqueline's reproduction of her playmate's temper tantrum 24 hours later. Piaget believed that older infants are capable of deferred imitation because they are now constructing mental symbols, or images, of a model's behavior that are stored in memory and retrieved later to guide the child's recreation of the modeled sequence. Other investigators disagree with Piaget, arguing that deferred imitation begins much earlier. Andrew Meltzoff, for example, has found that some 9-month-olds can imitate very simple acts (for example, button-pressing to activate a noise-making toy) 24 hours after observing them (Meltzoff, 1988c), and that most 14-month-olds can imitate at least some simple acts displayed by a live model after a delay of one week (Meltzoff, 1988b). So a capacity for deferred imitation—imitation requiring the infant to construct, store, and then retrieve mental symbols—is present much earlier than Piaget had thought.

Development of Object Permanence

One of the more notable achievements of the sensorimotor period is the development of **object permanence**—the idea that objects continue to exist when they are no longer visible or detectable through the other senses. Were you to remove your watch and cover it with a mug, you would be well aware that the watch continues to exist. But because very young infants rely so heavily on their senses and motor skills to "understand" an object, they seem to operate as if objects exist only if they can be sensed or acted upon. Indeed, Piaget (1954) and others have found that 1–4-month-olds will not search for attractive objects that are hidden from view: If a watch that interests them is covered by a mug, they soon lose interest, almost as if they believe that the watch no longer exists or has been transformed into a mug (Bower, 1982). At age 4 to 8 months, infants will retrieve toys that are partially concealed or placed beneath a semitransparent cover; but their continuing failure to search for objects that are *completely* concealed suggested to Piaget that, from the infant's perspective, disappearing objects may no longer exist.

Clearer signs of an emerging object concept appear by 8 to 12 months of age. However, object permanence is far from complete, as we see in Piaget's demonstration with his 10-month-old daughter:

deferred imitation: the ability to reproduce a modeled activity that has been witnessed at some point in the past.

object permanence: the realization that objects continue to exist when they are no longer visible or detectable through the other senses.

Playing peek-a-boo is an exciting activity for infants who are acquiring object permanence.

Jacqueline is seated on a mattress without anything to ... distract her ... I take her [toy] parrot from her hands and hide it twice ... under the mattress, on her left [point A]. Both times Jacqueline looks for the object immediately and grabs it. Then I take it from her hands and move it very slowly *before her eyes* to the corresponding place on her right, under the mattress [point B]. Jacqueline watches this movement ... but at the moment when the parrot disappears [at point B] she turns to her left and looks where it was before [at point A]. (Piaget, 1954, p. 51; italics added)

Jacqueline's response is typical of 8–12-month-olds, who will search for a hidden object *where they found it previously* rather than where they saw it last. Piaget's account of this **A, not B, error** was straightforward: Jacqueline acted as if her *behavior* determines where the object will be found; consequently, she does not treat the object as if it exists independent of her own activity.

Between 12 and 18 months of age, the object concept improves. Infants will now track the visible movements of objects and search for them *where they were last seen*. However, object permanence is not complete, because the child cannot make the mental inferences necessary to understand *invisible* displacements. So if you conceal a toy in your hand, place your hand behind a barrier and deposit the toy there, remove your hand, and then ask the child to find the toy, 12–18-month-olds will search *where the toy was last seen* (in your hand) rather than looking behind the barrier.

By 18 to 24 months of age, infants are capable of *mentally representing* such invisible displacements and using these mental inferences to guide their search for objects that have disappeared. At this point, they fully understand that objects have a "permanence" about them and take great pride at locating their objectives in sophisticated games of hide-and-seek.

Before we summarize the developments of the sensorimotor period, a caution is in order. In recent years, investigators have questioned several of Piaget's ideas about object permanence because they began to discover that young infants seem to understand much more about objects than Piaget had assumed. In Box 7-1, we consider a portion of this intriguing research and see why many of Piaget's ideas about object permanence have now been revised.

A, not B, error: tendency of 8–12-month-olds to search for a hidden object where they previously found it even after they have seen it moved to a new location.

BOX 7-1
Why Infants Know More about Objects Than Piaget Assumed

*D*o very young infants really believe that vanishing objects cease to exist? Renee Baillargeon (1987) doubts it, and her research illustrates a theme that has been echoed by many contemporary researchers: Young infants know more about objects than Piaget thought they did; in fact, they may never be totally ignorant about the permanence of objects.

Baillargeon suggests that the young infants tested by Piaget failed to display object permanence simply because Piaget equated searching for an object with an understanding that it exists. Would young infants show object permanence if procedures were used that do not require active searching to assess their knowledge? To find out, Baillargeon (1987) first habituated 3½–4½-month-old infants to a screen that moved back and forth like a drawbridge. After the infants had lost interest in this moving screen, a yellow box appeared to be placed behind it so that the screen would obscure the box as it neared its most upright position (actually, the box was an illusion created by a mirror). Then, as illustrated in the figure here, the screen was rotated to produce either a *possible* event (the screen would stop as if blocked by the box) or an *impossible* event (the screen rotated 180°, passing through the box). Baillargeon reasoned that if babies thought the box still existed, even when hidden by the screen, they should stare longer at the screen and be more surprised when it appeared to pass through the solid box (impossible event) than when it bumped the box and stopped its forward motion (possible event). This is precisely what most of the 4½-month-olds and many of the 3½-month-olds did—taking great interest in the impossible event. Clearly, these infants expected the screen to hit the box, thus illustrating their knowledge that the box continued to exist when blocked from view. In a similar vein, Thomas Bower (1982) has shown that even 1–4-month-old infants are often surprised if a toy hidden behind a screen is no longer there when the screen is lifted a few seconds later. If the delay in lifting the screen is too long, however, infants are *not* surprised when the object is missing. These observations imply that very young infants are not ignorant about the permanence of objects; instead, they simply *forget* that the object is behind the screen if the object is hidden too long.

It was once thought that memory deficits also explained the *A, not B, error* that 8–12-month-olds display. But we now know that infants this old have reasonably good memories and are actually quite surprised if a hidden object turns out *not* to be where they have last seen it (at point B) (Baillargeon & Graber, 1988). So 8–12-month-olds who commit A, not B, errors will often remember that an object has been hidden at new location B; what they may lack is the ability to *inhibit* the tendency to search where they have

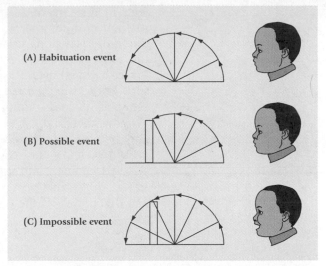

Representations of the habituation stimulus and the possible and impossible events shown to young infants in Baillargeon's (1987) experiment. Babies took great interest in the "impossible" event, thus suggesting that they knew that the box continues to exist and that the screen shouldn't have passed through it. Based on Baillargeon, 1987.

previously found the object. Indeed, Adele Diamond (1985) claims that some infants who search inappropriately for hidden objects at point A hardly look there at all, as if they realize that this is not the right place to search but simply cannot stop themselves. Diamond (1991) now believes maturational changes in the frontal lobes of the cerebral cortex during the second six months of life permit infants to gain more control over their motor responses, thus allowing them to inhibit an impulse to search for hidden objects at locations they know are incorrect. And she may be right. Using the evoked-potential method, Martha Bell and Nathan Fox (1992) found that 7–12-month-olds who *avoid* making A, not B, errors show far more frontal lobe electrical activity while performing the task than their age-mates who search less appropriately.

Though we've considered only a portion of the evidence, it is clear that Piaget's reliance on active search procedures caused him to (1) badly underestimate what very young infants know about objects and (2) misinterpret why infants display the A, not B, error. However, recent research continues to support Piaget's view that a mature understanding of object permanence does not emerge until 18–24 months of age, when the child is capable of mentally representing *invisible* displacements of objects that have disappeared (Wishart & Bower, 1985).

An Overview and Evaluation of Piaget's Sensorimotor Stage

The child's intellectual achievements during the sensorimotor period are truly remarkable. In two short years, infants have evolved from reflexive and largely immobile creatures into planful thinkers who can move about on their own, solve some problems in their heads, form concepts, and even communicate many of their thoughts to their companions. Clearly, deferred imitation emerges earlier than Piaget had thought, and young infants know far more about objects than he gave them credit for. Moreover, babies try to control their external environment much earlier than Piaget had assumed. In Chapter 6, for example, we learned that even newborns will suck vigorously on a special pacifier if this behavior allows them to reproduce interesting sights and sounds.

Why, then, did Piaget often underestimate the infant's cognitive capabilities? Probably because he inferred what infants know from their motor activities and thereby missed some of the schemes they construct through purely *perceptual learning*—by simply looking at and listening to objects and events (Gibson, 1992). But despite the shortcomings in Piaget's methods and the abilities he failed to detect, Piaget's general description of the sequencing of sensorimotor development is still considered a

Table 7-2 Summary of the Substages and Intellectual Accomplishments of the Sensorimotor Period

Substage	Methods of solving problems or producing interesting outcomes	Imitation	Object concept
1. Reflex activity (0–1 month)	Exercising and accommodation of inborn reflexes	Some reflexive imitation of motor responses*	Tracks moving object but ignores its disappearance
2. Primary circular reactions (1–4 months)	Repeating interesting acts that are centered on one's own body	Repetition of own behavior that is mimicked by a companion	Looks intently at the spot where an object disappeared[†]
3. Secondary circular reactions (4–8 months)	Repeating interesting acts that are directed toward external objects	Same as in Substage 2	Searches for partly concealed object
4. Coordination of secondary schemes (8–12 months)	Combining actions to solve simple problems (first evidence of intentionality)	Gradual imitation of novel responses; deferred imitation of very simple motor acts after a brief delay	Clear signs of emerging object concept; searches for and finds concealed object that has *not* been visibly displaced
5. Tertiary circular reactions (12–18 months)	Experimenting to find new ways to solve problems or reproduce interesting outcomes	Systematic imitation of novel responses; deferred imitation of simple motor acts after a long delay	Searches for and finds object that has been *visibly* displaced
6. Invention of new means through mental combinations (18–24 months)	First evidence of insight as the child solves problems at an internal, symbolic level	Deferred imitation of complex behavioral sequences	Object concept is complete; searches for and finds objects that have been hidden through *invisible* displacements

*Imitation of simple motor acts (such as tongue protrusions, head movements, and the opening and closing of one's lips or hands) is apparently an inborn, reflexlike ability that bears little relation to the voluntary imitation that appears later in the first year (Kaitz et al., 1988; Meltzoff & Moore, 1989; Reissland, 1988).

[†] Many researchers now believe that object permanence may be present very early and that Piaget's reliance on search procedures badly underestimated what young infants know about objects (see Box 7-1).

reasonably good overview of how the human mind changes over the first two years of life (Bjorklund, 1995; Flavell et al., 1993; see Table 7-2 for a brief summary).

The Preoperational Stage (2–7 Years)

As children enter Piaget's **preoperational stage,** we see a dramatic increase in their use of mental symbols (words and images) to represent the objects, situations, and events they encounter. But despite this important new strength, Piaget's descriptions of preoperational intelligence focus mainly on the limitations or deficiencies in children's thinking. Indeed, he called this period "preoperational" because he believed that preschool children have not yet acquired the cognitive operations (and operational schemes) that would enable them to think logically. Let's consider Piaget's thoughts about the intellectual capabilities of preschool children and then contrast his somewhat negative viewpoint with a more positive outlook that has emerged from recent research.

Piaget divided the preoperational period into two substages: the *preconceptual* period (2–4 years of age) and the *intuitive* period (4–7 years).

The Preconceptual Period

Emergence of symbolic thought. The **preconceptual period** is marked by the appearance of the **symbolic function:** the ability to make one thing—a word or an object—stand for, or represent, something else. This transition from the curious hands-on-everything toddler to the contemplative, symbolic preschool child is remarkable indeed. Consider, for example, that because 2–3-year-olds can use words and images to represent their experiences, they are now quite capable of reconstructing the past and thinking about or even comparing objects that are no longer present. And just how much does the ability to construct mental symbols transform a child's thinking? David Bjorklund (1995) answers by noting that the average, symbolic 3-year-old probably has more in common intellectually with a 21-year-old adult than with a 12-month-old infant. Although a 3-year-old's thinking changes in many ways over the next several years, it is similar to an adult's in that both preschool children and adults think by manipulating mental symbols.

Language is perhaps the most obvious form of symbolism that young children display. Although most infants utter their first meaningful word by the end of the first year, it is not until about 18 months of age—the point at which they show other signs of symbolism such as inner experimentation—that they combine two (or more) words to form simple sentences. Does the use of language promote cognitive development? Piaget said no, arguing instead that language merely reflects what the child *already knows* and contributes little to new knowledge. In other words, he believed that cognitive development promotes language development, not vice versa. Consistent with Piaget's view are numerous demonstrations that prelinguistic infants can form conceptual categories long before they have words to describe them (see, for example, Younger, 1990; 1993). In one such study (Roberts, 1988), 9-month-olds who had habituated to drawings of one particular kind of bird (for example, a hawk) were later shown drawings of other birds (for example, toucans, robins, and hummingbirds) as well as an out-of-category animal—a horse (see Figure 7-1). These infants explored the horse intently but paid little attention to the other birds, which they recognized as similar to the hawk. Clearly, the formation of this "bird" category could not have been based on language because 9-month-olds neither understand nor use the word "bird." But having first formed a *conceptual* category for these feathery creatures, these youngsters are primed to acquire and use the word "bird" when they do begin to talk.

A second major hallmark of the early preconceptual period is the blossoming of *pretend play:* Toddlers often pretend to be people they are not (mommies, superheroes), and they may play these roles with props such as a shoe box or a stick that

preoperational stage: Piaget's second stage of cognitive development, lasting from about ages 2–7 years, when children are thinking at a symbolic level but are not yet using cognitive operations.

preconceptual period: the early substage of preoperations, from ages 2–4 years, characterized by the appearance of primitive ideas, concepts, and methods of reasoning.

symbolic function: the ability to use symbols (for example, images and words) to represent objects and experiences.

Figure 7-1
Category stimuli used in
Roberts's study.
From Roberts, 1988.

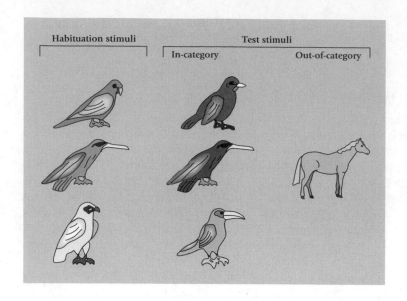

symbolize other objects such as a baby's crib or a ray gun. Although some parents are concerned when their preschool children immerse themselves in a world of make-believe and begin to invent imaginary playmates, Piaget felt that these are basically healthy activities. In Box 7-2, we focus briefly on children's play and see how these "pretend" activities may contribute in a positive way to the child's social, emotional, and intellectual development.

Deficits in preconceptual reasoning. Piaget called this period "preconceptual" because he believed that the ideas, concepts, and cognitive processes of 2–4-year-olds are rather primitive by adult standards. He claimed, for example, that young children often display **animism**—a willingness to attribute life and lifelike qualities (for example, motives and intentions) to inanimate objects. The 4-year-old who believed that the setting sun was alive, angry, and hiding behind the mountain provides a clear example of the animistic logic that children are likely to display during the preconceptual period.

Several other illogical schemes, or "preconcepts," were said to stem from the child's **precausal** or **transductive reasoning.** The transductive thinker reasons from the particular to the particular: When any two events occur together (covary), the child is likely to assume that one has caused the other. One day when Piaget's daughter had missed her usual afternoon nap, she remarked "I haven't had a nap, so it isn't afternoon." In this case, Lucienne reasoned from one particular (the nap) to another (the afternoon) and erroneously concluded that her nap determined when it was afternoon.

According to Piaget, the most striking deficiency in children's preoperational reasoning—a deficiency that contributes immensely to the other intellectual shortcomings they display—is their **egocentrism:** a tendency to view the world from one's own perspective and to have difficulty recognizing another person's point of view. Piaget demonstrated this by first familiarizing children with an asymmetrical mountain scene (see Figure 7-2, page 258) and then asking them what an observer would see as he gazed at the scene from a vantage point other than their own. Often, 3–4-year-olds said the other person would see exactly what they saw, thus failing to consider the other's divergent perspective. Other examples of this self-centered thinking appear in the statements young children make. On page 258 is a sample conversation in which the egocentrism of a 4-year-old named Sandy comes through as she describes an event she has witnessed.

animism: attributing life and lifelike qualities to inanimate objects.

precausal or transductive reasoning: reasoning from the particular to the particular, so that events that occur together are assumed to be causally related.

egocentrism: the tendency to view the world from one's own perspective while failing to recognize that others may have different points of view.

BOX 7-2
Play Is Serious Business

Play is an intrinsically satisfying activity—something young children do for the sheer fun of it (Rubin, Fein, & Vandenberg, 1983). In contrast to earlier views that childhood play activities were a frivolous waste of time, Piaget (1951) was fascinated by the young child's play. He believed that play provided a glimpse of children's emerging cognitive schemes in action while allowing young players to practice and strengthen whatever competencies they possess.

Sensorimotor play begins very early and develops in much the same way in all cultures (Sigman & Sena, 1993). Infants progress from playing with their own bodies (for example, sucking their thumbs), to manipulating external objects such as rattles and stuffed animals, to fully *functional play*—using objects to serve the functions they normally serve—which appears by the end of the first year. So a 12-month-old is now more inclined to turn the dial on a toy phone rather than merely sucking on or banging the toy.

Perhaps the most exciting breakthrough in play activities is the emergence of *symbolic (or pretend) play* at 11 to 13 months of age. The earliest "pretend" episodes are simple ones in which infants pretend to engage in familiar activities such as eating, drinking, or sleeping. But by 18–24 months of age, toddlers have progressed to a point where they will pretend to perform multiple acts in a meaningful sequence; they can also coordinate their actions with those of a play partner, making social games of imitating each other and sometimes even cooperating to achieve a goal (Brownell & Carriger, 1990; Howes & Matheson, 1992). Parents can foster this development by providing toddlers with a secure base of affection and by playing along with their child's little dramas (O'Reilly & Bornstein, 1993; Slade, 1987).

Symbolic play truly blossoms during Piaget's preoperational period. By age 2, toddlers can use one object (a block) to symbolize another (a car) and are now using language in inventive ways to create rich fantasy worlds for themselves. They clearly understand pretense: If you hand them a towel and suggest that they wipe up the imaginary tea you just spilled, they will do it (Harris, Kavanaugh, & Meredith, 1994). Think about this: Since there is no tea in sight, the child's willingness to clean it up suggests that he can construct a mental representation of someone else's pretend event and then act according to this representation. Pretend play becomes increasingly social and complex between ages 2 and 5. More importantly, children combine their capacity for increasingly social play and their capacity for understanding pretense to cooperate with each other at *planning* their pretend activities: They name and assign roles that each player will enact, propose play scripts, and may even stop playing to modify the script if necessary (Howes & Matheson, 1992). Indeed, play episodes are among the most complex social interactions that preschoolers have.

What good is play? Intellectually, play provides a context for using language to communicate and using the mind to fantasize, plan strategies, and solve problems. Children often show more advanced intellectual skills during pretend play than they do when performing other activities, suggesting that play fosters cognitive development (Lillard, 1993). Indeed, preschool children who engage in a great deal of pretend play (or who are trained to do so) perform better on tests of Piagetian cognitive development, language skills, and creativity than children who "pretend" less often (Fisher, 1992; Johnsen, 1991).

Preschool pretend activities may also promote social development. To be successful at social pretend play, children must adopt different roles, coordinate their activities, and resolve any disputes that may arise. Children may also learn about and prepare for adult roles by "playing house" or "school" and stepping into the shoes of their mothers, fathers, or nursery school teachers. Perhaps due to the social skills they acquire (for example, an ability to cooperate) and the role-playing experiences they have, preschool children who participate in a lot of *social* pretend play tend to be more socially mature and more popular with peers than age-mates who often play without partners (Connolly & Doyle, 1984; Howes & Matheson, 1992).

The reciprocal roles children enact during pretend play promote the growth of social skills and interpersonal understanding.

Finally, play may foster healthy emotional development by allowing children to express feelings that bother them or to resolve emotional conflicts (Fein, 1986). If Jennie, for example, has been scolded at lunch for failing to eat her peas, she may gain control of the situation at play as she scolds her doll for picky eating or persuades the doll to "eat healthy" and consume the peas. Indeed, playful resolutions of such emotional conflicts may even be an important contributor to children's understanding of authority and the rationales that underlie all those rules they must follow (Piaget & Inhelder, 1969).

Let it never be said, then, that play is useless. Although children play because it is fun, not because it sharpens their skills, players indirectly contribute to their own social, emotional, and intellectual development, enjoying themselves all the while. In this sense, play truly is the child's work—and is serious business indeed!

Figure 7-2
Piaget's three-mountain problem. Young preoperational children are egocentric. They cannot easily assume another person's perspective and will often say that another child viewing the mountain from a different vantage point will see exactly what they see from their own location.

Sandy: Uncle David, it got on your car and scratched it.

Adult: What did?

Sandy: Come, I'll show you. (She takes her uncle outside and shows him a scratch on the top of his new car.)

Adult: Sandy, what made the scratch?

Sandy: Not me!

Adult (laughing): I know, Sandy, but how did the scratch get there?

Sandy: It got on the car and scratched it with his claws.

Adult: What did?

Sandy (looking around): There! (She points to a cat that is walking across the street.)

Adult: Oh, a cat! Why didn't you tell me that in the first place?

Sandy: I did!

In this case, Sandy assumed that her uncle shared her perspective and must already know what had caused the scratch on his car. Consequently, her speech is not adapted to the needs of her listener, reflecting instead her egocentric point of view.

Finally, Piaget claimed that the young child's egocentric focus on the way things appear to be makes it nearly impossible for her to distinguish appearances from reality. Consider Rheta DeVries' (1969) classic study of the **appearance/reality distinction.** Children 3 to 6 years of age were first introduced to a cat named Maynard. After the children had petted Maynard, DeVries hid Maynard's head and shoulders behind

appearance/reality distinction: ability to keep the true properties or characteristics of an object in mind despite the deceptive appearance that the object has assumed; notably lacking among young children during the preconceptual period.

Figure 7-3
Maynard the cat, without and with a dog mask. Three-year-olds who met Maynard before his change in appearance nonetheless believed that he had become a dog.

a screen while she strapped a realistic mask of a dog's face onto Maynard's head (see Figure 7-3). The children were then asked such questions about Maynard's identity as "What kind of animal is it now?" and "Does it bark or meow?" Even though Maynard's back half and tail remained in full view during the transformation, nearly all the 3-year-olds focused on Maynard's new appearance and concluded that he really was a dog. By contrast, most 6-year-olds could distinguish appearances from reality, correctly noting that Maynard the cat now merely *looked* like a dog.

John Flavell and his colleagues have conducted extensive research on the appearance/reality distinction and have concluded that 3-year-olds (and some 4- and 5-year-olds) truly do not understand the distinction between misleading appearances and reality (Flavell, Flavell, & Green, 1983; Flavell, Miller, & Miller, 1993). However, this confusion is stronger for visual than for tactile incongruities, as most 3-year-olds know that an ice cube that is held in a gloved hand *really is* cold even though it doesn't *feel* cold (Flavell, Green, & Flavell, 1989). Moreover, 3-year-olds recognize *pretend/real distinctions* before appearance/reality distinctions. So, when making judgments about a decorative candle that looks like an apple, 3-year-olds are more likely to say that it really and truly is *not* an apple if they have pretended that it was an apple than if they have not (Flavell, Flavell, & Green, 1987). This observation suggested to Flavell that children's use of objects in creative ways during pretend play (for example, allowing a large box to represent a fort) may underlie their growing awareness (between ages 3 and 6) that objects are not always what they seem and that appearances can be deceiving. Yet, we will see in the following section that many 6- and even 7-year-olds sometimes allow misleading visual appearances to dominate their thinking as they attempt to solve logical problems that are unfamiliar to them.

The Intuitive Period

Piaget calls the phase between age 4 and age 7 the **intuitive period**. Intuitive thought is little more than an extension of preconceptual thought, although children are now somewhat less egocentric and much more proficient at classifying objects on the basis of shared perceptual attributes such as size, shape, and color. Indeed, the child's thinking is called "intuitive" because his understanding of objects and events is still largely based, or "centered," on their single most salient perceptual feature—the way things appear to be—rather than on logical or rational thought processes.

Classification and whole/part relations. The limitations of a perceptually based, intuitive logic are apparent when 4–7-year-olds work on **class inclusion** problems that require them to think about whole/part relations. One such problem presents children with a set of wooden beads, most of which are brown, with a few white ones thrown in. If the preoperational child is asked whether these are all wooden beads, he answers yes. If asked whether there are more brown beads than white beads, he will again answer correctly. However, if he is then asked "Are there more brown beads or more wooden beads?" he will usually say "More brown beads." Notice that

intuitive period: the later sub-stage of preoperations, from ages 4–7 years, when the child's thinking about objects and events is dominated by salient perceptual features.

class inclusion: the ability to compare a class of objects with its subclasses without confusing the two.

the child can conceive of a whole class (wooden beads) when responding to the first question and of two distinct classes (brown and white beads) when responding to the second. Yet the third question, which requires him to *simultaneously* relate a whole class to its component parts, is too difficult. The child's approach to class inclusion seems to be **centered thinking** on the one most salient perceptual feature—the color of the beads—so that he fails to consider that brown beads and white beads can be combined to form a larger class of wooden beads.

Failures to conserve. Other examples of children's intuitive reasoning come from Piaget's famous conservation studies (Flavell, 1963). One of these experiments begins with the child adjusting the volumes of liquid in two identical containers until each is said to have "the same amount to drink." Next, the child sees the experimenter pour the liquid from one of these tall, thin containers into a short, broad container. He is then asked whether the remaining tall, thin container and the shorter, broader container have the same amount of liquid (see Figure 7-4 for an illustration of the procedure). Children younger than 6 or 7 will usually say that the tall, thin receptacle contains *more* liquid than the short, broad one. The child's thinking about liquids is apparently *centered* on one perceptual feature: the relative heights of the columns (tall column = more liquid). In Piaget's terminology, preoperational children are incapable of **conservation**: They do not yet realize that certain properties of objects (such as volume, mass, or number) remain unchanged when the objects' appearances are altered in some superficial way.

Why do preschool children fail to conserve? The answer, according to Piaget, is that these *preoperational* children lack both of the cognitive operations that would help them to overcome their perceptually based intuitive reasoning. The first of these operations is **compensation** (or **decentration**)—the ability to concentrate on more than one aspect of a problem at the same time. Children at the intuitive stage are unable to attend *simultaneously* to both height and width when trying to solve the liquid conservation problem. Consequently, they fail to recognize that increases in the width of a column of liquid compensate for decreases in its height to preserve its absolute amount. Preschoolers also lack **reversibility**—the ability to mentally undo or reverse an action. So an intuitive 5-year-old faced with the conservation-of-liquids problem is unable to reverse mentally what he has seen to conclude that the liquid in the short, broad beaker is still the same amount of water and would attain its former height if it were poured back into its original container.

Does Piaget Underestimate the Preoperational Child?

Are preschool children really as intuitive, illogical, and egocentric as Piaget assumed? Can a child who has no understanding of cognitive operations be taught to conserve? Let's see what later research tells us.

New evidence on egocentrism. Several experiments indicate that Piaget badly underestimated the ability of preschool children to recognize and appreciate another person's point of view. In one study, John Flavell and his associates (1981) showed 3-year-olds a card with a dog on one side and a cat on the other. The card was then held vertically between the child (who could see the dog) and the experimenter (who could see the cat), and the child was asked which animal the experimenter could see. The 3-year-olds performed flawlessly, indicating that they could assume the experimenter's perspective and infer that he must see the cat rather than the animal they could see.

Flavell's study investigated young children's *perceptual* perspective taking—that is, the ability to make correct inferences about what another person can see or hear. Can preoperational children engage in *conceptual* perspective taking by making correct inferences about what another person may be thinking or feeling when these mental states differ from their own? The answer is a qualified yes, and recent experiments

centered thinking (centration): the tendency to focus on only one aspect of a problem when two or more aspects are relevant.

conservation: the recognition that the properties of an object or substance do not change when its appearance is altered in some superficial way.

compensation (or decentration): the ability to consider more than one aspect of a problem at a time.

reversibility: the ability to reverse, or negate, an action by mentally performing the opposite action.

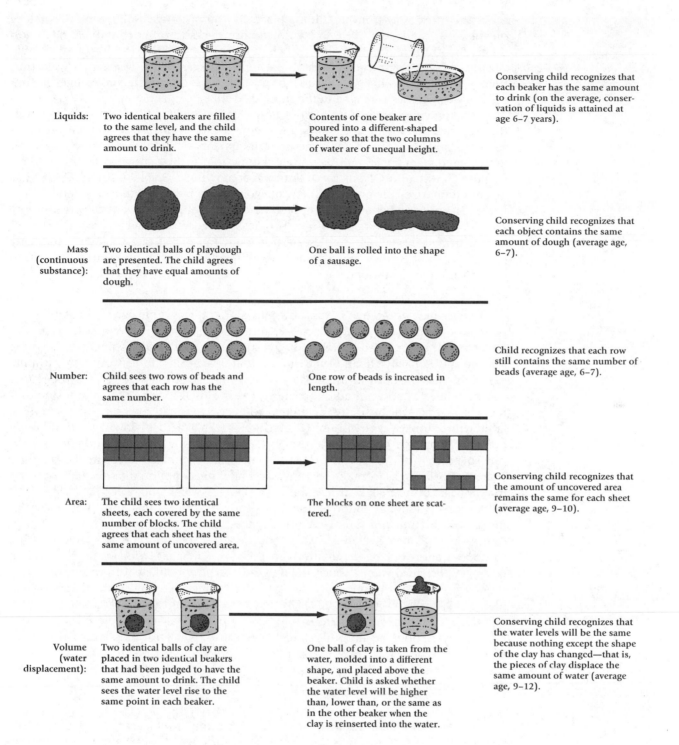

Liquids: Two identical beakers are filled to the same level, and the child agrees that they have the same amount to drink.

Contents of one beaker are poured into a different-shaped beaker so that the two columns of water are of unequal height.

Conserving child recognizes that each beaker has the same amount to drink (on the average, conservation of liquids is attained at age 6–7 years).

Mass (continuous substance): Two identical balls of playdough are presented. The child agrees that they have equal amounts of dough.

One ball is rolled into the shape of a sausage.

Conserving child recognizes that each object contains the same amount of dough (average age, 6–7).

Number: Child sees two rows of beads and agrees that each row has the same number.

One row of beads is increased in length.

Child recognizes that each row still contains the same number of beads (average age, 6–7).

Area: The child sees two identical sheets, each covered by the same number of blocks. The child agrees that each sheet has the same amount of uncovered area.

The blocks on one sheet are scattered.

Conserving child recognizes that the amount of uncovered area remains the same for each sheet (average age, 9–10).

Volume (water displacement): Two identical balls of clay are placed in two identical beakers that had been judged to have the same amount to drink. The child sees the water level rise to the same point in each beaker.

One ball of clay is taken from the water, molded into a different shape, and placed above the beaker. Child is asked whether the water level will be higher than, lower than, or the same as in the other beaker when the clay is reinserted into the water.

Conserving child recognizes that the water levels will be the same because nothing except the shape of the clay has changed—that is, the pieces of clay displace the same amount of water (average age, 9–12).

Figure 7-4
Some common tests of the child's ability to conserve.

suggest that this ability may first emerge much earlier than Piaget could have imagined. In one study, 2¹/₂–4-year-olds were asked to hide the driver of a toy truck underneath one of five containers in a sandbox so that an adult seated outside the room would not be able to find him. An experimenter took care to explain that this truck would leave telltale tracks wherever it went. Could these young children spontaneously generate deceptive strategies in the hope of misleading the adult about the driver's hiding place? Most 2¹/₂–3-year-olds were not especially deceptive: They required explicit prompts and reminders to even smooth over the tire tracks or to move the truck away from the hiding place. By contrast, 4-year-olds took these steps on their own and were likely to lay down false tracks to other containers or to volunteer incorrect information about where the driver was hiding (Sodian et al., 1991). Clearly, these 4-year-old con artists were trying to create *false beliefs* and were thus keenly aware that other people do not always share their own knowledge or conceptual perspectives (see also Ruffman et al., 1993).

So preoperational children are not nearly as egocentric as Piaget thought. Nevertheless, Piaget was right in claiming that young children often rely on their own perspectives and thus fail to make accurate judgments about other people's motives, desires, and intentions; and they often assume that if they know something, others will too (Ruffman & Olson, 1989; Ruffman et al., 1993). Rochel Gelman (1978) has nicely summarized the prevailing view of egocentrism by noting that children become less egocentric and better able to appreciate others' points of view as they learn more and more—particularly about other people and causes of their behavior. In other words, perspective-taking abilities are not totally absent at one stage and suddenly present at another; they are gradually developing and becoming more refined from early in life into adulthood.

Another look at children's causal reasoning. Piaget was quite correct in stating that preschool children are likely to provide animistic answers to many questions and to make logical errors when thinking about cause-and-effect relationships. Yet, Christine Massey and Rochel Gelman (1988) found that 3-year-olds do *not* routinely attribute life or lifelike qualities to inanimate objects, even such inanimates as a robot that can be made to move. In addition, most 4-year-olds recognize that plants and animals grow and will heal after an injury, whereas inanimate objects (for example, a table with a broken leg) will not (Backschneider, Shatz, & Gelman, 1993). Although preschool children occasionally display animistic responses, these judgments stem not so much from a general belief that moving inanimates have lifelike qualities (Piaget's position) as from the (typically accurate) presumption that *unfamiliar* objects that appear to move *on their own* are alive (Dolgin & Behrend, 1984).

Are preoperational children truly "precausal" beings? Apparently not. Even 10-month-old infants find causal event sequences more worthy of attention than noncausal ones (Cohen & Oakes, 1993). And by age 2, children are already expressing some awareness of causal intentions in their own language (for example, "I left it open [TV] *because* I wanna watch it") and are much more likely to recall causal event sequences rather than noncausal ones two weeks after observing them (Bauer & Mandler, 1989; Miller & Aloise, 1989). By age 3, children already know that (1) causes precede rather than follow effects and (2) an event that always precedes an effect (100% covariation) is more likely to be its cause than are other events that occasionally precede it (Sedlak & Kurtz, 1981). So even younger preschool children have some understanding of basic causal principles and will not always resort to transductive reasoning.

Can preoperational children conserve? According to Piaget (1970b), children younger than 6 or 7 cannot solve conservation problems, because they have not yet acquired reversibility or compensation—the two cognitive operations that would enable them to discover the constancy of attributes such as mass and volume. Piaget has also argued that one cannot teach conservation to subjects younger than 6 or 7, for these *pre*operational children are much too intellectually immature to understand and use logical operations such as reversibility and compensation.

Early attempts to teach the logical operations of reversibility and compensation produced only modest improvements in young children's performance on conservation tests (Sigel, Roeper, & Hooper, 1968). However, other investigators have had much greater success with **identity training**—teaching children to recognize that the object or substance transformed in a conservation task is still the *same* object or sub-

identity training: an attempt to promote conservation by teaching nonconservers to recognize that a transformed object or substance is the same object or substance, regardless of its new appearance.

stance, regardless of its new appearance. For example, a child being trained to recognize identities on a conservation-of-liquids task might be told "It may look like less water when we pour it from a tall, thin glass into this shorter one, but it is the *same* water, and there has to be the same amount to drink." Dorothy Field (1981) has shown that 4-year-olds who received this training not only conserved on the training task but could also use their new knowledge about identities to solve a number of conservation problems on which they had not been trained. Field also reports that nearly 75% of the 4-year-olds who had received some kind of identity training were able to solve at least three (out of five) conservation problems that were presented to them 2½–5 months *after* their training had ended. So contrary to Piaget's viewpoint, many preoperational children can learn to conserve, and their initial understanding of this "law of nature" seems to depend more on their ability to recognize identities than on their use of reversibility and compensation (see also Acredolo, 1982; Field, 1987).

Summing up. Taken together, the evidence we have reviewed suggests that preschool children are not nearly as illogical or egocentric as Piaget assumed. Today, many researchers believe that Piaget underestimated the abilities of preschool children because his problems were too complex to allow them to demonstrate what they actually knew. If I were to ask you, "What do quarks do?" you probably couldn't tell me unless you are a physics major. Surely, this is an unfair test of your "causal logic," just as Piaget's tests were when he questioned preschool children about phenomena (for example, "What causes the wind?") that were equally unfamiliar to them. Even when they were thinking about familiar concepts, Piaget required children to justify their answers verbally by stating rationales that these young, relatively inarticulate preschoolers were often incapable of providing (to Piaget's satisfaction, at least). Yet later research consistently indicates that Piaget's subjects may have had a reasonably good understanding of many ideas that they couldn't articulate (for example, class inclusion; distinctions between animates and inanimates) and would easily have displayed such knowledge if asked different questions or given nonverbal tests of the same concepts (Bullock, 1985; Waxman & Hatch, 1992).

Clearly, Piaget was right in arguing that preschool children are more intuitive, egocentric, and illogical than older, grade school children. Yet, it is now equally clear that (1) preschoolers are capable of reasoning logically about simple problems or concepts that are familiar to them and (2) a number of factors other than lack of cognitive operations may account for their poor performances on Piaget's cognitive tests.

The Concrete-Operational Stage (7–11 Years)

During Piaget's **concrete-operational** period, children are rapidly acquiring cognitive operations and applying these important new skills when thinking about objects, situations, and events that they have seen, heard, or otherwise experienced. Recall from our earlier discussion that a cognitive operation is an internal mental activity that enables the child to modify and reorganize her images and symbols to reach a logical conclusion (Flavell et al., 1993). With these powerful new operations in their cognitive arsenal, grade school children progress far beyond the static and centered thinking of the preoperational stage. For every limitation of the preoperational child, we can see a corresponding strength in the concrete operator (see Table 7-3).

Some Examples of Concrete-Operational Thought

Conservation. Concrete-operational children can easily solve several of Piaget's conservation problems. Faced with the conservation-of-liquids puzzle, for example, a 7-year-old concrete operator can *compensate* by focusing simultaneously on both the height and width of the two containers. She also displays *reversibility*—the ability to

concrete operations: Piaget's third stage of cognitive development, lasting from about ages 7–11 years, when children are acquiring cognitive operations and thinking more logically about real objects and experiences.

Table 7-3   A Comparison of Preoperational and Concrete-Operational Thought

Concept	Preoperational thought	Concrete-operational thought
Egocentrism	Children typically assume that others share their point of view.	Children may respond egocentrically at times but are now much more aware of others' divergent perspectives.
Animism	Children are likely to assume that unfamiliar objects that move on their own have lifelike qualities.	Children are more aware of the biological bases for life and do not attribute lifelike qualities to inanimates.
Causality	Limited awareness of causality. Children occasionally display transductive reasoning, assuming that one of two correlated events must have caused the other.	Children have a much better appreciation of causal principles (although this knowledge of causality continues to develop into adolescence and beyond).
Perception-bound thought/centration	Children make judgments based on perceptual appearances and focus on a single aspect of a situation when seeking answers to a problem.	Children can ignore misleading appearances and focus on more than one aspect of a situation when seeking answers to a problem (compensation).
Irreversibility/reversibility	Children cannot mentally undo an action they have witnessed. They cannot think back to the way an object or situation was before the object or situation changed.	Children can mentally negate changes they have witnessed to make before/after comparisons and consider how changes have altered the situation.
Performance on Piagetian tests of logical reasoning	Their egocentrism and their perception-bound, centered reasoning means that children often fail conservation tasks, have difficulty grouping objects into hierarchies of classes and subclasses, and display little ability to order objects *mentally* along such quantitative dimensions as height or length.	Their declining egocentrism and acquisition of reversible cognitive operations permit concrete-operational children to conserve, correctly classify objects on several dimensions, and mentally order objects on quantitative dimensions. Conclusions are now based on logic (the way things *must* necessarily be) rather than on the way they appear to be.

mentally undo the pouring process and imagine the liquid in its original container. Armed with these cognitive operations, then, the concrete operator now *knows* that the two different containers each have the same amount of liquid; she uses *logic*, not misleading appearances, to reach her conclusion.

Classification. Concrete-operational children now find Piaget's class inclusion problems to be much simpler exercises. The operation of *compensation* helps them to recognize that objects may vary on more than one dimension and thus may be grouped or classified in many different ways. And confusing classes with subclasses is now a thing of the past. Why? Because the operations of cognitive *addition* and *subtraction* permit the concrete operator to discover the logical relation between the two by mentally adding subclasses to form a superordinate whole and then quickly reversing this action (subtraction) to once again think of the whole class as a collection of subclasses (Flavell, 1963; Ricco, 1989).

Relational logic. An important hallmark of concrete-operational thinking is a better understanding of quantitative relations and relational logic. Do you remember an occasion when your gym teacher said "Line up by height from tallest to shortest"? Carrying out such an order is really quite easy for concrete operators, who are now

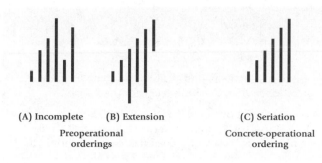

(A) Incomplete   (B) Extension

Preoperational
orderings

(C) Seriation

Concrete-operational
ordering

Figure 7-5
Children's performance on a simple seriation task. If asked to
arrange a series of sticks from shortest to longest, preoperational
children often line up one end of the sticks and create an incomplete ordering (A) or order them so the top of each successive
stick extends higher than the preceding stick (B). Concrete operators, by contrast, can use the inverse cognitive operations greater
than (>) and less than (<) to quickly make successive comparisons and create a correct serial ordering.

capable of **seriation**—the ability to *mentally* arrange items along a quantifiable
dimension such as height or weight. By contrast, preoperational youngsters perform
miserably on seriation tasks (see Figure 7-5) and would struggle to comply with the
gym teacher's request.

Concrete-operational thinkers have also mastered the related concept of **transitivity,** which describes the necessary relations among elements in a series. If, for example, John is taller than Mark, and Mark is taller than Sam, who is taller, John or Sam?
It follows *logically* that John must be taller than Sam, and the concrete operator grasps
the transivity of these size relationships. Lacking the concept of transitivity, the preoperational child will need to rely on perceptions to answer the question and might
insist that John and Sam stand next to each other so that it can be determined who
is taller. Preoperational children probably have a better understanding of such transitive relations than Piaget gave them credit for (Gelman, 1978; Trabasso, 1975), but
they still have difficulty grasping the logical necessity of transitivity (Chapman & Lindenberger, 1988).

The Sequencing of Concrete Operations

While examining Figure 7-4, you may have noticed that some forms of conservation
(for example, mass) are understood much sooner than others (area or volume). Piaget
was aware of this and other developmental inconsistencies, and he coined the term
horizontal decalage to describe them.

Why does the child display different levels of understanding on a series of conservation tasks that seem to require the same mental operations? According to Piaget,
horizontal decalage occurs because problems that appear quite similar may actually
differ in complexity. For example, conservation of volume (see Figure 7-4) is not
attained until age 9 to 12 because it is a complex task that requires the child to simultaneously consider the operations involved in the conservation of both liquids and
mass *and* then to determine whether there are any meaningful interactions between
these two phenomena. Although we have talked as if concrete operations were a set
of skills that appeared rather abruptly over a brief period, this is not Piaget's view.
Piaget always maintained that operational abilities evolve gradually and sequentially
as the simpler skills that appear first are consolidated, combined, and reorganized
into increasingly complex mental structures.

Carol Tomlinson-Keasey and her associates (1979) studied the growth of logical
reasoning between ages 6 and 9. In this longitudinal study, they found that various
concrete-operational abilities developed very gradually and in roughly the same
sequence for all the children they studied (for example, seriation appeared before
conservation of number and weight, which, in turn, seemed to be necessary for the
development of class-inclusion skills and the conservation of volume). However,
other investigators have found much less coherence, or consistency, to development
during the concrete-operational period (Case, 1985; Kuhn, 1992). Apparently, some
children breeze through class-inclusion problems before they can seriate or conserve
weight, whereas others acquire these skills in exactly the opposite order. So the
sequencing of different concrete-operational skills is highly variable—a finding that

seriation: a cognitive operation
that allows one to order a set of
stimuli along a quantifiable
dimension such as height or
weight.

transitivity: the ability to recognize relations among elements
in a serial order (for example, if
A > *B* and *B* > *C*, then *A* > *C*).

horizontal decalage: Piaget's
term for a child's uneven cognitive performance; an inability to
solve certain problems even
though one can solve similar
problems requiring the same
mental operations.

BOX 7-3

Piaget on Education

Late in his career, Piaget (1971; 1976) wrote about education, offering several suggestions for change that impressed educators and have had a major impact on preschool and early grade school curricula (Gallagher & Easley, 1978; Ginsburg & Opper, 1988). Among the more widely accepted of Piaget's ideas are:

1. *Tailor education to children's readiness to learn.* Appropriate learning experiences build on existing schemes. Piaget stresses that children profit most from *moderately novel* educational experiences—information that piques their curiosity, challenges their current understandings, and forces them to reevaluate what they already know. If the experiences one provides are too complex, students will be unable to assimilate (much less accommodate to) them, and no new learning will occur.

2. *Be sensitive to individual differences.* Because children differ in their rates of intellectual development, they will not all be ready to learn precisely the same lessons. In a Piagetian-based curriculum, these individual differences are accepted by teachers, who plan activities for individual students or for small groups, rather than the whole class (Ginsburg & Opper, 1988).

3. *Promote discovery-based education.* Piaget criticized traditional educational programs for relying much too heavily on passive, verbal forms of instruction that emphasize rote learning. He reminded us that young children are naturally inquisitive souls who will learn best when they act directly on their environments, probing

objects and participating in situations that will allow them to *construct* new knowledge for themselves.

Based on these principles, Piaget advised educators against lecturing or demonstrating to students who sit listening passively; instead, he argued that children should be encouraged to explore a variety of educational props—storybooks, arts and crafts, puzzles, and games—that will enable them to learn by doing. Piaget insisted that even formal lessons can be structured to promote active learning. For example, he believed that basic arithmetic operations are best illustrated by having children add and substract buttons rather than showing them how to solve problems on a blackboard. He advocated "teaching" the concepts of space and distance by allowing children to measure their heights or the widths of their desks, as opposed to lecturing them on the relations between inches, feet, and yards. In other words, Piaget stressed that the teacher's job is not so much to transmit facts and concepts or to actively reinforce correct answers as to provide the setting, materials, and guidance that will enable curious children to experience the *intrinsic* satisfaction of *discovering* this knowledge for themselves. Piaget saw a "discovery-based" education as critical because he believed that "the principal goal of education is to create [adults] who are capable of doing new things, not simply of repeating what other generations have done—[people] who are creative, inventive, discoverers" (Piaget, as cited in Elkind, 1977, p. 171).

challenges Piaget's notion that the operational proficiencies acquired early are simpler schemes that serve as prerequisities for those developing later.

After reviewing the intellectual accomplishments of the concrete-operational period, we can see why many societies begin to formally educate their young at 6 to 7 years of age. According to Piaget, this is precisely the time when children are decentering from perceptual illusions and acquiring the cognitive operations that will enable them to comprehend arithmetic, think about language and its properties, classify animals, people, objects, and events, and understand the relations between upper- and lower case letters, letters and the printed word, and words and sentences. Although Piaget was a basic scientist, not an educator, we can see in Box 7-3 that he had some very interesting ideas about the kinds of education that young children should receive.

An Important Limitation of Concrete-Operational Thought

Surely, since Piaget proposed a fourth stage of cognitive development, there must be at least one important limitation to concrete-operational reasoning. And there is. Piaget called this period *concrete* operations because he believed that children can apply their operational schemes only to objects, situations, or events that are real or imaginable. The transitive inferences of concrete operators, for example, are likely to be accurate only for real objects that are (or have been) *physically present*. Seven- to 11-year-olds cannot yet apply this relational logic to *abstract* signifiers such as the *X*s, *Y*s, and *Z*s that we use in algebra.

The Formal-Operational Stage (11–12 Years and Beyond)

By age 11 or 12, many children are entering the last of Piaget's intellectual stages—**formal operations.** Recall that concrete operations are mental actions performed on material aspects of experience and that concrete operators can think quite logically about tangible objects and events. By contrast, formal operations are mental actions performed on *ideas* and *propositions.* No longer is thinking tied to the factual or observable, for formal operators can reason quite logically about hypothetical processes and events that may have no basis in reality.

Reactions to Hypothetical Propositions

One way to determine whether a preadolescent has crossed over into the stage of formal operations is to present a thought problem that violates her views about the real world. The concrete operator, whose thinking is tied to objective reality, will often balk at hypothetical propositions. In fact, she may even reply that it is impossible to think logically about objects that don't exist or events that could never happen. By contrast, formal operators enjoy thinking about hypotheticals and are likely to generate some very creative yet logical responses. In Box 7-4, we can see the differences between concrete-operational and formal-operational thinking as children consider a hypothetical proposition that was presented in the form of an art assignment.

Hypothetical-Deductive Reasoning: The Systematic Search for Answers

The formal operator's approach to problem solving becomes increasingly systematic and abstract—much like the **hypothetical-deductive reasoning** of a scientist. We can easily compare the reasoning of formal operators with that of their younger counterparts by examining their responses to Piaget's *pendulum* problem (Inhelder & Piaget, 1958). Given strings of different lengths, objects of different weights to attach to one end of the strings, and a hook on which to hang the other end, the subject's task is to discover which factor influences how fast the string pendulum oscillates (that it, swings back and forth during a set time period). Is it the length of the string that matters? The heaviness of the weight? The force with which the weight is pushed? The height from which the weight is released? Or might two or more of these variables be important?

The key to solving this problem is first to identify the four factors that might control the pendulum's oscillation and then to systematically test each of these "hypotheses,"

formal operations: Piaget's fourth and final stage of cognitive development, from age 11 or 12 and beyond, when the individual begins to think more rationally and systematically about abstract concepts and hypothetical events.

hypothetical-deductive reasoning: a style of problem solving in which all possible solutions to a problem are generated and then systematically evaluated to determine the correct answer.

A systematic approach to problem solving is one of the characteristics of formal-operational thinking.

BOX 7-4
Children's Responses to a Hypothetical Proposition

Piaget (1970a) has argued that the thinking of concrete operators is reality bound. Presumably most 9-year-olds would have a difficult time thinking about objects that don't exist or events that could never happen. By contrast, children entering the stage of formal operations were said to be quite capable of considering hypothetical propositions and carrying them to a logical conclusion. Indeed, Piaget suspected that many formal operators would even enjoy this type of cognitive challenge.

Several years ago, a group of concrete operators (9-year-old fourth-graders) and a group of children who were at or rapidly approaching formal operations (11–12-year-old six-graders) completed the following assignment:

Suppose that you were given a third eye and that you could choose to place this eye anywhere on your body. Draw me a picture to show where you would place your "extra" eye, and then tell me why you would put it there.

All the 9-year-olds placed the third eye *on the forehead between their two natural eyes.* It seems as if these children called on their concrete experiences to complete their assignment: Eyes are found somewhere around the middle of the face in all people. One 9-year-old boy remarked that the third eye should go between the other two because "that's where a cyclops has his eye." The rationales for this eye placement were rather unimaginative. Consider the following examples:

Jim (age 9½): I would like an eye beside my two other eyes so that if one eye went out, I could still see with two.
Vickie (age 9): I want an extra eye so I can see you three times.
Tanya (age 9½): I want a third eye so I could see better.

In contrast, the older, formal-operational children gave a wide variety of responses that were not at all dependent on what they has seen previously. Furthermore, these children thought out the advantages of this hypothetical situation and provided rather imaginative rationales for placing the "extra" eye in unique locations. Here are some sample responses:

Ken (age 11½) (*draws the extra eye on top of a tuft of hair*): I could revolve the eye to look in all directions.
John (age 11½) (*draws his extra eye in the palm of his left hand*): I could see around corners and see what kind of cookie I'll get out of the cookie jar.

Tony (age 11) (*draws a close-up of a third eye in his mouth*): I want a third eye in my mouth because I want to see what I am eating.

When asked their opinions of the "three eye" assignment, many of the younger children considered it rather silly and uninteresting. One 9-year-old remarked, "This is stupid. Nobody has three eyes." However, the 11–12-year-olds enjoyed the task and continued to pester their teacher for "fun" art assignments "like the eye problem" for the remainder of the school year (Shaffer, 1973).

So the results of this demonstration are generally consistent with Piaget's theory. Older children who are at or rapidly approaching the stage of formal operations are more likely than younger, concrete operators to generate logical and creative responses to a hypothetical proposition and to enjoy this type of reasoning.

Tanya's, Ken's, and John's responses to the "third eye" assignment.

varying one factor at a time while holding all the other factors constant. Each successive hypothesis is tested in an if–then fashion: "*If* the weight on the string matters, *then* I should see a difference in oscillation when I compare a string with a heavy weight to a same-length string with a light weight, while holding other factors constant." Formal operators, who rely on this systematic approach to hypothesis generation and testing, eventually discover that the "weight hypothesis" is wrong and that the pendulum's oscillation depends on only one factor: the length of the string.

By contrast, 9–10-year-old concrete operators are not able to generate and systematically test the full range of possibilities that would permit them to draw the appropriate conclusion. They often begin with a reasonable hypothesis ("maybe string length matters"), but they can't isolate the effects of each variable. For example, they may test the "string length" hypothesis without holding weight constant; should they find that a short string with a heavy weight oscillates faster than a longer one with a lighter weight, they are likely to conclude erroneously that both string length and weight control the pendulum's oscillation. Older concrete operators can be trained to think more like formal operators when seeking solutions to problems (Adey & Shayer, 1992; Fabricius & Steffe, 1989), but they are unable to generate these rational and methodical problem-solving strategies on their own.

In sum, formal-operational thinking is rational, systematic, and abstract. The formal operator can now think planfully about thinking and can operate on ideas and hypothetical concepts, including those that contradict reality. This may be one reason that adolescents come to appreciate absurd humor, as we see in Box 7-5.

Personal and Social Implications of Formal Thought

Even in its earliest stages, formal-operational thinking is a powerful tool that may change adolescents in many ways—some good, and some not so good. First the good news. As we will see in Chapter 12, formal operations may pave the way for thinking about what is possible in one's life, forming a stable identity, and achieving a much richer understanding of other people's psychological perspectives and the causes of their behavior. The formal-operational thinker is also better equipped to make difficult personal decisions that involve weighing alternative courses of action and their probable consequences for oneself and other people (see Chapter 14, for example, on the development of moral reasoning). So advances in cognitive growth help to lay the groundwork for changes in many other aspects of development.

Now the bad news: Formal operations may also be related to some of the more painful aspects of the adolescent experience. Unlike younger children who tend to accept the world as it is and to heed the dictates of authority figures, formal operators, who can imagine hypothetical alternatives to present realities, may begin to question everything from their parents' authority to impose strict curfews to the need for spending billions on Star Wars technology when so many people are hungry and homeless. Indeed, the more logical inconsistencies and other flaws that adolescents detect in the real world, the more confused they become and the more inclined they are to become frustrated with or even to display rebellious anger toward the agents (for example, parents, the government) they hold responsible for these imperfect states of affairs. Piaget (1970a) viewed this idealistic fascination with the way things "ought to be" as a perfectly normal outgrowth of the adolescent's newly acquired abstract reasoning abilities, and he thus proclaimed formal operations the primary cause of the "generation gap."

According to Piaget, adolescents can be so "centered" on themselves and their thinking that they actually appear more egocentric than they were during the grade school years. Indeed, David Elkind (1967; 1981a) has identified two kinds of "egocentrism" that adolescents often display. The **imaginary audience** phenomenon refers to the adolescent's feeling that she is constantly "on stage" and that everybody around her is just as concerned with and as critical of her actions or appearance as she is. Thus, a teenage girl who has spent hours making up her face to hide a few pimples may be absolutely convinced that her date is repulsed by them whenever he looks away—when, in truth, the equally self-conscious boy may be turning away because he's convinced that her looks of concern imply that his mouthwash has failed him.

The second form of adolescent egocentrism is what Elkind calls the **personal fable**—a belief in the *uniqueness* of oneself and one's experiences. For example, a

imaginary audience: allegedly a form of adolescent egocentrism that involves confusing your own thoughts with those of a hypothesized audience and concluding that others share your preoccupations.

personal fable: allegedly a form of adolescent egocentrism that involves thinking that oneself and one's thoughts and feelings are special or unique.

BOX 7-5

Children's Humor and Cognitive Development

Where does the fish keep its money?
Answer: In the riverbank.

Do you remember going through a phase in early elementary school of telling terrible jokes like this one? A preschooler hearing this joke may laugh at the silly idea of a fish having money. But, if asked to rephrase the joke, the child is likely to say the answer was "In the bank." A child of this age misses the whole idea that the humor of the joke depends on the double meaning of "bank." Anything that looks or sounds silly may amuse preschoolers—calling a "shoe" a "floo" or a "poo," for example. Once children realize that everything has a correct name, mislabeling things becomes funny (McGhee, 1979).

With the onset of concrete-operational thought and advances in awareness of the nature of language, children come to appreciate jokes and riddles that involve linguistic ambiguities. The riverbank joke boils down to a classification task: There is a large category of banks, with at least two subclasses, financial institutions and the banks of streams. School-age children who have mastered the concept of class inclusion can keep the class and subclasses in mind at once and move back and forth mentally between the two meanings of bank. Appreciation of such puns is high among second-graders (7–8-year-olds) and continues to grow until fourth or fifth grade (McGhee & Chapman, 1980; Yalisove, 1978).

Children's tastes in humor change again when they enter the stage of formal operations at about age 11 or 12 (Yalisove, 1978). Simple riddles and puns are no longer cognitively challenging enough, it seems, and are likely to elicit loud groans (McGhee, 1979). Adolescents do, however, appreciate jokes that involve an absurd or contrary-to-fact premise and a punchline that is quite logical if the absurd premise is accepted. The humor in "How do you fit six elephants into a Volkswagen?" depends on appreciating that "Three in the front and three in the back" is a perfectly logical answer only if one accepts the hypothetical premise that multiple elephants could fit into a small car (Yalisove, 1978). Reality-oriented school-age children might simply judge this joke stupid; after all, elephants *can't* fit into cars. Clearly, then, children cannot appreciate certain forms of humor until they have the required cognitive abilities. Research on children's humor seems to suggest that children and adolescents are most attracted to jokes that challenge them intellectually by requiring them to use the cognitive skills they are just beginning to master (Bjorklund, 1995; McGhee, 1979).

An adolescent may feel that others are as preoccupied with her appearance or her conduct as she is—a form of "egocentrism" known as the "imaginary audience" phenomenon.

teenager who has just been "dumped" by his first love may feel that no one in human history has ever experienced anything quite like *his* crushing agony. According to Elkind, the personal fable may also explain the risks adolescents take. After all, they are *unique* and are unlikely to be harmed by reckless driving or having unsafe sex: The negative consequences only happen to others, so why bother with seat belts or contraception (Arnett, 1990)?

Elkind believed that both forms of adolescent egocentrism would increase as youngsters are first acquiring formal operations and would gradually decline as older adolescents enter adult roles that require them to consider others' perspectives more carefully. However, the data are not always consistent with this point of view. Apparently, teenagers perceive just as many personal dangers in risky acts such as drug use, driving while intoxicated, and having sex as middle-age adults do, thus challenging the idea that adolescents feel especially unique or invulnerable (Beyth-Marom et al., 1993). Indeed, much of adolescent risk taking reflects a desire to have exciting experiences rather than feelings of invulnerability (Arnett & Balle-Jensen, 1993). And although the imaginary audience phenomenon is stronger among 13–15-year-olds than among older adolescents, it is often the 13–15-year-olds still functioning at the *concrete-operational* level who show more of this self-consciousness (Gray & Hudson, 1984; O'Conner & Nikolic, 1990)—the reverse of what Elkind would expect. Consequently, some developmentalists now believe that the apparent self-centeredness that adolescents display may be linked less closely to formal-operational thinking than to the development of advanced social perspective-taking skills (discussed in Chapter 12) that allow teenagers to contemplate how *other people* might perceive them or react to their behavior (Jahnke & Blanchard-Fields, 1993; Lapsley et al., 1986). Viewed in this way, adolescent egocentrism is not very "egocentric" after all.

Does the Formal Operations Stage Conclude Cognitive Development?

Piaget (1970b) believed that the child's transition from concrete-operational to formal operational reasoning takes place very gradually. For example, 11–13-year-olds who are entering formal operations are able to consider simple hypothetical propositions such as the three-eye problem (see Box 7-4). However, they are not yet proficient at generating and testing hypotheses, and it may be another three to four years before they are capable of the planful, systematic reasoning that is necessary to deduce what determines how fast a pendulum will swing. Piaget never identified a stage of reasoning beyond formal operations, and he believed that most people reach this highest level of intellect by age 15–18.

Does everyone reach formal operations? Other investigators find that adolescents are much slower to acquire formal operations than Piaget had thought. In fact, Edith Neimark's (1979) review of the literature suggests that a sizable percentage of American adults do not reason at the formal level, and apparently there are some cultures—particularly those where formal schooling is rare or nonexistent—in which no one solves Piaget's formal-operational problems (Dasen, 1977; Dasen & Heron, 1981).

Why do some people fail to attain formal operations? Dasen's cross-cultural research provides one clue: They may not have had sufficient exposure to the kinds of schooling that stress logic, mathematics, and science—experiences that Piaget believed help the child to reason at the formal level. Another possibility is that some individuals, even those who have been educated, may lack the intellectual capacity to move from concrete to formal operations. Indeed, adolescents and adults who score even slightly below average on intelligence tests rarely if ever reason at the formal level (Inhelder, 1966; Jackson, 1965).

In the later stages of his career, Piaget (1972) suggested another possibility: Perhaps nearly all adults are capable of reasoning at the formal level but will do so only on problems that hold their interest or are of vital importance to them. Indeed, Tulkin and Konner (1973) found that preliterate Bushman hunters who fail Piaget's test problems often reason at the formal level on at least one task—tracking prey. Clearly, this is an activity of great importance to them that requires the systematic testing of inferences and hypotheses. A similar phenomenon has been observed among high school and college students: Not only do 12th-graders reason more abstractly about relevant everyday issues with which they are already familiar (Overton et al., 1987; Ward & Overton, 1990), but, as we see in Figure 7-6, physics,

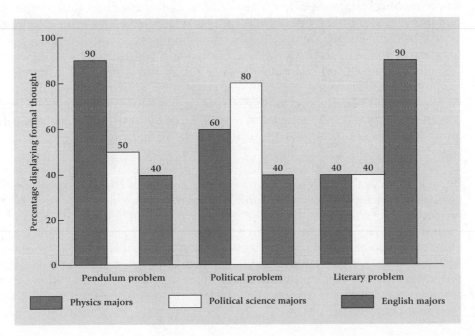

Figure 7-6
Expertise and formal operations. College students show the greatest command of formal-operational thought in the subject area most related to their major.
Adapted from De Lisi & Staudt, 1980.

English, and social science majors are all much more likely to perform at the formal level on problems that fall squarely within their own academic domains (De Lisi & Staudt, 1980).

It seems likely, then, that each person has an optimal or "highest" level of cognitive performance that will show itself in familiar or well-trained content domains (Fischer, 1980; Fischer, Kenny, & Pipp, 1990). However, performance is likely to be inconsistent across domains unless the person has had a chance to build knowledge and to practice reasoning in all these content areas (Marini & Case, 1994). So we must be careful not to underestimate the cognitive capabilities of adolescents and adults who fail Piaget's formal-operational tests, for their less-than-optimal *performances* on these *physical science* problems may simply reflect either a lack of interest or a lack of experience with the subject matter rather than an inability to reason at the formal level.

Are there higher stages of intellectual development? According to Piaget, formal-operational thinking is the structural equivalent of adult intelligence—the most mature form of reasoning of which human beings are capable. Not everyone agrees. Patricia Arlin (1975, 1977) has called formal operations a *problem-solving* stage that describes how bright adolescents and adults think about problems that someone else presents to them. However, she believes that truly creative and insightful thinkers—people like Aristotle, Einstein, and Piaget himself—operate on a higher plane that enables them to rethink or reorganize existing knowledge and then to ask important questions or define totally new problems. Arlin refers to this ability as a **problem-finding stage.**

Several other kinds of reasoning have been proposed as examples of postformal thought. Michael Basseches (1984) cites **dialectical reasoning**—the ability to resolve logical inconsistencies or paradoxes—as one such skill. Michael Commons and his associates (1982; Richards & Commons, 1990) cite **systematic reasoning** as another. Should your professor ask you to compare and contrast the premises of several developmental theories (each of which is an abstract "system") for purposes of constructing a single, comprehensive theory (or higher-order "supersystem"), he or she is asking you to try your hand at systematic reasoning.

It turns out that college faculty members and graduate students are much more proficient at both dialectical and systematic reasoning than undergraduate students are (Basseches, 1984; Commons, Richards, & Kuhn, 1982). Do these findings indicate that there are stages of intellectual development beyond formal operations? Basseches and Commons believe they do, although a Piagetian could argue that the inability of some formal-operational undergraduates to resolve paradoxes or to construct abstract "systems" and "supersystems" simply represents a form of horizontal decalage comparable to that of a concrete operator who conserves liquids and mass but not volume. In other words, the cognitive abilities that Arlin, Basseches, and Commons have described may represent very complex formal-operational proficiencies rather than higher stages of intellect that are qualitatively different from formal reasoning (Fischer, 1980). Or alternatively, some of these advanced skills may develop alongside formal-operational thought without actually replacing it (Chandler & Boutilier, 1992).

So it is not entirely clear whether any of these unusual and highly abstract cognitive abilities really qualify as a new and higher *stage* of cognitive development that evolves out of formal-operational thinking. However, we do know that these noteworthy cognitive skills are more likely to emerge among adults with advanced educations who live in a culture that encourages them to entertain new ideas (Irwin, 1991). It is also clear that cognitive development does not end in adolescence (Kitchner et al., 1993). During adulthood, many people become better able to define and think through "real-life" problems that require making sense of contradictory and ambiguous information that can be viewed from several perspectives and may not have one right answer.

problem-finding stage: according to Arlin, a stage beyond formal operations in which the individual is now capable of reorganizing knowledge to ask questions and define new problems.

dialectical reasoning: the ability to resolve logical inconsistencies or paradoxes; thought by some to be a stage of reasoning beyond formal operations.

systematic reasoning: the ability to operate on abstract systems to construct higher-order structures (or supersystems).

Concept Check 7-2 ⌄ Understanding Piaget's Stages of Cognitive Development

Check your understanding of some aspects of children's thinking that are said to characterize each of Piaget's four cognitive stages. The answers appear in the Appendix.

1. John knows that the amount of water remains unchanged when poured into a different beaker, and he understands the relation between classes of objects (trucks) and their sub-classes (red vs. green trucks). However, he has trouble with _____, or the ability to recognize relations among elements in a serial order. According to Piaget, John is at the _____ stage of cognitive development, and his uneven performance across these three problems is an example of _____ _____.

2. A child who searches for an object where it was found previously rather than where she last saw it has an incomplete sense of _____ _____, which is thought to be an important prerequisite for the establishment of emotional _____s. According to Piaget, this child's errors in searching stem from her belief that _____.

3. According to Piaget, a formal operator should be able to think logically about _____ propositions and to display _____-_____ reasoning by generating and systematically testing all possible solutions to a problem. Yet, adolescents and adults are most inclined to reason at the formal level on problems that are _____ to them.

4. According to Piaget, children's failure to _____ such properties as mass or liquids stems from their inability to understand and use cognitive operations such as _____ or _____. These children are at Piaget's _____ stage and may not even recognize that their _____ is an unchanging attribute.

 # AN EVALUATION OF PIAGET'S THEORY

Now that we have examined Piaget's theory of cognitive development, it is time to evaluate it. Let us start by giving credit where credit is due before considering the challenges to Piaget's viewpoint.

Piaget's Contributions

Piaget is a giant in the field of human development. As one scholar quoted by Harry Beilin (1992) put it, "assessing the impact of Piaget on developmental psychology is like assessing the impact of Shakespeare on English literature or Aristotle on philosophy—impossible" (p. 191). It is hard to imagine that we would know even a fraction of what we know about intellectual development had Piaget pursued his early interests in zoology and never worked with developing children.

We can credit Piaget with some major developmental insights that are widely accepted today. For example, he convinced us that human beings are active in their own development—that from birth they seek to master the environment and to understand the incomprehensible. This perspective on human nature was a dramatic departure from the then-traditional view of children as passive recipients of environmental influence who must be taught the ways of the world and trained to think for themselves. Piaget also taught us that young human beings do indeed think differently than older ones and that there is great value in looking at *how* people of different ages reason, not just whether they give right or wrong answers.

Let's also note that Piaget was largely right in his basic overview of cognitive development. The broad developmental *sequences* he proposed seem to describe the general course of intellectual development for children and adolescents from the hundreds of cultures and subcultures that have now been studied (Bjorklund, 1995; Flavell et al., 1993). Although cultural factors do influence the *rate* of cognitive growth, the direction of development is always from sensorimotor intellect, to preoperational thinking, to concrete operations, to (in many cases) formal operations.

Finally, the richness of Piaget's thinking drew literally thousands of researchers to the study of cognitive development. Thus Piaget's theory has been the focal point for an enormous amount of research; and as often happens when heuristic theories are repeatedly scrutinized, some of this research led to important new insights while pointing to problems with Piaget's original formulations.

Challenges to Piaget

Over the past 20 years, critics have pointed to several apparent shortcomings of Piaget's theory. We will briefly consider five of these criticisms.

Piaget Underestimated Developing Minds

One frequent charge is that Piaget was often incorrect about when individuals can be expected to master a concept or enter a particular stage of development. Most notably, Piaget seems to have underestimated the cognitive capabilities of infants and preschool children; but he also claimed that concrete operators are incapable of reasoning abstractly, when training studies suggest otherwise, and he seems to have erred in assuming that cognitive growth is complete by midadolescence. When researchers have turned to more familiar problems than Piaget used or have reduced Piaget's tasks to their bare essentials, the true competencies of young children—and of adolescents and adults too—come through more clearly.

Piaget Failed to Distinguish Competence from Performance.

Piaget was concerned with identifying the underlying *competencies*, or cognitive structures, that presumably determine how children perform on various cognitive tasks. He tended to assume that a child who failed one of his problems simply lacked the underlying concepts, or thought structures, he was testing.

We now know that this latter assumption is not valid because many factors other than a lack of critical competencies might undermine one's performance on a cognitive test. We've seen, for example, that 4- and 5-year-olds who seem to know the differences between animates and inanimates were failing Piaget's tests largely because Piaget required them to explain principles they understood (critical competency) but could not articulate. Late in his career, Piaget (1972) realized that he may have erred when he observed that adolescents are more likely to display formal-operational reasoning on familiar problems that interest them and concluded that *motivation* also influences intellectual performance. But his earlier tendency to equate task performances with competencies (and to ignore motivation, task familiarity, and all other factors that influence performance) is a major reason that his age norms for various cognitive milestones were often so far off target.

Does Cognitive Development Really Occur in Stages?

Piaget maintained that his stages of intellectual development are *holistic structures*— that is, coherent modes of thinking that are applied across a broad range of tasks. To say that a child is concrete operational, for example, implies that he relies on cognitive operations and thinks logically about the vast majority of intellectual problems that he encounters.

Recently, this "holistic structures" assumption has been challenged by researchers who question whether cognitive development is at all stagelike (Bjorklund, 1995; Flavell et al., 1993). From their perspective, a "stage" of intellect implies that abrupt changes in intellectual functioning occur as the child acquires several new competencies over a relatively brief period. Yet, we've seen that cognitive growth doesn't happen that way: Major transitions in intellect occur quite gradually, and there is often very little consistency in the child's performance on tasks that presumably measure the abilities that define a given stage. For example, it may be years before a 7-year-old who can seriate or conserve number will be able to conserve area or volume (see Figure 7-4). And when we recall that different concrete- and formal-operational problems are mastered in different orders by different children, there seems to be much less consistency and coherence to cognitive growth than Piaget assumed.

So is cognitive development truly stagelike? The issue is still hotly debated and far from being resolved. Some theorists insist that cognitive development is coherent and does progress through a series of stages, although not necessarily through the same stages that Piaget proposed (Case, 1985; 1992; Flavell et al., 1993). Yet, many other theorists believe that intellectual development is a complex, multifaceted process in which children gradually acquire skills in many different content areas such as deductive reasoning, mathematics, visual-spatial reasoning, verbal skills, and moral reasoning, to name a few (Bjorklund, 1995; Fischer et al., 1990). Although development within each of these domains may occur in small, orderly steps, there is no assumption of consistency across domains. Thus, a 10-year-old who enjoys solving word puzzles and playing verbal games might outperform most age-mates on tests of verbal reasoning but function at a much lower level in less-familiar domains, such as hypothesis testing or mathematical reasoning.

In sum, cognitive development is orderly and coherent (and some would say stagelike) *within particular intellectual domains*. Yet, there is very little evidence for strong consistencies in development across domains or for broad, holistic cognitive stages of the kind Piaget described.

Does Piaget "Explain" Cognitive Development?

Even those researchers who claim that cognitive growth is stagelike are bothered by Piaget's account of how children move from one stage of intellect to the next. Recall Piaget's interactionist viewpoint: Presumably, children are (1) constantly assimilating new experiences in ways that their level of maturation allows, (2) accommodating their thinking to these experiences, and (3) reorganizing their structures into increasingly complex mental schemes that enable them to reestablish cognitive equilibrium with novel aspects of the environment. As children continue to mature, assimilate more complex information, and alter and reorganize their schemes, they eventually come to view familiar objects and events in new ways and move from one stage of intellect to the next.

Clearly, this rather vague explanation of cognitive growth raises more questions than it answers. What maturational changes are necessary before children can progress from sensorimotor to preoperational intellect or from concrete operations to formal operations? What kinds of experiences must a child have before he will construct mental symbols, use cognitive operations, or operate on ideas and think about hypotheticals? Piaget is simply not very clear about these or any other mechanisms that might enable a child to move to a higher stage of intellect. As a result, growing number of researchers now look on his theory as an elaborate *description* of cognitive development that has limited explanatory power (Gelman & Baillargeon, 1983; Kuhn, 1992).

Piaget Devoted Too Little Attention to Social and Cultural Influences

Children live in very different social and cultural contexts that affect the way their world is structured. Although Piaget admitted that cultural factors may influence the rate of cognitive growth, developmentalists now know that culture influences *how* children think as well (Rogoff, 1990). Piaget also paid too little attention to the ways that children's minds develop through their *social interactions* with more competent individuals. From Piaget's descriptions, we picture the child as an isolated scientist, exploring the world and making critical discoveries largely on her own. Yet we now know that children develop many of their competencies by collaborating with parents, teachers, older siblings, and peers. Indeed, a belief in the importance of social interaction for cognitive growth is a cornerstone of the *sociocultural perspective* on cognitive development offered by one of Piaget's early critics, Lev Vygotsky.

The sociocultural theory of Lev Vygotsky (1896–1934) views cognitive development as a socially mediated process that may vary from culture to culture.

► VYGOTSKY'S SOCIOCULTURAL PERSPECTIVE

In order to view Piaget's work from a new vantage point, let's consider a perspective on cognitive development that has aroused a great deal of interest lately—the **socio-cultural viewpoint** of Lev Vygotsky (1934/1962; 1930–1935/1978; and see Wertsch & Tulviste, 1992). This Russian developmentalist was an active scholar in the 1920s and 1930s when Piaget was formulating his theory. Unfortunately, Vygotsky died at the age of 38 before his work was complete. Nevertheless, he left us with important food for thought by insisting that (1) cognitive growth occurs in a sociocultural context that influences the form it takes, and (2) many of a child's most noteworthy cognitive skills evolve from *social interactions* with parents, teachers, and other more competent associates.

The Role of Culture in Intellectual Development

Vygotsky (1930–1935/1978) claimed that infants are born with a few *elementary mental functions*—attention, sensation, perception, and memory—that are eventually transformed by the culture into new and more sophisticated mental processes that he called *higher mental functions*. Take memory, for example. A young child's early memorial capabilities are limited by biological constraints to the images and impressions she can produce. However, each culture provides its children with **tools of intellectual adaptation** that permit them to use their basic mental functions more adaptively. Thus, children in Western societies may learn to remember more efficiently by taking notes on what to remember, whereas their age-mates in preliterate societies may have learned other memory strategies, such as representing each chore or object that they must remember by tying a knot in a string or by tying a string around their finger. Such socially transmitted memory strategies and other cultural tools teach children how to use their minds; in short, *how* to think. And since each culture also transmits specific beliefs and values, it teaches children *what* to think as well.

In sum, Vygotsky claimed that human cognition, even when carried out in isolation, is inherently *sociocultural* because it is affected by the beliefs, values, and tools of intellectual adaptation passed to individuals by their culture. And since these values and intellectual tools may vary dramatically from culture to culture, Vygotsky believed that neither the course nor the content of intellectual growth was as "universal" as Piaget had assumed.

The Social Origins of Early Cognitive Competencies

Vygotsky agreed with Piaget that young children are curious explorers who are actively involved in learning and discovering new principles. However, he placed much less emphasis than Piaget did on *self*-initiated discovery, choosing instead to stress the importance of *social* contributions to cognitive growth.

According to Vygotsky, many of the truly important "discoveries" that children make occur within the context of cooperative or collaborative *dialogues* between a skillful tutor, who may model the activity and transmit verbal instructions, and a novice pupil, who first seeks to understand the tutor's instruction, and eventually internalizes this information, using it to regulate his own performance.

To illustrate collaborative (or guided) learning as Vygotsky envisioned it, let's imagine that Annie, a 4-year-old, has just received her first jigsaw puzzle as a birthday present. She attempts to work the puzzle but gets nowhere until her father comes along, sits down beside her, and gives her some tips. He suggests that it would be a good idea to put together the corners first, points to the pink area at the edge of one corner piece, and says, "Let's look for another pink piece." When Annie seems frustrated, he places two interlocking pieces near each other so that she will notice them,

sociocultural theory: Vygotsky's perspective on cognitive development, in which children acquire their culture's values, beliefs, and problem-solving strategies through collaborative dialogues with more knowledgeable members of society.

tools of intellectual adaptation: Vygotsky's term for methods of thinking and problem-solving strategies that children internalize from their interactions with more competent members of society.

and when Annie succeeds, he offers words of encouragement. As Annie gradually gets the hang of it, he steps back and lets her work more and more independently. This kind of social interaction, claimed Vygotsky, fosters cognitive growth.

How? First, Annie and her father are operating in what Vygotsky called the **zone of proximal development**—the difference between what a learner can accomplish independently and what he or she can accomplish with the guidance and encouragement of a more skilled partner. It is the zone in which sensitive instruction should be aimed and in which new cognitive growth can be expected to occur. Annie obviously becomes a more competent puzzle solver with her father's help than without it. More important, she will internalize the problem-solving techniques that she uses in collaboration with him and will ultimately use them on her own, rising to a new level of independent mastery.

Vygotsky's theory has some rather obvious implications for education. Like Piaget, Vygotsky would stress active, rather than passive, learning and would take great care to assess what the learner already knows, thereby estimating what he is now capable of learning. The major difference in approaches concerns the role of the instructor. Whereas students in Piaget's classroom would spend more time in independent, discovery-based activities, teachers in Vygotsky's classroom would favor *guided participations* in which they structure the learning activity, provide helpful hints or instructions that are carefully tailored to the child's current abilities, and then monitor the learner's progress, gradually turning over more of the mental activity to their pupils. Teachers may also arrange *cooperative learning exercises* in which students are encouraged to assist each other; the idea here is that the less competent members of the team are likely to benefit from the instruction they receive from their more skillful peers.

Is there any evidence that Vygotsky's guided-learning approach might be a particularly effective educational strategy? Consider what Lisa Freund (1990) found when she had 3–5-year-olds help a puppet decide which furnishings (for example, sofas, beds, bathtubs, and stoves) should be placed in each of six rooms of a dollhouse that the puppet was moving into. First, children were tested to determine what they already knew about proper furniture placement. Then, each child worked at a similar task, either alone (as might be the case in Piaget's discovery-based classroom) or with his or her mother (Vygotsky's guided learning). Then, to assess what they had learned, children performed a final, rather complex, furniture-sorting task. The results were clear: Children who had sorted furniture with help from their mothers showed dramatic improvements in sorting ability, whereas those who had practiced on their own showed little improvement at all, even though they had received some corrective feedback from the experimenter (see also Diaz et al., 1991; Rogoff, 1990). Similar advances in problem-solving skills have been reported when children collaborate with peers as opposed to working alone (Azmitia, 1992; Gauvain & Rogoff, 1989), and the youngsters who gain the most from these collaborations are those who were initially much less competent than their partners (Azmitia, 1988; Tudge, 1992).

So children do not always learn more when they function as solitary explorers, seeking discoveries on their own; often, conceptual growth springs more readily from children's interactions with other people—particularly with competent people who provide just the amount of guidance and encouragement that the individual needs.

The Role of Language in Cognitive Development

From Vygotsky's viewpoint, language plays two critical roles in cognitive development by (1) serving as the primary vehicle through which adults pass culturally valued modes of thinking and problem solving on to their children, and (2) eventually becoming one of the more powerful "tools" of intellectual adaptation in its own right. As it turns out, Vygotsky's perspective on language and thinking contrasts sharply with that of Piaget.

zone of proximal development: Vygotsky's term for the range of tasks that are too complex to be mastered alone but can be accomplished with guidance and encouragement from a more skillful partner.

Piaget's Theory of Language and Thought

Piaget was very interested in children's language, and he observed that infants' first words were typically centered on objects and activities that they already understood through nonverbal sensorimotor processes. He then concluded that language clearly illustrates the child's *existing* schemes but plays no meaningful role in shaping thought or helping the child to construct new knowledge.

As he recorded the chatterings of preschool children, Piaget (1926) noticed that they often talk *to themselves* as they go about their daily activities, almost as if they were play-by-play announcers ("Put the big piece in the corner. Not that one, the pink one"). Indeed, two preschool children playing close to each other sometimes carried on their own separate monologues rather than truly conversing. Piaget called these self-directed utterances **egocentric speech**—talk that is not addressed to anyone in particular nor adapted in any meaningful way so that a companion might understand it. What part might such speech play in a child's cognitive development? Very little, according to Piaget, who saw egocentric speech as merely reflecting the child's ongoing mental activity. However, he did observe that speech becomes progressively more "social" and less egocentric toward the end of the preoperational stage, which he attributed to the child's increasing ability to assume the perspective of others and thus adapt her speech so that listeners might understand. So here was another example of how cognitive development (a decline in egocentrism) was said to promote a language development (a shift from egocentric to communicative speech), rather than the other way around.

Vygotsky's Theory of Language and Thought

Vygotsky agreed with Piaget that the child's earliest thinking is prelinguistic and that early language often reflects what the child already knows. However, he argued that thought and language eventually merge and that many of the nonsocial utterances that Piaget called "egocentric" actually illustrate the transition from prelinguistic to verbal reasoning.

According to Vygotsky, a preschool child's self-directed monologues occur more often in some contexts than in others. Specifically, Vygotsky observed that children are more likely to talk to themselves as they attempt to solve problems or achieve important goals, and he claimed that this nonsocial speech increased dramatically whenever these young problem solvers encountered obstacles as they pursued their objectives. He then concluded that nonsocial speech is not egocentric, but communicative—it is a "speech for self," or **private speech,** that helps young children to plan strategies and regulate their behavior so that they are more likely to accomplish their goals. Viewed through this theoretical lens, language may thus play a critical role in cognitive development by making children more organized and efficient problem solvers! Vygotsky also claimed that private speech becomes more abbreviated with age, progressing from the whole phrases that 4-year-olds produce, to single words, to simple lip movements that are more common among 7–9-year-olds. His view was that private speech never completely disappears; instead, it simply goes underground, becoming silent or *inner speech*—the covert verbal thought that we use to organize and regulate our everyday activities.

Which Viewpoint Should We Endorse?

Studies conducted by Vygotsky and other researchers (see Berk, 1992) tend to confirm Vygotsky's theory over that of Piaget. It seems that the *social speech* that occurs during guided learning episodes (for example, the conversation between Annie and her father as they worked jointly on a puzzle) is what gives rise to much of the *private speech* (Annie's talking aloud as she tries to work the puzzle on her own) that preschool children display. Also consistent with Vygotsky's claims, children rely more heavily on private speech when facing difficult rather than easy tasks and when deciding how to proceed after making errors (Berk, 1992), and their performance often improves after turning to self-instruction (Behrend, Rosengren, & Perlmutter, 1989;

According to Vygotsky, new skills are often easier to acquire if children receive guidance and encouragement from a more competent associate.

egocentric speech: Piaget's term for the subset of a young child's utterances that are nonsocial— that is, neither directed to others nor expressed in ways that listeners might understand.

private speech: Vygotsky's term for the subset of a child's verbal utterances that serve a self-communicative function and guide the child's thinking.

According to Vygotsky, private speech is an important self-instructional tool used by preschool and young grade-school children to plan and regulate their problem-solving activities.

Bivens & Berk, 1990). Moreover, it is the brighter preschool children who rely most heavily on private speech—a finding that links this "self-talk" to cognitive *competence* rather than the cognitive immaturity (egocentrism) that Piaget claimed it represents (Berk, 1992; Kohlberg, Yaeger, & Hjertholm, 1968). Finally, private speech does eventually go underground, progressing from words and phrases, to whispers and mutterings, to inner speech (Frauenglass & Diaz, 1985), and this internalization process occurs earlier among the brighter members of an elementary school class (Berk & Landau, 1993; Kohlberg et al., 1968).

So private speech does appear to be an important tool of intellectual adaptation—a means by which children plan and regulate their mental activities to solve problems and make new discoveries (Vygotsky, 1934/1962).

Concept Check 7-3 ⌄ Understanding Vygotsky's Sociocultural Theory

Check your understanding of some of the basic premises of Vygotsky's theory by matching each of the following concepts with the descriptions listed below. The concepts are (a) tools of intellectual adaptation; (b) private speech; (c) zone of proximal development; (d) elementary mental functions; (e) collaborative verbal dialogues. The answers appear in the Appendix.

_____ 1. Important means of planning and self-regulation.

_____ 2. Problems children can master with skillful guidance.

_____ 3. Means by which culturally significant cognitive processes are transferred across generations.

_____ 4. That which is transformed in the context of collaborative activities with more skillful associates.

_____ 5. Culturally significant cognitive processes and methods of problem solving.

Vygotsky in Perspective: Summary and Evaluation

Vygotsky's sociocultural theory offers a new lens through which to view cognitive development by stressing the importance of specific social processes that Piaget (and others) largely overlooked. According to Vygotsky, children's minds develop as they

(1) take part in cooperative dialogues with skilled partners on tasks that are within their zone of proximal development and (2) incorporate what skillful tutors say to them into what they say to themselves. As social speech is translated into private speech and then inner speech, the culture's preferred methods of thinking and problem solving—or tools of intellectual adaptation—work their way from the language of competent tutors into the child's own thinking.

Vygotsky's theory has recently attracted a lot of attention among Western developmentalists, whose own research efforts tend to support his ideas. Yet many of Vygotsky's writings are only now being translated from Russian to other languages (Wertsch & Tulviste, 1992), and his theory has not received the intense scrutiny that Piaget's theory has. Nevertheless, at least some of his ideas have already been challenged. Barbara Rogoff (1990), for example, argues that guided participations that rely heavily on verbal instruction may be less adaptive in some cultures or less useful for some forms of learning than for others. A young child learning to stalk prey in Australia's outback or to plant, tend, and harvest rice in Southeast Asia may profit more from observation and practice than from joint participation and verbal instruction (see also Rogoff et al., 1993). Other investigators are finding that collaborative problem solving among peers does not always benefit the collaborators and may actually *undermine* task performance if the more competent collaborator is not very confident about what he knows or fails to adapt his instruction to a partner's level of understanding (Levin & Druyan, 1993; Tudge, 1992). But despite whatever criticism his theory generates in the years ahead, Vygotsky has provided a valuable service by reminding us that cognitive growth, like all other aspects of development, is best understood when studied in the cultural and social contexts in which it occurs.

SUMMARY

We began this chapter by examining Piaget's influential theory of cognitive development—a theory that evolved from his naturalistic observations and conversations (clinical interviews) with developing children. Influenced by his early training in zoology, Piaget defined intellectual activity as a basic life function that helps the child to adapt to the environment. He described children as active, inventive explorers who construct knowledge (schemes) and modify these cognitive structures through the processes of organization and adaptation. Organization is the process by which children rearrange their existing knowledge into higher-order structures, or schemes. Adaptation consists of two complementary activities: Assimilation and accommodation. Assimilation is the process by which the child attempts to fit new experiences to existing schemes. Accommodation is the process of modifying existing schemes in response to new experiences. Presumably, cognitive growth results from the interplay of these intellectual processes: Assimilations stimulate accommodations, which induce the reorganization of schemes, which allow further assimilations, and so on.

Piaget believed that intellectual growth proceeds through an invariant sequence of stages that can be summarized as follows:

Sensorimotor period (0–2 years). Over the first two years, infants come to know and understand objects and events by acting on them. The sensorimotor schemes that a child creates to adapt to his or her surroundings are eventually internalized to form mental symbols that enable the child to understand the permanence of objects, imitate the actions of absent models, and solve simple problems at a mental level without resorting to trial and error. Although Piaget's general sequences of sensorimotor development have been confirmed, recent evidence indicates that infants achieve such milestones as deferred imitation and object permanence earlier than Piaget had thought.

Preoperational period (roughly 2–7 years). Symbolic reasoning becomes increasingly apparent during the preoperational period as children begin to use words and images in inventive ways in their play activities. Although 2–7-year-olds are becoming more and more knowledgeable about the world around them, Piaget described their thinking as animistic, egocentric, and governed by appearances. Thus, he claimed that preschool children cannot think logically and will fail to solve problems that require them to consider the implications of several pieces of information or to assume another person's point of view. Yet, recent research has challenged Piaget's characterization by illustrating that preschool children are much more logical and less egocentric when thinking about familiar issues or about simplified versions of Piaget's tests. Moreover, preoperational children can be trained to solve complex problems such as Piaget's conservation tasks. So preschool children possess an early capacity for logical reasoning that Piaget overlooked.

Concrete operations (roughly 7–11 years). During the period of concrete operations, children can think logically and systematically about concrete objects, events, and experiences. They can now add and subtract in their heads, and they recognize that the effects of many physical actions are reversible. The acquisition of these and other cognitive operations permits the child to conserve, seriate, make transitive inferences, and understand the logical necessity of class inclusion and whole/part relations. However, concrete operators can only apply their logic to real or tangible aspects of experience and cannot reason abstractly.

Formal operations (age 11–12 and beyond). Formal-operational reasoning is rational, abstract, and much like the hypothetical-deductive reasoning of a scientist. Attainment of formal operations may sometimes contribute to confusion, idealism, rebellion, and self-consciousness. However, not all adolescents and adults reason at this level. Formal operations may elude those who score below average on intelligence tests or who have not been exposed to the kinds of educational experiences that promote this highest form of intellect. Yet, intellectual performance, even at this level, is uneven. Adults are most likely to display formal-operational reasoning in their areas of expertise. And some adults may go beyond basic formal-operational logic, displaying problem-finding abilities, dialectical thinking, and the ability to construct innovative systems and supersystems.

Although Piaget seems to have adequately described the general sequencing of intellectual development, his tendency to infer underlying competencies from children's intellectual performances often led him to underestimate the child's cognitive capabilities. Some investigators have challenged Piaget's assumption that development occurs in stages, and others have criticized his theory for failing to specify how children progress from one "stage" of intellect to the next, and for underestimating the effects of social and cultural influences on intellectual development.

Vygotsky's sociocultural perspective emphasizes social and cultural influences on intellectual growth. Each culture transmits beliefs, values, and preferred methods of thinking or problem solving—its *tools of intellectual adaptation*—to each successive generation. Thus, culture teaches children what and how to think. Children acquire cultural beliefs and problem-solving strategies in the context of collaborative dialogues with more skillful partners as they gradually internalize their tutor's instructions to master tasks within their zone of proximal development.

Unlike Piaget, who argued that cognitive development reflects language development and plays little if any role in constructing new knowledge, Vygotsky claimed that a child's *private speech* regulates problem-solving activities and is eventually internalized to become covert, verbal thought. Recent research favors Vygotsky's position over Piaget's, thus suggesting that language plays a very important role in children's intellectual development.

Although Vygotsky's theory has fared well to date, it has yet to receive the intense scrutiny that Piaget's theory has.

Key Terms

A, not B, error [252]

accommodation [247]

adaptation [247]

animism [256]

appearance/reality
distinction [258]

assimilation [247]

behavioral schemes [245]

centered thinking
(centration) [260]

class inclusion [259]

clinical method [243]

cognition [243]

cognitive
development [243]

cognitive
equilibrium [244]

cognitive operation [246]

compensation
(decentration) [260]

concrete operations [263]

conservation [260]

constructivist [244]

deferred imitation [251]

dialectical reasoning [272]

egocentric speech [278]

egocentrism [256]

formal operations [267]

horizontal decalage [265]

hypothetical-deductive
reasoning [267]

identity training [262]

imaginary audience [269]

inner
experimentation [250]

intelligence [244]

intuitive period [259]

invariant developmental
sequence [248]

object permanence [251]

organization [247]

personal fable [269]

precausal or transductive
reasoning [256]

preconceptual
period [255]

preoperational stage [255]

primary circular
reaction [249]

private speech [278]

problem-finding
stage [272]

reversibility [260]

scheme [244]

secondary circular
reaction [249]

sensorimotor stage [249]

seriation [265]

sociocultural theory [276]

symbolic function [255]

symbolic schemes [245]

systematic reasoning [272]

tertiary circular
reaction [250]

tools of intellectual
adaptation [276]

transitivity [265]

zone of proximal
development [277]

Learning and Information Processing

- What did you learn at school today?

- Why can't you grasp that simple principle?

- Her name was . . . ah . . . ah . . . JULIE!

- Excellent solution! How did you arrive at it?

- I can't recall.

Undoubtedly you've heard statements like those at the left because they occur frequently: learning, remembering, problem solving, and yes, failing to learn and forgetting are everyday experiences that all of us have had. In this chapter, our examination of cognitive development continues, but from a perspective very different than Piaget's or Vygotsky's. Our first objective is to understand the process of *learning* and to appreciate the prominent role it plays in many aspects of human development. You may recall from Chapter 2 that John B. Watson, the father of behaviorism, described the infant as a *tabula rasa* (blank slate) who is "written upon" by experience. Indeed, Watson (1928) believed that developing children had little if any control over their own destiny; he argued that they are extremely malleable organisms who are constantly being taught how to feel, think, and act by their parents, teachers, and other adults. Yet, few theorists continue to subscribe to this passive, mechanistic portrayal of learning and development. Why? Simply because children are not the passive pawns of environmental influence that Watson described; instead, they are more accurately characterized as *active information processors* who have had a hand in creating the very environments that will influence their growth and development.

The modern view of learning as an active, *cognitive* process was heavily influenced by Piaget's characterization of children as busy, motivated explorers, and it is partially responsible for the emergence of a new information-processing analysis of children's intelligence—a theory that many would argue is now a dominant approach to the study of cognitive development. As we examine this exciting new perspective, we will see that its proponents liken the human mind to a sophisticated computer that encodes, categorizes, stores, and retrieves information that is then used to solve problems or otherwise adapt to the environment. Their primary goals are to (1) describe how children process information to make sense of their surroundings, (2) specify how information processing changes with age, and (3) understand how these changes in cognitive-processing skills contribute to developmental changes in learning, thinking, and problem solving.

Let's now begin our review of learning and information processing by trying to determine what learning is—and what it is not.

 ## WHAT IS LEARNING?

Learning is one of those deceptively simple terms that are actually quite complex and difficult to define. Most psychologists think of learning as a change in behavior (or behavior potential) that meets the following three requirements (Domjan, 1993):

1. The individual now thinks, perceives, or reacts to the environment in a *new way.*
2. This change is clearly the result of one's *experiences*—that is, attributable to repetition, study, practice, or the observations one has made, rather than to hereditary or maturational processes or to physiological damage resulting from injury.
3. The change is *relatively permanent.* Facts, thoughts, and behaviors that are acquired and immediately forgotten have not really been learned; and temporary changes due to fatigue, illness, or drugs do not qualify as learned responses.

Let's now consider four fundamental ways in which children learn: habituation, classical conditioning, operant conditioning, and observational learning.

learning: a relatively permanent change in behavior (or behavioral potential) that results from one's experiences or practice.

Habituation: Early Evidence of Information Processing

In Chapter 6, we introduced one very simple and often-overlooked form of learning called **habituation**—the process by which we stop attending or responding to a stimulus that is repeated over and over. Habituation might be thought of as learning to be bored by the familiar (for example, the ticking of a clock or humming of an appliance) and may first occur even before a baby is born. Lynda Madison and her associates (1986), for example, applied vibrating stimuli to the abdomens of pregnant women and monitored fetal movements with ultrasound. After 40 repetitions, all but one of these 27–36-week-old fetuses had stopped moving in response to the vibrations (habituated) as if they processed this stimulus as "old hat"—a familiar event that was no longer worthy of their attention.

How do we know that an infant is not merely fatigued when he stops responding to a familiar stimulus? We know because when a baby has habituated to one stimulus, he often **dishabituates**—that is, attends to or even reacts vigorously to a slightly different stimulus. In so doing, he is telling us that (1) his sensory receptors are not simply fatigued and (2) he can discriminate the familiar from the unfamiliar.

Developmental trends. Habituation improves dramatically throughout the first year. Infants less than 4 months old may require many exposures to a stimulus before they habituate and are slow to dishabituate to novel stimuli; by contrast, 5–12-month-olds are much quicker to habituate and dishabituate (Bornstein & Sigman, 1986). This trend toward rapid habituation is probably related to the maturation of the sensory areas of the cerebral cortex. As the brain and the senses continue to mature, infants process information faster and detect more and more about a stimulus during any given exposure (Rovee-Collier, 1984). Indeed, 5–12-month-olds may recognize something as familiar after only one or two brief exposures, and they are likely to retain that "knowledge" for weeks (Fagan, 1984).

Individual differences. Infants reliably differ in the rate at which they habituate and dishabituate (Bornstein & Sigman, 1986; McCall & Carriger, 1993). Some infants are efficient information processors: They quickly recognize repetitive sensory inputs and are very slow to forget what they have experienced. Others are much less efficient:

habituation: a simple form of learning in which an organism eventually stops responding to a stimulus that is repeated over and over.

dishabituation: recovery of a habituated response that results from a change in the eliciting stimulus.

By 6 months of age, infants are quick to discriminate novel objects and events from familiar ones, and once they brand a stimulus as familiar, they may retain this knowledge for months.

They require many more exposures to brand a stimulus as "familiar" and may soon forget what they have learned. Might these early individual differences in learning and information processing have any implications for later development?

Apparently so. Infants who habituate rapidly during the first 6–8 months of life are quicker to understand and use language during the second year (Tamis-LeMonda & Bornstein, 1989) and reliably outscore their slower-habituating age-mates on standardized intelligence tests later in childhood (Bornstein & Sigman, 1986; McCall & Carriger, 1993). In fact, measures of early habituation and dishabituation are actually much better predictors of intellectual performance during the preschool and grade-school years than are the more traditional tests of infant intelligence (McCall & Carriger, 1993). Why should this be? Joseph Fagan (1985) believes that the ability to detect the familiar and to retain such information may be *the fundamental intellectual process* that underlies complex mental activities such as the analogical reasoning and problem-solving skills that are normally measured on intelligence tests. Although more research is needed to properly evaluate Fagan's claim, the strong links between infants' early information-processing abilities and their later intellectual performance imply that habituation is indeed a most important form of learning.

Classical Conditioning

classical conditioning: a type of learning in which an initially neutral stimulus is repeatedly paired with a meaningful stimulus so that the neutral stimulus comes to elicit the response originally made only to the meaningful stimulus.

unconditioned stimulus (UCS): a stimulus that elicits a particular response without any prior learning.

unconditioned response (UCR): the unlearned response elicited by an unconditioned stimulus.

conditioned response (CR): a learned response to a stimulus that was not originally capable of producing the response.

conditioned stimulus (CS): an initially neutral stimulus that comes to elicit a particular response after being paired with a UCS that always elicits the response.

stimulus generalization: the fact that one stimulus can be substituted for another and produce the same response that the former stimulus did.

discrimination: the process of differentiating and responding differently to stimuli that vary on one or more dimensions.

extinction: gradual weakening and disappearance of a learned response that occurs because the CS is no longer paired with the UCS (in classical conditioning) or the response is no longer reinforced (in operant conditioning).

A second way that young children learn is through **classical conditioning**. In classical conditioning, a neutral stimulus that initially has no effect on the child comes to elicit a response of some sort by virtue of its association with a second stimulus that always elicits the response. To illustrate, consider how Russian physiologist Ivan Pavlov originally discovered classical conditioning. In the course of his work on digestive processes in dogs, Pavlov noticed that his dogs would often salivate at the appearance of a caretaker who had come to feed them. Since it was unlikely that the dogs hoped to eat the caretaker, Pavlov wondered why they were salivating. He speculated that they had probably associated the caretaker (an initially neutral stimulus) with food, a nonneutral stimulus that ordinarily makes dogs salivate (an unlearned, or "reflexive," response to food). In other words, salivation at the sight of the caretaker was said to be a learned response that the dogs acquired as they made a connection between the caretaker and the presentation of food.

Pavlov then designed a simple experiment to test his hypothesis. Dogs first listened to a bell, a neutral stimulus in that bells do not ordinarily make them salivate. Then this neutral stimulus was sounded just before the dogs were fed. Of course, food normally elicits salivation: In the language of classical conditioning, food is an **unconditioned stimulus (UCS),** and salivation is an unlearned or **unconditioned response (UCR)** to food. After the bell and the food had been paired several times, Pavlov then sounded the bell, withheld the food, and observed that the dogs now salivated to the sound of the bell alone. Clearly, their behavior had changed as a result of their experiences. In the terminology of classical conditioning, the dogs were now emitting a **conditioned response (CR),** salivation, to an initially neutral or **conditioned stimulus (CS)**—the bell (see Figure 8-1).

As Pavlov continued to experiment with his dogs, he discovered a number of additional rules or characteristics of the conditioning process. One such rule was the principle of **stimulus generalization:** stimuli that are very similar to a CS (for example, a bell with a slightly different ring) will also elicit the conditioned response. The opposite of generalization is the principle of **discrimination:** If a stimulus is very different from the original CS (for example, a bell with a much higher- or much lower-pitched ring), the subject apparently notices the difference and will not emit the conditioned response. Finally, conditioned responses that occur repeatedly without occasionally being followed by the unconditioned stimulus will diminish in strength and eventually disappear. This gradual weakening and elimination of a conditioned response is called **extinction.**

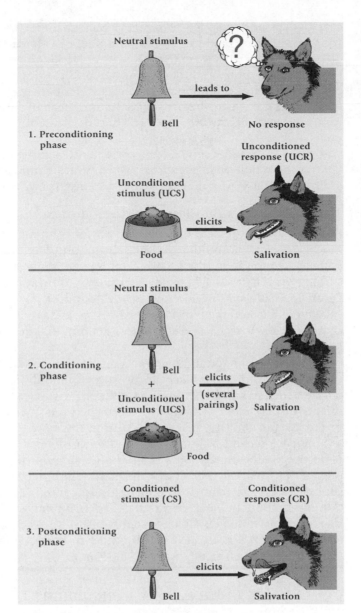

Figure 8-1
The three phases of classical conditioning. In the preconditioning phase, the unconditioned stimulus (UCS) always elicits an unconditioned response (UCR), whereas the conditioned stimulus (CS) never does. During the conditioning phase, the CS and UCS are paired repeatedly and eventually associated. At this point, the learner passes into the postconditioning phase, in which the CS alone will elicit the original response (now called a conditioned response, or CR).

Classical Conditioning of Emotions and Attitudes

Although the salivary responses that Pavlov conditioned may seem rather mundane, it is quite likely that every one of us has learned many things through classical conditioning, including some of our fears, phobias, and attitudes. Consider the plight of little Albert (Watson & Raynor, 1920)—the 11-month-old we met in Chapter 2—who had learned to fear a white rat because every time he reached for it, he heard a loud, startling bang behind him (the experimenter striking a rod with a hammer). In this case, the loud banging noise was the unconditioned stimulus (UCS) because it elicited fearful behavior (the UCR) without any learning having taken place. And as the noise and the rat (an initially neutral stimulus) were repeatedly paired, Albert soon detected their association, coming to *fear* his furry companion (the conditioned response, or CR). By today's standards, this experiment would be considered unethical, but Watson had made his point: Emotional responses can be acquired through classical conditioning.

Perhaps you can identify a fear or phobia you learned when an object or event that is not fearsome in itself became associated with a frightening experience. As a young child, I came to fear and avoid one particular playground because of two dogs

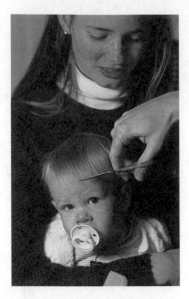

Those first haircuts are fearful events for many young children. With gentle treatment from the hairdresser—and perhaps a lollipop after the job is done—fear of the barbershop (or beauty parlor) will be weakened by counterconditioning.

counterconditioning: a treatment based on classical conditioning in which the goal is to extinguish an undesirable response and replace it with a new and more adaptive one.

operant conditioning: a form of learning in which freely emitted acts (or operants) become either more or less probable, depending on the consequences they produce.

reinforcer: any consequence of an act that increases the probability that the act will recur.

positive reinforcer: any stimulus whose presentation, as the consequence of an act, increases the probability that the act will recur.

that barked and snapped at me as I walked there from my home. Yet, classical conditioning may produce favorable attitudes or behavioral responses as well (Staats, 1975). Consider what Mary Cover Jones (1924) found when she tried to treat a young boy's existing phobia through **counterconditioning**—a therapeutic intervention based on classical conditioning procedures. Her patient was a 2-year-old named Peter who, like little Albert, had acquired a strong fear of furry objects. While Peter was eating some of his favorite foods (a UCS for pleasant feelings), he was exposed to a dreaded rabbit (for him, a strong CS for fear). The rabbit was gradually moved closer and closer until (after several sessions) Peter was able to hold it on his lap. Thus, by pairing the rabbit with *pleasurable stimuli*, Jones eliminated Peter's conditioned fear and replaced it with a more desirable response (playing with the rabbit).

Can Neonates Be Classically Conditioned?

Although it is extremely difficult and was once thought impossible, even neonates can be classically conditioned. Lewis Lipsitt and Herbert Kaye (1964), for example, paired a neutral tone (the CS) with the presentation of a nipple (a UCS that elicits sucking) to infants 2–3 days old. After several of these conditioning trials, the infants began to make sucking motions at the sound of the tone—before the nipple was presented. Clearly, their sucking qualifies as a classically conditioned response because it is now elicited by a stimulus (the tone) that does not normally elicit sucking behavior.

Yet there are important limitations on classical conditioning in the first few weeks of life. Conditioning is likely to be successful only for biologically programmed reflexes, such as sucking or breathing, that have survival value. Moreover, very young infants display more conditioning when the time interval between the presentation of the CS and the UCS is lengthened from the 0.5 second used in studies of adults to about 1.5 seconds (Little, Lipsitt, & Rovee-Collier, 1984). This latter finding makes perfectly good sense after reviewing the habituation literature. Recall that neonates process information very slowly and may simply require more time than an older subject to associate the conditioned and unconditioned stimuli in classical conditioning experiments. But despite these early limitations in information processing, classical conditioning is almost certainly one of the ways in which very young infants learn important lessons such as that bottles or breasts give milk or that other people (notably caregivers) signify warmth and comfort.

Operant (or Instrumental) Conditioning

In classical conditioning, learned responses are *elicited* by a conditioned stimulus. **Operant conditioning** is quite different: The learner first *emits* a response of some sort (that is, *operates* on the environment) and then associates this action with the pleasant or unpleasant consequences it produces. It was B. F. Skinner (1953) who made this form of conditioning famous. He argued that most human responses are behaviors that we emit voluntarily (that is, *operants*) and that become more or less probable, depending on their consequences. This basic principle makes a good deal of sense: We tend to repeat behaviors that have favorable consequences and to limit those that produce unfavorable outcomes. Through operant conditioning, then, we learn new skills and acquire many, many habits, both good and bad.

Some Possible Consequences of Operant Responses

In the language of operant conditioning, a **reinforcer** is any consequence that *strengthens* a response by making it more likely to occur in the future. If a child washes his dirty face and then receives a hug, the hug will probably serve as a **positive reinforcer** for face washing and make it more likely in the future. *Positive* here means that something has been *added* to the situation (the hug), and *reinforcement* means that the behavior (face washing) was strengthened. So a positive reinforcer is an event that, when introduced following a behavior, makes that behavior more probable in

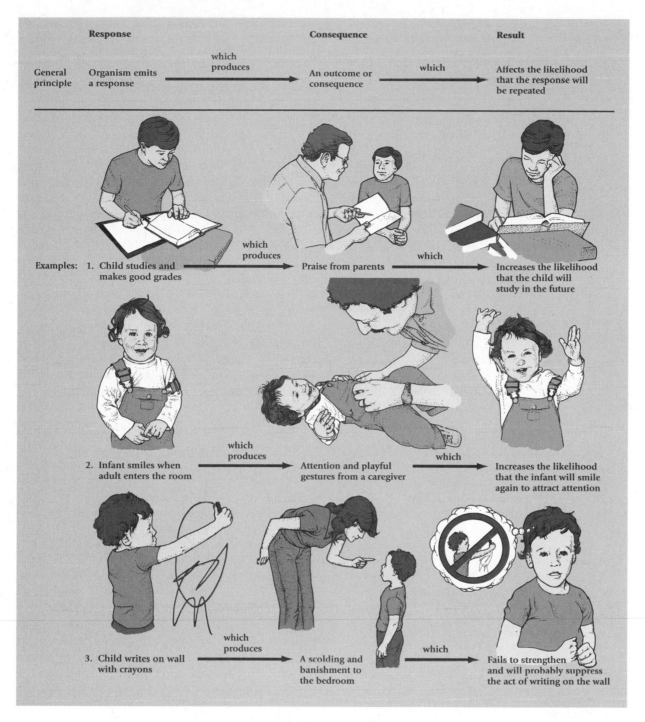

	Response		Consequence		Result
General principle	Organism emits a response	which produces	An outcome or consequence	which	Affects the likelihood that the response will be repeated

Examples:

1. Child studies and makes good grades → which produces → Praise from parents → which → Increases the likelihood that the child will study in the future

2. Infant smiles when adult enters the room → which produces → Attention and playful gestures from a caregiver → which → Increases the likelihood that the infant will smile again to attract attention

3. Child writes on wall with crayons → which produces → A scolding and banishment to the bedroom → which → Fails to strengthen and will probably suppress the act of writing on the wall

Figure 8-2
Basic principles of operant conditioning.

the future. **Negative reinforcers** also strengthen behaviors, but the behavior is strengthened because something unpleasant is *removed* from the situation (or avoided) after the behavior occurs. We have all been in cars in which an obnoxious buzzer sounds until we buckle our seat belts. The idea here is that "buckling up" will become a stronger habit through *negative reinforcement:* We learn to fasten the belt because this act ends the irritating noise. Indeed, the desire to terminate, escape, or avoid unpleasant consequences is the basis for many of our habits. If a child finds that she can prevent an aversive scolding by picking up her crayons after using them, this kind of "tidying up" should become more probable. If you find that you can avoid an incredibly boring teacher by transferring into another instructor's 8:00 A.M. section of the course, you are likely to become an early riser. In each of these examples, a

negative reinforcer: any stimulus whose removal or termination, as the consequence of an act, increases the probability that the act will recur.

behavior is strengthened through negative reinforcement—through the removal or elimination of something unpleasant.

Is *negative reinforcement* merely a fancy name for punishment? *No, it is not!* People tend to confuse the two because they generally think of pleasant stimuli as reinforcers and unpleasant ones as punishments. This source or confusion can be overcome if we keep in mind that reinforcers and punishers are defined not by their "pleasantness" or "unpleasantness" but by their *effects*: reinforcers always *strengthen* responses, whereas **punishers** inhibit or *suppress* them. There are actually two forms of punishment that parallel the two forms of reinforcement. **Positive punishment** occurs when an unpleasant consequence is *added* to the situation following a behavior (for example, a mother scolds her son for his roughhousing antics), whereas **negative punishment** occurs when something pleasant is *removed from* the situation following the behavior (for example, the mother punishes roughhousing by refusing to allow the boy to watch his favorite TV show). Both of these forms of punishment are designed to suppress behaviors and decrease the likelihood that they will be repeated.

These four possible consequences of a behavior are summarized in Table 8-1. Which of these outcomes is the most important for shaping a child's behavior? Skinner (1953) and other behavioral theorists emphasize the power of reinforcement, particularly *positive* reinforcement. They argue that punishment is less effective at producing desirable changes in behavior because it merely suppresses ongoing or established responses without really teaching anything new. For example, a toddler who is scolded for grabbing food with her hands is likely to stop eating altogether rather than to learn to use her spoon. A much simpler way to promote the use of silverware is to positively reinforce this desirable response with lots of attention and praise (Skinner, 1953).

Timing and scheduling of reinforcement. Both the timing of reinforcement and the *frequency* with which it is given will affect the success of operant conditioning in young children. With respect to timing, reinforcement is most effective when administered imediately after a response (Domjan, 1993). This is especially true for infants and toddlers who haven't the information-processing skills to associate their actions with an outcome unless the interval between these events is very short (Millar & Watson, 1979). Frequency (or scheduling) of reinforcement is also important. When a child is first being taught a new habit such as saying "please," "thank you," or learning to use the toilet, it is best to provide **continuous reinforcement**—reinforcing the behavior *every time it occurs*. Once the new behavior is established, it is best maintained by **partial** (or intermittent) **reinforcement**—reinforcing only some instances of the behavior, ideally on an unpredictable schedule. Why switch reinforcement schedules? Because children may quickly notice when continuous reinforcement comes to an abrupt halt, and the desirable behavior that parents have worked to instill may soon fade or *extinguish*. But if a child never quite knows when another dose of parental approval (or some other reinforcer) might be forthcoming, she may continue to display the desirable behavior until it becomes a well-ingrained habit and will persist, even after all reinforcement ceases (Domjan, 1993).

Why do reinforcers "reinforce"? An informational perspective. We have defined a reinforcer as any stimulus that *strengthens* a response by making it more likely to occur in the future. But *how* do reinforcers work? *How* do they strengthen a response? One possibility is that reinforcers "reinforce" because (1) they are pleasant and (2) we are motivated to repeat behaviors that produce pleasant outcomes. Another possibility is that reinforcers provide *information* about the consequences of our behavior that we can use to respond adaptively to the environment and *control* our own fate.

Information-processing theorists favor the latter interpretation, based on the results of several interesting studies of operant conditioning with young infants. In one such study (Watson & Ramey, 1972), a group of 8-week-old infants learned to

punisher: any consequence of an act that suppresses the response and decreases the probability that it will recur.

positive punishment: a punishing consequence that involves the presentation of something unpleasant following a behavior.

negative punishment: a punishing consequence that involves the removal of something pleasant following a behavior.

continuous reinforcement: a schedule of reinforcement in which every occurrence of an act is reinforced.

partial reinforcement: a schedule of reinforcement in which only some of the occurrences of an act are reinforced.

Table 8-1 Four Common Consequences of an Operant Behavior.

Julio comes into the TV room and sees his father joking with his sister Rita as the two watch a gymnastics meet. Soon Julio begins to whine, louder and louder, that he wants to use the TV set to play Nintendo. Here are four possible consequences of Julio's whining behavior.

	Positive stimulus (pleasant)	*Negative stimulus (unpleasant)*
Administered	*Positive reinforcement (strengthens the response)* Dad gives in to the whining and lets Julio use the TV, making whining more likely in the future.	*Positive punishment (weakens the response)* Dad calls Julio a "crybaby," which violates Julio's image of himself as a "big boy" and makes him less inclined to whine in the future.
Withdrawn	*Negative punishment (weakens the response)* Dad confiscates Julio's treasured Nintendo game to discourage such whining in the future.	*Negative reinforcement (strengthens the response)* Dad stops joking with Rita when Julio's whining becomes rather obvious. Since Julio gets jealous when Dad attends to Rita, his whining has enabled him to bring this unpleasant state of affairs to an end (and is thus reinforced).

turn their heads on a pressure-sensitive pillow, an act that closed an electrical switch in the pillow and caused a brightly colored mobile to rotate. These infants clearly enjoyed the activity, for they smiled and cooed whenever they caused the mobile to turn. A second group of infants was exposed to the same pleasant stimulus, with one important difference: They had *no* control over their mobiles, which rotated periodically on their own. Infants in this second group were just as fascinated at first by the rotating mobile but soon became rather apathetic; they now rarely smiled at this object and were no longer interested in watching it turn. Later, the investigators exposed all their young subjects to mobiles that they could control by moving their heads. Children who had previously learned to control the mobiles were soon turning their heads and exercising control once again. However, the infants who had not been able to control the mobiles in the earlier session made *no* further attempts to exercise control—even though they now had an opportunity to do so. Apparently, these children had learned that they were powerless to influence their environment, so they simply stopped trying, thus displaying a state of **learned helplessness.**

What does the Watson and Ramey experiment tell us about reinforcement? It suggests that an initially pleasant stimulus (in this case, the rotating mobile) is unlikely to reinforce anything merely because it is pleasant. However, a pleasant stimulus can become a reinforcer if it provides *information* that allows the learner to *control* its appearance or to otherwise determine his own fate (see also Box 8-1). Surely this was true of the rotating mobile in Watson and Ramey's experiment: What the infants liked most about the mobile was not that it moved but that *they* could make it move.

learned helplessness: the failure to learn how to respond appropriately in a situation because of previous exposures to uncontrollable events in the same or a similar situation.

BOX 8-1
Turning Fun into Work with Unnecessary Incentives

*M*any of the habits that parents hope to instill are responses that children find somewhat distasteful. Few youngsters are thrilled at the prospect of washing dishes, cleaning their rooms, or breaking away from a favorite TV program to finish their homework. How might adults persuade children to perform such chores and to develop an interest in initially unrewarding activities (such as homework)?

Operant learning theorists have repeatedly demonstrated that the offering and presentation of such incentives as money, privileges, praise, and recognition can motivate children to undertake and complete activities that are *not* intrinsically satisfying to them (Danner & Lonky, 1981; Loveland & Olley, 1979; McLoyd, 1979). For example, a teacher who offers her "nonreaders" a gold star for every ten minutes that they spend reading may well increase the reading activities of these children, who would not ordinarily read on their own. But would this incentive further motivate the class "bookworms," who read avidly because reading is *intrinsically* satisfying?

Although most parents would say yes (Boggiano et al., 1987), Mark Lepper (1983) strongly disagrees. Lepper contends that children who perform *intrinsically satisfying* activities as a means of obtaining an external incentive will come to like these activities *less*. Presumably, an incentive conveys the wrong *information* to a child who is intrinsically motivated to perform: She may now decide that she is undertaking the activity *not because she likes it*, but merely to obtain a reward! Ironically, then, the "incentive" could have the effect of undermining her intrinsic interest in the rewarded activity, making her see it as only worth doing if it "pays off."

An experiment by Lepper, Greene, and Nisbett (1973) confirms this hypothesis. Preschool children who showed considerable intrinsic interest in drawing with colored felt pens were promised a special certificate if they would draw a picture for a visiting adult (expected-reward condition). Other preschoolers who were equally interested in drawing with felt pens engaged in the same drawing activities and either received an unexpected certificate for their work (unexpected-reward condition) or did not receive a certificate (no-reward condition). Then, 7 to 14 days later, the children were observed during free-play periods to determine whether they still wanted to draw with the felt pens. Lepper et al. found that children who had contracted to draw a picture for an extrinsic reinforcer now spent less of their free time drawing with the pens (8.6%) than did the children who had received no reward (16.7%) or those who had received the reward as a surprise (18.1%). Note that the reward itself did not undermine intrinsic motivation, for children in the unexpected-reward condition continued to show as much intrinsic interest in drawing as those who were not rewarded. It was only when children believed they were drawing *in order to obtain a reward* that the incentive undermined intrinsic interest.

Undermining one's interest in intrinsically satisfying activities is not the only undesirable effect that external incentives can have. Children who are offered such incentives for undertaking activities they already enjoy may subsequently lower their aspirations, displaying less creativity in their work (Amabile & Hennessey, 1988) or choosing to work at easy rather than difficult assignments so as not to miss out on the rewards (Condry & Chambers, 1982). And unfortunately, this tendency to lower one's aspirations is most apparent among those children who had initially displayed the most intrinsic interest in the rewarded activities (Pearlman, 1984).

Do these findings mean that parents and teachers should never reward a child's noteworthy accomplishments at activities that she enjoys? No, they do not! Rewards can sustain and even increase intrinsic interest in an activity, provided that they are given for *successful* task performance rather than for merely working at the task (Lepper & Hodell, 1988; Pallak et al., 1982). Why? Because rewards given for *successes* or for diligent effort that has led to noticeable improvements in performance convey different information: They allow the child to attribute her outcomes to her *competence* in that activity rather than to a desire to obtain the reward. So unlike the case in which the child is rewarded for merely working at the task and feels that her performance is controlled by the incentive (that is, "I have to perform or I miss out on rewards"), a rewarded success informs her that she *controls* her own fate through the quality of her efforts. Of course, rewards for successes or for improvements in performance should also make the child feel efficacious at the activity—a perception that increases rather than undermines intrinsic interest (Bandura, 1989).

So the theoretical implications of this line of research are clear: Incentives offered for task performance convey information to the child, and it is the child's *interpretation* of this information (rather than the pleasantness of the incentives) that determines whether the incentive will "reinforce" (that is, strengthen or sustain) the activity. Of course, the practical lesson for parents, teachers, and other social agents is to guard against creating unnecessary and misinformative reward systems that are likely to reduce children's intrinsic interest in enjoyable activities and turn fun into work.

Operant Conditioning in Infancy

Watson and Ramey's (1972) experiment clearly demonstrates that 8-week-old infants are susceptible to operant conditioning. So too are full-term neonates and even babies born prematurely (Thoman & Ingersoll, 1993), especially when learning a response that results in being fed or is otherwise significant biologically (Rovee-Collier, 1987). However, very young infants are inefficient information processors who learn very slowly. So if you hoped to teach 2-day-old infants to turn their heads to the right and offered them a nippleful of milk every time they did so, you would find that they took about 200 trials, on average, to acquire this simple head-turning response (Papousek, 1967). Older infants learn much faster: A 3-month-old requires only about 40 trials to display a simple head-turning response, and 5-month-olds can acquire this habit in fewer than 30 trials. Apparently, these older subjects are quicker to associate their behavior (in this case, head turning) with its consequences (a tasty treat)—an advance in information processing that seems to explain infants' increasing susceptibility to operant conditioning over the first few months of life.

Can infants remember what they have learned? Earlier, we noted that very young infants seem to have very short memories. Minutes after they have habituated to a stimulus, they may begin to respond once again to that stimulus, as if they no longer recognize it as familiar. Yet, the simple act of recognizing a stimulus as "familiar" may not be terribly meaningful to a neonate, or even a 2-month-old. Might young infants be better at remembering behaviors they have performed that have proved to be reinforcing in the past?

Yes, indeed, and a program of research by Carolyn Rovee-Collier (1984; 1987) makes this point quite clearly. Rovee-Collier's procedure is to place an attractive mobile over the cribs of 2–3-month-old infants and to run a ribbon from the mobile to the infants' ankles (see Figure 8-3). Within a matter of minutes, these young subjects discover that they can make the mobile move by kicking their legs, and they take great pleasure in doing so. But will they remember how to make the mobile move a week later? To succeed at this memory task, the infant not only must *recognize* the mobile, but must also *recall* that it moves and that kicking is the way to get it to move. So how well do young infants remember?

The standard procedure for testing an infant's memory is to place the child back in the crib to see whether kicking occurs when he or she sees the mobile. Rovee-Collier

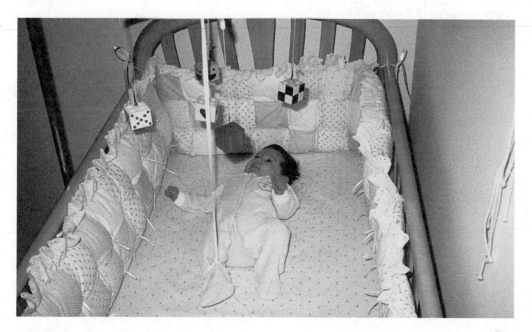

Figure 8-3
When ribbons are attached to their ankles, 2–3-month-old infants soon learn to make a mobile move by kicking their legs. But do they remember how to make the mobile move when tested days or weeks after the original learning? These are the questions that Rovee-Collier has explored in her fascinating research on infant memory.

and her associates find that 2-month-old infants remember how to make the mobile move for up to three days after the original learning, whereas 3-month-olds can recall this kicking response for more than a week. Clearly, a young infant's memory is much more impressive than habituation studies would have us believe.

But why do infants eventually forget how to make the mobile move? Is it that they simply have a limited capacity for storing such information, so that their previous learning is lost? Or is it that the learning is still there but that young infants can't retrieve this information from memory? To find out, Janet Davis and Carolyn Rovee-Collier (1983) first taught 2-month-old infants how to make the mobile move, and after 18 days, attempted to *"remind"* some of them of the kicking response *by rotating the mobile for them.* If the infants' previous learning had been lost, they should have treated the mobile as a novel stimulus, staring intently at it without kicking. But this is not what they did. Instead, they looked very *briefly* at the rotating mobile (thus indicating that they recognized it) and then kicked up a storm as soon as the ribbon was attached to their ankles. By contrast, infants who received no reminder of their previous learning did not try to make the mobile move when given an opportunity to do so. The implication, then, is that even young infants can retain meaningful information for weeks, if not longer. Yet, they have difficulties *retrieving* what they have learned from memory if they are not given explicit reminders or if the context in which they are tested is even slightly different from the context in which they learned a response (Howe & Courage, 1993; Rovee-Collier et al., 1992). So a baby's early memories are relatively fragile ones.

Significance of early operant learning. What impact might early learning have on infants and their companions? Since even newborns are capable of associating their responses with various outcomes, they should soon learn that they can make some interesting things happen. For example, a baby may discover that crying brings forth her mother (or some other caregiver), who then provides food, attention, warmth, or comfort. Gazing, smiling, and babbling are yet other sociable gestures on which the infant may learn to rely in order to attract the attention or nurturance of caregivers. As the child is acquiring these habits, her caregivers are also learning how to react to her, so that their social interactions gradually become smoother and more satisfying for both the infant and her companions. It is fortunate, then, that babies can learn, for in so doing, they are likely to become more responsive to other people, who, in turn, are becoming more responsive to them. As we will see in Chapter 11, these early reciprocal exchanges provide a foundation for the strong emotional attachments that often develop between infants and their closest companions.

Punishment as a Tactic for Controlling Behavior

Although parents generally do not like to harm their children or see them unhappy, they will at least occasionally resort to punishment to restrain a child's unacceptable conduct (Hoffman, 1988; Sears, Maccoby, & Levin, 1957). And there is a case to be made for its use, particularly if the prohibited act is something dangerous like playing with matches or probing electrical sockets with metallic objects. Yet many theorists believe that punishment is a two-edged sword that may prove counterproductive and even harmful in the long run.

Operant theorists are among the strongest critics of punitive controls. They believe that punishment merely suppresses an undesirable response without teaching anything new. Moreover, they argue that punishment may engender anger, hostility, or resentment, and, at best, a *temporary* suppression of the behavior it is designed to eliminate. Their point is that a fear of aversive consequences can never be a totally effective deterrent, because the child may simply inhibit unacceptable conduct until it is unlikely to be detected and punished.

Despite these criticisms, research indicates that punishment, properly applied, can be an effective method of controlling undesirable behavior. Turn first to Box 8-2,

BOX 8-2
Using Punishment Effectively

Although operant researchers emphasize the use of positive reinforcement to shape children's conduct, most parents use punishment at least occasionally to suppress undesirable behaviors. They can use it more effectively by following these guidelines, derived from the research literature (Domjan, 1993; Parke, 1977):

- *Punish as soon as possible.* It is best to punish as the child prepares to misbehave or at least during the act. Postponing punishment ("Wait til Daddy comes home") is bad practice. Young children may conclude that Daddy is punishing them for whatever they are doing at the moment—for example, putting toys back in the toy box. If delayed punishment cannot be avoided, it can be made more effective by carefully explaining to the child why she is being punished.

- *Punish firmly (but not with too much intensity).* Laboratory research with young children suggests that strong punishment, in the form of loud buzzers or noises, is more effective than mild punishment; that is, a loud "No" or "Stop that" is likely to be more effective than softer versions of the same commands. But we should not be misled into thinking that severe physical punishment is a good idea. Severe spankings, in particular, have several disadvantages. They create high levels of anxiety that can interfere with "learning one's lesson," and they may make the child learn to fear and avoid the disciplinarian. Harsh physical punishment may also teach the child to rely on aggression as a way of dealing with problems (Weiss, Dodge, Bates, & Pettit, 1992). So firm punishment can be effective as long as it is not so intense that it has these sorts of negative side effects.

- *Punish consistently.* Acts that are punished only now and then will persist. Why? Because if the child *enjoys* the prohibited act, he is being partially reinforced when the act goes unpunished, and we've learned that partially reinforced behaviors are extremely resistant to extinction.

- *Be otherwise warm and accepting.* Children respond better to punishment when it is administered by an otherwise warm and caring person, with whom they might regain approval by behaving appropriately, than by a cold, aloof disciplinarian who has never shown them much approval.

- *Consider alternatives to physical punishment.* Although spanking a child seems to be the first punishment that many parents think of when a child misbehaves, punishment can also involve taking away desirable commodities or privileges that the child already has (for example, candy) or would ordinarily receive in the future (a movie next Saturday). Another effective alternative to physical punishment is a procedure called *time out*, in which the

Improperly applied, physical punishment can have many undesirable side effects, including an increase in the child's aggressiveness.

adult removes children from the situation in which their misbehavior is positively reinforced. A boy who thoroughly enjoys dominating his little sister might be sent to a quiet room where he is cut off from the pleasure he receives from his bullying behavior. When misbehavior is no longer reinforced, it weakens through extinction.

- *Reinforce alternative behavior.* Since punishment alone tells a child what not to do, but not *what* to do, it makes sense to strengthen acceptable alternatives to the misbehavior. The parent who does not want a toddler to play with an expensive vase might punish that behavior but also reinforce play with an unbreakable plastic pot.

- *Explain yourself.* If there is a "most important" recommendation here, this may be it. Virtually all forms of punishment become more effective if the disciplinarian explains to children why their conduct was wrong and helps them to control their behavior in the future. Older children and adolescents, in particular, want and benefit from these *cognitive rationales* that point out the harmful consequences of misbehavior (although preschool children too may benefit from rationales that are carefully tailored to their ability to understand).

which presents several guidelines for using punishment effectively. We will then discuss why these findings make sense from a modern, information-processing perspective.

When researchers first began to study punishment and its effects, they generally favored a *conditioning viewpoint*. According to conditioning theorists, punishment produces fear or anxiety. And since a particular transgression may be detected and punished on several occasions, it is likely that the anxiety resulting from punishment will soon become conditioned to the punished act. Once this conditioning occurs, the child should then resist the temptation to commit the act in order to avoid the unpleasant consequences (conditioned fear or anxiety) now associated with its performance (Aronfreed, 1976; Parke, 1972). So conditioning theorists view punitive suppression as nothing more than a conditioned avoidance response.

Yet the recommendations presented in Box 8-2, particularly the finding that all forms of punishment become more effective when accompanied by a good cognitive rationale, eventually led many researchers to reject the conditioning viewpoint in favor of an *information-processing model* of punishment. Information-processing theorists agree that punishment can make children rather anxious or emotionally aroused. However, they argue that it is not the amount of anxiety or apprehension that the child experiences that determines whether she will inhibit a punished act; rather, the most critical determinant of a child's future conduct is her *interpretation* of the uneasiness she is experiencing, which, in turn, depends on the kind of rationale she has heard for modifying her conduct. To illustrate, let's imagine a child who is given no rationale with her punishment or, alternatively, hears a rationale that focuses her attention on her own negative consequences (for example, "I'll blister your rear if I catch you again"). If this child interprets her uneasiness as a fear of getting caught or a fear of the disciplinarian, she may well inhibit the punished act in the presence of authority figures but feel quite free to perform it when there is no one else around to detect these antics (see Figure 8-4).

By contrast, a second child who hears rationales specifying why a punished act is wrong and why he should feel bad for having performed it may be just as aroused

Figure 8-4
An information-processing model of the suppressive effects of punishment.

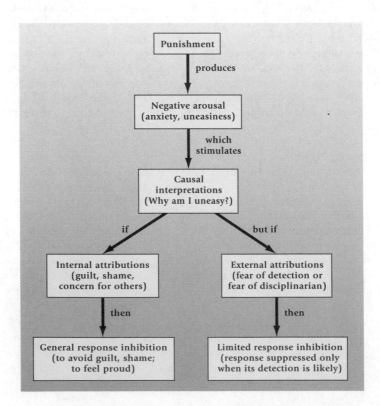

by the punishment he receives. But he has different information to process. He may now feel rather immature and even ashamed of himself for even contemplating this harmful act and, thus, be *internally* motivated to inhibit it in the future—even when there is no one else around to monitor his conduct.

In sum, punitive episodes provide children with a rich array of information to process, and it is the child's *interpretation* of this input, rather than the sheer amount of anxiety he experiences, that determines the effectiveness of punitive controls. Ross Parke, an expert on punitive suppression and former proponent of the conditioning viewpoint, now stresses the *informational* value of punishment and favors the information-processing viewpoint. He argues that the establishment of true *self*-restraint and long-term inhibitory controls "may require the use of cognitively-oriented training procedures. Punishment techniques that rely solely on anxiety induction, such as the noxious noises employed . . . in many experiments . . . or the more extreme forms of physical punishment sometimes used by parents may be effective mainly in securing only [temporary response] inhibition" (1972, p. 274).

Observational Learning

The last form of basic learning that we will consider is **observational learning,** which results from observing the behavior of other people. Almost anything can be learned by watching (or listening to) others. For example, a child may learn how to speak the language and tackle math problems, as well as how to swear, snack between meals, and smoke, by imitating his parents. As we saw in Chapter 2, this form of learning takes center stage in Albert Bandura's social learning theory.

How Do We "Learn" by Observation?

In 1965, Bandura made what was then considered a radical statement: Children can learn by merely observing the behavior of a social model, *even though they have never attempted the responses that they have witnessed or received any reinforcement for performing them.* Note the implications here: Bandura is proposing a type of "no trial" learning in which the learned response is neither elicited by a conditioned stimulus nor strengthened by a reinforcer. Impossible, said many learning theorists, for Bandura's proposition seems to ignore important principles of both classical and operant conditioning.

An example of "no trial" learning without reinforcement. But Bandura was right, although he had to conduct what is now considered a classic experiment to prove his point (Bandura, 1965). At the beginning of this experiment, nursery school children were taken one at a time to a semidarkened room to watch a short film. As they watched, they saw an adult model direct an unusual sequence of aggressive responses toward an inflatable Bobo doll, hitting the doll with a mallet while shouting "Sockeroo," throwing rubber balls at the doll while shouting "Bang, bang, bang," and so on. There were three experimental conditions:

1. Children in the *model-rewarded* condition saw a second adult give the aggressive model some candy and a soft drink for a "championship performance."
2. Children in the *model-punished* condition saw a second adult scold and spank the model for beating up on Bobo.
3. Children in the *no-consequences* condition simply saw the model behave aggressively.

When the film ended, each child was left alone in a playroom that contained a Bobo doll and many of the props that the model had used to work Bobo over. Hidden observers then watched the child, recording all instances in which he or she imitated one or more of the model's aggressive acts. These observations revealed how willing the children were to *perform* the responses they had seen the model display.

observational learning: learning that results from observing the behavior of others.

Figure 8-5
Average number of aggressive responses imitated during the performance test and the learning test for children who had seen a model rewarded, punished, or receive no consequences for his actions.
Adapted from Bandura, 1965.

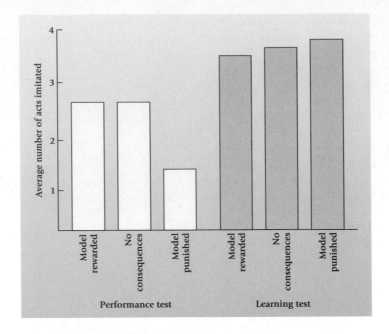

The results of this "performance" test appear on the left-hand (lighter) side of Figure 8-5. Here we see that children in the model-rewarded and the no-consequences conditions imitated more of the model's aggressive acts than children who had seen the model punished for aggressive behavior. At the very least, these results indicate that subjects in the first two conditions had learned some rather novel aggressive responses without being reinforced and without having had a previous opportunity to perform them. This looks very much like the kind of no-trial observational learning that Bandura had proposed.

The learning/performance distinction. But one question remained: Had the children in the model-rewarded and the no-consequences conditions actually *learned more* from observing the model than children who had seen the model punished? To find out, Bandura devised a second test in which he persuaded children to show just how much they had learned. Each child was offered some juice and trinkets for reproducing all of the model's behaviors that he or she could recall. The results of this *"learning"* test, which appear in the right-hand (darker) portion of Figure 8-5, clearly indicate that children in each of the three conditions learned about the same amount by observing the model. Apparently, children in the model-punished condition had imitated fewer of the model's responses on the initial "performance" test because they felt that they too might be punished for striking Bobo. But when offered a reward, they showed that they had learned much more than their initial performances implied.

In sum, it is important to distinguish between what children *learn* by observation and their willingness to *perform* these responses. Bandura's (1965) experiment shows that reinforcement is not necessary for observational learning. What reinforcement does is to increase the likelihood that the child will perform that which he or she has already learned by observing the model's behavior.

What do children acquire in observational learning? In many cases, young children will not imitate a model's behavior for days or even weeks after observing it. For example, a boy who wants to "shave" himself after watching his father may have to wait patiently until he can be alone, for few parents permit their youngsters to play with razors. What do children acquire that enables them to reproduce the behavior of an absent model at some point in the future—often the distant future?

Bandura's position on deferred imitation is very similar to Piaget's: A child who carefully observes a model will acquire *symbolic representations* of the model's behavior, which are stored in memory and retrieved later to guide his or her own attempts to imitate. These symbolic representations may be *images* of the model's actions or *verbal labels* that describe these responses in an economical way. Verbal representation is particularly important, for it enables the observer to retain information that would be difficult or impossible to remember by any other method. Imagine how hard it would be to open a combination safe if you simply formed images of the model turning the dials and did not translate these actions into a verbal label such as "L49, R37, L18"!

Developmental Trends in Imitation and Observational Learning

Bandura's theory of observational learning assumes that an observer can construct images or other symbolic representations of a model's behavior and then use these mediators to reproduce what he or she has witnessed. When do these abilities first emerge?

Origins of imitation and imitative learning. Although these findings remain highly controversial (Anisfeld, 1991), several investigators have reported that babies less than 7 days old are able to imitate a limited number of motor responses, such as sticking out their tongues (Meltzoff & Moore, 1983, 1989), moving their heads as an adult model does (Meltzoff & Moore, 1989), opening and closing their lips and their hands (Reissland, 1988; Vinter, 1986), and possibly even making facial expressions such as happiness and sadness (Field, Woodson, Greenberg, & Cohen, 1982). Yet, these kinds of imitative displays are much harder to elicit from a 1-month-old infant and are no longer observed at 20–21 weeks of age (Abravanel & Sigafoos, 1984). So the limited capacity for mimicry that neonates display may be a largely involuntary, *reflexive* scheme that disappears with age (just as many other early reflexes do), only to be replaced later by voluntary imitative responses (Kaitz et al., 1988; Vinter, 1986).

As we learned in Chapter 7, voluntary imitation of novel responses emerges and becomes much more reliable between 8 and 12 months of age (Piaget, 1951). Initially, the model must be present and must continue to perform a response before the child is able to imitate. But by age 9 months, some infants can imitate very simple acts (such as closing a wooden flap) up to 24 hours after they first witness them (Meltzoff, 1988c). This *deferred imitation*—the ability to reproduce the actions of a model at some point in the future—develops rapidly during the second year. By age 14 months, nearly half the infants in one study imitated the simple actions of a *televised* model after a 24-hour delay (Meltzoff, 1988a), and nearly all the 14-month-olds in a second experiment were able to imitate at least three (of six) novel behaviors displayed by a live model *after a delay of one week* (Meltzoff, 1988b). In fact, 14–18-month-olds who observe a *peer* operating a new toy in one context (a day-care center) are likely to imitate the model's behavior two days later when they finally have an opportunity to play with the toy at home (Hanna & Meltzoff, 1993).

Clearly, deferred imitation is an important developmental milestone, indicating that children can not only construct symbolic representations of their experiences, but can also retrieve this information from memory to guide their reproduction of past events. So 14–24-month-old infants should now be prepared to learn a great deal by observing the behavior of their companions. But do they take advantage of this newly acquired ability?

Yes, indeed! Leon Kuczynski and his associates (1987) asked mothers to record the immediate and the delayed reactions of their 16- and 29-month-old infants and toddlers to the behavior of parental and peer models. The results were quite interesting. All the children imitated their models a fair percentage of the time, but there were age differences in the content of these imitations. Although we've seen that 14–18-month-olds are capable of acquiring some skillful behaviors by observing

 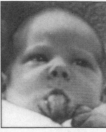    

Sample photographs from videotaped recordings of 2- and 3-week-old infants imitating tongue protrusion, mouth opening, and lip protrusion.

either adult or peer models (see Hanna & Meltzoff, 1993), the 16-month-olds in Kuczynski's study were more inclined to imitate affective displays, such as laughing and cheering, as well as other high-intensity antics such as jumping, shaking the head to and fro, and pounding their fists on the table. By contrast, older infants and toddlers more often imitated *instrumental* behaviors, such as household tasks and self-care routines, and their imitations had more of a self-instructional quality to them, as if the older children were now making an active attempt to (1) acquire skills their models had displayed or (2) understand the events they had witnessed. When imitating disciplinary encounters, for example, 16-month-olds simply repeated verbal prohibitions and physical actions such as hand slapping, usually directing these responses to themselves. However, older infants and toddlers tended to reenact the entire scenario, including the social influence strategies that the disciplinarian had used, and they usually directed these responses to another person, an animal, or a doll. So not only are older infants and toddlers making use of their imitative capabilities, but it appears that observational learning is already an important means by which they acquire basic personal and social competencies and gain a richer understanding of the routines and regulations that they are expected to follow (see also Rogoff et al., 1993).

By age 2, toddlers are already acquiring important personal and social skills by imitating the adaptive acts of social models.

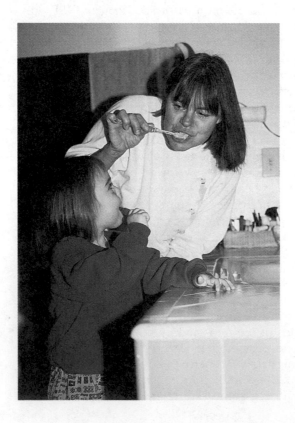

A later development in observational learning: Use of verbal mediators. Although preschool children are rapidly acquiring language and becoming accomplished conversationalists, they are less likely than older children to rely on verbal labels as a means of representing their experiences. This point is made quite clearly in a study by Coates and Hartup (1969) that we discussed earlier in Chapter 1 (p. 26). Recall that 4–5-year-olds and 7–8-year-olds watched a short film in which an adult model displayed a number of unusual responses. Some of the children from each age group were told to describe the model's actions as they observed them (induced-coding condition); others simply watched the model without having received any instructions (passive-observation condition). As we saw, the 4–5-year-olds who described what they were observing were later able to reproduce much more of the model's behavior than their age-mates in the passive-observation condition. By contrast, 7–8-year-olds reproduced the same number of the model's responses whether or not they had been told to describe what the model was doing. This latter finding suggests that 7–8-year-olds use verbal labels to describe what they have seen, even if they are not told to. One important implication of this study is that preschool children may learn less from social models because they, unlike older children, do not spontaneously produce the verbal mediators that would help them retain what they have observed.

In sum, children can learn any number of new responses by merely attending to others' behavior and retaining mental representations of what they have witnessed. Since observational learning requires neither formal instruction nor reinforcement, it probably occurs daily, even when models are simply pursuing their own interests and are not trying to teach the child anything in particular. Bandura (1977; 1986; 1989) reminds us that all developing children learn from a variety of social models and that no two children are exposed to exactly the same pattern of modeling influences. Thus, children should never be expected to emerge as carbon copies of their parents, siblings, or the child next door; individual differences are an inevitable consequence of observational learning.

Concept Check 8-1 ⌄ Basic Learning Processes

Check your understanding of some basic learning processes by completing the table below. For each vignette, decide what kind of learning is involved and identify the factor or type of consequence (if any) that is responsible for this learning. The answers appear in the Appendix.

Vignette	Kind of learning	Consequence responsible for learning
1. The Scumbags, a rock group, receive little response from their audience when they play new material. Consequently, they gradually begin to rely on their old "hits," which bring cheers from their fans.	_____	_____
2. Whenever Geri walks her dog, she puts on a yellow jacket. Soon she notices her dog becoming excited whenever he sees that jacket.	_____	_____
3. Having overheard a group of strangers agree that politicians are dishonest, Fred comes to look for the ulterior motive in every statement he hears a politician make.	_____	_____
4. Mosquitos consistently attack Jo in the outdoors until she applies insect repellent. Eventually, she comes to apply repellent before leaving the house.	_____	_____
5. After a week of work, Jim no longer notices the aromas that seemed so apparent when he first took his job at a bakery.	_____	_____

Learning and Development Reconsidered

Having now reviewed basic learning processes, we are ready to draw two conclusions that summarize the modern view of human learning and its contribution to child and adolescent development.

Learning Is a Fundamental Developmental Process

Had you already read the remaining chapters of this text, it would be rather obvious why we have taken the time to examine the fundamentals of human learning. Simply stated, many changes in behavior that occur as people develop are the result of learning. We learn not to dwell too long on stimuli that are already familiar (habituation). We may come to like, dislike, or fear almost anything if our encounters with these objects and events have occurred under pleasant or unpleasant circumstances (classical conditioning). We form habits, some good and some bad, by associating various actions with their reinforcing and punishing consequences (operant conditioning). We acquire new attitudes, values, and patterns of conduct by observing the behaviors and listening to the pronouncements of social models (observational learning). Clearly, learning is an important developmental process. And when we recall that even neonates are capable of learning and will change in response to their experiences, it is easy to see how the behaviorists of yesteryear might champion learning as the most important developmental process—the mechanism by which we become like other human beings and, at the same time, develop our own idiosyncrasies.

Human Learning Is an Active, Cognitive Process

Now let's contrast the modern view of human learning and development with that of the early behaviorists. Recall that John Watson, the father of behaviorism, believed that neonates are *tabulae rasae* (blank slates) who are *passively* molded, like lumps of clay, into purposeful and adaptive beings by parents, teachers, and other social agents. Radical behaviorists such as B. F. Skinner largely agreed with Watson, arguing that one form of learning in particular—operant conditioning—was the central developmental process. The radical behaviorists were called "radicals" because they stressed that one need not emphasize cognitive activities to understand operant learning and its contributions to human development. Presumably, new and more adaptive behaviors would evolve and persist because they were reinforced, whereas old and less adaptive habits would eventually wane if they were no longer reinforced or were punished.

Almost no one today takes this passive, mechanistic theory of human development very seriously, and some of the reasons for this skepticism should be apparent from our review of the literature. Consider first that learning is often (and some would say always) an *active*, rather than a passive, process. Habituation and observational learning, for example, require subjects to actively attend to the environment and to retain what they have experienced to show any evidence of learning. Moreover, human learning is often (and some would say always) a *cognitive* process rather than a noncognitive, reactive one in which responses are "stamped in" or "stamped out" by their reinforcing or punishing consequences. Nowhere is this any more apparent than in Bandura's classic research, for observational learning is clearly a cognitive activity that takes place as the observer attends to and **encodes** the model's behavior. Reinforcement (or the promise of reinforcement) may make observers more inclined to *perform* responses that they have already acquired through observation, but reinforcement is not necessary for this learning to occur in the first place. Even in operant learning, children seem to treat reinforcers and punitive events as "bits of information" that help them to decide whether various acts should be performed or inhibited.

encoding: process by which external stimulation is converted to a mental representation.

In sum, human beings are hardly the passive pawns of environmental influence that Watson and Skinner described. Instead, they are more accurately characterized as active information processors whose own *interpretations* of their experiences determine the impact of these events on their conduct and their eventual development.

Where have all the behaviorists gone? Although contemporary researchers generally agree that one must know how children learn in order to understand human development, very few of them continue to focus exclusively on basic learning processes in their own research. The primary interest of learning researchers today centers on the growth of mental strategies and information-processing skills that enable developing children and adolescents to learn more efficiently, to grasp increasingly complex ideas or concepts, to retain more of what they know or have experienced, and to become more adept at retrieving and using this information to answer questions, to solve problems, and to achieve other important objectives. In a word, many developmentalists from the behaviorist tradition have become information-processing researchers.

 # AN OVERVIEW OF THE INFORMATION-PROCESSING PERSPECTIVE

The information-processing perspective on cognition and cognitive development arose as a reaction to the many shortcomings of both Piaget's theory (problems we discussed in Chapter 7) and behavioral theories of basic and complex learning processes. Clearly, a fresh outlook on human cognition seemed necessary. Then came the digital computer—a wondrous new invention that intrigued many scientists with its capacity for rapidly and systematically converting input (data) into output (answers or solutions). Indeed, the computer seemed to provide a good analogy to the human mind (Klahr, 1992; Newell & Simon, 1961). Both the mind and the computer have a limited capacity for processing information, associated with their hardware and software. Computer *hardware* is the machine itself—its keyboard (or input system), storage capacity, and logic units. The mind's "hardware" is the nervous system, including the brain, the sensory receptors, and their neural connections. The computer's *software* consists of the programs used to store and manipulate information—word-processing and statistics programs and the like. The mind, too, has its software—rules, strategies, and other "mental programs" that specify how information is registered, interpreted, stored, retrieved, and analyzed.

This mind/computer analogy, then, provided the framework that information-processing theorists used to explain how children of different ages gather and use information about objects and events to "construct" knowledge and solve problems. Over the years, computers have become much more sophisticated: Not only do modern machines have a far greater storage (or memory) capacity than their predecessors, but they can also perform more operations more efficiently because of improvements in computer software. Information-processing theorists suggest that the same may be true of the developing mind: As children's brains and nervous systems mature (hardware improvements) and as children adopt new strategies for attending to stimuli, interpreting them, and remembering what they have experienced (software improvements), they should be able to perform increasingly complex cognitive feats with greater speed and accuracy (Kail & Bisanz, 1992; Klahr, 1992).

In the pages that follow, we will first consider a working model of the human information-processing system that was proposed nearly 30 years ago and is still useful today. We will then trace the development of three cognitive-processing skills that are thought to have a profound influence on the course and character of children's intellectual development: (1) the ability to gather task-relevant information (attention),

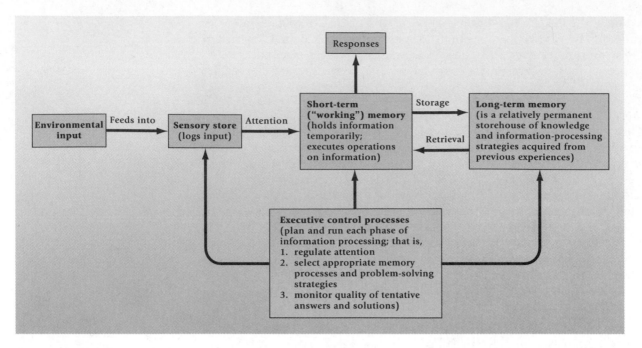

Figure 8-6
A schematic model of human information processing.
Adapted from Atkinson & Shiffrin, 1968.

(2) the ability to retain and retrieve this input (memory), and (3) the strategies or rules that children use when operating on or evaluating information they have gathered and retained (hypothesis testing and problem solving).

A Model of Human Information Processing

What happens as a person notices information and retains it for future use? Richard Atkinson and Richard Shiffrin (1968) assumed that humans process information in much the same way that computers do, and they formulated a **store model** to describe the process. A slightly modified and updated version of this important and influential model appears in Figure 8-6.

As we see in the figure, incoming information is thought to flow through a number of separate but interrelated processing units. The first of these components is the **sensory store** (or sensory register). This is the system's log-in unit; it simply holds raw sensory input for a very brief period (perhaps less than a second) as a kind of "afterimage" (or echo) of what has been sensed. The contents of our sensory stores are thus extremely volatile and will soon disappear without further processing. Should we attend to this information, however, it will pass into **short-term memory (STM)**, a processing unit that can store a limited amount of information (perhaps four to seven pieces) for several seconds. Thus, the capacity of short-term memory is sufficient to allow you to retain a telephone number for perhaps as long as it takes you to dial it. But unless this information is rehearsed or otherwise operated on, it too will soon be lost. Short-term memory is sometimes called *working memory* because all conscious intellectual activity is thought to take place here. So short-term, or "working," memory has two functions: (1) to store information temporarily so that (2) we can do something with it.

Finally, new information that is operated on while in short-term memory will pass into **long-term memory (LTM)**—a vast and relatively permanent storehouse of information that includes our knowledge of the world, our impressions of past experiences and events, and the strategies that we use to process information and solve problems.

An example will illustrate how the system is thought to work. Suppose that you are taking notes in your history class and you hear your instructor mention that the U.S. Constitution was ratified in 1789. Since this date is one you may need to remember, you attend to it. Consequently, the information flows from your sensory register into short-term memory, where it is *encoded* and remains long enough for you to

store model: information-processing model that depicts information as flowing through three processing units (or stores)—the sensory register, short-term memory, and long-term memory.

sensory store: first information-processing store, in which stimuli are noticed and are briefly available for further processing.

short-term memory (STM): second information-processing store, in which stimuli are retained for several seconds and operated upon (also called working memory).

long-term memory (LTM): third information-processing store, in which information that has been examined and interpreted is permanently stored for future use.

record it in your notebook. As you later study your notes in preparation for an upcoming exam, you will probably review this information several times and eventually register it in long-term memory, where it remains until you need it while taking your test.

If you are later asked a multiple-choice question about when the Constitution was ratified, you need not actively retrieve the correct date; you merely need to recognize it among the alternatives. This is an example of **recognition memory.** But assume that the question was a "fill-in" which asked "When was the Constitution ratified?" This would be a test of **recall memory,** which requires active retrieval of information without the aid of cues. Most people, children and adults alike, find questions requiring recognition memory easier to answer than those requiring active retrieval and recall.

Now imagine that you are asked how many years had passed between the signing of the Declaration of Independence (1776, remember?) and the ratification of the Constitution. Here we have a simple example of **problem solving,** or use of the information-processing system to arrive at a decision or achieve a goal (in this case, to find a correct answer for the question). The first step, of course, is to log in, attend to, and correctly interpret the problem. You must then search long-term memory for the two dates in question and also locate your stored knowledge of the mathematical operation of subtraction. Now you must transfer all this information to short-term, or working, memory so that you can "execute" your subtraction program (1789 minus 1776) to derive the correct answer.

Notice that to process information successfully and use it to solve problems, you have to know what you are doing and make the right decisions. Had you not known to log the significance of the year 1789 in your notebook, this information would have soon been lost under the barrage of names and dates that followed in your history lecture. Had you lacked any knowledge of subtraction or failed to retrieve this "program" from long-term memory, you would have been unable to determine the number of years that passed between the signing of the Declaration of Independence and the ratification of the Constitution. So, information does not simply "flow" on its own through the various stores, or processing units, of the system; instead, we actively channel this input and make it flow. This is why the model includes **executive control processes**—the processes involved in planning and monitoring what we attend to and what we do with this input.

Our executive control processes are thought to be largely under voluntary control and are, in fact, what most clearly distinguish human information processors from computers. When solving a problem, a computer does a whole lot less than we humans do. After all, the task-relevant information has already been logged into the machine, which solves problems that are assigned to it using strategies that are called up by a human "executive" (the programmer). All that the machine does is the necessary computations. By contrast, we humans, through our executive control processes, must initiate, organize, and monitor our own cognitive activities. We decide what to attend to; we select our own strategies for retaining and retrieving this input; we call up our own "programs" for solving problems; and last but not least, we are often free to choose the very problems that we will attempt to solve. Clearly, we humans are rather versatile information processors indeed.

An Alternative Model

One influential alternative to the Atkinson-Shiffrin store model is the **levels of processing** approach (Craik & Lockhart, 1972). This model assumes that what we are able to retain and use is limited not by constraints in the capacity of our sensory registers or short-term memory but, rather, by the levels at which incoming information is processed. Consider your processing of this page of text. If *shallow processing* occurs, you may notice that there are words printed here and no figures, but you would retain this information briefly, if at all. But if you process the text very deeply, you will understand its meaning, or semantic content, may integrate it with existing knowledge, and

recognition memory: realizing that an object or event that one experiences has been experienced before.

recall memory: recollecting objects, events, and experiences when examples of these bits of information are not available for comparative purposes.

problem solving: use of the information-processing system to achieve a goal or arrive at a decision.

executive control processes: the processes involved in regulating attention and determining what to do with information just gathered or retrieved from long-term memory.

levels of processing model: an information-processing model that suggests that retention of information, and thus its availability for use in problem solving is a function of the depth to which this input is encoded and analyzed.

may retain it indefinitely (so that you may be able to compare and contrast the store model with the levels of processing model if asked to do so).

According to the levels of processing model, limitations on information processing stem more from software than from hardware deficiencies. In other words, less-skilled information processors don't simply have smaller computers; instead, they either lack the necessary cognitive strategies for processing information deeply, or, if they know about these strategies, they apply them inefficiently. If a 7-year-old, for example, is asked "What is 5 + 39?" she may start with 5 and count out 39 more numbers until she arrives at an answer. In so doing, she is telling us that she lacks a "min rule" that we adults would apply by adding the smaller number to the larger number (Siegler, 1991). Moreover, the mathematical operation of addition is likely to be a laborious one for a 7-year-old, who may count out each successive number on her fingers. By contrast, addition has become **automatized** for adults, which means that the operation is performed quickly and almost effortlessly. So when faced with the problem of adding 5 + 39, we apply our min rule and quickly add the two numbers in our heads.

What, then, is happening as children develop intellectually? The *store model* contends that both the child's hardware (that is, the physical capacity of information-processing stores) and software (strategies; control processes) improve with age. By contrast, the *levels of processing* model suggests that the most important cognitive developments are *software* improvements that allow us to make better use of the limited space, or hardware, that we have (Siegler, 1983). And the research we will review tends to favor the levels of processing model. That is, children's cognitive strategies and control processes change dramatically over time, whereas there is much less conclusive evidence for changes in the *physical capacity* of our information-processing stores.

Comparisons with Piaget's Theory

The information-processing approach is similar to Piaget's in at least two important respects. First, many information-processing researchers, inspired by Piaget, study the growth of logical problem solving and attempt to specify the underlying schemes and strategies on which children rely to generate their solutions. Moreover, at least some information-processing theorists believe that cognitive development occurs in stages (Case, 1986, 1992; Fischer, 1980; Marini & Case, 1994), although the stages proposed are often specific to particular intellectual skills, or domains, rather than the very broad, holistic stages that Piaget described (Carey & Gelman, 1991; Wellman & Gelman, 1992).

Other information-processing theorists totally reject the notion of cognitive stages, choosing instead to depict cognitive development as a *continuous* process in which children's information-processing skills gradually become more and more efficient. Another critical distinction between Piaget and virtually everyone in the information-processing camp centers on their interpretations of children's intellectual shortcomings. Consider a child who fails a conservation-of-liquids problem, claiming that the taller of two containers now has more liquid. From an information-processing perspective, there are several possible contributors to this logical error. Perhaps the child has not attended to and encoded the most pertinent information. Or he might not be able to hold all the relevant information in short-term memory so that he can operate on it. He might also lack certain strategies that would enable him to transfer encoded information to long-term memory or would aid in retrieving knowledge already stored there. Of course, he may not have acquired and retained the critical rules or logical operations needed to solve the problem. And finally, he may lack the executive control processes that would enable him to coordinate all the necessary phases of problem solving to arrive at a logical conclusion. Clearly, this cognitive-processing analysis of the errors people make is much richer and more elaborate than that of Piaget, who generally assumed that the reason people fail at problems is that they lack the "cognitive structures" to solve them.

automatization: an increase in the efficiency with which cognitive operations are executed.

In the remaining portions of the chapter, we will trace the development of three crucial information-processing skills—attention, memory, and problem solving—and comment on the practical as well as the theoretical significance of these developments.

Concept Check 8-2 ⌄ Modeling Human Information Processing

Check your understanding of information-processing models by matching each of the descriptions below to one of the following ideas and concepts: (a) sensory store; (b) short-term memory; (c) long-term memory; (d) executive control processes; (e) levels of processing model; (f) store model. The answers appear in the Appendix.

_____ 1. Vast storehouse of acquired information.

_____ 2. Views cognitive development as improvements in mental software.

_____ 3. Log-in unit of the information-processing system.

_____ 4. Means by which we plan and monitor what we do with incoming or stored information.

_____ 5. Views cognitive development as improvements in mental hardware and software.

_____ 6. Site of conscious intellectual activity.

ATTENTIONAL PROCESSES: GETTING INFORMATION INTO THE SYSTEM

Obviously, a person must first detect, attend to, and encode information before this input can be retained or used to solve problems. Since the nervous system is developing rapidly early in life, it seems reasonable to assume that the sensory register might become more efficient at gathering and holding sensory input for our attention. However, research indicates that preschool children can hold just as much information in their sensory stores as older children and adults do (Bjorklund, 1995; House, 1982). So it is unlikely that the intellectual shortcomings that young children display are attributable to an immature or inefficient sensory register.

The Development of Attentional Strategies

Earlier in Chapter 6, we learned that perceptual development in childhood depends very critically on the growth of attentional processes. As children's **attention spans** increase and they are better able to *plan* what they will attend to and to ignore distractions, they detect more and more information about objects and events (that is, *invariants*, or *distinctive features*) and make finer perceptual discriminations (Gibson, 1992). Here, we will take a closer look at the development of two important aspects of attention: its planfulness and selectivity.

Early Planning of Appropriate Attentional Strategies

By age 4 or 5, children are becoming more persistant in their attempts to solve problems and are showing some signs of deliberation as they gather relevant information. For example, Patricia Miller and Yvette Harris (1988) asked 3- and 4-year-olds to compare two rows of objects to determine whether the rows were identical or different. Each object in each row was covered by a door, thereby preventing the child from quickly scanning all the objects. Thus, the most efficient strategy for gathering task-relevant information was a vertical comparison precedure in which the child examines vertically aligned pairs of objects (one in each row) as she proceeds across the rows. Three-year-olds rarely used this strategy, choosing instead to look first at all objects within a particular row before examining the second row. By contrast, the planful, vertical-comparison strategy was often employed by 4-year-olds, whose "same–different" judgments were more likely to be correct on the trials they used this procedure.

attention span: capacity for sustaining attention to a particular stimulus or activity.

However, the use of planful search strategies often breaks down when young children encounter similar but more complex tasks that require them to process information deeply or to adapt their search procedures to answer different questions. Alice Vlietstra (1982), for example, had 5-, 8-, and 11-year-olds examine a mock-up of a house. She then asked the children to search six similar houses until they found (1) *one* difference between the sample house and the comparison houses or (2) *all* differences between the sample and the comparison houses. The 5-year-olds in this experiment clearly failed to follow the instructions, choosing instead to explore the stimuli in a haphazard way. The 8-year-olds searched the stimulus displays much more systematically than the 5-year-olds did, but they failed to limit their attention to "one difference" when asked to find a single difference between the sample and the comparison houses. Only the 11-year-olds were very planful; they followed the two sets of instructions equally well by directing their visual search to the information that was necessary to perform each task. So the planful, adaptive gathering of information that would help children to solve problems develops gradually over the course of middle childhood.

Ignoring Information That Is Clearly Irrelevant

Would young children perform as well as older children if they were told in advance which information was relevant to the task at hand? Apparently not. Patricia Miller and Michael Weiss (1981) told 7-, 10-, and 13-year-olds to remember the locations of a number of *animals,* each of which was hidden behind a different cloth flap. When each flap was lifted to reveal an animal, the children could also see a household object positioned either above or below the animal. Here, then, is a learning task that requires the child to attend selectively to certain information (the animals), while ignoring other potentially distracting input (the household objects). When the children were tested to see whether they had learned where each animal was located, the 13-year-olds outperformed the 10-year-olds, who, in turn, performed slightly better than the 7-year-olds. Miller and Weiss then tested to see whether children had attended to the incidental (irrelevant) information by asking them to recall which household object had been paired with each animal. They found exactly the opposite pattern on this incidental learning test: 13-year-olds recalled *less* about the household objects than either 7- or 10-year-olds. In fact, both of the younger groups recalled as much about the irrelevant objects as about the locations of the animals. Taken together, these findings indicate that older children are much better than younger ones at concentrating on relevant information and filtering out extraneous input that may interfere with task performance.

What Do Children Know about Attention?

Do young children know more about attentional processes than their behavior might indicate? It often seems that they do. Even though 4-year-olds generally cannot overcome distractions when performing "selective attention" tasks, they are apparently aware that distractions are a problem, for they realize that two stories will be harder to understand if the storytellers speak simultaneously rather than taking turns (Pillow, 1988). By contrast, 3-year-olds would just as soon listen to stories told simultaneously as to have the storytellers take turns. In other research, Miller and Weiss (1982) asked 5-, 7-, and 9-year-olds to answer a series of questions about factors known to affect performance on an incidental-learning task (that is, a task like the "animals and objects" test described above. Although knowledge about attentional processes generally increased with age, even the 5-year-olds realized that one should at least *look first* at task-relevant stimuli and then *label* these objects as an aid to remembering them. The 7- and 10-year-olds further understood that one must *attend selectively* to task-relevant stimuli and *ignore* irrelevant information in order to do well on these problems.

Although the ability to concentrate improves dramatically during middle childhood, grade school students are not always successful at overcoming distractions.

Why, then, do younger children not follow their own advice when actually working at incidental learning (or other similar) tasks? Recent research by Miller and her associates (DeMarie-Dreblow & Miller, 1988; Miller & Seier, 1994; Miller, Woody-Ramsey, & Aloise, 1991) provides some clues. It seems that when children first acquire an appropriate attentional strategy, they go through a *transitional phase* in which they employ the strategy sporadically. Why not use appropriate strategies all of the time if children are aware of them? According to DeMarie-Dreblow and Miller (1988), the cognitive effort required in executing a new, unpracticed strategy may so tax the limited capacity of working memory that the transitional child has little capacity left to encode the information she is supposed to retain. So she fails to profit from using the strategy and will fall back on less-efficient procedures that seem to work better *for her*. But as transitional children become more practiced at executing a strategy, the cognitive effort to do so should decline, thus leaving them more space in short-term memory to gather the information they need to perform their tasks. And once such an attentional strategy consistently proves to be effective, the child will routinely access and implement it, thus showing large improvements on problems that would benefit from its use (DeMarie-Dreblow & Miller, 1988; Flavell et al., 1993).

In sum, the development of attention is apparently a lengthy process in which a child first learns to translate what she knows into appropriate actions and then gradually comes to rely on these strategies as they become more routinized and effective means of gathering information to achieve her objectives.

Despite these "normal" trends, a fair number of grade school children find it nearly impossible to sustain their attention for long or to develop planful attentional strategies. In Box 8-3, we will take a closer look at this **attention deficit–hyperactivity disorder** and its implications for children's academic, social, and emotional development.

 ## MEMORY PROCESSES: RETAINING AND RETRIEVING INFORMATION

Once children have attended to information of some kind, they must find a way to remember it if they are to learn from their experiences or use this input to solve a problem. Thus, the development of **memory**—the processes by which we store and retrieve information—is central to information-processing theories of intellectual development. We begin our review where memory begins—very early in infancy.

attention deficit–hyperactivity disorder: an attentional disorder involving distractibility, hyperactivity, and impulsive behavior that often leads to academic difficulties, poor self-esteem, and social/emotional problems.

memory: the processes by which people retain information and later retrieve it for use.

BOX 8-3

Attention Deficit–Hyperactivity Disorder

They can't sit still; they don't pay attention to the teacher; they mess around and get into trouble; they try to get others into trouble; they are rude; they get mad when they don't get their way . . . [Henker & Whalen, 1989; p. 216].

*T*hese and other similar descriptions are widely endorsed by classmates of those 3%–5% of grade school children (mostly boys) diagnosed as having *attention deficit–hyperactivity disorder (ADHD)*. ADHD youngsters display three major symptoms: (1) they are highly *impulsive*, often acting before thinking and blurting out whatever is on their minds; (2) they are *inattentive*, frequently failing to listen and displaying an inability to concentrate or to finish tasks; and (3) they are *hyperactive*, as they constantly fidget, squirm, or move about (American Psychiatric Association, 1987). As you might expect, these youngsters perform miserably on tests of sustained and selective attention (Landau, Milich, & Lorch, 1992). They also do poorly in school and often alienate both teachers and classmates by their failure to comply with requests and their disruptive and aggressive behavior (Henker & Whalen, 1989; Silver, 1992).

It was once believed that hyperactive children simply outgrew their problems after reaching puberty. Although they do generally become less fidgety and overactive during the teenage years, many people diagnosed in childhood as having ADHD will continue to display serious adjustment problems later in life. For example, attention-disordered adolescents are likely to struggle both socially and academically, and they frequently drop out of high school or impulsively commit reckless, delinquent acts without thinking about the consequences (Fischer et al., 1990). The picture is somewhat more positive by early adulthood, as about half of all ADHD individuals seem to be functioning well in their jobs. But for many with ADHD, young adulthood is characterized by above-average rates of job changes (or dismissals), marital disruptions, traffic accidents, legal infractions, and other personality problems or emotional disorders (Fischer et al., 1993; Mannuzza et al., 1993).

What causes ADHD? Unfortunately, we do not yet have a clear answer. Some people may be genetically predisposed to develop the disorder, in that 20%–30% of families with an ADHD child have a parent who has ADHD (Silver, 1992). Environment also matters. The incidence of ADHD is higher among children who were exposed *prenatally* to alcohol, drugs, and the disease rubella (Silver, 1992), and a harsh, highly controlling style of parenting may also contribute to, or at least aggravate, the problem in some cases (Jacobvitz & Sroufe, 1987). However, earlier theories linking the syndrome to food additives, excessive dietary intake of sugar, lead poisoning, and brain damage have received little support (Henker & Whalen, 1989).

What can be done to help hyperactive children? One treatment that seems to help 70%–80% of them is to administer stimulant drugs such as Ritalin (DuPaul et al., 1991). Although it may seem odd to give overactive children drugs that increase their heart rates and respiratory levels, stimulants work because they also make ADHD children better able to focus their attention and less distractable and disruptive (Tannock et al., 1993). Important side benefits of this increased attentional focusing is that both academic performances and peer relations are likely to improve (Pelham et al., 1993; Henker & Whalen, 1989). Gains in scholastic performance have also been achieved through cognitive-behavioral programs that teach ADHD children how to set academic goals that require sustained attention while allowing these youngsters to reinforce their successes with tokens that can be exchanged for prizes. Indeed, ADHD children seem to benefit most from a *combination* of drug and behavior therapies that is also supplemented by family therapy designed to help parents understand and cope with these often-difficult youngsters (DuPaul & Barkley, 1993; Whalen & Henker, 1991).

A final note: Although therapeutic interventions do improve the self-esteem, social behaviors, and academic performance of ADHD children, many of these "treated" individuals are no better adjusted as adults than hyperactive peers who received no therapy (Wilens & Biederman, 1992). Undoubtedly, the long-term prognosis will improve as we learn more about this disorder. At present, we can say that the many problems associated with ADHD clearly illustrate just how important the regulation of attention is, not only to cognitive development and academic performance, but to one's social and emotional development as well.

Development of Memory in the First Three Years

Earlier, we noted that the ability to *recognize* the familiar is apparently inborn, for neonates who habituate to the repeated administration of a stimulus are telling us that they remember this object or event as something they have experienced before. Moreover, very young infants even show a limited ability to *recall* their experiences in tests of **cued recall memory,** and we need only recall Rovee-Collier's work to make this point. By 2 to 3 months of age, babies who have been taught to make a mobile move by kicking their legs will recall this act several days later if placed back into the *same context* in which the learning took place (thus, the context "cues" the memory).

cued recall memory: a recollection that is prompted by a cue associated with the setting in which the recalled event originally occurred.

Indeed, infants this young will even recall how to make the mobile move nearly three weeks later if given a stronger "reminder" of their previous learning by seeing the mobile move (Rovee-Collier, 1984; 1987).

When do infants first display *pure recall* by actively retrieving information from memory when no cues to remind them of these experiences are available? Piaget's (and others') work provides some clues. For example, 8–9-month-old infants will search for objects that are completely concealed in tests of object permanence, a finding that suggests that they *recall* the object exists. *Deferred imitation*, the ability to imitate a novel act after a delay, also provides evidence of recall memory. As early as 9 months of age, many infants are able to imitate novel actions of an adult model (for example, pushing a button on a box to produce a beep) after a 24-hour delay (Meltzoff, 1988c).

Recall memory steadily improves throughout the first three years. By age 2, infants will occasionally recall interesting events that happened months ago and can even relate them in the form of a story (Howe & Courage, 1993; Nelson, 1984). Moreover, 2-year-olds show some signs of their emerging **prospective memory** by deliberately remembering to do things they consider important, such as reminding mother to buy them some candy as she is about to depart on a shopping trip (Somerville, Wellman, & Cultice, 1983). And by age 2½ to 3, some children can even remember some experiences that they had had nearly two years ago (Myers, Clifton, & Clarkson, 1987; Perris, Myers, & Clifton, 1990). Why, then, do most of us display **infantile amnesia**—an inability to recall anything that happened to us during the first few years? Though the answers remain elusive, some ideas about this fascinating "memory lapse" are presented in Box 8-4.

As toddlers become preschoolers, they begin to represent familiar experiences in terms of **scripts**—general impressions of what occurs and when in particular situations. When asked to tell what happens when he goes to the supermarket, a 3-year-old might say "You drive there, go in, get food and ice-cream, pay, and go home." Children's first scripts may mention only the highlights of what happens in many situations, but these highlights are almost always recalled in their correct order (Fivush, Kuebli, & Clubb, 1992). Eventually, scripts are formed to represent a large number of familiar events in children's lives, such as going to a restaurant, a nursery school, a birthday party, or even to bed at night (Flavell et al., 1993; Nelson, 1986). And these event schemes become more elaborate with age. In comparison with the barebones script offered by a 3-year-old, a 5-year-old might describe a trip to the supermarket as follows: "You park, go in, pick up fruit and vegetables, get your meat, go down the rows, fill up the cart, pay, and go right home to put the food in the fridge."

Forming scripts thus appears to be a basic *strategy* on which children rely to organize and interpet their everyday experiences (Flavell et al., 1993; Hudson, 1990). And once formed, scripts influence how *new* experiences are processed and interpreted. New information that follows a familiar script is easier to recall (see Bjorklund, 1995; Hudson & Nelson, 1983), perhaps explaining why young preschool children show clear improvements in recall memory. Yet, interestingly enough, children will often recall information that *violates* a script as *more consistent* with their scheme than it really is (Hudson & Nelson, 1983). As we will see in Chapter 13, such recall distortions are one of the primary reasons that unfounded social stereotypes about gender and sex differences are so slow to die out.

Memory Development in Childhood

Despite the impressive memorial capabilities that 3-year-olds display, the most dramatic improvements in recall memory occur between ages 3 and 12. One clear sign of the memory limitations of preschool children is that recognition memory is way ahead of recall memory. If a 4-year-old had two minutes to study the 12 items in Figure 8-7, she would later *recognize* nearly all of them if asked to select these objects from a larger set of pictures (Brown, 1975). But if asked to *recall* the objects, she

Figure 8-7
Imagine that you have 120 seconds in which to learn the 12 objects pictured here for an upcoming recall test. Chances are you could recall 10 or 11 of these objects when tested several minutes later, whereas an 8-year-old would recall 7–9 of them and a 4-year-old only 2–4. What tricks or strategies might you use to make your task easier? Why do you think 4-year-olds perform so poorly on this task?

prospective memory: memory directed to the performance of future activities.

infantile amnesia: a lack of memory for the early years of one's life.

script: a general representation of the typical sequencing of events (that is, what occurs and when) in some familiar context.

BOX 8-4
What Happened to Our Early Childhood Memories?

Although infants are quite capable of remembering, most adults recall almost nothing that happened to them before the age of 3—or, if they do have memories, many turn out to be pure fiction. Recently, JoNell Usher and Ulric Neisser (1993) studied this lack of memory for the early years, or *infantile amnesia*, by questioning college students about experiences they had had early in life—such as the birth of a younger sibling, a stay in the hospital, a family move, or the death of a family member. To assess recall, a series of questions were asked about each event that the subject had experienced (for example, Who told you your mother was going to the hospital to give birth? What were you doing when she left? Where were you when you first saw the new baby?). As we see in the figure, the percentage of questions subjects could answer increased dramatically the older the person was when he or she had experienced the event. Usher and Neisser concluded that the earliest age of *any* meaningful recall was about age 2 for the birth of a sibling or a hospitalization, and age 3 for the death of a family member or a family move. In an earlier study, only 3 of 22 college students who were younger than 3 at the time of a sibling's birth remembered anything at all about the event (Sheingold & Tenney, 1982). Even 9- and 10-year-olds who are shown photographs of their day-care classmates from 6–7 years earlier have difficulty discriminating these youngsters, who were once very familiar to them, from other young day-care children they have never seen before (Newcombe & Fox, 1994). So if infants can remember their experiences, why can't grade school children and adults remember much about what their lives were like as infants and toddlers?

Sigmund Freud thought infantile amnesia simply reflected our tendency to repress the emotional conflicts of early childhood. However, contemporary researchers have rejected Freud's view in favor of more cognitive explanations. For example, infants do not use language and adults do, so it is possible that early memories are stored in some nonverbal code that we cannot retrieve once we become language users (Sheingold & Tenney, 1982; Siegler, 1991). Or possibly, we must develop the capacity to create verbal narratives of our experiences in order to remember them well (Nelson, 1993). Mark Howe and Mary Courage (1993) suggest yet another interesting possibility: Maybe what is lacking in infancy is not cognitive or language ability, but a sense of "self" around which personal experiences can be organized. Once an infant gains a firm sense of self at about 18 to 24 months of age,* events may become more memorable when encoded as things that happened to *me*. Though we still cannot pinpoint the exact cause (or causes) of infantile amnesia, it is quite clear that a period of life (infancy) that is so critically important to later development is a blank for most of us.

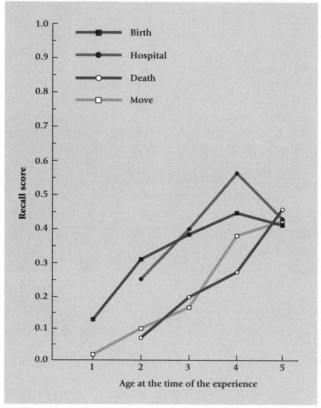

College students' recall of early life events increases as a function of their age at the time of the event. *From Usher & Neisser, 1993.*

*The development of a sense of self will be explored in detail in Chapter 12.

might remember only two to four of them, a far cry from the seven to nine items that an 8-year-old would recall. Preschoolers do display better memory for interesting, real-life events than for simple lists of objects; but even so, they are still much better at *recognizing* those events (or at retrieving them with the aid of hints) than they are at recalling them on their own (Baker-Ward et al., 1993).

Why do you suppose young children recall so little about new information or about objects they recognize as familiar? And why does recall memory improve so dramatically between the preschool years and early adolescence? Information-processing theorists have proposed four possible answers for these questions:

1. *Changes in basic capacities.* Older children have higher-powered "hardware" than young children do; their brains have more "working memory space" for manipulating information and can process information faster.
2. *Changes in memory strategies.* Older children have better "software;" they have learned and consistently use effective methods for getting information into long-term memory and retrieving it when they need it.
3. *Increased knowledge about memory.* Older children know more about memory (for example, about how long they must study to learn things thoroughly, which kinds of memory tasks take more effort, which strategies best fit each task, and so on).
4. *Increased knowledge about the world.* Older children know more about the world in general than young children do. This knowledge, or expertise, makes material to be learned more familiar, and familiar material is easier to learn and remember than unfamiliar material.

Do Basic Capacities Change?

Do older children remember more than younger children do because they have a better "computer"—an information-processing system that has a larger capacity or is more efficient? Those who have explored this hypothesis have ruled out the idea that the capacity of long-term memory changes much over time. Basically, both young children and older ones have more long-term storage than they can possibly use, and there is no consistent evidence for an enlarging of this capacity after the first month of life (Perlmutter, 1986). A more promising idea is that the capacity of *short-term* (working) *memory* might increase with age, so that older children and adults can keep more information in mind and perform mental operations more rapidly than a younger child can.

This latter notion has been featured in recent revisions of Piaget's theory proposed by two *neo-Piagetian* theorists, Juan Pascual-Leone (1984; 1988) and Robbie Case (1985; 1992), who have been strongly influenced by the information-processing approach. Both Case and Pascual-Leone believe that more advanced stages of cognitive development are made possible by increases in working memory space (or **M-space**). The traditional method of estimating the capacity of short-term memory is to assess one's **memory span.** This is done by measuring the number of items (for example, numbers) that a person can recall accurately, in order, immediately after hearing them. Studies consistently indicate that memory span increases throughout childhood: 5-year-olds can hold four or five numbers in mind, whereas 9-year-olds can recall six numbers, and adults recall an average of seven or eight (Dempster, 1981). Since short-term memory is also the site where mental operations are performed, Case prefers measures such as his **counting span** task that require subjects to operate on the information they are trying to remember. In Case's procedure, subjects are given a series of cards with different numbers of dots on them. They must count the dots on each card and remember the sum as the next card is counted, then the next, and so on. Like memory span, counting span increases with age: 5-year-olds remember an average of less than two "card sums," whereas 9-year-olds recall about three, and 12-year-olds can keep nearly four of them in mind (Case, 1985).

What develops: Physical capacity or operating efficiency? Obviously, short-term storage capacity increases with age. But why? One possibility is that the *physical capacity* of short-term memory increases: Older children and adults have bigger "containers" than younger children do. Another possibility is that the physical parameters of short-term memory remain relatively constant and that children become more *efficient* information processors—that is, they are quicker to recognize items on memory-span or counting-span tasks and are more skilled at performing cognitive operations on them. If less time or effort is needed to encode and operate on the stimuli

M-space: mental space; number of separate schemes or concepts that a child can manipulate simultaneously.

memory span: a measure of the amount of information that can be held in short-term memory.

counting span: a measure of M-space that requires individuals to operate on the information they have in short-term memory.

in a memory task, then more of one's *limited* working memory space can be used to store these items (Case, 1985; 1992; and see Figure 8-8).

At this point, there is no solid evidence that the *physical capacity* of short-term memory (that is, the size of the container) increases much over childhood (Dempster, 1985). Indeed, this "capacity hypothesis" cannot explain why young children (who would presumably have small storage capacities) are able to remember much more about lists of familiar children's items than adults do (Lindberg, 1980). Robbie Case's **operating efficiency hypothesis** fares much better: Children who are quick to identify and to operate on items in a memory task have longer memory spans than those who are slow to recognize or to operate on these stimuli (Case, 1985; 1992; Dempster, 1981; Howard & Polich, 1985). It seems that many information-processing skills that take a great deal of time and effort early in life become *automatized*—that is, they are accomplished with little effort later in life. Thus, you may quickly (and almost effortlessly) arrive at an answer of 225 for the problem $9 \times 25 = \_\_\_$, whereas a 10-year-old might have to laboriously perform each step of the operation (that is, $9 \times 5 = 45$; leave the 5, carry the 4; $9 \times 2 = 18 + 4 = 22$; 22 and 5 = 225) and probably could not do this problem in his head.

Increases in operating efficiency may be due in part to *hardware* improvements—to such maturational changes as increasing myelinization of the brain and nervous system and the elimination of unnecessary (or excess) neural synapses that could interfere with efficient information processing (Case, 1985; 1992; Hale, Fry, & Jessie, 1993). But *software* improvements are also involved. With practice or experience, children become more familiar with items they must remember and more skilled at performing mental operations on them (Bjorklund, 1995; Flavell et al., 1993). Although the exact causes are not clear, there is general agreement that older children are in many ways *faster* and more *efficient* information processors than younger children are (Hale et al., 1993; Kail, 1991; 1992; Kee, 1994). So increases in operating efficiency are one reason that memory improves over the course of childhood.

Implications for problem solving. Piaget did not emphasize memory or memory development in his theory. He felt that improvements in memory stemmed from the growth of operational schemes and logical reasoning. Neo-Piagetians such as Robbie Case (1985; 1992) argue just the opposite: Improvements in logical reasoning are largely attributable to the development of memory. In fact, Case believes that increases in short-term storage that result from the automatization of information processing are what underlies the growth of logical reasoning.

Consider a 5-year-old who is struggling with a *transitivity* task. To answer correctly, the child must first detect and remember the critical properties of three stimuli, *A*, *B*, and *C*, as well as the *A*-to-*B* relation and the *B*-to-*C* relation. Clearly, this is a lot of information to keep in mind for a 5-year-old who encodes information and performs mental operations very slowly. Should the child hold all this information in short-term storage, he may not have any space left over to make the appropriate transitive inference (that is, $A >$ or $< C$). Yet, if we reduce the memory demands of this problem (or indeed, other logical puzzles such as conservation problems) by training the child what to look for and think about, he may well answer correctly (Gelman & Baillargeon, 1983). This is not to imply that increases in short-term storage guarantee logical thinking: Case is a neo-Piagetian who agrees with Piaget that children must actively construct logical schemes from their own experiences with objects and events if they are ever to think logically. His point is simply that without sufficient short-term storage to gather the necessary information, young children are unable to "execute" their logical schemes to think rationally about many everyday events.

Development of Memory Strategies

In order to remember something for more than a few seconds, you must transfer this information from short-term to long-term memory. Of course, information stored in long-term memory is of little use if you are unable to retrieve it when you need it.

operating efficiency hypothesis: the notion that M-space increases with age because we come to process information faster or more efficiently.

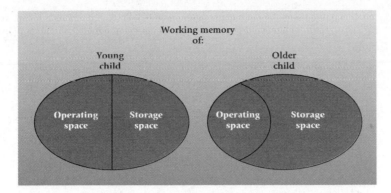

Figure 8-8
Robbie Case's "operating efficiency" hypothesis. With age, children process information much faster and more efficiently, thus requiring less operating space and leaving more storage space.
Adapted from Case, 1985.

Could some of the memory deficits that young children display stem from a failure to use planful strategies that could help them to store new information and later retrieve this input? Let's explore this idea by looking at the ways in which children of different ages approach the task of remembering.

Rehearsal. One very simple yet *effective* strategy that we adults can use to retain new information is to **rehearse** it—to repeat it over and over until we think we will remember it.

When instructed to try to remember a group of toys they have been shown, 3–4-year-olds will look very carefully at the objects and will often label them (once), but they rarely rehearse (Baker-Ward, Ornstein, & Holden, 1984). By contrast, John Flavell and associates (reviewed in Flavell et al., 1993) gave 5–10-year-olds similar memory instructions and found that spontaneous use of rehearsal (as indicated by children's lip movements) increased with age. Whereas only 10% of the 5-year-olds repeated information that they were asked to recall, more than half the 7-year-olds and 85% of the 10-year-olds adopted this rehearsal strategy. In addition, the children who actively rehearsed performed much better than nonrehearsers on this recall task.

Older children also rehearse more *efficiently* than younger children do. If asked to recall a list of words presented one at a time, 5–8-year-olds usually rehearse each word in just that way—one at a time. By contrast, 12-year-olds are more likely to rehearse word clusters, repeating the earlier items over and over again as they rehearse each successive word (Ornstein, Naus, & Liberty, 1975; Kunzinger, 1985). Apparently, this latter form of rehearsal is a much more effective strategy, for the children who use it perform better on recall tests than those who rehearse each item singly, as it is presented.

Why do young children not rehearse more efficiently? Possibly because their attempts to execute the more complex clustering strategy require so much of their limited working memory space that they are unable to *retrieve* enough information to form useful clusters. A study by Peter Ornstein and his associates (1985) supports this interpretation. Ornstein et al. tried to teach 7-year-olds to use the "clustering" rehearsal strategy and found that the children did so *only if earlier items on the list remained visible.* So when these younger children were able to form item clusters without having to expend effort retrieving the items, they were able to execute the complex clustering strategy. By contrast, 12-year-olds relied on the clustering strategy *regardless of whether earlier items were visually displayed.* Apparently, this efficient rehearsal technique has become so automatized for most 12-year-olds that they implement it almost effortlessly, thus leaving themselves ample space in working memory for retrieving items to rehearse.

In sum, the preschooler's general failure to rehearse, coupled with the young grade school child's less-effective use of this skill, implies that the development of memory strategies is a very gradual process that may depend on both the development of

rehearsal: a strategy for remembering that involves repeating the items that one is trying to retain.

working memory and the many opportunities children have to practice these techniques. Indeed, John Flavell and his associates (1993) have concluded that rehearsal and other memory strategies develop through four phases:

1. **Mediation deficiency.** At this stage, the child lacks the cognitive skills to execute or to benefit from the strategy; attempts to coach the child in its use will be ineffective.
2. **Production deficiency.** Now the child may use the strategy if she is coached in its use and is encouraged to do so, but she will not *spontaneously* produce and use the strategy.
3. **Utilization deficiency.** This is a transitional stage in which the child spontaneously produces and uses the strategy; but he gains little benefit from its use and often reverts to less-effective tactics.
4. **Mature strategy use.** Finally, the strategy is used spontaneously and *effectively* to improve learning and memory.

Apparently, these four phases characterize the development of many kinds of information-processing skills, for we've already seen that the growth of attentional strategies follows a similar developmental path (see also Bjorklund & Coyle, 1994).

Semantic organization. In one sense, rehearsal is a rather unimaginative memory device because it is simply a form of mimicry or imitation. If a rehearser merely repeats the names of items to be remembered, he or she may fail to notice certain meaningful relations among the stimuli that should make them easier to recall. Consider the following example:

List 1: boat, match, hammer, coat, grass, sentence, pencil, dog, cup, painting
List 2: knife, shirt, car, fork, boat, pants, sock, truck, spoon, plate

Although these ten-item lists should be equally difficult to recall if one simply rehearses them, the second list is actually much easier for many people. The reason is that its items can be grouped into three semantically distinct categories (eating utensils, clothes, and vehicles) that can serve as cues for storage and retrieval. Until about age 9 to 10, children are not any better at recalling items that can be **semantically organized** (such as list 2) than those that are difficult to categorize (such as list 1) (Hasselhorn, 1992). This finding suggests that young children make few attempts to organize information for later recall.

How do children learn to organize materials in ways that could help them to remember? If we think back to Vygotsky's perspective about how many new skills are socially mediated, we might immediately suspect that organizational strategies evolve from experiences children have had (1) categorizing highly related objects and events under a teacher's direction at school or (2) watching as the teacher presents materials in a highly organized fashion. Interestingly, elementary school instructors in the United States spend little time teaching children explicit memory strategies, although those who provide more in the way of strategic suggestions do have students who tend to rely more on organizational strategies and who perform better on recall tests (Moely et al., 1992). But even in the absence of explicit instruction, children may eventually discover the benefits of organization for themselves from experiences they have categorizing highly related objects and events at school. Deborah Best (1993; Best & Ornstein, 1986) found that 9-year-olds who were instructed to sort "easily categorizable" items in any way they wished were more likely to organize their materials into semantically distinct clusters than were control subjects, who were told to sort less categorizable items that could be organized, but with some difficulty. And there is more: Compared with the control subjects, those who had sorted the "easily categorizable" items later (1) were more inclined to organize subsequent lists that were difficult to categorize, (2) performed better on recall tests of these materials, and (3) were more likely to preach the virtues of organizational strategies when asked to teach 6-year-olds how to remember.

mediation deficiency: inability to learn and use effective memory strategy.

production deficiency: a failure to spontaneously generate and use known strategies that could improve learning and memory.

utilization deficiency: a failure to rely on effective memory strategies that one has spontaneously produced; thought to occur in the early phases of strategy acquisition when executing the strategy requires much mental effort.

mature strategy use: consistent production and use of an effective memory strategy.

semantic organization: a strategy for remembering that involves grouping or classifying stimuli into meaningful categories that are easier to retain.

Few experiences may contribute more to the development of effective memory skills than playing strategic games with a more competent opponent.

Yet important as schooling experience may be, memory strategies may also be fostered at home through collaborative or guided learning experiences that children have with their parents. For example, Martha Carr and her associates (1989) find that 8–9-year-olds who rely heavily on organizational strategies and perform well on recall tests tend to have parents who often (1) play strategy-related games with them, and (2) show them how to be planful and strategic when completing and checking their homework. So it seems that such pleasurable and strategic pursuits as chess, card games, Concentration, and the like are not only effective ways of promoting togetherness and passing leisure time but are likely to contribute to a youngster's intellectual growth as well!

Elaboration. Another effective strategy for improving recall is to add to, or *elaborate* on, the information that we hope to remember. **Elaboration** is particularly useful whenever our task is to associate two or more stimuli, such as a foreign word and its English equivalent. For example, one way to remember the Spanish word for "duck," *pato* (pronounced "pot-ō"), is to elaborate on the word *pato* by creating an image of a pot that is in some way linked to a duck (see Figure 8-9 for an example).

In a review of the literature, Wolfgang Schneider and Michael Pressley (1989) found that the spontaneous use of elaborative techniques is a "latecomer to the memorizer's bag of tricks" that is rarely seen before adolescence. Moreover, a sizable percentage of adolescents do not elaborate as a strategy for improving their recall, and these "nonelaborators" typically perform at lower levels on tests of associative learning than their counterparts who use elaborative techniques.

Why is elaboration so late in developing? One reason may be that the very limited capacity of a younger child's working memory may prevent her from generating complex elaborative mediators (Pressley et al., 1987). However, others believe that adolescents are more proficient at elaboration because they simply know more about the world than younger children do and are better able to imagine how any two (or more) stimuli might be linked (Bjorklund, 1987; Bjorklund & Harnishfeger, 1990). And as we will soon see, there is now some rather dramatic evidence that a person's "knowledge base" does indeed affect his or her performance on memory tasks.

Culture and memory strategies. Cultures clearly differ in the extent to which they support and encourage particular memory strategies (Kurtz, 1990; Rogoff, 1990). Rehearsal, organization, and elaboration, for example, are especially helpful to children

elaboration: a strategy for remembering that involves adding something to (or creating meaningful links between) the bits of information one is trying to retain.

Figure 8-9
An example of an elaborative image that one might create to associate *pato* (pronouned "pot-o"), the Spanish word for "duck," with its English translation.

from Western industrialized societies, whose school activities involve a great deal of rote memorization and list learning. Yet, these same strategies may not be so useful to unschooled children from nonindustrialized societies, whose most important memory tasks might involve recalling the location of objects (water; game animals) in a natural setting or remembering instructions passed along in the context of proverbs or stories. In list-learning experiments, Western children rely heavily on strategies acquired at school and clearly outperform their unschooled peers from nonindustrialized societies (Cole & Scribner, 1977). Yet, their superior performance does not extend to other kinds of memory tasks. Unschooled Australian aboriginal children, for example, are better than their Anglo-Australian peers at remembering the location of objects in natural settings (Kearins, 1981), and African adolescents display a better recall for orally transmitted stories than American adolescents do (Dube, 1982). Indeed, Western children actually remember less if they try to rehearse or to organize information in these latter kinds of memory tasks (Rogoff, 1990).

These findings make perfectly good sense when viewed through the "lens" of Vygotsky's *sociocultural theory:* Cognitive development always occurs within a particular cultural context, which not only defines the kinds of problems that children must solve, but also dictates the strategies (or "tools of intellectual adaptation") that will enable them to master these challenges.

Retrieval processes. We have talked about rehearsal, organization, and elaboration as if they were only methods of *storing* information in long-term memory. Yet, these and other memory strategies can also help us to search for and *retrieve* information from long-term storage—a fact that younger children may fail to understand. Consider the following examples.

Michael Pressley and Joel Levin (1980) prompted 6- and 11-year olds to *elaborate* on 18 pairs of stimuli that they were trying to learn. When later taking a recall test, half the children from each age group were told to use their elaborative images to help them remember the items; the remaining children were not given any retrieval instructions. Pressley and Levin found that 11-year-olds recalled nearly 65% of the items, regardless of whether they had been told to use their elaborative images to help them remember. By contrast, the 6-year-olds recalled nearly twice as many items when given retrieval instructions (42.5%) as when left to their own devices (23%). Strange as it may seem, it apparently did not occur to the latter group of 6-year-olds to use the images they had worked so hard to create as part of their retrieval strategy. In a similar study, Daniel Kee and Terace Bell (1981) found that 7-year-olds who had categorized materials they were trying to remember later failed to take full advantage of these categories as aids for recall *unless they were explicitly reminded to.* So the message that emerges from these studies is an important one: Even when younger children do "organize" or "elaborate" in order to register information in long-term memory, they may still perform worse than older children on recall tests because they fail to rely on these same strategies to retrieve what they have worked so hard to store.

But why? One gets the feeling that younger children simply know less about memory aids and the circumstances under which it is appropriate to use them. In recent years, investigators have begun to study what children know about memory and how this knowledge may influence their performance on memory tests. Let's consider what they have learned.

Metacognition and the Development of Metamemory

metacognition: one's knowledge about cognition and about the regulation of cognitive activities.

Metacognition is a term that cognitive psychologists use to refer to what we know of the human mind and its capabilities, including our awareness of our own mental strengths and liabilities and the ways in which we monitor and control our cognitive processes. Your own store of metacognitive knowledge might include an understanding that you find it easier to understand psychology than chemistry; that you must selectively attend to the most relevant information if you hope to solve difficult problems; or that it is wise to double check a proposed solution to a problem before concluding that it is correct.

One important aspect of metacognition is **metamemory**—one's knowledge of memory and memory processes. Children are displaying metamemory if they recognize, for example, that there are limits to what they can remember; that some things are easier to remember than others; or that certain strategies are more effective than others at helping them to remember (Flavell et al., 1993).

When do children first show any evidence of metamemory? Earlier, perhaps, than you might suspect. If instructed to remember where a stuffed animal (Big Bird) has been hidden so that they can later wake him up from his nap, even 2–3-year-olds will go stand near the spot where the object was placed or at least will look repeatedly at or point to that location—activities that they do not display as often if the toy is visible and they do not need to recall where it is (DeLoache, Cassidy, & Brown, 1985). So by about age 2, children have learned one simple bit of knowledge about memory: If you hope to remember something, you have to work at it! But even so, 2- and 3-year-olds apparently know little about *forgetting*; not until age 4, for example, do children understand it is harder to remember something over a long rather than a short period of time (Lyon & Flavell, 1993). It almost seems as if young preschool children view information that they have retained as a mental "copy" of reality that is filed away in one of the mind's drawers and will be available for use when they need it (Pillow, 1989).

Knowledge about memory increases dramatically between ages 4 and 12 as children come to regard the mind as an active, constructive agent that stores only *interpretations* (rather than copies) of reality that may fade over time (Flavell et al., 1993). Yet, this understanding of the limitations of one's mind and memory is acquired very gradually. Although a 4-year-old may know that very short lists are easier to remember than long ones and that it will take more effort to remember the longer list (Wellman, Collins, & Glieberman, 1981), children younger than age 7 consistently overestimate how well they will perform on memory tasks, while underestimating the amount of study that is necessary to learn the materials (Kreutzer, Leonard, & Flavell, 1975; Schneider & Pressley, 1989). Not until about age 7 do children recognize that related items that can be organized into categories are easier to recall than unrelated items (Kreutzer et al., 1975). And although 7–9-year-olds know that rehearsing and categorizing information are more effective memory strategies than simply looking at the items or labeling them once, not until age 11 do they seem to recognize that organization is more effective than rehearsal (Justice, 1985).

Finally, it appears that younger children know very little about mental strategies for *retrieving* information from long-term memory. Instead, they tend to rely on *external* prompts such as written notes to help them remember. But even though 5–7-year-olds may recognize that a written note or other tangible retrieval cues can help them to remember something, they are less likely than older children to know where to place such "reminders" to ensure their effectiveness (Fabricius & Wellman, 1983; Flavell et al., 1993).

What is the relation between memory and metamemory? Does a person's knowledge of memory processes determine how well he or she will perform on various memory tests? The answer is not as straightforward as we might hope. Two reviews of the literature have found only low to moderate positive correlations between memory and metamemory (Cavanaugh & Perlmutter, 1982; Schneider & Pressley, 1989), thus implying that *good metamemory is not always required for good recall*. David Bjorklund & Barbara Zeman (1982), for example, found that 7–9-year-olds were able to recall the names of more than 75% of their classmates, even though they claimed to have no preexisting strategies that might help them to retrieve this information.

metamemory: one's knowledge about memory and memory processes.

William Fabricius and Lynn Cavalier (1989) have proposed that the aspect of metamemory that is most closely related to actual memory behavior is not merely knowledge that a strategy works but, rather, knowledge of *why* that strategy works. To test this hypothesis, Fabricius and Cavalier first questioned 4-, 5-, and 6-year-olds to determine whether they (1) knew that labeling objects they hoped to remember could improve recall and (2) had a mental explanation for *why* labeling is an effective technique. Then the children were observed to see if they would actually use the labeling strategy when instructed to try to remember a series of pictures that the experimenter showed them. The results clearly supported the hypotheses—that is, children who knew that labeling could help them recall rarely labeled the objects they were trying to remember unless they also knew *why* labeling would improve recall.

These findings dovetail nicely with studies that have attempted to help children to improve their reading comprehension by training them to use effective memory aids and other metacognitive strategies (for example, identifying the most important information in a passage; evaluating the text for clarity and monitoring how well the material has been understood). Briefly, the training studies show that merely teaching strategies is not enough; to be effective, the training must also inform the child *why* each strategy is better than others she might use and *when* it will be advantageous to use it. Indeed, children who receive this "informed training" when learning ways to extract and retain more information from their reading materials soon rely on the strategies they have learned and usually show distinct improvements in reading comprehension (a measure of retention) and other academic skills (Brown et al., 1983; Brown & Campione, 1990; Paris, 1988).

So a child's understanding of how memory strategies work seems to be the best metacognitive predictor of her use of these techniques. Indeed, the finding that measures of metamemory and memory are often more highly correlated among children 10 years of age and older (Schneider & Pressley, 1989) undoubtedly reflects the fact that older children have had more time to discover *why* various memory strategies can make remembering easier.

Does Increased General Knowledge Contribute to Improvements in Memory?

Twelve-year-olds obviously know more about the world in general than 8-year-olds or 5-year-olds do. That is, they have a much richer **knowledge base** and may outperform younger children on many memory tests because they are much more familiar with the information they are asked to retain.

Perhaps the most dramatic illustration of the powerful influence of knowledge base on memory was provided by Michelene Chi (1978). She demonstrated that children could outperform adults at a memory task—something that children virtually never do. How? She simply recruited children who were expert chess players and compared them with adults who were familiar with the game but lacked expertise. On a test of memory for sequences of digits, the children recalled fewer than the adults did, as is typical. But on a test of memory for the locations of *chess pieces*, the child "experts" clearly beat the adults (see Figure 8-10). In a similar study, Mark Lindberg (1980) obtained similar results: Third-graders recalled more than college students about items that third-graders know more about (for example, cartoon characters and children's games), whereas college students recalled more than third-graders about items that are generally more familar to young adults (for example, types of music and natural earth formations). Even children with low intellectual ability but high expertise sometimes understand and remember as much or more about stories in their "specialty areas" than children with high intellectual ability but low expertise (Schneider & Bjorklund, 1992; Schneider, Korkel, & Weinert, 1989).

Consider the implications of these findings. On most tasks, younger children are the "novices" and older ones are the "experts." So if knowledge base affects memory performance, older children will generally outperform younger ones on many recall tests because they simply *know more* about most topics than younger children do.

knowledge base: one's existing information about a topic or content area; significant for its influence on how well one can learn and remember.

Why do we remember more about familiar information? Chi's hypothesis is that familar information is easier to *encode;* our knowledge of the material allows us to process it *faster* and may suggest ways that the items can be organized, stored, and retrieved from memory. So another reason why older children may begin to generate and use more effective memory strategies is that their ever-expanding knowledge base makes it easier for them to see how information they must remember can be rehearsed, organized, or elaborated (Bjorklund, 1987; 1995; Bjorklund & Harnishfeger, 1990).

Summing Up

How, then, can we briefly summarize the ground we have covered? One way is to review Table 8-2, which describes four general conclusions about the development of learning and memory that have each gained widespread support.

We should also recognize that these four aspects of development probably *interact* with each other rather than evolve independently. For example, the automatization of information processing may leave the child with enough working memory space to use effective memory strategies that were just too mentally demanding earlier in childhood (Case, 1985; Kee, 1994; Miller et al., 1991). Or a child's expanding knowledge base may permit faster information processing and suggest ways that information can be categorized and elaborated (Bjorklund, 1995). So there is no one "best" explanation for the growth of memorial skills. All of the developments that we have discussed seem to contribute in important ways to the dramatic improvements in recall memory that occur over the course of childhood.

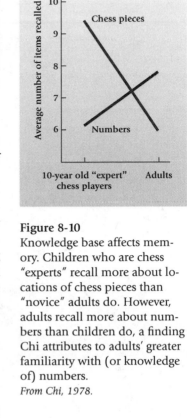

Figure 8-10
Knowledge base affects memory. Children who are chess "experts" recall more about locations of chess pieces than "novice" adults do. However, adults recall more about numbers than children do, a finding Chi attributes to adults' greater familiarity with (or knowledge of) numbers.
From Chi, 1978.

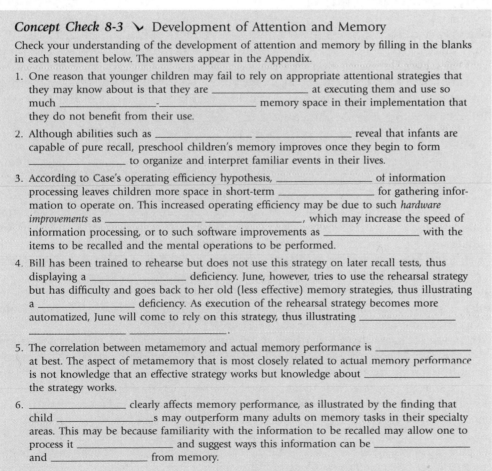

Concept Check 8-3 ⌄ Development of Attention and Memory

Check your understanding of the development of attention and memory by filling in the blanks in each statement below. The answers appear in the Appendix.

1. One reason that younger children may fail to rely on appropriate attentional strategies that they may know about is that they are _____ at executing them and use so much _____-_____ memory space in their implementation that they do not benefit from their use.

2. Although abilities such as _____ _____ reveal that infants are capable of pure recall, preschool children's memory improves once they begin to form _____ to organize and interpret familiar events in their lives.

3. According to Case's operating efficiency hypothesis, _____ of information processing leaves children more space in short-term _____ for gathering information to operate on. This increased operating efficiency may be due to such *hardware improvements* as _____ _____, which may increase the speed of information processing, or to such software improvements as _____ with the items to be recalled and the mental operations to be performed.

4. Bill has been trained to rehearse but does not use this strategy on later recall tests, thus displaying a _____ deficiency. June, however, tries to use the rehearsal strategy but has difficulty and goes back to her old (less effective) memory strategies, thus illustrating a _____ deficiency. As execution of the rehearsal strategy becomes more automatized, June will come to rely on this strategy, thus illustrating _____ _____.

5. The correlation between metamemory and actual memory performance is _____ at best. The aspect of metamemory that is most closely related to actual memory performance is not knowledge that an effective strategy works but knowledge about _____ the strategy works.

6. _____ clearly affects memory performance, as illustrated by the finding that child _____s may outperform many adults on memory tasks in their specialty areas. This may be because familiarity with the information to be recalled may allow one to process it _____ and suggest ways this information can be _____ and _____ from memory.

Table 8-2 Four Major Contributors to the Development of Learning and Memory

Contributor	Developmental trends
1. Working memory capacity	Older children have greater information-processing *capacity* than younger children do, particularly in the sense that they process information faster (or more automatically), leaving more of their limited working memory space for storage and other cognitive processes.
2. Memory strategies	Older children use more effective *memory strategies* for encoding, storing, and retrieving information.
3. Metamemory	Older children know more about memory processes, and their greater *metamemory* allows them to select the most appropriate strategies for the task at hand and to carefully monitor their progress.
4. Knowledge base	Older children know more in general, and their greater *knowledge base* improves their ability to learn and remember.

PROBLEM SOLVING: MAKING USE OF INFORMATION ONE HAS ENCODED AND RETAINED

Like Piaget, cognitive-processing theorists believe that children of different ages will show qualitatively different levels of performance when trying to solve various problems. However, they argue that Piaget was often vague in his description of children's levels or "stages" of problem solving, largely because his clinical method was simply too subjective and imprecise to ever provide a complete account of the growth of problem-solving skills.

Siegler's Rule-Assessment Approach

Robert Siegler's (1981; 1983; 1991) **rule assessment** approach nicely illustrates how information-processing theorists have studied the development of logical reasoning and problem-solving skills and how their approach differs from Piaget's. Siegler's most basic assumption is straightforward: When children are faced with a puzzling new experience or a problem to solve, they will first gather information and then formulate a *rule* to account for what they have witnessed. Presumably, the kind of rule that the child generates and applies to the task at hand will depend largely on the type of information that he has encoded (that is, noticed and interpreted). According to Siegler, an investigator who hopes to understand the development of problem-solving skills must first identify the rules that children use to solve problems and then determine *how* and *why* these rules change over time.

Among the tasks that Siegler uses in his rule-assessment approach is a set of balance-scale problems similar to those used by Inhelder and Piaget (1958) to assess formal-operational reasoning. The balance-scale apparatus (Figure 8-11) has four equally spaced pegs on each of its arms. Once weights are placed on various pegs, the child is asked to predict what will happen (for example, will the arms remain balanced? Will the left arm go up? down?) when a brake that holds the arms motionless is released. Clearly, two aspects of this problem are important: the number of weights on each arm and the distance of those weights from the fulcrum. To his credit, Piaget adequately described how formal-operational adolescents were able to

rule assessment: a method of assessing a child's level of cognitive functioning (or problem solving) by noting the information that he encodes and the principle, or rule, he uses to operate on this information and draw conclusions.

master these balance-scale problems. What he did not provide, however, was a very satisfactory account of how younger children approach these problems, and why they fail to master them.

According to Siegler (1981), younger children's attempts to solve balance-scale problems are clearly *rule-governed* rather than hit-or-miss. The reason they typically fail at this task is that they fail to encode all of the critical information and, thus, are guided by faulty rules. What rules might they adopt? The following four are possible for balance-state problems:

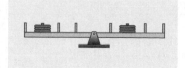

Figure 8-11
The balance-scale apparatus used by Siegler to study the development of children's problem-solving abilities.

Rule 1: The child considers only the *number of weights* and concludes that the arm with more weight will drop. If the number of weights on each arm is the same, the child concludes that the scale will remain balanced.
Rule 2: The child pays more attention to weight and consistently predicts that the arm with more weight will drop. Only when the weight on each arm is equal will the child consider the distance of the weights from the fulcrum.
Rule 3: The child always considers both weight and distance when making a prediction. But if one side has more weight while the other has its weights farther from the fulcrum, the child is conflicted and simply guesses at what will happen.
Rule 4: The child always considers both the weight and distance and seems to understand that the torque on each arm is a function of weight × distance. For example, if there are three weights on the second peg to the left and two weights on the fourth peg to the right, then left torque = 3 × 2 = 6; right torque = 2 × 4 = 8; therefore, the right arm will go down.

To assess which rule a child favors, Siegler presents him or her with the six balance-scale problems in Table 8-3 and notes the patterning of answers across all six tasks. If a child consistently uses one of the four rules, his or her answers will conform to one of the four patterns shown in the columns of the table. For example,

Table 8-3   **Six Balance-Scale Problems and the Patterning of Answers that Follows from Using Each of Siegler's Four Rules for Solving Such Problems**

Problem	Correct answer	Siegler's rule			
		1	2	3	4
1. 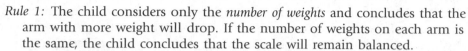	Balance	100% correct	100% correct	100% correct	100% correct
2.	Left down	100% correct	100% correct	100% correct	100% correct
3.	Left down	0% correct (will say balance)	100% correct	100% correct	100% correct
4.	Left down	100% correct	100% correct	33% correct (chance responding)	100% correct
5.	Left down	0% correct (will say right down)	0% correct (will say right down)	33% correct (chance responding)	100% correct
6.	Balance	0% correct (will say right down)	0% correct (will say right down)	33% correct (chance responding)	100% correct

Source: Adapted from Siegler, 1981.

children who rely on Rule 1 will solve problems 1, 2, and 4 but will erroneously conclude that the scale will balance in problem 3 and that the right arm will drop in problems 5 and 6. By contrast, a user of Rule 3 will correctly solve problems 1, 2, and 3 and respond at chance levels (guess) to problems 4, 5, and 6.

When Siegler (1981) administered these tasks to individuals aged 3 to 20, he found that 91% appeared to be using one or the other of the four rules, but with pronounced age differences. Almost no 3-year-olds used any kind of rule, suggesting that the very young child has limited problem-solving skills and tends to proceed in a haphazard rather than a logical way when solving problems (see also Klahr & Robinson, 1981). By contrast, 4- and 5-year-olds were rule governed, more than 80% of them using Rule 1 and encoding weight but ignoring distance. By age 8, children were generally using Rule 2 or 3; by age 12, the vast majority had settled on Rule 3. And, although most 20-year-olds continued to use Rule 3, 30% of them had discovered the weight-times-distance principle reflected in Rule 4.

What Is New about the Rule-Assessment Approach?

At first glance, Siegler's rule-assessment approach seems remarkably similar to Piaget's earlier work on age differences in problem solving. Yet there are some crucial distinctions between the two approaches. For example, Piaget viewed his logical operations as very general schemes that children would apply to most of the problems they face. By contrast, Siegler and other information-processing theorists assume that rules are more domain-specific and that the rules a child uses may vary for different kinds of problems. Second, Siegler places much more attention than did Piaget on the roles that *attention* and *encoding* play in problem solving, and this emphasis on what the child encodes and how he interprets this information often leads to a richer understanding of the child's problem-solving abilities and shortcomings. Consider the following example.

Siegler (1976) studied a group of 5- and 8-year-olds, all of whom were using Rule 1 (consider only weight) to answer balance-scale problems. If we were to infer their problem-solving abilities solely from the *answers* they gave (as Piaget tended to do), we would have to conclude that these children all had comparable "cognitive structures." Yet when Siegler provided these youngsters with feedback and demonstrations that their Rule 1 logic was inadequate, 8-year-olds often moved to Rule 2 or Rule 3, whereas the 5-year-olds did not. Why did all children not benefit from the demonstrations if they used the same rule?

Siegler then devised an encoding test to find out. Five-year-old and 8-year-old Rule 1 users studied the arrangement of weights on a balance scale for 10 seconds. Then the apparatus was covered, another scale was brought forward, and the children were asked to reproduce the arrangement of weights they had just seen. The 5-year-olds could reproduce the number of weights on each side of the scale but not their distances from the fulcrum. By contrast, the 8-year-old Rule 1 users reproduced (and had thus encoded) both weight and distance information. Here, then, is why Siegler had observed age differences in response to training. When shown that the weight-only rule was inadequate, 8-year-olds began to consider the distance information they had encoded, moving from Rule 1 to Rule 2 (or Rule 3). By contrast, 5-year-olds, who had encoded only weight, could not profit from the training demonstrations because they had no other information to consider when their weight-only rule proved to be wrong.

Can these 5-year-olds be taught to use Rule 2 or Rule 3 when solving balance-scale problems? Yes, indeed, but only if they are first trained to encode distance information (as the 8-year-olds already do) so that they will consider this input once they see that their weight-only rule is faulty (Siegler, 1976). Note the implication here: The ability of 5-year-olds to learn a new rule depends not just on their current rule (or cognitive structure for problem solving), but on their encoding activities as well.

In sum, Siegler and his associates agree with Piaget that children progress through a series of "alternative understandings" before mastering various problems and concepts. However, they believe that their rule-assessment approach is more precise than Piaget's theory at indicating why a child's thinking takes the form it does and at specifying the information that the child must now consider in order to move from one level of understanding to the next.

Educational Applications of Rule Assessment

Imagine how effective educators might be if they could accurately diagnose their pupils' information-processing strategies to determine exactly what each child is noticing (or failing to notice) about a problem and exactly what rule or strategy each child is using. It turns out that the rule-assessment approach has proved quite fruitful at specifying why individual children are having trouble comprehending their reading lessons or are failing to solve various arithmetic problems (Mayer, 1985; Siegler, 1988). If Johnny, for example, works the subtraction problem 350 − 131 and answers 221 rather than 219, he is using a faulty rule—one that says, "When subtracting from 0, enter the bottom digit." He will require different instruction than Susie who works the same problem and comes up with an answer of 119. Can you diagnose the problematic rule Susie is using? (If not, the answer appears at the bottom of the page.)

The rule-assessment approach is but one of several cognitive-processing strategies that can help teachers help their students to learn. In Box 8-5, we will consider several other important educational implications that stem from the work of information-processing researchers.

Some Limitations of Rule Assessment

Task limitations. Could we rely on the rule-assessment approach to help children solve such ordinary or everyday problems as locating a toy they have misplaced, finding their way when "lost" in a crowd at the Easter parade, or making their meager allowances last for an entire week? A number of critics (for example, Strauss & Levin, 1981) think not, arguing that Siegler's model may apply *only* to tightly circumscribed "logic" problems that *can* be solved by gathering objective information and formulating a rule. Moreover, rule-assessment theory makes little of abilities such as *advance planning* (particularly, the capacity to adapt one's planning activities to the requirements of different tasks) that also develop over the course of childhood (see Gardner & Rogoff, 1990) and may be crucial to determining the success that one attains on problems of any kind. So as fruitful an approach as rule assessment has been, it may apply to only a limited number of problems that children actually encounter.

Contextual limitations. One of the major claims that Vygotsky made in his *sociocultural theory* was that cognitive development occurs in a cultural context that will influence the way one thinks. If he is correct, then we might wonder whether applying a rule-assessment analysis based on the problem-solving activities of Western children might not underestimate the competencies of youngsters raised in other cultural (or subcultural) contexts.

Wonder no more: The answer is yes, and we can illustrate the point through cross-cultural studies of children's numerical reasoning. For example, uneducated 10–15-year-old street vendors in Brazil perform miserably when trying to interpret and compare large multidigit numbers or when working relatively simple paper-and-pencil

Susie uses an inappropriate borrowing rule. She thinks that whenever she needs to borrow she must borrow from every column—that is,

$$\begin{array}{r} 2\,4 \\ \cancel{3}\cancel{5}0 \\ -131 \\ \hline 119 \end{array}$$

Although unschooled street vendors may often fail at paper-and-pencil math problems, they display sophisticated arithmetic skills by quickly and accurately making change during sales transactions.

arithmetic problems requiring them to add and subtract (for example, "What is 510 + 90?"). Using rule assessment to compare their performance with that of grade school children would imply that these vendors have few if any basic mathematical skills. And yet, these unschooled youths are sophisticated mathematicians indeed when applying numerical concepts and operations to their everyday activities. For example, they are able to quickly and accurately identify numerical relations among bills and coins and to add and subtract currency values *in their heads* (just as they must when conducting street transactions) (Saxe, 1988; 1991; Schliemann, 1992). Clearly, we underestimate these children by using rule-based performance standards from scholastic settings to gauge their mathematical competencies. These findings also illustrate Vygotsky's most basic sociocultural premise: Cognitive development always occurs in a cultural (or subcultural) context that affects the problem-solving strategies that children acquire, as well as the kinds of problems to which they apply their competencies.

In sum, Siegler's rule-assessment analysis of children's problem-solving activities *is* an important extension of Piaget's earlier work that has clear implications for educators (see Box 8-5). Nevertheless, this model does not adequately explain all kinds of goal-directed reasoning in all contexts and, thus, falls far short of being a comprehensive theory of children's problem solving.

 ## CURRENT STATUS OF THE INFORMATION-PROCESSING APPROACH

Over the past 20 years, the information-processing perspective has become a dominant approach to the study of children's intellectual development. And the reasons for its rise to a position of prominence should be quite clear from your reading of this chapter. Simply stated, information-processing researchers have been able to provide us with reasonably detailed descriptions of how such cognitive processes as attention, encoding, and memory—processes that Piaget did not emphasize—not only change with age but also influence children's thinking and problem-solving activities.

Yet problems remain with the information-processing approach (Kail & Bisanz, 1992; Kuhn, 1992). To date, information-processing theorists have paid relatively little attention to the kinds of social and cultural influences on cognition that Vygotsky and others (for example, Rogoff, 1990) have emphasized (but see Case, 1985; 1992). And those who favor the elegant coherence of Piaget's stage model question what they see as the "fragmented" approach of information-processing theorists, who focus intently on specific cognitive processes and view development as the gradual acquisition of processing skills (and problem-solving strategies) in many different domains. Of course, information-processing theorists would reply by noting that it was the many, many problems with Piaget's broad-brush account of cognitive development that helped to stimulate their work in the first place. Although many information-processing theorists are neo-Piagetians who readily acknowledge the prodigious contributions that Piaget has made, they are quite correct in their assessment that children's thinking is not nearly so homogeneous across problems or domains as Piaget's theory implies. Moreover, they would challenge the assertion that their study of intellectual development is disorderly or chaotic—and with ample justification, for attention, memory, and problem solving all develop through predictable sequences and become increasingly planful and systematic from infancy through adolescence. And even although much relevant research remains to be conducted, these important developments in information processing are helping to provide richer and more detailed explanations for the appearance and refinement of such Piagetian abilities as deferred imitation, object permanence, seriation, classification, perspective taking, conservation, and hypothetical-deductive reasoning (Bjorklund, 1995; Flavell et al., 1993).

BOX 8-5

Some Educational Implications of Information-Processing Research

*R*ecall that Piaget offered educators several suggestions for helping their pupils to learn. First and foremost, he argued that teachers should view children as naturally inquisitive beings who learn best by constructing their *own* knowledge from *moderately novel* aspects of experience—that is, information that challenges their current understanding and forces them to reevaluate what they already know. Indeed, if the concepts that one hopes to teach are too complex, children will be unable to assimilate or accommodate to this instruction, and no new learning will occur. Moreover, Piaget stressed that a teacher's job is not so much to transmit facts, to actively structure problems, or to reinforce correct answers as to provide the climate, setting, and materials that will allow curious children the intrinsic satisfaction of discovering important concepts for themselves.

Information-processing theorists can certainly agree with Piaget that children are active and curious explorers who learn best by constructing knowledge from experiences that are just beyond current levels of understanding. However, their own guidelines for effective instruction are much more explicit than Piaget's and come closer to the views of Lev Vygotsky (1978), implying that teachers should take a more *active, directive* role than Piaget had envisioned. The following six implications for instruction flow directly from the information-processing research that we have reviewed.

1. *Analyze the requirements of problems that you present to your pupils.* Know what information must be encoded and what mental operations must be performed to arrive at a correct answer or to otherwise grasp the lesson to be learned. Without such knowledge, it may be difficult to tell why students are making errors or to help them overcome their mistakes.
2. *Reduce short-term memory demands to a bare minimum.* Problems that require young grade school children to encode more than three or four bits of information are likely to overload their short-term storage capacity and prevent them from thinking logically about this input. The simplest possible version of a new problem or concept is what teachers should strive to present. If a problem involves several steps, students might be encouraged to break it down into parts (or subroutines) and perhaps to record the solutions to these parts in their notes in order to reduce demands on their short-term storage. Once children grasp a concept and their information processing becomes more "automatized," they will have the short-term storage capacity to succeed at more complex versions of these same problems (Case, 1985; 1992).

3. *Treat the child's incorrect answers as opportunities to promote new learning.* Devise ways of (1) determining whether the child is encoding *all* the task-relevant information and (2) assessing the "rule" that she is using to arrive at her incorrect solution. Failures to encode pertinent information must first be overcome before the child can profit from experiences that illustrate that the rule she favors is inadequate (Siegler, 1976).
4. *Encourage children to "have fun" using their memories.* Strategic games such as 20 Questions or Concentration not only are enjoyable to grade school children but help them to appreciate the advantages of being able to retain information and to retrieve it for a meaningful purpose.
5. *Provide opportunities to learn effective memory strategies.* A teacher can do this by grouping materials into distinct categories as she talks about them or by giving children easily categorizable sets of items to sort and classify (Best, 1993). Question-and-answer games of the form "Tell me why leopards, lions, and house cats are alike" or "How do dragonflies and hummingbirds differ from helicopters and missiles?" are challenging to young children and make them aware of conceptual similarities and differences on which organizational strategies depend.
6. *Structure lessons so that children are likely to acquire metacognitive knowledge and to understand why they should plan, monitor, and control their cognitive activities.* Simply teaching appropriate information-processing strategies does not guarantee that your pupils will use them. If these skills are to transfer to settings other than the training task, it is important that children understand *why* these strategies will help them to achieve their objectives and *when* it is appropriate to use them. As an instructor, you can help by making your own metacognitive knowledge more explicit ("I'll have to read this page more than once to understand it"), offering suggestions to the child ("You might find it easier to remember the months of the year if you group them according to seasons. Summer includes . . ."), or asking questions that remind children of strategies already taught ("Why is it important to summarize what you've read?", "Why do you need to double-check your answer?"). All these approaches have proved quite successful at furthering children's metacognitive skills and persuading them to apply this knowledge to the intellectual challenges they face (Brown et al., 1983; Brown & Campione, 1990; Paris, 1988).

Others have argued that the mind–computer analogy on which the information-processing model is based clearly underestimates the richness of human cognitive activity: After all, people can dream, speculate, create, and reflect on their own (and other people's) cognitive activities and mental states, whereas computers most certainly cannot (Kuhn, 1992). And in some ways, the information-processing approach is just as vague in its explanations of developmental change as Piaget's theory is. Recall that Piaget attributed the growth of logical reasoning in middle childhood to the child's ability to construct and use operational schemes, which, in turn, was said to reflect the influence of maturation, experience, and the reorganization of earlier schemes. Too vague, say information-processing theorists, who choose instead to attribute the growth of logic to increases in the storage capacity of working memory, which result from the automatization of information processing. But how do information-processing theorists explain automatization? They point to factors such as . . . oops! . . . maturation, the growth of one's knowledge base (experience), and the richer organizational and elaborative representations that greater expertise allows (reorganization of schemes)! So if Piaget's theory can be criticized as being vague and imprecise about the underlying causes of development, then current versions of the information-processing approach are obviously subject to some of the same criticisms.

In sum, the information-processing approach is itself a developing theory that has clearly advanced our understanding of children's intellectual growth while experiencing some "growing pains" of its own. I like to think of this model as a necessary complement to, rather than a replacement for, Piaget's earlier framework. And my guess is that this "new look" at cognitive development will continue to evolve, filling in many of the gaps that remain within its own framework and that of Piaget, thereby contributing to a comprehensive theory of intellectual growth that retains the best features of both approaches.

SUMMARY

Learning, a relatively permanent change in behavior resulting from experience, is the process by which we acquire many of our attitudes, habits and abilities. The simplest form of learning is habituation—a process in which infants come to recognize and cease responding to stimuli that are presented over and over. Although habituation may be possible even before birth, this early form of learning improves dramatically over the first few months of life.

In classical conditioning, an initially neutral, or conditioned, stimulus (for example, a bell) is repeatedly paired with a nonneutral, or unconditioned, stimulus (for example, food) that always elicits an unconditioned response (salivation). After several such pairings, the conditioned stimulus alone will acquire the capacity to evoke what is now called a "conditioned" response (in this case, salivation). Although neonates can be classically conditioned, they process information very slowly and are less susceptible to this kind of learning than older infants are. It is important to understand classical conditioning because many of our fears, attitudes, and prejudices may be acquired in this way.

In operant conditioning, the subject first emits a response and then associates this action with a particular outcome. Reinforcers are outcomes that increase the probability that a response will be repeated; punishments are outcomes that suppress an act and decrease the likelihood that it will be repeated. Even very young infants are susceptible to operant conditioning and will recall what they have learned for a period of weeks if subtly reminded of the consequences of their actions.

Punishment, properly applied, can be an effective means of suppressing undesirable conduct. Factors that influence the effectiveness of punishment include its timing, intensity, consistency, and underlying rationale, as well as the relationship between the subject and the punitive agent. When applied improperly, punishment may produce a number of undesirable side effects that limit its usefulness.

Much of what children learn is acquired by observing the behavior of social models. This "observational learning" occurs as the child attends to the model and constructs symbolic representations of the model's behavior. These symbolic codes are then stored in memory and may be retrieved at a later date to guide the child's attempts to imitate the behavior he or she has witnessed. Reinforcement is not necessary for observational *learning;* reinforcement increases the likelihood that children will *perform* that which they have already learned by observing a model. By the end of the first year, children are beginning to imitate social models, and their capacity for observational learning continues to improve throughout childhood.

Although learning is clearly an important developmental process, the behaviorists of yesteryear were incorrect in assuming that children are passive pawns of environmental influence. Human learning is an *active* process that occurs at a *cognitive* level. As learning theorists gradually became more interested in the cognitive aspects of learning and problem solving, many began to study the growth of children's cognitive-processing skills, thereby contributing to a new, information-processing theory of intellectual development.

Information-processing theorists approach the topic of intellectual growth by charting the development of cognitive-processing skills such as attention, memory, and problem solving. Many analogies are drawn between human information processing and the functioning of computers. The human "system" is said to consist of a sensory register to detect or "log in" input; short-term (or working) memory, where information is stored temporarily until we can operate on it; long-term memory, where input that we operate on will remain until we retrieve it to solve problems; and executive control processes by which we plan, monitor, and control all phases of information processing.

In order to understand one's experiences or to solve a problem, one must first attend to the right kinds of information. Between the preschool period and adolescence, children become better able to sustain attention for longer periods, more planful and systematic in their search for information, and more knowledgeable about and practiced in using strategies that permit them to focus selectively on task-relevant information and ignore sources of distraction.

Memory also improves over the course of childhood. Four explanations for these improvements that have received some support are that older children (1) process information faster (or more automatically) than younger children, thus leaving more space in short-term memory for storing task-relevant information; (2) use more effective strategies (rehearsal, organization, and elaboration) for transferring information to long-term memory and retrieving this input; (3) know more about memory processes (metamemory), which helps them to select appropriate memory strategies and to monitor their performance; and (4) have larger knowledge bases than younger children, which improves their ability to learn and remember.

Like Piaget, information-processing theorists have sought to explain how developing children generate hypotheses and solve problems. As children mature, they encode more and more task-relevant information and formulate increasingly sophisticated problem-solving strategies, or *rules,* that are based largely on the information they are encoding. Cognitive-processing theorists agree with Piaget that children progress through a series of "alternative understandings" before mastering certain concepts, but they argue that their rule-assessment approach is better able than Piaget's theory to specify why children of different ages approach problems in different ways.

Despite its many strengths, the information-processing approach has been criticized for underemphasizing social contributions to cognitive growth, failing to produce a broad, integrative theory of children's intelligence, underestimating the richness and diversity of human cognitive activities, and being vague in its *explanation* of cognitive development.

Key Terms

attention deficit–hyperactivity disorder [309]

attention span [307]

automatization [306]

classical conditioning [286]

conditioned response (CR) [286]

conditioned stimulus (CS) [286]

counterconditioning [288]

counting span [313]

continuous reinforcement [290]

cued recall memory [310]

discrimination [286]

dishabituation [285]

elaboration [317]

encoding [302]

executive control processes [305]

extinction [286]

habituation [285]

infantile amnesia [311]

knowledge base [320]

learned helplessness [291]

learning [284]

levels of processing model [305]

long-term memory (LTM) [304]

mature strategy use [316]

mediation deficiency [316]

memory [309]

memory span [313]

M-space [313]

metacognition [318]

metamemory [318]

negative punishment [290]

negative reinforcer [289]

observational learning [297]

operant conditioning [288]

operating efficiency hypothesis [314]

partial reinforcement [290]

positive punishment [290]

positive reinforcer [288]

problem solving [305]

production deficiency [316]

prospective memory [311]

punisher [290]

recall memory [305]

recognition memory [305]

rehearsal [315]

reinforcer [288]

rule assessment [322]

script [311]

semantic organization [316]

sensory store [304]

short-term memory STM [304]

stimulus generalization [286]

store model [304]

unconditioned response (UCR) [286]

unconditioned stimulus (UCS) [286]

utilization deficiency [316]

Intelligence: Measuring Mental Performance

What does it mean to say that someone is intelligent? To Piaget, it suggested that the individual has acquired a number of cognitive structures that enable him or her to solve problems and adapt successfully to the environment. Piaget thought of intelligence as a particular type of logic that people use when answering questions and thinking about everyday issues. He believed that these logical structures change with age and that all children go through the same stages of reasoning as they progress toward intellectual maturity.

By contrast, the person on the street often thinks of intelligence as an indication of how smart someone is *compared with other people*. The implication is that intelligence is a "quantity" that reflects a person's ability to learn new material or to solve various problems. Several years ago, a group of Cornell undergraduates were asked to list the characteristics of "intelligent people." They attributed a wide range of qualities to the intellectually exceptional person, including broad general knowledge, an ability to think logically, common sense, wit, creativity, openness to new experience, and a sensitivity to one's own limitations (Neisser, 1980). Presumably, these students would have mentioned roughly the opposite attributes had they been asked to list the characteristics of "dull," or unintelligent, persons.

Our focus in this chapter is on *individual differences* in intelligence. We will begin by introducing yet another perspective on intellectual development—the *psychometric approach*—that has led to the creation and widespread use of intelligence tests. Unlike the Piagetian and information-processing approaches, which focus on cognitive processes, psychometricians are more *product oriented*. They seek to determine how many and what kinds of questions children can answer *correctly* at different ages and whether or not this index of intellectual performance can predict such developmental outcomes as scholastic achievement, occupational attainments, and even health and life satisfaction.

There may be some surprises ahead as we consider what a person's score on an intelligence test implies about his or her ability to learn, to perform in academic settings, or to succeed at a job. Perhaps the biggest surprise for many people is to learn that intelligence test scores, which can vary dramatically over the course of one's life, are assessments of intellectual *performance* rather than innate potential, or intellectual *capacity*. True, heredity does affect intellectual performance. But so too do a variety of environmental factors that we will examine, including one's cultural and socioeconomic background, the character of one's home environment, the schooling one receives, and even social and emotional factors surrounding the testing situation itself. We will then evaluate the merits of preschool educational programs, such as *Project Head Start*, designed to promote the intellectual development of children who perform poorly on intelligence tests. Finally, we will conclude by exploring the growth of highly valued *creative* talents that are not adequately represented on our current intelligence tests.

 ## WHAT IS INTELLIGENCE?

Although few topics in psychology have generated as much research as intelligence and intelligence testing, even today there is no clear consensus about what intelligence is (Weinberg, 1989). Piaget (1950) defined intelligence as "adaptive thinking or action." Other experts have offered different definitions, but virtually all of them center in some way on the ability to think abstractly or to solve problems effectively (Sternberg, 1991). Before 1960, the prevailing view was that intelligence was an innate capacity for thinking and problem solving that is genetically determined and fixed at conception. Yet, this "fixed capacity" hypothesis waned once it became quite clear that intellectual performance is often not very stable over time and is subject to many sources of environmental influence.

So why is there still no singular definition of intelligence? Because different theorists make very different assumptions about the structure and the stability of those attributes that they view as indications of "intelligent" behavior. Let's now consider some of the more influential viewpoints on the nature of intelligence, beginning with the psychometric approach.

Psychometric Views of Intelligence

The research tradition that spawned the development of standardized intelligence tests has come to be known as the **psychometric approach.** According to psychometric theorists, intelligence can be thought of as a trait or a set of traits that characterizes some people to a greater extent than others. Indeed, the psychometrician's major goals are to identify exactly what these traits are and to *measure* them so that intellectual differences among individuals can be detected and described.

One of the earliest debates among psychometricians centered on the *structure* of intelligence: Was intelligence a single ability that was likely to influence how people perform on all cognitive tests; or, alternatively, was it a number of separate and distinct mental abilities that are only loosely related to each other?

Alfred Binet (1857–1911), the father of intelligence testing.

Alfred Binet's Singular Component Approach

French psychologist Alfred Binet and a colleague, Theodore Simon, produced the forerunner of our modern intelligence tests. In 1904, Binet and Simon were commissioned by the French government to devise a test that would identify "dull" children—slow learners who might profit from remedial instruction. Since their task was a practical one—to predict success at school—Binet and Simon began by constructing a large battery of cognitive tasks that measured skills presumed necessary for classroom learning: processes such as attention, perception, memory, numerical reasoning, and verbal comprehension. These problems were then administered to normal schoolchildren and to those described by their instructors as dull or retarded. Items that did not discriminate between dull and normal children (for example, measures of motor skills) were systematically eliminated from the battery. After several such refinements, Binet and Simon produced a test of "general mental ability" that sampled several kinds of reasoning, could be administered in a little more than an hour, and reliably discriminated children described as dull, average, and bright by their teachers.

Binet's early observations convinced him that intelligence develops with age and that older children and adolescents should be able to perform a wider variety of intellectual tasks than their younger counterparts. In 1908, the Binet-Simon test was revised and all test items were age-graded. For example, problems that were passed by most 6-year-olds but few 5-year-olds were assumed to reflect the mental performance of a typical 6-year-old; those passed by most 12-year-olds but few 11-year-olds were said to measure the intellectual skills of an average 12-year-old; and so on. This age-grading of test items for ages 3–13 allowed a more precise assessment of a child's level of intellectual functioning. A child who passed all items at the 5-year-old level but none at the 6-year-old level is said to have a **mental age (MA)** of 5 years. A child who passed all items at the 10-year-old level and half of those at the 11-year-old level would have an MA of 10½ years.

In sum, Binet had created a test that enabled him to identify slow learners and to estimate their levels of intellectual development with a single score, or mental age. This information proved particularly useful to school administrators, who began to use children's mental ages as a guideline for planning curricula for both normal and retarded students.

Factor Analysis and the Multicomponent View of Intelligence

Other psychometric theorists were quick to challenge the notion that a single score, such as mental age, adequately represents human intellectual performance. Their point was that intelligence tests (even Binet's earliest versions) require people to

psychometric approach: a theoretical perspective that portrays intelligence as a trait (or set of traits) on which individuals differ; psychometric theorists are responsible for the development of standardized intelligence tests.

mental age (MA): a measure of intellectual development that reflects the level of age-graded problems that a child is able to solve.

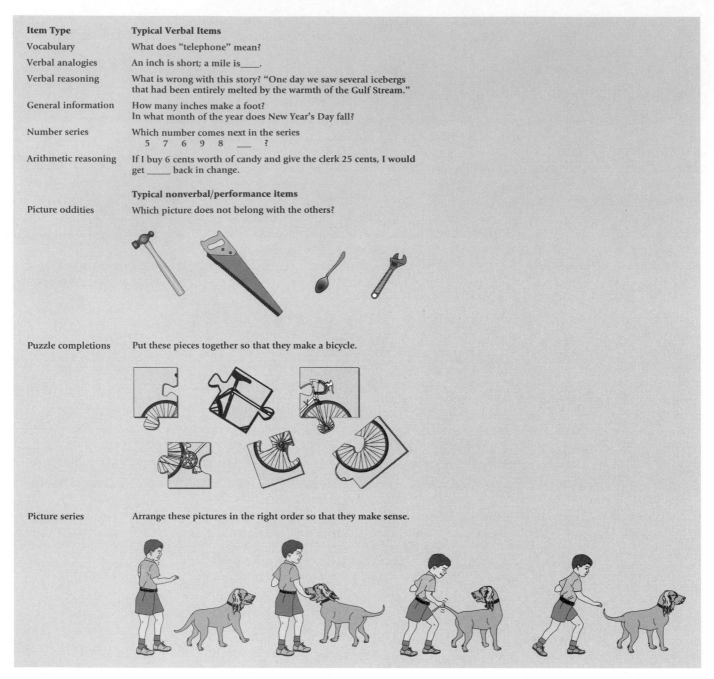

Item Type	Typical Verbal Items
Vocabulary	What does "telephone" mean?
Verbal analogies	An inch is short; a mile is____.
Verbal reasoning	What is wrong with this story? "One day we saw several icebergs that had been entirely melted by the warmth of the Gulf Stream."
General information	How many inches make a foot? In what month of the year does New Year's Day fall?
Number series	Which number comes next in the series 5 7 6 9 8 ___ ?
Arithmetic reasoning	If I buy 6 cents worth of candy and give the clerk 25 cents, I would get _____ back in change.

Typical nonverbal/performance items

Picture oddities   Which picture does not belong with the others?

Puzzle completions   Put these pieces together so that they make a bicycle.

Picture series   Arrange these pictures in the right order so that they make sense.

Figure 9-1
Items similar but not identical to those appearing on intelligence tests for children.

factor analysis: a statistical procedure for identifying clusters of tests or test items (called factors) that are highly correlated with one another and unrelated to other test items.

perform a *variety* of tasks such as defining words or concepts, extracting meaning from written passages, answering general information questions, reproducing geometric designs with blocks, and solving arithmetic puzzles (see Figure 9-1 for some sample items). Weren't these different "subtests" measuring a number of distinct mental abilities rather than a single, overarching ability?

One way of determining whether intelligence is a single attribute or many different attributes is to ask a group of subjects to perform a large number of mental tasks and then analyze their performances using a statistical procedure called **factor analysis.** Simply stated, factor analysis is a correlational technique for finding groups of test items or problems that are highly correlated with one another and yet unrelated to all the remaining items on the test. Clusters of related items are called *factors*, and each factor (if more than one are found) presumably represents a distinct mental ability. Suppose, for example, we found that examinees performed very similarly on four items that require verbal skills and on three items that require mathematical skills, but that their "verbal skill" score was only marginally related to their score on the math items. Under these circumstances, we might conclude that verbal ability and mathematical ability are distinct intellectual factors. But if subjects' verbal and math scores were highly correlated with each other and with scores for all other kinds of mental problems on the test, we might conclude that intelligence is a singular attribute rather than a number of distinct mental abilities.

Early applications of factor analysis. Charles Spearman (1927) was among the first to use factor analysis to try to determine whether intelligence was one or many abilities. He found that a child's scores across a variety of cognitive tests were moderately correlated and thus inferred that there must be a *general mental factor,* which he called *g,* that affects one's performance on most cognitive tasks. However, he also noticed that intellectual performance was often inconsistent: A student who excelled at most tasks, for example, might perform poorly on a particular test, such as verbal analogies or musical aptitude. So Spearman proposed that intellectual performance has two aspects: *g,* or general ability, and *s,* or special abilities, each of which is specific to a particular test.

Several years later, Louis Thurstone (1938; Thurstone & Thurstone, 1941) factor-analyzed some 50 mental tests that he administered to eighth-graders and college students. In contrast to Spearman's results, Thurstone obtained *seven* factors that he called **primary mental abilities**: spatial ability, perceptual speed (quick processing of visual information), numerical reasoning, verbal meaning (defining words), word fluency (speed at recognizing words), memory, and inductive reasoning (forming a rule that describes a set of observations). He thus concluded that Spearman's *g* really consists of seven distinct mental abilities.

Later factor-analytic models. Spearman's and Thurstone's early work implied that there must be a relatively small number of basic mental abilities that make up what we call "intelligence." A very different point of view has been voiced by J. P. Guilford (1967; 1988), who proposes that there are more than 100 distinct mental abilities. He arrived at this figure by first classifying cognitive tasks along three major dimensions: (1) *content* (what must the person think about), (2) *operations* (what kind of thinking is the person asked to perform), and (3) *products* (what kind of answer is required). Guilford argued that there are five kinds of intellectual contents, six kinds of mental operations, and six kinds of intellectual products. Thus, his **"structure of intellect" model** allows for as many as 180 primary mental abilities, based on all the possible combinations of the various intellectual contents, operations, and products (that is, $5 \times 6 \times 6 = 180$).

Guilford then set out to construct tests to measure each of his 180 mental abilities. For example, the test of "social intelligence" illustrated in Figure 9-2 measures the mental ability that requires the test taker to act on a *behavioral* content (the figure's facial expression), using a particular operation, *cognition,* to produce a particular product, the probable *implication* of that expression. To date, tests have been constructed to assess more than 100 of the 180 mental abilities in Guilford's model of intellect. However, the scores that people make on these presumably independent intellectual factors are often correlated, suggesting that these abilities are not nearly so independent as Guilford assumed (Brody, 1992).

So what have we learned from factor-analytic studies of intelligence? Perhaps that both Spearman and Thurstone were partially correct. Indeed, many psychometricians today favor a **hierarchical model of intellect** in which intelligence is viewed as consisting of (1) a general ability factor at the top of the hierarchy, which influences one's performance on most cognitive tests, and (2) a number of specialized ability factors (something similar to Thurstone's primary mental abilities) that influence how well one performs in particular intellectual domains (for example, on tests of

g: Spearman's abbreviation for *neogenesis,* which, roughly translated, means one's ability to understand relations (or general mental ability).

s: Spearman's term for mental abilities that are specific to particular tests.

primary mental abilities: seven mental abilities, identified by factor analysis, that Thurstone believed to represent the structure of intelligence.

"structure of intellect" model: Guilford's factor-analytic model of intelligence, which proposes that there are 180 distinct mental abilities.

hierarchical model of intelligence: model of the structure of intelligence in which a broad, general ability factor is at the top of the hierarchy, with a number of specialized ability factors categorized underneath.

Figure 9-2
An item from one of Guilford's tests of social intelligence. The task is to read the characters' expressions and to decide what the person marked by the arrow is most probably saying to the other person. You may wish to try this item yourself (the correct answer appears below).
Adapted from Guilford, 1967.

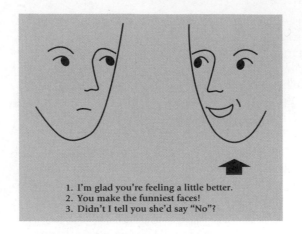

1. I'm glad you're feeling a little better.
2. You make the funniest faces!
3. Didn't I tell you she'd say "No"?

numerical reasoning or tests of verbal skills; see Carroll, 1992; Gardner & Clark, 1992). This model thus depicts children as having particular intellectual strengths and weaknesses, depending upon the patterns of specialized abilities they display. It also explains how a child of average general ability might actually excel in one particular area (for example, verbal analogies or visual-spatial tasks) if she displays an unusually high special ability for that kind of reasoning.

Another modern psychometric view of intelligence. Finally, Raymond Cattell and John Horn have influenced current thinking about intelligence by proposing that Spearman's *g* and Thurstone's primary mental abilities can be divided into two major dimensions of intellect: *fluid intelligence* and *crystallized intelligence* (Cattell, 1963; Horn & Cattell, 1982; Horn & Hofer, 1992). **Fluid intelligence** refers to one's ability to solve novel and abstract problems of the sort that are not taught and are relatively free of cultural influences. Examples of the kinds of problems that tap fluid intelligence are the verbal analogies and number series tests from Figure 9-1, as well as tests of one's ability to recognize relationships among otherwise meaningless geometric figures (see Figure 9-7 on page 361 for an example). By contrast, **crystallized intelligence** is the ability to solve problems that depend on knowledge acquired as a result of schooling and other life experiences. Tests of general information ("At what temperature does water boil?"), word comprehension ("What is the meaning of *duplicate?*"), and numerical abilities are all measures of crystallized intelligence.

The Cattell/Horn theory has a distinct developmental flavor. Crystallized intelligence is said to increase throughout the life span, since it is primarily a reflection of one's cumulative learning experiences. Fluid intelligence, in contrast, is said to increase gradually throughout childhood and adolescence as the nervous system matures. It should then level off during young adulthood and gradually decline with age. Many investigators have found that individuals do improve with age on measures of crystallized intelligence but show age-related declines (primarily after age 60) on measures of fluid intelligence (Schaie & Hertzog, 1986). Yet, much of the eventual decline that people display on tests of fluid intelligence results not from a loss of reasoning ability but from a gradual slowing of information processing in old age (Hertzog, 1989; Salthouse, 1993). And even better news is that elderly people who have remained intellectually active often retain their mental prowess well into their 70s, or even their 80s (Schaie, 1990).

The concepts of fluid and crystallized intelligence have proved useful, but there are those who believe that none of the psychometric theories of intelligence have fully described what it means to be an intelligent person. Let's now examine two new

fluid intelligence: the ability to perceive relationships and solve relational problems of a type that are not taught and are relatively free of cultural influences.

crystallized intelligence: the ability to understand relations or solve problems that depend on knowledge acquired from schooling and other cultural influences.

Answer to task in Figure 9-2: 3.

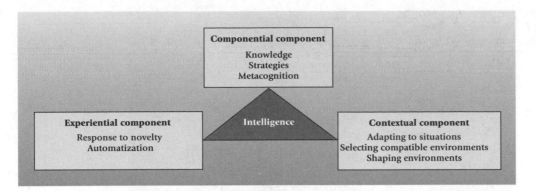

Figure 9-3
Sternberg's triarchic theory of
intelligence.

perspectives on intelligence that are quite different from those of psychometric theorists—perspectives that should help us to appreciate some of the limitations of today's intelligence tests.

A Modern Information-Processing Viewpoint

One recurring criticism of psychometric definitions of intelligence is that they are very narrow—focusing primarily on intellectual content, or *what* the child knows, rather than on the processes by which this knowledge is acquired, retained, and used to solve problems. Moreover, psychometric assessments of intelligence (that is, intelligence tests) measure one's proficiency at mathematical, verbal, and spatial reasoning while ignoring other attributes that people commonly think of as indications of intelligence, such as common sense, social and interpersonal skills, and the talents that underlie creative accomplishments in music, drama, and athletics (Gardner, 1983).

Recently, Robert Sternberg (1985; 1991) has proposed a **triarchic theory of intelligence** that emphasizes three aspects, or components, of intelligent behavior: *context, experience,* and *information-processing* skills (see Figure 9-3). As we will see in reviewing this model, Sternberg's view of intelligence is much, much broader than that of psychometric theorists.

Context

The contextual component of Sternberg's model is a relatively simple idea: Whether an act qualifies as "intelligent" behavior depends to a large extent on the social or sociocultural context in which it is displayed. According to Sternberg, intelligent people are those who can successfully adapt to their environments or who are successful at shaping their environments to suit them better. In everyday language, we might describe this kind of intelligence as practical wisdom or "street smarts." Unfortunately, this ability to tailor one's behavior to the demands of the environment is not assessed in traditional intelligence tests.

Notice that from this "contextual" perspective, what is meant by intelligent behavior may vary from one culture or subculture to another, from one historical epoch to another, and from one period of the life span to another. Sternberg describes an occasion when he attended a conference in Venezuela and showed up on time, at 8:00 A.M., only to find that he and four other North Americans were the only ones there. In North American society, it is considered "smart" to be punctual for important engagements. However, strict punctuality is not so important in Latin cultures, where people are rather lax (by our standards, at least) about being on time. And consider the effects of history on assessments of intelligence. Thirty years ago, it was considered "intelligent" indeed to be able to perform arithmetic operations quickly and accurately. However, an individual who spends countless hours perfecting these same skills today might be considered somewhat less than intelligent given that computers and calculators can perform these computations much faster. Finally, what is

triarchic theory: a recent information-processing theory of intelligence that emphasizes three aspects of intelligent behavior not normally tapped by IQ tests: the context of the action, the person's experience with the task (or situation), and the information-processing strategies that the person applies to the task (or situation).

The sophisticated ability that this child displays is considered intelligent in his culture, but is not measured by traditional IQ tests.

The sophisticated ability that this child displays is considered intelligent in his culture, but is not measured by traditional IQ tests.

considered intelligent depends to no small extent on the age of the actor. An 8-month-old who delights at making a jack-in-the-box work might be considered rather curious, creative, and intelligent. But were you to spend 10 minutes performing the very same actions, many observers would undoubtedly conclude that you are a bit slow, or even retarded.

The Experiential Component

According to Sternberg, one's experience with a task helps to determine whether one's actions or performance qualify as intelligent behavior. He believes that relatively novel tasks require active and conscious information processing and are the best measures of children's reasoning abilities—as long as these tasks are not so totally foreign that the child is unable to apply what he may know (as would be the case if geometry problems were presented to 5-year-olds). *Responses to novelty*, then, are an indication of the person's ability to generate good ideas or fresh insights.

In daily life, however, people also perform more or less intelligently on familiar tasks (such as driving, balancing a checkbook, or quickly extracting the most interesting or important content from a newspaper). This second kind of intelligence reflects *automatization*, or increasing efficiency of information processing with practice. According to Sternberg, it is a sign of intelligence when we develop automatized routines or "programs of the mind" for performing our everyday tasks accurately and efficiently, so that we don't have to waste much time thinking about them.

The experiential component of Sternberg's theory has a most important implication for intelligence testers: In order to properly assess a person's intellectual prowess from the answers he gives, you have to know how familiar the task is to the test taker and, thus, which aspect of intelligence—response to novelty or automatization—his answer reflects. A child who struggles with and finally solves a problem after 2–3 minutes might be considered highly intelligent if the problem is novel, but rather dull if this task is like others he has performed many, many times before. Similarly, if the items on an intelligence test are familiar to members of one cultural group but unfamiliar to members of another, the second group will perform much worse than the first, thereby reflecting a **cultural bias** in the test itself. So if one is seeking to compare the intellectual performances of people from diverse cultural backgrounds, one's test items must be equally familiar (or unfamiliar) to all test takers.

The Componential (or Information-Processing) Component

Sternberg's major criticism of psychometric theorists is that they estimate a person's intelligence from the quality, or correctness, of her answers while completely ignoring *how* she produces intelligent responses. Sternberg is an information-processing

cultural bias: the situation that arises when one cultural or subcultural group is more familiar with test items than is another group and therefore has an unfair advantage.

theorist who believes that we must now begin to focus on the componental aspects of intelligent behavior—that is, the cognitive processes by which we size up the requirements of problems, formulate strategies to solve them, and then monitor our cognitive activities until we've accomplished our goals. He argues that some people process information more efficiently than others and that our cognitive tests could be improved considerably were they to measure these differences and treat them as an important aspect of intelligence.

In sum, Sternberg's triarchic theory provides us with a very rich view of the nature of intelligence. It suggests that if you want to know how intelligent Charles, Chico, and Chenghuan are, you had better consider (1) the *context* in which they are performing (that is, the culture and historical period in which they live; their ages); (2) their *experience* with the tasks and whether their behavior qualifies as responses to novelty or automatized processes, and (3) the *information-processing skills* that reflect how each of them is approaching these tasks. Unfortunately, the most widely used intelligence tests are not based on such a broad and sophisticated view of intellectual processes.

Gardner's Theory of Multiple Intelligences

Howard Gardner is another theorist who criticizes the psychometricians for trying to describe a person's intelligence with a single score. In his book *Frames of Mind*, Gardner (1983) outlines his **theory of multiple intelligences,** which proposes that human beings display at least seven distinctive kinds of intelligence (described in Table 9-1).

Gardner does not claim that these seven abilities represent *the* list of intelligences. But he makes the case that each ability is distinct, is linked to a specific area of the brain, and follows a different developmental course. As support for these ideas, Gardner cites evidence that injury to a particular area of the brain usually influences only one ability (linguistic or spatial, for example), leaving others unaffected. As further evidence for the independence of these abilities, Gardner notes that some individuals are truly exceptional in one ability but poor in others.

This is dramatically clear in individuals known as **idiot savants,** who have an extraordinary talent but who are otherwise mentally retarded. Leslie Lemke is one such individual. He is blind, has cerebral palsy, and is mentally retarded, and he could not talk until he was an adult. Yet he can hear a musical piece once and play it flawlessly on the piano or imitate songs in German or Italian perfectly even though his own speech in his native language, English, is still primitive. Other idiot savants,

---

Concept Check 9-1 ⌄ Recognizing Different Perspectives on Intelligence

Check your understanding of various theories on the nature of intelligence by matching the names of their originators with the brief descriptions of the theories' main themes that appear below. Choose from among the following theorists: (a) Raymond Cattell/John Horn; (b) Howard Gardner; (c) J. P. Guilford; (d) Charles Spearman; (e) Robert Sternberg; (f) Louis Thurstone. The answers appear in the Appendix.

_____ 1. This theorist proposes that there may be as many as 180 distinct mental abilities.

_____ 2. This theorist claims that intelligence consists of a general mental factor, or *g*, and a number of special abilities, *s*, each of which is specific to a particular kind of reasoning.

_____ 3. This theorist thinks that there are seven distinctive kinds of intelligence, several of which (for example, musical intelligence) are not measured on intelligence tests.

_____ 4. This psychometrician also claims that there are seven forms of intelligence that he identified through factor analysis and called *primary mental abilities*.

_____ 5. This theory claims that *g*, or general mental ability, and the so-called primary mental abilities can be divided into two kinds of intelligence: *fluid* and *crystallized*.

_____ 6. This person's theory emphasizes three aspects of intelligence: the *contextual, experiential,* and *componental* (or information-processing) components.

theory of multiple intelligences: Gardner's theory that humans display at least seven distinct kinds of intelligence, each linked to a particular area of the brain, and several of which are not measured by IQ tests.

idiot savant: a person who has an extraordinary talent but is otherwise mentally retarded.

Table 9-1 Gardner's Multiple Intelligences

Type of intelligence	Intellectual processes	Vocational end-states
Linguistic	Sensitivity to the meaning and sounds of words, to the structure of language, and to the many ways language can be used.	Poet, novelist, journalist
Spatial	Ability to perceive visual-spatial relationships accurately, to transform these perceptions, and to re-create aspects of one's visual experience in the absence of the pertinent stimuli.	Engineer, sculptor, cartographer
Logical-mathematical	Ability to operate on and to perceive relationships in abstract symbol systems and to think logically and systematically in evaluating one's ideas.	Mathematician, scientist
Musical	Sensitivity to pitch, melody; ability to combine tones and musical phrases into larger rhythms; understanding of the emotional aspects of music.	Musician, composer
Body-kinesthetic	Ability to use the body skillfully to express oneself or achieve goals; ability to handle objects skillfully.	Dancer, athlete
Interpersonal	Ability to detect and respond appropriately to the moods, temperaments, motives, and intentions of others.	Therapist, minister, public relations specialist
Intrapersonal	Sensitivity to one's own inner states; recognition of personal strengths and weaknesses and ability to use information about the self to behave adaptively.	Contributes to success in almost any walk of life

Source: Adapted from Gardner, 1983.

despite their abysmal performance on intelligence tests, can draw well enough to gain admittance to art school or calculate almost instantaneously what day of the week January 16, 1909 was (O'Connor & Hermelin, 1991). Finally, different intelligences do seem to develop at different rates. Many of the great composers and athletes, for example, began to display their immense talents in childhood, whereas logical-mathematical intelligence often shows up much later in life.

Gardner's ideas have had an impact, particularly on investigators who study the development of creativity and special talents—a topic we will explore at the end of this chapter. Nevertheless, his theory has been criticized on several grounds. Perhaps the major criticism is that Gardner's seven intelligences are nowhere near as independent as he claims them to be. For example, individuals who are exceptionally talented in one area (for example, in music) are often talented in several other areas as well (Feldman & Goldsmith, 1991). Moreover, current intelligence tests do tap Gardner's linguistic, spatial, and logical-mathematical intelligences, which are moderately correlated rather than highly distinct. Perhaps it is too early, then, to reject the concept of g, or general mental ability. Yet Gardner is almost certainly correct in arguing that we misrepresent and underestimate the talents of many individuals by trying to characterize their "intelligence" with a single test score.

One final point: It may say something about Western cultures that we seem to value some of Gardner's intelligences far more than others. We provide gifted programs to children who score high on traditional IQ tests and compensatory or remedial education to those who don't show much talent in reading, math, or science. By contrast, recent American immigrants from Asia and Mexico have a different perspective, often viewing such attributes as motivation, self-regulation, and social skills as every bit as important to defining "intelligence" as the more traditional cognitive skills measured by our intelligence tests (Okagaki & Sternberg, 1993). Perhaps as we learn more about such abilities as musical, bodily, and inter- or intrapersonal intelligences, we will do more to foster these talents as well.

 ## HOW IS INTELLIGENCE MEASURED?

When psychologists began to construct intelligence tests at the beginning of this century, their concern was not with defining the nature of intelligence but with the more practical goals of determining which schoolchildren were likely to be slow learners. Recall that Binet and Simon produced a test that accomplished this goal and characterized each child's intellectual development with a single score, or *mental age*. Among the more popular of our contemporary intelligence tests for children is a direct descendant of Binet and Simon's early test.

The Stanford-Binet Intelligence Scale

In 1916, Lewis Terman of Stanford University translated and published a revised version of the Binet scale for use with American children. This test came to be known as the *Stanford-Binet Intelligence Scale*.

Like Binet's scale, the original version of the Stanford-Binet consisted of a series of age-graded tasks designed to measure the average intellectual performance of subjects aged 3 through 13. Terman first gave his test to a sample of about 1000 middle-class American schoolchildren in order to establish performance norms against which the individual child could be compared. But unlike Binet, who classified children according to mental age, Terman favored the use of a ratio measure of intelligence that came to be known as an **intelligence quotient,** or **IQ.** The child's IQ, which was conceptualized as a measure of his brightness or rate of intellectual development, was calculated by dividing his mental age by his chronological age and then multiplying by 100:

$$IQ = MA/CA \times 100$$

Notice that an IQ of 100 indicates average intelligence; it means that the child has passed all the items that age-mates typically pass and none of the items at the next higher level, so that *her mental age is exactly equal to her chronological age.* An IQ greater than 100 indicates that the child's performance is comparable with that of people who are older than she is, whereas an IQ less than 100 means that her intellectual performance matches that of children somewhat younger than herself.

A much revised version of the Stanford-Binet is still in use (Thorndike, Hagen, & Sattler, 1986). Its **test norms** are now based on representative samples of people from many socioeconomic and racial backgrounds rather than merely reflecting the performance of white, middle-class schoolchildren. And unlike earlier versions, which were appropriate for 3–13-year-olds, the modern Stanford-Binet is suitable for testing individuals between 2 and 18 years of age. The test continues to measure those abilities thought to be most important for academic success: verbal reasoning, quantitative (or numerical reasoning), spatial reasoning, and short-term memory.

Interestingly, neither the Stanford-Binet nor any other widely used intelligence test continues to rely on mental age to calculate IQs. The major criticism of the mental age concept was that it led to inappropriate conclusions. Are, for example, an 8-year-old with a mental age of 12 and a 12-year-old with the same mental age equally intelligent? Probably not. Being four years younger and far less knowledgeable, the

intelligence quotient (IQ): a numerical measure of a person's performance on an intelligence test relative to the performance of other examinees.

test norms: standards of normal performance on psychometric instruments that are based on the average scores and the range of scores obtained by a large, representative sample of test takers.

first child may have trouble keeping up with the second in many academic subjects, particularly those requiring an appreciation of abstract concepts (Piaget, 1970; Sattler, 1988). Furthermore, using mental ages to calculate IQs means that the same IQ will have different meanings at different ages (Bjorklund, 1995). To illustrate, a 4-year-old needs to score only 1 year above her chronological age to attain an IQ of 125, whereas an 8-year-old must score a full 2 years beyond his chronological age to attain the same IQ.

These and other problems have led IQ testers to rely on a new scoring procedure known as the **deviation IQ.** A child's test performance is now compared with that of *other children his own age* and not with the performances of younger and older children. Using this procedure, an 8-year-old would be considered bright, average, or dull depending on how far his or her test score deviates from the average performance of other 8-year-olds. An IQ of 100 is still average, and the higher (or lower) an IQ score an individual attains, the better (or worse) his performance is in comparison with age-mates.

The Wechsler Scales

Professor David Wechsler of the New York University–Bellevue Medical School has constructed two intelligence tests for children, both of which are now widely used. The *Wechsler Intelligence Scale for Children–III (WISC–III)* is appropriate for school-children aged 6 to 16, whereas the *Wechsler Preschool and Primary Scale of Intelligence–Revised (WPPSI–R)*, is designed for preschoolers between ages 3 and 8 (Wechsler, 1989; 1991).

One reason that Wechsler constructed his own intelligence tests is that he believed the Stanford-Binet was too heavily loaded with items that require verbal skills. Wechsler suggested that many intellectual skills are predominantly *nonverbal*—abilities that were not adequately represented on earlier versions of Binet-type scales. He also argued that the heavy verbal bias of the Stanford-Binet test discriminates against children who have certain language handicaps—for example, those for whom English is a second language or those who have reading difficulties or are hard of hearing.

Wechsler tried to overcome these problems by constructing intelligence scales that contain both verbal subtests and nonverbal, or "performance," subtests. Items on the verbal subtests are very similar to those on the Stanford-Binet. They are designed to measure the child's vocabulary, general knowledge, understanding of ideas and concepts, arithmetic reasoning, and the like. By contrast, items on the performance subtests are designed to assess predominantly nonverbal skills, such as the ability to assemble puzzles, solve mazes, reproduce geometric designs with colored blocks, and rearrange sets of pictures so that they tell a meaningful story. When the examinee's performance is evaluated, he or she is assigned three scores: a verbal IQ, a performance IQ, and a full-scale IQ based on a combination of the first two measures.

The Wechsler scales soon became quite popular. Not only did they tap a wider variety of intellectual skills than did earlier versions of the Stanford-Binet but they were also sensitive to inconsistencies in intellectual performance that may be early signs of brain damage or learning disorders. (For example, children with reading disorders often do much worse on the verbal component of the WISC.)

Distribution of IQ Scores

If a young girl scores 130 on the Stanford-Binet or the WISC, we know that her IQ is above average. But how bright is she? To tell, we would have to know something about the way IQs are distributed in the population at large.

One interesting feature of all modern IQ tests is that people's scores are **normally distributed** around an IQ of 100 (see Figure 9-4). This patterning of scores is hardly an accident. By definition, the average score made by examinees from each age group is set at 100, and this is the most common score that people make. Note that

deviation IQ: an IQ score based on the extent to which a child's test performance deviates from the average performance of age-mates.

normal distribution: a symmetrical, bell-shaped curve that describes the variability of certain characteristics within a population; most people fall at or near the average score, with relatively few at the extremes of the distribution.

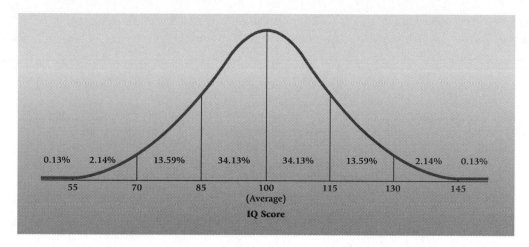

Figure 9-4
The approximate distribution of IQ scores people make on contemporary intelligence tests. These tests are constructed so that the average score made by examinees in each age group is equivalent to an IQ of 100. Note that more than two-thirds of all examinees score within 15 points of this average (that is, IQs of 85–115) and that 95% of the population score within 30 points of average (IQs of 70–130).
Adapted from Sattler.

approximately half the population scores below 100 and half above. Moreover, roughly equal numbers of examinees obtain IQs of 85 and 115 (15 points from the average) or 70 and 130 (30 points from average). To determine the meaning of an IQ of 130, we can look at Table 9-2, which shows what percentage of the population the person outperforms by scoring at that level. Here we see that an IQ of 130 equals or exceeds the IQs of 97% of the population; it is a very high IQ indeed. Similarly, fewer than 3% of all test takers obtain IQs below 70, a cutoff that is commonly used today to define mental retardation.

Group Tests of Mental Performance

Both the Stanford-Binet and the Wechsler scales are expensive and time consuming. These tests must be administered individually by a professional examiner, and assessing the IQ of a single examinee can take more than an hour. The costs of administering individual intelligence tests to a large number of people—army recruits, job applicants, or thousands of students in a city's public schools—can become prohibitive.

During World War I, psychologists were commissioned by the U.S. Army to develop a paper-and-pencil intelligence test that could be administered to large

Table 9-2   The Meaning of Different IQ Scores

An IQ of	Equals or exceeds—% of the population	An IQ of	Equals or exceeds—% of the population
160	99.99	100	50
140	99.3	95	38
135	98	90	27
130	97	85	18
125	94	80	11
120	89	75	6
115	82	70	3
110	73	65	2
105	62	62	1

groups of inductees to quickly weed out the very dull and to place the others into military occupations in accordance with their mental capabilities. Once developed, this first "group" test, or *Army Alpha*, was routinely used to classify and assign military personnel. As Wrightsman and Sanford (1975, p. 124) have noted, "Many of our . . . grandfathers had their military careers—and perhaps their lives—determined by their performance on this test."

It is likely that you have taken a group test of intelligence (or scholastic aptitude) at some point in your academic career. Among the more widely used of these tests are the Lorge-Thorndike Test, which is designed for grade school and high school students, the Scholastic Aptitude Test (SAT) and the American College Test (ACT), taken by many college applicants, and the Graduate Record Examination (GRE), often required of applicants to graduate school. These instruments are sometimes called "achievement" tests because they call for specific information that the examinee has learned at school (that is, what Cattell and Horn call *crystallized intelligence*) and are designed to predict future academic achievement.

Newer Approaches to Intelligence Testing

Although both the Stanford-Binet and the Wechsler scales are widely used today, new tests are constantly being developed. For example, there are now intelligence scales based on Piagetian concepts and developmental milestones (see Humphreys, Rich, & Davey, 1985). The *Kaufman Assessment Battery for Children* (K-ABC), another recent test, is based on modern information-processing theory. The test is heavily nonverbal in content, primarily measuring what Cattell and Horn call *fluid intelligence*. Several features have been incorporated in an attempt to reduce cultural bias and make the K-ABC fairer than other tests to minority, low-income, and handicapped youngsters. For example, test items were carefully selected so as to be equally familiar (or unfamiliar) to all test takers. And unlike other tests, the examiner has considerable flexibility in administering the K-ABC, even to the point of providing prompts or hints to get children to respond (Kaufman & Kaufman, 1983). But despite these strengths, information-processing theorists have criticized the K-ABC for its heavy emphasis on the most basic processing skills, namely rote learning and short-term memory (Sternberg, 1984).

Other investigators, disenchanted with the ways in which intelligence has been defined and measured, have developed entirely new approaches to intellectual assessment. One promising approach called **dynamic assessment** attempts to evaluate how well children actually learn new material when an examiner provides them with competent instruction (Campione, Brown, Ferrara, & Bryant, 1984; Frisby & Braden, 1992). Reuven Feuerstein and his colleagues (1979), for example, have argued that, even though intelligence is often defined as a *potential* to learn from experience, IQ tests typically assess *what has been learned*, not what can be learned. Thus, the traditional psychometric approach may be biased against children from culturally diverse or disadvantaged backgrounds who lack opportunities to learn what the tests measure. Feuerstein's *Learning Potential Assessment Device* asks children to learn new things with the guidance of an adult who provides increasingly helpful cues—precisely the kind of social learning that Vygotsky emphasizes in his sociocultural theory. This test interprets intelligence as the ability to learn quickly with minimal guidance. Robert Sternberg (1985, 1991) uses a similar approach in a test he has constructed based on his triarchic theory of intelligence. To better understand the information processes involved in verbal ability, for example, Sternberg does not ask people to define words they learned in the past, as IQ testers so often do. Instead, he places an unfamiliar word in a set of sentences and asks people to learn, from *context*, what the new word means, just as they must do in real life.

In sum, modern perspectives on intelligence are now beginning to be reflected in the content of intelligence tests. However, these new tests and testing procedures have a very short history, and it remains to be seen whether they will eventually

dynamic assessment: an approach to assessing intelligence that evaluates how well individuals learn new material when an examiner provides them with competent instruction.

replace more traditional assessments of mental performance, such as the WISC and the Stanford-Binet.

Assessing Infant Intelligence

None of the standard intelligence tests can be used with children much younger than 2½ because the test items require verbal skills and attention spans that infants do not have. However, attempts have been made to measure infant "intelligence" by assessing the rate at which babies achieve important developmental milestones. Perhaps the best known and most widely used of the infant tests is the *Bayley Scales of Infant Development* (Bayley, 1969; 1993). This instrument, designed for infants aged 2 to 30 months, has three parts:

1. The *motor* scale (which assesses such motor capabilities as grasping a cube, throwing a ball, or drinking from a cup).
2. The *mental* scale (which includes adaptive behaviors such as reaching for a desirable object, searching for a hidden toy, and following directions).
3. The *Infant Behavioral Record* (a rating of the child's behavior on dimensions such as goal directedness, fearfulness, and social responsivity).

On the basis of the first two scores, the infant is given a **DQ**, or **developmental quotient,** rather than an IQ. The DQ summarizes how well or poorly the infant performs in comparison with a large norm group of infants the same age.

Do DQs Predict Later IQs?

Infant scales are very useful for charting babies' developmental progress and for diagnosing neurological disorders and other signs of mental retardation—even when these conditions are fairly mild and difficult to detect in a standard neurological exam (Honzik, 1983). Yet, these instruments generally fail to predict a child's later IQ or scholastic achievements (Honzik, 1983; McCall, 1983; Rose et al., 1989). In fact, a DQ measured early in infancy may not even predict the child's DQ later in infancy!

Why do infant tests not do a better job at predicting children's later IQs? Perhaps the main reason is that infant tests and IQ tests tap very different kinds of abilities. Infant scales are designed to measure sensory, motor, language, and social skills, whereas standardized IQ tests such as the WISC and the Stanford-Binet emphasize more abstract abilities such as verbal reasoning, concept formation, and problem solving. So to expect an infant test to predict the later results of an IQ test is like expecting a yardstick to tell us how much someone weighs. There may be some correspondence between the two measures (a yardstick indicates height, which is correlated with weight; DQ indicates developmental progress, which is related to IQ), but the relationship is not very great.

New Evidence for Continuity in Intellectual Performance

Is it foolish, then, to think that we might ever accurately forecast a child's later IQ from his or her behavior during infancy? Maybe not. As we learned in Chapter 8, information processing theorists have discovered that certain measures of infant attention and memory are much better at predicting IQ during the preschool and early grade school years than are the Bayley scales or other measures of infant development. Two attributes appear especially promising: the speed at which infants *habituate* to repetitive stimuli and the extent to which they prefer novel stimuli to familiar ones *(preference for novelty)*. Indeed, measures of these two information-processing skills obtained during the first 6–8 months have an average correlation of .45 with IQ in childhood, particularly verbal IQ and memory skills (Bornstein & Sigman, 1986; McCall & Carriger, 1993; Thompson, Fagan, & Fulker, 1991). These same measures also predict the later intellectual performance of premature infants (Rose

developmental quotient (DQ): a numerical measure of an infant's performance on a developmental schedule relative to the performance of other infants of the same age.

et al., 1992) and are the basis for a new infant test, the *Fagan Test of Infant Intelligence*, which is as good (or better) than the Bayley scales at diagnosing mental retardation (Fagan, 1985; Fagan, Shepherd, & Knevel, 1991).

So there is some continuity between infant intelligence and childhood intelligence after all. Perhaps we can now characterize the "smart" infant as one who prefers and seeks out novel experiences and who soaks up new information quickly—in short, an efficient information processor.

Stability of IQ in Childhood and Adolescence

It was once assumed that a person's IQ reflected his or her genetically determined intellectual *capacity* and would remain quite stable over time. In other words, a child with an IQ of 120 at age 5 was expected to obtain a similar IQ at age 10, 15, or 20.

How much support is there for this idea? As we have seen, infant DQs do not predict later IQ test scores very well at all. But starting at about age 4, there is a fairly strong relationship between early and later IQs (see, for example, Sameroff et al., 1993), and the relationship grows even stronger during middle childhood. Table 9-3 summarizes the results of a longitudinal study of more than 250 children conducted at the University of California (Honzik, Macfarlane, & Allen, 1948). In examining these data, we see that the shorter the interval between two testings, the higher the correlations between children's IQ scores. But even when a number of years have passed, IQ seems to be a very stable attribute. After all, the scores that children obtain at age 8 are still clearly related to those they obtain 10 years later at age 18.

There is something that these correlations are not telling us, however. Each of them is based on a large group of children, and they do not necessarily mean that the IQs of *individual children* will remain stable over time. Robert McCall and his associates looked at the IQ scores of 140 children who had taken intelligence tests at regular intervals between age 2½ and 17 (McCall, Applebaum, & Hogarty, 1973). Their findings were remarkable. More than half of these individuals displayed fluctuations in IQ over time, and the average range of variation in the IQ scores of these "fluctuators" was a whopping 28.5 points. One child in seven showed changes of at least 40 points, and changes of more than 70 points are not unknown (Hindley & Owen, 1978).

So it seems that IQ is more stable for some children than for others. Clearly, these findings challenge the notion that IQ is a reflection of one's absolute potential for learning or intellectual capacity; if it were, the intellectual profiles of virtually all children would be highly stable, showing only minor variations due to errors of measurement.

What, then, does an IQ represent, if not one's intellectual competence or ability? Today, many experts believe that an IQ score is merely an estimate of the examinee's intellectual *performance* at one particular point in time—an estimate that may or may not be a good indication of the examinee's intellectual capacity. And the fact that IQs can vary upward or downward suggests that environment must play a crucial role in determining intellectual performance. Indeed, the authors of the California longitudinal study were intrigued to find that the children whose IQ scores fluctuated the most were those from unstable home environments—that is, youngsters whose life experiences had also fluctuated between periods of happiness and turmoil (Honzik et al., 1948).

 # WHAT DO INTELLIGENCE TESTS PREDICT?

We have seen that IQ tests measure intellectual performance rather than capacity and that a person's IQ may vary considerably over time. At this point, it seems reasonable to ask whether IQ scores can tell anything very meaningful about the people

	Correlation with	Correlation with
Age of child	IQ at age 10	IQ at age 18
4	.66	.42
6	.76	.61
8	.88	.70
10	—	.76
12	.87	.76

Table 9-3 Correlations of IQs Measured during the Preschool Years and Middle Childhood, with IQs Measured at Ages 10 and 18

Source: Adapted from Honzik, MacFarlane, & Allen, 1948.

who were tested. For example, does IQ predict future academic accomplishments? Is it in any way related to a person's health, occupational status, or general life satisfaction? Let's first consider the relationship between IQ and academic achievement.

IQ as a Predictor of Scholastic Achievement

Since the original purpose of IQ testing was to estimate how well children would perform at school, it should come as no surprise that modern intelligence tests do predict academic achievement. The average correlation between children's IQ scores and their *current* grades at school is about .50 (Minton & Schneider, 1980). Moreover, assessments of IQ (or scholastic aptitude) can predict *future* academic performance. In one longitudinal study, children's IQs measured in the fourth grade were highly correlated (+.73) with their scores on standardized achievement tests in the sixth grade (Crano, Kenny, & Campbell, 1972). Scholastic aptitude tests such as the ACT or SAT are also reliable predictors of the grades that high school students will make in college.

Not only do children with high IQs tend to do better in school, but they stay there longer (Brody, 1992): Students who perform well on IQ tests are less likely to drop out of high school and more likely than other high school graduates to attend and to complete college.

So intelligence test scores do predict academic achievements. Yet, it is important to note that the correlational findings we have reviewed are based on large numbers of students and that the IQ score of any individual student may not be a very good indicator of her current or future academic accomplishments. When trying to predict how well a particular student will perform in the future, a well-trained guidance counselor would surely consider the student's IQ score. However, a counselor would also want to know about other variables that are related to academic success, such as the student's work habits, interests, and motivation to succeed (Zigler & Seitz, 1982). So even though IQ (and aptitude) tests predict academic achievement better than *any other type of test*, judgments about a student's prospects for future success *should never be based on a test score alone*. Indeed, studies have consistently shown that the best single predictor of a student's future grades is not an IQ or aptitude score but, rather, the grades the student has previously earned (Minton & Schneider, 1980).

IQ as a Predictor of Vocational Outcomes

Do people with higher IQs land the better jobs? Are they more successful in their chosen occupations than co-workers who test lower in intelligence?

The answer to the first question seems to be yes. In one study of military personnel during World War II, recruits' IQ scores on the Army General Classification Test were clearly related to the prestige of their civilian occupations (Harrell & Harrell, 1945). Table 9-4 shows the rank order (from most to least prestigious) of some of the civilian occupations, as well as the average IQs and the range of IQs that characterized the men who worked at those jobs. Notice that the average IQ score increases as the prestige of the occupation increases—that is, the more prestigious jobs were generally held by the more intelligent men (see also Gottfredson, 1986). The reason for this relationship is clear: It undoubtedly takes more intellectual ability to complete law school and become a lawyer than it does to be a farmhand. But also notice the "range of IQ" column. There were some very bright men working in low-status occupations. Apparently, a high IQ does not guarantee a prestigious job.

Does IQ predict job *performance?* Are bright lawyers, electricians, or farmhands more successful or productive than their less intelligent colleagues? The answer here is also yes. The correlations between mental test scores and such indications of job performance as supervisor ratings average about +.50—about as high as IQ correlates with academic achievement (Gottfredson, 1986; Hunter & Hunter, 1984). Yet an astute manager or personnel officer would never rely exclusively on IQ scores to decide which job applicants to hire or to determine who among her existing workers is best suited for assuming additional responsibility. And the reasons for looking beyond IQ are straightforward: Other variables such as workers' family experiences, prior job performance, and motivation to succeed are also important predictors of future job performance.

IQ as a Predictor of Health, Adjustment, and Life Satisfaction

Are bright people any healthier, happier, or better adjusted than those of average or below-average intelligence? Let's see what researchers have learned by considering the life outcomes of people at opposite ends of the IQ continuum: the *intellectually gifted* and the *mentally retarded.*

In 1922, Lewis Terman began a most interesting longitudinal study (Fincher, 1973; Terman, 1954; Terman & Oden, 1959). The subjects for Terman's study were more than 1500 California schoolchildren who had IQs of 140 or higher. The purpose of the project was to collect as much information as possible about the abilities and personal characteristics of these "gifted" children and to follow up on them every few years to see what they were accomplishing.

It soon became apparent that these children were exceptional in many respects other than intelligence. For example, they had learned to walk and talk much sooner than most toddlers and their general health, as determined from physicians' reports, was much better than average. The gifted children were rated by teachers as better adjusted emotionally and more morally mature than their less intelligent peers. And although they were no more popular, on average, than their classmates, the gifted children were quicker to take charge and assume positions of leadership. Taken together, these findings demolish the stereotype of child prodigies as frail, sickly youngsters who are socially inadequate and emotionally immature.

Another convincing demonstration of the personal and social maturity of gifted individuals comes from a study of high-IQ children who skipped high school entirely and entered the University of Washington as part of a special program to accelerate their education (Robinson & Janos, 1986). Contrary to the common wisdom that gifted children will suffer socially and emotionally if they skip grades and are required to fit in with much older students, these youngsters showed no signs at all of maladjustment (see also Richardson & Benbow, 1990). Indeed, on several measures of psychological and social adjustment, they equalled their much older college classmates, as well as similarly gifted students who attended high school. Many of them thrived in college, finding for the first time friends like themselves—and friends who "got their jokes" (Noble, Robinson, & Gunderson, 1993).

Some gifted children as young as 9 or 10 thrive as college students, particularly if they have the support and encouragement of their parents.

Table 9-4   Average IQs and Range of IQs for Enlisted Military Personnel Who Had Worked at Various Civilian Occupations

Occupation	Average IQ	Range of IQs
Accountant	128.1	94–157
Lawyer	127.6	96–157
Engineer	126.6	100–151
Chemist	124.8	102–153
Reporter	124.5	100–157
Teacher	122.8	76–155
Pharmacist	120.5	76–149
Salesman	115.1	60–153
Artist	114.9	82–139
Machinist	110.1	38–153
Electrician	109.0	64–149
Carpenter	102.1	42–147
Chauffeur	100.8	46–143
Cook and baker	97.2	20–147
Truck driver	96.2	16–149
Barber	95.3	42–141
Farmhand	91.4	24–141
Miner	90.6	42–139

Source: Adapted from Harrell & Harrell, 1945.

What becomes of gifted children as adults? Most of Terman's gifted subjects were still remarkable in many respects. Fewer than 5% were rated as seriously maladjusted, and the incidence of problems such as ill health, psychiatric disturbance, alcoholism, and delinquent behavior was but a fraction of that normally observed in the general population (Terman, 1954). The marriage rate for these individuals was as high as it is for the population as a whole, and members of the gifted sample were more satisfied with their marriages and better adjusted sexually than were husbands and wives in general.

Finally, the occupational attainments of the gifted men in Terman's sample were impressive. By age 40, the vast majority (86%) were working in professional or semi-professional jobs. Many of these men were listed in *Who's Who* and *American Men of Science*, and, as a group, they had taken out more than 200 patents and written some 2000 scientific reports, 100 books, 375 plays or short stories, and more than 300 essays, sketches, magazine articles, and critiques. Due to the influence of gender-role expectations during the period covered by Terman's study, most of the gifted women sacrificed career aspirations to raise families (Schuster, 1990; Tomlinson-Keasey & Little, 1990). However, more recent cohorts of gifted women are pursuing careers more vigorously and seem to have a greater sense of well-being than Terman's gifted women did (Schuster, 1990; Subotnik, Karp, & Morgan, 1989).

In short, the majority of Terman's gifted sample were very well-adjusted people living happy, healthy, and (in many cases) highly productive lives. But was it their giftedness that accounted for these positive life outcomes? Maybe not. As David

BOX 9-1
Mental Retardation: A Closer Look

According to the American Association on Mental Retardation (1992), *mental retardation* is defined as significantly below-average general intellectual functioning associated with limitations in adaptive behavior that originated during childhood or adolescence. Specifically, to be diagnosed as mentally retarded, an individual must obtain an IQ score below 70 *and* have difficulties meeting age-appropriate expectations in everyday life. By these criteria, about 6 to 7 million people in the United States, or 3% of the population, are retarded.

Four levels of mental retardation are recognized: mild, moderate, severe, and profound. An adult who is *mildly retarded* (IQ 50 or 55 to 70) is likely to have a mental age comparable to an 8–12-year-old child. Mildly retarded persons can learn both academic and practical skills in school, although they may require special instruction. And as adults, they can often work and live independently. By contrast, *profoundly retarded* adults (IQs below 20 or 25) have mental ages of 3 years or less. They show major delays in all aspects of development and must be cared for throughout life, often in institutional settings. So we see that there are major differences among those individuals who have been classified as "retarded."

There are many, many causes of mental deficiencies. Most severely or profoundly retarded persons (IQs below 40) have a form of *organic retardation*; that is, their retardation stems from an injury or from some biological cause such as disease or a hereditary disorder. In Chapter 3, we discussed several organic deficiencies that are hereditary, including Down syndrome, the fragile-X syndrome, and phenylketonuria (PKU). Other forms of organic retardation are associated with prenatal and perinatal risk factors that we

reviewed in Chapter 4—for example, an alcoholic mother, exposure to rubella, or severe anoxia during childbirth. Because children with organic deficiencies often have physical defects and show serious mental impairments early in life, they are usually identified and labeled as mentally retarded at some point during infancy.

The second major form of mental deficiency—*cultural-familial retardation*—is not usually detected until a child performs very poorly on an IQ test at school. These children are mildly retarded, usually come from poverty-stricken areas, and are apt to have a parent or sibling who is also mildly retarded. Cultural-familial retardation often appears to be due to a combination of low genetic potential and a poor (unstimulating) environment, although other factors such as perinatal stress that passed undetected may sometimes be involved. Probably 50%–75% of mental retardation is of this type, and its exact cause is always difficult to pinpoint (Zigler & Hodapp, 1991).

We learned from Terman's study that gifted children experience predominantly positive outcomes later in life. What happens to mentally retarded children? We get some indication from a follow-up study of mildly retarded individuals (average IQ = 67) who had been placed in segregated special education classes for the mentally retarded during the 1920s and 1930s—the same era when Terman began his study of gifted children (Ross et al., 1985). Nearly 40 years later, their life outcomes were compared with those of siblings and nonretarded age-mates, and with the highly favorable attainments of Terman's gifted sample.

What did the data reveal? As you might expect, the mentally retarded adults had less favorable life outcomes than the nonretarded groups (see also Schalock et al., 1992). The

McClelland (cited in Fincher, 1973) points out, it could be that these gifted individuals succeeded not because of their high IQs, but because they came from affluent, highly educated families, thereby ensuring that they would receive good health care, an excellent education, and direct access to the more prestigious occupations.

Indeed, there are data to support McClelland's "family environment" hypothesis. Terman's sample (*n* = 1500) was rather large, and hundreds of these gifted children were not particularly happy or successful as adults (Terman, 1954; Shurkin, 1992). In an analysis of some of the factors that predicted the paths that gifted children's lives took over a 40-year period, Carolyn Tomlinson-Keasey and Todd Little (1990) found that the most well-adjusted and successful subjects had highly educated parents who offered them both love and intellectual stimulation; by contrast, the least successful of the group were more likely to have experienced disruption of family ties due to their parents' divorce and less support and encouragement (see also Terman, 1954). So we see that a high IQ, by itself, does not guarantee health, happiness, or success. Even among a select sample of children with superior IQs, the quality of the home environment contributes in important ways to future outcomes and accomplishments.

What about the other end of the IQ continuum? Do mentally retarded individuals have much hope of succeeding in life or achieving happiness? Although our

BOX 9-1 (continued)
Mental Retardation: A Closer Look

accompanying table brings this home by comparing the jobs held in middle age by the mentally retarded men with those of their nonretarded peers. (Like the females in Terman's gifted sample, retarded women tended to marry and become homemakers.) Although about 80% of the retarded men were gainfully employed, they usually wound up in jobs that required little education or intellectual ability. Compared directly with nonretarded peers, retarded men and women fared worse on almost all counts. For example, they had lower incomes, less adequate housing, and poorer adjustment in social relationships, and they displayed greater dependency on other people.

Although at first glance these outcomes may seem rather dismal, the authors of this study found plenty of reasons for optimism. Consider, for example, that the vast majority of the mentally retarded males did work, and that fewer than 20% of these workers were in the lowest job classifications, which society labels as menial. Moreover, the mentally retarded subjects were generally *self*-supporting; only about

one in five reported having *any* need for public assistance in the 10 years before being interviewed. Most of these mentally retarded individuals did marry, and most expressed some satisfaction with their accomplishments. So even though their life outcomes are poorer than those of nonretarded adults, these people were doing much better than common stereotypes about the mentally retarded would lead us to believe.

In sum, this study, like others before it, suggests that children who are labeled mildly or moderately retarded by the schools—and who do indeed have difficulty mastering academic lessons—often simply "melt" into the adult population after they leave school. Apparently, they can adapt to the demands of adult life, displaying a fair amount of the "contextual" intelligence or "street smarts" that Sternberg talks about—and that is not measured by standardized IQ tests. As the authors put it, "It does not take as many IQ points as most people believe to be productive, to get along with others, and to be self-fulfilled" (Ross et al., 1985, p. 149).

Midlife Occupations of Mentally Retarded, Nonretarded, and Gifted Males

Occupational classification	Mentally retarded subjects (*n* = 54), %	Nonretarded siblings (*n* = 31), %	Nonretarded peers (*n* = 33), %	Terman's gifted sample (*n* = 757), %
Professional, managerial	1.9	29.1	36.4	86.3
Retail business, skilled trade, agricultural	29.6	32.3	39.4	12.5
Semiskilled, minor or business, clerical	50.0	25.8	15.2	1.2
Slightly skilled, unskilled	18.5	13.0	9.4	0.0

Source: Adapted from Ross, Begab, Dondis, Giampiccolo, & Meyers, 1985.

stereotypes about mental retardation might persuade us to say no, the research presented in Box 9-1 suggests a very different conclusion.

 ## FACTORS THAT INFLUENCE IQ SCORES

Why do people differ so dramatically in the scores that they make on IQ tests? In the pages that follow, we will briefly review the evidence for hereditary and environmental influences on intelligence and will then take a closer look at several important social and cultural correlates of intellectual performance.

The Evidence for Heredity

In Chapter 3, we reviewed two major lines of evidence indicating that heredity affects intellectual performance and that about half of the variation in IQ scores within a particular population of test takers is due to genetic differences among these individuals.

Concept Check 9-2 ⌄ On the Stability and Predictive Power of Assessments of Mental Performance

Check your understanding of the meaning and usefulness of various assessments of mental performance by filling in the blanks in the statements below. The answers appear in the Appendix.

1. Although infant intelligence tests are useful for diagnosing _____ _____s, the DQs that infants make generally fail to predict their _____s later in childhood. However, two infant information-processing skills, _____ and _____, are moderately good predictors of childhood intellectual performances.

2. More than _____ of all children who are repeatedly tested show meaningful _____ in their IQs over time. These data imply that an IQ score is best interpreted as an estimate of the examinee's mental _____ at one point in time, rather than an indication of innate mental _____.

3. At the group level, IQs are _____ correlated with current and future academic performance and with current and future vocational performances. Yet, an astute counselor or manager never bases decisions _____ on IQ scores, because intelligence tests do not measure other contributors to academic/vocational performance, such as one's work _____, _____, and _____ to succeed.

4. Very bright children generally experience _____ life outcomes, compared with other people whose IQs are lower. But even among samples of high-IQ individuals, the quality of one's _____ _____ contributes importantly to future outcomes and accomplishments.

5. Mildly retarded adults experience _____ life outcomes than nonretarded adults do. Yet, most of these individuals are _____-_____ and are _____ with their accomplishments, thus _____ common stereotypes about the mentally retarded.

Twin studies. The intellectual resemblance between pairs of individuals living in the same home increases as a function of their kinship (that is, genetic similarity). For example, the IQ correlation for identical twins, who inherit identical genes, is substantially higher than the IQ correlations for fraternal twins and normal siblings, who have half their genes in common.

Adoption studies. Adopted children's IQs are more highly correlated with the IQs of their biological parents than with those of their adoptive parents. This finding can be interpreted as evidence for a genetic influence on IQ, for adoptees share genes with their biological parents but not with their adoptive caregivers.

We also learned in Chapter 3 that a person's genotype may influence the type of environment that he or she is likely to experience. Indeed, Scarr and McCartney (1983) have proposed that people seek out environments that are compatible with their genetic predispositions, so that identical twins (who share identical genes) will select and experience more similar environments than fraternal twins or ordinary siblings do. This is a major reason that identical twins resemble each other intellectually throughout life, whereas the intellectual resemblances between fraternal twins or ordinary siblings become progressively smaller over time (Scarr & McCartney, 1983).

Do these latter observations imply that a person's genotype *determines* his environment and thereby exerts the primary influence on his intellectual development? *No, they do not!* A child who has a genetic predisposition to seek out intellectual challenges could hardly be expected to develop a high IQ if she is raised in a barren environment that offers few such challenges for her to meet. Alternatively, a child who does not gravitate toward intellectual activities might nevertheless obtain an average or above-average IQ if raised in a stimulating environment that continually provides him with cognitive challenges that he must master. So it seems that a person's environment may either foster or inhibit the outward expression of genetic predispositions. Stated another way, heredity and environment interact to influence most human attributes—including intelligence and the course of intellectual development.

The Evidence for Environment

The evidence for environmental effects on intelligence comes from a variety of sources. For example, we learned in Chapter 3 that there is a small to moderate intellectual resemblance between pairs of genetically unrelated children who live in the same household. And earlier in this chapter, we saw that unstable home environments are associated with fluctuations in children's IQ scores. There are also data to indicate that a barren intellectual environment is likely to inhibit cognitive growth, whereas a stimulating environment can have the opposite effect.

Effects of an Impoverished Environment

Several investigators have studied the intellectual development of children who live in poverty-stricken communities where the literacy rate among adults is low and the educational facilities are substandard. Youngsters living in these impoverished settings scored far below average on standardized intelligence tests, and their IQs actually decreased with age (Ascher, 1935; Sherman & Key, 1932; Wheeler, 1932). Otto Klineberg (1963) has proposed a **"cumulative deficit" hypothesis** to explain these findings. According to cumulative-deficit theory, impoverished environments inhibit intellectual growth, and these inhibiting effects accumulate over time. Consequently, the longer children remain in a barren intellectual environment, the worse they will perform on IQ tests.

Arthur Jensen (1977) tested the cumulative-deficit hypothesis by comparing the intellectual performance of economically disadvantaged African-American siblings living in California and Georgia. Jensen proposed that if a "cumulative deficit" mechanism is operating, older siblings should obtain lower IQs than their younger brothers and sisters. This is precisely what he found for children in the Georgia sample, whose environmental disadvantages were markedly greater than those of the California group (see also Ramey & Ramey, 1992). Moreover, children who have *always* lived in poverty score lower on IQ tests than those whose poverty status is not so consistent (Duncan et al., 1994)—another finding that suggests that poverty has cumulative effects on children's intellectual performance.

Effects of Environmental Enrichment

Can we promote intellectual development by enriching the environments in which children live? Apparently so, if the results of two studies of isolated mountain children are any guide (Wheeler, 1932, 1942). When children from a mountain community in eastern Tennessee were first tested in the early 1930s, they obtained an average IQ of 82. Ten years later, the children in this same community were retested. During the interval between testings, this community had changed in many ways: Roads had been built, the school system had been modernized, and economic conditions had improved to the point that most people could now afford radios. In other words, this formerly isolated and impoverished community had entered into the social and economic mainstream of American life. As a result, the average IQ of children there rose by 11 points (to 93) in the 10 years between testings. Other studies conducted in Hawaii and the American Midwest found similar increases in children's intellectual performance in communities where dramatic social and educational improvements had taken place (Finch, 1946; Smith, 1942).

Other investigators have charted the intellectual growth of adopted children who left disadvantaged family backgrounds and were placed with highly educated adoptive parents (Scarr & Weinberg, 1983; Skodak & Skeels, 1949). By the time these adoptees were 4–7 years old, they were scoring well above average on standardized IQ tests (about 110 in Scarr and Weinberg's study and 112 in Skodak and Skeels's). In fact, their intellectual performance was considerably higher than what one would expect on the basis of the IQs and educational levels of their biological parents or the IQs of other children from disadvantaged backgrounds. Since the adopting parents

"cumulative-deficit" hypothesis: the notion that impoverished environments inhibit intellectual growth and that these inhibiting effects accumulate over time.

were known to be highly educated and above average in intelligence, it seems reasonable to assume that they were providing enriched, intellectually stimulating home environments that fostered the cognitive development of their adoptees.

As these studies clearly indicate, the environment is a powerful force that may either promote or inhibit intellectual growth. Yet the term *environment* is a very global concept, and the evidence that we have reviewed does not really tell us which of the many life experiences that children have are most likely to affect their intellectual development. In the next section of this chapter, we will concentrate on environmental influences and see that a child's performance on IQ tests depends to some extent on parental attitudes and child-rearing practices, the structure and socioeconomic status of the family, and perhaps even the racial or ethnic group to which the family belongs.

 ## SOCIOCULTURAL CORRELATES OF INTELLECTUAL PERFORMANCE

Home Environment and IQ

Earlier, we suggested that the quality or character of the home environment may play an important role in determining children's intellectual performance and eventual life outcomes. Recently, Arnold Sameroff and his colleagues (1993) provided a broad overview of some of the environmental factors that place some children at risk of performing poorly on IQ tests. These researchers assessed the IQ risk factors shown in Table 9-5 at age 4, and again when the children in their sample were 13 years old. Every one of these "risk factors" was related to IQ at age 4, and most also predicted IQ at age 13. In addition, the greater the number of these risk factors affecting a child,

Table 9-5   **Ten Environmental Risk Factors Associated with Low IQ and Mean IQs at Age 4 of Children Who Did or Did Not Experience Each Risk Factor**

	Mean IQ at age 4	
Risk factor	*Child experienced risk factor*	*Child did not experience risk factor*
Child is member of minority group	90	110
Head of household is unemployed or low-skilled worker	90	108
Mother did not complete high school	92	109
Family has four or more children	94	105
Father is absent from family	95	106
Family experienced many stressful life events	97	105
Parents have rigid child-rearing values	92	107
Mother is highly anxious/distressed	97	105
Mother has poor mental health/diagnosed disorder	99	107
Mother shows little positive affect toward child	88	107

Source: Data and descriptions compiled from Sameroff et al., 1993.

the lower his or her IQ, and which particular risk factors a child experienced were less important than how many he or she experienced. It is clearly not conducive to intellectual development to grow up in a disadvantaged home with an adult who may be unable to provide much intellectual stimulation.

Exactly how, then, and in what ways do parents influence a child's intellectual development? In an attempt to find out, Bettye Caldwell and Robert Bradley have developed a widely used instrument, called the **HOME inventory** (*Home Observation* for *Measurement* of the *Environment*), that allows an interviewer/observer to visit an infant, a preschooler, or a school-age child at home and to determine how intellectually stimulating (or impoverished) that home environment is (Caldwell & Bradley, 1984). The infant version of the HOME inventory consists of 45 statements, each of which is scored *yes* (the statement is true of this family) or *no* (the statement is not true of this family). To gather the information necessary to complete the inventory, the researcher (1) asks the child's parent (usually the mother) to describe her daily routine and child-rearing practices, (2) carefully observes the parent as she interacts with her child, and (3) notes the kinds of play materials that the parent makes available to the child. The 45 bits of information collected are then grouped into the six categories in Table 9-6. The home then receives a score on each subscale. The higher the scores across all six subscales, the more intellectually stimulating the home environment.

Table 9-6 Subscales and Sample Items for the HOME Inventory (Infant Version)

Subscale 1: Emotional and verbal responsivity of parent (11 items)

Sample items: Parent responds verbally to child's vocalizations or verbalizations
Parent's speech is distinct, clear, and audible
Parent caresses or kisses child at least once

Subscale 2: Avoidance of restriction and punishment (8 items)

Sample items: Parent neither slaps nor spanks child during visit
Parent does not scold or criticize child during visit
Parent does not interfere with or restrict child more than three times
during visit

Subscale 3: Organization of physical and temporal environment (6 items)

Sample items: Child gets out of house at least four times a week
Child's play environment is safe

Subscale 4: Provision of appropriate play materials (9 items)

Sample items: Child has a push or pull toy
Parent provides learning facilitators appropriate to age: mobile, table and
chairs, highchair, playpen, and so on
Parent provides toys for child to play with during visit

Subscale 5: Parental involvement with child (6 items)

Sample items: Parent talks to child while doing household work
Parent structures child's play periods

Subscale 6: Opportunities for variety in daily stimulation (5 items)

Sample items: Father provides some care daily
Child has three or more books of his or her own

Source: Adapted from Caldwell & Bradley, 1984.

HOME inventory: a measure of the amount and type of intellectual stimulation provided by a child's home environment.

Does the HOME Predict IQ?

Robert Bradley and his colleagues (1989) have found that scores on the HOME predict children's intellectual performance quite well. Moreover, gains in IQ from age 1 to age 3 are likely to occur among children from stimulating homes, whereas children from families with low HOME scores often experience drops in IQ over the same period. All of this is truer for Anglo- and African-American children than for Mexican-American children, though. The early IQ scores of Mexican-American children are not as closely related to their families' HOME scores, suggesting that the HOME inventory may not be capturing the ways in which Latino parents foster their children's intellectual development.

Which aspects of the home environment matter most? Although each of the HOME subscales is moderately correlated with children's IQ scores, longitudinal studies reveal that the best predictors of children's later IQs (and scholastic achievement) are the HOME subscales measuring *parental involvement* with the child, provision of *age-appropriate play materials,* and opportunities for *variety in daily stimulation* (Bradley, Caldwell, & Rock, 1988; Gottfried, 1984). Other researchers would add that the sheer amount of stimulation that parents provide is less important than whether that stimulation is *warm and responsive*—for example, a smile in return for a smile or an answer cheerfully given in response to a question (Crockenberg, 1983; Estrada et al., 1987).

In sum, an intellectually stimulating home environment is one in which parents are warm, verbally engaging, and eager to be involved with their child (Hart & Risley, 1992; MacPhee, Ramey, & Yeates, 1984). Parents describe new objects, concepts, and experiences clearly and accurately, and they provide the child with a variety of challenges that are appropriate for her age or developmental level. They encourage the child to ask questions, to solve problems, and to think about what she is learning. As the child matures and enters school, parents stress the importance of academic achievement and expect her to get good grades. When you stop and think about it, it is not at all surprising that children from these "enriched" home settings often have high IQs; after all, their parents are obviously concerned about their cognitive development and have spent several years encouraging them to acquire new information and to practice many of the cognitive skills that are measured on intelligence tests.

A Hidden Genetic Effect?

Interestingly, brighter parents are likely to provide more intellectually stimulating home environments (Coon et al., 1990; Longstreth et al., 1981). Is it possible, then, that any correlation between the quality of the home environment and children's IQ scores simply reflects the fact that bright parents transmit genes for high intelligence to their children?

There is some support for this idea in that correlations between HOME scores and IQ scores are higher for biological children, who share genes with their parents, than for adopted children, who are genetically unrelated to other members of their family (Braungart, Fulker, & Plomin, 1992). So does the quality of the home environment really have its own unique (or independent) effects on children's intellectual development?

The answer is yes, and there are two lines of evidence that tell us so. First, adopted children's IQ scores rise considerably when they are moved from less stimulating to more stimulating homes (Turkheimer, 1991). Clearly, this change in IQs has to be an *environmental* effect because adoptees share no genes with their adoptive parents. Even more revealing are the results of a longitudinal study of 112 mothers and their 2–4-year-old children conducted by Keith Yeates and his associates (1983). These investigators measured the mothers' IQs, the IQ of each child at ages 2, 3, and 4, and the quality of the families' home environment (as assessed by the HOME). The best predictor of a child's IQ at age 2 was the mother's IQ, just as a genetic hypothesis

would suggest. But the picture had changed by the time children were 4 years old; now the quality of the home environment was a strong predictor of children's IQs, even *after* the influence of mothers' IQ was taken into account (see also Sameroff et al., 1993).

So it appears that the quality of the home environment is truly an important contributor to a child's intellectual development. It also seems that these environmental effects may accumulate over time, so that the full impact of the home setting on a child's intellectual performance may not be apparent until later in the preschool period, when IQ becomes a more stable attribute (Sameroff et al., 1993; Yeates et al., 1983).

Birth Order, Family Size, and IQ

Two other "family" characteristics that seem to affect children's performance on IQ tests are *family size* and the child's position within the family, or *birth order*. These effects are clearly illustrated in a large-scale study based on military records of almost all males born in the Netherlands between 1944 and 1947 (Belmont & Marolla, 1973). As shown in Figure 9-5, the brighter children tended to come from *smaller* families. Moreover, the figure also reveals a "birth order" effect: On average, first-borns outperformed second-borns, who outperformed third-borns, and so on down the line. These findings are not unique to Dutch males; they have now been replicated in samples of males and females from several countries (Markus & Zajonc, 1977).

Robert Zajonc (1975; Zajonc & Markus, 1975) has offered an interesting explanation for these birth-order and family-size effects. According to Zajonc's **confluence hypothesis,** a child's intellectual development depends on the *average intellectual level of all family members,* including the child himself. Clearly, first-borns should have an advantage because they are initially exposed *only* to adults, whose intellectual levels are very high. By contrast, a second child experiences a less stimulating intellectual environment because she must deal with a cognitively immature older sibling as well as with her parents. The third child is further disadvantaged by the presence of *two* relatively immature older siblings. Zajonc (1975) suggests that

> with each additional child, the family's intellectual environment depreciates. . . . Children who grow up surrounded by people with higher intellectual levels have a better chance to achieve their maximum intellectual powers than . . . children from large families who spend more time in a world of child-sized minds . . . develop more slowly, and therefore attain lower IQs [p. 39].

Contrasting home environments. The photograph at the left shows an orderly home environment, and one in which family members are warm, responsive, and eager to be involved with one another. This is precisely the kind of setting that seems to promote children's intellectual development. In the photograph at the right, we see an example of a barren, disorderly, and unattractive home environment—one that is likely to inhibit intellectual development.

confluence hypothesis: Zajonc's notion that a child's intellectual development depends on the average intellectual level of all family members.

Figure 9-5
Average scores on a nonverbal measure of intelligence as a function of the examinee's birth order and the size of his family. Note that subjects from smaller families score higher on this test than do subjects from large families. We also see that, within a given family size, children born early tend to obtain higher IQs than those born late.
Adapted from Zajonc & Marcus, 1975.

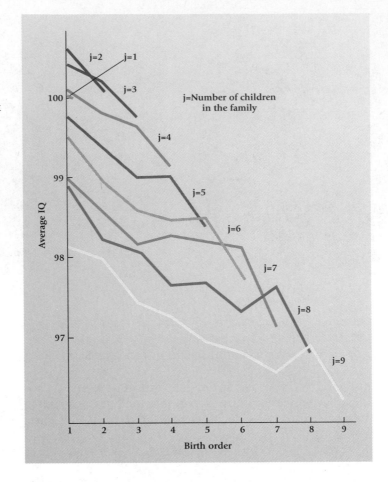

The confluence hypothesis predicts that first-borns and children from small families will receive more intellectual stimulation from parents than later-borns and children from larger families do. This is precisely what Bradley & Caldwell (1984) found when they used the HOME inventory to assess the quality of the home environment for first-born and later-born infants (see also Rothbart, 1971). Yet many other confluence predictions do not ring true. For example, the model predicts that children who grow up in homes with *three* mature adults (say, two parents and a grandparent) should score higher on IQ tests than those who are exposed only to their parents, yet they don't (Brackbill & Nichols, 1982). Moreover, children who live with only one parent (rather than two) do not always show the poorer intellectual performances that confluence theory predicts (Duncan et al., 1994; Entwisle & Alexander, 1990). So even though Zajonc's theory is an interesting explanation for birth-order and family-size effects on intelligence, it remains for future research to firmly establish its usefulness.

Finally, a caution is in order. These birth-order and family-size effects tend to be quite small and are observed only when large numbers of families are compared. Thus, the trends that emerge for the population as a whole may not apply to the members of any *particular* family. Clearly, not all first-borns are brighter than average, nor do all later-borns score lower in IQ than their older brothers and sisters.

Social-Class, Racial, and Ethnic Differences in IQ

One of the most reliable findings in the intelligence literature is a social-class effect: Children from lower- and working-class homes average some 10–15 points below their middle-class age-mates on standardized IQ tests. Infants are apparently the only exception to this rule, as there are no reliable social class differences on infant mea-

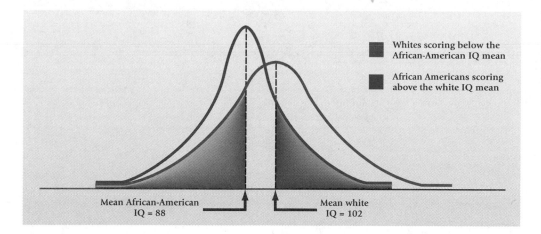

Figure 9-6
Approximate distributions of IQ scores for African-American and white children reared by their biological parents.
Based on Brody, 1992, and Kennedy, van de Reit, & White, 1963.

Legend within figure:
Whites scoring below the African-American IQ mean
African Americans scoring above the white IQ mean
Mean African-American IQ = 88
Mean white IQ = 102

sures of habituation and preference for novelty (McCall & Carriger, 1993) or in the developmental quotients (DQs) that infants make on infant "intelligence" tests (Golden et al., 1971).

There are also racial and ethnic differences in intellectual performance. In the United States, for example, children of African-American, Native American, or Latino ancestry score, on average, about 12–15 points below their Anglo-American classmates on standardized IQ tests, whereas Asian Americans score slightly higher, on average, than Anglos do (Brody, 1992; Minton & Schneider, 1980). Moreover, different subcultural groups may also show distinctive patterns of mental abilities. African-American children, for example, often perform better on verbal tasks than on other subtests, whereas Latino children may do particularly well on nonverbal items assessing spatial abilities (Saccuzzo, Johnson, & Russell, 1992; Taylor & Richards, 1991).

Before we try to interpret these social-class, racial, and ethnic differences, an important truth is worth stating here—one that is often overlooked when people discover that white and Asian-American children outperform their African-American or Latino classmates on IQ tests: We cannot predict anything about the IQ or the future accomplishments of an *individual* on the basis of his ethnicity or color. As we see in Figure 9-6, the IQ distributions for samples of African Americans and white Americans overlap considerably. So even though the average IQ of African Americans is somewhat lower than that of whites, the overlapping distributions mean that many African-American children obtain higher IQ scores than many white children do. In fact, approximately 15%–25% of the African-American population scores higher—in many cases, substantially higher—than *half* of the white population (Shuey, 1966).

Why Do Groups Differ in Intellectual Performance?

Over the years, developmentalists have proposed three hypotheses to account for racial, ethnic, and social-class differences in IQ: (1) a *test bias* hypothesis that standardized IQ tests assess proficiency in white, middle-class cultural experiences and thereby underestimate the intellectual capabilities of disadvantaged children or those from minority subcultures; (2) a *genetic* hypothesis that group differences in IQ are hereditary; and (3) an *environmental* hypothesis that the groups scoring lower in IQ come from intellectually impoverished backgrounds—that is, neighborhoods and home environments that are far less conducive to intellectual growth than those typically experienced by members of the middle class.

The Test Bias Hypothesis

Those who favor the **"test bias" hypothesis** believe that group differences in IQ are an artifact of our testing procedures (Helms, 1992). To illustrate, they point out that IQ tests currently in use were designed to measure cognitive skills (for example,

"test bias" hypothesis: the notion that IQ tests have a built-in, middle-class bias that explains the substandard performance of children from lower-class and minority subcultures.

Table 9-7 Sample Items from Dove's Counterbalance General "Intelligence" Test (the "Chitling Test")

1. Cheap chitlings (not the kind you purchase at a frozen food counter) will taste rubbery unless they are cooked long enough. How soon can you quit cooking them to eat and enjoy them? (A) 45 minutes, (B) 2 hours, (C) 24 hours, (D) one week (on a low flame), (E) 1 hour

2. A "handkerchief head" is: (A) a cool cat, (B) a porter, (C) an Uncle Tom, (D) a preacher

3. A "gas head" is a person who has a: (A) fast-moving car, (B) stable of "lace," (C) "process," (D) habit of stealing cars, (E) long jail record for arson

4. "Hully Gully" came from (A) East Oakland, (B) Fillmore, (C) Watts, (D) Harlem, (E) Motor City

5. If you throw the dice and a seven is showing on the top, what is facing down? (A) seven, (B) snake eyes, (C) boxcars, (D) little Joes, (E) eleven

6. T-Bone Walker got famous for playing what? (A) trombone, (B) piano, (C) "T-flute," (D) guitar, (E) "Hambone"

Source: Adapted from Dove, 1968. (Answers appear at the bottom of the page.)

assembling puzzles), general information (for example, "What is a 747?"), and cultural values (for example, "What do you do if another boy hits you?"; correct answer: Say, "That's all right; it was probably accidental") that white, middle-class children are more likely to have acquired. They note that subtests measuring vocabulary and word usage may be harder for blacks and Latinos, who often speak a different English dialect from that of the white middle class. Not only might these children be working under a linguistic handicap while trying to understand the test instructions, but many common words do not even have the same meanings for African Americans and Latinos as they do for whites. Even the way language is used varies across ethnic groups. For example, white parents ask a lot of "knowledge-training" questions ("What does a doggie say?"; "Where do Eskimos live?") that require brief answers and are similar to the kinds of questions asked on IQ tests. By contrast, African-American parents are more inclined to ask real questions that they may not know the answers to—questions that often require elaborate, story-type responses that are quite unlike those called for at school or on an IQ test (Heath, 1982; 1989). Adrian Dove (1968), an African-American sociologist, has attempted to illustrate the kinds of biases that minority children encounter on IQ tests by constructing his own humorous example of a "culturally biased" test that relies very heavily on the language and experiences of African Americans (see Table 9-7). If this test were to be interpreted as a valid measure of intellectual performance, the average African American of Dove's era would have undoubtedly obtained a higher IQ score than most whites.

Does "test bias" explain group differences in IQ? Even though standardized intelligence tests have a distinct middle-class flavor, many developmentalists believe that group differences in IQ are not solely attributable to test bias. Several attempts have now been made to construct **"culture fair" IQ tests** that do not place poor people or those from minority subcultures at an immediate disadvantage. For example, the *Raven Progressive Matrices Test* requires the examinee to scan a series of abstract designs, each of which has a missing section. The examinee's task is to complete each design by selecting the appropriate section from a number of alternatives (see Figure 9-7).

"culture fair" tests: intelligence tests constructed to minimize any irrelevant cultural biases in test content that could influence test performance.

Answers: 1. C; 2. C; 3. C; 4. C; 5. A; 6. D. How did you do on this test?

These problems are assumed to be equally familiar (or unfamiliar) to people from all ethnic groups and social classes. There is no time limit on the test, and the instructions are very simple. But despite such attempts to eliminate cultural bias from the test content, middle-class whites continue to outperform their lower-class and/or African-American age-mates on these "culture fair" measures of intelligence (Jensen, 1980). Translating existing tests into the African-American English dialect spoken by urban African-American children also does not appear to increase the scores that these children achieve (Quay, 1971). And finally, IQ tests and various tests of intellectual aptitude (such as the Scholastic Aptitude Test) predict future academic successes just as well for African Americans and other minorities as for whites (Anastasi, 1988; Barrett & Depinet, 1991; Oakland & Parmelee, 1985). Taken together, these findings imply that group differences in IQ are not solely attributable to biases in the *content* of our tests or the dialect in which they are administered. But another possibility remains.

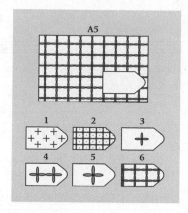

Figure 9-7
An item similar to those appearing in the Raven Progressive Matrices Test.

Zigler's motivational hypothesis. Edward Zigler and his associates (Zigler, Abelson, Trickett, & Seitz, 1982; Zigler & Finn-Stevenson, 1992) believe that social-class and ethnic differences in IQ are due largely to motivational factors. Presumably, lower-class and minority children score lower than they should on IQ tests because they tend to be wary of strange examiners and strange testing situations and may see little point in trying to do well on abstract and seemingly irrelevant test items, particularly if they have a history of academic failure and are anxious in testing situations.

Attempts to increase the motivation of these children by first allowing them time to become acquainted with a friendly examiner (or by mixing easy items with harder ones to prevent examinees from becoming discouraged by a long string of errors) have a clear effect on test performance: Disadvantaged children score some 7–10 points higher than they normally would when tested in the traditional way by a strange examiner (Zigler et al., 1982). Although most children do better when tested by a friendly examiner (Sacks, 1952; Zigler et al., 1982), it still seems that African-American children, even those from middle-class homes, are often less comfortable in testing situations than white, middle-class children are (Moore, 1986).

How much test bias? At least one recent IQ test, the K-ABC, was carefully constructed to reduce test bias. Not only were test items selected to be equally familiar or unfamiliar to all ethnic groups, but the test's flexible administration procedures allow the examiner to minimize children's wariness and maximize motivation by (1) behaving in a warm, responsive manner and (2) providing hints and prompts that prevent the defeatism that minority children often show after an early failure. These procedures have cut in half the typical IQ discrepancies between African Americans and whites (Kaufman, Kamphaus, & Kaufman, 1985), suggesting that possibly as much as half the racial and ethnic differences in intellectual performance are the result of biases in our testing procedures.

The Genetic Hypothesis

By far the most controversial explanation for group differences in intelligence is that they are hereditary. Those who favor the **genetic hypothesis** note that members of various social-class, ethnic, and racial groups tend to marry within their own populations rather than mating with outsiders. Although this selective mating is obviously not universal, it will nevertheless result in a restriction in the gene flow between groups if it continues over many generations. In other words, the argument is that people in various racial, ethnic, and social-class groupings have genotypes drawn from different gene pools. Presumably, these gene pools differ in the frequency and distribution of the genes that affect mental performance.

Perhaps the strongest proponent of this genetic interpretation is Arthur Jensen of the University of California (Jensen, 1969, 1980). Jensen believes that there are two

genetic hypothesis: the notion that group differences in IQ are hereditary.

kinds of intellectual abilities, which are equally heritable within different subgroups of the population. **Level I abilities** include attentional processes, short-term memory, and associative skills, which are important for simple kinds of rote learning. **Level II abilities** are those that allow one to reason abstractly and to manipulate words and symbols to form concepts and solve problems. According to Jensen, Level II abilities are highly correlated with school achievement, whereas Level I abilities are not. Of course, it is predominantly Level II abilities that are measured on IQ tests.

Jensen (1985) finds that Level I tasks are performed equally well by children from all races, ethnic groups, and social classes. However, middle-class and white children outperform lower-class and African-American children on the more advanced Level II tasks. Since Level I and Level II tasks are equally heritable *within* each social class and ethnic group, Jensen proposes that the IQ differences *between* groups must be hereditary (see also Herrnstein & Murray, 1994).

Criticisms of the genetic hypothesis. Although Jensen's arguments may sound convincing, there are reasons to believe that genetic influences do not explain group differences in IQ. For example, Jensen's critics have noted that within-group heritability estimates imply absolutely nothing about between-group variability in an attribute (Lewontin, 1976). As we see in Box 9-2, it is possible for individual differences *within* a group to be entirely genetic in character, whereas differences *between* two groups are largely the result of the environments in which they are raised.

Data available on mixed-race children also fail to support the genetic hypothesis. Eyferth (as cited in Loehlin et al., 1975) obtained the IQ scores of illegitimate German children fathered by African-American servicemen. These mixed-race children were then compared with a group of illegitimate white children of the same age and social background. Clearly, the mixed-race group should have scored lower than their white agemates if their African-American fathers had had fewer IQ-determining genes to pass along to them. However, Eyferth found that these two groups of illegitimate children did not differ in IQ. Similarly, extremely bright African-American children have no higher percentage of white ancestors than is typical of the African-American population as a whole (Scarr et al., 1977).

In sum, even though IQ is a moderately heritable attribute for all racial and ethnic groups, there is simply no evidence that conclusively demonstrates that *group differences* in IQ are genetically determined (Plomin, 1990).

The Environmental Hypothesis

A third explanation for group differences in IQ is the **environmental hypothesis** that poor people and members of various minority groups tend to grow up in environments that are much less conducive to intellectual development than those experienced by most whites and other members of the middle class.

Recently, developmentalists have carefully considered how a low-income or poverty-stricken lifestyle is likely to influence a family's children, and several of these findings bear directly on the issue of children's intellectual development (Duncan et al., 1994; Garrett, Ng'andu, & Ferron, 1994; Huston, McLoyd, & Garcia-Coll, 1994). Consider, for example, that a family's poverty status and lack of adequate income may mean that many children from low-income families are undernourished—a circumstance that may inhibit brain growth and make them listless and inattentive (Pollitt, 1994). Moreover, economic hardship creates psychological distress—a strong dissatisfaction with life's conditions that makes lower-income adults edgy and irritable and reduces their capacity to be sensitive, supportive, and highly involved in their children's learning activities (Conger et al., 1992; McLoyd, 1990). Finally, low-income parents are often poorly educated themselves and may have neither the knowledge nor the money to provide their children with age-appropriate books, toys, or other experiences that contribute to an intellectually stimulating home environment. Indeed, scores on the HOME inventory are consistently lower in low-income than in

Level I abilities: Jensen's term for lower-level intellectual abilities (such as attention and short-term memory) that are important for simple association learning.

Level II abilities: Jensen's term for higher-level cognitive skills that are involved in abstract reasoning and problem solving.

environmental hypothesis: the notion that groups differ in IQ because the environments in which they are raised are not equally conducive to intellectual growth.

BOX 9-2
Why Heritability Estimates Do Not Explain Group Differences in IQ

*L*et's suppose that a group of white children obtains an average IQ of 101 and their African-American classmates average 87 on the same test. Further, we will assume that the heritability estimates for the African-American and white populations are comparable. Jensen might use these data to argue that the 14-point difference in IQ between the white and African-American children is attributable to the genetic differences between African Americans and whites. On the surface, this reasoning seems to make sense, because IQ is equally heritable within each group.

However, the argument is flawed. Let's recall that heritability is the amount of variation in a trait that is attributable to genetic factors. If two groups have comparable heritability estimates for a trait, this simly means that, *within* each group, the amount of variability on that trait that is attributable to genetic factors is approximately the same. It says nothing about any differences *between* the groups on that trait.

An example should clarify the point. Suppose a farmer randomly draws corn seed from a bag containing several genetic varieties. He then plants half the seed in a barren field and half in soil that is quite fertile. When the plants are fully grown, the farmer discovers that those *within* each field have grown to different heights. Since all plants within each field were grown in the same soil, their different heights reflect the genetic variability among the seeds that were planted. Therefore, the heritability estimates for plants within each plot should be very high. But notice that the plants grown in the fertile soil are taller, on the average, than those grown in the barren soil. The most logical explanation for this *between-field variation* is an environmental one: Plants grown in fertile soil simply grew taller than those grown in barren soil, and this is true even though the heritability estimates for the heights of the plants *within* each field are comparable (Lewontin, 1976).

The same argument can be applied in explaining group differences in intellectual performance. Even though the heritability estimates for IQ are comparable *within* our samples of African-American and white schoolchildren, the 14-point differences in average IQ *between* the groups may reflect differences in the home environments of African Americans and whites rather than a genetic difference between the races.

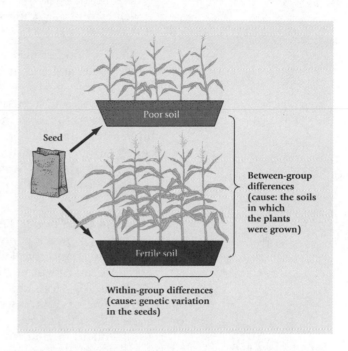

Why within-group differences do not necessarily imply anything about between-group differences. Here we see that the difference in the heights of the plants within *each field reflects the genetic variation in the seeds that were planted there, whereas the difference in the* average *heights of the plants across the fields is attributable to an environmental factor: the soils in which they were grown. Adapted from Gleitman, 1991.*

middle-class homes (Bradley et al., 1989; Gottfried, 1984). And children who have always lived in poverty and whose parents have the fewest financial resources are the ones who experience the least stimulating home environments (Garrett et al., 1994). So there are ample reasons for suspecting that social-class differences in intellectual performance are primarily *environmental* in origin.

Carefully conducted adoption studies lead to a similar conclusion. Sandra Scarr and Richard Weinberg (1983; Weinberg, Scarr, & Waldman, 1992) have studied 99 African-American (or interracial) children who were adopted during the first year of life by white, middle-class families. The adoptive parents in these families were above average in IQ and highly educated, and many had biological children of their own. Although Scarr and Weinberg found that the African-American children averaged about 6 points lower on IQ tests than the white offspring of these same families, this small racial difference seems rather insignificant when we look at the *absolute* performance of the transracial adoptees. As a group, the African-American adoptees obtained an average IQ of 110—10 points above the average for the population as a whole and 20 points above comparable children who are raised in low-income African-American communities. Moreover, the African-American adoptees from these middle-class families also scored well above the national average on standardized achievement tests at school. Scarr and Weinberg (1983) concluded that:

> the high IQ scores for the black and interracial children . . . mean that (a) genetic differences do not account for a major portion of the IQ performance difference between racial groups, and (b) black and interracial children *reared in the [middle class] culture of the tests and the schools* perform as well as other . . . children in similar families [p. 261, italics added].

There is another message in this transracial adoption study—namely, that much of the intellectual and academic discrepancies that have been attributed to race or ethnicity may actually reflect *ethnic differences in socioeconomic status.* Indeed, Charlotte Patterson and her associates (1990) found that variation in family income is a better predictor of the academic competencies of African-American and white school-children than race is. And the research described in Box 9-3 proceeds one step further by suggesting that almost all of the difference in IQ test performance between African-American and white preschool children reflects differences in the social and economic environments in which these children are raised.

A cultural influence? Finally, Elsie Moore (1986) believes that cultural differences in intellectual performance may still be found, even after differences in socioeconomic status are controlled. Moore extended Scarr and Weinberg's research by comparing African-American children adopted into middle-class white homes with similar African-American children adopted into middle-class African-American homes. Both groups of African-American adoptees obtained above-average IQs when tested at age 7 to 10. But even though the two groups were from the same social class, African-American children in white homes had an average IQ of 117, whereas the average IQ of adoptees in African-American homes was only 104. Why should this be?

Moore tried to find out by carefully observing the children during the session in which the IQ test was administered and noting how their mothers interacted with them as the children tried to perform a difficult cognitive task. What she found was what she believes to be cultural differences in parenting and in test taking, even within the same social class. For example, African-American children who had been placed into white homes seemed to enjoy the IQ testing session more than those from African-American homes did: They were more eager to answer questions; they persisted longer at the tasks; and they seemed much more confident. By contrast, children from African-American homes often seemed to want to escape the testing situation, and they sometimes shook their heads, as if to say that they didn't know an answer, even before a question was completed. These styles of test taking appeared to be linked to the parenting practices that mothers used while supervising their children's problem-solving activities. Compared with the African-American mothers, white mothers provided a great deal of positive encouragement. They joked to relieve tension and they often cheered when their children showed some progress. African-American mothers were more inclined to urge their children onward by showing signs of mild displeasure at a child's *lack of progress* (for example, "You could do better at this if you really tried!"), and their evaluations of their children's performance were somewhat more negative than those of white mothers. Perhaps this is why their children were less comfortable during the IQ testing session than children of white mothers were.

In sum, Moore's (1986) findings suggest that even when children of different racial and ethnic groups all grow up in advantaged homes, there may still be subtle cultural differences in parenting styles that contribute to group differences in IQ.

BOX 9-3

Do Socioeconomic Differences between the Races Explain Race Differences in IQ?

In 1991, nearly 22% of American children—some 14.3 million in all—were living in families in which total income was not sufficient to meet the families' most basic needs (U. S. Bureau of the Census, 1992). Moreover, children from minority groups are much more likely to be living under these marginal conditions than white youngsters are—especially African-American children, for whom living in poverty is more the rule than the exception (Duncan et al., 1994).

To what extent do socioeconomic differences between African Americans and whites account for race differences in IQ? One way to approach this question is to (1) select a large number of African-American and white families, (2) carefully measure several indicators and correlates of each family's socioeconomic status, and (3) determine whether any race differences in these socioeconomic variables are associated with (and thus might conceivably explain) race differences in children's intellectual performance.

Greg Duncan and his associates (1994) conducted such a study as part of a larger longitudinal investigation of low-birth-weight children. All of the children in this sample, who were now healthy 5-year-olds, had recently taken a standardized IQ test. In addition, data on such social class indicators and correlates as family (and average neighborhood) income, mother's educational level, number of parents living at home, and quality of the home environment (as assessed by the HOME inventory) were available for the family of each child. Like other investigators, Duncan et al. found that African-American children obtained lower IQs, on average, than white children did. Moreover, the African-American families scored lower on each of the above indicators and correlates of socioeconomic status. So how close was the association between race *differences* in IQ and race *differences* in socioeconomic status?

To find out, Duncan and his associates submitted their data to a sophisticated correlational analysis that allowed them to estimate how much of the race difference in intellectual performance is accounted for by each indicator/correlate of socioeconomic status. This is accomplished statistically by holding each socioeconomic variable constant for all children and then estimating what the IQ difference between African Americans and whites would be had they been raised under the same conditions—that is, under the same financial circumstances, in the same home environments, and so on.

The results of this analysis appear in the accompanying table. Since African-American children and white children differed in ways other than socioeconomic status that are known to affect intellectual performance (for example, their birth weights), it was necessary to first estimate the contribution of these demographic variables to race differences in intellectual performance. As we see in the table, race differences in IQ drop from the 13.6 points actually observed to an estimated 10.7 points after controlling for demographic differences between the races. After adjusting for the lower levels of maternal education and the greater number of single-parent families that African Americans experience, estimated race differences in IQ drop further, to 7.8 points. Adjusting next for the lower average incomes of African-American families reduces the estimated race differences in IQ to 4.8 points. And when the data are further adjusted for the less stimulating home environments in which African-American children live, there remains an IQ difference of only 2.9 points that is not accounted for by race differences in the demographic and socioeconomic variables!

Estimated Differences in Intellectual Performance of African-American and White Preschool Children after Adjusting for Race Differences in Demographic Variables and Socioeconomic Status

Analysis performed	Race difference in IQ (points)
Unadjusted (actual IQ scores)	13.6
After adjusting for race differences in:	
Demographic variables	10.7
Mother's education and number of parents living at home	7.8
Family/neighborhood income	4.8
Home environment	2.9

Of course, these findings are correlational data that we must interpret cautiously. Nevertheless, they strongly suggest that much of the IQ difference between African Americans and whites is really a "social-class" effect and that African-American children would perform comparably to whites if raised under similar socioeconomic circumstances. Indeed, we have reviewed other evidence that supports this conclusion—namely, Scarr and Weinberg's transracial adoption study: When raised in similar middle-class environments, African-American children and white children differ only minimally in intellectual performance and score above the national average on IQ tests.

Let's note, however, that neither Scarr and Weinberg nor Elsie Moore is suggesting that white parents are better parents or that disadvantaged children would be "better off" if they were routinely placed in middle-class homes. As Scarr and Weinberg (1976) point out, many traits other than a high IQ are necessary for successful adaptation to the natural environment, and they've gone so far as to speculate that white, middle-class caregivers may be less successful than other parents at fostering some of these competencies.

Even if we developmentalists were to assume that a high IQ is the ultimate human attribute, it would obviously be impractical (not to mention morally objectionable) to recommend that disadvantaged youths be taken from their parents and placed in more stimulating adoptive homes. However, there are other, less objectionable strategies that researchers have used to supplement the life experiences of disadvantaged children in the hope of furthering their intellectual and academic accomplishments. We will now consider these cognitive interventions, or attempts at compensatory education.

Concept Check 9-3 ⌄ Understanding Social and Cultural Influences on Intellectual Performance

Check your understanding of social and cultural contributors to IQ test performance by matching each descriptive statement below with one of the following concepts or hypotheses: (a) quality of home environment; (b) socioeconomic risk factors; (c) parenting styles; (d) unequal rearing environments; (e) "cumulative deficit" hypothesis; (f) confluence hypothesis; (g) genetic hypothesis for group differences in IQ; (h) "test bias" hypothesis. The answers appear in the Appendix.

_____ 1. Attempt to explain why first-borns outperform later-borns on IQ tests.

_____ 2. When held constant, race differences in intellectual performance are greatly attenuated.

_____ 3. The impact of this contributor to IQ becomes more apparent during the preschool period.

_____ 4. Posits that the inhibiting effects of impoverished environments on intellectual development will accumulate over time.

_____ 5. Attributes group differences in IQ to differences in examinees' motivation to perform and familiarity with the test items.

_____ 6. May contribute to group differences in IQ, even after group differences in socioeconomic status are taken into account.

_____ 7. Data on mixed-race youngsters and very bright minority children fail to support this notion.

_____ 8. Perhaps the strongest contributor to group differences in intellectual performance.

▶ IMPROVING COGNITIVE PERFORMANCE THROUGH COMPENSATORY EDUCATION

During the 1960s, a number of preschool educational programs were launched in an attempt to enrich the learning experiences of disadvantaged children. Project Head Start is perhaps the best known of these **compensatory interventions.** Simply stated, the goal of **Head Start** (and similar programs) was to provide disadvantaged children with the kinds of educational experiences that middle-class youngsters were presumably getting in their homes and nursery school classrooms. It was hoped that these early interventions would compensate for the disadvantages that these children might have already experienced and place them on a roughly equal footing with their middle-class peers by the time they entered first grade.

The earliest reports suggested that Head Start and comparable programs were a smashing success. Children participating in compensatory education were posting an average gain of about 10 points on IQ tests, whereas the IQs of nonparticipants from similar social backgrounds remained unchanged. However, this initial optimism soon began to wane. When program participants were reexamined after completing a year or two of grade school, the gains they had made on IQ tests had largely disappeared (Gray & Klaus, 1970). In other words, few if any lasting intellectual benefits seemed to be associated with these interventions, thus prompting Arthur Jensen (1969, p. 2) to conclude that "compensatory education has been tried and it apparently has failed" (see also Herrnstein & Murray, 1994).

compensatory interventions: special educational programs designed to further the cognitive growth and scholastic achievements of disadvantaged children.

Head Start: a large-scale preschool educational program designed to provide children from low-income families with a variety of social and intellectual experiences that might better prepare them for school.

However, many developmentalists were reluctant to accept this conclusion. They felt that it was shortsighted to place so much emphasis on IQ scores as an index of program effectiveness. After all, the ultimate goal of compensatory education is not so much to boost IQ as to improve children's academic performance. Others have argued that the impact of these early interventions might be cumulative, so that it may be several years before children who have participated in compensatory education begin to outperform their disadvantaged classmates who did not participate.

Long-Term Follow-Ups

As it turns out, Jensen's critics may have been right on both counts. In 1982, Irving Lazar and Richard Darlington reported on the *long-term* effects of 11 early intervention programs initiated during the 1960s. The program participants were disadvantaged preschool children from several areas of the United States. At regular intervals throughout the grade school years, the investigators examined the participants' scholastic records and administered IQ and achievement tests. The participants and their mothers were also interviewed to determine the children's feelings of self-worth, attitudes about school and scholastic achievement, and vocational aspirations, as well as the mothers' aspirations for their children and their feelings about the children's progress at school. Other follow-ups of Head Start and similar early education programs for disadvantaged children have been conducted since then (Berrueta-Clement et al., 1984; Darlington, 1991; Lee, Brooks-Gunn, & Schnur, 1988; Lee et al., 1990). Taken together, these longitudinal studies suggest that:

1. Children who participate in early intervention programs show immediate gains on IQ tests and other indicators of cognitive development, whereas nonparticipants from similar social backgrounds do not. Although the cognitive gains may persist for three to four years after the program has ended, participants and nonparticipants do not differ in IQ by the time they reach junior high school.
2. Program participants are more likely to meet their school's basic requirements than nonparticipants are. They are less likely to be assigned to special education classes, to be retained in a grade, or to drop out of high school.
3. Compensatory education improves both children's and mothers' attitudes about achievement. When asked to describe something that has made them feel proud of themselves, program participants are more likely than nonparticipants to mention scholastic achievements or (in the case of 15–18-year-olds) job-related successes. Mothers of program participants tend to be more satisfied with their children's school performance and to hold higher occupational aspirations for their children.
4. There is even some evidence (though not in all studies) that teens who have participated in early compensatory education are *less* likely than nonparticipants to become pregnant, require welfare assistance, and be involved in delinquent activities.

In sum, the longitudinal evaluations suggest that compensatory education has been tried and *apparently it works!* Although these programs rarely produce long-term gains in IQ, they clearly foster positive attitudes about achievement and improve children's chances of succeeding in the classroom. However, some programs (particularly those where parents are involved) are more effective than others.

The Importance of Parental Involvement

Comparisons of the effectiveness of early intervention programs suggest that the most effective ones almost always involve the child's parents in one way or another. Indeed, one particularly effective **home-based intervention** has focused more on the mothers

home-based interventions: compensatory interventions that take place in the home and provide services designed to make parents more confident and competent as caregivers.

Home-based interventions that target disadvantaged parents can lead to changes in parenting style that benefit all children in the family.

of disadvantaged infants and toddlers than on the children themselves (Seitz & Apfel, 1994b; Seitz et al., 1985) This 30-month program targeted mothers living in poverty who had delivered healthy first-born children. The program provided mothers with pediatric care, day care for the child, and monthly home visits by a psychologist, nurse, or social worker, who gave mothers social support, information about child rearing and other family matters, and assistance in obtaining vocational training or education that might help them to obtain a job (or a better-paying job). Other mothers of first-borns from the same socioeconomic background received no intervention and served as the control group. When Seitz and her associates (1985) followed up on the first-born children of these families 10 years later, they found that children in the intervention group were more likely to be making normal school progress, had better school attendance, and were less likely to require such costly remedial services as special education than children in the control group. Even more interesting was the finding that these same differences in scholastic adjustment were also found for *younger* siblings of these two groups—siblings who were not even born until *after the intervention was over* (Seitz & Apfel, 1994b)! Apparently, the early intervention had made mothers who participated more confident and effective in their parenting—a change that benefited their first-born child and all subsequent children as well (see also Madden, Levenstein, & Levenstein, 1976).

Parental involvement also seems to be important to the success of interventions that begin later in the preschool period and take place in nursery school or kindergarten settings. Joan Sprigle and Lyn Schaefer (1985) recently evaluated the long-term benefits of two such programs: *Head Start* (planned and administered by teachers and policy advisory councils) and *Learning to Learn*—an intervention that educated parents about the goals of the program, provided them with information about their children's progress, and repeatedly emphasized that a partnership between home and school was necessary to ensure the program's success. When the disadvantaged students who had participated in these interventions were later observed in the fourth, fifth, and sixth grades, the outcomes consistently favored the Learning to Learn (LTL) program, in which parents had been heavily involved. Although LTL students did not necessarily outperform those from Head Start on IQ tests, they were making better grades in basic academic subjects (such as reading) and were less likely to have failed a grade in school or to have been placed in costly special education classes for the learning disabled. And even though these two programs differed in ways other than degree of parental involvement, Sprigle and Schaefer believe that the greater participation of LTL parents in their children's learning activities at home contributed substantially to the success of this particular intervention.

Limitations of Compensatory Education and Implications for the Future

Now let's note what compensatory education has failed to accomplish. To date, none of these interventions has succeeded in transforming a disadvantaged population into a group of "high achievers" who score significantly above average in IQ or scholastic aptitude. The more typical finding is that children who take part in an enrichment program continue to score slightly below the national average on IQ tests and somewhat below their grade level on measures of academic achievement (Haskins, 1989; Ramey, 1982). But even though these interventions do not place program participants at the same intellectual level as their middle-class age-mates, they do serve a critically important function by helping to prevent the progressive decline in IQ and academic achievement so often observed among children from disadvantaged backgrounds.

Can we ever expect to do better than this in the future? Perhaps we can if we routinely provide parents with the kinds of home-based interventions that Seitz and her associates (1985; 1994b) did and combine such treatments with quality preschool education that begins *very early* and continues *over a period of several years*. One example of such an ambitious preschool program is the Carolina Abecedarian Project

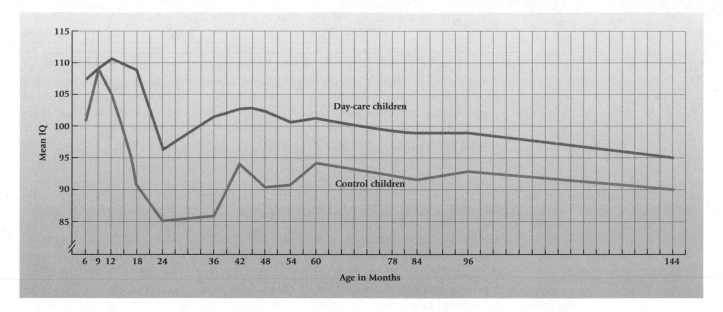

Mean IQ

Day-care children

Control children

Age in Months

Figure 9-8
IQ scores of day-care and control children from the Abecedarian Project between 6 months and 12 years of age.
Adapted from Campbell & Ramey, 1991.

(Ramey & Ramey, 1992; Campbell & Ramey, 1994). Program participants were selected from families considered to be "at risk" for producing mildly retarded children. Many of these families were on welfare, and most were headed by a single parent (the mother). The project began when the participating children were only 6 to 12 *weeks* old, and it continued for the next five years. Half of the high-risk children took part in a special day-care program designed to promote their intellectual development. The program was truly a full-time endeavor, running from 7:15 A.M. to 5:15 P.M., five days a week for 50 weeks each year, until the child entered school. The remaining children received dietary supplements for the first year, social services, and pediatric care comparable to that given to their age-mates in the experimental group, but they did not attend day care. At regular intervals over the next 12 years, the progress of these two groups of "high-risk" children was assessed by administering IQ tests. Periodic tests of academic achievement were also given at school.

Figure 9-8 summarizes the IQ data. Notice that the "high-risk" day-care children began to outperform their counterparts in the control group by 18 months of age and *maintained* this IQ advantage at age 12. Here, then, is evidence that high-quality preschool education that begins very early can have *lasting* intellectual benefits. Such programs can have lasting educational benefits, too, for the day-care children outperformed the control group in all areas of academic achievement from the third year of school onward (Campbell & Ramey, 1994).

Treatments such as Seitz's home-based intervention and the Abecedarian project are expensive to administer, and there are critics who claim that these programs would be not worth their high costs were we to provide them to all disadvantaged families (see, for example, Herrnstein & Murray, 1994). However, such an attitude may be "penny wise and pound foolish," for Victoria Seitz and her associates (1985) found that extensive *family* interventions emphasizing quality day care often pay for themselves by (1) allowing more parents to get away from full-time child care to work, thereby reducing their need for public assistance, and (2) providing the foundation for cognitive growth that enables most disadvantaged children to avoid special education in school—a service that costs in excess of $1500 per pupil per year (see also Zigler & Styfco, 1994). And when we consider the long-term economic benefits that could accrue later in life, when gainfully employed adult "graduates" of highly successful interventions pay more taxes than disadvantaged nonparticipants, need less welfare, and are less often maintained at public expense in penal institutions, the net return on each dollar invested in compensatory education could be impressive indeed (Haskins, 1989).

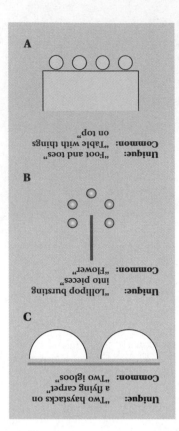

Figure 9-9
Are you creative? Indicate what you see in each of the three drawings. Below each drawing you will find examples of unique and common responses, drawn from a study of creativity in children.

Adapted from Wallach & Kogan, 1965.

A
Unique: "Foot and toes"   **Common:** "Table with things on top"

B
Unique: "Lollipop bursting into pieces"   **Common:** "Flower"

C
Unique: "Two haystacks on a flying carpet"   **Common:** "Two igloos"

giftedness: the possession of unusually high intellectual potential or other special talents.

creativity: the ability to generate novel ideas or works that are valued by others.

divergent thinking: thinking that requires a variety of ideas or solutions to a problem when there is no one correct answer.

ideational fluency: the most common measure of creativity; the sheer number of different ideas or solutions one can generate.

convergent thinking: thinking that requires one to come up with a single correct answer to a problem; what IQ tests measure.

Currently, we are a long way from routinely providing the kinds of compensatory assistance that disadvantaged children need. Indeed, fewer than half of all children eligible to participate in Head Start are currently enrolled, and some states do not even have statewide kindergarten programs. Recent plans to make Head Start available earlier to all eligible children and to upgrade its quality are steps in the right direction (Zigler & Styfco, 1994). But if we are to ever create truly equal intellectual opportunities for children born into poverty, we must seek to provide *long-term* interventions emphasizing quality preschool education (Campbell & Ramey, 1994) *and* the social supports that will help disadvantaged parents become more confident and competent as caregivers (Seitz & Apfel, 1994b).

▶ CREATIVITY AND SPECIAL TALENTS

What do we mean when we say that a child or an adolescent is *gifted?* In earlier years, the term was limited to people, such as those in Terman's famous longitudinal study, with IQs of 140 or higher. Yet, despite their lofty IQs and happy life outcomes, not one of Terman's gifted children ever became truly eminent. Recent definitions of **giftedness** have been broadened to include not only a high IQ but special talents in particular areas such as music, art, literature, or science. Over the years, we have learned that certain mental abilities not tapped by traditional IQ tests may enable some people to become innovators in their chosen fields. In other words, some gifted individuals are not only bright but also "creative."

What Is Creativity?

Creativity may be more important than a high IQ in permitting a Mozart, an Einstein, or a Piaget to break new ground. What is this special mental ability? Debates about the meaning of creativity have provoked nearly as much controversy as those about the meaning of intelligence (Mumford & Gustafson, 1988). Yet, almost everyone agrees that **creativity** represents an ability to generate novel ideas and innovative solutions—products that are not merely new and unusual but are also appropriate in context and *valued* by others. In his structure-of-intellect model, J. P. Guilford (1967; 1988) proposed that creativity represents divergent, rather than convergent, thinking. **Divergent thinking** requires one to generate a variety of ideas or solutions to problems when there is no one right answer. Indeed, the most common measure of creativity, at least for children, is what is called **ideational fluency**—the sheer number of different ideas that one can generate when asked, for example, to think of all the possible uses for a cork or to list all the words that can be made from the letters in BASEBALL. By contrast, **convergent thinking** requires a person to generate the one best answer to a problem and is precisely what IQ tests measure.

Interestingly, children's scores on creativity tests are not highly correlated with their scores on IQ tests, thus suggesting that creativity and general intelligence are independent attributes (Kogan, 1983). However, highly creative people rarely have below-average IQs, so that some minimal level of intelligence seems to be necessary before a person can be truly creative (Wallach, 1985; Runco, 1992). Among people with above-average IQs (college students, for example), general intelligence and creativity are essentially uncorrelated. So the IQ scores of you and your classmates would not necessarily predict who among you would be most creative on the exercises in Figure 9-9.

How Does Creativity Develop?

Why are some people creative while others are not? Because creativity is an intellectual ability, we might immediately suspect that it is a heritable attribute. Yet, twin studies have consistently shown that fraternal twins are about as similar to one

Parents of creative children encourage their intellectual curiosity and allow them to explore their interests in depth.

another in divergent thinking as identical twins are—a finding that suggests that (1) genetic influences play little if any part in the development of creativity, and (2) aspects of the home environment that siblings *share* are especially important in shaping creative potential (Plomin, 1990).

Although the evidence is not extensive, research on home environments reveals that parents of creative children tend to value nonconformity, to accept their children as they are (rather than trying to change them), to encourage intellectual curiosity, and to grant them a good deal of freedom to select their own interests and to explore them in depth (Getzels & Jackson, 1962; Harrington, Block, & Block, 1987; Runco, 1992). Perhaps these findings help to explain why creative children tend to be very playful and imaginative, very broad in their interests, and yet, *less* concerned than other bright classmates about making top grades or winning the approval of adults (Runco, 1992; Wallach, 1985).

How does creativity change with age? Apparently, the pattern varies somewhat from culture to culture. In summarizing his own cross-cultural research, Paul Torrance (1975) suggested that creativity declines temporarily during periods when children experience societal pressures to conform, as when they first enter school. Howard Gardner and his associates (1990) agree. They suggest that preschool children are much more uninhibited and original than their school-age counterparts, who instead are attempting to master the "right" (that is, culturally appropriate) way of expressing themselves in music, dance, art, and other endeavors. But learning to do things right may have its costs; Gardner believes that many adolescents simply give up any desire to express themselves creatively because they feel that their work is not original enough. However, some adolescents do regain the innovativeness and spontaneity they displayed as preschoolers and go on to produce highly creative works.

Could we predict whom these innovators are likely to be from their performance on childhood tests of creativity? Apparently, there are some links (see Runco, 1992). For example, researchers have occasionally found a modest relationship between scores on creativity tests administered in either elementary or secondary school and actual creative accomplishments, such as inventions and novels, in adulthood (Howieson, 1981; Torrance, 1988). However, his own review of the literature convinced Nathan Kogan (1983) that scores on creativity tests are better predictors of *current* creative achievements than of later accomplishments. Indeed, later accomplishments

Truly creative people have a passion to excel in their areas of special talent.

in a particular domain such as art or science are much more closely correlated with *early accomplishments in the same field* than with scores on creativity tests (Richards, Holland, & Lutz, 1967).

So researchers are now trying to understand the development of special creative abilities by locating individuals who have already shown exceptional talent in a particular domain and then contrasting their experiences with those of other youngsters. David Feldman (1982; 1986; Feldman & Goldsmith, 1991), for example, has studied child "prodigies" in such areas as chess, music, and mathematics. Surprisingly, perhaps, these children are generally similar to other children in domains outside their area of special talent.

What, then, contributed to their exceptional accomplishments? They were, of course, talented, but they also seemed to have a powerful motivation to develop their special talents, a burning passion for what they were trying to accomplish. The Olympic gymnast Olga Korbut put it well: "If gymnastics did not exist, I would have invented it" (Feldman, 1982, p. 35).

Equally important, however, was that these youngsters were blessed with an *environment* that nurtured their talent and motivation (see also Hennessey & Amabile, 1988; Monass & Engelhard, 1990). They were strongly encouraged by their families and *intensively tutored or coached by experts.* Early development of expertise in one's area is thought to be particularly important. According to Feldman, the child with creative potential must first become intimately familiar with the current state of his field if he is ever to advance or transform it, as the groundbreaking artist, musician, or scientist does. As Howard Gruber (1982) puts it, "Insight comes to the prepared mind . . ." (p. 22). To further emphasize the importance of environment, Feldman notes that his child prodigies were lucky enough to live in a culture and time that recognized and valued their special abilities. His point is simply that talents such as Olga Korbut's might not have bloomed had gymnastics not been so highly valued in Russian society when she was growing up.

In sum, the development of special or creative talent seems to be closely related to two factors: the individual's exceptional motivation to develop it and a supportive environment for its growth, including prolonged training at the hands of experts. Armed with this knowledge, perhaps we parents and educators can be a little more encouraging whenever one of our young charges displays an unusual passion for an offbeat or otherwise nontraditional interest. By providing such support (and exposure to experts if any are available), we just may be helping to nurture the creative potential of our future innovators.

SUMMARY

The psychometric, or testing, approach defines intelligence as a trait (or set of traits) that allows some people to think and solve problems more effectively than others. Alfred Binet developed the first successful intelligence test, which conceived of intelligence as a general mental ability. Yet, other researchers who rely on the factor-analytic techniques argue that intelligence is not a singular trait. Spearman viewed intelligence as consisting of a general mental ability (or *g*) and special abilities (or *s*), each of which was specific to a particular test. Thurstone claimed that intelligence consists of seven *primary mental abilities*, and at least one modern theorist believes that there may be 180 separate abilities. Cattell and Horn have argued that Spearman's *g* and Thurstone's primary mental abilities can be divided into two major dimensions of intellect: *fluid intelligence* and *crystallized intelligence*.

Two new viewpoints on intelligence are becoming increasingly influential. Robert Sternberg's triarchic theory criticizes psychometric theories of intelligence for their failure to consider the *contexts* in which intelligent acts are displayed, the test taker's *experience* with test items, and the *information-processing strategies* on which people rely when thinking or solving problems. And Gardner's *theory of multiple intelligences,* which is currently influencing research on creativity and special talents, contends that human beings display at least seven distinctive kinds of intelligence, several of which are not assessed by traditional intelligence tests.

The first intelligence tests were designed to predict children's academic performance and to identify slow learners who might profit from special education. Today, there are literally hundreds of intelligence tests, and instruments such as the *Stanford-Binet Intelligence Scale* and the *Wechsler Intelligence Scale for Children–III* are widely respected and used. The *Kaufman Assessment Battery for Children (K-ABC)* was the first major test guided by information-processing theory, and new tests that are based on this theory and compatible with Vygotsky's theory are beginning to appear. Intelligence tests differ considerably in format and content, but most of them present the examinee with a variety of cognitive tasks and then evaluate his or her performance by comparing it with the average performance of age-mates. An examinee whose performance equals that of the average age-mate is assigned an intelligence quotient (IQ) of 100. An IQ greater than 100 indicates that the child's performance is superior to that of other children her age; an IQ less than 100 means that the child's intellectual performance is below that of a typical age-mate.

IQ is a relatively stable attribute for some individuals. However, many others show wide variations in their IQ scores over the course of childhood. The fact that IQ can vary upward or downward over time suggests that IQ tests measure intellectual *performance* rather than an inborn capacity for thinking and problem solving.

When we consider trends for the population as a whole, IQ scores seem to predict important outcomes such as future academic accomplishments, occupational status, and even health and happiness. But at the individual level, an IQ score is not always a reliable indicator of one's future health, happiness, or success. Besides IQ, one's family background, work habits, education, and motivation to succeed are important contributors to the successes and happiness that one attains.

Both hereditary and environmental forces contribute heavily to intellectual performance. The evidence from twin studies and studies of adopted children indicates that about half the variation among individuals in IQ is attributable to hereditary factors. But regardless of one's genetic predispositions, barren intellectual environments clearly inhibit cognitive growth, whereas enriched, intellectually stimulating environments can clearly promote it.

Parents who create a stimulating home environment by becoming involved in their child's learning activities, carefully explaining new concepts, providing age-appropriate challenges, and consistently encouraging the child to achieve are likely to have children who score relatively high on IQ tests. Two other family characteristics that affect intellectual performance are family size and birth order: First-borns and children from smaller families tend to obtain slightly higher IQs than later-borns and children from large families.

On average, children from lower-class and minority backgrounds score lower on IQ tests than white children and other members of the middle class. Apparently, these group differences in IQ are not solely an artifact of our tests and testing procedures. Nor is there any conclusive evidence that they result from genetic differences among the various social-class, racial, and ethnic groups. The best explanation for group differences in IQ is the environmental hypothesis: Many poor people and minority group members score lower on IQ tests because they grow up in impoverished environments that are much less conducive to intellectual development than those of their middle-class age-mates.

Several compensatory education programs for disadvantaged preschoolers have now been evaluated. Although these early interventions do not ordinarily produce long-term gains in IQ, they do improve children's chances of succeeding in the classroom, and they help to prevent the progressive decline in intellectual performance so often observed among students from disadvantaged backgrounds. Outcomes are best when the programs begin earlier, last longer, and involve the child's parents.

Creativity, the ability to produce novel and socially valued ideas and solutions, is a distinct talent that requires divergent rather than convergent thinking. Creativity is largely independent of IQ, although a minimum level of intelligence is necessary for one to be very creative. Children who score high on creativity tests come from homes in which independence and intellectual curiosity are valued. Interestingly, neither tests of general intelligence nor tests of general creativity are very accurate at forecasting exceptional accomplishments in a specific field. The development of special talents and abilities seems to require a special motivation to develop one's skills and a special environment—namely, the encouragement of close companions and prolonged training in one's area of interest under the supervision of experts.

Key Terms

compensatory interventions [366]

confluence hypothesis [357]

convergent thinking [370]

creativity [370]

crystallized intelligence [336]

cultural bias [338]

"culture fair" tests [360]

"cumulative-deficit" hypothesis [353]

developmental quotient (DQ) [345]

deviation IQ [342]

divergent thinking [370]

dynamic assessment [344]

environmental hypothesis [362]

factor analysis [334]

fluid intelligence [336]

g [335]

genetic hypothesis [361]

giftedness [370]

Head Start [366]

hierarchical model of intelligence [335]

home-based interventions [367]

HOME inventory [355]

ideational fluency [370]

idiot savant [339]

intelligence quotient (IQ) [341]

Level I abilities [362]

Level II abilities [362]

mental age (MA) [333]

normal distribution [342]

primary mental abilities [335]

psychometric approach [333]

s [335]

"structure of intellect" model [335]

"test bias" hypothesis [359]

test norms [341]

theory of multiple intelligences [339]

triarchic theory [337]

Development of Language and Communication Skills

One truly remarkable achievement that sets us humans apart from the rest of the animal kingdom is our creation and use of **language**. Although animals can **communicate** with one another, their limited number of calls and gestures are merely isolated signals that convey very specific messages (for example, a greeting, a threat, a summons to congregate) in much the same way that single words or stereotyped phrases do in a human language. By contrast, human languages are amazingly *flexible* and *productive*. From a small number of individually meaningless sounds, a person who is proficient in a language can generate thousands of meaningful auditory patterns (syllables, words) that can then be combined according to a set of grammatical rules to produce an infinite number of messages. Language is also an *inventive* tool. Most of what people say or hear in any given situation is not merely a repetition of what they have said or heard before; speakers create novel utterances on the spot, and the topics they talk about may have nothing to do with their current situation or the stream of ongoing events. Indeed, language is the only form of communication by which we can easily produce a variety of messages that are blatantly untrue (as in a lie or a sarcastic utterance) or otherwise figurative in nature (as in the simile "She's like a breath of fresh air"). Yet, creative as we may be in generating new messages, other people who know the language will be able to understand any and all of our ideas as long as each of our statements adheres to the rules and conventions of the language we are speaking.

Although language is one of the most abstract bodies of knowledge we will ever acquire, children in all cultures come to understand and use this intricate form of communication very early in life. In fact, many infants are talking before they can walk. How is this possible? Are infants biologically programmed to acquire language? What kinds of linguistic input must they receive in order to become language users? Is there any relation between a child's cooing, gesturing, or babbling and the later production of meaningful words? How do infants and toddlers come to attach meaning to words? Do all children pass through the same steps or stages as they acquire their native language? And what practical lessons must children learn to become truly effective communicators? These are but a few of the issues we will consider as we trace the development of children's linguistic skills and try to determine how youngsters become so proficient in using language at such an early age.

▶ FOUR COMPONENTS OF LANGUAGE

Perhaps the most basic question that **psycholinguists** have tried to answer is the "what" question: What must children learn in order to master the intricacies of their native tongue? After many years and literally thousands of studies, researchers have concluded that four kinds of knowledge underlie the growth of linguistic proficiency: a knowledge of *phonology*, a knowledge of *semantics*, a knowledge of *syntax*, and a knowledge of *pragmatics*.

Phonology

Phonology refers to the basic units of sound, or **phonemes,** that are combined to produce words and sentences. Each language uses only a subset of the sounds that human beings are capable of generating. For example, English makes use of 45 phonemes, and no language uses more than 60. Each language has rules for combining phonemes and for pronouncing these phonemic combinations. Thus, speakers of English recognize that it is quite permissible to begin a word with *st-* (*stop, student*) or *sk-* (*skit, skull*) but not *sb-* or *sg-*. Although English-speaking people immediately discriminate the phonemic combinations "zip" and "sip," Spanish speakers may not, because the Spanish language does not make auditory distinctions between the phonemes *z* and *s*. The point for our purposes is that children must learn to discriminate and to pronounce a number of these speechlike sounds in order to make sense of the speech they hear and to be understood when they try to speak.

language: a small number of individually meaningless symbols (sounds, letters, gestures) that can be combined according to agreed-on rules to produce an infinite number of messages.

communication: the process by which one organism transmits information to and influences another.

psycholinguists: those who study the structure, meaning, and development of children's language.

phonology: the sound system of a language and the rules for combining these sounds to produce meaningful units of speech.

phonemes: the basic units of sound that are used in a spoken language.

Animals communicate through a series of calls and gestures that convey a limited number of very specific messages.

Semantics

Semantics refers to the *meanings* expressed in words and sentences. The most basic meaningful units of language are called **morphemes;** they include words and grammatical markers such as the suffix *-ed* for past tense, the suffix *-s* to signify a plural noun, and other prefixes and suffixes. Clearly, children must recognize that words convey meanings—that they symbolize particular objects, actions, and relations and can be combined to form larger and more complex meanings—before they can comprehend the speech of others or be understood when they speak.

Syntax

Language also involves **syntax,** or the rules that specify how words are to be combined to form meaningful phrases and sentences. Consider these three sentences:

> Garfield Odie bit.
> Garfield bit Odie.
> Odie bit Garfield.

Even very young speakers of English recognize that the first sentence violates the rules of English sentence structure (or syntax), although this word order would be perfectly acceptable in other languages, such as French. The second and third sentences are grammatical English sentences that contain the same words but convey very different meanings. They also illustrate how word meanings (semantics) interact with sentence structure (word order) to give the entire sentence a meaning. This basic principle is true of all languages, even though the rules of sentence construction (syntax) vary considerably from language to language. Clearly, children must acquire a basic understanding of the syntactical features of their native tongue before they can become very proficient at speaking or understanding that language.

Pragmatics

A knowledge of phonology, semantics, and syntax will enable children to produce grammatical sentences but is no guarantee that the speech they generate will be appropriate for the setting in which they find themselves. Language learners must also master the **pragmatics** of language—rules specifying how language is to be used to communicate effectively. Imagine a 6-year-old who is trying to explain a new game to her 2-year-old brother. Clearly, she cannot speak to the toddler as if he were an adult or an age-mate; she will have to adjust her speech to his linguistic capabilities if she hopes to be understood.

Pragmatics also involve *sociolinguistic knowledge*—culturally specified rules that dictate how language should be used in particular social context. A 3-year-old may not

semantics: the expressed meaning of words and sentences.

morphemes: the smallest meaningful units of language; these include words and grammatical markers such as prefixes, suffixes, and verb-tense modifiers (for example, *-ed*, *-ing*).

syntax: the structure of a language; the rules specifying how words and grammatical markers are to be combined to produce meaningful sentences.

pragmatics: principles that underlie the effective and appropriate use of language in social contexts.

A pragmatic error: Messages can have unintended consequences when we fail to adapt them to the social or situational context.

Reprinted with special permission of King Features Syndicate, Inc.

yet realize that the best way of obtaining a cookie from Grandma is to say "Grandma, may I please have a cookie?" rather than stating in a demanding tone "Gimme a cookie, Grandma!" In order to communicate most effectively, children must become "social editors" and take into account where they are, with whom they are speaking, what the listener already knows, and what the listener needs or wants to hear.

In short, mastering a language is an incredible challenge, for it requires mastering phonology, semantics, syntax, and pragmatics. Moreover, human communication involves not only language use, but *nonverbal communication* (facial expressions, intonational cues, gestures, and so on). Children must learn these nonverbal signals as well, for they often help to clarify the meaning of a verbal message and are an important means of communicating in their own right.

This brings us to a second basic question: *How* do young, cognitively immature preschool children acquire all this knowledge so quickly?

THEORIES OF LANGUAGE DEVELOPMENT

As psycholinguists began to chart the course of language development, they were amazed that children could learn such a complex symbol system at such a breathtaking pace. After all, many babies are using abstract signifiers (words) to refer to objects and activities before they can walk. And by age 5, children already seem to know and use most of the syntactical structures of their native tongue, even though they have yet to receive their first formal lesson in grammar. How do they do it?

In addressing the "how" question, we once again run headlong into a nativist/empiricist (nature/nurture) controversy. Learning theorists represent the empiricist point of view. From their perspective, language is obviously *learned:* After all, Japanese children acquire Japanese, French children acquire French, and profoundly deaf children of hearing parents may acquire few formal communication skills unless they receive instruction in sign language. However, other theorists point out that children the world over seem to display similar linguistic achievements at about the same age: They all babble by 4–6 months of age, utter their first meaningful word by age 12–13 months, begin to combine words by the end of the second year, and know the meanings of many thousands of words and are constructing a staggering array of grammatical sentences by the tender age of 4 or 5. These **linguistic universals** suggested to *nativists* that language acquisition is a *biologically programmed* activity that (1) is largely governed by maturation and (2) may even involve highly specialized linguistic processing capabilities that operate most efficiently early in childhood.

Interestingly, this nature/nurture debate is not settled, and, even today, we have no truly definitive answers to many "how" questions about early language development. However, an increasing number of psycholinguists believe that both the nativists and the empiricists are partially correct and that language acquisition reflects a complex *interaction* between the child's biological predispositions, her cognitive development, and the characteristics of her unique linguistic environment.

linguistic universal: an aspect of language development that all children share.

The Learning (or Empiricist) Perspective

Ask most adults how children learn language and they are likely to say that children imitate what they hear, are praised (that is, reinforced) when they use proper grammar, and are corrected when they say things wrong. Indeed, learning theorists have emphasized these same processes—imitation and reinforcement—in their own theories of language learning.

Skinner's reinforcement model. In 1957, B. F. Skinner published a book entitled *Verbal Behavior* in which he argued that children learn to speak appropriately because they are reinforced for grammatical speech. Skinner believed that adults begin to shape a child's language by selectively reinforcing those aspects of babbling that are most like adult speech, thereby increasing the probability that these sounds will be repeated. Once they have "shaped" sounds into words, adults then withhold further reinforcement (attention or approval) until the child begins combining words—first into primitive sentences and then into longer grammatical utterances. So caregivers are said to teach language by reinforcing successive approximations of grammatical speech until the child talks like an adult.

Another way that parents and other companions might subtly reinforce language is to correctly interpret what the child is trying to say. According to the **communication pressure hypothesis,** children learn to speak more clearly and grammatically because they need to communicate their needs to others (Dale, 1976). The idea here is that adults are most likely to understand grammatical speech and then unwittingly reinforce these interpretable utterances by attending to the child's requests and satisfying his needs.

The role of imitation. Other learning theorists (for example, Bandura, 1971; Whitehurst & Vasta, 1975) believe that children acquire much of their linguistic knowledge—phonology, word meanings (semantics), sentence structure (syntax), and even pragmatic rules—by carefully listening to and imitating the speech of their companions. Indeed, it is easy to imagine how a child might quickly acquire language by imitation, especially if his companions also "reinforce" his grammatical speech with attention and praise or by granting requests and satisfying needs.

Problems with the Empiricist Viewpoint

How well does the learning perspective account for language development? Obviously, imitation must play some role, for children end up speaking the same language that their parents speak, down to the same regional accent. Moreover, young children rapidly learn the meaning of many words spoken by other people, even new words introduced on television (Rice & Woodsmall, 1988). Finally, it seems that pressure to communicate effectively is sometimes involved in learning new *words* (semantics), for children are quicker to acquire and use the proper names for various toys when "reinforced" for doing so by receiving the toy to play with (Whitehurst & Valdez-Menchaca, 1988).

However, learning theorists have had an easier time explaining the development of phonology and semantics than accounting for the growth of syntax. If parents really "shaped" grammar, as Skinner contends, then they ought to reliably praise a child's grammatical speech while taking great pains to discourage ungrammatical utterances. Yet, Roger Brown and Camille Hanlon (1970) found that a mother's approval or disapproval of her child's speech depends more on its *semantics* or truth value than on its grammatical properties. For example, when one child said "Her curling my hair," her mother approved of this truthful but grammatically incorrect statement. When another child called attention to a lighthouse by stating "There's the animal farmhouse" (syntactically correct but untruthful), her mother quickly corrected her (see also de Villiers & de Villiers, 1992; Penner, 1987). Moreover, parents can

communication pressure hypothesis: the idea that children learn to speak clearly and grammatically because clear, grammatical statements will effectively communicate their needs and desires.

easily understand a child's *ungrammatical* utterances and are just as likely to reward a grammatically primitive request ("Want milk") as a well-formed version of the same idea (Brown & Hanlon, 1970). Clearly, these findings cast doubt on the notion that parents' selective reinforcement of appropriate grammar is the primary mechanism by which children learn syntax.

Do children acquire syntax by imitating their older companions? Probably not. Many of a child's earliest sentences are highly creative statements, such as "Allgone cookie" or "It broked," that do not appear in adult speech and could not have been learned by imitation. And when children do try to imitate an adult utterence, they usually condense the statement so that it conforms to their existing level of grammatical competence (Baron, 1992). For example, a 2½-year-old's imitation of "Look, the kitty is climbing the tree" is likely to be "Kitty climb tree." Indeed, Lois Bloom and her colleagues (1974) reported that young children do not readily imitate a grammatical rule until they have already used that principle at least once in their spontaneous speech. So imitation may help a child to properly apply rules that he partially understands and is beginning to use, but it is probably not the mechanism by which these rules are learned in the first place (Slobin, 1979).

How Do a Child's Companions Promote Language Learning?

Now we begin to see why the task of explaining language development is so challenging. If a child does not directly imitate parental speech, and if parents do not "shape" the child's language by selectively reinforcing grammatical utterances, then just what roles do others play in language learning? In recent years, psycholinguists have tried to answer this question by carefully analyzing the ways that adults and older children talk to younger children. Let's see what they have learned.

Opportunities to communicate. As we will see later in the chapter, even very young infants are learning important lessons about language and communication in the context of mutual play, vocal turn-taking, and other joint activities with their close companions. How important are these shared activities to the child's language development? Apparently, they are very important. Michael Tomasello and Jeff Farrar (1986) recorded and analyzed linguistic interactions between 24 mothers and their infants when the infants were 15 and 21 months of age. They found that very general measures of the mothers' speech to their infants (such as total amount of speech and speech complexity) did *not* predict the infants' language proficiency or language development. Yet, one specific measure, the extent to which mothers spoke about objects to which they and their infants were *jointly attending* (such as toys that they were sharing), was a strong predictor of early language: The mothers who referred to such objects the most had children with the largest vocabularies. Clearly, these findings make a good deal of sense, for if a child is already interested in objects that the mother is talking about, he should be highly motivated to decipher the meaning of his mother's speech (see also Dunham, Dunham, & Curwin, 1993).

Is the child's language development affected by the willingness of close companions to initiate and maintain conversations? Apparently so, for parents who frequently encourage vocal dialogues by asking questions, making requests, or issuing commands that invite verbal responses have children who are quicker to acquire syntactical rules, who recognize more letters and numbers and have larger vocabularies, and who score higher on academic achievement tests in elementary school, compared with children from similar backgrounds whose parents are less conversant (Hart & Risley, 1992; Huttenlocher et al., 1991; Valdez-Menchaca & Whitehurst, 1992; Walker et al., 1994).

But interesting as these findings may be, several questions remain. How do children come to understand grammatical rules as they converse with others? Does it matter what close companions are saying, or, rather, could infants and toddlers learn to talk just as well if they spent thousands of hours listening to people on television? Let's see whether we can shed some light on these issues by considering what parents seem to be doing when they talk to their children.

Reprinted with special permission of King Features Syndicate, Inc.

Talking the child's language. Cross-cultural research points to a nearly universal tendency of parents and older siblings to address infants and toddlers with very short, simple sentences that psycholinguists call "babytalk" or **motherese** (Gelman & Shatz, 1977; Grieser & Kuhl, 1988). Typically, these utterances are spoken slowly and in a high-pitched voice, with an emphasis on certain key words (Fernald & Mazzie, 1991). Much of motherese consists of questions ("Where's the ball?") or simple imperatives ("Throw it") that may be paraphrased or repeated several times in order to attract the child's attention and help him to understand. From the earliest days of life, infants pay more attention to the high-pitched sounds and varied intonational patterns of motherese than to the "flatter" speech that adults use when communicating with each other (Cooper & Aslin, 1990; Pegg, Werker, & McLeod, 1992). Indeed, infants even seem to grasp certain messages carried in their parents' intonational patterns (for example, "Pay attention" or "Good for you!") long before they can make out a word about what is being said (Fernald, 1989; 1993).

Cultural beliefs about child rearing clearly affect the content of motherese. When talking about a stuffed animal, for example, Japanese mothers often engage the infant in *social* routines designed to promote interpersonal harmony ("Give the doggie love"), whereas American mothers are more inclined to treat the interaction as an opportunity to teach the infant about objects and their characteristics ("It's a doggie! Look at his big ears.") (Fernald & Morikawa, 1993; see also Bornstein et al., 1992). But regardless of content, parents gradually increase both the length and complexity of their own sentences as their children's language becomes more elaborate (Newport, Gleitman, & Gleitman, 1977; Shatz, 1983). And at any given point in time, the adult's sentences are slightly longer and slightly more complex than the child's (Bohannon & Warren-Leubecker, 1989; Sokolov, 1993). Here then, is a situation that might seem to be ideal for language learning. The child is constantly exposed to new semantic relations and grammatical rules that appear in simple utterances that he will probably understand—particularly if older companions frequently repeat or paraphrase the ideas they are trying to communicate (Harris, 1992). Clearly, this is a form of modeling by the parent. However, children do not acquire new grammatical principles by mimicking them directly, nor do adults often attempt to teach these principles by illustration. Parents speak in "motherese" for one main reason—to communicate effectively with their children (Fernald & Morikawa, 1993; Penner, 1987).

Expansions, recasts, and topic extensions. Parents often react to syntactical or phonological errors in ways that (1) subtly communicate that a mistake has been made and (2) provide information that might be used to correct such errors (Bohannon & Stanowicz, 1988). For example, if a child says "Doggie go," an adult may respond with an **expansion**—a grammatically correct and enriched version of the child's ungrammatical statement ("Yes, the doggie is going away"). A slightly different form of expansion occurs when adults **recast** the child's sentences into new grammatical forms. For example, a child who says "Doggie eat" might have his sentence

motherese: the short, simple, high-pitched (and often repetitive) sentences that adults use when talking with young children.

expansions: responding to a child's ungrammatical utterance with a grammatically improved form of that statement.

recasts: responding to a child's ungrammatical utterance with a nonrepetitive statement that is grammatically correct.

restructured as "What is the doggie eating?" or "Yes, the doggie is hungry." These recasts are moderately novel utterances that will probably command the child's attention and thereby increase the likelihood that he will notice the new grammatical forms that appear in the adult's speech. Finally, parents are likely to respond to grammatically *appropriate* sentences by simply maintaining and extending the conversation *(topic extension)*. By carrying on without revising the child's utterance, adults are providing a strong clue that the utterance was grammatical (Bohannon & Stanowicz, 1988; Penner, 1987).

Do children profit from these experiences? Many psycholinguists think so. Although young children rarely mimic new grammatical forms immediately, there is clear evidence that they tend to imitate expansions and recasts more readily than other kinds of adult utterances (Bohannon & Stanowicz, 1988; Farrar, 1992). Moreover, adults who frequently expand, recast, or otherwise extend their children's speech (or those who have been trained to do so) have youngsters who are quicker to acquire syntactical principles and who score relatively high on standardized tests of expressive language ability, compared with children from similar backgrounds whose parents rely less on these conversational techniques (Hoff-Ginsberg, 1986; Valdez-Menchaca & Whitehurst, 1992; Whitehurst et al., 1988).

Do parents expand or recast their child's utterances as part of a *conscious* attempt to teach language? It might seem that way, for adults regularly modify the child's ungrammatical statements, while responding to grammatical statements with topic extensions. Yet, Sharon Penner (1987) found that parents are not even aware that they do this and, in fact, insist that they respond in the same way to grammatical and ungrammatical statements. Why are parents unaware of their tendency to repair ungrammatical utterances? Simply because their expansions and recasts are ploys to communicate more effectively with their children rather than deliberate attempts to improve children's grammar (Penner, 1987).

Are environmental props necessary? Adults who speak motherese and who expand and recast their child's sentences may be providing an ideal environment for language learning—one that contains a rich variety of sentences that are moderately novel but, at the same time, are related to the ideas that the child is currently expressing. Are these modifications of adult speech really necessary for normal language acquisition? Would children learn to talk just as well if adults spoke to them as if they were adults? Could they acquire language by merely listening to adults converse with one another?

Let's consider evidence bearing on the first question. There are cultures and subcultures (namely, the Kaluli of New Guinea, the natives of American Samoa, and the Trackton people of the Piedmont Carolinas) that allegedly do not address children in motherese or restructure children's primitive sentences, choosing instead to converse with them as though they were adults. And yet, children in these cultures do acquire language without notable delays (Gordon, 1990; Ochs, 1982; Schieffelin, 1986). So even though environmental props such as motherese and adult expansions may make a language a bit easier for the young child to decipher, they are not absolutely necessary for normal language development (Marcus, 1993).

Could children, then, acquire language by merely listening to others converse? Apparently not. Catherine Snow and her associates (1976) studied a group of Dutch children who happened to watch a great deal of German television. Despite their prolonged exposure to the German language, these Dutch-speaking subjects did not acquire any German words or grammar. De Villiers and de Villiers (1979) also cite the case of a hearing child of deaf parents who saw his parents sign to each other (but not to him) and who had little opportunity to hear any oral speech other than that on television. At age 4, this boy was combining words into highly idiosyncratic strings (for example, "That enough two wing") that clearly reflected his ignorance of most grammatical principles. By contrast, hearing children of profoundly deaf parents often show an approximately normal pattern of language development if they spend at least 5–10 hours a week in the company of a hearing/speaking adult, such as a grandparent (Schiff-Myers, 1988). So the evidence seems to imply that opportunities to *converse* with speakers of the language are necessary for normal language acquisition (Bohannon, MacWhinney, & Snow, 1990; de Villiers & de Villiers, 1979).

In sum, parents and other companions play a crucial role in the child's language development by conversing with him or her and thereby introducing new linguistic principles in sentences that are tailored to the child's level of understanding. (Indeed, this tailoring of speech to the child's comprehension occurs even within those cultures where companions rarely restructure the child's utterances or talk in motherese.) But let's recall that young children do not immediately mimic new linguistic forms nor do they need to produce grammatical utterances in order to be understood. What, then, prompts them to generate increasingly complex sentences? A number of linguists have proposed a biological theory of language development—*nativism*—in an attempt to answer this question.

Noam Chomsky's nativist theory dominated thinking about language development in the 1960s and 1970s.

The Nativist Perspective

According to the nativists, human beings are biologically programmed to acquire language. Linguist Noam Chomsky (1959; 1968) has argued that the structure of even the simplest of languages is incredibly elaborate—far too complex, he believes, to be either taught by parents (as Skinner proposed) or discovered via simple trial-and-error processes by cognitively immature toddlers and preschool children. Instead, Chomsky proposed that we humans (and only humans) come equipped with a **language acquisition device (LAD)**—an innate linguistic processor that is activated by verbal input. According to Chomsky, the LAD contains a *universal grammar*, or knowledge of rules that are common to all languages. So regardless of the language (or languages) that a child has been listening to, the LAD should permit any child who has acquired a sufficient vocabulary to combine words into novel, rule-bound utterances and to understand much of what he hears.

Other nativists make similar claims. Dan Slobin (1985), for example, does not assume that children have any innate knowledge of language (as Chomsky does), but he thinks that they have an inborn **language-making capacity (LMC)**—a set of cognitive and perceptual abilities that are highly specialized for language learning. Presumably, these innate mechanisms (a LAD or LMC) enable young children to process linguistic input and to infer the phonological regularities, semantic relations, and rules of syntax that characterize whatever language they are listening to. These inferences about the meaning and structure of linguistic information represent a "theory" of language that children construct for themselves and use to guide their own attempts to communicate (see Figure 10-1). Of course, young children are likely to make some erroneous inferences because their linguistic data base is not terribly extensive; but as they continue to process more and more input, their underlying theories of language become increasingly sophisticated until they eventually approximate those used by adults. For the nativists, then, language acquisition is quite natural and almost automatic, as long as children have linguistic data to process.

language acquisition device (LAD): Chomsky's term for the innate knowledge of grammar that humans were said to possess—knowledge that might enable young children to infer the rules governing others' speech and to use these rules to produce language.

language-making capacity (LMC): a hypothesized set of specialized linguistic processing skills that enable children to analyze speech and to detect phonological, semantic, and syntactical relationships.

Figure 10-1
A model of language acquisition proposed by nativists.

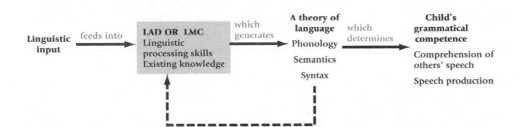

Support for the Nativist Perspective

Are children biologically programmed to acquire language? Several observations seem to suggest that they are. For example, we've noted that children the world over reach certain linguistic milestones at about the same age, despite cultural differences in the structure of language and in the types of speech that adults display when talking to them. Nativists interpret these *linguistic universals* as clear evidence that language must be guided by some species-specific biological blueprint. Even retarded children who perform very poorly on a broad range of cognitive tasks nevertheless acquire a near-normal knowledge of syntax and become quite adequate conversationalists (Flavell et al., 1993; Pinker, 1991).

Also consistent with the nativist approach is the observation that language is species-specific. Although animals can communicate with each other, no species has ever devised anything in the wild that closely resembles an abstract, rule-bound linguistic system. Is this because they lack a LAD (or LMC)? Are animals truly incapable of acquiring a language? Box 10-1 explores this intriguing issue.

Brain specialization and language. As we learned in Chapter 5, the brain is a lateralized organ with major language centers in the left cerebral hemisphere. Damage done to one of these language areas typically results in **aphasia**—a loss of one or more language functions, and the symptoms that an aphasic displays depend on the site and the extent of the injury. Injuries to Broca's area, near the frontal region of the left hemisphere, typically affect speech production rather than comprehension (Slobin, 1979). By contrast, patients who suffer an injury to Wernicke's area, at the back of the left hemisphere, may speak fairly well but will have difficulty understanding speech.

Apparently, the left hemisphere is sensitive to some aspects of language from birth. In the first day of life, speech sounds already elicit more electrical activity from the left side of an infant's brain, while music and other nonspeech sounds produce greater activity from the right cerebral hemisphere (Molfese, 1977). Moreover, we learned in Chapter 6 that infants are quite capable of discriminating important phonetic contrasts in the first few days and weeks of life (Eimas, 1982). These findings would seem to imply that the neonate is "wired" for speech and is prepared to analyze speechlike sounds.

The sensitive-period hypothesis. It often seems as if preschool children acquire their first language far more easily than college students learn a foreign tongue. Is this really the case? Nativists believe it is: They have argued that human beings are most proficient at language learning during the period between age 2 and puberty.

Eric Lenneberg (1967) is perhaps the strongest proponent of the **sensitive-period hypothesis** for language learning. Lenneberg claims that prepubescent children can easily acquire two (or more) languages simultaneously and speak each tongue without a trace of an accent from the other language(s). By contrast, he argues that people who acquire a second language after puberty must study intently to become fluent in that language, and they are likely to speak their new tongue with a "foreign" accent. In addition, Lenneberg claims that the prognosis for recovering from traumatic aphasia depends on the age at which the injury was sustained. Children who suffer brain damage before puberty will recover most if not all of their lost language functions without special therapy, particularly if their injury occurred before age 5. By contrast, adolescent and adult aphasics often require extensive therapy to regain even a portion of their lost language skills. If these observations are reliable, they would imply that the brain is particularly well suited for language acquisition before the onset of puberty. But why?

According to nativists, the sensitive period for language learning is a product of biological maturation. Lenneberg (1967) proposed that the brain is not fully specialized for language functions until it is fully mature, at puberty. Presumably, a young aphasic can recover lost language skills because the right hemisphere of his or her relatively unspecialized (immature) brain is able to assume the functions that would

aphasia: loss of one or more language functions due to an injury to the brain.

sensitive-period hypothesis (of language acquisition): the notion that human beings are most proficient at language learning before they reach puberty.

BOX 10-1
Language Learning in Chimpanzees

Perhaps it is only natural for humans to wonder whether chimpanzees and other primates who look so much like us could ever express themselves through some form of language. Earlier in this century, attempts were made to raise chimpanzees like children and to teach them to speak English (see Savage-Rumbaugh et al., 1993 for a review). Unfortunately, these projects were destined to fail, for the vocal apparatus of a chimpanzee is structurally incapable of producing the many phonemes of human speech.

In recent years, however, a number of researchers have shown that chimpanzees (and at least one gorilla) can learn to use linguistic signs and symbols to communicate a variety of messages. For example, several chimps have each acquired more than 100 signs from American Sign Language for the deaf (ASL) and can combine these signs to describe objects and events (for example, referring to a duck as a "water bird"), to make requests (such as "Give milk"), and to both ask and answer questions (for example, correctly answering "bed" in response to the question "What is that?" and answering "red" in response to the follow-up question "What color is it?") (Gardner & Gardner, 1974; Slobin, 1979). Other chimps introduced to linguistic hieroglyphics printed on computer keys have demonstrated similar communicative skills and have even used the code to type messages that permit trained chimpanzee companions to comply with their simple requests (such as "Give [chimp's own name] spoon") (Savage-Rumbaugh, Rumbaugh, & Boysen, 1978). Clearly, these accomplishments represent a form of *communication* that relies on abstract symbols and is far more elaborate than the calls and gestures that chimpanzees use in the wild (see Goodall, 1986). But is it language?

Remarkable as these achievements may be, nativists conclude that none of the so-called "linguistic" apes has acquired a language. One of the more vocal skeptics, Herbert Terrace (1979) actually began as an advocate of chimp language. But after attempting to teach sign language to a chimp pupil named Nim Chimpsky (an obvious play on the name of nativist Noam Chomsky), Terrace discovered that the internal structure of Nim's sign sentences was essentially arbitrary. To illustrate, Nim often produced blatantly ungrammatical constructions such as "Give banana, banana, banana" or "Play me Nim play" that were (1) highly similar to the "sentences" produced by all other "linguistic" apes and (2) very different from the speech of a 2-year-old child (Terrace at al., 1980). Lieberman (1984) reached a similar conclusion, noting that, after years of hard work, an ape may grasp many semantic relations but will display little if any knowledge of syntax—a critical feature of a true language.

These conclusions may have to be revised, however, in light of Sue Savage-Rumbaugh's recent findings when testing language *comprehension* in highly sociable pygmy chimps (Savage-Rumbaugh et al., 1993). In one study, Savage-Rumbaugh and her associates compared the linguistic abilities of a 2-year-old child, Alia, with those of Kanzi, an 8-year-old pygmy chimp who had been spoken to like a child since infancy. Two-year-olds respond appropriately to commands a majority of time. Could Kanzi comprehend the *verbal* instructions he received? Yes, indeed! In fact, he performed slightly better than 2-year-old Alia did, and his correct responses to hundreds of *novel* commands (for example, "Get the tomato that's in the microwave," "Put the egg in the juice") implies that he correctly interpreted both the semantics *and* the syntax of these statements. Nevertheless, it took years in a language-rich environment for Kanzi to attain an understanding of grammar comparable to that of a typical 2–3-year-old. Apparently, apes lack something that humans have that allows even severely retarded children who receive no formal training to easily surpass the linguistic accomplishments of the brightest chimpanzees.

Is that "something" we humans have a specialized linguistic processor—a LAD or LMC? Nativists say yes and offer several additional observations (described in the text) that they believe to be consistent with their biological perspective on language development.

This figure illustrates the array in front of Kanzi (top left) as he hears the sentence "Put the egg in the juice" (top right). It is possible for Kanzi either to put the juice in the egg, to put the egg in the juice, or to do something else entirely. Kanzi responds to this sentence by picking up the bowl containing the egg (bottom left) and tilting it until the egg falls into the juice (bottom right).

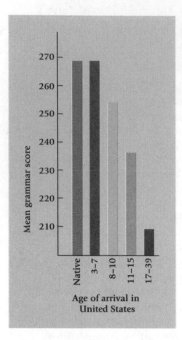

Figure 10-2
As shown here, there is a clear relationship between the age at which immigrants arrived in the United States and their eventual adult performance in English grammar. Those who arrived early in childhood end up performing like native speakers of English, whereas those who arrived as teenagers or adults perform much more poorly.

Adapted from Johnson & Newport, 1989.

normally be served by the damaged areas of the left hemisphere. At puberty, the prognosis changes. The brain is now completely specialized for language (and other neurological duties), so that the right hemisphere can no longer assume the linguistic functions that are lost when a person suffers an injury to the left side of the brain.

If the sensitive-period hypothesis is correct, then individuals who were largely deprived of a normal linguistic environment before puberty should find it difficult to acquire language later in life. Two excellent case studies reflect nicely on this idea. One is the case of Genie, a child who was locked away alone in a back room as an infant, not to be discovered by the authorities until she was nearly 14 years old. While confined, Genie heard very little language; no one was permitted to talk to her, and she was likely to be beaten by an abusive father if she made any noise (Curtiss, 1977). Then there is Chelsea, a deaf woman who, because of her deafness and her family's isolation, was 32 years old before she was ever exposed to a formal language system. Extensive efforts were undertaken to teach these women language, and each made remarkable progress, learning the meaning of many words and even producing lengthy sentences that were rich in their semantic content. Yet neither woman mastered the rules of syntax that virtually all children acquire without formal instruction (Curtiss, 1977; 1988), thus suggesting that first language learning is easier early in life.

What about second language learning? Is acquiring a foreign language a tougher task for a postpubertal adolescent whose "sensitive period" for language learning is over? Recent research by Jacqueline Johnson and Elissa Newport suggests that this may be the case. In one study (Johnson & Newport, 1989), native speakers of Korean or Chinese who had emigrated to the United States at different ages were tested as adults for mastery of English grammar. As we see in Figure 10-2, immigrants who began to learn English between 3 and 7 years of age were as proficient in English as native speakers are. By contrast, immigrants who arrived after puberty (particularly after age 15) performed rather poorly. Similarly, deaf adults show much better mastery of sign language if they were exposed to it as young children than if their training began later in life (Newport, 1991).

Finally, nativists interpret the research presented in Box 10-2 as a rather dramatic illustration that language acquisition is a fundamental human characteristic—even if children must "invent" the language they acquire.

Problems with the Nativist Approach

Today, almost everyone agrees that language development is influenced by biological development. However, many contemporary researchers seriously question the idea that human beings have any innate knowledge of language (LAD) or specialized language processor (LMC). Others are skeptical of findings that nativists take as support for their model. For example, recent research challenges Lenneberg's sensitive-period notion that young children (who allegedly have the benefit of a specialized linguistic processor) are any more likely to recover from traumatic aphasia than adults are (Bishop, 1988, Piacentini & Hynd, 1988). Moreover, it is by no means impossible for an adult to achieve near-native levels of proficiency when learning a foreign language. In fact, carefully controlled studies often find that adults are no worse and occasionally even better than younger children at the phonological aspects of second language learning (Reich, 1986).

Several other arguments for nativism fall by the wayside on closer examination. For example, human infants are said to be "wired" for language by virtue of their ability to make important phonological discriminations in the first few days and weeks of life. Is this really evidence for the existence of a LAD? If so, then rhesus monkeys and even chinchillas must have LADs, for members of these species show similar powers of auditory discrimination (Passingham, 1982). Even the seemingly amazing linguistic inventions that young children display (see Box 10-2) have been challenged. For example, no one has yet observed the language acquisition of children whose parents speak pidgins; thus, it is not completely clear that children transform pidgins to creole languages by themselves, without the assistance of adults (Bohannon, MacWhinney, & Snow, 1990).

BOX 10-2

On the "Invention" of Language by Children

Suppose that ten children were raised in isolation by an adult caregiver who attended to their basic needs but never talked or even gestured to them in any way. Would these youngsters devise some method of communicating among themselves? No one can say for sure, for children such as these have never been studied. However, the results of two recent programs of research suggest that our hypothetical children not only would learn to communicate but might even invent their own language.

Home sign among the deaf. Susan Goldin-Meadow and Carolyn Mylander (1984) have observed the progress of ten deaf children aged 1½ to 3 years, all of whom had hearing parents who knew little if anything about sign language. Clearly, these children were exposed to very atypical linguistic environments in that they couldn't hear oral speech and their parents were unable to instruct them in the use of signs. Would these youngsters invent a system of communicating in the absence of a language model? Could they create their own unique sign language?

Maybe so, for each of these children not only came to use signs and gestures to represent *actions* (for example, a fist at the mouth accompanied by chewing to represent eating), *objects* (for example, digging motions to refer to a snow shovel), and *attributes* (for example, a thumb and forefinger joined to signify "roundness"), but they soon began to combine their individualized signs into "sentences" that their companions could easily understand. However, critics have argued that these competencies may not reflect the child's inventiveness at all, for they may have resulted from subtle gestural exchanges with parents (Bohannon & Warren-Leubecker, 1989). So let's consider a second set of observations.

Transforming pidgins to true languages. When adults from different cultures migrate to the same area, they often begin to communicate in *pidgin*—a hybrid of their various languages that enables them to convey basic meanings and thus "understand" each other. In the 1870s, for example, large numbers of immigrants from China, Korea, Japan, the Philippines, Portugal, and Puerto Rico migrated to Hawaii to work in the sugar fields. What evolved from this influx was Hawaiian Pidgin English, a communication system with a small vocabulary and a few basic rules for combining words that enabled residents from different linguistic communities to communicate well enough to get by. Yet in the course of a generation, this pidgin was transformed into a *creole*—that is, a true language that evolves from a pidgin. Indeed, Hawaiian Creole English was a rich language with a vocabulary that sprang from the pidgin and its foreign language predecessors and had formal syntactical rules. How did this transformation from marginal pidgin to true language occur so rapidly?

Linguist Derek Bickerton (1983; 1984) claims that children of pidgin-speaking parents do not continue to speak pidgin. Instead, they spontaneously "invent" syntactical rules that creolize the pidgin to make it a true language that future generations in these multilingual communities will use. How did he decide that children were responsible? One clue was that whenever pidgins arise, they are quickly transformed into creoles—usually within a single generation. But the more important clue was that creole syntax closely resembles the (often inappropriate) sentences that young children construct when acquiring virtually any language. For example, questions of the form "Where he is going?" and double negatives such as "I haven't got none" are perfectly acceptable in creole languages. Finally, the structure of different creoles is similar the world over—so similar that it cannnot be attributed to chance. Bickerton believes that only a nativist model can account for these observations. In his own words: "The most cogent explanation of this similarity . . . is that it derives from . . . a species-specific program for language, genetically coded and expressed . . . in the structures . . . and operation of the human brain" (1984, p. 173).

So it seems that children who lack a formal linguistic model—be they deaf or subjected to marginally linguistic pidgins—will create languagelike codes to communicate with their companions. Apparently, they have some linguistic predispositions that serve them well.

Finally, the most damning critique of the nativist approach may be more conceptual than empirical: We don't really *explain* language development by attributing it to a built-in language-making capacity. Recall that the concept of a LAD arose as researchers began to discover that learning theories could not adequately explain language development. That being the case, the nativists concluded that the mechanism for language learning must be innate. Unfortunately, they have never specified *how* an inborn language processor might sift through linguistic input and infer the rules that govern language; they merely assume that these rules and relationships are eventually detected (in some unknown way) and applied to the child's own speech (for an especially lucid critique, see Moerk, 1989). Thus, the major shortcoming of the nativist approach can be illustrated by analogy: Attributing advances in linguistic competence to the mysterious workings of a LAD or LMC is like saying that physical growth is biologically programmed—*and then failing to identify the underlying variables (nutrition, hormones, and so forth) that explain why growth follows the course it takes. Clearly, the nativist approach is woefully incomplete; it is really more a description of language learning than a true explanation.*

The Interactionist Perspective

Although neither learning theory nor the nativist approach provides a complete explanation of language development, each of these perspectives may be partly correct. We know that children must have opportunities to *converse* with others before they become proficient users of a language. Imitation obviously plays some part in the language-learning process, for children acquire the same language (and even the same accent) that their companions use. Reinforcement must also play some role, for we've seen that children talk more (and become better readers) if their parents frequently encourage verbal interactions. Yet, if language were learned through imitation and reinforcement, it would be difficult to explain why children who hear varying kinds and amounts of linguistic input proceed through roughly the same steps when acquiring their first language. These "linguistic universals" suggest that language learning is related in some meaningful way to biological processes. But must we attribute language development to the mysterious workings of an inborn LAD (or LMC) in order to explain the similarities in children's early speech?

Apparently not. In recent years, cognitive theorists such as Jean Piaget (1970) and social-communication theorists such as Elizabeth Bates (1993; Bates & MacWhinney, 1982) and Neil Bohannon (see Bohannon & Warren-Leubecker, 1989) have argued that biological factors, cognitive development, and the linguistic environment interact to influence language development. According to this **interactionist theory,** young children the world over may talk alike because they are all members of the same species *who share many common experiences.* What may be innate is not any specialized linguistic knowledge or processing skills but, rather, a sophisticated brain and central nervous system that *matures* very slowly and predisposes children to develop similar ideas at about the same age—ideas that they are then motivated to express in their own speech (Bates, 1993).

However, the interactionist position also emphasizes—as Vygotsky did, but Piaget did not—ways in which *social interactions* with older, more competent individuals contribute to both cognitive and language development. We have noted, for example, that mothers apparently promote the growth of their infants' vocabularies if they pay close attention to what their infant is attending to and then talk to him or her about these objects and events (Dunham et al., 1993; Tomasello & Farrar, 1986). And as children develop intellectually, they express their new ideas and concepts in increasingly sophisticated utterances—statements that interactionists tell us will prompt a close companion to increase the complexity of her own speech as she addresses her child (Sokolov, 1993). This novel linguistic input then provides children with information they can use to form new linguistic hypotheses, produce even more complex utterances, and thereby influence the speech of their companions once again. Clearly, the pattern of influence is reciprocal: The child's speech influences the speech of older companions, which, in turn, influences the child's speech, and so on. Stated another way, the interactionists are proposing that the language of young children is influenced by a rich linguistic environment that they have had a hand in creating.

As we chart the course of language development in the pages that follow, we will review many findings that support this interactionist theory. Consider the relationship between general cognitive development and language development. Words are symbols, and it stands to reason that infants will not use them until they first display some capacity for symbolism. Indeed, infants begin to utter meaningful words at about 12 months of age, shortly after they first show some capacity for deferred imitation—a symbolic ability that emerges at about age 9 months (Meltzoff, 1988c). Moreover, we will see that infants' first words center heavily on objects they have

interactionist theory: the notion that biological factors and environmental influences interact to determine the course of language development.

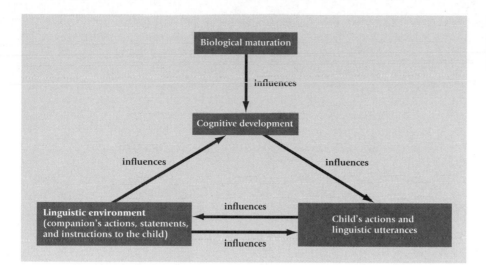

Figure 10-3
An overview of the interactionist perspective on language
development.

manipulated or on actions they have performed—in short, on aspects of experience they can understand through their sensorimotor schemes. Finally, words like "gone" and "oh oh" emerge during the second year, at about the same time that infants are mastering object permanence problems and appraising the success or failure of their problem-solving activities (Gopnik & Meltzoff, 1986; 1987). Thus, infants and tod-dlers often seem to talk about whatever cognitive concepts and competencies they are acquiring at the moment.

Similar links between cognitive growth and child language are apparent through-out the preschool period. For example, children rarely produce hypothetical state-ments such as "If it is cold, we will shiver" or "If it had rained, we would have been soaked" until age 4 or 5 (de Villiers & de Villiers, 1979). Indeed, these are reason-ably complex statements that require (1) the capacity to think about possibilities rather than actualities and (2) an ability to shift one's frame of reference to the future or the past. In English, the syntax required to express hypotheticals is reasonably com-plex, much more so than the grammatically simple forms used in Russian. Never-theless, Russian children do not begin to produce hypothetical statements until about the same age as English-speaking children do (Slobin, 1966). So the appearance of hypotheticals in children's speech depends more on an understanding of the *concept* of the hypothetical than on the intricacies of the grammar necessary to produce these utterances.

In sum, the interactionist perspective is both a synthesis and an extension of the learning and the nativist theories and is probably more accurate than either of these approaches. Like the nativists, the interactionists believe that children are biologically prepared for language learning. However, they stress that the "universals" in children's language reflect a basic interplay among biological maturation, cognitive develop-ment, and the linguistic environment rather than the workings of an inborn and highly specialized language processor (see Figure 10-3).

What distinguishes the interactionist approach from nativism and learning theory is (1) its focus on general cognitive development (rather than on the workings of a LAD or LMC) and (2) its emphasis on social/communicative factors (other than mim-icry and reinforcement) that promote language learning. The focus on cognition is not to imply that cognitive development explains language development; it merely places some limits on what children are likely to talk about and on what they will understand as they listen to others' speech. And even when children do grasp new concepts such as object permanence or hypotheticals, they must still discover how to express this knowledge in their own speech.

How do they make those discoveries? Here is where the interactionists propose that companions play a critically important role by promoting conversations in which they are continually introducing new concepts and linguistic principles in sentences that are generally tailored to the child's level of understanding (Sokolov, 1993). Could we educators ever devise any more effective "grammar" lessons? Probably not! And after several years (or by one estimate, more than 9000 hours) of interacting with these responsive linguistic models, the average 6-year-old has acquired most of the important principles of her native language and speaks in much the same way that her older companions do.

Although the interactionist perspective is the theory that many developmentalists favor, the question of *how* children acquire language is by no means resolved. We still know much more about *what* children are acquiring as they learn a language than about how they acquire this knowledge (Rice, 1989). So let's now chart the course of language development—a process that is well under way long before children utter their first meaningful word.

Concept Check 10-1 ⌄ Theories of Language Development

Check your understanding of theories of language development by matching each descriptive statement below with one of the following concepts or hypotheses: (a) communicative pressure hypothesis; (b) recasts; (c) language acquisition device; (d) sensitive-period hypothesis; (e) creolizing of pidgins by children; (f) universals in cognitive development; (g) conversations with language users. The answers appear in the Appendix.

_____ 1. Explains why adolescents have a harder time acquiring foreign languages than children do.

_____ 2. A means by which companions introduce new linguistic forms to young children.

_____ 3. Essential input for language learning.

_____ 4. Offered as support for the *nativist* perspective on language acquisition.

_____ 5. Claims that children's "grammatical" utterances are more likely to be correctly interpreted and reinforced.

_____ 6. Mechanism that *interactionist* theorists cite to explain cross-cultural similarities in language acquisition.

_____ 7. Proposed inborn linguistic processor containing a universal grammar common to all languages.

▶ BEFORE LANGUAGE: THE PRELINGUISTIC PERIOD

For the first 10 to 13 months of life, children are said to be in the **prelinguistic period** of language development—the period before speaking their first meaningful words. But even though young infants are preverbal, they are quite responsive to language from the day they are born.

Early Reactions to Language

In Chapter 6, we learned that newborns may be programmed to "tune in" to human speech. When spoken to, neonates often open their eyes, gaze at the speaker, and sometimes even vocalize themselves (Rheingold & Adams, 1980; Rosenthal, 1982). By 3 days of age, an infant already recognizes his or her mother's voice and clearly prefers it to the voice of a female stranger (DeCasper & Fifer, 1980), and newborns suck faster to hear recorded speech than to hear instrumental music or other rhythmic sounds (Butterfield & Siperstein, 1972). So babies can discriminate speech from other sound patterns, and they pay particularly close attention to speech from the very beginning.

Do different samples of speech all sound alike to the very young infant? Apparently not. Peter Eimas (1982) found that 1-month-old infants are about as capable as adults of discriminating consonant sounds such as *ba* and *pa* or *da* and *ta*. And

prelinguistic period: the period before children utter their first meaningful words.

by age 2 months, babies can reliably discriminate the vowel sounds /a/ and /i/ and even recognize that a particular vowel (an /a/, for example) is still the same sound when spoken at different pitches or intensities by different speakers (Marean, Werner, & Kuhl, 1992).

It seems, then, that the abilities to discriminate speech from nonspeech and to differentiate a variety of speechlike sounds are either (1) innate or (2) acquired in the first few days and weeks of life. In either case, it appears that young infants are remarkably well prepared for the task of decoding the speech they hear.

Producing Sounds: The Infant's Prelinguistic Vocalizations

All normal, healthy infants are capable of vocalizing at birth, and their prelinguistic vocalizations develop in predictable sequence over the first 10 to 12 months of life. As we noted in Chapter 5, neonates cry to signal their distress and may even emit different kinds of cries to communicate different needs. The next vocal milestone, at about 3 to 5 weeks of age, is **cooing**: repeating vowel-like sounds such as "oooooh" and "aaaaah." At about 3 to 4 months of age infants begin to add consonant sounds to their vocal repertoires and soon start to babble. This **babbling**, which may begin at any time between 4 and 6 months of age, is easily recognizable. A baby will repeat vocal/consonant combinations such as "mama" or "papapapa" that may sound like words, but are not used meaningfully. Interestingly, deaf infants whose parents are deaf and communicate in sign language will themselves babble manually, experimenting with gestures in much the same way that hearing infants experiment with sounds (Petitto & Marentette, 1991).

For the first 6 months of life, infants the world over (even deaf ones) sound pretty much alike, which suggests that early babbling is heavily influenced by maturation of the brain and the muscles controlling verbal articulation (Sachs, 1985). Yet, the effects of experience soon come into play. Deaf infants, who hear no speech, begin to fall far behind hearing infants in their ability to produce well-formed, language-like phonemes (Oller & Eilers, 1988). By contrast, 8-month-old hearing infants attend very carefully to others' speech and have even begun to babble in something of an accent—enough so that adults can often tell from their babbling whether the infants have been listening to English, Arabic, French, or Chinese (Boysson-Bardies, Sagart, & Durand, 1984). So advanced babblers seem to match the intonation of their babbles to the tonal qualities of the language they hear, and they actually begin to sound as if they are speaking that language. Apparently, babies are "learning the tune before the words" (Bates, O'Connell, & Shore, 1987, p. 157).

As their babbling progresses, infants begin to use particular babbling sounds selectively in certain situations. For example, one infant began to use the *m* sound (mmmm) when making requests and various vowel sounds (aaaaah) when manipulating objects (Blake & Boysson-Bardies, 1992). According to Charles Ferguson (1977), infants who produce these **vocables** are now aware that certain speech sounds have consistent meanings and are about ready to talk.

What Do Prelinguistic Infants Know about Language and Communication?

Do young infants know more about language than they can possibly tell? It now appears that they do and that one of the first things they learn about speech is a practical lesson. During the first six months, babies often coo or babble *while* their caregivers are speaking (Rosenthal, 1982). It is almost as if very young infants view "talking" as a game of noisemaking in which the object is to "harmonize" with their speaking companions. But by 7–8 months of age, infants are typically silent while a companion speaks and will wait to respond with a vocalization until their partner

coos: vowel-like sounds that young infants repeat over and over during periods of contentment.

babbles: vowel/consonant combinations that infants begin to produce at about 4 to 6 months of age.

vocables: unique patterns of sound that a prelinguistic infant uses to represent objects, actions, or events.

stops talking. Apparently, they have learned their first rule in the pragmatics of language: Don't talk while someone else is speaking, for you'll soon have an opportunity to have your say.

Vocal turn-taking may come about because parents typically say something to the baby, wait for the infant to smile, cough, burp, coo, or babble, and address the infant again, thereby inviting another response (Snow & Ferguson, 1977). Of course, infants may also learn about the importance of turn-taking from other contexts, or **formats,** in which they assume reversible roles with their companions (Bruner, 1983). Examples of these reciprocal exchanges might include bouts of nose touching, face making, and sharing toys. By 9 months of age, infants clearly understand the alternation rules of many games, and if such activities are interrupted by the adult's failure to take her turn, the infant is likely to vocalize, to urge the adult to resume by offering her a toy, or to wait for a second or two and take the adult's turn before looking once again at the adult (Ross & Lollis, 1987). So it seems that the ways caregivers structure their interactions with an infant may indeed help the child to recognize that many forms of social discourse, including "talking," are patterned activities that follow a definite set of rules.

The Importance of Intonational Cues

Earlier, we noted that adults typically speak to infants in a highly intonated "motherese" that attracts babies' attention. Moreover, adults reliably vary their tone of voice when trying to communicate different "messages" to their preverbal infants (Fernald, 1989; Stern et al., 1982). Rising intonations (for example, Look at mom^{my}) are used to recapture the attention of a baby who looks away, whereas falling intonations such as HEY $_{there}$! are often used to *elicit positive affect* (smiles, bright eyes) from a somber baby. These intonational prompts are often successful at affecting a baby's mood or behavior (Fernald, 1989; 1993), and 2–6-month-old infants frequently produce a vocalization in return that matches the intonation of what they have just heard (Masataka, 1992). So it is tempting to conclude that preverbal infants not only discriminate different intonational patterns, but soon recognize that certain tones of voice have a particular meaning. In fact, some researchers believe that a young infant's successful interpretation of intonational cues may provide some of the earliest evidence that speech is a *meaningful* enterprise that she might try to perfect (Fernald, 1989; 1993).

The characteristic "rhythm" of a language may also help preverbal infants to segment what they hear into words and phrases. By 7 to 10 months of age, infants clearly prefer to listen to speech that contains natural breaks and pauses to that in which pauses are inserted at unnatural places, such as the middle of a clause (Hirsh-Pasek et al., 1987). By 9 months of age, infants who have been exposed to English already prefer to listen to speech in which the predominant stress is on the first syllable of most words, as it is in English (Jusczyk, Cutler, & Redanz, 1993). Peter Jusczyk and his associates (1993) believe that this preference for a "strong/weak" stress pattern (which is not apparent in 6-month-olds) reflects the older infants' increasing familiarity with the "sound" of the English language and may even provide important clues about which sound patterns in an ongoing stream of speech represent individual words.

Gestures and Nonverbal Responses

By 8 to 10 months of age, preverbal infants begin to use gestures and other nonverbal responses (for example, facial expressions) to communicate with their companions (Acredolo & Goodwyn, 1990). Two kinds of preverbal gestures are common: *declarative gestures,* in which the infant directs others' attention to an object by pointing at or touching it, and *imperative gestures,* in which the infant tries to convince others to grant his requests through such actions as pointing at candy he wants or tugging at a caregiver's pantleg when he hopes to be picked up. Eventually, some of these gestures become entirely representational and function like words. For example, a

formats: interactions in which a young child and an older companion assume separate but reversible (reciprocal) roles.

Pointing is an early but very effective means of communication. By the end of the first year, children are calling attention to interesting objects and activities by pointing at them with the index finger.

1–2-year-old might raise her arms to signify that she wishes to be picked up, hold her arms out to signify an airplane, or even pant heavily to represent the family dog (Acredolo & Goodwyn, 1990; Bates et al., 1989). Once children begin to speak, they often supplement their one- and two-word utterances with a gesture or an intonational cue to ensure that their messages are understood (Ingram, 1989). However, the use of gestures eventually declines as parents encourage their children to talk, and children learn that their words are more likely to be understood.

Do Preverbal Infants Understand the Meaning of Words?

Although most babies do not speak their first meaningful words until the end of the first year, parents are often convinced that their preverbal infants can understand at least some of what is said to them. How can we tell whether preverbal infants really understand the meaning of particular words?

One way is to see if young infants attend to an object when told to look at the object by a parent who is out of sight and hence cannot point or use other gestures to direct the child's attention. In one such study (Thomas et al., 1981), 11–13-month-old infants were placed in a highchair facing four objects (for example, toys and cookies). One of these objects had a name that the child's mother was sure her infant recognized and understood. Seated behind her infant, the mother then instructed her child to (1) "look at the [known word]" on some trials and (2) look at objects designated by nonsense words that the child would *not* understand (for example, "look at the dosh") on other trials. Clearly, 13-month-olds did understand the meaning of the "known" word, for they looked intently at its referent when told to do so, and they gazed very little at any of the stimuli when told to look at unknown objects such as a "dosh." By contrast, most 11-month-olds did *not* understand the meaning of the "known" word, for they did not restrict their gazing to its referent when told to do so; in fact, they were just as likely to gaze at this object when told to look at the nonsense word! In a similar study, Sharon Oviatt (1980) reported a similar outcome: Few infants understood the meanings of individual words before their first birthday.

Why, then, are parents often deceived about their infants' understanding of particular words? Simply because 8–10-month-olds can often obey verbal commands such as "get the *ball*" by correctly interpreting the speaker's nonverbal gestures and other contextual cues—in much the same way a cocker spaniel might when given a similar command. By age 12 to 13 months, however, infants are beginning to realize that individual words have meaning. Indeed, Sharon Oviatt (1980) found that 12–17-month-olds understand the meaning of many nouns and verbs long before they use them in their own speech. So infants seem to know much more about language than they can possibly say. Apparently, **receptive language** (comprehension) is ahead of **productive language** (expression) from the 12th or 13th month of life and possibly even sooner.

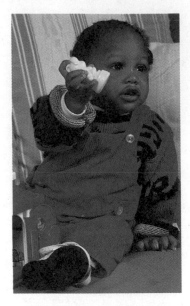

A large percentage of children's "first words" are the names of objects that move or can be acted on.

ONE WORD AT A TIME: THE HOLOPHRASTIC PERIOD

In the first stage of meaningful speech, the **holophrastic period**, infants utter single words that often seem to represent an entire sentence's worth of meaning (that is, **holophrases**). At first, the child's productive vocabulary is constrained, in part, by the sounds she can produce, so that her very first words may be intelligible only to close companions—for example, "ba" (for "ball") or "awa" (for "I want," as the child points to a cookie). Sounds that begin with consonants and end with vowels are easiest for infants, whose longer words are often repetitions of the syllables they can pronounce (for example, "mama," "bye-bye"). Yet, phonological development occurs very rapidly. By the middle of the second year, infants' cute and creative pronunciations are already guided by rules, or strategies, that enable them to produce simplified but more intelligible versions of adult words (Ingram, 1986). For example, they often delete the unstressed syllable of a multisyllable word (saying "ghetti" for "spaghetti") or replace an ending consonant syllable with a vowel (saying "appo" for "apple"). However, these errors become much less frequent during the preschool period as the vocal tract matures and children have more and more opportunities to decipher phonemic combinations in the speech of their companions. Indeed, most 4–5-year-olds are already pronouncing most words in pretty much the same way that adults do.

Early Semantics: Developing a Vocabulary

As infants begin to speak, the growth of their vocabularies literally proceeds one word at a time (Bloom, 1973). In fact, three to four months may pass before most children have a vocabulary of 10 words. But the pace of word learning quickens dramatically between 18 and 24 months of age, when infants may add anywhere from 10 to 40 new words a week (Dromi, 1987; Reznick & Goldfield, 1992). This vocabulary spurt is sometimes called the **naming explosion,** for as many parents will attest, toddlers seem to arrive at the wonderful realization that everything has a name and they want to learn all the names they can (Reznick & Goldfield, 1992). A typical 2-year-old may now produce nearly 200 words (Nelson, 1973) and may comprehend a far greater number (Benedict, 1979).

What do infants talk about? Katherine Nelson (1973) studied 18 infants as they learned their first 50 words and found that nearly two-thirds of these early words referred to *objects*, including familiar people (see Table 10-1). Moreover, these objects were nearly all either manipulable by the child (for example, balls or shoes) or capable of moving themselves (for example, animals, vehicles); rarely do infants mention objects such as plates or chairs that simply sit there without doing anything. Toddlers' first words include many references to familiar *actions* as well (Nelson, Hampson, & Shaw, 1993; see Table 10-1). So it seems that infants talk mostly about those aspects of experience that they already understand through their sensorimotor activities.

Attaching Meaning to Words

How do toddlers come to infer the meaning of words? In many cases, they seem to employ a **fast-mapping** process, quickly acquiring (and retaining) new words after hearing them applied to their referents only a time or two (Taylor & Gelman, 1988;

receptive language: that which the individual comprehends when listening to others' speech.

productive language: that which the individual is capable of expressing (producing) in his or her own speech.

holophrastic period: the period when the child's speech consists of one-word utterances, some of which are thought to be holophrases.

holophrase: a single-word utterance that represents an entire sentence's worth of meaning.

naming explosion: term used to describe the dramatic increase in the pace at which infants acquire new words in the latter half of the second year; so named because many of the new words acquired are the names of objects.

fast mapping: process of linking a word with its referent after hearing the word a time or two.

Table 10-1   Types of Words Used by Children with Productive Vocabularies of 50 Words

Word category	Description and examples	Percentage of utterances
Object words	Words used to refer to classes of objects (*car, doggie, milk*) Words used to refer to unique objects (*Mommy, Rover*)	65
Action words	Words used to describe or accompany actions or to demand attention (*bye-bye, up, go*)	13
Modifiers	Words that refer to properties or quantities of things (*big, hot, mine, allgone*)	9
Personal/social words	Words used to express feelings or to comment about social relationships (*please, thank you, no, ouch*)	8
Function words	Words that have a grammatical function (*what, where, is, to, for*)	4

Source: Adapted from Nelson, 1973.

1989; see also Woodward, Markman, & Fitzsimmons, 1994). In one study, toddlers were observed to pay closer attention to labeled objects, both at the time of labeling *and afterward,* than they did when the same objects were simply pointed out to them without being labeled (Baldwin & Markman, 1989; see also Baldwin, 1993). So early fast mapping may occur because language labels make objects more noteworthy and interesting, thereby encouraging young children to attend to and retain the words.

Common errors in word use. Despite their remarkable fast-mapping capabilities, children often attach meanings to words that differ from those of adults. One kind of error that they frequently make is to use a word to refer to a wider variety of objects or events than an adult would. This phenomenon, called **overextension,** is illustrated by a child's use of the term *doggie* to refer to all furry, four-legged animals. **Underextension,** the opposite of overextension, is the tendency to use a general word to refer to a smaller range of objects than an adult would—for example, applying the term *cookie* only to chocolate chip cookies. Why young children overextend or underextend particular words is not always clear, but it is likely that fast mapping contributes to these errors. Suppose, for example, that a mother points to a collie and says "doggie," and then turns toward a fox terrier and says "Look, another doggie." Her toddler may note that about the only things these two beasts seem to have in common are four legs and a hairy exterior, thus leading him to fast map the word doggie onto these perceptual attributes. And having done so, he may then be inclined to *overextend* the word *doggie* to all other animals (cats, horses) that share similar perceptual (semantic) features (Clark, 1973). Fast mapping could lead to underextensions as well. If the only dog a toddler has ever seen is the family pet, which he has heard his mother refer to as "doggie" a couple of times, he may assume that *doggie* is the proper name of this particular companion and use the term only when referring to his pet.

Of course, deciphering the meaning of new words is often more difficult than the above examples imply. For example, if mother sees a cat walking alongside a car and exclaims "Oh, there is a kitty!" the child must first decide whether mom is referring to the car or to the animal. If he rules out the car, it is still not obvious whether the word *kitty* refers to four-legged animals, to this particular animal, to the cat's pointed ears, leisurely gait, or even the meowing sound it made. How does the child decide among these many possibilities—all of which may seem plausible to him?

overextension: the young child's tendency to use relatively specific words to refer to a broader set of objects, actions, or events than adults do (for example, using the word *car* to refer to all motor vehicles).

underextension: the young child's tendency to use general words to refer to a smaller set of objects, actions, or events than adults do (for example, using *candy* to refer only to mints).

Table 10-2   Some Processing Strategies, or Constraints, That Guide Young Children's Inferences about the Meaning of New Words

Constraint	Description	Example
Object scope constraint	The assumption that words refer to whole objects rather than to parts of the objects or to object attributes.	The child concludes that the word *kitty* refers to the animal he sees rather than to the animal's ears, tail, meowing vocalizations, or color.
Taxonomic constraint	The assumption that words label categories of *similar* objects that share common perceptual features.	The child concludes that the word *kitty* refers to the animal he has seen *and* to other small, furry, four-legged animals.
Lexical contrast constraint	The assumption that each word has a unique meaning.	The child who already knows the meaning of *doggie* assumes that a label such as "dalmatian," applied to a dog, refers to that particular kind of dog (subordinate class).
Mutual exclusivity	The assumption that each object has one label and that different words refer to separate, nonoverlapping categories.	The child who already knows the word for *doggie* assumes that the word *kitty* refers to the fleeing animal should he hear "Look at the doggie chasing the kitty."

Some New Ideas about Early Semantic Development

Determining how young children figure out what new words mean when their referents are *not* immediately obvious (as in the previous "kitty" example) has proved to be a challenging task indeed—and one that is far from complete. Yet researchers are finding that even 2-year-olds display a number of strategies, or **processing constraints,** to help them to narrow down what a new word might possibly mean (de Villiers & de Villiers, 1992; Golinkoff et al., 1992; Hall & Waxman, 1993; Littschwager & Markman, 1994). Several of the more basic constraints that seem to guide children's inferences about word meaning are described in Table 10-2.

Of course, these constraints may often work together to help children infer the meaning of new words. For example, when 2-year-olds hear the words *horn* and *clip* applied to two very different objects, they assign each word correctly to a whole object, rather than to its parts or attributes **(object scope constraint),** and they display **mutual exclusivity** by almost never calling the horn a *clip* (or vice versa) when tested in the future (Waxman & Senghas, 1992).

However, the mutual exclusivity constraint is not very helpful when adults use more than one word to refer to the same object (for example, "Oh, there is a *doggie*—a *cocker spaniel*"). Under these circumstances, 2-year-olds who already know the word doggie often apply the **lexical contrast constraint** and assume that *cocker spaniel* must refer to a particular kind of dog that has the distinctive features (long floppy ears; heavy coat) that this one displays (Taylor & Gelman, 1988, 1989; Waxman & Hatch, 1992). Indeed, this tendency to contrast novel with familiar words may explain how children form hierarchical linguistic categories, eventually recognizing, for example, that a dog is also an animal and a mammal (superordinate designations) as well as a cocker spaniel who may have a proper name such as Pokey (subordinate designations).

Syntactical clues to word meaning. Finally, young language learners may often infer meanings by paying close attention to the *contexts* in which unfamiliar words are used (Nelson et al., 1993; Tomasello & Barton, 1994), including the way that the word is used in a sentence. For example, a child who hears a new word, *zav*, used as a noun to refer to a toy ("This is a *zav*") is likely to conclude that this new word

processing constraint: cognitive biases or tendencies that lead infants and toddlers to favor certain interpretations of the meaning of new words over other interpretations.

object scope constraint: the notion that young children assume that a new word applied to an object refers to the whole object rather than to parts of the object or to object attributes (for example, its color).

mutual exclusivity constraint: notion that young children assume that each object has but one label and that different words refer to separate and nonoverlapping categories.

lexical contrast constraint: notion that young children make inferences about word meanings by contrasting new words with words they already know.

refers to the toy itself. However, a child who hears *zav* used as an adjective ("This is a *zav* one") is more likely to conclude that *zav* refers to some characteristic of the toy, such as its shape or color (Taylor & Gelman, 1988).

Notice that the child is inferring word meanings from sentence structure, or *syntactical* clues. Indeed, this **syntactical bootstrapping** may be particularly important in helping children to decipher the meaning of new verbs (Gleitman, 1990). Consider the following two sentences:

The duck is gorping the bunny. (Gorping refers to a causitive action.)
The duck and the bunny are gorping. (Gorping is a synchronized action.)

When 2-year-olds hear one or the other of these sentences, they prefer to look at a video that matches what they have heard—for example, looking at a duck *causing* a rabbit to bend over after hearing the first sentence (Naigles, 1990). Clearly, the verb's syntax—the form that it takes in a sentence—provides important clues as to what it means (see also, Naigles & Kako, 1993).

Summing up. Even 2-year-olds have some reasonably sophisticated strategies for figuring out what new words mean. By this age, they already produce nearly 200 words—a sufficient baseline for lexical contrast. And, apparently, they already understand enough about sentence structure (syntax) to determine whether many new words are nouns, verbs, or adjectives—a second important clue to word meaning. While it is true that toddlers make many semantic errors, they often seem to know much more about the meaning of words than their errors might indicate. For example, 2-year-olds who call all four-legged animals "doggie" can usually discriminate dogs from other animals if they are given a set of animal pictures and asked to "show the doggie" (Thompson & Chapman, 1977). Why, then, might they choose to call a horse a doggie when they can easily tell the animals apart?

One possibility is that toddlers who know relatively few words may use overextension as yet another strategy for learning the names of new objects and activities. A child who sees a horse may call it a "doggie," not because he believes that it is a dog, but because he has no better word in his vocabulary to describe this new four-legged animal, and he has learned from experience that an incorrect label is likely to elicit reactions such as "No, Johnny, that's a *horse*. Can you say *horsie*? C'mon, say *horsie*" (Baron, 1992; Ingram, 1989).

When a Word Is More Than a Word

Many psycholinguists characterize an infant's one-word utterances as *holophrases* because they often seem less like labels and more like attempts to convey an entire sentence's worth of meaning. These single-word "sentences" can serve different communication functions depending on how they are said and the context in which they are said (Greenfield & Smith, 1976). For example, 17-month-old Shelley used the word *ghetti* (spaghetti) three times over a five-minute period. First, she pointed to the pan on the stove and seemed to be *asking* "Is that spaghetti?" Later, the function of her holophrase was to *name* the spaghetti when shown the contents of the pan, as in "It is spaghetti." Finally, she left little question that she was *requesting* spaghetti when she tugged at her companion's sleeve as he was eating and used a whining tone.

Of course, there are limits to the amount of meaning that can be packed into a single word, but infants in the holophrastic stage of language development seem to display such basic language functions as naming, questioning, requesting, and demanding—functions that they will later serve by producing different kinds of sentences. They are also learning an important pragmatic lesson: that their one-word messages are often ambiguous and may require an accompanying gesture or intonational cue if they are to be understood (Ingram, 1989).

syntactical bootstrapping: notion that young children make inferences about the meaning of words by analyzing the way words are used in sentences and inferring whether they refer to objects (nouns), actions (verbs), or attributes (adjectives).

Reprinted with special permission of
King Features Syndicate, Inc.

▶ FROM HOLOPHRASES TO SIMPLE SENTENCES:
THE TELEGRAPHIC PERIOD

At about 18 to 24 months of age, children begin to combine words into simple "sentences" such as "Daddy cat," "Go kitty," and "Mommie drink milk" that are remarkably similar across languages as diverse as English, German, Finnish, and Samoan (see Table 10-3). These early sentences have been called **telegraphic speech** because, like telegrams, they contain only critical content words, such as nouns, verbs, and adjectives, and leave out such frills as articles, prepositions, and auxiliary verbs.

Although it is clearly ungrammatical in adult English to say "No wet" or "There ball," these two-word sentences represent far more than strings of holophrases or random word combinations. Even in their earliest sentences, children show some evidence of following grammatical rules. English-speaking children, for example, usually say "Mommy drink" rather than "Drink Mommy" or "My ball" rather than "Ball my," thus suggesting that they already realize that some word orders are better than others for conveying meaning (de Villiers & de Villiers, 1992).

Why are children's earliest sentences incomplete? What kinds of messages and meanings are they trying to communicate in these telegraphic statements? And what have they learned about the pragmatics of language over the first two years? These are issues to which we now turn.

Why Are Early Sentences Incomplete?

Why do children stress nouns and verbs and omit most other parts of speech in their early sentences? It was once thought that toddlers spoke in "telegraphese" because memory limitations prevented them from generating longer sentences. But this "memory hypothesis" was rejected once researchers noted that 2 to 2½-year-olds were capable of producing three-, four-, and even five-word "telegraphic" utterances. Nor do the data imply that the omitted function words serve no function: Children clearly encode these words in others' speech, for they respond more appropriately to fully grammatical sentences (for example, "Get the ball") than to telegraphic (or otherwise ungrammatical) versions of the same idea (such as "Get ball" or "Point to gub ball") (Gerken & McIntosh, 1993; Petretic & Tweney, 1977). Lou Anne Gerken and her associates (1990) believe that young children treat function words such as *a, on,* and *the* as markers or spacers that separate and highlight the more heavily stressed content words in the speech they hear. So why do telegraphic children omit these important linguistic cues in their own speech? Probably because of their own production constraints: A child who can generate only very short utterances will choose to deemphasize lightly stressed function words in favor of those heavily stressed nouns and verbs that they view as essential for effective communication.

telegraphic speech: early sentences that consist of content words and omit the less meaningful parts of speech, such as articles, prepositions, pronouns, and auxiliary verbs.

Table 10-3   Similarities in Children's Spontaneous Two-Word Sentences in Four Languages

Function of sentence	Language			
	English	Finnish	German	Samoan
To locate or name	There book	Tuossa Rina (there Rina)	Buch da (book there)	Keith lea (Keith there)
To demand	More milk Give candy	Annu Rina (give Rina)	Mehr milch (more milk)	Mai pepe (give doll)
To negate	No wet Not hungry	Ei susi (not wolf)	Nicht blasen (not blow)	Le'ai (not eat)
To indicate possession	My shoe Mama dress	Täti auto (aunt's car)	Mein ball (my ball) Mamas hut (Mama's hat)	Lole a'u (candy my)
To modify or qualify	Pretty dress Big boat	Rikki auto (broken car)	Armer wauwau (poor dog)	Fa'ali'i pepe (headstrong baby)
To question	Where ball	Missa pallo (where ball)	Wo ball (where ball)	Fea Punafu (where Punafu)

Source: Adapted from Slobin, 1979.

Interestingly, telegraphic speech is not nearly as "universal" as earlier researchers had thought. Russian and Turkish children, for example, produce short but reasonably grammatical sentences from the very beginning. Why? Because their languages place more stress on small grammatical markers and have less rigid rules about word order than other languages do (de Villiers & de Villiers, 1992; Slobin, 1985). So it seems that whatever is most noticeable about the structure of a language is what children acquire first. And if content words and word-order rules are most heavily stressed, then young children will include this information and omit the lightly stressed grammatical markers to produce what appear to be "telegraphic" utterances.

A Semantic Analysis of Early Speech

Psycholinguists have approached early child language as if it were a foreign language and have tried to describe the rules that young children use to form their sentences. Early attempts were made to specify the structural characteristics, or syntax, of telegraphic speech, but it soon became clear that analyses based on syntax alone grossly underestimated the young child's linguistic capabilities. Why? Because young children often use the *same* two-word utterance to convey *different* meanings (or semantic relations) in different contexts. For example, one of Lois Bloom's (1970) young subjects said "Mommy sock" on two occasions during the same day—once when she picked up her mother's sock and once while her mother was putting a sock on the child's foot. In the first instance, "Mommy sock" seems to imply a possessive relationship ("Mommy's sock"). But in the second instance, the child was apparently expressing a different idea—namely, "Mommy is putting on my sock." So to properly interpret telegraphic statements, one must determine the child's *meaning* or *semantic intent* by considering not only the words that she generates but also the contexts in which these utterances take place.

Roger Brown (1973) has analyzed the "telegraphese" of several young children from around the world and written a **semantic grammar** to describe the basic

semantic grammar: an analysis of the semantic relations (meanings) that children express in their earliest sentences.

Table 10-4 Common Meanings (Semantic Relations) Expressed in Children's Earliest Sentences

Semantic relation	Examples
Agent + action	Mommy come; Daddy sit
Action + object	Drive car; eat grape
Agent + object	Mommy sock; baby book
Action + location	Go park; sit chair
Entity + location	Cup table; toy floor
Possessor + possession	My teddy; Mommy dress
Entity + attribute	Box shiny; crayon big
Demonstrative + entity	Dat money; dis telephone
Notice + noticed object	Hi belt; Hi Mommy
Recurrence	More milk
Nonexistence	Allgone cookie; No wet

Source: From Brown, 1973.

categories of meaning that they often express in their two-word sentences. The most common of these semantic relations appear in Table 10-4.

The child's next accomplishment is to combine these semantic relations into longer telegraphic utterances. For example, an agent/action relation such as "Mommy drink" might be added to an action/object relation such as "drink milk" to yield an agent/action/object relation of the form "Mommy drink milk." Once children reach this milestone, they are about ready to acquire and use some of the rules of syntax that will make their sentences more "grammatical" within the framework of the language they are learning.

The Pragmatics of Early Speech

Because early sentences are incomplete and their meanings often ambiguous, children continue to supplement their words with gestures and intonational cues to ensure that their messages are understood. Although we adults who are proficient with the spoken language may consider nonverbal gestures a rather limited and inefficient form of communication, such an attitude is extremely shortsighted. Indeed, many deaf children come to know and use a rather sophisticated language that is based entirely on nonverbal signs and gestures (see Box 10-3).

Toddlers are also becoming more aware of many of the social and situational determinants of effective communication. For example, 2-year-olds have become rather proficient at vocal turn-taking; they know that speakers "look up" at the listener when they are about to yield the floor, and they now use this same nonverbal cue to signal the end of their own utterances (Rutter & Durkin, 1987). By age 2 to 2½, children know they must either stand close to a listener or compensate for distance by raising their voices if they are to communicate with that person (Johnson et al., 1981; Wellman & Lempers, 1977). And when talking to another toddler about some object or activity, the 2-year-old knows that he must stand close to the referent before his message is likely to be understood (Wellman & Lempers, 1977).

Finally, young children are becoming more aware of certain sociolinguistic prescriptions, such as the need to be polite when making requests, and they are beginning to understand what is polite and what isn't in other people's speech (Baroni &

BOX 10-3
Learning a Gestural Language

Children who are born deaf or who lose their hearing very early in childhood have a difficult time learning to use an oral language. Contrary to popular opinion, the deaf do not learn much from lipreading. In fact, many deaf children learn no language at all until they go to school and are exposed to a gestural system known as American Sign Language (ASL).

Even though ASL is produced by the hands rather than orally, it is a remarkably flexible medium that is similar to an oral language (Bellugi, 1988). For example, ASL has a distinct sign for each morpheme. Some signs represent entire words; others stand for grammatical morphemes such as the progressive ending *-ing*, the past tense *-ed*, and auxiliaries. Each sign is constructed from a limited set of gestural components in much the same way that the spoken word is constructed from a finite number of distinctive sounds (phonemes). In ASL, the components that make up a sign are (1) the position of the signing hand(s), (2) the configuration of the hand(s) and fingers, and (3) the motions of the hand(s) and fingers. Syntactical rules specify how signs are combined to form declarative sentences, ask questions, and negate a proposition. And like an oral language, ASL permits the user to sign plays on words (puns), metaphorical state-

ments, and poetry. So people who are proficient in this gestural system can transmit and understand an infinite variety of highly creative messages; they are true language users.

Deaf children learn ASL in much the same way that hearing children acquire an oral language. Indeed, signs are readily visible to the infant and grow from sensorimotor schemes, perhaps explaining why many children produce their first truly referential sign or gesture at about the same time or slightly before hearing children utter their first meaningful words (Folven & Bonvillian, 1991; Goodwyn & Acredolo, 1993). The deaf child usually begins by "babbling" in sign—that is, forming rough approximations of signs that parents use—before proceeding to one-word, or "holophrastic," phrases, in which a single sign is used to convey a number of different messages. Moreover, the kinds of signs that the child first uses (nominals, action words, modifiers) are virtually identical to the categories of words that speaking children first acquire (Bonvillian et al., 1983). When deaf children begin to combine signs, their two-sign sentences are "telegraphic" statements that express the same set of semantic relations that appears in the early speech of hearing children. Finally, deaf children learning ASL and hearing children learning an oral tongue pass through roughly the same stages as they begin to acquire and use the grammatical rules of their respective languages (Bellugi, 1988).

What do these striking parallels tell us about theories of language acquisition? They surely imply that language learning depends, in part, on biological processes (Dale, 1976). What isn't clear, however, is whether the linguistic milestones and abilities that deaf children share with hearing children reflect (1) the operation of a specialized linguistic capacity that enables children to acquire any and all languages (nativist position) or (2) the gradual maturation of the human brain and achievement of *general* cognitive milestones that children are then motivated to express in their own language (interactionist position).

Today, many educators believe that deaf children should be exposed to both ASL and oral language as early as possible so that they can develop a broad range of general linguistic skills. Although this "total communication" training does not necessarily make it easier for deaf children to use the spoken language, it does make them more knowledgeable about communicating (see MacKay-Soroka, Trehub, & Thorpe, 1987; 1988) and may improve the quality of their social interactions with both their deaf and their hearing companions.

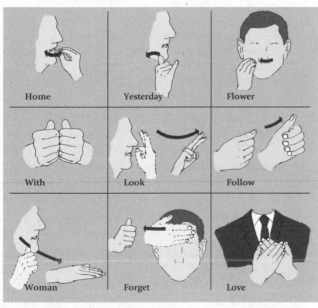

Some signs in American Sign Language.
From Reikehof, 1963.

Axia, 1989; Garton & Pratt, 1990). Although we have seen that parents do not intentionally teach grammar to their children, they *do* instruct them in etiquette (Flavell et al., 1993). Such common parental prompts as "What do you say?" or "Say the magic word and the cookie is yours" play an important part in this learning.

In sum, most 2–2½-year-olds have learned many practical lessons about language and communication even before they begin to use many of the grammatical rules of their native tongue. But even though toddlers can converse with adults and older children, their communication skills pale in comparison with those of a 5-year-old, a 4-year-old, or even many 3-year-olds. Our next task is to determine what it is that preschool children are learning that will enable them to become rather sophisticated users of language by the ripe old age of 5, when they are about ready to enter kindergarten.

Concept Check 10-2 ⌄ Language Learning among Infants and Toddlers

Check your understanding of *selected aspects* of early language learning by filling in the blanks in each statement below. The answers appear in the Appendix.

1. Although early babbling is heavily influenced by _____ _____, environmental influences come into play by age _____, when infants begin to match the _____ of their babbles to the tonal qualities of the language they hear.

2. Some psycholinguists believe that a caregiver's _____ cues provide infants with early evidence that speech is a _____ activity. The characteristic "rhythm" of a language may also help 7–10-month-olds to segment what they hear into _____s and _____s.

3. By age _____, most infants have uttered their first meaningful word. Vocabulary grows _____ until 18 to 24 months, when infants enter the _____ _____. If the referent for a new word is clear, infants may quickly learn that word through a _____-_____ process.

4. When the referents for new words are not clear, young children have _____ _____ that help them to infer word meanings. For example, they display _____ _____ by assuming that every new word has a unique meaning and _____ _____ by assuming that different words refer to separate, nonoverlapping categories. Young children may also infer word meanings from _____ _____s—the way the word is used in a sentence.

5. Children's early sentences are called _____ _____ because they contain only the most highly stressed content words such as_____s, _____s, and _____s. Less stressed "function" words may be omitted because they are viewed as less essential for effective _____.

6. Because their earliest sentences are incomplete and their meanings often _____, toddlers often supplement their words with nonverbal _____ and _____ cues to ensure that their messages are understood.

▶ ## LANGUAGE LEARNING DURING THE PRESCHOOL PERIOD

In the short period from age 2½ to 5, children come to produce sentences that are remarkably complex and adultlike. Table 10-5 gives an inkling of how fast things move in the brief span of 7 to 10 months. What are children acquiring that accounts for this language explosion? Surely, they are mastering basic syntax: As we see in Table 10-5, a child of 35–38 months is now inserting articles, auxiliary verbs, and grammatical markers (for example, *-ed*, *-ing*) that were previously omitted, as well as negating propositions and occasionally asking a well-formed question (de Villiers & de Villiers, 1992). And although it is not as obvious from the table, we will see that preschool children are also beginning to understand much more about the pragmatics of language and communication.

Grammatical Development

Development of Grammatical Morphemes

Grammatical morphemes are modifiers that give more precise meaning to the sentences we construct. These meaning modifiers usually appear sometime during the third year as children begin to pluralize nouns by adding *-s*, to signify location with the preposi-

grammatical morphemes: prefixes, suffixes, prepositions, and auxiliary verbs that modify the meaning of words and sentences.

Table 10-5 Samples of One Boy's Speech at Three Ages

Age		
28 months (telegraphic speech)	**35 months**	**38 months**
Somebody pencil	No—I don't know	I like a racing car
Floor	What dat feeled like?	I broke my racing car
Where birdie go?	Lemme do again	It's broked
Read dat	Don't—don't hold with me	You got some beads
Hit hammer, Mommy	I'm going to drop it—inne dump truck	Who put dust on my hair?
Yep, it fit	Why—cracker can't talk?	Mommy don't let me buy some
Have screw	Those are mines	Why it's not working?

Source: Adapted from McNeill, 1970.

tional morphemes *in* and *on*, to indicate verb tense with the present progressive *-ing* or the past tense *-ed*, and to describe possessive relations with the inflection *'s*.

Roger Brown (1973) kept records on three children as they acquired 14 grammatical morphemes that frequently appear in English sentences. He found that these three children varied considerably with respect to (1) the age at which they began to use grammatical markers and (2) the amount of time it took them to master all 14 rules. However, all three children in this longitudinal study learned the 14 grammatical morphemes in precisely the order in which they appear in Table 10-6—a

Table 10-6 Order of Acquisition of English Grammatical Morphemes

Morpheme	Example
1. Present progressive: *-ing*	He is sit*ting* down.
2. Preposition: *in*	The mouse is *in* the box.
3. Preposition: *on*	The book is *on* the table.
4. Plural: *-s*	The dog*s* ran away.
5. Past irregular: for example, *went*	The boy *went* home.
6. Possessive: *-'s*	The girl*'s* dog is big.
7. Uncontractible copula *be*: for example, *are, was*	*Are* they boys or girls? *Was* that a dog?
8. Articles: *the, a*	He has *a* book.
9. Past regular: *-ed*	He jump*ed* the stream.
10. Third person regular: *-s*	She run*s* fast.
11. Third person irregular: for example, *has, does*	*Does* the dog bark?
12. Uncontractible auxiliary *be*: for example, *is, were*	*Is* he running? *Were* they at home?
13. Contractible copula *be*: for example, *-'s, -'re*	That*'s* a spaniel.
14. Contractible auxiliary *be*: for example, *-'s, -'re*	They*'re* running very slowly.

Source: Adapted from Clark & Clark, 1977.

Figure 10-4
A linguistic puzzle used to determine young children's understanding of the rule for forming plurals in English.
From Berko, 1958.

finding that was confirmed in a cross-sectional study of 21 additional children (de Villiers & de Villiers, 1973).

Why do children who have very different vocabularies learn these 14 grammatical markers in one particular order? Brown (1973) soon rejected a "frequency of mention" hypothesis when he found that the grammatical morphemes learned first appear no more often in parents' speech than morphemes acquired later. What he did discover is that the morphemes acquired early are less semantically and syntactically complex than those acquired late. For example, the present progressive *-ing*, which describes an ongoing action, appears before the past regular *-ed*, which describes both action and a sense of "earlier in time." Moreover, *-ed*, which conveys two semantic features, is acquired earlier than the uncontractible forms of the verb *to be* (*is, are, was, were*), all of which are more structurally complex and specify *three* semantic relations: number (singular or plural), tense (present or past), and action (ongoing process).

Once young children have acquired a new grammatical morpheme, they will apply this rule to novel as well as to familiar contexts. For example, if the child realizes that the way to pluralize a noun is to add the grammatical inflection *-s*, he or she will have no problem solving the puzzle in Figure 10-4—these two funny-looking creatures are obviously wugs (Berko, 1958).

Overregularization. Interestingly, children occasionally overextend new grammatical morphemes to cases in which the adult form is irregular—a phenomenon known as **overregularization.** Statements such as "I brushed my *tooths*," "She *goed*," or "It *runned* away" are common examples of the kind of overregularization errors that 2½–3-year-olds make. Oddly enough, children have often memorized and used the *correct* forms of many irregular nouns and verbs (for example, "It *ran* away," "My *feet* are cold") *before* they learn any grammatical morphemes (Brown, 1973; Mervis & Johnson, 1991); and even after acquiring a new rule, a child's overregularizations are relatively rare, occurring on only about 2½–5% of those occasions in which irregular verbs are used (Marcus et al., 1992). So overregularization is not a serious grammatical defect that must be unlearned. Instead, these errors are merely evidence that the child has acquired a new linguistic principle that she will occasionally apply in a "creative" way in her own speech.

Why, then, do children ever overregularize irregular words? Probably because they occasionally fail to retrieve the irregular form of a noun or a verb from memory and must then apply their new morpheme (overregularize) to communicate the idea they are trying to express (Marcus et al., 1992).

Mastering Transformational Rules

In addition to grammatical morphemes, each language has rules for creating variations of the basic declarative sentence. For example, people who speak English learn to transform declaratives into *wh-* questions by placing an appropriate *wh-* word (*who, what, when, where, why*) at the beginning of the sentence and then inverting the order of the subject and the auxiliary verb. Applying these rules, the declarative statement "I was eating pizza" can be modified to produce the question "What was I eating?" Other rules of **transformational grammar** allow us to generate *negative* sentences ("I was *not* eating pizza"), *imperatives* ("Eat the pizza!"), *relative clauses* ("I, who hate cheese, was eating pizza"), and *compound sentences* ("I was eating pizza, and John was eating spaghetti").

Between the ages of 2 and 2½, most children begin to produce some variations of declarative sentences, many of which rest on their mastery of the auxiliary verb *to be* (de Villiers & de Villiers, 1992). However, children acquire transformational rules in a step-by-step fashion, so that their earliest transformations are very different from those of an adult. We can easily illustrate this point by considering the phases that children go through as they learn to ask questions, negate propositions, and generate complex sentences.

overregularization: the overgeneralization of grammatical rules to irregular cases where the rules do not apply (for example, saying "mouses" rather than "mice").

transformational grammar: rules of syntax that allow one to transform declarative statements into questions, negatives, imperatives, and other kinds of sentences.

Curious 3–5-year-olds display their knowledge of transformational grammar by asking many "who," "what," and "why" questions of their companions.

Asking questions. There are two kinds of questions that are common to virtually all languages. *Yes/no questions,* the simpler form which is mastered first, ask whether particular declarative statements are true or false (for example, "Is that a doggie?"). By contrast, *wh- questions* call for responses other than a simple yes or no. These latter queries are called *wh-* questions because, in English, they almost always begin with a *wh-* word such as *who, what, where, when,* or *why.*

The child's earliest questions often consist of nothing more than a declarative sentence uttered with a rising intonation that transforms it into a yes/no question (for example, "See doggie?"). However, *wh-* words are occasionally placed at the beginning of telegraphic sentences to generate simple *wh-* questions such as "Where doggie?" or "What Daddy eat?" During the second phase of question asking, children begin to use the proper auxiliary, or helping, verbs, but their questions are of the form "What Daddy is eating?" or "Where doggie is going?" Finally, children learn the transformational rule that calls for moving the auxiliary verb ahead of the subject, and they begin to produce adultlike questions such as "What is Daddy eating?"

Interestingly, children begin to ask "what," "where," and "who" questions long before they are requesting information about "why," "when," and "how" (Bloom, Merkin, & Wootten, 1982; Tyack & Ingram, 1977). One explanation for this finding ties it to general cognitive development: "What," "where," and "who" questions have concrete referents (objects, locations, and persons) that a cognitively immature toddler can easily understand, whereas "when," "why," and "how" questions require an appreciation of *abstract* concepts, such as time and causality, that develops a little later, between ages 3 and 5 (French, 1989).

Producing negative sentences. Like questions, children's negative sentences develop in a steplike fashion. Children the world over initially express negations by simply placing a negative word in front of the word or statement they wish to negate, producing such utterances as "No mitten" or "No I go." Notice, however, that these first negatives are ambiguous: "No mitten" can convey *nonexistence* ("There's no mitten"), *rejection* ("I won't wear a mitten"), or *denial* ("That's not a mitten")(Bloom, 1970). This ambiguity is clarified once the child begins to insert the negative word inside the sentence, in front of the word that it modifies (for example, "I not wear mitten" or "That not mitten"). Finally, children learn to combine negative markers with the proper auxiliary verbs to negate sentences in much the same way adults do. Indeed, Peter and Jill de Villiers (1979) describe a delightful experiment in which young children were persuaded to argue with a talking puppet. Whenever the puppet made a declarative statement, such as "He likes bananas," the child's task was to negate the proposition (argue) in any way he or she could. Most 3–4-year-olds thoroughly enjoyed this escalating verbal warfare between themselves and the puppet. But more

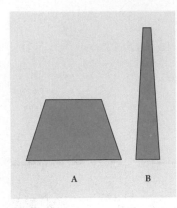

Figure 10-5
If asked to pick the "tall" one, 3–5-year-olds quickly select stimulus B, thus showing that they know what *tall* means. But when asked to pick the "big" one, they once again select stimulus B (whereas adults choose stimulus A, which occupies more area). Apparently, preschoolers often interpret *big* to mean tall, thus illustrating that they do not fully appreciate the meaning of the big/little relational contrast.
Adapted from Sena & Smith, 1990.

important, these young children were quite capable of using a wide variety of negative auxiliaries—including *wouldn't*, *wasn't*, *hasn't*, and *mustn't*—to properly negate almost any sentence the puppet produced.

Producing complex sentences. By age 3, most children have begun to produce complex sentences. Their first complex utterances usually involve use of (1) relative clauses that modify nouns (for example, "That's the box *that they put it in*"), and (2) conjunctions to join simple sentences ("He was stuck *and* I got him out"). Somewhat later, children begin to produce embedded sentences (for example, "The man *who fixed the fence* went home") and more intricate forms of questions as well (for example, "John will come, won't he?"; "Where did you say you put my doll?") (de Villiers & de Villiers, 1992). By the end of the preschool period, at age 5 to 6, children are using most of the grammatical rules of their language and speaking much like adults do, even though they have never had a formal lesson in grammar.

Semantic Development

Another reason that preschoolers' language becomes more complex is that 2½–5-year-olds are beginning to understand and express relational contrasts such as big/little, tall/short, in/on, before/after, here/there, and I/you (de Villiers & de Villiers, 1979; 1992). *Big* and *little* are usually the first spatial adjectives to appear, and these terms are soon used to specify a variety of relations. By age 2 to 2½, for example, children can use *big* and *little* to draw proper *normative* conclusions (a 10-cm egg, viewed by itself, is "big" relative to other eggs the child remembers seeing) and *perceptual* inferences (a 10-cm egg placed next to a larger egg is "little") (Ebeling & Gelman, 1988; 1994). By age 3, children are even capable of using these terms to make appropriate *functional* judgments such as deciding that an oversized article of doll clothing, which is little relative to what the child wears, is nonetheless too "big" to fit the doll in question (Gelman & Ebeling, 1989). And yet, even 4–5-year-olds occasionally interpret *big* to mean "tall" (see Figure 10-5) rather than using *big* as adults do to refer to the relative amount of area that an object occupies (Coley & Gelman, 1989; Sena & Smith, 1990).

Several researchers have devised linguistic games such as the argumentative-puppet technique to test children's knowledge and use of relational opposites such as big/little, tall/short, long/short, wide/narrow, and deep/shallow. They have found that children acquire these spatial contrasts in the following order:

$$
\text{big/little} \rightarrow
\begin{matrix}
\text{tall/short} \\
\text{long/short}
\end{matrix}
\rightarrow \text{high/low} \rightarrow
\begin{matrix}
\text{wide/narrow} \\
\text{thick/thin}
\end{matrix}
\rightarrow \text{deep/shallow}
$$

There appear to be two reasons that spatial adjectives are learned in this particular order. First, children hear some adjectives more than others: *Big* and *little* are by far the most frequent spatial terms in English, and even we adults seem to pay more attention to heights and lengths than to widths or thickness (for example, we are more apt to describe ourselves as tall or short than to mention whether we are thick or thin). Furthermore, the adjectives acquired first are less semantically precise than those acquired later. For example, *big* and *little* are broadly applicable, referring to variations in size along any and all dimensions, whereas *wide* and *narrow* are limited in meaning, pertaining only to variations on the horizontal dimension (Flavell et al., 1993).

Although preschoolers are becoming increasingly aware of a variety of meaningful relations and are rapidly learning how to express them in their own speech, their incomplete knowledge of syntax leads them to make some interesting semantic errors.

Consider the following sentences:

1. The girl hit the boy.
2. The boy was hit by the girl.

Children younger than 5 or 6 frequently misinterpret *passive* constructions, such as sentence 2 above. They can easily understand the *active* version of the same idea—that is, sentence 1. But if asked to point to a picture that shows "The boy was hit by the girl," preschoolers will usually select a drawing that shows a boy hitting a girl. What they have done is to assume that the first noun is the agent of the verb and that the second is the object; consequently, they interpret the passive construction as if it were an active sentence. Passive sentences based on mental state verbs such as *like* and *know* (for example, "Goofy was liked by Donald") are particularly difficult and are not understood until later in grade school (Sudhalter & Braine, 1985). Yet, preschoolers can often interpret *irreversible* passives that make little sense if processed as an active sentence. For example, even a 3-year-old might correctly interpret "The candy was eaten by the girl" because it is nonsense to assume that the candy was doing the eating (de Villiers & de Villiers, 1979).

Development of Pragmatics and Communication Skills

During the preschool period, children acquire a number of conversational skills that help them to communicate more effectively and accomplish their objectives. For example, 3-year-olds are already beginning to understand *illocutionary intent*—that the real underlying meaning of an utterance may not always correspond to the literal meaning of the words speakers use. Notice how the 3-year-old in the following example uses this knowledge to her advantage as she turns a declarative statement into a successful command (Reeder, 1981, p. 135):

Sheila: Every night I get an ice cream.
Babysitter: That's nice, Sheila.
Sheila: Even when there's a babysitter, I get an ice cream.
Babysitter (to himself): [B]acked into a corner by a 3-year-old's grasp of language as a social tool!

Three- to five-year-olds are also learning that they must tailor their messages to their audience if they hope to communicate effectively. Marilyn Shatz and Rochel Gelman (1973) recorded the speech of several 4-year-olds as they introduced a new toy to either a 2-year-old or an adult. An analysis of the tapes revealed that 4-year-old children are already proficient at adjusting their speech to their listener's level of

Communication skills develop rapidly in the preschool years. Four-year-olds are already quite proficient at adjusting their messages to a listener's level of understanding.

understanding. When talking to a 2-year-old, the children used short sentences and were careful to choose phrases such as "Watch," "Look, Perry," and "Look here" that would attract and maintain the toddler's attention. By contrast, 4-year-olds explaining how the toy worked to an adult used complex sentences and were generally more polite.

Referential Communication

An effective communicator is one who not only produces clear, unambiguous messages, but is able to detect any ambiguities in others' speech and ask for clarification. These aspects of language are called **referential communication skills.**

It was once generally assumed that preschool children lacked the abilities to detect uninformative messages and to resolve most problems in communication. Indeed, if asked to evaluate the quality of an ambiguous message such as "Look at *that* horse" when a number of horses are in view, preschool children are more likely than their grade school counterparts to say that this is an *informative* message. Apparently, they often fail to detect linguistic ambiguities because they are focusing on what they *think* the speaker means rather than on the (ambiguous) *literal* meaning of the message (Beal & Belgrad, 1990; Flavell et al., 1993). Why do preschoolers guess at the meaning of uninformative messages? Possibly because they are often quite successful at inferring the true meaning of ambiguous utterances from other "contextual" cues, such as their knowledge of a particular speaker's attitudes, preferences, and past behaviors (see Ackerman, Szymanski, & Silver, 1990). Four-year-olds are also less likely than 7-year-olds to detect and rephrase their own uninformative messages. In fact, they often assume that their own statements are perfectly informative and that failures to communicate should be blamed on their listeners (Flavell et al., 1993).

However, most 3–5-year-olds do display better referential communication skills (1) in the natural environment than on laboratory tasks (Warren-Leubecker & Bohannon, 1989) and (2) when there are few contextual cues to clarify an otherwise ambiguous message (Ackerman, 1993; Beal & Belgrad, 1990). Furthermore, even 3-year-olds know that they cannot carry out a request made by a yawning adult whose speech is unintelligible, and they quickly realize that other impossible requests (such as "Bring me the refrigerator") are problematic as well (Revelle, Wellman, & Karabenick, 1985). Indeed, these young children also know how they might resolve such breakdowns in communication, for they will often say "What?" or "Huh?" to a yawning adult or will ask "How? It's too heavy!" when told to retrieve a refrigerator.

In sum, 3–5-year-olds are not very good at detecting ambiguities in the *literal* meaning of oral messages. Nevertheless, they are better communicators than many laboratory studies of comprehension monitoring might suggest because they are often successful at inferring what an ambiguous message must mean from nonlinguistic contextual information.

 ## LANGUAGE LEARNING DURING MIDDLE CHILDHOOD AND ADOLESCENCE

Although 5-year-olds have learned a great deal about language in a remarkably brief period, many important strides in linguistic competence are made from ages 6 to 14—the grade school and junior high school years. Not only do schoolchildren use bigger words and produce longer and more complex utterances, they also begin to think about and manipulate language in ways that were previously impossible.

Later Syntactic Development

During middle childhood, children correct many of their previous syntactical errors and begin to use a number of complex grammatical forms that did not appear in their earlier speech. For example, 5–8-year-olds are beginning to iron out the kinks

referential communication skills: abilities to generate clear verbal messages, to recognize when others' messages are unclear, and to clarify any unclear messages that one transmits or receives.

in their use of personal pronouns, so that sentences such as "Him and her went" become much less frequent (Dale, 1976). By age 7–9, children understand and may occasionally even produce such complex *passive* sentences as "Goofy was liked by Donald" (Sudhalter & Braine, 1985) and *conditional sentences* such as "If Goofy had come, Donald would have been delighted" (Boloh & Champaud, 1993).

So middle childhood is a period of syntactical refinement: Children are learning subtle exceptions to grammatical rules and coming to grips with the more complex syntactical structures of their native tongue. However, this process of syntactic elaboration occurs very gradually, often continuing well into adolescence (Clark & Clark, 1977).

Semantics and Metalinguistic Awareness

Children's knowledge of semantics and semantic relations continues to grow throughout the grade school years. Vocabulary development is particularly impressive. Six-year-olds already understand approximately 10,000 words and will continue to expand their **receptive vocabularies** at the rate of about 20 words a day—until they comprehend some 40,000 words by age 10 (Anglin, 1993). Of course, grade school children do not use all these new words in their own speech and may not even have heard many of them before. What they have gained is **morphological knowledge**—knowledge of the meaning of morphemes that make up words—which enables them to analyze the structure of such unfamiliar words as "sourer," "custom-made," or "hopelessness" and quickly figure out what they mean (Anglin, 1993). Finally, adolescents' capacity for formal-operational reasoning permits them to further expand their vocabularies, adding a host of abstract words (for example, "ironic," "eradicate") that they had rarely heard (or didn't understand) during the grade school years (McGhee-Bidlack, 1991).

Grade school children are also becoming more proficient at *semantic integrations*—that is, at drawing linguistic inferences that enable them to understand more than is actually said. For example, if 6–8-year-olds hear "John did not see the rock; the rock was in the path; John fell," they are able to infer that John must have tripped over the rock. Interestingly, however, 6–8-year-olds often assume that the story explicitly described John tripping and are not consciously aware that they have drawn an inference (Beal, 1990a). By age 9–11, children are better able to make these kinds of linguistic inferences and recognize them as *inferences* (Beal, 1990a; Casteel, 1993), even when the two or more pieces of information that are necessary to draw the "appropriate" conclusion are separated by a number of intervening sentences (Johnson & Smith, 1981; van den Broek, 1989). And once children begin to integrate different kinds of linguistic information, they are able to detect *hidden* meanings that are not immediately obvious from the content of an utterance. For example, if a noisy 8-year-old hears her teacher quip "My, but you're quiet today," the child will probably note the contradiction between the literal meaning of the sentence and its satirical intonation or its context and thereby detect the *sarcasm* in her teacher's remark (Capelli, Nakagawa, & Madden, 1990).

One reason that school-age children are able to "go beyond the information given" when making linguistic inferences is that they are rapidly developing **metalinguistic awareness**—an ability to think about language and to comment on its properties. This reflective ability is present to some degree among preschoolers, particularly 5-year-olds, who are beginning to display much more *phonemic awareness* (for example, if you take the *s* sound out of scream, what's left?) and *grammatical awareness* (for example, is "I be sick" the right or wrong way to say it?) than younger children do (de Villiers & de Villiers, 1979). Yet, the metalinguistic competencies that 5-year-olds display are limited compared with those of a 9-year-old, a 7-year-old, or even a 6-year-old (Bialystock, 1986; Ferreira & Morrison, 1994).

An emerging awareness that language is an arbitrary and rule-bound system may have important educational implications, for children who score relatively high in

receptive vocabulary: words that a child already knows or can quickly define based on his or her knowledge of morphological rules.

morphological knowledge: one's knowledge of the meaning of morphemes that make up words.

metalinguistic awareness: a knowledge of language and its properties; an understanding that language can be used for purposes other than communicating.

By reading to young children, a parent promotes phonemic awareness—an important contributor to the development of reading skills.

metalinguistic awareness (particularly phonemic awareness) at ages 5 and 6 are likely to be the most proficient readers during the first and second grades (Warren-Leubecker & Carter, 1988; Wolf & Dickinson, 1985). So metalinguistic skills are related to reading abilities—but how? Some think that reading instruction and other early literary experiences promote metalinguistic awareness, whereas others argue that the development of a certain amount of metalinguistic knowledge makes reading easier. Amye Warren-Leubecker and Beth Carter (1988) think that both views may be correct. They found that (1) informal literary experiences (for example, having stories read to them) do predict 5–6-year-olds' levels of phonemic awareness, but (2) phonemic awareness was a better predictor of future reading achievement than were informal literary experiences or traditional tests of reading readiness, thus implying that some degree of phonological awareness may be necessary before a child can learn to read. Indeed, 7-year-olds who are poor readers tend to display poor phonemic awareness and phonological processing skills (Hansen & Bowey, 1994; Hatcher et al., 1994). And one particularly effective way of improving their reading is a program that combines phonological awareness training with reading instruction, thus highlighting the connections between the phonemic aspects of oral language and the decoding of written words (Hatcher et al., 1994).

Further Development of Communication Skills

Earlier, we examined a study (Shatz & Gelman, 1973) in which preschool children adjusted the style and content of their speech to match a listener's level of understanding. Recall that the 4-year-olds in this study were face to face with their 2-year-old or their adult companion and thus could see whether or not the listener was responding appropriately to their messages or following their instructions. Could children this young have communicated effectively with their partners if they had been asked to deliver their messages over a telephone?

Probably not. In one early study of children's referential communication abilities, 4–10-year-olds were asked to describe blocks with unfamiliar graphic designs on them to a peer on the other side of an opaque screen in such a way that the peer could identify them (Krauss & Glucksberg, 1977). As shown in Table 10-7, preschool children described these designs in highly idiosyncratic ways that neither meant much to their listeners nor enabled them to identify which blocks the speaker was talking about. By contrast, 8–10-year-olds provided much more informative messages. They realized that their listener could not see what they were referring to, thus requiring

Table 10-7 Typical Idiosyncratic Descriptions Offered by Preschool Children When Talking about Unfamiliar Graphic Designs in the Krauss and Glucksberg Communication Game

Form	Child				
	1	*2*	*3*	*4*	*5*
	Man's legs	Airplane	Drapeholder	Zebra	Flying saucer
	Mother's hat	Ring	Keyhold	Lion	Snake
	Daddy's shirt	Milk jug	Shoe hold	Coffeepot	Dog

Source: Adapted from Krauss & Glucksberg, 1977.

them to somehow *differentiate* these objects and make each distinctive if their messages were to be understood (see also Kahan & Richards, 1986, for similar age-related improvements in referential communication).

The dramatic improvement in referential communication skills over the early grade school years is due, in part, to the growth of cognitive skills, metacognitive abilities, and sociolinguistic understanding. Young children's *metacommunication*—their knowledge about how to communicate effectively—is very limited: 4-year-olds know that speech conveys information, but they believe that unclear or ambiguous messages are just as informative as unambiguous messages are (Flavell et al., 1993; Montgomery, 1993). Not until age 6 do children consciously recognize that the informativeness of a message depends on its quality (Sodian, 1988; 1990). As grade school children are recognizing the importance of generating clear messages, they are also becoming less egocentric and acquiring some role-taking skills—two *cognitive developments* that help them to adapt their speech to the needs of their listeners in such highly demanding situations as talking on the phone (or participating in a referential communication experiment), where it may be difficult to tell whether one's message has been interpreted correctly. Finally, *sociolinguistic understanding* is required to make the right kinds of speech adjustments, because messages that are clear for one listener may not be for others. For example, a listener who is unfamiliar with the stimuli in a referential communication task may require more differentiating information and more message redundancy than a second person who is already familiar with these objects. Six- to 10-year-olds do provide longer messages to "unfamiliar" than to "familiar" listeners. Yet, only the 9- and 10-year-olds adjust the *content* of their communications to the listeners' needs by providing richer *differentiating* information to an "unfamiliar" listener (Sonnenschein, 1986b, 1988).

Becoming a Better Listener

Of course, difficulties in communication can also arise if *listeners* fail to detect uninformative messages or, having detected them, fail to ask that they be clarified. Recently, investigators have been finding that younger grade school children are reasonably proficient at repairing or revising the uninformative messages that they happen to judge as problematic; however, these younger listeners were less likely than older children to detect uninformative messages in the first place (Beal, 1987, 1990b; Bonitatibus, 1988). Like preschoolers, it seems that 6–7-year-olds often overlook problematic messages because they have at least a vague idea of what the speaker means and assume that his intentions are clearly stated, particularly if the speaker is an adult (Beal & Flavell, 1984; Sonnenschein, 1986a). By contrast, 8–10-year-olds are much more likely to monitor the *literal* meaning of the message they hear, detect its ambiguity, and request that it be clarified.

How, then, might we encourage young listeners to stop guessing at what a speaker might mean and to question him instead about messages they don't fully understand? One seemingly effective approach is to teach them how to play *Twenty Questions*—a game that requires listeners to ask categorical questions and to carefully scrutinize the answers they receive if they are to solve the riddle posed to them. Not only do young children enjoy this game, but Mary Courage (1989) finds that 4–7-year-olds who are trained at Twenty Questions soon show noticeable (and sometimes dramatic) improvements in their ability to seek clarifying information on a referential communication task. Are such listening and questioning skills related to speaking skills? Apparently so, for children who know how (or have been trained) to listen effectively are generally able to monitor their own speech and produce informative messages (Pratt & Bates, 1982).

In sum, we cannot help but be awed by the pace at which children master the fundamentals of language and become effective communicators. Table 10-8 briefly summarizes the ground we have covered in tracing evolution of young human beings from preverbal creatures who are prepared for language learning to highly articulate adolescents, who can generate and understand an infinite number of messages.

Concept Check 10-3 ∨ Language Development from Toddlerhood to Adolescence

Check your understanding of *selected aspects* of language development from the preschool period through early adolescence by filling in the blanks in each statement below. The answers appear in the Appendix.

1. By age 2½, children's sentences are becoming more complex and adultlike as they begin to use _____ _____s to modify the meaning of their sentences and acquire rules of _____ _____ that enable them to create variations of the basic declarative sentence. By age _____, children are using most of the grammatical rules of their language.

2. Middle childhood and early adolescence is a period of syntactical _____ in which children are correcting their _____ errors and are beginning to understand the more _____ syntactical structures of their native language.

3. Expansion of children's _____ vocabularies is dramatic between ages 6 and 10. What they are acquiring is _____ _____ which allows them to analyze the structure of unfamiliar words and quickly infer their _____.

4. Starting at about age 5, children begin to show some _____ _____, or an ability to think about language and to comment on its properties. It seems as if a certain level of _____ awareness may be necessary before a child can learn to read.

5. Grade school children become much better communicators due, in part, to the growth of such cognitive abilities as _____-_____ skills, and to advances in _____ _____, which helps them to tailor their messages to the needs and characteristics of their listeners.

▶ BILINGUALISM: CHALLENGES AND CONSEQUENCES OF LEARNING TWO LANGUAGES

Most American children speak only English. However, many children around the world grow up bilingual, acquiring two (or more) languages by the time they reach puberty. Indeed, some 2.3–3.5 *million* American schoolchildren speak a language

Table 10-8 Important Milestones in Language Development

Age	Phonology	Semantics	Grammar/syntax	Pragmatics	Metalinguistic awareness
0–1 year	Receptivity to speech and discrimination of speech sounds. Babbling begins to resemble the sounds of native language.	Some interpretation of intonational cues in others' speech. Preverbal gestures appear. Vocables appear. Little if any understanding of words.	Preference for phrase structure and stress patterns of native language.	Joint attention with caregiver to objects and events. Turn-taking in games and vocalizations. Appearance of preverbal gestures.	None
1–2 years	Appearance of strategies to simplify word pronunciations.	First words appear. Rapid expansion of vocabulary after age 18 months. Overextensions and underextensions of word meanings.	Holophrases give way to 2-word telegraphic speech. Expression of distinct semantic relations. Acquisition of some grammatical markers.	Use of gestures and intonational cues to clarify messages. Richer understanding of vocal turn-taking rules. First signs of etiquette in children's speech.	None
3–5 years	Pronunciations improve.	Vocabulary expands. Understanding of spatial relations and use of spatial words in speech.	Grammatical morphemes added in regular sequence. Awareness of most rules of transformational grammar.	Beginning understanding of illocutionary intent. Some adjustment of speech to different audiences. Some attempts at clarifying obviously ambiguous or uncertain messages.	Some phonemic and grammatical awareness.
6–adolescence	Pronunciations become adultlike.	Acquisition of morphological knowledge. Dramatic expansion of vocabulary, including abstract words during adolescence. Appearance and refinement of semantic integrations.	Correction of earlier grammatical errors. Acquisition of complex syntactical rules.	Referential communication improves, especially the ability to detect and repair uninformative messages one sends and receives.	Metalinguistic awareness blossoms and becomes more extensive with age.

other than English at home, and many of them display at least some limitations in their use of the English language.

Does learning two languages rather than one hinder a child's language proficiency or slow her intellectual development? Before 1960, many researchers claimed that it did, pointing to several demonstrations that bilingual children score significantly lower than their monolingual peers on tests of linguistic knowledge and general

Contrary to popular belief, learning two (or more) languages rather than one neither hinders a child's language proficiencies nor retards her intellectual growth. Indeed, recent research suggests that there are cognitive advantages to bilingualism.

intelligence (Hakuta, 1988). Yet, these early studies were fatally flawed. The bilinguals were often first- or second-generation immigrants from lower socioeconomic backgrounds who were not very proficient in English. Moreover, the tests they took were administered in English (rather than in their language of greatest proficiency), and their performances were compared with samples largely comprised of middle-class, English-speaking monolinguals (Diaz, 1983). No wonder the bilinguals performed so poorly! Unfortunately, these findings were often taken at face value by educators and lawmakers, who have used them as justification for prohibiting the teaching of foreign languages until after age 10, so as not to ". . . distract from [students'] ability to assimilate their normal studies in the English language and . . . cause serious emotional disturbances . . ." (Kendler, as cited in Hakuta, 1988, p. 303).

Spurred on in part by the nativist contention that young children should easily acquire any language that they hear regularly, psycholinguists in the 1960s began to look more carefully at the process of becoming bilingual. Their findings were clear. Children exposed early (before age 3) to two languages were having little difficulty becoming proficient in both. Bilingual toddlers did occasionally mix phonologies and would apply the grammar and vocabulary of one language to the second tongue they were acquiring. But by age 3, they were well aware that the two languages were independent systems and that each was associated with particular contexts in which it was to be spoken (Lanza, 1992; Reich, 1986). By age 4, they displayed normal language proficiency in the language of their community and solid-to-excellent linguistic skills in the second language, depending on how much they had been exposed to it. Even when preschool children acquired a second language *sequentially* (that is, after age 3, when they are already conversant in their native tongue), it often took no more than a year to achieve near-native abilities in that language (Reich, 1986).

What about the cognitive consequences of bilingualism? Recent well-controlled studies that have matched bilinguals and monolinguals on important variables such as socioeconomic status are consistently finding that there are cognitive *advantages* to bilingualism. Not only do bilingual children score as high or higher than monolingual peers on tests of language proficiency, concept formation, and nonverbal intelligence (see, for example, Diaz, 1985), but they also outperform monolinguals on measures of metalinguistic awareness (Bialystock, 1986; 1988)—particularly those that call for them to recognize that words and their phonological components are arbitrary symbols, or to detect grammatical errors in speech and written prose (Galambos & Goldwin-Meadow, 1990). The metalinguistic advantages that bilinguals display may stem from the many experiences they have had translating messages back and forth across two linguistic systems—an activity that young bilinguals often treat as a game and will perform for the fun of it (Reich, 1986).

Despite these positive findings and increased federal support for bilingual education in the United States, public opinion in this country does not support this policy. In fact, some states have even passed laws making English the official language and thereby providing a strong argument for instructing non-native English speakers only in English. This is indeed unfortunate for at least two reasons. First, a total immersion in English-speaking classrooms causes students whose English is poor to lose some proficiency in their native language, thus placing them at risk of becoming *semilingual*—that is, less than fully competent, or literate, in either language. Second, and even more important, there appear to be clear benefits to **two-way bilingual education**—programs in which majority and limited-English-proficient (LEP) minority students are taught half of the day in English and half in a second language. Not only does this two-way bilingualism foster the academic achievement of LEP students, but the English-speaking students (1) perform just as well academically (or slightly better) than other comparable children who receive English-only instruction, and (2) often achieve near-native proficiency in the second language as well (Sleek, 1994). Moreover, both English-speaking and minority-language students in two-way bilingual programs are more optimistic about their academic and personal competencies than their counterparts who receive English-only instruction (Sleek, 1994).

It is rather ironic than an American educational system that so often tries to convert its LEP bilinguals into English-speaking monolinguals also deplores American citizens' lack of competence in foreign languages. Perhaps we could resolve this paradox by providing all children with two-way bilingual education—a strategy that may not only promote linguistic proficiency and better academic performance, but may also foster a greater appreciation of ethnic diversity and address our increasing societal need for a bilingually competent workforce (Hakuta & Garcia, 1989; Sleek, 1994).

two-way bilingual education: programs in which English-speaking (or other majority language) children and children who have limited proficiency in that language are instructed half of the day in English and the other half in a second language.

SUMMARY

Students of language development have tried to answer two basic questions. The first is the "what" question: What is the normal course of language development, and just what are children acquiring that enables them to become language users? The four aspects of language that children acquire are *phonology,* a knowledge of the phonemes used in producing language; *semantics,* an understanding of the meaning of words and sentences; *syntax,* the rules that specify how words are combined to produce sentences; and *pragmatics,* the principles governing how language is used in different social situations.

The second basic question about language development is the "how" question: How do young, relatively immature children acquire a working knowledge of language so quickly? There are three major theoretical perspectives on language acquisition: the learning (or empiricist) approach, nativism, and the interactionist viewpoint.

Learning theorists propose that children acquire language as they imitate others' speech and are reinforced for their grammatically correct utterances. However, careful analyses of conversations between parents and their young children reveal that children do not mimic the sentences they hear, nor do adults selectively reinforce their children's grammatical statements.

Nativists believe that human beings are innately endowed with linguistic processing capabilities (that is, a language acquisition device or language-making capacity) that function most efficiently prior to puberty. Presumably, children require nothing other than speech to analyze in order to learn any and all languages to which they are exposed. The identification of linguistic universals is consistent with the nativist viewpoint, as are the recent observations that deaf children of hearing parents and other children exposed to ungrammatical pidgins may create languages of their own. Moreover, both first- and second-language learning do seem to proceed more smoothly during the "sensitive period" prior to puberty. Yet many of these findings have been challenged; and unfortunately, nativists are not very clear about how children sift through verbal input and make the crucial discoveries that further their linguistic competencies.

Proponents of the interactionist position acknowledge that children are biologically prepared to acquire language. However, they suggest that what may be innate is not any specialized linguistic processor but, rather, a nervous system that gradually matures and predisposes children to develop similar ideas at about the same age. Thus, biological maturation is said to affect cognitive development, which, in turn, influences language development. However, interactionists stress that the environment plays a crucial role in language learning, for companions continually introduce new linguistic rules and concepts in engaging conversations that are tailored to the child's level of understanding.

Although babies respond to speech at birth and are soon capable of discriminating a variety of speechlike sounds, they do not utter their first meaningful words for about a year. During this prelinguistic phase, infants vocalize by crying, cooing, and babbling. As infants continue to babble, they begin to match the intonation of their babbles to the tonal qualities of the language they hear and eventually use sounds to represent objects and experiences, producing their own unique words, or "vocables." Although babies less than 1 year of age may not understand the meaning of individual words, they have already learned that (1) people take turns when vocalizing to each other, (2) a speaker's tone of voice conveys meaningful messages, and (3) speech has a "rhythm" which they come to appreciate (and which may help them to segment language into words and phrases). Near the end of the first year, infants develop preverbal gestures to communicate and to influence the behavior of their companions.

At about 1 year of age, infants produce their first recognizable words and enter the holophrastic phase of language development. For the next several months, children talk in one-word utterances and expand their vocabularies one word at a time. They talk most about those things that interest them: objects that move, make noise, or can be manipulated. At age 18–24 months comes a vocabulary spurt known as the *naming explosion*. Infants have a variety of processing strategies to help them figure out what new words mean, including *fast mapping,* contrasting new words with what they already know *(lexical contrast),* assuming that word meanings are *mutually exclusive,* and forming hypotheses about meaning from the way the word is used in a sentence *(syntactical bootstrapping).* Yet despite these strategies, toddlers frequently make such semantic errors as *overextension* and *underextension.* Many psycholinguists believe that a child's single words are often intended as *holophrases*—one-word messages that represent an entire sentence's worth of meaning.

At about 18–24 months of age, children enter the telegraphic phase of language development as they begin to combine words into two- and three-word sentences. These utterances are called "telegraphic" because they typically include only nouns, verbs, and occasionally adjectives, omitting prepositions, auxiliary verbs, articles, conjunctions, and other grammatical markers. Although telegraphic sentences are not grammatical by adult standards, they represent far more than random word combinations. Not only do children follow certain rules of word order when combining words, but they also express the same categories of meaning (semantic relations) in their earliest sentences.

During the preschool period (ages 2½ to 5), the child's language becomes much more similar to an adult's. As children produce longer utterances, they begin to add grammatical morphemes such as the -s for plurality, the -ed for past tense, the -ing for present progressive, articles, prepositions, and auxiliary verbs. Although individual children acquire grammatical markers at different rates, there is a striking uniformity in the order in which these morphemes appear. The preschool period is also the time when a child learns basic transformational rules that enable him or her to change declarative statements into questions, negations, imperatives, relative clauses, and compound sentences. By the time they enter school, children have mastered most of the syntactical rules of their native language and can produce a variety of sophisticated, adultlike messages. Another reason that language becomes increasingly complex during the preschool years is that youngsters are beginning to appreciate semantic and relational contrasts such as big/little, wide/narrow, more/less, and before/after. Preschool children also communicate more effectively as they begin to detect at least some of the uninformative messages they receive and to ask for clarification. Moreover, they have learned another important pragmatic lesson: If you hope to be understood, you must tailor your message to the listener's level of understanding.

Middle childhood and early adolescence is a period of linguistic refinement: Children learn subtle exceptions to grammatical rules and begin to understand even the most complex syntactical structures of their native language. Vocabulary grows rapidly, as does metalinguistic awareness—an ability to think about language and to comment on its properties—which is a good predictor of reading achievement. School-age children are also becoming much better communicators as they attend more carefully to literal meanings of ambiguous utterances and are more likely to clarify the uninformative messages they send and receive.

Bilingualism is becoming increasingly common in the United States, and children exposed early and regularly to two languages can easily acquire them both. There are cognitive advantages to bilingualism, and recent *two-way bilingual education* progams appear to promote the language skills and the self-perceived academic and social competencies of both majority-language and minority-language students.

Key Terms

aphasia [384]

babbles [391]

communication [376]

communication pressure hypothesis [379]

coos [391]

expansions [381]

fast mapping [394]

formats [392]

grammatical morphemes [402]

holophrase [394]

holophrastic period [394]

interactionist theory [388]

language [376]

language acquisition device (LAD) [383]

language-making capacity (LMC) [383]

lexical contrast constraint [396]

linguistic universal [378]

metalinguistic awareness [409]

morphemes [377]

morphological knowledge [409]

motherese [381]

mutual exclusivity constraint [396]

naming explosion [394]

object scope constraint [396]

overextension [395]

overregularization [404]

phonemes [376]

phonology [376]

pragmatics [377]

prelinguistic period [390]

processing constraint [396]

productive language [394]

psycholinguistics [376]

recasts [381]

receptive language [394]

receptive vocabulary [409]

referential communication skills [408]

semantic grammar [399]

semantics [377]

sensitive-period hypothesis (of language acquisition) [384]

syntactical bootstrapping [397]

syntax [377]

telegraphic speech [398]

transformational grammar [404]

two-way bilingual education [415]

underextension [395]

vocables [391]

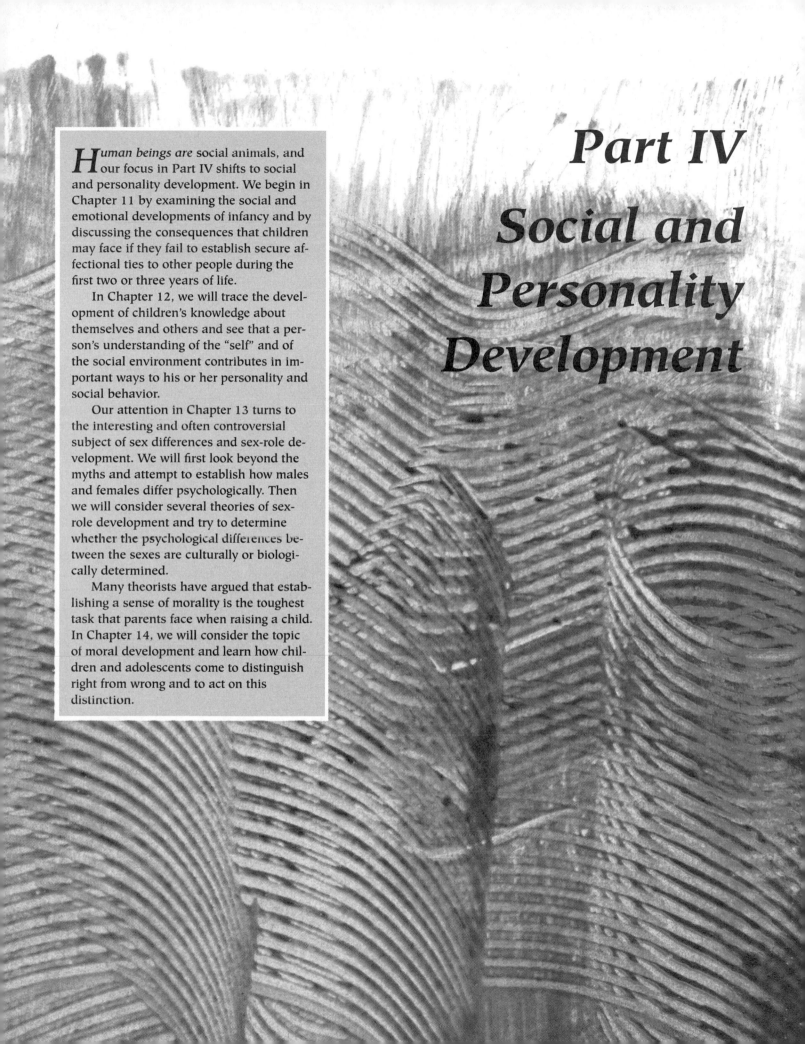

Part IV

Social and Personality Development

Human beings are social animals, and our focus in Part IV shifts to social and personality development. We begin in Chapter 11 by examining the social and emotional developments of infancy and by discussing the consequences that children may face if they fail to establish secure affectional ties to other people during the first two or three years of life.

In Chapter 12, we will trace the development of children's knowledge about themselves and others and see that a person's understanding of the "self" and of the social environment contributes in important ways to his or her personality and social behavior.

Our attention in Chapter 13 turns to the interesting and often controversial subject of sex differences and sex-role development. We will first look beyond the myths and attempt to establish how males and females differ psychologically. Then we will consider several theories of sex-role development and try to determine whether the psychological differences between the sexes are culturally or biologically determined.

Many theorists have argued that establishing a sense of morality is the toughest task that parents face when raising a child. In Chapter 14, we will consider the topic of moral development and learn how children and adolescents come to distinguish right from wrong and to act on this distinction.

Emotional Development and the Establishment of Intimate Relations

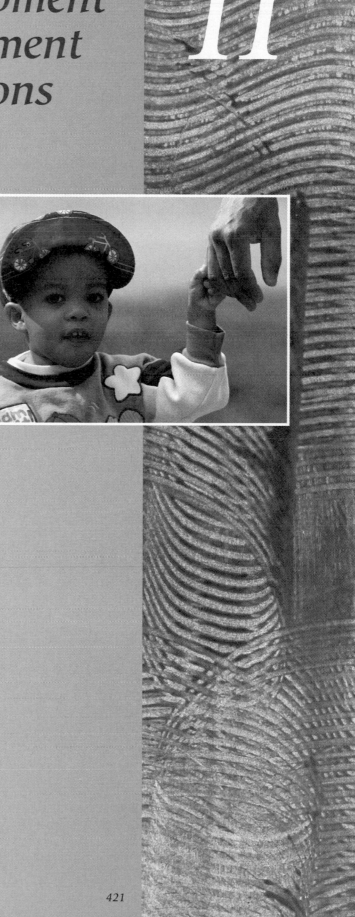

In 1891, G. Stanley Hall stated that adolescence is the most crucial period of the life span for the development of personality. Hall characterized the teenage years as a time when interests are solidified, long-lasting friendships emerge, and important decisions are made about one's education, career, and (in those days) choice of a mate. In other words, he viewed adolescence as the period when individuals assume personal and interpersonal identities that will carry them through their adult lives.

This viewpoint was soon challenged by Sigmund Freud (1905/1930), who believed that many of the decisions that an adolescent makes about the future are predetermined by his or her reactions to earlier life experiences. In fact, Freud proclaimed that the foundations of the adult personality are laid during the first five to six years of life and that personality development begins the moment that a baby is first handed to his or her parents.

Today, we know that Freud was right in at least one respect: Social and emotional development does begin very early in life. Though few contemporary theorists believe that our personalities are "set in stone" during the first few years, we know that the kinds of emotional relationships that infants develop with their close companions can affect the ways they relate to other people later in life. Early social experiences are important experiences—and infancy is truly a sensitive period for personality development.

Our primary focus in this chapter is on a major social and emotional milestone of infancy: the development of affectional ties between children and their closest companions. We will begin by briefly examining the growth of emotions and some of the roles that emotions play in early social and personality development. We will then turn to emotional *attachments*, first defining the term as developmentalists do and then exploring the process by which infants and their close companions establish these intimate affectional ties. Finally, we will review a rapidly expanding base of evidence suggesting that the kind of emotional attachments infants are able to establish (or the lack thereof) can have important implications for their later social, emotional, and intellectual development.

▶ AN OVERVIEW OF EMOTIONAL DEVELOPMENT

Do babies have feelings? Do they experience and display specific emotions such as happiness, sadness, fear, and anger the way older children and adults do? Most parents think they do. In one study, more than half the mothers of 1-month-old infants said that their babies displayed at least five distinct emotional expressions: interest, surprise, joy, anger, and fear (Johnson et al., 1982). Although one might argue that this is simply a case of proud mothers reading much too much into the behavior of their babies, there is now reliable evidence that even very young infants are indeed emotional creatures.

Displaying Emotions: The Development (and Control) of Emotional Expressions

Carroll Izard and his colleagues at the University of Delaware have studied infants' emotional expressions by videotaping babies' responses to such events as grasping an ice cube, having a toy taken away, or seeing their mothers return after a separation (Izard, 1982; 1993). Izard's procedure is straightforward: He asks raters, who are unaware of the events that an infant has experienced, to tell him what emotion the child is experiencing from the facial expression that the child displays. These studies reveal that different adult raters observing the same expressions reliably see the same emotion in a baby's face (see Figure 11-1). Other investigators find that adults can easily tell what *positive* emotion a baby is experiencing (for example, interest versus joy) from facial expressions, but that negative emotions (fear versus anger, for example)

Interest: brows raised; mouth may be rounded; lips may be pursed.

Fear: mouth retracted; brows level and drawn up and in; eyelids lifted.

Disgust: tongue protruding; upper lip raised; nose wrinkled.

Joy: bright eyes; cheeks lifted; mouth forms a smile.

Sadness: corners of mouth turned down; inner portion of brows raised.

Anger: mouth squared at corners; brows drawn together and pointing down; eyes fixed straight ahead.

Figure 11-1
Young infants display a variety of emotional expressions.

are much more difficult to discriminate on the basis of facial cues alone (Matias & Cohn, 1993; Oster, Hegley, & Nagel, 1992). Nevertheless, most researchers agree that babies communicate a variety of feelings through their facial expressions, and that each expression becomes a more recognizable sign of a particular emotion with age (Camras et al., 1992; Malatesta et al., 1989).

Sequencing of Discrete Emotions

Various emotions appear at different times over the first two years. At birth, babies show interest, distress, disgust, and contentment (as indicated by a rudimentary smile). Other **primary** (or **basic**) **emotions** that emerge between 2½ and 7 months of age are anger, sadness, joy, surprise, and fear. These so-called primary emotions seem to be biologically programmed, for they emerge in all normal infants at roughly the same ages and are displayed and interpreted similarly in all cultures (Camras et al., 1992; Izard, 1982; 1993; Malatesta et al., 1989). Yet some learning (or cognitive development) may be necessary before babies experience any emotion that is not present at birth. Indeed, one of the strongest elicitors of surprise and joy among 2–8-month-olds is their discovery that they can exert some control over objects and events. And disconformation of these *learned* expectancies (as when someone or something prevents them from exerting control) is likely to *anger* many 2–4-month-olds and may *sadden* 4–6-month-olds as well (Lewis, Alessandri, & Sullivan, 1990; Sullivan, Lewis, & Alessandri, 1992).

Later in the second year, infants begin to display such **secondary** (or **complex**) **emotions** as embarrassment, shame, guilt, envy, and pride. These feelings are sometimes called *self-conscious emotions* because each involves some damage to or embarrassment of our sense of self. Michael Lewis and his associates (Lewis, Sullivan, Stanger, & Weiss, 1989) believe that embarrassment, the simplest self-conscious emotion, does not emerge until the child recognizes herself in a mirror or photograph (a self-referential milestone we will discuss in detail in Chapter 12), whereas *self-*

primary (or basic) emotions: the set of emotions present at birth or emerging early in the first year that some theorists believe to be biologically programmed.

secondary (or complex) emotions: self-conscious or self-evaluative emotions that emerge in the second year and depend, in part, on cognitive development.

evaluative emotions such as shame, guilt, and pride may require both self-recognition *and* an understanding of rules or standards for evaluating one's conduct.

Most of the available evidence is quite consistent with Lewis's theory. For example, the only toddlers who become noticeably embarrassed by lavish praise or by requests to "show off" for strangers are those who display self-recognition (Lewis, Sullivan, Stanger, & Weiss, 1989). By about age 3, when children are better able to evaluate their performances as good or bad, they begin to show clear signs of *pride* (smiling, applauding, or shouting "I did it") when they succeed at a difficult task, as well as *shame* (a downward gaze with a slumped posture, often accompanied by statements such as "I'm no good at this") should they fail at an easy task (Lewis, Alessandri, & Sullivan, 1992; and see Stipek, Recchia, & McClintic, 1992). Let's note, however, that toddlers and young preschool children are most likely to display self-evaluative emotions when someone else is present to observe their behavior. Indeed, it may be well into the elementary school period before children feel especially prideful or shameful about their conduct in the absence of external surveillance (Bussey, 1992; Harter & Whitesell, 1989).

Socialization of Emotions and Emotional Self-Regulation

Each society has a set of **emotional display rules** that specify the circumstances under which various emotions should or should not be expressed (Gross & Ballif, 1991; Harris, 1989). Children in the United States, for example, learn that they are supposed to express happiness or gratitude when they receive a gift from grandma and, by all means, to suppress any disappointment they may feel should the gift turn out to be underwear. In some ways, these emotional "codes of conduct" are similar to the pragmatic rules of language: Children must acquire and use them in order to get along with other people and to maintain their approval. When does this learning begin?

Earlier than you might imagine! Consider that when mothers play with 7-month-old infants, they restrict themselves mainly to displays of joy, interest, and surprise, thus serving as models of positive emotions for their babies (Malatesta & Haviland, 1982). Mothers also respond selectively to their infants' emotions; over the first several months, they become increasingly attentive to babies' expressions of interest or surprise and less responsive to the infants' negative emotions (Malatesta et al., 1986). Through basic learning processes, then, babies are being trained to display more pleasant faces and fewer unpleasant ones, and they do just that over time.

However, the emotions that are considered socially acceptable may be quite different in one culture than in another. American parents love to stimulate their babies until they reach peaks of delight. By contrast, Gusii mothers in Kenya hardly ever take part in face-to-face play with their babies, seeking instead to keep young infants as calm and contented as possible (Dixon et al., 1981; LeVine & LeVine, 1988). So American babies learn that intense emotion is okay as long as it is positive, whereas Gusii babies learn to restrain both positive and negative emotions.

Regulating emotions. To comply with these emotional lessons, however, babies must devise strategies for **regulating** and controlling their emotions. This is a difficult task indeed for very young infants, who do manage to reduce at least some of their negative arousal by turning away from unpleasant stimuli or by sucking vigorously on objects. Nevertheless, young infants must often depend on caregivers to soothe them when they are experiencing strong emotional distress (Cole, Michel, & Teti, 1994). By the end of the first year, infants develop other strategies for reducing negative arousal as they rock themselves to and fro, chew on objects, and reach for and explore toys as a form of distraction (Kopp, 1989). And during the second year, infants begin to knit their brows or to bite or compress their lips as they actively attempt to suppress their anger or sadness (Malatesta et al., 1989).

The growth of cognitive and linguistic skills during the preschool period leads to new means of emotional regulation. Now parents and other close companions may

emotional display rules: culturally defined rules specifying which emotions should or should not be expressed under which circumstances.

emotional self-regulation: strategies for managing emotions or adjusting emotional arousal to a comfortable level of intensity.

Preschool children typically display their true feelings and are not very masterful at the art of emotional deceit.

attempt to moderate negative emotions by mentally *distracting* children from the most distressing aspects of unpleasant situations or by interjecting humor or otherwise helping children to *reinterpret* frightening, frustrating, or disappointing experiences (Thompson, 1994). These supportive interventions are a form of guided instruction of the kind that Vygotsky wrote about—experiences that should help preschoolers to devise strategies for regulating their own emotions. Indeed, 2–6-year-olds do gradually become more proficient at coping with unpleasant emotional arousal by directing their attention away from frightening events ("I scared of the shark. Close my eyes"), by thinking pleasant thoughts to overcome unpleasant ones ("Mommy left me; but when she comes back, we are going to the movies"), and by reinterpreting the cause of their distress in a more satisfying way ("He [story character] didn't *really* die . . . it's just pretend") (Thompson, 1994).

Interestingly, adaptive regulation of emotions may often involve *maintaining* or *intensifying* one's feelings rather than suppressing them. For example, children may learn that *conveying* their anger helps them to stand up to a bully (Thompson, 1994). And as we will see in Chapter 14, parents often call attention to (and thereby seek to maintain) the uneasiness young children experience after causing another person distress or breaking a rule. Why? Because they hope to persuade youngsters to *reinterpret* these feelings in ways that cause them to (1) *sympathize* with victims of distress and to act on this concern, or (2) feel *guilty* about their transgressions and become less inclined to repeat them. Another form of emotional arousal that we may seek to maintain or enhance is *pride* in our accomplishments—an important contributor to a healthy sense of achievement motivation and to the development of a positive academic self-concept (see Chapter 12 for further discussion of this point). So effective regulation of emotions involves an ability to suppress, maintain, or even intensify our emotional arousal in order to remain productively engaged with the challenges we face or the people we encounter (Thompson, 1994).

Acquiring emotional display rules. An ability to regulate emotions is only the first skill that children must acquire in order to comply with a culture's emotional display rules. Indeed, these prescriptions often dictate that we not only suppress whatever "unacceptable" emotions that we are actually experiencing, but also *replace* them (outwardly, at least) with whatever feeling that the display rule calls for in that situation (for example, acting happy rather than sad upon receiving a disappointing gift). Thus, complying with display rules is often an exercise in emotional deceit.

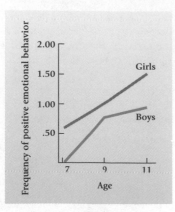

Figure 11-2
With age, children are better able to display positive emotional reactions after receiving a disappointing gift.
Adapted from Saarni, 1984.

By about age 3, children are beginning to show some limited ability to hide their true feelings. Michael Lewis and his associates (Lewis, Stanger, and Sullivan, 1989), for example, found that 3-year-olds who had lied about peeking at a forbidden toy showed subtle signs of anguish (detectable on film played in slow motion); however, they were able to mask their feelings well enough to make it impossible for uninformed adult judges to discriminate them from other children who truthfully reported that they hadn't peeked. Preschool children get a little better at lying and other deceptive ploys with each passing year (Peskin, 1992; Ruffman et al., 1993). Now inner feelings and outward expressions are not so clearly matched as they were in infancy. Still, preschoolers are quite inept compared with older children at disguising their true emotions; they typically wear their feelings on their face and express them freely.

Not until later in the elementary school years are children very masterful in the art of emotional deceit. Throughout childhood, they are becoming increasingly aware of socially sanctioned display rules, learning more about which emotions to express (and which to hide) in particular social situations (Harris, 1989). They are also motivated to comply with these emotional codes of conduct for precisely the same reasons they hide their guilt: to avoid punishment and maintain others' approval (Saarni, 1989; 1990). Yet even simple display rules may take some time to master. As we see in Figure 11-2, many 7–9-year-olds (especially boys) are still unable to act thrilled and to mask their disappointment upon receiving a lousy gift. And even many 12–13-year-olds will fail to suppress all their anger when a respected adult exercises authority and thwarts their plans (Underwood, Coie, & Herbsman, 1992).

Although we may not like the idea that children are trained to mask and alter their true feelings in many social situations, in all likelihood, this socialization of emotions works for the good of society. Indeed, life might be nearly unbearable if we adults were typically as honest about our feelings as most toddlers and preschool children are.

Recognizing and Interpreting Emotions

Currently, there is some debate about when babies begin to recognize and interpret the emotional expressions that others display. Although 3-month-olds prefer to look at photos of happy faces rather than at photos of neutral, sad, or angry ones (LaBarbera et al., 1976; Kuchuk, Vibbert, & Bornstein, 1986), their looking preferences may simply reflect their powers of visual discrimination and do not necessarily imply that infants this young *interpret* various expressions as "happy," "angry," or "sad" (Ludemann, 1991; Nelson, 1987). Yet, evidence is rapidly accumulating to suggest that young infants do attend carefully and react appropriately to more natural displays of emotion. For example, 3-month-olds will only discriminate their mother's happy, sad, or angry expressions when these facial configurations are accompanied by a happy, sad, or angry tone of voice, but they also become rather gleeful in response to a happy expression and distressed by their mothers' anger or sadness (Haviland & Lelwica, 1987; Tronick, 1989).

Social Referencing

social referencing: the use of others' emotional expressions to infer the meaning of otherwise ambiguous situations.

The ability of infants to *interpret* emotional expressions becomes more obvious between 8 and 10 months of age—the point at which they begin to monitor their parents' emotional reactions to uncertain situations and then use this information to regulate their own behavior (Feinman, 1992). This **social referencing** becomes more common with age (Walden & Baxter, 1989) and may soon extend to strangers as well: By the end of the first year, infants will typically approach and play with unfamiliar toys if a nearby stranger is smiling, but are apt to avoid these objects if the stranger displays a fearful expression (Klinnert et al., 1986). And during the second year, infants will often look to their companions *after* they have appraised a new object or situation, thus suggesting that they are now using others' emotional reactions to assess the accuracy of their *own* judgments (Hornik & Gunnar, 1988).

Conversations about Emotions

Once toddlers begin to talk about emotions at 18 to 24 months of age, family conversations that center on emotional experiences can help them achieve a much richer understanding of their own and others' feelings. In fact, Judy Dunn and her associates (1991) found that the more often 3-year-olds had discussed emotional experiences with other family members, the better they were at interpreting others' emotions three years later in grade school (see also Denham, Zoller, & Couchoud, 1994). Of course, the ability to identify how others are feeling and to understand why they feel that way is a central aspect of social cognition—and one that may have important social consequences in that kindergarten and first-grade children who score high on tests of emotional understanding tend to be rated high in social competence by teachers and to enjoy especially good relations with their peers (Cassidy et al., 1992; Garner, Jones, & Miner, 1994).

Later Milestones in Emotional Understanding

Children's ability to recognize and interpret others' emotional displays steadily improves throughout the preschool period. By age 4 to 5, children can offer explanations for why playmates are happy, angry, or sad, although they tend to focus more *external* events as causes of emotions than on internal needs, desires, moods, or motives (Fabes et al., 1988; 1991). As grade school children gradually begin to rely more on both internal and external information to interpret emotions, they achieve several important breakthroughs in emotional understanding. For example, they eventually recognize at about age 8 that many situations (for example, the approach of a big dog) will elicit different emotional reactions from different individuals (Gnepp & Klayman, 1992). Moreover, 7–9-year-olds are also beginning to understand that a person can experience more than one emotion (for example, excitement and wariness) at the same time (Arsenio & Kramer, 1992; Wintre, Polivy, & Murray, 1990), and they are displaying some ability to integrate contrasting facial, behavioral, and situational cues to infer what those emotions might be (Hoffner & Badzinski, 1989; see also Friend & Davis, 1993).

Notice that these latter advances in emotional understanding emerge at about the same age that children can integrate more than one piece of information (for example, the height and width of a column of liquid) in Piagetian conservation tasks, and they may depend, in part, on the same underlying cognitive developments. However, it is also likely that such relevant social experiences as having personally felt mixed emotions and having discussed them with friends and family members are important contributors to advanced emotional understandings as well (Harter & Buddin, 1987).

Emotions and Early Social Development

What role do emotions play in early social development? Clearly, a baby's feelings serve a *communicative* function that is likely to affect the behavior of caregivers. For example, cries of distress summon close companions. Early suggestions of a smile or expressions of interest may convince caregivers that their baby is willing and even eager to strike up a social relationship with them. Later expressions of fear or sadness may indicate that the infant is insecure or feeling blue and needs some attention or comforting. Anger may imply that the infant wishes her companions to cease whatever they are doing that is upsetting her, whereas joy serves as a prompt for caregivers to prolong an ongoing interaction or perhaps signals the baby's willingness to accept new challenges. So infant emotions are adaptive in that they promote social contact and help caregivers to adjust their behavior to the infant's needs and goals. Stated another way, the emotional expressions of infancy help infants and their close companions "get to know each other" (Tronick, 1989).

At the same time, the infant's emerging ability to recognize and interpret others' emotions is an important achievement that enables the child to infer how he should be feeling or behaving in a variety of situations. The beauty of this "social referencing" is that children can quickly acquire *knowledge* in this way. For example, a sibling's joyful reaction to the family pooch should indicate that this "ball of fur" is a friend rather than an unspeakable monster. A mother's pained expression and accompanying vocal concern might immediately suggest that the knife in one's hand is an implement to be avoided. And given the frequency with which expressive caregivers direct an infant's attention to important aspects of the environment or display their feelings about an infant's appraisal of objects and events, it is likely that the information contained in their emotional displays contributes in a major way to the child's understanding of the world in which he lives (Rosen, Adamson, & Bakeman, 1992).

▶ WHAT ARE EMOTIONAL ATTACHMENTS?

Although babies can communicate many of their feelings right from the start, their social lives change rather dramatically as they become emotionally attached to their caregivers. What is an emotional **attachment**? John Bowlby (1969) used the term to describe the strong affectional ties that bind a person to an intimate companion. According to Bowlby, people who are attached interact often and try to *maintain proximity* to each other. Thus, a 12-month-old boy who is attached to his mother may show his attachment by doing whatever it takes—crying, clinging, approaching, or following—in order to establish or to maintain contact with her. Leslie Cohen (1974) added that attachments are *selective* in character and imply that the company of some people **(attachment objects)** is more pleasant or reassuring than that of others. For example, a 2-year-old girl who is attached to her mother should prefer the mother's company to that of a mere acquaintance whenever she is upset, discomforted, or afraid.

Although our focus in this chapter is on the attachments that develop between infants and their close companions, there are many other kinds of attachments that individuals may form. Older children, adolescents, and adults may not "cling" to their intimate companions in the same way that infants do, but we can certainly see some similarities between an infant's strong ties to his mother, a child's or adolescent's involvement with a particularly close friend, and an adult's emotional commitment to a spouse or a lover (Hazan & Shaver, 1987; Simpson, Rholes, & Nelligen, 1992). Indeed, people even develop intense attachments to cuddly kittens, puppies, or other house pets that respond to them and seem to enjoy their company. All these ties are

---

attachment: a close emotional relationship between two persons, characterized by mutual affection and a desire to maintain proximity.

attachment object: a close companion to whom one is attached.

Concept Check 11-1 ⌄ Milestones in Early Emotional Development

Check your understanding of selected aspects of early emotional development by matching each descriptive statement below with one of the following concepts: (a) emotional self-regulation; (b) self-recognition; (c) social referencing; (d) disconfirmed expectancies; (e) ability to interpret emotions (emotional understanding); (f) infant emotional expressions. The answers appear in the Appendix.

_____ 1. Thought to be necessary for the development of all complex emotions.

_____ 2. Communicative prompt that affects the behavior of caregivers.

_____ 3. Correlate of social competence/peer relations in first-grade children.

_____ 4. Using others' emotional expressions to regulate one's conduct.

_____ 5. May underlie early expressions of anger, surprise, and sadness.

_____ 6. Necessary to comply with emotional display rules.

similar in that the attachment object is someone (or something) special with whom we are motivated to maintain contact (Ainsworth, 1989).

How do infants and caregivers become attached to each other? Let's address this important issue by looking first at caregivers' reactions to infants.

 ## THE CAREGIVER'S ATTACHMENT TO THE INFANT

People sometimes find it hard to understand how a parent might become attached to a neonate. After all, newborn infants can be demanding little creatures who drool, spit up, fuss, cry, dirty their diapers on a regular basis, and often require a lot of attention at all hours of the day and night. Since babies are associated with so many unpleasant consequences, why don't their parents learn to dislike them?

One reason is simply that many parents have already begun to form emotional ties to their infant before they experience the unpleasantries of parenthood. Even before a baby is born, parents often display their readiness to become attached by talking blissfully about the baby, formulating grand plans for him or her, and expressing delight in such milestones as feeling their fetus kick or hearing her heart beat with the aid of a stethoscope (Grossman, Eichler, Winickoff, & Associates, 1980). And as we learned in Chapter 4, parents who have close, skin-to-skin contact with their newborn in the first few hours after birth are often fascinated by the infant's behavior—an experience that can maintain and intensify any positive feelings that they may already display toward their baby (Klaus & Kennell, 1976; 1982). However, it is important to emphasize that these early contact or "bonding" effects are not nearly as strong or as long-lasting as earlier theorists believed (Eyer, 1992; Goldberg, 1983). True, parents *can* become emotionally involved with their babies in the first few hours after birth; but early contact is neither crucial nor sufficient for the development of strong parent-to-infant attachments. Instead, these attachments develop slowly from parent-child interactions that take place over many weeks and months. So there is absolutely no reason for parents who have not had early skin-to-skin contact with their infant to assume that they will have problems establishing a warm and loving relationship with the baby.

Young children and caregivers who are securely attached interact often and try to maintain proximity.

How Infants Promote Attachments

Since newborn infants spend so much time sleeping, crying, or in a drowsy, semiconscious state, it is tempting to think of them as inherently asocial creatures. However, ethologists John Bowlby (1969) and Konrad Lorenz (1943) have challenged this point of view, arguing that babies are highly *sociable* companions who are born with a number of endearing qualities that should make them easy to love. Let's explore this idea further.

Oh, Baby Face: The Kewpie-Doll Syndrome

Konrad Lorenz (1943) suggested that a baby's **"kewpie doll"** appearance (that is, large forehead, chubby cheeks, and soft, rounded features; see Figure 11-3) makes the infant appear cute or lovable to caregivers. Thomas Alley (1981) agrees. Alley found that adults judged line drawings of infant faces (and profiles) to be "adorable"— much cuter than those of 4-year-old children. Younger boys and girls also react positively to babyish facial features, although girls begin to show an even stronger interest in infants after reaching menarche (Goldberg, Blumberg, & Kriger, 1982).

Do adults respond more frequently and more favorably to attractive babies than to unattractive ones? Indeed they do—even when the babies in question are their own (Barden et al., 1989; Field & Vega-Lahr, 1984). One study found that mothers of "unattractive" 3-month-olds reported *more* satisfaction with parenting than did mothers of "attractive" age-mates; and yet, filmed observations revealed that these same mothers were *less* likely than mothers of attractive infants to cuddle or play with

kewpie-doll effect: the notion that infantlike facial features are perceived as cute and lovable and elicit favorable responses from others.

Figure 11-3
Infants of many species display the "kewpie-doll" effect that makes them appear lovable and elicits caregivers' attention.
Adapted from Lorenz, 1943.

their babies or to respond to their bids for attention (Barden et al., 1989). Furthermore, mothers expect infants with *fewer* babylike features to be capable of *more* behaviors than other infants of the same age, possibly because these infants look "older" than their baby-faced age-mates (Ritter, Casey, & Langlois, 1991; Zebrowitz & Montepare, 1992). Although these latter studies are early returns, they seem to imply that (1) babyish facial features may indeed elicit the kinds of positive attention from others that promote social attachments, and (2) nonbabyish features may inhibit such contact and contribute to the development of unrealistically high expectations for an infant, without the parent even being aware of these effects.

Innate Responses as Sociable Gestures

Not only do infants have "cute" faces, but many of their early reflexive behaviors may have an endearing quality about them (Bowlby, 1969). For example, the rooting, sucking, and grasping reflexes may lead parents to believe that their infant enjoys being close to them. Smiling, which is initially a reflexive response to almost any pleasing stimulus, seems to be a particularly potent signal to caregivers, as are cooing, excitable blurting, and spontaneous babbling (Keller & Scholmerich, 1987). In fact, an adult's typical response to a baby's smiles and positive vocalizations is to smile at (or vocalize to) the infant (Gewirtz & Petrovich, 1982; Keller & Scholmerich, 1987), and parents often interpret their baby's grins, laughs, and babbles as an indication that the child is contented and that they are effective caregivers. So, a smiling or babbling infant can reinforce caregiving activities and thereby increase the likelihood that parents or other nearby companions will want to attend to this happy little person in the future.

Even the reflexive cry, which is often described as aversive, can promote caregiver-to-infant attachments. Bowlby views the cry as a "distress signal" that elicits the approach of those who are responsible for the infant's care and safety. Presumably, responsive caregivers who are successful at quieting their babies will then become the beneficiaries of positive responses, such as smiling and babbling, that should reinforce their caregiving behavior and make them feel even closer to their contented infants.

Interactional Synchrony

One interesting feature of early face-to-face interactions between infants and caregivers is that babies cycle between periods of attention or interest, in which they may smile and make eye contact, and periods of inattention or avoidance, in which they quickly become overaroused and are likely to evade social overtures. Many infant-

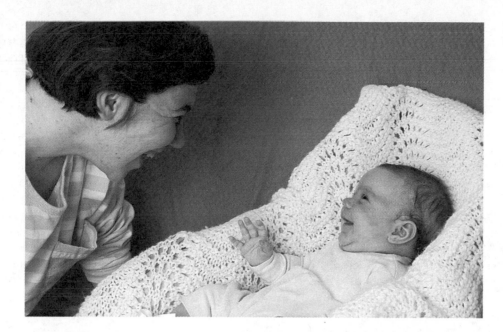

Few signals attract as much attention as a baby's social smile.

watchers now believe that these cycles of alert attention and inattention are important in establishing patterns of communication between babies and their caregivers. Should a caregiver attend carefully to a baby's cycles and limit social stimulation to those periods when the baby is alert and receptive, she and her infant may soon develop **synchronized routines** that both parties will probably enjoy. Developmentalists who have observed these interactions have likened them to "dances" in which the partners take turns responding to each other's leads. Edward Tronick (1989, p. 112) has described one such "dance" as a mother plays peek-a-boo with her infant.

> . . . The infant abruptly turns away from his mother as the game reaches its "peek" of intensity and begins to suck on his thumb and stare into space with a dull facial expression. The mother stops playing and sits back watching. . . . After a few seconds the infant turns back to her with an inviting expression. The mother moves closer, smiles, and says in a high-pitched, exaggerated voice, "Oh, now you're back!" He smiles in response and vocalizes. As they finish crowing together, the infant reinserts his thumb and looks away. The mother again waits. [Soon] the infant turns . . . to her and they greet each other with big smiles.

This is indeed an exquisite (synchronous) exchange in which each participant sends messages to which the other responds appropriately. By turning away and sucking, the excited infant is saying "Hey, I need to slow down and regulate my emotional state." His mother tells him she understands by patiently awaiting his return. As he returns, mom tells him she's glad he's back, and he acknowledges that signal with a smile and an excited blurt. And when the baby becomes overexcited a minute or two later, his mother waits for him to calm once again, and he communicates his thanks by smiling wide for her when he turns back the second time. Clearly, this is a dyad that not only interacts smoothly but quickly repairs any interactive errors.

How important are synchronous exchanges to the establishment of affectional ties? We can get some idea by contrasting synchronous interactions with conflictual, nonsynchronous ones. Suppose the mother in the example had been less patient when her infant turned away, choosing instead to click her tongue to attract his attention and to follow up by sticking her face in the baby's line of vision. According to Tronick (1989), what might well happen is that the baby would grimace, turn further away, and perhaps even push at his mother's face. The mother's intrusive actions have communicated something like "Cut the coy stuff and come play with me,"

synchronized routines: generally harmonious interactions between two persons in which each participant adjusts his or her behavior in response to the partner's actions.

whereas the infant's negative response implies "No, you cool it and give me some space." Here, then, is an exchange in which messages go unheeded and interactive errors persist and that is undoubtedly much less pleasant for both the mother and her baby than the highly affectionate, synchronous interplay described above.

In sum, infants play a major role in persuading other people to love them. Babies are physically appealing; they come equipped with a number of reflexes and response capabilities that capture the attention and warm the hearts of their companions; and last but not least, they are responsive to social overtures and may soon be capable of synchronizing their behavior with that of a caregiver. Daniel Stern (1977) believes that synchronized interactions between infants and their companions may occur several times a day and are particularly important contributors to emotional attachments. As an infant continues to interact with a particular caregiver, he will learn what this person is like and how he can regulate her attention. Of course, the caregiver should become better at interpreting the baby's signals and learn how to adjust her behavior to successfully capture and maintain his attention. As the caregiver and the infant practice their routines and become better "dance partners," their relationship should become more satisfying for both parties and eventually blossom into a strong reciprocal attachment (Isabella, 1993; Isabella & Belsky, 1991).

Problems in Establishing Caregiver-to-Infant Attachments

Although we have been talking as if caregivers invariably become closely attached to their infants, this does not always happen. As we will see, some babies are hard to love, some caregivers are hard to reach, and some environments are not very conducive to the establishment of secure emotional relationships.

Some Babies May Be Hard to Love

Unfortunately, some babies display characteristics that could annoy and even alienate their companions. For example, premature infants are alert less often than full-term infants, are more quickly overaroused by social stimulation, and often avoid a caregiver's bids for attention (Field, 1987; Lester, Hoffman, & Brazelton, 1985). Babies born addicted to a variety of narcotic agents also display abnormal behaviors that could disrupt the establishment of synchronous routines with their caregivers. Infants born to cocaine users, for example, are sometimes extremely irritable and susceptible to overarousal and at other times are withdrawn, sluggish, and unresponsive. Of course, the problems that drug-addicted babies face in endearing themselves to their caregivers may stem, in part, from the less-than-adequate care they often receive from their drug-using parents (Lester et al., 1991). Finally, some full-term and otherwise healthy infants have very difficult temperaments: They are at risk for alienating their companions by squirming, fussing, and generally resisting a caregiver's social overtures (Crockenberg, 1981).

Fortunately, most parents eventually establish satisfying routines and secure relationships with their difficult or unresponsive infants (Easterbrooks, 1989), particularly when they feel competent, or efficacious, about their parenting behavior (Teti & Gelfand, 1991) and when they have the support and encouragement of a spouse, a grandparent, or another close associate (Belsky, 1981; Jacobson & Frye, 1991; Spieker & Bensley, 1994). One way to help the process along is to identify *neonates* who may be difficult to love and then to teach their caregivers how to elicit favorable responses from these sluggish or irritable companions. The Brazelton testing and training programs reviewed in Chapter 5 (see Box 5-1) were designed with these objectives in mind.

Some Caregivers Are Hard to Reach

Caregivers sometimes have personal quirks or characteristics that seriously hinder them in establishing close emotional ties to their infants. For example, insecure attachments are the *rule* rather than the exception when a child's primary caregiver has been diagnosed as clinically depressed (Radke-Yarrow et al., 1985). The problem is that depressed parents are often not sufficiently responsive to a baby's social signals to establish a satisfying and synchronous relationship. And unfortunately, young infants of depressed mothers soon begin to match their mothers' depressive symptoms (Field et al., 1990; Pickens & Field, 1993) and often maintain this unresponsive, depressive demeanor, even when interacting with other *nondepressed* adults (Field et al., 1988)! Clearly, depressed parents are likely to require more than Brazelton training if they are to become more involved with their infants and establish secure emotional relationships with them. One intervention that has achieved good success is a program in which depressed mothers are visited regularly by a professional who (1) establishes a friendly, supportive relationship with the mother, (2) teaches her how to elicit more favorable responses from her baby, and (3) encourages her to participate in weekly parenting groups—a second important source of parenting information and social support (Lyons-Ruth et al., 1990.)

Other parents who could benefit from focused interventions are those who themselves felt unloved, neglected, or abused as children. Formerly mistreated caregivers often start out with the best intentions, vowing never to do to their children what was done to them, but they often expect their infants to be "perfect" and to love them right away. So when their babies are irritable, fussy, or inattentive (as all infants are at times), these emotionally insecure adults are apt to feel as if they are being rejected once again (Steele & Pollack, 1974). They may then back off or withdraw their own affection (see Biringen, 1990; Crowell & Feldman, 1991), sometimes to the point of neglecting or even abusing their babies.

Finally, some caregivers may be disinclined to love their babies because their pregnancies were unplanned and their infants unwanted. In one longitudinal study conducted in Czechoslovakia (Matejcek, Dytrych, & Schuller, 1979), mothers who had been denied permission to abort an unwanted pregnancy were judged to be less closely attached to their children than a group of same-aged mothers of similar marital and socioeconomic status who had not requested an abortion. Although both the "wanted" and the "unwanted" children were physically healthy at birth, over the next nine years, the unwanted children were more frequently hospitalized, made lower grades in school, had less stable family lives and poorer relations with peers, and were generally more irritable than the children whose parents had wanted them. Follow-up observations in young adulthood tell much the same story: Compared with their "wanted" peers, the formerly "unwanted" children were now much less satisfied with their marriages, jobs, friendships, and general mental health, having more often sought treatment for a variety of psychological disorders (David, 1992; 1994). Taken together, these data suggest that the failure of a caregiver to become emotionally attached to an infant can have long-term effects on the child's physical, social, emotional, and intellectual well-being.

Some Ecological Constraints on Attachment

To this point, we have seen that the character of an adult's attachment to an infant is influenced by the adult's characteristics as well as those of the infant. However, we should also recognize that interactions between infants and caregivers take place within a broader social and emotional context that may affect how a particular caregiver and infant react to each other. For example, mothers who must care for several small children with little or no assistance may find themselves unwilling or unable to devote much attention to their newest baby, particularly if the infant is at all irritable or unresponsive (Belsky, 1981; Crockenberg, 1981). Indeed, researchers have consistently reported that the more children a woman has had, the more negative her attitudes toward children become, and the more difficult she thinks her children are to raise (Garbarino & Sherman, 1980; Hurley & Hohn, 1971).

The quality of a caregiver's relationship with his or her spouse can also have a dramatic effect on parent/infant interactions and attachments. Consider that parents who were unhappily married *prior* to the birth of their child (1) are less sensitive caregivers after the baby is born, (2) express less favorable attitudes about their infants and the parenting role, and (3) establish less secure ties with their infants and toddlers, compared with other parents from similar socioeconomic backgrounds whose marriages are close and confiding (Cox et al., 1989; Howes & Markman, 1989). Unhappily married parents are often stressed to the point that it is difficult for them to respond warmly and sensitively to their infants. Indeed, the unpleasantries at home may even color their impressions of the baby, for unhappily married parents are more likely than happily married ones to describe their infants as temperamentally difficult (Easterbrooks & Emde, 1988).

Happily married couples, on the other hand, are likely to receive active encouragement from their mates as they undertake the responsibilities of parenthood, and this positive social support may be particularly important if the baby has already shown a tendency to be irritable and unresponsive. In fact, Jay Belsky (1981) found that neonates who are "at risk" for later emotional difficulties (as indicated by their poor performance on the Brazelton Neonatal Behavioral Assessment Scale) are likely to have nonsynchronous interactions with their parents *only when the parents are unhappily married.* So it seems that a stormy marriage is a major environmental hazard that can hinder or even prevent the establishment of close emotional ties between parents and their infants.

 # THE INFANT'S ATTACHMENT TO CAREGIVERS

Although adults may feel emotionally drawn to an infant very soon after the baby is born, the infant requires a little more time to form a genuine attachment to caregivers. Many theories have been proposed to explain how and why infants become emotionally involved with the people around them. But before we consider these theories, we should briefly discuss the stages that babies go through in becoming attached to a close companion.

Development of Primary Social Attachments

Many years ago, Rudolph Schaffer and Peggy Emerson (1964) studied the development of social attachments by following a group of Scottish infants from early infancy to 18 months of age. Once a month, mothers were interviewed to determine (1) how the infant responded when separated from close companions in seven situations (for example, being left in a crib; being left in the presence of strangers) and (2) the persons to whom the infant's separation responses were directed. A child was judged to be attached to someone if separation from that person reliably elicited a protest.

Schaffer and Emerson found that infants pass through the following steps, or stages, as they develop close ties with their caregivers:

1. **Asocial stage** *(0–6 weeks).* The very young infant is somewhat "asocial" in that many kinds of social and nonsocial stimuli produce a favorable reaction, and few produce any kind of protest. By the end of this period, infants are beginning to show a preference for social stimuli.

2. **Stage of indiscriminate attachments** *(6 weeks to 6–7 months).* Now infants clearly enjoy human company but tend to be somewhat indiscriminate: They smile more at people than at such lifelike objects as talking puppets (Ellsworth, Muir, & Hains, 1993) and are likely to fuss whenever *any* adult puts them down. Although 3–6-month-olds reserve their biggest grins for familiar companions (Watson et al., 1979) and are more quickly soothed by a regular caregiver, they seem to enjoy the attention they receive from just about anyone (including strangers).

3. **Stage of specific attachments** *(about age 7–9 months).* At about 7–9 months of age, infants begin to protest only when separated from one particular individual, usually the mother (see Figure 11-4). Now able to crawl, an infant often tries to fol-

asocial stage (of attachment): approximately the first six weeks of life, in which infants respond in an equally favorable way to interesting social and nonsocial stimuli.

stage of indiscriminate attachments: period between 6 weeks and 6–7 months of age in which infants prefer social to nonsocial stimulation and are likely to protest whenever any adult puts them down or leaves them alone.

stage of specific attachments: period between 7 and 9 months of age when infants are attached to one close companion (usually the mother).

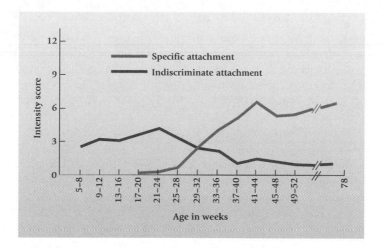

Figure 11-4
The developmental course of
attachment during infancy.
From Schaffer & Emerson, 1964.

low along behind her mother to stay close and will greet her warmly when she returns. Infants also become somewhat wary of strangers. According to Schaffer and Emerson, these babies have established their first true attachments.

The formation of a strong attachment to a caregiver has another important consequence: It promotes the development of exploratory behavior. Mary Ainsworth (1979) emphasizes that an attachment figure serves as a **secure base** for exploration—a point of safety from which an infant can feel free to venture away. Thus Juan, a securely attached infant visiting a neighbor's home with Mom, may be quite comfortable exploring the far corners of the living room so long as he can check back occasionally to see that Mom is still seated there, on the sofa. But should she disappear into the bathroom, Juan may become wary and reluctant to explore (Sroufe, 1977). Paradoxical as it may seem, then, infants apparently need to rely on another person in order to feel confident about acting independently.

4. **Stage of multiple attachments.** Within weeks after forming their initial attachments, about half the infants in Schaffer and Emerson's study were becoming attached to other people (fathers, siblings, grandparents, or perhaps a regular babysitter). By 18 months of age, very few infants were attached to only one person, and some were attached to five or more.

Schaffer and Emerson originally believed that infants who are multiply attached have a "hierarchy" of attachment objects and that the individual at the top of the list is their most preferred companion. However, later research indicates that each of the infant's attachment objects may serve different functions, so that the person whom an infant prefers most may depend on the situation. For example, most infants clearly prefer the mother's company if they are upset or frightened (Lamb & Oppenheim, 1989). However, fathers are often preferred as playmates, possibly because much of the time they spend with their infants is "play time" (Lamb, 1981; Roopnarine et al., 1990). Schaffer (1977) eventually concluded that "being attached to several people does not necessarily imply a shallower feeling toward each one, for an infant's capacity for attachment is not like a cake that has to be [divided]. Love, even in babies, has no limits" (p. 100).

Theories of Attachment

If you have ever had a kitten or a puppy, you may have noticed that pets often seem especially responsive and affectionate to the person who feeds them. Might the same be true of human infants? Developmentalists have long debated this very point, as we will see in examining the four most influential theories of infant attachment: psychoanalytic theory, learning theory, cognitive-developmental theory, and ethological theory.

For many infants, fathers
assume the role of special
playmate.

secure base: use of a caregiver as
a base from which to explore
the environment and to which
to return for emotional support.

stage of multiple attachments:
term used to describe infants
who have formed attachments to
two or more close companions.

Psychoanalytic Theory: I Love You Because You Feed Me

According to Freud, young infants are "oral" creatures who derive satisfaction from sucking and mouthing objects and should be attracted to any person who provides oral pleasure. Since it is usually mothers who "pleasure" oral infants by feeding them, it seemed logical to Freud that the mother would become the baby's primary object of security and affection, particularly if she was relaxed and generous in her feeding practices.

Erik Erikson also believed that a mother's feeding practices influence the strength or security of her infant's attachments. However, he suggested that a mother's *overall responsiveness* to her child's needs is more important than feeding itself. According to Erikson, a caregiver who consistently responds to an infant's needs will foster a sense of *trust* in other people, whereas unresponsive or inconsistent caregiving breeds mistrust. He added that an untrusting child may well become overdependent and "lean on" others, not necessarily out of love or a desire to be near but solely to ensure that his needs are met. Presumably, children who have not learned to trust others during infancy are likely to avoid close mutual-trust relationships throughout life.

Before we examine the research on feeding practices and their contribution to primary social attachments, we need to consider another viewpoint that assumes that feeding is important: learning theory.

Learning Theory: Rewardingness Leads to Love

For quite different reasons, some learning theorists have also assumed that infants become attached to persons who feed them and gratify their needs. Feeding was thought to be particularly important for two reasons (Sears, 1963). First, it should elicit positive responses from a contented infant (smiles, coos) that are likely to increase a caregiver's affection for the baby. Second, and more important to our discussion here, mothers are often able to relax with their infants while feeding and to provide them with *many comforts*—food, warmth, tender touches, soft and reassuring vocalizations, changes in scenery, and even a dry diaper (if necessary)—*all in one sitting.* What will a baby make of all this? According to learning theorists, an infant will eventually associate the mother with pleasant feelings and pleasurable sensations, so that the mother herself becomes a source of reinforcement. Once the mother (or any other caregiver) has attained this status as a **secondary reinforcer**, the infant is attached; he or she will now do whatever is necessary (smile, cry, coo, babble, or follow) in order to attract the caregiver's attention or to remain near this valuable and rewarding individual.

Just how important *is* feeding? In 1959, Harry Harlow and Robert Zimmerman reported the results of a study designed to compare the importance of feeding and tactile stimulation for the development of social attachments in infant monkeys. The monkeys were separated from their mothers in the first day of life and reared for the next 165 days by two surrogate mothers. As you can see in Figure 11-5, each surrogate mother had a face and well-proportioned body constructed of wire. However, the body of one surrogate (the "cloth mother") was wrapped in foam rubber and covered with terrycloth. Half the infants were always fed by this warm, comfortable cloth mother, the remaining half by the rather uncomfortable "wire mother."

The research question was simple: Would these infants become attached to the "mother" who fed them, or would they instead prefer the soft, cuddly terrycloth mother? It was no contest! Infants clearly preferred the cloth mother, *regardless of which mother had fed them.* Indeed, monkeys fed by the wire mother spent more than 15 hours a day clutching the *cloth* mother, compared with only an hour or so (mostly at mealtimes) with the wire mother. Moreover, all infants ran directly to the cloth mother when they were frightened by novel stimuli (marching toy bears, wooden spiders) that were placed in their cages. Clearly, the implication of Harlow and Zimmerman's classic study is that feeding is *not* the most important determinant of an infant's attachment to caregivers.

secondary reinforcer: an initially neutral stimulus that acquires reinforcement value by virtue of its repeated association with other reinforcing stimuli.

Figure 11-5
The "wire" and "cloth" surrogate mothers used in Harlow's research. This infant remains with the cloth mother even though it must stretch to the wire mother in order to feed.

Although Harlow's subjects were monkeys, research with human infants paints a similar picture. In their study of Scottish infants, Schaffer and Emerson (1964) asked each mother the age at which her child had been weaned, the amount of time it had taken to wean the child, and the feeding schedule (regular interval or demand feeding) that she had used with her baby. None of these feeding practices predicted the character of an infant's attachment to his or her mother. In fact, Schaffer and Emerson found that, in 39% of cases, the person who usually fed, bathed, and changed the child (typically the mother) was not even the child's primary attachment object! These findings are clearly damaging to any theory that states that feeding and feeding practices are the primary determinants of the child's first social attachment.

Current viewpoints. Although today's learning theorists no longer stress the importance of feeding, they continue to argue that *reinforcement* is the mechanism responsible for social attachments (Gewirtz & Petrovich, 1982). They have, in fact, ended up by adopting a viewpoint similar to that of Erik Erikson: Infants should be attracted to those individuals who are quick to respond to (and thereby reinforce) their social signals and who provide them with a variety of pleasant or rewarding experiences. Indeed, Schaffer and Emerson (1964) found that the two aspects of a mother's behavior that predicted the character of her infant's attachment to her were her *responsiveness* to the infant's behavior and the *total amount of stimulation* that she provided. Mothers who responded reliably and appropriately to their infants' bids for attention and who often played with their babies had infants who were closely attached to them.

Cognitive-Developmental Theory: To Love You, I Must Know You Will Always Be There

Cognitive-developmental theory has little to say about which adults are most likely to appeal to infants, but it does remind us of the holistic character of development by suggesting that the ability to form attachments depends, in part, on the infant's level of intellectual development. Before an attachment can occur, the infant must be able to discriminate familiar persons (that is, potential attachment objects) from strangers. He must also recognize that familiar companions have a "permanence" about them (object permanence), for it would be difficult indeed to form a stable relationship with a person who ceases to exist whenever she passes from view (Schaffer, 1971). So perhaps it is no accident that attachments first emerge at age 7–9 months—precisely the time that infants begin to show *clear* evidence of acquiring an object concept. Rudolph Schaffer (1971) went so far as to propose that attachments cannot occur until the *fourth sensorimotor substage*—the point at which infants first begin to search for and find objects hidden behind a screen.

Barry Lester and his associates (1974) evaluated Schaffer's hypothesis by giving 9-month-old infants a test of object permanence before exposing them to brief separations from their mothers, their fathers, and a stranger. They found that 9-month-olds who scored high (substage 4 or above) in object permanence only protested when separated from their mothers, whereas age-mates who scored lower (substage 3 or lower) showed little evidence of *any* separation protest. So only the cognitively advanced 9-month-olds had formed a primary attachment (to their mothers)—a finding that implies that the timing of this important emotional milestone does depend, in part, on the infant's level of object permanence.

Ethological Theory: Perhaps I Was Born to Love

Ethologists have proposed a most interesting and influential explanation for social attachments that has distinct evolutionary overtones. A major assumption of the ethological approach is that all species, including human beings, are born with a number of innate behavioral tendencies that have in some way contributed to the survival of the species over the course of evolution. Indeed, John Bowlby (1969; 1980) proposed that many of these built-in behaviors are specifically designed to promote attachments between infants and their caregivers. Even the attachment relationship itself is said to have adaptive significance, serving to protect the young from predators and other natural calamities and to ensure that their needs are met. Of course, ethologists would argue that the long-range purpose of the primary attachment is to permit members of each successive generation to live long enough to reproduce, thereby enabling the species to survive.

Origins of the ethological viewpoint. How did ethologists ever come up with their evolutionary theory of attachment? Interestingly enough, their insights were prompted by observations of young fowl. In 1873, Spaulding first noted that chicks would follow almost any moving object—another chicken, a duck, or a human being—as soon as they were able to walk. Konrad Lorenz (1937) observed this same "following response" in young goslings, a behavior he labeled **imprinting** (or stamping in). Lorenz also noted that imprinting (1) is automatic (young fowl do not have to be taught to follow), (2) occurs only within a narrowly delimited **critical period** after the bird has hatched, and (3) is irreversible (once the bird begins to follow a particular object, it will remain attached to it).

Lorenz then concluded that imprinting was an adaptive response. Young birds should generally survive if they stay close to their mothers so that they are led to food and afforded protection. Those that wander away may starve or be eaten by predators and thus fail to pass their genes to future generations. So over the course of many, many generations, the imprinting response eventually became an inborn, **preadapted characteristic** that attaches a young fowl to its mother, thereby increasing its chances of survival.

Attachment in humans. Although human infants do not imprint on their mothers in the same way that young fowl do, Bowlby (1969) claimed that they have inherited a number of behaviors that help them to maintain contact with others and to elicit caregiving. What preadapted behaviors do they display? In addition to crying, the signal that often brings caregivers running, infants also suck, grasp, smile, coo,

imprinting: an innate or instinctual form of learning in which the young of certain species follow and become attached to moving objects (usually their mothers).

critical period: a (typically) brief period in the development of an organism when it is particularly sensitive to certain environmental influences; outside this period, the same influences have little, if any, effect.

preadapted characteristic: an innate attribute that is a product of evolution and serves some function that increases the chances of survival for the individual and the species.

and babble—the very responses that were described earlier as having an endearing quality about them. In fact, Bowlby believes that adults are just as biologically predisposed to respond to a baby's signals as the baby is to emit them. It is difficult indeed for parents to ignore an urgent cry or to fail to warm up to a baby's big grin. In sum, human infants and their caregivers are said to have evolved in ways that predispose them to respond favorably to each other and form close attachments, thus enabling infants (and ultimately, the species) to survive.

Does this mean that attachments are automatic? No, indeed! Bowlby claimed that secure attachments develop gradually as parents become more proficient at reading and reacting appropriately to the baby's signals and the baby is *learning* what his parents are like and how he might regulate their behavior. Yet, the process can easily go awry, as illustrated by the finding that an infant's preprogrammed signals eventually wane if they fail to produce favorable reactions from an unresponsive companion, such as a depressed mother or an unhappily married father (Ainsworth et al., 1978). So while Bowlby claimed that human beings are biologically *prepared* to form close attachments, he also stressed that secure emotional bonds will not develop unless each participant has *learned* how to respond appropriately to the behavior of the other.

Ample close contact between infants and caregivers promotes mutual responsiveness and secure attachments.

Perhaps the most basic of all ethological hypotheses is that the more close physical contact a mother has with her baby early in infancy, the more responsive she should become to the baby and the more secure the infant should feel with her. This hypothesis was tested in an interesting experiment by Elizabeth Anisfeld and her colleagues (1990). On the second day after delivering their babies, mothers were randomly assigned to two conditions. Half received soft, pouchlike baby carriers for transporting their infants and were encouraged to use these products (close contact group), whereas the remaining mothers were instructed in the use of more common plastic infant seats—implements that permit less close contact than soft carriers do (control group). Follow-up sessions conducted to see how mothers and their infants were doing provided striking support for the "close contact" hypothesis. At age $3^{1}/_{2}$ months, mothers in the close contact group were significantly more responsive to their infants' bids for attention than were mothers in the control group. And when the babies were 13 months old, those who had had ample close contact early in infancy were more likely to be securely attached to their mothers than were babies in the control group. Of course, ethologists would explain these results by noting that the heightened "togetherness" of the close contact pairs had provided them more opportunity to learn how to adjust to each other and to develop the interactional synchrony from which secure relationships build.

Comparing the Four Theoretical Approaches

Although the four theories we have reviewed differ in many respects, each has something to offer. Even though feeding practices are not as important as psychoanalysts had originally thought, it was Freud who stressed that we need to know more about mother-infant interactions if we hope to understand how babies form attachments. Erik Erikson and the learning theorists pursued Freud's early leads and concluded that caregivers do play an important role in the infant's emotional development. Presumably, infants are likely to view a responsive companion who provides many comforts as a trustworthy and rewarding individual who is worthy of affection. Ethologists can agree with this point of view, but they add that infants are *active participants* in the attachment process who emit preprogrammed responses that enable them to promote the very interactions from which attachments are likely to develop. Finally, cognitive theorists have contributed by showing that the timing of emotional attachments is related to the child's level of intellectual development. So it makes little sense to tag one of these theories as "correct" and to ignore the others, for each theory has helped us to understand how infants become attached to their most intimate companions.

► TWO COMMON FEARS OF INFANCY

At about the same time that infants are establishing close affectional ties to a caregiver, they often begin to display negative emotional outbursts that may puzzle or perhaps even annoy their companions. In this section, we will look at two of the common fears of infancy—*stranger anxiety* and *separation anxiety*—and try to determine why these negative reactions are likely to emerge during the second half of the first year.

Stranger Anxiety

Nine-month-old Billy is sitting on the floor in the den when his mother leads a strange person into the room. The stranger suddenly walks closer, bends over, and says "Hi, Billy! How are you?" If Billy is like many 9-month-olds, he may stare at the stranger for a moment and then turn away, whimper, and crawl toward his mother.

This wary reaction to a stranger, or **stranger anxiety,** stands in marked contrast to the smiling, babbling, and other positive greetings that infants often emit when approached by a familiar companion. Most infants react positively to strangers until they form their first attachment, and then become apprehensive shortly thereafter (Schaffer & Emerson, 1964). Wary reactions to strangers—which are often mixed with signs of interest—peak at 8–10 months of age and gradually decline in intensity over the second year (Sroufe, 1977). However, even an 8–10-month-old is not afraid of every strange face she sees and may occasionally react rather positively to strangers. In Box 11-1, we will consider the circumstances under which stranger anxiety is most likely to occur and see how medical personnel and other child-care professionals might use this knowledge to head off outbreaks of fear and trembling in their offices.

Separation Anxiety

Not only do infants become wary of strangers, but they also begin to display obvious signs of discomfort when separated from their mothers or other familiar companions. For example, 10-month-old Tony, restrained in his playpen, is likely to cry if he sees his mother put on a coat and pick up a purse as she prepares to go shopping. If unrestrained and exposed to the same scene, 15-month-old Ben might run and cling to his mother or at least follow her to the door. As she leaves and closes the door behind her, Ben will probably cry. These reactions reflect the infants' **separation anxiety.** Separation anxiety normally appears during the latter half of the first year (at about the time infants are forming primary social attachments), peaks at 14–20 months, and gradually becomes less frequent and less intense throughout infancy and the preschool period (Kagan, Kearsley, & Zelazo, 1978; Weinraub & Lewis, 1977).

Why Do Infants Fear Strangers and Separations?

We have seen that both stranger anxiety and separation anxiety emerge at about the same time as the primary social attachment and follow a predictable developmental course. Why do infants who are just beginning to appreciate the pleasures of love now suddenly experience the gripping agony of fear? Let's consider two viewpoints that have received some support.

The ethological viewpoint. Ethologist John Bowlby's (1973) explanation for both stranger anxiety and separation anxiety is remarkably straightforward. He claims that there are a number of events that qualify as *natural clues to danger*—that is, situations that have been so frequently associated with danger throughout a species' evolutionary history that a fear or avoidance response has become "biologically programmed." Among the events that infants may be programmed to fear, once they can readily discriminate familiar objects and events from unfamiliar ones, are strange

stranger anxiety: a wary or fretful reaction that infants and toddlers often display when approached by an unfamiliar person.

separation anxiety: a wary or fretful reaction that infants and toddlers often display when separated from the person(s) to whom they are attached.

BOX 11-1
Combating Stranger Anxiety: Some Helpful Hints for Doctors and Child-Care Professionals

*I*t is not at all unusual for toddlers visiting the doctor's office to break into tears and to cling tenaciously to their parents. Some youngsters who remember previous visits may be suffering from "shot anxiety" rather than stranger anxiety, but many are simply reacting fearfully to the approach of an intrusive physician who may poke, prod, and handle them in ways that are atypical and upsetting. Fortunately, there are steps that caregivers and medical personnel (or any other stranger) can take to make such encounters less terrifying for an infant or toddler. What can we suggest?

1. *Keep familiar companions available.* Infants react much more negatively to strangers when they are separated from their mothers or other close companions. Indeed, most 6–12-month-olds are not particularly wary of an approaching stranger if they are sitting on their mother's laps; however, they will frequently whimper and cry at the stranger's approach if seated only a few feet from their mothers (Morgan & Ricciuti, 1969; and see Bohlin & Hagekull, 1993). Clearly, doctors and nurses can expect a more constructive response from their youngest patients if they can avoid separating them from their caregivers.

2. *Arrange for companions to respond positively to the stranger.* Stranger anxiety is less likely to occur if the caregiver issues a warm greeting to the stranger or uses a positive tone of voice when talking to the infant about the stranger (Feinman, 1992). These actions permit the child to engage in *social referencing* and to conclude that maybe the stranger really isn't all that scary if mom and dad seem to like him. It might not hurt, then, for medical personnel to strike up a pleasant conversation with the caregiver before directing their attention to the child.

3. *Make the setting more "familiar."* Stranger anxiety occurs less frequently in familiar settings than in unfamiliar ones. For example, few 10-month-olds are especially wary of strangers at home, but most react negatively to strange companions when tested in an unfamiliar laboratory (Sroufe, Waters, & Matas, 1974). Although it may be unrealistic to advise modern physicians to make home visits, they could make at least one of their examination rooms more homelike for young children, perhaps by placing an attractive mobile in one corner and posters of cartoon characters on the wall, or by having a stuffed toy or two available for the child to play with. The infant's familiarity with a strange setting also makes a difference: Whereas the vast majority (90%) of 10-month-olds become upset if a stranger approaches them within a minute after being placed in an unfamiliar room, only about half will react negatively to the stranger when they have had 10 minutes to grow accustomed to this setting (Sroufe et al., 1974). Perhaps trips to the doctor would become more tolerable for an in-

fant or a toddler if medical personnel gave the child a few minutes to familiarize himself with the examination room before making their entrance.

4. *Be a sensitive, unobtrusive stranger.* Not surprisingly, an infant's response to a stranger depends on the stranger's behavior (Sroufe, 1977). The meeting is likely to go best if the stranger initially keeps his or her distance and then approaches slowly while smiling, talking, and offering a familiar toy or suggesting a familiar activity (Bretherton, Stolberg, & Kreye, 1981; Sroufe, 1977). It also helps if the stranger, like any sensitive caregiver, takes his or her cues from the infant (Mangelsdorf, 1992). Babies prefer strangers they can control! Intrusive strangers who approach quickly and force themselves on the child (for example, by trying to pick infants up before they have time to adjust) probably get the response they deserve.

Most toddlers respond favorably to a friendly stranger—even a doctor—who offers a toy.

5. *Try looking a little less strange to the child.* Stranger anxiety depends, in part, on the stranger's physical appearance. Jerome Kagan (1972) has argued that infants form mental representations, or *schemas,* for the faces that they encounter in daily life and are most likely to be afraid of people whose appearance is not easily assimilated into these existing schemas. So a doctor in a sterile white lab coat with a strange stethoscope around her neck (or a nurse with a pointed hat that may give her a "witchlike" look) can make infants and toddlers rather wary indeed! Pediatric professionals may not be able to alter various physical features (for example, a huge nose or a facial scar) that might make children wary; but they can and often do shed their strange instruments and white uniforms in favor of more "normal" attire that will help their youngest patients to recognize them as members of the human race. Babysitters who favor the "punk" look might also do well to heed this advice if establishing rapport with their young companions is a priority.

faces, strange settings, and the "strange circumstance" of being separated from familiar companions.

Several observations are consistent with this ethological viewpoint. For example, infants show stronger fear of strangers and separations when these events take place in an unfamiliar laboratory than at home (Rinkoff & Corter, 1980; Sroufe et al., 1974). Why? Because the "strangeness" of the laboratory setting magnifies the apprehension they ordinarily experience upon encountering a stranger or having to endure a separation. Moreover, the ethological view also explains why infants from many nonindustrialized countries, who are nearly always in close contact with their mothers, begin to protest separations much earlier than do infants in some of the industrialized nations. Presumably, these infants are quick to protest because separations from a caregiver are so unusual that they represent very "strange" and fear-provoking events (Ainsworth, 1967).

Why, then, do stranger anxiety and separation anxiety become less intense during the second year—declining to the point where the infant actually *initiates* separations and is often able to tolerate strangers, even after her mother has left the room? Mary Ainsworth (1979) believes that infants become less wary of strangers and separations as they begin to use their attachment objects as *secure bases* for exploration. As the infant ventures away from his secure base to explore, he should eventually become more tolerant of separations and much less wary of novel stimuli (strangers and unfamiliar settings) that have previously been a source of concern.

The cognitive-developmental viewpoint. Cognitive theorists view both stranger anxiety and separation anxiety as natural outgrowths of the infant's perceptual and cognitive development. Jerome Kagan (1972) suggests that 6–8-month-olds have finally developed stable schemas for the faces of familiar companions and that a strange face now represents a discrepant and potentially fear-provoking stimulus. He notes that babies this age typically stare at a stranger before protesting, as if they are *hypothesizing*, trying to explain who this is or what has become of familiar faces that match their schemas for caregivers. Failing to answer these questions, the child becomes apprehensive and may cry in an attempt to summon familiar company.

Kagan's (1972; 1976) explanation of separation anxiety is equally interesting. He suggests that infants develop not only schemas for familiar faces (caregivers) but also schemas for a familiar person's probable whereabouts. Moreover, he claims that violations of these "familiar faces in familiar places" schemas are the primary cause of separation distress. Consider the implications of this viewpoint. If a mother proceeds to the kitchen, leaving her 10-month-old son on the living-room floor, the infant may watch her depart but should then resume his previous activity *without protesting her*

> *Concept Check 11-2* ∨ Understanding Theories of Attachment
>
> Check your understanding of various theories of attachment by matching each descriptive statement below to one of the following theories or theorists: (a) Sigmund Freud; (b) Erik Erikson; (c) learning perspective; (d) John Bowlby; (e) Mary Ainsworth; (f) cognitive-developmental perspective. The answers appear in the Appendix.
>
> _____ 1. Believes that stranger/separation anxieties gradually decline as infants use their attachment objects as secure bases for exploration.
>
> _____ 2. Proposes that infants are "attached" once the caregiver attains the status of a secondary reinforcer.
>
> _____ 3. Claims that infants protest separations when they cannot account for the caregiver's whereabouts.
>
> _____ 4. Proposes that caregiver's feeding practices determine the strength or character of infant attachments.
>
> _____ 5. Thinks that strange faces and separations from attachment objects are "natural clues to danger" that infants are programmed to fear.
>
> _____ 6. Emphasizes caregiver responsiveness and the infant's feelings of trust as the primary determinants of attachment security.

BOX 11-2
On Easing the Pain of Separation

At some point, most parents find it necessary to leave their infants and toddlers in an unfamiliar setting (such as a nursery or a day-care center) or in the company of a stranger (for example, a babysitter) for hours at a time. How can they make these necessary separations easier for their child to bear? Here are three simple recommendations:

1. *Provide an explanation for the separation.* Cognitive-developmental theorists tell us that separations are most upsetting when infants and toddlers cannot explain where caregivers have gone or when they will return. Thus, an explanation for the separation may help immensely. Indeed, toddlers who are left in unfamiliar settings cry less and play much more constructively if their mothers have taken a moment to explain that they are leaving and will soon return (Weinraub & Lewis, 1977). Brief explanations work better than lengthy ones (Adams & Passman, 1981), and one need not prepare a toddler days in advance for an upcoming separation. In fact, 2-year-olds who are prepared in advance often worry in advance; moreover, they protest more and play less constructively once the separation actually occurs than do age-mates who have received little advance preparation (Adams & Passman, 1980).
2. *Provide some reminder of home.* Ethologists tell us that separations involving a *strange* caregiver in a *strange* setting are likely to be particularly upsetting. Not surpris-

ingly, then, separations can be made less painful for older infants and toddlers if they have some reminder of home with them, such as a favorite stuffed animal or a security blanket (Passman & Weisberg, 1975). Indeed, giving the toddler a sharply focused photograph of his mother (or having one available for the substitute caregiver to show the child) may also help him to respond more constructively to a necessary separation (Passman & Longeway, 1982).
3. *Choose a sensitive substitute caregiver.* Finally, all developmentalists advise parents to select a substitute caregiver who enjoys children and is sensitive to their concerns. Although infants 8 months of age and older are likely to become visibly upset when first left with an unfamiliar sitter, their adjustment to this arrangement clearly depends on the sitter's behavior (Gunnar et al., 1992). If the sitter assumes a "caretaker" role by first settling the child in and then pursuing her own interests, most infants and toddlers will continue to display signs of distress. But if the sitter acts as a "playmate" by providing toys and attracting the child's interest, most infants and toddlers will quickly stop protesting and join in the fun (Gunnar et al., 1992). Clearly, a sitter who enjoys interacting with young children is a far better choice than one who sees her function as quickly attending to the child's most basic needs before heading to the telephone or refrigerator.

departure. He knows where his mother has gone because he has previously developed a schema for mother-in-the-kitchen. But should she pick up her coat and purse and walk out the front door, the child should find it difficult to account for her whereabouts and will probably cry. In sum, cognitive theorists believe that infants are most likely to protest separations when they cannot understand where their absent companions may have gone.

Indeed, infants observed at home are more likely to protest when mothers depart through an unfamiliar doorway (such as the entry to the cellar) than through a familiar one (Littenberg, Tulkin, & Kagan, 1971). And 9 month-old infants who have played quietly during a separation soon become extremely upset after looking for their mother and discovering that she is not where they thought she was (Corter et al., 1980). Clearly, these observations support Kagan's theory: Infants are most likely to protest separation from a caregiver when they are uncertain of her whereabouts.

In sum, stranger anxiety and separation anxiety are relatively complex emotional responses that stem, in part, from an infant's *general apprehension of the unfamiliar* (the ethological viewpoint) and inability to *explain* who a stranger may be or what has become of familiar companions (cognitive-developmental viewpoint). In Box 11-2, we will see how parents might use this knowledge to make necessary separations easier for their infants and toddlers to bear.

Now we come to an important issue: Do the emotional events of infancy have any *long-term* effects on developing children? Most developmentalists believe that they do. In fact, Sigmund Freud (1905/1930) argued that the formation of a stable mother-infant emotional bond is *absolutely necessary* for normal social and personality development, a sentiment shared by ethologist John Bowlby and the best-known psychoanalyst of recent times, Erik Erikson. Though not all theorists make such bold claims, almost everyone agrees that the emotional events of infancy are important in shaping future development.

There are at least two ways to evaluate this **early-experience hypothesis.** First, we could try to determine whether infants who fail to become securely attached to their parents turn out any different from those who do. Second, one could look at what happens to infants who have had little or no contact with a mother figure during the first two years and do not become attached to anyone. In the pages that follow, we will consider the findings and implications of both these lines of inquiry.

▶ INDIVIDUAL DIFFERENCES IN ATTACHMENT QUALITY

Mary Ainsworth and her associates (1978) have found that infants differ in the type (or quality) of attachments they establish with their caregivers. Ainsworth measures the quality of an infant's attachment by exposing the child to a **strange-situations test** consisting of a series of eight episodes (summarized in Table 11-1) that attempt to simulate (1) naturalistic caregiver-infant interactions in the presence of toys (to see if the infant uses the caregiver as a *secure base* from which to explore); (2) brief separations from the caregiver and encounters with strangers (which often stress the infant); and (3) reunion episodes (to determine whether a stressed infant derives any comfort and reassurance from the caregiver and can once again become involved with toys). By recording and analyzing an infant's responses to these episodes—that is, exploratory activities, reactions to strangers and to separations, and, in particular, behaviors when reunited with the close companion—it is usually possible to characterize his or her attachment to the caregiver in one of four ways:

1. **Secure attachment.** About 65% of 1-year-old North American infants fall into this category. The securely attached infant actively explores while alone with the mother and is visibly upset by separation. The infant *greets the mother warmly when she returns and welcomes physical contact with her.* The child is outgoing with strangers while the mother is present.

2. **Resistant attachment.** About 10% of 1-year-olds show this type of "insecure" attachment. These infants try to stay close to their mother but explore very little while she is present. They become very distressed as the mother departs. But when she returns, the infants are ambivalent: They *remain near her,* although they seem to resent her for having left them and are likely to *resist physical contact initiated by the mother.* Resistant infants are quite wary of strangers, even when their mothers are present.

3. **Avoidant attachment.** These infants (about 20% of 1-year-olds) also display an "insecure" attachment. They often show little distress when separated from the mother and generally *turn away so as to ignore or avoid contact with her when she returns.* Avoidant infants are not particularly wary of strangers but may sometimes avoid or ignore them in much the same way that they avoid or ignore their mothers.

4. **Disorganized/disoriented attachment.** This recently discovered attachment pattern characterizes about 5%–10% of American infants and seems to reflect the greatest insecurity. It appears to be a curious combination of the resistant and the avoidant patterns that reflects confusion about whether to approach or avoid the caregiver (Main & Solomon, 1990). When reunited with their mothers, these infants may act dazed and freeze; or they may move closer but then abruptly move away as the mother draws near; or they may show both patterns in different reunion episodes.

From these descriptions, it seems that securely attached infants are reasonably happy babies who have established an affectionate relationship with their primary caregiver. By contrast, resistant infants are drawn to their caregivers but seem not to trust them; avoidant babies seem to derive little if any comfort from their caregivers; and disorganized/disoriented infants appear extremely confused and uncertain about whether to approach or avoid their caregivers.

early-experience hypothesis: the notion that the social and emotional events of infancy are very influential in determining the course of one's future development.

strange-situations test: a series of eight separation and reunion episodes to which infants are exposed in order to determine the quality of their attachments to one or more close companions.

secure attachment: an infant/caregiver bond in which the child welcomes contact with a close companion and uses this person as a secure base from which to explore the environment.

resistant attachment: an insecure infant/caregiver bond, characterized by strong separation protest and a tendency of the child to resist contact initiated by the caregiver, particularly after a separation.

avoidant attachment: an insecure infant/caregiver bond, characterized by little separation protest and a tendency of the child to avoid or ignore the caregiver.

disorganized/disoriented attachment: an insecure infant/caregiver bond, characterized by the infant's dazed appearance on reunion or a tendency to first seek and then abruptly avoid the caregiver.

Table 11-1 The Eight Episodes That Make Up the Strange-Situations Test

Episode number	Persons present	Brief description of action	Behaviors observed
1	Mother, baby, and observer	Observer introduces mother and baby to experimental room, then leaves. (Room contains many appealing toys scattered about.)	
2	Mother and baby	Mother is nonparticipant while baby explores; if necessary, play is stimulated after 2 minutes.	Exploration (use of parent as secure base)
3	Stranger, mother, and baby	Stranger enters. First minute: stranger silent. Second minute: stranger converses with mother. Third minute: stranger approaches baby. After 3 minutes, mother leaves unobtrusively.	Reactions to stranger
4	Stranger and baby	First separation episode. Stranger's behavior is geared to that of baby.	Separation anxiety
5	Mother and baby	First reunion episode. Mother greets and/or comforts baby, then tries to settle him again in play. Mother then leaves, saying "bye-bye."	Reunion behaviors
6	Baby alone	Second separation episode.	Separation anxiety
7	Stranger and baby	Continuation of second separation. Stranger enters and gears her behavior to that of baby.	Ability to be comforted by stranger
8	Mother and baby	Second reunion episode. Mother enters, greets baby, then picks him up. Meanwhile stranger leaves unobtrusively.	Reunion behaviors

Note: All episodes except the first last approximately 3 minutes. The strange-situations test can also be used to measure the kinds of attachments that infants have established with other close companions, such as fathers or regular sitters.
Source: Ainsworth, Blehar, Waters, & Wall, 1978.

Cultural Variations in Attachment Classifications

The percentages of infants who fall into the various attachment categories differ somewhat from culture to culture and seem to reflect cultural variations in child rearing. For example, German parents deliberately encourage their infants to be independent and tend to discourage clingy close contact, perhaps explaining why more German babies show reunion behaviors characteristic of the avoidant attachment pattern (Grossmann et al., 1985). Moreover, intense separation and stranger anxieties, which characterize resistant attachments, are much more common in cultures such as Japan, where caregivers rarely leave their infants with substitute caregivers, and Israel, where communally reared kibbutz children sleep in infant houses under the care of a stranger without their parents being accessible to them at night (Sagi et al., 1994). But despite these cultural variations, all of the major attachment classifications have been observed in all cultures studied to date, and more babies around the world fall into the secure attachment category than into any of the "insecure" categories (van !Jzendoorn & Kroonenberg, 1988).

How Do Infants Become Securely or Insecurely Attached?

Ainsworth's Caregiving Hypothesis

Ainsworth (1979) believes that the quality of an infant's attachment to his mother (or any other close companion) depends largely on the kind of attention he has received. According to this **caregiving hypothesis,** mothers of *securely attached* infants are thought to be responsive caregivers from the very beginning. And evidently they are, for Ainsworth (1979) found that these mothers enjoy close contact with their babies, are emotionally expressive, are highly sensitive to their infants' social signals, and are quick to encourage their infants to explore (see also Isabella, 1993). Her view is that infants' impressions of other people are shaped by their early experiences with primary caregivers. And when a caregiver is sensitive to the infant's needs and easily accessible, the infant should derive comfort and pleasure from their interactions and become securely attached.

Babies who show a *resistant* rather than secure pattern of attachment sometimes have irritable and unresponsive temperaments (Cassidy & Berlin, 1994; Waters et al., 1980), but more often they have parents who are *inconsistent* in their caregiving — reacting enthusiastically or indifferently depending on their moods and being unresponsive a good deal of the time (Ainsworth, 1979; Isabella, 1993; Isabella & Belsky, 1991). The infant copes with this inconsistent caregiving by trying desperately—through clinging, crying, and other attachment behaviors—to obtain emotional support and comfort and then becomes both saddened and resentful when these efforts often fail.

There may be at least two patterns of caregiving that place infants at risk of developing *avoidant* attachments. Ainsworth and others (for example, Isabella, 1993) find that some mothers of avoidant infants are often impatient with their babies and unresponsive to their signals, are likely to express negative feelings about their infants, and seem to derive little pleasure from close contact with them. Ainsworth (1979) believes that these mothers are rigid, self-centered people who are likely to *reject* their babies. In other cases, however, avoidant babies have overzealous parents who chatter endlessly and provide high levels of stimulation even when their babies do not want it (Belsky et al., 1984; Isabella & Belsky, 1991). Infants may be responding quite adaptively by learning to avoid adults who seem to dislike their company or who bombard them with stimulation they do not want and cannot handle. Whereas resistant infants make vigorous attempts to gain emotional support, avoidant infants seem to have learned to do without it (Isabella, 1993).

What about infants who develop *disorganized/disoriented* attachments? Mary Main believes that these very insecure infants are drawn to their caregivers but may also *fear* them because of past episodes in which they were neglected or physically abused (Main & Solomon, 1990). Indeed, the infant's approach/avoidance (or totally dazed demeanor) at reunion is quite understandable if she has experienced cycles of acceptance and abuse (or neglect) and doesn't know whether to approach the caregiver for comfort or to retreat from her to safety. Available research supports Main's theorizing: Although disorganized/disoriented attachments are occasionally observed in any research sample, they seem to be the *rule* rather than the exception among groups of abused infants (Carlson et al., 1989). And this same curious mixture of approach and avoidance, coupled with sadness upon reunion, also characterizes many infants of severely depressed mothers, who may be inclined to ignore and neglect their babies (Lyons-Ruth et al., 1990).

Caregivers or Infants as Architects of Attachment Quality? The Temperament Hypothesis

To this point, we have talked as if mothers were primarily responsible for the kinds of attachments their infants form. Not everyone agrees. Jerome Kagan (1984), for example, believes that the strange-situations test may really measure individual differences in infants' temperaments rather than the quality of their attachments. Recall

caregiving hypothesis:
Ainsworth's notion that the type of attachment that an infant develops with a particular caregiver depends primarily on the kind of caregiving he has received from that person.

Table 11-2 Comparison of the Percentages of Young Infants Who Can Be Classified as Temperamentally "Easy," "Difficult," and "Slow to Warm Up" with the Percentages of 1-Year-Olds Who Have Established Secure, Resistant, and Avoidant Attachments with Their Mothers

Temperamental profile	Percentage of "classifiable" infants*	Attachment classification	Percentage of 1-year-olds
Easy	60	Secure	65
Difficult	15	Resistant	10
Slow to warm up	23	Avoidant	20

*These percentages are based only on the 65% of young infants who clearly exhibited one of the three temperamental profiles; hence they exclude the 35% of Thomas and Chess's sample who could not be classified.
Source: Ainsworth, Blehar, Waters, & Wall, 1978; Thomas & Chess, 1977.

from Chapter 3 that a majority of young infants display one of three temperamental profiles: *easy, difficult,* and *slow to warm up.* And as we see in Table 11-2, the percentages of 1-year-olds who have established secure, resistant, and avoidant attachments correspond closely to the percentages of classifiable infants who fall into the easy, difficult, and slow-to-warm-up categories. Is this merely a coincidence?

Kagan doesn't think so. He suggests that a temperamentally "difficult" infant who resists changes in routine and is upset by novelty may become so distressed by the strange-situations procedure that he is unable to respond constructively to his mother's comforting and is thus classified as *resistant.* By contrast, a friendly, easygoing child is apt to be classified as *"securely attached,"* whereas one who is shy or "slow to warm up" may appear distant or detached in the strange situations and will probably be classified as *avoidant.* So Kagan's **temperament hypothesis** implies that infants, not caregivers, are the primary architects of their attachment classifications. Presumably, the attachment behaviors that a child displays reflect his or her own temperament.

Which Hypothesis Should We Endorse?

Although such components of temperament as irritability and negative emotionality do predict certain attachment behaviors (for example, intensity of separation protests) and have some bearing on the quality of an infant's attachments (Goldsmith & Alansky, 1987; Izard et al., 1991; Vaughn et al., 1992), most experts view Kagan's temperament hypothesis as far too extreme. Consider, for example, that many infants are securely attached to one close companion and insecurely attached to another—a pattern that we would not expect to see if attachment classifications were merely reflections of the child's relatively stable temperamental characteristics (Goossens & van IJzendoorn, 1990; Sroufe, 1985). Moreover, several longitudinal studies have measured infant temperament and maternal caregiving over the first year to see which of these factors best predicts the quality of attachments that infants establish with their mothers. Both temperament and caregiving play a part, but the caregiver's behavior has more to do with whether a secure attachment forms than the infant's temperament does (Belsky, Rovine, & Taylor, 1984; Goldberg et al., 1986; Mangelsdorf et al., 1990; Vaughn et al., 1989).

So it seems that caregivers, not infants, are the *primary* architects of the quality of infant attachments. This is not to say that infant temperament is unimportant, for we've seen that it is harder for a caregiver to be consistently sensitive and responsive to a temperamentally difficult infant than to an easygoing one. However, it should

temperament hypothesis: Kagan's view that the strange-situations test measures individual differences in infants' temperaments rather than the quality of their attachments.

be emphasized that a clear majority of temperamentally difficult babies will establish *secure* attachments with caregivers who display lots of patience and adapt their caregiving to their babies' temperamental characteristics (Mangelsdorf et al., 1990; van den Boom, 1994; van IJzendoorn et al., 1992). By contrast, even many babies who are good-natured will end up establishing shaky, insecure relationships with mothers who are experiencing serious psychological difficulties that prevent them from being sensitive, responsive companions (van IJzendoorn et al., 1992).

Perhaps these findings are best summarized in terms of Thomas and Chess's (1977) *goodness-of-fit model* that we introduced in Chapter 3: secure attachments evolve from relationships in which there is a "good fit" between the caregiving that a baby receives and his or her own temperament, whereas insecure attachments are more likely to develop when highly stressed or otherwise inflexible caregivers fail to accommodate to their infants' temperamental qualities (van den Boom, 1994). Indeed, one reason why "caregiver sensitivity" so consistently predicts attachment security is that the very notion of *sensitive* care implies an ability to tailor one's routines to whatever temperamental quirks a baby might display (Sroufe, 1985).

To this point, we have focused only on the quality of the infant's attachment to his or her mother. Does the kind of attachment an infant has to the mother have any effect on the infant's relationship with the father? In Box 11-3, we will explore this issue as we consider some of the ways fathers respond to their infants and contribute to their social and emotional development.

Attachment Quality and Later Development

Both psychoanalytic theorists (Erikson, 1963; Freud, 1905/1930) and ethologists (Bowlby, 1969) believe that the feelings of warmth, trust, and security that infants gain from secure attachments set the stage for healthy psychological development later in life. Of course, one implication of this viewpoint is that insecure attachments may forecast less-than-optimal developmental outcomes in the years ahead.

Long-Term Correlates of Secure and Insecure Attachments

Although the existing data are somewhat limited in that they focus almost exclusively on infants' attachments to their mothers, it seems that infants who have established secure primary attachments are likely to display more favorable developmental outcomes. For example, babies who were securely attached at age 12–18 months are better problem solvers as 2-year-olds (Frankel & Bates, 1990), are more complex and creative in their symbolic play (Pipp, Easterbrooks, & Harmon, 1992), and are more attractive to toddlers as playmates (Jacobson & Wille, 1986) than children who were insecurely attached. Indeed, infants whose primary attachments are disorganized/disoriented are at risk of becoming hostile and aggressive preschoolers whom peers are likely to reject (Lyons-Ruth, Alpern, & Repacholi, 1993).

Longer-term studies of securely and insecurely attached children paint a similar picture. Everett Waters and his associates (1979), for example, first measured the quality of children's attachments at 15 months of age and then observed these children in a nursery school setting at age 3½. Children who had been securely attached to their mothers at age 15 months were now social leaders in nursery school: They often initiated play activities, were generally sensitive to the needs and feelings of other children, and were very popular with their peers. Observers described these children as curious, self-directed, and eager to learn. By contrast, children who had been insecurely attached at age 15 months were socially and emotionally withdrawn, and hesitant to engage other children in play activities, and were described by observers as less curious, less interested in learning, and much less forceful in pursuing their goals. By age 4 to 5, children who were securely attached as infants continue to be more curious, more responsive to peers, and less dependent on adults than classmates who were insecurely attached (Sroufe, Fox, & Pancake, 1983). And at age 10 to 11, they still enjoy better peer relations and are more likely to have close friends than

BOX 11-3
Fathers as Attachment Objects

In 1975, Michael Lamb described fathers as the "forgotten contributors to child development." And he was right. Until the mid-1970s, fathers were treated as biological necessities who played only a minor role in the social and emotional development of their infants and toddlers. One reason for overlooking or discounting the father's early contributions may have been that fathers spend less time interacting with babies than mothers do (Belsky, Gilstrap, & Rovine, 1984; Parke 1981). However, fathers appear to be just as "engrossed" with their newborn infants as mothers are (Parke, 1981), and they become increasingly involved with their babies over the first year of life (Belsky et al., 1984), spending an average of nearly an hour a day interacting with their 9-month-olds (Ninio & Rinott, 1988). Fathers are most highly involved with their infants and hold more favorable attitudes about them when they are happily married (Cox et al., 1989; 1992; Levy-Shiff & Israelashvili, 1988) and when their wives encourage them to become an important part of their babies' lives (Palkovitz, 1984).

Many infants form secure attachments to their fathers during the latter half of the first year (Lamb, 1981), particularly if the father has a positive attitude about parenting, spends a lot of time with them, and is a sensitive caregiver (Cox et al., 1992). And how do fathers compare to mothers as companions? In his classic early work on fathering, Lamb (1981) found that mothers and fathers tend to play somewhat different roles in a baby's life. Mothers are more likely than fathers to hold their infants, soothe them, play traditional games, and care for their physical needs; fathers are more likely than mothers to provide playful physical stimulation and initiate unusual or unpredictable games that infants often enjoy (Lamb, 1981). Although most infants prefer their mothers' company when upset or afraid (Lamb & Oppenheim, 1989), fathers are often preferred as playmates.

However, the playmate role is but one of many that modern fathers fulfill, particularly if their wives are working and they must necessarily assume at least some of the caregiving burden (Cox et al., 1992). And what kinds of caregivers do dads make? Many of them are (or soon become) rather skillful at virtually all phases of routine care (including diapering, bathing, and soothing a distressed infant). Moreover, once fathers become objects of affection, they begin to serve as a secure base from which their babies will venture to explore the environment (Hwang, 1986; Lamb, 1981). So fathers are rather versatile companions who can assume any and all functions normally served by the other parent (of course, the same is true of mothers).

Although many infants form the same kind of attachment with their fathers that they have previously established with their mothers (Fox, Kimmerly, & Schafer, 1991; Rosen & Rothbaum, 1993), it is not at all unusual for a child to be securely attached to one parent and insecure with the other (Cox et al., 1992; Goossens & van IJzendoorn, 1990). For example, when Mary Main and Donna Weston (1981) used the strange-situations test to measure the quality of 44 infants' attachments to their mothers and their fathers, they found that 12 infants were securely attached to both parents, 11 were secure with the mother but insecure with the father, 10 were insecure with the mother but secure with the father, and 11 were insecurely attached to both parents.

What does the father add to a child's social and emotional development? One way to find out is to compare the social behavior of infants who are securely attached to their fathers and infants whose relationships with their fathers are insecure. Main and Weston adopted this strategy by exposing their four groups of infants to a friendly stranger in a clown outfit who spent several minutes trying to play with the child and then turned around and cried when a person at the door told the clown he would have to leave. As the clown went through his routine, the infants were each observed and rated for (1) the extent to which they were willing to establish a positive relationship with the clown (low ratings indicated that the infant was wary or distressed) and (2) signs of emotional conflict (that is, indications of psychological disturbance such as curling up in the fetal position on the floor or vocalizing in a "social" manner to a wall). The table shows the results of this stranger test. Note that infants who were securely attached to both parents were the most socially responsive group. Equally important is the finding that infants who were securely attached to *at least one parent* were more friendly toward the clown and less emotionally conflicted than infants who had insecure relationships with both parents. In sum, this study illustrates the important role that fathers play in their infants' social and emotional development. Not only are infants more socially responsive when securely attached to *both* the mother and the father, but it also appears that a secure attachment to the father can help to prevent harmful consequences (emotional disturbances, an exaggerated fear of other people) that could otherwise result when infants are insecurely attached to their mothers (see also Biller, 1993).

Average Levels of Social Responsiveness and Emotional Conflict Shown by Infants Who Were Either Securely or Insecurely Attached to Their Mothers and Fathers

Measure	Patterns of attachment			
	Securely attached to both parents	Secure with mother, nonsecure with father	Nonsecure with mother, secure with father	Nonsecurely attached to both parents
Social responsiveness	6.04	4.87	3.30	2.45
Emotional conflict	1.17	1.00	1.80	2.50

Note: Social responsiveness ratings could vary from 1 (wary, distressed) to 9 (happy, responsive). Conflict ratings could vary from 1 (no conflict) to 5 (very conflicted). *Source:* Adapted from Main & Weston, 1981.

age-mates whose primary attachments were insecure (Elicker, Englund, & Sroufe, 1992; Grossmann & Grossmann, 1991). So it seems that children can be influenced by the quality of their early attachments for many years to come. And one reason is that attachments are often stable over time: Most children experience the same kind of attachment relationships with their parents during the grade school years that they did in infancy (Main & Cassidy, 1988; Wartner et al., 1994). Indeed, young adults who characterize their early attachments as secure, resistant, or avoidant tend to establish the same kind of attachment relationships with their current romantic partners (Feeney & Noller, 1990; Hazan & Shaver, 1987).

Why Might Attachment Quality Forecast Later Behavior?

Why does the quality of one's early attachments remain so stable over time for many individuals? And *how* might attachments shape one's behavior and influence the character of one's future interpersonal relationships?

Erikson's viewpoint. Erik Erikson answered by emphasizing how attachments might foster or inhibit the child's sense of "trust" in other people. Perhaps securely attached infants who have learned to trust an easily accessible and responsive caregiver become curious problem solvers later in life because they feel comfortable about venturing away from an attentive parent to explore and, as a result, they learn how to answer questions and solve problems on their own. Moreover, securely attached infants may become quite sociable and rather popular with their peers because they have already established pleasant relationships with responsive caregivers and have learned from these experiences that people are likely to react positively to their social overtures. By contrast, an anxious, insecure infant who has not learned to trust her caregivers may be reluctant to either (1) explore the environment and gain the initiative that would help her to answer questions or (2) completely trust other people with whom she may have dealings, including her closest romantic partners later in life.

The ethological viewpoint. Ethologists can agree in principle with Erikson's analyses but have chosen to explain any enduring effects of early attachment histories in a different way. John Bowlby (1969, 1988) and Inge Bretherton (1985, 1990) have proposed that, as infants continue to interact with primary caregivers, they will develop **internal working models**—that is, cognitive representations of *themselves* and *other people*—that are used to interpret events and to form expectations about the character of human relationships. Sensitive, responsive caregiving, for example, may lead the child to conclude that people are dependable (positive working model of others), whereas insensitive, neglectful, or abusive caregiving may lead to insecurity and a lack of trust (negative working model of others). Although this sounds very similar to Erikson's theory, the ethologists further propose that an infant will also develop a working model of the *self*—either a positive or a negative one, based largely on *his ability* to elicit (or fail to elicit) attention and comfort *when he needs it.* Presumably, these two working models combine to influence the quality of the child's primary attachments and the expectations he has about future relationships. And what kinds of expectations might he form?

A recent version of this "working models" theory appears in Figure 11-6. As shown, infants who construct positive working models of themselves and their caregivers are the ones who should (1) form secure primary attachments, (2) have the self-confidence to approach and to master new challenges, and (3) be predisposed to establish secure, mutual-trust relationships with friends and spouses later in life. By contrast, a positive model of self coupled with a negative model of others (as might result when infants can successfully attract the attention of an insensitive, overintrusive caregiver) is thought to predispose the infant to form *avoidant* attachments and to "dismiss" the importance of close emotional bonds. A negative model of self and a positive model of others (as might result when infants sometimes can

internal working models: cognitive representations of self, others, and relationships that infants construct from their interactions with caregivers.

MODEL OF OTHERS	MODEL OF SELF: Positive	MODEL OF SELF: Negative
Positive	SECURE (Secure primary attachments)	PREOCCUPIED (Resistant primary attachments)
Negative	DISMISSING (Avoidant primary attachments)	FEARFUL (Disorganized/disoriented primary attachments)

Figure 11-6
Four perspectives on close emotional relationships that evolve from the positive or negative "working models" of self and others that people construct from their experiences with intimate companions.
Adapted from Bartholomew & Horowitz, 1991.

but often cannot attract the attention they need) should be associated with *resistant* attachments and a "preoccupation" with establishing secure emotional ties. Finally, a negative working model of both the self and others is thought to underlie *disorganized/disoriented* attachments and an emerging "fear" of being hurt (either physically or emotionally) in intimate relationships (Bartholomew & Horowitz, 1991).

Of course, caregivers also have working models of themselves and others that are based on their own life experiences and that color their perceptions of children (Rholes, Simpson, & Blakely, in press) and can clearly affect the working models that their babies construct. Peter Fonagy and his associates (1991), for example, found that English mothers' working models of attachment relationships measured *before their babies were born* accurately predicted about 75% of the time whether their infants would establish secure or insecure attachments with them; and similar results have now been reported in studies conducted in Canada, Germany, the Netherlands, and the United States (Benoit & Parker, 1994; Crowell & Feldman, 1991; Grossmann & Grossmann, 1991; van IJzendoorn, 1992). So it seems that cognitive representations of intimate relationships are often transmitted from generation to generation. Indeed, Bowlby (1988) proposed that, once formed, working models may stabilize, becoming an aspect of personality that continues to influence the character of one's close emotional ties throughout life.

Is Attachment History Destiny?

Although it appears that early working models of relationships can be long lasting, and that there are some clear advantages to having formed secure emotional attachments early in life, the future is not always so bleak for infants who are insecurely attached. As we learned in Box 11-3, a secure relationship with another person such as the father (or perhaps a grandparent or a day-care provider) can help to offset whatever undesirable consequences might otherwise result from an insecure attachment to the mother (Clarke-Stewart, 1989). Moreover, the character of one's social relationships later in childhood and adolescence will also influence one's ultimate social adjustment. In fact, one longitudinal study found that adult social outcomes were actually predicted as well or better by peer relations during adolescence as by early attachment histories (Skolnick, 1986).

Let's also note that secure attachments can quickly become insecure should a mother return to work, place her infant in day care, or experience such life stresses as marital problems, a major illness, or financial woes that drastically alter the ways that she and her infant respond to each other (Thompson, Lamb, & Estes, 1982). Indeed, one reason why Bowlby (and later Bretherton) used the term "*working* models" was to underscore that a child's cognitive representations of self, others, and close emotional relationships are dynamic and can change (for better or for worse) if later experiences with caregivers, close friends, romantic partners, or spouses imply that a revision is necessary. Finally, such major life disruptions such as the divorce of one's parents or the death of a sibling can quickly undermine a child's psychological well-being, regardless of the quality of his early emotional ties.

So secure attachment histories are no guarantee of positive adjustment later in life; nor are insecure early attachments a certain indicator of poor life outcomes (Fagot & Kavanagh, 1990). Yet, we should not underestimate the adaptive significance of secure early attachments, for children who have functioned adequately as infants but very poorly during the preschool period are more likely to recover and to display good social skills and self-confidence during the grade school years if their early attachment histories were secure rather than insecure (Sroufe, Egeland, & Kreutzer, 1990).

 ## THE UNATTACHED INFANT

Some infants have very limited contacts with adults during the first year or two of life and do not appear to become attached to anyone. Occasionally, these socially deprived youngsters are reared at home by very abusive or neglectful caregivers, but most of them are found in understaffed institutions where they may see a caregiver only when it is time to be fed, changed, or bathed. Will these "unattached" infants suffer as a result of their early experiences? Must infants form attachments to develop normally, as Freud and some ethologists (for example, Bowlby, 1973) have argued?

Effects of Social Deprivation in Infancy and Childhood

In the 1940s, physicians and psychologists began to discover and study infants who were living under conditions of extreme social deprivation. For example, it was not uncommon for the impoverished institutions in which these infants lived to have but one caregiver for every 10–20 infants. Moreover, these caregivers rarely interacted with the infants except to bathe and change them or to prop a bottle against the infant's pillow at feeding time. Infants were often housed in separate cribs with sheets hung over the railings so that, in effect, they were isolated from the world around them. To make matters worse, babies in the more impoverished of these settings had no crib toys to manipulate and few if any opportunities to get out of their cribs and practice motor skills. Compared with babies raised in a typical home setting, these institutionalized infants received little in the way of social or sensory stimulation.

Babies raised under these conditions appear quite normal for the first three to six months of life: They cry for attention, smile and babble at caregivers, and make the proper postural adjustments when they are about to be picked up. But in the second half of the first year, their behavior changes. Now they seldom cry, coo, or babble; they become rigid and fail to respond to the handling of caregivers; and they often appear rather depressed and uninterested in social contact (Goldfarb, 1943; Provence & Lipton, 1962; Ribble, 1943; Spitz, 1945). Here is a description of one such infant:

> Outstanding were his soberness, his forlorn appearance, and lack of animation. . . . He did not turn to adults to relieve his distress. . . . He made no demands. . . . As one made active and persistent efforts at a social exchange he became somewhat more responsive, animated and . . . active, but lapsed into his depressed . . . appearance when the adult became less active. . . . If you crank his motor you can get him to go a little; but he can't start on his own (Provence & Lipton, 1962, pp. 134–135).

What are these institutionalized infants like as schoolchildren and adolescents? The answer depends, in part, on how long they remain in the institution. William Goldfarb (1943; 1947) compared children who left an understaffed orphanage during the first year with similar children who spent their first three years at the orphanage before departing for foster homes. After interviewing, observing, and testing these

Children raised in barren, understaffed institutions show many signs of developmental retardation.

children at ages 3½, 6½, 8½, and 12, Goldfarb found that the youngsters who had spent three years in the institution lagged behind the early adoptees in virtually all aspects of development. They scored poorly on IQ tests, were socially immature and remarkably dependent on adults, had poor language skills, and were prone to behavior problems such as aggression and hyperactivity. By early adolescence, they were often loners who had a difficult time relating to peers or family members.

Barbara Tizard (1977; Hodges & Tizard, 1989) recently compared similar groups of long-institutionalized and early-adopted children and found that many of the developmental impairments described by Goldfarb also characterized her sample of late adoptees. The institutions in which Tizard's children lived were adequately staffed. But because staff turnover was so high, children were cared for by as many as 80 different caregivers, and they rarely became attached to any one adult over the first few years of life. By age 8, Tizard's late adoptees were intellectually normal, socially outgoing, and many had even formed close emotional ties to a housemother or an adoptive parent. But despite these encouraging signs, children who had spent at least four years in the institution were more restless, disobedient, and unpopular in elementary school and were much more emotionally troubled and antisocial at age 16 than were children adopted early in life. So it seems that prolonged institutionalization can have adverse effects that are difficult to overcome.

Why Is Early Deprivation Harmful?

The Maternal Deprivation Hypothesis

Many psychologists (for example, Bowlby, 1973; Spitz, 1965) believe that infants will not develop normally unless they receive the warm, loving attention of one consistent mother figure to whom they can become attached. Presumably, children raised in understaffed institutions are developmentally impaired because they have not had an opportunity to become emotionally involved with a primary caregiver.

Popular as this **maternal deprivation hypothesis** once was, there is little evidence that infants need to be "mothered" by a single caregiver in order to develop normally. Studies of adequately staffed institutions in Russia, the People's Republic of China,

maternal deprivation hypothesis: the notion that socially deprived infants develop abnormally because they have failed to establish attachments to a primary caregiver.

Children raised in communal settings, such as this Israeli kibbutz, develop quite normally, even though they have been cared for since early infancy by a variety of responsive adults.

and Israel reveal that infants who are cared for by many responsive caregivers appear quite normal and are as well adjusted later in childhood as are infants who are reared at home (Bronfenbrenner, 1970; Kessen, 1975; Oppenheim, Sagi, & Lamb, 1988). Similarly, Efe (Pygmy) infants in Zaire seem to thrive from birth on being cared for and even nursed by a variety of caregivers besides their mothers (Tronick, Morelli, & Ivey, 1992). So infants need not first form a strong attachment to one mother figure in order to develop normally.

The Social Stimulation Hypothesis

Could it be that understaffed institutions are breeding grounds for developmental abnormalities because they provide the infant with a monotonous *sensory* environment where there is little stimulation *of any kind* to encourage any sort of responsiveness? Or, rather, is it a lack of *social* stimulation that accounts for the unusual behavior and abnormal development of institutionalized children?

Most developmentalists today favor the latter explanation, or **social stimulation hypothesis,** arguing that institutionalized children develop abnormally because they have very little contact with anyone who responds to their social signals. Indeed, mere lack of sensory stimulation is probably not involved, for institutionalized children who have lots of toys and can see and hear other infants are still developmentally delayed if they have little contact with adult caregivers (Provence & Lipton, 1962). If we contrast this finding with the normal development of Chinese, Russian, Israeli, and Efe infants who are raised by a multitude of caregivers, we can draw a meaningful conclusion: Infants need *sustained interactions with sensitive, responsive companions*, whether one or several, in order to develop normally.

Why are interactions with responsive caregivers so important? Probably because the social stimulation that an infant receives is likely to depend, in part, on the infant's own behavior: People often attend to the infant *when* he or she cries, smiles, babbles, or gazes at them. This kind of association between one's own behavior and the behavior of caregivers may lead an infant to believe that she has some *control* over the social environment. She then becomes more outgoing as she learns that she can use her social signals to attract the attention and affection of her companions.

Now consider the plight of institutionalized infants who may emit many signals and rarely receive a response from their overburdened or inattentive caregivers. What are these children likely to learn from their early experiences? Probably that attempts to attract the attention of others are useless, for nothing they do seems to matter to anyone. Consequently, they may develop a sense of **"learned helplessness"** and simply stop trying to elicit responses from other people (Finkelstein & Ramey, 1977). Here, then, is a very plausible reason why socially deprived infants are often rather passive, withdrawn, and apathetic.

Can Children Recover from Early Deprivation Effects?

social stimulation hypothesis: the notion that socially deprived infants develop abnormally because they have had little contact with companions who respond contingently to their social overtures.

learned helplessness: the failure to learn how to respond appropriately in a situation because of previous exposures to uncontrollable events in the same or similar situations.

Fortunately, socially deprived institutionalized children can overcome many of their initial handicaps if placed in homes where they receive lots of attention from affectionate and responsive caregivers (Clarke & Clarke, 1976; Rutter, 1981). Recovery seems to go especially well if deprived children are placed with *highly educated, relatively affluent* parents. Audrey Clark and Jeannette Hanisee (1982), for example, studied a group of Asian orphans who had lived in institutions, foster homes, or hospitals before coming to the United States. Many were war orphans who had early histories of malnutrition or serious illness. But despite the severe environmental insults they had endured, these children made remarkable progress. After only two to three years in their highly stimulating, middle-class adoptive homes, the Asian adoptees scored significantly *above* average on both a standardized intelligence test and an assessment of social maturity.

The prognosis for recovery also depends on the *amount of time* that a child has spent in a depriving early environment. Children whose deprivation lasts for the first three years or longer are likely to display some lingering social, emotional, or intellectual difficulties, even after spending the next several years in stable adoptive homes (Dennis, 1973; Goldfarb, 1947) and showing some evidence of being able to form attachments to an adoptive parent later in childhood (Hodges & Tizard, 1989). Are late adoptees incapable of making *complete* recoveries? Do their lingering deficiencies imply that the first three years of life is a *critical period* for human social and emotional development, as Bowlby (1973) and others have argued?

Other researchers say no, suggesting that even though infancy may be a *sensitive period* for emotional development, recovery may still be possible (Rutter, 1981). It stands to reason that children who develop severe problems when deprived for long periods will take longer to overcome their handicaps than children whose early deprivation was relatively brief. Moreover, we have to wonder how Goldfarb's or Tizard's late adoptees would have fared had they been adopted into enriched home environments such as those of the Asian adoptees in Clark and Hanisee's (1982) study. Clearly, the fact that late adoptees continued to show some deficiencies as adolescents in no way establishes that they were *incapable* of recovery, as proponents of the critical-period hypothesis might have us believe.

In sum, infants who have experienced social and emotional deprivation over the first two years show a strong capacity for recovery when they are placed in a stimulating home environment and receive individualized attention from responsive caregivers. Even severely disturbed children who are adopted after spending several years in understaffed institutions show dramatic improvements, compared with their counterparts who remain in a barren institutional setting (Dennis, 1973; Rutter, 1981). And rather than being discouraged by handicaps that continue to plague many late adoptees, we could just as easily treat their partial recoveries as an encouraging sign that may lead to the discovery of environmental interventions and therapeutic techniques that will enable these victims of prolonged social deprivation to put their lingering deficiencies behind them.

Concept Check 11-3 ⌄ Understanding Individual Differences in Attachment

Check your understanding of individual differences in attachment by matching each descriptive statement below with one of the following models/hypotheses: (a) Ainsworth's caregiving hypothesis; (b) Kagan's temperament hypothesis; (c) Thomas & Chess's goodness-of-fit model; (d) the Bowlby/Bretherton "internal working models" hypothesis; (e) maternal deprivation hypothesis; (f) social stimulation hypothesis. The answers appear in the Appendix.

_____ 1. Best summarizes how characteristics of infants and caregivers combine to influence attachment quality.

_____ 2. Has difficulty explaining why an infant might be securely attached to one parent and insecure with the other.

_____ 3. Easily explains why institutionalized infants show no developmental impairments when exposed to many responsive caregivers.

_____ 4. Claims that babies may be responding adaptively by forming avoidant attachments with unresponsive caregivers who seem to dislike their company.

_____ 5. Explains how early attachments can affect the character of one's interpersonal relationships later in life.

_____ 6. Now-discredited explanation for the developmental delays shown by children in understaffed institutions.

We will now conclude our discussion of early emotional development with a topic that has been widely debated in both the popular and the scholarly presses. The question is simple, but the answers are not: Do maternal employment and alternative caregiving arrangements undermine children's emotional well-being?

MATERNAL EMPLOYMENT, ALTERNATIVE CARE, AND EARLY EMOTIONAL DEVELOPMENT

In recent years, an important question has arisen about the ways in which infants in our society spend their time. Should they be cared for at home by a parent, or can they pursue their developmental agendas just as well in a day-care setting? Now that more than half of all mothers work outside the home at least part time, more and more young children are receiving alternative forms of care. According to recent U.S. Department of Labor statistics, only 25% of infants and toddlers are cared for by their parents, whereas 27% are with other relatives, 7% at home with a sitter, 25% in day-care homes (typically run by a woman who takes a few children into her own home for payment), and 16% in large day-care centers (Clarke-Stewart, 1993).

Do infants who attend day-care homes or centers suffer in any way compared with infants who stay at home with a parent? Research to date suggests that they usually do not (Clarke-Stewart, 1993; Scarr & Eisenberg, 1993). In fact, we learned in Chapter 9 that high-quality day care promotes both the social responsiveness and the intellectual development of children from disadvantaged backgrounds, who are otherwise at risk of experiencing developmental delays (Campbell & Ramey, 1994; and see Caughy, DiPietro, & Strobino, 1994). In some studies, children in alternative care actually proved to be more socially mature and independent than children cared for at home (Clarke-Stewart, 1993; Scarr & Eisenberg, 1993). Apparently, then, day care is not *necessarily* damaging to young children.

However, this broad generalization does not tell the full story. Let's briefly consider three factors that are likely to influence how an infant or toddler adjusts to maternal employment and day care.

Age at Entry in Alternative Care

Over the years, some developmentalists have feared that babies placed into day care very early in life are at risk of forming shaky, insecure relationships with their parents. Indeed, infants who spend a great deal of time in alternative care during the first year of life are *somewhat* less likely to form secure attachments with their mothers and fathers than those who are cared for at home by their parents (Barglow, Vaughn, & Molitor, 1987; Belsky & Rovine, 1988; Lamb, Sternberg, & Prodromidis, 1992; but see Roggman et al., 1994). But in analyzing this research, Michael Lamb and his colleagues (1992) found that, on average, 71% of infants cared for exclusively by their mothers develop secure attachments with them, compared with 65% of infants receiving regular alternative care. So the risk of insecurity associated with alternative care is *very small*, and most infants in day care do form *secure* attachments with their parents. Nevertheless, some researchers continue to be concerned about possible negative effects of too much day care early in life (Bates et al., 1994; Belsky & Braungart, 1991).

Quality of Alternative Care

Compared with the day care available in many Western European countries, the quality of alternative care in the United States is very uneven. Large numbers of American infants and toddlers are cared for by sitters who have little knowledge of or training in child development, or are in unlicensed day-care homes that often fail to meet minimum health and safety standards (Zigler & Gilman, 1993).

According to experts on alternative care, a high-quality day-care facility is one that has (1) a reasonable child-to-caregiver ratio (no more than three infants, four toddlers, or eight preschoolers per adult), (2) caregivers who are warm, emotionally expressive, and responsive to children's bids for attention, (3) little staff turnover so that children become familiar and feel comfortable with their new adult companions,

High-quality day care can have beneficial effects on children's social, emotional, and intellectual development.

(4) a curriculum made up of toys, games, and activities that are age appropriate, and (5) an administration that is willing (or better yet, eager) to confer with parents about the child's progress (Howes, 1990; Howes, Phillips, & Whitebook, 1992). Given adequate training and resources, and some effort on the substitute caregiver's part, all these criteria can be achieved by a relative or a regular sitter providing in-home care, by a nonrelative operating a day-care home, or a group day-care center (Howes, 1988).

Regardless of the setting in which care is given, it is now apparent that the quality of alternative care that children receive clearly matters. Apparently, there is little risk of emotional insecurity (or any other adverse outcome) when children receive excellent alternative care—*even when that care begins very early.* Jerome Kagan and his associates (1978), for example, found that infants who entered a high-quality, university-sponsored day-care program at age 3½ to 5½ months not only developed secure attachments to their mothers but were just as socially, emotionally, and intellectually mature over the first two years of life as children from similar backgrounds who had been cared for at home. Studies conducted in Sweden (where day care is government subsidized, closely monitored, and typically of high quality) report similar positive outcomes (Lamb et al., 1988), and it seems that the earlier that Swedish infants enter high-quality day care, the better their cognitive, social, and emotional development 6 to 8 years later in elementary and junior high school (Andersson, 1989, 1992; see also Field, 1991). Finally, Carollee Howes's (1990) longitudinal study of middle-class families in California indicates that early entry into day care is associated with poor social, emotional, and intellectual outcomes later in childhood *only* when the care that children received was of low quality (see also Vandell, Henderson, & Wilson, 1988).

Unfortunately, infants who receive the poorest and most unstable day care are often those whose parents are living complex, stressful lives of their own that may prevent them from becoming highly involved with or closely attached to their children (Howes, 1990; Scarr & Eisenberg, 1993). So a child's poor progress in day care may often stem as much from a disordered home life, in which parents are not all that enthused about parenting, as from the less-than-optimal alternative care that he or she receives. Let's explore this idea further.

Parents' Attitudes about Work and Parenting

According to Hoffman (1989), a mother's attitudes about working and child care may be as important to her child's social and emotional well-being as her actual employment status. Mothers tend to be much happier and more sensitive as caregivers when their employment status matches their attitudes about working (Crockenberg & Litman, 1991; Hock & DeMeis, 1990; Stuckey, McGhee, & Bell, 1982). So, if a woman wants to work, it may make little sense to pressure her into staying home to care for her child when she might be depressed, hostile, or otherwise unresponsive in that role.

Even when children receive less-than-optimal alternative care, their outcomes depend greatly on their parents' attitudes and behaviors. Outcomes are likely to be better if a working mother has positive attitudes *both* about working and about being a mother (Belsky & Rovine, 1988; Crockenberg & Litman, 1991). And it also helps immensely if her spouse approves of her working and supports her in her parenting role (Spitze, 1988). Ultimately, parents' attitudes about being parents and the quality of care they provide at home may have much more to do with an infant's development than the kind of alternative care he receives (Lamb et al., 1988).

In sum, we cannot draw simple conclusions about the effects of maternal employment and alternative care on infant development, for these effects range from beneficial to damaging. It does seem, however, that alternative care is least likely to disrupt development if infants are old enough to have already formed attachments to their parents. And, not surprisingly, infants from all social backgrounds are likely to fare rather well if they receive sensitive, responsive care both at home and from their alternative caregivers.

What can be done to help working parents establish more secure emotional ties with their infants and to promote these infants' early social and personality development? A national policy governing parental leave for child care is one step in the right direction. In early 1993, the United States finally adopted a parental-leave policy that guaranteed workers in firms with 50 or more employees the right to take 12 weeks of unpaid leave to spend time with their newborn infants, without jeopardizing their jobs. Yet this guarantee (1) does not apply to the *majority* of American workers (who are employed by firms with fewer than 50 employees) and (2) seems almost miserly compared with the often-generous parental-leave policies that many other industrialized societies have enacted (see Table 11-3).

Table 11-3 Sample Parental-Leave Policies in Modern Industrialized Nations

Denmark:	Mothers receive 14 weeks' paid maternity leave after childbirth; at their option, either the mother or father may take an additional 10 weeks without pay.
Finland:	Leave for a mother or a father consists of 70 working days at full pay and an additional 188 working days at 70% pay. Unpaid leave may be extended for 3 years without jeopardizing the parent's employment.
France:	Working mothers receive 16 weeks of leave at 85% pay.
Israel:	Working mothers receive 12 weeks' paid leave and up to 40 weeks' unpaid leave.
Japan:	Working mothers receive 14 weeks' paid leave.
Poland:	Working mothers can take up to 6 months' leave with full pay and up to $2^{1}/_{2}$ additional years with partial pay.
Sweden:	Working mothers receive 6 months' leave at 90% pay and an additional 6 months' unpaid leave. Mothers and fathers may share leave benefits if they wish.
United States:	Either parent may take 12 weeks of unpaid leave in firms of 50 or more employees.

Source: Adapted from Bjorklund & Bjorklund, 1992.

A national policy on day care might be even more important. At present, middle-class families are the ones who are caught most directly in a day-care squeeze. Upper-income families have the resources to purchase excellent day care; and the compensatory education (or other subsidized alternative care) that many lower-income children receive is typically of higher quality than that which middle-class parents can afford to purchase (Phillips et al., 1994). Meanwhile, parents from all social backgrounds must often struggle to find and keep competent sitters or other high-quality day-care placements, which are in short supply, due in part to the continuing reluctance of the U.S. government to subsidize day care for all citizens and carefully monitor its quality, as many European countries have done. Sandra Scarr (1984) finds this puzzling since the U.S. government is quite willing to invest in children once they are old enough to attend public school. Increasingly, employers are realizing that it is in their best interest to help workers obtain quality day care, and a few have even established day-care centers at the work site (Hymes, 1990). But until more options are available, working parents will continue to face the challenges of finding good alternative care at a cost they can afford.

SUMMARY

Human infants are clearly emotional beings. At birth, babies reliably display interest, distress, disgust, and contentment (as indicated by their facial expressions), with the remaining *primary emotions* (that is, anger, sadness, surprise, and fear) normally appearing by the middle of the first year. Such *secondary emotions* as embarrassment, pride, guilt, and shame emerge in the second (or third) year, after children reach such cognitive milestones as self-recognition and have acquired standards for evaluating their conduct.

The socialization of emotions and emotional self-regulation begin very early, as parents model positive emotions for their infants, attend carefully to and try to prolong their infants' pleasant feelings, and become less responsive to infants' negative emotional displays. By the end of the first year, infants develop simple strategies for regulating aversive arousal; soon thereafter, they make active attempts to suppress their sadness or anger. However, the ability to regulate and control emotions develops very slowly, and it may be well into the grade school years before children become proficient at complying with culturally defined *emotional display rules*.

The infant's ability to recognize and interpret others' emotions improves dramatically over the first year of life. During the first six months, infants begin to discriminate and respond appropriately to their mother's naturalistic displays of emotion, and by age 8–12 months, they are actively seeking emotional information from their companions. The ability to identify and interpret others' emotions continues to improve throughout the preschool and early grade school years, aided, in part, by cognitive development and by family conversations that center on the child's emotional experiences and those of her companions.

Emotions play at least two important roles in an infant's social development. The child's own emotional expressions are adaptive in that they promote social contact with others and assist caregivers in adjusting their behavior to the infant's needs and goals. At the same time, the infant's ability to recognize and interpet the emotions of other people serves an important *social-referencing* function by helping the child to infer how he or she should feel, think, or behave in a wide variety of situations.

Infants begin to form affectional ties to their close companions during the first year of life. These *attachments* serve many purposes and are important contributors to social and emotional development. Attachments are usually reciprocal relationships, for parents and other intimate companions typically become attached to the infant.

Parents may begin to feel emotionally involved with a neonate during the first few hours if they have close contact with their baby during this period. This initial *bonding* may then be strengthened as the infant begins to emit social signals (smiles, vocalizations) that attract the attention of caregivers and make them feel that the baby enjoys their company. If the caregiver adjusts his or her behavior to the infant's cycles of attention and inattention, eventually he (or she) and the baby will establish highly synchronized interactive routines that are satisfying to both parties and are likely to blossom into a reciprocal attachment. However, some parents may have a difficult time becoming attached to their baby if the child is irritable, unresponsive, or unwanted; if they are clinically depressed or unhappily married; or if they have other problems that prevent them from being sensitive and responsive to the infant.

Most infants have formed a primary social attachment to a close companion by 6–8 months of age, and within weeks they are establishing these affectional ties with other regular companions. Many theories have been proposed to explain how and why infants form attachments. Among the most influential theories of attachment are the *psychoanalytic*, the *learning-theory*, the *cognitive-developmental*, and the *ethological* viewpoints. Although these theories make different assumptions about the roles that infants and caregivers play in the formation of attachments, each viewpoint has contributed to our understanding of early social and emotional development.

At about the time that infants are becoming attached to a close companion, they often begin to display two kinds of fear. *Stranger anxiety* refers to the child's wariness of unfamiliar people. It is by no means a universal reaction and is most likely to occur in response to an intrusive stranger who appears in an unfamiliar setting where loved ones are unavailable. *Separation anxiety* is the discomfort infants may feel when separated from the person or persons to whom they are attached. As infants develop intellectually and begin to move away from attachment objects to explore the environment, they will become increasingly familiar with strangers and better able to account for the absences of familiar companions. As a result, both stranger anxiety and separation anxiety decline in intensity during the second year.

Research with Ainsworth's *strange-situations test* (which assesses a baby's responses to strangers, brief separations, and reunions with a caregiver) reveals that infants typically establish one of four kinds of attachment to their mothers. One kind of attachment is labeled *secure*, whereas the other three (that is, *avoidant*, *resistant*, and *disorganized/disoriented*) are thought to be emotionally insecure. Sensitive, responsive caregiving is consistently associated with the development of secure attachments, whereas inconsistent, neglectful, overintrusive, and abusive styles of caregiving predict insecure attachments. However, infant temperament may also influence the quality of early attachments by affecting the character of caregiver-infant interactions. Although most babies form primary attachments to their mothers, fathers play an important role in many infants' lives.

Research consistently indicates that people with an early history of secure attachments are more socially skilled and intellectually competent later in life than are their counterparts with insecure attachment histories. However, children's *working models* of attachment relationships can change over time. Thus, a secure attachment history is *no* guarantee of positive adjustment later in life, nor are initially insecure attachments a certain indicator of poor life outcomes.

Some infants have had very limited contacts with caregivers during the first year or two of life; as a result, they do not become attached to anyone. Children who are socially deprived during infancy are likely to be withdrawn and apathetic and may display intellectual deficiencies. The longer infants experience such social/emotional deprivation, the more disturbed they become. However, socially deprived children have a strong capacity for recovery and often overcome many of their handicaps if placed in homes where they receive ample amounts of individualized attention from sensitive and responsive companions.

It was once feared that regular separations from working parents might prevent infants from establishing secure attachments. However, there is little evidence that either a mother's employment outside the home or alternative caregiving will have such an effect, provided that the day care is of good quality and that parents are sensitive and responsive caregivers when they are at home.

Key Terms

asocial stage (of attachment) [434]

attachment [428]

attachment object [428]

avoidant attachment [444]

caregiving hypothesis [446]

critical period [438]

disorganized/disoriented attachment [444]

early-experience hypothesis [444]

emotional display rules [424]

emotional self-regulation [424]

imprinting [438]

internal working models [450]

kewpie-doll effect [429]

learned helplessness [454]

maternal deprivation hypothesis [453]

preadapted characteristic [438]

primary (or basic) emotions [423]

resistant attachment [444]

secondary (or complex) emotions [423]

secondary reinforcer [436]

secure attachment [444]

secure base [435]

separation anxiety [440]

social referencing [426]

social stimulation hypothesis [454]

stage of indiscriminate attachments [434]

stage of multiple attachments [435]

stage of specific attachments [434]

stranger anxiety [440]

strange-situations test [444]

synchronized routines [431]

temperament hypothesis [447]

12

Development of the Self and Social Cognition

How would you answer the "Who am I?" question in the margin? If you are like most adults, you would probably respond by mentioning some of your noteworthy personal characteristics (honesty, friendliness), some roles you play in life (student, hospital volunteer), your religious or moral views, and perhaps your political leanings. In doing so, you would be describing that elusive concept that psychologists call the **self.**

Although no one else knows you as well as you do, it is a safe bet that much of what you know about yourself stems from your contacts and experiences with other people. When a college sophomore tells us that he is a friendly, outgoing person who is active in his fraternity, the Young Republicans, and the Campus Crusade for Christ, he is saying that his past experiences with others and the groups to which he belongs are important determinants of his personal identity. Many years ago, sociologists Charles Cooley (1902) and George Herbert Mead (1934) proposed that the self-concept evolves from social interactions and undergoes many changes over the course of a lifetime. Cooley used the term **looking-glass self** to emphasize that a person's understanding of self is a reflection of how other people react to him: The self-concept is the image cast by a social mirror.

Cooley and Mead believed that the self and social development are completely intertwined, that they emerge together and that neither can progress far without the other. Presumably, newborns experience people and events as simple "streams of impressions" and have absolutely no concept of "self" until they realize that they exist independently of the objects and individuals that they encounter regularly. Once infants make this important distinction between self and nonself, they establish interactive routines with close companions (that is, develop socially) and learn that their behavior elicits predictable reactions from others. In other words, they are acquiring information about the "social self" based on the ways people respond to them. Mead (1934) concluded that

> the self has a character that is different from that of the physiological organism proper. The self is something which . . . is not initially there at birth but arises in the process of social development. That is, it develops in a given individual as a result of his relations to that process as a whole and to other individuals within the process.

Do babies really have no sense of self at birth? This issue is explored in the first section of the chapter, where we will trace the growth of the self-concept from infancy through adolescence. We will then consider how children and adolescents evaluate the self and construct a sense of *self-esteem.* Our focus next shifts to the development of one very important contributor to self-esteem, as we explore how children develop an interest (or disinterest) in achievement and form positive or negative academic self concepts. We will then discuss a major developmental hurdle faced by adolescents: the need to establish a firm, future-oriented self-portrait, or *identity*, with which to approach the responsibilities of young adulthood. Our examination of the self will then conclude with the growth of *self-control*—an attribute that figures prominently in determining what we will be able to accomplish in life and how well we will get along with other people. Finally, we will consider what developing children know about other people and interpersonal relationships and will see that this aspect of **social cognition,** which parallels the development of the self-concept, nicely illustrates Cooley's and Mead's point that personal (self) and social aspects of development are intricately intertwined.

Of course, there are other important aspects of the self and social cognition that warrant chapters of their own. In Chapter 13, for example, we will examine the *sex-typing* process and see that a child's growing conception of self as a male or a female can (and often does) exert a powerful influence on his or her goals in life and patterns of social conduct. Our focus in Chapter 14 then shifts to moral and ethical issues—including the growth of aggressive, antisocial tendencies as well as the more

WHO AM I?

I'm a person who says what I think . . . not [one] who's going to say one thing and do the other. I'm really lucky. I've never [drunk or] done drugs, but I'm always high. I love life. I've got a lot of different business interests . . . a construction company, oil wells, land . . . I'm trying everything. I travel a lot . . . it's difficult to be traveling and in school at the same time. [People] perceive me as being unusual . . . very mysterious, and I hope they see me as being a competitor, because I do all my talking on the field.

Herschel Walker, former college student and Olympic bobsledder, and now running back of the New York Giants (as quoted by Blount, 1986)

self: the combination of physical and psychological attributes that is unique to each individual.

looking-glass self: the idea that a child's self-concept is largely determined by the ways other people respond to him or her.

social cognition: the thinking that people display about the thoughts, feelings, motives, and behaviors of themselves and other people.

altruistic, or prosocial, aspects of self—as we follow the child's transformation from an egocentric and reputedly self-indulgent organism to a moral philosopher of sorts who may have strongly internalized certain ethical principles to guide her conduct and to evaluate the behavior of others.

Now let's return to the starting point and see how children come to know this entity we call the "self."

 ## DEVELOPMENT OF THE SELF-CONCEPT

When do infants first distinguish themselves from other people, objects, and environmental events? At what point do they sense their uniqueness and form self-images? What kinds of information do young children use to define the self? And how do their self-images and feelings of self-worth change over time? These are some of the issues we will explore as we trace the development of the **self-concept** from infancy through adolescence.

The Emerging Self: Differentiation and Self-Recognition

Like Mead, many developmentalists believe that infants are born without a sense of self. Psychoanalyst Margaret Mahler (Mahler, Pine, & Bergman, 1975) likens the newborn to a "chick in an egg" who has no reason to differentiate the self from the surrounding environment. After all, every need that the child has is soon satisfied by his or her ever-present companions, who are simply "there" and have no identities of their own. So when do infants first gain a sense of themselves as beings separate from the world around them?

This is not an easy question to answer, but it is helpful to recall Piaget's (and others') descriptions of cognitive development early in infancy. During the first two months, babies are exercising their reflexive schemes and repeating pleasurable acts centered in their own bodies (for example, sucking their thumbs and waving their arms). But the picture soon changes. As we saw in Chapters 8 and 11, infants only 2 months old delight at producing interesting sights and sounds by kicking their legs or pulling their arms to tug on strings attached to mobiles or to audiovisual machinery (Lewis, Alessandri, & Sullivan, 1990; Rovee-Collier, 1987). Moreover, even an 8-week-old infant can recall how to produce these interesting events for two or three days; and if the strings are disconnected so she can no longer exert any control, she may pull or kick all the harder and become rather *angry* (Lewis et al., 1990; Sullivan et al., 1992). Thus, it seems that 2-month-old infants may have some limited sense of **personal agency,** or understanding that *they* are responsible for at least some of the events that so fascinate them. Of course, Piaget emphasized this very point in noting that 4–8-month-olds in his stage of *secondary circular reactions* are reliably manipulating *external* objects (for example, noisemaking toys) to reproduce interesting results. It is certainly possible, then, that infants learn the limits of their own bodies during the first month or two and differentiate this "physical self" from the external objects they can control shortly thereafter (Samuels, 1986). So if a 2–6-month-old could talk, he might answer the "Who am I?" question by saying "I am a looker, a chewer, a reacher, and a grabber who acts on objects and makes things happen."

Self-Recognition

Once infants know that they *are* (that they exist independent of other entities), they are in a position to find out *who* or *what* they are (Harter, 1983). When, for example, do infants recognize themselves as distinct individuals and become able to tell themselves apart from other infants?

Michael Lewis and Jeanne Brooks-Gunn (1979) have studied the development of self-recognition by asking mothers to surreptitiously apply a spot of rouge to their

self-concept: one's perceptions of one's unique attributes or traits.

personal agency: the recognition or understanding that one can be the cause of events.

infants' noses (under the pretext of wiping the infants' faces) and then place the infants before a mirror. If infants have a scheme for their own faces and recognize their mirror images as themselves, they should soon notice the new red spot and reach for or wipe their *own* noses. When infants 9 to 24 months old were given this rouge test, the younger ones showed no self-recognition: They seemed to treat the image in the mirror as if it were "some other kid." Signs of self-recognition were observed among a few of the 15–17-month olds, but only among the 18–24-month-olds did a majority of infants touch their own noses, apparently realizing that they had a strange mark on their faces. They knew exactly who that kid in the mirror was (see also Bullock & Lukenhaus, 1990)!

Interestingly, infants from nomadic tribes, who have no experience with mirrors, begin to display self-recognition on the rouge test at the same age as city-reared infants (Priel & deSchonen, 1986). And many 18–24-month-olds can even recognize themselves in photographs and will often use a personal pronoun ("me") or their own name to label their photographic image (Lewis & Brooks-Gunn, 1979). Recall that this is precisely the age when the object concept is maturing and infants are internalizing their sensorimotor schemes to form mental images. So it seems that the ability to recognize the self is closely related to the child's level of cognitive development. Even children with Down syndrome and a variety of other mental deficiencies can recognize themselves in a mirror if they have attained a mental age of at least 18–20 months (Hill & Tomlin, 1981).

Although a certain level of cognitive development may be necessary for self-recognition, social experiences are probably of equal importance. Gordon Gallup (1979) finds that adolescent chimpanzees can easily recognize themselves in a mirror (as shown by the rouge test) unless they have been reared in complete social isolation. In contrast to normal chimps, social isolates react to their mirror images as if they were looking at another animal! So the term *looking-glass self* may apply to chimpanzees as well as to humans: Reflections in a "social mirror" enable normal chimps to develop some self-awareness, whereas a chimpanzee that is denied these experiences will fail to acquire a clear self-image.

What kinds of social experiences might contribute to self-recognition in humans? Secure attachments seem to. When Sandra Pipp and her associates (1992) administered a complex test of self-knowledge to 2- and 3-year-olds (a test assessing the child's awareness of his name and gender as well as self-recognition), they found that (1) securely attached 2-year-olds were already outperforming their insecurely attached age-mates on the test and (2) differences in self-knowledge between secure and insecure children were even greater among the 3-year-olds. Securely attached infants and toddlers also knew more *about their mothers* than insecure children did. So secure attachments may not only promote the growth of self-awareness but may also be an important contributor to other aspects of social cognition (for example, knowing about others) as well.

The ability to distinguish oneself from other people has both social and emotional consequences for toddlers. For example, we saw in Chapter 11 that the ability to experience such self-conscious emotions as embarrassment and pride depends on self-recognition. Moreover, toddlers who have reached this self-referential milestone soon become more outgoing and socially skilled—to the point that they now take great pleasure in imitating each other's play activities (Asendorph & Baudonniere, 1993) and will occasionally even *cooperate* (as illustrated by one child's operating a handle so that another can retrieve toys from a container) to achieve shared goals (Brownell & Carriger, 1990).

Categorical Self

Shortly after toddlers can recognize themselves in a mirror or a photograph, they begin to notice some of the ways that people differ and to categorize themselves on these dimensions (Stipek, Gralinski, & Kopp, 1990)—a classification called the **categorical self**. Age, sex, and evaluative dimensions are the first social categories that

Recognizing one's mirror image as "me" is a crucial milestone in the development of "self."

categorical self: a person's classification of the self along socially significant dimensions such as age and sex.

toddlers incorporate into their self-concepts, as illustrated by such statements as "I *big boy*, not a *baby*" or "Jennie *good girl.*"

Interestingly, young children are even becoming aware of racial and ethnic categories, although it takes a while before they can classify themselves correctly. Native American 3–5-year-olds, for example, can easily discriminate Native Americans from Anglos in photographs but are less often accurate in specifying which category they most resemble (Spencer & Markstrom-Adams, 1990). A similar "misidentification" phenomenon has been observed among African-American preschoolers, who show a clear pro-white bias and associate fewer positive attributes with the color black or with African-American people (Cross, 1985; Spencer, 1988). Do these "misidentifications" and pro-majority opinions imply that minority preschoolers are uncertain of their racial identity or, alternatively, that they know which group to which they belong and are critical of themselves? Probably neither assumption is correct, for African-American children often display both a pro-white bias *and* a highly favorable *self*-concept (Powell, 1985). Thus, minority preschoolers are more likely displaying (1) the same early awareness of negative social stereotypes about minorities that white children display (see Bigler & Liben, 1993) and (2) a desire to be a part of what they think is the most desirable group (Spencer & Markstrom-Adams, 1990).

Who Am I? Responses of Preschool Children

Until recently, developmentalists believed that the self-concepts of preschool children were concrete, physicalistic, and nearly devoid of any *psychological* self-awareness. Why? Because when 3–5-year-olds are asked to describe themselves, they talk mostly about their physical attributes ("I have blue eyes"), their possessions ("I have a new bike"), or about *actions* of which they feel especially proud, such as hitting a baseball or walking to nursery school on their own. By contrast, psychological descriptors such as "I'm happy," "I'm good at sports," or "I like people" are rarely used by children this young (Damon & Hart, 1982; Keller, Ford, & Meachum, 1978).

Do Preschoolers Display any Psychological Self-Awareness?

However, not everyone agrees that preschoolers' self-concepts are so concrete and "physicalistic." Rebecca Eder (1989; 1990), for example, finds that 3½–5-year-olds know how they usually behave in various contexts (saying, for example, "I like to play by myself at nursery school"), and she believes that these "habit" statements are an early *psychological* characterization of self that provides the basis for later traitlike conceptions that older children express (for example, "I'm not very sociable"). Indeed, 3–5-year-olds can quickly characterize themselves on psychological dimensions such as achievement if asked the appropriate contrasting questions (for example, choosing between "mostly doing things that are hard" versus "mostly doing things that are easy"). Moreover, they characterize themselves differently on different dimensions, and these self-characterizations are stable over a one-month period (Eder, 1990). Although preschool children may not be consciously aware of what it means to be "sociable" or to be an "achiever," Eder's research implies that they have rudimentary psychological conceptions of self long before they can express this knowledge in traitlike terminology (see also Flavell et al., 1993).

Origins of the Private Self: Young Children's Theory of Mind

When adults think about the self, they know that they have a **public self** (or **me**) that others can see and a **private self** (or **I**) that has an inner, reflective (thinking) character not available to others. Are young children aware of this distinction between public and private selves?

One way to find out is to assess their **theory of mind**—their understanding of how the mind works and their knowledge that humans are cognitive beings with a

public self (or me): those aspects of self that others can see or infer.

private self (or I): those inner, or subjective, aspects of self that are known only to the individual and are not available for public scrutiny.

theory of mind: an understanding that people are cognitive beings with rich mental lives that are available to themselves but not to others.

Preschool children are already aware of their behavioral patterns and preferences and are using this information to form an early portrait of the self.

rich mental life that is accessible to themselves but not to others. Research on children's theory of mind has expanded in recent years and revealed much about children's growing conceptions of mental life (see Flavell et al., 1993, for an excellent review). By age 2 to 3, for example, children often talk about mental states such as needs, emotions, and desires, and they think that people's actions always reflect their desires. Three-year-olds also know that the mind is separate from the physical world and that other people can't actually observe their thoughts (Flavell et al., 1993). What 3-year-olds don't seem to understand is that beliefs are only mental representations of reality that may differ from person to person and may be *inaccurate.* Stated another way, 3-year-olds act as if beliefs *are* reality and think that if they hold a particular belief then others must as well. Consider children's reactions to the following story:

> A boy puts some chocolate in a blue cupboard and goes out to play. In his absence, his mother moves the chocolate to the green cupboard. When the boy returns, he wants his chocolate. Where does he look for it?

Three-year-olds say "in the green cupboard." They do not yet understand that a person will act on the basis of what he believes to be true rather than on what they themselves know to be true. By contrast, 4–5-year-olds display a **belief-desire theory** of mind: They understand that beliefs are merely mental representations of reality that may be inaccurate and that someone else may not share; thus, they know that the boy will look for his chocolate in the blue cupboard where he believes it is (beliefs determine behavior, even if they are false) rather than in the green cupboard where they know it is (Wellman & Woolley, 1990).

Once children recognize that people will act on the basis of false beliefs, they may use this knowledge to their own advantage by lying or attemping other deceptive ploys. In Chapter 7, for example, we noted that 4-year-olds (but not 3-year-olds) who are playing hide-the-object games will spontaneously generate false clues, trying to mislead their opponent about the object's true location (Sodian et al., 1991). Apparently, 4-year-olds are making a clear distinction between public and private self, for they recognize that their deceptive *public* behavior will lead their opponent to adopt a belief that differs from their own *private* knowledge.

belief-desire theory: theory of mind that develops around age 4; the child now realizes that beliefs are only mental constructions rather than copies of reality and that people will act on these constructions, even if they are inaccurate.

In sum, older preschool children are beginning to appreciate how the mind works and to discriminate the private self-as-knower from the public self they present to others. How important are these developments? John Flavell and his colleagues (1993) answer by saying that if children had no theory of mind or no awareness that public appearances do not necessarily reflect private realities, they would be largely incapable of drawing meaningful *psychological* inferences about their own or others' behavior; in other words, the rich social-cognitive abilities that humans display would be impossible.

Conceptions of Self in Middle Childhood and Adolescence

During the grade school years, children's self-descriptions gradually evolve from listings of their physical, behavioral, and other "external" attributes to sketches of their enduring inner qualities—that is, their traits, values, beliefs, and ideologies (Damon & Hart, 1988; Livesley & Bromley, 1973). This developmental shift toward a more abstract or "psychological" portrayal of self can be seen in the following three responses to the "Who am I?" question (Montemayor & Eisen, 1977, pp. 317–318):

9-year-old: My name is Bruce C. I have brown eyes. I have brown hair. I love! sports. I have seven people in my family. I have great! eye site. I have lots! of friends. I live at . . . I have an uncle who is almost 7 feet tall. My teacher is Mrs. V. I play hockey! I'm almost the smartest boy in the class. I love! food . . . I love! school.

11½-year-old: My name is A. I'm a human being . . . a girl . . . a truthful person. I'm not pretty. I do so-so in my studies. I'm a very good cellist. I'm a little tall for my age. I like several boys . . . I'm old fashioned. I am a very good swimmer . . . I try to be helpful . . . Mostly I'm good, but I lose my temper. I'm not well liked by some girls and boys. I don't know if boys like me . . .

17-year-old: I am a human being . . . a girl . . . an individual . . . I am a Pisces. I am a moody person . . . an indecisive person . . . an ambitious person. I am a big curious person . . . I am lonely. I am an American (God help me). I am a Democrat. I am a liberal person. I am a radical. I am conservative. I am a pseudoliberal. I am an Athiest. I am not a classifiable person (i.e., I don't want to be).

Although grade-school children and young adolescents are coming to rely more and more on psychological labels to describe the self, they tend to apply them in an absolute way, viewing these attributes as stable and unchanging. For example, 8–13-year-olds who say that they are "kind" are apt to believe that kindness is an enduring aspect of their personalities that will always characterize their interactions with others (Harter, 1986; Mohr, 1978).

By contrast, 15-year-olds are often aware that they are not the same person in all situations and they may be confused by these inconsistencies. To illustrate, consider an interesting study by Susan Harter and Ann Monsour (1992) in which 13-, 15-, and 17-year-olds were asked to describe themselves when they are with parents, with friends, in romantic relationships, and in the classroom. These adolescents were then asked to sort through their four self-descriptions, identify any inconsistencies, and indicate which inconsistencies confused or upset them. As we see in Figure 12-1, the 13-year-olds were quite unaware of inconsistencies and were not bothered much by the few they did detect. By contrast, 15-year-olds listed many such oppositional attributes and were quite bothered by them. One 15-year-old who was upset about several major inconsistencies talked about her tendency to be happy with friends but depressed at home. "I really think of myself as a happy person, and I want to be that way with everyone because I think that's my true self, but I get depressed with my

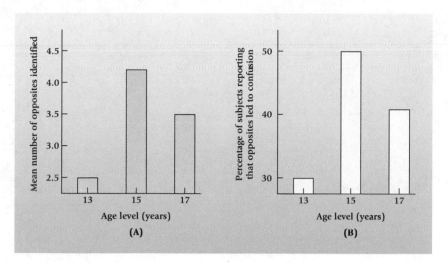

Figure 12-1
Average number of oppositional attributes reported by 13-, 15-, and 17-year-olds (panel A) and the percentages of 13-, 15-, and 17-year-olds who said they were confused or "mixed up" by these inconsistencies in their self-portraits (panel B).
Adapted from Harter & Monsour, 1992.

family and it bugs me because that's not what I want to be like" (Harter & Monsour, 1992, p. 253). These 15-year-olds, girls especially, seemed to feel that there were several different selves inside them and were concerned about finding the "real me."

It was not until their later high school years that adolescents were able to feel more comfortable about the inconsistencies they display, often integrating them into a higher-order and more coherent view of themselves. For example, a 17-year-old boy might conclude that it is perfectly understandable to be relaxed and confident in most situations but nervous on dates if one has not yet had much dating experience, or that being "moody" can explain his being cheerful with friends on some occasions but irritable on others. Harter and Monsour believe that cognitive development—specifically, the formal-operational ability to compare abstract trait concepts and ultimately integrate them into higher-order concepts like "moodiness"—is behind this change in self-perceptions.

In sum, one's self-concept becomes more psychological, more abstract, and more of a coherent, integrated self-portrait from childhood to adolescence and over the course of adolescence. Truly, the adolescent becomes a sophisticated self-theorist who can reflect on and understand the workings of his or her personality.

 ## SELF-ESTEEM: THE EVALUATIVE COMPONENT OF SELF

As children develop, they not only come to understand more and more about themselves and to construct more intricate self-portraits, but they also begin to *evaluate* the qualities that they perceive themselves as having. This evaluative aspect of self is called **self-esteem.** Children with high self-esteem are fundamentally satisfied with the type of person they are; they recognize their strong points, can acknowledge their weaknesses (often hoping to overcome them), and generally feel quite positive about the characteristics and competencies they display. By contrast, children with low self-esteem view the self in a less favorable light, often choosing to dwell on perceived inadequacies rather than on any strengths they may happen to display (Dweck & Elliott, 1983; Zupan, Hammen, & Jaenicke, 1987).

Measuring Self-Esteem

Many early studies of self-esteem attempted to characterize one's self-worth with a single score. However, subsequent research (see Harter, 1982, 1988, 1990) indicates that children first evaluate their competencies in many different domains and only

self-esteem: one's evaluation of one's worth as a person based on an assessment of the qualities that make up the self-concept.

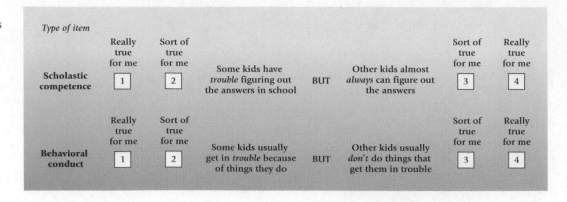

later integrate these impressions into an overall self-evaluation. Susan Harter (1986, 1990) has developed a 36-item scale, called the *Self-Perception Profile for Children,* that assesses subjects' opinions of their overall self-worth as well as their evaluations of their competencies in five separate domains: *scholastic competence, athletic competence, behavioral conduct, social acceptance,* and *physical appearance.* Each of the six subscales contains six items, and each item requires the child to (1) select one of two statements that best describes the self and (2) indicate whether that statement is "sort of true for me" or "really true for me." Figure 12-2 illustrates sample items from the scholastic competence and the behavioral conduct subscales. As shown in the figure, each item is scored from 1 to 4, with higher scores indicating higher perceived competence on that item. Responses to the six items on each subscale are then summed to determine how positively the child evaluates his or her competencies in each of the six areas.

Even kindergarten and first-grade children recognize that they are better at some activities than at others. However, these 4–7-year-olds might be accused of having inflated egos, for they rate themselves as relatively competent in most areas and are probably displaying their *desires* to be liked or to be good at various activities rather than a firm set of beliefs about their actual competencies (Eccles et al., 1993; Harter & Pike, 1984).

Starting at about age 8, children's self-evaluations become more realistic and are more accurate reflections of how others perceive them (Harter, 1982). For example, children with high scholastic self-esteem are rated quite high in intellectual competence by their teachers. Children's ratings of social self-esteem are confirmed by peers who had been asked to rate their classmates' social competencies. And children with high athletic self-esteem are more frequently chosen for team sports and are rated higher in physical competence by gym teachers than classmates who feel physically inadequate. Taken together, these findings suggest that both self-knowledge and self-esteem may depend to a large extent on the way others perceive and react to our behavior. This is precisely the point that Charles Cooley (1902) was making when he coined the term *looking-glass self* to explain how we construct a self-image.

Harter (1986) also finds that children differ in the *importance* they assign to the five competency domains assessed by her scale. Moreover, youngsters who rate themselves as very competent in the areas that *they* see as most important tend to be highest in overall self-worth. So it seems that older children and adolescents' feelings of self-esteem depend both on how they think others evaluate them (that is, the social looking glass) and on how they choose to evaluate themselves (Harter, 1990).

Does Self-Esteem Change at Adolescence?

How stable are one's feelings of self-worth? Is a child who enjoys high self-esteem as an 8-year-old likely to feel especially good about himself as an adolescent? Or is it more reasonable to assume that the stresses and strains of adolescence cause most teenagers to doubt themselves and their competencies, thereby undermining their self-esteem?

Erikson (1963) favored the latter point of view, arguing that young adolescents are likely to experience at least some erosion of self-esteem as they begin to seek a stable identity. He proposed that the many physical, cognitive, and social changes that occur at puberty force the young adolescent to conclude "I ain't what I ought to be, I ain't what I'm gonna be, but I ain't what I was" (1950 , p. 139). In other words, 12–15-year-olds face an **"identity crisis"** in that they are no longer sure of who they are and yet must also grapple with the question "Who will I become?" A failure to answer these questions leaves them confused and uncertain about their self-worth. However, Erikson believed that adolescents would eventually view themselves in more positive terms if they achieved a stable identity with which to approach the tasks of young adulthood.

Apparently, some young adolescents do experience a decline in self-esteem as they leave elementary school as the oldest and most revered students and enter junior high, where they are the youngest and least competent (Seidman et al., 1994; Simmons et al., 1987; Wigfield et al., 1991). This dip in self-esteem is likely to be greatest when multiple stressors pile up—for example, when adolescents are not only making the transition to junior high school but coping with pubertal changes, beginning to date, and perhaps dealing with family changes, such as a move, all at the same time (Simmons et al., 1987). Indeed, young adolescents do experience more daily hassles and other negative events, both at home and at school, than younger children do, and these stresses largely account for the increased sulkiness and other negative emotions that seventh–ninth graders display (Larson & Ham, 1993; Seidman et al., 1994). So early adolescence can be a painful experience—one that can even drive some teenagers to consider taking their own lives (see Box 12-1).

But before we conclude that adolescence is hazardous to our sense of self-worth, let's note that *most* 11–14-year-olds show no appreciable decline in self-worth (Nottelmann, 1987; Peterson, 1988). In fact, teenagers generally display gradual, though modest, *increases* in self-esteem over the course of adolescence (Marsh, 1989; Mullis, Mullis, & Normandin, 1992; Savin-Williams & Demo, 1984). Perhaps owing to the greater autonomy they are granted, boys are more likely than girls to show such increases in self-esteem; but most youths emerge from their teenage years with their self-worth intact, particularly if they enjoyed good self-esteem upon entering adolescence (Block & Robins, 1993).

Contributors to Self-Esteem

Why do some children enjoy higher self-esteem than others? One answer is that some children are in fact more competent and more socially attractice than others are. As early as age 5 or 6, children begin to make these discoveries on their own as they use **social comparison** information to tell them whether they perform better or worse than their peers (Ruble, Eisenberg, & Higgins, 1994). For example, they glance at each other's papers and say "How many did you miss?" or make such statements as "I'm faster than you" after winning a footrace (Frey & Ruble, 1985). This kind of comparison increases with age (Stipek & Mac Iver, 1989) and apparently plays a very important role in shaping children's self-esteem, particularly in cultures where competition and individual accomplishments are stressed. Interestingly, this preoccupation with evaluating oneself in comparison with others is not nearly as strong among communally reared kibbutz children in Israel, perhaps because cooperation and teamwork are so strongly emphasized there (Butler & Ruzany, 1993).

Parents may also play a crucial role in shaping a child's self-esteem. Specifically, children with high self-esteem tend to have parents who are warm and democratic (Coopersmith, 1967; Isberg et al., 1989; Lamborn et al., 1991). These parents are loving and supportive, they set clear standards for their children to live up to, and they

identity crisis: Erikson's term for the uncertainty and discomfort that adolescents experience when they become confused about their present and future roles in life.

social comparison: the process of defining and evaluating the self by comparing oneself to other people.

BOX 12-1

Adolescent Suicide: The Tragic Destruction of Self

Surprising as it may seem to anyone who has never contemplated taking his or her own life, suicidal thoughts are shockingly common among adolescents and young adults (Dubow et al., 1989). In one recent survey of high school students, nearly 63% reported at least one instance of suicidal thinking, and 10.5% had actually attempted suicide (Smith & Crawford, 1986). Moreover, the suicide rate among 15–24-year-olds has increased dramatically over the past 30 years—so much so that suicide is now the third leading cause of death for this age group, ranking behind only accidents and homicides (U.S. Bureau of the Census, 1993). Among some Native American groups, suicidal thoughts and behaviors are even more widespread (Garland & Zigler, 1993); in one sample of Zuni adolescents, for example, fully 30% had attempted suicide, most of them more than once (Howard-Pitney et al., 1992). Overall, females *attempt* suicide more often than males do; but males are more often successful in their attempts—by a ratio of about 3 to 1, a difference that holds up across most cultures studied (Girard, 1993). Males succeed more often simply because they shun slower-acting pills in favor of more abruptly lethal techniques such as nooses and guns.

Unfortunately, there is no sure way to identify young people who will try to kill themselves: Suicidal adolescents come from all racial and ethnic groups and all social classes, and even popular adolescents of superior intelligence may take their own lives. Yet, there are some telltale warning signs. Suicidal adolescents are often severely depressed, are abusing drugs, or displaying other psychological disorders (Felts, Chenier, & Barnes, 1992; Garland & Zigler, 1993). They have often experienced deteriorating relationships with parents, peers, or romantic partners, suffered academic failures, and lost all interest in hobbies or other enjoyable activities as they sink into a state of hopelessness and despair and feel incapable of coping with their problems (Berman & Jobes, 1991; Rubenstein et al., 1989). Because adolescents are far less successful than adults at killing themselves when they try (see figure), some researchers believe that their suicide attempts are often a desperate "cry for help." Unlike suicidal adults, who are often determined to end it all, many suicidal adolescents are hoping to *improve* their lives; they may see their suicide attempts as a way of forcing others to take their problems seriously, but by miscalculation or sudden impulse, they often die before they can be helped (Berman & Jobes, 1991; Rubenstein et al., 1989).

What can be done to prevent adolescent suicides? Friends and associates can play an important role in recognizing the warning signs of suicidal thinking and urging their depressed young companions to talk about their problems. If an adolescent divulges suidical thoughts, companions should try to convince him or her that there are ways other than suicide to cope with distress. But perhaps the most important thing friends and associates can do is to communicate the situation to other people who are in a better position to help, such as the adolescent's parents, a teacher, or a school counselor. Clearly, it is better to break a confidence than to let the person die.

As for parents, perhaps the best advice is to take all suicidal thinking seriously, for perhaps as many as one in six teenagers who have such thoughts will actually attempt to kill themselves (Smith & Crawford, 1986). And professional assistance is definitely called for after an unsuccessful suicide attempt, for adolescents who try once are at risk of succeeding in the future if they receive little help and continue to feel incapable of coping with their problems (Berman & Jobes, 1991).

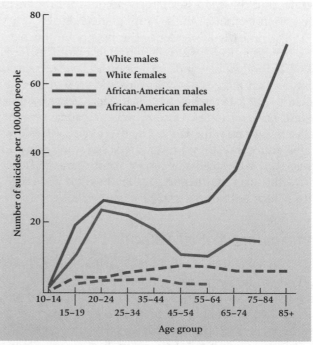

Number of suicides per 100,000 people by age and sex among whites and African Americans in the United States. Data about the oldest African Americans are not shown because too few cases were studied. Data from U.S. Bureau of the Census, 1992.

allow their children to state their opinions and participate in decision making. Indeed, the relationship between high self-esteem and this nurturing, democratic parental style is much the same in Taiwan and Australia as it is in the United States and Canada (Scott, Scott, & McCabe, 1991). Although these child-rearing studies are correlational data and we cannnot be sure that warm, supportive parenting *causes* high self-esteem, it is easy to imagine such a causal process at work. Certainly, sending a message that "You're a good kid whom I trust to follow rules and make good decisions" is apt to promote higher self-esteem than more aloof or more controlling styles in which parents may be saying, in effect, "Your inadequacies turn me off" (Isberg et al., 1989).

One major aspect of self-esteem that has been studied in some depth is the development of children's perceptions of their academic competencies—a topic to which we will now turn.

Concept Check 12-1 ⌄ Development of the Self-Concept

Check your understanding of important processes and milestones in the development of the self-system by matching each descriptive statement below with one of the following concepts: (a) categorical self; (b) self-esteem; (c) looking-glass self; (d) belief-desire theory of mind; (e) private self; (f) social comparison; (g) self-recognition. The answers appear in the Appendix.

_____ 1. Evaluative component of self that becomes more realistic by age 8.

_____ 2. Inner, reflective component of the self.

_____ 3. Portrait of oneself based on other's reactions to one's attributes and behaviors.

_____ 4. Thought to be an early contributor to socially skilled play activities.

_____ 5. Early description of self along such socially significant dimensions as age and sex.

_____ 6. Appears to underlie children's use of deceptive ploys.

_____ 7. Important contributor to self-worth in cultures where individual accomplishments are emphasized.

► DEVELOPMENT OF ACHIEVEMENT MOTIVATION AND ACADEMIC SELF-CONCEPTS

In Chapter 9, we learned that even though intelligence predicts academic achievement, the relationship is far from perfect. Why? Because children also differ in **achievement motivation**—their willingness to strive to succeed at challenging tasks and to meet high standards of accomplishment. Although the meaning of achievement varies somewhat from society to society, one survey conducted in 30 cultures revealed that people around the world value personal attributes such as self-reliance, responsibility, and a willingness to work hard to attain important objectives (Fyans et al., 1983).

Must these valued attributes be taught? Social-learning theorists think so, but others disagree. Psychoanalyst Robert White (1959) proposes that children are intrinsically motivated to "master" their environments. He calls this **effectance motivation**— a desire to have an effect on or to cope successfully with the environment and the people within it. We see this effectance, competence, or mastery motive in action as we watch infants struggle to turn knobs, open cabinets, and operate toys and then notice their pleasure when they succeed (Mayes & Zigler, 1992). White argued that it is quite natural for human beings to seek out challenges just for the joy of mastering them. Of course, his position is very similar to that of Piaget, who believed that children are intrinsically motivated to adapt to the environment by assimilating new experiences and then accommodating to these experiences.

But even though the basic propensity for competence or mastery may be innate, it is obvious that some children try harder than others to master their school assignments, their music lessons, or the positions they play on the neighborhood softball team. How do we explain these individual differences? Let's begin by tracing the development of achievement motivation early in life and examining some of the factors that promote (and inhibit) its growth.

achievement motivation: a willingness to strive to succeed at challenging tasks and to meet high standards of accomplishment.

effectance motivation: an inborn motive to explore, understand, and control one's environment (sometimes called *mastery motivation*).

Three-year-olds are highly motivated to master challenges and can take pride in their accomplishments.

The Early Origins of Achievement Motivation

How does a baby's effectance motivation evolve into a grade school child's achievement motivation? Deborah Stipek and her associates (Stipek, Recchia, & McClintic, 1992) have conducted an interesting series of studies with 1–5-year-olds to find out when children develop the capacity to evaluate their accomplishments against performance standards, which is central to achievement motivation. In Stipek's research, children were observed as they undertook activities that had clear-cut achievement goals (for example, hammering pegs into pegboards, working puzzles, knocking down plastic pins with a bowling ball). Some tasks were structured so that children either could or could not master them, in order to observe reactions to success or failure. Based on this research, Stipek and her colleagues suggest that children progress through three stages in learning to evaluate their performances in achievement situations: *joy in mastery, approval seeking,* and *use of standards.*

Stage 1: Joy in mastery. Before the age of 2, infants are visibly pleased to master challenges, displaying the effectance motivation that White (1959) wrote about. However, they do not call other people's attention to their triumphs or otherwise seek recognition, and, rather than being bothered by failures, they simply shift goals and attempt to master other toys. They are not yet evaluating their outcomes in relation to performance standards that define success and failure.

Stage 2: Approval seeking. As they near age 2, toddlers begin to anticipate how others will evaluate their performances. They seek recognition when they master challenges and expect disapproval when they fail. For example, children as young as 2 who succeeded on a task often smiled, held their heads and chins up high, and made such statements as "I did it" as they called the experimenter's attention to their feats. Meanwhile, 2-year-olds who failed to master a challenge often turned away from the experimenter as though they hoped to avoid criticism. It seems, then, that 2-year-olds are already appraising their outcomes as mastery successes or nonsuccesses and have already learned that they can expect approval after successes and disapproval after failures (see also Bullock & Lutkenhaus, 1988).

Stage 3: Use of standards. Another important breakthrough occurred around age 3 as children began to react more independently to their successes and failures. They seemed to have adopted objective standards for appraising their performance and were not as dependent on others to tell them when they had done well or poorly.

Figure 12-3
Scenes like this one were used by David McClelland and his associates to measure achievement motivation.

These Stage 3 children seemed capable of experiencing real *pride* (rather than mere pleasure) in their achievements and real *shame* (rather than mere disappointment) after failure (see also Lewis, Alessandri, & Sullivan, 1992).

In sum, infants are guided by an effectance or mastery motive and take pleasure in their everyday accomplishments; 2-year-olds begin to anticipate other's approval or disapproval of their performances; and children 3 and older evaluate their accomplishments against performance standards and are capable of experiencing pride or shame depending on how successfully they meet those standards.

Achievement Motivation during Childhood and Adolescence

In their pioneering studies of achievement motivation, David McClelland and his associates (1953) gave children and adolescents a series of four somewhat ambiguous pictures and asked them to write stories about them as part of a test of creative imagination. Assuming that people will project their own motives into their stories, one can measure their achievement motivation by counting the number of achievement-related themes they mention. What kind of story would you tell about the scene portrayed in Figure 12-3? A person high in achievement motivation might respond by saying that this woman has been working for months on a new scientific breakthrough that will revolutionize the field of medicine, whereas a person who scores low might say that the worker is glad the day is over so that she can go home and relax. Early research revealed that children who scored high in achievement motivation on this and other measures did indeed tend to receive better grades in school than those who scored low (McClelland et al., 1953). This prompted investigators to look more closely at parent-child interactions, seeking to determine how the home setting influences achievement motivation.

Home and Family Influences on Mastery Motivation and Achievement

By 6 months of age, infants already differ in their willingness to explore the environment and their attempts to control objects, situations, and the actions of other people. Which infants are most "mastery oriented" early in life? Leon Yarrow and his associates (1984) found that those who score highest in mastery motivation have parents who frequently provide *sensory stimulation* designed to amuse them and arouse their curiosity—experiences such as tickling, bouncing, and games of pat-a-cake.

Important as these observations may be, instilling a strong sense of achievement motivation requires much more than tickling a child or bouncing her on one's knee. Other especially potent influences on mastery motivation and achievement are the

Table 12-1	Relation between Quality of Home Environment at 12 Months of Age and Children's Grade School Academic Achievement Five to Nine Years Later	
	Academic achievement	
Quality of home environment at age 12 months	Average or high (top 70%)	Low (bottom 30%)
Stimulating	20 children	10 children
Unstimulating.	6 children	14 children

Source: Adapted from van Doorninck, Caldwell, Wright, & Frankenberg, 1981.

quality of the child's attachments, the character of the home environment, and the child-rearing practices that parents use, which can either foster or inhibit a child's will to achieve.

Quality of attachment. In Chapter 11, we learned that children who were securely attached to primary caregivers at age 12–18 months are more likely than those who were insecurely attached to solve problems successfully as 2-year-olds and to display a strong sense of curiosity, self-reliance, and an eagerness to solve problems some 4–5 years later as they enter elementary school. It is not that securely attached preschoolers are any more intellectually competent; instead, they seem to be more *eager* than insecurely attached children to *apply* their competencies to the new problems they encounter (Belsky, Garduque, & Hrncir, 1984). So children apparently need the "secure base" provided by a loving, responsive parent to feel comfortable about taking risks and *seeking* challenges.

The home environment. The young child's tendency to explore, acquire new skills, and solve problems also depends on the character of the home environment and the challenges it provides. In one study (van Doorninck, Caldwell, Wright, & Frankenberg, 1981), investigators visited the homes of fifty 12-month-old infants from lower-income families and used the **HOME inventory** (described in Chapter 9) to classify each child's early environment as intellectually stimulating or unstimulating. Five to nine years later, the research team followed up on these children by looking at their standardized achievement test scores and the grades they had earned at school. As we see in Table 12-1, the quality of the home environment at 12 months of age predicted children's academic achievement several years later. Two out of three children from stimulating homes were now performing quite well at school, whereas 70% of those from unstimulating homes were doing very poorly (see also Bradley, Caldwell, & Rock, 1988). Although the seeds of mastery motivation may well be innate, it seems that the joy of discovery and problem solving is unlikely to blossom in a barren home environment where the child has few problems to solve and limited opportunities for learning.

Child rearing and achievement. What kinds of child-rearing practices foster achievement motivation? In their book *The Achievement Motive*, McClelland and his associates (1953) proposed that parents who stress *independence training*—doing things on one's own—and who warmly reinforce such self-reliant behavior will contribute in a positive way to achievement motivation. And research bears this out (Grolnick & Ryan, 1989; Winterbottom, 1958). Moreover, direct *achievement training*—setting *high standards* and encouraging children to do things *well*—also fosters achievement motivation (Rosen & D'Andrade, 1959). Finally, patterns of praise (or punishment) that accompany the child's accomplishments are also important: Chil-

HOME inventory: a measure of the amount and type of intellectual stimulation provided by a child's home environment.

dren who seek challenges and display high levels of achievement motivation have parents who *praise their successes and are not overly critical of an occasional failure;* by contrast, children who shy away from challenges and are low in achievement motivation have parents who are slow to acknowledge their successes (or who do so in a "matter-of-fact" way) and are inclined to *punish* their failures (Baumrind, 1973; Teeven & McGhee, 1972).

We see, then, that parents of youngsters high in achievement motivation possess three characteristics: (1) they are warm, accepting, and quick to praise the child's accomplishments; (2) they provide guidance and control by setting standards for the child to live up to and then monitoring her progress to ensure that she does; and (3) they permit the child some independence or autonomy, allowing her a say in deciding how best to master challenges and meet their expectations. Diana Baumrind calls this warm, firm, but democratic parenting an **authoritative parenting** style—a style that she and others have found to foster positive attitudes about achievement and considerable academic success among grade school children and adolescents in both Western societies (Baumrind, 1973; Lamborn et al., 1991; Steinberg, Elmen, & Mounts, 1989) and the Orient (Lin & Fu, 1990). If children are encouraged and supported in a positive manner as they tackle their schoolwork, they are likely to enjoy new challenges and feel confident of mastering them (Connell, Spencer, & Aber, 1994). By contrast, parents can undermine a child's school performance and motivation to succeed if they are (1) uninvolved and offer little in the way of guidance or (2) highly controlling and do such things as nag continually about homework, offer tangible bribes for good grades, or harp incessantly about bad ones (Ginsburg & Bronstein, 1993).

Parents who encourage achievement and who respond warmly to successes are likely to raise mastery-oriented children who enjoy challenges.

Peer-Group Influences

Peers are also an important source of influence on grade school children and adolescents and can sometimes undermine parents' efforts to encourage academic achievement. When James Coleman (1961) asked high school students how they would like to be remembered, only 31% of the boys and 28% of the girls wanted to be remembered as bright students. They were more concerned with having the athletic and social skills that lead to popularity (see also Seidman et al., 1994). Since peer acceptance is highly important to most adolescents, perhaps it is not surprising that some of them emphasize academic goals less and social goals more than they did as grade school children, particularly if they attend schools where few students are highly achievement oriented.

The problem of peer pressures that interfere with academic achievement motivation may be especially acute for many lower-income African-American and Latino students and may help explain why they often lag behind Anglo-American and Asian-American students in school achievement (Slaughter-Defoe et al., 1990; Tharp, 1989). Lawrence Steinberg and his colleagues (Steinberg, Dornbusch, & Brown, 1992) note that the African-American and Latino peer cultures in many low-income areas actively discourage academic achievement, whereas Anglo- and Asian-American peer groups tend to value and encourage it. High-achieving African-American students in some inner-city schools actually run the risk of rejection by their African-American peers if their academic accomplishments cause them to be perceived as "acting white" (Fordham & Ogbu, 1986). Overall, then, achievement motivation is influenced by a number of contextual factors. It is nurtured more in some families, peer groups, schools, and neighborhoods than in others.

Beyond Achievement Motivation: Cognitive Contributors to Academic Self-Concepts

Does a high need for achievement ensure that a child will master all important challenges and live up to his potential? Not necessarily. While acknowledging that the concept of achievement motivation has some value, many researchers now think that it is naive to presume that this one global motive will predict behavior in all achievement

authoritative parenting: flexible, democratic style of parenting in which warm, accepting parents provide guidance and control while allowing the child some say in deciding how best to meet challenges and obligations.

Table 12-2 Weiner's Classification of the Causes of Achievement Outcomes (and Examples of How You Might Explain a Terrible Test Grade)

| | Locus of causality | |
	Internal cause	External cause
Stable cause	Ability "I'm hopeless in math."	Task difficulty "That test was incredibly hard and much too long."
Unstable cause	Effort "I should have studied more instead of going out to the concert."	Luck "What luck! Every question seemed to be about information taught on the days of class I missed."

situations. Why? Because they have also discovered that children's achievement behavior and academic self-concepts depend very heavily on how they *interpret* their successes and failures.

Weiner's Attribution Theory

Bernard Weiner (1974; 1986) has proposed an **attribution theory** of achievement in which he argues that the explanations **(causal attributions)** that we offer for our outcomes influence our future expectancies of success and our future motivation to succeed. Weiner has emphasized four possible causes of success or failure: *ability* (or lack thereof), *effort, task difficulty,* and *luck* (either good or bad).

Two of these causes, ability and effort, are *internal* causes or qualities of the individual, whereas the other two, task difficulty and luck, are *external* or environmental factors. In other words, Weiner proposes that causal attributions can be grouped along a locus dimension (internal versus external). Here, Weiner's thinking corresponds to earlier work on a dimension of personality called **locus of control** (Crandall, 1967, 1969). Individuals with an *internal locus of control* assume that they are personally responsible for what happens to them. For example, they might credit an *A* grade on a paper to superior writing ability or hard work. Individuals with an *external locus of control* believe that their outcomes depend more on luck, fate, or the actions of others than on their own abilities and efforts. They might say that their *A*s are due to luck ("The teacher just happened to like my paper topic"), indiscriminate grading, or some other external cause. Children with an internal locus of control earn higher grades and higher scores on academic achievement tests than children with an external locus of control do (Findley & Cooper, 1983), perhaps because they believe their efforts will pay off and therefore they work harder.

But Weiner claims that causal attributions also differ along a *stability* dimension. Ability and task difficulty are reasonably stable or unchangeable. If one has low math ability today, one is likely to have the same low ability tomorrow, and if algebra problems are difficult today, similar algebra problems are likely to be difficult tomorrow. By contrast, the amount of effort one expends and the workings of luck are highly unstable or variable from situation to situation (see Table 12-2).

Why is it useful to categorize causes of success and failure along both a locus of causality and a stability dimension? Mainly, because it is not *always* adaptive to attribute what happens to internal causes, as research on locus of control would lead us to believe. It is indeed healthy to conclude that your *successes* must be due to high ability; this will not only make you feel proud but should lead you to expect more success in the future, since ability is relatively stable and should therefore continue

attribution theory: a social-cognitive theory specifying that the explanations that we construct for social experiences largely determine how we respond to those experiences.

causal attributions: inferences made about the underlying causes of one's own or another person's behavior.

locus of control: personality dimension that distinguishes people who assume that they are personally responsible for their life outcomes (internal locus) from those who believe that their outcomes depend more on circumstances beyond their control (external locus).

to affect your performance. But is it healthy to conclude from a failure that you are seriously lacking in ability? Hardly! Low ability may be an internal cause of poor performance, but because it is also a stable cause, attributing failure to low ability is an admission that you can do little to improve on your poor performance. Not only would you have low expectancies of future success and little motivation to strive, but you would lose self-esteem by admitting that you are "incompetent" at this kind of challenge.

If you were to critique Weiner's theory as a little too cognitive and too abstract to explain the achievement attributions that young children display, you would be right. Before age 7 or so, children tend to be unrealistic optimists who think that they have the ability to succeed in almost any novel task (Dweck & Elliott, 1983; Stipek & Mac Iver, 1989). This rosy optimism is based in part on wishful thinking; the more young children want to succeed, the more they believe they will succeed, even on tasks that they have repeatedly failed at in the past (Stipek, Roberts, & Sanborn, 1984). Kindergarten and primary-grade teachers may contribute to this outlook by setting mastery goals and by praising children more for their efforts than for the quality of their work, thus leading them to believe that they can accomplish much and "be smart" by working hard (Rosenholtz & Simpson, 1984; Stipek & Mac Iver, 1989). Indeed, young children do seem to have an **incremental view of ability:** They believe that ability is changeable, not stable, and that they can get smarter or become more capable through increased effort and lots of practice (Droege & Stipek, 1993; Dweck & Leggett, 1988).

When do children begin to distinguish ability from effort? When do they adopt an **entity view of ability**—a perspective that ability is a fixed or stable trait that is not influenced much by effort or practice? It turns out that many 8–12-year-olds are beginning to distinguish effort from ability (Nicholls & Miller, 1984) due, in part, to the changing character of their experiences at school. As children progress through grade school, teachers place more and more emphasis on *ability* appraisals; they assign grades that reflect the quality of work students perform rather than the amount of effort expended, and these performance evaluations are supplemented by such competitive activities as science fairs and spelling bees, which also place a premium on the *quality* rather than the quantity of students' work. Moreover, older grade school children are often tracked into "ability groups" based on the teacher's appraisal of their competencies (Rosenholtz & Simpson, 1984; Stipek & Mac Iver, 1989). So all these practices, coupled with children's increased use of social comparison to appraise their outcomes (Butler, 1990), help to explain why older grade school students begin to distinguish effort from ability and to make the kind of causal attributions for their successes and failures that Weiner's theory anticipates.

Interestingly, the late elementary school period (fourth to sixth grades) is also the time when many students begin to value academic achievement less and to develop rather negative academic self-concepts, a trend that becomes even stronger during the junior high school years (Eccles et al., 1993; Seidman et al., 1994). And as we are about to see, children's tendency to distinguish effort from ability and to adopt an *entity view* of ability is a major contributor to these trends.

Dweck's Learned-Helplessness Theory

Carol Dweck and her colleagues (Dweck & Elliott, 1983; Dweck & Leggett, 1988) find that middle-school children clearly differ in the attributions they offer for their achievement outcomes, particularly for their failures. Some children are **mastery oriented:** They attribute their successes to their high ability but tend to externalize the blame for their failures ("That test was ambiguous and unfair") or to attribute them to *unstable* causes that they can easily overcome ("I'll do better if I try harder"). These students are called "mastery oriented" because they persist in the face of failure, believing that their increased effort will allow them to succeed. Although they see their ability as a reasonably stable attribute that doesn't fluctuate radically from day to day (which allows them to feel confident about repeating their successes), they

incremental view of ability: belief that one's ability can be improved through increased effort and practice.

entity view of ability: belief that one's ability is a highly stable trait that is not influenced much by effort or practice.

mastery orientation: a tendency to persist at challenging tasks because of a belief that one has high ability and/or that earlier failures can be overcome by trying harder.

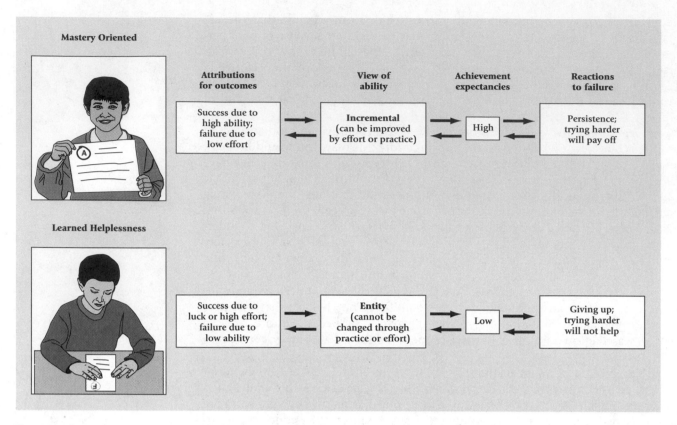

Mastery Oriented

Attributions for outcomes	View of ability	Achievement expectancies	Reactions to failure
Success due to high ability; failure due to low effort	Incremental (can be improved by effort or practice)	High	Persistence; trying harder will pay off

Learned Helplessness

Attributions for outcomes	View of ability	Achievement expectancies	Reactions to failure
Success due to luck or high effort; failure due to low ability	Entity (cannot be changed through practice or effort)	Low	Giving up; trying harder will not help

Figure 12-4
Characteristics of the mastery-oriented and learned-helplessness achievement orientations.

still think that they can improve their competencies (an *incremental* viewpoint) by trying harder after a failure. So mastery-oriented youngsters are highly motivated to "master" new challenges, regardless of whether they have previously succeeded or failed at similar tasks (see Figure 12-4).

By contrast, other children often attribute their successes to the *unstable* factors of hard work or luck; they do not experience the pride and self-esteem that come from viewing themselves as highly competent. Yet they often attribute their failures to a stable and internal factor—namely, their *lack of ability*—that causes them to form low expectations of future successes and to give up. It appeared to Dweck as if these youngsters were displaying a **learned helplessness orientation:** If failures are attributed to a *stable* cause—lack of ability—that the child thinks he can do little about (an *entity view* of competence), he becomes frustrated and sees little reason to try to improve. So he stops trying and acts helpless.

It is important to note that children who display this learned helplessness syndrome are *not* merely the least competent members of a typical grade school classroom. Even highly talented students may adopt this unhealthy attributional style (Phillips, 1984); and, once established, learned helplessness tends to persist over time and eventually undermine the child's academic performance in subjects for which she feels incompetent (Fincham, Hokada, & Sanders, 1989).

How does learned helplessness develop? According to Dweck (1978), parents and teachers may unwittingly foster the development of a helpless achievement orientation if they praise the child for *being neat* or for *working hard* when she succeeds but criticize her *lack of ability* when she fails. Apparently, even 4–6-year-olds can begin to develop a helpless orientation if their failures are criticized in ways that cause them to doubt their abilities (Heyman, Dweck, & Cain, 1992; see also Smiley & Dweck, 1994). By contrast, if parents and teachers praise the child's *abilities* when she succeeds but emphasize her *lack of effort* when she fails, the child may conclude that she is certainly smart enough and would do even better if she tried harder—precisely the

learned helplessness orientation: a tendency to give up or to stop trying after failing because these failures have been attributed to a lack of ability that one can do little about.

viewpoint adopted by mastery-oriented youngsters. In one experiment, Dweck and her associates (1978) demonstrated that fifth-graders who received the *helplessness-producing* pattern of evaluation while working at unfamiliar problems did indeed begin to attribute their failures to a lack of ability, whereas classmates who received the *mastery-oriented* evaluative pattern attributed their failures to a lack of effort, saying, in effect, "I need to try harder." These strikingly different attributional styles were created in less than one hour in this experiment, thus implying that similar patterns of evaluative feedback from parents or teachers, given consistently over a period of months or years, might well contribute to the development of the contrasting "helpless" and "mastery" orientations so often observed among grade school (and older) students.

On helping the helpless to achieve. Obviously, giving up as soon as one begins to founder is not the kind of achievement orientation that adults would hope to encourage. What can be done to help these "helpless" children to persist at tasks they have failed? According to Dweck, the most effective therapy might be a form of **attribution retraining** in which helpless children are persuaded to attribute their failures to unstable causes—namely, insufficient effort—that they can do something about, rather than continuing to view them as stemming from their lack of ability, which is not so easy to change.

Dweck (1975) tested her hypothesis by exposing children who had become helpless after failing a series of tough math problems to either of two "therapies." Over a period of 25 therapy sessions, half the children received a *success-only* therapy in which they worked problems they could solve and received tokens for their successes. The other half received *attribution retraining;* they experienced nearly as many successes over the 25 sessions as did the children in the other group but were also told after each of several prearranged failures that they had not worked fast enough and *should have tried harder.* Thus, an explicit attempt was made to convince these youngsters that failures can reflect a lack of effort rather than a lack of ability. Did this therapy work? Yes, indeed! At the end of the experiment, helpless children in the attribution-retraining condition now performed much better on the tough math problems they had initially failed; and when they did fail one, they usually attributed their outcome to a lack of effort and tried all the harder. By contrast, children in the success-only condition showed no such improvements, giving up once again after failing the original problems. So merely showing helpless children that they are capable of succeeding is not enough! To alleviate learned helplessness, one must teach children to respond more constructively to their *failures* by viewing these experiences as something that they can overcome if they try harder.

Can we do better than this? Certainly we can by taking steps to *prevent* learned helplessness before it happens. Parents and teachers can play a major part in these preventive efforts by simply praising the child's *abilities* when she succeeds and taking care not to undermine her self-worth by suggesting that failures reflect a lack of ability. Indeed, one of the reasons that *authoritative parenting* is so consistently linked to high achievement is that these warm, supportive adults (1) convince their child that he has the *ability* to meet high standards, while (2) praising successes and not becoming overly concerned about occasional failures, thereby fostering the development of a *mastery-oriented* attributional style. Yet another preventive measure that educators might wish to consider is described in Box 12-2.

Reflections on Achievement Motivation and Academic Self-Concepts

Clearly, children's academic self-concepts involve far more than the workings of an innate mastery motive or a global achievement motive. Although McClelland and his associates made an important contribution by showing that people reliably differ in their *motivation* to achieve and by suggesting how this motive might be nurtured by

attribution retraining: therapeutic intervention in which helpless children are persuaded to attribute failures to their lack of effort rather than a lack of ability.

Theory. Elaine Elliott and Carol Dweck (1988) have argued that children pursue either of two goals in achievement situations: (1) *performance goals*, in which they seek to display their competencies (or avoid looking incompetent), and (2) *learning goals*, in which they seek to *increase* their abilities or master new tasks. According to Elliott and Dweck, mastery-oriented students favor learning goals: When seeking to master a challenge or to improve their competencies, these youngsters treat initial failures as evidence that their learning strategies are inadequate; consequently, they adopt new strategies and keep working. By contrast, helpless children seem to be pursuing performance goals: They give up after failing because their failure has *immediately* undermined their objective, which was to display their competencies. Would children who are prone to helplessness be more persistent at achievement tasks if they adopted a "learning goal" to *improve* their abilities—a goal that is not immediately undermined by an early mistake or two?

Research. To test the plausibility of their goal-based model of helplessness, Elliott and Dweck had fifth-graders perform a novel task, led them to believe they had either high or low ability, and then told them they would soon be performing similar tasks, some of which would be rather difficult (thus leading the children to anticipate errors). Half the children worked under a *performance goal*, having been told that their performances were going to be compared with those of other kids and evaluated by an expert. The remaining children were induced to adopt a *learning goal:* Their instructions suggested that, although they would make many mistakes, working at the tasks would "sharpen the mind" and help them at school. As anticipated, children made many errors on the new tasks they performed. And

also as anticipated, the only children who displayed telltale signs of helplessness (that is, deteriorating performances, low ability attributions) were those who thought they had low ability *and* were pursuing a *performance* goal. By contrast, even "low-ability" students persisted after initial failures and showed remarkably little distress if they were pursuing a learning goal in which the focus was on *improving* their competencies rather than displaying them.

Applications. As presently structured, most classrooms stress performance goals: Students undertake the same assignments, their performances are compared, and they receive recognition (praise, gold stars, grades, and the like) that places undue attention on their relative abilities—information that seems to undermine many students' intrinsic interest in the subject matter (Butler, 1989, 1990) and may seriously depress the self-esteem of slower learners, who compare so unfavorably with their peers (Butler, 1990; Ruble & Flett, 1988). Might we prevent these undesirable consequences by restructuring classroom goals—by emphasizing *individual mastery* of particular learning objectives (learning goals) rather than continuing to place children in direct competition (as teachers often do by saying "Let's see who can finish first," ". . . come up with the best answer," and so on) and making comparative appraisals of their progress? Many contemporary researchers think so (see Butler, 1989, 1990; Stipek & Mac Iver, 1989). And if Elliott and Dweck's results are any guide, it would seem that an emphasis on individual mastery would be particularly beneficial to the slower learners, who should begin to view their initial mistakes as evidence that they must change strategies to *improve* their competencies rather than treating these errors as proof that they have little ability and simply cannot master their lessons.

adults, their notion that this one global motive would predict a person's reactions to all challenges was grossly overstated. Weiner's attribution theory broke new ground by illustrating that people's reactions to significant challenges depend very heavily on the explanations, or *causal attributions*, that they offer for their prior successes and failures. Finally, Dweck's learned-helplessness theory demonstrates how different attributional styles that children adopt lead to positive or negative academic self-concepts that affect children's *motivation* to persist at challenges they have initially failed to master. So, as we concluded when reviewing the various theories of attachment in Chapter 11, it makes no sense to brand any single achievement theory as "correct" and to ignore the others. Each of these theories has helped us to understand why children differ so dramatically when responding to the challenges they face.

 ## WHO AM I TO BE? FORGING AN IDENTITY

identity: a mature self-definition; a sense of who one is, where one is going, and how one fits into society.

According to Erik Erikson (1963), the major developmental hurdle that adolescents face is establishing an **identity**—a firm and coherent sense of who they are, where they are heading, and where they fit into society. Forging an identity involves grap-

Concept Check 12-2 ⌄ Understanding Achievement Motivation and Academic Self-Concepts

Check your understanding of the development of children's achievement motivation and academic self-concepts by filling in the blanks in each statement below. The answers appear in the Appendix.

1. Very young infants take pleasure in their accomplishments, as if guided by a(n) _____ motive that White wrote about. About age _____, toddlers begin to anticipate others' _____ or _____ when they succeed or fail; and by age _____, children are beginning to evaluate their accomplishments against _____ standards—a capacity central to _____ motivation.

2. Parents of high achievers tend to possess three characteristics: They are _____, _____, and _____. However, the influence of this _____ parenting style can be undermined by _____ against academic achievement motivation.

3. Weiner's achievement theory claims that the explanations, or _____ _____s, that we offer for our successes and failures affect our expectancies of future success or failure. He claims that our achievement expectancies are more likely to be healthy if we attribute our successes to _____ causes and our failures to _____ ones.

4. Carol Dweck finds that _____-_____ children do display the healthy attributional style that Weiner describes. By contrast, children with a _____-_____ orientation tend to attribute their failures to a stable cause: low _____. They have adopted an _____ view of ability, and _____ _____ in the face of failure, thinking that there is little they can do to improve their performances. One way to help these children is through _____ _____—a program that attempts to persuade them to attribute failures to a lack of _____, which they can do something about.

pling with many important choices: What kind of career do I want? What religious, moral, and political values should I adopt? Who am I as a man or a woman, and as a sexual being? Just where do I fit in the world? All this is, of course, a lot for teenagers to have on their minds, and Erikson used the term "identity crisis" to capture the sense of confusion, and even anxiety, that adolescents may feel as they think about who they are today and try to decide "What kind of self can (or should) I be?"

Can you recall a time during the teenage years when you were confused about who you were, what you should be, and what you were likely to become? Is it possible that you have not yet resolved these identity issues and are still seeking answers? If so, does that make you abnormal or maladjusted?

James Marcia (1980) has developed a structured interview that enables researchers to classify adolescents into one of four *identity statuses* based on whether or not they have explored various alternatives and made firm commitments to an occupation, a religious ideology, a sexual orientation, and a set of political values. These identity statuses are as follows:

1. **Identity diffusion.** Adolescents classified as "diffuse" have not yet thought about identity issues or, having thought about them, have failed to make any firm future-oriented commitments.

2. **Foreclosure.** Persons classified as "foreclosures" have made future commitments without ever experiencing the "crisis" of deciding what really suits them best. This can easily occur if parents suggest an identity to the adolescent (for example, "You'll go to med school, Johnny"), who then adopts this viewpoint without carefully evaluating its implications.

3. **Moratorium.** This status describes the person who is experiencing what Erikson referred to as an identity crisis. He or she has made no definite commitments, but is actively exploring a number of values, interests, ideologies, and careers in search of a stable identity.

identity diffusion: identity status characterizing individuals who are not questioning who they are and have not yet committed themselves to an identity.

foreclosure: identity status characterizing individuals who have prematurely committed themselves to occupations or ideologies without really thinking about these commitments.

moratorium: identity status characterizing individuals who are currently experiencing an identity crisis and are actively exploring occupational and ideological positions in which to invest themselves.

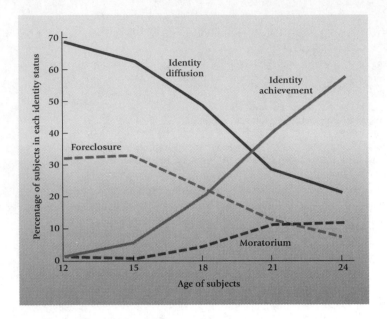

Figure 12-5
Percentages of subjects in each of Marcia's four identity statuses as a function of age. Note that resolution of the identity crisis occurs much later than Erikson assumed: Only 4% of the 15-year-olds and 20% of the 18-year-olds had achieved a stable identity.
From Meilman, 1979.

4. **Identity achievement.** The identity achiever has resolved his or her identity crisis by making relatively strong *personal* commitments to an occupation or an ideology (or both).

Developmental Trends in Identity Formation

Although Erikson assumed that the identity crisis occurs in early adolescence and is often resolved by age 15–18, it appears that his age norms were overly optimistic. When Philip Meilman (1979) measured the identity statuses of college-bound (or college-educated) males between the ages of 12 and 24, he observed a clear developmental progression. But as shown in Figure 12-5, the vast majority of 12–18-year-olds were identity diffused or foreclosed, and not until age 21 or older had the majority of participants reached the moratorium status or achieved stable identities.

Is the identity formation process different for females than it is for males? In most respects, no (Archer, 1992). Females make progress toward achieving a clear sense of identity at about the same ages that males do (Streitmatter, 1993). However, one intriguing sex difference has been observed: Although today's college women are just as concerned about establishing a career identity as men are, they attach greater importance to the aspects of identity that center on interpersonal relationships, gender roles, and sexuality (Bilsker, Schiedel, & Marcia, 1988; Kroger, 1988; Patterson, Sochting, & Marcia, 1992). They are also more concerned than males with the issue of how to balance career and family goals (Archer, 1992; Matula et al., 1992).

Judging from this research, identity formation takes quite a bit of time. Not until late adolescence—during the college years—do many young men and women move from the diffusion or foreclosure status into the moratorium status and then achieve a sense of identity (Waterman, 1982). But this is by no means the end of the identity formation process. Many adults are *still* struggling with identity issues or have reopened the question of who they are after thinking they had all the answers earlier in life (Waterman & Archer, 1990). A divorce, for example, may cause a woman to rethink what it means to be a woman and raise new questions about other aspects of her identity as well.

The process of achieving identity is also quite uneven (Archer, 1982; Kroger, 1988). For example, Sally Archer (1982) assessed the identity statuses of sixth to twelfth graders in four domains: occupational choice, gender-role attitudes, religious beliefs, and political ideologies. Only 5% of her adolescents were in the same iden-

identity achievement: identity status characterizing individuals who have carefully considered identity issues and have made firm commitments to an occupation and ideologies.

tity status in all four areas, and more than 90% were in two or three categories across the four domains. So adolescents can achieve a strong sense of identity in one area and still be searching in others.

How Painful Is Identity Formation?

Perhaps it is unfortunate that Erikson used the term "crisis" to describe the adolescent's active search for an identity (or identities), because adolescents in the moratorium status do not appear all that "stressed out." In fact, James Marcia (1980) found that these active identity seekers feel much better about themselves and their futures than do age-mates in the diffusion and foreclosure statuses. Yet, Erikson was right in characterizing identity achievement as a very healthy and adaptive development, for identity achievers do enjoy higher self-esteem and are less self-conscious or preoccupied with personal concerns than their counterparts in the other three identity statuses (Adams, Abraham, & Markstrom, 1987).

What may be most painful or "crisislike" about identity seeking is a long-term failure to establish one. Erikson believed that these individuals would eventually become depressed and lacking in self-confidence as they drift aimlessly, trapped in the "diffusion" status. Or alternatively, they might heartily embrace what Erikson called a *negative identity*, becoming a "black sheep," a "delinquent," or a "loser." Why? Because for these foundering souls, it is better to become everything that one is not supposed to be than to have no identity at all (Erikson, 1963). Indeed, many adolescents who are stuck in the diffusion status are highly apathetic and do express a sense of hopelessness about the future (Waterman & Archer, 1990). Others who enter high school with very low self-esteem often drift into delinquency and view their deviant self-image as having provided them with a boost in self-worth (Brynner, O'Malley, & Bachman, 1981; Wells, 1989). So it seems that a minority of adolescents and young adults experience what might be termed an identity *crisis* after all.

Influences on Identity Formation

The adolescent's progress toward identity achievement is influenced by at least four factors: cognitive growth, parenting, schooling, and the broader social-cultural context.

Cognitive Influences

Cognitive development plays an important role in identity achievement. Adolescents who have achieved solid mastery of formal-operational thought are now better able to imagine and contemplate future identities and are more likely to raise and resolve identity issues than those who are less intellectually mature (Boyes & Chandler, 1992; Waterman, 1992). Moreover, Michael Berzonsky (1992) finds that adolescents in the moratorium and achievement statuses adopt an information-processing style that involves actively seeking out relevant information rather than relying on others for guidance (as foreclosed adolescents tend to do) or putting off decisions and making impulsive choices at the last minute (as adolescents in the diffusion status tend to do). Adolescents in the moratorium status also seem to be especially open to the playful and creative experimenting that is so critical to identity formation (Bilsker & Marcia, 1991).

Parenting Influences

The relationships that adolescents have with their parents can affect their progress at forging an identity (Markstrom-Adams, 1992; Waterman, 1982). Adolescents in the diffusion status of identity formation are more likely than those in the other categories to be neglected or rejected by their parents and to be distant from them. Perhaps it is difficult to establish one's own identity without first having the opportunity to identify with respected parental figures and take on some of their desirable qualities. At the other extreme, adolescents categorized as being in the identity fore-closure status appear to be extremely close—possibly too close—to their relatively controlling parents. Foreclosed adolescents may never question parental authority or feel any need to forge a separate identity.

By contrast, students who are classified in the moratorium and identity achieve-ment statuses appear to have a solid base of affection at home, combined with con-siderable freedom to be individuals in their own right (Grotevant & Cooper, 1986). In family discussions, for example, these adolescents experience a sense of closeness and mutual respect while feeling free to disagree with their parents. So the same lov-ing and democratic style of parenting that fosters academic achievement and helps children gain a strong sense of self-esteem is also associated with healthy and adap-tive identity outcomes in adolescence.

Scholastic Influences

Does attending college help one to forge an identity? The answer is yes—and no. Attending college does seem to push people toward setting career goals and making stable occupational commitments (Waterman, 1982); but college students are often far behind their working peers in terms of establishing firm political and religious identities (Munro & Adams, 1977). In fact, some collegians will regress from iden-tity achievement to the moratorium or even the diffusion status in certain areas, most notably religion. But let's not be too critical of the college environment, for, like col-lege students, many adults later reopen the question of "who they are" if exposed to people or situations that challenge old viewpoints and offer new alternatives (Water-man & Archer, 1990).

Social-Cultural Influences

Finally, identity formation is strongly influenced by the broader social and historical context in which it occurs—a point that Erikson himself emphasized. Indeed, the idea that adolescents should choose a personal identity after carefully exploring many options may well be peculiar to industrialized societies of the 20th century (Cote & Levine, 1988). As in past centuries, adolescents in many nonindustrialized societies today will simply adopt the adult roles they are expected to adopt, without any soul-searching or experimentation: Sons of farmers will become farmers; the children of fishermen will become (or perhaps marry) fishermen, and so on. For many of the world's adolescents, then, what Marcia calls identity foreclosure is probably the most adaptive route to adulthood.

On the other hand, the process of forging an identity may be especially difficult for members of minority racial and ethnic groups in modern industrialized societies. As Box 12-3 indicates, they face the additional task of establishing a positive ethnic identity.

 ## DEVELOPMENT OF SELF-CONTROL

Now that we have considered how developing children and adolescents gain infor-mation about the self, evaluate this information, and achieve an identity (or identi-ties), we will now examine yet another critical aspect of self: the development of *self-control*.

Developmentalists use the term **self-control** to refer to our ability to regulate our conduct and to *inhibit* actions (for example, rule violations) that we might otherwise be inclined to perform. Self-control is unquestionably an important attribute. If we had never learned to control our immediate impulses, we would constantly be at odds with other people for violating their rights, breaking rules, and failing to dis-play the patience and self-sacrifice that would permit us to achieve important *long-range* objectives (for example, earning a diploma). Although many theorists have commented on the development of self-control (for example, Bandura, 1986; Freud,

self-control: ability to regulate one's conduct and to inhibit actions that are unacceptable or that conflict with a goal.

BOX 12-3
Identity Formation among Minority Adolescents

*I*n addition to the identity issues that confront all adolescents, members of ethnic minority groups must also establish an *ethnic identity*—a personal identification with an ethnic group and its values and traditions (Phinney & Rosenthal, 1992). This is not always an easy task. As we saw earlier, some minority children may even identify at first with the culture's ethnic majority, apparently wanting to affiliate themselves with the group that has the most status in society (Spencer & Markstrom-Adams, 1990). One Latino adolescent who had done this said, "I remember I would not say I was Hispanic. My friends . . . were white and Oriental and I tried so hard to fit in with them" (Phinney & Rosenthal, 1992, p. 158).

The process of forming an ethnic identity seems to involve the same steps, or stages, as forming a vocational or a religious identity (Phinney & Rosenthal, 1992). Children and young adolescents often say that they identify with their racial or ethnic group because their parents and other members of the group influenced them to do so (foreclosure status) or because that is what they are and they have not given the issue much thought (diffusion status). But between ages 16 and 19, many minority youths move into the moratorium or achievement phases of ethnic identity. And this is a very positive development, for minority adolescents who have explored and committed themselves to the values of their ethnic group tend to enjoy higher self-esteem and better peer relations than those who are still ethnically "diffuse" or "foreclosed" (Phinney, 1989; Phinney & Rosenthal, 1992).

Interestingly, minority adolescents often lag behind their majority-group peers at resolving other, more traditional identity issues. Why is this? Spencer and Markstrom-Adams (1990) suggest several possibilities. For one thing, minority adolescents may come to realize that prejudice and discrimination in society may limit their educational and vocational prospects, thus causing them to be less than optimistic about the future and hindering their establishment of an occupational identity (Ogbu, 1988). In addition, minority youths frequently encounter conflicts between the values of their subculture and those of the majority culture, and members of their subcultural communities (especially peers) often discourage identity explorations that clash with the social traditions of their own group. Virtually all North American minorities have a term for community members who are "too white" in orientation, be it the "apple" (red on the outside, white on the inside) for Native Americans, the Hispanic "coconut," the Asian "banana," or the African-American "Oreo." Minority adolescents must decide what

they are inside. Biracial adolescents sometimes face even greater dilemmas: They may, for example, be pressured to choose between African-American and white peer groups and not allowed to achieve an identity as *both* African-American and Anglo (Kerwin, Ponterotto, Jackson, & Harris, 1993). In view of these conflicts, many minority youths may find it more adaptive in the short run to "foreclose" on identity issues and simply adopt the beliefs of their own group. Here is where the process of forming a mature *ethnic* identity is so very important, for minority adolescents who have already resolved these majority/minority value conflicts and achieved a stable ethnic identity are likely to resolve other identity issues successfully as well (Phinney & Rosenthal, 1992).

How can we help minority youths to forge positive ethnic identities? Their parents can play a major role by (1) teaching them about their group's cultural traditions and fostering ethnic pride, (2) preparing them to deal constructively with the prejudices and value conflicts they may encounter, and (3) simply being warm and democratic confidants (Knight et al., 1993; Rosenthal & Feldman, 1992). Schools and communities can also help by promoting a greater understanding and appreciation of ethnic diversity, starting early in the preschool years, and by continuing their efforts to ensure that educational and economic opportunities are extended to all (Spencer & Markstrom-Adams, 1990).

Forging a positive ethnic identity is an adaptive development for minority youths.

1935/1960; Kopp, 1987; Mischel, 1986), all of them make two assumptions: (1) young children's behavior is almost completely controlled by external agents (for example, parents); (2) over time, some of this control is *internalized* as children adopt standards, or norms, that stress the value of self-control and acquire self-regulatory skills that permit them to adhere to these prescriptions.

Emergence of Self-Control in Early Childhood

When do children first display any evidence of self-regulation and self-control? Most theorists assume that these milestones occur at some point during the second year, after infants realize that they are separate, autonomous beings and that their actions have consequences that *they* have produced. In Chapter 11, we discussed one such example of early *self-regulation*: lip compressing and brow knitting by 1–2-year-olds who are attempting to *control* their sadness and anger (Malatesta et al., 1989). But, on the whole, the 1–2-year-old's ability to monitor her behaviors and adjust them as necessary is very limited indeed (Bullock & Lutkenhaus, 1988).

By age 2, children are showing clear evidence of **compliance.** They are now aware of a caregiver's wishes and expectations and can voluntarily follow her requests and commands (Crockenberg & Litman, 1990; Schneider-Rosen & Wenz-Gross, 1990). They are also beginning to show clear signs of distress when they break things or otherwise do something that is prohibited, such as snitching a forbidden cookie (Cole, Barrett & Zahn-Waxler, 1992; Kochanska, 1993). Yet, their behavior is still largely *externally* controlled by the approval they anticipate for compliance and the disapproval they associate with noncompliance.

However, anyone who has ever spent much time with 2–3-year-olds knows that they can become extremely uncooperative and noncompliant upon entering a phase that parents sometimes call the "terrible twos." Indeed, 2–3-year-olds often appear *defiant*, ignoring or actively spurning others' commands and instructions and insisting that they can accomplish tasks on their own (Bullock & Lutkenhaus, 1990; Erikson, 1963). According to Erikson, these toddlers are struggling with the psychosocial conflict of **autonomy versus shame and doubt:** They are resolved to display their independence and self-determination by doing things their own way, even if that means being noncompliant and risking others' disapproval.

An autonomy-seeking toddler who refuses to comply may do so through **self-assertion** (simply refusing a command or request) or **defiance** (saying "NO!" and becoming angry or intensifying one's ongoing behavior). Susan Crockenberg and Cindy Litman (1990) find that the strategies that a caregiver uses to resolve autonomy conflicts with a self-assertive toddler play a major role in determining whether the child becomes negative and defiant toward authority figures or adopts a more cooperative and compliant posture that is likely to promote self-control. Specifically, mothers who reacted to their 2-year-olds' self-assertive refusals by intervening physically or threatening and criticizing were likely to elicit *defiance*, whereas those who took an initial "NO" as an opportunity to remain firm in their demands while offering a rationale for complying were likely to elicit *compliance*.

Young children's emerging ability to control their impulses becomes much clearer by the middle of the third year. In one *delay of gratification* study, Brian Vaughn and his associates (Vaughn, Kopp, & Krakow, 1984) presented 18–30-month-old toddlers with three challenges: (1) to refrain from touching a nearby toy telephone, (2) to not eat raisins hidden under a cup until told that they could, and (3) to not open a gift until the experimenter had finished her work. The child was then observed to see how long he or she could wait before succumbing to these powerful temptations. As shown in Figure 12-6, delay of gratification increased dramatically between 18 and 30 months of age. Moreover, there were clear individual differences in the ability of 30-month-olds to defer gratification; the single best predictor of this capacity for self-control was their level of language development: Linguistically advanced children delayed longer.

What Role Does Language Play in the Development of Self-Control?

While examining Vygotsky's *sociocultural theory* in Chapter 7, we learned that preschool children begin to use *private speech* to plan and regulate their problem-solving activities. Alexander Luria (1961), a student of Vygotsky's, was interested in determining the age at which children could first use language to *inhibit* a response when they tell themselves to. Of course, an ability to voluntarily inhibit behaviors is

compliance: the act of willfully obeying the requests or commands of others.

autonomy versus shame and doubt: the second of Erikson's psychosocial stages, in which toddlers either assert their wills and attend to their own basic needs or else become passive, dependent, and lacking in self-confidence.

self-assertion: noncompliant acts that are undertaken by children in the interest of doing things for themselves or otherwise establishing autonomy.

defiance: active resistance to others' requests or demands; noncompliant acts that are accompanied by anger and an intensification of ongoing behavior.

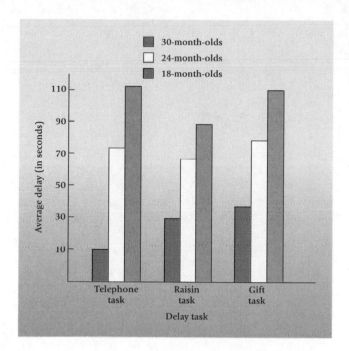

Figure 12-6
Average delay of gratification (in seconds) of 18-, 24-, and 30-month-olds exposed to three strong temptations.
Adapted from Vaughn, Kopp, & Krakow, 1984.

an important accomplishment that allows children to resist temptations and to forgo immediate gratifications in the service of more valuable long-term goals.

In Luria's research on language and self-control, 1½–5-year-olds were given a rubber bulb that they were to squeeze whenever the experimenter said "press" or instructed them to say "press." When the experimenter said "don't press," or instructed them to say "don't press," they were to quit squeezing the bulb. What Luria discovered is that children younger than 3 could not respond appropriately to their own self-instructions. In fact, if they were squeezing the bulb and heard "don't press" (either from themselves or from the experimenter), they often squeezed even faster! It is not that the young child intends to disobey, but rather that the inhibitory command "don't press" has a positive instructional component (the verb *press*) that seems to energize the ongoing response (Luria, 1961). Indeed, Eli Saltz and his associates (Saltz, Campbell, & Skotko, 1983) found that, the louder an adult's instruction to inhibit a response, the greater the likelihood that 3- and even 4-year-olds will continue to perform it, at least for short periods (see Figure 12-7). By contrast, 5–6-year-olds are more likely to respond appropriately to an adult's inhibitory commands, particularly if the command is loud or forceful.

So when do children begin to follow their *own* instructions to inhibit a response? Not until about age 5, according to Luria, who concluded that this is the time when language becomes a powerful instrument of *self*-control. Yet, Luria's research may well underestimate the self-regulating function of private speech. As Grazyna Kochanska (1993) points out, even 2–2½-year-olds will occasionally say things like "No" or "Don't" and then stop when they are about to commit a prohibited act, such as jumping on the sofa. And recall that the 2½-year-olds who were best able to delay immediate gratification in Vaughn's study were those who had progressed furthest in their language development. Nevertheless, we will see that Luria was right in one important respect: Older children are much better than younger ones at tailoring their self-instructions to the requirements of the task so that they can *effectively* regulate their conduct.

Delay of Gratification in Childhood and Adolescence

One of the more fruitful approaches for studying the development of self-control has been the **delay of gratification** paradigm. In a typical delay of gratification study, participants are offered a choice between a small incentive available immediately and a

delay of gratification: a form of self-control involving the capacity to inhibit impulses to seek small rewards that are available immediately in the interest of obtaining larger, delayed incentives.

Figure 12-7
Average number of impulsive responses by younger (3–4-year-old) and older (5–6-year-old) children as a function of the intensity of the verbal command not to respond.

From Saltz, Campbell, & Skotko, 1983.

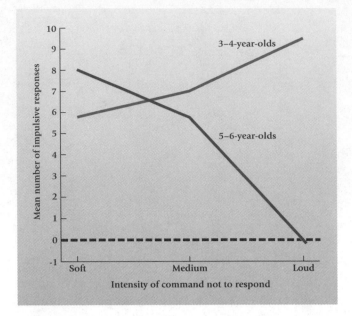

larger (or more desirable) incentive for which they must wait. What these studies find is that (1) preschool children find it exceedingly difficult to be patient when the smaller incentives they must resist are in plain sight, although (2) they do become better and better at delaying gratification over the grade school years, eventually showing a strong preference to wait for larger delayed incentives by age 10 to 12 (Mischel, 1986). Why does this aspect of self-control improve so dramatically with age? Let's consider two possibilities.

Knowledge of Delay Strategies

In an early delay of gratification study, Walter Mischel and Ebbe Ebbesen (1970) found that 3–5-year-olds simply cannot keep their minds off tempting objects for long. The children in this study were told that, if they waited 15 minutes, they would receive a very attractive snack; but, if they couldn't wait that long, they could signal the experimenter by ringing a bell and would receive a less desirable snack. When both kinds of snacks were visible during the delay period, preschoolers waited an average of only a minute or two before losing their patience, signaling the experimenter, and receiving the less desirable treat. Indeed, only a handful of children were able to wait the entire 15-minute delay period to earn the more valuable incentive. How did they do it? By covering their eyes, singing songs, inventing games, or otherwise *distracting* themselves from the temptations they faced.

However, it should be emphasized that the vast majority of preschoolers do *not* know that distraction can help them to resist immediate temptations. They can be *taught* by adults to use distractive strategies (Mischel & Patterson, 1976)—even very complex ones that require them to mentally transform tempting objects (for example, marshmallows) into less tempting stimuli (for example, white, puffy clouds)—to help them maintain their resolve (Mischel & Baker, 1975). But they do not generate these distractive strategies on their own. In fact, if it is suggested to them that they might become more patient by choosing a self-instructional strategy, preschoolers are much more inclined to focus attention on the *desirable qualities* of the incentives they are trying to resist (Toner, 1981)—a very ineffective means of coping with the frustrations of a delay.

By age 6–8 most children realize that creating physical distractions (for example, by covering their eyes or the tempting objects) can help them to be more patient. And by age 11–12, they know that *abstract ideation* (that is, cognitive distractions such as the marshmallows-are-clouds transformation or even such untrue self-instructions

Instructing children that they can be patient is an important step parents can take to foster self-control and delay of gratification.

as "I hate marshmallows") can reduce their frustrations and make waiting easier (Mischel & Mischel, 1983). Why does awareness of abstract ideation take so long to develop? Probably because it rests on hypothetical transformations of present realities—a formal-operational ability. Younger children can use abstract ideation if adults supply these distractors for them, but they will not generate them on their own. So one reason why self-control improves over the grade school years is that children learn more about *effective* means of regulating their thinking and conduct.

Self-Control as a Valued Attribute

Another reason why older children and adolescents are better able to delay gratification, to comply with rules, or to otherwise control their impulses is that they are internalizing norms that stress the value of self-regulation and self-control. Evidence of this can be seen in the self-descriptions of preadolescents and adolescents. When asked what they like about themselves, adolescents often mention conduct that reflects their self-discipline (for example, being persistent at pursuing their goals or being slow to lose their tempers), and teenagers are often quite concerned about breakdowns in self-control (for example, blowing up at someone over nothing or failing to complete their homework) (Rosenberg, 1979). So by early adolescence, a capacity for self-control is viewed as a highly desirable and almost obligatory attribute that many teenagers hope to incorporate into their own self-concepts.

Could we, then, foster children's self-control by working on their self-concepts—that is, by trying to convince them that they can be patient, persistent, honest, and even-tempered whenever they have shown some signs of displaying these attributes? Might children who are labeled "honest" or "patient" incorporate these attributions into their self-concepts and try to live up to this new self-image? Indeed, they may. Nace Toner and his associates (1980) attempted to influence children's self-concepts by labeling them as "patient" individuals. Before commencing a typical delay of gratification experiment, the experimenter casually mentioned to half of the 5½–9-year-old participants "I hear that you are patient because you can wait for nice things when you can't get them right away." The remaining children heard a task-irrelevant attribution: "I hear that you have some very nice friends." The results were clear: Even when no one was present to monitor their conduct, children who had been labeled as "patient" were able to delay gratification far longer than those who had been labeled as having nice friends. So in addition to suggesting effective self-instructional strategies for regulating conduct, it appears that adults can promote self-control by bolstering children's images of themselves as patient, honest, or otherwise self-disciplined individuals (see also Casey & Burton, 1982).

Early Self-Control as a Predictor of Later Life Outcomes

Developmentalists who study self-control cannot help but notice that some children are much more self-disciplined than others. Indeed, individual differences in compliance with rules and requests are already quite apparent by age 2; and relatively noncompliant toddlers with mothers who are either emotionally unresponsive or are critical and forceful with them (and who remain that way over time) are likely to become *defiant* and will often continue to display undercontrolled aggressive and disruptive behaviors from the preschool period throughout early adolescence (Beckwith, Rodning, & Cohen, 1992; Shaw, Keenan, & Vondra, 1994). So there is reason to believe that a lack of self-discipline early in life can be a very maladaptive attribute. Do children who display early evidence of self-control experience more favorable life outcomes?

Indeed they may. Walter Mischel and his associates have recently conducted 10-year follow-up studies of subjects who had participated as preschoolers in Mischel's early delay of gratification experiments. In the follow-ups, parents of Mischel's subjects completed questionnaires in which they described the competencies and shortcomings of their adolescent sons and daughters. These descriptions were highly informative. Apparently, self-control is a reasonably stable attribute, for adolescents who had been unable to delay gratification for long during the preschool years were the ones whom parents were now most likely to characterize as impatient and impulsive (Shoda, Mischel, & Peake, 1990). Adolescents who had been better at delaying gratification 10 years earlier were generally described in more favorable terms (that is, more academically competent, more socially skilled, more confident and self-reliant, and better able to cope with stress) than their counterparts who had shown less self-control as preschoolers (Mischel, Shoda, & Peake, 1988; Shoda et al., 1990). And, consistent with the parents' reports of their teenagers' academic competencies, adolescents who had displayed the most self-control as preschoolers were the ones who made the highest scores on the Scholastic Aptitude Test (SAT) (Shoda et al., 1990).

Perhaps we can now appreciate why developmentalists consider the establishment of self-regulatory skills and the emergence of self-control to be such important devel-

---

Concept Check 12-3 ∨ Establishing an Identity and a Sense of Self-Control

Check your understanding of identity formation and the development of self-control by matching each descriptive statement below with one of the following concepts: (a) moratorium; (b) identity foreclosure; (c) identity diffusion; (d) ethnic identity achievement; (e) self-assertion; (f) defiance; (g) delay of gratification; (h) private speech/self-instructions. Answers appear in the Appendix.

_____ 1. Thought to be an adaptive route to identity formation in many nonindustrialized cultures.

_____ 2. Healthier form of noncompliance among autonomy-seeking toddlers.

_____ 3. Noncompliance fostered by parents' threatening or forceful disciplinary styles.

_____ 4. Adolescents displaying this identity status often feel neglected or rejected by their parents.

_____ 5. Mechanism used by children to regulate and control their conduct.

_____ 6. Early predictor of favorable life outcomes.

_____ 7. Solid mastery of formal operations may promote this identity status.

_____ 8. Adaptive development that helps those who attain it to resolve other identity issues.

opmental hurdles. Not only is self-control a reasonably stable characteristic (see also Block & Block, 1980), but it is reliably associated with the very attributes (cognitive competencies, social skills, self-confidence, self-reliance) that forecast high self-esteem in adolescence (Harter, 1990) and occupational success and general life satisfaction throughout adulthood (Hunter & Hunter, 1984; Vaillant, 1983). So one's capacity for self-control does appear to be a crucial component of this entity we call the "self"— a conclusion we will reach over and over again as we discuss such topics as aggression, altruism, moral development, and peer relations.

 ## THE OTHER SIDE OF SOCIAL COGNITION: KNOWING ABOUT OTHERS

Being appropriately "social" requires us to interact with other people, and these interactions are more likely to be harmonious if we know what our social partners are thinking or feeling and can predict how they are likely to behave. The development of children's knowledge about other people—their descriptions of others' characteristics and the inferences that they make about others' thoughts and behaviors—constitutes perhaps the largest area of social-cognitive research. And there are so many questions to be answered. For example, what kinds of information do children use to form impressions of others? How do these impressions change over time? And what skills do children acquire that might explain such changes in person perception? These are the issues that we will now explore.

Age Trends in Person Perception

Children younger than 7 or 8 are likely to characterize people they know in the same concrete, observable terms that they use to describe the self (Livesley & Bromley, 1973; Peevers & Secord, 1973). Five-year-old Jenny, for example, said: "My daddy is big. He has hairy legs and eats mustard. Yuck! My daddy likes dogs—do you?" Not much of a personality profile there! When young children do use a psychological term to describe others, it is typically a very general attribute such as "He's *nice*" or "She's *mean*" that they may use more as a label for the other person's recent behavior than as a description of the person's enduring qualities (Rholes, Jones, & Wade, 1988; Rholes & Ruble, 1984).

It's not that preschoolers have *no* appreciation for the inner qualities that people possess. Three- to 5-year-olds typically assume that others' actions reflect definite motives or intentions (Miller & Aloise, 1989), and they are well aware of how their closest peer companions typically behave in a variety of different situations (Eder, 1989). For example, kindergarteners already know that their classmates differ in academic competencies and social skills; moreover, they reliably choose the "smart" ones as teammates for academic competitions and the "socially skilled" classmates as partners for play activities (Droege & Stipek, 1993; see also Dozier, 1991). Nevertheless, it appears that traitlike descriptions are often less meaningful for younger children than for older ones. Five- to 7-year-olds are not especially interested in playing with a child merely because he is "nice"; but describe the same child as owning an attractive toy and his popularity skyrockets. By contrast, 9-year-olds are much more inclined to want to play with a child described as "nice" than with one whose most noteworthy quality is owning an attractive toy (Boggiano, Klinger, & Main, 1986).

Between ages 7 and 16, children come to rely less and less on concrete attributes and more on psychological descriptors to characterize their friends and acquaintances. These changes are nicely illusrated in a program of research by Carl Barenboim (1981), who asked 6–11-year-olds to describe three persons they know well. Rather than simply listing the behaviors that close companions display, 6–8-year-olds often *compared* others on noteworthy behavioral dimensions, making such statements as "Billy *runs faster* than Jason" or "She *draws the best* pictures in our whole class." As

Figure 12-8

Percentages of descriptive statements classified as behavioral comparisons, psychological (traitlike) constructs, and psychological comparisons for children between the ages of 6 and 11.

From Barenboim, 1981.

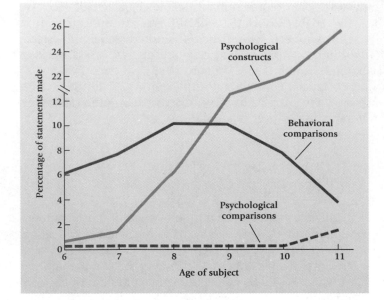

shown in Figure 12-8, use of these **behavioral comparisons** increased between ages 6 and 8 and declined rapidly after age 9. One outgrowth of the behavioral comparison process is that children become increasingly aware of regularities in a companion's behavior and eventually begin to attribute them to stable **psychological constructs,** or traits, that the person is now presumed to have. So a 10-year-old who formerly described one of her acquaintances as drawing best of anyone in her class may now convey the same impression by saying that the acquaintance is "very artistic." Notice in reexamining the figure that children's use of these psychological constructs increased rapidly between ages 8 and 11—the same period when behavioral comparisons became less common. Eventually, children begin to compare and contrast others on important psychological *dimensions,* making statements such as "Bill is more shy than Ted" or "Susie is the most artistic person in our class." Although few 11-year-olds generate these **psychological comparisons** when describing others, the majority of 12–16-year-olds in Barenboim's second study were actively comparing their associates on noteworthy psychological dimensions.

By age 14 to 16, adolescents are not only aware of the dispositional similarities and dissimilarities that characterize their acquaintances, they are also beginning to recognize that any number of situational factors (for example, illness, family strife) can cause a person to act "out of character" (Damon & Hart, 1988). So by midadolescence, young people are becoming sophisticated "personality theorists" who are able to look both inside and outside a companion to explain her conduct and form coherent impressions of her character.

Why do children progress from behavioral comparisons, to psychological constructs, to psychological comparisons? Why do their own self-concepts and their impressions of others become increasingly integrated and abstract over time? In addressing these issues, we will first examine two "cognitive" points of view before considering how social forces might contribute, both directly and indirectly, to the growth of social cognition.

Theories of Social-Cognitive Development

Cognitive Theories of Social Cognition

The two cognitive theories that are most often used to explain developmental trends in social cognition are Piaget's cognitive-developmental approach and Robert Selman's role-taking analysis.

behavioral comparisons phase: the tendency to form impressions of others by comparing and contrasting their overt behaviors.

psychological constructs phase: tendency to base one's impressions of others on the stable traits these individuals are presumed to have.

psychological comparisons phase: tendency to form impressions of others by comparing and contrasting these individuals on abstract psychological dimensions.

Cognitive-developmental theory. According to cognitive-developmental theorists, the ways that children think about the self and other people largely depend on their own levels of cognitive development. Recall that the thinking of 3–6-year-old "pre-operational" children tends to be static and to center on the most salient perceptual aspects of stimuli and events. So it would hardly surprise a Piagetian to find that 4–6-year-olds describe their associates in very concrete, observable terms, mentioning their appearances and possessions, their likes and dislikes, and the actions that they can perform.

The thinking of 7–10-year-olds will change in many ways as these youngsters enter Piaget's concrete-operational stage. For example, egocentrism is becoming less pronounced, so that children may begin to appreciate that other people have points of view that differ from their own. Concrete operators are also *decentering* from perceptual illusions, becoming more proficient at *classifying* objects and events, and beginning to recognize that certain properties of an object remain unchanged despite changes in the object's appearance *(conservation)*. Clearly, these emerging abilities to look beyond immediate appearances and to infer underlying invariances might help to explain why 7–10-year-olds, who are actively comparing themselves with their peers, become more attuned to regularities in their own and others' conduct and use psychological constructs, or traits, to describe these patterns.

By age 12 to 14, children are entering formal operations and are now able to think more logically and systematically about abstractions. Although the concept of a psychological trait is itself an abstraction, it is based on regularities in concrete, observable behaviors, perhaps explaining why *concrete* operators can think in these terms. However, a trait *dimension* is even more of a mental inference or abstraction that has few if any concrete referents. Thus, the ability to think in dimensional terms and to reliably order people along these continua (as is necessary in making psychological comparisons) implies that a person is able to operate on abstract concepts—a formal-operational ability (O'Mahoney, 1989).

Although children do begin to make behavioral comparisons at ages 6–8 and psychological comparisons at age 12—precisely the times that Piaget's theory implies that they should—Robert Selman (1980) believes that there is one particular aspect of cognitive development that underlies a mature understanding of the self and other people—the growth of **role-taking** skills.

Selman's role-taking theory. According to Selman (1980; Yeates & Selman, 1989), children gain much richer understandings of themselves and other people as they acquire the ability to discriminate their own perspectives from those of their companions and to see the relationships between these potentially discrepant points of view. Simply stated, Selman believes that, in order to "know" a person, one must be able to assume his perspective and understand his thoughts, feelings, motives, and intentions—in short, the *internal* factors that account for his behavior. If a child has not yet acquired these important role-taking skills, she may have little choice but to describe her acquaintances in terms of their external attributes—that is, their appearance, their activities, and the things they possess.

Selman has studied the development of role-taking skills by asking children to comment on a number of interpersonal dilemmas. Here is one example (from Selman, 1976, p. 302):

> Holly is an 8-year-old girl who likes to climb trees. She is the best tree climber in the neighborhood. One day while climbing down from a tall tree, she falls . . . but does not hurt herself. Her father sees her fall. He is upset and asks her to promise not to climb trees any more. Holly promises.
>
> Later that day, Holly and her friends meet Shawn. Shawn's kitten is caught in a tree and can't get down. Something has to be done right away or the kitten may fall. Holly is the only one who climbs trees well enough to reach the kitten and get it down but she remembers her promise to her father.

role taking: the ability to assume another person's perspective and understand his or her thoughts, feelings, and behaviors.

Table 12-3   Selman's Stages of Social Perspective Taking

Stage of role taking	Typical responses to the "Holly" dilemma
0. Egocentric or undifferentiated perspective (roughly 3 to 6 years) Children are unaware of any perspective other than their own. They assume that whatever they feel is right for Holly to do will be agreed on by others.	Children often assume that Holly will save the kitten. When asked how Holly's father will react to her transgression, these children think he will be "happy because he likes kittens." In other words, these children like kittens themselves, and they assume that Holly and her father also like kittens.
1. Social-informational role taking (roughly 6 to 8 years) Children now recognize that people can have perspectives that differ from their own but believe that this happens *only* because these individuals have received different information.	When asked whether Holly's father will be angry because she climbed the tree, the child may say "If he didn't know why she climbed the tree, he would be angry. But if he knew why she did it, he would realize that she had a good reason."
2. Self-reflective role taking (roughly 8 to 10 years) Children now know that their own and others' points of view may conflict even if they have received the same information. They are now able to consider the other person's viewpoint. They also recognize that the other person can put himself in their shoes, so that they are now able to anticipate the person's reactions to their behavior. However, the child cannot consider his own perspective and that of another person at the same time.	If asked whether Holly will climb the tree, the child might say "Yes. She knows that her father will understand why she did it." In so doing, the child is focusing on the father's consideration of Holly's perspective. But if asked whether the father would want Holly to climb the tree, the child usually says no, thereby indicating that he is now assuming the father's perspective and considering the father's concern for Holly's safety.
3. Mutual role taking (roughly 10 to 12 years) The child can now simultaneously consider her own and another person's points of view and recognize that the other person can do the same. The child can also assume the perspective of a disinterested third party and anticipate how each participant (self and other) will react to the viewpoint of his or her partner.	At this stage, a child might describe the outcome of the "Holly" dilemma by taking the perspective of a disinterested third party and indicating that she knows that both Holly and her father are thinking about what each other is thinking. For example, one child remarked: "Holly wanted to get the kitten because she likes kittens, but she knew that she wasn't supposed to climb trees. Holly's father knew that Holly had been told not to climb trees, but he couldn't have known about [the kitten]."
4. Societal role taking (roughly 12 to 15 and older) The adolescent now attempts to understand another person's perspective by comparing it with that of the social system in which he operates (that is, the view of the "generalized other"). In other words, the adolescent expects others to consider and typically assume perspectives on events that most people in their social group would take.	When asked if Holly should be punished for climbing the tree, the stage 4 adolescent is likely to say "No" and claim that the value of humane treatment of animals justifies Holly's act and that most fathers would recognize this point.

Source: Adapted from Selman, 1976.

To assess how well a child understands the perspectives of Holly, her father, and Shawn, Selman asks: Does Holly know how Shawn feels about the kitten? How will Holly's father feel if he finds out that she climbed the tree? What does Holly think her father will do if he finds out that she climbed the tree? What would you do? Children's responses to these probing questions led Selman to conclude that role-taking skills develop in a stagelike manner, as shown in Table 12-3.

Notice in examining the table that children progress from largely egocentric beings, who may be unaware of any perspective other than their own (stage 0), to sophisticated social-cognitive theorists, who can keep several perspectives in mind and compare each with the viewpoint that "most people" would adopt (stage 4). Apparently, these role-taking skills represent a true developmental sequence, for 40

Table 12-4 Percentages of Children and Adolescents at Each of Selman's Role-Taking Stages as a Function of Their Level of Cognitive Development

| | Role-taking stage | | | | |
Piaget's stage	0 Egocentric	1 Social-informational	2 Self-reflective	3 Mutual	4 Societal
Preoperational	80	20	0	0	0
Concrete operations	0	14	32	50	4
Transitional (late concrete)	1	3	42	43	10
Early formal operations	0	6	6	65	24
Consolidated formal operations	0	12	0	38	50

Sources: Based on Keating & Clark, 1980; and Selman & Byrne, 1974.

of 41 boys who were repeatedly tested over a five-year period showed a steady forward progression from stage to stage with no skipping of stages (Gurucharri & Selman, 1982). Perhaps the reason that they develop in one particular order is that they are closely related to Piaget's invariant sequence of cognitive stages (Keating & Clark, 1980). As we see in Table 12-4, preoperational children are at Selman's first or second level of role taking (stage 0 or 1), whereas most concrete operators are at the third or fourth level (stage 2 or 3), and many formal operators have reached the fifth and final level of role taking (stage 4).

Role taking and thinking about relationships. As children acquire role-taking skills, their understandings of the meaning and character of human relationships begin to change. Consider what children of different ages say about the meaning of *friendship.*

Preschoolers at Selman's egocentric stage (stage 0) think that virtually any pleasant interactions between themselves and available playmates qualify those playmates as "friends." Thus, 5-year-old Chang might describe Terry as a close friend simply because "He lives next door and plays games with me" (Damon, 1977).

Common activity continues to be the principal basis for friendship among 6–8-year-olds (Hartup, 1992). But because these youngsters have reached Selman's stage 1 and recognize that others may not always share their perspectives, they begin to view a friend as someone who *chooses* to "do nice things for me." Friendships are often one-way at this stage, for the child feels no strong pressure to reciprocate these considerations. And should a friend fail to serve the child's interests (for example, by spurning an invitation to camp out in the backyard), she may quickly become a nonfriend.

Later, at Selman's stage 2, 8–10-year-olds show increasing concern for the needs of a friend and begin to see friendships as reciprocal relationships, based on *mutual trust,* in which two people exchange respect, kindness, and affection (Furman & Bierman, 1983; Selman, 1980). No longer are common activities sufficient to brand someone a friend; as children appreciate how their own interests and perspectives and those of their peers can be similar or different, they insist that their friends be *psychologically* similar to themselves.

By early adolescence, many children have reached Selman's stage 3 or 4. Although they still view friends as psychologically similar people who like, trust, and assist each other, they have expanded their notions of the obligations of friendship to emphasize the exchange of *intimate* thoughts and feelings (Berndt & Perry, 1990). They increasingly expect their friends to stick up for them and be *loyal,* standing ready to provide close emotional support whenever they may need it (Berndt & Perry, 1990; Buhrmester, 1990).

So, with the growth of role-taking skills, children's conceptions of friendship gradually change from the one-sided, self-centered view of friends as "people who benefit me" to a harmonious, reciprocal perspective in which each party truly understands the other, enjoys providing him or her with emotional support and other niceties, and expects these same considerations in return. Perhaps because they rest on a firmer basis of intimacy and interpersonal understanding, the close friendships of older children and adolescents are viewed as more important and are more stable, or long-lasting, than those of younger children (Berndt, 1989; Berndt & Hoyle, 1985; Furman & Buhrmester, 1992).

Role taking and social status. A child's role-taking skills may also affect his or her general status in the peer group. Lawrence Kurdek and Donna Krile (1982) found that the most popular children among groups of third- to eighth-graders are those who have well-developed role-taking skills. Moreover, highly sociable children and those who have established intimate friendships score higher on tests of role-taking abilities than their less sociable classmates and those without close friends (LeMare & Rubin, 1987; McGuire & Weisz, 1982).

Why might mature role takers enjoy such a favorable status in the peer group? A study by Lynne Hudson and her associates (Hudson, Forman, & Brion-Meisels, 1982) provides one clue. Second-graders who had tested either high or low in role-taking ability were asked to teach two kindergarten children how to make caterpillars out of construction paper. As each tutor worked with the kindergartners, his or her behavior was videotaped for later analysis. Hudson et al. found that all the older tutors were willing to assist their younger pupils if the kindergartners *explicitly asked for help*. However, good role takers were much more likely than poor role takers to respond to a kindergartner's subtle or *indirect* requests for help. For example, exaggerated straining with scissors and frequent glances at the tutor usually elicited a helpful response from a good role taker but nothing more than a smile from a poor role taker. Apparently, good role takers are better able to infer the needs of their companions so that they can respond accordingly—an ability that may help to explain why they are so popular with their peers and quite successful at establishing close friendships.

Social Influences on Social-Cognitive Development

Recently, developmentalists have wondered whether the growth of children's self-awareness and their understanding of other people are as closely tied to cognitive development as social-cognitive theorists have assumed. Consider, for example, that even though children's role-taking abilities are related to their performances on Piagetian measures and IQ tests (Pellegrini, 1985), it is quite possible for a child to grow less egocentric and to mature intellectually without becoming an especially skillful role taker (Shantz, 1983). Thus, there must be other, *noncognitive* factors that contribute to the growth of role-taking skills and that may even exert their own unique effects on children's social-cognitive development. Might social experiences play such a role? No less an authority than Jean Piaget thought so.

Social experience as a contributor to role taking. Many years ago, Piaget (1965) argued that playful interactions among grade school children promote the development of role-taking skills and mature social judgments. Piaget's view was that, by assuming different roles while playing together, young children become more aware of discrepancies between their own perspectives and those of their playmates. When conflicts arise in play, children must learn to coordinate their points of view with those of their companions (that is, compromise) in order for play to continue. So Piaget assumed that equal-status contacts among peers are an important contributor to social perspective taking and the growth of interpersonal understanding.

Equal-status contacts with peers are important contributors to role-taking skills and the growth of interpersonal awareness.

Not only has research consistently supported Piaget's viewpoint (see, for example, Bridgeman, 1981), but it appears that some forms of peer contact may be better than others at fostering the growth of interpersonal understanding. Specifically, Janice Nelson and Francis Aboud (1985) propose that disagreements among *friends* are particularly important because children tend to be more open and honest with their friends than with mere acquaintances. As a result, disagreeing friends should be more likely than disagreeing acquaintances to provide each other with the information needed to understand and appreciate their conflicting points of view.

Nelson and Aboud tested their hypothesis by first administering a test of social awareness to two groups of 8–10-year-olds—pairs of friends and pairs of acquaintances. They then asked these friends and acquaintances to discuss one of the interpersonal issues on which they initially disagreed and retested the participants' social awareness after the discussions were over. As predicted, friends responded differently to their conflict than acquaintances did. Friends were much more critical of their partners but were also more likely to carefully explain the rationales for their own points of view—precisely the kind of information that might be expected to promote an understanding (and perhaps an appreciation) of each other's perspectives. Prior to the the discussions, pairs of friends and pairs of acquaintances made comparable scores on the social awareness test. But after the discussions, friends' final answers to the issue they had discussed were at a higher level of social understanding than their original answers, whereas the answers of acquaintances hadn't changed from pretest to posttest. So the results of this study seem to suggest that equal-status contacts among friends may be particularly important to the development of role-taking skills and interpersonal understanding.

Social experience as a direct contributor to person perception. Social contacts with peers not only contribute *indirectly* to person perception by fostering the development of role-taking skills, but they are also a form of *direct experience* by which children can learn what others are like. In other words, the more experience that a child has with peers, the more *motivated* she should be to try to understand them and the more *practiced* she should become at appraising the causes of their behavior (Higgins & Parsons, 1983).

Popularity is a convenient measure of social experience; that is, popular children interact more often with a wider variety of peers than do their less popular age-mates

(LeMare & Rubin, 1987). So, if the amount of direct experience that a child has with peers exerts its own unique influence on his or her social-cognitive judgments, then popular children should outperform less popular age-mates on tests of social understanding, *even when their cognitive abilities are comparable.* This is precisely what Jackie Gnepp (1989) found when she tested the ability of popular and less popular 8-year-olds to make personalized (psychological) inferences about an unfamiliar child from a small sample of the child's previous behaviors. So it seems that both social experience (as indexed by popularity) and cognitive competence (role-taking skills) contribute in their own way to the development of children's understanding of other people. Apparently, Cooley (1902) and Mead (1934) were quite correct in suggesting that social cognition and social experience are completely intertwined, that they develop together, are reciprocally related, and that neither can progress very far without the other.

SUMMARY

This chapter has traced the development of children's knowledge about the self and other people (that is, social cognition) and has focused on the growth of two personal attributes—achievement orientation and capacity for self-control—that are very important contributors to one's self-concept.

Most developmentalists believe that infants are born without a sense of self and gradually come to distinguish themselves from the external environment over the first 2–6 months of life. By 18–24 months of age, toddlers have formed stable self-images and have begun to categorize themselves along socially significant dimensions such as age and sex.

During the preschool period, children develop a *theory of mind*—an understanding of how the human mind works—that enables them to begin to distinguish their "public" self from their inner "private" self that is not available to others. Though preschoolers know how they typically behave in many contexts, their self-descriptions are typically very concrete, focusing on their physical features, possessions, and the activities they can perform. By about age 8, children begin to describe themselves in terms of their inner psychological attributes, and adolescents have an even more integrated and abstract conception of self that includes not only their dispositional qualities (that is, traits, beliefs, attitudes, and values) but a knowledge of how these characteristics might interact with each other and with situational influences to affect their behavior.

Self-esteem, the evaluative component of self, begins to crystalize at about age 8, as children evaluate their academic, social, behavioral, and physical competencies and construct a sense of general self-worth. Although children differ somewhat in the competencies that they consider most important, they frequently base their overall self-worth on their perceived academic, athletic, and social competencies. Some adolescents experience a decline in self-esteem; however, most teenagers cope rather well with the biological and social changes of adolescence, showing no decrease or even a modest increase over time in their perceived self-worth. Children are most likely to develop high self-esteem if (1) their parents are warm, supportive, and democratic in enforcing rules and (2) they fare well (in comparison with peers) in the competencies that they consider most important.

Children clearly differ in achievement motivation—that is, their willingness to strive for success and to master new challenges. Infants who are securely attached to responsive companions who provide them with a stimulating home environment are likely to become curious nursery school children who will later do well at school. Parents may also foster the development of achievement motivation by encouraging their children to do things on their own and to do them well and by reinforcing a child's successes without becoming overly distressed about an occasional failure. Parents who combine all of these practices into one parenting style (*authoritative par-*

enting) tend to raise children who seek challenges and who achieve considerable academic success.

Although children differ in achievement motivation, their academic self-concepts also depend very heavily on the causal attributions that they make for their successes and failures. Mastery-oriented children tend to attribute their successes to stable, internal causes (such as high ability) and their failures to unstable ones (lack of effort); consequently, they feel quite competent and will work hard to overcome failures. By contrast, helpless children often stop trying after a failure because they attribute their failures to stable, internal factors—most notably a lack of ability—that they feel they can do little about. Fortunately, these helpless children can become more mastery oriented if they are taught (through *attribution retraining*) that their failures can and often should be attributed to unstable causes, such as a lack of effort, that they can overcome.

One of the more challenging tasks of adolescence is forming a stable *identity* (or identities) with which to embrace the responsibilities of young adulthood. From the diffusion and foreclosure statuses, many college-age youths progress to the moratorium status (where they are experimenting to find an identity) and ultimately to identity achievement. Identity formation is an uneven process that often continues into adulthood and is fostered by such social experiences as interactions with warm, supportive parents who encourage individuality. Minority youths may be slower to achieve personal identities, owing, in part, to the conflicts they experience between their subcultures and the majority culture. But the vast majority of adolescents eventually forge a positive identity that helps them to face the challenges of adulthood.

Children's capacity for *self-control* is a major achievement that represents a shift from external, or environmental, control to internal *self-regulation* of conduct. Although 2-year-olds voluntarily comply with others' directives, their conduct is still largely externally controlled by the consequences that they anticipate for *compliance* (or noncompliance). But, by the middle of the third year, children are displaying an increasing capacity to regulate and control their own thinking and behavior—aided, in part, by private speech as a regulatory mechanism.

Delay of gratification is an important aspect of self-control that improves dramatically with age as children become more knowledgeable about effective delay strategies and internalize norms that stress the value of self-regulation and self-control. Indeed, self-control becomes an important component of adolescents' self-concepts. And preschoolers who have already developed a relatively strong capacity for delaying gratification tend to become self-disciplined adolescents whom parents describe as displaying attributes that contribute to high self-esteem and to favorable outcomes later in life.

Children younger than 7 or 8 are likely to describe friends and acquaintances in the same concrete observable terms (physical attributes and activities) that they use to describe the self. But as they compare themselves and others on noteworthy behavioral dimensions, they become more attuned to regularities in their own and others' conduct and begin to rely on stable psychological constructs, or traits, to describe these patterns. As they approach adolescence, their impressions of others become more abstract as they begin to compare and contrast their friends and acquaintances on a number of psychological dimensions. And by age 14 to 16, adolescents are becoming sophisticated "personality theorists" who know that any number of situational influences can cause a person to act "out of character."

The growth of children's social-cognitive abilities is related to cognitive development in general and to the emergence of role-taking skills in particular: To truly "know" a person, one must be able to assume her perspective and understand her thoughts, feelings, motives, and intentions. However, equal-status contacts with friends and peers are crucial to social-cognitive development: They contribute indirectly by fostering the growth of role-taking skills and directly by providing the experiences children need to learn what others are like.

Key Terms

achievement
  motivation [473]
attribution
  retraining [481]
attribution theory [478]
authoritative
  parenting [477]
autonomy versus shame
  and doubt [488]
behavioral comparisons
  phase [494]
belief-desire theory [467]
categorical self [465]
causal attributions [478]

compliance [488]
defiance [488]
delay of gratification [489]
effectance
  motivation [473]
entity view of ability [479]
foreclosure [483]
HOME inventory [476]
identity [482]
identity achievement [484]
identity crisis [471]
identity diffusion [483]
incremental view of
  ability [479]

learned helplessness
  orientation [480]
locus of control [478]
looking-glass self [463]
mastery orientation [479]
moratorium [483]
personal agency [464]
private self (or I) [466]
psychological comparisons
  phase [494]
psychological constructs
  phase [494]
public self (or me) [466]

role taking [495]
self [463]
self-assertion [488]
self-concept [464]
self-control [486]
self-esteem [469]
social comparison [471]
social cognition [463]
theory of mind [466]

Sex Differences and Sex-Role Development

13

Sex-role socialization begins very early as parents provide their infants with "gender-appropriate" clothing, toys, and hairstyles.

H ow important is a child's gender to his or her eventual development? The answer seems to be "Very important!" Often the first bit of information that parents receive about their child is his or her sex, and the question "Is it a boy or a girl?" is the very first one that most friends and relatives ask when proud new parents telephone to announce the birth of their baby (Intons-Peterson & Reddel, 1984). Indeed, the ramifications of this gender labeling are normally swift in coming and rather direct. In the hospital nursery or delivery room, parents often call an infant son things like "big guy" or "tiger," and they are likely to comment on the vigor of his cries, kicks, or grasps. By contrast, female infants are more likely to be labeled "sugar" or "sweetie" and described as soft, cuddly, and adorable (Maccoby, 1980; MacFarlane, 1977). A newborn infant is usually blessed with a name that reflects his or her sex, and in many Western societies children are immediately adorned in either blue or pink. Mavis Hetherington and Ross Parke (1975, pp. 354–355) describe the predicament of a developmental psychologist who "did not want her observers to know whether they were watching boys or girls":

> Even in the first few days of life some infant girls were brought to the laboratory with pink bows tied to wisps of their hair or taped to their little bald heads. . . . When another attempt at concealment of sex was made by asking mothers to dress their infants in overalls, girls appeared in pink and boys in blue overalls, and "Would you believe overalls with ruffles?"

This gender indoctrination continues during the first year as parents provide their children with "sex-appropriate" clothing, toys, and hairstyles (Pomerleau et al., 1990). Moreover, they often play differently with and expect different reactions from their young sons and daughters (Caldera, Huston, and O'Brien, 1989). So it is clear that a child's companions view gender as an important attribute and that gender often determines how they respond to him or her.

Why do people react differently to males and females—especially *infant* males and females? One explanation centers on the biological differences between the sexes. Recall that fathers determine the gender of their offspring. A zygote that has received an X chromosome from each parent is a genetic (XX) female that will develop into a baby girl, whereas a zygote that has received a Y chromosome from the father is a genetic (XY) male that will normally assume the appearance of a baby boy. Could it be that this basic genetic difference between the sexes is ultimately responsible for *sex differences in behavior* that might explain why parents often do not treat their sons and daughters alike? We will explore this interesting idea in some detail in a later section of the chapter.

However, there is more to sex differences than biological heritage. Virtually all societies expect males and females to behave differently and to assume different roles. In order to conform to these expectations, the child must understand that he is a boy or that she is a girl and must incorporate this information into his or her self-concept. In this chapter, we will concentrate on the interesting and controversial topic of **sex typing**—the process by which children acquire not only a gender identity but also the motives, values, and behaviors considered appropriate in their culture for members of their biological sex.*

We begin the chapter by summarizing what people generally believe to be true about sex differences in cognition, personality, and social behavior. As it turns out,

sex typing: the process by which a child becomes aware of his or her gender and acquires motives, values, and behaviors considered appropriate for members of that sex.

---

*Some writers have used the term *sex* when talking about biological differences between males and females, and the term *gender* when discussing masculine and feminine traits and behavioral preferences that are heavily influenced by social forces. This usage is *not* adopted here on the assumption that differences between males and females on any (and all) psychological attribute(s) could conceivably result from an interaction between biological predispositions and social influences. Thus, we use the terms *sex* and *gender* interchangeably and will reserve the term *sexual* for behavior that is directly linked to mating and genital activities.

some of these beliefs have an element of truth to them, although many others are best described as fictions or fables that have no basis in fact. We will then look at developmental trends in sex typing and see that youngsters are often well aware of sex-role stereotypes and display sex-typed patterns of behavior long before they are old enough to go to kindergarten. And how do children learn so much about the sexes and sex roles at such an early age? We will address this issue by reviewing several influential theories of sex typing that indicate how biological forces, social experiences, and cognitive development might combine or interact to influence the sex-typing process. And after examining a new perspective on sex typing that asserts that traditional sex roles have outlived their usefulness in today's modern society, we will conclude by briefly considering yet another aspect of development that is central to our concepts of self as males or females—the growth of human sexuality.

 ## CATEGORIZING MALES AND FEMALES: SEX-ROLE STANDARDS

Most of us have learned a great deal about males and females by the time we enter college. In fact, if you and your classmates were asked to jot down ten psychological dimensions on which men and women are thought to differ, it is likely that every member of the class could easily generate such a list. Here's a head start: Which gender is more likely to display emotions? to be tidy? to be competitive? to use harsh language?

A **sex-role standard** is a value, a motive, or a class of behavior that is considered more appropriate for members of one sex than the other. Taken together, a society's sex-role standards describe how males and females are expected to behave and, thus, reflect the stereotypes by which we categorize and respond to members of each sex.

The female's role as childbearer is largely responsible for the sex-role standards that have prevailed in many societies, including our own. Girls have typically been encouraged to assume an **expressive role** that involves being kind, nurturant, cooperative, and sensitive to the needs of others (Parsons, 1955). These psychological traits, it was assumed, prepare girls to play the wife and mother roles, keep the family functioning, and raise children successfully. By contrast, boys have been encouraged to adopt an **instrumental role,** for as a traditional husband and father, a male would face the tasks of providing for the family and protecting it from harm. Thus, young boys are expected to become dominant, assertive, independent, and competitive. Similar norms and role prescriptions are found in many, though certainly not all, societies (Williams & Best, 1990; Whiting & Edwards, 1988). In one rather ambitious project, Herbert Barry, Margaret Bacon, and Irving Child (1957) analyzed the sex-typing practices of 110 nonindustrialized societies, looking for sex differences in the socialization of five attributes: nurturance, obedience, responsibility, achievement, and self-reliance. The results are summarized in Table 13-1. Note that achievement and self-reliance were more often expected of young boys, whereas young girls were encouraged to become nurturant, responsible, and obedient.

Children in modern industrialized societies also face strong sex-typing pressures, though not always to the same extent and in the same ways that children in nonindustrialized societies do. (For example, parents in many Western societies place roughly equal emphasis on achievement for sons and for daughters; Lytton & Romney, 1991). Moreover, the findings in Table 13-1 do not imply that female self-reliance is frowned on or that disobedience by young males is acceptable. In fact, all five attributes that Barry et al. studied were encouraged of *both* boys and girls, but with different emphases on different attributes depending on the sex of the child (Zern, 1984). So it appears that the first goal of socialization is to encourage children to acquire those traits that will enable them to become well-behaved, contributing members of society. A second goal (but one that adults view as important nevertheless)

sex-role standard: a behavior, value, or motive that members of a society consider more typical or appropriate for members of one sex.

expressive role: a social prescription, usually directed toward females, that one should be cooperative, kind, nurturant, and sensitive to the needs of others.

instrumental role: a social prescription, usually directed toward males, that one should be dominant, independent, assertive, competitive, and goal oriented.

Table 13-1	Sex Differences in the Socialization of Five Attributes in 110 Societies	
	Percentage of societies in which socialization pressures were greater for:	
Attribute	**Boys**	**Girls**
Nurturance	0	82
Obedience	3	35
Responsibility	11	61
Achievement	87	3
Self-reliance	85	0

Note: The percentages for each attribute do not add to 100, because some of the societies did not place differential pressures on boys and girls with respect to that attribute. For example, 18% of the societies for which pertinent data were available did not differentiate between the sexes in the socialization of nurturance.
Source: Adapted from Barry, Bacon, & Child, 1957.

is to "sex type" the child by stressing the importance of relationship-oriented (or expressive) attributes for females and individualistic (or instrumental) ones for males.

Because cultural norms demand that females play an expressive role and males an intrumental role, we may be inclined to assume that females actually display expressive traits and that males possess instrumental traits (Broverman et al., 1972; Eagly, 1987; Williams & Best, 1990). If you are thinking these stereotypes have disappeared as attention to women's rights has increased and as more women have entered the labor force, think again. Although some change has occurred, adolescents and young adults still endorse most traditional stereotypes about men and women (Bergen & Williams, 1991; Lewin & Tragos, 1987; and test yourself in Box 13-1). Might these beliefs about sex differences have a basis in fact, then? Let's see if they do.

 ## SOME FACTS AND FICTIONS ABOUT SEX DIFFERENCES

The old French maxim "Vive la différence" reflects a fact that we all know to be true: Males and females are anatomically different. Adult males are typically taller, heavier, and more muscular than adult females, while females may be hardier in the sense that they live longer and are less susceptible to many diseases. But although these physical variations are fairly obvious, the evidence for sex differences in psychological functioning is not as clear as most of us might think.

Actual Psychological Differences between the Sexes

In a classic review of more than 1500 studies comparing males and females, Eleanor Maccoby and Carol Jacklin (1974) concluded that few traditional sex-role stereotypes have any basis in fact. Indeed, their review pointed to only four *small* but reliable

BOX 13-1
What Traits Characterize Males and Females?

Several recent surveys have asked college students to respond to lists of various mannerisms and personal characteristics by saying which of these traits characterize the "typical" man or "typical" woman (or by judging which are clearly "masculine" or clearly "feminine" attributes). Although you may not agree with peer consensus, see if you can anticipate how they have responded by indicating whether each trait in the list below is more characteristic of men or more characteristic of women. (The results of the survey are given at the bottom of the page.)

More characteristic of:

Trait	Men	Women
1. Active	___	___
2. Aware of others' feelings	___	___
3. Adventurous	___	___
4. Considerate	___	___
5. Aggressive	___	___
6. Creative	___	___
7. Ambitious	___	___
8. Cries easily	___	___
9. Competitive	___	___
10. Other-oriented	___	___
11. Dominant	___	___
12. Emotional	___	___

Trait	Men	Women
13. Independent	___	___
14. Artistic	___	___
15. Displays leadership	___	___
16. Excitable	___	___
17. Mathematical	___	___
18. Empathic	___	___
19. Makes decisions easily	___	___
20. Feelings hurt easily	___	___
21. Mechanical	___	___
22. Gentle	___	___
23. Outspoken	___	___
24. Kind	___	___
25. Persistent	___	___
26. Neat	___	___
27. Self-confident	___	___
28. Seeks approval	___	___
29. Skilled in business	___	___
30. Tactful	___	___
31. Takes a stand	___	___
32. Understanding	___	___

differences between the sexes that were consistently supported by research. Here are their conclusions, with some updates and amendments:

1. *Verbal ability.* Females have greater verbal abilities than males. Girls develop verbal skills at an earlier age than boys and display a small but consistent verbal advantage on tests of reading comprehension and speech fluency throughout childhood. However, girls' advantage on tests of general verbal ability has become smaller over the past 20 years—so small, in fact, that recent reviewers have branded it as negligible (Feingold, 1988; Hyde & Linn, 1988).

2. *Visual/spatial abilities.* Males outperform females on tests of **visual/spatial abilities**—that is, the ability to draw inferences about or to otherwise mentally manipulate pictorial information (see Figure 13-1 for two kinds of visual/spatial tasks on which sex differences have been found). The male advantage in spatial abilities is not large, although it is detectable by middle childhood and persists across the life span (Kerns and Berenbaum, 1991; Linn & Petersen, 1985).

Answers for Box 13-1: College students generally indicate that the even-numbered traits characterize women, whereas the odd-numbered ones are more characteristic of men. (Source for these traits: Ruble, 1983.)

visual/spatial abilities: the ability to mentally manipulate or otherwise draw inferences about pictorial information.

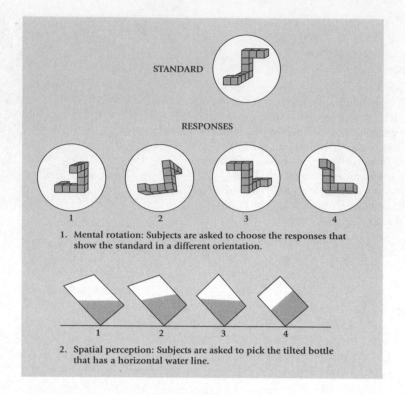

STANDARD

RESPONSES

1   2   3   4

1. **Mental rotation:** Subjects are asked to choose the responses that show the standard in a different orientation.

1   2   3   4

2. **Spatial perception:** Subjects are asked to pick the tilted bottle that has a horizontal water line.

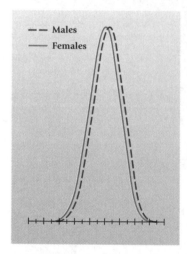

Figure 13-2
These two distributions of scores—one for males, one for females—give some idea of the size of the gap between the sexes in abilities for which sex differences are consistently found. Despite a small difference in average performance, the scores of males and females overlap considerably.
Adapted from Hyde, Fennema, & Lamon, 1990.

3. *Mathematical ability.* Beginning in adolescence, boys show a small but consistent advantage over girls on tests of *arithmetic reasoning* (Feingold, 1988; Hyde, Fennema, & Lamon, 1990; and see Figure 13-2). Girls actually exceed boys in computational skills; but boys have acquired more mathematical problem-solving strategies that enable them to outperform girls on complex word problems (Byrnes & Takahira, 1993). Interestingly, sex differences in math performance are most apparent at the *extremes* of the distribution, where more boys than girls are exceptionally talented and exceptionally poor in mathematics achievement (Feingold, 1992; Hyde et al., 1990).

4. *Aggression.* Finally, males are more physically and verbally *aggressive* than females, starting as early as age 2 (see also Eagly & Steffen, 1986).

Other researchers were quick to criticize Maccoby and Jacklin's review, claiming that the procedures they used to gather and tabulate their results led them to underestimate the number of sex differences that actually exist (Block, 1976; Huston, 1983). More recent research points to several additional sex differences that seem to be accurate.

5. *Activity level.* Boys are more physically active than girls (Eaton & Enns, 1986; Eaton & Yu, 1989), particularly when interacting with peers. Indeed, the heightened activity that boys display may help to explain why they are more likely than girls to initiate and to be receptive to bouts of nonaggressive, rough-and-tumble play (DiPietro, 1981; Humphreys & Smith, 1987).

6. *Fear, timidity, and risk-taking.* Girls consistently *report* being more fearful or timid in uncertain situations than boys do. Girls are also more cautious in such situations, taking far fewer risks than their male age-mates (Christophersen, 1989; Ginsburg & Miller, 1982).

7. *Developmental vulnerability.* From conception, boys are more physically vulnerable than girls to prenatal and perinatal stress and to the effects of disease. Boys are also more likely than girls to display a variety of developmental disorders, including reading disabilities, speech defects, hyperactivity, emotional disorders, and mental retardation (Henker & Whalen, 1989; Jacklin, 1989).

8. *Emotional sensitivity/expressivity.* From about age 4–5 on, girls and women appear to be more interested in and more responsive to infants than boys and men

Rough-and-tumble play is more common among boys than among girls.

are (Berman & Goodman, 1984; Reid, Tate, & Berman, 1989), and they rate themselves higher in nurturance and empathy as well (although they often appear no more empathic than boys and men in naturalistic settings; see, for example, Fabes, Eisenberg, & Miller, 1990). Parents talk more with girls than with boys about emotions and memorable emotional events (Kuebli & Fivush, 1992; Reese & Fivush, 1993), and girls and women characterize their emotions as deeper or more intense and feel freer to express them than do boys and men (Diener, Sandvik, & Larson, 1985; Fuchs & Thelen, 1988).

9. *Compliance.* Girls are more compliant than boys to the requests and demands of parents, teachers, and other authority figures (Maccoby, 1990). Moreover, girls are more likely to rely on tact and polite suggestions, rather than forceful or demanding strategies, when trying to persuade others to comply with them (Maccoby, 1990; Cowan & Avants, 1988).

In reviewing the evidence for "real" sex differences, we must keep in mind that the data reflect *group averages* that may or may not characterize the behavior of any particular individual. For example, gender accounts for about 5% of the variation children display in aggressive behavior (Hyde, 1984), so that the remaining 95% is due to differences between people other than their sex. Moreover, the sex differences in verbal, spatial, and mathematical abilities that Maccoby and Jacklin identified are also small—even smaller today than they were 20 years ago (Feingold, 1988; Hyde et al., 1990; and review Figure 13-2). Finally, gender variations that emerge in one cultural or social context may not be evident elsewhere (Daubman, Heatherington, & Ahn, 1992). For example, women do better on tests of mathematical ability, sometimes even outperforming men, in societies like Israel, where women have excellent opportunities in technical training and technical occupations (Baker & Jones, 1992). Findings such as these imply that sex differences in abilities are not biologically inevitable and that cultural influences play an important role in the development of males and females.

What, then, should we conclude about psychological differences between the sexes? Although contemporary scholars may quibble at times about which sex differences are real or meaningful (Eagly, 1995; Hyde & Plant, 1995), most developmentalists agree on this: *Males and females are far more psychologically similar than they are different*, and most of the well-documented differences seem to be modest. So it is impossible to accurately predict the aggressiveness, mathematical skills, activity level, or emotional expressivity of any individual simply by knowing his or her gender. Only when group averages are computed do the sex differences emerge.

Table 13-2 Some Unfounded Beliefs about Sex Differences

Beliefs	Facts
1. Girls are more "social" than boys.	The two sexes are equally interested in social stimuli, equally responsive to social reinforcement, and equally proficient at learning from social models. At certain ages, boys actually spend more time than girls with playmates.
2. Girls are more "suggestible" than boys.	Most studies of children's conformity find no sex differences. However, sometimes boys are more likely than girls to accept peer-group values that conflict with their own.
3. Girls have lower self-esteem than boys.	The sexes are highly similar in their overall self-satisfaction and self-confidence throughout childhood and adolescence. More boys than girls show gains in self-esteem over the course of adolescence, possibly reflecting the greater freedom and encouragement that males receive to pursue instrumental roles (Block & Robins, 1993). Yet, the personality characteristics that are associated with high and low levels of self-esteem among older adolescents are highly similar for the two sexes.
4. Girls are better at simple repetitive tasks, whereas boys excel at tasks that require higher-level cognitive processing.	The evidence does not support these assertions. Neither sex is superior at rote learning, probability learning, or concept formation.
5. Boys are more "analytic" than girls.	With the exception of the *small* sex differences in cognitive abilities that we have already discussed, boys and girls do *not* differ on tests of analytical or logical reasoning.
6. Girls lack achievement motivation.	No such differences exist! Perhaps the myth of lesser achievement motivation for females has persisted because males and females have generally directed their achievement strivings toward different goals.

Source: Adapted from Maccoby & Jacklin, 1974.

Cultural Myths

Another conclusion that most developmentalists now endorse is Maccoby and Jacklin's (1974) proposition that most popular sex-role stereotypes are "cultural myths" that have no basis in fact. Among the most widely accepted of these "myths" are those in Table 13-2.

Why do these inaccuracies persist? Maccoby and Jacklin (1974) propose that:

a . . . likely explanation for the perpetuation of "myths" is the fact that stereotypes are such powerful things. An ancient truth is worth restating here: if a generalization about a group of people is believed, whenever a member of the group behaves in the expected way the observer notes it and his belief is confirmed and strengthened; when a member of the group behaves in a way that is not consistent with the observer's expectations, the instance is likely to pass unnoticed, and the observer's generalized belief is protected from disconfirmation. . . . [This] well-documented [selective attention] . . . process . . . results in the perpetuation of myths that would otherwise die out under the impact of negative evidence (p. 355).

In other words, sex-role stereotypes are well-ingrained cognitive schemes that we use to interpret and often to distort the behavior of males and females (Martin & Halverson, 1981; see also Box 13-2). People even use these schemes to classify the behavior of infants. In one study (Condry & Condry, 1976), college students watched a videotape of a 9-month-old child who was introduced as either a girl ("Dana") or

BOX 13-2

Do Sex Stereotypes Color Children's Interpretations of Counterstereotypic Information?

Maccoby and Jacklin (1974) proposed that, once people learn sex stereotypes, they are more likely to attend to and remember events that are consistent with these beliefs than events that would disconfirm them. Carol Martin and Charles Halverson (1981) agree, arguing that gender stereotypes are well-ingrained schemes or naive theories that people use to organize and represent experience. Once established, these gender schemes should have at least two important effects on a child's (or an adult's) cognitive processes: (1) an *organizational* effect on memory, such that information consistent with the scheme will be easier to remember than counterstereotypic events, and (2) a *distortion* effect, such that counterstereotypic information will tend to be remembered as much more consistent with one's gender scheme than the information really is. For example, it should be easier for people to remember that they saw a girl at the stove cooking (sex-consistent information) than a boy partaking in the same activity (sex-inconsistent information). And if people were to witness the latter event, they might distort what they had seen to make it more consistent with their stereotypes—perhaps by remembering the actor as a girl rather than a boy or by reconstructing the boy's activities as *fixing* the stove rather than cooking.

Martin and Halverson (1983) tested their hypotheses in an interesting study with 5- and 6-year-olds. During a first session, each child was shown 16 pictures, half of which depicted a child performing *gender-consistent* activities (for example, a boy playing with a truck) and half showing

children displaying *gender-inconsistent* behaviors (for example, a girl chopping wood). One week later, children's memory for what they had seen was assessed.

The results of this experiment were indeed interesting. Children easily recalled the sex of the actor for scenes in which actors had performed gender-consistent activities. But when the actor's behavior was gender *inconsistent*, these youngsters often distorted the scene by saying that the actor's sex was consistent with the activity they recalled (for example, they were likely to say that it had been a boy rather than a girl who had chopped wood). As predicted, children's *confidence* about the sex of the actors was greater for gender-consistent scenes than for gender-inconsistent ones, suggesting that counterstereotypic information is harder to remember. But it was interesting to note that, when children actually distorted a gender-inconsistent scene, they were just as confident about the sex of the actor (which they recalled *incorrectly*) as they were for the gender-consistent scenes in which they correctly recalled the actor's sex. So it seems that children are likely to distort counterstereotypic information to be more consistent with their stereotypes and that these memory distortions are as "real" to them as stereotypical information that has not been distorted.

Why, then, do inaccurate sex stereotypes persist? Because we find disconfirming evidence harder to recall and, in fact, often distort that information in ways that will confirm our initial (and inaccurate) beliefs.

a boy ("David"). As the students observed the child at play, they were asked to interpret his/her reactions to toys such as a teddy bear or a jack-in-the-box. The resulting impressions of the infant's behavior clearly depended on his or her presumed sex. For example, a strong reaction to the jack-in-the-box was labeled "anger" when the child was presumed to be a male and "fear" when the child had been introduced as a female (see also Burnham & Harris, 1992).

As it turns out, the persistence of unfounded or inaccurate sex-role stereotypes has important consequences for both males and females. Some of the more negative implications of these cultural myths are discussed in the following section.

Do Cultural Myths Contribute to Sex Differences in Ability (and Vocational Opportunity)?

In 1968, Phillip Goldberg asked female college students to judge the merits of several scientific articles that were attributed to a male author ("John McKay") or to a female author ("Joan McKay"). Although these manuscripts were identical in every other respect, subjects perceived the articles written by a male to be of higher quality than those by a female.

These young women were reflecting a belief, common to people in many societies, that girls and women lack the potential to excel in either math and science courses or in occupations that require this training. Kindergarten and first-grade girls already believe that they are not as good as boys are in arithmetic; and throughout the grade school years, children increasingly come to regard reading, art, and music as girls' domains and mathematics, athletics, and mechanical subjects as more appropriate for boys (Eccles, et al., 1990; 1993; Entwisle and Baker, 1983). Moreover, an examination of the percentages of male and female practioners in various occupations reveals that women are overrepresented in fields that call for verbal ability (for example, library science, elementary education) and seriously underrepresented in most other professions, particularly the sciences and other technical fields (for example, engineering) that require a math/science background (Associated Press, 1994a; U.S. Bureau of the Census, 1992). How do we explain these dramatic sex differences? Are the small sex-related differences in verbal, mathematical, and visual/spatial performances responsible? Or rather, do sexist stereotypes create a **self-fulfilling prophecy** that *promotes* sex differences in cognitive performance and steers males and females along different career paths? Today, many developmentalists favor the latter viewpoint. Let's take a closer look.

Home Influences

Parents may often contribute to sex differences in ability and self-perceptions by treating their sons and daughters differently. Jacquelynne Eccles and her colleagues (1990) have conducted a number of studies aimed at understanding why girls tend to shy away from math and science courses and are underrepresented in occupations that involve math and science. They find that parental expectations about sex differences in mathematical ability do become self-fulfilling prophecies. The plot goes something like this:

1. Parents, influenced by societal stereotypes about sex differences in ability, expect their sons to outperform their daughters in math. Indeed, before their children have even received any formal math instruction, mothers in the United States, Japan, and Taiwan express a belief that boys have more mathematical ability than girls (Lummis & Stevenson, 1990).
2. Parents attribute their sons' successes in math to ability but credit their daughters' successes to hard work (Parsons, Adler, & Kaczala, 1982). These attributions further reinforce the belief that girls lack mathematical talent and turn in respectable performances only through plodding effort.
3. Children begin to internalize their parents' views, so that girls come to believe that they are "no good" in math (Jacobs & Eccles, 1992).
4. Thinking they lack ability, girls become less interested than boys in math and less likely to take math courses or pursue career possibilities that involve math after high school (Associated Press, 1994a; Benbow & Arjmand, 1990).

In short, parents who expect their daughters to have trouble with numbers get what they expect. In their research, Eccles and her colleagues have ruled out the possibility that parents (and girls themselves) expect less of girls because girls actually do worse in math than boys do. The negative effects of low parental expectancies on girls' self-perceptions are evident even when boys and girls perform *equally well* on tests of math aptitude and attain similar grades in math (Eccles et al., 1990). Parental beliefs that girls excel in English and that boys excel in sports contribute to sex differences in interests and competencies in these areas as well (Eccles et al., 1990).

Scholastic Influences

Interestingly, teachers also have stereotyped beliefs about the relative abilities of boys and girls in particular subjects. Sixth-grade math teachers, for example, believe that boys have more ability in math but that girls try harder at it (Jussim & Eccles, 1992). And even though these teachers often reward girls' greater efforts by assigning them equal or higher grades than they give to boys (Jussim & Eccles, 1992), their message that girls must try harder to succeed in math may nonetheless convince many girls

self-fulfilling prophecy: phenomenon whereby people cause others to act in accordance with the expectations they have about those others.

that their talents might be best directed toward other, nonquantitative achievement domains for which they are better suited—like music or English.

In sum, unfounded beliefs about sex differences in cognitive abilities may indeed contribute to the small sex-related ability differences that we have discussed and, ultimately, to the large underrepresentation of women in the sciences and other occupations requiring quantitative skills. Even as we approach the 21st century, young boys and girls are still being steered toward different social and vocational roles in society (Associated Press, 1994a; Ruble, 1988), and most high school students continue to aspire toward occupations that are dominated by members of their own sex (Hannah & Kahn, 1989). These findings may not surprise you, particularly after we examine the sex-typing process and see just how powerful the forces are that push males and females in different directions. Nevertheless, there are some signs that the times are changing. Although we still see relatively few females among the engineering graduates of most colleges, women now make up nearly 50% of the first-year law class and about 40% of the enrollment in the School of Business at my home institution (*University of Georgia Fact Book*, 1994). So there is some reason to suspect that many of the constraining stereotypes about women's competencies will eventually crumble as women achieve, in ever-increasing numbers, in politics, professional occupations, skilled trades, and virtually all other walks of life. To oppose such a trend is to waste a most valuable resource: the abilities and efforts of more than half the world's population.

Now let's explore the sex-typing process to see why it is that males and females come to view themselves so differently and often choose to assume complementary roles.

 DEVELOPMENTAL TRENDS IN SEX TYPING

Sex-typing research has traditionally focused on three separate but interrelated topics: (1) the development of **gender identity,** or the knowledge that one is either a boy or a girl and that gender is an unchanging attribute, (2) the development of *sex-role stereotypes,* or ideas about what males and females are supposed to be like, and (3) the development of *sex-typed* patterns of *behavior*—that is, the child's tendency to favor same-sex activities over those normally associated with the other sex. Let's look first at the child's understanding of gender and its implications.

Development of the Gender Concept

The first step in the development of a gender identity is to discriminate males from females and to place oneself into one of these categories. By 6 months of age, infants are using differences in vocal pitch to discriminate female speech from that of males, (Miller, 1983); and by the end of the first year, they can reliably discriminate photographs of male and female adults (females are the long-haired ones) and are beginning to match male and female voices with faces in tests of intermodal perception (Leinbach & Fagot, 1993; Poulin-Dubois et al., 1994).

Between ages 2 and 3, children begin to tell us what they know about gender as they acquire and correctly use such labels as "mommy" and "daddy" and (slightly later)"boy" and "girl" (Leinbach & Fagot, 1986). By age 2½ to 3, almost all children can accurately label themselves as either boys or girls (Thompson, 1975), although it will take longer for them to grasp the fact that gender is a permanent attribute. Indeed, many 3–5-year-olds think that boys could become mommies or girls daddies if they really wanted to, or that a person who changes clothing and hairstyles can become a member of the other sex (Fagot, 1985b; Marcus & Overton, 1978; Slaby & Frey, 1975). Children normally begin to understand that sex is an unchanging attribute between the ages of 5 and 7, so that most youngsters have a stable identity as a male or a female by the time they enter grade school.

gender identity: one's awareness of one's gender and its implications.

By age 2½ to 3, children know that boys and girls prefer different kinds of activities, and they have already begun to play in sex-stereotyped ways.

Development of Sex-Role Stereotypes

Remarkable as it may seem, toddlers begin to acquire sex-role stereotypes at about the same time that they become aware of their basic identities as boys or girls. Deanna Kuhn and her associates (Kuhn, Nash, & Brucken, 1978) showed a male doll ("Michael") and a female doll ("Lisa") to 2½–3½-year-olds and then asked each child which of the two dolls would engage in sex-stereotyped activities such as cooking, sewing, playing with dolls, trucks, or trains, talking a lot, giving kisses, fighting, or climbing trees. Almost all the 2½-year-olds had some knowledge of sex-role stereotypes. For example, boys and girls agreed that girls talk a lot, never hit, often need help, and like to play with dolls and help their mothers with chores such as cooking and cleaning. By contrast, these young children felt that boys like to play with cars, help their fathers, and build things, and are apt to make statements such as "I can hit you." The 2–3-year-olds who know the most about gender stereotypes are those who can correctly label photographs of other children as boys and girls (Fagot, Leinbach, and O'Boyle, 1992). So an understanding of gender labels seems to accelerate the process of sex-role stereotyping.

Over the preschool and early grade school years, children learn more and more about the toys, activities, and achievement domains considered appropriate for boys and for girls (Serbin, Powlishta, and Gulko, 1993). Eventually, grade school children draw sharp distinctions between the sexes on *psychological* dimensions, learning first the positive traits that characterize their own gender and the negative traits associated with the other sex (Serbin et al., 1993). By age 10–11, children's stereotyping of personality traits is beginning to rival that of adults. In one well-known cross-cultural study, Deborah Best and her colleagues (1977) found that fourth- and fifth-graders in England, Ireland, and the United States generally agree that women are weak, emotional, softhearted, sophisticated, and affectionate, whereas men are ambitious, assertive, aggressive, dominating, and cruel.

How seriously do children take the sex-role prescriptions that they are rapidly learning? Do they believe that they must conform to those stereotypes? Many 3–7-year-olds do; they often reason like little chauvinists, treating sex-role standards as blanket rules that are not to be violated (Biernat, 1991; Martin, 1989; but see Lobel & Menashri, 1993). Consider the reaction of one 6-year-old when commenting on a boy named George who likes to play with dolls:

(Why do you think people tell George not to play with dolls?) Well, he should only play with things that boys play with. The things that he is playing with now is girls' stuff . . . *(Can George play with Barbie dolls if he wants to?)* No sir! . . . *(What should George do?)* He should stop playing with girls' dolls and start playing with G.I. Joe. *(Why can a boy play with G.I. Joe and not a Barbie doll?)* Because if a boy is playing with a Barbie doll, then he's just going to get people teasing him . . . and if he tries to play more, to get girls to like him, then the girls won't like him either (Damon, 1977, p. 255; italics added).

Why are young children so rigid and intolerant of sex-role transgressions? Possibly because gender-related issues are very important to them between ages 3 and 7: After all, this is the time when they are firmly classifying themselves as boys or girls and beginning to suspect that they will *always* be boys and girls. Thus, they may exaggerate sex-role stereotypes to "get them cognitively clear" so that they can live up to their self-images (Maccoby, 1980).

By age 8 to 9, however, children are becoming much more flexible and less chauvinistic in their thinking about sex-role stereotypes (Damon, 1977; Martin, 1989; Serbin et al., 1993). Notice how 9-year-old James makes a clear distinction between moral rules that people are obligated to obey and sex-role standards that are customary but *nonobligatory.*

(What do you think his parents should do?) They should . . . get him trucks and stuff, and see if he will play with those. *(What if . . . he kept on playing with dolls? Do you think they would punish him?)* No. *(How come?)* It's not really doing anything bad. *(Why isn't it bad?)* Because . . . if he was breaking a window, and he kept on doing that, they could punish him, because you're not supposed to break windows. But if you want to you can play with dolls. *(What's the difference? . . .)* Well, breaking windows you're not supposed to do. And if you play with dolls, you can, but boys usually don't (Damon, 1977, p. 263; italics added).

Interestingly, many 12–15-year-olds once again become very intolerant of certain cross-sex behaviors (such as a male wearing nail polish or a female sporting a crew cut), even though they remain flexible about the hobbies or occupations that males and females might pursue (Carter & McCloskey, 1983–1984; Sigelman, Carr, & Begley, 1986; Stoddart & Turiel, 1985; and see Figure 13-3). How can we account for this second round of gender chauvinism?

Apparently, the young teen's sudden intolerance of cross-sex mannerisms and behaviors is tied to a larger process of **gender intensification**—a magnification of sex differences associated with increased pressure to conform to sex roles as adolescents reach puberty (Boldizar, 1991; Galambos, Almeida, & Petersen, 1990; Hill & Lynch, 1983). Boys begin to see themselves as more masculine; girls emphasize their feminine side. Why might this gender intensification occur? Phyllis Katz (1979) suggests that adolescents increasingly find that they must conform to traditional gender norms in order to succeed in the dating scene. A girl who is a tomboy and thinks nothing of it may find during adolescence that she must dress and behave in more "feminine" ways to attract boys, and a boy may find that he is more popular if he projects a more sharply "masculine" image. Social pressures on adolescents to conform to traditional roles may even help to explain why sex differences in cognitive abilities sometimes become noticeable as children enter adolescence (Hill & Lynch, 1983; Roberts et al., 1990). Later in adolescence, teenagers become much more comfortable with their identities as men and women and more flexible in their thinking once again (Urberg, 1979).

gender intensification: a magnification of sex differences early in adolescence; associated with increased pressure to conform to traditional sex roles.

Figure 13-3

Children's rankings of the wrongness of gender-role transgressions (such as a boy's wearing nail polish) and violations of moral rules (such as pushing another child from a swing). Notice that children of all ages deplore immoral acts but that only kindergartners and adolescents view gender-role violation as wrong. Elementary school children come to think about gender-role standards in a more flexible way than they did earlier in life, but adolescents become concerned about the psychological implications of deviating from one's "proper" gender identity.

Adapted from Stoddart & Turiel, 1985.

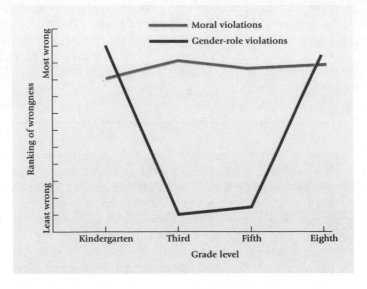

Development of Sex-Typed Behavior

The most common method of assessing the "sex-appropriateness" of children's behavior is to observe whom and what they like to play with. Sex differences in toy preferences develop very early, even before the child has established a clear gender identity or can correctly label various toys as "boy things" or "girl things" (Blakemore, LaRue, & Olejnik, 1979; Fagot, Leinbach, & Hagan, 1986; Weinraub et al., 1984). Boys aged 14 to 22 months usually prefer trucks and cars to other objects, whereas girls of this age would rather play with dolls and soft toys (Smith & Daglish, 1977). In fact, 18–24-month-old toddlers often refuse to play with cross-sex toys, even when there are no other objects available for them to play with (Caldera, Huston, & O'Brien, 1989).

Gender Segregation

Children's preferences for same-sex playmates also develop very early. In nursery school, 2-year-old girls already prefer to play with other girls (La Freniere, Strayer, & Gauthier, 1984), and by age 3, boys are reliably selecting boys rather than girls as companions. This **gender segregation,** which has been observed in a variety of cultures (Whiting & Edwards, 1988), becomes progressively stronger with each passing year (Serbin et al., 1993). By age 6½, children already spend more than ten times as much time with same-sex as with opposite-sex companions (Maccoby, 1988), and both boys and girls have developed rather clear prejudices against playmates of the other sex (Powlishta et al., 1994). Alan Sroufe and his colleagues (1993) find that those 10–11-year-olds who insist most strongly on maintaining clear gender boundaries and who avoid consorting with the "enemy" tend to be viewed as socially competent and popular, whereas children who violate gender segregation rules tend to be much less popular and less well adjusted. This bias against other-sex companions declines in adolescence, however, when the social and physiological events of puberty trigger an interest in members of the opposite sex (Serbin et al., 1993).

Why does gender segregation occur? Eleanor Maccoby (1990) argues that it is largely due to incompatibilities between boys' and girls' play styles. In one study (Jacklin and Maccoby, 1978), pairs of 33-month-old toddlers dressed in gender-neutral clothing (T-shirts and pants) were placed in a laboratory playroom that contained several interesting toys. Some of these dyads were same-sex pairs (two boys or two girls), and others were mixed-sex pairs (a boy and a girl). As the children played, an adult observer recorded how often they engaged in solitary activities and in socially directed play. As we see in Figure 13-4, social play varied as a function of the sex of one's playmate: Boys directed more social responses to boys than to girls, while girls were more sociable with girls than with boys. Interactions between playmates in the same-sex dyads were lively and positive in character. By contrast, girls tended to withdraw from boys in the mixed-sex dyads. Maccoby (1988; 1990) believes that these findings do reflect basic incompatibilities in boys' and girls' play styles, with boys being too boisterous and domineering to suit the taste of many girls, who prefer less roughhousing and would rather rely on polite negotiations rather than demands or shows of force when settling disputes with their playmates (see also Alexander & Hines, 1994; Bukowski et al., 1993).

Sex Differences in Sex-Typed Behavior

Many cultures, including our own, assign greater status to the male sex role (Rosenblatt & Cunningham, 1976), and boys face stronger pressures than girls to adhere to sex-appropriate codes of conduct (Bussey & Bandura, 1992; Lobel & Menashri, 1993). Consider that fathers of baby girls are generally willing to offer a truck to their 12-month-old daughters, whereas fathers of baby boys are likely to withhold dolls from their sons (Snow, Jacklin, & Maccoby, 1983). Indeed, boys are quicker than girls to adopt sex-typed toy preferences. Judith Blakemore and her associates (1979), for example, found that 2-year-old boys clearly favor sex-appropriate toys, whereas some 2-year-old girls may not. And by age 3 to 5, boys (1) are much more likely than girls to say that they *dislike* opposite-sex toys (Bussey & Bandura, 1992; Eisenberg, Murray, & Hite, 1982) and (2) *may* even prefer a girl playmate who likes "boy" toys to a boy playmate who prefers girls' activities (Alexander & Hines, 1994).

Between the ages of 4 and 10, both boys and girls are becoming more aware of what is expected of them and conforming to these cultural prescriptions (Huston, 1983). Yet, girls are more likely than boys to retain an interest in cross-sex toys, games, and activities. Consider what John Richardson and Carl Simpson (1982) found when recording the toy preferences of 750 5–9-year-olds as expressed in their letters to Santa Claus. Although most requests were clearly sex typed, we see in Table 13-3 that more girls than boys were asking for "opposite-sex" items (see also Etaugh & Liss, 1992). With respect to their actual sex-role preferences, young girls often wish

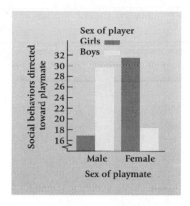

Figure 13-4
Two- to 3-year-old toddlers already prefer playmates of their own sex. Boys are much more sociable with boys than with girls, whereas girls are more outgoing with girls than with boys.
Adapted from Jacklin & Maccoby, 1978.

Table 13-3	Percentages of Boys and Girls Who Requested Popular "Masculine" and "Feminine" Items from Santa Claus	
	Percentage of boys requesting	*Percentage of girls requesting*
Masculine items		
Vehicles	43.5	8.2
Sports equipment	25.1	15.1
Spatial/temporal toys	24.5	15.6
(construction sets, clocks, and so on)		
Race cars	23.4	5.1
Real vehicles	15.3	9.7
(tricycles, bikes, motorbikes)		
Feminine items		
Dolls (adult female)	.6	27.4
Dolls (babies)	.6	23.4
Domestic accessories	1.7	21.7
Dollhouses	1.9	16.1
Stuffed animals	5.0	5.4

Source: Adapted from Richardson & Simpson, 1982.

that they were boys, but it is unusual for a boy to wish that he were a girl (Martin, 1990; Goldman & Goldman, 1982).

There are probably several reasons that girls are drawn to male activities and the masculine role during middle childhood. For one thing, they are becoming increasingly aware that masculine behavior is more highly valued, and perhaps it is only natural that girls would want to be what is "best" (or at least something other than a second-class citizen) (Frey and Ruble, 1992). Moreover, girls are given much more leeway than boys are to partake in cross-sex activities; it is okay to be a "tomboy," but it is a sign of ridicule and rejection for a boy to be labeled a "sissy" (Martin, 1990). Finally, fast-moving masculine games and "action" toys may simply be more interesting than the playthings and pastimes (dolls, dollhouses, dish sets, cleaning and caretaking utensils) often imposed on girls to encourage their adoption of a nurturant, expressive orientation. Consider the reaction of Gina, a 5-year-old who literally squealed with delight when she received an "action garage" (complete with lube racks, gas pumps, cars, tools, and spare parts) from Santa one Christmas. At the unveiling of this treasure, Gina and her three female cousins (aged 3, 5, and 7) immediately ignored their dolls, dollhouses, and unopened gifts to cluster around and play with this unusual and intriguing toy.

In spite of their earlier interest in masculine activities, most girls come to prefer (or at least to comply with) many of the prescriptions for the feminine role by early adolescence. Why? Probably for biological, cognitive, and social reasons. Once they reach puberty and their bodies assume a more womanly appearance *(biological growth)*, girls often feel the need to become more "feminine" if they hope to be attractive to members of the other sex (Katz, 1979). Moreover, these young adolescents are also attaining formal operations and advanced role-taking skills *(cognitive growth)*, which may help to explain why they become (1) self-conscious about their changing body images (Von Wright, 1989), (2) so concerned about other people's evaluation of them (Elkind, 1981a; remember the *imaginary audience* phenomenon), and thus (3) more inclined to conform to the *social* prescriptions of the female role.

In sum, sex-role development proceeds at a remarkable pace. By the time they enter school, children have long been aware of their basic gender identities, have acquired many, many stereotypes about how the sexes differ, and have come to prefer gender-appropriate activities and same-sex playmates. During middle childhood, their knowledge continues to expand as they learn more about gender-stereotyped *psychological* traits, and they become more flexible in their thinking about gender roles. Yet their *behavior,* especially if they are boys, becomes even more sex typed, and they segregate themselves even more from the other sex. Now the most intriguing question: How does all this happen so fast?

Concept Check 13-1 ∨ Sex Differences and Sex-Role Development

Check your understanding of sex differences and selected aspects of sex-role development by matching each descriptive statement below with one of the following terms: (a) achievement motivation; (b) gender identity; (c) gender intensification; (d) gender segregation; (e) reading comprehension; (f) self-fulfilling prophecy; (g) sex-role standard; (h) visual/spatial ability. The answers appear in the Appendix.

_____ 1. Attribute for which girls show a small but consistent advantage.

_____ 2. Knowledge about one's gender and its permanence.

_____ 3. Value, belief, motive, or behavior considered more appropriate for members of one sex than the other.

_____ 4. Process by which others' expectancies may promote sex differences in behavior.

_____ 5. Attribute for which boys show a small but consistent advantage.

_____ 6. Affiliative preference that becomes stronger with age during early childhood.

_____ 7. Attribute on which boys and girls do not differ.

_____ 8. Process that seems responsible for young teens' renewed intolerance of cross-sex mannerisms and behaviors.

THEORIES OF SEX TYPING AND SEX-ROLE DEVELOPMENT

Several theories have been proposed to account for sex differences and the development of sex roles. Some theories emphasize the role of biological differences between the sexes, whereas others emphasize *social* influences on children. Some emphasize what society does to children, others what children do to themselves as they try to understand gender and all its implications. Let's briefly examine a biologically oriented theory and then consider the more "social" approaches offered by psychoanalytic theory, social-learning theory, cognitive-developmental theory, and gender-schema theory.

Money and Ehrhardt's Biosocial Theory

Many scholars once believed that virtually all sex differences were largely (if not entirely) attributable to biological variations between males and females. What biological differences might be so important? For one, males have a Y chromosome and hence some genes that all females lack. For another, the sexes clearly differ in hormonal balance, with males having higher concentrations of androgens (including testosterone) and lower levels of estrogen than females do. But do these biological *correlates* of gender and gender differences actually cause sex differences in behavior? Do they predispose boys and girls to prefer and to adopt different sex roles?

Today, even biologically oriented theorists take a softer stance, arguing that biological and social influences *interact* to determine a person's behaviors and role preferences. Nowhere is this interactive emphasis any more apparent than in the *biosocial theory* proposed by John Money and Anke Ehrhardt (1972). Although biosocial theory concentrates on biological forces that may channel and constrain the development of boys and girls, it also acknowledges that early biological developments affect other people's *reactions* to the child and suggests that these social forces play a major part in steering the child toward a particular sex role. Let's take a closer look at this influential theory.

An Overview of Gender Differentiation and Sex-Role Development

Money and Ehrhardt (1972) proposed that there are a number of critical episodes or events that affect a person's eventual preference for the masculine or the feminine sex role. The first critical event occurs at conception as the child inherits either an X or a Y chromosome from the father. Over the next six weeks, the developing embryo has only an undifferentiated gonad, and the sex chromosomes determine whether this structure becomes the male testes or the female ovaries. If a Y chromosome is present, the embryo develops testes; otherwise, ovaries will form.

These newly formed gonads then determine the outcome of episode 2. The testes of a male embryo secrete two hormones: *testosterone*, which stimulates the development of a male internal reproductive system, and *mullerian inhibiting substance (MIS)*, which inhibits the development of female organs. In the absence of these hormones, the embryo develops the internal reproductive system of a female.

At a third critical point, three to four months after conception, secretion of testosterone by the testes normally leads to the growth of a penis and scrotum. If testosterone is absent (as in normal females) or if the male fetus has inherited a rare recessive disorder, called **testicular feminization syndrome (TFS)** that makes his body insensitive to male sex hormones, female external genitalia (labia and clitoris) will form. At this juncture, testosterone also alters the development of the brain and nervous system. For example, it signals the male brain to stop secreting hormones in a cyclical pattern so that males do not experience menstrual cycles at puberty.

Once a biological male or female is born, *social* factors immediately come into play. Parents and other people label and begin to react to the child based on the

testicular feminization syndrome (TFS): a genetic anomaly in which a male fetus is insensitive to the effects of male sex hormones and develops female-like external genitalia.

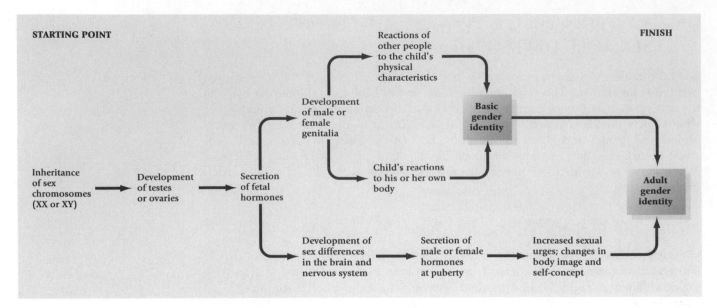

Figure 13-5
Critical events in Money and
Ehrhardt's biosocial theory of
sex typing.
From Money & Ehrhardt, 1972.

appearance of his or her genitals. If a child's genitals are abnormal so that he or she is labeled as a member of the other sex, this incorrect label and the corresponding reactions of other people will greatly affect his or her future development. For example, if a biological male were consistently labeled and treated as a girl (as a boy with TFS syndrome and female external genitalia might be), he would, by about age 2½ to 3, acquire the gender identity (though not the biological characteristics) of a girl. Normally, babies are correctly labeled and acquire a gender identity that matches their biological sex.

Finally, biological factors enter the scene again at puberty when large quantities of hormones are released, stimulating the growth of the reproductive system, the appearance of secondary sex characteristics, and the development of sexual urges. These events, in combination with one's earlier self-concept as a male or a female, provide the basis for adult gender identity and sex-role preference (see Figure 13-5).

Evidence for Biological Influences on Sex-Role Development

How much influence *do* biological factors have on the behavior of males and females? To answer this question, we must consider what investigators have learned about genetic and hormonal influences.

Genetic influences. Corinne Hutt (1972) believes that genetic differences between the sexes may help to explain why boys are more vulnerable to problems such as reading disabilities, speech defects, various emotional disorders, and certain forms of mental retardation. Since genetic [XY] males have but one X chromosome, they are necessarily more susceptible to any X-linked recessive disorder for which their mother is a carrier (recall from our discussion in Chapter 3 that genetic [XX] females would have to inherit a recessive gene from each parent to show the same disorder). Psychological theories of sex typing cannot easily explain why males often appear to be the "weaker sex," susceptible to many developmental disorders. Hutt's theory is an interesting explanation for this puzzling sex difference—one that should be investigated further.

Although it was once thought that sex differences in visual/spatial abilities and verbal skills might be directly attributable to genetic differences between the sexes, two major reviews of the literature provide little support for this notion (Huston, 1983; Linn & Petersen, 1985). **Timing of puberty**—a *biological* variable regulated in part by one's genes—has a *slight* effect on visual/spatial performances: Both boys and girls who mature *late* tend to outperform early maturers of their own sex on at least

timing-of-puberty effect: the finding that people who reach puberty late perform better on visual/spatial tasks than those who mature early.

Girls who often play with visual/spatial toys tend to perform better on tests of spatial ability.

some tests of visual/spatial ability (see Newcombe & Dubas, 1987). However, there are two other important influences on the visual/spatial performances of both males and females: (1) the person's previous *involvement* in spatial activities and (2) the extent to which the person has acquired masculine personality traits—that is, a masculine self-concept (Signorella & Jamison, 1986; Signorella, Jamison, & Krupa, 1989). These two variables are not closely related to timing of puberty and may, in fact, be *socially* mediated. What, then, contributes most to the development of spatial skills? Nora Newcombe and Judith Dubas (1992) believe that having a masculine self-concept is the most critical factor. Indeed, they found that the strength of girls' masculine self-concepts at age 11 predicted both their involvement in spatial activities and their performance on visual/spatial tests five years later at age 16. Interestingly, neither timing of puberty nor involvement in spatial activities *at age 11* could reliably forecast girls' visual/spatial abilities *at age 16*. Finally, girls who had strong *feminine* self-concepts at age 11 performed more poorly on visual/spatial tests five years later than those who had viewed themselves as less feminine. So it seems that having a strong masculine self-concept promotes interest in spatial activities and the growth of spatial skills, whereas a strong feminine self-concept may inhibit these attributes.

How closely are our masculine and feminine self-concepts related to the genes that we have inherited? Results from behavioral genetics studies of adolescent twins suggest that genotype accounts for about 50% of the variability in people's masculine self-concepts but only 0%–20% of the variability in their feminine self-concepts (Loehlin, 1992; Mitchell, Baker, & Jacklin, 1989). So even though genes determine our biological sex and have some influence on the outcome of sex typing, it appears that at least half the variability in people's masculine and feminine self-concepts is attributable to environmental influences.

Hormonal influences. Biological influences on development are also evident in studies of children who have been exposed to the "wrong" hormones during the prenatal period (Ehrhardt & Baker, 1974; Money & Ehrhardt, 1972; and see Gandelman, 1992). Before the consequences were known, some mothers who had had problems carrying pregnancies to term were given drugs contining progestins, which are converted to the male hormone testosterone by the body. These drugs had the effect of masculinizing female fetuses so that, despite their XX genetic endowment and female internal organs, they were born with external genitalia that resembled those of a boy (for example, a large clitoris that looked like a penis and fused labia that resembled a scrotum).

Money and Ehrhardt (1972; Ehrhardt & Baker, 1974) have followed several of these **androgenized females** whose external organs were surgically altered and who

androgenized females: females who develop malelike external genitalia because of exposure to male sex hormones during the prenatal period.

were then raised as girls. Compared with their sisters and other girls, it became apparent that many more androgenized girls were tomboys who often played with boys and who preferred boys' toys and activities to traditionally feminine pursuits (see also Berenbaum & Hines, 1992; Berenbaum & Snyder, 1995; Hines & Kaufman, 1994). As adolescents, they began dating somewhat later than other girls and felt that marriage should be delayed until they had established their careers. A high proportion (37%) described themselves as homosexual or bisexual (Money, 1985; see also Dittman, Kappes, & Kappes, 1992). Androgenized females also perform better than most females on tests of spatial ability, further suggesting that early exposure to male hormones has "masculinizing" effects on a female fetus (Kimura, 1992; Resnick et al., 1986). Yet it is still not entirely clear that the masculine interests and abilities these girls display are a direct result of their prenatal exposure to androgen. Many of those girls received cortisone therapy to control their androgen levels and prevent further masculinization of their bodies, and one side effect of cortisone is to dramatically increase a person's activity level. Thus, a plausible alternative interpretation is that the high-intensity "masculine" behaviors and the interest patterns that androgenized girls display are really due more to the cortisone they received than to their prenatal exposure to male sex hormones (Huston, 1983).

It has also been suggested that males are more aggressive than females because of their higher levels of testosterone—the male sex hormone that is thought to promote heightened activity, a readiness to anger, and hence, a predisposition to behave aggressively (Archer, 1991; Jacklin, 1989). The evidence seems quite convincing when experiments are conducted with animals. For example, female rhesus monkeys exposed prenatally to the male hormone testosterone later display patterns of social behavior more characteristic of males: They often threaten other monkeys, initiate rough-and-tumble play, and try to "mount" a partner as males do at the beginning of a sexual encounter (Young, Goy, & Phoenix, 1964). By contrast, genetically male rat pups that are castrated and cannot produce testosterone tend to be passive and to display feminine sexual behavior (Beach, 1965).

What about humans? Dan Olweus and his associates (1980) found that 16-year-old boys who label themselves as physically and verbally aggressive do have higher testosterone levels than boys who view themselves as nonaggressive, and men with extremely high testosterone levels tend to display higher rates of delinquency, abusiveness, and violence (Dabbs & Morris, 1990). Yet we must be extremely cautious in interpreting these correlational findings, because a person's hormonal level may depend on his or her experiences. To illustrate, Irwin Bernstein and his associates (Rose, Bernstein, & Gordon, 1975) found that the testosterone levels of male rhesus monkeys rose after they had won a fight but fell after they had been defeated. So it appears that higher concentrations of male sex hormones might be either a cause or an effect of aggressive behavior, and it is difficult to establish conclusively that these hormones either *cause* one to act aggressively or explain sex differences in aggression (Archer, 1991).

Evidence for the "social" component of biosocial theory. Although biological forces may steer males and females toward different patterns of behavior, Money and Ehrhardt (1972) believe that social influences are also important—so important, in fact, that they can modify or even *reverse* biological predispositions. Indeed, some of the evidence for this seemingly radical claim comes from Money's own work with androgenized females.

Recall that Money's androgenized females were born with the internal reproductive organs of a normal female even though their external genitalia resembled a penis and scrotum. These children are sometimes labeled boys at birth and raised as such until their abnormalities are detected. Money (1965) reports that the discovery and correction of this condition (by surgery and gender reassignment) presents few if any adjustment problems for the child, provided that the sex change occurs *before age 18 months*. But after age 3, gender reassignment is exceedingly difficult because these

BOX 13-3
Is Biology Destiny?

When biological sex and social labeling conflict, which wins out? Consider the case of a male identical twin whose penis was damaged beyond repair during circumcision (Money & Tucker, 1975). After seeking medical advice and considering the alternatives, the parents agreed to a surgical procedure that made their 21-month-old son a girl anatomically. After the operation, the family began to actively sex type this boy-turned-girl by changing her hairstyle, dressing her in frilly blouses, dresses, and the like, purchasing feminine toys for her to play with, and teaching such feminine behaviors as sitting to urinate. By age 5, the girl twin was quite different from her *genetically identical* brother: She most definitely knew she was a girl, had developed distinct preferences for feminine toys, activities, and apparel, and was far neater and daintier than her brother. Here, then, was a case in which assigned sex and sex-role socialization seemed to overcome biological predispositions. Or did they?

Milton Diamond (1982) describes what had happened by age 13, when the BBC followed up on this twin, attempting to produce a program about her life. According to her psychiatrists, she was a very maladjusted young lady who was unhappy and uncomfortable in her female role and who very much wanted to become a mechanic. And despite taking estrogen to prevent further masculinization of her body, she looked somewhat masculine and was rejected by peers, who had been known to call her "cavewoman." Perhaps, then, we should reassess the position that sex-role socialization is all that matters. Apparently, biology matters, too.

A second source of evidence that biology matters is a study of 18 biological males in the Dominican Republic with a genetic condition (TFS syndrome) that made them insensitive prenatally to male sex hormones and caused them to be born with ambiguous genitals (Imperato-McGinley, Peterson, Gautier, & Sturla, 1979). These children were labeled girls and raised as such throughout childhood. But without female hormone therapy at puberty, their male sex hormones caused them to sprout beards and to assume a muscular, masculine appearance. Can a person adjust to becoming a young man at puberty after leading an entire childhood as a girl?

Amazingly, 16 of these 18 individuals seemed quite capable of accepting their late conversion from female to male and adopting masculine lifestyles, including the establishment of heterosexual relationships! One retained a female identity and sex role, while the remaining individual switched to a male gender identity but still dressed as a female. Clearly, this research casts some doubt on the notion that socialization during the first three years is "critical" to later sex-role development. In fact, it seems to suggest that hormonal influences are more important than social influences (Imperato-McGinley et al., 1979).

However, Imperato-McGinley's conclusions have been challenged (Ehrhardt, 1985). Little information was reported about how these individuals were raised, and it is quite possible that Dominican parents, knowing that this genetic disorder was common in their society, treated these girls-turned-boys differently from other "girls" when they were young. Moreover, the girls-turned-boys had genitals that were not completely normal in appearance, and the practice of river bathing in Dominican culture almost certainly means that these youngsters compared themselves to normal girls (and boys) and may have recognized early on that they were "different." So these children may not have received an exclusively feminine upbringing and may never have fully committed themselves to being girls. Nor should we automatically assume that their later incorporation of the masculine role was due to hormones. One study of TFS males raised as females among the Sambia of New Guinea found that *social pressures*—namely, the argument that they could not bear children—is what appeared most responsible for the gender switches that occurred after puberty (Herdt & Davidson, 1988).

Considering all the evidence, then, is social experience during the first three years (Money's critical period) really so powerful that it overrides biological influences? What studies of people with genital and other hormonal abnormalities (including Money and Ehrhardt's clinical samples) seem to suggest is this: The first three years is a *sensitive* period, rather than a critical period, for sex-role development; and both biology and society influence a child's gender identity and sex-role preferences. Stated another way, neither biology nor social labeling is "destiny."

genetic females have experienced prolonged masculine sex typing and have already labeled themselves as boys. These data led Money to conclude that there is a "critical period" between 18 months and 3 years of age for the establishment of gender identity. As illustrated in Box 13-3, it may be more accurate to call the first three years a *sensitive* period, for other investigators have claimed that it is possible to assume a new identity later in adolescence. Nevertheless, Money's findings indicate that early social labeling and sex-role socialization can play a very prominent role in determining a child's gender identity and sex-role preferences.

Margaret Mead's (1935) cross-cultural observations of three New Guinea tribes lead to the same conclusion. Mead noted that both males and females of the Arapesh tribe were taught to be cooperative, nonaggressive, and sensitive to the needs of others. This behavioral profile would be considered "expressive" or "feminine" in Western cultures. By contrast, both men and women of the Mundugumor tribe were expected to be hostile, aggressive, and emotionally unresponsive in their interpersonal relationships—a masculine pattern of behavior by Western standards. Finally, the Tchambuli displayed a pattern of sex-role development opposite to that of Western societies: Males were passive, emotionally dependent, and socially sensitive, whereas females were dominant, independent, and assertive. In sum, members of these three tribes developed in accordance with the sex roles prescribed by their culture—even when these roles were quite inconsistent with sex-linked biological predispositions. Clearly, social forces contribute heavily to sex typing.

In sum, Money and Ehrhardt's biosocial theory stresses the importance of early biological developments that influence how parents and other social agents label a child at birth and that possibly also affect behavior more directly. However, the theory also holds that children's socialization as boys or girls strongly influences their sex-role development—in short, that biological and social forces *interact*. What biosocial theory does *not* do is to specify the precise social processes through which children acquire gender identities and sex-typed patterns of behavior. Let's turn now to the "social" theories of sex typing, the first of which was Sigmund Freud's psychoanalytic approach.

Freud's Psychoanalytic Theory

Freud believed that sex-role development is a product of both biological and social forces. Recall from our discussion of psychoanalytic theory in Chapter 2 that sexuality (the sex instinct) was said to be innate. Freud also believed that everyone is constitutionally bisexual, having inherited, in varying proportions, the biological attributes of both sexes. What, then, is responsible for the child's adoption of a gender identity consistent with his or her (predominant) biological sex?

Freud's answer was that sex typing occurs through the process of **identification.** Recall that identification is the child's tendency to emulate another person, usually the parent of the same sex. Freud argued that a 3–6-year-old boy in the **phallic stage** of development internalizes masculine attitudes and behaviors when he is forced to identify with his father (the aggressor) as a means of renouncing his incestuous desires for his mother, reducing his **castration anxiety,** and thus resolving the **Oedipus complex.** However, Freud believed that sex typing is more difficult for a young girl, who already feels castrated and experiences no overriding fear that would compel her to identify with her mother and resolve her **Electra complex.** Why, then, would a girl ever develop a preference for the feminine role? Freud offered several suggestions, one of which was that the object of a girl's affection, her father, was likely to encourage her feminine behavior—an act that increases the attractiveness of the mother, who serves as the girl's model of femininity. So by trying to please her father (or to prepare for relationships with other males after she recognizes the implausibility of possessing her father), the girl should be motivated to incorporate her mother's feminine attributes and will eventually become sex typed (Freud, 1924/1961a).

Some of the evidence that we have reviewed is generally consistent with Freudian theory. Children are rapidly acquiring sex-role stereotypes and developing sex-typed activity preferences at roughly the same age that Freud says they will (3 to 6). Moreover, boys whose fathers are absent from the home (because of divorce, military service, or death) during the Oedipal period frequently have no male role model to emulate and, indeed, are often found to be less masculine in their sex-role behaviors than boys from homes where the father is present (Stevenson & Black, 1988). Finally, the notion that fathers play an important role in the sex typing of their daughters has now been confirmed (Huston, 1983).

Yet, on other counts, psychoanalytic theory has not fared well at all. Many preschool children are so ignorant about differences between male and female

identification: Freud's term for the child's tendency to emulate another person, usually the same-sex parent.

phallic stage: Freud's third stage of psychosexual development (from 3 to 6 years of age) in which children gratify the sex instinct by fondling their genitals and developing an incestuous desire for the parent of the other sex.

castration anxiety: in Freud's theory, a young boy's fear that his father will castrate him as punishment for his rivalrous conduct.

Oedipus complex: Freud's term for the conflict that 3–6-year-old boys experience when they develop an incestuous desire for their mothers and, at the same time, a jealous and hostile rivalry with their fathers.

Electra complex: female version of the Oedipus complex, in which a 3–6-year-old girl was believed to envy her father for possessing a penis and to seek him as a sex object in the hope of sharing the valuable organ that she lacked.

According to psychoanalytic theory, children become appropriately "masculine" or "feminine" by identifying with the same-sex parent.

genitalia that it is hard to see how most boys could fear castration or how most girls could feel castrated and envy males for having a penis (Bem, 1989; Katcher, 1955). Moreover, Freud assumed that a boy's identification with his father is based on fear; but most researchers find that boys identify more strongly with fathers who are warm and nurturant rather than with those who are overly punitive and threatening (Hetherington & Frankie, 1967; Mussen & Rutherford, 1963). Finally, studies of parent-child resemblances reveal that school-age children and adolescents are not all that similar psychologically to either parent (Maccoby & Jacklin, 1974). Clearly, these findings are damaging to the Freudian notion that children acquire important personality traits by identifying with the same-sex parent.

In sum, Freud's explanation of sex typing has not fared very well even though children do begin to develop sex-role preferences at about the time that he specified. Let's now consider the social-learning interpretation of sex typing to see whether this approach looks any more promising.

Social-Learning Theory

Prominent social-learning theorists (Bandura, 1989; Mischel, 1970) have argued that children acquire their gender identities, sex-role preferences, and sex-typed behaviors in two ways: through direct tuition and observational learning. **Direct tuition** (or differential reinforcement) refers to the tendency of parents, teachers, and other social agents to "teach" boys and girls how they should behave by encouraging and reinforcing sex-appropriate behaviors and by punishing or otherwise discouraging those actions considered more appropriate for members of the other sex. In addition, every child is thought to acquire a large number of sex-typed attitudes and behaviors by observing the activities of a variety of same-sex models, including peers, teachers, older siblings, and media personalities, as well as the mother or the father. Walter Mischel (1970) has noted that children do not necessarily identify with (that is, hope to emulate) all the models who contribute to their sex-role development. Indeed, imitative responses that psychoanalysts call "identification" are just as easily described as examples of *observational learning*.

Direct Tuition of Sex Roles

Are parents actively involved in the sex typing of their children? Yes, indeed (Lytton & Romney, 1991), and the shaping of sex-typed behaviors begins rather early. As part of a longitudinal study of sex-role development, Beverly Fagot and Mary Leinbach (1989) found that parents are already encouraging sex-appropriate play and responding more negatively to cross-sex behaviors during the second year, *before* the child acquires a basic gender identity or displays a clear preference for male or female activities. By age 20–24 months, daughters are consistently reinforced for such behaviors

direct tuition: process of teaching young children how to behave by reinforcing appropriate behaviors and by punishing or otherwise discouraging inappropriate conduct.

as dancing, dressing up (as women), following parents around, asking for help, and playing with dolls, and they are likely to be discouraged from manipulating objects, running, jumping, and climbing; by contrast, sons are often punished for "feminine" behaviors (such as doll play or seeking help) and are actively encouraged to play with masculine items such as blocks, trucks, and push-and-pull toys that require large-muscle activity (Fagot, 1978).

Are children influenced by the "gender curriculum" that their parents provide? They certainly are! In fact, parents who show the clearest patterns of differential reinforcement have children who are relatively quick to (1) label themselves as boys or girls, (2) develop strongly sex-typed toy and activity preferences, and (3) acquire an understanding of gender stereotypes (Fagot & Leinbach, 1989; Fagot, Leinbach, & O'Boyle, 1992). It turns out that fathers are even more likely than mothers to reinforce "sex-appropriate" behaviors and to punish or otherwise discourage behavior considered more appropriate for the other sex (Langlois & Downs, 1980; Lytton & Romney, 1991). And, apparently, *peer pressure* for sex-appropriate play also begins very early: Even before they establish a basic gender identity, 21–25-month-old boys often belittle or disrupt each other for playing with feminine toys or with a girl, and girls of this same age are critical of other girls who choose to play with boys (Fagot, 1985a).

So it seems that the child's earliest preferences for sex-typed toys and activities may result from the tendency of parents (particularly fathers) to actively encourage sex-appropriate behavior and to discourage acts that they consider sex inappropriate. As the child grows older, other people, such as teachers, Scout leaders, and especially peers, become increasingly important as sources of reinforcement for sex-typed attitudes and behaviors.

Observational Learning

According to Bandura (1989), children acquire many of their sex-typed attributes and interests by observing and imitating a variety of same-sex models. By observing peers or older siblings, for example, children may quickly learn which toys and activities are "for boys" and "for girls," and they may often be encouraged to imitate same-sex models as well. Indeed, you have probably heard a proud parent make such statements as "That's my little man; you're just like daddy!" or "Oh, you're as pretty as your mommy when you get all dressed up."

Yet there is some question about just how much social models contribute to sex typing during the preschool years. Although some investigators find that preschoolers do pay closer attention to same-sex models (Bussey & Bandura, 1984), others report that the model's sex is of little consequence until relatively late—about 6 to 7 years of age (Ruble, Balaban, & Cooper, 1981; Slaby & Frey, 1975). In fact, John Masters and his associates (1979) found that preschool children are much more concerned about the sex appropriateness of the *behavior* they are observing than the sex of the model who displays it. For example, 4–5-year-old boys will play with objects labeled "boys' toys" even after they have seen a girl playing with them. However, these youngsters are reluctant to play with "girls' toys" that boy models have played with earlier. So children's toy choices are affected more by the labels attached to the toys than by the sex of the child who served as a model. But once children recognize that gender is an unchanging aspect of their personalities (at age 6 to 7), they do begin to attend more selectively to same-sex models and are now likely to avoid toys and activities that other-sex models seem to enjoy (Frey & Ruble, 1992; Ruble et al., 1981).

Media influences. Not only do children learn by observing other children and adult models with whom they interact, but they also learn about sex roles from reading stories and watching television. Although sexism in children's books has declined over the past 50 years, male characters are still more likely than female characters to engage in active, instrumental pursuits such as riding bikes or making things, whereas female characters are often depicted as passive and dependent individuals who spend much of their time playing quietly indoors and "creating problems that require masculine solutions" (Kortenhaus & Demarest, 1993). It is similar in the world of television: Males are usually featured as the central characters who work at professions, make important decisions, respond to emergencies, and assume positions of leadership, whereas females are often portrayed as relatively passive and emotional creatures who manage a home or work at "feminine" occupations such as waitressing or nursing (Liebert & Sprafkin, 1988).

Are children influenced by these highly sexist media portrayals? Apparently so, for those who watch a lot of television are more likely to prefer sex-typed activities and to hold highly stereotyped views of men and women than their classmates who watch little television (McGhee & Frueh, 1980; Signorielli & Lears, 1992). But as more women play detectives and more men raise families on television, children's perceptions of male and female roles are likely to change. Indeed, children who regularly watch *The Cosby Show* and other relatively nonsexist programs do hold less stereotyped views of the sexes (Rosenwasser, Lingenfelter, & Harrington, 1989).

In sum, there is a lot of evidence that differential reinforcement and observational learning contribute to sex-role development. However, social-learning theorists have often portrayed children as *passive pawns* in the process: Parents, peers, and TV characters show them what to do and reinforce that behavior. Might this perspective miss something—namely, the child's *own* contribution to sex-role socialization? Consider, for example, that children do not always receive gender-stereotyped Christmas presents because their sexist parents force these objects upon them. Instead, many parents who would rather buy gender-neutral or educational toys end up "giving in" to sons who beg for machine guns or daughters who want tea sets (Robinson & Morris, 1986).

Kohlberg's Cognitive-Developmental Theory

Lawrence Kohlberg (1966) has proposed a cognitive theory of sex typing that is quite different from the other theories we have considered and helps to explain why boys and girls adopt traditional sex roles even when their parents may not want them to. Kohlberg's major themes are:

1. Sex-role development depends on cognitive development; children must acquire certain understandings about gender before they will be influenced by their social experiences.
2. Children *actively socialize themselves*; they are not merely passive pawns of social influence.

According to both psychoanalytic theory and social-learning theory, children first learn to do "boy" or "girl" things because their parents encourage these activities; then, they come to identify with or habitually imitate same-sex models, thereby acquiring a stable gender identity. By contrast, Kohlberg suggests that children *first* establish a stable gender identity and then *actively* seek out same-sex models and other information to learn how to act like a boy or a girl. To Kohlberg, it's not "I behave like a boy; therefore, I must be one" (social-learning position). It's more like "Hey, I'm a boy; therefore, I'd better do everything I can to find out how to behave like one" (cognitive–self-socialization position).

Kohlberg believes that children pass through the following three stages as they acquire a mature understanding of what it means to be a male or a female:

1. **Basic gender identity.** By age 3, children have labeled themselves as boys or girls.
2. **Gender stability.** Somewhat later, gender is perceived as *stable over time.* Boys invariably become men, and girls grow up to be women.
3. **Gender consistency.** The gender concept is complete when the child realizes that one's sex is also *stable across situations.* Six- to 7-year-olds who have

basic gender identity: the stage of gender identity in which the child first labels the self as a boy or a girl.

gender stability: the stage of gender identity in which the child recognizes that gender is stable over time.

gender consistency: the stage of gender identity in which the child recognizes that a person's gender is invariant despite changes in the person's activities or appearance (also known as gender constancy).

reached this stage are no longer fooled by appearances. They know, for example, that one's sex cannot be altered by cross-dressing or taking up cross-sex activities.

When do children become motivated to socialize themselves—that is, to seek out same-sex models and learn how to act like males and females? According to Kohlberg, self-socialization begins only after children reach *gender consistency*. So for Kohlberg, a mature understanding of gender (1) instigates true sex typing and (2) is the *cause*, rather than the consequence, of attending to same-sex models.

Support for Kohlberg's Viewpoint

Several observations are consistent with various aspects of Kohlberg's theory. For example, studies conducted in more than 20 different cultures reveal that (1) preschool children do proceed through Kohlberg's three stages of gender identity in the sequence that he describes, and (2) their attainment of gender consistency (that is, conservation of gender) is clearly associated with other relevant aspects of cognitive development, such as the conservation of mass and liquids (Marcus & Overton, 1978; Munroe, Shimmin, & Munroe, 1984; Slaby & Frey, 1975). Moreover, children who have reached gender consistency do begin to pay closer attention to a model's gender: They are now more likely to attend to same-sex rather than other-sex models in a movie (Slaby & Frey, 1975); and they (particularly boys) now favor novel toys that same-sex models prefer (and shun those that models of the other sex like)—even when the toys that they are passing up are the *more attractive objects* (Frey & Ruble, 1992; Ruble et al., 1981). Thus, it seems that children with a mature gender identity (especially boys) feel that they had better play it safe and select the "gender-correct" toy rather than other less appropriate options.

Limitations of Kohlberg's Theory

Of course, the major problem with Kohlberg's cognitive approach is that sex typing is already well under way before the child acquires a mature gender identity. As we have noted, 2-year-old boys prefer masculine toys before they are even aware that these playthings are more appropriate for boys than for girls. Moreover, 3-year-olds of each sex have learned many sex-role stereotypes and already prefer same-sex activities and playmates long before they begin to attend more selectively to same-sex models. It seems that only a rudimentary understanding of gender is necessary before children learn about sex-role stereotypes and display sex-appropriate toy preferences and that measures of gender consistency tell us very little about how "sex typed" children are (Bussey & Bandura, 1992; Carter & Levy, 1988; Levy & Carter, 1989; Lobel & Menashri, 1993; Martin & Little, 1990). Finally, let's not forget the work of John Money (1965), who found that gender reassignment is exceedingly difficult once children have reached the age of 3 (or Kohlberg's basic identity stage) and have initially categorized themselves as boys or girls. So, it appears that Kohlberg clearly overstates the case in arguing that a mature understanding of gender is necessary for sex typing and sex-role development.

Gender-Schema Theory

Carol Martin and Charles Halverson (1981; 1987) have proposed a somewhat different cognitive theory of sex typing (actually, an information-processing theory) that appears quite promising (see Bem, 1983, for a similar viewpoint). Like Kohlberg, Martin and Halverson believe that children are intrinsically motivated to acquire interests, values, and behaviors that are consistent with their "boy" or "girl" self-images. But unlike Kohlberg, they argue that this "self-socialization" begins as soon as the child acquires a *basic gender identity* at age 2½ or 3 and thus is well under way by age 6 to 7, when the child achieves gender consistency.

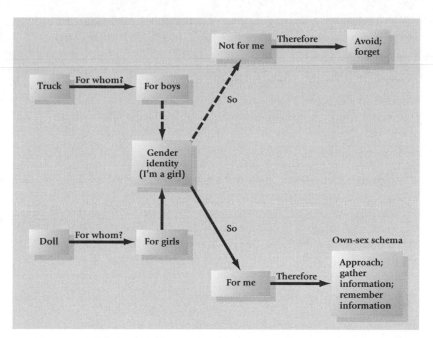

Figure 13-6
Gender-schema theory in action. A young girl classifies new information according to an "in-group/out-group schema" as either "for boys" or "for girls." Information about boys' toys and activities is ignored, but information about toys and activities for girls is relevant to the self and so is added to an ever-larger "own-sex schema."
Adapted from Martin & Halverson, 1987.

According to Martin and Halverson's "gender-schema" theory, establishment of a basic gender identity motivates a child to learn about the sexes and to incorporate this information into **gender schemas**—that is, organized sets of beliefs and expectations about males and females that influence the kinds of information he attends to, elaborates, and remembers. First, children acquire a simple **"in-group/out-group" schema** that allows them to classify some objects, behaviors, and roles as "for males" and others as "for females" (for example, trucks are for boys; girls can cry but boys should not, and so on). This is the kind of information that investigators normally tap when studying children's knowledge of sex-role stereotypes. In addition, children are said to construct an **own-sex schema,** which consists of detailed plans of action that one needs to perform various gender-consistent behaviors and enact one's sex role. So a girl who has a basic gender identity might first learn that sewing is "for girls" and building model airplanes is "for boys." Then, because she is a girl and wants to act consistently with her own self-concept, she will gather a great deal of information about sewing to add to her own-sex schema, while largely ignoring information about building model airplanes (see also Figure 13-6).

Once formed, gender schemas serve as scripts for processing social information. We learned in Chapter 8 that preschool children often have a difficult time recalling information that deviates from their scripted knowledge of everyday events. And so it goes with gender-related knowledge: Children are likely to encode and remember information consistent with their gender schemas and to forget schema-inconsistent information or to otherwise distort it so that it becomes more consistent with their stereotypes (Liben & Signorella, 1993; Martin & Halverson, 1983). Support for this idea was presented in Box 13-2; recall that children who heard stories in which actors performed cross-sex behaviors (for example, a girl chopping wood) tended to recall the action but to alter the scene to conform to their gender stereotypes (saying that a boy had been chopping). Surely, these strong tendencies to forget or to distort counterstereotypic information help to explain why unfounded beliefs about males and females are so slow to die.

Also consistent with this schematic-processing theory, children do seem to be especially interested in learning about objects and activities that fit their "own-sex" schemas. In one study, 4–9-year-olds were given boxes of gender-neutral objects (for example, hole punches, burglar alarms, and pizza cutters) and were told that the objects were either "boy" items or "girl" items (Bradbard et al., 1986). Boys explored

gender schemas: organized sets of beliefs and expectations about males and females that guide information processing.

"in-group/out-group" schema: one's general knowledge of the mannerisms, roles, activities, and behaviors that characterize males and females.

own-sex schema: detailed knowledge or plans of action that enable a person to perform gender-consistent activities and to enact his or her sex role.

"boy" items more than girls did, whereas girls explored more than boys when the objects were described as things that girls enjoy. One week later, children easily recalled whether these objects were "boy" or "girl" items; they had apparently sorted the objects according to their "in-group/out-group" schemas. However, boys recalled much more in-depth information about "boy" items than did girls, whereas girls recalled more than boys about these very same objects if they had been labeled "girl" items. If children's information-gathering efforts are consistently guided by their own-sex schemas in this way, we can easily see how boys and girls might acquire very different stores of knowledge and develop different interests and competencies as they mature.

In sum, Martin and Halverson's gender schema theory is an interesting "new look" at the sex-typing process. Not only does this model describe how sex-role stereotypes might originate and persist over time, but it also indicates how these emerging "gender schemas" might contribute to the development of strong sex-role preferences and sex-typed behaviors long before the child realizes that gender is an unchanging attribute.

An Attempt at Integration

The biosocial, social-learning, cognitive-developmental, and gender-schema perspectives have each contributed in important ways to our understanding of sex differences and sex-role development (Huston, 1983; Serbin et al., 1993). In fact, the processes that different theories emphasize seem to be especially important at different periods of sex-role development. Biosocial theory accounts for the major biological developments that occur before birth—the events that induce people to label the child as a boy or a girl and to treat him or her accordingly. The differential reinforcement process that social-learning theorists emphasize seems to account rather well for early sex typing: Young children display gender-consistent behaviors because other people encourage these activities and often discourage behaviors considered more appropriate for members of the other sex. As a result of this early socialization and the growth of categorization skills, $2^{1}/_{2}$–3-year-olds acquire a basic gender identity and form *gender schemas* that tell them (1) what boys and girls are like and (2) how they, as boys and girls, are supposed to think and act. And when they finally understand, at age 6 or 7, that their sex will never change, children begin to focus less exclusively on gender schemas and to pay more and more attention to same-sex models to decide which attitudes, activities, interests, and mannerisms are most appropriate for members of their own sex (Kohlberg's viewpoint). Of course, summarizing developments in an integrative model such as this one (see Table 13-4 for an overview) does not mean that biological forces play no further role after the child is born or that differential reinforcement ceases to affect development once the child acquires a basic gender identity. But an integrative theorist would emphasize that, from age 3 on, children are active *self-socializers* who try very hard to acquire the masculine or feminine attributes that they view as consistent with their male or female self-images. This is why parents who hope to discourage their children from adopting traditional gender roles are often amazed that their sons and daughters seem to become little "sexists" all on their own.

One more point: All theories of sex-role development would agree that what children actually learn about being a male or a female depends greatly on what their society offers them in the way of a "gender curriculum." In other words, we must view sex-role development through an *ecological* lens and appreciate that there is nothing inevitable about the patterns of male and female development that we see in our society today. (Indeed, recall the gender-role reversals that Mead observed among the Tchambuli tribe of New Guinea.) In another era, in another culture, the sex-typing process can produce very different kinds of boys and girls.

Should we in Western cultures be trying to raise different kinds of boys and girls? As we will see in our next section, some theorists would answer this question with a resounding YES!

Table 13-4 An Overview of the Sex-Typing Process from the Perspective of an Integrative Theorist

Developmental period	Events and outcomes	Pertinent theory(ies)
Prenatal period	The fetus develops the morphological characteristics of a male or a female, which others will react to once the child is born.	Biosocial
Birth to 3 years	Parents and other companions label the child as a boy or a girl, frequently remind the child of his or her gender, and begin to encourage gender-consistent behavior while discouraging cross-sex activities. As a result of these social experiences and the development of very basic classification skills, the young child acquires some sex-typed behavioral preferences and the knowledge that he or she is a boy or a girl (basic gender identity).	Social learning (differential reinforcement)
3 to 6 years	Once children acquire a basic gender identity, they begin to seek information about sex differences, form gender schemas, and become intrinsically motivated to perform those acts that are viewed as "appropriate" for their own sex. When acquiring gender schemas, children attend to *both* male and female models. Once their gender schemas are well established, these youngsters are likely to imitate behaviors considered appropriate for their sex, regardless of the gender of the model who displays them.	Gender schema
7 to puberty	Children finally acquire a sense of gender consistency—a firm, future-oriented image of themselves as boys who must necessarily become men or as girls who will obviously become women. At this point, they begin to rely less exclusively on gender schemas and more on the behavior of same-sex models to acquire those mannerisms and attributes that are consistent with their firm categorization of self as a male or female.	Cognitive-developmental (Kohlberg)
Puberty and beyond	The biological upheavals of adolescence, in conjunction with new social expectations (gender intensification), cause teenagers to reexamine their self-concepts, forming an adult gender identity.	Biosocial; social learning; gender schema; cognitive-developmental

PSYCHOLOGICAL ANDROGYNY: A PRESCRIPTION FOR THE FUTURE?

Throughout this chapter, we have used the term *sex appropriate* to describe the mannerisms and behaviors that societies consider more suitable for members of one sex than the other. Today, many developmentalists believe that these rigidly defined sex-role standards are actually harmful because they constrain the behavior of both males and females. Indeed, Sandra Bem (1978) has stated that her major purpose in studying sex roles is "to help free the human personality from the restrictive prison of sex-role stereotyping and to develop a conception of mental health that is free from culturally imposed definitions of masculinity and femininity."

For many years, psychologists assumed that masculinity and femininity were at opposite ends of a single dimension. If one possessed highly masculine traits, one must be very unfeminine; being highly feminine implied being unmasculine. Bem (1974) challenged this assumption by arguing that individuals of either sex can be characterized by psychological **androgyny**—that is, by a balancing or blending of both desirable masculine-stereotyped traits (for example, being assertive, analytical, forceful, and independent) and desirable feminine-stereotyped traits (for example, being affectionate, compassionate, gentle, and understanding). In Bem's model, then, masculinity and femininity are *two separate dimensions* of personality. A male or female who has many desirable masculine-stereotyped traits and few feminine ones is defined as a *masculine sex-typed* person. One who has many feminine- and few

androgyny: a sex-role orientation in which the individual has incorporated a large number of both masculine and feminine attributes into his or her personality.

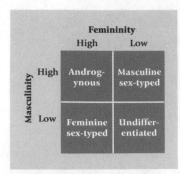

Figure 13-7
Categories of sex-role orientation based on viewing masculinity and femininity as separate dimensions of personality.

masculine-stereotyped traits is said to be *feminine sex-typed*. The androgynous person possesses both masculine and feminine traits, whereas the *undifferentiated* individual lacks both of these kinds of attributes (see Figure 13-7).

Do Androgynous People Really Exist?

Bem (1974) and other investigators (Spence & Helmreich, 1978) have developed self-perception inventories that contain both a masculinity (or instrumentality) scale and a femininity (or expressivity) scale. In one large sample of college students (Spence & Helmreich, 1978), roughly 33% of the test takers proved to be "masculine" men or "feminine" women, about 30% were androgynous, and the remaining individuals were either undifferentiated or "sex-reversed" (masculine sex-typed females or feminine sex-typed males). Janet Boldizar (1991) has developed a similar sex-role inventory for grade school children (see Table 13-5 for sample items) and finds that approximately 25%–30% of third- through seventh-graders can be classified as androgynous (see also Hall & Halberstadt, 1980). So androgynous individuals do exist, and in sizable numbers.

Are There Advantages to Being Androgynous?

When we consider the idea that a person can be both assertive and sensitive, both independent and understanding, we can't help but think that being androgynous is psychologically healthy. Is it? Bem (1975, 1978) demonstrated that androgynous men and women behave more flexibly than more sex-typed individuals. For example, androgynous people, like masculine sex-typed people, can display the "masculine," instrumental trait of *independence* by resisting social pressure to judge very unamusing cartoons as funny just because their companions do. Yet they are as likely as feminine sex-typed individuals to display the "feminine," expressive quality of *nurturance* by interacting positively with a baby. Androgynous people seem to be highly adapt-

Table 13-5	**Sample Items from a Sex-Role Inventory for Grade School Children**

Personality trait	Question
Masculine	
Dominant	I can control a lot of the kids in my class.
Authoritative	I am a leader among my friends.
Analytical	I like to think about and solve problems.
Self-sufficient	I can take care of myself.
Ambitious	I am willing to work hard to get what I want.
Masculine	I like to do what boys and men do.
Feminine	
Compassionate	I care about what happens to others.
Cheerful	I am a cheerful person.
Loyal	I am faithful to my friends.
Nurturant	I like babies and small children a lot.
Flatterable	I feel good when people say nice things about me.
Feminine	I like to do what girls and women do.

Format: The child is asked to respond to each item on a four-point scale, with options ranging from 1 = "not at all true of me" to 4 = "very true of me."

Source: Adapted from Boldizar, 1991.

able, able to adjust their behavior to the demands of the situation at hand (Shaffer, Pegalis, & Cornell, 1992). Moreover, androgynous children and adolescents appear to enjoy higher self-esteem and are perceived as more likable and better adjusted than their traditionally sex-typed peers (Allgood-Merten & Stockard, 1991; Boldizar, 1991; Massad, 1981; O'Heron & Orlofsky, 1990). It has also become clear that androgynous men can still feel quite masculine and androgynous women appropriately feminine even though they sometimes express traits traditionally associated with the other sex (Spence, 1993).

But before we conclude that androgyny is a thoroughly desirable attribute, let's note some contrary evidence. It appears that it is the possession of "masculine" traits rather than androgyny per se that is most strongly associated with good adjustment and high self-esteem (Orlofsky & O'Heron, 1987; Whitley, 1983). The finding should not surprise us, for people in many societies value masculine attributes more highly than feminine attributes (Rosenblatt & Cunningham, 1976). But even so, there are signs that the times may be changing. In her recent study of grade school children, Boldizar (1991) found that (1) androgyny was by far the best single predictor of children's impressions of their global self-worth, and (2) femininity predicted some aspects of self-esteem (physical attractiveness; behavioral conduct) just as well or better than masculinity did.

So it may be premature to conclude that one is better off in *all* respects to be androgynous rather than masculine or feminine in orientation. But given the behavioral flexibility that androgynous people display and the strong contribution that androgyny makes to children's perceived self-worth, we can safely assume that it is probably adaptive and certainly not harmful for girls and women to become a little more "masculine" and for boys and men to become a little more like women.

Concept Check 13-2 ∨ Theories of Sex-Role Development

Check your understanding of theories of sex-role development by matching each descriptive statement below with one of the following concepts or viewpoints on sex typing: (a) Money and Ehrhardt's biosocial theory; (b) Freud's psychoanalytic theory; (c) social-learning theory; (d) Kohlberg's cognitive-developmental theory; (e) Martin and Halverson's gender schema theory; (f) basic gender identity; (g) gender consistency; (h) gender schemas; (i) androgenized females; (j) andogynous females. The answers appear in the Appendix.

_____ 1. Starting point for self-socialization of sex-roles, according to cognitive-developmental theory.

_____ 2. Accounts for joint influence of genes and environment on psychological masculinity and femininity.

_____ 3. Claims that children adopt sex roles by identifying with the same-sex parent.

_____ 4. Starting point for self-socialization of sex roles, according to gender schema theory.

_____ 5. Cited as evidence for biological influences on sex-role development.

_____ 6. Claims that early sex typing largely reflects the gender curriculum that a child's parents provide.

_____ 7. Personalities consist of a blending of both masculine and feminine attributes.

_____ 8. Explains why unfounded beliefs about males and females often persist.

_____ 9. Cannot easily explain why gender reassignment is usually unsuccessful with 3–5-year-olds.

_____ 10. Scripts for social information processing that influence the interests that boys and girls come to display.

On Changing Sex-Role Attitudes and Behavior

Today, many people believe that the world would be a better place if sexism were eliminated and if boys and girls were no longer steered toward adopting the confining "masculine" or "feminine" roles. In a nonsexist culture, women would no longer suffer from a lack of assertiveness and confidence in the world of work, and men

By encouraging and engaging in counterstereotypic activities, parents may deter their children from developing rigid gender stereotypes.

would be freer to display their sensitive, nurturant sides that many now suppress in the interest of appearing "masculine." How might we reduce sexism and encourage children to be more flexible about the interests and attributes that they might display?

Bem (1983; 1989) believes that parents must take an active role by (1) teaching their young children about genital anatomy as part of a larger lesson that one's sex is unimportant outside the domain of reproduction, and (2) delaying children's exposure to gender stereotypes by encouraging cross-sex as well as same-sex play and by dividing household chores more equitably (with fathers sometimes cooking and cleaning and mothers gardening or making repairs). If preschoolers come to think of sex as a purely biological attribute and often see themselves and their parents pursuing cross-sex interests and activities, they should be less inclined to construct the rigid gender stereotypes that might otherwise evolve in a highly sexist early environment. Indeed, research suggesting that androgynous parents tend to raise androgynous children is consistent with Bem's prescriptions for change (Orlofsky, 1979; see also Weisner & Wilson-Mitchell, 1990), as are findings that daughters of employed mothers perceive fewer psychological differences between the sexes and are more likely to be androgynous themselves, compared with daughters of mothers who are not employed (Hoffman, 1989).

How might we reach children from more traditional backgrounds, who have already received thousands of sex-stereotyped messages from family members, television, and their peers? Apparently, interventions that simply show children the benefits of cross-sex cooperation or that praise them for playing with other-sex toys and play partners have no lasting effect: Children soon retreat to same-sex play and continue to prefer same-sex peers after the interventions are over (see Lockheed, 1986; Maccoby, 1988). One particularly ambitious program (Guttentag & Bray, 1976) exposed kindergarten, fifth-grade, and ninth-grade students to age-appropriate readings and activities designed to teach them about the capabilities of women and about the problems created by stereotyping and sexism. This program worked quite well with the younger children, particularly the girls, who often became outraged about what they had learned about sexism. However, it actually had a boomerang effect among ninth-grade boys, who seemed to resist the new ideas they were being taught and actually expressed more stereotyped views after the training than before. And although ninth-grade girls took many of the lessons to heart, they still tended to cling to the idea that women should run the family and that men should be the primary breadwinners.

This study and others (see Katz & Walsh, 1991, for a review) suggest that efforts to change sex-role attitudes are more effective with younger children than with older ones and possibly with girls than with boys. It makes some sense that it is easier to alter children's thinking before their stereotypes have become fully crystallized; and many researchers now favor *cognitive interventions* that either attack the stereotypes directly or remove constraints on children's thinking that permit them to construct these rigid gender schemas. Rebecca Bigler and Lynn Liben (1990; 1992) have tried this approach with 5–11-year-olds. The children who participated in this research were assigned to one of three conditions:

1. *Rule training*. Through a series of problem-solving discussions, children were taught that (1) the most important considerations in deciding who would perform well at such traditionally masculine and feminine occupations as construction worker and beautician are the person's interests and willingness to learn, and (2) that the person's gender was irrelevant.

2. *Classification training*. Children were given multiple classification tasks that required them to sort objects into two categories at once (for example, men and women engaged in masculine and feminine activities). This training was designed to illustrate that objects can be classified in many ways, with the hope of helping children to see that occupations can be classified independently of the kinds of people who normally enact these roles.

3. *Control group.* Children were given lessons on the contributions of various occupations to the community.

Compared with children in the control group, those who either received rule training or who improved in classification skills showed clear declines in occupational stereotyping. Moreover, later tests of information processing provided further evidence for the weakening of children's stereotypes. Specifically, children who received rule training or who had gained in classification skills after the classification training were much more likely than "control" children to remember counterstereotypic information in stories (for example, recalling that the garbage man in a story was actually a woman). It seems, then, that gender stereotypes can be modified by directly attacking their accuracy (rule training) or by promoting the cognitive skills (classification training) that help children to see the fallacies in their own rigid gender schemas.

Finally, there is some evidence that programs designed to modify children's sex-stereotyped attitudes and behaviors may be more effective when the adult in charge is a male (Katz & Walsh, 1991). Why? Possibly because adult males make stronger distinctions between "gender-appropriate" and "gender-inappropriate" behaviors than adult females do; thus, they may be particularly noteworthy as *agents of change*. In other words, children may feel that cross-sex activities and aspirations are quite legitimate if it is a man who encourages (or fails to discourage) these pursuits.

So new gender-role attitudes can be taught, although it remains to be seen whether such change will persist and generalize to new situations if these attitudes are not reinforced at home or in the culture at large. Our society is slowly changing, however, and some people believe that these changes have already had an impact on children (Etaugh, Levine, & Mennella, 1984). Judith Lorber (1986) sees much hope in her 13-year-old's response to her inquiry about whether a pregnant acquaintance of theirs had delivered a boy or girl: "Why do you want to know?" this child of a new era asked (p. 567).

Concept Check 13-3 ∨ On Altering Sexist Attitudes

You are an educator who hopes to modify children's rigid gender stereotypes. Design a program based on the research literature that should help you to achieve this objective. One such program is described in the Appendix.

 # DEVELOPMENT OF SEXUALITY AND SEXUAL BEHAVIOR

As children acquire knowledge about males and females and about the roles that society expects males and females to assume, they are also becoming increasingly aware of their own **sexuality**—an aspect of development that will have a major effect on their concepts of self as men or women. In this final section of the chapter, we will briefly consider the growth of human sexuality and discuss some of the changes in adolescent sexual attitudes (and behavior) over the past 70 years.

Origins of Sexual Activities

When do children first display signs of sexuality? Might we humans really be "sexual" beings from birth, as Freud assumed? Although this claim might seem a bit outrageous, consider that both male babies (Kinsey, Pomeroy, & Martin, 1948) and female babies (Bakwin, 1973) have been observed to (1) fondle their genitals, (2) display the grunting, flushing, and sweating that accompany intense sexual arousal, and (3) have what appear to be orgasms before becoming pale and more tranquil. In fact, parents in some cultures are well aware of the pleasure that babies receive

sexuality: aspect of self referring to one's erotic thoughts, actions, and orientation.

Preschoolers are naturally curious about the human body.

from sexual gratification and occasionally use genital stimulation as a means of soothing a fussy or distressed infant (Ford & Beach, 1951).

Of course, infants are "sexual" beings only in the sense that their genitals are sensitive and their nervous systems allow sexual reflexes and responses. However, it will not be very long before they begin to learn what human sexuality is about and how the members of their society react to sexual behavior.

Sexual Behavior during Childhood

According to Freud, preschoolers in the *phallic stage* of psychosexual development are very interested in the functioning of their genitals and seek bodily pleasure through masturbation. However, Freud assumed that the traumas associated with the resolution of their Oedipus or Electra complexes would force school-age children to (1) repress their sexuality and (2) rechannel their energies into schoolwork and other nonerotic social activities during the long **latency period** of middle childhood. It turns out that Freud was partly right and partly wrong.

Freud was right about the sexual curiosity and sexual activities of preschool children. However, he was quite incorrect in assuming that sexuality declines during the grade school years. In fact, masturbation and other forms of sexual experimentation (including cross-sex exploits such as "playing doctor") actually *increase* with age (Rosen & Hall, 1984). In one large survey of 4–14-year-olds, more than half the boys and about one-third of the girls reported having masturbated and having engaged in some form of erotic play with same-sex peers (for example, manipulating each other's genitals); and about one-third of the respondents of each sex admitted that they had fondled the genitals of an other-sex playmate (Elias & Gebhard, 1969). Perhaps Freud was misled by the fact that preschoolers, often unaware of society's rules of etiquette, are more likely to get caught at their sex play than older children are. As Rosen and Hall (1984) put it, older children are very discreet, playing "by adult sexual rules, behaving around adults in the sexless manner that leads observers to believe that they are sexually inactive" (p. 287).

Cultural Influences on Childhood Sexuality

Perhaps Freud would not have been misled about the sexuality of grade school children had his patients come from *permissive* cultures, where children are free to express their sexuality and are even encouraged to prepare for their roles as mature sexual beings (Ford & Beach, 1951). On the island of Ponape, for example, 4- and 5-year-

latency period: Freud's fourth stage of psychosexual development (age 6 to puberty), in which sexual desires are repressed and the child's available libido is channeled into socially acceptable outlets such as schoolwork or vigorous play.

olds receive a thorough "sex education" from adults and are encouraged to experiment with one another. Among the Chewa of Africa, parents believe that practice makes perfect; so, with the blessings of their parents, older boys and girls build huts and play at being husbands and wives in trial marriages. Of course, Freud might have concluded that humans are largely sexless *throughout childhood* had he worked with people from *restrictive* cultures, in which all overt expressions of sexuality are actively suppressed. In New Guinea, for example, Kwoma boys are simply not allowed to touch themselves, and a boy caught having an erection is apt to have his penis beaten with a stick!

Where do the United States and other modern Western societies fall on this continuum of sexual restrictiveness and permissiveness? Most can be classified as "semi-restrictive." There are unspoken rules against childhood masturbation and sex play, but adults ignore many violations. Mainly, adults leave the task of preparing for adult sexual relations up to children themselves, and children end up learning from their peers how they should relate to the other sex.

As Barrie Thorne's (1993) observations in elementary schools demonstrate, boys and girls may be segregated by gender, but they are hardly oblivious to each other. They talk constantly of who "likes" whom, and who is "cute"; they play kiss-and-chase games in which girls attempt to catch boys and infect them with "cooties"; and they have steady boyfriends and girlfriends (if only for a few days). At times, boys and girls seem like mortal enemies, but by loving and hating each other, kissing and running away, they are grooming themselves for the establishment of heterosexual relationships later in life (Thorne, 1993).

Adolescent Sexuality

Sexuality assumes far greater importance once children experience puberty and become sexually mature: Now adolescents must incorporate concepts of themselves as sexual beings into their male or female self-concepts. They must also figure out how to properly express their sexuality. These tasks have never been easy. But they may now be more difficult than ever given the "new morality" that has emerged over the past several decades in Western societies. What are the sexual values of today's teenagers? What is "normal" sexual behavior during adolescence? And why do some adolescents display homosexual rather than heterosexual orientations (see Box 13-4)? Let's see what recent research can tell us.

Adolescent Sexual Morality

Have today's teenagers adopted a new morality that is dramatically different from the standards that their parents and grandparents held? In one sense they have, for adolescents have become increasingly liberal in their thinking about sex throughout this century—especially during the 1960s and 1970s. It seems that sexual *attitudes* may now be reverting ever so slightly in a conservative direction, largely as a result of the AIDS epidemic (Carroll, 1988). But even before the specter of AIDS, it was clear that few teenagers had completely abandoned the "old" (or traditional) morality.

In his review of the literature on teenage sexuality, Philip Dreyer (1982) noted three major changes in teenagers' sexual attitudes that describe what the "new morality" means to them (see also Abler & Sedlacek, 1989). First, most adolescents now believe that *sex with affection* is acceptable. Thus, today's youth are rejecting the maxim that premarital intercourse is always immoral, but they still believe that casual or exploitative sex is wrong (even though they may themselves have had such experiences). Still, only a surprisingly small percentage of sexually active adolescents in one national survey (6% of the males and 11% of the females) mentioned love as the major reason they first had intercourse; instead, nearly 75% of the girls and 80% of the boys attributed their loss of virginity to strong social pressures to initiate sexual relations, while also citing curiosity and sexual desire as important reasons for becoming sexually active (Harris & Associates, 1986).

BOX 13-4

On Sexual Orientation and the Origins of Homosexuality

Part of the task of establishing one's sexual identity is becoming aware of one's *sexual orientation*—one's preference for sexual partners of the same or other sex. Sexual orientation exists on a continuum, and not all cultures categorize sexual preferences as ours does (Paul, 1993), but we commonly describe people as having primarily heterosexual, homosexual, or bisexual orientations. Most adolescents establish a heterosexual sexual orientation without much soul-searching. For the 2% to 4% of youths who are attracted to members of their own sex, the process of accepting that they have a homosexual orientation and establishing a positive identity in the face of negative societal attitudes can be a long and torturous one. It is not that homosexual youths are especially critical of themselves, for their levels of general self-esteem are quite comparable to those of heterosexual peers (Savin-Williams, 1995). Yet, they often do not feel good about their gay or lesbian orientation, or gather the courage to "come out" until their mid-20s (Garnets & Kimmel, 1991).

How do adolescents become homosexual or heterosexual in orientation? In addressing this issue, John Money (1988) emphasizes that sexual orientation is *not* a choice we make but, rather, something that happens to us. In other words, we do not *prefer* to be gay or straight; we simply turn out that way. How, then, do homosexual individuals become homosexual?

Part of the answer lies in the genetic code, it seems. Michael Bailey and his colleagues (Bailey & Pillard, 1991; Bailey et al., 1993) find that identical twins are more alike in sexual orientation than fraternal twins are. But as we see in the table, only about half of identical twin pairs share the same sexual orientation. This means that environment contributes *at least as much as genes* to the development of sexual orientation.

What environmental factors might help to determine whether a person with a genetic predisposition toward homosexuality actually becomes attracted to same-sex companions? We really don't know as yet. The old psychoanalytic view that male homosexuality stems from having a domineering mother and a weak father has received little support (Bell, Weinberg, & Hammersmith, 1981). Nor is there any compelling evidence for the long-standing "seduction hypothesis"—the idea that homosexuals have been lured into the lifestyle by an older same-sex companion. Although many children and adolescents (perhaps 20%–40%) participate in at least one homosexual act, the vast majority do so with peers and turn out to be *heterosexual* anyway (Money, 1988). Even the once-popular notion that fathers who reject their sons will make them effeminate and push them toward homosexuality has failed to gain much support (Bell et al., 1981; Green, 1987). A more promising hypothesis is that hormonal influences during the prenatal period may be important (Meyer-Bahlburg et al., 1995; Witelson as cited by Hendrick, 1994a). For example, the fact that androgenized females are more likely than most women to adopt a lesbian or bisexual orientation suggests that high doses of male hormones prenatally may predispose at least some females to homosexuality (Dittman et al., 1992; Money, 1988). However, the fact is that no one yet knows exactly which factors in the prenatal or postnatal environment contribute, along with genes, to a homosexual orientation (Berenbaum & Snyder, 1995; Paul, 1993).

If one twin is gay (or lesbian), in what percentage of twin pairs does the other twin also have a homosexual or bisexual sexual orientation? Higher rates of concordance (similarity) for identical twin pairs than for fraternal twin pairs provide evidence of genetic influence on homosexuality, but less-than-perfect concordance points to the operation of environmental influences as well.

	Identical twins	Fraternal twins
Both male twins are gay/bisexual if one is	52%	22%
Both female twins are lesbian/bisexual if one is	48%	16%

Source: Male figures from Bailey & Pillard, 1991. Female figures from Bailey et al., 1993.

A second major change in teenage attitudes about sex might be termed the decline of the **double standard**—the idea that many sexual practices viewed as appropriate for males (for example, premarital sex, promiscuity) are less appropriate for females. The double standard hasn't disappeared, for fathers often seem to condone (or, at least, not to strongly discourage) the sexual exploits of their sons (Brooks-Gunn & Furstenberg, 1989), and college students of recent times still believed that a woman who has many sexual partners is more immoral than an equally promiscuous man (Robinson et al., 1991). But Western societies have been moving for some time toward a single standard of sexual behavior for both males and females.

Finally, a third change in adolescents' sexual attitudes might be described as *increased confusion about sexual norms.* As Dreyer (1982) notes, the "sex with affection"

double standard: the view that sexual behavior that is appropriate for members of one gender is inappropriate for the other.

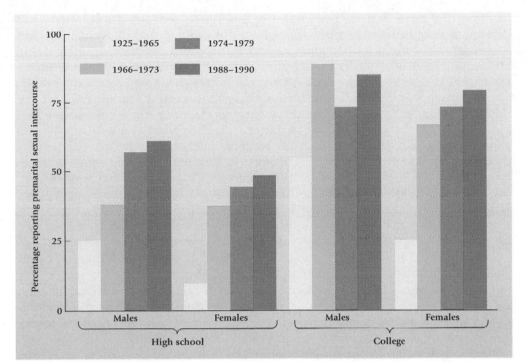

Figure 13-8
Historical changes in the percentages of high school and college students reporting premarital sexual intercourse.

Data for first three time periods adapted from Dreyer, 1982; data for most recent period from Baier, Rosenzweig, & Whipple, 1991; Centers for Disease Control, 1992; Reinisch et al., 1992.

idea is very ambiguous: Must one truly be in love, or is mere liking enough to justify sexual intercourse? It is now up to the individual(s) to decide. Yet these decisions are tough because adolescents receive mixed messages from many sources. On the one hand, they are often told by parents, the clergy, and advice columnists to value virginity and to avoid such consequences as pregnancy and sexually transmitted diseases. On the other hand, adolescents are strongly encouraged to be popular and attractive, and the more than 9,000 glamorous sexual innuendos and behaviors that they see annually on television (most of which occur between *unmarried* couples) may convince them that sexual activity is one means to these ends (American Academy of Pediatrics, 1986). Apparently, the behavior of older siblings adds to the confusion, for younger brothers and sisters of a sexually active teenager tend to be even more sexually involved at an earlier age than the older siblings were (Rodgers & Rowe, 1988). One young adolescent, lamenting the strong social pressures she faced to become sexually active, offered this amusing definition of a virgin: "An awfully ugly third grader" (Gullotta, Adams, & Alexander, 1986, p. 109). In years gone by, the norms of appropriate behavior were much simpler: Sex was fine if you were married (or perhaps engaged), but it should otherwise be avoided. This is not to say that our parents or grandparents always resisted the temptations they faced; but they probably had a lot less difficulty than today's adolescents in deciding whether what they were doing was acceptable or unacceptable.

Adolescent Sexual Behavior

Not only have sexual attitudes changed over the years, but so have patterns of sexual behavior. Today's teenagers are involved in more intimate forms of sexual activity (masturbation, petting, and intercourse) at earlier ages than adolescents of past eras were (Forrest & Singh, 1990; Hendrick, 1994b). Figure 13-8 shows the percentages of high school and college students from four historical periods who reported ever having experienced premarital intercourse. Clearly, the percentages of young people who have had intercourse increase over the adolescent years. About half of high school females and 60% of high school males have had intercourse (Centers for Disease Control, 1992; Hendrick, 1994b); among college students, the rate is now more like 70%–80% (Baier, Rosenzweig, & Whipple, 1991; Reinisch et al., 1991). Notice

Sexual involvement has become an integral component of the adolescent's search for an adult identity and emotional fulfillment.

also from the figure that the percentages of both males and females who have had intercourse have increased steadily throughout this century. And the sexual behavior of females has changed more than that of males—so much so that sex differences in adolescent sexual activity have all but disappeared (Wielandt & Boldsen, 1989). Apparently, the decline of the double standard reflects changes not only in attitudes but in behaviors as well. Finally, it is clearly a myth to assume that today's boys and girls are having sex as early and as often as circumstances permit. Only about 30% of U.S. teenagers have had sex by age 15, and their experiences are usually limited to one partner (Hendrick, 1994b). Girls are more likely than boys to insist that sex and love—physical and emotional intimacy—go together, and they are more likely than boys to have been in a steady relationship with their first sexual partner (Darling, Davidson, & Passarello, 1992). This attitudinal gap between the sexes can sometimes create misunderstandings and hurt feelings, and it may partially explain why females are less likely than males to describe their first sexual experience as satisfying (Coles & Stokes, 1985; Darling et al., 1992).

In sum, both the sexual attitudes and the sexual behaviors of adolescents have changed dramatically in this century—so much so that sexual involvement is now part of the normal adolescent's experience, a part of his or her search for an adult identity and emotional fulfillment (Dreyer, 1982). This is true of all major ethnic groups and social classes, and differences in sexual activity among social groups are shrinking dramatically (Forrest & Singh, 1990; Hendrick, 1994b).

Sadly, large numbers of sexually active adolescents fail to use contraception, largely because they are (1) uninformed about reproductive issues, (2) too cognitively immature to take seriously the possibility that their behavior could have serious long-term consequences, and (3) concerned that other people (including their partners) will think negatively of them if they appear prepared and thus "ready" to have sex (Brooks-Gunn & Furstenberg, 1989; Loewenstein & Furstenberg, 1991). Unfortunately, for the adolescent who gives birth, the consequences of teenage sexuality are likely to include an interrupted education, low income, and a difficult start for both the new mother and her child. And compared with children of older mothers, children born to teenagers show small but consistent cognitive decrements in the preschool and early grade school years and markedly lower academic achievement thereafter (Furstenberg, Brooks-Gunn, & Chase-Lansdale, 1989). The young mother's life situation and her child's developmental status sometimes improve, especially if she goes back to school and limits her family size; but she (and her children) are likely to remain economically disadvantaged compared with peers who postpone parenthood until their 20s (Furstenberg, Brooks-Gunn, & Chase-Lansdale, 1989).

What effect has the threat of AIDS had on adolescent sexual behavior? Most studies find some change, but not enough. One review of several recent surveys found that more than 70% of sexually active teens *report* using condoms regularly as a prevention against unwanted pregnancies and sexually transmitted diseases (Hendrick, 1994b). However, very few of them (only 1% of college students by one count) are actually doing what they would need to do to protect themselves from HIV infection: using a condom (latex, with a spermicide) *every* time (Maticka-Tyndale, 1991). And some adolescents continue to put themselves at risk by having sex with multiple partners (Forrest & Singh, 1990; Maticka-Tyndale, 1991). No wonder many educators are now calling for stronger programs of sex education and distribution of free condoms at school. There is little chance of preventing the unwanted consequences of teenage sexuality unless more adolescents either postpone sex or practice safer sex.

SUMMARY

Differences between males and females can be detected in the physical, psychological, and social realms. Some sex differences are biological in origin, whereas many others arise from socialization pressures. Interests, activities, and attributes that are considered more appropriate for members of one sex than the other are called sex-role standards (or sex-role stereotypes). Sex typing is the process by which children acquire a gender identity and assimilate the motives, values, and behaviors considered appropriate in their culture for members of their biological sex.

Research comparing males and females indicates that the two sexes are far more similar than they are different psychologically. Males tend to be more active, aggressive, and vulnerable to developmental disorders than females and to outperform females on tests of spatial abilities and arithmetic reasoning; females are more emotionally expressive and compliant than males, and they tend to outperform males on tests of verbal abilities. But on the whole, these sex differences are quite small. Among the beliefs that have no basis in fact are the notions that females are more sociable, suggestible, and illogical and less analytical and achievement-oriented than males. The persistence of these "cultural myths" can create self-fulfilling prophecies that (1) promote sex difficulties in cognitive performance, and (2) steer males and females along different career paths.

Sex typing begins very early. Infants begin to respond to males and females as different sorts of people by the end of the first year. By age 2½, most children know whether they are boys or girls; they tend to favor sex-typed toys and activities, and they are already aware of several sex-role stereotypes. By the time they enter school (or shortly thereafter), they know that gender is an unchanging aspect of their personalities, and they have learned most of the sex-role standards of their society. Boys face stronger sex-typing pressures than girls do, and consequently males are quicker to develop a preference for sex-appropriate patterns of behavior.

Several theories have been proposed to account for sex differences and sex-role development. Money and Ehrhardt's biosocial theory emphasizes the biological developments that occur before a child is born—developments that parents and other social agents react to when deciding how to socialize the child. Other theorists have focused more intently on the socialization process itself. Psychoanalytic theorists suggest that sex typing is a result of the child's identification with the same-sex parent. Social-learning theorists offer two mechanisms to explain how children acquire sex-typed attitudes and behaviors: (1) direct tuition (reinforcement for sex-appropriate behaviors and punishment for sex-inappropriate ones) and (2) observational learning. Cognitive-developmental theorists point out that the course of sex-role development depends, in part, on the child's cognitive development. And proponents of gender-schema theory have shown how children's active construction of gender schemas foster the continuance of unwarranted gender stereotypes and contribute to the development of sex-typed interests, attitudes, and patterns of behavior.

The psychological attributes "masculinity" and "femininity" are generally considered to be at opposite ends of a single dimension. However, one "new look" at sex roles proposes that masculinity and femininity are two separate dimensions and that the *androgynous* person is someone who possesses a fair number of masculine *and* feminine characteristics. Recent research shows that androgynous people do exist, are relatively popular and well adjusted, and may be adaptable to a wider variety of environmental demands than people who are traditionally sex typed. Parents and teachers (particularly males) may prevent rigid sex typing by emphasizing that one's sex is largely irrelevant outside the domain of reproduction, by encouraging and modeling other-sex as well as same-sex activities, and by highlighting and discussing the many exceptions to any unfounded gender stereotypes that their children may have acquired.

As Freud had thought, infants are sexual beings from the start, reacting physiologically to genital stimulation even though they have no awareness that their responses are "sexual" ones. Moreover, Freud's portrayal of preschool children as sexually curious beings was also correct, although he was very wrong in assuming that school-age children had repressed their sexual urges; in fact, sexual activity actually increases rather than declines during Freud's so-called latency period. Sexual matters become very important to adolescents, who, having reached sexual maturity, must incorporate their sexuality into their changing self-concepts. During this century, sexual attitudes have become much more permissive. The belief that premarital sex is immoral has given way to the view that sex with affection is acceptable; the double standard has weakened, and conflicting norms have increased confusion about what constitutes acceptable sexual conduct. Sexual behavior has increased as well, as more adolescents are engaging in various forms of sexual activity at earlier ages than in the past, despite the AIDS scare.

Key Terms

androgenized females [521]

androgyny [531]

basic gender identity [527]

castration anxiety [524]

direct tuition [525]

double standard [538]

Electra complex [524]

expressive role [505]

gender consistency [527]

gender identity [513]

gender intensification [515]

gender schemas [529]

gender stability [527]

identification [524]

"in-group/out-group" schema [529]

instrumental role [505]

latency period [536]

Oedipus complex [524]

own-sex schema [529]

phallic stage [524]

self-fulfilling prophecy [512]

sex-role standard [505]

sex typing [504]

sexuality [535]

testicular feminization syndrome (TFS) [519]

timing-of-puberty effect [520]

visual/spatial abilities [507]

Aggression, Altruism, and Moral Development

uppose that a large sample of parents was asked "What is the most important aspect of a child's social development?" Surely this is a question that could elicit any number of responses. However, it's a good bet that many parents would hope above all that their children would acquire a strong sense of morality—right and wrong—to guide their everyday interactions with other people.

What sort of moral principles and premises do parents and other adults hope to instill? We can get some clues by observing the ways they react to the behavior of young children. For example, adults often spring into action when they observe one child who appears to be harming another. Few parents would stand idly by as their 3-year-old "punches out" a playmate to gain control over a toy the other child is using. Few teachers would fail to comment on the inappropriateness of taunting, teasing, or otherwise insulting a classmate just because he shuns rough-and-tumble games in favor of more solitary activities. So children's unprovoked and intentional acts of harmdoing—or *aggression*—make up one class of behavior that many adults strive to suppress as they attempt to instill the principle that it is inappropriate and a violation of another person's rights to purposely attempt to harm that person.

Another value that many adults try to impart and hope their children will eventually acquire is *altruism*—that is, a selfless concern for the welfare of other people and a willingness to act on that concern. In fact, it is not at all unusual to see parents encouraging altruistic acts such as sharing, cooperating, or helping others while their children are still in diapers.

Finally, adults spend a considerable amount of time (1) describing various rules and regulations that children must obey and (2) carefully monitoring children's activities to ensure that these rules are followed (or, alternatively, that rule violations do not pass without comment). At first, parents' attempts to instill these rules of appropriate conduct may take the form of reinforcing praiseworthy behaviors and disrupting or punishing inappropriate acts while explaining why these transgressions are wrong. Of course, the ultimate goal of this *moral socialization* is to help the child to acquire a set of *personal* values, or moral principles, that will enable her to distinguish right from wrong and to do the "right" things, even when there may be no one else present to monitor and evaluate her conduct.

In this chapter, we will explore three interrelated aspects of social development that are often considered when making judgments about a child's moral character. We begin with the topic of aggression, asking how it develops and changes over time and then considering some of the ways that adults might effectively control such conduct. Our focus will then shift from harmdoing to a seemingly incompatible form of social activity—altruism and prosocial behavior—as we consider how young and reputedly selfish children might come to make personal sacrifices to benefit others. Finally, we will concentrate on the broader issue of moral development as we trace the child's evolution from a seemingly self-indulgent creature who appears to respect no rules to a moral philosopher of sorts who has internalized certain ethical principles to evaluate his own and others' conduct.

Let's now turn to the topic of aggression.

 THE DEVELOPMENT OF AGGRESSION

Although toddlers and preschool children often play together cooperatively, they may also fight over toys, punch, kick, or tease their companions, or call them names. Why do children behave aggressively? How does aggression change over time? And what can adults do to control these hostilities? These are some of the issues that we will consider in the pages that follow.

What Is Aggression?

What are we really referring to when we talk about aggression? Could it be an instinct—a basic part of human nature? Freud thought so (remember the Thanatos), as did ethologist Konrad Lorenz (1966), who argued that human beings (particularly males) are biologically programmed to fight over sources of food, territories, and members of the other sex. Yet, most contemporary researchers have rejected this instinctual view, choosing instead to think of human aggression as a particular category of goal-driven behaviors. According to this widely accepted *"intentional"* definition of **aggression,** an aggressive act is any form of behavior designed to harm or injure a living being who is motivated to avoid such treatment (Baron & Byrne, 1994). Notice that the actor's intentions are what define an act as "aggressive," not the act's consequences. Thus, the intentional definition would classify as aggressive all acts in which harm was intended but not done (for example, a violent kick that misses its target) while excluding accidental injuries or activities such as rough-and-tumble play in which participants are enjoying themselves with no harmful intent.

Aggressive acts are often divided into two categories: **hostile aggression** and **instrumental aggression.** If an actor's major goal is to harm a victim, his or her behavior qualifies as hostile aggression. By contrast, instrumental aggression describes those situations in which one person harms another as a means to some other end. Clearly, the same overt act could be classified as either hostile or instrumental aggression depending on the circumstances. If a young boy clobbered his sister and then teased her for crying, we might consider this hostile aggression. But these same actions could be labeled instrumentally aggressive (or a mixture of hostile and instrumental aggression) had the boy also grabbed a toy that his sister was using.

Origins of Aggression in Infancy

Although young infants do get angry and may occasionally strike people, it is difficult to think of these actions as having an aggressive intent. Piaget (1952) describes an incident in which he frustrated 7-month-old Laurent by placing his hand in front of an interesting object that Laurent was trying to reach. The boy then smacked Piaget's hand, as if it merely represented an obstruction that must be removed.

However, the picture soon changes. Marlene Caplan and her associates (1991) find that 1-year-old infants can be quite forceful with each other when one infant controls a toy that the other wants. Even when duplicate toys are available, 12-month-olds occasionally ignored these unused objects and tried to overpower a peer in order to control *that child's* toy. And the intimidators in these tussles appeared to be treating the other child as an *adversary* rather than an inanimate obstacle—implying that the seeds of instrumental aggression may already have been sown by the end of the first year.

Although 2-year-olds have just as many (or more) conflicts over toys as 1-year-olds do, they are more likely than 1-year-olds to resolve these disputes by negotiating and sharing than by fighting, particularly when toys are in short supply (Caplan et al., 1991). So early conflicts need not be training grounds for aggression. Indeed, Dale Hay (1984) thinks that these squabbles can be quite adaptive, serving as a context in which infants and toddlers can learn how to negotiate and thereby achieve their aims without having to resort to shows of force.

Age-Related Changes in the Nature of Aggression

The character of children's aggression changes dramatically with age. In her classic study of the development of aggression among preschoolers, Florence Goodenough (1931) asked mothers of 2–5-year-olds to keep diaries in which they recorded the details of their children's angry outbursts. In examining these data, Goodenough found that unfocused temper tantrums became less and less common between ages 2 and 3 as children began to *physically retaliate* (by hitting or kicking) when playmates frustrated or attacked them. However, physical aggression gradually declined between ages 3 and 5, only to be replaced by teasing, tattling, name calling, and other forms of verbal aggression. What were these preschoolers squabbling about? Goodenough found that they fought most often over toys and other possessions, so that their aggression was usually *instrumental* in character. And although the majority of

aggression: behavior performed with the intention of harming a living being who is motivated to avoid this treatment.

hostile aggression: aggressive acts for which the actor's major goal is to harm or injure a victim.

instrumental aggression: aggressive acts for which the actor's major goal is to gain access to objects, space, or privileges.

The squabbles of young children usually center around toys, candy, or other treasured resources and qualify as acts of instrumental aggression.

As children mature, an increasing percentage of their aggressive acts qualify as examples of hostile aggression.

tussles among older (4–7-year-old) children are still centered around the control of objects, Willard Hartup (1974) found that an increasing percentage of their aggressive outbursts are *hostile* exchanges designed primarily to harm an adversary.

It is easy to imagine why physical aggression might peak early and decline with age: Not only are adults apt to respond negatively to these high-intensity antics, either to maintain their own sanity or to prepare their older preschoolers for a structured kindergarten environment (Emmerich, 1966), but older children may have also learned from their own experiences that negotiation can be a relatively painless and efficient method of achieving the same instrumental objectives that they used to attempt through a show of force (Shantz, 1987). Why, then, would hostile aggression *increase* with age? Hartup's view is that older children are acquiring important role-taking skills that will enable them to infer the motives and intentions of other people. So when a companion behaves in a deliberately harmful way, a grade school child is more likely to detect the aggressive intent and retaliate against the harmdoer.

Yet, it is important to note that 7–11-year-olds, who can easily discriminate accidental from deliberate harmdoing, may react aggressively to almost any provocation, even those that they know were unintentional (Sancilio, Plumert, & Hartup, 1989). Why? Because grade school children (particularly boys) are reluctant to condemn **retaliatory aggression,** often viewing it as an understandable (though not necessarily moral) response to provocation (Astor, 1994; Coie et al., 1991; Ferguson & Rule, 1988). So another reason why hostile aggression may increase with age is that peers informally sanction the practice of fighting back; they view it as a normal reaction to harmdoing (Sancilio et al., 1989).

From aggression to antisocial conduct. The incidence of hostile and other retaliatory forms of aggression peaks early in adolescence (that is, at age 13–15) and declines thereafter (Cairns et al., 1989; Loeber, 1982). However, this does not necessarily mean that adolescents are becoming any better behaved. Teenage girls begin to conceal their hostilities, turning to *social ostracism*—that is, malicious gossip and exclusion—as a means of dealing with adversaries (Bjorkqvist, Lagerspetz, & Kaukiainen, 1992; Cairns et al., 1989). And boys are now more likely to express their anger and frustrations through such delinquent acts as theft, truancy, substance abuse, and sexual misconduct (Newcomb & Bentler, 1989; U.S. Department of Justice, 1992). So it seems that adolescents who are becoming less overtly aggressive may simply turn to more *covert* forms of antisocial conduct to express their aggressive impulses.

retaliatory aggression: aggressive acts elicited by real or imagined provocations.

Individual Differences in Aggression

Children of all ages differ, and differ dramatically, in aggression. In fact, some investigators who have charted aggressive exchanges among grade school children find that a small minority of youngsters are involved in a large majority of the conflicts (Perry, Kusel, & Perry, 1988). Who is involved? In many groups, the participants are a handful of highly aggressive children and the 10%–15% of their classmates who are regularly abused by these bullies (Olweus, 1984; Perry et al., 1988).

How do highly aggressive children differ from their less aggressive classmates? For one thing, they have more positive *expectancies* about the outcomes of aggression; compared with nonaggressive peers, they are (1) more confident that aggression will yield tangible rewards (such as control of a disputed toy), (2) more certain that aggression will be successful at terminating others' noxious behavior, and (3) more inclined to believe that aggression will enhance their self-esteem and will not cause their victims any permanent harm (Perry, Perry, & Rasmussen, 1986; Quiggle et al., 1992; Slaby & Guerra, 1988). Second, aggressive children are more likely than nonaggressive children to *value* the outcomes of aggression; that is, they attach much significance to their ability to dominate and control their victims, and they are not particularly concerned about the suffering they may cause or the possibility of being rejected by their peers (Boldizar, Perry, & Perry, 1989; Coie et al., 1991). Finally, Kenneth Dodge (1980; 1986) has argued that highly aggressive children display a **hostile attributional bias** that causes them to overattribute harmful intentions to their peers, thus viewing them as belligerent adversaries who *deserve* to be dealt with in a forceful manner (see also Astor, 1994). Let's take a closer look.

According to Dodge's social-cognitive theory of aggression, highly aggressive youngsters who have a history of bickering and fighting with their peers are likely to carry in memory a powerful expectancy that "other people are often hostile to me." Thus, whenever aggressive children are harmed, they may be predisposed to search for social cues that will confirm this expectancy. Should they then experience truly *ambiguous* harmdoing (such as being hit by a ball while walking across the playground), aggressive children should be more likely than nonaggressive ones to attribute hostile intent to the harmdoer, which makes them *angry* and predisposes them to retaliate (see Graham, Hudley, & Williams, 1992). The aggressive child's hostile reaction may then trigger counteraggression from his victim, which, as we see in Figure 14-1, should reinforce the aggressive child's impression that others are hostile, thus starting the vicious cycle all over again.

hostile attributional bias: tendency to view harm done under ambiguous circumstances as having stemmed from a hostile intent on the part of the harmdoer; characterizes highly aggressive children and adolescents.

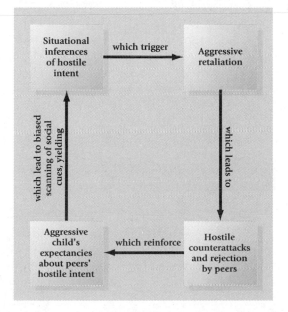

Figure 14-1
A social-cognitive model of the aggressive child's biased attributions about ambiguous harmdoing and their behavioral outcomes.

Tests of Dodge's theory. Do aggressive children really interpret ambiguous information about harmdoing as implying a hostile intent? To find out, Dodge (1980) had highly aggressive and nonaggressive boys from the second, fourth, and sixth grades each work on a jigsaw puzzle in one room while a peer worked on a similar puzzle in a second room. During a break when the boys had switched rooms to check on each other's progress, the subject heard a voice on the intercom. The voice (supposedly that of the peer who was examining the subject's puzzle) then expressed either a *hostile* intent ("Gee, he's got a lot done—I'll mess it up"), a *benign* intent ("I'll help him—Oh, no, I didn't mean to drop it"), or an *ambiguous* intent ("Gee, he's got a lot done") just before a loud crash (presumably the subject's puzzle being scattered). How did the subjects respond? Dodge found that both aggressive and nonaggressive boys reacted much more aggressively (as measured by disassembling the harmdoer's puzzle or making verbal threats) to a hostile intent than to a benign intent. So aggressive boys did not distort social cues when the harmdoer's intentions were obvious. But when the intent was ambiguous, cue distortion was apparent: Aggressive boys quickly retaliated as if the peer had acted with a hostile intent, whereas nonaggressive boys typically did nothing or said something positive, as if the peer's intentions were honorable. Later research indicates that highly aggressive girls distort cues about ambiguous harmdoing in roughly the same way that aggressive boys do (Dodge et al., 1984; Guerra & Slaby, 1990).

Are the expectancies of aggressive children valid ones? As it turns out, aggressive youngsters may have some very good reasons for attributing hostile intentions to others: Not only do aggressive children provoke a large number of conflicts, but they are also more likely than nonaggressive children to be disliked (Dodge, Coie, Pettit, & Price, 1990), to experience negative interactions with teachers (see Trachtenberg & Viken, 1994), and to become targets of peer aggression. In fact, *nonaggressive* children who are harmed under ambiguous circumstances are much more likely to retaliate *if the harmdoer has a reputation as an aggressive child* (Dodge & Frame, 1982; Sancilio et al., 1989). So by virtue of their own hostile inclinations, highly aggressive children ensure that they will often elicit unfavorable reactions from adults and other children.

Earlier, we noted that most acts of aggression in children's groups involve a highly aggressive child and one of his (her) chronic victims. In Box 14-1, we will see what researchers have learned about that small minority of youngsters who are habitually abused by their peers.

Sex Differences in Aggression

In Chapter 13, we learned that males are more aggressive than females. Data from more than 100 studies conducted in countries all over the world reveal that boys and men are clearly more physically aggressive than girls and women and may be more verbally aggressive as well (Bogard, 1990; Harris, 1992; Maccoby & Jacklin, 1974). The probability of becoming a *target* of aggression also depends on one's sex: Conflicts of all kinds are more common in boy-boy than in boy-girl or girl-girl dyads (Barnett, 1979), and even though boys can be quite verbally abusive toward girls, it seems that they are less likely to physically assault a harmdoer if that person is a girl (Barnett, 1979; Cairns et al., 1989). Perhaps boys do take to heart the cultural maxim that it is inappropriate to clobber little girls (Cairns et al., 1989), although their reluctance to do so may also stem from a fear of offending their parents (Herzberger & Hall, 1993; Perry, Perry, & Weiss, 1989).

We also noted in Chapter 13 that hormonal and other biological differences may contribute to sex differences in aggression. Yet, proponents of a social viewpoint are quick to point out that *very* young boys are *not* more aggressive than girls. In fact, Marlene Caplan and her associates (1991) found that forceful, aggressive resolutions of disputes over toys were actually more numerous among 1-year-olds when the play

BOX 14-1
Victims of Peer Aggression

*E*ach of us has probably known at least one victimized child—a youngster who repeatedly serves as a target for other children's hostile acts. Who are these children? Why are they singled out for abuse?

Dan Olweus's (1978, 1984) studies of 13–16-year-old Swedish "toughs" and their "whipping boys" provide some clues. Based on ratings made by their teachers, about 10% of Olweus's subjects could be described as habitual bullies who regularly subjected another 10% of the sample (their whipping boys) to physical and verbal harassment. Comparing the personality profiles of bullies, victims, and other well-adjusted male classmates, Olweus found that whipping boys showed a number of distinctive characteristics. They were (1) highly anxious, (2) low in self-esteem, (3) socially isolated, (4) physically weak, and (5) afraid to be assertive or to defend themselves. Most of these chronic patsies were "passive victims" who were quick to submit to their peers and who appeared to do nothing (other than being "easy marks") to invite the hostilities that they received (see also Schwartz, Dodge, & Coie, 1993). But about one victimized adolescent in five could be described as a "provocative victim"—one who was restless, hot-tempered, inclined to irritate or tease others, and who would at least attempt to fight back (unsuccessfully) when attacked by a peer.

David Perry and his associates (1988; Perry, Williard, & Perry, 1990) have studied patterns of aggression and victimization in American elementary schools, finding that, even among third-graders, about 1 child in 10 was repeatedly abused by highly aggressive classmates. Perry, like Olweus, found that there are two kinds of victims—passive and provocative—and he discovered that both groups are disliked and rejected by their peers. Interestingly, girls are victimized almost as often as boys, although female victims are more likely to be verbally harassed and less likely to be physically assaulted than male victims are. Finally, being a victim is apparently a stable attribute, for children who were highly victimized at the beginning of the study were still viewed as extreme victims three months later by their teachers and peers (and, indeed, Olweus found that his 13-year-old whipping boys were likely to retain that status when observed at age 16).

How are victimized children perceived by their classmates? Why might they be chosen as victims? Perry et al. (1990) addressed these issues by asking fourth- through seventh-graders to contemplate acts of aggression against victimized and nonvictimized peers and to estimate the consequences of these actions. They found that classmates of chronic victims hold very *positive expectancies* about attacking a victimized peer—that is, they felt that victimized children were "easy marks" who would reinforce them by surrendering tangible resources and by showing signs of dis-

tress (or defeat). Moreover, peers seemed to *value* tangible rewards more when taken from a victimized rather than a nonvictimized child, and they were relatively unconcerned about the prospect of harming (or being harmed by) these targets of abuse. So both aggressive and nonaggressive peers expect good things to follow from their attacks on chronic victims, and they even *exaggerate* the importance of obtaining these outcomes! Given the high probability of defeating a victimized child and the value attached to dominating these "whipping boys" (and girls), it is easy to see why the field of potential victims narrows considerably (to about 10% of a typical grade school class) over the course of middle childhood.

A large percentage of aggressive episodes in children's peer groups involve chronic victims and the highly aggressive youngsters who regularly torment them.

Clearly, there is much that we still don't know about the causes and consequences of prolonged victimization. Why, for example, are "passive" victims so disliked that their tormentors relish the prospect of dominating them and are relatively unconcerned about the suffering these children may experience? Are these young whipping boys (and girls) at risk of becoming depressed, untrusting adolescents and young adults who are likely to experience serious adjustment problems later in life? And how might we help victimized children become less inviting targets for their peers? Obviously, these are important questions that developmentalists will be trying to answer in the years ahead.

groups were dominated *by girls!* Even at age 2, groups dominated by boys were more likely than those dominated by girls to negotiate and share when toys were scarce. It is not until age 2½ to 3 that sex differences in aggression are reliable, and this is clearly enough time for social influences to have steered boys and girls in different directions (see Fagot, Leinbach, & O'Boyle, 1992).

Of course, there are many social influences that might conspire to make boys more aggressive than girls. For example, parents play rougher with boys than with girls; they react more negatively to the aggressive antics of daughters than to those of sons (Mills & Rubin, 1990; Parke & Slaby, 1983), and they are more likely to side with their sons than with their daughters in disputes with peers (Ross, Tesla, Kenyon, & Lollis, 1990). The toy guns, tanks, missile launchers, and other symbolic implements of destruction that parents buy their sons encourage the enactment of aggressive themes and actually promote aggressive behavior (see Feshbach, 1956; Turner & Goldsmith, 1976), whereas the dolls, dollhouses, and miniature tea sets that daughters receive promote their adoption of a nurturant, expressive (nonaggressive) orientation. By the time they enter grade school, children have categorized aggression as a male attribute in their gender schemas, and their ability to recall information about previous aggressive episodes is much better if the perpetrators were boys rather than girls (Bukowski, 1990). And by age 9 to 12, boys expect less parental and peer disapproval for aggression than girls do; they also think that aggression will provide them more tangible rewards, and they value these outcomes more than girls do (Boldizar et al., 1989; Herzberger & Hall, 1993; Perry et al., 1989). So even though biological factors may contribute, it is clear that sex differences in aggression depend to no small extent on the sex-typing process and sex differences in social learning.

Is Aggression a Stable Attribute?

We've seen that the kinds of aggression and antisocial conduct that children display change over time. But what about aggressive dispositions? Do aggressive preschoolers remain highly aggressive throughout the grade school years, during adolescence, and as young adults?

Apparently, aggression is a reasonably stable attribute. Not only are aggressive toddlers likely to become aggressive 5-year-olds (Cummings, Iannotti, & Zahn-Waxler, 1989), but the amount of physical and verbal aggression that a child displays at ages 6 to 10 is a fairly good predictor of his or her aggressive or other antisocial inclinations later in life (Cairns et al., 1989; Kagan & Moss, 1962). Rowell Huesmann and his associates (1984), for example, tracked one sample of 600 subjects for 22 years. They found that highly aggressive 8-year-olds often became relatively hostile 30-year-olds who were likely to batter their spouses or children and to be convicted of criminal offenses (see Figure 14-2). Similarly, Avshalom Caspi and his colleagues (1987) found that both boys and girls who had been moody, aggressive, and ill-tempered at age 10 tended to become ill-tempered young adults whose relations with their spouses and children were generally unpleasant and conflictual.

Of course, these findings reflect group trends and do not necessarily imply that a highly aggressive individual cannot become relatively nonaggressive over time, or vice versa. Yet we should not be surprised to find that aggression is a reasonably stable attribute for many children. Twin studies suggest that some individuals are genetically predisposed to have irritable temperaments and to engage in aggressive behavior and other antisocial acts (Plomin, 1990; Rushton et al., 1986). And regardless of their genetic predispositions, some children remain highly aggressive because they have been raised in social environments that can be described as "training grounds" for the establishment and *maintenance* of aggressive habits (Bandura, 1991; Dodge, 1993). Let's now consider two important kinds of social influences that help to explain why some children and adolescents are more aggressive than others: (1) the norms and values endorsed by their societies and subcultures and (2) the family settings in which they are raised.

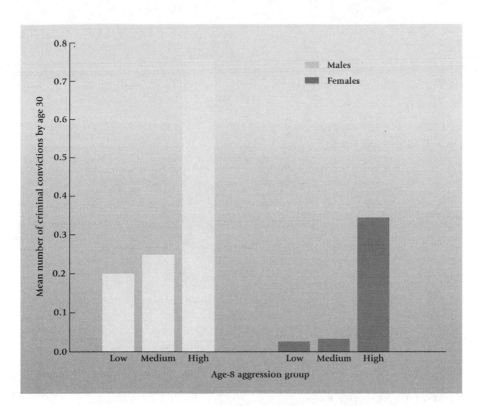

Figure 14-2
Aggression in childhood predicts criminal behavior in
adulthood for both males and
females.
*From Huesmann, Eron, Lefkowitz, &
Walder, 1984.*

Cultural and Subcultural Influences on Aggression

Cross-cultural studies consistently indicate that some societies and subcultures are more violent and aggressive than others. Peoples such as the Arapesh of New Guinea, the Lepchas of Sikkim, and the Pygmies of central Africa all use weapons to hunt but rarely show any kind of interpersonal aggression. When these peace-loving societies are invaded by outsiders, their members retreat to inaccessible regions rather than stand and fight (Gorer, 1968).

In marked contrast to these groups is the Ik tribe of Uganda, whose members live in small bands and steal from, deceive, or even kill one another in order to ensure their own survival (Turnbull, 1972). Another aggressive society is the Gebusi of New Guinea, who teach their children to be combative and emotionally unresponsive to the needs of others and who show a murder rate that is more than 50 times higher than that of any industrialized nation (Scott, 1992). The United States is also an "aggressive" society. On a percentage basis, the incidence of rape, homicide, and assault is higher in the United States than in any other industrialized nation (see Figure 14-3), and the United States ranks a close second to Spain (and far above third-place Canada) in the incidence of armed robbery (Wolff, Rutten, & Bayer, 1992).

Studies conducted in the United States and in England also point to social-class differences in aggression: Children and adolescents from the lower socioeconomic strata (SES)—particularly males from larger urban areas—exhibit more aggressive behavior and higher levels of delinquency than their age-mates from the middle class (see Atwater, 1992, and Feshbach, 1970, for reviews). African-American males, in particular, are overrepresented among school-age children labeled as aggressive and among juveniles arrested for delinquency—so much so that researchers who study childhood aggression often include large numbers of black males in their samples (Graham et al., 1992). Yet, this finding may simply reflect the fact that more African Americans live in poverty, for other researchers are finding that economically disadvantaged white children and adolescents are every bit as aggressive and are just as inclined to commit violent crimes as disadvantaged African Americans are (Dodge, Pettit, & Bates, 1994; Farrington, 1987).

Figure 14-3
Frequencies of three major violent crimes in modern industrialized societies.
Adapted from Wolff, 1992.

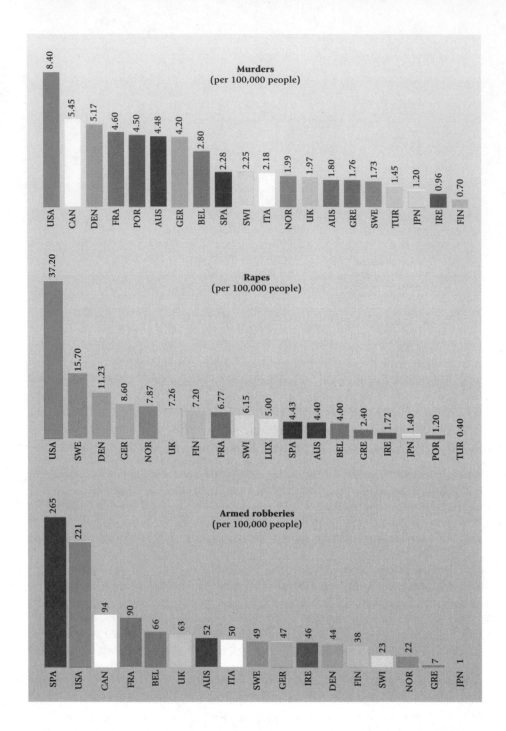

What accounts for these social-class differences in aggression and antisocial conduct? One important contributor seems to be social-class differences in parenting (Dodge et al., 1994). Parents from the lower socioeconomic strata tend to display a number of attitudes and child-rearing practices that previous child-rearing studies have found to be strong correlates of childhood and adolescent aggression. For example, they often display less warmth and more hostility toward their children than middle-class parents do; they also tend to rely more on physical punishment to discipline aggression and noncompliance, thus *modeling aggression* even as they are trying to suppress it (Dodge et al., 1994; Patterson, DeBaryshe, & Ramsey, 1989; Sears et al., 1957; Weiss et al., 1992). Indeed, a child who learns that he will be hit, kicked, or shoved when he displeases his parents will probably direct the same kinds of responses toward playmates who displease him (Hart, Ladd, & Burleson, 1990). Low-

Antisocial or delinquent conduct is rather common among teenagers whose parents fail to monitor their activities, whereabouts, and choice of friends.

SES parents are also more inclined to endorse aggressive solutions to conflict and to encourage their children to respond forcefully when provoked by peers (Dodge et al., 1994)—practices that may foster the development of the *hostile attributional bias* that highly aggressive youngsters so often display. Finally, low-SES parents are often less inclined to manage or monitor their child's whereabouts, activities, and choice of friends, and this *lack* of parental monitoring is consistently associated with such aggressive or delinquent adolescent behaviors as fighting with peers, sassing teachers, destroying property, abusing drugs, and generally breaking rules outside the home (Capaldi & Patterson, 1991; Patterson & Stouthamer-Loeber, 1984).

In sum, a person's aggressive or antisocial inclinations depend, in part, on the extent to which the culture or subculture encourages and condones such behavior. Yet not all people in pacifistic societies are kind, cooperative, and helpful, and the vast majority of people raised in "aggressive" societies or subcultures are not especially prone to violence. Why are there such dramatic individual differences in aggression within a given culture or subculture? Gerald Patterson and his associates answer by claiming that highly aggressive children often live in homes that can be described as "breeding grounds" for hostile, antisocial conduct. Let's take a closer look.

Coercive Home Environments: Breeding Grounds for Aggression and Delinquency

Patterson (1982; Patterson et al., 1989) has observed patterns of interaction among children and their parents in families that have at least one highly aggressive child. The aggressive children in Patterson's sample seemed "out of control"; they fought a lot at home and at school and were generally unruly and defiant. These families were then compared with other families of the same size and socioeconomic status that had no problem children.

Families as Social Systems

Patterson soon discovered that one could not explain "out of control" behavior by merely focusing on the child-rearing practices that parents use. Instead, it seemed that highly aggressive children were living in rather atypical family environments that were characterized by a social climate that *they had helped to create*. Unlike most homes, where people frequently display approval and affection, the highly aggressive problem child usually lives in a setting in which family members are constantly struggling with one another: They are reluctant to initiate conversations, and, when they do talk, they tend to needle, threaten, or otherwise irritate other family members rather than converse positively. Patterson called these settings **coercive home environments** because a high percentage of interactions centered on one family member's attempts to force another to stop irritating him or her. He also noted that **negative reinforcement** was important in maintaining these coercive interactions: When one family member makes life unpleasant for another, the second learns to whine, yell, scream, tease, or hit because these actions often force the antagonist to stop (and thus are reinforced). Consider the following sequence of events, which may be fairly typical in a coercive home environment:

1. A girl teases her older brother, who makes her stop teasing by yelling at her (yelling is negatively reinforced).
2. A few minutes later, the girl calls her brother a nasty name. The boy then chases and hits her.
3. The girl stops calling him names (which negatively reinforces hitting). She then whimpers and hits him back, and he withdraws (negatively reinforcing her hits). The boy then approaches and hits his sister again, and the conflict escalates.
4. At this point, the mother intervenes. However, her children are too emotionally disrupted to listen to reason, so she finds herself applying punitive and coercive tactics to make them stop fighting.
5. The fighting stops (thus reinforcing the mother for using coercive methods). However, the children now begin to whine, cry, or yell at the mother. These countercoercive techniques are then reinforced if the mother backs off and accepts peace at any price. Unfortunately, backing off is only a temporary solution. The next time that the children antagonize each other and become involved in an unbearable conflict, the mother is likely to use even more coercion to get them to stop. The children once again apply their own methods of countercoercion to induce her to "lay off," and the family atmosphere becomes increasingly unpleasant for everyone.

Patterson finds that mothers of problem children rarely use social approval as a means of behavior control, choosing instead to largely ignore prosocial conduct, to interpret many innocuous acts as antisocial, and to rely almost exclusively on coercive tactics to deal with perceived misconduct. Perhaps the overwhelmingly negative treatment that these problem children receive at home (including parents' tendency to label ambiguous events as antisocial) helps to explain why they generally mistrust other people and display the *hostile attributional bias* so commonly observed among highly aggressive children (Dishion, 1990; see also Weiss et al., 1992). And ironically, children from highly coercive home environments eventually become resistant to punishment. They have learned to fight coercion with countercoercion and often do so by defying the parent and *repeating the very act that she is trying to suppress*. Why? Because this is one of the few ways that the child can be successful at commanding the attention of an adult who rarely offers praise or shows any signs of affection. No wonder Patterson calls these children "out of control"! By contrast, children from noncoercive families receive much more positive attention from siblings and parents, so that they don't have to irritate other family members to be noticed (Patterson, 1982).

So we see that the flow of influence in the family setting is *multidirectional:* Coercive *interactions* between parents and their children and the children themselves affect the behavior of *all* parties and may contribute to the development of a hostile family environment—a true breeding ground for aggression. Unfortunately, these problem families may never break out of this destructive pattern of attacking and counterattacking one another unless they receive help. In Box 14-2, we will look at one particularly effective approach to this problem—a method that necessarily focuses on the entire family as a social system rather than solely on the aggressive child who has been referred for treatment.

coercive home environment: a home in which family members often annoy one another and use aggressive or otherwise antisocial tactics as a method of coping with these aversive experiences.

negative reinforcer: any stimulus whose removal or termination, as the consequence of an act, increases the probability that the act will recur.

BOX 14-2

Helping Children (and Parents) Who Are "Out of Control"

How does one treat a problem child who is hostile, defiant, and "out of control"? Rather than focusing on the problem child, Gerald Patterson's (1981, 1982) approach is to work with the entire family. Patterson begins by carefully observing the family's interactions and determining just how family members are reinforcing one another's coercive activities. The next step is to describe the nature of the problem to parents and to teach them a new approach to managing their children's behavior. Some of the principles, skills, and procedures that Patterson stresses are the following:

1. Don't give in to the child's coercive behavior.
2. Don't escalate your own coercion when the child becomes coercive.
3. Control the child's coercion with the *time-out* procedure—a method in which the child is sent to her room (or some other location) until she calms down and stops using coercive tactics.
4. Identify those of the child's behaviors that are most irritating, and then establish a point system in which the child can earn credits (rewards, privileges) for acceptable conduct or lose them for unacceptable behavior. Parents with older problem children are taught how to formulate "behavioral contracts" that specify how the child is expected to behave at home and at school, as well as how deviations from this behavioral code will be punished. Whenever possible, children should have a say in negotiating these contracts.

5. Be on the lookout for occasions when you can respond to the child's prosocial conduct with warmth and affection. Although this is often difficult for parents who are accustomed to snapping at their children and accentuating the negative, Patterson believes that parental affection and approval will reinforce good conduct and eventually elicit displays of affection from the child—a clear sign that the family is on the road to recovery.

A clear majority of problem families respond quite favorably to these methods. Not only do problem children become less coercive, defiant, and aggressive, but the mother's depression fades as she gradually begins to feel better about herself, her child, and her ability to resolve family crises (Patterson, 1981). Some problem families show an immediate improvement. Others respond more gradually to the treatment and may require periodic "booster shots"—that is, follow-up treatments in which the clinician visits the family, determines why progress has slowed (or broken down), and then retrains the parents or suggests new procedures to correct the problems that are not being resolved. Clearly, this therapy works because it recognizes that "out of control" behavior stems from a *family system* in which both parents and children are influencing each other and contributing to the development of a hostile family environment. Therapies that focus exclusively on the problem child are not enough!

Coercive Home Environments as Contributors to Chronic Delinquency

How serious are the risks faced by "out of control" children who grow up in a coercive home environment? Patterson and his associates (1989) have addressed this issue by reviewing the literature on problem children and drawing some strong conclusions. As shown in Figure 14-4, coercive parenting early in childhood contributes to the development of children's hostile attributional biases, defiant, aggressive behaviors, and general lack of self-restraint (see also Feldman & Weinberger, 1994), which, in turn, can cause these youngsters to be rejected by grade school peers, to be criticized by teachers, and to founder academically. These poor outcomes may then cause parents to feel less invested in their children and less inclined to closely monitor their activities (Patterson et al., 1989; Vuchinich et al., 1992).

Moreover, the rejection that problem children experience from peers, coupled with their likely placement in classes or study groups with other academically deficient children, often means that they have lots of exposure to other relatively defiant, aggressive, and socially unskilled youngsters like themselves. Indeed, Thomas Dishion and his associates (1991) found that aggressive preadolescent boys who had been rejected by peers earlier in childhood were now associating mainly with other hostile, antisocial classmates and were much more likely than nonrejected boys to be involved in antisocial conduct. In other words, aggressive preadolescents were banding together to form deviant cliques (see Cairns et al., 1988, for evidence that aggressive girls also form such alliances) that tend to devalue academics, encourage aggression, and

Figure 14-4

A model of the development of chronic antisocial behavior.

Adapted from Patterson, DeBaryshe, & Ramsey, 1989.

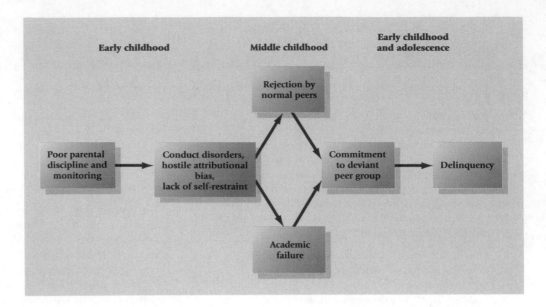

promote such dysfunctional adolescent activities as sexual misconduct, substance abuse, dropping out of school, and a variety of other kinds of delinquent or criminal behaviors (Cairns, Cairns, & Neckerman, 1989; Newcomb & Bentler, 1989; Patterson et al., 1989, 1992). So, to return to the question raised above, Patterson et al. (1989) think that living in a coercive home environment poses serious risks indeed, for such an experience is often a crucial first step along the road to chronic antisocial or delinquent behavior.

Although more boys than girls complete the developmental progression described in Figure 14-4 and become chronic delinquents, the delinquency "gender gap" is narrowing (*Uniform Crime Reports,* 1989). Male delinquents still dominate the violent crime statistics, but females are about as likely as males to be involved in larcenies, sexual misconduct, and substance abuse, and they are more likely than males to be arrested for such status offenses as running away from home and engaging in prostitution (*Uniform Crime Reports,* 1989). Although it does seem to take a more disordered home environment to push girls along the path to delinquency (Thornburg, 1986), females can become just as chronically antisocial as males can.

Family interventions of the kind described in Box 14-2 can be quite effective at modifying the antisocial tendencies of preadolescent (and younger) children; however, once antisocial patterns continue into adolescence, so many factors conspire to maintain them that interventions are usually unsuccessful (Kazdin, 1987; Patterson et al., 1989). Note the implication here: To cope with the problem of chronic delinquency, we must think in terms of *preventive* interventions with programs that would ideally (1) teach parents more effective child-management techniques, (2) foster children's social skills to prevent them from being rejected by their peers, and (3) provide any academic remediation that may be necessary to keep children on track at school and to lessen the likelihood that they will fall in with deviant peer groups and/or become high school dropouts. Of course, any intervention that makes aggressive, antisocial conduct a less viable or attractive option for young children would be a step in the right direction. Let's now consider some of the procedures that developmentalists have used in attemping to control children's hostilities.

Methods of Controlling Aggression and Antisocial Conduct

What methods other than family therapy might help parents and teachers to suppress the aggressive antics of young children so that antisocial approaches to conflict do not become habitual? A variety of solutions have been offered over the years, but few have been so highly touted as the one we will consider first: offering children harmless ways to express their anger or frustrations.

Catharsis: A Dubious Strategy

Psychoanalyst Sigmund Freud believed that hostile, aggressive urges build over time, and he urged people to find *harmless* ways to release them every now and then (that is, to experience *catharsis*) before they reach dangerous levels and trigger a truly violent outburst. The implications of this **catharsis hypothesis** are clear: If we encourage young children to vent their anger or frustrations on inanimate objects such as inflatable dolls, they should drain away their aggressive energies and become less inclined to harm other people.

Popular as this **cathartic technique** has been, it does *not* work and *may even backfire*. In one study (Walters & Brown, 1963), children who had been encouraged to slap, punch, and kick an inflatable doll were found to be much *more* aggressive in their later interactions with peers than were classmates who had not had an opportunity to beat on the doll. Other investigators report that children who are first angered by a peer and then given an opportunity to aggress against an inanimate object become no less aggressive toward the peer who had angered them in the first place (Mallick & McCandless, 1966). So cathartic techniques do not reduce children's aggressive urges. In fact, they may teach youngsters that hitting and kicking are acceptable methods of expressing their anger or frustrations.

Eliminating the Payoffs for Aggression

Parents and teachers can reduce aggression by identifying and then eliminating its reinforcing consequences. For example, if 5-year-old Lennie were to dominate his 3-year-old sister Gail in order to take possession of a toy, Lennie's mother could teach him that this instrumental aggression doesn't pay by simply returning the toy to Gail and denying him his objective. But this strategy wouldn't work if Lennie is an insecure child who feels neglected and has attacked his sister *in order to attract his mother's attention;* under these circumstances, the mother would be reinforcing Lennie's aggression if she attended to it at all! So what is she to do?

One proven method that she might use is the **incompatible-response technique:** a strategy of *ignoring* all but the most serious of Lennie's aggressive antics (thereby denying him an "attentional" reward) while reinforcing such acts as cooperation and sharing that are incompatible with aggression. Teachers who have tried this strategy find that it quickly produces an increase in children's prosocial conduct and a corresponding decrease in their hostilities (Brown & Elliot, 1965; see also Slaby & Crowley, 1977). And how might adults handle *serious* acts of harmdoing without "reinforcing" them with their attention? One effective approach is the **time-out technique** that Patterson favors: a technique in which the adult removes the offender from the situation in which his aggression is reinforced (for example, by sending the aggressor to his room until he is ready to behave appropriately). Although this approach may generate some resentment, the adult in charge is not physically abusing the child, is not serving as an aggressive model, and is not likely to unwittingly reinforce the child who misbehaves as a means of attracting attention. The time-out procedure is most effective at controlling children's hostilities when adults also reinforce cooperative or helpful acts that are incompatible with aggression (Parke & Slaby, 1983).

Modeling and Coaching Strategies

Responses that are incompatible with aggression may also be instilled by modeling or by coaching strategies. When children see a model choose a nonaggressive solution to a conflict or are explicitly coached in the use of nonaggressive methods of problem solving, they become more likely to enact similar solutions to their own problems (Shure, 1989; Zahavi & Asher, 1978). Indeed, coaching of effective methods of conflict resolution is particularly useful with chronically aggressive children, who often resort to aggressive tactics because they overattribute hostile intentions to others and are not very skilled at generating amiable solutions on their own (Rabiner, Lenhart, & Lochman, 1990; Shure, 1989). In one study (Guerra & Slaby, 1990), a group of violent adolescent offenders was coached in such skills as (1) looking

catharsis hypothesis: the notion that aggressive urges are reduced when people commit real or symbolic acts of aggression.

cathartic technique: a strategy for reducing aggression by encouraging children to vent their anger or frustrations on inanimate objects.

incompatible-response technique: a nonpunitive method of behavior modification in which adults ignore undesirable conduct while reinforcing acts that are incompatible with these responses.

time-out technique: a strategy in which the disciplinary agent controls a child's conduct by disrupting or preventing the prohibited activity that the child seems to enjoy.

for nonhostile cues that might be associated with harmdoing, (2) controlling their impulses (or anger), and (3) generating nonaggressive solutions to conflict. Not only did these violent offenders show dramatic improvements in their social problem-solving skills, but they also became less inclined to endorse beliefs supporting aggression and less aggressive in their interactions with authority figures and other inmates. Yet it is important to note that any reduction in hostilities that results from these elaborate social-cognitive training programs could be short-lived if the principles that subjects have learned are quickly undermined in a coercive home environment (Pettit, Dodge, & Brown, 1988) or in the company of chronically aggressive friends who value and endorse aggression (Cairns et al., 1988).

Creating "Nonaggressive" Environments

Another method that adults may use to reduce children's aggression is to create play areas that minimize the likelihood of conflict. For example, parents and teachers might remove (or refuse to buy) such "aggressive" toys as guns, tanks, and rubber knives that are known to provoke hostilities. Providing ample space for vigorous play also helps to eliminate the accidental bumps, shoves, and trips that often escalate into full-blown hostilities (Hartup, 1974). Finally, shortages of play materials sometimes contribute to conflicts and aggression; yet, children are likely to play quite harmoniously if adults have provided enough balls, slides, swings, and other toys to keep them from having to compete for scarce resources (Smith & Connolly, 1980).

Training Children to Empathize with Victims

Grade school children, adolescents, and adults will normally back off and stop attacking a victim who shows signs of pain or suffering. However, many preschool children and *highly aggressive* grade school boys may continue to attack a suffering victim (Perry & Perry, 1974) and express little concern about the harm they have done (Boldizar et al., 1989). One possible explanation for this seemingly sadistic behavior is that preschoolers and other highly aggressive individuals do not *empathize* with their victims. In other words, they may feel little sympathy or remorse when they have harmed another person.

Does **empathy** inhibit aggression? Apparently so. Grade school children who score high in empathy are rated low in aggression by their teachers, whereas classmates who test very low in empathy tend to be more aggressive (Bryant, 1982; see also Miller & Eisenberg, 1988). Moreover, Michael Chandler (1973) found that highly aggressive 11–13-year-old delinquents who participated in a ten-week program designed to make them more aware of other people's feelings subsequently became less hostile and aggressive, compared with a second group of delinquents who had not participated in the program (see also Feshbach & Feshbach, 1982, for similar results in an empathy-training program with 9–11-year-olds).

In the home setting, parents can foster the development of empathy by modeling empathic concern and by using disciplinary techniques that (1) point out the harmful consequences of the child's aggressive actions while (2) encouraging the child to put himself in the victim's place and imagine how the victim feels. In the next section of the chapter, we will see that parents who rely mainly on these rational, nonpunitive disciplinary techniques tend to raise sympathetic children who seem genuinely concerned about the welfare of others.

 ALTRUISM: DEVELOPMENT OF THE PROSOCIAL SELF

As we noted in opening this chapter, most parents hope that their children will acquire a sense of **altruism**—that is, a selfless concern for the welfare of other people and a willingness to act on that concern. In fact, many parents are already encour-

empathy: the ability to experience the same emotions that someone else is experiencing.

Concept Check 14-1 ⌄ Understanding Aggression and Antisocial Conduct

Check your understanding of the development of aggression and antisocial conduct by matching each descriptive statement below with one of the following concepts or processes: (a) cathartic technique; (b) deviant peer cliques; (c) hostile aggression; (d) hostile attributional bias; (e) instrumental aggression; (f) coercive home environment; (g) physical punishment (parents' use of); (h) peer rejection; (i) time-out technique; (j) negative reinforcement. The answers appear in the Appendix.

_____ 1. Thought to be an important contributor to social-class differences in aggression.

_____ 2. This kind of aggression becomes more common with age.

_____ 3. Process by which unpleasant interactions are maintained in coercive home environments.

_____ 4. Thought to be a strong and *direct* contributor to chronically antisocial conduct.

_____ 5. This kind of aggression is the first to appear, often by age 12 months.

_____ 6. Notably ineffective method of controlling children's aggression.

_____ 7. Characteristic that helps to perpetuate the aggression shown by highly aggressive children.

_____ 8. Effective method of controlling children's aggression.

_____ 9. Thought to be a strong and *direct* contributor to one's association with deviant peer cliques.

_____ 10. Often the *first step* on the road to chronic delinquency.

aging altruistic acts such as sharing, cooperating, or helping while their children are still in diapers! Until recently, experts in child development would have claimed that these well-intentioned adults were wasting their time, for infants and toddlers were thought to be incapable of considering the needs of anyone other than themselves. But the experts were wrong!

Origins of Altruism and Altruistic Concern

Long before children receive any formal moral or religious training, they may act in ways that resemble the prosocial behavior of older people. Twelve- to 18-month-olds, for example, occasionally offer toys to companions (Hay et al., 1991) and even attempt to help their mothers with such household chores as sweeping or dusting (Rheingold, 1982). And the prosocial conduct of very young children even has a certain "rationality" about it. For example, 2-year-olds are more likely to offer toys to a peer when playthings are scarce than when they are plentiful (Hay et al., 1991). Moreover, a type of *reciprocity* appears by the end of the third year. In one study (Levitt et al., 1985), 29–36-month-old toddlers who had previously received a toy from a peer when they had had none of their own typically returned the favor when they later found themselves with several toys to play with and the peer without any. Yet, if that peer had earlier refused to share, the toddlers almost invariably hoarded the toys when it was their turn to control them.

Are toddlers capable of expressing sympathy and behaving compassionately toward their companions? Yes, indeed, and these displays of prosocial concern are not all that uncommon (see Radke-Yarrow et al., 1983; Zahn-Waxler et al., 1992). Consider the reaction of 21-month-old John to his distressed playmate, Jerry:

> Today Jerry was kind of cranky; he just started . . . bawling and he wouldn't stop. John kept coming over and handing Jerry toys, trying to cheer him up. . . . He'd say things like "Here Jerry," and I said to John "Jerry's sad; he doesn't feel good; he had a shot today." John would look at me with his eyebrows wrinkled together like he really understood that Jerry was crying because he was unhappy. . . . He went over and rubbed Jerry's arm and said "Nice Jerry," and continued to give him toys (Zahn-Waxler, Radke-Yarrow, & King, 1979, pp. 321–322).

altruism: a selfless concern for the welfare of others that is expressed through prosocial acts such as sharing, cooperating, and helping.

Preschool children must often be coaxed to share.

Clearly, John was concerned about his little playmate and did what he could to make him feel better.

Although some toddlers often try to comfort distressed companions, others rarely do. These individual differences are due, in part, to cognitive development, for 23–25-month-olds who have achieved self-recognition (as assessed by the rouge test and other similar measures) are more likely than those who haven't to display sympathy for and to try to comfort a victim of distress (Zahn-Waxler et al., 1992). By contrast, younger infants often became *personally distressed* (rather than concerned) by others' distress and were less inclined to show compassion, sometimes even behaving aggressively.

Individual differences in early compassion also depend on parents' reactions to occasions in which their toddler has harmed another child. Carolyn Zahn-Waxler and her associates (1979) found that mothers of less compassionate toddlers typically used coercive tactics such as verbal rebukes or physical punishment to discipline harmdoing. By contrast, mothers of highly compassionate toddlers frequently disciplined harmdoing with *affective explanations* that may foster sympathy (and perhaps some remorse) by helping the child to see the relation between his or her own acts and the distress they have caused (for example, "You made Doug cry; it's not nice to bite!").

Developmental Trends in Altruism

Although many 2–3-year-olds will show some sympathy and compassion toward distressed companions, they are not particularly eager to make truly self-sacrificial responses, such as sharing a treasured cookie with a peer. Sharing and other benevolent acts are more likely to occur if adults instruct a toddler to consider others' needs (Levitt et al., 1985), or if a peer should actively elicit sharing through a request or a threat of some kind, such as "I won't be your friend if you won't gimme some" (Birch & Billman, 1986). But, on the whole, acts of *spontaneous* self-sacrifice in the interest of others are relatively infrequent among toddlers and young preschool children. Is this because toddlers are largely oblivious to others' needs and to the good they might do by sharing or helping their companions? Probably not, for at least one observational study in a nursery school setting found that 2½–3½-year-olds often took pleasure in performing acts of kindness for others during *pretend play*; by contrast, 4–6-year-olds performed more *real* helping acts and rarely "play acted" the role of an altruist (Bar-Tal, Raviv, & Goldberg, 1982).

Many studies conducted in cultures from around the world find that sharing, helping, and most other forms of prosocial conduct become more and more common from the early elementary school years onward (see, for example, Underwood & Moore, 1982; Whiting and Edwards, 1988). Indeed, much of the research that we will examine seeks to explain why older children and adolescents tend to become more prosocially inclined.

Before turning to this research, let's address one other issue that developmentalists have pondered: Are there sex differences in altruism? Although people commonly assume that girls are (or will become) more helpful, generous, and compassionate than boys (see Shigetomi, Hartmann, & Gelfand, 1981; Zarbatany et al., 1985), two major reviews of the literature strongly dispute this notion (Radke-Yarrow et al., 1983; Rushton, 1980). Girls sometimes emit stronger *facial* expressions of sympathy than boys do (Eisenberg et al., 1988; Fabes, Eisenberg, & Miller, 1990; Zahn-Waxler et al., 1992). However, the vast majority of studies find that girls and women do not reliably differ from boys and men in either the amount of sympathy that they *say* they experience or in their willingness to comfort, help, or share resources with people in need. In fact, boys are occasionally more helpful than girls on certain measures, such as active rescue behaviors.

Does the sex of the person who needs help or comforting affect children's altruism? Apparently so, at least for young children. Rosalind Charlesworth and Willard

Hartup (1967) observed the interactions of nursery school children over a five-week period and found that these youngsters generally directed their acts of kindness to playmates of the same sex. However, the sex of a prospective recipient becomes a less important consideration during the grade school years. In one study (Ladd, Lange, & Stremmel, 1983), kindergartners and first-, third-, and fourth-graders were given an opportunity to help other children complete some schoolwork. Some of these potential recipients clearly needed more help than others. Ladd et al. found that kindergartners and first-graders often disregarded recipients' apparent needs, choosing instead to help children of their own sex. However, this same-sex bias was much less apparent among third- and fourth-graders, who typically based their helping decisions on a recipient's need for help rather than on his or her gender.

Cognitive and Affective Contributors to Altruism

In Chapter 12, we saw that children with well-developed role-taking skills appear to be more charitable or helpful than poor role takers because they are better able to infer a companion's needs for assistance or comforting. Indeed, evidence for a causal link between *affective* and *social* perspective taking (recognizing what another person is feeling, thinking, or intending) and altruism is quite clear in studies showing that children and adolescents who receive training to further these role-taking skills subsequently become more charitable, more cooperative, and more concerned about the needs of others when compared with age-mates who receive no training (Chalmers & Townsend, 1990; Iannotti, 1978). However, role taking is only one of several personal attributes that play a part in the development of altruistic behavior. Three other contributors are children's level of **prosocial moral reasoning,** their empathic reactions to the distress of other people, and their emerging self-concepts as altruistic individuals.

Prosocial Moral Reasoning

Recently, researchers have begun to chart the development of children's reasoning about prosocial issues and its relationship to altruistic behavior. Nancy Eisenberg and her colleagues, for example, have presented children with stories in which the central character has to decide whether or not to help or comfort someone when the prosocial act would be personally costly to the helper. The following story illustrates the kinds of dilemmas that children were asked to think about (Eisenberg-Berg & Hand, 1979):

> One day a girl named Mary was going to a friend's birthday party. On her way she saw a girl who had fallen down and hurt her leg. The girl asked Mary to go to her house and get her parents so that [they] could come and take her to a doctor. But if Mary did . . . , she would be late to the party and miss the ice cream, cake, and all the games. What should Mary do?

As illustrated in Table 14-1, reasoning about these prosocial dilemmas may progress through as many as five levels between early childhood and adolescence. Notice that preschoolers' responses are frequently *self-serving:* These youngsters often say that Mary should go to the party so as not to miss out on the goodies. But as children mature, they tend to become increasingly responsive to the needs and wishes of others, so much so that some high school students feel that they could no longer respect themselves were they to ignore the appeal of a person in need in order to pursue their own interests (Eisenberg, 1983; Eisenberg, Miller, et al., 1991).

Does a child's level of prosocial moral reasoning predict his or her altruistic behavior? To some extent, it does. Eisenberg-Berg and Hand (1979) found that preschoolers who had begun to consider the needs of others when responding to prosocial dilemmas later displayed more *spontaneous* sharing with peers than did their nursery school classmates whose prosocial reasoning was more hedonistic. And in a

prosocial moral reasoning: the thinking that people display when deciding whether to help, share with, or comfort others when these actions could prove costly to themselves.

Table 14-1 Levels of Prosocial Moral Reasoning

Level	Brief description	Age range
1. Hedonistic (self-centered)	Concern is for oneself; help giving is most likely when it will in some way benefit the self.	Preschool and young elementary school children
2. Needs oriented	Will base helping decisions on the needs of others; not much evidence of sympathy or guilt for not helping at this level.	Elementary school children and a few preschoolers
3. Approval oriented	Concern is for performing altruistic acts that other people see as good or praiseworthy; being good or socially appropriate is important.	Elementary school and some high school students
4. Empathic or transitional	Judgments now include evidence of sympathetic responding, guilt for failing to respond, and feeling good for having done the right thing; vague references are made to abstract principles, duties, and values.	High school students and some older elementary school children
5. Strongly internalized	Justifications for helping are based on strongly internalized values, norms, convictions, and responsibilities; to violate one's internalized principles will now undermine self-respect.	A small minority of high school students and virtually no elementary school children

Source: Adapted from Eisenberg, Lennon, & Roth, 1983.

later study of older subjects, Eisenberg (1983) found that mature moral reasoners among her high school sample might even help someone they *disliked* if that person really needed their assistance, whereas immature moral reasoners were apt to ignore the needs of a person they did not like (see also Eisenberg, Miller, et al., 1991).

Why are mature moral reasoners so sensitive to the needs of others—even *disliked* others? Eisenberg's view is that the child's growing ability to *empathize* with others contributes heavily to mature prosocial reasoning and to the development of a self-less concern for promoting the welfare of *whomever* might require one's assistance (Eisenberg et al., 1987; Eisenberg, Miller, et al., 1991). Let's now consider what researchers have learned about the relationship between empathy and altruism.

Empathy: An Important Affective Contributor to Altruism

Empathy refers to a person's ability to experience the emotions of other people. According to Martin Hoffman (1981, 1993), empathy is a universal human response that has a neurological basis and can be either fostered or suppressed by environmental influences. Hoffman believes that empathic arousal will eventually become an important mediator of altruism. Why else, Hoffman asks, would we set aside our own selfish motives to help other people or to avoid harming them unless we had the capacity to share their emotions?

Although infants and toddlers do seem to recognize and will often react to the distress of their companions (Zahn-Waxler et al., 1979, 1992; see also Box 2-4), their responses are not always helpful ones. Indeed, some young children experience *personal* distress upon witnessing the distress or misfortunes of others (this may be the predominant response early in life) and may turn away from a person in need, or even attack him or her, in order to relieve their *own* discomfort. Yet other children (even some young ones) are more inclined to interpret their empathic arousal as concern for distressed others, and it is this **sympathetic empathic arousal,** rather than **self-oriented distress,** that should eventually promote altruism (Batson, 1987; Eisenberg et al., 1992; Hoffman, 1993).

Socialization of empathy. As we noted earlier when discussing the origins of compassion in toddlers, parents can help to promote sympathetic empathic arousal by (1) modeling empathic concern and (2) relying on affectively oriented forms of discipline that help young children to understand the harmful *effects* of any distress they may have caused others (Barnett, 1987; Eisenberg, Fabes, et al., 1991; Zahn-Waxler et al., 1979; 1992). Interestingly, mothers who use more *positive* facial expressions while modeling sympathy have children who act more sympathetically—probably because the mother's positivity helps to counteract the negative reactions that young children may have to others' misfortunes, thus making them less inclined to interpret their arousal as *personal* distress (Fabes et al., 1994). And mothers who *explicitly verbalize* their own sympathetic reactions are also contributing to the development of sympathy, particularly for boys, who seem to be somewhat less sensitive than girls to mothers' sympathetic facial displays (Eisenberg et al., 1992).

As children mature and develop better role-taking skills, they are more likely to sympathize with distressed companions and to provide them with comfort or assistance.

Age trends in the empathy-altruism relationship. So what is the relationship between empathy and altruism? The answer depends, in part, on how empathy is measured and how old the research participants are. In studies that assess empathy by having children report their own feelings about the misfortunes of story characters, researchers have found little association between empathy and altruism. However, teacher ratings of children's empathic sensitivities and children's own *facial* expressions of emotion in response to others' misfortunes are better predictors of prosocial behavior (Chapman et al., 1987; Eisenberg et al., 1990). Overall, it seems that the evidence for a link between empathy and altruism is modest at best for preschool and young grade school children but stronger for preadolescents, adolescents, and adults (Underwood and Moore, 1982).

One possible explanation for these age trends is that it simply takes some time for children to become better at suppressing personal distress to others' misfortunes so that they can respond more sympathetically. And it is likely that cognitive development plays an important part in this process, for younger children may lack the role-taking skills to fully understand and appreciate (1) *why* others are distressed and, thus, (2) *why* they are experiencing empathic arousal. For example, when kindergartners see a series of slides showing a boy becoming depressed after his dog runs away, they usually attribute his sadness to an external cause (the dog's disappearance) rather than to a more "personal" or internal one, such as the boy's longing for his pet (Hughes, Tingle, & Sawin, 1981). And, although kindergartners report that they feel sad after seeing the slides, they usually provide egocentric explanations for their empathic arousal that seem to reflect *personal distress* (for example, "I might lose my dog"). However, 7–9-year-olds are beginning to associate their own empathic emotions with those of the story character as they put themselves in his place and infer the psychological basis for his sadness (for example, "I'm sad because he's sad . . . because, if he really liked the dog, then . . ."). So empathy may become an important mediator of altruism once children become more proficient at inferring others' points of view (role taking) and understanding the causes of their own empathic emotions—causes that can help them to feel *sympathy* for distressed or needy companions (see also Strayer, 1993).

The felt-responsibility hypothesis. Now an important question: *How* exactly does empathy promote altruism? One possibility is that a child's *sympathetic* empathic arousal causes him to reflect on altruistic lessons that he has learned—such as the Golden Rule, the *norm of social responsibility* (that is, help others who need help), or

sympathetic empathic arousal: feelings of sympathy or compassion that may be elicited when we experience the emotions of (that is, empathize with) a distressed other; thought to become an important mediator of altruism.

self-oriented distress: feeling of *personal* discomfort or distress that may be elicited when we experience the emotions of (that is, empathize with) a distressed other; thought to inhibit altruism.

Figure 14-5
How empathy promotes altruism: A "felt responsibility" interpretation.

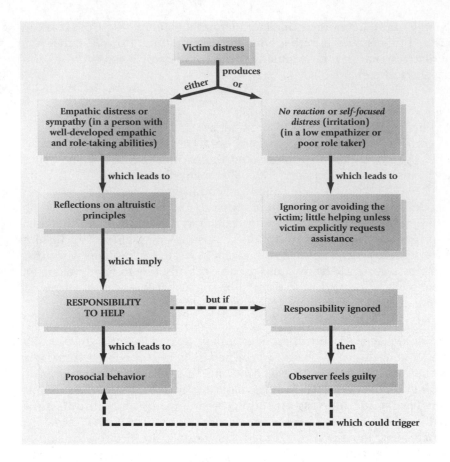

even the knowledge that other people approve of helping behavior. As a result of this reflection, the child is likely to assume some personal *responsibility* for aiding a victim in distress (see Figure 14-5) and would now feel guilty for callously ignoring that obligation (Chapman et al., 1987; Williams & Bybee, 1994). Notice that this **"felt responsibility" hypothesis** is reflected in Eisenberg's higher stages of prosocial moral reasoning (see Table 14-1) and may help to explain why the link between empathy and altruism becomes stronger with age. Since older children are likely to have learned (and internalized) more altruistic principles than younger children, they should have much more to reflect on as they experience empathic arousal. Consequently, they are more likely than younger children to feel responsible for helping a distressed person and to follow through by rendering the necessary assistance.

Viewing Oneself as Altruistic

Research consistently indicates that adults with strong altruistic self-concepts are more prosocially inclined than those who do not view themselves as particularly compassionate, charitable, or helpful (see Baron & Byrne, 1994). Might the same be true of children? Could we promote altruism by persuading youngsters to think of themselves as generous or helpful individuals?

Indeed, we can. Joan Grusec and Erica Redler (1980) found that 8-year-olds who had been told that they were "nice" or "helpful" persons after they had shared with or helped others (self-concept training) were more inclined than those who were simply praised for their generosity (control group) to donate toys and craft materials to hospitalized children ten days later. However, this same self-concept training was less effective with 5-year-olds. Why? The research we reviewed in Chapter 12 provides a strong clue. Recall that 8-year-olds (but not 5-year-olds) are beginning to describe the self in *psychological* terms and to see these "traits" as stable aspects of their character.

"felt responsibility" hypothesis: the theory that empathy may promote altruism by causing one to reflect on altruistic norms and, thus, to feel some obligation to help distressed others.

Thus, when told that they were "nice" or "helpful," Grusec and Redler's 8-year-olds apparently incorporated these traitlike attributions into their self-concepts and were trying to live up to this new, more altruistic self-image by generously volunteering assistance when help was needed.

So encouraging youngsters to think of themselves as altruistic is one way to promote acts of kindness—at least among children old enough to understand and appreciate the implications of traitlike attributions. In our next section, we will consider a number of other social and cultural factors that have a bearing on how altruistic children are likely to become.

Concept Check 14-2 ⌄ Understanding Cognitive and Affective Contributors to Altruism

Check your understanding of cognitive and affective contributors to prosocial conduct by matching each of the descriptive statements below with one of the following concepts or processes: (a) altruistic lessons (or norms); (b) felt responsibility; (c) role-taking ability; (d) self-concept (or attribution) training; (e) self-oriented distress; (f) sympathetic empathic arousal. The answers appear in the Appendix.

_____ 1. Promotes altruism by persuading children to think of themselves as kind or helpful after they have performed prosocial acts.

_____ 2. Empathic arousal that is thought to *inhibit* altruism.

_____ 3. What empathizers may focus on when experiencing others' distress.

_____ 4. May be the most *direct* contributor to an empathizer's prosocial conduct.

_____ 5. Helps children to interpret empathic arousal as sympathy rather than personal distress.

_____ 6. Empathic arousal that is thought to *promote* altruism.

Cultural and Social Influences on Altruism

Cultural Influences

Cultures clearly differ in their endorsement or encouragement of altruism. In one interesting cross-cultural study, Beatrice and John Whiting (1975) observed the altruistic behavior of 3–10-year-olds in six cultures: Kenya, Mexico, the Philippines, Okinawa, India, and the United States. As we see in Table 14-2, the cultures in which children were most altruistic were the less industrialized societies where people tend to live in large families and *everyone* contributes to the family welfare. The Whitings concluded that children who are assigned important responsibilities, such as producing and processing food or caring for infant brothers and sisters, are likely to develop a cooperative, altruistic orientation at an early age.

Table 14-2 **Prosocial Behavior in Six Cultures: Percentages of Children in Each Culture Who Scored above the Median Altruism Score for the Cross-Cultural Sample as a Whole**

Type of society	Percentage scoring high in altruism	Type of society	Percentage scoring high in altruism
Nonindustrialized		*Industrialized*	
Kenya	100	Okinawa	29
Mexico	73	India	25
Philippines	63	United States	8

Source: Based on Whiting & Whiting, 1975.

Another possible explanation for the very low altruism scores among children from industrialized nations is that many Western societies place a tremendous emphasis on competition and stress individual rather than group goals. By contrast, Native American and Mexican children (and those raised in such communal settings as the Israeli kibbutz) are taught to suppress individualism, to cooperate with others for the greater good of the group, and to avoid interpersonal conflicts. The impact of these cultural teachings is apparent in a number of contexts. For example, Anne Marie Tietjen (1986) found that children from a communal society in New Guinea typically become less other-oriented and more self-centered in their thinking about prosocial issues once they have spent three years attending Westernized schools. And even within the same society (Israel), communally reared kibbutz children are much more inclined to cooperate with one another and to *seek* assistance than are their city-dwelling age-mates, whose environment stresses typical Western attitudes calling for self-reliance and individual achievement (Nadler, 1986; 1991).

Although cultures may differ in the emphasis that they place on altruism, most people in most societies endorse the norm of social responsibility—the rule of thumb prescribing that one should help others who need help. Let's now consider some of the ways that adults might persuade young children to adopt this important value and to become more concerned about the welfare of other people.

Reinforcing Altruism

Might we promote altruism by offering children tangible rewards for their generous or helpful acts? Probably not. Although the practice of giving children toys or bubble gum for acts of kindness does increase the frequency of such behavior in the short run (Fischer, 1963), rewarded children are actually *less likely* than other "nonrewarded" peers to make sacrifices for others once the rewards stop (Fabes et al., 1989). Why? Because children who are "bribed" with tangible incentives for prosocial conduct come to attribute their acts of kindness to the rewards rather than to the recipient's needs or to their own inclinations to be kind to others. Consequently, tangible rewards can undermine children's altruistic motivation in much the same way that rewards can undermine interest in other intrinsically satisfying activities (see Box 8-1). Apparently, parents understand that a strong concern for others is not easily established through bribery, for mothers of 4–7-year-olds report that they rarely use tangible rewards to promote prosocial behavior (Grusec, 1991).

On the other hand, *verbal reinforcement* can promote altruism if it is administered by a warm and charitable person whom children respect and admire (Yarrow, Scott, & Waxler, 1973). Perhaps verbal approval is effective under these circumstances because children hope to live up to standards set by a liked and respected person, and praise that accompanies their kindly acts suggests that they are accomplishing that objective.

Another way that adults might subtly reinforce altruism is to structure play activities so that children are likely to discover the benefits of cooperating and helping one another. Terry Orlick (1981) found that preschool children who have been trained to play cooperative games in which they must join forces to achieve various goals are later more cooperative in other contexts (for example, with peers on the playground) than age-mates who have spent an equal amount of time playing very similar but individualistic games that do not require cooperation. Orlick also found that youngsters in his "cooperative activities" program usually became more generous about sharing treats and possessions—even when the peers who would benefit from their acts of kindness were unknown to them. By contrast, children who participated in traditional (individualistic) activities often became stingier with their possessions over time. So it seems that a program designed to teach children to cooperate not only accomplishes that objective but may also promote completely different forms of altruism, such as sharing.

Practicing and Preaching Altruism

Social-learning theorists have assumed that adults who encourage altruism and who practice what they preach will affect children in two ways. By practicing altruism, the adult model may induce the child to perform similar acts of kindness. In addition, regular exposure to the model's **altruistic exhortations** provides the child with opportunities to internalize principles such as the norm of social responsibility that should contribute to the development of an altruistic orientation.

Laboratory experiments consistently indicate that young children who observe charitable or helpful models become more charitable or helpful themselves, especially if the model has established a warm relationship with them, provides a compelling justification (rationale) for his acts of kindness, and regularly *practices what he preaches* (Rushton, 1980; Yarrow et al., 1973). Moreover, it appears that exposure to these altruistic models can have *long-term* effects on children's behavior that generalize to new situations. For example, Elizabeth Midlarsky and James Bryan (1972) found that a model who donated valuable tokens to a charity increased children's willingness to donate candy to the same charity, even though the candy donations were solicited ten days later in a different setting by a person the children had never seen. Other investigators have noted that children who observe charitable models are more generous than those who observe selfish models, even when they are tested *two to four months later* (Rice & Grusec, 1975; Rushton, 1980). So it seems that encounters with altruistic models may indeed promote the development of prosocial habits and altruistic values.

Now let's turn to the child-rearing literature to see if the variables that promote altruism in the laboratory have similar effects on children in the natural environment.

Who Raises Altruistic Children?

Studies of unusually charitable adults indicate that these "altruists" have enjoyed a warm and affectionate relationship with parents who themselves were highly concerned about the welfare of others. For example, Christians who risked their lives to save Jews from the Nazis during World War II reported that they had had close ties to moralistic parents who always acted in accordance with their ethical principles (London, 1970). And interviews of white "freedom riders" from the U.S. civil rights movement of the 1960s reveal that "fully committed" activists (volunteers who gave up their homes and/or careers to work full-time for the cause) differed from "partially committed" (part-time) activists in two major ways: They had enjoyed warmer relations with their parents, and they had had parents who advocated altruism and backed up these exhortations by performing many kind and compassionate deeds. By contrast, parents of partially committed activists had often preached but rarely practiced altruism (Rosenhan, 1970; see also Clary & Snyder, 1991). Clearly, these findings are consistent with the laboratory evidence we have reviewed, which indicates that warm and compassionate models who practice what they preach are especially effective at eliciting prosocial responses from young children.

Parental reactions to a child's harmdoing also play an important role in the development of altruism. We've already noted that mothers of less compassionate infants and toddlers react to harmdoing in punitive or forceful ways, whereas mothers of compassionate toddlers rely more heavily on nonpunitive, affective explanations in which they persuade the child to accept personal responsibility for her harmdoing and urge her to direct some sort of comforting or helpful response toward the victim (Zahn-Waxler et al., 1979; 1992). Research with older children paints a similar picture: Parents who continue to rely on rational, nonpunitive disciplinary techniques in which they regularly display sympathy and concern for others tend to raise children who are sympathetic and self-sacrificing, whereas frequent use of forceful and punitive discipline appears to inhibit altruism and to lead to the development of self-centered values (Brody & Shaffer, 1982; Eisenberg et al., 1992; Fabes et al., 1990).

If we think about it, there are several reasons that rational, affectively oriented discipline that is heavy on reasoning might inspire children to become more altruistic.

Children learn many prosocial lessons by observing the behavior of prosocial models.

altruistic exhortations: verbal encouragements to help, comfort, share, or cooperate with others.

First, it encourages the child to assume another person's perspective (role taking) and to experience that person's distress (empathy training). It also teaches the child to perform helpful or comforting acts that make both the self and the other person feel better. And last but not least, these reparative responses might convince older (grade school) children that they are "nice" or "helpful" people, thus promoting a *positive self-image* that they may try to live up to by performing other acts of kindness in the future.

Now that we have looked at the development of aggressive inclinations and the growth of prosocial concerns, we will focus on a broader aspect of social development—one that encompasses both the encouragement of altruistic values and the inhibition of hostile, antisocial impulses. Of course, I am referring to the child's *moral development.*

 ## WHAT IS MORALITY (AND MORAL MATURITY)?

We all have some idea of what **morality** is, although the ways we define the term may depend, in part, on our backgrounds and general outlooks on life. A theologian, for example, might mention the relationship between human beings and their Creator. A philosopher's definition of morality may depend on the assumptions that he or she makes about human nature. When college students are asked what morality means to them, they generally agree that it implies *an ability to* (1) *distinguish right from wrong,* (2) *act on this distinction,* and (3) *experience pride in virtuous conduct and guilt or shame over acts that violate one's standards* (Quinn, Houts, & Graesser, 1994; Shaffer, 1994).

Implicit in this definition is the idea that *morally mature* individuals do not submit to society's dictates because they expect tangible rewards for complying or fear punishments for transgressing. Rather, they eventually *internalize* the moral principles that they have learned and will conform to these ideals, even when authority figures are not present to enforce them. As we will see, many contemporary theorists consider **internalization**—the shift from externally controlled actions to conduct that is governed by internal standards and principles—to be a most crucial milestone along the road to moral maturity.

How developmentalists look at morality. Interestingly, developmental theorizing and research have centered on the same three moral components that college students mention in their consensual definition of morality:

1. An *affective,* or emotional, component that consists of the feelings (guilt, concern for others' feelings, and so on) that surround right or wrong actions and that motivate moral thoughts and actions.
2. A *cognitive* component that centers on the way we conceptualize right and wrong and make decisions about how to behave.
3. A *behavioral* component that reflects how we actually behave when, for example, we experience the temptation to lie, cheat, or violate other moral rules.

As it turns out, each of the three major theories of moral development has focused on a different component of morality. Psychoanalytic theorists emphasize the affective component, or powerful **moral affects.** They believe that children are motivated to act in accordance with their ethical principles in order to experience positive affects such as pride and to avoid such negative moral emotions as guilt and shame. Cognitive-developmental theorists have concentrated on the cognitive aspects of morality, or **moral reasoning,** and have found that the ways children think about right and wrong may change rather dramatically as they mature. Finally, the research of social-learning and social information-processing theorists has helped us to understand how children learn to resist temptation and to practice **moral behavior,** inhibiting actions such as lying, stealing, and cheating that violate moral norms.

morality: a set of principles or ideals that help the individual to distinguish right from wrong, to act on this distinction, and to feel pride in virtuous conduct and guilt (or shame) for conduct that violates one's standards.

internalization: the process of adopting the attributes or standards of other people; taking these standards as one's own.

moral affect: the emotional component of morality, including feelings such as guilt, shame, and pride in ethical conduct.

moral reasoning: the cognitive component of morality; the thinking that people display when deciding whether various acts are right or wrong.

moral behavior: the behavioral component of morality; actions that are consistent with one's moral standards in situations where one is tempted to violate them.

Resisting temptation is a difficult feat for young children to accomplish, particularly when there is no one around to help the child exercise will power.

We will begin by examining each of these theories and the research it has generated. As we see how each theory approaches the topic of moral development, we will be looking at the relationships among moral affect, moral reasoning, and moral behavior. This information should help us to decide whether a person really has a unified "moral character" that is stable over time and across situations. Finally, we will consider how various child-rearing practices may affect a child's moral development and, in so doing, will attempt to integrate much of the information we have reviewed.

 ## PSYCHOANALYTIC EXPLANATIONS OF MORAL DEVELOPMENT

According to Freud (1935/1960), the personality consists of three basic components: the id, ego, and superego. Recall from Chapter 2 that the sole purpose of the impulsive id is to gratify instinctual needs. The ego's function is to restrain the id until "realistic" means for satisfying needs can be worked out. Finally, the superego serves as the child's moral arbiter, or *internal* censor, by monitoring the acceptability of the ego's thoughts and deeds. Freud argued that a well-developed superego is a harsh master that will punish the ego for moral transgressions by producing feelings of guilt, shame, or loss of self-esteem. So a child who is morally mature should resist temptation to violate moral norms in order to avoid these dreaded forms of negative moral affect.

Freud's Theory of Oedipal Morality

According to Freud, the superego develops during the phallic stage (age 3–6), when children were said to experience an emotional conflict with the same-sex parent that stemmed from their incestuous desire for the other-sex parent. To resolve this *Oedipus complex*, a boy was said to *identify* with and pattern himself after his father, particularly if his father is a threatening figure who arouses fear. Not only does he learn his masculine role in this manner, but he also internalizes his father's moral standards. Similarly, a girl resolves her *Electra complex* by identifying with her mother and internalizing her mother's moral standards. However, Freud believed that girls, because they do not experience the intense fear of castration that boys experience, develop weaker superegos than boys do.

Evaluation of Freud's Theory

We might applaud Freud for pointing out that moral emotions such as pride, shame, and guilt are potentially important determinants of ethical conduct and that the internalization of moral principles is a crucial step along the way to moral maturity. Yet, the "specifics" of his theory are largely unsupported. For example, threatening and punitive parents do not raise children who are morally mature. Quite the contrary; parents who rely on punitive forms of discipline tend to have children who often misbehave and who rarely express feelings of guilt, remorse, shame, or self-criticism (Brody & Shaffer, 1982; Hoffman, 1988). Furthermore, there is simply no evidence that males develop stronger superegos than females. Finally, Freud's proposed age trends for moral development are actually rather pessimistic. Two-year-olds, for example, are already beginning to show clear signs of distress when they violate rules they have learned (Kochanska et al., 1994), and they will sometimes try to correct any mishaps they think they have caused—*even when no one else is present to tell them to* (Cole, Barrett, & Zahn-Waxler, 1992). In addition, 2–3-year-olds are already displaying complex emotions that look very much like *pride* when they live up to a standard and *shame* when they fail to do so (Lewis et al., 1992; Stipek et al., 1992). These kinds of observations suggest that the process of moral internalization may have already begun long before young children would have even experienced much of an Oedipus or Electra complex, much less having resolved it or established a mature superego. So even though Freud's broader themes about the significance of moral emotions have some merit, perhaps it is time to lay his theory of **oedipal morality** to rest.

Indeed, this is exactly what modern psychoanalytic theorists have done. They argue that moral internalization may often begin late in infancy if children are *securely attached* to their caregivers. Within the context of a *warm* (rather than fear-provoking) emotional relationship, toddlers are (1) motivated to comply with parental standards of conduct, (2) responsive to parents' emotional signals indicating whether they have done right or wrong, and (3) beginning to internalize these parental reactions to their triumphs and transgressions, coming to experience the pride, shame, and (later) guilt that will help them to evaluate and regulate their conduct (Emde et al., 1991; Kochanska, 1993).

Unfortunately, modern psychoanalytic theorists have little to say about moral development beyond the preschool period or about children's moral reasoning—the very issue that cognitive-developmentalists emphasize.

 ## COGNITIVE-DEVELOPMENTAL THEORY: THE CHILD AS A MORAL PHILOSOPHER

Cognitive-developmentalists study morality by charting the development of *moral reasoning*—the thinking children display when deciding whether various acts are right or wrong. A major assumption of the cognitive approach is that moral development depends very heavily on cognitive development. Moral reasoning is said to progress through an *invariant sequence* of "stages," each of which is a consistent way of thinking about moral issues that differs from the stages preceding or following it. Presumably, each moral stage evolves from and replaces its immediate predecessor, so that there can be no "skipping" of stages. If these assumptions sound familiar, they should, for they are the same ones that Piaget made about his stages of intellectual development.

In this section of the chapter, we will consider two cognitive-developmental theories of morality: Jean Piaget's model and Lawrence Kohlberg's revision and extension of Piaget's approach.

Piaget's Theory of Moral Development

According to Piaget (1932/1965), moral maturity implies both a respect for rules and a sense of social justice—that is, a concern that all people be treated fairly and equitably under the socially defined rules of order. Piaget studied the development of a respect for rules by rolling up his sleeves and playing marbles with a large number of Swiss children. As he played with children of different ages, Piaget would ask them

oedipal morality: Freud's theory that moral development occurs during the phallic period (ages 3 to 6) when children internalize the moral standards of the same-sex parent as they resolve their Oedipus or Electra conflicts.

questions about the rules of the game, such as "Where do these rules come from? Must everyone obey a rule? Can these rules be changed?" Once he had identified developmental stages in the understanding and use of rules, he proceeded to study children's conceptions of social justice by presenting them with moral dilemmas in the form of stories. Here is one example:

> *Story A.* A little boy who is called John is in his room. He is called to dinner. He goes into the dining room. But behind the door there was a chair, and on the chair there was a tray with 15 cups on it. John couldn't have known that there was all this behind the door. He goes in, the door knocks against the tray, bang go the 15 cups, and they all get broken.

> *Story B.* Once there was a little boy whose name was Henry. One day when his mother was out he tried to reach some jam out of the cupboard. He climbed onto a chair and stretched out his arm. But the jam was too high up, and he couldn't reach it. . . . While he was trying to get it, he knocked over a cup. The cup fell down and broke (Piaget, 1932/1965, p. 122).

Having heard the stories, subjects were asked "Are these children equally guilty?" and "If not, which child is naughtier? Why?" Subjects were also asked how the naughtier child should be punished. Through the use of these research techniques, Piaget formulated a theory of moral development that includes a premoral period and two moral stages.

The Premoral Period

According to Piaget, preschool children show little concern for or awareness of rules. In a game of marbles, these **premoral** children do not play systematically with the intent of winning. Instead, they seem to make up their own rules, and they think the point of the game is to take turns and have fun.

The Stage of Moral Realism or Heteronomous Morality

Between the ages of 6 and 10, children develop a strong respect for rules as they enter Piaget's stage of **heteronomous morality** ("heteronomous" means "under the rule of another"). Children now believe that rules are laid down by authority figures such as God, the police, or their parents, and they think that these regulations are sacred and unalterable. Try breaking the speed limit with a 6-year-old at your side and you may see what Piaget was talking about. Even if you are rushing to the hospital in a medical emergency, the young child may note that you are breaking a "rule of the road" and consider your behavior unacceptable conduct that deserves to be punished. In sum, heteronomous children think of rules as *moral absolutes.* They believe that there is a "right" side and a "wrong" side to any moral issue, and right always means following the rules.

Heteronomous children are also likely to judge the naughtiness of an act by its objective consequences rather than by the actor's intent. For example, Piaget found that many 5–9-year-olds judged John, who broke 15 cups while performing a well-intentioned act, to be naughtier than Henry, who broke one cup while stealing jam.

Heteronomous children also favor *expiatory punishment*—punishment for its own sake with no concern for its relation to the nature of the forbidden act. For example, a 6-year-old might favor spanking a boy who had broken a window rather than making the boy pay for the window from his allowance. Moreover, the heteronomous child believes in **immanent justice**—the idea that violations of social rules will invariably be punished in one way or another (see, for example, Dennis's warning to Joey in the cartoon on the next page). So if a 6-year-old boy were to fall and skin his knee while stealing cookies, he might conclude that this injury was the punishment he deserved for his transgression. Life for the heteronomous child is fair and just.

premoral period: in Piaget's theory, the first five years of life, when children have little respect for or awareness of socially defined rules.

heteronomous morality: Piaget's first stage of moral development, in which children view the rules of authority figures as sacred and unalterable.

immanent justice: the notion that unacceptable conduct will invariably be punished and that justice is ever present in the world.

Dennis the Menace® used by permission of Hank Ketcham and © by North American Syndicate.

"HEY, CAREFUL, JOEY! GOD SEES EVERYTHING WE DO, THEN HE GOES AN' TELLS SANTA CLAUS!"

The Stage of Moral Relativism or Autonomous Morality

By age 10 or 11, most children have reached Piaget's second moral stage: the stage of moral relativism, or **autonomous morality**. Older, autonomous children now realize that social rules are arbitrary agreements that can be challenged and even changed with the consent of the people they govern. They also feel that rules can be violated in the service of human needs. Thus, a driver who speeds during a medical emergency will no longer be considered a wrongdoer, even though she is breaking the law. Judgments of right and wrong now depend more on the actor's intent to deceive or to violate social rules rather than the objective consequences of the act itself. So 10-year-olds reliably say that Henry, who broke one cup while stealing some jam (bad intent), is naughtier than John, who broke 15 cups while coming to dinner (good or neutral intent).

When deciding how to punish transgressions, the morally autonomous child usually favors *reciprocal punishments*—that is, treatments that tailor punitive consequences to the "crime" so that the rule breaker will understand the implications of a transgression and perhaps be less likely to repeat it. So an autonomous child may decide that the boy who deliberately breaks a window should pay for it out of his allowance (and learn that windows cost money) rather than simply submitting to a spanking. Finally, autonomous youngsters no longer believe in immanent justice, because they have learned from experience that violations of social rules often go undetected and unpunished.

Moving from Heteronomous to Autonomous Morality

According to Piaget, both cognitive maturation and social experience play a role in the transition from heteronomous to autonomous morality. The cognitive advances that are necessary for this shift are a general decline in egocentrism and the development of role-taking skills that enable the child to view moral issues from several perspectives. The kind of social experience that Piaget considers important is *equal status* contact with peers. As we noted in Chapter 12, peers must learn to take each other's perspectives and resolve their disagreements in mutually beneficial ways, often

autonomous morality: Piaget's second stage of moral development, in which children realize that rules are arbitrary agreements that can be challenged and changed with the consent of the people they govern.

without any adult intervention, if they are to play cooperatively or accomplish other group goals. So equal-status contacts with peers may lead to a more flexible, autonomous morality because they (1) lessen the child's respect for adult authority, (2) increase his or her self-respect and respect for peers, and (3) illustrate that rules are arbitrary agreements that can be changed with the consent of the people they govern.

And what role do parents play? Interestingly, Piaget claimed that unless parents relinquish some of their power, they may *slow* the progress of moral development by reinforcing the child's respect for rules and authority figures. If, for example, a parent enforces a demand with a threat or a statement such as "Do it because I told you to!" it is easy to see how the young child might conclude that rules are "absolutes" that derive their "teeth" from the parent's power to enforce them.

An Evaluation of Piaget's Theory

Many researchers have used Piaget's methods in an attempt to replicate his findings, and much of the evidence they have collected is consistent with his theory. In Western cultures, there is a clear relationship between children's ages and stages of moral reasoning: Younger children are more likely than older children to display such aspects of heteronomous morality as a strong belief in immanent justice and a tendency to weigh the consequences of an act much more heavily than the actor's intentions when making moral judgments (Jose, 1990; Lickona, 1976). In addition, moral reasoning is related to cognitive development: Children with higher IQs and better role-taking skills tend to make more advanced moral judgments than age-mates whose cognitive abilities are less well-developed (Ambron & Irwin, 1975; Selman, 1971). And there is even some support for Piaget's "peer participation" hypothesis: Popular children who often take part in social activities and who assume positions of leadership in the peer group tend to make mature moral judgments (Bear & Rys, 1994; Keasey, 1971).

Nevertheless, there are reasons to believe that Piaget's theory clearly underestimates the moral capacities of preschool and grade school children. Let's take a closer look.

Do Younger Children Ignore an Actor's Intentions?

Recent research indicates that younger children may often consider an actor's intentions when evaluating his conduct. Two problems with Piaget's moral-decision stories are that they (1) confounded intentions and consequences by asking whether a person who caused little harm with a bad intent was naughtier than one who caused a larger amount of harm while serving good intentions and (2) made information about the consequences of an act *much clearer* (or easier to detect) than information about the actor's intentions.

Sharon Nelson (1980) overcame these flaws in an interesting experiment with 3-year-olds. Each child listened to stories in which a character threw a ball to a playmate. The actor's motive was described as *good* (his friend had nothing to play with) or *bad* (the actor was mad at his friend), and the consequences of his act were either *positive* (the friend caught the ball and was happy to play with it) or *negative* (the ball hit the friend in the head and made him cry). To ensure that these young subjects would understand the actor's intentions, Nelson showed them drawings such as Figure 14-6, which depicts a negative intent.

How did these 3-year-olds evaluate the actor's behavior? As we see in Figure 14-7, they did judge acts that had positive consequences more favorably than those that produced negative outcomes. Yet the more interesting finding was that the well-intentioned child who had wanted to play was evaluated much more favorably than the child who intended to hurt his friend, *regardless of the consequences of his actions* (see also Bussey, 1992; Nelson-LeGall, 1985). So even *preschool* children consider an

Figure 14-6
Example of drawings used by Nelson to convey an actor's intentions to preschool children.
Adapted from Nelson, 1980.

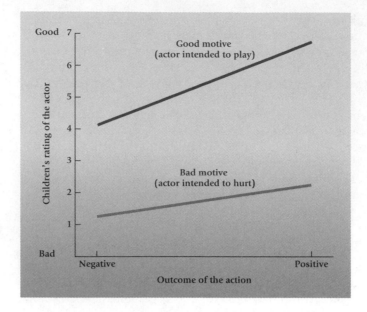

Figure 14-7
Average ratings of an actor's behavior for actors who produced positive or negative outcomes while serving either good or bad intentions.
Adapted from Nelson, 1980.

actor's intentions when making moral judgments; in fact, young children frequently attempt to escape punishment by pleading, "I didn't *mean* it, mommy!" But Piaget was right in one respect: Younger children do assign more weight to consequences and less weight to intentions than older children do, even though both younger and older children consider both sources of information when evaluating others' conduct (Olthof, Ferguson, & Luiten, 1989; Surber, 1982).

Do Younger Children Respect All Rules (and Adult Authority)?

According to Piaget, young children think of rules as sacred and obligatory prescriptions that are laid down by respected authority figures and are not to be questioned or changed. However, Elliot Turiel (1983) notes that children actually encounter two kinds of rules: (1) **moral rules,** which focus on the rights and privileges of individuals, and (2) **social-conventional rules,** which are determined by consensus and tell us what is appropriate in a particular social setting. Moral rules include rules against hitting, lying, stealing, or otherwise violating other people's rights. Social-conventional rules are more like rules of social etiquette and include rules of games as well as school rules that forbid snacking in class or using the restroom without permission. Do children treat these two kinds of rules as equivalent?

Apparently not. Judith Smetana (1981; 1985; Smetana, Schlagman, & Adams, 1993) finds that even 2½–3-year-olds consider moral transgressions such as hitting, stealing, and refusing to share to be much more serious and more deserving of punishment than social-conventional violations such as snacking in class or not saying please when requesting a toy. And when asked whether a violation would be okay if there were no rule against it, children said that moral transgressions are always wrong but social-conventional violations are okay in the absence of any explicit rule. Although preschoolers may not always feel guilty about violating a moral rule (Nunner-Winkler & Sodian, 1988), they do indeed understand the need for and importance of these prescriptions by age 2½ to 3—much sooner than Piaget had assumed they would.

Moreover, 6–10-year-olds in Piaget's heteronomous stage of morality, who should be even more likely than younger children to respect pronouncements laid down by adults, are nonetheless quite capable of questioning adult authority (Laupa, 1991; Tisak & Tisak, 1990). These children believe that parents are justified in enforcing rules against stealing and other *moral* transgressions, but they feel that a parent is clearly abusing authority should he arbitrarily impose rules that restrict their choice of friends or leisure activities—areas that they perceive as under their own *personal*

moral rules: standards of acceptable and unacceptable conduct that focus on the rights and privileges of individuals.

social-conventional rules: standards of conduct determined by social consensus that indicate what is appropriate within a particular social context.

jurisdiction (Tisak & Tisak, 1990). Perhaps the best illustration that older heteronomous children are not particularly cowed by authority is this: Ten-year-olds who are relatively religious believe that not even the endorsement of the ultimate authority figure—God—would make a *moral* transgression (such as stealing) morally right (Nucci & Turiel, 1993). So young children do have ideas about what constitutes *legitimate* authority, and those ideas are not based solely on an unwavering respect for the sanctity or wisdom of adult authority figures as Piaget had assumed.

Do Parents Impede Children's Moral Development?

Finally, Piaget was partially right and partially wrong in his views of parents as agents of moral socialization. He was right in assuming that parents can impede moral growth by adopting a heavy-handed, authoritarian approach in which they *challenge* the child's moral reasoning and present their own ideas in a lecturelike format as lessons to be learned (Walker & Taylor, 1991a). But he was very wrong in assuming that parents typically operate in this way when discussing moral issues with their children. Consider that 6–7-year-olds, who should be at Piaget's heteronomous stage, often make *autonomous* moral judgments—*as long as their parents do* (Leon, 1984). How is this possible? Research by Lawrence Walker and John Taylor (1991a) suggests an answer: By carefully tailoring their own reasoning to the child's ability to understand and by presenting new moral perspectives in a supportive (rather than challenging) way, parents may often *promote* their children's moral development (see also Speicher, 1994).

Developmentalists are indebted to Piaget for suggesting that children's moral reasoning develops in stages that are closely tied to cognitive growth. His early theory stimulated an enormous amount of research and several new insights, including the findings above, which indicate that children younger than age 10 are considerably more sophisticated in their moral reasoning than Piaget made them out to be. But is moral reasoning fully developed by age 10 to 11, as Piaget had assumed? Lawrence Kohlberg certainly didn't think so.

Kohlberg's Theory of Moral Development

Kohlberg* (1963, 1984; Colby & Kohlberg, 1987) refined and extended Piaget's theory of moral development by asking 10-, 13-, and 16-year-old boys to resolve a series of "moral dilemmas." Each dilemma challenged the respondent by requiring him to choose between (1) obeying a rule, law, or authority figure and (2) taking some action that conflicts with these rules and commands while serving a human need. The following story is the best known of Kohlberg's moral dilemmas:

> In Europe, a woman was near death from a special kind of cancer. There was one drug that doctors thought might save her. It was a form of radium that a druggist in the same town had recently discovered. The drug was expensive to make, but the druggist was charging $2000, or 10 times the cost of the drug, for a small (possibly life-saving) dose. Heinz, the sick woman's husband, borrowed all the money he could, about $1000, or half of what he needed. He told the druggist that his wife was dying and asked him to sell the drug cheaper or to let him pay later. The druggist replied "No, I discovered the drug, and I'm going to make money from it." Heinz then became desperate and broke into the store to steal the drug for his wife. Should Heinz have done that?

---

*Lawrence Kohlberg was born in 1927 and died in 1987. As a youth, he put his own moral principles into action by helping to transport Jewish refugees from Europe to Israel after World War II. He devised his theory of moral development as a doctoral student at the University of Chicago and then spent most of his career at Harvard University, studying moral development and promoting moral education.

Kohlberg was actually less interested in the subject's decision (that is, what Heinz should have done) than in the underlying rationale, or "thought structures," that the subject used to justify his decision. So, if a subject responded "Heinz should steal the drug to save his wife's life," it is necessary to determine why her life is so important. Is it because she cooks and irons for Heinz? Because it's a husband's duty to save his wife? Or because the preservation of life is among the highest of human values? To determine the "structure" of a subject's moral reasoning, Kohlberg asked probing questions: Does Heinz have an obligation to steal the drug? If Heinz doesn't love his wife, should he steal it for her? Should Heinz steal the drug for a stranger? Is it important for people to do everything they can to save another life? Is it against the law to steal? Does that make it morally wrong? Of course, the purpose of the probes is to clarify how individual participants reason about obedience and authority on the one hand and about human needs, rights, and privileges on the other.

Through his use of these elaborate *clinical interviews*, Kohlberg's first discovery was that moral development is far from complete at age 10 to 11, or Piaget's autonomous stage. Indeed, moral reasoning seems to evolve and become progressively more complex throughout adolescence and into young adulthood. Careful analyses of his subjects' responses to several dilemmas led Kohlberg to conclude that moral growth progresses through an *invariant sequence* of three moral levels, each of which is composed of two distinct moral stages. According to Kohlberg, the order of these moral levels and stages is invariant because each depends on the development of certain cognitive abilities that evolve in an invariant sequence. Like Piaget, Kohlberg assumed that each succeeding stage evolves from and replaces its predecessor; once the individual has attained a higher stage of moral reasoning, he or she should never regress to earlier stages.

Before looking at Kohlberg's sequence of stages, it is important to emphasize that each stage represents a particular perspective, or *method of thinking* about moral dilemmas, rather than a particular type of moral decision. As we will see, decisions are not very informative in themselves, because subjects at each moral stage might well endorse either of the alternative courses of action when resolving one of these ethical dilemmas. (There is, however, a strong tendency for subjects at Kohlberg's highest moral level to favor serving human needs over complying with rules or laws that conflict with such needs.)

The basic themes and defining characteristics of Kohlberg's three moral levels and six stages are as follows:

Level 1: Preconventional Morality

For the person at the level of **preconventional morality**, rules are truly external to the self rather than internalized. The child conforms to rules imposed by authority figures to avoid punishment or obtain personal rewards. Morality is self-serving: what is right is what one can get away with or what is personally satisfying.

Stage 1: Punishment-and-obedience orientation. The goodness or badness of an act depends on its consequences. The child will obey authorities to avoid punishment, but may not consider an act wrong if it will not be detected and punished. The greater the harm done or the more severe the punishment is, the more "bad" the act is. The following two responses reflect a "punishment-and-obedience" orientation to the Heinz dilemma:

Protheft: It isn't really bad to take the drug—he did ask to pay for it first. He wouldn't do any other damage or take anything else, and the drug he'd take is only worth $200, not $2000.

Antitheft: Heinz doesn't have permission to take the drug. He can't just go and break through a window. He'd be a bad criminal doing all that damage . . . and stealing anything so expensive would be a big crime.

preconventional morality: Kohlberg's term for the first two stages of moral reasoning, in which moral judgments are based on the tangible punitive consequences (Stage 1) or rewarding consequences (Stage 2) of an act for the actor rather than on the relationship of that act to society's rules and customs.

Calvin and Hobbes copyright 1990
Universal Press Syndicate. Reprinted
with permission. All rights reserved.

Stage 2: Naive hedonism. A person at this second stage conforms to rules in order to gain rewards or satisfy personal objectives. There is some concern for the perspective of others, but other-oriented behaviors are ultimately motivated by the hope of benefit in return. "You scratch my back and I'll scratch yours" is the guiding philosophy. Here are two samples of this hedonistic, self-serving morality (see also Calvin's moral philosophy in the cartoon).

Protheft: Heinz isn't really doing any harm to the druggist, and he can always pay him back. If he doesn't want to lose his wife, he should take the drug.

Antitheft: Hey, the druggist isn't wrong, he just wants to make a profit like everybody else. That's what you're in business for, to make money.

Level 2: Conventional Morality

The individual at the level of **conventional morality** strives to obey rules and social norms in order to win others' approval or to maintain social order. Social praise and the avoidance of blame have now replaced tangible rewards and punishments as motivators of ethical conduct. The perspectives of other people are clearly recognized and given careful consideration.

Stage 3: "Good boy" or "good girl" orientation. Moral behavior is that which pleases, helps, or is approved of by others. Actions are evaluated on the basis of the actor's intent. "He means well" is a common expression of moral approval at this stage. As we see in the responses below, the primary objective of a Stage 3 respondent is to be thought of as a "good" person.

Protheft: Stealing is bad, but Heinz is only doing something that is natural for a good husband to do. You can't blame him for doing something out of love for his wife. You'd blame him if he didn't save her.

Antitheft: If Heinz's wife dies, he can't be blamed. You can't say he is heartless for failing to commit a crime. The druggist is the selfish and heartless one. Heinz tried to do everything he really could.

Stage 4: Social-order-maintaining morality. At this stage, the individual considers the perspectives of the generalized other—that is, the will of society as reflected in law. Now what is right is what conforms to the rules of *legal* authority. The reason for conforming is not a fear of punishment, but a belief that rules and laws maintain a social order that is worth preserving. As we see in the following responses, laws always transcend special interests for the Stage 4 respondent:

Protheft: The druggist is leading the wrong kind of life if he just lets somebody die; so it's Heinz's duty to save [his wife]. But Heinz just can't go around breaking laws—he must pay the druggist back and take his punishment for stealing.

conventional morality: Kohlberg's term for the third and fourth stages of moral reasoning, in which moral judgments are based on a desire to gain approval (Stage 3) or to uphold laws that maintain social order (Stage 4).

Antitheft: It's natural for Heinz to want to save his wife, but it's still always wrong to steal. You have to follow the rules regardless of your feelings or the special circumstances.

Level 3: Postconventional (or Principled) Morality

A person at the level of **postconventional morality** defines right and wrong in terms of broad principles of justice that could conflict with written laws or with the dictates of authority figures. Morally right and legally proper are not always one and the same.

Stage 5: Morality of contract, individual rights, and democratically accepted law. At this "social contract" stage, the individual is now aware that the purpose of just laws is to express the will of the majority and further human values. Laws that accomplish these ends and are impartially applied are viewed as social contracts that one has an obligation to follow; but imposed laws that compromise human rights or dignity are considered unjust and worthy of challenge. (By contrast, the person at Stage 4 will not ordinarily challenge the sanctity of an established law and may by suspicious of those who do.) Notice how distinctions between what is legal and what is moral begin to appear in the following Stage 5 responses to Heinz's dilemma:

Protheft: Before you say stealing is morally wrong, you've got to consider this whole situation. Of course, the laws are quite clear about breaking into a store. And . . . Heinz would know that there were no *legal* grounds for his actions. Yet it would be reasonable for anybody, in that kind of situation, to steal the drug.

Antitheft: I can see the good that would come from illegally taking the drug. But the ends don't justify the means. The law represents a consensus of how people have agreed to live together, and Heinz has an obligation to respect these agreements. You can't say Heinz would be completely wrong to steal the drug, but even these circumstances don't make it right.

Stage 6: Morality of individual principles of conscience. At this "highest" moral stage, the individual defines right and wrong on the basis of the self-chosen ethical principles of his or her own conscience. These principles are not concrete rules such as the Ten Commandments. They are abstract moral guidelines or principles of universal justice (and respect for individual rights) that *transcend* any law or social contract that may conflict with them. Kohlberg (1981) described Stage 6 thinking as a kind of "moral musical chairs" in which the person facing a moral dilemma is able to take the perspective of each and every person who could potentially be affected by a decision and arrive at a solution that would be regarded as just by all. Here are two Stage 6 responses to the Heinz dilemma:

Protheft: When one must choose between disobeying a law and saving a human life, the higher principle of preserving life makes it morally right to steal the drug.

Antitheft: With many cases of cancer and the scarcity of the drug, there may not be enough to go around to everybody who needs it. The correct course of action can only be the one that is "right" by all people concerned. Heinz ought to act, not on emotion or the law, but according to what he thinks an ideally just person would do in this case.

Stage 6 is Kohlberg's vision of ideal moral reasoning. But because it is so very rare and virtually no one functions consistently at this level, Kohlberg came to view it as

postconventional morality:
Kohlberg's term for the fifth and sixth stages of moral reasoning, in which moral judgments are based on social contracts and democratic law (Stage 5) or on universal principles of ethics and justice (Stage 6).

a hypothetical construct—that is, the stage to which people would progress were they to develop beyond Stage 5. In fact, the later versions of Kohlberg's manual for scoring moral judgments no longer attempt to measure Stage 6 reasoning (Colby & Kohlberg, 1987).

An Evaluation of Kohlberg's Theory

Although Kohlberg believes that his stages form an invariant and universal sequence of moral growth that is closely tied to cognitive development, he also claims that cognitive growth, by itself, is not sufficient to guarantee moral development. In order to move beyond the preconventional level of moral reasoning, children must be exposed to persons or situations that introduce *cognitive disequilibria*—that is, conflicts between existing moral concepts and new ideas that will force them to reevaluate their viewpoints. So, like Piaget, Kohlberg believes that both cognitive development and *relevant social experiences* underlie the growth of moral reasoning.

How much support is there for these ideas? Let's review the evidence, starting with data bearing on Kohlberg's invariant-sequence hypothesis.

Are Kohlberg's Stages an Invariant Sequence?

If Kohlberg's stages represent a true developmental sequence, we should find a strong positive correlation between age and maturity of moral reasoning. Kohlberg reports such a relationship in his original work with 10–16-year-olds, and similar findings have emerged from studies in Mexico, the Bahamas, Taiwan, Turkey, Honduras, India, Nigeria, and Kenya (see Colby & Kohlberg, 1987, for a review). In all these cultures, adolescents and young adults typically reason about moral issues at higher levels than preadolescents and younger children do. So it seems that Kohlberg's levels and stages of moral reasoning are "universal" structures that are age-related—just as we would expect them to be if they formed a developmental sequence. But do these studies establish that Kohlberg's stages form a fixed, or *invariant*, sequence?

No, they do not! The problem is that subjects at each age level were *different* people, and we cannot be certain that a 25-year-old at Stage 5 has progressed through the various moral levels and stages in the order specified by Kohlberg's theory.

The longitudinal evidence. Clearly, the most compelling evidence for Kohlberg's invariant-sequence hypothesis would be a demonstration that individual children progress through the moral stages in precisely the order that Kohlberg says they should. Ann Colby and her associates (1983) have reported the results of a 20-year longitudinal study of 58 American males who were 10, 13, or 16 years old at the beginning of the project. These boys responded to Kohlberg's moral dilemmas when the study began and again in five follow-up sessions administered at 3–4-year intervals. As shown in Figure 14-8, moral reasoning developed very gradually, with use of preconventional reasoning (Stages 1 and 2) declining sharply in adolescence—the same period in which conventional reasoning (Stages 3 and 4) is on the rise. Conventional reasoning remained the dominant form of moral expression in young adulthood, with very few subjects ever moving beyond it to postconventional morality (Stage 5). But even so, Colby et al. found that, as subjects proceeded through the stages, they did so in precisely the order Kohlberg predicted and that no subject ever skipped a stage. Similar results have been reported in a 9-year longitudinal study of adolescents in Israel and a 12-year longitudinal project conducted in Turkey (Colby & Kohlberg, 1987). So Kohlberg's moral stages do seem to represent an invariant sequence (see also Walker & Taylor, 1991b). However, the notion that people show an orderly progression from Stages 1 to 4 is better supported than the idea that people continue to progress from Stage 4 to Stage 5. Stage 3 or 4 is the end of the developmental journey for most individuals worldwide (Snarey, 1985).

Figure 14-8

Use of Kohlberg's moral stages at ages 10 through 36 by male participants studied longitudinally over a 20-year period.

Adapted from Colby, Kohlberg, Gibbs, & Lieberman, 1983.

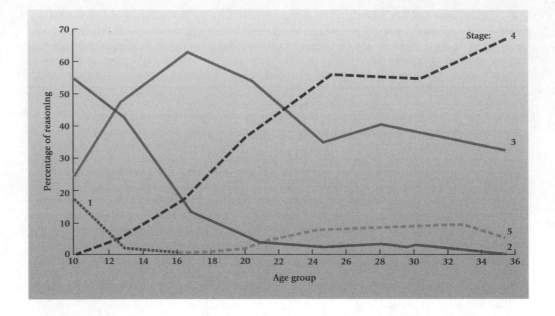

The Relationship of Kohlberg's Stages to Cognitive Development

According to Kohlberg (1963), the young, preconventional child reasons about moral issues from an egocentric point of view. At Stage 1, the child thinks that certain acts are bad because they are punished. At Stage 2, the child shows a limited awareness of the needs, thoughts, and intentions of others but still judges self-serving acts as "right," or appropriate. However, conventional reasoning clearly requires some role-taking abilities. A person at Stage 3, for example, must necessarily recognize others' points of view before she will evaluate intentions that would win their approval as "good" or morally acceptable. Furthermore, postconventional, or "principled," morality would seem to require much more than a decline in egocentrism and a capacity for mutual role taking: The person who bases moral judgments on abstract principles must be able to reason abstractly and take all possible perspectives on a moral issue rather than simply adhering to the rule of law or to concrete moral norms. So Kohlberg believes that the highest level of intellect, *formal operations*, is necessary for principled moral reasoning (Stage 5).

Much of the available research is consistent with Kohlberg's hypotheses. For example, Lawrence Walker's (1980) study of 10–13-year-olds found that all subjects who had reached Kohlberg's third stage of moral reasoning ("good boy/good girl" morality) were proficient at mutual role taking. However, not all the proficient role takers had reached Stage 3 in their moral reasoning. So Walker's results imply that mutual role-taking skills are *necessary but not sufficient* for the development of conventional morality.

Carol Tomlinson-Keasey and Charles Keasey (1974) administered Kohlberg's moral dilemmas and tests of cognitive development to sixth-grade girls (ages 11–12) and to college women. An interesting pattern emerged. All the subjects who reasoned at the postconventional level (Stage 5) on the dilemmas showed at least some formal-operational thinking on the cognitive tests. But not all the formal operators reasoned at the postconventional level on the dilemmas test. This same pattern also emerged in a later study by Deanna Kuhn and her associates (1977). So it seems that formal operations are *necessary but not sufficient* for the development of postconventional morality.

In sum, Kohlberg's moral stages are clearly related to one's level of cognitive development. Proficiency at mutual role taking may be necessary for the onset of conventional morality, and formal operations appear to be necessary for postconventional, or "principled," morality. Yet, it is important to emphasize, as Kohlberg himself has, that intellectual growth does not guarantee moral development, for a person who has reached the highest stages of intellect (or role taking) may continue to reason at the preconventional level about moral issues. The implication, then, is that both *intellectual growth* and *relevant social experiences* (exposure to persons or situations that force a reevaluation of one's current moral concepts) are necessary before children can progress from preconventional morality to Kohlberg's higher stages.

Evidence for Kohlberg's "Social-Experience" Hypothesis

Does research support the proposition that social experience contributes to moral development? Indeed it does, and we've already discussed an important example: the fact that parents can promote the growth of moral reasoning if they are sensitive to the child's viewpoint when discussing moral issues and present their own perspectives in a supportive (and nonthreatening) way.

Discussing important ethical issues with peers often promotes the growth of moral reasoning.

Peer interactions. Like Piaget, Kohlberg felt that interactions with peers probably contribute more to moral growth than one-sided discussions with adult authority figures, in which children are expected to defer to the adult. Even though we've seen that parents can foster moral growth, Piaget and Kohlberg were right to call attention to the role that peers play as agents of moral socialization. Children do seem to think more actively and deeply about their own and their partners' moral ideas in discussions with peers than in talks with their mothers or other adults; moreover, discussions with peers are more likely to stimulate moral growth (Kruger, 1992; Kruger & Tomasello, 1986).

Interestingly, the participants who seem to benefit most from peer discussions are those whose moral reasoning was least mature before the discussions began. And the changes in moral reasoning that they display are not merely a modeling effect. Berkowitz and Gibbs (1983) report that change is unlikely to occur unless the discussions include **transactive interactions**—that is, exchanges in which each discussant performs mental operations on the reasoning of his or her partner (for example, "Your reasoning misses an important distinction"; "Here's an elaboration of your position"; "We can combine our positions into a common view"). This latter finding is important, for it reinforces Kohlberg's contention that social experiences promote moral growth by introducing cognitive challenges to one's current reasoning—challenges to which the *less mature* individual will adapt by assimilating and accommodating to the other person's logic. Why do the more mature discussants not move in the direction of their less mature partners? Because the challenges introduced by their less mature counterparts are based on reasoning that they have already rejected. Indeed, their failure to regress in the face of such logic provides additional support for Kohlberg's invariant-sequence hypothesis.

Now an important issue. We've seen that parents who *directly challenge* a child's moral judgments through the kinds of transactive interactions that Berkowitz and Gibbs (1983) describe do *not* seem to foster growth, but peers do! How might we explain this inconsistency? Walker and Taylor (1991a) believe that there is a simple explanation. Cognitive conflict introduced in a challenging way by a parent (who then offers his or her own discrepant point of view) is likely to be perceived as hostile criticism and thus to arouse defensiveness in a child or adolescent. By contrast, the same kind of criticism is less likely to be perceived as threatening when voiced by a social equal; in fact, children may be especially inclined to listen carefully and to accommodate to a peer's position because they are so highly motivated to establish and maintain good relations with peers. Although more research is needed to confirm this explanation, it seems that parents and peers do promote moral growth in very different ways.

Advanced education. Another kind of social experience that promotes moral growth is receiving an advanced education. Consistently, adults who go on to college and receive many years of education reason more complexly about moral issues than

transactive interactions: verbal exchanges in which individuals perform mental operations on the reasoning of their discussion partners.

those who are less educated (Boldizar, Wilson, & Deemer, 1989; Pratt et al., 1991; Speicher, 1994), and differences in the moral reasoning between college students and their nonstudent peers become greater with each successive year of school that the college students complete (Rest & Thoma, 1985). Advanced education may foster moral growth in two ways: (1) by contributing to cognitive growth and (2) by exposing students to diverse moral perspectives that produce cognitive conflict and soul-searching (Kohlberg, 1984; Mason & Gibbs, 1993).

Cultural influences. Finally, simply living in a complex, diverse, and democratic society can stimulate moral development. Just as we learn the give-and-take of mutual perspective taking by discussing issues with our friends, we learn in a diverse democracy that the opinions of many groups must be weighed and that laws reflect a consensus of the citizens rather than the arbitrary rulings of a dictator. Indeed, cross-cultural studies suggest that postconventional moral reasoning emerges primarily in Western democracies and that people in rural villages in many nonindustrialized countries show no signs of it (Harkness, Edwards, & Super, 1981; Snarey & Keljo, 1991; Tietjen & Walker, 1985). People in these homogeneous communities may have less experience with the kinds of political conflicts and compromises that take place in a more complex society and so may never have any need to question conventional moral standards. By adopting a contextual perspective on development, we can appreciate that the conventional (mostly Stage 3) reasoning typically displayed by adults in these societies—with its emphasis on cooperation and loyalty to the immediate social group—is adaptive and mature within their own social systems (Harkness et al., 1981).

In sum, Kohlberg not only devised a stage sequence that appears to have universal applicability, but he correctly identified some of the major factors that determine how far an individual progresses in the sequence. Advanced moral reasoning is most likely if the individual has acquired the necessary cognitive skills (particularly perspective-taking skills and, later, the ability to reason abstractly). Moreover, an individual's moral development is highly influenced by social experiences, including interactions with parents but perhaps even more so by opportunities to be exposed to diverse perspectives through discussions with peers, exposure to higher education, or participation in democracy.

Is Kohlberg's theory of moral development sound, then? Not entirely, say the critics. Whenever a theory arouses the enormous interest that Kohlberg's has, you can bet that it will also provoke an enormous amount of criticism. Many of the criticisms have centered on the possibility that Kohlberg's theory is biased against certain groups of people and on the fact that it says much about moral reasoning but little about moral affect and behavior.

Is Kohlberg's Theory Biased?

Cultural bias. Although research indicates that children and adolescents in the many cultures that have been studied proceed through the first three or four of Kohlberg's stages in order, we have seen that postconventional morality as Kohlberg defines it simply does not exist in some societies. Critics have charged that Kohlberg's highest stages reflect a Western ideal of justice and that the stage theory is therefore biased against people who live in non-Western societies or who do not value individualism and individual rights highly enough to want to challenge society's rules (Gibbs & Schnell, 1985; Shweder, Mahapatra, & Miller, 1990). People in societies that emphasize social harmony and place the good of the group ahead of the good of the individual may be viewed as conventional moral thinkers in Kohlberg's system but may actually have very sophisticated concepts of justice (Snarey & Keljo, 1991; Vasudev & Hummel, 1987). Although there are some aspects of moral development that do seem to be common to all cultures, the research presented in Box 14-3 indicates that other aspects of moral growth vary considerably from society to society.

BOX 14-3
Cultural Differences in Moral Thinking

*I*s each of the following acts wrong? If so, how serious a violation is it?

1. A young married woman is beaten black and blue by her husband after going to a movie without his permission despite having been warned not to do so again.
2. A brother and sister decide to get married and have children.
3. The day after his father died, the oldest son in a family has a haircut and eats chicken.

These are three of 39 acts presented by Richard Shweder, Manamahan Mahapatra, and Joan Miller (1990, pp. 165– 166) to children ages 5 to 13 and adults in India and the United States. You may be surprised to learn that Hindu children and adults rated the son's having a haircut and eating chicken after his father's death as among the very most morally offensive of the 39 acts they rated, and the husband's beating of his disobedient wife as not wrong at all. American children and adults, of course, viewed wife beating as far more serious than breaking seemingly arbitrary rules about appropriate mourning behavior. Although Indians and Americans could agree that a few acts like brother-sister incest were serious moral violations, they did not agree on much else.

Moreover, Indian children and adults viewed the Hindu ban against behavior that is disrespectful of one's dead father as a *universal moral rule*; they thought it would be best if *everyone in the world* followed it (see also Wainryb, 1993) and strongly disagreed that it would be acceptable to change the rule if most people in their society wanted to change it. Hindus also believed that it is a serious moral offense for a widow to eat fish or wear brightly colored clothes or for a woman to cook food for her family during her menstrual period. To orthodox Hindus, rules against such behavior are required by natural law; they are not just arbitrary social conventions created by members of society. Hindus also regard it as morally necessary for a man to beat his disobedient wife in order to uphold his obligations as head of the family.

What effects do cultural beliefs of this sort have on moral development? The developmental trend in moral thinking that Shweder detected in India was very different from the developmental trend he observed in the United States, as the figure here shows. With age, Indian children saw more and more issues as matters of universal moral principle, whereas American children saw fewer and fewer issues in the same light (and more and more as matters of arbitrary social convention that can legitimately differ from society to society). Moreover, even the youngest children in both soci-

eties expressed moral outlooks that were very similar to those expressed by adults in their own society and very different from those expressed by either children or adults in the other society.

Based on these cross-cultural findings, Shweder calls into question Kohlberg's claims that all children everywhere construct similar moral codes at similar ages and that certain universal moral principles exist. Moreover, Shweder questions Turiel's claim that children everywhere distinguish from an early age between moral rules and social-conventional rules, for Shweder found that the concept of social-conventional rules was simply not very meaningful to Indians of any age.

Overall, then, these findings challenge the cognitive-developmental position that *all* important aspects of moral growth are universal. Instead, they tend to support a contextual perspective on moral development by suggesting that children's moral judgments are shaped by the culture in which they live (see also Haidt, Koller, & Dias, 1993). Perhaps children all over the world think in more and more complex ways about issues of morality and justice as they get older, as Kohlberg claimed, but at the same time adopt quite different notions about what is right and what is wrong, as Shweder claims.

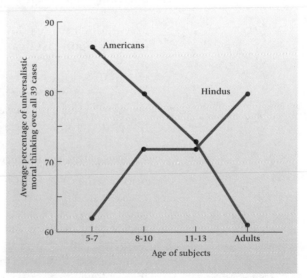

Universalistic moral thinking—the tendency to view rules of behavior as universally valid and unalterable—increases with age among Hindu children in India but decreases with age in the United States. The course of moral development is likely to be different in different societies. Adapted from Shweder, Mahapatra, & Miller, 1987.

Is Kohlberg's theory biased against women? No criticism of Kohlberg has stirred more heat than the charge that his theory is biased against women. Carol Gilligan (1977, 1982, 1993) has been disturbed by the fact that Kohlberg's stages were based on interviews with males and that, in some studies, women seemed to be the moral inferior of men, typically reasoning at Stage 3 of Kohlberg's sequence while men usually reasoned at Stage 4. Her response was to argue that (1) females develop a different moral orientation than males do—one that is not adequately represented in Kohlberg's theory—and that (2) these different moral orientations are a product of sex typing. According to Gilligan, the independence and assertiveness training that boys receive encourage them to consider moral dilemmas as inevitable conflicts of interest between *individuals* that laws and other social conventions are designed to resolve. She calls this orientation the **morality of justice**—a perspective that approximates Stage 4 in Kohlberg's scheme. By contrast, girls are taught to be nurturant, empathic, and concerned about others—in short, to define their sense of "goodness" in terms of their interpersonal *relationships*. So for females, morality implies a sense of caring or compassionate concern for human welfare—a **morality of care** that may seem to represent Stage 3 in Kohlberg's scheme. However, Gilligan insists that the morality of care that females adopt can become quite abstract or "principled," even though Kohlberg's scheme might place it at Stage 3 because of its focus on interpersonal obligations.

At this point, there is little support for Gilligan's claim that Kohlberg's theory is systematically biased against women. Most studies indicate that women reason just as complexly about moral issues as men do when their answers are scored by Kohlberg's criteria (Kahn, 1992; Pratt et al., 1991; Walker, 1991). Nor is there much evidence for sex differences in moral orientations: When reasoning about real-life moral dilemmas they have faced, *both* males and females raise issues of compassion and interpersonal responsibility about *as often as* or *more often than* they talk about issues of law, justice, and individual rights; the only seemingly reliable sex differences discovered thus far is that adolescent girls and women are more likely than adolescent boys and men to discuss and to feel guilty about problems that arise in their personal relationships (Pratt et al., 1988, 1991; Walker, 1989; Williams & Bybee, 1994).

Although her hypothesis about sex differences in moral reasoning has not received much support, Gilligan's work *has* increased our awareness that both men and women often think about moral issues—especially real-life as opposed to hypothetical moral issues—in terms of their responsibilities for the welfare of other people. Kohlberg emphasized only one way, a very legalistic way, of thinking about right and wrong. There seems to be merit in tracing the development of *both* a morality of justice and a morality of care in *both* males and females (Brabeck, 1983; Gilligan, 1993).

Is Kohlberg's Theory Incomplete?

Another major criticism of Kohlberg's theory is that it focuses too heavily on moral reasoning and neglects moral affect and behavior. Clearly, this criticism has some merit. As we have already noted, a person at any of Kohlberg's moral stages might decide to uphold or break a law. What distinguishes one stage from another is the "structure" of a person's reasoning, not the specific decisions that she reaches. Nonetheless, Kohlberg argued that people at the higher stages of moral reasoning are more likely than those at lower stages to behave in accordance with widely accepted moral standards that preserve individual rights and serve human needs.

Does moral reasoning predict moral conduct? So how well does a person's stage of moral reasoning predict that person's behavior? Many researchers have found that the moral judgments of young children do *not* predict their actual behavior in situations where they are induced to cheat or violate other moral norms (Nelson, Grinder, & Biaggio, 1969; Santrock, 1975; Toner & Potts, 1981). However, studies of older grade school children, adolescents, and young adults often find at least some consistency between moral reasoning and moral conduct. Individuals at higher stages of moral reasoning are more likely than those at lower stages to behave altruistically and conscientiously and are less likely to cheat or take part in delinquent or criminal activity (Blasi, 1980; Colby & Kohlberg, 1987; Rest, 1993). Kohlberg (1975), for exam-

morality of justice: Gilligan's term for what she presumes to be the dominant moral orientation of males, focusing more on socially defined justice as administered through law than on compassionate concerns for human welfare.

morality of care: Gilligan's term for what she presumes to be the dominant moral orientation of females, focusing more on compassionate concerns for human welfare than on socially defined justice as administered through law.

ple, found that only 15% of those students who reasoned at the postconventional level actually cheated on a test when given an opportunity, compared with 55% of the "conventional" students and 70% of those at the preconventional level. Yet the relationship between stage of moral reasoning and moral behavior is typically quite modest. For example, even though many juvenile delinquents reason at the preconventional level, a fair number of them are conventional moral reasoners who break the law anyway (Blasi, 1980). So there must be personal qualities other than one's level of moral reasoning, and many situational factors as well, that influence a person's moral conduct in daily life (Kurtines, 1986; Thoma, Rest, & Davison, 1991). One such influence is moral affect.

Kohlberg ignores moral emotions. Norma Haan and her associates (1985) point out that moral dilemmas in everyday life arouse powerful emotions (moral affects). We care about moral issues and how our decisions will affect other people; we agonize about what to do and want to feel that we are moral beings; and we often feel guilty or remorseful when we violate moral norms. These moral emotions play a central role in morality by motivating our actions, and any theory that overlooks the role of emotions, as Kohlberg's tends to, would seem to be woefully incomplete (see also Haidt et al., 1993; Hart & Chmiel, 1992).

Kohlberg underestimates young children. Finally, Kohlberg's focus on legalistic dilemmas that laws were designed to resolve caused him to overlook other "nonlegalistic" forms of moral reasoning that influence the behavior of grade school children. For example, we've seen that young elementary school children do often consider the needs of others or will do whatever they think people will approve of when resolving Eisenberg's *prosocial* moral dilemmas—even though these youngsters are hopelessly mired in Stage 1 (or Stage 2) when tested using Kohlberg's criteria. Moreover, 8–10-year-old Stage 1 reasoners have often developed some sophisticated notions about **distributive justice**—deciding what is a "fair and just" allocation of limited resources (toys, candies, etc.) among a group of deserving recipients (see Damon, 1977; Sigelman & Waitzman, 1991)—reasoning that is not adequately represented in Kohlberg's theory. Interestingly, fear of punishment, deference to authority, and other legalistic themes that Kohlberg believes to characterize the moral judgments of 8–10-year-olds do not even appear in children's distributive-justice reasoning. So by focusing so heavily on legalistic concepts, Kohlberg has clearly underestimated the moral sophistication of grade school children.

In sum, Kohlberg's theory of moral development has become prominent for good reason. It does indeed describe a universal sequence of changes in moral reasoning extending from childhood through adulthood. Moreover, the evidence supports Kohlberg's view that both cognitive growth and social experiences contribute to moral development. However, there is also some merit to the criticisms. Kohlberg's theory may not adequately describe the morality of people who live in non-Western societies or who emphasize a "morality of care" rather than a "morality of justice," and it clearly underestimates the moral reasoning of young children. And because Kohlberg concentrates so heavily on moral reasoning, we must rely on other perspectives to help us to understand how moral affect and moral behavior develop, and how thought, emotions, and behavior interact to make us the moral beings that most of us ultimately become.

MORALITY AS A PRODUCT OF SOCIAL LEARNING (AND SOCIAL INFORMATION PROCESSING)

Social-learning theorists such as Albert Bandura (1986; 1991) and Walter Mischel (1974) have been primarily interested in the behavioral component of morality— what we actually do when faced with temptation. They claim that moral behavior is

distributive justice: conceptions of what is "fair" or "just" concerning the allocation of resources among the members of a group.

Concept Check 14-3 ⌄ Strengths and Shortcomings of Kohlberg's Cognitive-Developmental Theory

Check your understanding of some of the strengths and the criticisms of Kohlberg's theory of moral development by filling in the blanks in each of the following statements. The answers appear in the Appendix.

1. Kohlberg assumed that his levels and stages of moral development form an _____ sequence and that no subject should ever _____ a stage or _____ to a lower level or stage of moral reasoning. Support for this hypothesis comes from _____ studies, in which subjects progress through the stage sequence in precisely the _____ Kohlberg predicts.

2. Kohlberg believed that moral development is closely tied to cognitive development. Presumably, the onset of conventional morality requires a certain level of _____-_____ skills, whereas _____ _____s are necessary for postconventional morality. Research _____ these predictions.

3. In addition, Kohlberg claimed that social experiences that cause one to _____ one's current moral perspective are necessary for moral growth. Among the social experiences that seem to promote such growth are _____ _____ with peers and receiving a(n) _____ education.

4. Cross-cultural studies suggest that moral development is not nearly as _____ as Kohlberg claimed. Gilligan's work on morality of _____ also points to a moral perspective that Kohlberg did not emphasize, and critics argue that Kohlberg's theory ignores powerful _____ _____s that people experience and that motivate many moral behaviors.

5. Finally, research on children's resolutions of _____ moral dilemmas and on children's _____ _____ reasoning when deciding how to justly divide resources among a group of deserving recipients suggests that Kohlberg's theory _____s the moral sophistication of young grade school children.

learned in the same way that other social behaviors are learned: through the operation of reinforcement and punishment and through observational learning. They also consider moral behavior to be strongly influenced by the nature of the specific situations in which people find themselves: It is not at all surprising, they say, to see a person behave morally in one situation but transgress in another situation or to proclaim that nothing is more important than honesty but then lie.

How Consistent Are Moral Conduct and Moral Character?

Perhaps the most extensive study of children's moral conduct is one of the oldest: the Character Education Inquiry reported by Hugh Hartshorne and Mark May (1928–1930). The purpose of this five-year project was to investigate the moral "character" of 10,000 children aged 8–16 by tempting them to lie, cheat, or steal in a variety of situations. The most noteworthy finding of this massive investigation was that children tended *not* to be consistent in their moral behavior; a child's willingness to cheat in one situation did not predict his willingness to lie, cheat, or steal in other situations. Of particular interest was the finding that children who cheated in a particular setting were just as likely as those who did not to state that cheating is wrong! Hartshorne and May concluded that "honesty" is largely specific to the situation rather than a stable character trait.

This **"doctrine of specificity"** has been questioned by other researchers. Roger Burton (1963; 1976) reanalyzed Hartshorne and May's data using newer and more sophisticated statistical techniques. His analyses provide some support for behavioral consistency. For example, a child's willingness to cheat or not cheat in one context (for example, on tests in class) is reasonably consistent, although the same child might behave very differently in highly unrelated contexts (for example, at competitive games on the playground; see also Nelson, Grinder, & Mutterer, 1969). Rushton (1980) drew a similar conclusion after finding that children who help (or share) in one situation are more likely than their nonaltruistic age-mates to help (or share) in

doctrine of specificity: a viewpoint shared by many social-learning theorists that holds that moral affect, moral reasoning, and moral behavior may depend as much or more on the situation one faces than on an internalized set of moral principles.

other *similar* situations. So it seems that moral behaviors *of a particular kind* (for example, cheating on exams; helping needy others) are not nearly so situationally specific as Hartshorne and May had thought. Furthermore, it appears that both the consistency of moral behaviors and the correlations among measures of moral affect, moral reasoning, and moral conduct become progressively stronger between the grade school years and young adulthood (Blasi, 1980).

In sum, the "doctrine of specificity" is clearly an overstatement, for all three aspects of morality become more consistent and more highly interrelated over time. However, this is not to imply that morality ever becomes a wholly stable and unitary attribute, for one's willingness to lie, cheat, or violate other moral norms may always depend to some extent on contextual factors, such as the importance of the goal one might achieve by transgressing or the amount of encouragement provided by peers for deviant conduct (Burton, 1976). In other words, the moral character of even the most mature of adults is unlikely to be perfectly consistent across all situations.

Learning to Resist Temptation

From society's standpoint, one of the more important indexes of morality is the extent to which an individual is able to resist pressures to violate moral norms, *even when the possibility of detection and punishment is remote* (Hoffman, 1970). A person who resists temptation in the absence of external surveillance not only has learned a moral rule but also is *internally* motivated to abide by that rule. How do children acquire moral standards, and what motivates them to obey these learned codes of conduct? Social-learning theorists have attempted to answer these questions by studying the effects of reinforcement, punishment, and social modeling on children's moral behavior.

Reinforcement as a Determinant of Moral Conduct

We have seen on several occasions that the frequency of many behaviors can be increased if these acts are reinforced. Moral behaviors are certainly no exception. For example, David Perry and Ross Parke (1975) found that children were more likely to obey a prohibition against touching attractive toys if they had been reinforced for playing with other, less attractive items. So the practice of rewarding alternative behaviors that are incompatible with prohibited acts (that is, the *incompatible-response* technique) can be an effective method of instilling moral controls. In addition, punishment administered by a warm, loving (socially reinforcing) parent is more successful at producing resistance to temptation than the same punishment given by a cold, rejecting parent (Sears et al., 1957). Thus, the effectiveness of punishment as a means of establishing moral prohibitions depends, in part, on the disciplinarian's past history as a *reinforcing* agent.

The Role of Punishment in Establishing Moral Prohibitions

Although reinforcing acceptable behaviors is an effective way to promote desirable conduct, adults often fail to recognize that a child has resisted a temptation and is deserving of praise. By contrast, people are quick to inform a child of his or her misdeeds by *punishing* moral transgressions. Is punishment an effective way to foster the development of **inhibitory controls?** As we will see, the answer depends very critically on the child's *interpretation* of these aversive experiences.

Early research. Ross Parke (1977) used the **"forbidden toy" paradigm** to study the effects of punishment on children's resistance to temptation. During the first phase of a typical experiment, subjects were punished (by hearing a noxious buzzer) whenever they touched an attractive toy; however, nothing happened when they played with unattractive toys. Once the child learned the prohibition, the experimenter left and the child was surreptitiously observed to determine whether he or she played with the forbidden toys.

Sometimes it is difficult to tell whether children are working together, helping each other, or using each other's work. Although there is some consistency to moral behavior, a child's conduct in any particular situation is likely to be influenced by factors such as the importance of the goal that might be achieved by breaking a moral rule and the probability of being caught should he or she commit a transgression.

inhibitory control: an ability to display acceptable conduct by resisting the temptation to commit a forbidden act.

"forbidden toy" paradigm: a method of studying children's resistance to temptation by noting whether youngsters will play with forbidden toys when they believe that this transgression is unlikely to be detected.

Recall from our discussion in Chapter 8 (see Box 8-2) that *stronger* (rather than mild) punishments administered *immediately* (rather than later) and *consistently* by a *warm* (rather than an aloof) disciplinarian proved most effective at inhibiting the child's undesirable conduct after the adult had left the room. Yet, Parke's most important discovery was that all forms of punishment become more effective when accompanied by a cognitive rationale that provides the transgressor with reasons for inhibiting a forbidden act.

Explaining the effects of cognitive rationales. Why do rationales increase the effectiveness of punishment, even mild or delayed punishments that produce little moral restraint by themselves? Probably because rationales provide children with information specifying why the punished act is wrong and why *they* should feel guilty or shameful were they to repeat it. So when these youngsters think about committing the forbidden act in the future, they should experience a general uneasiness (stemming from previous disciplinary encounters), should be inclined to make an *internal* attribution for this arousal (for example, "I'd feel guilty were I to deviate"; "I'd violate my positive self-image"), and should now be more likely to inhibit the forbidden act and to feel rather good about their "mature and responsible" conduct. By contrast, children who receive no rationales or who have been exposed to reasoning that focuses their attention on the negative consequences they can expect for future transgressions (for example, "You'll be spanked again if you do it") will experience just as much uneasiness when they think about committing the forbidden act. However, these youngsters should tend to make *external* attributions for their emotional arousal (for example, "I'm worried about getting caught and punished")—attributions that might make them comply with moral norms in the presence of authority figures but should do little to inhibit deviant conduct if there is no one around to detect a transgression.

We see, then, that fear of detection and punishment is not enough to persuade children to resist temptations in the absence of external surveillance. In order to establish truly internalized *self*-controls, adults must structure disciplinary encounters to include an appropriate rationale that informs the child why the prohibited act is wrong and why *she* should feel guilty or otherwise less than virtuous were she to repeat it (Hoffman, 1988). Stated another way, true *self*-restraint is largely under *cognitive* control; the ability to resist temptation depends on what's in children's heads rather than on the amount of fear or uneasiness in their guts.

Moral self-concept training. The idea that moral self-restraint is heavily influenced by the attributions we make implies that we should be able to promote compliance with moral rules by convincing children that they are "good" or "honest" people who are inhibiting the temptation to lie, cheat, or steal because they want to (an internal attribution). This kind of moral self-concept training really does work. William Casey and Roger Burton (1982) found that 7–10-year-olds became much more honest while playing games if being "honest" was stressed and the players had learned to remind themselves to follow the rules. Yet when honesty was *not* stressed, the players were likely to cheat—even if they had been told to periodically remind themselves to comply with the rules. Moreover, David Perry and his associates (1980) found that 9–10-year-olds who had been told that they were especially good at carrying out instructions and following rules (moral self-concept training) behaved very differently after succumbing to a nearly irresistible temptation (leaving a boring task to watch an exciting TV show) than did peers who had not been told they were especially good. Specifically, children who had heard positive attributions about themselves were more inclined than control subjects to *punish their own transgressions* by giving back many of the valuable prize tokens they had been paid for working at the boring task. So it seems that labeling children as "good" or "honest" may not only increase the likelihood that they will resist temptations but also contributes to children's feelings of guilt or remorse should they behave inappropriately and violate their positive self-images. Indeed, Perry believes that the expectation of feeling guilty or remorseful over deviant conduct may be what motivates children with positive self-concepts to resist temptations in the first place.

In sum, moral self-concept training can be a rather effective alternative to punishment as a method of establishing inhibitory controls—one that should help to convince the child that "I'm resisting temptation because *I* want to" and thus lead to the development of truly *internalized* controls rather than a response inhibition based on a fear of detection and punishment. Furthermore, this positive, nonpunitive approach should produce none of the undesirable side effects (for example, resentment) that often accompany punishment.

Effects of Social Models on Children's Moral Behavior

Social-learning theorists have generally assumed that modeling influences play an important role in the child's moral development. And they are correct, for as we have seen, young children often imitate the compassionate and helpful acts of altruistic models. But helpful acts are *active* responses that will capture a child's attention. Will children learn *inhibitory controls* from models who exhibit socially desirable behavior in a "passive" way by failing to commit forbidden acts?

Indeed they will, as long as they recognize that the "passive" model is actually resisting the temptation to violate a moral norm (Toner, Parke, & Yussen, 1978). Joan Grusec and her associates (1979) found that a temptation-resisting model can be particularly effective at inspiring children to behave in kind if he clearly verbalizes that he is following a rule and states a rationale for not committing the deviant act. Moreover, rule-following models whose rationales match the child's customary level of moral reasoning are more influential than models whose rationales are well beyond that level (Toner & Potts, 1981).

Finally, an experiment by Nace Toner and his associates (1978) produced a very interesting outcome: 6–8-year-olds who were persuaded to *serve* as models of moral restraint for other children became more likely than age-mates who had not served as exemplary models to obey rules during later tests of resistance to temptation. It was almost as if serving as a model had produced a change in children's self-concepts, so that they now defined themselves as "people who follow rules." The implications for child rearing are clear: Perhaps parents could establish inhibitory controls in their older children by appealing to their maturity and persuading them to serve as models of self-restraint for their younger brothers and sisters.

WHO RAISES CHILDREN WHO ARE MORALLY MATURE?

Many years ago, Martin Hoffman (1970) reviewed the child-rearing literature to see whether the disciplinary techniques that *parents* use have any effect on the moral development of their children. Three major approaches were compared:

1. **Love withdrawal:** withholding attention, affection, or approval after a child misbehaves—or in other words, creating anxiety over a loss of love.
2. **Power assertion:** use of superior power to control the child's behavior (includes techniques such as forceful commands, physical restraint, spankings, and withdrawal of privileges—techniques that may generate fear, anger, or resentment).
3. **Induction:** explaining why a behavior is wrong and should be changed by emphasizing how it affects other people; often suggests how the child might undo any harm done.

Suppose that little Suzie has just terrorized the family dog by chasing him with a lit sparkler during a Fourth of July celebration. Using *love withdrawal*, a parent might say "How could you? Get away! I can't bear to look at you." Using *power assertion*, a parent might spank Suzie or say "That's it! No movie for you this Saturday." Using

love withdrawal: a form of discipline in which an adult withholds attention, affection, or approval in order to modify or control a child's behavior.

power assertion: a form of discipline in which an adult relies on his or her superior power (for example, by administering spankings or withholding privileges) to modify or control a child's behavior.

induction: a nonpunitive form of discipline in which an adult explains why a child's behavior is wrong and should be changed by emphasizing its effects on others.

Table 14-3 Relationships between Parents' Use of Three Disciplinary Strategies and Children's Moral Development

Direction of relationship between parents' use of a disciplinary strategy and children's moral maturity	Type of discipline		
	Power assertion	Love withdrawal	Induction
+ (positive correlation)	7	8	38
− (negative correlation)	32	11	6

Note: Table entries represent the number of occasions on which a particular disciplinary technique was found to be associated (either positively or negatively) with a measure of children's moral affect, reasoning, or behavior.
Source: Adapted from Brody & Shaffer, 1982.

induction, the parent might say "Suzie, look how scared Pokey is. You could have set him on fire, and you know how sad we'd all be if he died." Induction, then, is a matter of providing rationales that focus special attention on the consequences of one's wrongdoing for other people (or dogs, as the case may be).

Although only a limited number of child-rearing studies had been conducted by 1970, their results suggested that (1) neither love withdrawal nor power assertion were particularly effective at promoting moral maturity, but that (2) induction seemed to foster the development of all three aspects of morality—moral emotions, moral reasoning, and moral behavior (Hoffman, 1970). Table 14-3 summarizes the relationships among the three patterns of parental discipline and various measures of children's moral maturity that emerged from a later review of the literature which included many more studies (Brody & Shaffer, 1982). Clearly, these data confirm Hoffman's conclusions: Parents who rely on inductive discipline tend to have children who are morally mature, whereas frequent use of power assertion is more often associated with moral *immaturity* than with moral maturity. The few cases in which induction was *not* associated with moral maturity all involved children under age 4. However, other recent research indicates that induction can be highly effective with 2–5-year-olds, reliably promoting sympathy and compassion for others as well as a willingness to comply with parental requests; by contrast, use of such high-intensity, power-assertive tactics as becoming angry and physically restraining or spanking the child is already associated with and seems to promote noncompliance, defiance, and a lack of concern for others (Crockenberg & Litman, 1990; Hart et al., 1992; Kuczynski & Kochanska, 1990; Zahn-Waxler et al., 1979).

Why Is Inductive Discipline Effective?

Hoffman believes there are several reasons that the use of inductive tactics is such an effective disciplinary strategy. First, the inductive disciplinarian provides *cognitive standards* (or rationales) that children can use to evaluate their conduct. Second, use of inductive discipline helps children to sympathize with individuals whom they may have wronged, and it allows parents to talk about such moral emotions as pride, guilt, and shame that are not easily discussed with a child who is made emotionally insecure by love withdrawal or angry by power-assertive techniques. Finally, parents who use inductive discipline are likely to explain to the child (1) what he or she *should have done* when tempted to violate a prohibition and (2) what he or she *can now do* to make up for a transgression. So induction may be an effective method of moral socialization because it calls attention to the cognitive, affective, and behavioral aspects of morality and may help the child to integrate them.

Finally, it is important to note that few if any parents are totally inductive, love oriented, or power assertive in their approach to discipline; most make at least some use of all three disciplinary techniques. Although parents classified as "inductive" rely

Dennis the Menace® used by permission of Hank Ketcham and © by North American Syndicate.

"IF YOU'RE TRYIN' TO GET SOMETHING INTO MY HEAD, YOU'RE WORKIN' ON THE WRONG END!"

heavily on inductive methods, they occasionally take punitive measures whenever punishment is necessary to command the child's attention or to discipline repeated transgressions. So the style of parenting that Hoffman calls induction may be very similar to the "rationale plus mild punishment" treatment that is so effective in laboratory studies of resistance to temptation.

Criticisms of Hoffman's Ideas about Discipline

Several investigators have wondered whether Hoffman's conclusions about the effectiveness of inductive discipline might not be overstated. For example, inductive discipline used by white, middle-class mothers is consistently associated with measures of children's moral maturity; however, the same findings don't always hold for fathers or for parents from other socioeconomic backgrounds (Brody & Shaffer, 1982; Grusec & Goodnow, 1994). And since inductive disciplinarians rely on other forms of discipline as well as on reasoning, it is possible that their effectiveness as agents of moral socialization reflects their ability to tailor discipline to the nature of the transgression rather than their use of reasoning itself (see Grusec & Goodnow, 1994).

Other critics have raised the *direction-of-effects* issue: Does induction promote moral maturity; or, rather, do morally mature children elicit more inductive forms of discipline from their parents? Since child-rearing studies are correlational in nature, either of these possibilities can explain Hoffman's findings. Hoffman (1975) responds by claiming that parents exert far more control over their children's behavior than children exert over parents. In other words, he believes that parental use of inductive discipline promotes moral maturity rather than the other way around. And there is some *experimental* support for Hoffman's claim in that induction is much more effective than other forms of discipline at persuading children to keep their promises and to comply with rules imposed by *unfamiliar* adults (Kuczynski, 1983). Moreover, parents have preexisting attitudes about child rearing or implicit theories of discipline that play a major part in determining how they react to children's undesirable conduct (Dix, Ruble, & Zambarano, 1989). For example, mothers who believe that they can do little to control problem behaviors are the ones who react most negatively and coercively to such antics, regardless of whether they are overseeing their own or someone else's child (Bugental, Blue, & Cruzcosa, 1989; Bugental, Blue, & Lewis, 1990).

And yet, children clearly have a hand in determining how they are treated by their overseers. As Grazyna Kochanska (1993) points out, a child's *temperament* may influence how he or she responds to different kinds of discipline, which, in turn, may affect how he or she is treated by parents. Some children are, by temperament, more *emotionally reactive* or arousable; they may become anxious when disciplined and susceptible to interpreting their arousal as sympathy or guilt (depending on the context). Some children are also less *impulsive* than others and better able to inhibit their urges to commit transgressions (Kochanska et al., 1994). How might these components of temperament influence parents' moral socialization? Kochanska (1993) proposes that children who are relatively high in emotionality and low in impulsivity should respond most favorably to rational disciplinary techniques such as induction. By contrast, an emotionally unreactive but highly impulsive child who is not easily led to empathize with others or to experience negative emotions over his or her transgressions may drive parents to use more power-assertive (and less effective) disciplinary techniques (see also Anderson, Lytton, & Romney, 1986; Lytton, 1990).

So moral socialization at home is a two-way street: Although inductive discipline may indeed promote moral development, children who are most temperamentally responsive to these rational, nonpunitive techniques are the ones who are most likely to be treated this way by their parents.

A Child's-Eye View of Discipline

What do children think about various disciplinary strategies? Do they feel (as many developmentalists do) that physical punishment and love withdrawal are ineffective methods of promoting moral restraint? Would they favor inductive techniques? Or is it conceivable that children would prefer their parents to adopt a more permissive attitude and not be so quick to discipline transgressions?

Michael Siegal and Jan Cowen (1984) addressed these issues by asking 100 children and adolescents between the ages of 4 and 18 to listen to stories describing different kinds of misdeeds and to evaluate strategies that mothers had used to discipline these antics. Five kinds of transgressions were described: (1) simple disobedience (the child refused to clean his room), (2) causing physical harm to others (the child punched a playmate), (3) causing physical harm to oneself (ignoring an order not to touch a hot stove), (4) causing psychological harm to others (making fun of a physically disabled person), and (5) causing physical damage (breaking a lamp while roughhousing). The four disciplinary techniques on which mothers were said to have relied were *induction* (reasoning with the culprit by pointing out the harmful consequences of his or her actions), *physical punishment* (striking the child), *love withdrawal* (saying she wanted nothing more to do with the culprit), and *permissive nonintervention* (ignoring the incident and assuming that the child would learn important lessons on his or her own). Each participant heard 20 stories that resulted from pairing each of the four maternal disciplinary strategies with each of the five transgressions. After listening to or reading each story, the subject indicated whether the mother's approach to the problem was "very wrong," "wrong," "half right–half wrong," "right," or "very right."

Although the perceived appropriateness of each disciplinary technique varied somewhat across transgressions, the most interesting findings overall were that (1) induction was the most preferred disciplinary strategy for subjects of all ages (even preschoolers), and (2) physical punishment was the next most favorably evaluated technique, although older children evaluate it less favorably than young children do (see also Catron & Masters, 1993). So all participants seemed to favor a rational disciplinarian who relies heavily on reasoning that is occasionally backed by power assertion. By contrast, love withdrawal and permissiveness were favorably evaluated by no age group. In fact, the younger children in the sample (that is, the 4–9-year-olds) favored *any* form of discipline, even love withdrawal, over a permissive attitude on the mother's part (which they viewed as "wrong" or "very wrong"). Apparently, young children see the need for adults to step in and restrain their inappropriate conduct, for they were quite bothered by the stories in which youngsters were generally free to do their own thing, largely unencumbered by adult constraints.

We see, then, that the disciplinary style that children favor (induction backed by occasional use of power assertion) is the one most closely associated with measures of moral maturity in the child-rearing studies and with resistance to temptation in the laboratory. Perhaps another reason that inductive discipline may promote moral maturity is simply that children view this approach as the "right" way to deal with transgressions, and they may be highly motivated to accept influence from a disciplinarian whose "world view" matches their own. By contrast, children who favor induction but are usually disciplined in other ways may see little justification for internalizing the values and exhortations of a disciplinarian whose very methods of inducing compliance seem unwise, unjust, and hardly worthy of their respect.

SUMMARY

This chapter focuses on three interrelated aspects of social development that are often considered when making judgments about a child's moral character: the emergence and control of aggressive behavior, the development of altruism and prosocial behavior, and the broader (or more inclusive) topic of moral socialization and moral development.

Aggression is defined as any act designed to harm or injure another living being who is motivated to avoid such treatment. It emerges by the end of the first year as infants begin to quarrel with siblings and peers over toys and other possessions. During early childhood, aggression becomes less physical and increasingly verbal, and somewhat less instrumental and increasingly hostile. Although the overall incidence of aggression declines with age, adolescents are not necessarily any "better behaved," as they often turn instead to more covert forms of antisocial conduct to express their anger or frustrations.

Compared with nonaggressive peers, highly aggressive children (1) expect aggression to be personally rewarding, (2) value these outcomes highly, and (3) display a *hostile attributional bias* that predisposes them to favor aggressive solutions to conflict. One's characteristic level of aggression (aggressiveness) is a reasonably stable attribute for both boys and girls; however, boys are more aggressive than girls and are more likely than girls to become targets of aggression. These small but well-established sex differences in aggression seem to reflect the contribution of biological and social forces.

A person's aggressive inclinations depend, in part, on the cultural, subcultural, and family settings in which he or she is raised. Due in part to social class differences in parenting, children and adolescents from disadvantaged backgrounds are more aggressive and display higher rates of delinquency than their middle-class peers. However, children from any social background can become highly aggressive and find themselves on a path leading to chronic delinquency if they live in a coercive home environment where family members are constantly struggling with one another. In order to help these highly combative children, it is often necessary to treat the entire family. Yet, once highly aggressive individuals reach adolescence, family therapy and other treatments are generally unsuccessful at modifying their antisocial conduct.

Thus, many developmentalists now believe that delinquency must be *prevented* rather than remediated. In addition to family therapy, a number of other strategies for reducing young children's antisocial conduct have been attempted. Proceeding in accordance with the *catharsis hypothesis*—the belief that children become less aggressive after letting off steam against an inanimate object—is an *ineffective* control tactic that may *instigate* aggressive behavior. Some proven methods of controlling children's aggression are (1) using the *incompatible response technique*, (2) using the *time-out* procedure to control aggression, (3) modeling and coaching nonaggressive solutions to conflict, (4) creating play environments that minimize the likelihood of conflict, and (5) encouraging children to recognize the harmful effects of their aggressive acts and to *empathize* with the victims of aggression.

Although infants and toddlers occasionally offer toys to playmates, help their parents with household chores, and try to soothe distressed companions, examples of altruism become increasingly common over the course of childhood. The growth of altruistic concern is closely linked to the development of role-taking skills, empathy, and prosocial moral reasoning; and children who have incorporated altruism into their self-concepts are inclined to perform many acts of kindness in order to live up to their positive self-images.

Like aggression, a person's altruistic tendencies are influenced by the cultural and family settings in which he or she is raised. Parents can promote altruistic behavior by encouraging their child to perform acts of kindness, by showing approval for such kindly deeds, and by practicing themselves the prosocial lessons they have preached. Moreover, parents who discipline harmdoing with nonpunitive, affective explanations that point out the negative effects of misconduct for the child's victims are likely to raise children who become sympathetic, self-sacrificing, and concerned about the welfare of others.

Morality has been defined in many ways, although almost everyone agrees that it implies a set of principles or ideals that help the individual to distinguish right from wrong and to act on this distinction. Morality has three basic components: moral affect, moral reasoning, and moral behavior.

Psychoanalytic theorists emphasize the affective, or "emotional," aspects of morality. According to Freud, the character of the parent-child relationship largely determines the child's willingness to internalize the moral standards of his or her parents. This internalization is said to occur during the phallic stage and to result in the development of the superego. Once formed, the superego functions as an internal censor that rewards the child for virtuous conduct and punishes moral transgressions by making the child feel anxious, guilty, or shameful. Although Freud's broader themes about the importance of moral emotions have some merit, recent psychoanalytic ideas and research suggest that moral internalization begins much earlier than Freud had thought and is fostered by a warm (rather than threatening) parent-child relationship.

Cognitive-developmental theorists have emphasized the cognitive component of morality by studying the development of moral reasoning. Jean Piaget formulated a two-stage model of moral development based on changes that occur in children's conceptions of rules and their sense of social justice. Although Piaget identified some important processes and basic trends in the development of moral reasoning, recent research suggests that his theory badly underestimated the moral sophistication of preschool and young grade school children.

Lawrence Kohlberg's revision and extension of Piaget's theory views moral reasoning as progressing through an invariant sequence of three levels, each composed of two distinct stages. According to Kohlberg, the order of progression through the levels and stages is invariant because each of these modes of thinking depends, in part, on the development of cognitive abilities that evolve in a fixed sequence. Yet, Kohlberg also claimed that no moral growth occurs in the absence of social experiences that would cause a person to reevaluate her existing moral concepts.

Research indicates that Kohlberg's stages do form an invariant sequence and that both cognitive development and such relevant social experiences as exposure to divergent moral perspectives in the context of discussions with parents, peers, and partners in higher education or democratic activities do contribute to the growth of moral reasoning. However, Kohlberg's theory may not adequately describe the morality of people who live in many non-Westernized societies or who emphasize a "morality of care" rather than a morality of justice; and like Piaget, Kohlberg clearly underestimates the moral reasoning of young children. Critics also claim that the theory says too little about moral affect and moral behavior.

Social-learning theorists emphasize the behavioral component of morality, and their research has helped us to understand how children are able to resist temptation and to inhibit acts that violate moral norms. Among the processes that are important in establishing inhibitory controls are reinforcing the child for virtuous conduct and punishing transgressions. The most effective punitive tactics are those that include cognitive rationales explaining why the punished act is wrong and why the child should want to inhibit such conduct. Nonpunitive techniques such as convincing the child that she is a "good" or "honest" person are also quite effective at promoting moral self-restraint. Indeed, any technique that induces children to make *internal attributions* for their uneasiness in the face of temptation or for their compliance with rules is likely to contribute to their moral maturity. Children may also acquire inhibitory controls by observing models who show moral restraint and by serving as rule-following models for other children.

Martin Hoffman has looked at the relationship between parental disciplinary practices and children's moral development. His findings indicate that parents who rely mainly on inductive discipline tend to raise children who are morally mature. Induction is an effective method of moral socialization because it often illustrates and may help the child to integrate the affective, cognitive, and behavioral aspects of morality. And because children generally prefer induction to other disciplinary techniques, viewing it as the wise choice for handling most transgressions, they may be highly motivated to accept influence from an inductive adult whose methods they can respect.

Key Terms

aggression [545]

altruism [559]

altruistic exhortations [567]

autonomous morality [572]

catharsis hypothesis [557]

cathartic technique [557]

coercive home environment [554]

conventional morality [577]

distributive justice [585]

doctrine of specificity [586]

empathy [558]

"felt responsibility" hypothesis [564]

"forbidden toy" paradigm [587]

heteronomous morality [571]

hostile aggression [545]

hostile attributional bias [547]

immanent justice [571]

incompatible-response technique [557]

induction [589]

inhibitory control [587]

instrumental aggression [545]

internalization [568]

love withdrawal [589]

moral affect [568]

moral behavior [568]

moral reasoning [568]

moral rules [574]

morality [568]

morality of care [584]

morality of justice [584]

negative reinforcer [554]

oedipal morality [570]

postconventional morality [578]

power assertion [589]

preconventional morality [576]

premoral period [571]

prosocial moral reasoning [561]

retaliatory aggression [546]

self-oriented distress [563]

social-conventional rules [574]

sympathetic empathic arousal [563]

time-out technique [557]

transactive interactions [581]

Part V

The Ecology of Development

You may have heard the saying that we are products of our environments and are influenced by the company we keep. The truth in this assertion will become quite apparent as we explore in this final section of the book the contexts or settings in which people develop.

Virtually all children are raised in a family setting, although families differ considerably and no two individuals ever experience exactly the same family environment. Chapter 15 concentrates on the family as an agent of socialization and outlines the many ways in which families (and the cultural contexts in which families live) influence the social, emotional, and intellectual development of their young.

Of course, the family is only one source of influence for developing children, who soon reach a point in their lives when they spend many of their waking hours away from the watchful eyes of parents and other family members. In our 16th and final chapter, we will look beyond the family to see how children and adolescents react to the messages they receive from television, their schooling, and the society of their peers.

The Family

Have humans always been social animals? Although no one can answer this question with absolute certainty, the archeological record provides some strong clues. Apparently, our closest evolutionary ancestors (dating back before the Neanderthals) were already living in small bands, or tribal units, that provided increased protection against common enemies and allowed individuals to share the many labors necessary for their survival (Weaver, 1985). Of course, there are no written records of social life among these early collectives. But it is clear that, at some point during the prehistoric era, early human societies (and perhaps even the proto-human aggregations) evolved codes of conduct that defined the roles of various tribal members and sanctioned certain motives and practices while prohibiting others. Once a workable social order was established, it then became necessary to "socialize" each succeeding generation.

Socialization is the process by which children acquire the beliefs, values, and behaviors deemed significant and appropriate by the older members of their society. The socialization of each generation serves society in at least three ways. First, it is a means of regulating children's behavior and controlling their undesirable or antisocial impulses. Second, socialization promotes the personal growth of the individual. As children interact with and become like other members of their culture, they acquire the knowledge, skills, motives, and aspirations that should enable them to adapt to their environment and function effectively within their communities. Finally, socialization perpetuates the social order. Socialized children become socialized adults who impart what they have learned to their own children.

All societies have developed various institutions for socializing their young. Examples of these socializing institutions are the family, the church, the educational system, children's groups (for example, Boy and Girl Scouts), and the mass media.

Central among the many social agencies that influence children's lives is that institution we call the family. More than 99% of children in the United States are raised in a family of one kind or another (U.S. Bureau of the Census, 1993), and most children in most societies grow up in a home setting with at least one biological parent or other relative. Often, children have little exposure to people outside the family for several years until they are placed in day care or nursery school or until they begin formal schooling. So the family has a clear head start on other institutions when it comes to socializing a child. And since the events of the early years are so very important to the child's social, emotional, and intellectual development, it is perhaps appropriate to think of the family as society's primary instrument of socialization.

Our focus in this chapter is on the family as a *social system*—an institution that both influences and is influenced by its young. What is a family, and what functions do families serve? How does the birth of a child affect other family members? Do the existing (or changing) relationships among other members of the family have any effect on the care and training that a young child receives? Are some patterns of child rearing better than others? Do parents decide how they will raise their children—or do children influence their parents? Does the family's cultural heritage and socioeconomic status affect parenting and parent-child interactions? How important are siblings as socialization agents? How do children adjust to divorce, maternal employment, or a return to the two-parent family when a single parent remarries? And why do some parents mistreat their offspring? These are some of the major issues that we will consider as we look at the important roles that families play in the cognitive, social, and emotional development of their children.

 ## FUNCTIONS OF THE FAMILY

Families serve society in many ways. They produce and consume goods and services, thereby playing a role in the economy. Traditionally, the family has served as an outlet for the sexual urges of its adult members and as the means of replenishing the population. And historically, families have cared for their elderly, although this func-

socialization: the process by which children acquire the beliefs, values, and behaviors considered desirable or appropriate by the society to which they belong.

tion is now less common in Western societies with the advent of institutions such as Social Security, socialized medical care, and nursing homes. But perhaps the most widely recognized functions of the family—those that are common to all societies—are the caregiving and training that parents and other family members provide for young children.

Three Goals of Parenting

After studying the child-rearing practices of many diverse cultures, Robert LeVine (1974, p. 238) concluded that families in all societies have three basic goals for their children:

1. The **survival goal:** to promote the physical survival and health of the child, ensuring that he or she will live long enough to have children too.
2. The **economic goal:** to foster the skills and behavioral capacities that the child needs for economic self-maintenance as an adult.
3. The **self-actualization goal:** to foster behavioral capabilities for maximizing other cultural values (for example, morality, religion, achievement, wealth, prestige, and a sense of personal satisfaction).

According to LeVine, these universal goals of parenting form a hierarchy. Parents and other caregivers are initially concerned about maximizing the child's chances of survival, and all higher-order goals are placed on the back burner until it is clear that the youngster is healthy and is likely to survive. When physical health and security can be taken for granted, then parents begin to encourage those characteristics that are necessary for economic self-sufficiency. Only after survival and the attributes necessary for economic productivity have been established do parents begin to encourage the child to seek status, prestige, and self-fulfillment.

LeVine's ideas stem from observations of child-rearing practices in societies where infants often die before their second birthday. Regardless of whether one is observing African Bushmen, South American Indians, or Indonesian tribes, parents in societies where infant mortality is high tend to maintain close contact with their infants 24 hours a day, often carrying them on their hips or their backs in some sort of sling, pouch, or cradleboard. These practices increase the infants' chances of survival by protecting them against such environmental stressors as extreme heat or cold and by reducing the likelihood of their becoming ill or dehydrated, crawling into the river or the campfire, or ambling off to be captured by a predator (LeVine, 1974; Tronick, Thomas, & Daltabuit, 1994). Sleeping with parents is also a common practice in these cultures (Whiting & Edwards, 1988)—one that may promote survival by helping to alert parents to infants' breathing-control problems which, if not corrected, could otherwise result in *sudden infant death syndrome* (McKenna, 1986; Morelli et al., 1992). Although parents keep infants close at all times, they may rarely chat with or smile at them and may seem almost uninterested in their future psychological development. Could this pattern of psychologically reserved yet competent physical caregiving be a defensive maneuver that prevents parents from becoming overly attached to an infant who might well die? Perhaps so, for many cultures in which infant mortality is high still advocate practices such as not speaking to neonates as if they were human beings or not naming them until late in the first year, when it is more probable that they will survive (Brazelton, 1979).

The next task that parents face is to promote those characteristics and competencies that will enable children to care for themselves and their own future families. Anthropologist John Ogbu (1981) points out that the economy of a culture (that is, the way in which people support themselves, or subsist) influences how families socialize their young. To illustrate his point, he cites a well-known cross-cultural study by Herbert Barry and his associates (1959), who hypothesized that societies that depend on an agricultural or pastoral economy (those that accumulate food) would stress obedience, cooperation, and responsibility when raising their children. By

In many cultures, parents increase their babies' chances of survival by keeping them close at all times.

survival goal: LeVine's first priority of parenting—to promote the physical health and safety (survival) of young children.

economic goal: LeVine's second priority of parenting—to promote skills that children will need for economic self-sufficiency.

self-actualization goal: LeVine's third priority of parenting—to promote the child's cognitive and behavioral capacity for maximizing such cultural values as morality, achievement, prestige, and personal satisfaction.

contrast, hunter-gatherer societies that do not accumulate food were expected to train their children to be independent, assertive, and venturesome. In other words, both types of societies were expected to emphasize the values, competencies, and attributes that are necessary to maintain their way of life. Barry et al. used existing anthropological records to review the economic characteristics and child-rearing practices of 104 **preliterate societies** all over the world. As predicted, they found that agricultural and pastoral societies did place strong pressures on their children to be cooperative and obedient, whereas hunter-gatherer societies stressed assertiveness, self-reliance, and individual achievement.

Even in industrial societies such as the United States, a family's social position or socioeconomic status affects child-rearing practices. For example, parents from the lower socioeconomic strata, who typically work for a boss and must defer to his or her authority, tend to stress obedience, neatness, cleanliness, and respect for power—attributes that should enable their children to function effectively within a blue-collar economy. By contrast, middle-class parents, particularly those who work for themselves or who are professionals, are more likely to stress ambition, curiosity, creativity, and independence when raising their children (Kohn, 1979). The latter finding would hardly surprise LeVine, who would argue that middle-class parents who have the resources to promote their child's eventual economic security are freer to encourage his or her initiative, achievement, and personal self-fulfillment (the third set of parenting goals) at a very early age.

 THE FAMILY AS A SOCIAL SYSTEM

Our brief overview of LeVine's three parenting goals may make it sound as if parents consciously decide how they will raise their young and that their child-rearing practices determine how their children will behave and develop. Indeed, early family researchers focused almost entirely on the mother-child relationship, operating under the assumption that mothers (and to a lesser extent fathers) were the ones who molded children's conduct and character (Ambert, 1992). However, modern family theorists have rejected this simple, unidirectional model of family socialization in favor of a more comprehensive "systems" approach that is similar to Urie Bronfenbrenner's (1986; 1989) *ecological theory* that we discussed in Chapter 2. The "systems" approach recognizes that parents influence their children. But it also stresses that (1) children influence the behavior and child-rearing strategies of their parents, and (2) that families are complex **social systems**—that is, networks of reciprocal relationships and alliances that are constantly evolving and are greatly affected by the larger social context. Let's now consider some implications of this systems perspective.

Families Are Complex Entities

What does it mean to say that a family is a social system? To Jay Belsky (1981), it means that the family, much like the human body, is a *holistic structure* consisting of interrelated parts, each of which affects and is affected by every other part, and each of which contributes to the functioning of the whole.

To illustrate, let's consider the simplest of **nuclear families,** consisting of a mother, a father, and a first-born child. According to Belsky (1981), even this man-woman-infant "system" is quite complex. An infant interacting with his or her mother is already involved in a process of **reciprocal influence,** as is evident when we notice that the infant's smile is likely to be greeted by the mother's smile or that a mother's concerned expression often makes her infant wary. And what happens when Dad arrives? The mother-infant dyad is suddenly transformed into a *"family system* [comprising] a husband-wife as well as mother-infant and father-infant relationships" (Belsky, 1981, p. 17).

preliterate society: a society in which there is little or no formal schooling, so that many children never learn to read and write.

family social system: the complex network of relationships, interactions, and patterns of influence that characterize a family with three or more members.

nuclear family: a family unit consisting of a wife/mother, a husband/father, and their dependent child(ren).

reciprocal influence: the notion that each person in a social relationship influences and is influenced by the other person(s).

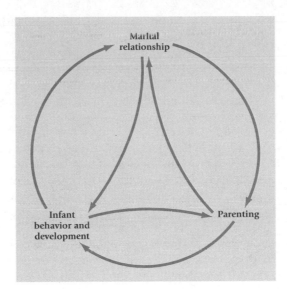

Figure 15-1
A model of the family as a social system. As implied in the diagram, a family is bigger than the sum of its parts. Parents affect infants, who affect each parent and the marital relationship. Of course, the marital relationship may affect the parenting that the infant receives, the infant's behavior, and so on. Clearly, families are complex social systems. As an exercise, you may wish to rediagram the patterns of influence within a family after adding a sibling or two.
From Belsky, 1981.

One implication of viewing the family as a system is that interactions between any two family members are likely to be influenced by attitudes and behaviors of a third family member—a phenomenon known as an **indirect,** or **third party, effect.** To illustrate, fathers clearly influence the mother-infant relationship: Happily married mothers who have close, supportive relationships with their husbands tend to interact much more patiently and sensitively with their infants than mothers who experience marital tension and feel that they are raising their children on their own (Cox et al., 1989; 1992). Meanwhile, mothers indirectly influence the father-infant relationship: Fathers tend to be more involved with their infants when their wives believe that a father should play an important role in a child's life (Palkovitz, 1984) and when the two parents talk frequently about the baby (Belsky, Gilstrap, & Rovine, 1984; Lamb & Elster, 1985). In sum, both mothers and fathers can affect their children indirectly through their interactions with their *spouses.* And overall, children appear to be best off when couples provide *mutual* support and encouragement that allows *both* to be more sensitive and responsive parents (Biller, 1993; Crnic et al., 1983). Of course, children also exert direct and indirect effects on their parents. A highly impulsive toddler who shows little inclination to comply with requests may drive a mother to punitive coercive methods of discipline (direct "child-to-mother" effect; see Kochanska, 1993), which, in turn, may make the child more defiant than ever (a direct "mother-to-child" effect; see Crockenberg and Litman, 1990). Alarmed by this state of affairs, the exasperated mother may then criticize her husband for his nonintervention, thereby precipitating an unpleasant discussion about parental obligations and responsibilities (an indirect effect of the child's impulsivity on the husband-wife relationship).

In short, every person and every relationship within the family affects every other person and relationship through pathways of reciprocal influence (see Figure 15-1). Now we begin to see why it was rather naive to think we might understand how families influence children by concentrating exclusively on the mother-child relationship.

Now think about how complex the family system becomes with the birth of a second child and the addition of sibling-sibling and sibling-parent relationships. Or consider the complexity of an **extended family** household, a nearly universal practice in some cultures in which parents and their children live with other kin—grandparents or aunts, uncles, nieces, and nephews. It turns out that living in extended families is a fairly common arrangement for African Americans—and an adaptive one in that large numbers of economically disadvantaged African American mothers must

indirect, or third party, effect: instances in which the relationship between two individuals in a family is modified by the behavior or attitudes of a third family member.

extended family: a group of blood relatives from more than one nuclear family (for example, grandparents, aunts, uncles, nieces, and nephews) who live together, forming a household.

Older members of extended families serve many useful functions. In addition to providing information and emotional support to young parents, grandmothers and even great-grandmothers may figure prominently in the care and guidance of the family's children.

work, are often supporting their offspring without the father, and can surely use the assistance they receive from grandparents, siblings, uncles, aunts, and cousins who may live with them and serve as surrogate parents for young children (Pearson et al., 1990; Wilson, 1989). Until recently, family researchers have largely ignored extended families or have looked upon them as unhealthy contexts for child rearing. That view is changing, thanks in part to research showing how support from members of extended families (particularly grandmothers) can help disadvantaged single mothers to cope with the stresses they face and to become more sensitive caregivers (Burton, 1990; Wilson, 1989). Indeed, disadvantaged African-American schoolchildren who receive ample kinship support also tend to receive competent parenting at home which, in turn, is associated with such positive outcomes as a strong sense of self-reliance, good psychological adjustment, competent academic performance, and fewer behavior problems (Taylor, Casten, & Flickinger, 1993; Wilson, 1986). And in cultures such as the Sudan, where social life is governed by ideals of communal interdependence and intergenerational harmony, children routinely display better patterns of psychological adjustment if raised in extended-family households than in Westernized, two-parent nuclear families (Al-Awad & Sonuga-Barke, 1992). So it seems that the healthiest family context for child development depends very heavily on both the needs of individual families and the values that families (within particular cultural and subcultural contexts) are trying to promote.

Families Are Developing Entities

Not only are families complex social systems, they are dynamic systems as well. Consider that every family member is a *developing* individual and that relationships between husband and wife, parent and child, and sibling and sibling will also change in ways that can influence the development of each family member. Many such changes are planned, as when parents allow toddlers to do more things on their own as a means of encouraging autonomy and the development of individual initiative. Yet, a host of unplanned or unforeseen changes (such as the death of a sibling or the souring of the husband-wife relationship) can greatly affect family interactions and the growth of its children. So a family is not only a system in which developmental change takes place; its dynamics also change with development of its members.

Families Are Embedded Entities

The social systems perspective also emphasizes that all families are embedded within larger cultural and subcultural contexts and that the ecological niche that a family occupies (for example, the family's religion, its socioeconomic status, and the values that prevail within a subculture, a community, or even a neighborhood) can affect family interactions and the development of a family's children (Bronfenbrenner, 1986; 1989). As we will see later in the chapter, economic hardship exerts a strong influence on parenting: Parents often become depressed over their financial situation, which, in turn, can cause them to become less nurturant toward and involved with their children (Conger et al., 1992, 1995; McLoyd, 1990). And yet, economically distressed parents who have close ties to a "community"—a church group, a volunteer organization, or a circle of close friends—experience far less stress and less disruption of their parenting routines (Hashima & Amato, 1994; Simons, Lorenz, et al., 1993). Clearly, the broader social contexts that families experience can greatly affect the ways that family functions are carried out.

In sum, even the simplest of families is a true social system that is much bigger than the sum of its parts. Not only does each family member influence the behavior of every other, but the relationship between any two family members can affect the interactions and relationships of all other family members. And when we consider that family members develop, relationships change, and that all family dynamics are influenced by the broader social contexts in which families are embedded, it becomes quite clear that socialization within the family is best described not as a two-way street between parents and children, but as the busy intersection of many, many avenues of influence.

A Changing Family System in a Changing World

Not only is the family a complex, developing system, but it exists and develops in a world that is constantly changing. During the last half of the 20th century, several dramatic social changes have affected the makeup of the typical family and the character of family life. Drawing on U.S. census data and other surveys, we highlight the following changes:

Increased numbers of single adults. More adults are living as singles today than in the past. In 1992, only 61% of American adults were married, down from 72% in 1971 (U.S. Bureau of the Census, 1993). Marriage isn't "out," however, as about 90% of today's young adults will eventually marry (Chadwick & Heaton, 1992).

Active postponement of marriage. Many young singles are postponing marriage to pursue educational and career goals. Although the average age of first marriage actually decreased during the first half of this century, it has risen again to about 24 for women and 26 for men (Chadwick & Heaton, 1992), despite the high rates of teenage pregnancy among lower-income groups.

Decreased childbearing. Today's adults are not only waiting longer after they marry to have children, they are also having fewer of them—about two on average. The Baby Boom period after World War II was an unusual departure from an otherwise consistent trend toward smaller family sizes. Increasing numbers of young women are also remaining childless, though often not by choice (Jacobson & Heaton, 1991).

Increased female participation in the labor force. In 1950, 12% of married women with children under age 6 worked outside the home; now the figure is 57%, a truly dramatic social change (Chadwick & Heaton, 1992). Although women still carry the lion's share of child rearing and housework responsibilities, fewer and fewer children have a mother whose full-time job is to be a mother.

Increases in divorce. The divorce rate has been increasing over the past several decades, to the point where an additional one *million* children each year are affected by their parents' divorce (Teegartin, 1994). By one estimate, up to 60% of newly married couples can expect to divorce (Bumpass, 1990).

Increased numbers of single-parent families. Nearly 60% of all children born in the 1980s and 90s will spend some time in a **single-parent family** (Teegartin, 1994). In 1960, only 9% of children lived with one parent, usually a widowed one; now 24% live with a single parent, usually a never-married or divorced one (see Figure 15-2). Father-headed single-parent homes are more common than they used to be, now accounting for about 15% of all single-parent families (Meyer & Garasky, 1993).

Increased numbers of children living in poverty. Unfortunately, the increase in the number of single-parent families has contributed to an increase in the proportion of children living below the poverty line; 54% of children living in female-headed homes live in poverty, compared with 10% of children living in two-parent homes (Eggebeen & Lichter, 1991). Poverty is the rule rather than the exception for African-American children (U.S. Bureau of the Census, 1993), 65% of whom live in single-parent homes (Teegartin, 1994).

single-parent family: a family system consisting of one parent (either the mother or the father) and the parent's dependent child(ren).

Figure 15-2
The single-parent, postdivorce family is a common phenomenon of the past two decades; now, however, the number of children living with single parents who never married is almost equal to the number living with single parents who are divorced. In 1970, just 7% of American children in single-parent homes had a never-married parent.

Source: U.S. Census data cited in Teegartin, 1994.

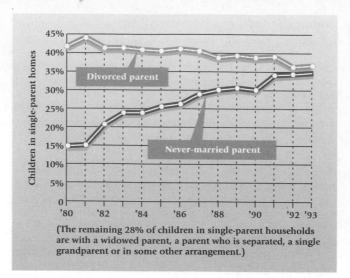

(The remaining 28% of children in single-parent households are with a widowed parent, a parent who is separated, a single grandparent or in some other arrangement.)

Increased remarriage. Because more married couples are divorcing, more adults (about 72% of divorced mothers and 80% of divorced fathers) are remarrying, forming **reconstituted families** that involve at least one child, his or her biological parent, and a stepparent and that often blend multiple children from two families into a new family system (Glick, 1989). About 25% of American children will spend some time in a stepparent family (Hetherington, 1989).

What these changes tell us is that modern families are much more diverse than ever. Our stereotyped image of the model family—the *Leave It to Beaver* nuclear aggregation with a breadwinning father, a housewife mother, and at least two children—is just that: a stereotype. By one estimate, this "typical" family represented 70% of American households in 1960, but only 11% in 1993 (Teegartin, 1994). Although the family is by no means dying, we must broaden our image of it to include the many dual-career, single-parent, and reconstituted families that exist today and are influencing the development of the *majority* of our children. Bear that in mind as we begin our excursion into family life, seeking to determine how families influence the development of their children.

 PARENTAL SOCIALIZATION DURING CHILDHOOD AND ADOLESCENCE

In previous chapters, we considered the results of a large body of research aimed at understanding how parents might affect the social, emotional, and intellectual development of their infants and toddlers. Recall that this work was remarkably consistent in its implications: Warm and sensitive parents who offer talk to their infants and try to stimulate their curiosity are contributing in a positive way to the establishment of secure emotional attachments as well as to the child's curiosity and willingness to explore, sociability, and intellectual development. It also helps if *both* parents are sensitive, responsive caregivers who can agree on how their infant should be raised and support each other in their roles as parents. Indeed, Jay Belsky (1981) has argued that caregiver warmth/sensitivity "is the most influential dimension of [parenting] in infancy. It not only fosters healthy psychological functioning during this developmental epoch, but also . . . lays the foundation on which future experiences will build" [p. 8].

During the second year, parents continue to be caregivers and playmates, but they also become much more concerned with teaching children how to behave (or how not to behave) in a variety of situations (Fagot & Kavanagh, 1993). According to Erik Erikson (1963), this is the period when socialization begins in earnest. Parents must

reconstituted families: new families that form after the remarriage of a single parent.

Concept Check 15-1 ⌄ Families and Their Functions

Check your understanding of family forms and functions by matching each descriptive statement below with one of the following principles or concepts: (a) economic goal of parenting; (b) extended family; (c) families are "developing" entities; (d) families are "embedded" entities; (e) single-parent family; (f) indirect (or third party) effect; (g) reconstituted family; (h) self-actualization goal of parenting; (i) survival goal of parenting. The answers appear in the Appendix.

_____ 1. A husband's hostility toward his son causes his wife to criticize his behavior, thus precipitating marital discord.

_____ 2. A mother carries her infant with her at all times and even sleeps with him at night.

_____ 3. Parents in an agricultural society socialize their children to be obedient and to cooperate with others.

_____ 4. Type of family in which children show better psychological adjustment in societies that stress communal interdependence.

_____ 5. Billy's parents allow him to dress himself as soon as he is able.

_____ 6. Living arrangement experienced by more than 50% of American children at one time or another.

_____ 7. Parents encourage a child to be ambitious, curious, and creative.

_____ 8. Child abuse is more common in cultures where the use of physical punishment is sanctioned.

_____ 9. Living arrangement in which a child lives with a biological parent and a nonbiological parent.

now manage the child's budding autonomy in the hope of instilling a sense of social propriety and self-control, while taking care not to undermine his or her curiosity, initiative, and feelings of personal competence.

Patterns of Parenting

Erikson and others (for example, Maccoby & Martin, 1983) claim that two aspects of parenting are especially important throughout childhood: *parental warmth* and *parental control* (sometimes called "demandingness" or *permissiveness-restrictiveness*).

Parental warmth (or **warmth/hostility**) refers to the amount of responsiveness and affection that a parent displays. Parents classified as warm and responsive often smile at, praise, and encourage their children, expressing a great deal of affection, even though they can become quite critical when a child misbehaves. By contrast, "hostile" (aloof/unresponsive) parents are often quick to criticize, belittle, punish, or ignore a child; they rarely communicate to children that they are valued or loved.

Parental control refers to the amount of regulation or supervision that parents undertake with their children. Controlling parents limit their children's freedom of expression by imposing many demands and actively surveying their children's behavior to ensure that these rules and regulations are followed. Uncontrolling parents are much less restrictive; they make fewer demands and allow children considerable freedom to pursue their interests, to express their opinions and emotions, and to make decisions about their own activities.

These two dimensions of child rearing are reasonably independent, so that we find parents who are warm and controlling, warm and uncontrolling, aloof and controlling, and aloof and uncontrolling (see Figure 15-3). How are these aspects of parenting related to a child's social, emotional, and intellectual development? Let's look first at the correlates of parental warmth.

Parental Warmth/Hostility

How important is it that a child be (or feel) accepted by his or her parents? You should already know the answer to this question, for throughout the text we have discussed many studies indicating that parental warmth and affection are powerful

warmth/hostility: a dimension of parenting that describes the amount of responsiveness and affection that a parent displays toward a child.

parental control: a dimension of parenting that describes how restrictive and demanding parents are.

Figure 15-3
Two major dimensions of parenting. When we cross the two dimensions, we come up with four parenting styles: warm/controlling (or "authoritative"); warm/uncontrolling (or "permissive"); aloof/controlling (or "authoritarian"); and aloof/uncontrolling (or "uninvolved"). Which parenting style do you think would be associated with the most favorable outcomes? The least favorable outcomes?
Data from Maccoby & Martin, 1983.

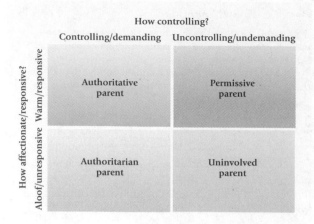

contributors to healthy cognitive, social, and emotional outcomes. By way of review, here are some of the attributes that children of warm, responsive parents tend to display:

1. They are securely attached to their caregivers. Of course, secure attachments are an important contributor to the growth of curiosity, exploratory competence, problem-solving skills, and positive social relations with both adults and peers (see Chapter 11).

2. They tend to be competent students during the grade school years and to make steady scholastic progress and score average or above on IQ tests (see Chapters 9 and 12).

3. They are relatively altruistic, especially when their parents preach altruistic values and practice what they preach (see Chapter 14).

4. They are generally obedient, noncoercive youngsters who get along reasonably well with parents and peers (see Chapter 12).

5. They tend to be high in self-confidence, self-esteem, and role-taking skills, and when they are disciplined, they usually feel that their parents' actions are justified (Brody & Shaffer, 1982; Kurdek & Fine, 1994; and see Chapter 12).

6. They are satisfied with their gender identities and are likely to be firmly sex typed or androgynous (see Chapter 13).

7. They often refer to internalized norms rather than fear of punishment as a reason for complying with moral rules (Brody & Shaffer, 1982).

Now compare this behavioral profile with that of the "unwanted" Czechoslovakian children we met in Chapter 11, whose mothers had tried repeatedly to gain permission to abort them (David, 1994). Compared with "wanted" children from similar family backgrounds, the unwanted children had less stable family ties; were described as anxious, emotionally frustrated, and irritable; had more physical health problems; made poorer grades in school (even though they were comparable in IQ to the "wanted" children); were less popular with peers; and were more likely to require psychiatric attention for serious behavior disorders throughout childhood, adolescence, and young adulthood. Other investigators are also finding that a primary contributor to clinical depression and other psychosocial problems later in life is a family setting in which one or both parents have treated the child as if he or she was unworthy of their love and affection (see, for example, Lefkowitz & Tesiny, 1984; MacDonald, 1992). Children simply do not thrive when they are rejected, nor are they apt to become happy, well-adjusted adults (MacDonald, 1992).

In sum, warmth and affection are clearly important components of effective parenting. As Eleanor Maccoby (1980) points out:

Parental warmth binds children to their parents in a positive way—it makes children responsive and more willing to accept guidance. If the parent-child relationship is close and affectionate, parents can exercise what control is needed without having to apply heavy disciplinary pressure. It is as if parents' responsiveness, affection, and obvious commitment to their children's welfare have earned them the right to make decisions and exercise control (p. 394).

Now what about parental control: Is it better for parents to be highly controlling, or, rather, should they impose few restrictions and grant their children considerable autonomy? To answer these questions, we need to be more specific about the degrees of restrictiveness that parents use and to look carefully at patterns of parental affection *and* control.

Styles of Child Rearing

Perhaps the best-known research on parenting styles is Diana Baumrind's (1967; 1971) studies of preschool children and their parents. Each child in Baumrind's sample was observed on several occasions in nursery school and at home. These data were used to rate the child on such behavioral dimensions as sociability, self-reliance, achievement, moodiness, and self-control. Parents were also interviewed and observed while interacting with their children at home. When Baumrind analyzed the parental data, she found that individual parents generally used one of three parenting styles, which can be summarized as follows:

1. **Authoritarian parenting**. A very restrictive pattern of parenting in which adults impose many rules, expect strict obedience, rarely if ever explain to the child why it is necessary to comply with all these regulations, and often rely on punitive, forceful tactics (that is, power assertion or love withdrawal) to gain compliance. Authoritarian parents are not sensitive to a child's conflicting viewpoints, expecting the child to accept their word as law and to respect their authority.
2. **Authoritative parenting**. A more flexible style of parenting in which adults allow their children considerable freedom but are careful to provide rationales for the restrictions they impose and to ensure that the children follow these guidelines. Authoritative parents are responsive to their children's needs and points of view and often seek their children's input in family decisions. However, they expect the child to comply with the restrictions they view as necessary and will use both power, if necessary, and reason (that is, inductive discipline) to ensure that he does.
3. **Permissive parenting**. A warm but lax pattern of parenting in which adults make relatively few demands, permit their children to freely express their feelings and impulses, do not closely monitor their children's activities, and rarely exert firm control over their behavior.

When Baumrind (1967) linked these three parenting styles to the characteristics of the preschool children who were exposed to each style, she found that children of authoritative parents were developing rather well. They were cheerful, socially responsible, self-reliant, achievement oriented, and cooperative with adults and peers. By contrast, children of authoritarian parents tended to be moody and seemingly unhappy much of the time, easily annoyed and unfriendly, relatively aimless, and generally not very pleasant to be around. Finally, children of permissive parents were often impulsive and aggressive, especially if they were boys. They tended to be bossy and self-centered, lacking in self-control, and low in independence and achievement.

Although Baumrind's findings clearly favor authoritative parenting, one might legitimately wonder whether children of authoritarian or permissive parents might

Warmth and affection are crucial components of effective parenting.

authoritarian parenting: a restrictive pattern of parenting in which adults set many rules for their children, expect strict obedience, and rely on power rather than reason to elicit compliance.

authoritative parenting: a flexible style of parenting in which adults allow their children autonomy, but are careful to explain the restrictions they impose and will ensure that their children follow these guidelines.

permissive parenting: a pattern of parenting in which adults make few demands of their children and rarely attempt to control their behavior.

eventually "outgrow" whatever shortcomings they displayed as preschoolers. Seeking to answer this question, Baumrind (1977) observed her subjects (and their parents) once again when the children were 8 to 9 years old. As we see in Table 15-1, children of authoritative parents were still relatively high in both *cognitive competencies* (that is, original thinking, high achievement motivation, and enthusiasm for intellectual challenges) and *social skills* (for example, sociability, active participation, and leadership in group activities), whereas children of authoritarian parents were generally average to below average in cognitive and social skills, and children of permissive parents were relatively unskilled in both areas. Indeed, the strengths of children exposed to authoritative parenting are still evident in adolescence; they are confident, achievement oriented, and socially competent, and they tend to stay clear of drug abuse and other problem behaviors (Baumrind, 1991). The link between authoritative parenting and positive developmental outcomes seems to hold for all racial and ethnic groups studied to date in the United States (Lamborn et al., 1991; Steinberg et al., 1991; 1994)* and in a variety of different cultures as well (Pinto, Folkers, & Sines, 1991; Scott, Scott, & McCabe, 1991).

The uninvolved parent. One interesting aspect of Baumrind's research is that almost all the parents in her sample were reasonably warm and accepting. Even her authoritarian parents, who could be described as more self-centered and unresponsive than child-centered and responsive, did not clearly reject their children. It turns out that the least successful parenting style is what might be termed **uninvolved parenting**—an extremely lax, uncontrolling approach displayed by parents who have either *rejected* their children or are so overwhelmed with their own stresses and problems that they haven't much time or energy to devote to child rearing (Becker, 1964; Maccoby & Martin, 1983). One major contributor to uninvolved parenting is parental depression (Radke-Yarrow et al., 1985); and as we noted in Chapter 11, infants of these emotionally detached caregivers are already showing clear signs of nonsynchronous social behaviors, even when given opportunities to interact with a *socially responsive* companion (Field et al., 1988). By age 3, children of uninvolved parents are relatively high in aggression and such externalizing behaviors as temper tantrums (Miller et al., 1993). Moreover, they tend to perform very poorly in the classroom later in childhood (Eckenrode, Laird, & Doris, 1993), and often become hostile, rebellious adolescents who are prone to commit such antisocial and delinquent acts as alcohol and drug abuse, sexual misconduct, truancy, and a wide variety of criminal offenses (Lamborn et al., 1991; Patterson et al., 1989; 1992; Pulkkinen, 1982). In effect, these youngsters have neglectful, "unattached" parents whose actions (or lack thereof) seem to be saying "I don't care about you or about what you do"—a message that undoubtedly breeds resentment and a willingness to strike back at these aloof adversaries or at other authority figures.

Explaining the Effectiveness of Authoritative Parenting

Why is authoritative parenting so consistently associated with positive social, emotional, and intellectual outcomes? Probably for several reasons. First, authoritative parents are warm and accepting; they communicate a sense of *caring concern* that may motivate their children to comply with the directives they receive in a way that children of more aloof and demanding (authoritarian) parents are not. Then there is the issue of how control is exercised. Unlike the authoritarian parent who sets inflexible standards and dominates the child, allowing little if any freedom of expression, the authoritative parent exercises control in a *rational* way, carefully explaining his or her

uninvolved parenting: a pattern of parenting that is both aloof (or even hostile) and overpermissive, almost as if parents neither care about their children nor about what they may become.

---

*Interestingly, the links between authoritative parenting and positive developmental outcomes seem to be strongest for European-American adolescents, possibly because this pattern of parenting is more common among European-American families and thus is more likely to be endorsed and amplified by European-American peers (Steinberg et al., 1994).

Table 15-1 Relationship between Patterns of Parental Control during the Preschool Period and Children's Cognitive and Social Competencies during the Grade School Years

Patterns of parenting during preschool period	Children's competencies at age 8–9	
	Girls	Boys
Authoritative	Very high cognitive and social competencies	High cognitive and social competencies
Authoritarian	Average cognitive and social competencies	Average social competencies; low cognitive competencies
Permissive	Low cognitive and social competencies	Low social competencies; very low cognitive competencies

Source: From Baumrind, 1977.

point of view, while also considering the child's viewpoint. Thus, demands that come from a warm, accepting parent and that appear to be fair rather than arbitrary are likely to elicit compliance rather than complaining or defiance. Finally, authoritative parents are careful to tailor their demands to the child's ability to regulate his or her own conduct. In other words, they set standards that children can *realistically* achieve and allow the child some freedom, or *autonomy*, in deciding how best to comply with these expectations. This kind of treatment carries a most important message—something like "You are a capable human being whom I trust to be self reliant and accomplish important objectives." Of course, we've seen in earlier chapters that feedback of this sort fosters the growth of self-reliance, achievement motivation, and high self-esteem in childhood, and is the kind of support that adolescents need to feel comfortable about exploring various roles and ideologies to forge a personal identity.

In sum, it appears that authoritative parenting—warmth combined with *moderate* and *rational* parental control—is the parenting style most closely associated with positive developmental outcomes. Children apparently need love *and* limits—a set of rules that help them to structure and to evaluate their conduct. Without such guidance, they may not learn self-control and may become quite selfish, unruly, and lacking in clear achievement goals, particularly if their parents are also aloof or uncaring (Steinberg et al., 1994). But, if they receive too much guidance and are hemmed in by restrictions, they may have few opportunities to become self-reliant and may lack confidence in their own decision-making abilities (Grolnick & Ryan, 1989; Steinberg et al., 1994).

Does authoritative parenting really foster positive traits in children? Or is it that easygoing, manageable children cause parents to be authoritative? Baumrind (1983, 1993) insists that authoritative parenting causes children to be well behaved rather than the other way around. She notes that children of authoritative parents often resist parental demands at first; but they eventually come around *because* parents are firm in their demands and sufficiently patient to allow their children time to comply without caving in to the children's unreasonable demands or turning to power-assertive tactics. Indeed, Crockenberg and Litman's (1990) study of disciplinary conflict among mothers and their 2-year-olds clearly supports Baumrind's view that an adult's approach to parenting has a greater impact on the child's behavior than the child has on the parent's. Specifically, authoritative mothers who dealt firmly but patiently with noncompliance had toddlers who became more compliant over time; by contrast, authoritarian mothers who used arbitrary, power-assertive control strategies had children who became more *defiant*.

Yet, it is also true that extremely stubborn and impulsive children who seem to have little self-control do tend to elicit more coercive forms of discipline and may eventually wear their parents out, causing them to become more lax, less affectionate, and possibly even hostile and uninvolved (Anderson et al., 1986; Lytton, 1990; see also Lerner, 1993). So as we concluded when considering the impact of discipline on moral development in Chapter 14, socialization within the family is a matter of *reciprocal* influence: Parents certainly influence their children, but children can also influence the parenting they receive.

Social Class, Economic Hardship, and Parenting

Social class, or socioeconomic status (SES), refers to one's position within a society that is stratified according to status or power. Unlike many countries such as India, where social standing is fixed at birth by the status of one's parents, we in the United States are fond of saying that anyone can rise above his or her origins if that person works hard enough to succeed. Indeed, this proverb is the cornerstone of the American dream.

However, sociologists tell us that the "American dream" is a belief that is more likely to be endorsed by members of the middle and upper classes—those elements of society that have the economic resources to maintain or improve on their lofty economic status (Hess, 1970). As we will see, many people from the lower and working classes face very different kinds of problems, pursue different goals, and often adopt different values. In short, they live in a different world than middle-class people do, and these ecological considerations may well affect the approaches they take when raising their children.

Social Class Differences in Child Rearing

How, then, do parenting styles differ by social class? Compared with middle- and upper-class parents, lower- and working-class parents tend to:

1. stress obedience and respect for authority more and to place somewhat less emphasis on fostering independence, curiosity, and creativity.
2. be more restrictive and authoritarian, more frequently using power-assertive discipline.
3. talk to and reason with their children less frequently.
4. show less warmth and affection (Maccoby, 1980; McLoyd, 1990).

According to Eleanor Maccoby (1980), these class-linked differences in parenting have been observed in many cultures and across racial and ethnic groups in the United States. Of course, we should keep in mind that what we are talking about here are *group trends* rather than absolute contrasts: Some middle-class parents are highly restrictive, power assertive, and aloof in their approach to child rearing, whereas many lower- and working-class parents function more like their typical counterparts in the middle class (Kelley, Power, & Wimbush, 1992; Laosa, 1981). But on average, it appears that lower- and working-class parents are somewhat more critical, punitive, and intolerant of disobedience than parents from the middle and upper socioeconomic strata.

Explaining Social Class Differences in Child Rearing

Undoubtedly, many factors contribute to social-class differences in child rearing, and economic considerations seem to head the list. Consider that a low income may mean that living quarters are crowded, that family members must occasionally make do without adequate food, clothing, or medical care, and that parents are constantly tense or anxious about living under these marginal conditions. Eleanor Maccoby (1980) suggests that low-income living is probably much more *stressful* for parents and that stress affects the ways in which parental functions are carried out. Vonnie McLoyd (1989; 1990) agrees. Her recent reviews of the literature suggest that economic hardship creates its own psychological distress—a most pervasive discomfort that makes lower-income adults more edgy and irritable and more vulnerable to all

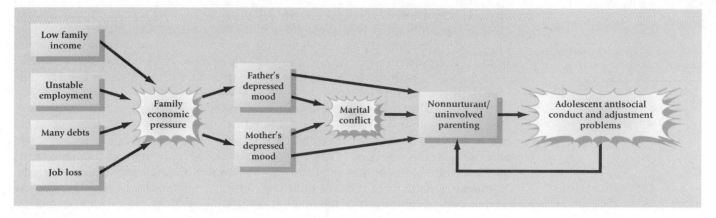

Figure 15 4
A model of the relationship among family economic stress, patterns of parenting, and adolescent adjustment.
Adapted from Conger, Conger, Elder, Lorenz, Simons, & Whitbeck, 1992.

negative life events (including the daily hassles associated with child rearing), thereby diminishing their capacity to be warm, supportive parents who are highly involved in their children's lives.

Recently, Rand Conger and his associates (1992, 1994, 1995; see also McLoyd et al., 1994) offered support for this "economic distress" hypothesis by finding clear links between family economic hardships, nonnurturant/uninvolved parenting, and poor adolescent outcomes. The causal sequence, shown in Figure 15-4, goes like this: Parents who are experiencing economic pressure or feeling that they cannot cope with their financial problems tend to become depressed, which increases marital conflict. Marital conflict, in turn, disrupts each parent's ability to be a supportive, involved parent and therefore contributes to such adolescent problems as low self-esteem, poor school performance, poor peer relations, and adjustment problems such as depression, hostility, and aggression. Many of the conflicts that economically distressed parents have with their adolescents center on money matters—a highly sensitive topic that can make a financially strapped parent feel downright hostile toward his or her children (Conger et al., 1994). And the adolescent adjustment problems and antisocial conduct that nonnurturant/uninvolved parenting helps to create may further exasperate parents, causing them to back away and become even less nurturant and less involved in the lives of their children (Vuchinich, Bank, & Patterson, 1992). So it seems that Maccoby and McLoyd were right in assuming that economic hardships are a very important contributor to the relatively aloof and coercive style of parenting often observed in low-income families.

Another explanation for the link between economic factors and parenting styles focuses on the skills needed by workers in white-collar and blue-collar jobs (Kohn, 1979; Ogbu, 1981). A large percentage of lower- and working-class breadwinners are blue-collar workers who must please a supervisor and defer to his or her authority. So many lower-income parents may emphasize obedience and respect for authority because these are precisely the attributes they view as critical for success in the blue-collar economy. By contrast, middle- and upper-class parents may reason and negotiate more with their children while emphasizing individual initiative, curiosity, and creativity because these are the skills, attributes, and abilities that matter in their own occupations as business executives, white-collar workers, or professionals.

When we consider the findings we have reviewed, it may seem that middle-class parenting is somehow "better" or more competent. After all, the authoritative parenting style so often observed in middle-class families produces highly sociable children who are curious, outgoing, intellectually capable, and well-behaved. Yet there is another side to this issue that researchers in Western societies sometimes fail to consider. Perhaps middle-class parenting is "better" for children who are expected to become productive members of a middle-class subculture. However, a middle-class pattern of parenting that stresses curiosity, independence, and individual accomplishments may actually represent "incompetent" parenting among the Temne of

Sierra Leone, a society in which everyone must pull together and suppress individualism if the community is to successfully plant, harvest, and ration the meager crops on which its livelihood absolutely depends (Berry, 1967). And since many children from Western societies will choose a career within the so-called blue-collar economy, it hardly seems reasonable to conclude that a lower-SES pattern of child rearing that prepares them for this undertaking is in some way deficient or "incompetent."

This brings us back to a point we have stressed repeatedly throughout this text: Development always takes place in a cultural or subcultural context, and we should not automatically assume that a particular style of child rearing that produces favorable outcomes in one context is the optimal pattern of parenting in all other cultures and subcultures. Louis Laosa (1981, p. 159) makes this same point, noting that "indigenous patterns of child care throughout the world represent largely successful adaptations to conditions of life that have long differed from one people to another. [Adults] are 'good [parents]' by the only relevant standards, those of their own culture."

The Quest for Autonomy: Renegotiating the Parent-Child Relationship during Adolescence

One of the most important developmental tasks that adolescents face is to achieve a mature and healthy sense of **autonomy**. This complex attribute has two major components: (1) *emotional autonomy,* or an ability to serve as one's own source of emotional strength rather than childishly depending on parents to provide comfort, reassurance, and emotional security, and (2) *behavioral autonomy,* or an ability to make one's own decisions, govern one's own affairs, and take care of oneself (Steinberg, 1985). If adolescents are to "make it" as adults, they can't be rushing home for consoling hugs after every little setback. Nor can they continue to rely on parents to get them to work on time or remind them of their duties and obligations. Indeed, parents want their adolescents to become autonomous, and adolescents actively seek the freedom to become autonomous.

So what happens within the family system when teenagers mature and begin to act more autonomously? Sparks fly! Conflicts between parents and children about self-governance issues become much more frequent, at least temporarily as children reach puberty (Holmeck & Hill, 1991; Paikoff & Brooks-Gunn, 1991; Steinberg, 1981). These squabbles are usually neither prolonged nor severe, often centering around such issues as the adolescent's physical appearance, her choice of friends, or her neglect of schoolwork and household chores. And much of the friction stems from the different perspectives that parents and adolescents adopt: Parents view conflicts through a *social-conventional* lens, feeling that they have a responsibility to monitor and regulate their child's conduct, whereas the adolescent, locked in his quest for autonomy, often views his nagging parents as infringing on *personal* rights and choices (Smetana & Asquith, 1994). As teenagers continue to assert themselves and parents slowly loosen the reins, the parent-child relationship gradually evolves from an enterprise in which the parent is dominant to one in which parents and adolescents are on a more equal footing (Feldman & Gehring, 1988; Furman & Buhrmester, 1992). Do these experiences undermine the closeness of the parent-child emotional bond?

Ideally, they do not. Although researchers once believed that establishing autonomy meant separating from one's parents—cutting the cords—they now realize that maintaining a close attachment to one's family may be just as important to an adolescent's psychological adjustment as the ability to fend for oneself (Grotevant & Cooper, 1986; Kobak et al., 1993; Lamborn & Steinberg, 1993). In other words, independence in the context of *inter*dependence should be one's goal, for it seems that adolescents who achieve autonomy while maintaining close attachments to family members show the best psychosocial outcomes. It is much more difficult to become competent and self-assured by distancing oneself from parents and thereby undermining a potentially important source of social support (Lamborn & Steinberg, 1993; Ryan & Lynch, 1989).

autonomy: the capacity to make decisions independently, to serve as one's own source of emotional strength, and to otherwise manage one's life tasks without depending on others for assistance; an important developmental task of adolescence.

As adolescents begin their quest for autonomy, conflicts with parents become more commonplace.

Recent research is providing a clearer picture of how parents might successfully promote adolescent autonomy and healthy psychosocial outcomes (Brown et al., 1993; Dishion et al., 1991; Lamborn et al., 1991; Youniss & Smollar, 1985). It seems that parents of well-adjusted teenagers gradually relinquish control as their teenagers display a readiness to accept more responsibility, but by no means do they cease to enforce rules or to keep tabs on their children's behavior. They give adolescents more freedom to venture away from home with friends, but they still watch closely to see that their youngsters are keeping up with schoolwork and are not developing any serious behavior problems. By viewing their adolescents as more mature, parents not only give them more freedom but also demand more of them in the way of self-governance. And although adolescents report that they stop treating their parents as all-knowing authority figures and begin to ask them to justify their rules and restrictions, they continue to respect parental opinions (particularly well-reasoned ones) and very much want their parents' approval (Galambos, 1992; Youniss & Smollar, 1985).

So it seems that adolescents are most likely to achieve a healthy sense of autonomy if their parents keep their rules and restrictions to a reasonable minimum, explain them, and continue to be warm and supportive. Does this parenting style sound familiar? It should, for this winning combination of parental warmth and a pattern of control that is neither too lax nor overly restrictive is an *authoritative* approach—the same style that fosters high self-esteem and healthy developmental outcomes in childhood. It is mainly when parents react negatively to a teenager's push for autonomy and become overly strict or overly permissive that adolescents are likely to experience personal distress or to rebel and get into trouble (Barber, Olsen, & Shagle, 1994; Koestner et al., 1991; Lamborn et al., 1991). Of course, we must remind ourselves that socialization within the family is a matter of reciprocal influence and that it may be much easier for a parent to respond authoritatively to a responsible, levelheaded adolescent than to one who is rude, hostile, and unruly.

In sum, the parent-adolescent relationship might be viewed as more of a partnership, the quality of which depends on what both parents and children do when renegotiating their ties. Although power struggles are an inevitable consequence of the adolescent's quest for autonomy, most parents and their teenagers are able to resolve their differences and maintain positive feelings for one another as they rework their relationship so that it becomes more equal (Furman & Buhrmester, 1992). As a result, most adolescents achieve autonomy and become more self-reliant while also developing a more "friendlike" attachment to their parents.

Might a teenager's experiences in the world of work help to foster a healthy sense of autonomy? As we will see in Box 15-1, there is a negative side to gaining early work experience, and many adolescents would be better off concentrating on their schooling rather than taking on major work responsibilities.

BOX 15-1

Does Part-Time Employment for Adolescents Foster a Healthy Sense of Autonomy (and Positive Developmental Outcomes)?

Many adolescents in the United States and Canada work at least part-time during their high school days, and it seems reasonable to assume that these early work experiences could have any number of effects on their development. On the positive side, the money that teenagers earn might foster a sense of self-sufficiency and economic autonomy from parents, which in turn could contribute to higher self-esteem. In addition, working youths just might be (1) quicker than nonworking peers to establish a positive work orientation (that is, pride in a job well done) and (2) more knowledgeable about the world of work, consumer issues, and financial management. Yet there are some potential disadvantages as well. For example, might hours spent working undermine teenagers' academic performance? Are teens who work long hours less closely monitored by parents, thus having both the freedom and the economic means (from their earnings) to partake heavily in such antisocial activities as drug or alcohol abuse?

Lawrence Steinberg and his associates have attempted to find out just how high school students are affected by their work experiences by comparing working and nonworking youths on such outcome measures as their autonomy from parents, self-esteem, attitudes about work, academic performance, psychological adjustment, and involvement in delinquent activities (Greenberger & Steinberg, 1986; Steinberg, 1984; Steinberg & Dornbusch, 1991; Steinberg, Fegley, & Dornbusch, 1993). Overall, this research reports far more bad news than good about teenagers who work, particularly about those who work more than 20 hours per week during the school year. Although working youths know more than their nonworking peers about consumer issues and financial management, there is no evidence that increasing involvement in the world of work fosters the development of a healthy orientation toward work; in fact, working adolescents often develop some rather cynical attitudes about work and become more tolerant of such unethical practices as overreporting work hours (to boost their pay).

Even more discouraging are the findings that adolescents who work more than 20 hours a week are less involved in school, make lower grades, and are *lower* in self-esteem than age-mates who worked 10 or fewer hours a week. Although these findings hold for all racial groups, the negative impact of long working hours on scholastic achievement is greatest for Caucasian and Asian-American students—the two groups that ordinarily do best at school.

And there is more. Adolescents who work more than 20 hours a week are granted much more autonomy over day-to-day decisions than are age-mates who work 10 hours a week or less. Yet this greater autonomy seems to be directed toward "cutting the cords" to parents—the less adaptive form of independence—for teenagers who work long hours are much less invested in family activities and are monitored less closely by older family members. And, as shown in the figure, the psychological and behavioral correlates of all this freedom are downright gloomy: Teenagers working more than 20 hours per week report higher levels of anxiety, depression, and somatic symptoms (for example, headaches, stomachaches, and colds) and more frequent alcohol and drug use and other delinquent activities than do age-mates working 10 or fewer hours a week (Steinberg & Dornbusch, 1991).

Now you may be thinking that students who work long hours already have more problems. There is an element of truth to this notion. But when Steinberg and his colleagues (1993) followed students over the course of a year to see what they were like before and after they began working, they found that working more than 20 hours a week leads to even *less* engagement in school activities, to *greater* distancing from parents, and to new problems that were not apparent before, including increased delinquency and substance abuse. Moreover, working students who quit working during the year improved their school performance after their employment ended (see also Bachman & Schulenberg, 1993). So even though problem-prone adolescents are the

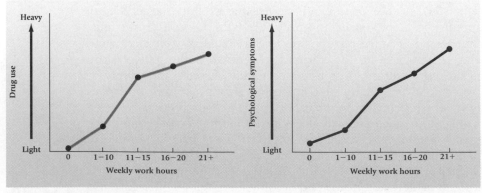

Relations between the number of hours worked per week and adolescents' drug use and reported psychological symptoms. Adapted from Steinberg & Dornbusch, 1991.

BOX 15-1 (continued)

Does Part-Time Employment for Adolescents Foster a Healthy Sense of Autonomy (and Positive Developmental Outcomes)?

ones who are most inclined to work long hours, their development is negatively affected by their heavy involvement in work activities.

Why is working not a more positive contributor to adolescent development? One major reason may be that teenagers typically work at relatively menial "fast food" or manual labor jobs that offer few opportunities for self-direction or decision making (Steinberg, 1984). By contrast, many German youths profit immensely from *work-study apprenticeships*. Starting at age 15 or 16, program participants spend two days a week in vocational classes geared to the

academic skills they will need *for their chosen vocation*, and three days a week apprenticing for (or learning) that vocation (Hamilton, 1990). These programs permit non-college-bound students to gain work skills that translate into economically viable careers as soon as they graduate from the program. But in the absence of such a broad and *effective* commitment to vocational training, students in other countries might be best served by postponing work, if possible, so that they can concentrate on their schooling and grow as individuals in the context of their relationships with family members and peers (Steinberg, 1984).

THE INFLUENCE OF SIBLINGS AND SIBLING RELATIONSHIPS

Although families are getting smaller, the majority of American children still grow up with at least one sibling, and there is certainly no shortage of speculation about the roles that brothers and sisters play in a child's life. For example, many parents, distressed by the fighting and bickering that their children display, often fear that such rivalrous conduct will undermine the growth of children's prosocial concerns and their ability to get along with others. At the same time, the popular wisdom is that only children are likely to be lonely, overindulged "brats" who would profit both socially and emotionally from having siblings to teach them that they are not nearly as "special" as they think they are (Falbo, 1992).

Although rivalries among siblings are certainly commonplace, we will see that siblings can play some very positive roles in a child's life, often serving as caregivers, teachers, playmates, and confidants. And yet, we will also see that only children may not be nearly as disadvantaged by their lack of sibling relationships as people have commonly assumed.

Changes in the Family System When a New Baby Arrives

Judy Dunn and Carol Kendrick (1982; see also Dunn, 1993) have studied how children adapt to a new baby, and the account they provide is not an entirely cheerful one. After the baby arrives, mothers typically devote less warm and playful attention to their older children, who may respond to this perceived "neglect" by becoming difficult and demanding, crying a lot, clinging to their mothers, and sometimes even hitting or pinching their tiny brother or sister (see also Stewart et al., 1987). So older siblings are not entirely thrilled to have an attention-grabbing new baby in the home. They resent losing the mother's attention, may harbor animosities toward the baby for stealing it, and will do whatever they can to make their feelings known and recapture the mother's love.

Thus, **sibling rivalry**—a spirit of competition, jealousy, or resentment between siblings—often begins as soon as a younger brother or sister arrives. How can it be minimized? Fathers can play an important role by increasing the time that they devote to older children as mothers are decreasing theirs (Stewart et al., 1987). Mothers can also help by talking to older children about the infant's feelings and competencies and by appealing to the older child's maturity, encouraging him or her to assist in caring for the baby (Dunn & Kendrick, 1982; Howe & Ross, 1990). Setting

sibling rivalry: the spirit of competition, jealousy, and resentment that may arise between two or more siblings.

Reprinted with special permission of King Features Syndicate.

a little "quality time" aside to let the older child know she is still loved and considered important is also a useful strategy for mothers to pursue. Yet some caution is required here, for Dunn and Kendrick (1982) found that older girls whose parents showered them with attention in the weeks after a baby was born were the ones who *played least* with and were *most negative* toward their baby brother or sister 14 months later. The older children who were most positive toward younger siblings (both 14 months later and at age 6) were those whose mothers had not permitted them to brood or respond negatively toward the baby (Dunn, 1984). We see, then, that parents may have to tread a thin line between two traps: becoming so attentive toward the new baby that they deprive the older child of attention or undermine his security, and becoming so indulgent of the older child that he resents any competition from the younger sib. Indeed, researchers are consistently finding that sibling relationships are friendlier and less conflictual when both mothers and fathers respond warmly and sensitively to *all* their children and do not consistently favor one child over the others (Brody, Stoneman, & McCoy, 1994; Dunn, 1993; Teti & Ablard, 1989; Volling & Belsky, 1992). Children pay close attention to what goes on between siblings and parents, are acutely sensitive to any signs of favoritism, and often resent it if they think that mom or dad "likes the other kid(s) best" (Dunn, 1993).

Sibling Relationships over the Course of Childhood

Fortunately, most older siblings adjust fairly quickly to having a new brother or sister, becoming much less anxious and less inclined to display the problem behaviors that they showed early on. But even in the best of sibling relationships, conflict is normal. Indeed, Judy Dunn (1993) reports that the number of skirmishes between very young siblings can range as high as 56 per hour! Confrontations often become more frequent and intense once the younger child reaches 18 to 24 months of age and is better to "hold his own" by hitting or teasing the older sib or by directing a parent's attention to an older sib's misconduct (Dunn & Munn, 1985).

Although rivalrous conduct among siblings continues throughout the preschool and grade school years, researchers who have observed siblings at home find that their interactions are more often positive and supportive than oppositional or conflictual (Abramovitch et al., 1986; Baskett & Johnson, 1982). There are some reliable differences in the behavior of older and younger siblings, with older siblings generally being the more domineering and aggressive parties, and younger siblings the more compliant (Abramovitch et al., 1986; Berndt & Bulleit, 1985). Yet, older sibs also initiate more helpful, playful, and other prosocial behaviors, a finding that may reflect the pressure that parents place on them to demonstrate their maturity by looking after a younger brother or sister.

In some ways, sibling relationships are truly paradoxical because they are often both *close* and *conflictual*. Wyndol Furman and Duane Buhrmester (1985a, 1985b), for example, found that grade school siblings who were similar in age reported more warmth and closeness than other sibling pairs—but, at the same time, more friction and conflict. Moreover, children viewed their sibling relations as more conflict-ridden and less satisfying than their relations with either parent, their grandparents, or their friends. Yet, when children were asked to rate the *importance* of different social relationships and the *reliability* of their various social alliances, siblings were viewed as more important and more reliable than friends!

As is true of parent-child relationships, sibling relationships become much more egalitarian during the adolescent years. Siblings now quarrel less frequently, and their relationships otherwise become less intense, probably because teenagers are spending less time with brothers and sisters who are, after all, part of the family from whom they want to develop some autonomy (Buhrmester & Furman, 1990; Furman & Buhrmester, 1992). But even though they are immersing themselves in close friendships and romantic relationships, adolescents continue to perceive their siblings as important and intimate associates—people to whom they can turn for support and companionship, despite the fact that relations with them have often been rather stormy (Buhrmester & Furman, 1990; Furman & Buhrmester, 1992).

Perhaps these seemingly paradoxical data make perfectly good sense if we carefully reexamine the findings on the nature of sibling-sibling interactions. Yes, rivalries and conflicts among siblings are a very normal part of family life. Yet the observational record consistently shows that brothers and sisters often do nice things for one another and that these acts of kindness and affection are typically much more common than hateful or rivalrous conduct.

Positive Aspects of Sibling Interaction

What positive roles might siblings play in one another's lives? One important contribution that older siblings make is to provide *caretaking* services for younger brothers and sisters. Indeed, one survey of child-rearing practices in 186 societies found that older children were the *principal* caregivers for infants and toddlers in 57% of the groups studied (Weisner & Gallimore, 1977). Even in industrialized societies such as the United States, older siblings (particularly girls) are often asked to look after their younger brothers and sisters (McHale & Gamble, 1989). Of course, their role as caregivers provides older children opportunities to influence their younger siblings in many ways, by serving as their teachers, playmates, and advocates, as well as important sources of emotional security.

Siblings as Attachment Objects

Do infants become attached to older brothers and sisters, viewing them as providers of security? To find out, Robert Stewart (1983) exposed 10–20-month-old infants to a variation of Ainsworth's "strange situations" test. Each infant was left with a 4-year-old sibling in a strange room that a strange adult soon entered. The infants typically showed signs of distress as their mothers departed, and they were wary in the company of the stranger. Stewart noted that these distressed infants often approached their older brother or sister, particularly when the stranger appeared. And most of the 4-year-olds offered some sort of comforting or caregiving to their baby brothers and sisters.

Other investigators have replicated these findings and have shown that the older children who are most inclined to comfort an infant sibling are those who themselves are securely attached to their mothers (Teti & Ablard, 1989) and who have developed the role-taking skills to understand the basis for the infant's distress (Garner, Jones, & Palmer, 1994; Stewart & Marvin, 1984). So it appears that older siblings can become important sources of emotional support who help younger sibs to cope with uncertain situations when their parents are not around. Moreover, Patricia East and Karen Rook (1992) found that a secure tie to a favorite sibling can help to prevent the anxiety, distress, and other adjustment problems that grade school children often display if they have few friends and are neglected or ignored by their peers (see also Dunn, Slomkowski, & Beardsall, 1994). So siblings can be meaningful sources of emotional support indeed.

Older siblings often serve as teachers for their younger brothers and sisters.

Siblings as Teachers

In addition to serving as caregivers, companions, and emotional confidants, older siblings frequently teach new skills to younger brothers and sisters. Even infants are attentive to older sibs, often choosing to imitate their behaviors or taking over toys that they have abandoned (Abramovitch, Corter, & Pepler, 1980). Younger children tend to admire their older siblings, who continue to serve as important models and tutors throughout childhood (Buhrmester & Furman, 1990). Given a problem to master, children are likely to learn more when they have an older sibling available to guide them than when they have access to an equally competent older peer (Azmitia & Hesser, 1993). Why? Because (1) older siblings feel a greater responsibility to teach if the pupil is a younger sibling (see also Brody, Stoneman, & MacKinnon, 1982), (2) older sibs provide more detailed instructions and encouragement than older peers do, and (3) younger children are more inclined to seek the older sibling's guidance. And the instruction that older siblings provide can be meaningful indeed. When they play "school" with younger brothers and sisters, for example, teaching them such lessons as the ABCs, younger siblings have an easier time learning to read (Norman-Jackson, 1982).

If we reexamine the ground we have covered, it may seem as if younger siblings are reaping all the benefits. Yet studies of peer tutoring, in which older children teach academic lessons to younger pupils, consistently find that the *tutors* show significant gains in academic achievement—bigger gains than those posted by age-mates who have not had an opportunity to tutor a younger child (Feldman, Devin-Sheehan, & Allen, 1976). Older siblings who often tutor younger ones seem to profit as well, for they score higher on tests of academic aptitude and achievement than peers who have not had such tutoring experiences (Paulhus & Shaffer, 1981; Smith, 1990). So the teacher-learner roles that siblings often assume are beneficial to *both* parties: Older siblings learn by tutoring their younger brothers and sisters, while their young tutees profit from the instruction they receive.

Sibling Effects on Social Competence

How do experiences with siblings affect a child's social relationships outside the family? Here is one area where developmentalists know relatively little. There is some evidence that later-born children tend to be somewhat *more popular*, on average, than firstborns are (see, for example, Miller & Maruyama, 1976). Why? One reason may be that some older siblings who reliably use their greater power to dominate a younger brother or sister employ these same coercive tactics with peers (Berndt & Bulleit, 1985)—a move that is not likely to enhance their popularity or status in the peer group. Yet another reason that later-borns may eventually become more popular than firstborns is that they have learned to defer to and to negotiate with their older and more powerful siblings, thereby acquiring cooperative and conciliatory interpersonal skills that should serve them well when interacting with peers (Miller & Maruyama, 1976).

However, it is important to add that these **ordinal position** effects on peer popularity are small in magnitude and that there are many, many exceptions to the rule. Some firstborns are immensely popular, whereas some later-borns lack social skills and are actually *rejected* by their peers. What these qualifications tell us, then, is that much more research is needed before we will fully understand how children's experiences with siblings affect their social standing outside the family.

Characteristics of Only Children

Are "only" children who grow up without siblings the spoiled, selfish, overindulged brats that people often presume them to be? Hardly! Two major reviews of hundreds of pertinent studies found that only children are (1) relatively high, on average, in self-esteem and achievement motivation, (2) more obedient and slightly more intellectually competent than children with siblings, and (3) likely to establish good relations with peers (Falbo, 1992; Falbo & Polit, 1986). Since only children enjoy an exclusive relationship with their parents, they may receive more quality time from parents and more direct achievement training than children with siblings do, perhaps explaining their tendency to be relatively friendly, well-behaved, and instrumentally competent (Baskett, 1985). Moreover, these singletons have no younger sibs that they can bully, and, like later-borns, they may soon learn that they must negotiate and be accommodating if they hope to play successfully with *peer* playmates, most of whom are probably at least as powerful as they are.

Might these findings simply reflect the fact that parents who choose to have only one child differ systematically from those who have more children? Probably not. In 1979, the People's Republic of China implemented a one-child family policy in an attempt to control its burgeoning population. So regardless of the number of children that parents may have wanted, most Chinese couples, in urban areas at least,

---

Concept Check 15-2 ∨ Understanding Parental and Sibling Influences on Children

Check your understanding of some of the influences that parents and siblings may have on developing children by matching each descriptive statement below with one of the following groups or concepts: (a) authoritarian parenting; (b) authoritative parenting; (c) economic distress; (d) emotional support; (e) increased academic aptitude; (f) later-born siblings; (g) older siblings; (h) only children; (i) uninvolved parenting; (j) unwanted children. The answers appear in the Appendix.

_____ 1. Can undermine a parent's ability to be a supportive, involved parent.

_____ 2. A benefit that older siblings may receive from interactions with younger siblings.

_____ 3. Their development dramatically illustrates that warmth is a crucial component of effective parenting.

_____ 4. Slightly more popular, on average, than their brothers and sisters.

_____ 5. Children exposed to this parenting style show average cognitive and social competencies.

_____ 6. Contrary to popular belief, they are not developmentally disadvantaged.

_____ 7. Very ineffective parenting style that is consistently associated with poor developmental outcomes.

_____ 8. Benefit that younger siblings may receive from interactions with older siblings.

_____ 9. More helpful, on average, than their brothers and sisters.

_____ 10. Pattern implying that *rational* exercise of control contributes to positive developmental outcomes.

ordinal position: the child's order of birth among siblings (also called birth order).

have been limited to one child. Contrary to the fears of many critics, there is no evidence that China's one-child policy has produced a generation of spoiled, self-centered brats who behave like "little emperors." Only children in China closely resemble only children in Western countries, scoring slightly higher than children with siblings on measures of intelligence and academic achievement and showing few meaningful differences in personality (Falbo & Polit, 1986; Falbo & Posten, 1993).

So evidence from very different cultural settings suggests that only children are hardly disadvantaged by having no brothers and sisters. Apparently, many singletons are able to gain through their friendships and peer alliances whatever they may miss by not having siblings at home.

 ## THE IMPACTS OF DIVORCE

Earlier, we noted that about half of today's marriages will end in divorce and that as many as 60% of all children born in the 1980s and 1990s will spend some time (about five years, on average) in a single-parent home—usually one headed by the mother (Teegartin, 1994). What effects might a divorce have on developing children? As we address this issue, let's first note that divorce is *not* a singular life event; instead, it represents a series of stressful experiences for the entire family that begins with marital conflict before the actual separation and includes a multitude of life changes afterward. As Mavis Hetherington and Kathleen Camara (1984) see it, families must often cope with "the diminution of family resources, changes in residence, assumption of new roles and responsibilities, establishment of new patterns of [family] interaction, reorganization of routines . . . , and [possibly] the introduction of new relationships [that is, stepparent-child and stepsibling relationships] into the existing family" (p. 398).

Developmentalists have known since the 1960s that a divorce is stressful for children. But only recently have investigators begun to conduct longitudinal studies to determine how family members cope with divorce and whether this dissolution of the nuclear family has any long-term effects on children's social, emotional, and intellectual development. Let's see what they have learned.

Immediate Effects: Crisis and Reorganization

Most families going through a divorce experience a *crisis period* of a year or more in which the lives of all family members are seriously disrupted (Booth & Amato, 1991; Hetherington, 1981, 1989; Hetherington, Cox, & Cox, 1982; Kitson & Morgan, 1990). Typically, both spouses experience emotional as well as practical difficulties. The wife, who obtains custody of any children in about 85% of divorcing families, may feel angry, depressed, lonely, or otherwise distressed, although often relieved as well. The husband is also likely to be distressed, particularly if he did not seek the divorce and feels shut off from his children. Having just become single adults, both parents often feel isolated from former married friends and other bases of social support on which they relied as a married couple. Divorced women with children usually face the added problem of getting by with less money—about half the family income they had before, on average (Smock, 1993). And life may seem especially difficult if they are forced to move to a lower-income neighborhood, and try to work and raise young children singlehandedly (Kitson & Morgan, 1990).

As you might suspect, psychologically distressed adults do not make the best parents. Hetherington and her associates (1982) found that custodial mothers, overwhelmed by responsibilities and by their own emotional reactions to divorce, often become edgy, impatient, and insensitive to their children's needs, and they typically adopt more restrictive and coercive methods of child rearing. Indeed, mothers often appear (to their children, at least) to have been transformed into more hostile, less caring parents (Fauber et al., 1990). Meanwhile, noncustodial fathers are likely to change in a different way, becoming somewhat overpermissive and indulgent during visits with their children.

We trust that you can imagine how these changes in parenting are likely to be received by the children of divorce, who themselves are often angry, fearful, and depressed about recent events and who may be feeling guilty as well, especially if they are preschoolers who are likely to think that they are somehow responsible for their parents' separation (Hetherington, 1981). What frequently happens is that these distressed youngsters react vigorously to their mother's seeming aloofness, impatience, and coercive parenting by becoming whiney, argumentative, disobedient, and downright disrespectful. Parent-child relationships during this crisis phase are best described as a vicious circle in which the child's emotional distress and problem behaviors and the adult's ineffective parenting styles feed on each other and make everyone's life unpleasant (Baldwin & Skinner, 1989).

The low point in mother-child relations often comes about a year after the divorce. One divorced mother described her family's ordeal as a "struggle for survival," while another characterized experiences with her children as like "getting bitten to death by ducks" (Hetherington et al., 1982, p. 258). For children, the stresses associated with a divorce and a breakdown in effective parenting often lead not only to problem behaviors at home but to strained relations with peers and to academic difficulties and conduct disorders at school (Allison & Furstenberg, 1989; Doherty & Needle, 1991; Fauber et al., 1990). And even though older children and adolescents are better able to understand the reasons for their parents' divorce, they seem to suffer no less than younger children do (Amato, 1993; Hetherington, Clingempeel, and Associates, 1992).

The Question of Sex Differences

Although the finding is by no means universal (see, for example, Allison & Furstenberg, 1989), many investigators report that the impact of marital strife and divorce is more powerful and enduring for boys than for girls. Even before the divorce occurs, boys are already showing more behavioral disruptions than girls (Block, Block, & Gjerde, 1986; 1988). And at least two longitudinal studies found that girls had largely recovered from their social and emotional disturbances two years after a divorce, whereas boys, who improved dramatically over this same period, were nevertheless continuing to show signs of emotional stress and problems in their relationships with parents, siblings, teachers, and peers (Hetherington et al., 1982; Wallerstein & Kelly, 1980).

Why might marital turmoil and divorce strike harder at boys? One explanation is that boys may feel closer to fathers than girls do, so that they experience more frustration and a deeper sense of loss when the father is no longer readily available to them (Lamb, 1981). And because boys are normally more active and less compliant than girls are (see Chapter 13), they may respond more negatively and vigorously to new restrictions imposed by the custodial parent—reactions that often elicit the kinds of coercive discipline that are likely to perpetuate their whiney, surly, and defiant behavior (Hetherington et al., 1982). However, some developmentalists believe that boys look so poorly adjusted because investigators have focused more on overt behavior problems that are easy to detect than on other, more subtle adjustment measures, such as covert psychological distress (Zaslow, 1989). Indeed, at least two recent studies suggest that even prior to a divorce (and for up to five years afterward), girls experience more *covert* distress than boys do (Allison & Furstenberg, 1989; Doherty & Needle, 1991). Moreover, a disproportionate number of girls from divorced families show precocious sexual activity at adolescence and a persistent lack of self-confidence in their relationships with boys and men (Hetherington, Stanley-Hagan, & Anderson, 1989; Wallerstein & Corbin, 1989). So divorce seems to affect boys and girls in different ways.

Another reason why boys may look bad is that most researchers have limited their studies to the most common custodial arrangement: mother-headed households.

Youngsters who live in conflict-ridden nuclear families often suffer physically and emotionally. In the long run, children of divorce are usually better adjusted than those whose unhappily married parents stay together "for the sake of the children."

Interestingly, boys whose fathers assume custody fare much better than boys who live with their mothers; in fact, children and adolescents of *both* sexes seem to be better adjusted and are less likely to drop out of high school when they live with their same-sex parent (Camara & Resnick, 1988; Zaslow, 1989; Zimiles & Lee, 1991).

So a divorce can strike very hard at children of either sex. Clearly, we would be overstating the case (not to mention being insensitive to girls) were we to conclude that this disruptive life experience is anything but a major struggle for the majority of boys *and* girls.

Long-Term Reactions to Divorce

Although many of the emotional and behavioral disturbances that accompany a divorce diminish considerably over the next two years, the whole experience is not forgotten. Compared with children in harmonious, two-parent families, children of divorce are still showing more evidence of psychological distress and academic difficulties four to six years later, especially if they were very young at the time of their parents' divorce (Allison & Furstenberg, 1989; Hetherington, 1989; Kurdek et al., 1981). Interestingly, children who show the most positive changes over time in their attitudes about the divorce often report that having friends whose parents were divorced had helped them to cope with their earlier feelings of bitterness and resentment (Kurdek et al., 1981).

Judith Wallerstein's (1987; Wallerstein & Blakeslee, 1989) studies of adolescents ten years after their parents' divorces found that few of them can recall the events that transpired when they were preschoolers; but many were still rather negative about what the divorce had done to their lives and often harbored fantasies that their parents would reconcile. Yet another interesting long-term reaction is that adolescents from divorced families are more likely than those from nondivorced families to fear that their own marriages will be unhappy (Franklin, Janoff-Bulman, & Roberts, 1990; Wallerstein & Blakeslee, 1989). It is not that children of divorce fear intimacy or think that they will be unable to find happiness in love relationships; rather, they differ from other respondents only in their optimism about the success of their *marriages* (Franklin et al., 1990). There may well be some basis for this concern, for adults whose parents divorced are more likely than adults from intact families to experience an unhappy marriage and a divorce themselves (Amato & Keith, 1991).

In sum, divorce tends to be a most unsettling and troubling life event—one that few children feel very positive about, even after ten years have elapsed. But despite the gloomy portrait of divorce that we have painted here, there are some more encouraging messages. The conventional wisdom used to be that unhappily married couples should try to remain together for the good of the children. However, researchers are consistently finding that children in stable, single-parent (or stepparent) homes are usually better adjusted than those who remain in conflict-ridden two-parent families (Hetherington, 1989; Long & Forehand, 1987). Indeed, many of the behavior problems that children display after a divorce are actually evident well *before* the divorce and may be related to longstanding family conflict rather than to divorce itself (Block et al., 1986; Cherlin et al., 1991). Take away the conflict and the breakdown in parenting often associated with divorce, and the experience, while always stressful, need not be damaging (Amato, 1993). So today's conventional wisdom holds that unhappily married couples who have irreconcilable differences might well *divorce* for the good of the children; that is, children are likely to *benefit* if the ending of a stormy marriage ultimately reduces the stress they are experiencing and enables either or both parents to be more sensitive and responsive to their needs (Barber & Eccles, 1992; Hetherington, 1989).

A second encouraging message is that not all divorcing families experience all the difficulties that we have described. In fact, some adults and children manage this transition quite well and may even grow psychologically as a result of it (Bursik, 1991; Hetherington, 1989). Who are these survivors? Box 15-2 provides some clues by exploring the factors that seem to promote a positive adjustment to divorce.

Remarriage and Reconstituted Families

Within three to five years after a divorce, about 75% of single-parent families experience yet another major change when the parent remarries and the children acquire a stepparent—and perhaps new siblings as well (Hetherington, 1989). Remarriage often improves the financial and other life circumstances of custodial parents, and most newly remarried adults report that they are satisfied with their second marriages. Yet, these reconstituted families introduce new challenges for children, who must now adjust not only to the parenting of an unfamiliar adult, but to the behavior of stepsiblings (if any) and to the possibility of receiving less attention from both their custodial and noncustodial parents (Hetherington, 1989). Moreover, second marriages are somewhat more likely to end in divorce than first marriages are (Booth & Edwards, 1992). Imagine, then, the stresses experienced by those adults and children who find themselves in a recurring cycle of marriage, marital conflict, divorce, single parenthood, and remarriage (Brody, Neubaum, & Forehand, 1988)! Indeed, one recent study found that the more marital transitions that grade school boys had experienced, the less well adjusted they were (see Figure 15-5).

How do children fare initially when their custodial parents remarry? At first, there is often a period of conflict and disruption as new family roles and relationships are ironed out (Hetherington, 1989). After this initial transition phase, an interesting sex difference emerges: Boys seem to benefit more than girls by gaining a *stepfather*, enjoying higher self-esteem, being less anxious and angered about their new living arrangements, and eventually overcoming most of the adjustment problems that they displayed before their mothers remarried (Clingempeel, Ievoli, & Brand, 1984; Hetherington, 1989; Zaslow, 1989). Why do girls not fare as well? Certainly *not* because stepfathers are treating stepdaughters any worse than stepsons; in fact, Hetherington and her associates (1989; Vuchinich et al., 1991) found that just the opposite is true during the early stages of remarried life, and that no matter how hard stepfathers tried, their stepdaughters rejected them! Apparently, girls view stepfathers as major threats to their relationships with their mothers, and they are likely to resent their mothers for remarrying and becoming less attentive to their needs (Hetherington, 1989; Vuchinich et al., 1991).

Less is known about children's reactions to *stepmothers* because stepmother families are still relatively uncommon (recall that fathers currently receive custody of their children in only about 15% of all custody hearings). What research there is indicates

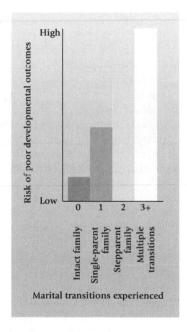

Figure 15-5
Boys' risk for poor adjustment outcomes (that is, antisocial behavior, low self-esteem, peer rejection, drug use, depression, poor academic performance, and deviant peer associations) as a function of number of marital transitions experienced.
From Capaldi & Patterson, 1991.

BOX 15-2
Smoothing the Rocky Road to Recovery from a Divorce

Some individuals adjust rather well to a divorce, whereas others suffer many negative and long-lasting effects. Let's note up front that children with difficult temperaments often fail to cope very well with the divorce experience and are likely to display stronger and more prolonged adjustment problems (Hetherington, Clingempeel & Associates, et al., 1992). However, several other factors can make the process of adjustment much easier, even for a difficult child.

Adequate financial support. Families fare much better after a divorce if they have adequate finances (Hetherington, 1989; Simons, Beaman, Conger, & Chao, 1993). Unfortunately, many mother-headed families experience a precipitous drop in income, which may necessitate a move to a lower-income neighborhood and the mother's return to work at precisely the time that her children need stability and increased attention. Moreover, a lack of money for trips, treats, and other amenities to which children may be accustomed can be a significant contributor to family quarrels and bickering. Recent efforts to ensure that more noncustodial parents pay their fair share of child support should help the cause.

Adequate parenting by the custodial parent. The custodial parent obviously plays a crucial role in the family's adjustment to divorce. If he or she can continue to respond in a warm, consistent, and authoritative manner, children are much less likely to experience serious problems (Hetherington et al., 1992; Kline et al., 1989). Of course, it is difficult to be an effective parent when one is depressed and under stress. Yet, both the custodial parent and the children can benefit immensely from receiving outside social support, not the least important of which is that provided by the *noncustodial* parent.

Social/emotional support from the noncustodial parent. If divorced parents continue to squabble and are hostile to each other, both are likely to be upset, the custodial parent's parenting is likely to suffer, and children will likely feel "caught in the middle" and torn in their loyalties, and will probably have difficulties adjusting (Amato, 1993; Buchanan, Maccoby, & Dornbusch, 1991). Children may also suffer by losing contact with the noncustodial parent, and, unfortunately, about one-third of those children who live with their mothers lose all contact with their fathers (Seltzer & Bianchi, 1988). By contrast, regular contact with a father who *supports* the mother in her parenting role helps children (particularly sons) to make a positive adjustment to life in a single-parent home (Amato, 1993; Camara & Resnick, 1985). Ideally, then, children should be permitted to maintain affectionate ties with *both* parents and should be shielded from any continuing conflict between parents.

Is *joint physical custody* the answer? Obviously, children will have regular contact with both parents when they live part of the time in each parent's home. Yet, this "contact advantage" may be offset by new kinds of instability (that is, changes in residence and, sometimes, in schools and peer

groups) that can leave some children distressed and confused (Kline et al., 1989). It may not really matter whether parents obtain joint custody if they both maintain high-quality relationships with their children (Emery & Tuer, 1993; Kline et al., 1989). But when the parents' relationship is hostile and conflictual, living in dual residences may heighten children's perceptions of being "caught in the middle"—an impression associated with high levels of stress and poor adjustment outcomes (Buchanan et al., 1991).

Additional social support. Divorcing adults are less depressed if they participate in support groups such as *Parents without Partners* (a national organization with local chapters that attempts to help single parents cope with their problems) or if they have close confidants to whom they can turn (Emery, 1988; Hetherington, 1989). Children also benefit from the support that they receive from close friends (Lustig, Wolchik, & Braver, 1992), as well as from participating in peer-support programs at school, in which they and other children of divorce are encouraged to share their feelings, correct their misconceptions, and learn positive coping skills (Grych & Fincham, 1992; Pedro-Carroll & Cowen, 1985). Adolescents in single-parent homes also appear to be less likely to engage in delinquent activities if a second adult (a grandmother, for example) lives in the home and bears some responsibility for child rearing and supervision (Dornbusch et al., 1985). In sum, friends, peers, school personnel, and other sources of social support outside the nuclear family can do much to help families adjust to divorce.

Minimizing additional stress. Generally, families respond more positively to divorce if additional disruptions are kept to a minimum—for example, if parents do not have to go through messy divorce trials and custody hearings, seek new jobs or residences, cope with the loss of their children, and so on (Buehler et al., 1986). One way to accomplish some of these aims is through *divorce mediation*—meetings prior to the divorce in which a trained professional tries to help divorcing parents reach amiable agreements on disputed issues such as child custody and property settlements. Divorce mediation increases the likelihood of out-of-court settlements and often promotes a better relationship between divorcing adults (Emery & Wyer, 1987); thus it may well have a beneficial effect on children's adjustment to the family breakup (although this latter effect remains to be confirmed by research).

Here, then, we have some effective first steps in the path toward a positive divorce experience, as well as a better understanding of why divorce is more disruptive for some families than for others. This research also serves as yet another excellent example of the family as a social system embedded in larger social systems. Mother, father, and children all influence one another's adjustment to divorce, and the family's experience also depends on the supports available within the neighborhood, the schools, the community, and the family members' own social networks.

that the introduction of a stepmother into the family system is somewhat more disruptive initially than the introduction of a stepfather, perhaps because stepmothers play more active roles as behavior monitors and disciplinarians than stepfathers do (Clingempeel et al., 1984; Furstenberg, 1988; Santrock & Sitterle, 1987). And it appears that transition from a father-headed, single-parent home to a two-parent *stepmother* family is once again more disruptive and difficult for girls than for boys, particularly if the biological mother maintains frequent contact with her children (Brand, Clingempeel, & Bowen-Woodward, 1988; Clingempeel & Segal, 1986). The problem seems to be that girls are often so closely allied with their mothers that they are bothered by either a stepfather competing for their mother's attention or a stepmother attempting to play a substitute-mother role. But the emotional disruption and resentment that daughters may initially experience in stepmother families is often short-lived, for "over time, the relative childrearing roles of biological mother and stepmother [are] effectively negotiated, and girls may benefit from a support system [with] a second mother figure" (Clingempeel & Segal, 1986, p. 482).

In sum, *stable* second marriages often work out well for two groups: custodial parents and their sons. Custodial parents gain the satisfaction of companionship, financial support, and some assistance in child rearing, and boys usually fare better in reconstituted families than in single-parent homes headed by their mothers. Yet, girls are not so clearly advantaged by gaining a stepparent, and it remains for future research to determine whether their long-range outcomes are any better (or worse) in reconstituted families than in single-parent homes.

A final note: Preadolescent and young adolescent children of both sexes find it much more difficult to adjust to life in a reconstituted family than younger children do (Hetherington, 1989). In fact, Mavis Hetherington and her associates (1992) found that, even after spending more than two years in a stepparent home, many adolescent males and females were less well adjusted than age-mates from intact homes and had shown little improvement over the 26-month course of the study. Of course, not all these adolescents were functioning poorly (see Maccoby, 1992), and authoritative parenting (by both the custodial parent and the stepparent) was associated with better adjustment outcomes than was authoritarian or uninvolved parenting. Nevertheless, there is clear evidence, both from this study and several others, that the incidence of deviant or delinquent behavior is higher among adolescents in stepparent homes than among age-mates living with both biological parents (see also Capaldi & Patterson, 1991; Dornbusch et al., 1985; Steinberg, 1987).

How might we explain this finding? One possibility is that adolescents, who are becoming increasingly autonomous, simply view any rules imposed by a *stepparent*

Concept Check 15-3 ⋁ Understanding Family Transitions

Check your understanding of some of the possible consequences of family transitions by matching each descriptive statement below with one of the following response options: (a) boys; (b) coercive parenting; (c) delinquent conduct; (d) girls; (e) better psychological adjustment; (f) joint physical custody; (g) noncustodial parental support; (h) unhappy marital relations. The answers appear in the Appendix.

_____ 1. More common among adolescents in reconstituted families than among those from intact homes.

_____ 2. Factor that may hinder rather than help children adjust to divorce.

_____ 3. Seem to adjust better to living with a custodial mother.

_____ 4. Factor that helps children adjust to a divorce.

_____ 5. Postdivorce change in family dynamics that may contribute to children's adjustment problems.

_____ 6. Long-term advantage of divorce for many children from conflict-ridden nuclear families.

_____ 7. Seem to adjust better to living in a reconstituted family.

_____ 8. Long-term risk of being a child of divorce.

as more intrusive or unwarranted than those coming from a biological parent. Another possibility that has received some support (see Fine & Kurdek, 1994; Hetherington et al., 1992) is that many stepparents are hesitant to impose restrictions on adolescents or to carefully monitor their activities, preferring to leave these tasks to the biological parent. And because grandparents often become less involved in their grandchildren's lives once a custodial parent remarries (Clingempeel et al., 1992), the biological parent may now have little social support for the rules that she imposes and may find it extremely difficult to adequately monitor the activities of adolescents on her own (Dornbusch et al., 1985; Steinberg, 1987). But before we get too carried away about the antisocial tendencies of adolescents in reconstituted families, an important truth should be stated here: Most adolescents who experience this marital transition turn out to be perfectly normal teenagers who may experience some initial problems adjusting but are unlikely to display any prolonged psychopathological tendencies (Maccoby, 1992).

 ## MATERNAL EMPLOYMENT—REVISITED

In Chapter 11, we learned that a clear majority of American mothers now work outside the home and that this arrangement need not undermine the emotional security of their children. Infants and toddlers are likely to become or to remain securely attached to their working parents if they have good day care and receive responsive caregiving when their parents are home from work.

Looking beyond primary attachments, research with older children suggests that maternal employment, by itself, is unlikely to impede a child's social and emotional development. In fact, the opposite may be true, for children of working mothers (particularly daughters) tend to be more independent, to enjoy higher self-esteem, and to hold higher educational and occupational aspirations and less stereotyped views of men and women than those whose mothers are not employed (Hoffman, 1989; Richards & Duckett, 1994). Moreover, studies of toddlers (Schachter, 1981), grade school children (Gold & Andres, 1978b), and adolescents (Gold & Andres, 1978a) consistently indicate that children of employed mothers are as confident in social settings as children whose mothers remain at home and are somewhat more sociable with peers. Finally, one recent study of a national sample of *low-income* families links maternal employment to children's cognitive *competence:* Second-graders whose mothers had worked a great deal outperformed those whose mothers had worked less (if at all) in mathematics, reading, and language achievement (Vandell & Ramanan, 1992; see also Williams & Radin, 1993). Although there have been reports that young children of working mothers are somewhat more aggressive and less obedient than children cared for at home by mothers who are not employed (Clarke-Stewart, 1989; Hoffman, 1989), these "negative returns" are generally small in magnitude (see, for example, Bates et al., 1994) and are often limited to children receiving low-quality day care where children's activities are not closely supervised (Howes, 1990; Vandell, Henderson, & Wilson, 1988).

Parenting of Employed Mothers

One reason that children of employed mothers often experience favorable (rather than unfavorable) developmental outcomes and appear to be so socially mature is that employed mothers are more inclined than unemployed mothers to grant their children independence and autonomy when their youngsters are ready for it (Hoffman, 1989). And, when mothers have stimulating jobs, receive adequate social support from their husbands and other close associates, and are highly committed to being a parent, they have generally favorable impressions of their children, rely less on power assertion to control their behavior, and are inclined to take an authoritative approach to child rearing—precisely the parenting style so often associated with favorable cognitive, social, and emotional outcomes (Crockenberg & Litman, 1991; Greenberger & Goldberg, 1989; Greenberger, O'Neil, & Nagel, 1994).

Of course, employed mothers may be less effective parents if they are dissatisfied with their jobs, are not highly committed to being a parent, or receive little support in their parenting role (Greenberger & Goldberg, 1989; and see Greenberger & O'Neil, 1993). Under these circumstances, working mothers can become rather aloof, impatient, and restrictive, which makes their children more argumentative and difficult (Hock, DeMeis, & McBride, 1988; Lerner & Galambos, 1988). But on the whole, the research we have reviewed suggests that maternal employment may often foster rather than impede children's development, as long as working mothers are committed to parenting and have the support they need to be effective parents.

The Importance of Good Day Care

As we noted in Chapter 11, one of the strongest supports that working parents could hope for is *high-quality* day care for their children. Recall that children who enter high-quality day-care centers early in life tend to display positive social, emotional, and intellectual outcomes from infancy through early adolescence (Andersson, 1989; 1992). Much of the research that points to the long-term benefits of excellent day care comes from Western European countries, where day care for toddlers and preschool children is often government subsidized, staffed with trained, well-paid child-care professionals, and widely available to all citizens at a modest fee (Scarr et al., 1993). By comparison, day care in the United States is woefully inadequate. Typically run as for-profit enterprises, U.S. day-care centers and day-care homes are generally staffed by poorly compensated caregivers who have little training or experience in early childhood education and who rarely stay in the profession long enough to gain much expertise (Zigler & Gilman, 1993). Moreover, American day care is expensive; providing one child with what is often far less than optimal care can run $3,000–$4,000 per year, or about 25%–30% of the annual income of a minimum-wage worker (U.S. Bureau of the Census, 1993). In 1990, the U.S. Congress passed a bill granting some tax relief to low-income parents to help offset the cost of day care. But until more strides are taken to ensure the availability of *high-quality* care at a *reasonable cost* to *all* who may need it, many American workers will have to struggle to find and finance the kinds of good alternative care that can help them to optimize the development of their children.

Self-Care

The importance of adequate alternative care raises another employment-related issue: the after-school care of children whose mothers work. In the United States, some 2 to 4 *million* grade school students between the ages of 6 and 13 qualify as **self-care (or latchkey) children** who care for themselves after school with little or no adult supervision (Zigler & Finn-Stevenson, 1993). Are these children at risk of such poor developmental outcomes as feelings of loneliness, neglect, and low self-esteem? Are they deficient academically? Is there a danger that, in the absence of adult supervision, self-care children will be prone to delinquent or antisocial conduct?

Research designed to answer these questions is often contradictory. Some studies report no differences between supervised children and self-care children in self-esteem, self-confidence, peer popularity, academic achievement, and antisocial behavior (see, for example, Galambos & Maggs, 1991; Vandell & Corasantini, 1988), whereas other research suggests that self-care children display higher levels of anxiety, poorer academic performances, and more delinquent or antisocial conduct than supervised youngsters do (Cole & Rodman, 1987; Posner & Vandell, 1994; Richardson et al., 1989).

How might we explain these inconsistent outcomes? Let's begin by noting that the risks of self-care do seem to be greater for lower-income children in urban

self-care (or latchkey) children: children who care for themselves after school or in the evenings while their parents are working.

neighborhoods that may present many opportunities for unsupervised children to associate with deviant peer groups and to take part in antisocial conduct (Posner & Vandell, 1994; Vandell & Ramanan, 1991). Lawrence Steinberg (1986) agrees that the effects of self-care may depend very heavily on the way self-care children spend their time and on whether parents are supervising them *in absentia*. Steinberg's own studies of 10–16-year-olds revealed that self-care children who were allowed to "hang out" after school were likely to describe themselves as willing to engage in delinquent or antisocial conduct with peers. By contrast, self-care children who came home after school and whose parents *monitored them from a distance* (by telephone or by assigning chores to be completed) were no more susceptible to deviant peer influences than children supervised at home by a parent. Moreover, Steinberg found that authoritative parenting greatly increased latchkey children's resistance to undesirable peer influences, even when they were not closely monitored in the afternoon and peer pressure for deviant conduct was reasonably strong (see also Galambos & Maggs, 1991).

So it appears that there are steps that working parents can take to minimize some of the potential risks of leaving schoolchildren to care for themselves—namely, requiring them to go home after school, supervising them *in absentia* to ensure that they do, and parenting them in an authoritative manner. Nevertheless, leaving children younger than 8 or 9 to fend for themselves may be asking for trouble. Not only is the practice illegal in many states, but 5–7-year-olds often lack the cognitive skills to avoid high-risk hazards such as swimming pools or heavy traffic or to cope with such emergencies as personal injuries or fires (Peterson, Ewigman, & Kivlahan, 1993). Younger children in self-care also appear to be more vulnerable to sexual abuse and to harm at the hands of burglars as well (Zigler & Finn-Stevenson, 1993).

At present, organized after-school care for school-age children is rare in American communities. This is indeed unfortunate, for Jill Posner and Deborah Vandell (1994) found that 9-year-olds from high-risk neighborhoods who attended *closely supervised* after-school programs providing reactional opportunities and/or academic assistance were more academically competent, were rated as better adjusted by teachers, and were much *less* likely to be involved in antisocial activities than age-mates who were not supervised after school by an adult. However, the same benefits of after-school care are not found if the programs that children attend are primarily custodial and provide little stimulation or adult guidance (Vandell & Corasantini, 1990). So the *quality* of day care that children receive is important at all ages; and given the success of the publicly funded programs that Posner and Vandell (1994) evaluated, we might encourage politicians and community leaders to look carefully at them as a potentially affordable means of (1) optimizing developmental outcomes and (2) preventing more children of working mothers from having to face the risks of being alone in the afternoon and early evening.

► WHEN PARENTING BREAKS DOWN: THE PROBLEM OF CHILD ABUSE

Family relationships can be our greatest source of nurturance and support, but they can also be a powerful source of anguish. Nowhere is this more obvious than in cases of **child abuse.** Every day, thousands of infants, children, and adolescents are burned, bruised, beaten, starved, suffocated, sexually molested, or otherwise mistreated by their caregivers. Other children are not targets of these "physical" forms of abuse, but suffer such *psychological abuse* as rejection, ridicule, or even being terrorized by their parents (Hart & Brassard, 1987). Still others are *neglected* and deprived of the basic care and stimulation that they need to develop normally. Although instances of severe battering are the most visible forms of child abuse and are certainly horrible, many investigators now believe that strong and recurrent psychological abuse and neglect

Children of working mothers may benefit, both socially and academically, from organized after-school care that is closely supervised by adults.

child abuse: term used to describe any extreme maltreatment of children, involving physical batterings, sexual molestations, psychological insults such as persistent ridicule, rejection, and terrorization, and physical or emotional neglect.

may prove to be even more harmful to children in the long run (Emery, 1989; Grusec & Walters, 1991).

Child abuse is a very serious problem. In 1985, over 1.9 *million* reports of child maltreatment of all sorts were filed in the United States (American Humane Association, as cited in U.S. Bureau of the Census, 1989). In a more recent national sample of families in the United States, almost 11% of the children had reportedly been kicked, bitten, punched, beaten up, hit with an object, or threatened with a knife or a gun by their parents in the past year (Wolfner & Gelles, 1993). Another national survey conducted in 1991 found that more than 400,000 American children a year are coerced into oral, anal, or genital intercourse (Finkelhor & Dziuba-Leatherman, 1994), usually by a father, a stepfather, an older sibling, or another male relative or family friend (Trickett & Putnam, 1993). It is not a pretty picture, is it? And since many cases of child abuse are never reported or detected, these figures may represent only the tip of the iceberg.

There are many, many factors that contribute to a social problem as widespread as child abuse. Fortunately, researchers are beginning to gain a better understanding of why abuse occurs by adopting a social systems perspective and recognizing that (1) some adults may be more inclined than others to abuse children, (2) some children may be more likely than others to be abused, and (3) abuse may be more likely to occur in some contexts, communities, and cultures than in others.

Who Are the Abusers?

Anyone examining a badly beaten child might immediately suspect that the abuser must be psychologically deranged. But strange as it may seem, only about one child abuser in ten appears to have a severe mental illness (Kempe & Kempe, 1978). An abusive parent tends most often to be a young, poverty-stricken mother who is unemployed and often has no spouse to share her burdens (Gelles, 1992; Wolfner & Gelles, 1993). However, child abusers come from all races, ethnic groups, and social classes, and many of them appear to be rather typical, loving parents—except for their tendency to become extremely irritated with their children and to do things they will later regret.

Yet there are at least some differences between parents who abuse their children and those who do not. Although most maltreated children do not abuse their own children when they become parents, roughly 30% do (Kaufman & Zigler, 1989). In other words, abusive parenting is often passed from generation to generation (Simons et al., 1991; van IJzendoorn, 1992). Second, many abusive parents are emotionally insecure themselves and can't seem to tolerate the normal behavior of young children. For example, Byron Egeland and his associates (1979; Egeland, Sroufe, & Erickson, 1983) found that when an infant cries to communicate needs such as hunger, nonabusive mothers correctly interpret these cries as signs of discomfort, whereas abusive mothers often infer that the baby is somehow *criticizing* or *rejecting* them. Indeed, many abusive parents reach a point where even a baby's smiles are unpleasantly arousing, and they are much less inclined than nonabusive parents to interact with a smiling baby (Frodi & Lamb, 1980). Finally, abusive parents generally favor authoritarian control and power-assertive forms of discipline over authoritative and inductive techniques (which they view as much less effective). Although abusive parents do not report using physical punishment any more often than nonabusive parents do, they do admit to relying heavily on the most severely punitive tactics such as yanking children's hair, hitting them in the face, or striking them with objects (Trickett & Susman, 1988).

In sum, we can construct a "profile" of the abusive parent: Typically, she is a younger parent who was exposed to harsh parenting herself, who believes that coercive discipline is more effective than reasoning, and who finds parenting more stressful, unpleasant, and ego threatening than nonabusive parents do (Bugental, Blue, &

The incidence of child abuse is relatively high in deteriorating neighborhoods that offer few services and little if any social support to financially troubled families.

Cruzcosa, 1989; Trickett & Susman, 1988). Still, there are many *nonabusive* parents who display all these characteristics, and it has been difficult to specify *in advance* exactly who will or will not become a child abuser (Trickett et al., 1991).

Who Is Abused?

Interestingly, abusive parents often single out only one child in the family as a target, thus implying that some children may bring out the worst in their parents (Gil, 1970). No one is suggesting that children are to *blame* for this abuse, but some children do appear to be more at risk than others. For example, infants who are emotionally unresponsive, hyperactive, irritable, or ill are far more likely to be abused than are quiet, healthy, and responsive babies who are easy to care for (Egeland & Sroufe, 1981; Sherrod et al., 1984). Similarly, temperamentally impulsive children who have trouble controlling their behavior may come to elicit stronger and stronger forms of physical punishment from their caregivers until the line between spanking and abuse is crossed (Parke & Lewis, 1981). Yet it is important to emphasize that many such "difficult" children are never abused, while many cheerful and seemingly easygoing children are mistreated. Just as caregiver characteristics cannot fully predict or explain why abuse occurs, neither can characteristics of abused children, although it is likely that the combination of a high-risk parent and a high-risk child spells trouble (see Bugental et al., 1989).

But even the match between high-risk children and caregivers does not invariably result in child abuse. As we will see, the broader social contexts in which families are embedded matter too.

Social-Contextual Triggers: The Ecology of Child Abuse

Child abuse is most likely to occur in families under stress. Consider, for example, that battered children often come from large families in which overburdened caregivers have many small children to attend to (Light, 1973). The probability of abuse under these stressful circumstances is further compounded if the mother is relatively young, is poorly educated, and receives little child-rearing assistance from the father, a friend or relative, or some other member of her social network (Crockenberg, 1987; Egeland et al., 1983, 1988). Other significant life changes such as divorce, the death of a family member, the loss of a job, or moving to a new home can disrupt social and emotional relationships within a family and thereby contribute to neglectful or abusive parenting (Bronfenbrenner, 1986; McLoyd, 1989; McLoyd et al., 1994; Wolfner & Gelles, 1993). Finally, children are much more likely to be abused or neglected if their parents are unhappily married (Belsky, 1980; Egeland et al., 1988).

High-Risk Neighborhoods

Of course, families are embedded in broader social contexts (for example, a neighborhood, a community, a culture) that may well affect a child's chances of being abused. Some residential areas can be labeled **high-risk neighborhoods** because they have much higher rates of child abuse than other neighborhoods with the same demographic and socioeconomic characteristics. What are these high-risk areas like? According to James Garbarino (1992; Garbarino & Sherman, 1980), they tend to be deteriorating neighborhoods that offer struggling parents little in the way of *community services*, such as parks, recreation centers, preschool programs, and churches, or *informal support systems*, such as contacts with friends and relatives. Consequently, socially isolated parents who live in these neighborhoods have nowhere to turn for advice and assistance during particularly stressful periods, and they often end up taking out their frustrations on their children. Interestingly, high-risk neighborhoods can be created by the actions of government or industry. For example, a local planning board's decision to rezone a stable residential area or to locate a highway there can lead to a destruction of play areas, declining property values, a loss of pride in the

high-risk neighborhood: a residential area in which the incidence of child abuse is much higher than in other neighborhoods with the same demographic and socioeconomic characteristics.

Table 15-2 Factors Contributing to Child Abuse and Neglect

Contributing factor	Examples
Parental characteristics	Younger age (under 25); low educational level; depression or other psychological disturbance; history of rejection or abuse as a child; belief in effectiveness of coercive discipline; general insecurity or low ego strength.
Child characteristics	Irritable or impulsive temperament; hyperactivity; prematurity; inattentiveness; sickliness or other chronic developmental problems.
Family characteristics	Financial strain or poverty; job loss; frequent moves; marital instability; lack of spousal support; many children to care for; divorce.
Neighborhood	High-risk areas characterized by few community services and little opportunity for informal social support from friends and relatives.
Culture	Approval of coercive methods of resolving conflicts and use of corporal punishment to discipline children.

neighborhood, and the eventual isolation of families from friends, community services (which may no longer exist), and other bases of social support. James Garbarino (1992) is one of many theorists who believe that large numbers of American children are likely to be mistreated because of political or economic decisions that have undermined the health and stability of low-risk, family oriented neighborhoods.

Cultural Influences

Finally, the broader cultural contexts in which families live can affect the likelihood that children will be abused by a highly stressed or overburdened caregiver. Some developmentalists believe that child abuse is rampant in the United States because people in that society (1) have a permissive attitude about violence and (2) generally sanction the use of physical punishment as a means of controlling children's behavior. There may well be some truth to these assertions, for cross-cultural studies reveal that children are less often abused in societies that discourage the use of physical punishment and advocate nonviolent ways of resolving interpersonal conflicts (Belsky, 1980; Levinson, 1989). In fact, several Scandinavian countries, where children are rarely abused, have *outlawed* the use of corporal punishment (spanking), even by parents (Finkelhor & Dziuba-Leatherman, 1994).

Clearly, child abuse is a very complex phenomenon with many causes and contributing factors (see Table 15-2 for a brief review). It is not easy to specify who will abuse their children and who will not, but we know that abuse is most likely to occur when a psychologically vulnerable parent faces overwhelming stress with insufficient support (Wolfner & Gelles, 1993).

Consequences of Abuse and Neglect

As you might expect, physically abused and otherwise maltreated children tend to display a number of problems. Intellectual deficits, academic difficulties, and disturbed social relationships with teachers and peers are particularly common (Malinosky-Rummell & Hansen, 1993; Salzinger et al., 1993; and see Box 15-3 for some

BOX 15-3
Effects of Childhood Sexual Abuse

*I*n the 1970s, developmentalists began to discover that the sexual abuse of children was nowhere near as rare as they had thought. We noted earlier that approximately 400,000 children a year are sexually abused in the United States. And if we count all those individuals who report that they were *ever* molested as children, as David Finkelhor and his associates (1989) did in a national survey, 27% of the women and 16% of the men had experienced some form of sexual abuse, ranging from being fondled in ways they considered inappropriate to actually being raped. Sexual abuse is a serious and widespread social problem.

What impacts might this kind of abuse have on its victims? After reviewing 45 studies, Kathleen Kendall-Tackett and her associates (1993) concluded that there is no one distinctive "syndrome" of psychological problems that characterizes all who experience sexual abuse. Instead, these victims display any number of problems commonly seen in emotionally disturbed individuals, including anxiety, depression, low self-esteem, acting out, aggression, withdrawal, and academic difficulties. Roughly 20% to 30% of sexual abuse victims experience each of these problems, and boys seem to display the same types and degrees of disturbance as girls do.

Many of these aftereffects boil down to feelings of shame, a lack of self-worth, and a reluctance to trust other people (Cole & Putnam, 1992). And there are two problems that seem to be uniquely associated with sexual abuse. First, about a third of the victims engage in "sexualized behaviors"—acting out sexually by placing objects in their vaginas, masturbating in public, behaving seductively or, if they are older, becoming sexually promiscuous (Kendall-Tackett et al., 1993). Perhaps it is not surprising, then, that adults who were sexually abused as children are more likely than nonabused individuals to be sexually victimized as adults (Wyatt, Guthrie, & Notgrass, 1992) and to report dissatisfac-

tion with their sexual relationships and marriages (Finkelhor et al., 1989). Second, about a third of abuse victims display the symptoms of *posttraumatic stress disorder*—a clinical syndrome that includes nightmares, flashbacks to the traumatizing events, and feelings of helplessness and anxiety in the face of danger (Kendall-Tackett et al., 1993). In addition, a small minority of sexual abuse victims display severe psychological problems, including multiple personality disorder—a splitting of the psyche into distinct personalities (Cole & Putnam, 1992). Such self-destructive acts as abusing drugs and even committing suicide are also more common among sexual abuse victims than among nonvictims (Artenstein, 1990; Haugaard & Reppucci, 1988). And yet, about a third of sexually abused children display no psychological symptoms at all (Kendall-Tackett et al., 1993)—although long-term follow-ups to see if they will experience problems later in life have not been conducted.

Overcoming the harmful effects of sexual abuse can be very difficult, particularly if it occurred frequently over a long period of time, if the perpetrator was a close relative such as the father, and if the child's mother looked the other way or otherwise failed to be a reliable source of social support (Kendall-Tackett et al., 1993; Trickett et al., 1993). Yet, many symptoms fade within a year or two, and recovery may proceed particularly well if the nonabusing parent believes the child's story, puts a stop to the abuse, and provides a stable and loving home environment thereafter (Kendall-Tackett, 1993). Psychotherapy aimed at treating the anxiety and depression that many victims experience and teaching them not to be revictimized can also contribute to the healing process (O'Donohue & Elliott, 1992). Recovery takes time but it can and does occur in many cases, particularly when the sexually victimized child is identified early and immediately receives the help that he or she needs.

noteworthy correlates of childhood sexual abuse). John Eckenrode and his associates (1993) found that the behavioral correlates of physical abuse differ somewhat from those of neglect. Children who are neglected are even more likely than those who are physically abused to display poor academic performances and to have to repeat a grade. Neglected children undoubtedly receive very few opportunities for guided, or collaborative, learning and little in the way of enriching intellectual stimulation from their aloof, uninvolved caregivers. By contrast, disordered social relationships are more common among physically abused children who, because of their hostile and highly aggressive behavior, often have lengthy records of discipline problems at school (Eckenrode et al., 1993) and are likely to be rejected by peers (Haskett & Kistner, 1991; Salzinger et al., 1993).

One of the most disturbing consequences of severe physical abuse is a lack of normal empathy in response to the distress of others. When Mary Main and Carol George (1985) observed the responses of abused and nonabused toddlers to the fussing and crying of peers, they found that nonabused children typically attended carefully to the distressed child, showed concern, or even attempted to provide comfort. But as shown in Figure 15-6, not one abused child showed appropriate concern; instead, abused toddlers were likely to become angry and attack the crying child (see also Klimes-Dougan & Kistner, 1990). So it seems that physically abused children are likely to become abusive companions who have apparently learned from their own experiences at home that distress signals are particularly irritating to others and often elicit angry responses rather than displays of sympathy and compassion. No wonder they are rejected by their peers!

Abused and neglected youngsters also tend to be fearful, anxious, depressed, and low in self-esteem (Emery, 1989; Sternberg et al., 1993; Trickett et al., 1991). Children of battered women display many of the same social and emotional problems that physically abused children do (Holden & Ritchie, 1991), although the adjustment problems of children who were abused themselves appear to be somewhat more severe than those of youngsters who have witnessed spouse abuse (see Sternberg et al., 1993). Moreover, the social and emotional consequences of abuse and neglect are often long-lasting: Adults who were maltreated as children tend to be violent, both inside and outside the family, and they show higher-than-average rates of criminal activity, substance abuse, depression, and other psychological problems (Finkelhor & Dziuba-Leatherman, 1994; Malinosky-Rummell & Hansen, 1993).

The good news is that many abused or neglected youngsters are remarkably resilient, especially if they are able to establish a warm, secure, and supportive relationship with a nonabusive parent, a grandparent, or some other member of the family (Egeland et al., 1988; Egeland & Sroufe, 1981). And even though abused children are at risk of becoming abusive parents, it is worth emphasizing once again that the majority of these maltreated individuals do *not* abuse their own children (Kaufman & Zigler, 1989). Abused parents who succeed at breaking this cycle of abuse are more likely than those who do not to (1) have received emotional support from a nonabusive parent (or parent substitute), a therapist, and their spouses and (2) have avoided severe stress as adults (Egeland et al., 1988; Vondra & Belsky, 1993).

Despite our better understanding of the causes of child abuse and observations that its often severe consequences can be lessened or even overcome, we are still a long way from solving the problem. Rather than conclude on that pessimistic note, let's consider some of the methods that have been used to assist the abused child and his or her abusers.

How Do We Solve the Problem?

It can be a bit discouraging to realize that so many factors contribute to the maltreatment of children. Where do we begin to intervene? Just how many problems must we correct before we can prevent or stop the violence and discourage the neglect? Despite the complexity of the problem, progress has been made. Let's look first at preventive measures.

Preventing Abuse and Neglect

In order to prevent child maltreatment before it begins, we must be able to identify high-risk families—a task that is greatly aided by the kinds of studies we have reviewed. For example, extremely irritable or unresponsive babies who are at risk of alienating their caregivers can be identified through neonatal assessment programs, and their parents can be taught how to help these infants respond more favorably to their caregiving. Indeed, we have already seen that Brazelton testing and training programs (see Box 5-1) are effective methods of preventing the "miscommunications" between infants and caregivers that can contribute to child abuse.

Other efforts to prevent abuse have been targeted directly at high-risk parents. Steven Schinke and his associates (1986), for example, worked with one high-risk group of mothers: single teenagers who were under a great deal of stress. The goal was to teach a wide range of stress-management skills: relaxation techniques, problem-solving strategies, communication skills that would enable mothers to request help and to refuse unreasonable demands, and even techniques for building stronger

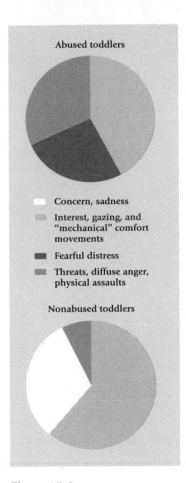

Figure 15-6
Responses to the distress of peers observed in abused and nonabused toddlers in the day-care setting. (The circles show the mean proportion of responses falling into each category for the nine abused and nine nonabused toddlers.)
Adapted from Main & George, 1985.

social support networks. Three months later, mothers who received the training out-performed those in a control group on several measures. They had improved their problem-solving skills, had established stronger support networks, now enjoyed higher self-esteem, and were more confident about their parenting skills. It seems likely that high-risk parents who have learned effective techniques for coping with stress are better able to deal with the sometimes overwhelming challenges that they face, without resorting to violence. These parents can also benefit from programs to teach them effective child-management skills (Wolfe et al., 1988).

The demonstrated success of these and other similar interventions has led child-welfare agencies in several states to develop family support and education programs designed to prevent child abuse (Zigler & Finn-Stevenson, 1993). For example, the **Ounce of Prevention program,** a collaborative effort of the Illinois Department of Children and Family Services and the Pittway Corporation, attempts to head off child abuse by offering parent-education classes that teach effective child-management techniques and by providing such support services (through churches, medical clinics, and schools) as child-care programs, medical assistance, and job training. Other similar family support systems, which are regularly evaluated to ensure that they are meeting families' needs, are now available in Arkansas, Iowa, Oregon, and Vermont (Zigler & Finn-Stevenson, 1993).

Controlling Abuse

How do we deal with parents who are already abusive? It seems clear that a few visits from a social worker are unlikely to solve the problem (Oates, 1986). Kempe and Kempe (1978) report that a fair percentage of abusive parents will stop physically maltreating their children if they can be persuaded to use certain services, such as 24-hour "hot lines" or crisis nurseries, that will enable them to discuss their hostile feelings with a volunteer or to get away from their children for a few hours when they are about to lose control. However, these are only stopgap measures that will probably not work for long unless the abuser also takes advantage of other services—such as **Parents Anonymous** or family therapy—that are designed to help the caregiver to understand his or her problem while providing the friendship and emotional support that an abusive parent so often lacks.* Ultimately, however, a comprehensive approach is likely to be most effective. Abusive parents need emotional support *and* opportunities to learn more effective parenting and coping skills, whereas the victims of abuse and neglect need stimulating day-care programs *and* specialized training to help them overcome the cognitive, social, and emotional problems associated with abuse (see Culp et al., 1991; Fantuzzo, 1990). In short, the ultimate goal in attempting to prevent or control child abuse must be to convert a pathological family system into a healthy one.

In recent years, another control tactic has become more common in cases of severe or repeated abuse: arresting and prosecuting parents for acts of violence that would qualify as criminal assault if they occurred between strangers (Emery, 1989). Yet, child abuse is often difficult to prove (beyond a reasonable doubt, as required for criminal conviction), and American courts are quite hesitant to take children from abusive parents, even when there is reason to suspect a child has been repeatedly abused. One reason for this reluctant attitude is that, historically, children have been treated as their parents' possessions (Hart & Brassard, 1987). Another is that abused children and their parents are often attached to each other, so that neither the abusive adult nor the battered child wishes to be separated. However, it is essential that we care-

Ounce of Prevention program: a comprehensive, community-based attempt to prevent child abuse by educating parents in effective child-management techniques and providing such family support services as child-care programs, job training, and medical assistance.

Parents Anonymous: an organization of reformed child abusers (modeled after Alcoholics Anonymous) that functions as a support group and helps parents to understand and overcome their abusive tendencies.

---

*Fortunately, these services are often free. Chapters of Parents Anonymous are now located in many cities and towns in the United States. (For the location of a nearby chapter, one can consult a telephone directory or write to Parents Anonymous, 6733 South Sepulveda Blvd., Suite 270, Los Angeles, CA 90045.) In addition, many cities and counties provide free family therapy to abusive parents. Often, the therapists are lay volunteers who have been trained to serve in this capacity and do so quite effectively.

SFPD 4502317 9-8-81

4 out of 5 convicts were abused children.

In the United States, an average of 80% of our prisoners were abused children. That is why we are working so hard to help these children today, before they develop into a threat to others tomorrow.

With your support, we can have a full staff of trained people available 24 hours a day. Abused children desperately need us. Please let us be there to help. Write for our free brochure, or send in your tax-deductible donation today.

San Francisco Child Abuse Council, Inc.
4093 24th Street, San Francisco, CA 94114

A number of programs and services have arisen as attempts to prevent or control the problem of child abuse.

fully weigh the child's rights against the rights and wishes of parents, for some abusive adults (slightly more than 2,000 per year in the United States) will eventually kill their children, regardless of the counseling they receive (Finkelhor & Dziuba-Leatherman, 1994; Hart, 1991).

Although some people may disagree, developmentalists the world over have argued that no caregiver has the right to abuse a child (Hart, 1991). And in cases of severe abuse or neglect, developmentalists generally agree that our first priority must be to provide for the health and safety of mistreated children, even if that means terminating the abusers' legal rights of parenthood and placing their children in foster care or adoptive homes. The challenge that we now face is to become much more successful at preventing and controlling child abuse so that the difficult decision of whether to separate children from their parents will need to be made less frequently than it is at present.

 ## REFLECTIONS ON THE FAMILY

If you do not yet fully appreciate the awesome significance of the family for children and adolescents, reflect for a moment on how very badly things can go when the family does not fulfill its important functions. Start with a neglected infant who may not only fail to thrive physically (see Chapter 5) but does not experience anything faintly resembling warm, sensitive, and responsive parenting. How is this child to form the secure attachments that serve as foundations for later social and intellectual competencies? Or think about the child whose parents are downright hostile and who either provide no guidance at all or who hem the child in with rules and punish his every misstep. How is this child to learn how to care about other people, become appropriately autonomous, and fit into society?

Regina Campos and her associates (1994) studied homeless street youths in Brazil whose families had failed them by neglecting, abusing, or otherwise dismissing them as unimportant. What were these homeless youngsters like? Compared with age-mates who worked on the streets but lived at home, youths "of the street" were faring very poorly. They struggle daily to survive, often begging if necessary to get by. Moreover, they live in constant fear of being victimized and are themselves heavily involved in such antisocial behaviors as prostitution, drug abuse, thievery, and a host of other criminal activities. In short, these youngsters who have no family life are pursuing a highly atypical and deviant lifestyle that might seem to place them on the fast track to psychopathology, as we see in one 16-year-old's account of his daily routine:

> When you go to sleep it's about 5 in the morning; we wake up around 2 or 3 in the afternoon . . . get up, wash your face, if you have money you have breakfast [then] go out to steal, then you start to sell the stuff and the money all goes on drugs, because in the street it's all drugs! . . . Then, you get high, you're all set, then you come down and sleep (Campos et al., 1994, p. 322).

What happens to these homeless street youths when they grow up? No one can say for sure because longitudinal studies of this or similar populations have not been conducted. But there is reason to suspect that their outcomes are likely to be grim, in view of the fact that 80% of the prison population of one major Brazilian city consisted of former street youth (Campos et al., 1994).

You get the picture. It is often easier to illustrate the grave importance of families by accentuating the negative; and fortunately, most of us have fared much better than this, even though we do not always acknowledge just how significant our families may have been in underwriting our developmental successes. So think about what you have learned in this chapter the next time you gather with the closest members of your own family. Chances are you will understand why children and adults who are asked to reflect on what or who is most important in their lives almost invariably speak of their families (Furman & Buhrmester, 1992; Whitbourne, 1986). Although we change and our families change as we get older, it seems that most of us never cease to affect, or to be affected by, those folks we call "family."

SUMMARY

The family is the primary agent of socialization—the context in which children begin to acquire the beliefs, attitudes, values, and behaviors considered appropriate in their society. Basic goals of parenting in all societies include (1) ensuring the child's survival, (2) preparing the child for economic self-sufficiency, and (3) encouraging the child to maximize other cultural values such as morality, religion, and achievement.

Whether nuclear or extended in form, families are best viewed as changing social systems embedded in larger social systems that are also changing. Social trends affecting family life today include greater numbers of single adults, later marriages, a decline in childbearing, more female participation in the workforce, and more divorces, single-parent families, and remarriages, as well as greater numbers of families living in poverty.

Parents differ along two broad child-rearing dimensions—*warmth/hostility* and *permissiveness/restrictiveness* (or control)—that, when considered together, yield four styles of parenting. Generally speaking, warm and restrictive (that is, *authoritative*) parents who appeal to reason in order to enforce their demands are likely to raise highly competent, well-adjusted children. Outcomes of other parenting styles are not as favorable; indeed, children of hostile and permissive (that is, *uninvolved*) parents are often deficient in virtually all aspects of psychological functioning.

Parents from different cultures and social classes have different values, concerns, and outlooks on life that influence their child-rearing practices. Lower-income parents tend to be more punitive and authoritarian than middle-class parents, due both to negative effects of economic hardship on parenting and to their desire to promote such attributes as obedience and respect, which they see as essential for success in a blue-collar economy. By contrast, middle-class parents are more likely to stress independence, creativity, ambition, and self-assertion—the attributes that their children will need to succeed in business or a profession. So, parents from all socioeconomic strata (and from different cultures) emphasize the characteristics that contribute to *success as they know it*, and it is inappropriate to conclude that one particular style of parenting is somehow "better" or more competent than all others.

Parent-child relationships are renegotiated as adolescents seek to become more autonomous. Although family conflict escalates during this period, adolescents are likely to become appropriately autonomous if their parents willingly grant them more freedom, explain the rules and restrictions that they do impose, and continue to be loving and supportive guides.

Sibling rivalries are a normal aspect of family life that may begin as soon as a younger sibling arrives; yet there is a positive side to having siblings. Siblings are typically viewed as intimate associates who can be counted on for support. Older sibs frequently serve as attachment objects, models, and teachers for their younger siblings, and they often profit themselves from the instruction and guidance they provide. Yet, sibling relationships are not essential for normal development, for only children are just as socially, emotionally, and intellectually competent (or slightly more so), on average, than children with siblings are.

Divorce represents a drastic change in family life that is stressful and unsettling for children and their parents. Children's initial reactions often include anger, fear, depression, and guilt—feelings that may last more than a year. The emotional upheaval that follows a divorce often influences the parent-child relationship. Children often become cranky, disobedient, or otherwise difficult, while the custodial parent may suddenly become more punitive and controlling. The stresses resulting from a divorce and this new coercive lifestyle often affect the child's peer relations and schoolwork. But in the long run, children of divorce are usually better adjusted than those who remain in conflict-ridden two-parent families. Girls adjust better than boys to life in a single-parent, mother-headed home, whereas after a period of initial disruption in which new roles are ironed out, boys seem to fare better than girls when the custodial parent remarries, forming a reconstituted family. Among the factors that help children to make positive adjustments to divorce are adequate financial and emotional support from the noncustodial parent, additional social support (from friends, relatives, and the community) for custodial parents and their children, and a minimum of additional stressors surrounding the divorce itself.

As long as working mothers are satisfied with their jobs, committed to parenting, and receiving adequate support from their spouses and other close associates, their employment is associated with such favorable child outcomes as self-reliance, sociability, competent intellectual and academic performances, and less stereotyped views of men and women. Given proper support, working mothers tend to grant their children autonomy when they are ready for it and to take an authoritative approach to parenting, which helps to explain the positive outcomes that their children display. One of the strongest supports that working parents could hope for is stimulating day care for their children—a support system that is woefully inadequate in the United States, compared with that provided by many other Western industrialized nations. In addition, large numbers of American grade school children whose mothers work must care for themselves after school. When monitored from a distance by authoritative parents, these self-care children fare well. Yet unmonitored self-care children may face a variety of risks, including peer pressure to engage in antisocial conduct. Although after-school day-care programs are rare in the United States, there is evidence that well-managed ones that offer children meaningful activities can help to optimize developmental outcomes and lessen the chances that children of working mothers will engage in antisocial conduct.

Child abuse and neglect are related to conditions within the family, the community, and the larger culture. Abusers come from all social strata and walks of life, although many of them were themselves abused as children and are rather intolerant of normal behaviors that children display. Highly impulsive children and those who are irritable, emotionally unresponsive, or ill are more vulnerable to abuse than healthy, even-tempered children who are easy to care for. The incidence of child abuse is highest when stressed caregivers live in neighborhoods where they are isolated from sources of social support. The long-term consequences of abuse are often severe and long-lasting. Programs designed to assist abused children and their abusive parents have achieved some noteworthy success. However, we are still a long way from solving the problem.

Key Terms

authoritarian parenting [609]

authoritative parenting [609]

autonomy [614]

child abuse [630]

economic goal [601]

extended family [603]

family social system [602]

high-risk neighborhood [632]

indirect, or third party, effect [603]

nuclear family [602]

ordinal position [621]

Ounce of Prevention program [636]

parental control [607]

Parents Anonymous [636]

permissive parenting [609]

preliterate society [602]

reciprocal influence [602]

reconstituted families [606]

self-actualization goal [601]

self-care (or latchkey) children [629]

sibling rivalry [617]

single-parent family [605]

socialization [600]

survival goal [601]

uninvolved parenting [610]

warmth/hostility [607]

Beyond the Family: Extrafamilial Influences

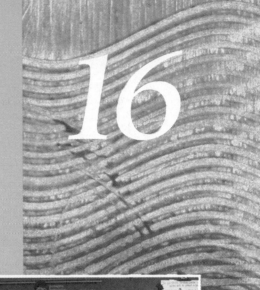

In Chapter 15, we focused on the family as an agent of socialization, looking at the ways that parents and siblings affect developing children. Although families have an enormous impact on their young, it is only a matter of time before other societal institutions begin to exert their influence. For example, infants and toddlers are often exposed to alternative caregivers and a host of new playmates when their working parents place them in some kind of day care. But even those toddlers who remain at home soon begin to learn about the outside world once they develop an interest in television. Between ages 2 and 5, many American children spend several hours of every weekday away from home as they attend nursery school. And by age 6 to 7, virtually all children in Western societies are going to elementary school, a setting that requires them to interact with other little people who are similar to themselves and to adjust to rules and regulations of a brave new world that may be very dissimilar to the home environment from which they came.

So as they mature, children are becoming increasingly familiar with the outside world and spend much less time under the watchful eyes of their parents. How do these experiences affect their lives? This is the issue to which we will now turn as we consider the impact of three **extrafamilial** agents of socialization: television, schools, and children's peer groups.

► THE EARLY WINDOW: EFFECTS OF TELEVISION ON CHILDREN AND YOUTH

It seems almost incomprehensible that the average American of only 50 years ago had never seen a television. Now more than 98% of American homes have one or more TV sets (Comstock, 1991), and children between the ages of 3 and 11 watch an average of two to four hours of TV a day (Huston et al., 1992; Liebert & Sprafkin, 1988). As we see in Figure 16-1, TV viewing begins in infancy, increases until about age 12, and then declines somewhat during adolescence—a trend that holds in Australia, Canada, and several European countries, as well as in the United States. By age 18, an average child born today will have spent more time watching television than in any other single activity except sleeping (Liebert & Sprafkin, 1988). Boys watch more TV than girls do, and ethnic minority children living in poverty are especially likely to be heavy viewers (Signorielli, 1991). Is all this time in front of the tube damaging to children's cognitive, social, and emotional development, as many critics have feared?

Television and Children's Lifestyles

One way to assess the global impact of television is to see whether children who have access to the medium differ systematically from those who live in remote areas not served by television. One such study of Canadian children gives some cause for concern (Corteen & Williams, 1986; Harrison & Williams, 1986). Prior to the coming of television, grade school children in "Notel" tested higher in both reading skills and creativity than did age-mates in other comparable Canadian towns served by television. But two to four years after television broadcasts became available in their village, these youngsters' creativity and reading proficiency scores had declined to the levels shown by children in the other towns. Moreover, the coming of television was associated with a dramatic rise in children's aggression during free play periods and with a sharp decline in adolescents' participation in community activities.

Although sobering, these findings may be somewhat unusual. Other investigators report that the biggest impact of the coming of television is to persuade children to substitute TV viewing for such other leisure activities as listening to the radio, reading comics, or going to movies (Huston et al., 1992; Liebert & Sprafkin, 1988), and TV viewers do not necessarily spend any less time playing with peers, interacting with parents, or doing homework than nonviewers do. Moreover, the introduction of tele-

extrafamilial influences: social agencies other than the family that influence a child's cognitive, social, and emotional development.

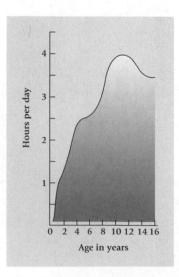

Figure 16-1
Average number of hours per day that American children and adolescents spend watching television.
From Liebert & Sprafkin, 1988.

vision to remote areas does not seem to affect children's cognitive development (Lonner et al., 1985); in fact, one review of the literature suggests that young children may actually learn a great deal of useful information from watching television, particularly educational programming (Anderson & Collins, 1988). So in moderate doses of 10–15 hours per week, television does not seem to deaden young minds or to impair one's social development. However, children who watch far more television than their peers do tend to perform less well in school (Fraser et al., 1987; Signorielli, 1991).

In sum, the overall effects of exposure to television do not appear to be as uniformly negative as some critics have charged unless children watch so much TV that they have little time left for more growth-inducing activities such as play or homework. But might we be missing something by focusing only on whether children have access to television? Shouldn't we be asking *what* they are watching? Viewing a steady diet of murder and carnage may have very different effects than watching educational programs such as *Sesame Street*. And, indeed it does!

Some Potentially Undesirable Effects of Television

Effects of Televised Violence

As early as 1954, complaints raised by parents, teachers, and experts in child development prompted Senator Estes Kefauver, then chairman of the Senate Subcommittee on Juvenile Delinquency, to question the need for violence in television programming. As it turns out, American television is incredibly violent. More than 80% of all prime-time television programs contain at least one incident of physical violence, and it is estimated that the average child of 16 has already witnessed more than 13,000 killings on television (Gerbner et al., 1986; Signorielli, 1991). In fact, some of the most violent TV programs are those designed for children, especially Saturday morning cartoons, which average more than 20 violent acts per hour (Signorielli, 1991).

Does TV violence instigate aggression? Even though many people have argued that the often-comical violence portrayed in children's television programming is unlikely to affect the behavior of young viewers, both anecdotal and research evidence suggests otherwise. Robert Liebert and Joyce Sprafkin (1988) provide several dramatic illustrations of how children have behaved in a violent or aggressive fashion after watching similar actions on television. Here is one example:

> In Los Angeles, a housemaid caught a 7-year-old boy in the act of sprinkling ground glass into the family's lamb stew. [The act] was purely experimental, having been inspired by curiosity to learn whether it would really work as well as it had on television (Liebert & Sprafkin, 1988, p. 9).

A large number of experimental studies and correlational surveys paint a similar picture: Children and adolescents who watch a lot of televised violence tend to be more aggressive than their classmates who watch little violence. Indeed, a positive relationship between the amount of violence that one observes on TV and aggressive behavior in naturalistic settings has been documented over and over with preschool, grade school, high school, and adult subjects in the United States and with grade school boys and girls in Australia, Canada, Finland, Great Britain, and Poland (Liebert & Sprafkin, 1988; Parke & Slaby, 1983). Moreover, longitudinal studies suggest that the link between TV violence and aggression is *reciprocal:* Viewing TV violence increases children's aggressive tendencies, which stimulates interest in violent programming, which promotes further aggression (Eron, 1982; Huesmann et al., 1984b). Although longitudinal surveys are correlational research and do *not* demonstrate causality, their results are at least consistent with the argument that early exposure to a heavy diet of televised violence can lead to the development of hostile, antisocial

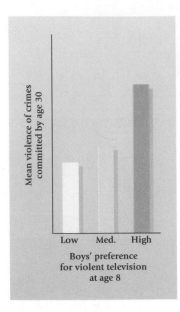

Figure 16-2
Relationship between boys' preference for violent TV programming at age 8 and mean violence of crimes committed by age 30.
Adapted from Huesmann, 1986.

habits that persist over time. Indeed, when Rowell Huesmann (1986) followed up on boys from an earlier study when they were 30 years old, he found that their earlier preferences for violent television at age 8 predicted not only their aggressiveness as adults, but their involvement in serious criminal activities as well (see Figure 16-2).

Other effects of televised violence. Even if children do not act out the aggression that they observe on television, they may be influenced by it nonetheless. For example, a steady diet of televised violence can instill **mean-world beliefs**—a tendency to view the world as a violent place inhabited by people who typically rely on aggressive solutions to their interpersonal problems (Comstock, 1991). Indeed, 7–9-year-olds who show the strongest preferences for violent television are the ones most likely to believe that violent shows are an accurate portrayal of everyday life.

In a similar vein, prolonged exposure to televised violence can *desensitize* children to violence—that is, make them less emotionally upset by violent acts and more willing to tolerate them in real life. Margaret Thomas and her colleagues (1977; Drabman & Thomas, 1974) have tested this **desensitization hypothesis** with 8–10-year-olds. Half the children in these studies watched a *violent* detective show, whereas children in a control condition watched a *nonviolent* but exciting film of a championship volleyball match. The viewers were hooked up to a physiograph that recorded their reactions to the films (which were equally arousing). Then each child was asked to watch a television monitor to ensure that two kindergarten children who were playing in another room didn't get into trouble while the experimenter was away at the principal's office. The experimenter took great care to explain to the child that he or she was to come to the principal's office for help should *anything* go wrong. Each child then observed the same videotaped sequence, in which the two kindergartners got into an intense battle. The tape ended with a loud crash that occurred shortly after the camera had been upset and the video had gone dead.

The results of these studies were quite clear: Children who had earlier watched the violent programming were much less physiologically aroused by what they believed to be a *real-life* altercation and were much slower to intervene or to seek help than were children who had watched nonviolent programming. Apparently, exposure to media violence does lessen a viewer's emotional sensitivity to later acts of aggression—a finding that may help to explain why children were more likely to *tolerate* aggression after witnessing violent acts on television.

Reducing the harmful effects of TV violence. Parents who are concerned about these negative effects can attempt to restrict their children's exposure to violent fare while interesting them in programs with prosocial or educational themes (Huston et al., 1992). Information about programs that experts consider too violent for children can be obtained from the *Foundation for the Improvement of Television* (Boston, MA; phone: [617] 523-6353).

Parents can also help their children to critically evaluate media violence by watching television with them and converting viewing sessions into positive learning experiences. For example, adults can point out subtleties that young viewers often miss, such as an aggressor's antisocial motives and intentions and the unpleasant consequences that perpetrators suffer as a result of their aggressive acts (Collins, Sobol, & Westby, 1981). When adults highlight this information while strongly criticizing a perpetrator's aggressive behavior, young children gain a much better understanding of media violence and are less affected by it, particularly if the adult also suggests how these perpetrators might have approached their problems in a more constructive way (Singer & Singer, 1990; St. Peters et al., 1991).

Television as a Source of Social Stereotypes

Another unfortunate effect that television may have on children is to reinforce a variety of potentially harmful social stereotypes. In Chapter 13, for example, we noted that sex-role stereotyping is common on television and that children who watch a

mean-world belief: a belief, fostered by televised violence, that the world is a more dangerous and frightening place than is actually the case.

desensitization hypothesis: the notion that people who watch a lot of media violence will become less aroused by aggression and more tolerant of violent and aggressive acts.

lot of commercial TV are likely to hold more traditional views of men and women than do their classmates who watch little television. Indeed, once television was introduced to the isolated Canadian village of "Notel," both boys and girls showed a sharp increase in sex-role stereotyping (Kimball, 1986). And it seems that the youngsters most affected by sex-role stereotypes on television are girls of above-average intelligence from middle-class homes—precisely the group that is otherwise least likely to hold traditionally sexist attitudes (Morgan, 1982).

Stereotyping of minorities. Prior to 1970, African Americans appeared infrequently on television and were usually cast in comical or subservient roles. Largely due to the influence of the civil rights movement, African Americans now appear on television in a much wider range of occupations, and their numbers approximate or exceed their proportions in the population. However, Latinos and other ethnic minorities remain underrepresented. And when non-African-American minorities do appear, they are usually portrayed in an unfavorable light, often cast as villains or victims (Associated Press, 1994c).

Surpringly, Liebert and Sprafkin's (1988) review found only one study (Graves, 1975) that has examined the effects of media stereotyping on children's racial attitudes. African-American and white children watched a series of cartoons in which African-American people were portrayed either positively (as competent, trustworthy, and hardworking) or negatively (as inept, lazy, and powerless). On a later test of racial attitudes, both African-American and white children became more favorable toward African Americans if they had seen the positive portrayals. But when the depictions of African Americans were negative, an interesting racial difference emerged: African-American children once again became more favorable in their racial attitudes, while whites became much *less* favorable. So the way that African Americans are portrayed on television may have a striking effect on the racial attitudes of non-African-American viewers, whereas the mere presence of African-American TV characters may be sufficient to produce more favorable attitudes toward African Americans among a young African-American audience.

Heavy exposure to media violence may blunt children's emotional reactions to real-life aggression and convince them that the world is a violent place populated mainly by hostile and aggressive people.

Countering stereotypes on television. Several attempts have been made to design programs for the younger set that counter inaccurate racial, sexual, and ethnic stereotypes while fostering goodwill among children from different social backgrounds. In 1969, *Sesame Street* led the way with positive portrayals of African Americans and Latinos. And one early study (Gorn, Goldberg, & Kanungo, 1976) found that white preschool children soon became more willing to include nonwhites in their play activities after watching episodes of *Sesame Street* that depicted minority youngsters as cheerful companions. Among the other shows that have been effective at fostering international awareness and reducing children's ethnic stereotypes are *Big Blue Marble*, a program designed to teach children about people in other countries, and *Vegetable Soup*, a show that portrays many ethnic groups in a favorable light (Liebert & Sprafkin, 1988).

Other programs designed to counteract gender stereotypes by showing girls and women excelling at traditionally masculine pastimes are enjoying at least some limited success (Johnston & Ettema, 1982; Rosenwasser, Lingenfelter, & Harrington, 1989). However, the effectiveness of these programs would undoubtedly be enhanced were they combined with the kinds of cognitive training efforts, described in Chapter 13, that directly undermine the erroneous *beliefs* on which gender stereotypes rest (Bigler & Liben, 1990; 1992).

Children's Reactions to Commercial Messages

In the United States, the average child is exposed to nearly 20,000 television commercials each year, many of which extol the virtues of toys, fast foods, and sugary treats that adults may not wish to purchase. Nevertheless, young children continue to ask for products that they have seen advertised on television, and conflicts often ensue when parents refuse to honor their requests (Atkin, 1978; Kunkel & Roberts,

1991). Young children may be so darn insistent because they rarely understand the manipulative (selling) intent of ads, often treating them more like public service announcements that are intended to be helpful and informative to viewers (Liebert & Sprafkin, 1988). By ages 9–11, most children realize that ads are designed to persuade and sell, and by 13–14, they have acquired a healthy skepticism about product claims and advertising in general (Linn, de Benedictis, & Delucchi, 1982; Robertson & Rossiter, 1974). Nevertheless, even adolescents are often persuaded by the ads they see, particularly if the product endorser is a celebrity or the appeals are deceptive and misleading (Huston et al., 1989).

Is it any wonder, then, that many parents are concerned about the impact of commercials on their children? Not only do children's ads often push products that are unsafe or of poor nutritional value, but the many ads for over-the-counter drugs and glamorous depictions of alcohol use may cause children to underestimate the consequences of such risky behaviors as drinking, self-medication, and drug use (Tinsley, 1992). Indeed, *Action for Children's Television*—an organization of parents that monitors and tries to change television's impact on children—considers the potentially harmful influence of TV commercials to be an even greater problem than televised violence! And policymakers are beginning to respond to the outcries, as evidenced by a recent law limiting the number of commercials on children's programs and requiring broadcasters to offer more educational programming or risk losing their licenses (Zigler & Finn-Stevenson, 1993).

Television as an Educational Tool

Thus far, we've cast a wary eye at television, talking mostly about its capacity to do harm. Yet, there is reason to believe that this "early window" could become a most effective way of teaching a number of valuable lessons if only its content were altered to convey such information. Let's examine some of the evidence to support this claim.

Educational Television and Children's Prosocial Behavior

Many TV programs—especially offerings such as *Sesame Street* and *Mister Rogers' Neighborhood* that are broadcast on public television—are designed, in part, to illustrate the benefits of such prosocial activities as cooperation, sharing, and comforting distressed companions. One major review of the literature found that young children who often watch prosocial programming do indeed become more prosocially inclined (Hearold, 1986). However, it is important to emphasize that merely parking young children in front of the tube to watch *Sesame Street, Mister Rogers,* or other programs with prosocial themes is not an effective training strategy, for this programming has few, if any, *lasting* benefits unless adults monitor the programs and encourage children to rehearse and enact the prosocial lessons they have learned (Friedrich & Stein, 1975; Friedrich-Cofer et al., 1979). Furthermore, young children are more likely to process and to act on the prosocial lessons that are broadcast when the programming is free of violent acts which will otherwise compete for their attention. But despite these important qualifications, it seems that the positive effects of prosocial programming greatly outweigh the negatives (Hearold, 1986), especially if adults encourage children to pay close attention to episodes that emphasize constructive methods of resolving interpersonal conflicts.

Television as a Contributor to Cognitive Development

In 1968, the U.S. government and a number of private foundations provided funds to create **Children's Television Workshop (CTW)**, an organization committed to producing TV programs that would hold children's interest and foster their intellectual development. CTW's first production, *Sesame Street,* became the world's most popular children's series—seen an average of three times a week by about half of America's preschool children and broadcast to nearly 50 other countries around the world (Liebert & Sprafkin, 1988). Targeted at 3–5-year-olds, *Sesame Street* attempts to foster important cognitive skills such as recognizing and discriminating numbers and

Children's Television Workshop (CTW): an organization committed to producing TV programs that hold children's interest and facilitate their social and intellectual development.

Children learn many valuable lessons from educational TV programs such as *Sesame Street*.

letters, counting, ordering and classifying objects, and solving simple problems. It was hoped that children from disadvantaged backgrounds would be much better prepared for school after viewing this programming on a regular basis. In 1969, *Sesame Street* was unveiled and became an immediate hit. But was it accomplishing its objectives?

Evaluating **Sesame Street.** During the first season that *Sesame Street* was broadcast, its impact was assessed by the Educational Testing Service. About 950 3–5-year-olds from five areas of the United States participated in the study. At the beginning of the project, children took a pretest that measured their cognitive skills and determined what they knew about letters, numbers, and geometric forms. At the end of the season, they took this test again to see what they had learned.

When the data were analyzed, it was clear that *Sesame Street* was achieving its objectives. As shown in Figure 16-3, children who watched *Sesame Street* the most

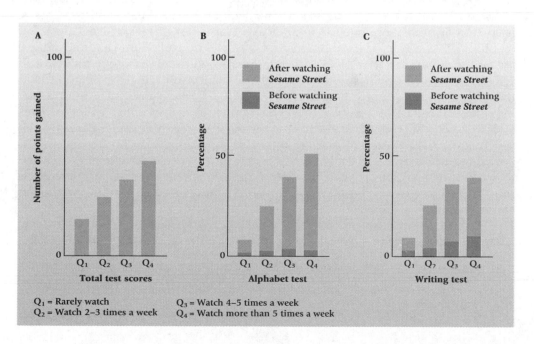

Figure 16-3
Relationship between amount of viewing of *Sesame Street* and children's abilities: **A,** improvement in total test scores for children grouped into different quartiles according to amount of viewing; **B,** percentage of children who recited the alphabet correctly, grouped according to quartiles of amount of viewing; **C,** percentage of children who wrote their first names correctly, grouped according to quartiles of amount of viewing. *From Liebert & Sprafkin, 1988.*

(groups Q^3 and Q^4, who watched four or more times a week) were the ones who showed the biggest improvements in their total test scores (panel A), their scores on the alphabet test (panel B), and their ability to write their names (panel C). The 3-year-olds posted bigger gains than the 5-year-olds, probably because the younger children knew less to begin with. The results of a second similar study that included only urban disadvantaged preschoolers paralleled those of the original study (Bogatz & Ball, 1972), and others have found that regular exposure to *Sesame Street* is associated with impressive gains in preschoolers' vocabularies and prereading skills as well (Rice et al., 1990). Finally, disadvantaged children who had been heavy viewers of *Sesame Street* were later rated by their first-grade teachers as better prepared for school and more interested in school activities than classmates who had rarely watched the program (Bogatz & Ball, 1972).

The Electric Company. In 1970 CTW consulted with reading specialists to create *The Electric Company*, a TV series designed to teach reading skills to young elementary school children. The programming was heavily animated, and to interest children in the content, well-known personalities such as Bill Cosby often appeared. The curriculum attempted to teach children the correspondence between letters (or letter combinations) and sounds—knowledge that should help them to decode words. Reading for meaning and syntax were also taught (Liebert & Sprafkin, 1988).

The success of *The Electric Company* was evaluated by administering a battery of reading tests to first- through fourth-grade children. Although home viewing had little or no effect on children's reading skills, those who watched *The Electric Company* at school attained significantly higher scores on the reading battery than nonviewers (Ball & Bogatz, 1973). In other words, *The Electric Company* was achieving many of its objectives when children watched the program with an adult, in this case the teacher, who could help them to apply what they had learned.[*]

Other educational programs. In recent years, CTW and other noncommercial producers have created children's programs to teach subjects such as math *(Square One)*, logical reasoning *(Think About)*, science *(3-2-1 Contact)*, and social studies *(Big Blue Marble)*. Although these offerings have been quite popular in the areas where they are broadcast, it remains to be seen how well they are achieving their objectives.

Criticisms of educational programming. One recurring criticism of educational television is that it is essentially a one-way medium in which the pupil is a passive recipient of information rather than an active constructor of knowledge. Critics fear that heavy TV viewing (be it educational TV or otherwise) will blunt children's curiosity, and they believe that a child's viewing time would be more profitably spent in active, imaginative activities under the guidance of an adult (Singer & Singer, 1990). Indeed, we've seen that programs such as *The Electric Company* (as well as those stressing prosocial behavior) are unlikely to achieve their objectives unless children watch *with an adult* who encourages them to apply what they have learned. Perhaps John Wright and Aletha Huston (1983) are correct in arguing that television's potential as a teaching device will be greatly enhanced once it becomes *computer integrated* and interactive, thereby allowing the viewer to be more actively involved in the learning process (see Box 16-1 for some early returns on the impact of computer technologies on developing children).

Although *Sesame Street* was primarily targeted at disadvantaged preschoolers in an attempt to narrow the intellectual gap between these youngsters and their advantaged

---

[*]In 1985, *The Electric Company* went off the air. However, episodes are still available to schools on videocassette for classroom use.

BOX 16-1
Child Development in the Computer Age

*L*ike television, the computer is a modern technology that has the potential to influence children's learning and lifestyles. But in what ways? If we take our cues from Hollywood, we might be led to believe that young computer "hackers" will grow up to be *brainy* but socially inept misfits like those curiously lovable characters from the movie *Revenge of the Nerds.* Indeed, many educators believe that the microcomputer is an effective supplement to classroom instruction—a tool that helps children to learn more and to have more fun doing so. And parents, many of whom may be "computer illiterates," are nevertheless rushing out to buy home computers, prompted, in part, by TV ads suggesting that they may be undermining their child's chances of success if they don't. Do computers really help children to learn, think, or create? Is there a danger that young "hackers" will become so enamored of computer technology and so reclusive or socially unskilled that they risk being ostracized by their peers?

Only recently have researchers begun to explore the impact of computers on children's lives, and the educational benefits of this new technology seem most promising indeed. For example, elementary school children do learn more and seem to enjoy school more when they receive at least some *computer-assisted instruction* (CAI) in the classroom (Clements & Nastasi, 1992; Lepper & Gurtner, 1989). Many CAI programs are simply drills that begin at a student's current level of mastery and present increasingly difficult problems, often intervening with hints or clues when progress breaks down. Other, more elaborate forms of CAI are guided tutorials that rely less on drill and more on the discovery of important concepts and principles in the context of highly motivating, thought-provoking games. Regular use of drill programs during the early grades does seem to improve children's basic reading and math skills, particularly for disadvantaged students and other low achievers (Clements & Nastasi, 1992; Lepper & Gurtner, 1989). Moreover, the benefits of CAI are strongest when children receive at least some exposure to highly involving tutorials as well as simple drills.

Douglas Clements (1990; 1991) believes that teaching students to *program* a computer has many advantages beyond those associated with the performance of computer-assisted academic exercises. In his own research, Clements gave first- and third-graders 22 weeks of training in *Logo,* a computer language that allows children to take drawings they've made and translate them into input statements so that they eventually succeed at reproducing their drawings on the computer monitor. Of what benefit is this kind of problem-solving activity? Although Clements's Logo children performed no better on achievement tests than agemates who participated in the more usual kinds of computer-assisted academic exercises, Logo users scored higher on tests of Piagetian concrete-operational abilities, metacognition (knowledge about thinking and thought

processes), and creativity. These data are intriguing, for they suggest that computers are useful not only for teaching children academic lessons but for helping them to *think* in new ways as well.

Aside from its instructional function, the computer is also a *tool* that can further children's basic writing and communications skills (Lepper & Gurtner, 1989). For example, word-processing programs eliminate the drudgery of handwriting and increase the likelihood that students will edit, revise, and polish their work (Clements & Nastasi, 1992). And it seems that computer-prompted metacognitive strategies can also help students to organize their thoughts into more coherent essays (Lepper & Gurtner, 1989).

But what about the social consequences? Are young computer users likely to become reclusive misfits who prefer solitary activities to playing with peers? Apparently not. Children often use home computers to attract playmates, as if the machine were like any other desirable toy; and classroom research reveals that children learning to solve problems by computer engage in more collaborative activities with classmates than students who are working on traditional assignments (Crook, 1992; Kee, 1986; Weinstein, 1991). In sum, computers seem to promote rather than inhibit social interaction. (Of course, it is possible that some withdrawn children with poor social skills could become even more reclusive should they find that their nonevaluative computer is more "user friendly" than most peers.)

(continued)

Learning by computer is an effective complement to classroom instruction and an experience that can teach young children to collaborate.

BOX 16-1 *(continued)*
Child Development in the Computer Age

Clearly, there is much more that we need to learn about the impacts of computers on developing children. For example, researchers have yet to determine whether the violent computer games that are so widely available might instigate aggression or cultivate aggressive habits in the same ways that televised violence does. Others are convinced that the computer revolution may leave some groups of children behind, lacking in skills required in our increasingly computer-dependent society. For example, children from economically disadvantaged families may be exposed to computers at school but are unlikely to have them at home (Lepper & Gurtner, 1989). Also, boys are far more likely than girls to take an interest in computers and to sign up for computer courses, probably because computers are often viewed as involving mathematics, a traditionally masculine subject, and many available computer games are designed with boys in mind (Lepper, 1985; Ogletree & Williams, 1990).

Perhaps computers, like television sets, will turn out to be either a positive or a negative force on development, depending on how they are used. Outcomes may be less than desirable if a child's primary use of the machine is to hole up by himself in the bedroom, zapping mutant aliens from space. But the news may be rather positive indeed for children who use computers to learn, to think in new ways, and to collaborate with siblings and peers.

peers, early research suggested that children from advantaged backgrounds were the ones who were more likely to watch the program. Thus, it was feared that *Sesame Street* might actually end up *widening* the intellectual and academic gaps between advantaged and disadvantaged youth (Cook et al., 1975). Yet, this particular concern now appears unfounded. Later research suggests that children from disadvantaged backgrounds are not only watching *Sesame Street* about as often as their advantaged peers (Pinon, Huston, & Wright, 1989) but are learning just as much from it (Rice et al., 1990). Moreover, children benefit from viewing this series even when they watch it alone (Rice et al., 1990). So *Sesame Street* appears to be a potentially valuable resource for *all* preschool children and a true educational bargain that costs about a penny a day per viewer (Palmer, 1984). The formidable task lies ahead: convincing more parents that episodes of *Sesame Street* (and other educational programs) are indeed rewarding and valuable experiences that they and their children should not be missing.

Should Television Be Used to Socialize Children?

Although television is often criticized as an instigator of violence or an "idiot box" that undermines the intellectual curiosity of our young, we have seen that the medium can have many positive effects on children's social, emotional, and intellectual development. Should we now harness television's potential as an "early window" for socializing our children? Many developmentalists think so, although not everyone agrees, as we see in the following newspaper account of a conference on behavioral control through the media. To set the stage, the conference participants were reacting to the work of Dr. Robert M. Liebert, a psychologist who had produced some 30-second TV spots to teach children cooperative solutions to conflict. Here is part of the account that appeared in the *New York Times:*

> The outburst that followed Liebert's presentation flashed around the conference table. Did he believe that he had a right to . . . impose values on children? Should children . . . be taught cooperation? Did ghetto kids perhaps need to be taught to slug it out in order to survive in this society? Was it not . . . immoral to create a TV ad . . . to influence kids' behavior? Liebert was accused of . . . manipulation and even brainwashing. One would have thought he had proposed setting up Hitler Youth Camps on Sesame Street.

However, I understand why the hackles had gone up around the . . . table. I am one of those people who [are] terrified of manipulation. A Skinnerian world filled with conditioned people scares the daylights out of me—even if those people do hate war and . . . love their fellow man. [Behavior control through technology may come] . . . at the cost of our freedom (Rivers, 1974, quoted in Liebert & Sprafkin, 1988, pp. 243–244).

The concern of those conference participants is perhaps understandable, for television is often used as a means of political indoctrination in many countries. And is the use of television for socialization not a subtle form of brainwashing? Perhaps it is. However, one could argue that television in this country already serves as a potent agent of socialization and that much of what children see in the media helps to create attitudes and to instigate actions that the majority of us may not condone. Perhaps the question we should be asking is "Can we somehow alter television to make it a more effective agent of socialization that joins forces with parents and educators in helping children to grow in positive directions?" Surely we can, although it remains to be seen whether we will.

 THE SCHOOL AS A SOCIALIZATION AGENT

Of all the formal institutions that children encounter in their lives away from home, few have as much opportunity to influence their development as the schools they attend. Obviously, students acquire a great deal of knowledge and many academic skills at school. But schooling also promotes cognitive and **metacognitive** growth by teaching children a variety of rules, strategies, and problem-solving skills (including an ability to concentrate and an appreciation for abstraction) that they can apply to many different kinds of information (Ceci, 1991). Consider what Frederick Morrison (1991) found when comparing the cognitive performance of children who had just made the age cutoff for entering first grade with that of youngsters who had just missed the cutoff and had spent the year in kindergarten. When tested at the end of the school year, the first-graders outperformed the nearly *identically aged* kindergartners in memory, language, and reading skills (see also Varnhagen et al., 1994). In a similar study of fourth-, fifth-, and sixth-graders in Israel (Cahan & Cohen, 1989), children at any given grade performed at higher levels on a variety of intellectual tests than their chronological *age-mates* in the next lower grade—another indication that intellectual performance is influenced, in part, by the *amount* of schooling one has had (see also Ceci, 1991).

In addition to the cognitive and academic challenges that they provide, schools expose children to an **informal curriculum** that teaches them how to fit into their culture. Students are expected to obey rules, cooperate with their classmates, respect authority, and become good citizens. Today, we see the schools providing information and moral guidance in an attempt to combat almost every social problem affecting children, including racism, teenage sex, and substance abuse (Comer, 1991; Linney & Seidman, 1989). And much of the influence that peers may have on developing children occurs in the context of school-related activities and may depend very critically on the type of school that a child attends and the quality of a child's school experiences. So it is quite proper to think of the school as a socialization agent that is likely to affect children's social and emotional development as well as imparting knowledge and helping to prepare students for a job and economic self-sufficiency.

The vast majority of children in our society now begin their school careers well before age 6—attending kindergarten as 5-year-olds and, in many cases, going to nursery school or day care before that (Clarke-Stewart, 1993). Is this a healthy trend? As we will see in Box 16-2, there are advantages as well as some possible disadvantages associated with early entry into a school-like environment.

metacognition: one's knowledge about cognition and about the regulation of cognitive activities.

informal curriculum: noncurricular objectives of schooling such as teaching children to cooperate, respect authority, obey rules, and become good citizens.

BOX 16-2
Should Preschoolers Attend School?

*I*n recent years, children in the United States have begun their schooling earlier and earlier. Not only is kindergarten compulsory in most states, but there is talk of requiring school for 4-year-olds (Zigler, 1987). And already many preschoolers spend 6–8-hour days in day-care settings or nursery schools that have a strong academic emphasis and attempt to ready them for the classroom. Indeed, some wealthy parents will do almost anything to get their youngsters into the "right" settings, including enrolling their toddlers in courses that prepare them for admission interviews with exclusive nursery schools (Geist, 1985)!

Is attending preschool beneficial? Developmentalists such as Edward Zigler (1987) and David Elkind (1981b), author of *The Hurried Child*, express some concerns, fearing that the current push for earlier and earlier education may be going too far. They feel that many young children today are not given enough time simply to be children—to play and socialize as they choose. Elkind even worries that children may lose their self-initiative and enjoyment of learning when their lives are orchestrated by parents who incessantly push them to achieve.

One study seems to confirm Elkind's concerns (Hyson, Hirsch-Pasek, & Rescorla, 1989). Four-year-olds in preschools with a very strong academic emphasis gained an initial advantage in such basic academic skills as knowledge of letters and numbers but had lost it by the end of kinder-

garten. What's more, they proved to be *less* creative, *more* anxious about tests, and *more* negative toward school than children who attended preschool programs with a social rather than an academic emphasis. So it may well be possible to overdo an emphasis on academics in the preschool years.

On the other hand, preschool programs that offer a healthy mix of play and academic skill-building activities can be very beneficial to young children, especially to disadvantaged children. Children who attend high-quality preschools often develop social skills at an earlier age than those who remain at home (Clarke-Stewart, 1993). And, although most children who attend preschool classes are no more or less intellectually advanced than those who remain at home, *disadvantaged* preschoolers who attend programs designed to prepare them for school do display more cognitive growth and achieve more success in school than other disadvantaged youngsters (Campbell & Ramey, 1994; Lee et al., 1990). So, as long as preschool programs allow plenty of time for play and group social interactions, they can help children from all social backgrounds to acquire social and communications skills, as well as an appreciation of rules and routines, that will smooth the transition from individual learning at home to group learning in an elementary school classroom (Zigler & Finn-Stevenson, 1993).

Determinants of Effective (and Ineffective) Schooling

One of the first questions that parents often ask when searching for a residence in a new town is "What are the schools like here?" or "Where should we live so that our children will get the best education?" These concerns reflect the common belief that some schools are "better" or "more effective" than others. But are they?

Michael Rutter (1983) certainly thinks so. According to Rutter, **effective schools** are those that promote academic achievement, social skills, polite and attentive behavior, positive attitudes toward learning, low absenteeism, continuation of education beyond the age at which attendance is mandatory, and acquisition of skills that will enable students to find and hold a job. Rutter argues that some schools are more successful than others at accomplishing these objectives, regardless of the students' racial, ethnic, or socioeconomic backgrounds. Let's examine the evidence for this claim.

In one study, Rutter and his associates (1979) conducted extensive interviews and observations in 12 high schools serving lower- to lower-middle-class populations in London, England. As the children entered these schools, they were given a battery of achievement tests to measure their prior academic accomplishments. At the end of high school, the pupils took another major exam to assess their academic progress. Other information, such as attendance records and teacher ratings of classroom behavior, was also available. When the data were analyzed, Rutter et al. found that the 12 schools clearly differed in "effectiveness": Students from the "better" schools exhibited fewer problem behaviors, attended school more regularly, and made more academic progress than students from the less effective schools. We get some idea of the importance of these "schooling effects" from Figure 16-4. The "bands" on the graph refer to the pupils' academic accomplishments *at the time they entered* high

effective schools: schools that are generally successful at achieving curricular and noncurricular objectives, regardless of the racial, ethnic, or socioeconomic background of the student population.

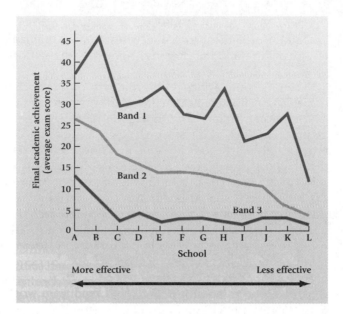

Figure 16-4
Average level of academic achievement in secondary school as a function of initial achievement at the time of entry (bands 1–3) and the school that pupils were attending (schools A–L). Note that pupils in all three bands performed at higher levels on this final academic assessment if they attended the more effective schools. Moreover, students in band 2 performed like band-1 students in the more effective schools but like band-3 students in the least effective schools.
From Rutter, Maughan, Mortimore, & Ouston, 1979.

school (band 3, low achievers; band 1, high achievers). In all three bands, students attending the "more effective" schools outperformed those in the "less effective" schools on the final assessment of academic achievement. Even more revealing is the finding that the initially poor students (band 3) who attended the "better" schools ended up scoring just as high on this final index of academic progress as the initially good (band 1) students who attended the least effective schools. Similar findings were obtained in other large studies of elementary and high schools in the United States. Even after controlling for important variables such as the racial composition and socioeconomic backgrounds of the student bodies and the type of communities served, some elementary schools were found to be much more "effective" than others (Brookover et al., 1979; Hill, Foster, & Gendler, 1990).

So the school that children attend can make a difference. And you may be surprised by some of the factors that do and do not have a bearing on how "effective" a school is.

Some Misconceptions about Effective Schooling

There are several variables that really contribute very little to a school's effectiveness, even though many people may think they are important. Let's briefly review some of the common misconceptions about effective schooling.

Monetary support. Surprising as it may seem, a school's *level* of support has little to do with the quality of the education that students receive. The amount of money spent per pupil, the number of books in the school library, teachers' salaries, and teachers' academic credentials play only a minor role in determining student outcomes (Rutter, 1983). To be sure, some minimal level of support must exist for a school to accomplish its objectives. But as long as adequate support is maintained, merely adding more dollars to the school's budget will not substantially improve the quality of education that students receive (Rutter, 1983).

School and class size. Another factor that has relatively little to do with a school's effectiveness is average class size: In typical elementary and secondary school classes ranging from 20 to 40 students, class size has little or no effect on academic achievement (Cooper, 1989; Odden, 1990). However, classes smaller than 15–20 pupils are beneficial in the primary grades (kindergarten through grade 3), and primary students in larger classes—especially disadvantaged or low-ability students—do much better in reading and math when they are tutored part of the day in smaller study groups

(Odden, 1990; Slavin, 1989). So if a school district has money available to hire a few additional instructors, the wisest course might be to devote these "personnel resources" to the primary grades—precisely the settings in which smaller classes promote academic achievement.

There is some evidence that the size of one's school affects older students' participation in structured extracurricular activities—settings in which such aspects of the "informal curriculum" as cooperation, fair play, and healthy attitudes toward competition are likely to be stressed. Roger Barker and Paul Gump (1964) surveyed the activities of high school students in schools ranging in size from 100 pupils to more than 2,000. Although the larger schools offered more extracurricular activities to their students, it was the pupils in the smaller schools who were (1) more heavily involved, (2) more likely to hold positions of responsibility or leadership, and (3) more satisfied with their after-school experiences. Moreover, there were few "isolates" in small schools, where almost everyone was encouraged to join in one or more activities. By contrast, students in larger schools received less encouragement to participate; they could easily get lost in the crowd and often felt isolated or even alienated from their peers—feelings that may help to explain why the incidence of truancy, delinquency, substance abuse, and dropping out of school is higher in large schools than in smaller ones (Dusek, 1991; Linney & Seidman, 1989). So to the extent that a sense of belonging and the lessons stemming from extracurricular activities are important aspects of schooling, there may be some clear advantages to attending smaller schools.

Ability tracking. The merits of **ability tracking**—a procedure in which students are grouped by IQ or academic achievement and then taught in classes made up of students of comparable "ability"—have been debated for years. Some educators believe that students learn more when surrounded by peers of equal ability. Others argue that ability tracking undermines the self-esteem of lower-ability students and contributes to their poor academic achievement and high dropout rate.

In his review of the literature, Rutter (1983) found that neither ability tracking nor mixed-ability teaching has decisive advantages: Both procedures are common in highly effective and less effective schools. Yet, recent research suggests some qualifications to this conclusion. Apparently, ability tracking does widen the gap between high and low achievers (Slavin, 1987), whereas mixed-ability instruction in elementary and middle schools seems to promote the academic achievement of less capable students without undermining the performance of their more capable peers (Associated Press, 1994c; Kulik & Kulik, 1992). Ability tracking *can* be beneficial, especially to high-ability students, *if* they are exposed to a curriculum tailored to their learning needs (Kulik & Kulik, 1992). However, lower-ability students are unlikely to benefit and may well suffer if they are stigmatized as "dummies" and are not challenged academically, or if they are denied access to the more effective instructors who might help them to master such challenges (Kulik & Kulik, 1992; Rutter, 1983).

Classroom organization. Chances are that you were educated in **traditional classrooms** where the seats were arranged in neat rows facing the teacher, who lectured or gave demonstrations at a desk or a chalkboard. In a traditional classroom, the curriculum is highly structured. Normally, students will all be studying the same subject at a given moment, and they are expected to interact with the teacher rather than with one another. One potential drawback to this classroom arrangement is that teachers end up interacting with some students more than others. As illustrated in Figure 16-5, students who sit "front and center" are more likely to catch the teacher's eye and to participate in classroom discussions (Adams & Biddle, 1970).

Over the past 30 years, many classrooms have become less formal or structured. "Open education" is a philosophy based on the premise that children are curious explorers who will achieve more by becoming *actively involved* in the learning process than by simply listening to a teacher recite facts, figures, and principles. In an **open classroom,** the children rarely do the same thing all at once. A more typical scenario

ability tracking: the educational practice of grouping students according to ability and then educating them in classes with students of comparable educational or intellectual standing.

traditional classroom: a classroom arrangement in which all pupils sit facing an instructor, who normally teaches one subject at a time by lecturing or giving demonstrations.

open classroom: a less structured classroom arrangement in which there is a separate area for each educational activity and children distribute themselves around the room, working individually or in small groups.

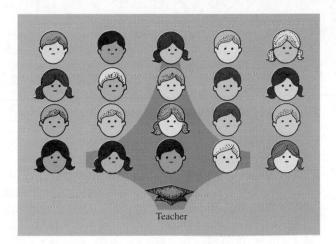

Figure 16-5
In a traditional classroom, the students in the shaded area are more likely to capture teachers' attention and to participate in classroom activities than their classmates who sit outside this "zone of activity."

is for students to distribute themselves around the room, working individually or in small groups at reading stories, playing word games, solving math puzzles, creating art, or working on the class's science project. And rather than being centers of attention or central authority figures, teachers in open classrooms help children to decide what they will learn about and circulate around the room, guiding and instructing students in response to their individual needs (Minuchin & Shapiro, 1983).

There are some clear social and emotional advantages associated with the open classroom: Students express more positive attitudes about school, are more self-directed in pursuing learning objectives, and display a greater ability to cooperate with classmates while creating fewer disciplinary problems than students in traditional classrooms (Minuchin & Shapiro, 1983). However, many investigators find no difference in the academic performance of students in open and traditional classrooms (Minuchin & Shapiro, 1983), and others have concluded that students actually learn more in a *traditional* classroom whenever the subject matter involves learning abstract concepts that may be difficult for students to grasp on their own (Good, 1979; Slavin, as cited in Associated Press, 1994a). After reviewing much of this literature, Rutter (1983, p. 21) concluded that "debates of whether 'open classrooms' are better than traditional [ones] . . . or whether formal methods are preferable to 'informal' methods . . . are misplaced. Neither system has overall superiority, but both include elements of good practice."

Factors that Contribute to Effective Schooling

Composition of the student body. To some extent, the "effectiveness" of a school is a function of what it has to work with. On average, academic achievement is lowest in schools with a preponderance of economically disadvantaged students (Brookover et al., 1979; Rutter, 1983), and it appears that *any* child is likely to make more academic progress if taught in a school with a higher concentration of intellectually capable peers. However, this does *not* mean that a school is only as good as the students it serves, for many schools that draw heavily from disadvantaged minority populations are highly effective at motivating students and preparing them for jobs or higher education (Reynolds, 1992).

The scholastic atmosphere of successful schools. So what is it about the learning environment of some schools that allows them to accomplish so much? Reviews of the literature (Linney & Seidman, 1989; Reynolds, 1992; Rutter, 1983) point to the following values and practices that characterize effective schools.

1. *Academic emphasis.* Effective schools have a clear focus on academic goals. Children are regularly assigned homework, which is checked, corrected, and discussed with them. Effective secondary schools require all students to complete a basic, or "core," curriculum rather than allowing pupils a great deal

of latitude in setting learning objectives (Hill et al., 1990). Teachers expect a lot from their students and devote a high proportion of their time to active teaching and planning lessons so that their expectations can be met.

2. *Classroom management.* In effective schools, teachers spend little time setting up equipment, handing out papers, and dealing with disciplinary problems. Lessons begin and end on time. Pupils are told exactly what is expected of them and receive clear and unambiguous feedback about their academic performance. The classroom atmosphere is comfortable; all students are actively encouraged to work to the best of their abilities, and ample praise acknowledges good work.

3. *Discipline.* In effective schools, the staff is firm in enforcing rules and does so on the spot rather than sending offenders off to the principal's office. Rarely do instructors resort to physical sanctions (slapping or spanking), which contribute to truancy, defiance, and a tense classroom atmosphere.

4. *Teamwork.* Effective schools have faculties that work as a team, jointly planning curricular objectives and monitoring student progress, under the guidance of a principal who provides active, energetic leadership.

In sum, the effective school environment is a *comfortable* but *businesslike* setting in which academic successes are expected and students are *motivated* to learn. After reviewing the literature, Rutter (1983) concluded that the task of motivating students is of critical importance, for "in the long run, good pupil outcomes were [nearly always] dependent on pupils *wanting* to participate in the educational process" (p. 23).

The "goodness of fit" between students and schools. There is another important point to make about effective schooling: Characteristics of the student and of the school environment often *interact* to affect student outcomes—a phenomenon Lee Cronbach and Richard Snow (1977) call **aptitude-treatment interaction (ATI)**. Over the years, much educational research has been based on the assumption that a particular teaching method, philosophy of education, or organizational system will prove superior for all students, regardless of their abilities, personalities, and cultural backgrounds. This assumption is often wrong. Instead, many approaches to education are highly effective with *some* kinds of students but quite ineffective with others. The secret to being effective is to find an appropriate fit between learners and educational practices.

For example, teachers tend to get the most out of *high-ability, middle-class* students by moving at a quick pace and insisting on high standards of performance—that is, by challenging these students (Brophy, 1979). By contrast, *low-ability* and *disadvantaged* students often respond more favorably to a teacher who motivates them by being warm and encouraging rather than intrusive and demanding.

Awareness of students' *cultural* traditions is also crucial for designing an effective instructional program. North American students of European ancestry come from cultures that stress individual learning, perhaps making them especially well-suited for the individual mastery expectations that are emphasized in traditional classrooms. By contrast, ethnic Hawaiians and other students from cultures that stress cooperation and collaborative approaches to learning often founder in traditional classrooms. They pay little attention to the teacher or their lessons and spend a lot of time seeking the attention of classmates—behaviors that are perceived by teachers as reflecting their lack of interest in school (Tharp, 1989). Yet, when instruction is made more culturally compatible for these youngsters, by having teachers circulate among small groups, instructing each group and encouraging group members to pull together and assist each other to achieve learning objectives, Hawaiian children become much more enthusiastic about school and achieve much more as well (see Figure 6-6).

Unfortunately, young adolescents from any social background may begin to lose interest in academics if they experience a mismatch between their school environments and their changing developmental needs—a point well illustrated by the findings presented in Box 16-3.

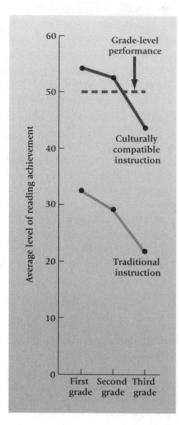

Figure 16-6
Reading achievement of ethnic Hawaiian first- through third-grade students who received traditional or culturally compatible classroom instruction. The students who received culturally compatible instruction read at grade level, whereas those receiving traditional instruction read far below grade level.
Adapted from Tharp & Gallimore, 1988.

aptitude-treatment interaction (ATI): phenomenon whereby characteristics of the student and of the school environment interact to affect student outcomes, such that any given educational practice may be effective with some students, but not with others.

BOX 16-3
On the Difficult Transition to Secondary Schools

For some time now, educators have been concerned about a number of negative changes that often occur when students make the transition from elementary school to junior high school: loss of interest in school, declining grades, and increased troublemaking, to name a few (Eccles et al., 1993; Seidman et al., 1994). Why is this a treacherous move?

One reason that the transition is difficult is because young adolescents are often experiencing major physical and psychological changes at the same time they are being asked to switch schools. Roberta Simmons and Dale Blyth (1987), for example, found that girls who were reaching puberty at the same time they were making the transition from sixth grade in an elementary school to seventh grade in a junior high school were more likely to experience drops in self-esteem and other negative changes than girls who remained in a K–8 school during this vulnerable period. Could it be, then, that more adolescents would remain interested in school if they did not have to change schools at the very same time they are experiencing pubertal changes? This has been part of the rationale for the development of *middle schools,* schools serving grades 6 to 8 and designed to make the transition from elementary school to high school easier for early adolescents. Middle schools are now more common than junior high schools in the United States (see Braddock & McPartland, 1993).

Yet Jacquelynne Eccles and her colleagues (Eccles, Lord, & Midgley, 1991; Eccles et al., 1993) have shown that students do not necessarily find the transition to middle school any easier than the transition to junior high school. This has led them to suspect that it is not as important *when* adolescents make a school change as *what* their new school is like.

Moving from small, close-knit elementary schools to highly bureaucratic and impersonal secondary schools is stressful for adolescents, many of whom lose interest in academics and become more susceptible to peer-group influences.

Specifically, they have offered a "goodness of fit" hypothesis stating that the transition to a new school is likely to be especially difficult when the new school, whether a junior high or middle school, is ill-matched to the developmental needs of early adolescents.

Eccles and her associates have found that the transition to junior high school often involves going from a small school with close student-teacher relationships, a good deal of choice regarding learning activities, and reasonable discipline to a larger, more bureaucratized environment where student-teacher relationships are impersonal, good grades are harder to come by, opportunities for choice are limited, assignments are not very intellectually stimulating, and discipline is rigid—all this at a time when adolescents are seeking more rather than less autonomy and are more intellectually capable.

Eccles and others have demonstrated that the "fit" between developmental needs and school environment is indeed an important influence on adolescent adjustment to school. In one study (Mac Iver & Reuman, 1988), the transition to junior high brought about a decline in intrinsic interest in learning mainly among students who wanted more involvement in classroom decisions but ended up with fewer such opportunities than they had had in elementary school. Moreover, the lack of close, supportive relations with teachers makes many autonomy-seeking adolescents in impersonal secondary schools much more susceptible to peer values and influences—which they often perceived as antisocial (Seidman et al., 1994). Finally, a third study (Midgley, Feldlaufer, & Eccles, 1989) illustrates just how important a *good* fit between students and school environments can be. Students experienced negative changes in their attitudes toward mathematics if their transition to junior high resulted in less personal and supportive relations with math teachers; but for those few students whose transition to junior high involved gaining more supportive teachers than they had in elementary school, interest in academics actually *increased.*

The message? Declines in academic motivation and performance are not inevitable as students move from elementary to secondary schools. These declines occur primarily when the fit between student and school environment goes from good to poor. How might we improve the fit? The Carnegie Council on Adolescent Development (1989) advises secondary schools to reorganize into smaller communities for learning in order to provide young adolescents with social support and to make them feel less invisible, or anonymous. The key elements of this "communities" approach involves creating (1) "schools within schools," in which subsets of students and teachers grouped together as "teams" become more familiar with (and, hopefully, supportive of) each other and (2) small group advisories to ensure that every student has access to at least one adult who knows him or her well.

In sum, the "goodness of fit" between students and their classroom environments is a crucial aspect of effective schooling (Lerner et al., 1989). Education that is highly individualized—that is, tailored to suit students' cultural backgrounds, personal characteristics, and developmental needs—is much more likely to succeed.

Do Our Schools Meet the Needs of All Our Children?

From the beginning, the American public school system was intended to be an instrument of social change. The push for compulsory education in the United States arose not so much from a desire to produce an educated workforce (most people were then employed as farmers or as unskilled laborers and required little education) as from the need to "Americanize" an immigrant population—to teach them the values and principles on which the country was founded so as to assimilate them into the mainstream of American society (Rudolph, 1965). Thus, public schools in the United States have traditionally been middle-class, white institutions staffed by middle-class, white instructors who preach middle-class, white values.

However, more and more of the students educated in our public schools come from nonwhite social backgrounds; in fact, a *majority* of students in California's public schools now belong to various "minority" groups (Garcia, 1993). How well are minority students being served by our schools? And how well are today's schools meeting the needs of students with developmental disabilities and bringing them into the mainstream of education?

Ethnic Differences in Academic Achievement

Many African-American, Latino, and Native American children earn poorer grades and make lower scores on standardized achievement tests than their Anglo-American classmates, whereas Asian Americans (at least Japanese and Chinese Americans) tend to outperform Anglo students at school (Slaughter-Defoe et al., 1990; Sue & Okazaki, 1990). These racial and ethnic differences in academic achievement are still found even after group differences in socioeconomic status are controlled, and they are not merely the product of group differences in intellectual ability (Alexander & Entwistle, 1988; Sue & Okazaki, 1990). Why do such differences exist?

Parental attitudes and involvement. One widely held notion is that parents of underachieving ethnic minority students do not value education or encourage school achievement as much as other parents do. This is a serious misconception. African-American and Latino parents seem to value education at least as much as Anglo-American parents do (Steinberg et al., 1992), and they are actually *more* likely to appreciate the value of homework, competency testing, and a longer school day (Stevenson, Chen, & Uttal, 1990). However, minority parents are often less knowledgeable about the school system and less involved in many school activities, and this lack of participation may partially counteract their message that school is important. But when minority parents *are* highly involved in school activities, their children feel more competent about mastering academic challenges and tend to do well in school (Connell, Spencer, & Aber, 1994; Slaughter-Defoe et al., 1990). So active parental involvement can make a big difference.

Patterns of parenting and peer influences. Although minority parents do play an important role in their children's school achievement, we cannot fully appreciate their contribution without also understanding how peers influence academic achievement. Lawrence Steinberg and his colleagues (1992) have conducted a large-scale study of school achievement among African-American, Latino, Asian-American, and Anglo-American high school students. They find that academic success and good personal adjustment are usually associated with *authoritative parenting* (the warm and firm yet democratic style discussed in Chapter 15). Interestingly, African-American parents typically provide authoritative parenting. But this positive influence on academic

Children are more likely to do well in school if their parents value education and are interested and involved in school activities.

achievement is often undermined by African-American peers, who devalue academic achievement and force many African-American students to choose between academic success and peer acceptance (see also Ogbu, 1990).

Latino parents tend to be strict and authoritarian, rather than authoritative. Thus, Steinberg and his colleagues suggest that Latino students may have relatively few opportunities at home to act autonomously and acquire decision-making skills that would serve them well in school. And they, like African-American students, tend to associate with peers who do not strongly value academics and who undercut parents' efforts to promote academic achievement. By contrast, Anglo-American students are more likely than either African-American or Latino students to have *both* authoritative parents and peer support for education working in their favor.

Interestingly, high-achieving Asian-American students often experience restrictive, authoritarian parenting at home. However, this controlling pattern, coupled with the very high achievement standards that many Asian-American parents set for their children, actually fosters academic success. Why? Because Asian-American children are also taught from a very early age to be loyal and to obey their elders, who have a duty to train them to be socially responsible and competent human beings (Chao, 1994). Given this kind of socialization in Asian-American homes, we should not be surprised to learn that the Asian-American peer group strongly endorses education and encourages academic success. And although Asian-American students are no more likely than other students to believe that getting an education will pay off in a good job, they do more strongly believe that educational *failure* will seriously hurt their vocational prospects. The result? Asian-American students study twice as much as other students, which undoubtedly accounts for much of their success (Steinberg et al., 1992). By contrast, their growing awareness of social prejudices and the limitations they may place on vocational opportunities causes many African-American students to conclude that their efforts in school are unlikely to pay off (Ogbu, 1990).

What these findings tell us, then, is that students from any ethnic background are likely to do better at school if they have (1) authoritative parents who value and are highly involved in their education, (2) friends who care about school and who endorse academic achievement, and (3) a personal set of values about education that motivate them to work hard for the sake of their futures.

Teacher expectancies. Finally, we must consider another hypothesis about ethnic differences in school achievement: the possibility that underachievement by some minority students is rooted in stereotyping and discrimination on the part of teachers.

According to social stereotypes, Asian Americans are expected to be bright and hardworking, whereas African-American and Latino students from low-income neighborhoods are expected to perform poorly in school. And teachers are hardly immune to these stereotypes. As early as the first couple of weeks of kindergarten, and before they know much about their students' competencies, many teachers are already placing children into "ability groups" on the basis of cues to their ethnicity and socioeconomic status: grooming, the quality of their clothing, and their mastery of standard English (Rist, 1970). In one study, teachers were asked to select from a checklist those attributes that best described their lower-income, minority pupils. Teachers consistently selected adjectives such as *lazy, fun-loving,* and *rebellious,* thus implying that they did not expect much of these students (Gottlieb, 1966). But are students influenced by teacher expectancies?

In a classic study, Robert Rosenthal and Lenore Jacobson (1968) demonstrated that a teacher's expectancies about a student can influence that student's ultimate achievement through what they called the **Pygmalion effect.** Students actually perform better when they are expected to do well than when they are expected to do poorly, so that teacher expectancies become *self-fulfilling prophecies.* To demonstrate this, Rosenthal and Jacobsen gave each elementary school teacher in their study a list of five students who were supposed to be "rapid bloomers." In fact, the so-called rapid bloomers had been randomly selected from class rosters. The only way they differed from other students is that their teachers expected more of them. Yet planting these high expectancies in the minds of first- and second-grade teachers was sufficient to cause the so-called rapid bloomers to show greater gains in IQ and reading achievement than their unlabeled classmates.

Although some investigators have failed to replicate Rosenthal and Jacobson's results (Cooper, 1979), many others have reported similar findings, showing that (1) students expected by teachers to do well are likely to live up to these positive expectancies, whereas (2) those expected to perform poorly often do earn lower grades and score lower on standardized tests than classmates of comparable ability for whom the teacher has no negative expectancies (see Harris & Rosenthal, 1986; Weinstein et al., 1987). Clearly, the positive or negative expectancies that most teachers form reflect *real* differences between students. Students who are expected to perform well (or poorly) in the future have typically performed well (or poorly) in the past (Jussim & Eccles, 1992). Still, even if two students have equal aptitude and motivation, the one whose teacher expects great things is likely to outperform the one whose teacher expects less (Jussim & Eccles, 1992).

How exactly does the Pygmalion effect work? It seems that teachers expose high-expectancy students to more challenging materials, demand better performances from them, and are more likely to praise these youngsters for answering questions correctly (perhaps leading them to infer that they have *high ability*). And when high-expectancy students do not answer correctly, they often hear the question rephrased so that they can get it right, thus implying that failures can be overcome by *persisting* and *trying harder* (Dweck & Elliott, 1983). Meanwhile, a Mexican-American or African-American student from a poor neighborhood might be tagged by a teacher as a low-ability student who may rarely be challenged or who is likely to be criticized if he does not know the answers to questions. Of course, these practices could convince the child that he has little ability, thereby undermining his will to achieve and causing him to confirm the teacher's low expectations (see Sorensen & Hallinan, 1986).

In sum, parents' values and styles of parenting, peers' support for academic achievement, and teacher expectancies probably all contribute to racial and ethnic differences in school achievement. Some theorists feel that children from lower-income, minority subcultures are at an immediate disadvantage when they enter the middle-class institutions we call schools and that schools must change dramatically if they are to motivate and better educate these children. Among the positive changes we see today are stronger bilingual education programs designed to meet the needs of children from the over 100 distinct language groups in the United States (Garcia,

Pygmalion effect: the tendency of teacher expectancies to become self-fulfilling prophecies, causing students to perform better or worse depending on their teacher's estimation of their potential.

1993) and multicultural education programs designed to bring the perspectives of many cultural and subcultural groups into the classroom so that all students feel more welcome there (Banks, 1993).

Making Integration and Mainstreaming Work

For many African-American students in the past, additional barriers to school success were created by school segregation. African-American children in many states were forced to attend "black schools" that were clearly inferior to "white schools." In its landmark decision in the case of *Brown v. Board of Education* in 1954, the Supreme Court ruled that segregated schools were "inherently unequal" and declared that they must be desegregated. What have we learned since this ruling?

Generally, the effects of school desegregation on children's racial attitudes, self-esteem, and school achievement have been disappointing (Stephan, 1978). White prejudice toward African-American students often does not decrease much at all, and the self-esteem of African-American children in integrated schools is often no higher than that of African-American children in segregated schools. The most encouraging news has been that minority students tend to achieve more in integrated classrooms, especially if they begin to attend them early in their academic careers (St. John, 1975; and see Entwisle & Alexander, 1992).

Meanwhile, other children with developmental disabilities (mental retardation, learning disabilities, physical and sensory handicaps, and other special learning needs) have had a somewhat similar history. They used to be placed in separate schools or classrooms—or, in some cases, were rejected as unteachable by the public schools—until the U.S. Congress passed the Education for All Handicapped Children Act in 1975. This law required school districts to provide an education comparable with that received by normal children to all youngsters with special needs. The intent of the law was to help children with special needs to acquire the full range of academic and social skills that normal children were acquiring at school. How might the law be served? Many school districts opted for **mainstreaming**—the practice of integrating special-needs children into regular classrooms for all or large parts of the day, as opposed to segregating them in special schools or classrooms.

Has mainstreaming accomplished its objectives? Not very well, it hasn't. Compared with other special-needs children who attend segregated special education classes, mainstreamed youngsters sometimes fare better academically and socially but often do not (Buysse & Bailey, 1993; Madden & Slavin, 1983). Moreover, their self-esteem often declines because normal children tend to ridicule them and are reluctant to choose them as friends or playmates (Guralnick & Groom, 1988; Taylor, Asher, & Williams, 1987).

What we seem to be learning about both racial integration and mainstreaming is that simply putting diverse students in the same schools and classrooms accomplishes little by itself. Instead, something special must be done to ensure that students do in fact interact in positive ways and also learn what they are supposed to be learning. What techniques for facilitating racial integration and mainstreaming *have* proved successful?

Robert Slavin (1986; 1991) and his colleagues have had much success using **cooperative learning methods** in which students of different races or ability levels are assigned to work teams and are reinforced for performing well *as a team*. For example, each member of a math team is given problems to solve that are appropriate to his or her ability level. Yet members of a work team also monitor one another's progress and offer one another aid when needed. To encourage this cooperation, the teams that complete the most math units are rewarded—for example, with special certificates that designate them as "superteams." Similarly, the "jigsaw method" of instruction developed by Elliot Aronson and his colleagues (1978) to facilitate racial integration involves giving each member of a small learning team one portion of the material to be learned and requiring him or her to teach it to teammates. Here, then, is a formula for ensuring that children of different races and ability levels will

mainstreaming: the educational practice of integrating developmentally disabled students into regular classrooms rather than placing them in segregated special education classes.

cooperative learning methods: an educational practice whereby children of different races or ability levels are assigned to teams; each team member works on problems geared to his or her ability level, and all members are reinforced for "pulling together" and performing well as a team.

By stressing teamwork to achieve shared goals, cooperative learning activities make integration and mainstreaming more fruitful experiences for children of all races and ability levels.

interact in a context where the efforts of even the least capable team members are important to the group's success.

Elementary school students come to like school better and learn more when they participate in cooperative learning groups than when they receive traditional instruction (Aronson et al., 1978; Slavin, 1986; 1991). Moreover, team members gain self-esteem from their successes, and minority group members and students with developmental disabilities are more fully accepted by their peers (see also Johnson, Johnson, & Maruyama, 1983; Weinstein, 1991). In short, racial integration and mainstreaming *can* succeed if educators deliberately design learning experiences that encourage students from different backgrounds to pool their efforts in order to achieve common goals.

How Well Educated Are Our Children? A Cross-Cultural Comparison

How successful are schools at imparting academic skills to their pupils? Large surveys of the reading, writing, and mathematical achievement of 9–17-year-old American students reveal that most of them do learn to read during the elementary school years and have acquired such mathematical proficiencies as basic computational skills and graph-reading abilities by the time they finish high school (Dossey et al., 1988; National Education Goals Panel, 1992; The Nation's Report Card, cited in White, 1994). However, American youths do not write very well; in fact, more than one-third of all 17-year-olds could not produce a well-formed and coherent paragraph. Are these findings cause for alarm?

Many educators think so (see National Education Goals Panel, 1992), especially in view of the results of several cross-national surveys of children's academic achievement indicating that the average scores obtained by American schoolchildren in mathematics, science, and verbal skills are consistently lower, and sometimes much lower, than those made by students in many other industrialized nations (McKnight et al., 1987; National Education Goals Panel, 1992; Stevenson, Chen, & Lee, 1993).

Cross-cultural research conducted by Harold Stevenson and his colleagues (Stevenson & Lee, 1990; Stevenson, Lee, & Stigler, 1986; Stevenson et al., 1993) leaves no doubt that schoolchildren in Taiwan, the People's Republic of China, and Japan outperform students in the United States in math, reading, and other school subjects. The gap in math performance is especially striking; in recent testings of fifth-graders,

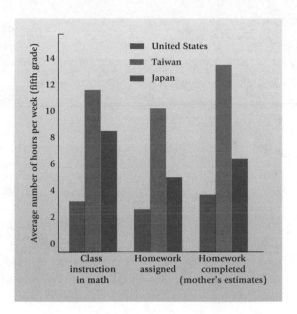

Figure 16-7
Average number of hours per week of class instruction in mathematics and of homework (of all kinds) that teachers assign and that mothers report their children completing.
Data from Chen and Stevenson, 1989.

for example, only 4% of Chinese children and 10% of Japanese students had scores on a math achievement test as low as those of the average American child (Stevenson et al., 1993). Achievement differences of this sort are evident from the time children enter school and grow larger as children progress from first to fifth to eleventh grade (Stevenson et al., 1993). Why do these differences exist, and what can they tell us about methods of improving American education?

The problem is not that American students are "dumber," for they enter school performing just about as well on IQ tests as their Asian counterparts (Stevenson et al., 1985), and they score at least as well as Japanese and Chinese students on general information tests covering material *not* typically covered in school (Stevenson et al., 1993). Instead, the achievement gap between American and Asian students seems to be rooted in cultural differences in educational attitudes and practices.

Classroom instruction. Asian students spend more time being educated than American students do. Elementary school teachers in Asian countries devote more class time to core academic subjects—for example, two to three times as many hours a week on math instruction (see Figure 16-7). The Asian classroom is a businesslike place where little time is wasted; Asian students spend about 95% of their time on "on-task" activities such as listening to the teacher and completing assignments, whereas American students spend only about 80% of their time "on task" (Stigler, Lee, & Stevenson, 1987). Asian students also attend school for more hours per day and more days per year (Stevenson et al., 1986).

Parental involvement. Asian parents are strongly committed to the educational process. They hold higher achievement expectancies for their children than American parents do, and even though their children are excelling by American standards, Asian parents are much less likely than American parents to be satisfied with their children's current academic performance (Stevenson et al., 1993). Asian parents think that homework is more important than American parents do, and they also receive frequent communications from their children's teachers in notebooks that children carry to and from school each day. These communications enable Asian parents to keep close tabs on how their children are progressing and to follow teachers' suggestions about how they can encourage and assist their children at home (Stevenson & Lee, 1990). By contrast, communications between U.S. parents and teachers are often limited to brief annual parent-teacher conferences.

Children in traditional Asian classrooms are required to stay in their seats working on assignments or paying close attention to their teacher.

Student involvement. Not only do Asian students spend more days of the year in class and more class time on academic assignments than American children do, but they are assigned and complete more homework as well (see Figure 16-7).

An emphasis on effort. Asian parents, teachers, and students share a strong belief that hard work or effort will pay off in better learning. Perhaps this belief is one major reason why Asian students are no more and often *less* anxious about school than American children are, despite the stronger pressures placed upon them to excel in the classroom (Crystal et al., 1994; Stevenson et al., 1993). By contrast, American parents, teachers, and students are more inclined to believe that a child's successes or failures reflect his or her native abilities. As a result, Americans may give up too quickly on children who are having difficulties at school.

So the formula for more effective education may not be so mysterious after all, judging from the success of the Chinese and Japanese educational systems. The secret is to get teachers, students, and parents working together to make education a top priority for youth, to set high achievement goals, and to invest the day-by-day effort

---

Concept Check 16-1 ∨ Schools as Socialization Agents

Check your understanding of the impacts of schools and educational practices on children by matching each descriptive statement below with one of the following terms, principles, or concepts: (a) ability tracking; (b) aptitude-treatment interaction (ATI); (c) cooperative learning methods; (d) group differences in IQ; (e) informal curriculum; (f) mainstreaming; (g) monetary support; (h) parental involvement; (i) Pygmalion effect; (j) school size. The answers appear in the Appendix.

_____ 1. May undermine the self-esteem of developmentally disadvantaged students.

_____ 2. Thought to be a contributor to ethnic differences in achievement.

_____ 3. Likely to undermine the academic achievement of low-ability students.

_____ 4. Lessons aimed at teaching students how to fit into their culture.

_____ 5. Weakly correlated with a school's "effectiveness."

_____ 6. Strong contributor to the academic successes of minority youth and students in Asian nations.

_____ 7. Correlate of adolescent students' involvement with school activities.

_____ 8. Factor that best describes the effectiveness (or ineffectiveness) of particular educational practices.

_____ 9. Factor that does *not* account for cross-cultural differences in academic achievement.

_____ 10. Successful technique for promoting the objectives of integration and mainstreaming.

required to attain those goals. Many states and local school districts have begun to respond to evidence that American schools are being outclassed by schools in other countries by strengthening curricula, tightening standards for teacher certification, raising standards for graduation and promotion from grade to grade, and even implementing alternative academic calendars that shorten summer vacation, thereby increasing student retention of previously learned material and giving teachers in the next grade a better chance of achieving their instructional goals. Moreover, educational reformers such as James Comer (1988; Anson et al., 1991) have been successful at forging closer ties between inner-city schools and the communities they serve and involving parents as partners with teachers in the educational process. These educational leaders recognize that improving the academic achievement and vocational preparation of America's youth is crucial if Americans are to maintain a leadership role in an ever-changing and increasingly competitive world (National Education Goals Panel, 1992).

 ## THE SECOND WORLD OF CHILDHOOD: PEERS AS SOCIALIZATION AGENTS

Although youngsters spend an enormous amount of time and energy socializing with each other, only within the past 25–30 years have developmentalists given much thought to how contacts with peers might influence developing children. Perhaps owing to early research on the behavior of adolescent gangs (see Hartup, 1983), peers have often been characterized as potentially subversive agents who may erode the influence of adults and lead the child into a life of delinquency and antisocial conduct. Popular novels and films such as *Lord of the Flies* and *A Clockwork Orange* reinforce this point of view.

However, this perspective on peer relations is distorted and unnecessarily negative. Although peers are occasionally "bad influences," they clearly have the potential to affect their playmates in positive ways. Try to imagine what your life would be like if other children had not been available as you were growing up. Would you have acquired the social skills to mix comfortably with others, to cooperate and to engage in socially acceptable forms of competition, or to make appropriate social (or sexual) responses to love objects other than your parents? No one can say for sure, but the following letter written by a farmer from the midwestern United States provides a strong clue that interactions with other children may be a most important aspect of the socialization process.*

Dear Dr. Moore:

I read the report in the Oct. 30 issue of _____ about your study of only children. I am an only child, now 57 years old, and I want to tell you some things about my life. Not only was I an only child, but I grew up in the country where there were no nearby children to play with. . . . [And] from the first year of school, I was teased and made fun of. . . . I dreaded to get on the school bus and go to school because the other children on the bus called me "Mommy's baby." In about the second grade I heard the boys use a vulgar word. I asked what it meant and they made fun of me. So I learned a lesson—don't ask questions. This can lead to a lot of confusion to hear talk one doesn't understand and not be able to learn what it means.

I never went out with a girl while I was in school—in fact I hardly talked to them. In our school the boys and girls did not play together. Boys were sent to one part of the playground and girls to another. So I didn't learn anything about girls. When we got into high school and boys and girls started dating, I could only listen to their stories about their experiences.

---

*This letter appears with the permission of its author and its recipient, Dr. Shirley G. Moore.

I could tell you a lot more, but the important thing is I have never married or had any children. I have not been very successful in an occupation or vocation. I believe my troubles are not all due to being an only child . . . but I do believe you are right in recommending playmates for preschool children, and I will add playmates for . . . school agers and not have them strictly supervised by adults. . . . Parents of only children should make special efforts to provide playmates for them.

Sincerely yours,

If we assume that peers are important agents of socialization, there are a number of questions that remain to be answered. For example, who qualifies as a peer? How do peers influence one another? What is it about peer influence that is unique? What are the consequences (if any) of poor peer relations? Is it important to have special peer alliances, or friendships? Do peers eventually become a more potent source of influence than parents or other adults? These are some of the issues that we will consider in this final section of the chapter.

Who or What Is a Peer, and What Functions Do Peers Serve?

Webster's New Collegiate Dictionary defines a **peer** as "one that is of equal standing with another." Developmentalists also think of peers as *"social equals"* or as individuals *who, for the moment at least, are operating at similar levels of behavioral complexity* (Lewis & Rosenblum, 1975). According to this activity-based definition, children who differ somewhat in age could still be considered "peers" as long as they can adjust their behaviors to suit one another's capabilities as they pursue common interests or goals.

Same-Age (or Equal-Status) Contacts

We can gain some idea about why peer contacts among age-mates may be important by contrasting them to exchanges that occur at home. A child's interactions with parents and older siblings are rarely equal-status contacts; typically children are placed in a subordinate position by an older member of the family who is instructing them, issuing orders, or otherwise overseeing their activities. By contrast, age-mates are much less critical and directive, and children are freer to try out new roles, ideas, and behaviors when interacting with someone of similar status. And in so doing, they are likely to learn important lessons about themselves and others, such as "She quits when I don't take turns," "He hits me when I push him," or "Nobody likes a cheater." Many theorists believe that peer contacts are important precisely because they are *equal-status* contacts—that is, they teach children to understand and appreciate the perspectives of people *just like themselves* and thereby contribute to the development of social competencies that are difficult to acquire in the nonegalitarian atmosphere of the home.

Mixed-Age Interactions

According to Hartup (1983), interaction among children of *different* ages is also a critically important context for development. Although cross-age interactions tend to be somewhat *asymmetrical*, with one child (typically the elder) possessing more power than the other, it is primarily these asymmetries that may help children to acquire certain social competencies. For example, the presence of younger peers may foster the development of compassion, caregiving and prosocial inclinations, assertiveness, and leadership skills in older children (see, for example, French et al., 1986). At the same time, younger children may benefit from mixed-age interactions by acquiring a variety of new skills from older playmates and by learning how to seek assistance and how to defer gracefully to the wishes and directives of these more powerful associates. In their survey of children's social contacts in several cultures, Whiting and Edwards (1988) found that mixed-age interactions do differ in important ways from

peers: two or more persons who are operating at similar levels of behavioral complexity.

Both older and younger children benefit from mixed-age interactions.

those among age-mates. Nurturant and prosocial behaviors occurred more frequently in mixed-age groups, whereas casually sociable acts (such as conversation and cooperative play) as well as antisocial ones (such as aggression) were more likely to occur among age-mates. Older children usually took charge of mixed-age interactions and adjusted their behavior to the competencies of their younger companions (see also Brody, Graziano, & Musser, 1983; Graziano et al., 1976). Even 2-year-olds show such powers of leadership and accommodation, for they are more inclined to take the initiative and to display simpler and more repetitive play routines when paired with an 18-month-old toddler than with an agemate (Brownell, 1990).

By the time that children enter grade school, they know that same-age and mixed-age interactions serve different purposes, and their preferences for associating with older, younger, or same-age peers clearly depend on the goals they are pursuing (French, 1984). Children aged 6–9, for example, prefer age-mates to younger or older children if their objective is to pick a friend. However, older children are preferred as companions over age-mates if the child feels the need for sympathy or guidance, whereas younger children are chosen in situations calling for compassion or teaching another child what they already know.

Perhaps you have noticed that mixed-age peer interactions are presumed to benefit older and younger children in many of the same ways that sibling interactions benefit older and younger siblings (see Chapter 15). But there is a crucial difference between sibling and peer contacts, for one's standing as either a younger or an older sibling is *fixed* by order of birth, whereas one's position among peers is *flexible*, depending on the associates one chooses. Thus, mixed-age *peer* interactions may provide children with experiences that they might otherwise miss in their mixed-age sibling interactions and, in fact, may be the primary context in which (1) a habitually domineering elder sibling learns to be more accommodating (when interacting with older peers), (2) an oppressed younger sib learns to lead and to show compassion (when dealing with even younger children), and (3) an only child (who has no sibs) acquires both sets of social competencies. Viewed in this way, mixed-age peer associations may be important experiences indeed.

Frequency of Peer Contacts

Between the ages of 2 and 12, children spend more and more time with peers and less and less time with adults. This trend is nicely illustrated in Figure 16-8, which summarizes what Sherri Ellis and her colleagues (1981) found while observing 436 children playing in their homes and around the neighborhood. Interestingly, this same study revealed that youngsters of all ages spent *less* time with age-mates (defined

Figure 16-8
Developmental changes in children's companionship with adults and other children.
Adapted from Ellis, Rogoff, & Cromer, 1981.

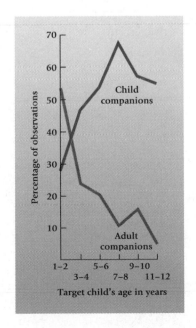

as children whose ages were within a year of their own) than with children who were more than a year older or younger than they were. Apparently, we must take seriously the idea that peers are "social equals" rather than age-mates.

Another finding of this study is a familiar one: Even 1–2-year-olds played more often with same-sex companions than with other-sex companions, and this *gender segregation* became increasingly strong with age (see also Maccoby, 1990, and Chapter 13). Once in their sex-segregated worlds, boys and girls experience different kinds of social relationships. Boys tend to form "packs," whereas girls form "pairs"; that is, a boy often plays competitive games or team sports in groups, whereas a girl more often establishes a cooperative relationship with one playmate (Archer, 1992; Maccoby, 1990).

Overall, then, children spend an increasing amount of time with peers, and those peers are typically *same*-sex children who are only *roughly similar* in age but who enjoy the same kinds of sex-typed activities.

How Important Are Peer Influences?

To this point, we have speculated that peer interactions may promote the development of many social and personal competencies that are not easily acquired within the decidedly nonegalitarian parent-child relationship. Is there truly any basis for such a claim? And, if so, just how important are these peer influences? Developmentalists became very interested in these questions once they learned of Harry Harlow's research with rhesus monkeys.

Harlow's work with monkeys. Will youngsters who have little or no contact with peers turn out to be abnormal or maladjusted? To find out, Harlow and his associates (Alexander & Harlow, 1965; Suomi & Harlow, 1978) raised groups of rhesus monkeys with their mothers and denied them the opportunity to play with peers. These **"mother-only" monkeys** failed to develop normal patterns of social behavior. When finally exposed to age-mates, the peer-deprived youngsters preferred to avoid them. On those occasions when they did approach a peer, these social misfits tended to be highly (and inappropriately) aggressive, and their antisocial tendencies often persisted into adulthood.

Is peer contact the key to normal social development? Not entirely. In later experiments, Harlow and his colleagues separated rhesus monkey infants from their mothers and raised them so that they had continuous exposure to their peers. These **"peer-only" monkeys** were observed to cling tenaciously to one another and to form strong mutual attachments. Yet their social development was somewhat atypical in that they became highly agitated over minor stresses or frustrations (see also Higley et al., 1992), and as adults they were unusually aggressive toward monkeys from outside their peer groups.

A human parallel. In 1951, Anna Freud and Sophie Dann reported a startling human parallel to Harlow's peer-only monkeys. During the summer of 1945, six 3-year-olds were found living by themselves in a Nazi concentration camp. By the time these children were 12 months old, their parents had been put to death. Although they received minimal caregiving from a series of inmates who were periodically executed, these children had, in effect, reared themselves.

When rescued at the war's end, the six orphans were flown to a special treatment center in England, where attempts were made to "rehabilitate" them. How did these "peer-only" children respond to this treatment? They began by breaking nearly all their toys and damaging their furniture. Moreover, they often reacted with cold indifference or open hostility toward the staff at the center. And like Harlow's monkeys, these children were strongly attached to each other and often became upset when separated from other members of the group—even for brief periods. They also displayed a remarkable prosocial concern for one another:

"mother-only" monkeys: monkeys who are raised with their mothers and denied any contact with peers.

"peer-only" monkeys: monkeys who are separated from their mothers (and other adults) soon after birth and raised with peers.

There was no occasion to urge the children to "take turns"; they did it spontaneously. They were extremely considerate of each other's feelings. . . . At mealtimes handing food to the neighbor was of greater importance than eating oneself (Freud & Dann, 1951, pp. 132–133).

Although these youngsters displayed many signs of anxiety and were highly suspicious of outsiders, they eventually established positive relationships with their adult caregivers and acquired a new language during their first year at the center. The story even has a happy ending, for 35 years later, these orphans were leading productive lives as middle-aged adults (Hartup, 1983).

Taken together, Harlow's monkey research and Freud and Dann's observations of their war orphans suggest that parents and peers each contribute something different and perhaps unique to a child's (or a monkey's) social development. Regular contacts with sensitive, responsive parents not only permit infants to acquire some basic interactive skills but also provide a sense of *security* that enables them to venture forth to explore the environment and to discover that other people can be interesting companions (Hartup, 1989; Higley et al., 1992). By contrast, contacts with peers may allow children to elaborate their basic interactive routines and to develop competent and adaptive patterns of social behavior with associates who are more or less similar to themselves. Indeed, Harlow's "peer-only" monkeys lacked the security of a mother-infant relationship, perhaps explaining why they clutched at one another, were reluctant to explore, and were terrified by (and aggressive toward) outsiders. But *within their own peer groups*, they developed competent interactive routines and displayed normal patterns of social and sexual behavior (Suomi & Harlow, 1978).

Just how important is it for human beings to establish and maintain *harmonious* relations with their peers? Apparently, it is very important. One review of more than 30 studies revealed that youngsters who had been rejected by their peers during grade school are much more likely than those who had enjoyed good peer relations to drop out of school, to become involved in delinquent or criminal activities, and to display serious psychological difficulties later in adolescence and young adulthood (Parker & Asher, 1987; see also Kupersmidt & Coie, 1990; Morison & Masten, 1991). So merely having contact with peer associates is not enough to ensure normal developmental outcomes; getting along with peers is important, too.

In sum, peers do seem to be significant agents of socialization, and the task of becoming *appropriately* sociable with peers is a most important developmental hurdle. In our next section, we will focus on the growth of peer sociability and on some of the factors that influence how appropriately (or inappropriately) sociable a child turns out to be.

Monkeys raised only with peers form strong mutual attachments and will often attack other monkeys from outside their peer group.

The Development of Peer Sociability

Sociability is a term that describes the child's willingness to engage others in social interaction and to seek their attention or approval. In Chapter 11, we learned that even young infants are sociable creatures: Months before forming their first attachments, they are already smiling, cooing, or otherwise trying to attract the attention of caregivers and are likely to protest whenever *any* adult puts them down or walks off and leaves them alone. But would they be so positively disposed to a peer?

Peer Sociability in Infancy

Although babies show an interest in other babies from the first months of life, they do not really *interact* until about the middle of the first year. By then, infants will often smile or babble at their tiny companions, vocalize, offer toys, and gesture to one another (Hay, Nash, & Pedersen, 1983; Vandell, Wilson, & Buchanan, 1980). At first, many of these friendly gestures go unnoticed and unreciprocated; interactions between infants and adults are a good deal smoother than interactions between two still-quite-socially-awkward infants (Hay, 1985; Vandell & Wilson, 1987).

sociability: one's willingness to interact with others and to seek their attention or approval.

Between 12 and 18 months of age, infants begin to react more appropriately to each other's behavior. However, there is some question about whether these action/reaction episodes qualify as true social discourse, for 12–18-month-olds often seem to treat peers as particularly responsive "toys" that they can control (Brownell, 1986). For example:

> Larry sits on the floor and Bernie turns and looks toward him. Bernie waves his hand and says "da," still looking at Larry. He repeats the vocalization three more times before Larry laughs. Bernie vocalizes again and Larry laughs again. This same sequence . . . is repeated twelve more times before Bernie . . . walks off (Mueller & Lucas, 1975, p. 241).

By 18 months of age, however, almost all infants are beginning to display *coordinated interactions* with age-mates that are clearly social in character. They now take great delight in *imitating* each other and will often gaze and smile at their partners as they turn their imitative sequences into social games (Eckerman & Stein, 1990; Howes & Matheson, 1992). By age 24 months, toddlers are assuming *complementary* roles, such as chaser and chasee in games of tag, and they will occasionally coordinate their actions (that is, cooperate) to achieve a shared goal, as illustrated by one child's operating a handle, thereby enabling the second to retrieve attractive toys from a container (Brownell & Carriger, 1990).

Both social and cognitive developments contribute to the growth of peer sociability over the first two years. In Chapter 11, for example, we learned that toddlers who are securely attached to their caregivers are generally more outgoing and even more "popular" as playmates than those who are insecurely attached, implying that the sensitive, responsive caregiving that securely attached infants receive contributes in a positive way to the development of social skills. And 18–24-month-olds are beginning to display truly coordinated, reciprocal interactions at precisely the time that they first recognize themselves in a mirror and can discriminate photographs of themselves from those of other infants (see Chapter 12). This may be no accident. Celia Brownell and Michael Carriger (1990) propose that infants must first realize that both they and their companions are autonomous causal agents who can make things happen before they are likely to play complementary games or try to coordinate their actions to accomplish a goal. Indeed, Brownell and Carriger found that toddlers who

With age, infants' interactions with one another become increasingly skilled and reciprocal.

cooperated successfully to achieve a goal did score higher on a test of self-other differentiation than their less cooperative age-mates, thus suggesting that infants' interactive skills may depend very heavily on their levels of social-cognitive development.

Sociability during the Preschool Period

Between the ages of 2 and 5, children not only become more outgoing but also direct their social gestures to a wider audience. Observational studies suggest that 2–3-year-olds are more likely than older children to remain near an adult and to seek physical affection, whereas the sociable behaviors of 4–5-year-olds normally consist of playful bids for attention or approval that are directed at *peers* rather than adults (Harper & Huie, 1985; Hartup, 1983).

Just as children are becoming more peer oriented during the preschool years, the character of their peer interactions is changing as well. Between ages 2 and 5, preschoolers become less inclined to stand around and watch a playmate or to take part in simple initiative games; instead, they engage in increasingly sophisticated, reciprocal exchanges, many of which require players not only to assume complementary roles but also to agree on how these roles are to be played if their play activities are to continue successfully.

Not only does play become increasingly social over the preschool years (Parten, 1932), it becomes more cognitively complex as well. Recently, Carolee Howes and Catherine Matheson (1992) proposed a developmental sequencing of young children's play based on the *cognitive complexity* of children's social interactions. Their six categories of preschool play (from least to most complex) are described in Table 16-1.

To determine whether these six forms of play really do develop sequentially, Howes and Matheson (1992) conducted a longitudinal study in which the play

Table 16-1 Changes in Social Play from Infancy through the Preschool Period

Play type	Age of appearance	Description
Parallel play	6–12 months	Two children perform similar activities without paying any attention to each other.
Parallel aware play	By age 1	Children engage in parallel play while occasionally looking at each other or monitoring each other's activities.
Simple pretend play	1–1½ years	Children engage in similar activities while talking, smiling, sharing toys, or otherwise interacting.
Complementary and reciprocal play	1½–2 years	Children display action-based role reversals in social games such as run-and-chase or peek-a-boo.
Cooperative social pretend play	2½–3 years	Children play complementary *nonliteral*, or "pretend," roles (for example, mommy and baby), but without any planning or discussion about the meaning of these roles or about the form that the play will take.
Complex social pretend play	3½–4 years	Children actively *plan* their pretend play. They name and explicitly assign roles for each player and propose a play script, and may stop playing to modify the script if play breaks down.

Source: Adapted from Howes & Matheson, 1992.

activities of a group of 1–2-year-olds were repeatedly observed (at six-month intervals) over the next three years. The observers also rated each child's social competencies with peers at each observation period. Howes and Matheson found that the categories of play described in the table did develop sequentially. Most infants were displaying simple social play soon after their first birthday and complementary and reciprocal play by ages 19–24 months. By age 2½ to 3, most children had progressed to cooperative social pretend play, and nearly half had displayed complex social pretend play by age 3½ to 4. Moreover, there was a clear relationship between the complexity of a child's play and the child's social competence with peers: Children who engaged in more complex play at any given age were rated as more outgoing and prosocially inclined and as less aggressive and withdrawn at the next observation period six months later. So it seems that the complexity of a child's play (particularly pretend play) is a reliable predictor of his or her future social competencies with peers (see also Connolly & Doyle, 1984; Doyle et al., 1992; Rubin, Fein, & Vandenberg, 1983).

Peer Interactions in Middle Childhood and Adolescence

Peer interactions become increasingly sophisticated throughout the grade school years. Not only do cooperative forms of complex social pretend play become more commonplace, but, by ages 6–10, children are becoming enthusiastic participants in games (such as jacks, marbles, and Monopoly) that are governed by formal sets of rules (Hartup, 1983; Piaget, 1965).

Another very noticeable way that peer interactions change during middle childhood is that contacts among 6–10-year-olds more often occur in true **peer groups.** When psychologists talk about peer groups, they are referring not merely to a collection of playmates but, rather, to a confederation that (1) interacts on a regular basis, (2) defines a sense of belonging, (3) shares implicit or explicit *norms* that specify how members are supposed to behave, and (4) develops a structure or hierarchical organization that enables the members to work together toward the accomplishment of shared goals. Older nursery school children do share common interests, assume different roles while playing together, and conform to loosely defined norms or rules of conduct. But the membership of these preschool "play groups" may fluctuate from day to day, and the guidelines to which the children conform are often laid down by adults. The group activities of elementary school children, however, are very different. Members now share norms that *they* have had a hand in creating, and they begin to assume stable roles or "statuses" within the group. Moreover, elementary school children clearly identify with their groups; to be a "Brownie," a "Blue Knight," or "one of Smitty's gang" is often a source of great personal pride. So between ages 6 and 10, children are exposing themselves to a most potent social context—the peer group—in which they are likely to discover the value of teamwork, develop a sense of commitment and loyalty to shared goals, and learn a number of other important lessons about how social organizations pursue their objectives (Hartup, 1983; Sherif et al., 1961).

By early adolescence, youngsters are spending more time with peers—particularly with small groups of close friends known as **cliques**—than with parents, siblings, or any other agent of socialization (Berndt, 1989; Medrich et al., 1982). Early peer cliques usually consist of four to eight *same-sex* members who share similar values and activity preferences; but by midadolescence, boy cliques and girl cliques begin to interact more frequently, eventually forming *heterosexual cliques* (Dunphy, 1963). Once formed, cliques often develop distinct and colorful dress codes, dialects, and behaviors—norms that set cliques apart from each other and help clique members to establish a firm sense of belonging, or a group identity.

Often several cliques with similar norms and values will form a new peer group structure called a **crowd.** Crowds do not replace cliques; they come into play mainly as a mechanism for defining an adolescent's niche within the larger social structure of their high schools and for arranging organized social activities on the weekend—parties, outings to the football game or the lake, and so on. The names may vary, but

peer group: a confederation of peers that interact regularly; defines a sense of membership and formulates norms that specify how members are supposed to look, think, and act.

clique: a small group of friends who interact frequently.

crowd: a large, loosely organized peer group made up of several cliques that share similar norms, interests, and values.

every school has its crowds of "brains," "populars," "jocks," "druggies," and "losers," each consisting of a loose aggregation of cliques that are similar to one another in some fundamental way (Brown et al., 1993; Brown & Lohr, 1987).

Not only do cliques and crowds permit adolescents to express their values and to try out new roles as they begin their quest to forge an identity apart from their families, but they also pave the way for the establishment of dating relationships (Brown, 1990; Dunphy, 1963). Gender segregation usually breaks down early in adolescence as members of boys' and girls' cliques begin to interact. Same-sex cliques provide what amounts to a "secure base" for exploring ways to behave with members of the other sex: Talking to girls when your other male buddies are there is far less threatening than doing so on your own. And as heterosexual cliques and crowds take shape, adolescents are likely to have many opportunities to get to know members of the other sex in casual social situations, without having to be intimate. Eventually, strong cross-sex friendships develop and couples form, often double-dating or spending time with a small number of other couples. At this point, the crowd gradually begins to disintegrate, having served its purposes of helping adolescents to establish a social identity and bringing the boys and girls together (Brown, 1990; Dunphy, 1963).

Parental Effects on Peer Sociability

Some children are drawn to peers and seem to thrive on social interaction, whereas others appear rather unsociable or even withdrawn. Although we learned in Chapter 3 that sociability is influenced to some extent by one's genotype, it is also clear that the path to positive or negative peer relations often begins at home and that parents might either foster or inhibit peer sociability.

Promoting peer contacts. There are many ways in which parents can influence the sheer amount of contact their children have with peers. Their choice of a residence is one such influence. If parents choose to live in a neighborhood where there are parks, playgrounds, and many young children, their sons and daughters may have ample opportunities to interact with peers. By contrast, a decision to reside in a neighborhood with big yards, widely spaced houses, and few playgrounds or available playmates could seriously restrict children's access to peers (Medrich et al., 1982).

The amount of contact that children have with peers also depends on whether parents act as "booking agents" for peer interaction: whether they arrange visits by playmates, enroll their children in day care or nursery school, or encourage their participation in other organized activities for children. As we noted earlier in Box 16-2, children who receive good day care or who attend nursery schools that emphasize a social curriculum do tend to develop social skills at an earlier age than those who remain at home. Why? Although the guidance offered by nursery school teachers and day care providers undoubtedly plays a part in improving children's social skills (Howes, Hamilton, & Matheson, 1994), children may also become more outgoing with day care or nursery school classmates because they have gotten to know them better. Indeed, play among preschoolers is much more cooperative and more complex when playmates are familiar companions rather than strangers (Doyle, Connolly, & Rivest, 1980; Harper & Huie, 1985), and collaborative problem solving proceeds much more smoothly among familiar than among unfamiliar playmates as well (Brody et al., 1983). So familiarity among preschool peers breeds sociability rather than contempt.

Monitoring and controlling play activities. Of course, parents who arrange home visits by peer playmates are also in a position to influence their child by monitoring his or her peer interactions to ensure that play proceeds smoothly and amiably, without major conflicts. This brings us to an interesting issue.

Should parents closely monitor or intrude upon playful interactions between young children? Gary Ladd and Beckie Golter (1988) attempted to answer this question by asking parents of preschool children how they had supervised any recent

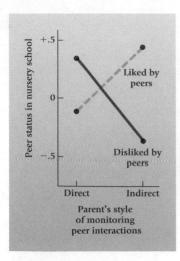

Figure 16-9
Nursery school children enjoy a more favorable status with peers when parents have indirectly monitored their interactions with playmates.
Based on Ladd & Golter, 1988.

interactions their child had had with peers at home. Some parents reported that they had closely watched over the children or had even participated in their play activities (direct monitoring), whereas others said they had checked occasionally on the children without often intruding or becoming involved as a playmate (indirect monitoring). Which form of monitoring is associated with successful and harmonious peer interactions? Ladd and Golter's findings clearly favor indirect parental monitoring. As we see in Figure 16-9, preschoolers whose parents had indirectly monitored their peer interactions were much better liked (and less often disliked) by their nursery school classmates than those whose parents closely monitored and often intruded on their play activities.

Perhaps direct monitoring inhibits peer sociability because an overly intrusive, controlling parent does not allow children enough autonomy to choose to play as they want to and to resolve minor squabbles on their own. Indeed, researchers who have observed playful interactions between 3–5-year-olds *and their parents* find that *directive, controlling* parents who are always issuing commands and who rarely allow their children to regulate their activities tend to have children who have poor social skills and nonharmonious peer interactions (MacDonald, 1987; Russell & Finnie, 1990; Youngblade & Belsky, 1992). A controlling parent who is always barking orders may inhibit sociability by simply taking all the fun out of play activities. Or, alternatively, these parents may be teaching their children to be bossy and dictatorial themselves—a style that is likely to elicit negative reactions from playmates and convince the child that contacts with peers are not all that pleasant (Kochanska, 1992; Russell & Finnie, 1990).

In sum, parents of appropriately sociable preschool children tend to be warm, accepting companions who (1) indirectly monitor their children's interactions with peers to ensure that they comply with rules of social etiquette while (2) allowing children considerable freedom to structure their own play activities and to resolve minor disputes on their own (Ladd & Hart, 1992). Clearly, this pattern of warmth, sensitivity, and moderate control sounds very much like the *authoritative* pattern of child rearing that we have commented favorably upon throughout the text. Indeed, investigators are consistently finding that authoritative parents who rely on reason (induction) rather than forceful coercive methods (power assertion) to control their children's conduct are likely to raise well-adjusted sons and daughters who (1) display many prosocial and few disruptive or antisocial behaviors toward peers and (2) are likely to be accepted by or even popular with their playmates (Baumrind, 1971; Dekovic & Janssens, 1992; Hart et al., 1992; Youngblade & Belsky, 1992). By contrast, highly authoritarian (or uninvolved) parents who rely heavily on power assertion as a control tactic tend to raise youngsters who (1) display the *hostile attributional bias* we discussed in Chapter 14, (2) are often disruptive and aggressive when interacting with other children, and (3) are likely to be *rejected* by their peers (Dekovic & Janssens, 1992; MacKinnon-Lewis et al., 1994; Weiss et al., 1992).

So it does seem as if the path to positive (or negative) peer interactions often begins at home. As Putallaz and Heflin have noted:

> Parental involvement, warmth, and moderate control appear to be important in terms of children's social competence. Within the social context of the family, children appear to learn certain interactional skills and behaviors that then transfer to their interactions with peers (1990, p. 204).

Peer Acceptance and Popularity

Perhaps no other aspect of children's social lives has received more attention than **peer acceptance**—the extent to which a child is viewed by peers as a worthy or likable companion. Typically, researchers assess peer acceptance through self-report instruments called **sociometric techniques.** In a sociometric survey, children might be asked to nominate several classmates whom they like and several whom they dis-

peer acceptance: a measure of a person's likability (or dislikability) in the eyes of peers.

sociometric techniques: procedures that ask children to identify those peers whom they like or dislike or to rate peers for their desirability as companions; used to measure children's peer acceptance (or nonacceptance).

Calvin and Hobbs copyright © 1994 by Universal Press Syndicate. Reprinted with permission. All rights reserved.

like; or they may be asked to rate each of their classmates with respect to their desirability as social companions (Terry & Coie, 1991). Even 3–5-year-olds can respond appropriately to sociometric surveys (Denham et al., 1990); and the choices (or ratings) that children provide correspond reasonably well to teacher ratings of peer popularity, thus suggesting that sociometric surveys provide *valid* assessments of children's social standing in their peer groups (Hymel, 1983).

When sociometric data are analyzed, it is usually possible to classify each child into one of the following categories: **popular children,** who are liked by many peers and disliked by few; **rejected children,** who are disliked by many peers and liked by a few; **neglected children,** who receive very few nominations as a liked or a disliked companion and who seem almost invisible to their peers; and **controversial children,** who are liked by many peers but disliked by many others. Together, these four types of children make up about two-thirds of the pupils in a typical elementary school classroom. The remaining one-third are **average-status children,** who are liked (or disliked) by a moderate number of peers (Coie, Dodge, & Coppotelli, 1982).

Notice that both neglected children and rejected children are low in acceptance and are not well received by their peers. Yet it is not nearly so bad to be ignored by other children as to be rejected by them. Neglectees do not feel as lonely as rejectees do (Cassidy & Asher, 1992; Crick & Ladd, 1993), and they are much more likely than rejected children to eventually attain a more favorable sociometric status should they enter a new class at school or a new play group (Coie & Dodge, 1983). Moreover, rejected children are the ones who face the greater risk of displaying deviant, antisocial behavior and other serious adjustment problems later in life (Asher & Coie, 1990; Morison & Masten, 1991; Parker & Asher, 1987).

However, there are at least two kinds, or categories, of rejected children: **aggressive rejected children,** who are highly and inappropriately aggressive, and **nonaggressive rejected children,** who are anxious and display few social skills and who may actively avoid peer contacts. Aggressive rejected children often misinterpret other children's behavior as hostile, even when it isn't, and are likely to display severe conduct disorders (Bierman, Smoot, & Aumiller, 1993; Crick & Ladd, 1993). These are the children who are at greater risk of becoming chronically hostile and antisocial and of performing criminal acts of violence or displaying other externalizing disorders in adolescence and adulthood (Parker & Asher, 1987). By contrast, nonaggressive rejected children are typically socially awkward companions who display unusual behaviors, are insensitive to peer-group expectations, and are hypersensitive to teasing, often interpreting this verbal banter as evidence that peers dislike them (Parkhurst & Asher, 1992; Rabiner, Keane, & MacKinnon-Lewis, 1993). Indeed, many of those nonaggressive rejectees begin to withdraw from peers and to feel especially lonely, and they appear to be at risk of experiencing very low self-esteem, clinical depression, and other emotional disorders (Hymel, Bowker, & Woody, 1993; Hymel et al., 1990). Moreover, Parkhurst and Asher (1992) find that nonaggressive rejectees are perceived by peers as "easy to push around," and they speculate that these youngsters may become especially inviting targets for bullies (recall from Box 14-1 that

popular children: children who are liked by many members of their peer group and disliked by very few.

rejected children: children who are disliked by many peers and liked by few.

neglected children: children who receive few nominations as either a liked or a disliked individual from members of their peer group.

controversial children: children who receive many nominations by peers as a liked individual and many as a disliked individual.

average-status children: children who receive a moderate number of nominations as a liked and/or a disliked individual from members of their peer group.

aggressive rejected children: a subgroup of rejected children who display high levels of hostility and aggression in their interactions with peers.

nonaggressive rejected children: a subgroup of rejected children who are often passive, socially unskilled, and insensitive to peer-group expectations.

chronically victimized children are typically passive youngsters who are clearly rejected by their peers). So it seems that there are some significant risks associated with the nonaggressive rejected social status after all.

Why Are Children Accepted, Neglected, or Rejected by Peers?

At several points throughout the text, we have discussed factors that seem to contribute to children's popularity with peers. By way of brief review, they are described below.

Parenting styles. Warm, sensitive, and authoritative parents who rely on reasoning rather than power to guide and control children's conduct tend to raise youngsters who are *liked* by adults and peers. By contrast, highly authoritarian and/or uninvolved parents who rely heavily on power assertion as a control tactic often have youngsters who are surly, uncooperative, and aggressive, and are actively *disliked* by peers.

Physical correlates. Both physique and rate of maturation are correlates of peer acceptance. Children with athletic or "mesomorphic" builds tend to be more popular than those with linear (ectomorphic) or rounded (endomorphic) physiques, and boys who mature early are more popular than boys who mature late (see Chapter 5).

Cognitive skills. Popular children tend to have well-developed role-taking skills (see Chapter 12). They also tend to do well in school and to score higher on IQ tests than less popular children do (Bukowski et al., 1993; Dishion et al., 1991).

Ordinal position effects. Later-born children who must learn to negotiate with older, more powerful siblings tend to be more popular than firstborns (see Chapter 15).

At least two additional characteristics seem to reliably predict children's standing among their peers: their physical attractiveness (particularly facial attractiveness) and their patterns of interpersonal behavior.

Facial attractiveness. Despite the maxim that "beauty is only skin deep," many of us seem to think otherwise. Even 6-month-old infants can easily discriminate attractive from unattractive faces (Langlois et al., 1991), and 12-month-old infants already prefer to interact with attractive rather than unattractive strangers (Langlois, Roggman, & Rieser-Danner, 1990). By the preschool period, attractive youngsters are often described in more favorable ways (that is, friendlier, smarter) than their less attractive classmates by both teachers and peers (Adams & Crane, 1980; Langlois, 1986), and attractive children are generally more popular than unattractive children from elementary school onward (Langlois, 1986). Indeed, this link between facial attractiveness and peer acceptance even begins to make some sense when we consider how attractive and unattractive children interact with their playmates. Although attractive and unattractive 3-year-olds do not yet differ a great deal in the character of their social behaviors, by age 5, unattractive youngsters are more likely than attractive ones to be active and boisterous during play sessions and to respond aggressively toward peers (Langlois & Downs, 1979). So unattractive children do seem to develop patterns of social interaction that could alienate other children.

Why might this happen? Some theorists have argued that parents, teachers, and other children may contribute to a self-fulfilling prophecy by subtly (or not so subtly) communicating their expectancies to attractive youngsters, letting them know that they are smart and are supposed to do well in school, behave pleasantly, and be likable. Information of this sort undoubtedly has an effect on children: Attractive youngsters may become progressively more confident, friendly, and outgoing, whereas unattractive children may resent the less favorable feedback that they receive and become more defiant and aggressive. This is precisely how a "beautiful is good" stereotype could become a reality (Langlois & Downs, 1979).

Behavioral contributors. Although physical characteristics and cognitive/scholastic/athletic prowess are all meaningfully related to peer acceptance, even the brightest and most attractive children may be unpopular if peers consider their behavior inappropriate or antisocial (Dodge, 1983). What behavioral characteristics are most important in influencing a child's standing with peers?

Several studies of preschool, elementary school, and middle school (young adolescent) children report pretty much the same findings. *Popular* children are observed to be relatively calm, outgoing, friendly, and supportive companions who can successfully initiate and maintain interactions and can resolve disputes amicably (see Coie, Dodge, & Kupersmidt, 1990; Denham et al., 1990; Ladd, Price, & Hart, 1988). Stated another way, these "sociometric stars" are warm, cooperative, and compassionate souls who display many prosocial behaviors and are seldom disruptive or aggressive (Hart et al., 1992; Parkhurst & Asher, 1992).

Neglected children, by contrast, often appear shy or withdrawn. They are not very talkative; they make fewer attempts than children of average status to enter play groups; and they seldom call attention to themselves (Coie et al., 1990; Coie & Kupersmidt, 1983). Nevertheless, these youngsters are no less socially skilled than children of average status, nor are they any more lonely or more distressed about the character of their social relationships (Cassidy & Asher, 1992; Parkhurst & Asher, 1992). Their withdrawn behavior appears to stem more from their own social anxieties and their beliefs that they are not socially skilled than from any active ostracism or exclusion by their peer groups (Cassidy & Asher, 1992; Younger & Daniels, 1992).

Rejected children display many characteristics that are likely to annoy or anger their peers. Aggressive rejected children often attempt to dominate and control other children and their resources (Coie et al., 1991; Dodge et al., 1990). They tend to be disruptive braggarts who are uncooperative and critical of peer group activities and who display very low levels of prosocial behavior (Coie et al., 1990; Parkhurst & Asher, 1992). By contrast, nonaggressive rejected children do not attempt to dominate and may even be withdrawn; but they are often thin-skinned, hypersensitive companions who irritate peers by their refusal to cooperate or to display socially condoned patterns of behavior (Bierman et al., 1993; Hymel et al., 1993; Parkhurst & Asher, 1992).

Do popular children become popular because they are friendly, cooperative, and nonaggressive? Or is it that children become friendlier, more cooperative, and less aggressive after achieving their popularity? One way to test these competing hypotheses is to place children in play groups with *unfamiliar* peers and then see whether the behaviors that they display will predict their eventual status in the peer group. Several studies of this type have been conducted (Coie & Kupersmidt, 1983; Dodge, 1983; Dodge et al., 1990; Ladd et al., 1988), and the results are reasonably consistent: The patterns of behavior that children display do predict the status they will achieve with their peers. Children who are ultimately accepted by unfamiliar peers are effective at initiating social interactions and at responding positively to others' bids for attention. When they want to join a group activity, for example, these socially skilled, *soon-to-be-accepted* children first watch and attempt to understand what is going on, and then comment constructively about the proceedings as they blend smoothly into the group. By contrast, children who are ultimately *rejected* are pushy and self-serving: They often criticize or disrupt group activities and may even threaten reprisals if they are not allowed to join in. Other children who end up being *neglected* by their peers tend to hover around the edges of a group, initiating few interactions and shying away from other children's bids for attention.

In sum, peer popularity is affected by many factors. It may help to be athletic or to have an attractive face and academic skills, but it is probably more important to display social-cognitive skills and to behave in socially competent ways. Definitions of desirable social behavior, of course, may vary from culture to culture and change over time. For example, children who are shy are likely to be unpopular in Canada but popular in China, where being quiet and reserved is a more socially desirable trait (Chen, Rubin, & Sun, 1992). The ingredients of popularity also change with age:

Although establishing close relationships with members of the other sex enhances popularity during adolescence, such consorting with "the enemy" violates norms of gender segregation during childhood and *detracts* from one's popularity (Sroufe et al., 1993). In short, contextual factors influence who is popular and who is not.

Unfortunately, children who are actively rejected by peers—particularly aggressive rejected children—are likely to retain their rejected status from grade to grade (Cillessen et al., 1992; Coie et al., 1990). In Box 16-4, we will examine some of the ways in which these youngsters might be helped to improve their social skills and their prospects for experiencing healthier psychological outcomes.

Concept Check 16-2 ∨ Understanding Peer Sociability and Peer Relations

Check your understanding of peer sociability and peer relations by matching each descriptive statement below with one of the following concepts or processes: (a) aggressive rejected children; (b) crowd; (c) indirect monitoring (of peer interactions); (d) neglected children; (e) nonaggressive rejected children; (f) parental dominance/control; (g) play complexity; (h) popular children; (i) same-sex peer clique; (j) social behaviors. The answers appear in the Appendix.

_____ 1. Apparent parental contributor to nonharmonious peer interactions.

_____ 2. At greater risk of retaining their unfavorable sociometric status.

_____ 3. Important mechanism for promoting cross-sex friendships.

_____ 4. Display many prosocial behaviors and are seldom disruptive or aggressive.

_____ 5. Apparent parental contributor to harmonious peer interactions.

_____ 6. Lonely children who are at risk of experiencing depression and low self-esteem.

_____ 7. Perhaps the strongest contributor to a child's sociometric status.

_____ 8. Form that peer groups take early in adolescence.

_____ 9. Personal characteristic that predicts a toddler/preschooler's future social competence with peers.

_____ 10. Shy youngsters who are not particularly lonely and will often improve their sociometric status.

Children and Their Friends

As young children become more outgoing and are exposed to a wider variety of peers, they typically form close ties to one or more playmates—bonds that we call **friendships.** Recall from Chapter 12 that children have some pretty firm ideas about what qualifies someone as a friend. Before age 8, the principal basis for friendship is *common activity:* Children view a friend as someone who likes them and who enjoys similar kinds of play activities. By contrast, 8–10-year-olds, equipped with more sophisticated social perspective-taking skills, begin to see friends as individuals who are *psychologically similar* and who can be trusted to be loyal, kind, cooperative, and sensitive to each other's feelings and needs (Berndt, 1986; Pataki, Shapiro, & Clark, 1994). And although adolescents continue to think that loyalty and shared psychological attributes are characteristics that friends display, their conceptions of friendship now focus much more intently on *reciprocal emotional commitments.* That is, friends are viewed as *intimate* associates who truly understand each other's strengths, can accept each other's weaknesses, and are willing to share their innermost thoughts and feelings (Hartup, 1992).

Social Interactions among Friends and Acquaintances

As early as age 1 to 2, children may become attached to a preferred play partner and respond very differently to these "friends" than to other playmates (Hartup, 1992; Zaslow, 1980). For example, friends display more advanced forms of pretend play than acquaintances do—as well as more affection and more approval (Howes, Droege, & Matheson, 1994; Whaley & Rubenstein, 1994). Moreover, friends often do nice things for each other, and many altruistic behaviors may first appear within these

friendship: a close and often enduring relationship between two individuals which may be characterized by loyalty and mutual affection.

coaching: method of social-skills training in which an adult displays and explains various socially skilled behaviors, allows the child to practice them, and provides feedback aimed at improving the child's performance.

social problem-solving training: method of social-skills training in which an adult helps children (through role playing or role-taking training) to make less hostile attributions about harm-doing and to generate nonaggressive solutions to conflict.

BOX 16-4
On Improving the Social Skills of Unpopular Children

The finding that peer rejection is a strong predictor of current and future psychological difficulties has prompted many investigators to devise interventions, or "therapies," aimed at improving the social skills of unpopular children. Here are some of the more effective techniques.

Reinforcement and modeling therapies. Many early approaches to social-skills training were based on learning theory and involved (1) reinforcing children (with tokens or praise) for displaying such socially appropriate behaviors as cooperation and sharing or (2) exposing children to social models who display a variety of socially skilled acts. Both approaches have been successful at increasing the frequency of children's socially skilled behaviors. But to be effective in the long run, reinforcement of socially appropriate acts should be administered on a regular basis to the *entire peer group*, which not only increases the frequency of the target child's desirable acts but also allows him or her to see others reinforced for similar conduct. And when teachers and peers are involved in the intervention, they are much more likely to notice changes in the rejected child's behavior and are more inclined to change their opinion of him or her (Bierman & Furman, 1984; White & Kistner, 1992). Similarly, some modeling therapies are more effective than others. It seems that the modeling approach works best when the model is similar to the target child and when his socially skillful actions are accompanied by some form of commentary that directs the child's attention to the purposes and benefits of behaving appropriately toward peers (Asher, Renshaw, & Hymel, 1982).

Cognitive approaches to social-skills training. The fact that modeling strategies work better when accompanied by verbal rationales and explanations implies that interventions that prompt the child to think about or to imagine the consequences of various social overtures are likely to be effective. Why? Because the child's active cognitive involvement in the social-skills training may increase her understanding and appreciation of the principles that are taught, thereby persuading her to internalize and then rely on these lessons when interacting with peers.

Coaching is a cognitive social-learning technique in which the therapist displays one or more social skills, carefully explains the rationales for using them, allows children to practice such behavior, and then suggests how the children might improve on their performances. Sherri Oden and Steven Asher (1977) coached third- and fourth-grade social isolates on four important skills: how to participate in play activities, how to take turns and share, how to communicate effectively, and how to give attention and help to peers. Not only did the children who were coached become more outgoing and positive, but follow-up measures a year later revealed that these former isolates had achieved even further gains in social status (see also Bierman, 1986; Schneider, 1992). Coaching can be effective with preschool as well as grade school children (Mize & Ladd, 1990), and

apparently the benefits of this approach are even greater when it is combined with other forms of social-skills training, such as encouraging children to work together toward the attainment of cooperative goals (Bierman & Furman, 1984).

Other cognitive interventions, firmly grounded in cognitive-developmental theory, include attempts to improve children's *role-taking* skills and *social problem-solving abilities* (Chandler, 1973; Rabiner, Lenhart, & Lochman, 1990). These techniques can be especially effective with aggressive rejectees who often display a *hostile attributional bias* (a tendency to overattribute hostile intentions to their companions) that has been acquired at home from coercive parents who mistrust other people and endorse aggression (Keane, Brown, & Crenshaw, 1990; Pettit, Dodge, & Brown, 1988). In order to help these aggressive rejectees, the training must not only emphasize that aggression is inappropriate but also help them to generate nonaggressive solutions to conflict. One approach that looks promising is the **social problem-solving training** that Myrna Shure and George Spivack (1978; Shure, 1989) devised to help preschoolers generate and then evaluate amicable solutions to interpersonal problems. Over a ten-week period, children role played conflict scenarios with puppets and were encouraged to discuss the impact of their solutions on the feelings of all parties involved in a conflict. Shure and Spivack found that the longer the children had participated in the program, the fewer aggressive solutions were offered. Moreover, the children's classroom adjustment (as rated by teachers) improved as they became better able to think through the social consequences of their own actions.

Academic-skills training. Children who are failing miserably at school are often rejected by their classmates (Dishion et al., 1991). Might we elevate their social status by improving their academic skills and bringing them back into the mainstream of school activities? One research team tried this approach, providing extensive academic-skills training to low-achieving, socially rejected fourth-graders (Coie & Krehbiel, 1984). This training not only improved the children's reading and math achievement but their social standing as well. One year after the intervention ended, these former rejectees were now "accepted" and enjoyed average status in their peer group.

So there are a variety of techniques on which adults might rely to improve the social skills of unpopular children and help them to establish a more favorable standing among their peers. Yet a caution is in order, for the long-term success of any intervention could easily be compromised if the new social skills and problem-solving strategies that children have acquired are likely to be undermined by coercive, mistrusting parents who endorse aggressive solutions to conflict or by highly aggressive friends. For these

(continued)

reasons, Gregory Pettit and his associates (1988) favor *preventive* therapies—family-based interventions in which parents who value and encourage aggression are identified early and retrained themselves, thus possibly preventing their children from ever being rejected by their peers. Moreover, academic-skills training is also a preventive strategy: Children who gain in scholastic competence not only become better liked by peers but are also less likely to select highly aggressive children as friends or to become members

of deviant peer cliques (Dishion et al., 1991). Today, we are seeing a much stronger emphasis on preventive interventions—programs that are undertaken as soon as a child's problems with peers become apparent. And such an emphasis is clearly warranted, for (as we learned in Chapter 14) social-skills training programs rarely succeed once a child's deviant, antisocial conduct has continued beyond the first few grades at school (Kazdin, 1987; Patterson, DeBaryshe, & Ramsey, 1989).

early alliances of the preschool era. Frederick Kanfer and his associates (1981), for example, found that 3–6-year-olds were generally willing to give up their own valuable play time to perform a dull task if their efforts would benefit a friend; yet, this same kind of self-sacrifice was almost never made for a mere acquaintance. Young children also express more sympathy in response to the distress of a friend than to that of an acquaintance, and they are more inclined to try to relieve the friend's distress as well (Costin & Jones, 1992; Farver & Branstetter, 1994). Notice, then, that even *preschool* friendships are characterized by a sense of mutual caring and emotional support (see also Dunn, 1993; Whaley & Rubenstein, 1994), even though years may pass before children *say* that these qualities are what define a good friendship.

It is often said that there is a "chemistry" to close friendships and that best friends seem to be "in tune with each other." Recent research provides some support for these notions. Tiffany Field and her associates (1992) filmed pairs of sixth-graders as they chatted for ten minutes on topics of their own choosing. They found that interactions between pairs of friends were much more lively and "in synch" than those between acquaintances. For example, friends were more attentive and involved in the conversations and appeared to be more relaxed and playful with each other than acquaintances were. Moreover, friends were more likely than acquaintances to display the same behavioral state (for example, playfulness) at the same time. Finally, a measure of participants' saliva cortisol levels (a physiological correlate of stress) taken after the interactions suggested that casual conversations between acquaintances are more stressful than those between friends.

So perhaps it is fair to say that interactions between friends have a favorable "chemistry" about them. This is not to say that friends never lock horns; in fact, they squabble about as often or even more often than acquaintances do (Hartup et al., 1988; 1993). But as we noted in Chapter 12, disagreeing friends are more likely than disagreeing acquaintances to fully explain the basis for their conflicting points of view, thus providing each other with information that might foster the development of role-taking skills (Nelson & Aboud, 1985) as well as an ability to compromise.

How long do children's friendships last? It may surprise you to learn that even preschool friendships can be highly stable. Carollee Howes (1988), for example, found that children who attend the same day-care center for several years often keep the same close friends for more than a year. *Best* friendships often remain highly stable from year to year during middle childhood, although friendship networks (the list of *all* individuals that a child might nominate as "friends") tend to shrink in size as children approach adolescence (Berndt, Hawkins, & Hoyle, 1986; Berndt & Hoyle, 1985). This loss of friends may simply reflect the young adolescent's growing awareness that the obligations of friendship—which now include the exchange of intimate information and the provision of emotional support—are easier to live up to if one selects a smaller circle of very close friends.

Sometimes nothing is as reassuring as the affection and encouragement of a friend.

Are There Distinct Advantages to Having Friends?

Do friends play a unique role in shaping a child's development? Do children who have established adequate peer relations but no close friends turn out any differently from those who have one or more of these special companions? Unfortunately, no one can answer these questions, for long-term studies of the effects of having (or not having) friends have not been conducted. Nevertheless, the available data permit some tentative conclusions about the roles that friends play as socializing agents.

Friends as promotors of social competence and personal adjustment. One strong clue that friends play an important role in children's lives is the recent finding that having at least one friend goes a long way toward reducing the loneliness of unpopular children who are excluded from the larger peer group (Parker & Asher, 1993). Indeed, Carollee Howes (1988a) found that rejected children were much more likely to gain entry into ongoing peer-group activities if they tried to join with a friend or if they had a friend in the group. Moreover, rejected children who had a close friend displayed greater social skills and more mature forms of social play than other rejectees who had no friends. One implication of these findings is that having a mutual friend, especially a socially competent one, may help an unpopular child to acquire better social skills—an important prerequisite for improving his or her standing among peers.

Friends as providers of security and social support. A close attachment to one or more friends may also provide an emotional safety net—a kind of security that not only helps children to deal more constructively with new challenges but may also make almost any other form of life stress (for example, coping with a divorce or with a rejecting parent) a little easier to bear. Indeed, Gary Ladd (1990; Ladd & Price, 1987) finds that children who enter kindergarten along with their friends seem to like school better and have fewer adjustment problems than those who enter school without many friends. Moreover, we saw in Chapter 15 that children who respond most constructively to their parents' divorce are often those who have the support of friends whose parents are also divorced. We can also gauge the security and support that young children derive from friendships by looking at what happens when they lose a close friend who moves away. Such a loss is often a devastating experience for preschool children—one that can quickly undermine their emotional security and the quality (or maturity) of their interactions with peers (Howes, 1988a).

So friends are potentially important sources of security and **social support,** and they become increasingly important in fulfilling this role as children grow older. Fourth-graders, for example, say that their parents are their primary sources of social support; however, friends are perceived to be (1) as supportive as parents by seventh-graders and (2) the most frequent providers of social support by tenth-grade adolescents (Furman & Buhrmester, 1992).

Friends as contributors to social problem-solving skills. Since friendships are usually described as pleasant and rewarding relationships that are worth preserving, children should be highly motivated to resolve any conflicts with these "special" companions (Hartup, 1992). And apparently they are: Even during the preschool period, disagreeing friends are more likely than disagreeing acquaintances to step away before the squabbles become intense, to make concessions by accepting equal outcomes, and to continue playing together after the conflict is over (Hartup et al., 1988). So the experience of amicably resolving conflicts with a friend is undoubtedly an important contributor to the growth of mature social problem-solving skills—one of the strongest predictors of a healthy sociometric status with peers.

Friendships as preparation for adult love relationships. We've seen that close friendships are characterized by increasing intimacy and mutuality from middle childhood through adolescence. Could these relatively intense and intimate ties to what are overwhelmingly *same-sex* companions be necessary for the development of the deep interpersonal sensitivity and commitment so often observed in stable adult love relationships? Harry Stack Sullivan (1953) thought so. Sullivan reported that many of his mentally disturbed patients had failed to form close friendships when they were young, and he concluded that the close bonds that develop between same-sex friends (or "chums") during preadolescence provide the foundation of caring and compassion that a person needs to establish and maintain intimate love relationships (as well as close friendships) later in life. Although many of Sullivan's ideas remain to be confirmed, Duane Buhrmester (1990) finds that adolescents who have succeeded at establishing *intimate* friendships are better adjusted (that is, more sociable, less hostile, anxious, and depressed, and higher in self-esteem) than those whose friendships are not as deep.

One more point—and an important one. Friendships clearly differ in quality, and the very children who tend to have poor social skills—those who are insecurely attached to their parents, who have dominating, controlling parents, or who are rejected by peers—also tend to have friendships that are conflictual, nonsupportive, and lacking in trust (Kerns, 1994; Park & Waters, 1989; Parker & Asher, 1993; Youngblade & Belsky, 1992). In view of the important roles that close, supportive friendships seem to play in a child's life, perhaps our interventions for at-risk, unpopular children ought to include lessons in how to make (and keep) close friends as well as more general kinds of social-skills training (Murphy & Schneider, 1994).

How Do Peers Exert Their Influence?

To this point, we have seen that it is important for children to establish good peer relations because they will acquire many competent and adaptive patterns of social behavior through their interactions with peers. How exactly do peers exert their influence? In many of the same ways that parents do: by reinforcing, modeling, discussing, and even pressuring one another to comply with the values and behaviors they condone.

Peer Reinforcement and Modeling Influences

It is easy to see that parents, teachers, and other powerful authority figures are in a position to reward or punish the behavior of children. Yet we might legitimately wonder whether a peer, who shares a similar status with the child, can become an effec-

social support: tangible and intangible resources provided by other people in times of uncertainty or stress.

tive agent of reinforcement. Wonder no longer—the evidence is clear: Peers are rather potent sources of reinforcement.

Consider what Michael Lamb and his associates found while observing the reactions of 3–5-year-olds to their playmates' sex-appropriate or sex-inappropriate (cross-sex) activities. Children generally reinforced their companions for sex-appropriate play and were quick to criticize or disrupt a playmate's cross-sex activities. But were these playmates influenced by the treatment they received? Indeed they were. Children who received approval for sex-appropriate play tended to keep playing, whereas those who were punished for sex-inappropriate play usually terminated this activity in less than a minute (Lamb, Easterbrooks, & Holden, 1980).

Many of the reinforcers that children provide one another are quite subtle or unintentional. For example, a child who "caves in" to a bully has not only reinforced the bully's aggressive tactics without meaning to, but has set herself up to be victimized again. Yet, when a potential victim "punishes" a tormentor by fighting back, she may persuade him to seek other victims and possibly even learn that fighting "pays off," thus becoming more aggressive herself (Patterson, Littman, & Bricker, 1967).

So peers *are* important sources of social reinforcement. Although we have sampled but two studies from a voluminous literature, the evidence clearly indicates that children's social behaviors are often strengthened, maintained, or virtually eliminated by the favorable or unfavorable reactions they elicit from peers.

Modeling influences. Peers also influence one another by serving as social models for a multitude of social behaviors—some good, and some not so good. Among the more desirable attributes and activities that are easily acquired by observing peer models are socially skilled behaviors (Cooke & Apolloni, 1976), achievement behaviors (Sagotsky & Lepper, 1982), moral judgments (Kruger, 1992), an ability to delay gratification (Stumphauzer, 1972), and sex-typed attitudes and behaviors (Ruble, Balaban, & Cooper, 1981), to name a few. You may recall that several of these findings were discussed at length in earlier chapters.

Peers as objects for social comparison. Finally, children often reach conclusions about their competencies and other personality attributes by comparing their behaviors and accomplishments with those displayed by peers. If a 10-year-old consistently outperforms all her classmates on math tests, she is apt to conclude that she is "smart" or at least "good in math." A 7-year-old who loses every footrace that he has with peers will soon come to think of himself as a slow runner. Because peers are similar in age (and are presumed to be reasonably similar in many other respects), the peer group is the most logical choice for these kinds of *social comparisons* (see Festinger, 1954; France-Kaatrude & Smith, 1985). It matters little to our "smart" 10-year-old that she knows less math than her teenage sister. And our "snaillike" 7-year-old is not at all comforted by the fact that he can run faster than his 4-year-old brother. In matters of social comparison and self-definition, peers simply have no peer.

The Normative Function of Peer Groups

Another reason that peers become more potent as agents of socialization is that, from middle childhood onward, an increasing percentage of peer interactions occur in true *peer groups*—confederations that influence their members by setting explicit or implicit norms specifying how group members are supposed to look, dress, think, and act. And children do become increasingly responsive to normative peer pressures as they grow older, although they are hardly blind conformists as people commonly assume.

In his study of **peer conformity,** Thomas Berndt (1979) asked third- through twelvth-graders to indicate the likelihood that they would bend to peer pressure when peers were advocating various prosocial or antisocial acts. He found that conformity to peer pressure for prosocial behaviors did not change much with age. Instead, the most striking developmental change was a sharp increase in conformity to peers

peer conformity: the tendency to go along with the wishes of peers or to yield to peer-group pressures.

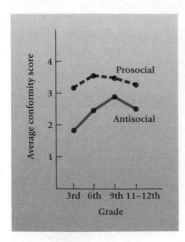

Figure 16-10
Average scores by grade for conformity to peer pressure for prosocial and antisocial behaviors.
Adapted from Berndt, 1979.

urging *antisocial* behavior. This receptivity to peer-sponsored misconduct peaked in the ninth grade (or about age 15; see Figure 16-10) and then declined throughout the high school years (see also Brown, Clasen, & Eicher, 1986; Steinberg & Silverberg, 1986). So parents may have some grounds for worrying that their 13–15-year-olds could wind up in trouble by going along with the crowd. Peer pressure of all kinds is especially strong at this age (Gavin & Furman, 1989), and there is nothing worse than being viewed as a "dork" or a "geek" who does not fit in (Kinney, 1993).

Why does conformity to peer-sponsored misconduct *decrease* by the end of high school? Perhaps this trend reflects the progress that older adolescents have made in their quest for autonomy: They are now better able to make their own decisions and are less dependent on the opinions of *either* parents or peers. According to Lawrence Steinberg and Susan Silverberg (1986), strong conformity to peer pressure early in adolescence may even be a necessary step in the development of autonomy: Young adolescents who are struggling to become less dependent on their parents may need the security that peer acceptance provides before they develop confidence to take their own stands and stick by them. And they are unlikely to gain such acceptance if they conform too closely to adult rules and values without taking a chance and going along with peers every now and then (Allen, Weissberg, & Hawkins, 1989). Although the parent whose teenager is nabbed with his friends for cherry bombing mailboxes or deflating tires may not be totally comforted by this thought, it does seem that a period of heavy peer influence may pave the way for later independence.

Peer versus Adult Influence: The Question of Cross-Pressures

In years gone by, adolescence was often characterized as a stormy period when all youths experience **cross-pressures**—strong conflicts that stem from differences in the values or practices advocated by parents and those favored by peers. How accurate is this "life portrait" of the teenage years? It may have some merit for some adolescents, especially those "rejected" youth who form deviant peer groups and endorse antisocial behaviors that are likely to alienate their parents, teachers, and most other peers (Dishion et al., 1991; Patterson et al., 1989). But there are several reasons to believe that the "cross-pressures problem" is not a problem for most adolescents.

One reason that parent-peer conflicts are kept to a minimum is that parents and peers tend to exert their influence in different domains. Hans Sebald (1986), for example, asked adolescents whether they would seek the advice of their parents or the advice of their peers on a number of different issues. *Peers* were likely to be more influential than parents on such issues as what styles to wear and which clubs, social events, hobbies, and other recreational activities to choose. By contrast, adolescents claimed that they would depend more on their *parents* when the issue involved scholastic or occupational goals or other future-oriented decisions (see also Wilks, 1986). Teenagers are unlikely to be torn between parent and peer pressures as long as parents and peers have different areas of influence.

A second and more important reason why parent-peer warfare is typically kept to a minimum is that parents have a good deal of influence on the kinds of friends their adolescents interact with. Authoritative parents who are warm, neither too controlling nor too lax, and consistent in their discipline generally find that their adolescents are closely attached to them and have internalized their values. These adolescents have little need to rebel or to desperately seek acceptance from peers when they are so warmly received at home (Brook et al., 1990; Brown et al., 1993; Fuligni & Eccles, 1993). In fact, they tend to associate with friends who share their values, which largely protects them from unhealthy peer influences (Fletcher et al., 1995).

Interestingly, problems for youths who do "fall in with the wrong crowd" and display antisocial behavior usually begin at home. One way parents can go wrong is by being too strict, failing to adjust to an adolescent's needs for greater autonomy. This may cause adolescents to become alienated from parents and overly susceptible to negative peer influences, to the point that they let schoolwork slide or break parental

cross-pressures: conflicts stemming from differences in the values and practices advocated by parents and those favored by peers.

rules to gain acceptance by their friends (Fuligni & Eccles, 1993). Parents can also go wrong by failing to provide enough discipline and by not monitoring their children's activities closely enough (Barber et al., 1994; Brown et al., 1993; Dishion et al., 1991). So parents have a good deal of power to influence, through their parenting, whether their adolescents end up in "good" or "bad" crowds and are exposed to healthy or unhealthy peer pressures. And contrary to prevailing stereotypes that minority youths often come from troubled families and are especially peer oriented, Peggy Giordano and her associates (1993) found that *most* African-American teenagers actually feel closer to their parents, attach less significance to their friendships, and are perhaps even less susceptible to deviant peer influences than white adolescents are.

Of course, there are some issues for which parental opinions are likely to conflict with those of many peers (for example, opinions about acceptable conduct on dates or about the harm involved in experimenting with tobacco, alcohol, or marijuana). But even so, peer-group values are rarely as deviant as adults commonly assume, and the adolescent's behavior is usually a product of *both* parental and peer influences. Denise Kandel (1973), for example, studied a group of adolescents whose best friends either did or did not smoke marijuana and whose parents either did or did not use psychoactive drugs. Among those teenagers whose parents used drugs but whose friends did not, only 17% were marijuana users. When parents did not use drugs but best friends did, 56% of the adolescents used marijuana. From these findings, we might conclude that the peer group is more influential than parents over marijuana use (see also Bentler, 1992). However, the highest rate of marijuana smoking (67%) occurred among teenagers whose parents and peers *both* used psychoactive drugs, and a similar pattern emerges when we look at parental and peer influences on use of alcohol, tobacco, and other illicit drugs (Newcomb & Bentler, 1989).

Concept Check 16-3 ⌄ Understanding the Influence of Close Friends and Peers

Check your understanding of some of the roles that friends and other peers play in a child's or an adolescent's development by filling in the blanks in each of the following statements. The answers appear in the Appendix.

1. By age _____ to _____, many children have become attached to a preferred play partner. During the preschool period, children are responding more _____ to friends than to acquaintances and display more _____ to a friend's distress. Later in childhood, interactions among friends have a more favorable _____ about them and are less _____ than interactions among acquaintances.

2. The fact that children with close friends find stresses easier to bear implies that friends serve as an important source of _____ _____. And because friendships are viewed as worth preserving, the experiences that friends have at _____ _____ amicably may promote the growth of mature social problem-solving skills—one of the strongest predictors of peer _____.

3. Intense and intimate ties to _____-_____ friends during preadolescence is thought by some to provide the sense of caring or compassion necessary for the maintenance of intimate _____ _____ later in life.

4. Peer groups are important sources of social influence. Studies of peer conformity show a sharp increase in children's conformity to peer-sponsored _____, which peaks by _____. Interestingly, going along with peers may be a necessary first step in the development of _____.

5. Cross-pressures can be a problem for _____ youth who form _____ cliques. However, they are not a problem for _____ adolescents. One reason that parent-peer conflicts are kept to a minimum is that parents and peers tend to exert their influence in different _____s. And by virtue of their child-rearing practices, parents exert a powerful influence over the _____s that their children fall into. Finally, even when peer norms differ from those of parents, the peer group values are rarely as _____ as people commonly assume.

Although teenagers are often characterized as wild or rebellious, typically their norms and values are a reflection of adult society.

In sum, adolescent socialization is not a continual war of parents *versus* peers; instead, these two important sources of influence *combine* to affect one's development. Most adolescents have cordial relationships with their parents, accept many of their parents' values, and are reluctant to stray too far from these guidelines and undermine their parents' approval. And most parents know how important it is for their children and adolescents to establish close relationships with their social equals. They seem to appreciate what the lonely farmer whose letter opened this section has learned the hard way: Many of the social competencies that will serve people well are the fruits of their alliances with close friends and peers.

SUMMARY

In this chapter, we have focused on three extrafamilial agents of socialization: television, schools, and children's peer groups.

Although children spend more time watching television than in any other waking activity, TV viewing, in moderate doses, is unlikely to impair their cognitive growth, academic achievement, or peer relations. However, television programming is often violent, and there is ample evidence that a heavy diet of televised violence can instigate aggressive behavior; cultivate aggressive, antisocial habits; and make children more tolerant of aggression. Television is also an important source of knowledge about people in the outside world. But, unfortunately, the information that children receive is often inaccurate and misleading—frequently consisting of stereotyped portrayals of men, women, and various racial and ethnic groups. Children are also influenced by television commercials, often developing preferences for unhealthy foods or unsafe toys and becoming angry or resentful if a parent refuses to buy a product they have requested.

Yet, the effects of television are not all bad. Children are likely to learn prosocial lessons and to put them into practice after watching acts of kindness on television. Parents can help by watching shows such as *Mister Rogers's Neighborhood* with their children and then encouraging them to verbalize or role play the prosocial lessons they have observed. Educational programs such as *Sesame Street* and *The Electric Company* have been quite successful at fostering basic cognitive skills, particularly when children watch with an adult who discusses the material with them and helps them to apply what they have learned.

Children seem to benefit, both intellectually and socially, from their use of computers. Computer-assisted instructional programs improve children's basic academic skills; word processing programs foster the growth of writing skills; and computer programming facilitates cognitive and metacognitive development. Moreover, computers promote rather than inhibit social interactions, for children tend to collaborate when using the machine to solve problems.

By age 6, children are spending several hours of each weekday at school. Schools seem to have two missions: to impart academic knowledge and to teach children how to become "good citizens." Schooling also appears to promote cognitive and metacognitive development by transmitting a variety of rules, strategies, and problem-solving skills that can be applied to many different kinds of information.

Some schools are more "effective" than others at producing positive outcomes such as low absenteeism, an enthusiastic attitude about learning, academic achievement, occupational skills, and socially desirable patterns of behavior. What makes a school effective is not its physical characteristics, classroom structure, or amount of money spent per pupil but, rather, its *human resources*. Effective schools are those in which (1) students are motivated to learn and become intellectually capable, (2) teachers create a classroom environment that is comfortable, engaging, and task oriented, and (3) there is a good "fit" between students' personal characteristics and the kinds of instruction they receive.

Racial and ethnic differences in academic achievement can often be traced to parental and peer influences and to teacher expectancies. At best, school desegregation and mainstreaming have led to modest improvements in the academic performance of minority students and those with developmental disabilities; but these practices have done little to reduce racial prejudice or to enhance the self-esteem of either handicapped pupils or minority youth. Among the steps that might be taken to better meet the educational needs of all of our students are creating stronger bilingual and multicultural educational programs and making greater use of *cooperative learning methods* in the classroom.

Cross-national surveys of academic achievement clearly brand American students as "underachievers," especially in math and science. American children are not any less intelligent than children from other countries. Instead, the achievement gap that exists between American schoolchildren and those in other industrialized societies centers around cultural differences in educational attitudes, educational practices, and the involvement of both parents and students in the learning process. Steps are now being taken at local, state, and national levels to try to bridge this achievement gap.

Peer contacts represent a second world for children—a world of equal-status interactions that is very different from the nonegalitarian environment of the home. Contacts with peers increase dramatically with age, and during the preschool or early elementary school years, children are spending at least as much of their leisure time with peers as with adults. The "peer group" consists mainly of *same-sex* playmates of somewhat *different ages*.

Research with monkeys and young children indicates that peer contacts are important for the development of competent and adaptive patterns of social behavior. Children who fail to establish and maintain adequate relations with their peers run the risk of experiencing any number of serious adjustment problems later in life.

Sociable gestures between peers begin by the middle of the first year. By age 18–24 months, infants' sociable interactions are becoming much more complex and coordinated as they reliably imitate each other, assume complementary roles in simple social games, and occasionally coordinate their actions to achieve shared goals. Play becomes increasingly social and more cognitively complex throughout the preschool years as children develop and refine the skills necessary to plan and monitor their enactment of *nonliteral* complementary roles during social pretend play. The maturity of a preschool child's play activities is a reasonably good predictor of his or her present and future social competencies and popularity with peers. During middle childhood, an increasing percentage of peer interactions occur in true *peer groups*—

confederations that associate regularly, define a sense of group membership, and formulate norms that specify how group members are supposed to behave. By early adolescence, youngsters are spending even more time with peers, particularly with their closest friends in small *cliques*, and in larger confederations of like-minded cliques known as *crowds*.

Several factors contribute to individual differences in peer sociability, including the child's genotype, parents' efforts to promote peer contacts, and the patterns of child-rearing practices that parents employ. Parents can directly influence their children's interactions with peers by virtue of the neighborhood in which they choose to live, their willingness to serve as "booking agents" for peer contacts, and their monitoring of peer interactions. Warm, sensitive, authoritative parents tend to raise appropriately sociable children who establish good relations with peers, whereas highly authoritarian or uninvolved parents—particularly those who rely on power assertion as a control tactic—tend to raise disruptive, aggressive youngsters whom peers often dislike.

Children clearly differ in popularity—the extent to which other youngsters view them as likable (or dislikable) companions. Using *sociometric techniques*, developmentalists find that there are five categories of peer acceptance: (1) *popular children* (liked by many and disliked by few), (2) *rejected children* (disliked by many and liked by few), (3) *controversial children* (liked by many and disliked by many), (4) *neglected children* (seldom nominated by others as likable or dislikable), and (5) *average-status children* (those who are liked or disliked by a moderate number of peers). Neither neglected children nor rejected children are well received by peers; however, it is the rejected child who is typically the lonelier of the two and at greater risk of displaying serious adjustment problems later in life. *Aggressive rejected* children are at risk of becoming chronically antisocial and displaying delinquent or criminal acts later in adolescence, whereas *nonaggressive rejected* children may become easy targets for bullies and experience low self-esteem, depression, and other emotional disorders.

Although a child's physical attractiveness, cognitive prowess, and ordinal position among siblings may contribute to his or her popularity with peers, one's patterns of social behavior are the strongest predictor of peer acceptance. Popular children are generally warm, cooperative, and compassionate companions who display many prosocial behaviors and are rarely disruptive or aggressive. Neglected children often have adequate social skills, but they may underestimate their social competencies or experience social anxieties that cause them to appear shy and to hover at the edge of peer-group activities, rarely calling attention to themselves. Rejected children display many unpleasant and annoying behaviors and few prosocial ones. Aggressive rejected children are highly uncooperative and aggressive, whereas nonaggressive rejected children are hypersensitive to criticism and actively isolate themselves from peers. Several techniques have been devised to improve the peer acceptance of rejected children. These social-skills training programs work better (1) with younger than with older children, and (2) when the target children's classmates also participate in the intervention.

Children typically form close ties, or friendships, with one or more members of their play groups. Younger children view a friend as a harmonious playmate, whereas older children and adolescents come to think of friends as close companions who share similar interests and values and are willing to provide them with intimate social and emotional support. Interactions among friends are warmer, more cooperative, more compassionate, and more synchronous (though not necessarily less conflictual) than those among acquaintances. Close friendships seem to promote positive developmental outcomes by (1) providing a sense of security and social support that enables children and adolescents to respond more constructively to stresses and challenges, (2) promoting the growth of social problem-solving skills and an ability to compromise, and (3) fostering caring and compassionate feelings which are the foundation of intimate love relationships later in life.

Peers influence a child in many of the same ways that parents do—by modeling, reinforcing, discussing, and pressuring associates to conform to the behaviors and values they condone. Conformity pressures peak at midadolescence, when teenagers are most susceptible to peer-sponsored misconduct. Yet, adolescents who have established warm relations with their parents have generally internalized many of their parents' values and continue to seek their parents' advice about scholastic matters and future-oriented decisions. Moreover, peer-group values are often very similar to those of parents, and peers are more likely to discourage than to condone antisocial conduct. So adolescent socialization is not a continual battle between parents and peers; instead, these two important influences *combine* to affect one's development.

Key Terms

ability tracking [654]

aggressive rejected children [675]

aptitude-treatment interaction (ATI) [656]

average-status children [675]

Children's Television Workshop (CTW) [646]

clique [672]

coaching [678]

controversial children [675]

cooperative learning methods [661]

cross-pressures [684]

crowd [672]

desensitization hypothesis [644]

effective schools [652]

extrafamilial influences [642]

friendship [678]

informal curriculum [651]

mainstreaming [661]

mean-world belief [644]

metacognition [651]

"mother-only" monkeys [668]

neglected children [675]

nonaggressive rejected children [675]

open classroom [654]

peer acceptance [674]

peer conformity [683]

peer group [672]

"peer-only" monkeys [668]

peers [666]

popular children [675]

Pygmalion effect [660]

rejected children [675]

sociability [669]

social problem-solving training [678]

social support [682]

sociometric techniques [674]

traditional classroom [654]

Appendix: Answers to Concept Checks

CHAPTER 1

Concept Check 1-1

1. **d.** *structured observation*. Obvious transgressions are events that children may not admit to in an interview, may not be detected by a case study, or may not occur while they are being monitored by an adult observer.

2. **a.** *structured interview*. If young children listening to the same vignettes regularly guess that the characters who display the most negative traits are the minority rather than majority group members, we might infer that they have already acquired some negative stereotyping about members of minority groups.

3. **c.** *case study*. Using a case study approach, you might interview clinically depressed adults, their parents, and perhaps their teachers to look for similarities in their childhood experiences. (As a second choice, you might ask clinically depressed adults to complete a structured interview or questionnaire about their childhood experiences.)

4. **d.** *naturalistic observation*. To answer this question, you would probably want to observe boys and girls in the natural environment where conflicts are likely to occur.

Note: Of course, any of the above research questions *can* be addressed by a variety of research methods.

Concept Check 1-2

1. **b. & d.** The other conclusions either equate correlation with causation (a & c) or describe the wrong kind of relationship (e).

2. **d.** Chang has failed to control for any potentially confounding variables. For example, the boys may have earned higher grades than the girls because they were smarter to begin with (intelligence is a confounding variable). Moreover, having boys in the treatment group and girls in the control group confounds treatment with gender. Had Chang wanted to see if increases in self-esteem *cause* increases in academic performance, he should have *randomly assigned* boys and girls to the treatment and control groups, thereby helping to ensure that all potentially confounding variables were roughly equivalent across these two conditions. If children in the treatment group subsequently earned higher grades than their counterparts in the control group, a causal inference would then be warranted.

Concept Check 1-3

1. **a.** *cross-sectional design*. Although either the longitudinal or the sequential design could provide similar information, neither of these alternatives is very quick.

2. **c.** *sequential design*. The researcher's question concerns the long-term effects of interventions given to children of different ages, thus calling for a sequential design.

3. **d.** *cross-cultural design*. The only way to determine whether there are any true "universals" in development is to conduct cross-cultural research to see whether children show the same developmental patterns despite differences in their rearing environments.

4. **b.** *longitudinal design*. Because our researcher is interested in the stability of children's intellectual performance relative to their peers

between ages 2 and 6, he could answer his question by following a group of 2-year-olds over a 4-year-period in a simple longitudinal comparison. The cross-section design is inappropriate here because each child is observed only once, thus providing no information about the *development* of individuals.

CHAPTER 2

Concept Check 2-1

1. **d.** *universal vs. particularistic development*. Although the sequencing of cognitive growth seems to be the same across cultures (universal), the rate of growth varies from child to child (particularistic development).

2. **a.** *nature vs. nurture*. Biological factors (nature) seem to account for half the variation in IQ test performance, whereas the environments that people experience (nurture) accounts for the other half.

3. **b.** *activity vs. passivity*. The "American Dream" assumes that humans are *active* beings who largely influence their own developmental outcomes. Watson's quote (see p. 43 of the text), by contrast, represents the opposite view, that humans are passive creatures shaped by their experiences.

4. **c.** *continuity vs. discontinuity*. Gradual growth of 1–2 in. per year over a period of 10 years is continuous development, whereas the growth spurt of adolescence (and other rapid biological changes that occur at puberty) represents discontinuous development.

Concept Check 2-2

1. **b.** *Erik Erikson* (1950, p. 32) explaining that humans are biological beings whose development is heavily influenced by the cultural contexts in which they live.

2. **d.** *Albert Bandura* (1977, p. 10) criticizing the radical behaviorist views of B. F. Skinner and emphasizing cognitive contributors to social learning.

3. **c.** *B. F. Skinner* (1971, p. 17) explaining why he thinks that free will is an illusion and that behavior is controlled by its external (reinforcing or punitive) consequences.

4. **a.** *Sigmund Freud* (1905, p. 78) arguing that it is possible to probe into the unconscious depths of the mind and reveal the conflicts that motivate many behaviors.

Concept Check 2-3

1. **c.** *Piaget's cognitive-developmental theory*

2. **b.** *learning theory* (particularly the behaviorist viewpoints of Watson and Skinner)

3. **d.** *the evolutionary viewpoint*

4. **a.** *psychoanalytic theory*

CHAPTER 3

Concept Check 3-1

1. **a.** *100%*. Monozygotic twins have 100% of their genes in common and are always the same sex.

2. *c. 50%.* Your mother cannot curl her tongue and can pass only recessive (non-tongue-curling) genes to her children. And because your sister cannot curl her tongue, she received a recessive gene from each parent. So your father is *heterozygous* for tongue curling. Half his sperm will carry the dominant tongue-curling gene, thus implying that your odds of being able to curl your tongue are 50%.

3. *b. heterozygous.* Your mother can transmit only recessive genes. So if you can curl your tongue, you necessarily have but one dominant gene for tongue curling (which came from your father).

4. *a. 100%.* Since both parents cannot curl their tongues, they can pass only recessive genes to their children.

Concept Check 3-2

1. identical twins; fraternal twins
2. biological; adoptive
3. kinship; trait similarity
4. together; live apart

Concept Check 3-3

1. *c. low.* $H = (r_{mz} - r_{dz}) \times 2 = (.61 - .50) \times 2 = .22$

2. *a.* This is a trait for which both SE and NSE contribute more than heredity does. The contribution of NSE (i.e., $1 - r_{m_3}$ twins, or $.39$) is about twice as large as the hereditary contribution. And a rough estimate of the contribution of SE (that is, $1 - (NSE \& H) = 1 - (.39 + .22)$, or $.39$ is comparable in magnitude to that of NSE.

CHAPTER 4

Concept Check 4-1

Event	Period	Time span	Name for organism
Implantation	germinal	0–2 weeks	zygote
Age of viability	fetal	2 mo.–birth	fetus
First heartbeats	embryonic	2 wks.–2 mo.	embryo
Kicks first felt by mother	fetal	2 mo.–birth	fetus
Organs form	embryonic	2wks.–2 mo.	embryo

Concept Check 4-2

1. the third trimester
2. the period of the embryo; sensitive period
3. rubella (see also Table 4-2 for other possible answers); thalidomide (see Table 4-3 for other possible answers)
4. Smoking fathers turn nonsmoking mothers into "passive smokers," which increases the risk of a low-birth-weight delivery; some drugs or other environmental toxins may bind to a father's sperm and may thus alter prenatal development from the moment of conception.

Concept Check 4-3

1. *d. sluggish, inattentive behavior for months after birth*
2. *a. cranial bleeding*
3. *c. respiratory distress syndrome* (Note: Alternative *d.* is also acceptable, for some preterm infants display a sluggish, inattentive demeanor for months after birth.)
4. *e. cerebral palsy*
5. *b. emotional bonding/engrossment*

CHAPTER 5

Concept Check 5-1

1. *c.* Establishment of *lateral preferences* is one consequence of cerebral lateralization.

2. *d.* Many subcortical *reflexes disappear* as the higher cortical centers mature.

3. *e.* The formation of glia and proliferation of synapses early in life are important contributors to the *brain growth spurt.*

4. *a.* With the loss of unused neural pathways, the brain becomes *less plastic.*

5. *b.* Increasing myelinization of the nervous system over the course of childhood is thought to underlie the *increases in attention span* that children display.

Concept Check 5-2

1. pursue goals
2. crawling; retreat to caregivers should they feel insecure
3. sex-role (and its encouragement of more sedentary activities); positive; anorexic; bulimic
4. Conflicts; advantage; disadvantage; fade (or become less clear)

Concept Check 5-3

1. *b. severe malnutrition*
2. *a. increase in GH production* (testosterone plays a secondary role for boys)
3. *d. stress-induced inhibition of GH*
4. *e. sedentary lifestyle*
5. *c. increase in testosterone/estrogen production*

CHAPTER 6

Concept Check 6-1

1. habituated; discriminates
2. discriminates Elvis from "rap" and prefers "rap"
3. identify his/her breast-feeding mother
4. Vision; 12 months
5. human voices

Concept Check 6-2

1. maturation; visual forms
2. kinetic (motion); form; spatial
3. depth; fear heights (or dropoffs)
4. experience (or language learning); better
5. integrated; upset; differentiation

Concept Check 6-3

1. *c. Strict, domineering parenting* is associated with the development of a field-dependent orientation.

2. *e. Learning a language* makes one insensitive to phonetic contrasts that are irrelevant to that language.

3. *b. Regular exposure to moving stimuli* that capture one's attention is crucial to the development of normal spatial abilities.

4. *a. Limited exposure to patterned visual stimuli* can alter the development of the visual areas of the brain, thereby impairing the ability to perceive visual forms.

5. *d. Living in a hunter-gatherer society,* where children are raised to be assertive and self-reliant, is associated with the development of a field-independent orientation.

CHAPTER 7

Concept Check 7-1

1. *e. disequilibrium*
2. *d. reversibility*
3. *c. accommodation*
4. *a. organization*
5. *b. assimilation*

Concept Check 7-2

1. transitivity; concrete-operational; horizontal decalage
2. object permanence; attachments; her behavior determines where the object will be found
3. hypothetical; hypothetical-deductive; familiar (or vitally important)
4. conserve; compensation; reversibility; preoperational; gender

Concept Check 7-3

1. *b. private speech*
2. *c. zone of proximal development*
3. *e. collaborative verbal dialogues*
4. *d. elementary mental functions*
5. *a. tools of intellectual adaptation*

CHAPTER 8
Concept Check 8-1

Vignette	Kind of learning	Consequence responsible for learning
1. Scumbags learn to stick with old hits.	Operant learning	Positive reinforcement for playing old hits.
2. Dog becomes excited at the sight of a yellow jacket.	Classical conditioning	By pairing the yellow jacket with a UCS (walking) that elicits excitement, the yellow jacket becomes a CS for excitement.
3. Fred distrusts politicians after hearing a group of strangers who are unanimous in questioning their integrity.	Observational learning	None. Learning occurs at a symbolic level, without reinforcement or punishment.
4. Jo comes to apply insect repellent before venturing outdoors.	Operant conditioning	Negative reinforcement (applying repellent ends the aversive insect attacks).
5. Jim no longer notices initially powerful odor.	Habituation	Becoming bored or disinterested in a now-familiar stimulus.

Concept Check 8-2

1. *c. long-term memory*
2. *e. levels of processing model*
3. *a. sensory store*
4. *d. executive control processes*
5. *f. store model*
6. *b. short-term (or working) memory*

Concept Check 8-3

1. unpracticed; short-term
2. deferred imitation; scripts
3. automatization; storage; brain maturation; familiarity (or practice)
4. production; utilization; mature strategy use
5. moderate; *why*
6. Knowledge base; experts; faster; stored; retrieved

CHAPTER 9
Concept Check 9-1

1. *c. J. P. Guilford (structure of intellect model)*
2. *d. Charles Spearman (early factor-analytic model of intelligence)*
3. *b. Howard Gardner (theory of multiple intelligences)*

4. *f. Louis Thurstone (early factor-analytic model of intelligence)*
5. *a. Raymond Cattell/John Horn (a modern psychometric view of intelligence)*
6. *e. Robert Sternberg (triarchic theory of intelligence)*

Concept Check 9-2

1. neurological disorders; IQs; speed of habituation; preference for novelty
2. half; fluctuations; performance; capacity
3. moderately; solely; habits; interests; motivation
4. favorable; home environment
5. poorer (or less favorable); self-supporting; satisfied; disconfirming

Concept Check 9-3

1. *f. confluence hypothesis*
2. *b. socioeconomic risk factors*
3. *a. quality of home environment*
4. *e. "cumulative deficit" hypothesis*
5. *d. "test bias" hypothesis*
6. *c. parenting styles*
7. *g. genetic hypothesis for group differences in IQ*
8. *d. unequal rearing environments*

CHAPTER 10
Concept Check 10-1

1. *d. sensitive-period hypothesis*
2. *b. recasts*
3. *g. conversations with language users*
4. *e. creolizing of pidgins by children*
5. *a. communication pressure hypothesis*
6. *f. universals in cognitive development*
7. *c. language acquisition device*

Concept Check 10-2

1. biological maturation; 8 months; intonation
2. intonational; meaningful; words; phrases
3. 12 months; slowly; naming explosion; fast-mapping
4. processing constraints; mutual exclusivity; lexical contrast; syntactical clues
5. telegraphic speech; nouns; verbs; adjectives; communication
6. ambiguous; gestures; intonational

Concept Check 10-3

1. grammatical morphemes; transformational grammar; 5 or 6
2. refinement; grammatical; complex
3. receptive; morphological knowledge; meaning
4. metalinguistic awareness; phonemic
5. role-taking; sociolinguistic understanding

CHAPTER 11
Concept Check 11-1

1. *b. self-recognition*
2. *f. infant emotional expressions*
3. *e. emotional understanding*
4. *c. social referencing*
5. *d. disconfirmed expectancies*
6. *a. emotional self-regulation*

Concept Check 11-2

1. **e.** Ainsworth's ethological viewpoint
2. **c.** learning perspective (Robert Sears)
3. **f.** cognitive-developmental perspective
4. **a.** Freud's psychoanalytic viewpoint
5. **d.** Bowlby's ethological viewpoint
6. **b.** Erikson's psychoanalytic viewpoint

Concept Check 11-3

1. **c.** Thomas and Chess's goodness-of-fit model
2. **b.** Kagan's temperament hypothesis
3. **f.** social stimulation hypothesis
4. **a.** Ainsworth's caregiving hypothesis
5. **d.** Bowlby/Bretherton "internal working models" hypothesis
6. **e.** maternal deprivation hypothesis

CHAPTER 12

Concept Check 12-1

1. **b.** self-esteem
2. **e.** private self
3. **c.** looking-glass self
4. **g.** self-recognition
5. **a.** categorical self
6. **d.** belief-desire theory of mind
7. **f.** social comparison

Concept Check 12-2

1. effectance (or mastery); 2 years; approval; disapproval; 3 years; performance; achievement
2. warm/supportive; firm/demanding; democratic (allowing the child some autonomy in deciding how to master challenges or comply with standards); authoritative; peer pressures
3. causal attributions; stable; unstable
4. mastery-oriented; learned-helplessness; ability; entity; give up; attribution retraining; effort

Concept Check 12-3

1. **b.** identity foreclosure
2. **e.** self-assertion
3. **f.** defiance
4. **c.** identity diffusion
5. **h.** private speech/self-instructions
6. **g.** delay of gratification
7. **a.** moratorium
8. **d.** ethnic identity achievement

CHAPTER 13

Concept Check 13-1

1. **e.** reading comprehension
2. **b.** gender identity
3. **g.** sex-role standard
4. **f.** self-fulfilling prophecy
5. **h.** visual/spatial ability
6. **d.** gender segregation
7. **a.** achievement motivation
8. **c.** gender intensification

Concept Check 13-2

1. **g.** gender consistency
2. **a.** Money and Ehrhardt's biosocial theory
3. **b.** Freud's psychoanalytic theory
4. **f.** basic gender identity
5. **i.** androgenized females
6. **c.** social learning theory
7. **j.** androgynous females
8. **e.** Martin and Halverson's gender schema theory
9. **d.** Kohlberg's cognitive-developmental theory
10. **h.** gender schemas

Concept Check 13-3

The program might target 3–6-year-olds whose gender stereotypes are just forming and are not entrenched. The program should encourage cross-sex as well as same-sex play activities, and its adult leaders should model both same- and cross-sex pursuits. Question and answer sessions about the gender stereotypes that children already hold should provide opportunities to point out that one's interests and willingness to learn, rather than one's gender, are the most important considerations in determining the activities that people should pursue (rule training). Giving children multiple classification tasks that require them to sort objects into more than one category (and illustrate that men and women often share similar interests and occupational goals) should also help children to break free of rigid gender stereotypes. Finally, at least part of the training might be conducted by an adult male, for it is males who normally make the stronger distinctions between what is "appropriate" for males and females and, thus, may be more noteworthy as agents of change.

CHAPTER 14

Concept Check 14-1

1. **g.** lower-SES parents rely more heavily on physical punishment
2. **c.** hostile aggression
3. **j.** negative reinforcement
4. **b.** deviant peer cliques
5. **e.** instrumental aggression
6. **a.** cathartic technique
7. **d.** hostile attributional bias
8. **i.** time-out technique
9. **h.** peer rejection
10. **f.** coercive home environment

Concept Check 14-2

1. **d.** self-concept (or attribution) training
2. **e.** self-oriented distress
3. **a.** altruistic lessons or norms
4. **b.** felt responsibility (or obligation to help)
5. **c.** role-taking ability
6. **f.** sympathetic empathic arousal

Concept Check 14-3

1. invariant; skip; regress; longitudinal; order (or sequence)
2. role-taking; formal operations; supports
3. reevaluate; transactive interactions; advanced (or college)
4. universal; care; moral emotions
5. prosocial; distributive justice; underestimates

CHAPTER 15

Concept Check 15-1

1. *f.* In this *indirect effect,* the father-son relationship influences the husband-wife relationship.

2. *i.* The mother is keeping the infant close and promoting his *survival.*

3. *a.* Parents are encouraging attributes necessary for maintaining the *economic welfare* of an agricultural society.

4. *b.* In communal societies, children living in *extended families* seem to fare better.

5. *c.* Family dynamics change with the *development* of family members.

6. *e.* Due to divorce and out-of-wedlock deliveries, *single-parent families* are common today.

7. *h.* These are attributes that reflect parental encouragement of *self-actualization.*

8. *d.* This finding illustrates that families are *embedded* in a larger social context that may influence parenting practices.

9. *g.* Such an arrangement is called a *reconstituted family.*

Concept Check 15-2

1. *c. economic distress*

2. *e. increased academic aptitude* (younger sibs may share this benefit if older sibs teach them academic lessons)

3. *j. unwanted children*

4. *f. later-born siblings*

5. *a. authoritarian parenting*

6. *h. only children*

7. *i. uninvolved parenting*

8. *d. emotional support*

9. *g. older siblings*

10. *b. authoritative parenting*

Concept Check 15-3

1. *c. delinquent conduct*

2. *f. joint physical custody* (option *b* is also an acceptable alternative)

3. *d. girls*

4. *g. support* (both emotional and financial) *from the noncustodial parent*

5. *b. coercive parenting* by the custodial parent (option *f* is also an acceptable alternative)

6. *e. better psychological adjustment*

7. *a. boys*

8. *h.* children of divorce are more likely than those from intact families to experience an *unhappy marriage* and a divorce themselves

CHAPTER 16

Concept Check 16-1

1. *f. mainstreaming*

2. *i. Pygmalion effect*

3. *a. ability tracking*

4. *e. informal curriculum*

5. *g. monetary support*

6. *h. parental involvement in scholastic activities*

7. *j. school size*

8. *b. aptitude-treatment interaction (ATI)*

9. *d. group differences in IQ*

10. *c. cooperative learning methods*

Concept Check 16-2

1. *f. parental dominance/control*

2. *a. aggressive rejected children*

3. *b. crowd*

4. *h. popular children*

5. *c. indirect monitoring* (of peer interactions)

6. *e. nonaggressive rejected children*

7. *j. social behaviors*

8. *i. same-sex cliques*

9. *g. play complexity*

10. *d. neglected children*

Concept Check 16-3

1. 1 to 2 years; positively (or prosocially); sympathy; chemistry; stressful

2. social support; resolving conflicts; acceptance

3. same-sex; love relationships

4. misconduct; midadolescence (or age 15); autonomy

5. rejected; deviant peer; most; areas or domains; crowds; deviant

Glossary

A, not B, error: tendency of 8- to 12-month-olds to search for a hidden object where they previously found it even after they have seen it moved to a new location.

ability tracking: the educational practice of grouping students according to ability and then educating them in classes with students of comparable educational or intellectual standing.

accommodation: Piaget's term for the process by which children modify their existing schemes in order to incorporate or adapt to new experiences.

achievement motivation: a willingness to strive to succeed at challenging tasks and to meet high standards of accomplishment.

acquired immune deficiency syndrome (AIDS): a viral disease that can be transmitted from a mother to her fetus or neonate and that results in a weakening of the body's immune system and, ultimately, death.

action system: a more advanced motor skill that arises as the child combines and reorganizes existing skills.

active genotype/environment correlations: the notion that our genotypes affect the types of environments that we prefer and will seek out.

activity/passivity issue: a debate among developmental theorists about whether children are active contributors to their own development or, rather, passive recipients of environmental influence.

adaptation: an inborn tendency to adjust to the demands of the environment.

adolescent growth spurt: the rapid increase in physical growth that marks the beginning of adolescence.

adoption design: study in which adoptees are compared with their biological relatives and their adoptive relatives to estimate the heritability of an attribute or attributes.

age of viability: a point between the 24th and 28th prenatal weeks when a fetus may survive outside the uterus if excellent medical care is available.

aggression: behavior performed with the intention of harming a living being who is motivated to avoid this treatment.

aggressive rejected children: a subgroup of rejected children who display high levels of hostility and aggression in their interactions with peers.

aging-ova hypothesis: the hypothesis that an older mother is more likely to have children with chromosomal abnormalities because her ova are degenerating as she nears the end of her reproductive years.

alleles: alternative forms of a gene that is coded for a particular trait.

alternative birth center: a hospital birthing room or other facility that provides a homelike atmosphere for childbirth but still makes medical technology available.

altruism: concern for the welfare of others that is expressed through such prosocial acts as sharing, cooperating, and helping.

altruistic exhortations: verbal encouragements to help, comfort, share, or cooperate with others.

amniocentesis: a method of extracting amniotic fluid from a pregnant woman so that fetal body cells within the fluid can be tested for chromosomal abnormalities and other genetic defects.

amnion: a watertight membrane that develops from the trophoblast and surrounds the developing embryo, serving to regulate its temperature and to cushion it against injuries.

anal stage: Freud's second stage of psychosexual development (from 1 to 3 years of age), in which anal activities such as defecation become the primary methods of gratifying the sex instinct.

androgenized females: females who develop male-like external genitalia because of exposure to male sex hormones during the prenatal period.

androgyny: a sex-role orientation in which the individual has incorporated a large number of both masculine and feminine attributes into his or her personality.

animism: attributing life and lifelike qualities to inanimate objects.

anorexia nervosa: a life-threatening eating disorder characterized by self-starvation and a compulsive fear of getting fat.

anoxia: a lack of sufficient oxygen to the brain; may result in neurological damage or death.

Apgar test: a quick assessment of the newborn's heart rate, respiration, color, muscle tone, and reflexes that is used to gauge perinatal stress and to determine whether a neonate requires immediate medical assistance.

aphasia: loss of one or more language functions due to an injury to the brain.

appearance/reality distinction: ability to keep the true properties or characteristics of an object in mind despite the deceptive appearance the object has assumed; notably lacking among young children during the preconceptual period.

aptitude-treatment interaction (ATI): phenomenon whereby characteristics of the student and of the school environment interact to affect student outcomes, such that any given educational practice may be effective with some students, but not with others.

asocial stage (of attachment): approximately the first six weeks of life, in which infants respond in an equally favorable way to interesting social and nonsocial stimuli.

assimilation: Piaget's term for the process by which children interpret new experiences by incorporating them into their existing schemes.

astigmatism: a refractive defect of the lens of the eye that prevents the formation of clear, distinct images.

attachment: a close emotional relationship between two persons, characterized by mutual affection and a desire to maintain proximity.

attachment object: a close companion to whom one is attached.

attention deficit-hyperactivity disorder: an attentional disorder involving distractibility, hyperactivity, and impulsive behavior that often leads to academic difficulties, poor self-esteem, and social/emotional problems.

attention span: a person's capacity for sustaining attention to a particular stimulus or activity.

attribution retraining: therapeutic intervention in which helpless children are persuaded to attribute failures to their lack of effort rather than a lack of ability.

attribution theory: a social-cognitive theory specifying that the explanations that we construct for social experiences largely determine how we respond to these experiences.

authoritarian parenting: a restrictive pattern of parenting in which adults set many rules for their children, expect strict obedience, and rely on power rather than reason to elicit compliance.

authoritative parenting: flexible, democratic style of parenting in which warm, accepting parents provide guidance and control while allowing the child some say in deciding how best to meet challenges and obligations.

automatization: an increase in the efficiency in which cognitive operations are executed.

autonomous morality: Piaget's second stage of moral development, in which children realize that rules are arbitrary agreements that can be challenged and changed with the consent of the people they govern.

autonomy: the capacity to make decisions independently, to serve as one's own source of emotional strength, and to otherwise manage one's life tasks without depending on others for assistance; an important developmental task of adolescence.

autonomy versus shame and doubt: the second of Erikson's psychosocial stages, in which toddlers either assert their wills and attend to their own basic needs or else become passive, dependent, and lacking in self-confidence.

autostimulation theory: a theory proposing that REM sleep in infancy is a form of self-stimulation that helps the central nervous system to develop.

average-status children: children who receive a moderate number of nominations as a liked and/or a disliked individual from members of their peer group.

avoidant attachment: an insecure infant/caregiver bond, characterized by little separation protest and a tendency of the child to avoid or ignore the caregiver.

babbles: vowel/consonant combinations that infants begin to produce at about 4 to 6 months of age.

baby biography: a detailed record of an infant's growth and development over a period of time.

basic gender identity: the stage of gender identity in which the child first labels the self as a boy or a girl.

basic trust versus mistrust: the first of Erikson's eight psychosocial stages, in which infants must learn to trust their closest companions or else run the risk of mistrusting other people later in life.

behavioral comparisons phase: the tendency to form impressions of others by comparing and contrasting their overt behaviors.

behavioral genetics: the scientific study of how one's hereditary endowment interacts with environmental influences to determine such attributes as intelligence, temperament, and personality.

behavioral inhibition: a temperamental characteristic reflecting one's tendency to withdraw from unfamiliar people or situations.

behavioral schemes: organized patterns of behavior that are used to represent and respond to objects and experiences.

behaviorism: a school of thinking in psychology that holds that conclusions about human development should be based on controlled observations of overt behavior rather than speculation about unconscious motives or other unobservable phenomena; the philosophical underpinning for the early theories of learning.

belief-desire theory: theory of mind that develops around age 4; the child now realizes that beliefs are only mental constructions rather than copies of reality and that people will act on these constructions, even if they are inaccurate.

blastocyst: a hollow sphere of about 100-150 cells that results from the rapid division of the zygote as it moves through the fallopian tube.

brain growth spurt: the period between the seventh prenatal month and 2 years of age when more than half of the child's eventual brain weight is added.

Brazelton Neonatal Behavioral Assessment Scale (NBAS): a test that assesses a neonate's neurological status and responsiveness to environmental stimuli.

breech birth: a delivery in which the fetus emerges feet first or buttocks first rather than head first, as is usual.

bulimia: a life-threatening eating disorder characterized by recurrent eating binges followed by such purging activities as heavy use of laxatives or vomiting.

canalization: genetic restriction of phenotype to a small number of developmental outcomes; a highly canalized attribute is one for which genes channel development along predetermined pathways, so that the environment has little effect on the phenotype that emerges.

caregiving hypothesis: Ainsworth's notion that the type of attachment that an infant develops with a particular caregiver depends primarily on the kind of caregiving he has received from that person.

case study: a research method in which the investigator gathers extensive information about the life of an individual and then tests developmental hypotheses by analyzing the events of the person's life history.

castration anxiety: in Freud's theory, a young boy's fear that his father will castrate him as punishment for his rivalrous conduct.

catch-up growth: a period of accelerated growth in which children who have experienced growth deficits grow very rapidly to "catch up" to the growth trajectory that they are genetically programmed to follow.

categorical self: a person's classification of the self along socially significant dimensions such as age and sex.

catharsis hypothesis: the notion that aggressive urges are reduced when people commit real or symbolic acts of aggression.

cathartic technique: a strategy for reducing aggression by encouraging children to vent their anger or frustrations on inanimate objects.

causal attributions: inferences made about the underlying causes of one's own or another person's behavior.

centered thinking (centration): the tendency to focus on only one aspect of a problem when two or more aspects are relevant.

cephalocaudal development: a sequence of physical maturation and growth that proceeds from the head (cephalic region) to the tail (or caudal region).

cerebral cortex: the outer layer of the brain's cerebrum that is involved in voluntary body movements, perception, and higher intellectual functions such as learning, thinking, and speaking.

cerebral lateralization: the specialization of brain functions in the left and the right cerebral hemispheres.

cerebrum: the highest brain center; includes both hemispheres of the brain and the fibers that connect them.

cesarean delivery: surgical delivery of a baby through an incision made in the mother's abdomen and uterus (also called cesarean section).

child abuse: term used to describe any extreme maltreatment of children, involving physical batterings, sexual molestations, psychological insults such as persistent ridicule, rejection, and terrorization, and physical or emotional neglect.

Children's Television Workshop (CTW): an organization committed to producing TV programs that hold children's interest and facilitate their social and intellectual development.

chorion: a membrane that develops from the trophoblast and becomes attached to the uterine tissues to gather nourishment for the embryo.

chorionic villus sampling (CVS): an alternative to amniocentesis in which fetal cells are extracted from the chorion for prenatal tests. CVS can be performed earlier in pregnancy than is possible through amniocentesis.

chromosome: a threadlike structure made up of genes; in humans there are 46 chromosomes in the nucleus of each body cell.

classical conditioning: a type of learning in which an initially neutral stimulus is repeatedly paired with a meaningful stimulus so that the neutral stimulus comes to elicit the response originally made only to the meaningful stimulus.

class inclusion: the ability to compare a class of objects with its subclasses without confusing the two.

clinical method: a type of interview in which a participant's response to each successive question (or problem) determines what the investigator will ask next.

clique: a small group of friends who interact frequently.

coaching: method of social-skills training in which an adult displays and explains various socially skilled behaviors, allows the child to practice them, and provides feedback aimed at improving the child's performance.

codominance: condition in which two heterozygous but equally powerful alleles produce a phenotype in which both genes are fully and equally expressed.

coercive home environment: a home in which family members often annoy one another and use aggressive or otherwise antisocial tactics as a method of coping with these aversive experiences.

cognition: the activity of knowing and the processes through which knowledge is acquired.

cognitive development: age-related changes that occur in mental activities such as attending, perceiving, learning, thinking, and remembering.

cognitive equilibrium: Piaget's term for the state of affairs in which there is a balanced, or harmonious, relationship between one's thought processes and the environment.

cognitive operation: an internal mental activity that one performs on objects of thought.

cohort effect: age-related difference among cohorts that is attributable to cultural/historical differences in cohorts' growing-up experiences rather than to true developmental change.

communication: the process by which one organism transmits information to and influences another.

communication pressure hypothesis: the idea that children learn to speak clearly and grammatically because clear, grammatical statements will effectively communicate their needs and desires.

comparative research: an approach whereby investigators compare behavior and/or development across species.

compensation: the ability to consider more than one aspect of a problem at a time (also called decentration).

compensatory interventions: special educational programs designed to further the cognitive growth and scholastic achievements of disadvantaged children.

compliance: the act of willfully obeying the requests or commands of others.

conception: the moment of fertilization, when a sperm penetrates an ovum, forming a zygote.

concordance rate: the percentage of cases in which a particular attribute is present for both members of a pair if it is present for one member.

concrete operations: Piaget's third stage of cognitive development, lasting from about ages 7–11 years, when children are acquiring cognitive operations and thinking more logically about real objects and experiences.

conditioned response (CR): a learned response to a stimulus that was not originally capable of producing the response.

conditioned stimulus (CS): an initially neutral stimulus that comes to elicit a particular response after being paired with a UCS that always elicits the response.

confluence hypothesis: Zajonc's notion that a child's intellectual development depends on the average intellectual level of all family members.

confounding variable: some factor other than the independent variable which, if not controlled by the experimenter, could explain any differences across treatment conditions in participants' performance on the dependent variable.

congenital defect: a problem that is present (thought not necessarily apparent) at birth; such defects may stem from genetic and prenatal influences or from complications of the birth process.

conservation: the recognition that the properties of an object or substance do not change when its appearance is altered in some superficial way.

constructivist: one who gains knowledge by acting or otherwise operating on objects and events to discover their properties.

contextual model: view of children as active entities whose developmental paths represent a continuous, dynamic interplay between internal forces (nature) and external influences (nurture). Represented (loosely) by ethologists and ecological systems theorists.

continuity/discontinuity issue: a debate among theorists about whether developmental changes are quantitative and continuous, or, rather, are qualitative and discontinuous (i.e., stagelike).

continuous reinforcement: a schedule of reinforcement in which every occurrence of an act is reinforced.

controversial children: children who receive many nominations by peers as a liked individual and many as a disliked individual.

cooperative learning methods: an educational practice whereby children of different races or ability levels are assigned to teams; each team member works on problems geared to his or her ability level, and all members are reinforced for "pulling together" and performing well as a team.

coos: vowel-like sounds that young infants repeat over and over during periods of contentment.

corpus callosum: the bundle of neural fibers that connects the two hemispheres of the brain and transmits information from one hemisphere to the other.

correlational design: a type of research design that indicates the strength of associations among variables; though correlated variables are systematically related, these relationships are not necessarily causal.

correlation coefficient: a numerical index, ranging from -1.00 to $+1.00$, of the strength and direction of the relationship between two variables.

conventional morality: Kohlberg's term for the third and fourth stages of moral reasoning, in which moral judgments are based on a desire to gain approval (Stage 3) or to uphold laws that maintain social order (Stage 4).

convergent thinking: thinking that requires one to come up with a single correct answer to a problem; what IQ tests measure.

counterconditioning: a treatment based on classical conditioning in which the goal is to extinguish an undesirable response and replace it with a new and more adaptive one.

counting span: a measure of M-space that requires individuals to operate on the information they have in short-term memory.

creativity: the ability to generate novel ideas or works that are valued by others.

critical period: a (typically) brief period in the development of an organism when it is particularly sensitive to certain environmental influences; outside this period, the same influences have little, if any, effect.

cross-cultural comparison: a study that compares the behavior and/or development of people from different cultural or subcultural backgrounds.

cross-generational problem: the fact that long-term changes in the environment may limit conclusions of a longitudinal project to that generation of children who were growing up while the study was in progress.

crossing over: a process in which genetic material is exchanged between pairs of chromosomes.

cross-pressures: conflicts stemming from differences in the values and practices advocated by parents and those favored by peers.

cross-sectional design: a research design in which subjects from different age groups are studied at the same point in time.

crowd: a large, loosely organized peer group made up of several cliques that share similar norms, interests, and values.

crystallized intelligence: the ability to understand relations or solve problems that depend on knowledge acquired from schooling and other cultural influences.

cued recall memory: a recollection that is prompted by a cue associated with the setting in which the recalled event originally occurred.

cultural bias: the situation that arises when one cultural or subcultural group is more familiar with test items than is another group and therefore has an unfair advantage.

"culture fair" tests: intelligence tests constructed to minimize any irrelevant cultural biases in test content that could influence test performance.

cumulative-deficit hypothesis: the notion that impoverished environments inhibit intellectual growth and that these inhibiting effects accumulate over time.

cytomegalovirus (CMV): a virus in the herpes group that produces few, if any, symptoms in mothers but is the most common infectious cause of congenital deafness and mental retardation.

deferred imitation: the ability to reproduce a modeled activity that has been witnessed at some point in the past.

defiance: active resistance to others' requests or demands; noncompliant acts that are accompanied by anger and an intensification of ongoing behavior.

delay of gratification: a form of self-control involving the capacity to inhibit impulses to seek small rewards that are available immediately in the interest of obtaining larger, delayed incentives.

deoxyribonucleic acid (DNA): long, double-stranded molecules that make up chromosomes.

dependent variable: the aspect of behavior that is measured in an experiment and assumed to be under the control of the independent variable.

deprivation dwarfism: Gardner's name for retardation in physical growth that is apparently triggered by emotional distress and/or a lack of love and attention.

desensitization hypothesis: the notion that people who watch a lot of media violence will become less aroused by aggression and more tolerant of violent and aggressive acts.

development: the process by which organisms grow and change over the course of their lives.

developmental quotient (DQ): a numerical measure of an infant's performance of a developmental schedule relative to the performance of other infants of the same age.

developmental psychology: branch of psychology devoted to the study of how individuals change over time and the factors that produce these changes.

developmental stage: a distinct phase within a larger sequence of development; a period characterized by a particular set of abilities, motives, behaviors, or emotions that occur together and form a coherent pattern.

deviation IQ: an IQ score based on the extent to which a child's test performance deviates from the average performance of age mates.

dialectical reasoning: the ability to resolve logical inconsistencies or paradoxes; thought by some to be a stage of reasoning beyond formal operations.

diethylstilbestrol (DES): a synthetic hormone, formerly prescribed to prevent miscarriage, that can produce cervical cancer in adolescent female offspring and genital-tract abnormalities (and sterility) in males.

differentiation theory: a theory specifying that perception involves detecting distinctive features or cues that are contained in the sensory stimulation we receive.

difficult temperament: temperament in which the child is irregular in daily routines and adapts slowly to new experiences, often responding negatively and intensely.

discrimination: the process of differentiating and responding differently to stimuli that vary on one or more dimensions.

direct tuition: process of teaching young children how to behave by reinforcing appropriate behaviors and by punishing or otherwise discouraging inappropriate conduct.

disequilibriums: imbalances or contradictions between one's thought processes and environmental events. By contrast, *equilibrium* refers to a balanced, harmonious relationship between one's cognitive structures and the environment.

dishabituation: recovery of a habituated response that results from a change in the eliciting stimulus.

disorganized/disoriented attachment: an insecure infant/caregiver bond, characterized by the infant's dazed appearance on reunion or a tendency to first seek and then abruptly avoid the caregiver.

distinctive features: characteristics of a stimulus that remain constant; dimensions on which two or more objects differ and can be discriminated (sometimes called *invariances* or *invariant features*).

distributive justice: conceptions of what is "fair" or "just" concerning the allocation of resources among the members of a group.

divergent thinking: thinking that requires a variety of ideas or solutions to a problem when there is no one correct answer.

dizygotic (or fraternal) twins: twins that result when a mother releases two ova at roughly the same time and each is fertilized by a different sperm, producing two zygotes that are genetically different.

doctrine of specificity: a viewpoint shared by many social-learning theorists that holds that moral affect, moral reasoning, and moral behavior may depend as much or more on the situation one faces than on an internalized set of moral principles.

dominant allele: a relatively powerful gene that is expressed phenotypically and masks the effect of a less powerful gene.

double standard: the view that sexual behavior that is appropriate for members of one gender is inappropriate for the other.

Down syndrome: a chromosomal abnormality (also known as trisomy 21) caused by the presence of an extra 21st chromosome; people with this syndrome have a distinct physical appearance and are moderately to severely retarded.

dynamic assessment: an approach to assessing intelligence that evaluates how well individuals learn new material when an examiner provides them with competent instruction.

dyslexia: a general label used to describe the abnormal impairments that some seemingly normal individuals experience when learning to read.

early-experience hypothesis: the notion that the social and emotional events of infancy are very influential in determining the course of one's future development.

easy temperament: temperament such that the child quickly establishes regular routines in infancy, is generally good natured, and adapts easily to new routines.

eclectics: those who borrow from many theories in their attempts to explain human development.

ecological systems model: Bronfenbrenner's view emphasizing that the developing person is embedded in a series of environmental systems that interact with one another and with the person to influence development.

ecological validity: state of affairs in which the findings of one's research are an accurate representation of processes that occur in the natural environment.

economic goal: LeVine's second priority of parenting—to promote skills that children will need for economic self-sufficiency.

effectance motivation: an inborn motive to explore, understand, and control one's environment (sometimes called *mastery motivation*).

effective schools: schools that are generally successful at achieving curricular and noncurricular objectives, regardless of the racial, ethnic, or socioeconomic background of the student population.

ego: psychoanalytic term for the rational component of the personality.

egocentric speech: Piaget's term for the subset of a young child's utterances that are nonsocial—that is, neither directed to others nor expressed in ways that listeners might understand.

egocentrism: the tendency to view the world from one's own perspective while failing to recognize that others may have different points of view.

elaboration: a strategy for remembering that involves adding something to (or creating meaningful links between) the bits of information one is trying to retain.

Electra complex: female version of the Oedipus complex, in which a 3- to 6-year-old girl was believed to envy her father for possessing a penis and to seek him as a sex object in the hope of sharing the organ that she lacks.

embedded figures test: a measure of the ability to locate hidden objects in a distracting visual context.

embryo: name given to the prenatal organism from the third through the eighth week after conception.

embryonic disk: inner cluster of cells of the blastocyst, from which the embryo develops.

emotional bonding: term used to describe the strong affectional ties that parents may feel toward their infant; some theorists believe that the strongest bonding occurs shortly after birth, during a sensitive period.

emotional display rules: culturally defined rules specifying which emotions should or should not be expressed under which circumstances.

emotional self-regulation: strategies for managing emotions or adjusting emotional arousal to a comfortable level of intensity.

empathic concern: a measure of the extent to which an individual recognizes the needs of others and is concerned about their welfare.

empathy: the ability to experience the same emotions that someone else is experiencing.

encoding: process by which external stimulation is converted to a mental representation.

engrossment: paternal analogue of maternal emotional bonding; term used to describe fathers' fascination with their neonates, including their desire to touch, hold, caress, and talk to the newborn baby.

enrichment theory: a theory specifying that we must "add to" sensory stimulation by drawing on stored knowledge in order to perceive a meaningful world.

entity view of ability: belief that one's ability is a highly stable trait that is not influenced much by effort or practice.

environmental determinism: the notion that children are passive creatures who are molded by their environments.

environmental hypothesis: the notion that groups differ in IQ because the environments in which they are raised are not equally conducive to intellectual growth.

Eros: Freud's name for instincts such as respiration, hunger, and sex that help the individual (and the species) to survive.

estrogen: female sex hormone, produced by the ovaries, that is responsible for female sexual maturation.

ethology: the study of the bioevolutionary bases of behavior and development.

evocative genotype/environment correlations: the notion that our heritable attributes will affect others' behavior toward us and thus will influence the social environment in which development takes place.

evoked potential: a change in patterning of the brain waves that indicates that an individual detects (senses) a stimulus.

executive control processes: the processes involved in regulating attention and determining what to do with information just gathered or retrieved from long-term memory.

exosystem: social system that children and adolescents do not directly experience but that may nonetheless influence their development; the third of Bronfenbrenner's environmental layers or contexts.

expansions: responding to a child's ungrammatical utterance with a grammatically improved form of that statement.

experimental control: steps taken by an experimenter to ensure that all extraneous factors that could influence the dependent variable are roughly equivalent in each experimental condition; these precautions must be taken before an experimenter can be reasonably certain that observed changes in the dependent variable were caused by the manipulation of the independent variable.

experimental design: a research design in which the investigator introduces some change in the participant's environment and then measures the effect of that change on the participant's behavior.

expressive role: a social prescription, usually directed toward females, that one should be cooperative, kind, nurturant, and sensitive to the needs of others.

extended family: a group of blood relatives from more than one nuclear family (for example, grandparents, aunts, uncles, nieces, and nephews) who live together, forming a household.

extinction: gradual weakening and disappearance of a learned response that occurs because the CS is no longer paired with the UCS (in classical conditioning) or the response is no longer reinforced (in operant conditioning).

extrafamilial influences: social agencies other than the family that influence a child's cognitive, social, and emotional development.

factor analysis: a statistical procedure for identifying clusters of tests or test items (called factors) that are highly correlated with one another and unrelated to other test items.

failure to thrive: a condition in which seemingly healthy infants fail to grow normally and are much smaller than their age-mates.

falsifiability: a criterion for evaluating the scientific merit of theories. A theory is falsifiable when it is capable of generating predictions that could be disconfirmed.

family social system: the complex network of relationships, interactions, and patterns of influence that characterize a family with three or more members.

fast mapping: process of linking a word with its referent after hearing the word a time or two.

"felt responsibility" hypothesis: the theory that empathy may promote altruism by causing one to reflect on altruistic norms and, thus, to feel some obligation to help distressed others.

fetal alcohol effects (FAE): a group of mild congenital problems that are sometimes observed in children of mothers who drink sparingly to moderately during pregnancy.

fetal alcohol syndrome (FAS): a group of serious congenital problems commonly observed in the offspring of mothers who abuse alcohol during pregnancy.

fetus: name given to the prenatal organism from the ninth week of pregnancy until birth.

field dependence/independence: a dimension of perceptual style—namely, the extent to which the surrounding context (the field) affects a person's perceptual judgments.

field experiment: an experiment that takes place in a naturalistic setting such as the home, the school, or a playground.

first stage of labor: the period of the birth process lasting from the first regular uterine contractions until the cervix is fully dilated.

fixation: arrested development at a particular psychosexual stage; often occurs as a means of coping with existing conflicts and preventing movement to the next stage, where stress may be even greater.

fluid intelligence: the ability to perceive relationships and solve relational problems of the type that are not taught and are relatively free of cultural influences.

"forbidden toy" paradigm: a method of studying children's resistance to temptation by noting whether youngsters will play with forbidden toys when they believe that this transgression is unlikely to be detected.

foreclosure: identity status characterizing individuals who have prematurely committed themselves to occupations or ideologies without really thinking about these commitments.

formal operations: Piaget's fourth and final stage of cognitive development, from age 11 or 12 and beyond, when the individual begins to think more rationally and systematically about abstract concepts and hypothetical events.

formats: interactions in which a young child and an older companion assume separate but reversible (reciprocal) roles.

fragile-X syndrome: a sex chromosome abnormality in which individuals have a compressed or broken X chromosome; affected individuals (particularly males) may show mild to severe mental retardation.

friendship: a close and often enduring relationship between two individuals that may be characterized by loyalty and mutual affection.

g: Spearman's abbreviation for *neogenesis*, which, roughly translated, means one's ability to understand relations (or general mental ability).

gender consistency: the stage of gender identity in which the child recognizes that a person's gender is invariant despite changes in the person's activities or appearance (also known as *gender constancy*).

gender identity: one's awareness of one's gender and its implications.

gender intensification: a magnification of sex differences early in adolescence; associated with increased pressure to conform to traditional sex roles.

gender schemas: organized sets of beliefs and expectations about males and females that guide information processing.

gender stability: the stage of gender identity in which the child recognizes that gender is stable over time.

genes: hereditary blueprints for development that are transmitted unchanged from generation to generation.

genetic counseling: a service designed to inform prospective parents about genetic diseases and to help them determine the likelihood that they would transmit such disorders to their children.

genetic hypothesis: the notion that group differences in IQ are hereditary.

genital herpes: a sexually transmitted disease that can infect infants at birth, causing blindness, brain damage, or even death.

genital stage: Freud's final stage of psychosexual development (from puberty onward), in which the underlying aim of the sex instinct is biological reproduction.

genotype: the genetic endowment that an individual inherits.

gentle birthing: Leboyer's method of childbirth, in which the neonate is comforted, massaged, shielded from unpleasant sensory stimulation, and bathed in warm water in an attempt to reduce any traumas associated with birth.

germinal period: first phase of prenatal development, lasting from conception until the developing organism becomes attached to the wall of the uterus (also called period of the zygote).

giftedness: the possession of unusually high intellectual potential or other special talents.

glia: nerve cells that nourish neurons and encase them in insulating sheaths of myelin.

"goodness of fit" model: Thomas and Chess's notion that development is likely to be optimized when parents' child-rearing practices are adapted to (or are compatible with) the child's temperamental characteristics.

grammatical morphemes: prefixes, suffixes, prepositions, and auxiliary verbs that modify the meaning of words and sentences.

growth hormone (GH): the pituitary hormone that stimulates the rapid growth and development of body cells; primarily responsible for the adolescent growth spurt.

habits: well-learned associations between various stimuli and responses that represent the stable aspects of one's personality.

habituation: a decrease in one's response to a stimulus that has become familiar through repetition.

Head Start: a large-scale preschool educational program designed to provide children from low-income families with a variety of social and intellectual experiences that might better prepare them for school.

heritability: the amount of variability in a trait that is attributable to hereditary factors.

heritability coefficient: a numerical estimate, ranging from .00 to +1.00, of the amount of variation in an attribute that is due to hereditary factors.

heteronomous morality: Piaget's first stage of moral development, in which children view the rules of authority figures as sacred and unalterable.

heterozygous: having inherited two alleles for an attribute that have different effects.

heuristic value: a criterion for evaluating the scientific merit of theories. An heuristic theory is one that continues to stimulate new research and new discoveries.

hierarchical model of intelligence: model of the structure of intelligence in which a broad, general ability factor is at the top of the hierarchy, with a number of specialized ability factors nested underneath.

high-amplitude sucking method: a method of assessing infants' perceptual capabilities that capitalizes on the ability of infants to make interesting events last by varying the rate at which they suck on a special pacifier.

high-risk neighborhood: a residential area in which the incidence of child abuse is much higher than in other neighborhoods with the same demographic and socioeconomic characteristics.

holistic perspective: a unified view of the developmental process that emphasizes the important interrelationships among the physical, mental, social, and emotional aspects of human development.

holophrase: a single-word utterance that represents an entire sentence's worth of meaning.

holophrastic period: the period when the child's speech consists of one-word utterances, some of which are thought to be holophrases.

home-based interventions: compensatory interventions that take place in the home and provide services designed to make parents more confident and competent as caregivers.

HOME inventory: a measure of the amount and type of intellectual stimulation provided by a child's home environment.

homozygous: having inherited two alleles for an attribute that are identical in their effects.

horizontal decalage: Piaget's term for a child's uneven cognitive performance; an inability to solve certain problems even though one can solve similar problems requiring the same mental operations.

hostile aggression: aggressive acts for which the actor's major goal is to harm or injure a victim.

hostile attributional bias: tendency to view harm done under ambiguous circumstances as having stemmed from a hostile intent on the part of the harmdoer; characterizes highly aggressive children and adolescents.

Huntington's disease: a genetic disease caused by a dominant allele that typically appears later in life and causes the nervous system to degenerate.

hypothesis: a theoretical prediction about some aspect of experience.

hypothetical-deductive reasoning: a style of problem solving in which all possible solutions to a problem are generated and then systematically evaluated to determine the correct answer.

id: psychoanalytic term for the inborn component of the personality that is driven by the instincts.

ideational fluency: the most common measure of creativity; the sheer number of different ideas or solutions one can generate.

identification: Freud's term for the child's tendency to emulate another person, usually the same-sex parent.

identity: a mature self-definition; a sense of who one is, where one is going, and how one fits into society.

identity achievement: identity status characterizing individuals who have carefully considered identity issues and have made firm commitments to an occupation and ideologies.

identity crisis: Erikson's term for the uncertainty and discomfort that adolescents experience when they become confused about their present and future roles in life.

identity diffusion: identity status characterizing individuals who are not questioning who they are and have not yet committed themselves to an identity.

identity training: an attempt to promote conservation by teaching nonconservers to recognize that a transformed object or substance is the same object or substance, regardless of its new appearance.

idiographic development: individual variations in the rate, extent, or direction of development.

idiot savant: a person who has an extraordinary talent but is otherwise mentally retarded.

imaginary audience: allegedly a form of adolescent egocentrism that involves confusing your own thoughts with those of a hypothesized audience and concluding that others share your preoccupations.

immanent justice: the notion that unacceptable conduct will invariably be punished and that justice is ever present in the world.

implantation: the burrowing of the blastocyst into the lining of the uterus.

imprinting: an innate or instinctual form of learning in which the young of certain species follow and become attached to moving objects (usually their mothers).

incompatible-response technique: a nonpunitive method of behavior modification in which adults ignore undesirable conduct while reinforcing acts that are incompatible with these responses.

incomplete dominance: condition in which a stronger allele fails to mask all the effects of a weaker allele; a phenotype results that is similar but not identical to the effect of the stronger gene.

incremental view of ability: belief that one's ability can be improved through increased effort and practice.

independent assortment: the principle stating that each pair of chromosomes segregates independently of all other chromosome pairs during meiosis.

independent variable: the aspect of the environment that an experimenter modifies or manipulates in order to measure its impact on behavior.

indifferent gonad: undifferentiated tissue that produces testes in males and ovaries in females.

indirect, or third party, effect: instances in which the relationship between two individuals in a family is modified by the behavior or attitudes of a third family member.

induction: a nonpunitive form of discipline in which an adult explains why a child's behavior is wrong and should be changed by emphasizing its effects on others.

infantile amnesia: a lack of memory for the early years of one's life.

infant states: levels of sleep and wakefulness that young infants display.

informal curriculum: noncurricular objectives of schooling such as teaching children to cooperate, respect authority, obey rules, and become good citizens.

"in-group/out-group" schema: one's general knowledge of the mannerisms, roles, activities, and behaviors that characterize males and females.

inhibitory control: an ability to display acceptable conduct by resisting the temptation to commit a forbidden act.

initiative versus guilt: the third of Erikson's psychosocial stages, in which preschool children either develop goals and strive to achieve them or feel guilty when their ambitions are thwarted by others.

innate purity: the idea that infants are born with an intuitive sense of right and wrong that is often misdirected by the demands and restrictions of society.

inner experimentation: the ability to solve simple problems on a mental, or symbolic, level without having to rely on trial-and-error experimentation.

instinct: an inborn biological force that motivates a particular response or class of responses.

instrumental aggression: aggressive acts for which the actor's major goal is to gain access to objects, space, or privileges.

instrumental role: a social prescription, usually directed toward males, that one should be dominant, independent, assertive, competitive, and goal oriented.

intelligence: in Piaget's theory, a basic life function that enables an organism to adapt to its environment.

intelligence quotient (IQ): a numerical measure of a person's performance on an intelligence test relative to the performance of other examinees.

interactionist theory: the notion that biological factors and environmental influences interact to determine the course of language development.

intermodal perception: the ability to use one sensory modality to identify a stimulus or pattern of stimuli that is already familiar through another modality.

internalization: the process of adopting the attributes or standards of other people, taking these standards as one's own.

internal working models: cognitive representations of self, others, and relationships that infants construct from their interactions with caregivers.

introversion/extroversion: the opposite poles of a personality dimension: Introverts are shy, anxious around others, and ready to withdraw from social situations; extroverts are highly sociable and enjoy being with others.

intuitive period: the later substage of preoperations, from ages 4–7 years, when the child's thinking about objects and events is dominated by salient perceptual features.

invariant developmental sequence: a series of developments that occur in one particular order because each development in the sequence is a prerequisite for the next.

iron deficiency anemia: a listlessness caused by too little iron in the diet that makes children inattentive and may retard physical and intellectual development.

karyotype: a chromosomal portrait created by staining chromosomes and then photographing them under a high-power microscope.

kewpie-doll effect: the notion that infantlike facial features are perceived as cute and lovable and elicit favorable responses from others.

kinship: the extent to which two individuals have genes in common.

knowledge base: one's existing information about a topic or content area; significant for its influence on how well one can learn and remember.

kwashiorkor: a growth-retarding disease affecting children who receive enough calories but little, if any, protein.

language: a small number of individually meaningless symbols (sounds, letters, gestures) that can be combined according to agreed-on rules to produce an infinite number of messages.

language acquisition device (LAD): Chomsky's term for the innate knowledge of grammar that humans were said to possess—knowledge that might enable young children to infer the rules governing others' speech and to use these rules to produce language.

language-making capacity (LMC): a hypothesized set of specialized linguistic processing skills that enable children to analyze speech and to detect phonological, semantic, and syntactical relationships.

latency period: Freud's fourth stage of psychosexual development (age 6 to puberty), in which sexual desires are repressed and the child's available libido is channeled into socially acceptable outlets such as schoolwork or vigorous play.

learned helplessness: the failure to learn how to respond appropriately in a situation because of previous exposures to uncontrollable events in the same or a similar situation.

learned helplessness orientation: a tendency to give up or to stop trying after failing because these failures have been attributed to a lack of ability that one can do little about.

learning: a relatively permanent change in behavior (or behavioral potential) that results from one's experiences or practice.

Level I abilities: Jensen's term for lower-level intellectual abilities (such as attention and short-term memory) that are important for simple association learning.

levels of processing model: an information-processing model that suggests that retention of information and, thus, its availability for use in problem solving is a function of the depth to which this input is encoded and analyzed.

Level II abilities: Jensen's term for higher-level cognitive skills that are involved in abstract reasoning and problem solving.

lexical contrast constraint: notion that young children make inferences about word meanings by contrasting new words with words they already know.

libido: Freud's term for the biological energy of the sex instinct.

linguistic universal: an aspect of language development that all children share.

locus of control: personality dimension that distinguishes people who assume that they are personally responsible for their life outcomes (internal locus) from those who believe that their outcomes depend more on circumstances beyond their control (external locus).

longitudinal design: a research design in which one group of subjects is studied repeatedly over a period of months or years.

long-term memory (LTM): third information processing store, in which information that has been examined and interpreted is permanently stored for future use.

looking chamber: an enclosed criblike apparatus used to study infants' visual preferences.

looking-glass self: the idea that a child's self-concept is largely determined by the ways other people respond to him or her.

love withdrawal: a form of discipline in which an adult withholds attention, affection, or approval in order to modify or control a child's behavior.

macrosystem: the larger cultural or subcultural context in which development occurs; Bronfenbrenner's outermost environmental layer or context.

mainstreaming: the educational practice of integrating developmentally disabled students into regular classrooms rather than placing them in segregated special education classes.

manic-depression: a psychotic disorder characterized by extreme fluctuations in mood.

marasmus: a growth-retarding disease affecting infants who receive insufficient protein and too few calories.

mastery orientation: a tendency to persist at challenging tasks because of a belief that one has high ability and/or that earlier failures can be overcome by trying harder.

maternal deprivation hypothesis: the notion that socially deprived infants develop abnormally because they have failed to establish attachments to a primary caregiver.

maturation: developmental changes in the body or behavior that result from the aging process rather than from learning, injury, illness, or some other life experience.

mature strategy use: consistent production and use of an effective memory strategy.

mean-world belief: a belief, fostered by televised violence, that the world is a more dangerous and frightening place than is actually the case.

mechanistic model: view of children as passive entities whose developmental paths are primarily determined by external (environmental) influences. Represented by learning theorists.

mediation deficiency: inability to learn and use an effective memory strategy.

meiosis: the process in which a germ cell divides, producing gametes (sperm or ova) that each contain half of the parent cell's original complement of chromosomes; in humans, the products of meiosis contain 23 chromosomes.

memory: the processes by which people retain information and later retrieve it for use.

memory span: a measure of the amount of information that can be held in short-term memory.

menarche: the first occurrence of menstruation.

mental age (MA): a measure of intellectual development that reflects the level of age-graded problems a child is able to solve.

mesosystem: the interconnections among an individual's immediate settings or microsystems. The second of Bronfenbrenner's environmental layers or contexts.

metacognition: one's knowledge about cognition and about the regulation of cognitive activities.

metalinguistic awareness: a knowledge of language and its properties; an understanding that language can be used for purposes other than communicating.

metamemory: one's knowledge about memory and memory processes.

microsystem: the immediate settings (including role relationships and activities) that the person actually encounters; the innermost of Bronfenbrenner's environmental layers or contexts.

mitosis: the process in which a cell duplicates its chromosomes and then divides into two genetically identical daughter cells.

monozygotic (or identical) twins: twins that result when a single zygote divides into two separate but identical cells that each develop independently. As a result, each member of a monozygotic twin pair has inherited exactly the same set of genes.

moral affect: the emotional component of morality, including feelings such as guilt, shame, and pride in ethical conduct.

moral behavior: the behavioral component of morality; actions that are consistent with one's moral standards in situations where one is tempted to violate them.

morality: a set of principles or ideals that help the individual to distinguish right from wrong, to act on this distinction, and to feel pride in virtuous conduct and guilt (or shame) for conduct that violates one's standards.

morality of care: Gilligan's term for what she presumes to be the dominant moral orientation of females, focusing more on compassionate concerns for human welfare than on socially defined justice as administered through law.

morality of justice: Gilligan's term for what she presumes to be the dominant moral orientation of males, focusing more on socially defined justice as administered through law than on compassionate concerns for human welfare.

moral reasoning: the cognitive component of morality; the thinking that people display when deciding whether various acts are right or wrong.

moral rules: standards of acceptable and unacceptable conduct that focus on the rights and privileges of individuals.

moratorium: identity status characterizing individuals who are currently experiencing an identity crisis and are actively exploring occupational and ideological positions in which to invest themselves.

morphemes: the smallest meaningful units of language; these include words and grammatical markers such as prefixes, suffixes, and verb-tense modifiers (for example, -ed, -ing).

morphological knowledge: one's knowledge of the meaning of morphemes that make up words.

motherese: the short, simple, high-pitched (and often repetitive) sentences that adults use when talking with young children.

"mother-only" monkeys: monkeys who are raised with their mothers and denied any contact with peers.

motion hypothesis: the notion that individuals must attend to objects that move in order to develop a normal repertoire of visual/spatial skills.

M-space: mental space; number of separate schemes or concepts that a child can manipulate simultaneously.

multiple sclerosis: a crippling loss of muscular control that occurs when the myelin sheaths surrounding individual neurons begin to disintegrate.

muscular dystrophy: a genetic disease that attacks the muscles and results in a gradual loss of motor capabilities.

mutation: a change in the chemical structure or arrangement of one or more genes that has the effect of producing a new phenotype.

mutual exclusivity constraint: notion that young children assume that each object has but one label and that different words refer to separate and nonoverlapping categories.

myelinization: the process by which neurons are enclosed in waxy myelin sheaths that will facilitate the transmission of neural impulses.

naming explosion: term used to describe the dramatic increase in the pace at which infants acquire new words in the latter half of the second year; so named because many of the new words acquired are the names of objects.

naturalistic observation: a method in which the scientist tests hypotheses by observing people as they engage in everyday activities in their natural habitats (for example, at home, at school, or on the playground).

natural (or quasi-) experiment: a study in which the investigator measures the impact of some naturally occurring event that is assumed to affect people's lives.

natural selection: an evolutionary process, proposed by Charles Darwin, stating that individuals with characteristics that promote adaptation to the environment will survive, reproduce, and pass these adaptive characteristics to offspring; those lacking these adaptive characteristics will eventually die out.

nature/nurture issue: the debate within developmental psychology over the relative importance of biological predispositions (nature) and environmental influences (nurture) as determinants of human development.

negative punishment: a punishing consequence that involves the removal of something pleasant following a behavior.

negative reinforcer: any stimulus whose removal or termination, as the consequence of an act, increases the probability that the act will recur.

neglected children: children who receive few nominations as either a liked or a disliked individual from members of their peer group.

neonate: a newborn infant from birth to approximately 1 month of age.

neural tube: the primitive spinal cord that develops from the ectoderm and becomes the central nervous system.

neurons: nerve cells that receive and transmit neural impulses.

neurotic disorder: an irrational pattern of thinking or behavior that a person may use to contend with stress or to avoid anxiety.

nonaggressive rejected children: a subgroup of rejected children who are often passive, socially unskilled, and insensitive to peer-group expectations.

nonrepresentative sample: a subgroup that differs in important ways from the larger group (or population) to which it belongs.

nonshared environmental influence (NSE): an environmental influence that people living together do not share and that makes these individuals different from one another.

normal distribution: a symmetrical, bell-shaped curve that describes the variability of certain characteristics within a population; most people fall at or near the average score, with relatively few at the extremes of the distribution.

normative development: developmental changes that characterize most or all members of a species; typical patterns of development.

nuclear family: a family unit consisting of a wife/mother, a husband/father, and their dependent child(ren).

obese: a medical term describing individuals who are at least 20% above the "ideal" weight for their height, age, and sex.

object permanence: the realization that objects continue to exist when they are no longer visible or detectable through the other senses.

object scope constraint: the notion that young children will assume that a new word applied to an object refers to the whole object rather than to parts of the object or to object attributes (for example, its color).

observational learning: learning that results from observing the behavior of others.

oedipal morality: Freud's theory that moral development occurs during the phallic period (ages 3 to 6) when children internalize the moral standards of the same-sex parent as they resolve their Oedipal or Electra conflicts.

Oedipus complex: Freud's term for the conflict that 3- to 6-year-old boys experience when they develop an incestuous desire for their mothers and, at the same time, a jealous and hostile rivalry with their fathers.

open classroom: a less structured classroom arrangement in which there is a separate area for each educational activity and children distribute themselves around the room, working individually or in small groups.

operant learning (or conditioning): a form of learning in which freely emitted acts (or operants) become either more or less probable, depending on the consequences they produce.

operating efficiency hypothesis: the notion that M-space increases with age because we come to process information faster or more efficiently.

oral stage: Freud's first stage of psychosexual development (from birth to 1 year), in which children gratify the sex instinct by stimulating the mouth, lips, teeth, and gums.

ordinal position: the child's order of birth among siblings (also called birth order).

organismic model: view of children as active entities whose developmental paths are primarily determined by forces from within themselves. Represented by psychoanalytic and cognitive-developmental theorists.

organization: an inborn tendency to combine and integrate available schemes into coherent systems or bodies of knowledge.

original sin: the idea that children are inherently negative creatures who must be taught to rechannel their selfish interests into socially acceptable outlets.

Ounce of Prevention program: a comprehensive, community-based attempt to prevent child abuse by educating parents in effective child management techniques and providing such family support services as child-care programs, job training, and medical assistance.

overextension: the young child's tendency to use relatively specific words to refer to a broader set of objects, actions, or events than adults do (for example, using the word **car** to refer to all motor vehicles).

overregularization: the overgeneralization of grammatical rules to irregular cases where the rules do not apply (for example, saying "mouses" rather than "mice").

ovulation: the process in which a female gamete (ovum) matures in one of the ovaries and is released into the fallopian tube.

own-sex schema: detailed knowledge or plans of action that enable a person to perform gender-consistent activities and to enact his or her sex role.

parental control: a dimension of parenting that describes how restrictive and demanding parents are.

Parents Anonymous: an organization of reformed child abusers (modeled after Alcoholics Anonymous) that functions as a support group and helps parents to understand and overcome their abusive tendencies.

parsimony: a criterion for evaluating the scientific merit of theories; a parsimonious theory is one that uses relatively few explanatory principles to explain a broad set of observations.

partial reinforcement: a schedule of reinforcement in which only some of the occurrences of an act are reinforced.

passive genotype/environment correlations: the notion that the rearing environments that biological parents provide are influenced by the parents' own genes, and hence are correlated with the child's own genotype.

peer acceptance: a measure of a person's likability (or dislikability) in the eyes of peers.

peer conformity: the tendency to go along with the wishes of peers or to yield to peer-group pressures.

peer group: a confederation of peers that interacts regularly; defines a sense of membership and formulates norms that specify how members are supposed to look, think, and act.

"peer-only" monkeys: monkeys who are separated from their mothers (and other adults) soon after birth and raised with peers.

peers: two or more persons who are operating at similar levels of behavioral complexity.

perception: the process by which we categorize and interpret sensory input.

perceptual learning: changes in one's ability to extract information from sensory stimulation that occur as a result of experience.

perinatal environment: the environment surrounding birth, including influences such as childbirth medication, obstetrical practices, and the social stimulation a baby may receive.

period of the embryo: second phase of prenatal development, lasting from the third through the eighth prenatal week, during which the major organs and anatomical structures take shape.

period of the fetus: third phase of prenatal development, lasting from the ninth prenatal week until birth; during this period, all major organ systems begin to function and the fetus grows rapidly.

permissive parenting: a pattern of parenting in which adults make few demands of their children and rarely attempt to control their behavior.

personal agency: the recognition or understanding that one can be the cause of events.

personal fable: allegedly a form of adolescent egocentrism that involves thinking that oneself and one's thoughts and feelings are special or unique.

phallic stage: Freud's third stage of psychosexual development (from 3 to 6 years of age), in which children gratify the sex instinct by fondling their genitals and developing an incestuous desire for the parent of the other sex.

phenotype: the ways in which a person's genotype is expressed in observable or measurable characteristics.

phenylketonuria (PKU): a genetic disease in which the child is unable to metabolize phenylalanine; if left untreated, it soon causes hyperactivity and mental retardation.

phocomelia: a prenatal malformation in which all or parts of the limbs are missing.

phonemes: the basic units of sound that are used in a spoken language.

phonology: the sound system of a language and the rules for combining these sounds to produce meaningful units of speech.

pictorial (perspective) cues: depth and distance cues, including linear perspective, texture gradients, sizing, interposition, and shading, that are monocular—that is, detectable with only one eye.

pincer grasp: a grasp in which the thumb is used in opposition to the fingers, enabling an infant to become more dexterous at lifting and fondling objects.

pituitary: a "master gland" located at the base of the brain that regulates the endocrine glands and produces growth hormone.

placenta: an organ, formed from the lining of the uterus and the chorion, that provides for respiration and nourishment of the unborn child and the elimination of its metabolic wastes.

plasticity: capacity for change; a developmental state that has the potential to be shaped by experience.

polygenic trait: a characteristic that is influenced by the action of many genes rather than a single pair.

popular children: children who are liked by many members of their peer group and disliked by very few.

positive punishment: a punishing consequence that involves the presentation of something unpleasant following a behavior.

positive reinforcer: any stimulus whose presentation, as the consequence of an act, increases the probability that the act will recur.

postconventional morality: Kohlberg's term for the fifth and sixth stages of moral reasoning, in which moral judgments are based on social contracts and democratic law (Stage 5) or on universal principles of ethics and justice (Stage 6).

postpartum depression: strong feelings of sadness, resentment, and despair that may appear shortly after childbirth and can linger for months.

power assertion: a form of discipline in which an adult relies on his or her superior power (for example, by administering spankings or withholding privileges) to modify or control a child's behavior.

pragmatics: principles that underlie the effective and appropriate use of language in social contexts.

preadapted characteristic: an innate attribute that is a product of evolution and serves some function that increases the chances of survival for the individual and the species.

precausal or transductive reasoning: reasoning from the particular to the particular, so that events that occur together are assumed to be causally related.

preconceptual period: the early substage of preoperations, from ages 2–4 years, characterized by the appearance of primitive ideas, concepts, and methods of reasoning.

preconventional morality: Kohlberg's term for the first two stages of moral reasoning, in which moral judgments are based on the tangible punitive consequences (Stage 1) or rewarding consequences (Stage 2) of an act for the actor rather than on the relationship of that act to society's rules and customs.

preference method: a method used to gain information about infants' perceptual abilities by presenting two (or more) stimuli and observing which stimulus the infant prefers.

prelinguistic period: the period before children utter their first meaningful words.

preliterate society: a society in which there is little or no formal schooling, so that many children never learn to read and write.

premoral period: in Piaget's theory, the first five years of life, when children have little respect for or awareness of socially defined rules.

prenatal development: development that occurs between the moment of conception and the beginning of the birth process.

preoperational stage: Piaget's second stage of cognitive development, lasting from about ages 2–7 years, when children are thinking at a symbolic level but are not yet using cognitive operations.

prepared or natural childbirth: a delivery in which physical and psychological preparations for the birth are stressed and medical assistance is minimized.

preterm babies: infants born more than three weeks before their normal due dates.

primary circular reaction: a pleasurable response, centered on the infant's own body, that is discovered by chance and performed over and over.

primary (or basic) emotions: the set of emotions present at birth or emerging early in the first year that some theorists believe to be biologically programmed.

primary mental abilities: seven mental abilities, identified by factor analysis, that Thurstone believed to represent the structure of intelligence.

primitive reflexes: reflexes controlled by subcortical areas of the brain that gradually disappear over the first year of life.

private self (or I): those inner, or subjective, aspects of self that are known only to the individual and are not available for public scrutiny.

private speech: Vygotsky's term for the subset of a child's verbal utterances that serve a self-communicative function and guide the child's thinking.

problem-finding stage: according to Arlin, a stage beyond formal operations in which the individual is now capable of reorganizing knowledge to ask questions and define new problems.

problem solving: use of the information-processing system to achieve a goal or arrive at a decision.

processing constraints: cognitive biases or tendencies that lead infants and toddlers to favor certain interpretations of the meaning of new words over other interpretations.

productive language: that which the individual is capable of expressing (producing) in his or her own speech.

production deficiency: a failure to spontaneously generate and use known strategies that could improve learning and memory.

proprioceptive information: sensory information from the muscles, tendons, and joints that help one to locate the position of one's body (or body parts) in space.

prosocial moral reasoning: the thinking that people display when deciding whether to help, share with, or comfort others when these actions could prove costly to themselves.

prospective memory: memory directed to the performance of future activities.

proximodistal development: a sequence of physical maturation and growth that proceeds from the center of the body (the proximal region) to the extremities (distal regions).

psycholinguists: those who study the structure, meaning, and development of children's language.

psychological comparisons phase: tendency to form impressions of others by comparing and contrasting these individuals on abstract psychological dimensions.

psychological constructs phase: tendency to base one's impressions of others on the stable traits these individuals are presumed to have.

psychometric approach: a theoretical perspective that portrays intelligence as a trait (or set of traits) on which individuals differ; psychometric theorists are responsible for the development of standardized intelligence tests.

puberty: the point at which a person reaches sexual maturity and is physically capable of fathering or conceiving a child.

public self (or me): those aspects of self that others can see or infer.

punisher: any consequence of an act that suppresses that act and/or decreases the probability that it will recur.

Pygmalion effect: the tendency of teacher expectancies to become self-fulfilling prophecies, causing students to perform better or worse depending on their teacher's estimation of their potential.

questionnaire: a research instrument that asks the persons being studied to respond to a number of written questions.

random assignment: a control technique in which participants are assigned to experimental conditions through an unbiased procedure so that the members of the groups are not systematically different from one another.

range of reaction principle: the idea that genotype sets limits on the range of possible phenotypes that a person might display in response to different environments.

reaction time: a measure of the time it takes for a person to respond motorically to a test stimulus (for example, the time between seeing a flash and pressing a button).

recall memory: recollecting objects, events, and experiences when examples of these bits of information are not available for comparative purposes.

recasts: responding to a child's ungrammatical utterance with a nonrepetitive statement that is grammatically correct.

receptive language: that which the individual comprehends when listening to others' speech.

receptive vocabulary: words that a child already knows or can quickly define based on his or her knowledge of morphological rules.

recessive allele: a less powerful gene that is not expressed phenotypically when paired with a dominant allele.

reciprocal determinism: the notion that the flow of influence between children and their environments is a two-way street; the environment may affect the child, but the child's behavior also influences the environment.

reciprocal influence: the notion that each person in a social relationship influences and is influenced by the other person(s).

recognition memory: realizing that an object or event that one experiences has been experienced before.

reconstituted families: new families that form after the remarriage of a single parent.

referential communication skills: abilities to generate clear verbal messages, to recognize when others' messages are unclear, and to clarify any unclear messages that one transmits or receives.

reflex: an unlearned and automatic response to a stimulus or class of stimuli.

regression: a defense mechanism whereby the ego copes with stress and conflict by producing behaviors more characteristic of an earlier stage of development.

rehearsal: a strategy for remembering that involves repeating the items one is trying to retain.

reinforcer: any consequence of an act that increases the probability that the act will recur.

rejected children: children who are disliked by many peers and liked by few.

reliability: the extent to which a measuring instrument yields consistent results, both over time and across observers.

REM sleep: a state of active or irregular sleep in which the eyes move rapidly beneath the eyelids and brain-wave activity is similar to the pattern displayed when awake.

repression: a type of motivated forgetting in which anxiety-provoking thoughts and conflicts are forced out of conscious awareness.

research ethics: standards of conduct that investigators are ethically bound to honor in order to protect their research participants from physical or psychological harm.

resistant attachment: an insecure infant/caregiver bond, characterized by strong separation protest and a tendency of the child to resist contact initiated by the caregiver, particularly after a separation.

respiratory distress syndrome: a serious condition in which a preterm infant breathes very irregularly and is at risk of dying (also called hyaline membrane disease).

retaliatory aggression: aggressive acts elicited by real or imagined provocations.

reticular formation: an area of the brain that serves to activate the organism and is thought to be important in regulating attention.

reversibility: the ability to reverse, or negate, an action by mentally performing the opposite action.

role taking: the ability to assume another person's perspective and understand his or her thoughts, feelings, and behaviors.

rubella (German measles): a disease that has little effect on a mother but may cause a number of serious birth defects in unborn children who are exposed in the first 3-4 months of pregnancy.

rule assessment: a method of assessing a child's level of cognitive functioning (or problem solving) by noting the information that he encodes and the principle, or rule, he uses to operate on this information and draw conclusions.

s: Spearman's term for mental abilities that are specific to particular tests.

scheme: an organized pattern of thought or action that a child develops to make sense of some aspect of his or her experience (also called cognitive structure).

schizophrenia: a serious form of mental illness characterized by disturbances in logical thinking, emotional expression, and interpersonal behavior.

scientific method: an attitude or value about the pursuit of knowledge that dictates that investigators must be objective and must allow their data to decide the merits of their theorizing.

script: a general representation of the typical sequencing of events (that is, what occurs and when) in some familiar context.

secondary circular reaction: a pleasurable response, centered on an external object, that is discovered by chance and performed over and over.

secondary (or complex) emotions: self-conscious or self-evaluative emotions that emerge in the second year and depend, in part, on cognitive development.

secondary reinforcer: an initially neutral stimulus that acquires reinforcement value by virtue of its repeated association with other reinforcing stimuli.

second stage of labor: the period of the birth process during which the fetus moves through the vaginal canal and emerges from the mother's body (also called the delivery).

secular trend: a trend in industrialized societies toward earlier maturation and greater body size now than in the past.

secure attachment: an infant/caregiver bond in which the child welcomes contact with a close companion and uses this person as a secure base from which to explore the environment.

secure base: use of a caregiver as a base from which to explore the environment and to which to return for emotional support.

selective attention: the focusing of attention on certain aspects of experience while ignoring irrelevant or distracting sensations.

self: the combination of physical and psychological attributes that is unique to each individual.

self-actualization goal: LeVine's third priority of parenting—to promote the child's cognitive and behavioral capacity for maximizing such cultural values as morality, achievement, prestige, and personal satisfaction.

self-assertion: noncompliant acts that are undertaken by children in the interest of doing things for themselves or otherwise establishing autonomy.

self-care (or latchkey) children: children who care for themselves after school or in the evenings while their parents are working.

self-concept: one's perceptions of one's unique attributes or traits.

self-control: ability to regulate one's conduct and to inhibit actions that are unacceptable or that conflict with a goal.

self-esteem: one's evaluation of one's worth as a person based on an assessment of the qualities that make up the self-concept.

self-fulfilling prophecy: phenomenon whereby people cause others to act in accordance with the expectations they have about those others.

self-oriented distress: feeling of *personal* discomfort or distress that may be elicited when we experience the emotions of (that is, empathize with) a distressed other; thought to inhibit altruism.

semantic grammar: an analysis of the semantic relations (meanings) that children express in their earliest sentences.

semantic organization: a strategy for remembering that involves grouping or classifying stimuli into meaningful categories that are easier to retain.

semantics: the expressed meaning of words and sentences.

sensation: detection of stimuli by the sensory receptors and transmission of this information to the brain.

sensitive period: a period during which an organism is quite susceptible to certain environmental influences; outside this period, the same environmental influences must be much stronger to produce comparable effects on development (weaker form of the critical period concept).

sensitive-period hypothesis (of language acquisition): the notion that human beings are most proficient at language learning before they reach puberty.

sensorimotor stage: Piaget's first intellectual stage, from birth to 2 years, when infants are relying on behavioral schemes as a means of exploring and understanding the environment.

sensory store: first information-processing store, in which stimuli are noticed and are briefly available for further processing.

separation anxiety: a wary or fretful reaction that infants and toddlers often display when separated from the person(s) to whom they are attached.

sequential design: a research design in which subjects from different age groups are studied repeatedly over a period of months or years.

seriation: a cognitive operation that allows one to order a set of stimuli along a quantifiable dimension such as height or weight.

sex-linked characteristic: an attribute determined by a gene that appears on only one of the two types of sex chromosomes, usually the X chromosome.

sex-role standard: a behavior, value, or motive that members of a society consider more typical or appropriate for members of one sex.

sex typing: the process by which a child becomes aware of his or her gender and acquires motives, values, and behaviors considered appropriate for members of that sex.

sexuality: aspect of self referring to one's erotic thoughts, actions, and orientation.

shared environmental influence (SE): an environmental influence that people living together share and that makes these individuals similar to one another.

short-term memory (STM): second information processing store, in which stimuli are retained for several seconds and operated upon (also called working memory).

sibling rivalry: the spirit of competition, jealousy, and resentment that may arise between two or more siblings.

sickle-cell anemia: a genetic blood disease that causes red blood cells to assume an unusual sickled shape and to become inefficient at distributing oxygen.

single gene-pair inheritance: genetic process through which a characteristic is influenced by only one pair of genes, one from the father and one from the mother.

single-parent family: a family system consisting of one parent (either the mother or the father) and the parent's dependent child(ren).

size constancy: the tendency to perceive an object as the same size from different distances despite changes in the size of its retinal image.

skeletal age: a measure of physical maturation based on the child's level of skeletal development.

slow-to-warm-up temperament: temperament in which the child is inactive and moody and displays mild passive resistance to new routines and experiences.

small-for-date babies: infants whose birth weight is far below normal, even when born close to their normal due dates.

sociability: one's willingness to interact with others and to seek their attention or approval.

social cognition: the thinking that people display about the thoughts, feelings, motives, and behaviors of themselves and other people.

social comparison: the process of defining and evaluating the self by comparing oneself to other people.

social-conventional rules: standards of conduct determined by social consensus that indicate what is appropriate within a particular social context.

socialization: the process by which children acquire the beliefs, values, and behaviors considered desirable or appropriate by the society to which they belong.

social problem-solving training: method of social skills training in which an adult helps children (through role playing or role-taking training) to make less hostile attributions about harmdoing and to generate nonaggressive solutions to conflict.

social referencing: the use of others' emotional expressions to infer the meaning of otherwise ambiguous situations.

social stimulation hypothesis: the notion that socially deprived infants develop abnormally because they have had little contact with companions who respond contingently to their social overtures.

social support: tangible and intangible resources provided by other people in times of uncertainty or stress.

sociobiology: a branch of biology that focuses on the evolutionary origins of social motives and behaviors.

sociocultural theory: Vygotsky's perspective on cognitive development, in which children acquire their culture's values, beliefs, and problem-solving strategies through collaborative dialogues with more knowledgeable members of society.

sociometric techniques: procedures that ask children to identify those peers whom they like or dislike or to rate peers for their desirability as companions; used to measure children's peer acceptance (or nonacceptance).

stage of indiscriminate attachments: period between 6 weeks and 6-7 months of age in which infants prefer social to nonsocial stimulation and are likely to protest whenever any adult puts them down or leaves them alone.

stage of multiple attachments: term used to describe infants who have formed attachments to two or more close companions.

stage of specific attachments: period between 7 and 9 months of age when infants are attached to one close companion (usually the mother).

stereopsis: fusion of two flat images to produce a single image that has depth.

stimulus generalization: the fact that one stimulus can be substituted for another and produce the same response that the former stimulus did.

store model: information-processing model that depicts information as flowing through three processing units (or stores): the sensory register, short-term memory, and long-term memory.

stranger anxiety: a wary or fretful reaction that infants and toddlers often display when approached by an unfamiliar person.

strange-situations test: a series of eight separation and reunion episodes to which infants are exposed in order to determine the quality of their attachments to one or more close companions.

structured interview or structured questionnaire: a technique in which all participants are asked the same questions in precisely the same order so that the responses of different participants can be compared.

structured observation: an observational method in which the investigator cues the behavior of interest and observes participants' responses in a laboratory.

"structure of intellect" model: Guilford's factor-analytic model of intelligence, which proposes that there are 180 distinct mental abilities.

sublimation: a defense mechanism by which the ego finds socially acceptable outlets for the id's undesirable impulses.

sudden infant death syndrome (SIDS): the unexplained death of a sleeping infant who suddenly stops breathing (also called crib death).

superego: psychoanalytic term for the component of the personality that consists of one's internalized moral standards.

survival goal: LeVine's first priority of parenting—to promote the physical health and safety (survival) of young children.

survival reflexes: inborn responses such as breathing, sucking, and swallowing that enable the newborn to adapt to the extrauterine environment.

symbolic function: the ability to use symbols (for example, images and words) to represent objects and experiences.

symbolic schemes: internal mental symbols (such as images or verbal codes) that one uses to represent aspects of experience.

sympathetic empathic arousal: feelings of sympathy or compassion that may be elicited when we experience the emotions of (that is, empathize with) a distressed other; thought to become an important mediator of altruism.

synapse: the connective space (juncture) between one nerve cell (neuron) and another.

synchronized routines: generally harmonious interactions between two persons in which each participant adjusts his or her behavior in response to the partner's actions.

syntactical bootstrapping: notion that young children make inferences about the meaning of words by analyzing the way words are used in sentences and inferring whether they refer to objects (nouns), actions (verbs), or attributes (adjectives).

syntax: the structure of a language; the rules specifying how words and grammatical markers are to be combined to produce meaningful sentences.

syphilis: a common venereal disease that may cross the placental barrier in the middle and later stages of pregnancy, causing miscarriage or serious birth defects.

systematic reasoning: the ability to operate on abstract systems to construct higher-order structures (or supersystems).

tabula rasa: the idea that the mind of an infant is a "blank slate" and that all knowledge, abilities, behaviors, and motives are acquired through experience.

Tay-Sachs disease: a genetic disease that attacks the nervous system, causing it to degenerate.

telegraphic speech: early sentences that consist of content words and omit the less meaningful parts of speech, such as articles, prepositions, pronouns, and auxiliary verbs.

temperament: a person's characteristic modes of response to the environment, including such attributes as activity level, irritability, fearfulness, and sociability.

temperament hypothesis: Kagan's view that the strange-situations test measures individual differences in infants' temperaments rather than the quality of their attachments.

teratogens: external agents such as viruses, drugs, chemicals, and radiation that can harm a developing embryo or fetus.

tertiary circular reaction: an exploratory scheme in which the infant devises a new method of acting on objects to reproduce interesting results.

"test bias" hypothesis: the notion that IQ tests have a built-in, middle-class bias that explains the substandard performance of children from lower-class and minority subcultures.

testicular feminization syndrome (TFS): a genetic anomaly in which a male fetus is insensitive to the effects of male sex hormones and develops femalelike external genitalia.

test norms: standards of normal performance on psychometric instruments that are based on the average scores and the range of scores obtained by a large, representative sample of test takers.

testosterone: male sex hormone, produced by the testes, that is responsible for male sexual maturation.

thalidomide: a mild tranquilizer that, taken early in pregnancy, can produce a variety of malformations of the limbs, eyes, ears, and heart.

Thanatos: Freud's name for inborn, self-destructive instincts that were said to characterize all human beings.

theory: a set of concepts and propositions designed to organize, describe, and explain an existing set of observations.

theory of mind: an understanding that people are cognitive beings with rich mental lives that are available to themselves but not to others.

theory of multiple intelligences: Gardner's theory that humans display at least seven distinct kinds of intelligence, each linked to a particular area of the brain, and several of which are not measured by IQ tests.

third stage of labor: expulsion of the placenta (afterbirth).

thyroxine: a hormone produced by the thyroid gland, essential for normal growth of the brain and the body.

timing-of-puberty effect: the finding that people who reach puberty late perform better on visual/spatial tasks than those who mature early.

time-out technique: a strategy in which the disciplinary agent controls a child's conduct by disrupting or preventing the prohibited activity that the child seems to enjoy.

tools of intellectual adaptation: Vygotsky's term for methods of thinking and problem-solving strategies that children internalize from their interactions with more competent members of society.

traditional classroom: a classroom arrangement in which all pupils sit facing an instructor, who normally teaches one subject at a time by lecturing or giving demonstrations.

transactive interactions: verbal exchanges in which individuals perform mental operations on the reasoning of their discussion partners.

transformational grammar: rules of syntax that allow one to transform declarative statements into questions, negatives, imperatives, and other kinds of sentences.

transitivity: the ability to recognize relations among elements in a serial order (for example, if A > B and B > C, then A > C).

triarchic theory: a recent information-processing theory of intelligence that emphasizes three aspects of intelligent behavior not normally tapped by IQ tests: the context of the action; the person's experience with the task (or situation); and the information-processing strategies that the person applies to the task (or situation).

trophoblast: outer cells of the blastocyst, which develop into tissues that protect and nourish the embryo.

twin study: study in which sets of twins that differ in zygosity (kinship) are compared to determine the heritability of an attribute or attributes.

two-way bilingual education: programs in which English-speaking (or other majority language) children and children who have limited proficiency in that language are instructed half the day in English and the other half in a second language.

ulnar grasp: an early manipulatory skill in which an infant grasps objects by pressing the fingers against the palm.

ultrasound: method of detecting gross physical abnormalities by scanning the womb with sound waves, thereby producing a visual outline of the fetus.

umbilical cord: a soft tube containing blood vessels that connects the embryo to the placenta.

unconditioned response (UCR): the unlearned response elicited by an unconditioned stimulus.

unconditioned stimulus (UCS): a stimulus that elicits a particular response without any prior learning.

unconscious motives: Freud's term for feelings, experiences, and conflicts that influence a person's thinking and behavior, but lie outside the person's awareness.

underextension: the young child's tendency to use general words to refer to a smaller set of objects, actions, or events than adults do (for example, using *candy* to refer only to mints).

uninvolved parenting: a pattern of parenting that is both aloof (or even hostile) and overpermissive, almost as if parents neither cared about their children nor about what they may become.

utilization deficiency: a failure to rely on effective memory strategies that one has spontaneously produced; thought to occur in the early phases of strategy acquisition when executing the strategy requires much mental effort.

validity: the extent to which a measuring instrument accurately reflects what the researchers intended to measure.

virtual object: an intangible object (optical illusion), produced by a shadow caster, that appears to occupy a particular location in space.

visual acuity: a person's ability to see small objects and fine detail.

visual cliff: an elevated platform that creates an illusion of depth, used to test the depth perception of infants.

visual contrast: the amount of light/dark transition in a visual stimulus.

visual looming: the expansion of the image of an object to take up the entire visual field as it draws very close to the face.

visual/spatial abilities: the ability to mentally manipulate or otherwise draw inferences about pictorial information.

vitamin and mineral deficiencies: a form of malnutrition in which the diet provides sufficient protein and calories but is lacking in one or more substances that promote normal growth.

vocables: unique patterns of sound that a prelinguistic infant uses to represent objects, actions, or events.

warmth/hostility: a dimension of parenting that describes the amount of responsiveness and affection that a parent displays toward a child.

X chromosome: the longer of the two sex chromosomes; normal females have two X chromosomes, whereas normal males have but one.

Y chromosome: the shorter of the two sex chromosomes; normal males have one Y chromosome, whereas females have none.

zone of proximal development: Vygotsky's term for the range of tasks that are too complex to be mastered alone but can be accomplished with guidance and encouragement from a more skillful partner.

zygote: a single cell formed at conception from the union of a sperm and an ovum.

References

Abel, E. L. (1981). Behavioral teratology of alcohol. *Psychological Bulletin, 90,* 564–581.

Abel, E. L. (1984). *Fetal alcohol syndrome and fetal alcohol effects.* New York: Plenum.

Abler, R. M., & Sedlacek, W. E. (1989). Freshman sexual attitudes and behaviors over a 15-year period. *Journal of College Student Development, 30,* 201–209.

Abma, J. C., & Mott, F. L. (1991). Substance use and prenatal care during pregnancy among young women. *Family Planning Perspectives, 23,* 117–122, 128.

Abramovitch, R., Corter, C., & Pepler, D. J. (1980). Observations of mixed-sex sibling dyads. *Child Development, 51,* 1268–1271.

Abramovitch, R., Corter, C., Pepler, D. J., & Stanhope, L. (1986). Sibling and peer interaction: A final follow-up and a comparison. *Child Development, 57,* 217–229.

Abramovitch, R., Freedman, J. L., Thoden, K., & Nikolich, C. (1991). Children's capacity to consent to participation in psychological research: Empirical findings. *Child Development, 62,* 1100–1109.

Abravanel, E., & Sigafoos, A. D. (1984). Exploring the presence of imitation during early infancy. *Child Development, 55,* 381–392.

Achenbach, T. M., Phares, V., Howell, C. T., Rauh, V. A., & Nurcombe, B. (1990). Seven-year outcome of the Vermont Intervention Program for low-birthweight infants. *Child Development, 61,* 1672–1681.

Ackerman, B. P. (1993). Children's understanding of the speaker's meaning in referential communication. *Journal of Experimental Child Psychology, 55,* 56–86.

Ackerman, B. P., Szymanski, J., & Silver, D. (1990). Children's use of common ground in interpreting ambiguous referential utterances. *Developmental Psychology, 26,* 234–245.

Acredolo, C. (1982). Conservation/nonconservation: Alternative explanations. In C. J. Brainerd (Ed.), *Progress in cognitive development* (Vol. 1). New York: Springer-Verlag.

Acredolo, L. P. (1978). Development of spatial orientation in infancy. *Developmental Psychology, 14,* 224–234.

Acredolo, L. P., & Goodwyn, S. W. (1990). Sign language in babies: The significance of symbolic gesturing for understanding language development. In R. Vasta (Ed.), *Annals of child development* (Vol. 7). Greenwich, CT: JAI Press.

Adams, G. R., Abraham, K. G., & Markstrom, C. A. (1987). The relations among identity development, self-consciousness, and self-focusing during middle and late adolescence. *Developmental Psychology, 23,* 292–297.

Adams, G. R., & Crane, P. (1980). An assessment of parents' and teachers' expectations of preschool children's social preference for attractive or unattractive children and adults. *Child Development, 51,* 224–231.

Adams, M. J. (1990). *Beginning to read: Learning and thinking about print.* Cambridge, MA: MIT Press.

Adams, R. E., & Passman, R. H. (1980, March). *The effects of advance preparation upon children's behavior during brief separation from their mother.* Paper presented at annual meeting of the Southeastern Psychological Association. Washington, D.C.

Adams, R. E., & Passman, R. H. (1981). The effects of preparing two-year-olds for brief separations from their mothers. *Child Development, 52,* 1068–1071.

Adams, R. S., & Biddle, B. J. (1970). *Realities of teaching.* New York: Holt, Rinehart & Winston.

Adey, P. S., & Shayer, M. (1992). Accelerating the development of formal thinking in middle and high school students. II: Postproject effects on science achievement. *Journal of Research in Science Teaching, 29,* 81–92.

Adler, A. (1964). *Problems of neurosis.* New York: Harper & Row. (Original work published 1929)

Adolph, K. E., Eppler, M. A., & Gibson, E. J. (1993). Crawling versus walking infants' perception of affordances for locomotion over sloping surfaces. *Child Development, 64,* 1158–1174.

Ainsworth, M. D. S. (1967). *Infancy in Uganda: Infant care and the growth of love.* Baltimore: Johns Hopkins University Press.

Ainsworth, M. D. S. (1979). Attachment as related to mother-infant interaction. In J. S. Rosenblatt, R. A. Hinde, C. Beer, & M. Busnel (Eds.), *Advances in the study of behavior* (Vol. 9). Orlando, FL: Academic Press.

Ainsworth, M. D. S. (1989). Attachments beyond infancy. *American Psychologist, 44,* 709–716.

Ainsworth, M. D. S., Bell, S. M., & Stayton, D. J. (1972). Individual differences in the development of some attachment behaviors. *Merrill-Palmer Quarterly, 18,* 123–143.

Ainsworth, M. D. S., Blehar, M., Waters, E., & Wall, S. (1978). *Patterns of attachment.* Hillsdale, NJ: Erlbaum.

Al-Awad, A. M., & Sonuga-Barke, E. J. (1992). Childhood problems in a Sudanese city: A comparison of extended and nuclear families. *Child Development, 63,* 906–914.

Alder, T. (1989). Cocaine babies face deficits. *The APA Monitor, 20,* 14.

Alegria, J., & Noirot, E. (1978). Neonate orientation behavior toward human voices. *International Journal of Behavioral Development, 1,* 291–312.

Alessandri, S. M., Sullivan, M. W., Imaizumi, S., & Lewis, M. (1993). Learning and emotional responsivity in cocaine-exposed infants. *Developmental Psychology, 29,* 989–997.

Alexander, B. K., & Harlow, H. F. (1965). Social behavior in juvenile rhesus monkeys subjected to different rearing conditions during the first 6 months of life. *Zoologische Jarbucher Physiologie, 60,* 167–174.

Alexander, G. M., & Hines, M. (1994). Gender labels and play styles: Their relative contribution to children's selection of playmates. *Child Development, 65,* 869–879.

Alexander, K. L., & Entwisle, D. R. (1988). Achievement in the first two years of school: Patterns and processes. *Monographs of the Society for Research in Child Development, 53*(2, Serial No. 218).

Allen, J. P., Weissberg, R. P., & Hawkins, J. A. (1989). The relation between values and social competence in early adolescence. *Developmental Psychology, 25,* 458–464.

Allen, M. C., & Capute, A. J. (1986). Assessment of early auditory and visual abilities of extremely premature infants. *Developmental Medicine and Child Neurology, 28,* 458–466.

Alley, T. R. (1981). Head shape and the perception of cuteness. *Developmental Psychology, 17,* 650–654.

Allgood-Merten, B., & Stockard, J. (1991). Sex role identity and self-esteem: A comparison of children and adolescents. *Sex Roles, 25,* 129–139.

Allison, P. D., & Furstenberg, F. F., Jr. (1989). How marital dissolution affects children: Variations by age and sex. *Developmental Psychology, 25,* 540–549.

Amabile, T. M., & Hennessey, B. A. (1988). The motivation for creativity in children. In A. K. Boggiano & T. Pittman (Eds.), *Achievement and motivation: A social developmental perspective.* New York: Cambridge University Press.

Amato, P. R. (1993). Children's adjustment to divorce: Theories, hypotheses, and empirical support. *Journal of Marriage and the Family, 55,* 23–38.

Amato, P. R., & Keith, B. (1991). Parental divorce and adult well-being: A meta-analysis. *Journal of Marriage and the Family, 53,* 43–58.

Ambert, A. (1992). *The effect of children on parents.* New York: Haworth.

Ambron, S. R., & Irwin, D. M. (1975). Role-taking and moral judgment in five- and seven-year-olds. *Developmental Psychology, 11,* 102.

American Academy of Pediatrics (1986). Sexuality, contraception, and the media. *Pediatrics, 71,* 535–536.

American Association on Mental Retardation (1992). *Mental retardation: Definition, classification, and systems of support* (9th ed.). Washington, D.C.: American Association on Mental Retardation.

American Psychiatric Association (1987). *Diagnostic and statistical manual of mental disorders* (3rd ed., revised). Washington, D.C.: American Psychiatric Association.

American Psychological Association. (1982). *Ethical principles in the conduct of research with human participants.* Washington, D.C.: American Psychological Association.

Anand, K. J., & Hickey, P. R. (1992). Halothane-morphine compared with high-dose sufentanil for anesthesia and postoperative analgesia in neonatal cardiac surgery. *New England Journal of Medicine, 326,* 1–9.

Anastasi, A. (1988). *Psychological testing* (6th ed.). New York: Macmillan.

Anderson, D. R., & Collins, P. A. (1988). *The impact on children's education: Television's influence on cognitive development.* Washington, D.C.: U.S. Department of Education.

Anderson, D. R., Lorch, E. P., Field, D. E., Collins, P. A., & Nathan, J. G. (1986). Television viewing at home: Age trends in visual attention and time with TV. *Child Development, 57,* 1024–1033.

Anderson, K. E., Lytton, H., & Romney, D. M. (1986). Mothers' interactions with normal and conduct-disordered boys: Who affects whom? *Developmental Psychology, 22,* 604–609.

Anderson, R. L., & Golbus, M. S. (1989). Chemical teratogens. In M. I. Evans, J. C. Fletcher, A. O. Dixler, and J. D. Schulman (Eds.), *Fetal diagnosis and therapy: Science, ethics, and the law.* Philadelphia: J. B. Lippincott.

Andersson, B. (1989). Effects of public day-care: A longitudinal study. *Child Development, 60,* 857–866.

Andersson, B. (1992). Effects of day-care on cognitive and socioemotional competence of thirteen-year-old Swedish schoolchildren. *Child Development, 63,* 20–36.

Anglin, J. M. (1993). Vocabulary development: A morphological analysis. *Monographs of the Society for Research in Child Development, 58*(10, Serial No. 238).

Anisfeld, E., Casper, V., Nozyce, M., & Cunningham, N. (1990). Does infant carrying promote attachment? An experimental study of the effects of increased physical contact on the development of attachment. *Child Development, 61,* 1617–1627.

Anisfeld, M. (1991). Neonatal imitation. *Developmental Review, 11,* 60–97.

Annas, G. J. (1984). Legal aspects of home birth. In S. E. Sagov, R. I. Feinbloom, P. Spindel, & A. Brodsky (Eds.), *Home birth: A practitioner's guide to birth outside the hospital.* Rockville, MD: Aspen.

Annis, L. F. (1978). *The child before birth.* Ithaca, NY: Cornell University.

Anson, A. R., Cook, T. D., Habib, F., Grady, M. K., Haynes, N., & Comer, J. P. (1991). The Comer school development program: A theoretical analysis. *Urban Education, 26,* 56–82.

Apgar, V., & Beck, J. (1974). *Is my baby all right?* New York: Pocket Books.

Archer, J. (1991). The influence of testosterone on human aggression. *British Journal of Psychology, 82,* 1–28.

Archer, J. (1992). Childhood gender roles: Social context and organization. In H. McGurk (Ed.), *Childhood social development: Contemporary perspectives.* Hove, England: Erlbaum.

Archer, S. L. (1982). The lower age boundaries of identity development. *Child Development, 53,* 1551–1556.

Archer, S. L. (1992). A feminist's approach to identity research. In G. R. Adams, T. P. Gullotta, & R. Montemayor (Eds.), *Advances in adolescent development. Vol. 4: Adolescent identity formation.* Newbury Park, CA: Sage.

Aries, P. (1962). *Centuries of childhood.* New York: Knopf.

Arlin, P. K. (1975). Cognitive development in adulthood: A fifth stage? *Developmental Psychology, 11,* 602–606.

Arlin, P. K. (1977). Piagetian operations in problem finding. *Developmental Psychology, 13,* 297–298.

Arnett, J. (1990). Contraceptive use, sensation seeking, and adolescent egocentrism. *Journal of Youth and Adolescence, 19,* 171–180.

Arnett, J., & Balle-Jensen, L. (1993). Cultural bases of risk behavior: Danish adolescents. *Child Development, 64,* 1842–1855.

Aro, H., & Taipale, V. (1987). The impact of timing of puberty on psychosomatic symptoms among fourteen- to sixteen-year-old Finnish girls. *Child Development, 58,* 261–268.

Aronfreed, J. (1976). Moral development from the standpoint of a general psychological theory. In T. Lickona (Ed.), *Moral development and behavior.* New York: Holt, Rinehart & Winston.

Aronson, E., Blaney, N., Stephan, C., Sikes, J., & Snapp, M. (1978). *The jigsaw classroom.* Beverly Hills, CA: Sage.

Aronson, E., & Rosenbloom, S. (1971). Space perception within a common auditory-visual space. *Science, 172,* 1161–1163.

Arsenio, W. F., & Kramer, R. (1992). Victimizers and their victims: Children's conceptions of mixed emotional consequences of moral transgressions. *Child Development, 63,* 915–927.

Artenstein, J. (1990). *Runaways in their own words: Kids talking about living on the street.* New York: Tor Books.

Arterberry, M., Yonas, A., & Bensen, A. S. (1989). Self-produced locomotion and the development of responsiveness to linear perspective and texture gradients. *Developmental Psychology, 25,* 976–982.

Ascher, E. J. (1935). The inadequacy of current intelligence tests for testing Kentucky mountain children. *Journal of Genetic Psychology, 46,* 480–486.

Asendorph, J. B., & Baudonniere, P. (1993) Self-awareness and other-awareness: Mirror self-recognition and synchronic imitation among unfamiliar peers. *Developmental Psychology, 29,* 88–95.

Asher, S. R., & Coie, J. D. (1990). *Peer rejection in childhood.* Cambridge, England: Cambridge University Press.

Asher, S. R., Renshaw, P. D., & Hymel, S. (1982). Peer relations and the development of social skills. In S. G. Moore (Ed.), *The young child: Reviews of research* (Vol. 3). Washington, DC: National Association for the Education of Young Children.

Aslin, R. N. (1987). Visual and auditory development in infancy. In J. D. Osofsky (Ed.), *Handbook of infant development* (2nd ed.). New York: Wiley.

Aslin, R. N., Pisoni, D. B., & Jusczyk, P. W. (1983). Auditory development and speech perception in infancy. In M. M. Haith & J. J. Campos (Eds.), *Handbook of child psychology. Vol. 2: Infancy and developmental psychobiology.* New York: Wiley.

Aslin, R. N., & Smith, L. B. (1988). Perceptual development. *Annual Review of Psychology, 39,* 435–473.

Associated Press (1993, March 4). NIH panel urges testing of newborns for deafness. *Washington Post,* A13.

Associated Press (1994a, July 30). Science: A man's domain. *Atlanta Constitution,* A6.

Associated Press (1994b, September 7). Study: TV ignores, maligns hispanics. *Fresno Bee,* F1, F4.

Associated Press (1994c, August 24). Which practices work best in today's schools? *Atlanta Constitution,* A1, A14.

Astor, R. A. (1994). Children's moral reasoning about family and peer violence: The role of provocation and retribution. *Child Development, 65,* 1054–1067.

Atkin, C. (1978). Observation of parent-child interaction in supermarket decision-making. *Journal of Marketing, 42,* 41–45.

Atkinson, R. C., & Shiffrin, R. M. (1968). Human memory: A proposed system and its control processes. In K. W. Spence & J. T. Spence (Eds.), *The psychology of learning and motivation: Advances in research and theory* (Vol. 2). Orlando, FL: Academic Press.

Atwater, E. (1992). *Adolescence* (2nd ed.). Englewood Cliffs, NJ: Prentice-Hall.

Austin, R. J., & Moawad, A. H. (1993). The very low birth weight fetus. In C. Lin, M. S. Verp, & R. E. Sabbagha (Eds.), *The high-risk fetus: Pathophysiology, diagnosis, management.* New York: Springer-Verlag.

Ayala, F. J., & Kiger, J. A. (1984). *Modern genetics.* Menlo Park, CA: Cummings.

Azmitia, M. (1988). Peer interaction and problem-solving: When are two heads better than one? *Child Development, 59,* 87–96.

Azmitia, M. (1992). Expertise, private speech, and the development of self-regulation. In R. M. Diaz & L. E. Berk (Eds.), *Private speech: From social interaction to self-regulation.* Hillsdale, NJ: Erlbaum.

Azmitia, M., & Hesser, J. (1993). Why siblings are important agents of cognitive development: A comparison of siblings and peers. *Child Development, 64,* 430–444.

Bachman, J. G., & Schulenberg, J. (1993). How part-time work intensity relates to drug use, problem behavior, time use, and satisfaction among high school seniors: Are these consequences or merely correlates? *Developmental Psychology, 29,* 220–235.

Backschneider, A. G., Shatz, M., & Gelman, S. A. (1993). Preschoolers' ability to distinguish living kinds as a function of regrowth. *Child Development, 64,* 1242–1257.

Bahrick, L. E. (1988). Intermodal learning in infancy: Learning on the basis of two kinds of invariant relations in audible and visible events. *Child Development, 59,* 197–209.

Bai, D. L., & Bertenthal, B. I. (1992). Locomotor status and the development of spatial search skills. *Child Development, 63,* 215–226.

Baier, J. L., Rosenzweig, M. G., & Whipple, E. (1991). Patterns of sexual behavior, coercion, and victimization of university students. *Journal of College Student Development, 32,* 310–322.

Bailey, J. M., & Pillard, R. C. (1991). A genetic study of the male sexual orientation. *Archives of General Psychiatry, 48,* 1089–1096.

Bailey, J. M., Pillard, R. C., Neale, M. C., & Agyei, Y. (1993). Heritable factors influence sexual orientation in women. *Archives of General Psychiatry, 50,* 217–223.

Baillargeon, R. (1987). Object permanence in 3½- and 4½-month-old infants. *Developmental Psychology, 23,* 655–664.

Baillargeon, R., & Graber, M. (1988). Evidence of location memory in 8-month-old infants in a nonsearch AB task. *Developmental Psychology, 24,* 502–511.

Baird, P. A., Anderson, T. W., Newcombe, H. B., & Lowry, R. B. (1988). Genetic disorders in children and young adults: A population study. *American Journal of Human Genetics, 42,* 677–693.

Baker, D. P., & Jones, D. P. (1992). Opportunity and performance: A sociological explanation for gender differences in academic mathematics. In J. Wrigley (Ed.), *Education and gender equality.* London: The Falmer Press.

Baker, L. A., & Daniels, D. (1990). Nonshared environmental influences and personality differences in adult twins. *Journal of Personality and Social Psychology, 58,* 103–110.

Baker, L. A., Mack, W., Moffitt, T. E., & Mednick, S. (1989). Sex differences in property crime in a Danish adoption cohort. *Behavior Genetics, 19,* 355–370.

Baker, R. L., & Mednick, B. R. (1984). *Influences on human development: A longitudinal perspective.* Boston: Kluwer Nijhoff.

Baker-Ward, L., Gordon, B. N., Ornstein, P. A., Larus, D. M., & Clubb, P. A. (1993). Young children's long-term retention of a pediatric examination. *Child Development, 64,* 1519–1533.

Baker-Ward, L., Ornstein, P. A., & Holden, D. J. (1984). The expression of memorization in early childhood. *Journal of Experimental Child Psychology, 37,* 555–575.

Bakwin, H. (1973). Erotic feelings in infants and young children. *American Journal of Diseases of Children, 126,* 52–54.

Baldwin, D. A. (1993). Early referential understanding: Infants' ability to recognize referential acts for what they are. *Developmental Psychology, 29,* 832–843.

Baldwin, D. A., & Markman, E. M. (1989). Establishing word-object relations: A first step. *Child Development, 60,* 381–398.

Baldwin, D. V., & Skinner, M. L. (1989). Structural model for antisocial behavior: Generalization to single-mother families. *Developmental Psychology, 25,* 45–50.

Ball, S., & Bogatz, C. (1970). *The first year of Sesame Street: An evaluation.* Princeton, NJ: Educational Testing Service.

Ball, S., & Bogatz, C. (1973). *Reading with television: An evaluation of The Electric Company.* Princeton, NJ: Educational Testing Service.

Baltes, P. B., Reese, H. W., & Lipsitt, L. P. (1980). Life-span developmental psychology. *Annual Review of Psychology, 31,* 65–110.

Bandura, A. (1965). Influence of models' reinforcement contingencies on the acquisition of imitative responses. *Journal of Personality and Social Psychology, 1,* 589–595.

Bandura, A. (1971). An analysis of modeling processes. In A. Bandura (Ed.), *Psychological modeling.* New York: Lieber-Atherton.

Bandura, A. (1977). *Social learning theory.* Englewood Cliffs, NJ: Prentice-Hall.

Bandura, A. (1986). *Social foundations of thought and action. A social cognitive theory.* Englewood Cliffs, NJ: Prentice-Hall.

Bandura, A. (1989). Social cognitive theory. In R. Vasta (Ed.), *Annals of child development. Vol. 6: Theories of child development: Revised formulations and current issues.* Greenwich, CT: JAI Press.

Bandura, A. (1991). Social cognitive theory of moral thought and action. In W. M. Kurtines, & J. L. Gewirtz (Eds.), *Handbook of moral behavior and development. Vol. 1: Theory.* Hillsdale, NJ: Erlbaum.

Banks, J. A. (1993). Multicultural education: Historical development, dimensions, and practice. *Review of Educational Research, 19,* 3–49.

Banks, M. S., & Ginsburg, A. P. (1985). Infant visual preferences: A review and new theoretical treatment. In H. W. Reese (Ed.), *Advances in child development and behavior* (Vol. 19). Orlando, FL: Academic Press.

Banks, M. S., & Salapatek, P. (1983). Infant visual perception. In M. M. Haith & J. J. Campos (Eds.), *Handbook of child psychology. Vol. 2: Infancy and developmental psychobiology.* New York: Wiley.

Barber, B. K., Olsen, J. E., & Shagle, S. C. (1994). Associations between parental psychological and behavioral control and youth internalized and externalized behaviors. *Child Development, 65,* 1120–1136.

Barber, B. L., & Eccles, J. S. (1992). Long-term influence of divorce and single parenting on adolescent family- and work-related values, behaviors, and aspirations. *Psychological Bulletin, 111,* 108–126.

Barden, R. C., Ford, M. E., Jensen, A. G., Rogers-Salyer, M., & Salyer, K. E. (1989). Effects of craniofacial deformity in infancy on the quality of mother-infant interactions. *Child Development, 60,* 819–824.

Barenboim, C. (1981). The development of person perception in childhood and adolescence: From behavioral comparisons to psychological constructs to psychological comparisons. *Child Development, 52,* 129–144.

Barglow, P., Vaughn, B. E., & Molitor, N. (1987). Effects of maternal absence due to employment on the quality of infant-mother attachment in a low-risk sample. *Child Development, 58,* 945–954.

Barker, R. G., & Gump, P. V. (1964). *Big school, small school.* Stanford, CA: Stanford University Press.

Barnard, K. E., & Bee, H. L. (1983). The impact of temporally patterned stimulation on the development of preterm infants. *Child Development, 54,* 1156–1167.

Barnett, M. A. (1987). Empathy and related responses in children. In N. Eisenberg & J. Strayer (Eds.), *Empathy and its development.* Cambridge, England: Cambridge University Press.

Baron, N. S. (1992). *Growing up with language: How children learn to talk.* Reading, MA: Addison-Wesley.

Baron, R. A., & Byrne, D. (1994). *Social psychology: Understanding human interaction* (7th ed.). Newton, MA: Allyn & Bacon.

Baroni, M. R., & Axia, G. (1989). Children's metapragmatic abilities and the identification of polite and impolite requests. *First Language, 9,* 285–297.

Barr, H. M., Streissguth, A. P., Darby, B. L., & Sampson, P. D. (1990). Prenatal exposure to alcohol, caffeine, tobacco, and aspirin: Effects on fine and gross motor performance in 4-year-old children. *Developmental Psychology, 26,* 339–348.

Barrera, M. E., & Maurer, D. (1981a). Discrimination of strangers by the three-month-old. *Child Development, 52,* 558–563.

Barrera, M. E., & Maurer, D. (1981b). Recognition of mother's photographed face by the three-month-old infant. *Child Development, 52,* 714–716.

Barrett, D. E. (1979). A naturalistic study of sex differences in children's aggression. *Merrill-Palmer Quarterly, 25,* 193–203.

Barrett, D. E., & Frank, D. A. (1987). *The effects of undernutrition on children's behavior.* New York: Gordon and Breach.

Barrett, D. E., Radke-Yarrow, M., & Klein, R. E. (1982). Chronic malnutrition and child behavior: Effects of early calorie supplementation on socioemotional functioning at school age. *Developmental Psychology, 18,* 541–556.

Barrett, G. V., & Depinet, R. L. (1991). A reconsideration of testing for competence rather than for intelligence. *American Psychologist, 46,* 1012–1024.

Barry, H., III, Bacon, M. K., & Child, I. L. (1957). A cross-cultural survey of some sex differences in socialization. *Journal of Abnormal and Social Psychology, 55,* 327–332.

Barry, H., Child, I. L., & Bacon, M. K. (1959). The relation of child training to subsistence economy. *American Anthropologist, 61,* 51–63.

Bar-Tal, D., Raviv, A., & Goldberg, M. (1982). Helping behavior among preschool children: An observational study. *Child Development, 53,* 396–402.

Bartholomew, K., & Horowitz, L. M. (1991). Attachment styles among young adults: A test of a four-category model. *Journal of Personality and Social Psychology, 61,* 226–244.

Baskett, L. M. (1985). Sibling status effects: Adult expectations. *Developmental Psychology, 21,* 441–445.

Baskett, L. M., & Johnson, S. M. (1982). The young child's interaction with parents versus siblings: A behavioral analysis. *Child Development, 53,* 643–650.

Basseches, M. (1984). *Dialectical thinking and adult development.* Norwood, NJ: Ablex.

Bates, E. (1993, March). *Nature, nurture, and language.* Invited address presented at the biennial meeting of the Society for Research in Child Development, New Orleans.

Bates, E., & MacWhinney, B. (1982). Functionalist approaches to grammar. In E. Wanner & L. Gleitman (Eds.), *Language acquisition: The state of the art.* Cambridge, England: Cambridge University Press.

Bates, E., O'Connell, B., & Shore, C. (1987). Language and communication in infancy. In J. D. Osofsky (Ed.), *Handbook of infant development* (2nd ed.). New York: Wiley.

Bates, E., Thal, D., Whitsell, K., Fenson, L., & Oakes, L. (1989). Integrating language and gesture in infancy. *Developmental Psychology, 25,* 1004–1019.

Bates, J. E. (1987). Temperament in infancy. In J. D. Osofsky (Ed.), *Handbook of infant development* (2nd ed.). New York: Wiley.

Bates, J. E., Marvinney, D., Kelly, T., Dodge, K. A., Bennett, D. S., & Pettit, G. S. (1994). Child-care history and kindergarten adjustment. *Developmental Psychology, 30,* 690–700.

Batson, C. D. (1987). Prosocial motivation: Is it ever truly altruistic? In L. Berkowitz (Ed.), *Advances in experimental social psychology* (Vol. 20). New York: Academic Press.

Bauer, P. J., & Mandler, J. M. (1989). One thing follows another: Effects of temporal structure on 1- to 2-year-olds' recall of events. *Developmental Psychology, 25,* 197–206.

Baumrind, D. (1967). Child care practices anteceding three patterns of preschool behavior. *Genetic Psychology Monographs, 75,* 43–88.

Baumrind, D. (1971). Current patterns of parental authority. *Developmental Psychology Monographs, 4*(1, Part 2).

Baumrind, D. (1973). The development of instrumental competence through socialization. In A. Pick (Ed.), *Minnesota symposium on child psychology* (Vol. 7). Minneapolis: University of Minnesota Press.

Baumrind, D. (1977, March). *Socialization determinants of personal agency.* Paper presented at the biennial meeting of the Society for Research in Child Development, New Orleans.

Baumrind, D. (1983). Rejoinder to Lewis's reinterpretation of parental firm control effects: Are authoritative families really harmonious? *Psychological Bulletin, 94,* 132–142.

Baumrind, D. (1991). Effective parenting during the early adolescent transition. In P. A. Cowan & M. Hetherington (Eds.), *Family transitions.* Hillsdale, NJ: Erlbaum.

Baumrind, D. (1993). The average expectable environment is not good enough: A response to Scarr. *Child Development, 64,* 1299–1317.

Bayley, N. (1969). *Bayley Scales of Infant Development.* New York: Psychological Corporation.

Bayley, N. (1993). *Bayley Scales of Infant Development* (2nd ed.). San Antonio, TX: Psychological Corporation.

Beach, F. A. (1965). *Sex and behavior.* New York: Wiley.

Beal, C. R. (1987). Repairing the message: Children's monitoring and revision skills. *Child Development, 58,* 401–408.

Beal, C. R. (1990a). Development of knowledge about the role of inference in text comprehension. *Child Development, 61,* 1011–1023.

Beal, C. R. (1990b). The development of text evaluation and revision skills. *Child Development, 61,* 247–258.

Beal, C. R., & Belgrad, S. L. (1990). The development of message evaluation skills in young children. *Child Development, 61,* 705–712.

Beal, C. R., & Flavell, J. H. (1984). Development of the ability to distinguish communicative intention and literal message meaning. *Child Development, 55,* 920–928.

Bear, G. G., & Rys, G. S. (1994). Moral reasoning, classroom behavior, and sociometric status among elementary school children. *Developmental Psychology, 30,* 633–638.

Becker, W. C. (1964). Consequences of different kinds of parental discipline. In M. L. Hoffman & L. W. Hoffman (Eds.), *Review of child development research* (Vol. 1). New York: Russell Sage Foundation.

Beckwith, L., Rodning, C., & Cohen, S. (1992). Preterm children at early adolescence and continuity and discontinuity in maternal responsiveness from infancy. *Child Development, 63,* 1198–1208.

Behrend, D. A., Rosengren, K., & Perlmutter, M. (1989). A new look at children's private speech: The effects of age, task difficulty, and parent presence. *International Journal of Behavioral Development, 12,* 305–320.

Beilin, H. (1992). Piaget's enduring contribution to developmental psychology. *Developmental Psychology, 28,* 191–204.

Bell, A. P., Weinberg, M. S., & Hammersmith, S. K. (1981). *Sexual preference: Its development in men and women.* Bloomington, IN: Indiana University Press.

Bell, M. A., & Fox, N. A. (1992). The relations between frontal brain electrical activity and cognitive development during infancy. *Child Development, 63,* 1142–1163.

Bell, R. Q. (1979). Parent, child, and reciprocal influences. *American Psychologist, 34,* 821–826.

Bellugi, U. (1988). The acquisition of a spatial language. In F. S. Kessel (Ed.), *The development of language and language researchers: Essays in honor of Roger Brown.* Hillsdale, NJ: Erlbaum.

Belmont, L., & Marolla, F. A. (1973). Birth order, family size, and intelligence. *Science, 182,* 1096–1101.

Belsky, J. (1980). Child maltreatment: An ecological integration. *American Psychologist, 35*, 320–335.

Belsky, J. (1981). Early human experience: A family perspective. *Developmental Psychology, 17*, 3–23.

Belsky, J. (1985). Experimenting with the family in the newborn period. *Child Development, 56*, 407–414.

Belsky, J., & Braungart, J. M. (1991). Are insecure-avoidant infants with extensive day-care experience less stressed by and more independent in the Strange Situation? *Child Development, 62*, 567–571.

Belsky, J., Garduque, L., & Hrncir, E. (1984). Assessing performance, competence, and executive capacity in infant play: Relations to home environment and security of attachment. *Developmental Psychology, 20*, 406–417.

Belsky, J., Gilstrap, B., & Rovine, M. (1984). The Pennsylvania Infant and Family Development Project. I: Stability and change in mother-infant and father-infant interaction in a family setting. *Child Development, 55*, 692–705.

Belsky, J., & Rovine, M. (1988). Nonmaternal care in the first year of life and the security of infant-parent attachment. *Child Development, 59*, 157–167.

Belsky, J., Rovine, M., & Taylor, D. G. (1984). The Pennsylvania Infant and Family Development Project. III: The origins of individual differences in infant-mother attachment—maternal and infant contributions. *Child Development, 55*, 718–728.

Bem, S. L. (1974). The measurement of psychological androgyny. *Journal of Consulting and Clinical Psychology, 42*, 155–162.

Bem, S. L. (1975). Sex-role adaptability: One consequence of psychological androgyny. *Journal of Personality and Social Psychology, 31*, 634–643.

Bem, S. L. (1978). Beyond androgyny: Some presumptuous prescriptions for a liberated sexual identity. In J. A. Sherman & F. L. Denmark (Eds.), *The psychology of women: Future directions in research.* New York: Psychological Dimensions.

Bem, S. L. (1983). Gender schema theory and its implications for child development: Raising gender aschematic children in a gender-schematic society. *Signs: Journal of Women in Culture and Society, 8*, 598–616.

Bem, S. L. (1989). Genital knowledge and gender constancy in preschool children. *Child Development, 60*, 649–662.

Benbow, C. P., & Arjmand, O. (1990). Predictors of high academic achievement in mathematics and science by mathematically talented students: A longitudinal study. *Journal of Educational Psychology, 82*, 430–441.

Bendersky, M., & Lewis, M. (1994). Environmental risk, biological risk, and developmental outcome. *Developmental Psychology, 30*, 484–494.

Benedict, H. (1979). Early lexical development: Comprehension and production. *Journal of Child Language, 6*, 183–200.

Benoit, D., & Parker, K. C. H. (1994). Stability and transmission of attachment across three generations. *Child Development, 65*, 1444–1456.

Bentler, P. M. (1992). Etiologies and consequences of adolescent drug use: Implications for prevention. *Journal of Addictive Diseases, 11*, 47–61.

Berenbaum, S. A., & Hines, M. (1992). Early androgens are related to childhood sex-typed toy preferences. *Psychological Science, 3*, 203–206.

Berenbaum, S. A., & Snyder, E. (1995). Early hormonal influences on childhood sex-typed activity and playmate preferences: Implications for the development of sexual orientation. *Developmental Psychology, 31*, 31–42.

Berg, W. K., & Berg, K. M. (1987). Psychophysiologic development in infancy: State, startle, and attention. In J. Osofsky (Ed.), *Handbook of infant development* (2nd ed.). New York: Wiley.

Bergen, D. J., & Williams, J. E. (1991). Sex stereotypes in the United States revisited: 1972–1988. *Sex Roles, 24*, 413–424.

Berk, L. E. (1992). Children's private speech: An overview of theory and the status of research. In R. M. Diaz & L. E. Berk (Eds.), *Private speech: From social interaction to self-regulation.* Hillsdale, NJ: Erlbaum.

Berk, L. E., & Landau, S. (1993). Private speech of learning disabled and normally achieving children in classroom academic and laboratory contexts. *Child Development, 64*, 556–571.

Berko, J. (1958). The child's learning of English morphology. *Word, 14*, 150–177.

Berkowitz, M. W., & Gibbs, J. C. (1983). Measuring the developmental features of moral discussion. *Merrill-Palmer Quarterly, 29*, 399–410.

Berman, A. L., & Jobes, D. A. (1991). *Adolescent suicide: Assessment and intervention.* Washington, D.C.: American Psychological Association.

Berman, P. W., & Goodman, V. (1984). Age and sex differences in children's responses to babies: Effects of adults' caretaking requests and instructions. *Child Development, 55*, 1071–1077.

Berndt, T. J. (1979). Developmental changes in conformity to peers and parents. *Developmental Psychology, 15*, 608–616.

Berndt, T. J. (1986). Children's comments about their friendships. In M. Perlmutter (Ed.), *Minnesota symposia on child psychology. Vol. 18: Cognitive perspectives on children's social and behavioral development.* Hillsdale, NJ: Erlbaum.

Berndt, T. J. (1989). Friendships in childhood and adolescence. In W. Damon (Ed.), *Child development today and tomorrow.* San Francisco: Jossey-Bass.

Berndt, T. J., & Bulleit, T. N. (1985). Effects of sibling relationships on preschoolers' behavior at home and at school. *Developmental Psychology, 21*, 761–767.

Berndt, T. J., Hawkins, J. A., & Hoyle, S. G. (1986). Changes in friendship during a school year: Effects on children's and adolescents' impressions of friendship and sharing with friends. *Child Development, 57*, 1284–1297.

Berndt, T. J., & Hoyle, S. G. (1985). Stability and change in childhood and adolescent friendships. *Developmental Psychology, 21*, 1007–1015.

Berndt, T. J., & Perry, T. B. (1990). Distinctive features and effects of early adolescent friendships. In R. Montemayor, G. R. Adams, & T. P. Gulotta (Eds.), *From childhood to adolescence: A transitional period.* Newbury Park, CA: Sage.

Berrueta-Clement, J. R., Schweinhart, L. J., Barnett, S. W., Epstein, A. S., & Weikart, D. P. (1984). *Changed lives: The effects of the Perry Preschool Program on youths through age 19.* Ypsilanti, MI: High/Scope Press.

Berry, J. W. (1967). Independence and conformity in subsistence-level societies. *Journal of Personality and Social Psychology, 7*, 415–418.

Berry, J. W., Poortinga, Y. H., Segall, M., & Dasen, P. R. (1992). *Cross-cultural psychology: Research and applications.* Cambridge, England: Cambridge University Press.

Berscheid, E., Walster, E., & Bohrnstedt, G. (1973, June). The happy American body: A survey report. *Psychology Today*, 119–131.

Bertenthal, B. I. (1993, March). *Emerging trends in perceptual development.* Paper presented at the biennial meeting of the Society for Research in Child Development, New Orleans, LA.

Bertenthal, B. I., Proffitt, D. R., & Cutting, J. E. (1984). Infant sensitivity to figural coherence in biomechanical motions. *Journal of Experimental Child Psychology, 37*, 213–230.

Bertenthal, B. I., Proffitt, D. R., Kramer, S. J., & Spetner, N. B. (1987). Infants' encoding of kinetic displays varying in relative coherence. *Developmental Psychology, 23*, 171–178.

Berzonsky, M. D. (1992). A process perspective on identity and stress management. In G. R. Adams, T. P. Gullotta, & R. Montemayor (Eds.), *Advances in adolescent development. Vol. 4: Adolescent identity formation.* Newbury Park, CA: Sage.

Best, D. L. (1993). Inducing children to generate mnemonic organizational strategies: An examination of long-term retention and materials. *Developmental Psychology, 29*, 324–336.

Best, D. L., & Ornstein, P. A. (1986). Children's generation and communication of mnemonic organizational strategies. *Developmental Psychology, 22*, 845–853.

Best, D. L., Williams, J. E., Cloud, J. M., Davis, S. W., Robertson, L. S., Edwards, J. R., Giles, H., & Fowlkes, J. (1977). Development of sex-trait stereotypes among young children in the United States, England, and Ireland. *Child Development, 48*, 1375–1384.

Beyth-Marom, R., Austin, L., Fischoff, B., Palmgren, C., & Jacobs-Quadrel, M. (1993). Perceived consequences of risky behaviors: Adolescents and adults. *Developmental Psychology, 29*, 549–563.

Bialystock, E. (1986). Factors in the growth of linguistic awareness. *Child Development, 57*, 498–510.

Bialystock, E. (1988). Levels of bilingualism and levels of metalinguistic awareness. *Developmental Psychology, 24*, 560–567.

Bickerton, D. (1983). Creole languages. *Scientific American, 249*, 116–122.

Bickerton, D. (1984). The language bioprogram hypothesis. *Behavioral and Brain Sciences, 7*, 173–221.

Bierman, K. L. (1986). Process of change during social skills training with preadolescents and its relation to treatment outcome. *Child Development, 57*, 230–240.

Bierman, K. L., & Furman, W. (1984). The effects of social skills training and peer involvement on the social adjustment of preadolescents. *Child Development, 55*, 157–162.

Bierman, K. L., Smoot, D. L., & Aumiller, K. (1993). Characteristics of aggressive-rejected, aggressive (nonrejected), and rejected (nonaggressive) boys. *Child Development, 64*, 139–151.

Biernat, M. (1991). Gender stereotypes and the relationship between masculinity and femininity: A developmental analysis. *Journal of Personality and Social Psychology, 61*, 351–365.

Bigler, R. S., & Liben, L. S. (1990). The role of attitudes and interventions in gender-schematic processing. *Child Development, 61*, 1440–1452.

Bigler, R. S., & Liben, L. S. (1992). Cognitive mechanisms in children's gender stereotyping: Theoretical and educational implications of a cognitive-based intervention. *Child Development, 63*, 1351–1363.

Bigler, R. S., & Liben, L. S. (1993). A cognitive-developmental approach to racial stereotyping and reconstructive memory in Euro-American children. *Child Development, 64*, 1507–1518.

Bijeljac-Babic, R., Bertoncini, J., & Mehler, J. (1993). How do 4-day-old infants categorize multisyllabic utterances? *Developmental Psychology, 29*, 711–721.

Biller, H. B. (1993). *Fathers and families: Paternal factors in child development.* Westport, CT: Auburn House.

Bilsker, D., & Marcia, J. E. (1991). Adaptive regression and ego identity. *Journal of Adolescence, 14*, 75–84.

Bilsker, D., Schiedel D., & Marcia, J. (1988). Sex differences in identity status. *Sex Roles, 18*, 231–236.

Birch, L. L. (1990). Development of food acceptance patterns. *Developmental Psychology, 26*, 515–519.

Birch, L. L., & Billman, J. (1986). Preschool children's food sharing with friends and acquaintances. *Child Development, 57*, 387–395.

Birch, L. L., Marlin, D. W., & Rotter, J. (1984). Eating as the "means" activity in a contingency: Effects on young children's food preference. *Child Development, 55*, 431–439.

Biringen, Z. (1990). Direct observation of maternal sensitivity and dyadic interactions in the home: Relations to maternal thinking. *Developmental Psychology, 26*, 278–284.

Birns, B., Blank, M., & Bridger, W. H. (1966). The effectiveness of various soothing techniques on human neonates. *Psychosomatic Medicine, 28,* 316–322.

Bishop, D. (1988). Language development after focal brain damage. In D. Bishop & K. Mogford (Eds.), *Language development in exceptional circumstances.* Edinburgh: Churchill Livingstone.

Bishop, J. E., & Waldholz, M. (1990). *Genome. The story of the most astonishing scientific adventure of our time—The attempt to map all the genes of the human body.* New York: Simon & Schuster.

Bivens, J. A., & Berk, L. E. (1990). A longitudinal study of the development of elementary school children's private speech. *Merrill-Palmer Quarterly, 36,* 443–463.

Bjorklund, D. F. (1987). How age changes in knowledge base contribute to the development of children's memory: An interpretive review. *Developmental Review, 7,* 93–130.

Bjorklund, D. F. (1995). *Children's thinking: Developmental function and individual differences* (2nd ed.). Pacific Grove, CA: Brooks/Cole.

Bjorklund, D. F., & Bjorklund, B. R. (1992). *Looking at children.* Pacific Grove, CA: Brooks/Cole.

Bjorklund, D. F., & Coyle, T. R. (1994). Utilization deficiencies in the development of memory strategies. In F. E. Weinert & W. Schneider (Eds.), *Research on memory development: State of the art and future directions.* Hillsdale, NJ: Erlbaum.

Bjorklund, D. F., & Harnishfeger, K. K. (1990). Children's strategies: Their definition and origins. In D. F. Bjorklund (Ed.), *Children's strategies: Contemporary views of cognitive development.* Hillsdale, NJ: Erlbaum.

Bjorklund, D. F., & Zeman, B. R. (1982). Children's organization and metamemory awareness in their recall of familiar information. *Child Development, 53,* 799–810.

Bjorkqvist, K., Lagerspetz, K. M. J., & Kaukiainen, A. (1992). Do girls manipulate and boys fight? Developmental trends in regard to direct and indirect aggression. *Aggressive Behavior, 18,* 117–127.

Blake, J., & Boysson-Bardies, B. de (1992). Patterns in babbling: A cross-linguistic study. *Journal of Child Language, 19,* 51–74.

Blakemore, J. E. O., LaRue, A. A., & Olejnik, A. B. (1979). Sex-appropriate toy preference and the ability to conceptualize toys as sex-role related. *Developmental Psychology, 15,* 339–340.

Blasi, A. (1980). Bridging moral cognition and moral action: A critical review of the literature. *Psychological Bulletin, 88,* 1–45.

Blass, E. M., & Ciaramitaro, V. (1994). A new look at some old mechanisms in human newborns: Taste and tactile determinants of state, affect, and action. *Monographs of the Society for Research in Child Development, 59*(1, Serial No. 239).

Block, J., & Robins, R. W. (1993). A longitudinal study of consistency and change in self-esteem from early adolescence to early adulthood. *Child Development, 64,* 909–923.

Block, J. H. (1976). Issues, problems, and pitfalls in assessing sex differences: A critical review of *The psychology of sex differences. Merrill-Palmer Quarterly, 27,* 283–308.

Block, J. H., & Block, J. (1980). The role of ego-control and ego-resiliency in the organization of behavior. In W. A. Collins (Ed.), *Minnesota symposium on child psychology* (Vol. 13). Hillsdale, NJ: Erlbaum.

Block, J. H., Block, J., & Gjerde, P. F. (1986). The personality of children prior to divorce: A prospective study. *Child Development, 57,* 827–840.

Block, J. H., Block, J., & Gjerde, P. F. (1988). Parental functioning and the home environment of families of divorce: Prospective and current analyses. *Journal of the American Academy of Child and Adolescent Psychiatry, 27,* 207–213.

Bloom, L. (1970). *Language development: Form and function in emerging grammars.* Cambridge, MA: MIT Press.

Bloom, L. (1973). *One word at a time: The use of single word utterances before syntax.* The Hague: Mouton.

Bloom, L., Hood, L., & Lightbown, P. (1974). Imitation in language development: If, when and why. *Cognitive Psychology, 6,* 380–420.

Bloom, L., Merkin, S., & Wootten, J. (1982). Wh-questions: Linguistic factors that contribute to the sequence of acquisition. *Child Development, 53,* 1084–1092.

Blount, R. (1986, May 4). "I'm about five years ahead of my age." *Atlanta Journal and Constitution,* C17–C20.

Bogard, N. (1990). Why we need gender to understand human violence. *Journal of Interpersonal Violence, 5,* 132–135.

Bogatz, G. A., & Ball, S. (1972). *The second year of Sesame Street: A continuing evaluation.* Princeton, NJ: Educational Testing Service.

Boggiano, A. K., Barrett, M., Weiher, A. W., McClelland, G. H., & Lusk, C. M. (1987). Use of the maximal-operant principle to motivate children's intrinsic interest. *Journal of Personality and Social Psychology, 53,* 866–879.

Boggiano, A. K., Klinger, C. A., & Main, D. S. (1986). Enhancing interest in peer interaction: A developmental analysis. *Child Development, 57,* 852–861.

Bohannon, J. N., MacWhinney, B., & Snow, C. (1990). No negative evidence revisited: Beyond learnability or who has to prove what to whom. *Developmental Psychology, 26,* 221–226.

Bohannon, J. N., & Stanowicz, L. (1988). The issue of negative evidence: Adult responses to children's language errors. *Developmental Psychology, 24,* 684–689.

Bohannon, J. N., & Warren-Leubecker, A. (1989). Theoretical approaches to language acquisition. In J. B. Gleason (Ed.), *The development of language.* Columbus, OH: Merrill.

Bohlin, G., & Hagekull, B. (1993). Stranger wariness and sociability in the early years. *Infant Behavior and Development, 16,* 53–67.

Boismier, J. D. (1977). Visual stimulation and the wake-sleep behavior in human neonates. *Developmental Psychobiology, 10,* 219–227.

Boldizar, J. P. (1991). Assessing sex-typing and androgyny in children: The children's sex-role inventory. *Developmental Psychology, 27,* 505–515.

Boldizar, J. P., Perry, D. G., & Perry, L. C. (1989). Outcome values and aggression. *Child Development, 60,* 571–579.

Boldizar, J. P., Wilson, K. L., & Deemer, D. K. (1989). Gender, life experience, and moral judgment development: A process-oriented approach. *Journal of Personality and Social Psychology, 57,* 229–238.

Boloh, Y., & Champaud, C. (1993). The past conditional verb form in French children: The role of semantics in late grammatical development. *Journal of Child Language, 20,* 169–189.

Bonitatibus, G. (1988). Comprehension monitoring and the apprehension of literal meaning. *Child Development, 59,* 60–70.

Bonvillian, J. D., Orlansky, M. D., & Novack, L. L. (1983). Developmental milestones: Sign language acquisition and motor development. *Child Development, 54,* 1435–1445.

Booth, A., & Amato, P. (1991). Divorce and psychological stress. *Journal of Health and Social Behavior, 32,* 396–407.

Booth, A., & Edwards, J. N. (1992). Starting over: Why remarriages are more unstable. *Journal of Family Issues, 13,* 179–194.

Bornstein, M. H. (1992). Perception across the lifespan. In M. H. Bornstein & M. E. Lamb (Eds.), *Developmental psychology: An advanced textbook* (3rd ed.). Hillsdale, NJ: Erlbaum.

Bornstein, M. H., Kessen, W., & Weiskopf, S. (1976). Color vision and hue categorization in young human infants. *Journal of Experimental Psychology: Human Perception and Performance, 2,* 115–129.

Bornstein, M. H., & Sigman, M. D. (1986). Continuity in mental development from infancy. *Child Development, 57,* 251–274.

Bornstein, M. H., Tal, J., Rahn, C., Galperin, C. Z., Pecheux, M., Lamour, M., Toda, S., Azuma, H., Ogino, M., & Tamis-LeMonda, C. S. (1992). Functional analysis of the contents of maternal speech to infants of 5 and 13 months in four cultures: Argentina, France, Japan, and the United States. *Developmental Psychology, 28,* 593–603.

Borstelmann, L. J. (1983). Children before psychology: Ideas about children from antiquity to the late 1800s. In P. H. Mussen (Ed.), *Handbook of child psychology* (Vol. 1). New York: Wiley.

Bouchard, T. J., Jr., Lykken, D. T., McGue, M., Segal, N. L., & Tellegen, A. (1990). Sources of human psychological differences: The Minnesota study of twins reared apart. *Science, 250,* 223–228.

Bouchard, T. J., Jr., & McGue, M. (1981). Family studies of intelligence: A review. *Science, 212,* 1055–1059.

Bower, T. G. R. (1982). *Development in infancy.* New York: W. H. Freeman.

Bower, T. G. R., Broughton, J. M., & Moore, M. K. (1970). The coordination of vision and tactile input in infancy. *Perception and Psychophysics, 8,* 51–53.

Bowlby, J. (1969). *Attachment and loss. Vol. 1: Attachment.* New York: Basic Books.

Bowlby, J. (1973). *Attachment and loss. Vol. 2: Separation, anxiety and anger.* New York: Basic Books.

Bowlby, J. (1980). *Attachment and loss. Vol. 3: Loss, sadness, and depression.* New York: Basic Books.

Bowlby, J. (1988). *A secure base: Clinical applications of attachment theory.* London: Routledge.

Boyes, M. C., & Chandler, M. (1992). Cognitive development, epistemic doubt, and identity formation in adolescence. *Journal of Youth and Adolescence, 21,* 277–304.

Boysson-Bardies, B. de, Sagart, L., & Durand, C. (1984). Discernible differences in the babbling of infants according to target language. *Journal of Child Language, 11,* 1–16.

Brabeck, M. (1983). Moral judgment: Theory and research on differences between males and females. *Developmental Review, 3,* 274–291.

Brackbill, Y. (1975). Continuous stimulation and arousal level in infancy: Effects of stimulus intensity and stress. *Child Development, 46,* 364–369.

Brackbill, Y. (1979). Obstetrical medication and infant behavior. In J. D. Osofsky (Ed.), *Handbook of infant development.* New York: Wiley.

Brackbill, Y., McManus, K., & Woodward, L. (1985). *Medication in maternity: Infant exposure and maternal information.* Ann Arbor: University of Michigan Press.

Brackbill, Y., & Nichols, P. L. (1982). A test of the confluence model of intellectual development. *Developmental Psychology, 18,* 192–198.

Bradbard, M. R., Martin, C. L., Endsley, R. C., & Halverson, C. F. (1986). Influence of sex stereotypes on children's exploration and memory: A competence versus performance distinction. *Developmental Psychology, 22,* 481–486.

Braddock, J. H., II, & McPartland, J. M. (1993). Education of early adolescents. *Review of Educational Research, 19,* 135–170.

Bradley, R. H., & Caldwell, B. M. (1984). 174 children: A study of the relationship between home environment and cognitive development during the first 5 years. In A. W. Gottfried (Ed.), *Home environment and early cognitive development: Longitudinal research.* Orlando, FL: Academic Press.

Bradley, R. H., Caldwell, B. M., & Rock, S. L. (1988). Home environment and school performance: A ten-year follow-up and examination of three models of environmental action. *Child Development, 59,* 852–867.

Bradley, R. H., Caldwell, B. M., Rock, S. L., Ramey, C. T., Barnard, K. E., Gray, C., Hammond, M. A., Mitchell, S., Gottfried, A. W., Siegel, L., & Johnson, D. L. (1989). Home environment and cognitive development in the first 3 years of life: A collaborative study involving six sites and three ethnic groups in North America. *Developmental Psychology, 25,* 217–235.

Bradley, R. H., Whiteside, L., Mundfrom, D. J., Casey, P. H., Kelleher, K. J. & Pope, S. K. (1994). Early indications of resilience and their relation to experiences in the home environments of low birthweight, premature children living in poverty. *Child Development, 65,* 346–360.

Brand, E., Clingempeel, W. G., & Bowen-Woodward, K. (1988). Family relationships and children's psychological adjustment in stepmother and stepfather families: Findings and conclusions from the Philadelphia Stepfamily Research Project. In E. M. Hetherington & J. D. Arasteh (Eds.), *Impact of divorce, single-parenting, and stepparenting on children.* Hillsdale, NJ: Erlbaum.

Braungart, J. M., Fulker, D. W., & Plomin, R. (1992). Genetic mediation of the home environment during infancy: A sibling adoption study of the HOME. *Developmental Psychology, 28,* 1048–1055.

Braungart, J. M., Plomin, R., DeFries, J. C., & Fulker, D. W. (1992). Genetic influence on tester-rated infant temperament as assessed by Bailey's Infant Behavior Record: Nonadoptive and adoptive siblings and twins. *Developmental Psychology, 28,* 40–47.

Brazelton, T. B. (1979). Behavioral competence of the newborn infant. *Seminars in Perinatology, 3,* 35–44.

Bretherton, I. (1985). Attachment theory: Retrospect and prospect. In I. Bretherton & E. Waters (Eds.), Growing points of attachment theory and research. *Monographs of the Society for Research in Child Development, 50*(1–2, Serial No. 209).

Bretherton, I. (1990). Open communication and internal working models: Their role in the development of attachment relationships. In R. A. Thompson (Ed.), Socioemotional development. *Nebraska Symposium on Motivation* (Vol. 36). Lincoln: University of Nebraska Press.

Bretherton, I., Stolberg, U., & Kreye, M. (1981). Engaging strangers in proximal interaction: Infants' social initiative. *Developmental Psychology, 17,* 746–755.

Bridgeman, D. L. (1981). Enhanced role-taking through cooperative interdependence: A field study. *Child Development, 51,* 1231–1238.

Brinich, E., Drotar, D., & Brinich, P. (1989). Security of attachment and outcome of preschoolers with histories of nonorganic failure to thrive. *Journal of Clinical Child Psychology, 18,* 142–152.

Brody, G. H., Graziano, W. G., & Musser, L. M. (1983). Familiarity and children's behavior in same-age and mixed-age peer groups. *Developmental Psychology, 19,* 568–576.

Brody, G. H., Neubaum, E., & Forehand, R. (1988). Serial marriage: A heuristic analysis of an emerging family form. *Psychology Bulletin, 103,* 211–222.

Brody, G. H., & Shaffer, D. R. (1982). Contributions of parents and peers to children's moral socialization. *Developmental Review, 2,* 31–75.

Brody, G. H., Stoneman, Z., & MacKinnon, C. E. (1982). Role asymmetries in interactions among school-aged children, their younger siblings, and their friends. *Child Development, 53,* 1364–1370.

Brody, G. H., Stoneman, Z., & McCoy, J. K. (1994). Forecasting sibling relationships in early adolescence from child temperaments and family processes in middle childhood. *Child Development, 65,* 771–784.

Brody, J. E. (1993, Feb 11). Prenatal exposure to DES linked to immune disorders. *Atlanta Journal,* E6.

Brody, N. (1992). *Intelligence* (2nd ed.). San Diego, CA: Academic Press.

Bronfenbrenner, U. (1970). *Two worlds of childhood: U.S. and U.S.S.R.* New York: Russell Sage Foundation.

Bronfenbrenner, U. (1977). Toward an experimental ecology of human development. *American Psychologist, 32,* 513–531.

Bronfenbrenner, U. (1979). *The ecology of human development.* Cambridge, MA: Harvard University Press.

Bronfenbrenner, U. (1986). Ecology of the family as a context for human development: Research perspectives. *Developmental Psychology, 22,* 723–742.

Bronfenbrenner, U. (1989). Ecological systems theory. In R. Vasta (Ed.) *Annals of child development. Vol. 6: Theories of child development: Revised formulations and current issues.* Greenwich, CT: JAI Press.

Bronson, G. W. (1991). Infant differences in rate of visual encoding. *Child Development, 62,* 44–54.

Brook, J. S., Brook, D. W., Gordon, A. S., Whiteman, M., & Cohen, P. (1990). The psychosocial etiology of adolescent drug use: A family interactional approach. *Genetic, Social, and General Psychology Monographs, 116,* 111–267.

Brookover, W., Beady, C., Flood, P., Schweitzer, J., & Wisenbaker, J. (1979). *School social systems and student achievement: Schools can make a difference.* New York: Praeger.

Brooks-Gunn, J. (1988). Antecedents and consequences of variation in girls' maturational timing. *Journal of Adolescent Health Care, 9,* 365–373.

Brooks-Gunn, J., & Furstenberg, F. F., Jr. (1989). Adolescent sexual behavior. *American Psychologist, 44,* 249–257.

Brooks-Gunn, J., Klebanov, P. K., Liaw, F., & Spiker, D. (1993). Enhancing the development of low birthweight, premature infants: Changes in cognition and behavior over the first three years. *Child Development, 64,* 736–753.

Brooks-Gunn, J., & Petersen, A. C. (1991). Studying the emergence of depression and depressive symptoms during adolescence. *Journal of Youth and Adolescence, 20,* 115–119.

Brooks-Gunn, J., & Warren, M. P. (1988). The psychological significance of secondary sexual characteristics in nine- to eleven-year-old girls. *Child Development, 59,* 1061–1069.

Brophy, J. E. (1979). Teacher behavior and its effects. *Journal of Educational Psychology, 71,* 733–750.

Broverman, I. K., Vogel, S. R., Clarkson, F. E., & Rosenkrantz, P. S. (1972). Sex-role stereotypes: A current appraisal. *Journal of Social Issues, 28,* 59–78.

Brown, A. L. (1975). The development of memory: Knowing, knowing about knowing, and knowing how to know. In H. W. Reece (Ed.), *Advances in child development and behavior* (Vol. 10). Orlando, FL: Academic Press.

Brown, A. L., Bransford, T. D., Ferrara, R. A., & Campione, J. C. (1983). Learning, remembering, and understanding. In P. H. Mussen (Ed.), *Handbook of child psychology. Vol. 3: Cognitive development.* New York: Wiley.

Brown, A. L., & Campione, J. C. (1990). Communities of learning and thinking, or a context by any other name. In D. Kuhn (Ed.), *Developmental perspectives on teaching learning and thinking skills.* Basel: Karger.

Brown, B. B. (1990). Peer groups. In S. Feldman & G. Elliott (Eds.), *At the threshold: The developing adolescent.* Cambridge, England: Cambridge University Press.

Brown, B. B., Clasen, D. R., & Eicher, S. A. (1986). Perceptions of peer pressure, peer conformity dispositions, and self-reported behavior among adolescents. *Developmental Psychology, 22,* 521–530.

Brown, B. B., & Lohr, M. J. (1987). Peer-group affiliation and adolescent self-esteem: An integration of ego-identity and symbolic-interaction theories. *Journal of Personality and Social Psychology, 52,* 47–55.

Brown, B. B., Mounts, N., Lamborn, S. D., & Steinberg, L. (1993). Parenting practices and peer group affiliation in adolescence. *Child Development, 64,* 467–482.

Brown, J. L. (1964). States in newborn infants. *Merrill-Palmer Quarterly, 10,* 313–327.

Brown, P., & Elliot, R. (1965). Control of aggression in a nursery school class. *Journal of Experimental Child Psychology, 2,* 103–107.

Brown, R. (1973). *A first language: The early stages.* Cambridge, MA: Harvard University Press.

Brown, R., & Hanlon, C. (1970). Derivational complexity and order of acquisition. In J. R. Hayes (Ed.), *Cognition and the development of language.* New York: Wiley.

Brown, S. S. (1988). *Prenatal care: Reaching mothers, reaching infants.* Washington, D.C.: National Academy Press.

Browne, J. C. M., & Dixon, G. (1978). *Antenatal care.* Edinburgh: Churchill Livingstone.

Brownell, C. A. (1986). Convergent developments: Cognitive-developmental correlates of growth in infant/toddler peer skills. *Child Development, 57,* 275–286.

Brownell, C. A. (1990). Peer social skills in toddlers: Competencies and constraints illustrated by same-age and mixed-age interaction. *Child Development, 61,* 838–848.

Brownell, C. A., & Carriger, M. S. (1990). Changes in cooperation and self-other differentiation during the second year. *Child Development, 61,* 1164–1174.

Bruner, J. S. (1983). *Child's talk: Learning to use language.* New York: Norton.

Bruner, J. S., & Goodman, C. C. (1947). Value and need as organizing factors in perception. *Journal of Abnormal and Social Psychology, 42,* 33–44.

Bryant, B. K. (1982). An index of empathy for children and adolescents. *Child Development, 53,* 413–425.

Buchanan, C. M., Eccles, J. S., & Becker, J. B. (1992). Are adolescents the victims of raging hormones? Evidence for activational effects of hormones on moods and behavior at adolescence. *Psychological Bulletin, 111,* 62–107.

Buchanan, C. M., Maccoby, E. E., & Dornbusch, S. M. (1991). Caught between parents: Adolescents' experiences in divorced homes. *Child Development, 62,* 1008–1029.

Buehler, C. A., Hogan, M. J., Robinson, B. E., & Levy, R. J. (1986). The parental divorce transition: Divorce-related stressors and well-being. *Journal of Divorce, 9,* 61–81.

Bugental, D. B., Blue, J., & Cruzcosa, M. (1989). Perceived control over caregiving outcomes: Implications for child abuse. *Developmental Psychology, 25,* 532–539.

Bugental, D. B., Blue, J., & Lewis, J. (1990). Caregiver beliefs and dysphoric affect directed to difficult children. *Developmental Psychology, 26,* 631–638.

Buhrmester, D. (1990). Intimacy of friendship, interpersonal competence, and adjustment during preadolescence and adolescence. *Child Development, 61,* 1101–1111.

Buhrmester, D., & Furman, W. (1990). Perceptions of sibling relationships during middle childhood and adolescence. *Child Development, 61,* 1387–1398.

Bukowski, W. M. (1990). Age differences in children's memory of information about aggressive, socially withdrawn, and prosocial boys and girls. *Child Development, 61,* 1326–1334.

Bukowski, W. M., Gauze, C., Hoza, B., & Newcombe, A. F. (1993). Differences and consistency between same-sex and other-sex peer relationships during early adolescence. *Developmental Psychology, 29,* 255–263.

Bullock, M. (1985). Animism in childhood thinking: A new look at an old question. *Developmental Psychology, 21,* 217–225.

Bullock, M., & Lutkenhaus, P. (1988). The development of volitional behavior in the toddler years. *Child Development, 59,* 664–674.

Bullock, M., & Lutkenhaus, P. (1990). Who am I? Self understanding in toddlers. *Merrill-Palmer Quarterly, 36,* 217–238.

Bumpass, L. L. (1990). What's happening to the family? Interactions between demographic and institutional change. *Demography, 27,* 483–498.

Burnham, D. K., & Harris, M. B. (1992). Effects of real gender and labeled gender on adults' perceptions of infants. *Journal of Genetic Psychology, 153,* 165–183.

Burns, G. W., & Bottino, P. J. (1989). *The science of genetics* (6th Ed.). New York: Macmillan.

Bursik, K. (1991). Adaptation to divorce and ego development in adult women. *Journal of Personality and Social Psychology, 60,* 300–306.

Burtley, S. H. (1980). *Introduction to perception.* New York: Harper & Row.

Burton, L. M. (1990). Teenage childrearing as an alternative life-course strategy in multigenerational black families. *Human Nature, 1,* 123–143.

Burton, R. V. (1963). The generality of honesty reconsidered. *Psychological Review, 70,* 481–499.

Burton, R. V. (1976). Honesty and dishonesty. In T. Lickona (Ed.), *Moral development and behavior.* New York: Holt, Rinehart & Winston.

Bushnell, E. W., & Boudreau, J. P. (1993). Motor development and the mind: The potential role of motor abilities as a determinant of aspects of perceptual development. *Child Development, 64,* 1005–1021.

Buss, A. H., & Plomin, R. (1984). Temperament: *Early developing personality traits.* Hillsdale, N.J.: Erlbaum.

Bussey, K. (1992). Lying and truthfulness: Children's definitions, standards, and evaluative reactions. *Child Development, 63,* 129–137.

Bussey, K., & Bandura, A. (1992). Self-regulatory mechanisms governing gender development. *Child Development, 63,* 1236–1250.

Butler, R. (1990). The effects of mastery and competitive conditions on self-assessment at different ages. *Child Development, 61,* 201–210.

Butler, R., & Ruzany, N. (1993). Age and socialization effects on the development of social comparison motives and normative ability assessment in kibbutz and urban children. *Child Development, 64,* 532–543.

Butterfield, E. C., & Siperstein, G. N. (1972). Influence of contingent auditory stimulation upon non-nutritional suckle. In J. F. Bosma (Ed.), *Third symposium on oral sensation and perception: The mouth of the infant.* Springfield, IL: Charles C. Thomas.

Buysse, V., & Bailey, D. B. (1993). Behavioral and developmental outcomes in young children with disabilities in integrated and segregated settings: A review of comparative studies. *Journal of Special Education, 26,* 434–461.

Bynner, J., O'Malley, P., & Bachman, J. (1981). Self-esteem and delinquency revisited. *Journal of Youth and Adolescence, 10,* 407–441.

Byrnes, J. P., & Takahira, S. (1993). Explaining gender differences on SAT-math items. *Developmental Psychology, 29,* 805–810.

Cahan, S., & Cohen, N. (1989). Age versus schooling effects on intelligence development. *Child Development, 60,* 1239–1249.

Cairns, R. B., Cairns, B. D., & Neckerman, H. J. (1989). Early school dropout: Configurations and determinants. *Child Development, 60,* 1437–1452.

Cairns, R. B., Cairns, B. D., Neckerman, H. J., Ferguson, L. L., & Gariepy, J. (1989). Growth and aggression: 1. Childhood to early adolescence. *Developmental Psychology, 25,* 320–330.

Cairns, R. B., Cairns, B. D., Neckerman, H. J., Gest, S. D., & Gariepy, J. (1988). Social networks and aggressive behavior: Peer support or peer rejection. *Developmental Psychology, 24,* 815–823.

Caldera, Y. M., Huston, A. C., & O'Brien, M. (1989). Social interactions and play patterns of parents and toddlers with feminine, masculine, and neutral toys. *Child Development, 60,* 70–76.

Caldwell, B. M., & Bradley, R. H. (1984). *Manual for the Home Observation for Measurement of the Environment.* Little Rock: University of Arkansas Press.

Camara, K. A., & Resnick, G. (1988). Interparental conflict and cooperation: Factors moderating children's postdivorce adjustment. In E. M. Hetherington & J. D. Arasteh (Eds.), *Impact of divorce, single-parenting, and stepparenting on children.* Hillsdale, NJ: Erlbaum.

Campbell, F. A., & Ramey, C. T. (1994). Effects of early intervention on intellectual and academic achievement: A follow-up study of children from low-income families. *Child Development, 65,* 684–698.

Campbell, S. B., Cohn, J. F., Flanagan, C., Popper, S., & Meyers, T. (1992). Course and correlates of postpartum depression during the transition to parenthood. *Development and Psychopathology, 4,* 29–47.

Campione, J. C., Brown, A. L., Ferrara, R. A., & Bryant, N. R. (1984). The zone of proximal development: Implications for individual differences and learning. In B. Rogoff & J. V. Wertsch (Eds.), *Children's learning in the "zone of proximal development"* (New Directions for Child Development, No. 23). San Francisco: Jossey-Bass.

Campos, J. J., Bertenthal, B. I., & Kermoian, R. (1992). Early experience and emotional development: The emergence of wariness of heights. *Psychological Science, 3,* 61–64.

Campos, J. J., Campos, R. G., & Barrett, K. C. (1989). Emergent themes in the study of emotional development and emotional regulation. *Developmental Psychology, 25,* 394–402.

Campos, J. J., Langer, A., & Krowitz, A. (1970). Cardiac responses on the visual cliff in prelocomotor human infants. *Science, 170,* 196–197.

Campos, R., Raffaelli, M., Ude, W., Greco, M., Ruff, A., Rolf, J., Antunes, C. M., Halsley, N., Greco, D., & Associates (1994). Social networks and daily activities of street youth in Belo Horizonte, Brazil. *Child Development, 65,* 319–330.

Campos, R. G. (1989). Soothing pain-elicited distress in infants with swaddling and pacifiers. *Child Development, 60,* 781–792.

Camras, L. A., Oster, H., Campos, J. J., Miyake, K., & Bradshaw, D. (1992). Japanese and American infants' responses to arm restraint. *Developmental Psychology, 28,* 578–583.

Capaldi, D. M., & Patterson, G. R. (1991). Relation of parental transitions to boys' adjustment problems. I: A linear hypothesis. II: Mothers at risk for transition and unskilled parenting. *Developmental Psychology, 27,* 489–504.

Capelli, C. A., Nakagawa, N., & Madden, C. M. (1990). How children understand sarcasm: The role of context and intonation. *Child Development, 61,* 1824–1841.

Caplan, M., Vespo, J., Pedersen, J., & Hay, D. F. (1991). Conflict and its resolution in small groups of one- and two-year-olds. *Child Development, 62,* 1513–1524.

Caputo, D. V., & Mandell, W. (1970). Consequences of low birth weight. *Developmental Psychology, 3,* 363–383.

Carey, G. (1992). Twin imitation for antisocial behavior: Implications for genetic and family environment research. *Journal of Abnormal Psychology, 101,* 18–25.

Carey, S., & Gelman, R. (1991). *The epigenesis of mind: Essays on biology and cognition.* Hillsdale, NJ: Erlbaum.

Carey, W. B., & McDevitt, S. C. (1980). Commentary: Measuring infant temperament. *Journal of Pediatrics, 96,* 423–424.

Carlson, V., Cicchetti, D., Barnett, D., & Braunwald, K. (1989). Disorganized/disoriented attachment relationships in maltreated infants. *Developmental Psychology, 25,* 525–531.

Carnegie Council on Adolescent Development (1989). *Turning points: Preparing American youth for the 21st century.* Washington, D.C.: Carnegie Council on Adolescent Development.

Carr, M., Kurtz, B. E., Schneider, W., Turner, L. A., & Borkowski, J. G. (1989). Strategy acquisition and transfer among American and German children: Environmental influences on metacognitive development. *Developmental Psychology, 25,* 765–771.

Carroll, J. B. (1992). Cognitive abilities: The state of the art. *Psychological Science, 3,* 266–270.

Carroll, L. (1988). Concern with AIDS and the sexual behavior of college students. *Journal of Marriage and the Family, 50,* 405–411.

Carson, S. A. (1993). Nongenetic causes of pregnancy loss. In C. Lin, M. S. Verp, & R. E. Sabbagha (Eds.), *The high-risk fetus: Pathophysiology, diagnosis, management.* New York: Springer-Verlag.

Carter, D. B., & Levy, G. D. (1988). Cognitive aspects of early sex-role development: The influence of gender schemas on preschoolers' memories and preferences for sex-typed toys and activities. *Child Development, 59,* 782–792.

Carter, D. B., & McCloskey, L. A. (1983–1984). Peers and the maintenance of sex-typed behavior: The development of children's conceptions of cross-gender behavior in their peers. *Social Cognition, 2,* 294–314.

Case, R. (1985). *Intellectual development: Birth to adulthood.* Orlando, FL: Academic Press.

Case, R. (1992). *The mind's staircase: Exploring the conceptual underpinnings of children's thought and knowledge.* Hillsdale, NJ: Erlbaum.

Casey, W. M., & Burton, R. V. (1982). Training children to be consistently honest through verbal self-instructions. *Child Development, 53,* 911–919.

Caspi, A., Elder, G. H., Jr., & Bem, D. J. (1987). Moving against the world: Life-course patterns of explosive children. *Developmental Psychology, 23,* 308–313.

Caspi, A., Elder, G. H., Jr., & Bem, D. J. (1988). Moving away from the world: Life-course patterns of shy children. *Developmental Psychology, 24,* 824–831.

Caspi, A., Lynam, D., Moffitt, T. E., & Silva, P. A. (1993). Unraveling girls' delinquency: Biological, dispositional, and contextual contributors to adolescent misbehavior. *Developmental Psychology, 29,* 19–30.

Cassidy, J., & Asher, S. R. (1992). Loneliness and peer relations in young children. *Child Development, 63,* 350–365.

Cassidy, J., & Berlin, L. J. (1994). The insecure/ambivalent pattern of attachment: Theory and research. *Child Development, 65,* 971–991.

Cassidy, J., Parke, R. D., Butkovsky, L., Braungart, J. M. (1992). Family-peer connections: The roles of emotional expressiveness within the family and children's understanding of emotions. *Child Development, 63,* 603–618.

Casteel, M. A. (1993). Effects of inference necessity and reading goal on children's inferential generation. *Developmental Psychology, 29,* 346–357.

Catherwood, D., Crassini, B., & Freiberg, K. (1989). Infant response to stimuli of similar hue and dissimilar shape: Tracing the origins of the categorization of objects by hue. *Child Development, 60,* 752–762.

Catron, T. F., & Masters, J. C. (1993). Mothers' and childrens' conceptualizations of corporal punishment. *Child Development, 64,* 1815–1828.

Cattell, R. B. (1963). Theory of fluid and crystallized intelligence: A critical experiment. *Journal of Educational Psychology, 54,* 1–22.

Caughy, M. O., DiPietro, J. A., & Strobino, D. M. (1994). Day-care participation as a protective factor in the cognitive development of low-income children. *Child Development, 65,* 457–471.

Cavanaugh, J. C., & Perlmutter, M. (1982). Metamemory: A critical examination. *Child Development, 53,* 11–28.

Ceci, S. J. (1991). How much does schooling influence general intelligence and its cognitive components? A reassessment of the evidence. *Developmental Psychology, 27,* 703–722.

Centers for Disease Control (1992). Sexual behavior among high-school students—United States, 1990. *Morbidity and Mortality Weekly Report, 40,* 885–888.

Cernoch, J. M., & Porter, R. H. (1985). Recognition of maternal axillary odors by infants. *Child Development, 56,* 1593–1598.

Chadwick, B. A., & Heaton, T. B. (1992). *Statistical handbook on the American family.* Phoenix, AZ: Onyx Press.

Chall, J. S. (1983). *Stages of reading development.* New York: McGraw-Hill.

Chalmers, J. B., & Townsend, M. A. R. (1990). The effects of training in social perspective taking on socially maladjusted girls. *Child Development, 61,* 178–190.

Chan, M. (1987). Sudden Infant Death Syndrome and families at risk. *Pediatric Nursing, 13,* 166–168.

Chandler, M. J. (1973). Egocentrism and antisocial behavior: The assessment and training of social perspective taking skills. *Developmental Psychology, 9,* 326–332.

Chandler, M. J., & Boutilier, R. G. (1992). The development of dynamic system reasoning. *Human Development, 35,* 121–137.

Chang, H. W., & Trehub, S. E. (1977). Infants' perception of temporal grouping in auditory patterns. *Child Development, 48,* 1666–1670.

Chao, R. K. (1994). Beyond parental control and authoritarian parenting style: Understanding Chinese parenting through the cultural notion of training. *Child Development, 65,* 1111–1119.

Chapman, M., & Lindenberger, U. (1988). Functions, operations, and decalage in the development of transitivity. *Developmental Psychology, 24,* 542–551.

Chapman, M., Zahn-Waxler, C., Cooperman, G., & Iannotti, R. J. (1987). Empathy and responsibility in the motivation of children's helping. *Developmental Psychology, 23,* 140–145.

Charlesworth, R., & Hartup, W. W. (1967). Positive social reinforcement in the nursery school peer group. *Child Development, 38,* 993–1002.

Charlesworth, W. R. (1992). Darwin and developmental psychology: Past and present. *Developmental Psychology, 28,* 5–16.

Chasnoff, I. J., Griffith, D. R., Freier, C., & Murray, J. (1992). Cocaine/polydrug use in pregnancy: Two-year follow-up. *Pediatrics, 89,* 284–289.

Chen, X., Rubin, K. H., & Sun, Y. (1992). Social reputation in Chinese and Canadian children: A cross-cultural study. *Child Development, 63,* 1336–1343.

Cherlin, A. J., Furstenberg, F. F., Jr., Chase-Lansdale, P. L., Kiernan, K. E., Robins, P. K., Morrison, D. R., & Teitler, J. O. (1991). Longitudinal studies of effects of divorce on children in Great Britain and the United States. *Science, 252,* 1386–1389.

Chess, S., & Thomas, R. (1984). *Origins and evolution of behavior disorders.* New York: Brunner/Mazel.

Chi, M. H. T. (1978). Knowledge structures and memory development. In R. S. Siegler (Ed.), *Children's thinking: What develops?* Hillsdale, NJ: Erlbaum.

Chomsky, N. (1959). A review of B. F. Skinner's *Verbal Behavior. Language, 35,* 26–129.

Chomsky, N. (1968). *Language and mind.* San Diego, CA: Harcourt Brace Jovanovich.

Christopherson, E. R. (1989). Injury control. *American Psychologist, 44,* 237–241.

Cillessen, A. H. N., van IJzendoorn, H. W., van Lieshout, C. F. M., & Hartup, W. W. (1992). Heterogeneity among peer-rejected boys: Subtypes and stabilities. *Child Development, 63,* 893–905.

Clark, E. A., & Hanisee, J. (1982). Intellectual and adaptive performance of Asian children in adoptive American settings. *Developmental Psychology, 18,* 595–599.

Clark, E. V. (1973). What's in a word? On the child's acquisition of semantics in his first language. In T. E. Moore (Ed.), *Cognitive development and the acquisition of language.* Orlando, FL: Academic Press.

Clark, H. H., & Clark, E. V. (1977). *Psychology and language: An introduction to psycholinguistics.* San Diego, CA: Harcourt Brace Jovanovich.

Clarke, A. M., & Clarke, A. D. B. (1976). *Early experience: Myth and evidence.* New York: Free Press.

Clarke-Stewart, A. (1989). Infant day care: Maligned or malignant? *American Psychologist, 44,* 266–273.

Clarke-Stewart, A. (1993). *Daycare.* Cambridge, MA: Harvard University Press.

Clarkson, M. G., & Berg, W. K. (1983). Cardiac orienting and vowel discrimination in newborns: Crucial stimulus parameters. *Child Development, 54,* 162–171.

Clary, E. G., & Snyder, M. (1991). A functional analysis of altruism and prosocial behavior: The case of volunteerism. *Review of Personality and Social Psychology, 12,* 119–148.

Clausen, J. A. (1975). The social meaning of differential physical maturation. In D. E. Drugastin & G. H. Elder (Eds.), *Adolescence in the life cycle.* New York: Halsted Press.

Clements, D. H. (1990). Metacomponential development in a Logo programming environment. *Journal of Educational Psychology, 82,* 141–149.

Clements, D. H. (1991). Enhancement of creativity in computer environments. *American Educational Research Journal, 28,* 173–187.

Clements, D. H., & Nastasi, B. K. (1992). Computers and early childhood education. In M. Gettinger, S. N. Elliott, & T. R. Kratochwill (Eds.), *Advances in school psychology: Preschool and early childhood treatment directions.* Hillsdale, NJ: Erlbaum.

Clifton, R. K., Muir, D. W., Ashmead, D. H., & Clarkson, M. G. (1993). Is visually guided reaching in early infancy a myth? *Child Development, 64,* 1099–1110.

Clingempeel, W. G., Colyar, J. J., Brand, E., & Hetherington, E. M. (1992). Children's relationships with maternal grandparents: A longitudinal study of family structure and pubertal status effects. *Child Development, 63,* 1404–1422.

Clingempeel, W. G., Ievoli, R., & Brand, E. (1984). Structural complexity and the quality of stepparent-stepchild relationships. *Family Processes, 23,* 547–560.

Clingempeel, W. G., & Segal, S. (1986). Stepparent-stepchild relationships and the psychological adjustment of children in stepmother and stepfather families. *Child Development, 57,* 474–484.

Coates, B., & Hartup, W. W. (1969). Age and verbalization in observational learning. *Developmental Psychology, 1,* 556–562.

Cohen, J. E., & Parmelee, A. H. (1983). Prediction of five-year Stanford-Binet scores in preterm infants. *Child Development, 54,* 1242–1253.

Cohen, L. B., DeLoache, J. S., & Strauss, M. S. (1979). Infant visual perception. In J. Osofsky (Ed.), *Handbook of infant development.* New York: Wiley.

Cohen, L. B., & Oakes, L. M. (1993). How infants perceive a simple causal event. *Developmental Psychology, 29,* 421–433.

Cohen, L. J. (1974). The operational definition of human attachment. *Psychological Bulletin, 4,* 207–217.

Cohn, J. F., Campbell, S. B., Matias, R., & Hopkins, J. (1990). Face-to-face interactions of postpartum depressed and nondepressed mother-infant pairs at 2 months. *Developmental Psychology, 26,* 15–23.

Coie, J. D., & Dodge, K. A. (1983). Continuities and changes in children's social status: A five-year longitudinal study. *Merrill-Palmer Quarterly, 19,* 261–282.

Coie, J. D., Dodge, K. A., & Coppotelli, H. (1982). Dimensions and types of social status: A cross-age perspective. *Developmental Psychology, 18,* 557–570.

Coie, J. D., Dodge, K. A., & Kupersmidt, J. B. (1990). Peer group behavior and social status. In S. R. Asher & J. D. Coie (Eds.), *Peer rejection in childhood.* Cambridge, England: Cambridge University Press.

Coie, J. D., Dodge, K. A., Terry, R., & Wright, V. (1991). The role of aggression in peer relations: An analysis of aggression episodes in boys' play groups. *Child Development, 62,* 812–826.

Coie, J. D., & Krehbiel, G. (1984). Effects of academic tutoring on the social status of low-achieving, socially rejected children. *Child Development, 55,* 1465–1478.

Coie, J. D., & Kupersmidt, J. B. (1983). A behavioral analysis of emerging social status in boys' groups. *Child Development, 54,* 1400–1416.

Colby, A., & Kohlberg, L. (1987). *The measurement of moral judgment. Vol. 1: Theoretical foundations and research validation.* Cambridge, England: Cambridge University Press.

Colby, A., Kohlberg, L., Gibbs, J., & Lieberman, M. (1983). A longitudinal study of moral judgment. *Monographs of the Society for Research in Child Development, 48*(1–2, Serial No. 200).

Cole, C., & Rodman, H. (1987). When school-age children care for themselves: Issues for family life educators and parents. *Family Relations, 26,* 92–96.

Cole, M., & Scribner, S. (1977). Cross-cultural studies of memory and cognition. In R. V. Kail & J. W. Hagen (Eds.), *Perspectives on the development of memory and cognition.* Hillsdale, NJ: Erlbaum.

Cole, P. M., Barrett, K. C., & Zahn-Waxler, C. (1992). Emotion displays in two-year-olds during mishaps. *Child Development, 63,* 314–324.

Cole, P. M., Michel, M. K., & Teti, L. O. (1994). The development of emotion regulation and dysregulation: A clinical perspective. In N. Fox (Ed.), The development of emotion regulation: Biological and behavioral considerations. *Monographs of the Society for Research in Child Development, 59*(2–3, Serial No. 240).

Cole, P. M., & Putnam, F. W. (1992). Effect of incest on self and social functioning: A developmental psychopathology perspective. *Journal of Consulting and Clinical Psychology, 60,* 174–184.

Coleman, J. S. (1961). *The adolescent society: The social life of the teenager and its impact on education.* Glencoe, IL: Free Press.

Coles, R., & Stokes, G. (1985). *Sex and the American teenager.* New York: Harper & Row.

Coley, J. D., & Gelman, S. A. (1989). The effects of object orientation and object type on children's interpretation of the word *Big. Child Development, 60,* 372–380.

Collins, W. A., Sobol, B. L., & Westby, S. (1981). Effects of adult commentary on children's comprehension and inferences about a televised aggressive portrayal. *Child Development, 52,* 158–163.

Colombo, J., & Horowitz, F. D. (1987). Behavioral state as a lead variable in neonatal research. *Merrill-Palmer Quarterly, 33,* 423–437.

Comer, J. (1988). Educating poor minority children. *Scientific American, 259*(5), 42–48.

Comer, J. (1991). The black child in school. In M. Lewis (Ed.), *Child and adolescent psychiatry: A comprehensive textbook.* Baltimore: Williams & Wilkins.

Commons, M. L., Richards, F. A., & Kuhn, D. (1982). Systematic and metasystematic reasoning: A case for levels of reasoning beyond Piaget's stage of formal operations. *Child Development, 53,* 1058–1069.

Comstock, G. (with H. Paik). (1991). *Television and the American child.* New York: Academic Press.

Condry, J., & Chambers, J. (1982). Intrinsic motivation and the process of learning. In D. Greene & M. R. Lepper (Eds.), *The hidden costs of rewards.* Hillsdale, NJ: Erlbaum.

Condry, J., & Condry, S. (1976). Sex differences: A study in the eye of the beholder. *Child Development, 47,* 812–819.

Conger, R. D., Conger, K. J., Elder, G. J., Jr., Lorenz, F. O., Simons, R. L., & Whitbeck, L. B. (1992). A family process model of economic hardship and adjustment of early adolescent boys. *Child Development, 63,* 526–541.

Conger, R. D., Ge, X., Elder, G. H., Jr., Lorenz, F. O., & Simons, R. L. (1994). Economic stress, coercive family processes, and developmental problems of adolescents. *Child Development, 65,* 541–561.

Conger, R. D., Patterson, G. R., & Ge, X. (1995). It takes two to replicate: A mediational model for the impact of parents' stress on adolescent adjustment. *Child Development, 66,* 80–97.

Connell, J. P., Spencer, M. B., & Aber, J. L. (1994). Educational risk and resilience in African-American youth: Context, self, action, and outcomes in school. *Child Development, 65,* 493–506.

Connolly, J. A., & Doyle, A. B. (1984). Relation of social fantasy play to social competence in preschoolers. *Developmental Psychology, 20,* 797–806.

Connolly, K., & Dalgleish, M. (1989). The emergence of tool use in infancy. *Developmental Psychology, 25,* 894–912.

Cook, T. D., Appleton, H., Conner, R. F., Shaffer, A., Tabkin, G., & Weber, J. S. (1975). *Sesame Street revisited.* New York: Russell Sage Foundation.

Cooke, T., & Apolloni, T. (1976). Developing positive social-emotional behaviors: A study of training and generalization effects. *Journal of Applied Behavior Analysis, 9,* 65–78.

Cooley, C. H. (1902). *Human nature and the social order.* New York: Scribner's.

Coon, H., Fulker, D. W., DeFries, J. C., & Plomin, R. (1990). Home environment and cognitive ability of 7-year-old children in the Colorado Adoption Project: Genetic and environmental etiologies. *Developmental Psychology, 26,* 459–468.

Cooper, H. M. (1979). Pygmalion grows up: A model for teacher expectation, communication, and performance influence. *Review of Educational Research, 49,* 389–410.

Cooper, H. M. (1989). Does reducing student-to-instructor ratios affect achievement? *Educational Psychologist, 24,* 79–98.

Cooper, R. P., & Aslin, R. N. (1990). Preference for infant-directed speech in the first month after birth. *Child Development, 61,* 1585–1595.

Coopersmith, S. (1967). *The antecedents of self esteem.* New York: W. H. Freeman.

Corah, N. L., Anthony, E. J., Painter, P., Stern, J. A., & Thurston, D. (1965). Effects of perinatal anoxia after seven years. *Psychological Monographs, 79*(3, Whole No. 596).

Corbin, C. (1973). *A textbook of motor development.* Dubuque, IA: William C. Brown.

Coren, S., Porac, C., & Duncan, P. (1981). Lateral preference behaviors in preschool children and young adults. *Child Development, 52,* 443–450.

Corteen, R. S., & Williams, T. (1986). Television and reading skills. In T. Williams (Ed.), *The impact of television: A natural experiment in three communities.* Orlando, FL: Academic Press.

Corter, C. M., Zucker, K. J., & Galligan, R. F. (1980). Patterns in the infant's search for mother during brief separation. *Developmental Psychology, 16,* 62–69.

Costin, S. E., & Jones, D. C. (1992). Friendship as a facilitator of emotional responsiveness and prosocial interventions among young children. *Developmental Psychology, 28,* 941–947.

Cote, J. E., & Levine, C. (1988). A critical examination of the ego identity status paradigm. *Developmental Review, 8,* 147–184.

Courage, M. L. (1989). Children's inquiry strategies in referential communication and in the game of Twenty Questions. *Child Development, 60,* 877–886.

Cowan, G., & Avants, S. K. (1988). Children's influence strategies: Structure, sex differences, and bilateral mother-child influences. *Child Development, 59,* 1303–1313.

Cowan, P. A. (1978). *Piaget: With feeling.* New York: Holt, Rinehart & Winston.

Cox, M. J., Owen, M. T., Henderson, V. K., & Margand, N. A. (1992). Prediction of infant-father and infant-mother attachment. *Developmental Psychology, 28,* 474–483.

Cox, M. J., Owen, M. T., Lewis, J. M., & Henderson, V. K. (1989). Marriage, adult adjustment, and early parenting. *Child Development, 60,* 1015–1024.

Craik, F. I. M., & Lockhart, R. S. (1972). Levels of processing: A framework for memory research. *Journal of Verbal Learning and Verbal Behavior, 11,* 671–684.

Crain-Thoreson, C., & Dale, P. S. (1992). Do early talkers become early readers? Linguistic precocity, preschool language, and emergent literacy. *Developmental Psychology, 28,* 421–429.

Crandall, V. C. (1967). Achievement behavior in young children. In *The young child: Reviews of research.* Washington, D.C.: National Association for the Education of Young Children.

Crandall, V. C. (1969). Sex differences in expectancy of intellectual and academic reinforcement. In C. P. Smith (Ed.), *Achievement-related motives in children.* New York: Russell Sage Foundation.

Crano, W. D., Kenny, J., & Campbell, D. T. (1972). Does intelligence cause achievement? A cross-lagged panel analysis. *Journal of Educational Psychology, 63,* 258–275.

Craton, L. G., & Yonas, A. (1988). Infants' sensitivity to boundary flow information for depth at an edge. *Child Development, 59,* 1522–1529.

Crick, N. R., & Ladd, G. W. (1993). Children's perceptions of their peer experiences: Attributions, loneliness, social anxiety, and social avoidance. *Developmental Psychology, 29,* 244–254.

Crnic, K. A., Greenberg, M. T., Ragozin, A. S., Robinson, N. M., & Basham, R. B. (1983). Effects of stress and social support on mothers and premature and full-term infants. *Child Development, 54,* 209–217.

Crnic, K. A., Ragozin, A. S., Greenberg, M. T., Robinson, N. M., & Basham, R. B. (1983). Social interaction and developmental competence of preterm and full-term infants in the first year of life. *Child Development, 54,* 1199–1210.

Crockenberg, S. (1981). Infant irritability, mother responsiveness, and social support influences on the security of infant-mother attachment. *Child Development, 52,* 857–865.

Crockenberg, S. (1983). Early mother and infant antecedents of Bayley Scale performance at 21 months. *Developmental Psychology, 19,* 727–730.

Crockenberg, S. (1987). Predictors and correlates of anger toward and punitive control of toddlers by adolescent mothers. *Child Development, 58,* 964–975.

Crockenberg, S., & Litman, C. (1990). Autonomy as competence in 2-year-olds: Maternal correlates of child defiance, compliance, and self-assertion. *Developmental Psychology, 26,* 961–971.

Crockenberg, S., & Litman, C. (1991). Effects of maternal employment on maternal and two-year-old child behavior. *Child Development, 61,* 930–953.

Cronbach, L. J., & Snow, R. E. (1977). *Aptitude and instructional methods: A handbook for research on interactions.* New York: Irvington.

Crook, C. (1992). Cultural artefacts in social development: The case of computers. In H. McGurk (Ed.), *Childhood social development: Contemporary perspectives.* Hove, England: Erlbaum.

Crook, C. K. (1978). Taste perception in the newborn infant. *Infant Behavior and Development, 1,* 52–69.

Cross, W. E. (1985). Black identity: Rediscovering the distinction between personal identity and reference group orientation. In M. B. Spencer, G. K. Brookins, & W. R. Allen (Eds.), *Beginnings: The social and affective development of black children.* Hillsdale, NJ: Erlbaum.

Crowell, J. A., & Feldman, S. S. (1991). Mothers' working models of attachment relationships and mother and child behavior during separation and reunion. *Developmental Psychology, 27,* 597–605.

Crystal, D. S., Chen, C., Fuligni, A. J., Stevenson, H. W., Hsu, C., Ko, H., Kitamura, S., & Kimura, S. (1994). Psychological maladjustment and academic achievement: A cross-cultural study of Japanese, Chinese, and American high school students. *Child Development, 65,* 738–753.

Culp, R. E., Little, V., Letts, D., & Lawrence, H. (1991). Maltreated children's self-concept: Effects of a comprehensive treatment program. *American Journal of Orthopsychiatry, 61,* 114–121.

Cummings, E. M., Iannotti, R. J., & Zahn-Waxler, C. (1989). Aggression between peers in early childhood: Individual continuity and developmental change. *Child Development, 60,* 887–895.

Curtiss, S. (1977). *Genie: A psycholinguistic study of a modern-day "wild child."* New York: Academic Press.

Curtiss, S. (1988). *The case of Chelsea: A new test case of the critical period for language acquisition.* Unpublished manuscript. University of California, Los Angeles.

Dabbs, J. M., & Morris, R. (1990). Testosterone, social class, and antisocial behavior in a sample of 4,462 men. *Psychological Science, 1,* 209–211.

Dale, P. S. (1976). *Language development: Structure and function.* New York: Holt, Rinehart & Winston.

Damon, W. (1977). *The social world of the child.* San Francisco: Jossey-Bass.

Damon, W., & Hart, D. (1988). *Self-understanding in childhood and adolescence.* New York: Cambridge University Press.

Daniels, D. (1986). Differential experiences of siblings in the same family as predictors of adolescent sibling personality differences. *Journal of Personality and Social Psychology, 51,* 339–346.

Daniels, D., & Plomin, R. (1985). Differential experience of siblings in the same family. *Developmental Psychology, 21,* 747–760.

Dannemiller, J. L. (1989). A test of color constancy in 9- and 20-week-old human infants following simulated illuminant changes. *Developmental Psychology, 25,* 171–184.

Dannemiller, J. L., & Stephens, B. R. (1988). A critical test of infant pattern preference models. *Child Development, 59,* 210–216.

Danner, F. W., & Lonky, E. (1981). A cognitive-developmental approach to the effects of rewards on instrinsic motivation. *Child Development, 52,* 1043–1052.

Darling, C. A., Davidson, J. K., & Passarello, L. C. (1992). The mystique of first intercourse among college youth: The role of partners, contraceptive practices, and psychological reactions. *Journal of Youth and Adolescence, 21,* 97–117.

Darlington, R. B. (1991). The long-term effects of model preschool programs. In L. Okagaki & R. J. Sternberg (Eds.), *Directors of development: Influences on the development of children's thinking.* Hillsdale, NJ: Erlbaum.

Darwin, C. A. (1877). A biographical sketch of an infant. *Mind, 2,* 285–294.

Dasen, P. R. (1977). *Piagetian psychology: Cross-cultural contributions.* New York: Gardner Press.

Dasen, P. R., & Heron, A. (1981). Cross-cultural tests of Piaget's theory. In H. C. Triandis & A. Heron (Eds.), *Handbook of cross-cultural psychology: Developmental psychology* (Vol. 4). Newton, MA: Allyn & Bacon.

Daubman, K., Heatherington, L., & Ahn, A. (1992). Gender and the self-presentation of academic achievement. *Sex Roles, 27,* 187–204.

David, H. P. (1992). Born unwanted: Long-term developmental effects of denied abortion. *Journal of Social Issues, 48,* 163–181.

David, H. P. (1994). Reproductive rights and reproductive behavior: Clash or convergence of private values and public policies. *American Psychologist, 49,* 343–349.

Davis, J. M., & Rovee-Collier, C. K. (1983). Alleviated forgetting of a learned contingency in 8-week-old infants. *Developmental Psychology, 19,* 353–365.

Day, R. H. (1987). Visual size constancy in infancy. In B. E. McKenzie & R. H. Day (Eds.), *Perceptual development in early infancy: Problems and issues.* Hillsdale, NJ: Erlbaum.

Day, R. H., & McKenzie, B. E. (1981). Infant perception of the invariant size of approaching and receding objects. *Developmental Psychology, 17,* 670–677.

DeCasper, A. J., & Fifer, W. P. (1980). Of human bonding: Newborns prefer their mother's voices. *Science, 208,* 1174–1176.

DeCasper, A. J., & Spence, M. J. (1986). Prenatal maternal speech influences newborns' perception of speech sounds. *Infant Behavior and Development, 9,* 133–150.

DeCasper, A. J., & Spence, M. J. (1991). Auditorily mediated behavior during the perinatal period: A cognitive view. In M. J. S. Weiss & P. R. Zelazo (Eds.), *Newborn attention: Biological constraints and the influence of experience.* Norwood, NJ: Ablex.

Dekovic, M., & Janssens, J. M. A. M. (1992). Parents' child-rearing style and children's sociometric status. *Developmental Psychology, 28,* 925–932.

De Lisi, R., & Staudt, J. (1980). Individual differences in college students' performance on formal operations tasks. *Journal of Applied Developmental Psychology, 1,* 163–174.

DeLoache, J. S., Cassidy, D. J., & Brown, A. L. (1985). Precursors of mnemonic strategies in very young children's memory. *Child Development, 56,* 125–137.

DeMarie-Dreblow, D., & Miller, P. H. (1988). The development of children's strategies for selective attention: Evidence for a transitional period. *Child Development, 59,* 1504–1513.

deMause, L. (1974). The evolution of childhood. In L. deMause (Ed.), *The history of childhood.* New York: Harper & Row.

Dempster, F. N. (1981). Memory span: Sources of individual and developmental differences. *Psychological Bulletin, 89,* 63–100.

Dempster, F. N. (1985). Short-term memory development in childhood and adolescence. In C. J. Brainerd & M. Pressley (Eds.), *Basic processes in memory development. Progress in cognitive development research.* New York: Springer-Verlag.

Denham, S. A., McKinley, M., Couchoud, E. A., & Holt, R. (1990). Emotional and behavioral predictors of preschool peer ratings. *Child Development, 61,* 1145–1152.

Denham, S. A., Zoller, D., & Couchoud, E. A. (1994). Socialization of preschoolers' emotion understanding. *Developmental Psychology, 30,* 928–936.

Denning, C. R., Kagan, B. M., Mueller, D. H., & Neu, H. C. (1991). The CF gene—one year later. *Cystic Fibrosis Currents, 6,* 1–19.

Dennis, W. (1960). Causes of retardation among institutional children: Iran. *Journal of Genetic Psychology, 96,* 47–59.

Dennis, W. (1973). *Children of the creche.* East Norwalk, CT: Appleton-Century-Crofts.

Dennis, W., & Dennis, M. G. (1940). The effect of cradling practices upon the onset of walking in Hopi children. *Journal of Genetic Psychology, 56,* 77–86.

Descartes, R. (1965). La dioptrique. In R. J. Herrnstein & E. G. Boring (Eds.), *A sourcebook in the history of psychology.* Cambridge, MA: Harvard University Press. (Original work published 1638)

Despert, J. L. (1965). *The emotionally disturbed child: Then and now.* New York: Brunner/Mazel.

de Villiers, J. G., & de Villiers, P. A. (1973). A cross-sectional study of the acquisition of grammatical morphemes in child speech. *Journal of Psycholinguistic Research, 2,* 267–278.

de Villiers, P. A., & de Villiers, J. G. (1979). *Early language.* Cambridge, MA: Harvard University Press.

de Villiers, P. A., & de Villiers, J. G. (1992). Language development. In M. H. Bornstein & M. E. Lamb (eds.), *Developmental psychology: An advanced textbook* (3rd ed.). Hillsdale, NJ: Erlbaum.

DeVries, R. (1969). Constancy of generic identity in the years three to six. *Monographs of the Society for Research in Child Development, 34* (3, Serial No. 127).

Diamond, A. (1985). Development of the ability to use recall to guide action, as indicated by the infant's performance on AB. *Child Development, 56,* 868–883.

Diamond, A. (1991). Frontal lobe involvement in cognitive changes during the first year of life. In K. R. Gibson & A. C. Petersen (Eds.), *Brain maturation and cognitive development: Comparative and cross-cultural perspectives.* New York: Aldine de Gruyter.

Diamond, M. (1982). Sexual identity, monozygotic twins reared in discordant sex-roles and a BBC follow up. *Archives of Sexual Behavior, 11,* 181–186.

Diaz, R. M. (1983). Thought and two languages: The impact of bilingualism on cognitive development. In E. W. Gordon (Ed.), *Review of research in education* (Vol. 10). Washington, D.C.: American Educational Research Association.

Diaz, R. M. (1985). Bilingual cognitive development: Addressing three gaps in recent research. *Child Development, 56,* 1376–1388.

Diaz, R. M., Neal, C. J., & Vachio, A. (1991). Maternal teaching in the zone of proximal development: A comparison of low- and high-risk dyads. *Merrill-Palmer Quarterly, 37,* 83–108.

Dick-Read, G. (1972). *Childbirth without fear: The original approach to natural childbirth.* New York: Harper & Row. (Original work published 1933)

Diener, E., Sandvik, E., & Larsen, R. J. (1985). Age and sex effects for emotional intensity. *Developmental Psychology, 21,* 542–546.

DiPietro, J. A. (1981). Rough and tumble play: A function of gender. *Developmental Psychology, 17,* 50–58.

Dishion, T. J. (1990). The family ecology of boys' peer relations in middle childhood. *Child Development, 61,* 874–892.

Dishion, T. J., Patterson, G. R., Stoolmiller, M., & Skinner, M. L. (1991). Family, school, and behavioral antecedents to early adolescent involvement with antisocial peers. *Developmental Psychology, 27,* 172–180.

Dittman, R. W., Kappes, M. E., & Kappes, M. H. (1992). Sexual behavior in adolescent and adult females with congenital adrenal hyperplasia. *Psychoneuroendocrinology, 17,* 153–170.

Dix, T., Ruble, D. N., & Zambarano, R. J. (1989). Mothers' implicit theories of discipline: Child effects, parent effects, and the attribution process. *Child Development, 60,* 1373–1391.

Dixon, R. A., & Lerner, R. M. (1992). A history of systems in developmental psychology. In M. H. Bornstein & M. E. Lamb (Eds.), *Developmental psychology: An advanced textbook* (3rd ed.). Hillsdale, NJ: Erlbaum.

Dixon, S., Tronick, E., Keefer, C., & Brazelton, T. B. (1981). Mother-infant interaction among the Gusii of Kenya. In T. M. Field, A. M. Sostek, P. Vietze, & P. H. Leiderman (Eds.), *Culture and early interactions.* Hillsdale, NJ: Erlbaum.

Dodge, K. A. (1980). Social cognition and children's aggressive behavior. *Child Development, 51,* 162–170.

Dodge, K. A. (1983). Behavioral antecedents of peer social status. *Child Development, 54,* 1386–1399.

Dodge, K. A. (1986). A social information processing model of social competence in children. In M. Perlmutter (Ed.), *Minnesota symposia on child psychology* (Vol. 18). Hillsdale, NJ: Erlbaum.

Dodge, K. A. (1993). Social-cognitive mechanisms in the development of conduct disorder and depression. *Annual Review of Psychology, 44,* 559–584.

Dodge, K. A., Coie, J. D., Pettit, G. S., & Price, J. M. (1990). Peer status and aggression in boys' groups: Developmental and contextual analyses. *Child Development, 61,* 1289–1309.

Dodge, K. A., & Frame, C. L. (1982). Social cognitive biases and deficits in aggressive boys. *Child Development, 53,* 620–635.

Dodge, K. A., Murphy, R. R., & Buchsbaum, K. (1984). The assessment of intention-cue detection skills in children: Implications for developmental psychopathology. *Child Development, 55,* 163–173.

Dodge, K. A., Pettit, G. S., & Bates, J. E. (1994). Socialization mediators of the relation between socioeconomic status and child conduct problems. *Child Development, 65,* 649–665.

Doherty, W. J., & Needle, R. H. (1991). Psychological adjustment and substance abuse among adolescents before and after a parental divorce. *Child Development, 62,* 328–337.

Dolgin, K. G., & Behrend, D. A. (1984). Children's knowledge about animates and inanimates. *Child Development, 55,* 1646–1650.

Domjan, M. (1993). *Principles of learning and behavior* (3rd ed.). Pacific Grove, CA: Brooks/Cole.

Dornbusch, S. M., Carlsmith, J. M., Bushwall, S. J., Ritter, P. L., Leiderman, P. H., Hastorf, A. H., & Gross, R. T. (1985). Single parents, extended households, and the control of adolescents. *Child Development, 56,* 326–341.

Dossey, J. A., Mullis, I. V. S., Lindquist, M. M., & Chambers, D. L. (1988). *The Mathematics Report Card: Are we measuring up?* Princeton, NJ: Educational Testing Service.

Dove, A. (1968, July 15). The Chitling Test. *Newsweek.*

Downey, J., Elkin, E. J., Ehrhardt, A. A., Meyer-Bahlburg, H. F., Bell, J. J., & Morishima, A. (1991). Cognitive ability and everyday functioning in women with Turner syndrome. *Journal of Learning Disabilities, 24,* 32–39.

Doyle, A. B., Connolly, J., & Rivest, L. (1980). The effects of playmate familiarity on the social interaction of very young children. *Child Development, 51,* 217–223.

Doyle, A. B., Doehring, P., Tessier, O., de Lorimier, S., & Shapiro, S. (1992). Transitions in children's play: A sequential analysis of states preceding and following social pretence. *Developmental Psychology, 28,* 137–144.

Dozier, M. (1991). Functional measurement assessment of young children's ability to predict future behavior. *Child Development, 62,* 1091–1099.

Drabman, R. S., & Thomas, M. H. (1974). Does media violence increase children's toleration of real-life aggression? *Developmental Psychology, 10,* 418–421.

Dreyer, P. H. (1982). Sexuality during adolescence. In B. B. Wolman (Ed.), *Handbook of developmental psychology.* New York: Wiley.

Drillien, C. M. (1969). School disposal and performance for children of different birthweight born 1953–1960. *Archives of Diseases in Childhood, 44,* 562–570.

Droege, K. L., & Stipek, D. J. (1993). Children's use of dispositions to predict classmates' behavior. *Developmental Psychology, 29,* 646–654.

Dromi, E. (1987). *Early lexical development.* Cambridge, England: Cambridge University Press.

Dubas, J. S., Graber, J. A., & Petersen, A. C. (1991). The effects of pubertal development on achievement during adolescence. *American Journal of Education, 99,* 444–460.

Dube, E. F. (1982). Literacy, cultural familiarity, and "intelligence" as determinants of story recall. In U. Neisser (Ed.), *Memory observed: Remembering in natural contexts.* San Francisco: W. H. Freeman.

Dubow, E. F., Kausch, D. F., Blum, M. C., Reed, J., & Bush, E. (1989). Correlates of suicidal ideation and attempts in a sample of junior high and high school students. *Journal of Clinical Child Psychology, 18,* 158–166.

Duke, P. M., Carlsmith, J. M., Jennings, D., Martin, J. A., Dornbusch, S. M., Gross, R. T., & Siegel-Gorelick, B. (1982). Educational correlates of early and late sexual maturation in adolescence. *Journal of Pediatrics, 100,* 633–637.

Duncan, G. J., Brooks-Gunn, J., & Klebanov, P. K. (1994). Economic deprivation and early childhood development. *Child Development, 65,* 296–318.

Dunham, P. J., Dunham, F., & Curwin, A. (1993). Joint-attentional states and lexical acquisition at 18 months. *Developmental Psychology, 29,* 827–831.

Dunn, J. (1984). Sibling studies and the developmental impact of critical incidents. In P. B. Baltes & O. G. Brim, Jr. (Eds.), *Life-span development and behavior* (Vol. 6). Orlando, FL: Academic Press.

Dunn, J. (1993). *Young children's close relationships. Beyond attachment.* Newbury Park, CA: Sage.

Dunn, J., Brown, J., & Beardsall, L. (1991). Family talk about feeling states and children's later understanding of children's emotions. *Developmental Psychology, 27,* 448–455.

Dunn, J., & Kendrick, C. (1982). *Siblings: Love, envy, and understanding.* Cambridge, MA: Harvard University Press.

Dunn, J., & Munn, P. (1985). Becoming a family member: Family conflict and the development of social understanding in the second year. *Child Development, 56,* 480–492.

Dunn, J., Slomkowski, C., & Beardsall, L. (1994). Sibling relationships from the preschool period through middle childhood and early adolescence. *Developmental Psychology, 30,* 315–324.

Dunphy, D. C. (1963). The social structure of urban adolescent peer groups. *Sociometry, 26,* 230–246.

DuPaul, G. J., & Barkley, R. A. (1993). Behavioral contributions to pharmaco-therapy: The utility of behavioral methodology in medication treatment of children with Attention Deficit Hyperactivity Disorder. *Behavior Therapy, 24,* 47–65.

DuPaul, G. J., Barkley, R. A., & McMurray, M. B. (1991). Therapeutic effects of medication on ADHD: Implications for school psychologists. *School Psychology Review, 20,* 203–219.

Dusek, J. B. (1991). *Adolescent development and behavior* (2nd ed.). Englewood Cliffs, NJ: Prentice Hall.

Dweck, C. S. (1975). The role of expectations and attributions in the alleviation of learned helplessness. *Journal of Personality and Social Psychology, 31,* 674–685.

Dweck, C. S. (1978). Achievement. In M. E. Lamb (Ed.), *Social and personality development.* New York: Holt, Rinehart & Winston.

Dweck, C. S., Davidson, W., Nelson, S., & Enna, B. (1978). Sex differences in learned helplessness: II. The contingencies of evaluative feedback in the classroom; and III. An experimental analysis. *Developmental Psychology, 14,* 268–276.

Dweck, C. S., & Elliott, E. S. (1983). Achievement motivation. In P. H. Mussen (Ed.), *Handbook of child psychology. Vol. 4: Socialization, personality, and social development.* New York: Wiley.

Dweck, C. S., & Leggett, E. L. (1988). A social-cognitive approach to motivation and personality. *Psychological Review, 95,* 256–273.

Dyer, K. F. (1977). The trend of male-female performance differential in athletics, swimming, and cycling 1948–1976. *Journal of Biosocial Science, 9,* 325–338.

Eagly, A. H. (1987). *Sex differences in social behavior: A social-role interpretation.* Hillsdale, NJ: Erlbaum.

Eagly, A. H. (1995). The science and politics of comparing men and women. *American Psychologist, 50,* 145–158.

Eagly, A. H., & Steffen, V. J. (1986). Gender and aggressive behavior: A meta-analytic review of the social psychological literature. *Psychological Bulletin, 100,* 309–330.

East, P. L., & Rook, K. S. (1992). Compensatory patterns of support among children's peer relationships: A test using school friends, nonschool friends, and siblings. *Developmental Psychology, 28,* 163–172.

Easterbrooks, A., & Emde, R. (1988). Marital and parent-child relationships: The role of affect in the family system. In R. Hinde & J. Stevenson-Hinde (Eds.), *Relationships within families: Mutual influences.* Oxford: Oxford University Press.

Easterbrooks, M. A. (1989). Quality of attachment to mother and to father: Effects of perinatal risk status. *Child Development, 60,* 825–830.

Eaton, W. O., & Enns, L. R. (1986). Sex differences in human motor activity level. *Psychological Bulletin, 100,* 19–28.

Eaton, W. O., & Yu, A. P. (1989). Are sex differences in child motor activity level a function of sex differences in maturational status? *Child Development, 60,* 1005–1011.

Ebeling, K. S., & Gelman, S. A. (1988). Coordination of size standards by young children. *Child Development, 59,* 888–896.

Ebeling, K. S., & Gelman, S. A. (1994). Children's use of context in interpreting "big" and "little." *Child Development, 65,* 1178–1192.

Eccles, J. S., Jacobs, J. E., & Harold, R. D. (1990). Gender role stereotypes, expectancy effects, and parents' socialization of gender differences. *Journal of Social Issues, 46,* 183–201.

Eccles, J. S., Lord, S., & Midgley, C. (1991). What are we doing to early adolescents? The impact of educational contexts on early adolescents. *American Journal of Education, 99,* 521–542.

Eccles, J. S., Midgley, C., Wigfield, A., Buchanan, C. M., Reuman, D., Flanagan, C., & Mac Iver, D. (1993). Development during adolescence: The impact of stage-environment fit on young adolescents' experiences in schools and in families. *American Psychologist, 48,* 90–101.

Eccles, J. S., Wigfield, A., Harold, R. D., & Blumefeld, P. (1993). Age and gender differences in children's self- and task perceptions during elementary school. *Child Development, 64,* 830–847.

Eckenrode, J., Laird, M., & Doris, J. (1993). School performance and disciplinary problems among abused and neglected children. *Developmental Psychology, 29,* 53–62.

Eckerman, C. O., & Stein, M. R. (1990). How imitation begets imitation and toddlers' generation of games. *Developmental Psychology, 26,* 370–378.

Eder, R. A. (1989). The emergent personalogist: The structure and content of 3½-, 5½-, and 7½-year-olds' concepts of themselves and other persons. *Child Development, 60,* 1218–1228.

Eder, R. A. (1990). Uncovering young children's psychological selves: Individual and developmental differences. *Child Development, 61,* 849–863.

Edwards, M., & Waldorf, M. (1984). *Reclaiming birth: History and heroines of American childbirth reform.* Trumansburg, NJ: Crossing Press.

Edwards, R. G. (1993). *Preconception and preimplantation diagnosis of human genetic disease.* Cambridge, England: Cambridge University Press.

Egeland, B. (1979). Preliminary results of a prospective study of the antecedents of child abuse. *International Journal of Child Abuse and Neglect, 3,* 269–278.

Egeland, B., Jacobvitz, D., & Sroufe, L. A. (1988). Breaking the cycle of abuse. *Child Development, 59,* 1080–1088.

Egeland, B., & Sroufe, L. A. (1981). Attachment and early maltreatment. *Child Development, 52,* 44–52.

Egeland, B., Sroufe, L. A., & Erickson, M. (1983). The developmental consequences of different patterns of maltreatment. *International Journal of Child Abuse and Neglect, 7,* 459–469.

Eggebeen, D. J., & Lichter, D. T. (1991). Race, family structure, and changing poverty among American children. *American Sociological Review, 56,* 801–817.

Ehrhardt, A. A. (1985). The psychobiology of gender. In A. S. Rossi (Ed.), *Gender and the life course.* New York: Adline.

Ehrhardt, A. A., & Baker, S. W. (1974). Fetal androgens, human central nervous system differentiation, and behavioral sex differences. In R. C. Friedman, R. M. Rickard, & R. L. Van de Wiele (Eds.), *Sex differences in behavior.* New York: Wiley.

Eichorn, D. H. (1979). Physical development: Current foci of research. In J. D. Osofsky (Ed.), *Handbook of infant development.* New York: Wiley.

Eimas, P. D. (1975a). Auditory and phonetic cues for speech: Discrimination of the (r-l) distinction by young infants. *Perception and Psychophysics, 18,* 341–347.

Eimas, P. D. (1975b). Speech perception in early infancy. In L. B. Cohen & P. Salapatek (Eds.), *Infant perception: From sensation to cognition.* Orlando, FL: Academic Press.

Eimas, P. D. (1982). Speech perception: A view of the initial state and perceptual mechanisms. In J. Mehler, M. Garrett, & E. Walker (Eds.), *Perspectives on mental representation.* Hillsdale, NJ: Erlbaum.

Eimas, P. D. (1985). The perception of speech in early infancy. *Scientific American, 252,* 46–52.

Eisenberg, N. (1983). Children's differentiations among potential recipients of aid. *Child Development, 54,* 594–602.

Eisenberg, N., Fabes, R. A., Carlo, G., Troyer, D., Speer, A. L., Karbon, M., & Switzer, G. (1992). The relations of maternal practices and characteristics to children's vicarious emotional responsiveness. *Child Development, 63,* 583–602.

Eisenberg, N., Fabes, R. A., Miller, P. A., Shell, R., Shea, C., & May-Plumlee, T. (1990). Preschoolers' vicarious emotional responding and their situational and dispositional prosocial behavior. *Merrill-Palmer Quarterly, 36,* 507–529.

Eisenberg, N., Fabes, R. A., Schaller, M., Carlo, G., & Miller, P. A. (1991). The relations of parental characteristics and practices in children's vicarious emotional responding. *Child Development, 62,* 1393–1408.

Eisenberg, N., Lennon, R., & Roth, K. (1983). Prosocial development: A longitudinal study. *Developmental Psychology, 19,* 846–855.

Eisenberg, N., Miller, P. A., Shell, R., McNalley, S., & Shea, C. (1991). Prosocial development in adolescence: A longitudinal study. *Developmental Psychology, 27,* 849–857.

Eisenberg, N., Murray, E., & Hite, T. (1982). Children's reasoning regarding sex-typed toy choices. *Child Development, 53,* 81–86.

Eisenberg, N., Schaller, M., Fabes, R. A., Bustamante, D., Mathy, R. M., Shell, R., & Rhodes, K. (1988). Differentiation of personal distress and sympathy in children and adolescents. *Developmental Psychology, 24,* 766–775.

Eisenberg, N., Shell, R., Pasternack, J., Lennon, R., Beller, R., & Mathy, R. M. (1987). Prosocial development in middle childhood: A longitudinal study. *Developmental Psychology, 23,* 712–718.

Eisenberg-Berg, N., & Hand, M. (1979). The relationship of preschoolers' reasoning about prosocial moral conflicts to prosocial behavior. *Child Development, 50,* 356–363.

Elder, G. H., Liker, J. K., & Cross, C. E. (1984). Parent-child behavior in the Great Depression: Life course and intergenerational influences. In P. B. Baltes & O. G. Brim (Eds.), *Life-span development and behavior* (Vol. 6). New York: Academic Press.

Elias, J., & Gebhard, P. (1969). Sexuality and sexual learning in childhood. *Phi Delta Kappan, 50,* 401–405.

Elias, S., & Simpson, J. L. (1992). Amniocentesis. In A. Milunsky (Ed.), *Genetic disorders and the fetus: Diagnosis, prevention, and treatment* (3rd ed.). Baltimore, MD: Johns Hopkins University Press.

Elicker, J., Englund, M., & Sroufe, L. A. (1992). Predicting peer competence and peer relationships in childhood from early parent-child relationships. In R. D. Parke & G. W. Ladd (Eds.), *Family-peer relationships: Modes of linkage.* Hillsdale, NJ: Erlbaum.

Elkind, D. (1967). Egocentrism in adolescence. *Child Development, 38,* 1025–1033.

Elkind, D. (1977). Giant in the nursery—Jean Piaget. In E. M. Hetherington & R. D. Parke (Eds.), *Contemporary readings in child psychology.* New York: McGraw-Hill.

Elkind, D. (1981a). *Children and adolescents: Interpretive essays on Jean Piaget* (3rd ed.). New York: Oxford.

Elkind, D. (1981b). *The hurried child: Growing up too fast too soon.* Reading, MA: Addison-Wesley.

Elliott, E. S., & Dweck, C. S. (1988). Goals: An approach to motivation and achievement. *Journal of Personality and Social Psychology, 54,* 5–12.

Ellis, S., Rogoff, B., & Cromer, C. C. (1981). Age segregation in children's social interactions. *Developmental Psychology, 17,* 399–407.

Ellsworth, C. P., Muir, D. W., & Hains, S. M. J. (1993). Social competence and person-object differentiation: An analysis of the still-face effect. *Developmental Psychology, 29,* 63–73.

Emde, R. N. (1992). Individual meaning and increasing complexity: Contributions of Sigmund Freud and Rene Spitz to developmental psychology. *Developmental Psychology, 28*, 347–359.

Emde, R. N., Biringen, Z., Clyman, R. B., & Oppenheim, D. (1991). The moral self of infancy: Affective core and procedural knowledge. *Developmental Review, 11*, 251–270.

Emde, R. N., Plomin, R., Robinson, J., Corley, R., DeFries, J., Fulker, D. W., Reznick, J. S., Campos, J., Kagan, J., & Zahn-Waxler, C. (1992). Temperament, emotion, and cognition at fourteen months: The MacArthur longitudinal twin study. *Child Development, 63*, 1437–1455.

Emery, R. E. (1988). *Marriage, divorce, and children's adjustment.* Beverly Hills, CA: Sage.

Emery, R. E. (1989). Family violence. *American Psychologist, 44*, 321–328.

Emery, R. E., & Tuer, M. (1993). Parenting and the marital relationship. In T. Luster & L. Okagaki (Eds.), *Parenting. An ecological perspective.* Hillsdale, NJ: Erlbaum.

Emery, R. E., & Wyer, M. M. (1987). Divorce mediation. *American Psychologist, 42*, 472–480.

Emmerich, W. (1966). Continuity and stability in early social development. II: Teacher's ratings. *Child Development, 37*, 17–27.

Entwisle, D. R., & Alexander, K. L. (1987). Long-term effects of cesarean delivery on parents' beliefs and children's schooling. *Developmental Psychology, 23*, 676–682.

Entwisle, D. R., & Alexander, K. L. (1990). Beginning school math competence: Minority and majority comparisons. *Child Development, 61*, 454–471.

Entwisle, D. R., & Alexander, K. L. (1992). Summer setback: Race, poverty, school composition, and mathematics achievement in the first two years of school. *American Sociological Review, 57*, 72–84.

Entwisle, D. R., & Baker, D. P. (1983). Gender and young children's expectations for performance in arithmetic. *Developmental Psychology, 19*, 200–209.

Epstein, L. H., McCurley, J., Wing, R. R., & Valoski, A. (1990). Five-year follow-up of family-based treatments for childhood obesity. *Journal of Consulting and Clinical Psychology, 58*, 661–664.

Epstein, L. H., Wing, R. R., Koeske, R., & Valoski, A. (1987). Long-term effects of family-based treatment of childhood obesity. *Journal of Consulting and Clinical Psychology, 55*, 91–95.

Erikson, E. H. (1950). In M. J. E. Senn (Ed.), *Symposium on the healthy personality.* New York: Josiah Macy, Jr., Foundation.

Erikson, E. H. (1963). *Childhood and society* (2nd ed.). New York: Norton.

Erikson, E. H. (1982). *The life cycle completed. A review.* New York: Norton.

Eron, L. D. (1982). Parent-child interaction, television violence, and aggression of children. *American Psychologist, 37*, 197–211.

Espenschade, A., & Eckert, H. (1974). Motor development. In W. R. Warren & E. R. Buskirk (Eds.), *Science and medicine of exercise and sport.* New York: Harper & Row.

Estrada, P., Arsenio, W. F., Hess, R. D., & Holloway, S. D. (1987). Affective quality of the mother-child relationship: Longitudinal consequences for children's school-relevant cognitive functioning. *Developmental Psychology, 23*, 210–215.

Etaugh, C., Levine, D., & Mennella, A. (1984). Development of sex biases in children: 40 years later. *Sex Roles, 10*, 911–922.

Etaugh, C., & Liss, M. B. (1992). Home, school, and playroom: Training grounds for adult gender roles. *Sex Roles, 26*, 129–147.

Evans, M. I., Fletcher, J. C., Dixler, A. O., & Shulman, J. D. (1989). *Fetal diagnosis and therapy: Science, ethics, and the law.* Philadelphia: J. B. Lippincott.

Evans, M. I., Robertson, J. A., & Fletcher, J. C. (1993). Legal and ethical issues in fetal therapy. In C. Lin, M. S. Verp, & R. E. Sabbagha (Eds.), *The high-risk fetus: Pathophysiology, diagnosis, management.* New York: Springer-Verlag.

Eyer, D. E. (1992). *Mother-infant bonding. A scientific fiction.* New Haven, CT: Yale University Press.

Fabes, R. A., Eisenberg, N., Karbon, M., Bernzweig, J., Speer, A. L., & Carlo, G. (1994). Socialization of children's vicarious emotional responding and prosocial behavior: Relations with mothers' perceptions of children's emotional reactivity. *Developmental Psychology, 30*, 44–55.

Fabes, R. A., Eisenberg, N., McCormick, S. E., & Wilson, M. S. (1988). Preschoolers' attributions of situational determinants of others' naturally occurring emotions. *Developmental Psychology, 24*, 376–385.

Fabes, R. A., Eisenberg, N., & Miller, P. A. (1990). Maternal correlates of children's vicarious emotional responsiveness. *Developmental Psychology, 26*, 639–648.

Fabes, R. A., Eisenberg, N., Nyman, M., & Michealieu, Q. (1991). Young children's appraisals of others' spontaneous emotional reactions. *Developmental Psychology, 27*, 858–866.

Fabes, R. A., Fultz, J., Eisenberg, N., May-Plumlee, T., & Christopher, F. S. (1989). Effects of rewards on children's prosocial motivation: A socialization study. *Developmental Psychology, 25*, 509–515.

Fabricius, W. V., & Cavalier, L. (1989). The role of causal theories about memory in young children's memory strategy choice. *Child Development, 60*, 298–308.

Fabricius, W. V., & Steffe, L. (1989, April). *Considering all possible combinations: The early beginnings of a formal-operational skill.* Paper presented at the biennial meeting of the Society for Research in Child Development, Kansas City, MO.

Fabricius, W. V., & Wellman, H. M. (1983). Children's understanding of retrieval cue utilization. *Developmental Psychology, 19*, 15–21.

Fagan, J. F., III (1979). The origins of facial pattern recognition. In M. H. Bornstein & W. Kessen (Eds.), *Psychological development from infancy: Image to intention.* Hillsdale, NJ: Erlbaum.

Fagan, J. F., III (1984). Infant memory: History, current trends, and relations to cognitive psychology. In M. Moscovitch (Ed.), *Infant memory: Its relation to normal and pathological memory in humans and other animals.* New York: Plenum.

Fagan, J. F., III (1985a). A new look at infant intelligence. In D. K. Detterman (Ed.), *Current topics in human intelligence, Vol. 1: Research methodology.* Norwood, NJ: Ablex.

Fagan, J. F., III (1985b, April). *Early novelty preferences and later intelligence.* Paper presented at the meeting of the Society for Research in Child Development, Toronto.

Fagan, J. F., III, Shepherd, P. A., & Knevel, C. R. (1991). *Predictive validity of the Fagan Test of Infant Intelligence.* Paper presented at the biennial meeting of the Society for Research in Child Development, Seattle, WA.

Fagot, B. I. (1978). The influence of sex of child on parental reactions to toddler children. *Child Development, 49*, 459–465.

Fagot, B. I. (1985a). Beyond the reinforcement principle: Another step toward understanding sex-role development. *Developmental Psychology, 21*, 1097–1104.

Fagot, B. I. (1985b). Changes in thinking about early sex-role development. *Developmental Review, 5*, 83–98.

Fagot, B. I., & Kavanagh, K. (1990). The prediction of antisocial behavior from avoidant attachment classifications. *Child Development, 61*, 864–873.

Fagot, B. I., & Kavanagh, K. (1993). Parenting during the second year: Effects of children's age, sex, and attachment classification. *Child Development, 64*, 258–271.

Fagot, B. I., & Leinbach, M. D. (1989). The young child's gender schema: Environmental input, internal organization. *Child Development, 60*, 663–672.

Fagot, B. I., Leinbach, M. D., & Hagan, R. (1986). Gender labeling and the adoption of sex-typed behaviors. *Developmental Psychology, 22*, 440–443.

Fagot, B. I., Leinbach, M. D., & O'Boyle, C. (1992). Gender labeling, gender stereotyping, and parenting behaviors. *Developmental Psychology, 28*, 225–230.

Falbo, T. (1992). Social norms and the one-child family: Clinical and policy implications. In F. Boer & J. Dunn (Eds.), *Children's sibling relationships.* Hillsdale, NJ: Erlbaum.

Falbo, T., & Polit, D. F. (1986). Quantitative review of the only child literature: Research evidence and theory development. *Psychological Bulletin, 100*, 176–189.

Falbo, T., & Poston, D. L., Jr. (1993). The academic, personality, and physical outcomes of only children in China. *Child Development, 64*, 18–35.

Fantuzzo, J. W. (1990). Behavioral treatment of the victims of child abuse and neglect. *Behavior Modification, 14*, 316–339.

Fantz, R. L. (1961). The origin of form perception. *Scientific American, 204*, 66–72.

Fantz, R. L. (1963). Pattern vision in newborn infants. *Science, 140*, 296–297.

Farber, S. L. (1981). *Identical twins reared apart: A reanalysis.* New York: Basic Books.

Farrar, M. J. (1992). Negative evidence and grammatical morpheme acquisition. *Developmental Psychology, 28*, 90–98.

Farrington, D. P. (1987). Epidemology. In H. C. Quay (Ed.), *Handbook of juvenile delinquency.* New York: Wiley.

Farver, J. M., & Branstetter, W. H. (1994). Preschoolers' prosocial responses to their peers' distress. *Developmental Psychology, 30*, 334–341.

Fauber, R., Forehand, R., Thomas, A. M., & Wierson, M. (1990). A mediational model of the impact of marital conflict on adolescent adjustment in intact and divorced families: The role of disrupted parenting. *Child Development, 61*, 1112–1123.

Faust, M. S. (1960). Developmental maturity as a determinant of prestige in adolescent girls. *Child Development, 31*, 173–184.

Feeney, J. A., & Noller, P. (1990). Attachment style as a predictor of adult romantic relationships. *Journal of Personality and Social Psychology, 58*, 281–291.

Fein, G. G. (1986). The affective psychology of play. In A. W. Gottfried & C. C. Brown (Eds.), *Play interactions. The contributions of play material and parental involvement to children's development.* Lexington, MA: Lexington Books.

Feingold, A. (1988). Cognitive gender differences are disappearing. *American Psychologist, 43*, 95–103.

Feingold, A. (1992). Sex differences in variability in intellectual abilities: A new look at an old controversy. *Review of Educational Research, 62*, 61–84.

Feinman, S. (1992). *Social referencing and the social construction of reality in infancy.* New York: Plenum.

Feldman, D. H. (1982). A developmental framework for research with gifted children. In D. H. Feldman (Ed.), *New directions for child development. No. 17: Developmental approaches to giftedness and creativity.* San Francisco: Jossey-Bass.

Feldman, D. H. (1986). *Nature's gambit: Child prodigies and the development of human potential.* New York: Basic Books.

Feldman, D. H., & Goldsmith, L. T. (1991). *Nature's gambit.* New York: Teacher's College Press.

Feldman, R. S., Devin-Sheehan, L., & Allen, V. L. (1976). Children tutoring children: A critical review of research. In V. L. Allen (Ed.), *Children as teachers: Theory and research on tutoring.* New York: Academic Press.

Feldman, S. S., & Gehring, T. M. (1988). Changing perceptions of family cohesion and power across adolescence. *Child Development, 59*, 1034–1045.

Feldman, S. S., & Weinberger, D. A. (1994). Self-restraint as a mediator of family influences on boys' delinquent behavior: A longitudinal study. *Child Development, 65*, 195–211.

Felts, W. M., Chenier, T., & Barnes, R. (1992) Drug use and suicide ideation and behavior among North Carolina public school students. *American Journal of Public Health, 82,* 870–872.

Fentress, J. C., & McLeod, P. J. (1986). Motor patterns in development. In E. M. Blass (Ed.), *Handbook of behavioral neurobiology. Vol. 8: Developmental psychobiology and developmental neurobiology.* New York: Plenum.

Ferguson, C. A. (1977). Learning to produce: The earliest stages of phonological development in the child. In F. D. Minifie & L. L. Lloyd (Eds.), *Communication and cognitive abilities: Early behavioral assessment.* Baltimore: University Park Press.

Ferguson, T. J., & Rule, B. G. (1988). Children's evaluations of retaliatory aggression. *Child Development, 59,* 961–968.

Fernald, A. (1989). Intonation and communicative intent in mothers' speech to infants: Is the melody the message? *Child Development, 60,* 1497–1510.

Fernald, A. (1993). Approval and disapproval: Infant responsiveness to vocal affect in familiar and unfamiliar languages. *Child Development, 64,* 657–674.

Fernald, A., & Mazzie, C. (1991). Prosody and focus in speech to infants and adults. *Developmental Psychology, 27,* 209–221.

Fernald, A., & Morikawa, H. (1993). Common themes and cultural variations in Japanese and American mothers' speech to infants. *Child Development, 64,* 637–656.

Ferreira, F., & Morrison, F. J. (1994). Children's metalinguistic knowledge of syntactical constituents: Effects of age and schooling. *Developmental Psychology, 30,* 663–678.

Feshbach, N., & Feshbach, S. (1982). Empathy training and the regulation of aggression: Potentialities and limitations. *Academic Psychology Bulletin, 4,* 399–413.

Feshbach, S. (1956). The catharsis hypothesis and some consequences of interaction with aggressive and neutral play objects. *Journal of Personality, 24,* 449–461.

Feshbach, S. (1970). Aggression. In P. H. Mussen (Ed.), *Carmichael's manual of child psychology* (Vol. 2). New York: Wiley.

Festinger, L. (1954). A theory of social comparison processes. *Human Relations, 7,* 117–140.

Feuerstein, R. (1979). *The dynamic assessment of retarded performers: The learning potential assessment device, theory, instruments, and techniques.* Baltimore, MD: University Park Press.

Field, D. (1981). Can preschool children really learn to conserve? *Child Development, 52,* 326–334.

Field, D. (1987). A review of preschool conservation training: An analysis of analyses. *Developmental Review, 7,* 210–251.

Field, J., Muir, D., Pilon, R., Sinclair, M., & Dodwell, P. (1980). Infants' orientation to lateral sounds from birth to three months. *Child Development, 51,* 295–298.

Field, T. (1990). *Infancy.* Cambridge, MA: Harvard University Press.

Field, T., Greenwald, P., Morrow, C., Healy, B., Foster, T., Guthertz, M., & Frost, P. (1992). Behavior state matching during interactions of preadolescent friends versus acquaintances. *Developmental Psychology, 28,* 242–250.

Field, T. M. (1979). Interaction patterns of preterm and term infants. In T. M. Field, A. M. Sostek, S. Goldberg, & H. H. Shuman (Eds.), *Infants born at risk.* New York: Spectrum.

Field, T. M. (1987). Affective and interactive disturbances in infants. In J. D. Osofsky (Ed.), *Handbook of infant development* (2nd ed.). New York: Wiley.

Field, T. M. (1991). Quality of infant day-care and grade school behavior and performance. *Child Development, 62,* 863–870.

Field, T. M., Healy, B., Goldstein, S., & Guthertz, M. (1990). Behavior-state matching and synchrony in mother-infant interactions of nondepressed versus depressed dyads. *Developmental Psychology, 26,* 7–14.

Field, T. M., Healy, B., Goldstein, S., Perry, S., Bendell, D., Schanberg, S., Zimmerman, E. A., & Kuhn, C. (1988). Infants of depressed mothers show "depressed" behavior even with nondepressed adults. *Child Development, 59,* 1569–1579.

Field, T. M., Sandberg, D., Garcia, R., Nitza, V., Goldstein, S., & Guy, L. (1985). Pregnancy problems, postpartum depression, and early mother-infant interactions. *Developmental Psychology, 21,* 1152–1156.

Field, T. M., & Vega-Lahr, N. (1984). Early interactions between infants with cranio-facial anomalies and their mothers. *Infant Behavior and Development, 7,* 527–530.

Field, T. M., Woodson, R., Greenberg, R., & Cohen, D. (1982). Discrimination and imitation of facial expressions by neonates. *Science, 218,* 179–181.

Finch, F. H. (1946). Enrollment increases and changes in the mental level of the high school population. *Applied Psychology Monographs,* No. 10.

Fincham, F. D., Hokoda, A., & Sanders, R., Jr. (1989). Learned helplessness, test anxiety, and academic achievement: A longitudinal analysis. *Child Development, 60,* 138–145.

Fincher, J. (1973). The Terman study is 50 years old: Happy anniversary and pass the ammunition. *Human Behavior, 2,* 8–15.

Findley, M. J., & Cooper, H. M. (1983). Locus of control and academic achievement: A literature review. *Journal of Personality and Social Psychology, 44,* 419–427.

Fine, M. A., & Kurdek, L. A. (1994). Parenting cognitions in stepfamilies: Differences between parents and stepparents and relations to parenting satisfaction. *Journal of Social and Personal Relationships, 11,* 95–112.

Finitzo, T., Gunnarson, A. D., & Clark, J. L. (1990). Auditory deprivation and early conductive hearing loss from otitus media. *Topics in Language Disorders, 11,* 29–42.

Finkelhor, D., & Dziuba-Leatherman, J. (1994). Victimization of children. *American Psychologist, 49,* 173–183.

Finkelhor, D., Hotaling, G. T., Lewis, I. A., & Smith, C. (1989). Sexual abuse and its relationship to later sexual satisfaction, marital status, religion, and attitudes. *Journal of Interpersonal Violence, 4,* 379–399.

Finkelstein, N. W., & Ramey, C. T. (1977). Learning to control the environment in infancy. *Child Development, 48,* 806–819.

Finster, M., Pedersen, H., & Morishima, H. O. (1984). Principles of fetal exposure to drugs used in obstetric anesthesia. In B. Krauer, F. Krauer, F. E. Hytten, & E. del Pozo (Eds.), *Drugs and pregnancy. Maternal drug handling—fetal drug exposure.* Orlando, FL: Academic.

Fischer, K. W. (1980). A theory of cognitive development: The control and construction of hierarchies of skills. *Psychological Review, 87,* 477–531.

Fischer, K. W., Kenny, S. L., & Pipp, S. L. (1990). How cognitive processes and environmental conditions organize discontinuities in the development of abstractions. In C. N. Alexander & E. J. Langer (Eds.), *Higher stages of human development. Perspectives on adult growth.* New York: Oxford University Press.

Fischer, M., Barkley, R. A., Edelbrock, C. S., & Smallish, L. (1990). The adolescent outcome of hyperactive children diagnosed by research criteria. II: Academic, attentional, and neuropsychological status. *Journal of Consulting and Clinical Psychology, 58,* 580–588.

Fischer, M., Barkley, R. A., Fletcher, K. E., & Smallish, L. (1993). The adolescent outcome of hyperactive children: Predictors of psychiatric, academic, social, and emotional adjustment. *Journal of the American Academy of Child and Adolescent Psychiatry, 32,* 324–332.

Fischer, W. F. (1963). Sharing in pre-school children as a function of the amount and type of reinforcement. *Genetic Psychology Monographs, 68,* 215–245.

Fisher, C. B., & Brone, R. J. (1991). Eating disorders in adolescence. In R. M. Lerner, A. C. Petersen, & J. Brooks-Gunn (Eds.), *Encyclopedia of adolescence* (Vol. 1). New York: Garland.

Fisher, E. P. (1992). The impact of play on development: A meta-analysis. *Play and Culture, 5,* 159–181.

Fivush, R., Kuebli, J., & Clubb, P. A. (1992). The structure of events and event representations: A developmental analysis. *Child Development, 63,* 188–201.

Flavell, J. H. (1963). *The developmental psychology of Jean Piaget.* New York: Van Nostrand Reinhold.

Flavell, J. H., Everett, B. H., Croft, K., & Flavell, E. R. (1981). Young children's knowledge about visual perception: Further evidence for the level 1–level 2 distinction. *Developmental Psychology, 17,* 99–103.

Flavell, J. H., Flavell, E. R., & Green, F. L. (1983). Development of the appearance-reality distinction. *Cognitive Psychology, 15,* 95–120.

Flavell, J. H., Flavell, E. R., & Green, F. L. (1987). Young children's knowledge about apparent-real and pretend-real distinctions. *Developmental Psychology, 23,* 816–822.

Flavell, J. H., Green, F. L., & Flavell, E. R. (1989). Young children's ability to differentiate appearance-reality and level 2 perspectives in the tactile modality. *Child Development, 60,* 201–213.

Flavell, J. H., Miller, P. H., & Miller, S. A. (1993). *Cognitive development* (3rd ed.). Englewood Cliffs, NJ: Prentice-Hall.

Fletcher, A. B. (1987). Pain in the neonate. *New England Journal of Medicine, 317,* 1347–1348.

Fletcher, A. C., Darling, N. E., Steinberg, L., & Dornbusch, S. M. (1995). The company they keep: Relation of adolescents' adjustment and behavior to their friends' perceptions of authoritative parenting in the social network. *Developmental Psychology, 31,* 300–310.

Folven, R. J., & Bonvillian, J. D. (1991). The transition for nonreferential to referential language in children acquiring American Sign Language. *Developmental Psychology, 27,* 806–816.

Fonagy, P., Steele, H., & Steele, M. (1991). Maternal representations of attachment during pregnancy predict the organization of infant-mother attachment at one year of age. *Child Development, 62,* 891–905.

Ford, C. S., & Beach, F. A. (1951). *Patterns of sexual behavior.* New York: Harper & Row.

Fordham, S., & Ogbu, J. (1986). Black students' school success: Coping with the "burden of 'acting white.'" *Urban Review, 18,* 176–206.

Forrest, J. D., & Singh, S. (1990). The sexual and reproductive behavior of American women, 1982–1988. *Family Planning Perspectives, 22,* 206–214.

Fox, N. A., Kimmerly, N. L., & Schafer, W. D. (1991). Attachment to mother/attachment to father: A meta-analysis. *Child Development, 62,* 210–225.

Fox, R., Aslin, R. N., Shea, S. L., & Dumais, S. T. (1980). Stereopsis in human infants. *Science, 207,* 323–324.

France-Kaatrude, A., & Smith, W. P. (1985). Social comparison, task motivation, and the development of self-evaluative standards in children. *Developmental Psychology, 21,* 1080–1089.

Frankel, K. A., & Bates, J. E. (1990). Mother-toddler problem-solving: Antecedents in attachment, home behavior, and temperament. *Child Development, 61,* 810–819.

Frankenberg, W. K., & Dodds, J. B. (1967). The Denver development screening test. *Journal of Pediatrics, 71,* 181–191.

Franklin, K. M., Janoff-Bulman, R., & Roberts, J. E. (1990). Long-term impact of parental divorce on optimism and trust: Changes in general assumptions or narrow beliefs? *Journal of Personality and Social Psychology, 59,* 743–755.

Fraser, B. J., Walberg, H. J., Welch, W. W., & Hattie, J. A. (1987). Synthesis of educational productivity research. *International Journal of Educational Research, 11,* 145–252.

Frauenglass, M. H., & Diaz, R. M. (1985). Self-regulatory functions of children's private speech: A critical analysis of recent challenges to Vygotsky's theory. *Developmental Psychology, 21,* 357–364.

Freedman, D. G. (1979). Ethnic differences in babies. *Human Nature, 2,* 36–43.

French, D. C. (1984). Children's knowledge of the social functions of younger, older, and same-age peers. *Child Development, 55,* 1429–1433.

French, D. C., Wass, G. A., Stright, A. L., & Baker, J. A. (1986). Leadership asymmetrics in mixed-age children's groups. *Child Development, 57,* 1277–1283.

French, L. A. (1989). Young children's responses to "when" questions: Issues of directionality. *Child Development, 60,* 225–236.

Freud, A., & Dann, S. (1951). An experiment in group upbringing. In R. Eisler, A. Freud, H. Hartmann, & E. Kris (Eds.), *The psychoanalytic study of the child* (Vol. 6). New York: International Universities Press.

Freud, S. (1930). *Three contributions to the theory of sex.* New York: Nervous and Mental Disease Publishing Co. (Original work published 1905)

Freud, S. (1933). *New introductory lectures in psychoanalysis.* New York: Norton.

Freud, S. (1960). *A general introduction to psychoanalysis.* New York: Washington Square Press. (Original work published 1935)

Freud, S. (1961a). Some physical consequences of the anatomical distinction between the sexes. In J. Strachey (Ed.), *The standard edition of the complete psychological works of Sigmund Freud* (Vol. 19). London: Hogarth Press. (Originally published 1924)

Freud, S. (1961b). The dissolution of the Oedipus complex. In J. Strachey (Ed.), *The standard edition of the complete psychological works of Sigmund Freud* (Vol. 19). London: Hogarth Press. (Original work published 1924)

Freud, S. (1964). An outline of psychoanalysis. In J. Strachey (Ed. and Trans.), *The standard edition of the complete psychological works of Sigmund Freud* (Vol. 23). London: Hogarth Press. (Original work published 1940)

Freud, S. (1974). *The ego and the id.* London: Hogarth Press. (Original work published 1923)

Freund, L. S. (1990). Maternal regulation of children's problem-solving behavior and its impact on children's performance. *Child Development, 61,* 113–126.

Frey, K. S., & Ruble, D. N. (1985). What children say when the teacher is not around: Conflicting goals in social comparison and performance assessment in the classroom. *Journal of Personality and Social Psychology, 48,* 550–562.

Frey, K. S., & Ruble, D. N. (1992). Gender constancy and the cost of sex-typed behavior: A test of the conflict hypothesis. *Developmental Psychology, 28,* 714–721.

Fried, P. A., O'Connell, C. M., & Watkinson, B. (1992). 60- and 72-month follow-up of children prenatally exposed to marijuana, cigarettes, and alcohol: Cognitive and language assessment. *Developmental and Behavioral Pediatrics, 13,* 383–391.

Friedrich, L. K., & Stein, A. H. (1973). Aggressive and prosocial television programs and the natural behavior of preschool children. *Monographs of the Society for Research in Child Development, 38*(4, Serial No. 51).

Friedrich, L. K., & Stein, A. H. (1975). Prosocial television and young children: The effects of verbal labeling and role-playing on learning and behavior. *Child Development, 46,* 27–38.

Friedrich-Cofer, L. K., Huston-Stein, A., Kipnis, D. M., Susman, E. J., & Clewett, A. S. (1979). Environmental enhancement of prosocial television content: Effects on interpersonal behavior. *Developmental Psychology, 15,* 637–646.

Friend, M., & Davis, T. L. (1993). Appearance-reality distinction: Children's understanding of the physical and affective domains. *Developmental Psychology, 29,* 907–914.

Frisby, C. L., & Braden, J. P. (1992). Feuerstein's dynamic assessment approach: A semantic, logical, and empirical critique. *Journal of Special Education, 26,* 281–301.

Frisch, R. E. (1983). Fatness, puberty, and fertility. The effects of nutrition and physical training on menarche and ovulation. In J. Brooks-Gunn & A. C. Petersen (Eds.), *Girls at puberty: Biological and psychosocial perspectives.* New York: Plenum.

Frodi, A. M., & Lamb, M. E. (1980). Child abusers' responses to infant smiles and cries. *Child Development, 51,* 238–241.

Frodi, A. M., Lamb, M. E., Leavitt, L. A., Donovan, W. L., Neff, C., & Sherry, D. (1978). Fathers' and mothers' responses to the faces and cries of normal and premature infants. *Developmental Psychology, 14,* 490–498.

Fuchs, D., & Thelen, M. H. (1988). Children's expected interpersonal consequences of communicating their affective state and reported likelihood of expression. *Child Development, 59,* 1314–1322.

Fuligni, A. J., & Eccles, J. S. (1993). Perceived parent-child relationships and early adolescents' orientation toward peers. *Developmental Psychology, 29,* 622–632.

Fullerton, J. T., & Severino, R. (1992). In-hospital care for low-risk childbirth. Comparison with results from the National Birth Center Study. *Journal of Nurse Midwifery, 37,* 331–340.

Furman, W., & Bierman, K. L. (1983). Developmental changes in young children's conceptions of friendship. *Child Development, 54,* 549–556.

Furman, W., & Buhrmester, D. (1985a). Children's perceptions of the personal relationships in their social networks. *Developmental Psychology, 21,* 1016–1024.

Furman, W., & Buhrmester, D. (1985b). Children's perceptions of the qualities of sibling relationships. *Child Development, 56,* 448–461.

Furman, W., & Buhrmester, D. (1992). Age and sex differences in perceptions of networks of personal relationships. *Child Development, 63,* 103–115.

Furstenberg, F. F., Jr. (1988). Child care after divorce and remarriage. In E. M. Hetherington & J. D. Arasteh (Eds.), *Impact of divorce, single-parenting, and stepparenting on children.* Hillsdale, NJ: Erlbaum.

Furstenberg, F. F., Jr., Brooks-Gunn, J., & Chase-Lansdale, L. (1989). Teenaged pregnancy and childbearing. *American Psychologist, 44,* 313–320.

Fyans, L. J., Jr., Salili, F., Maehr, M. L., & Desai, K. A. (1983). A cross-cultural exploration into the meaning of achievement. *Journal of Personality and Social Psychology, 44,* 1000–1013.

Gabiano, C., Tovo, P. A., de Martino, M., Galli, L., Giaquinto, C., Loy, A., Schoeller, M. C., Giovannini, M., Ferranti, G., Rancilio, L., Caselli, D., Segni, G., Livadiotti, S., Conte, A., Rizzi, M., Viggiano, D., Mazza, A., Ferrazzin, A., Tozzi, A. E., & Capello, N. (1992). Mother-to-child transmission of human immunodeficiency virus type 1: Risk of infection and correlates of transmission. *Pediatrics, 90,* 369–374.

Gaddis, A., & Brooks-Gunn, J. (1985). The male experience of pubertal change. *Journal of Youth and Adolescence, 14,* 61–69.

Galambos, N. L. (1992). Parent-adolescent relations. *Current Directions in Psychological Science, 1,* 146–149.

Galambos, N. L., Almeida, D. M., & Petersen, A. C. (1990). Masculinity, femininity, and sex role attitudes in early adolescence: Exploring gender intensification. *Child Development, 61,* 1905–1914.

Galambos, N. L., & Maggs, J. L. (1991). Out-of-school care of young adolescents and self-reported behavior. *Developmental Psychology, 27,* 644–655.

Galambos, S. J., & Goldin-Meadow, S. (1990). The effects of learning two languages on levels of metalinguistic awareness. *Cognition, 34,* 1–56.

Gallagher, J. M., & Easley, J. A., Jr. (1978). *Knowledge and development. Vol. 2: Piaget and education.* New York: Plenum.

Gallahue, D. L. (1989). *Understanding motor development* (2nd ed.). Carmel, ID: Benchmark Press.

Gallup, G. G., Jr. (1979). Self-recognition in chimpanzees and man: A developmental and comparative perspective. In M. Lewis & L. A. Rosenblum (Eds.), *Genesis of behavior. Vol. 2: The child and its family.* New York: Plenum.

Ganchrow, J. R., Steiner, J. E., & Daher, M. (1983). Neonatal facial expressions to different qualities and intensities of gustatory stimuli. *Infant Behavior and Development, 6,* 189–200.

Gandelman, R. (1992). *Psychobiology of behavioral development.* New York: Oxford University Press.

Garbarino, J. (1992). *Children and families in the social environment* (2nd ed). New York: Aldine de Gruyter.

Garbarino, J., & Sherman, D. (1980). High-risk neighborhoods and high-risk families: The human ecology of child maltreatment. *Child Development, 51,* 188–198.

Garcia, E. E. (1993). Language, culture, and education. *Review of Educational Research, 19,* 51–98.

Gardner, B. T., & Gardner, R. A. (1974). Comparing the early utterances of child and chimpanzee. In A. Pick (Ed.), *Minnesota Symposia on Child Psychology* (Vol. 8). Minneapolis: University of Minnesota Press.

Gardner, H. (1983). *Frames of mind: The theory of multiple intelligences.* New York: Basic Books.

Gardner, H., Phelps, E., & Wolf, D. (1990). The roots of adult creativity in children's symbolic products. In C. N. Alexander & E. J. Langer (Eds.), *Higher stages of human development. Perspectives on adult growth.* New York: Oxford University Press.

Gardner, L. J. (1972). Deprivation dwarfism. *Scientific American, 227,* 76–82.

Gardner, M. K., & Clark, E. (1992). The psychometric perspective on intellectual development in childhood and adolescence. In R. J. Sternberg & C. A. Berg (Eds.), *Intellectual development.* New York: Cambridge University Press.

Gardner, W., & Rogoff, B. (1990). Children's deliberateness of planning according to task circumstances. *Developmental Psychology, 26,* 480–487.

Garland, A., & Zigler, E. (1993). Adolescent suicide prevention: Current research and social policy implications. *American Psychologist, 48,* 169–182.

Garner, P. W., Jones, D. C., & Miner, J. L. (1994). Social competence among low-income preschoolers: Emotion socialization practices and social cognitive correlates. *Child Development, 65,* 622–637.

Garner, P. W., Jones, D. C., & Palmer, D. J. (1994). Social-cognitive correlates of preschool children's sibling caregiving behavior. *Developmental Psychology, 30,* 905–911.

Garnets, L., & Kimmel, D. (1991). Lesbian and gay male dimensions of the psychological study of human diversity. In J. D. Goodchilds (Ed.), *Psychological perspectives on human diversity in America.* Washington, D.C.: American Psychological Association.

Garrett, P., Ng'andu, N., & Ferron, J. (1994). Poverty experiences of young children and the quality of their home environments. *Child Development, 65,* 331–345.

Garton, A. F., & Pratt, C. (1990). Children's pragmatic judgments of direct and indirect requests. *First Language, 10,* 51–59.

Gauvain, M., & Rogoff, B. (1989). Collaborative problem solving and children's planning skills. *Developmental Psychology, 25,* 139–151.

Gavin, L. A., & Furman, W. (1989). Age differences in adolescents' perceptions of their peer groups. *Developmental Psychology, 25,* 827–834.

Gehorsam, J., & King, M. (1991, May 30). 9.9 ounces at birth, baby nears second birthday. *Atlanta Journal,* C3.

Geist, W. E. (1985, November 3). New Yorkers trying to stop nursery school madness. *Lexington Herald-Leader,* A14.

Gelles, R. J. (1992). Poverty and violence toward children. *American Behavioral Scientist, 35,* 258–274.

Gelman, R. (1978). Cognitive development. *Annual Review of Psychology, 29,* 297–332.

Gelman, R., & Baillargeon, R. (1983). A review of Piagetian concepts. In P. H. Mussen (Ed.), *Handbook of child psychology. Vol. 3: Cognitive development.* New York: Wiley.

Gelman, R., & Shatz, M. (1977). Appropriate speech adjustments: The operation of conversational constraints on talk to two-year-olds. In M. Lewis & L. A. Rosenblum (Eds.), *Interaction, conversation, and the development of language.* New York: Wiley.

Gelman, S. A., & Ebeling, K. S. (1989). Children's use of nonegocentric standards in judgments of functional size. *Child Development, 60,* 920–932.

Gerbner, G., Gross, L., Signorielli, N., & Morgan, M. (1986). *Television's mean world: Violence Profile No. 14 15.* Philadelphia, PA: University of Pennsylvania, Annenberg School of Communications.

Gerken, L., Landau, B., & Remez, R. E. (1990). Function morphemes in young children's speech perception and production. *Developmental Psychology, 26,* 204–216.

Gerken, L., & McIntosh, B. J. (1993). Interplay of function morphemes and prosody in early language. *Developmental Psychology, 24,* 448–457.

Gesell, A. (1933). Maturation and the patterning of behavior. In C. Murchison (Ed.), *A handbook of child psychology.* Worcester, MA: Clark University Press.

Gesell, A., Halverson, H. M., Thompson, H., Ilg, F. L., Costner, B. M., Ames, L. B., & Amatruda, C. S. (1940). *The first five years of life: A guide to the study of the preschool child.* New York: Harper & Row.

Gesell, A., & Thompson, H. (1929). Learning and growth in identical twins: An experimental study by the method of co-twin control. *Genetic Psychology Monographs, 6,* 1–123.

Getzels, J. W., & Jackson, P. W. (1962). *Creativity and intelligence: Explorations with gifted children.* New York: Wiley.

Gewirtz, J. L., & Pelaez-Nogueras, M. (1992). Skinner, B. F.: Legacy to human infant behavior and development. *American Psychologist, 47,* 1411–1422.

Gewirtz, J. L., & Petrovich, S. B. (1982). Early social and attachment learning in the frame of organic and cultural evolution. In T. M. Field, A. Huston, H. C. Quay, L. Troll, & G. E. Finley (Eds.), *Review of human development.* New York: Wiley.

Ghent, L. (1956). Perception of overlapping and embedded figures by children of different ages. *American Journal of Psychology, 69,* 575–587.

Ghim, H. (1990). Evidence for perceptual organization in infants: Perception of subjective contours by young infants. *Infant Behavior and Development, 13,* 221–248.

Gibbs, J. C., & Schnell, S. V. (1985). Moral development "versus" socialization. A critique. *American Psychologist, 40,* 1071–1080.

Gibson, D., & Harris, A. (1988). Aggregated early intervention effects for Down syndrome persons. *Journal of Mental Deficiency Research, 32,* 1–7.

Gibson, E. J. (1969). *Principles of perceptual learning and development.* East Norwalk, CT: Appleton-Century-Crofts.

Gibson, E. J. (1987). Introductory essay: What does infant perception tell us about theories of perception? *Journal of Experimental Psychology: Human Perception and Performance, 13,* 515–523.

Gibson, E. J. (1992). How to think about perceptual learning: Twenty-five years later. In J. L. Pick, P. Van den Broek, & D. C. Knoll (Eds.), *Cognitive psychology: Conceptual and methodological issues.* Washington, D.C.: American Psychological Association.

Gibson, E. J., Gibson, J. J., Pick, A. D., & Osser, H. A. (1962). A developmental study of the discrimination of letterlike forms. *Journal of Comparative and Physiological Psychology, 55,* 897–906.

Gibson, E. J., & Levin, H. (1975). *The psychology of reading.* Cambridge, MA: MIT Press.

Gibson, E. J., & Walk, R. D. (1960). The "visual cliff." *Scientific American, 202,* 64–71.

Gibson, E. J., & Walker, A. S. (1984). Development of knowledge of visual-tactile affordances of substance. *Child Development, 55,* 453–460.

Gil, D. G. (1970). *Violence against children.* Cambridge, MA: Harvard University Press.

Gilligan, C. (1977). In a different voice: Women's conceptions of self and morality. *Harvard Educational Review, 47,* 481–517.

Gilligan, C. (1982). *In a different voice: Psychological theory and women's development.* Cambridge, MA: Harvard University Press.

Gilligan, C. (1993). Adolescent development reconsidered. In A. Garrod (Ed.), *Approaches to moral development: New research and emerging themes.* New York: Teachers College Press.

Ginsburg, G. S., & Bronstein, P. (1993). Family factors related to children's intrinsic/extrinsic motivational orientation and academic performance. *Child Development, 64,* 1461–1474.

Ginsburg, H. J., & Miller, S. M. (1982). Sex differences in children's risk-taking behavior. *Child Development, 53,* 426–428.

Ginsburg, H. P., & Opper, S. (1988). *Piaget's theory of intellectual development* (3rd ed.). Englewood Cliffs, NJ: Prentice-Hall.

Giordano, P. C., Cernkovich, S. A., & DeMaris, A. (1993). The family and peer relations of black adolescents. *Journal of Marriage and the Family, 55,* 277–287.

Girard, C. (1993). Age, gender, and suicide: A cross-national analysis. *American Sociological Review, 58,* 553–574.

Gleitman, H. (1991). *Psychology* (3rd ed.). New York: Norton.

Gleitman, L. R. (1990). The structural sources of verb meanings. *Language Acquisition, 1,* 3–55.

Glick, P. C. (1989). Remarried families, stepfamilies, and stepchildren: A brief demographic profile. *Family Relations, 38,* 24–47.

Gnepp, J. (1989). Personalized inferences of emotions and appraisals: Component processes and correlates. *Developmental Psychology, 25,* 277–288.

Gnepp, J., & Klayman, J. (1992). Recognition of uncertainty in emotional inferences: Reasoning about emotionally equivocal situations. *Developmental Psychology, 28,* 145–158.

Golbus, M. S., & Fries, M. M. (1993). Surgical fetal therapy. In C. Lin, M. S. Verp, & R. E. Sabbagha (Eds.), *The high-risk fetus: Pathophysiology, diagnosis, management.* New York: Springer-Verlag.

Gold, D., & Andres, D. (1978a). Developmental comparisons between adolescent children with employed and nonemployed mothers. *Merrill-Palmer Quarterly, 24,* 243–254.

Gold, D., & Andres, D. (1978b). Developmental comparisons between 10-year-old children with employed and nonemployed mothers. *Child Development, 49,* 75–84.

Goldberg, P. (1968). Are women prejudiced against women? *Trans/Action, 5,* 28–30.

Goldberg, S. (1983). Parent-infant bonding: Another look. *Child Development, 54,* 1355–1382.

Goldberg, S., Blumberg, S. L., & Kriger, A. (1982). Menarche and interest in infants: Biological and social influences. *Child Development, 53,* 1544–1550.

Goldberg, S., Perrotta, M., Minde, K., & Corter, C. (1986). Maternal behavior and attachment in low-birth-weight twins and singletons. *Child Development, 57,* 34–46.

Golden, M., Birns, B., Bridger, W., & Moss, A. (1971). Social class differentiation in cognitive development among black preschool children. *Child Development, 42,* 37–46.

Goldfarb, W. (1943). The effects of early institutional care on adolescent personality. *Journal of Experimental Education, 12,* 107–129.

Goldfarb, W. (1947). Variations in adolescent adjustment in institutionally reared children. *Journal of Orthopsychiatry, 17,* 449–457.

Goldfield, E. C. (1989). Transition from rocking to crawling: Postural constraints on infant movement. *Developmental Psychology, 25,* 913–919.

Goldin-Meadow, S., & Mylander, C. (1984). Gestural communication in deaf children: The effects and noneffects of parental input on early language development. *Monographs of the Society for Research in Child Development, 49* (3–4, Serial No. 207).

Goldman, R., & Goldman, J. (1982). *Children's sexual thinking. A comparative study of children aged 5 to 15 years in Australia, North America, Britain and Sweden.* London: Routledge & Kegan Paul.

Goldman-Rakic, P. S., Isseroff, A., Schwartz, M. L., & Bugbee, N. M. (1983). The neurobiology of cognitive development. In M. M. Haith & J. J. Campos (Eds.), *Handbook of child psychology. Vol. 2: Infancy and developmental psychobiology* (4th ed.). New York: Wiley.

Goldsmith, H. H., & Alansky, J. A. (1987). Maternal and infant temperamental predictors of attachment: A meta-analytic review. *Journal of Consulting and Clinical Psychology, 55,* 805–816.

Goldsmith, H. H., Buss, A. H., Plomin, R., Rothbart, M. K., Thomas, A., Chess, S., Hinde, R. A., & McCall, R. B. (1987). Roundtable: What is temperament? Four approaches. *Child Development, 58,* 505–529.

Golinkoff, R. M., Hirsh-Pasek, K., Bailey, L.M., & Wenger, N. R. (1992). Young children and adults use lexical principles to learn new nouns. *Developmental Psychology, 28,* 99–108.

Gollin, E. S. (1960). Developmental studies of visual recognition of incomplete objects. *Perceptual and Motor Skills, 11,* 289–298.

Gollin, E. S. (1962). Factors affecting the visual recognition of incomplete objects: A comparative investigation of children and adults. *Perceptual and Motor Skills, 15,* 583–590.

Good, T. L. (1979). Teacher effectiveness in the elementary school: What do we know about it now? *Journal of Teacher Education, 30,* 52–64.

Goodall, J. (1986). *The chimpanzees of Gombe: Patterns of behavior.* Cambridge, MA: Harvard University Press.

Goodenough, F. L. (1931). *Anger in young children.* Minneapolis: University of Minnesota Press.

Goodwyn, S. W., & Acredolo, L. P. (1993). Symbolic gesture versus word: Is there a modality advantage for onset of symbol use? *Child Development, 64,* 688–701.

Goossens, F. A., & van IJzendoorn, M. H. (1990). Quality of infants' attachments to professional caregivers: Relation to infant-parent attachment and day-care characteristics. *Child Development, 61,* 832–837.

Gopnik, A., & Meltzoff, A. N. (1986). Relations between semantic and cognitive development in the one-word stage: The specificity hypothesis. *Child Development, 57,* 1040–1053.

Gopnik, A., & Meltzoff, A. N. (1987). Language and thought in the young child: Early semantic developments and their relationships to object permanence, means-ends understanding, and categorization. In K. Nelson & A. Van Kleeck (Eds.), *Children's language* (Vol. 6). Hillsdale, NJ: Erlbaum.

Gordon, P. (1990). Learnability and feedback. *Developmental Psychology, 26,* 217–220.

Goren, C. C., Sarty, M., & Wu, P. Y. K. (1975). Visual following and pattern discrimination of face-like stimuli by newborn infants. *Pediatrics, 56,* 544–549.

Gorer, G. (1968). Man has no "killer" instinct. In M. F. A. Montague (Ed.), *Man and aggression.* New York: Oxford University Press.

Gorn, G. J., Goldberg, M. E., & Kanungo, R. N. (1976). The role of educational television in changing the intergroup attitudes of children. *Child Development, 47,* 277–280.

Gotlib, I. H., Whiffen, V. E., Wallace, P. M., & Mount, J. (1991). Prospective investigation of postpartum depression: Factors involved in onset and recovery. *Journal of Abnormal Psychology, 100,* 122–132.

Gottesman, I. I. (1963). Genetic aspects of intelligent behavior. In N. Ellis (Ed.), *Handbook of mental deficiency.* New York: McGraw-Hill.

Gottesman, I. I., & Shields, J. (1982). *Schizophrenia: The epigenetic puzzle.* Cambridge, England: Cambridge University Press.

Gottfredson, L. S. (1986). Societal consequences of the g factor in employment. *Journal of Vocational Behavior, 29,* 379–410.

Gottfried, A. W. (1984). Home environment and early cognitive development: Integration, meta-analyses, and conclusions. In A. W. Gottfried (Ed.), *Home environment and early cognitive development: Longitudinal research.* Orlando, FL: Academic Press.

Gottlieb, D. (1966). Teaching and students: The views of Negro and white teachers. *Sociology of Education, 37,* 344–353.

Gottlieb, G. (1991a). Experiental canalization of behavioral development: Results. *Developmental Psychology, 27,* 35–39.

Gottlieb, G. (1991b). Experiential canalization of behavioral development: Theory and commentary. *Developmental Psychology, 27,* 4–13.

Gouin-DeCarie, T. (1969). A study of the mental and emotional development of the thalidomide child. In B. M. Foss (Ed.), *Determinants of infant behavior* (Vol. 4). London: Methuen.

Graham, S., Hudley, C., & Williams, E. (1992). Attributional and emotional determinants of aggression among African-American and Latino young adolescents. *Developmental Psychology, 28,* 731–740.

Granrud, C. E. (1987). Size constancy in newborn human infants. *Investigative Ophthalmology and Visual Science, 28,* 5.

Granrud, C. E., & Yonas, A. (1984). Infants' perception of pictorially specified interposition. *Journal of Experimental Child Psychology, 37,* 500–511.

Grantham-McGregor, S., Powell, C., Walker, S., Chang, S., & Fletcher, P. (1994). The long-term follow-up of severely malnourished children who participated in an intervention program. *Child Development, 65,* 428–439.

Graves, S. B. (1975, April). *How to encourage positive racial attitudes.* Paper presented at the biennial meeting of the Society for Research in Child Development, Denver.

Gray, S. W., & Klaus, R. A. (1970). The early training project: A seventh-year report. *Child Development, 41,* 909–924.

Gray, W. M., & Hudson, L. M. (1984). Formal operations and the imaginary audience. *Developmental Psychology, 20,* 619–627.

Graziano, W. G., French, D., Brownell, C. A., & Hartup, W. W. (1976). Peer interaction in same- and mixed-age triads in relation to chronological age and incentive condition. *Child Development, 47,* 707–714.

Green, R. (1987). *The "sissy boy syndrome" and the development of homosexuality.* New Haven, CT: Yale University Press.

Greenberg, M., & Morris, N. (1974). Engrossment: The newborn's impact upon the father. *American Journal of Orthopsychiatry, 44,* 520–531.

Greenberger, E., & Goldberg, W. A. (1989). Work, parenting, and the socialization of children. *Developmental Psychology, 25,* 22–35.

Greenberger, E., & O'Neil, R. (1993). Spouse, parent, worker: Role commitments and role-related experiences in the construction of adults' well-being. *Developmental Psychology, 29,* 181–197.

Greenberger, E., O'Neil, R., & Nagel, S. K. (1994). Linking workplace and homeplace: Relations between the nature of adults' work and their parenting behavior. *Developmental Psychology, 30,* 990–1002.

Greenberger, E., & Steinberg, L. (1986). *When teenagers work: The psychological and social costs of adolescent employment.* New York: Basic Books.

Greenfield, P. M., & Smith, J. H. (1976). *The structure of communication in early language development.* New York: Academic.

Greenough, W. T., Black, J. E., & Wallace, C. S. (1987). Experience and brain development. *Child Development, 58,* 539–559.

Greif, E. B., & Ulman, K. J. (1982). The psychological impact of menarche on early adolescent females: A review of the literature. *Child Development, 53,* 1413–1430.

Grieser, D. L., & Kuhl, D. K. (1988). Maternal speech to infants in a tonal language: Support for the universal prosodic features in motherese. *Child Development, 59,* 14–20.

Grolnick, W. S., & Ryan, R. M. (1989). Parents' styles associated with children's self-regulation and competence in school. *Journal of Educational Psychology, 81,* 143–154.

Gross, A. L., & Ballif, B. (1991). Children's understanding of emotion from facial expressions and situations: A review. *Developmental Review, 11,* 368–398.

Grossman, F. K., Eichler, L. S., Winickoff, S. A., & Associates (1980). *Pregnancy, birth, and parenthood: Adaptations of mothers, fathers, and infants.* San Francisco: Jossey-Bass.

Grossmann, K., Grossmann, K. E., Spangler, S., Suess, G., & Unzner, L. (1985). Maternal sensitivity and newborn responses as related to quality of attachment in Northern Germany. In I. Bretherton & E. Waters, Growing points of attachment theory. *Monographs of the Society for Research in Child Development, 50*(1–2, Serial No. 209).

Grossmann, K. E., & Grossmann, K. (1991). Attachment quality as an organizer of emotional and behavioral responses in a longitudinal perspective. In C. M. Parker, J. Stevenson-Hinde, & P. Marris (Eds.), *Attachment across the life cycle.* London: Tavistock/Routledge.

Grotevant, H. D., & Cooper, C. R. (1986). Individuation in family relations: A perspective on individual differences in the development of identity and role-taking skills in adolescence. *Human Development, 29,* 82–100.

Gruber, H. (1982). On the hypothesized relation between giftedness and creativity. In D. H. Feldman (Ed.), *New directions for child development. No. 17: Developmental approaches to giftedness and creativity.* San Francisco: Jossey-Bass.

Grusec, J. E. (1991). Socializing concern for others in the home. *Developmental Psychology, 27,* 338–342.

Grusec, J. E. (1992). Social learning theory and developmental psychology: The legacies of Robert Sears and Albert Bandura. *Developmental Psychology, 28,* 776–786.

Grusec, J. E., & Goodnow, J. J. (1994). Impact of parental discipline methods on the child's internalization of values: A reconceptualization of current points of view. *Developmental Psychology, 30,* 4–19.

Grusec, J. E., Kuczynski, L., Rushton, J. P., & Simutis, Z. (1979). Learning resistance to temptation through observation. *Developmental Psychology, 15,* 233–240.

Grusec, J. E., & Redler, E. (1980). Attribution, reinforcement, and altruism: A developmental analysis. *Developmental Psychology, 16,* 525–534.

Grusec, J. E., & Walters, G. C. (1991). Psychological abuse and childrearing belief systems. In R. H. Starr, Jr., & D. A. Wolfe (Eds.), *The effects of child abuse and neglect.* New York: Guilford.

Grych, J. H., & Fincham, F. D. (1992). Interventions for children of divorce: Toward greater integration of research and action. *Psychological Bulletin, 111,* 434–454.

Guerra, N. G., & Slaby, R. G. (1990). Cognitive mediators of aggression in adolescent offenders. 2: Intervention. *Developmental Psychology, 26,* 269–277.

Guilford, J. P. (1967). *The nature of human intelligence.* New York: McGraw-Hill.

Guilford, J. P. (1988). Some changes in the structure-of-the-intellect model. *Educational and Psychological Measurement, 40,* 1–4.

Gullotta, T. P., Adams, G. R., & Alexander, S. J. (1986). *Today's marriages and families. A wellness approach.* Monterey, CA: Brooks/Cole.

Gunderson, V., & Sackett, G. P. (1982). Paternal effects on reproductive outcome and developmental risk. In M. E. Lamb & A. L. Brown (Eds.), *Advances in developmental psychology* (Vol. 2). Hillsdale, NJ: Erlbaum.

Gunnar, M. R., Larson, M. C., Hertsgaard, L., Harris, M. L., & Brodersen, L. (1992). The stressfulness of separation among 9-month-old infants: Effects of social context variables and infant temperament. *Child Development, 63,* 290–303.

Gunnar, M. R., Malone, S., Vance, G., & Fisch, R. O. (1985). Coping with aversive stimulation in the neonatal period: Quiet sleep and plasma cortisol levels during recovery from circumcision. *Child Development, 56,* 824–834.

Guralnick, M. J., & Groom, J. M. (1988). Friendships of preschool children in mainstreamed playgroups. *Developmental Psychology, 24,* 595–604.

Gurucharri, C., & Selman, R. L. (1982). The development of interpersonal understanding during childhood, preadolescence, and adolescence: A longitudinal follow-up study. *Child Development, 53,* 924–927.

Gustafson, G. E., & Harris, K. L. (1990). Women's responses to young infants' cries. *Developmental Psychology, 26,* 144–152.

Guttentag, M., & Bray, H. (1976). *Undoing sex stereotypes. Research and resources for educators.* New York: McGraw-Hill.

Haan, N., Aerts, E., & Cooper, B. A. B. (1985). *On moral grounds. The search for practical morality.* New York: New York University Press.

Haidt, J., Koller, S. H., & Dias, M. G. (1993). Affect, culture, and morality, or is it wrong to eat your dog? *Journal of Personality and Social Psychology, 65,* 613–628.

Haith, M. M. (1980). Visual competence in early infancy. In R. Held, H. Liebowitz, & H. R. Teuber (Eds.), *Handbook of sensory physiology* (Vol. 8). Berlin: Springer-Verlag.

Haith, M. M., Bergman, T., & Moore, M. J. (1977). Eye contact and face scanning in early infancy. *Science, 198,* 853–855.

Hakuta, K. (1988). Why bilinguals? In F. S. Kessel (Ed.), *The development of language and language researchers: Essays in honor of Roger Brown.* Hillsdale, NJ: Erlbaum.

Hakuta, K., & Garcia, E. E. (1989). Bilingualism and education. *American Psychologist, 44,* 374–379.

Hale, S., Fry, A., & Jessie, K. A. (1993). Effects of practice on speed of information processing in children and adults: Age sensitivity and age invariance. *Developmental Psychology, 29,* 880–892.

Half our pregnancies are unintentional (1983, October 10). *Newsweek,* 37.

Hall, D. G., & Waxman, S. R. (1993). Assumptions about word meaning: Individuation and basic-level kinds. *Child Development, 64,* 1550–1570.

Hall, G. S. (1891). The contents of children's minds on entering school. *Pedagogical Seminary, 1,* 139–173.

Hall, G. S. (1904). *Adolescence.* New York: Appleton-Century-Crofts.

Hall, J. A., & Halberstadt, A. G. (1980). Masculinity and femininity in children: Development of the Children's Personal Attributes Questionnaire. *Developmental Psychology, 16,* 270–280.

Halverson, H. M. (1931). An experimental study of prehension in infants by means of systematic cinema records. *Genetic Psychology Monographs, 10,* 107–286.

Hamilton, S. F. (1990). *Apprenticeship for adulthood: preparing youth for the future.* New York: Free Press.

Hanna, E., & Meltzoff, A. N. (1993). Peer imitation by toddlers in the laboratory, home, and day-care contexts: Implications for social learning and memory. *Developmental Psychology, 29,* 701–710.

Hannah, J. S., & Kahn, S. E. (1989). The relationship of socioeconomic status and gender to the occupational choices of grade 12 students. *Journal of Vocational Behavior, 34,* 161–178.

Hansen, J., & Bowey, J. A. (1994). Phonological analysis skills, verbal working memory, and reading ability in second-grade children. *Child Development, 65,* 938–950.

Hanshaw, J. B., Dudgeon, J. A., & Marshall, W. C. (1985). *Viral diseases of the fetus and newborn* (2nd ed.). Philadelphia: Saunders.

Hardie, A. (1994, November 12). Age of discovery for Alzheimer's. *Atlanta Constitution*, E1.

Harkness, S., Edwards, C. P., & Super, C. M. (1981). Social roles and moral reasoning: A case study in a rural African community. *Developmental Psychology, 17*, 595–603.

Harlow, H. F., & Zimmerman, R. R. (1959). Affectional responses in the infant monkey. *Science, 130*, 421–432.

Harmon, T. M., Hynan, M. T., & Tyre, T. E. (1990). Improved obstetric outcomes using hypnotic analgesia and skill mastery combined with childbirth education. *Journal of Consulting and Clinical Psychology, 58*, 525–530.

Harper, L. V., & Huie, K. S. (1985). The effects of prior group experience, age, and familiarity on the quality and organization of preschoolers' social relationships. *Child Development, 56*, 704–717.

Harrell, T. W., & Harrell, M. S. (1945). Army General Classification Test scores for civilian occupations. *Educational and Psychological Measurement, 5*, 229–239.

Harrington, D. M., Block, J. H., & Block, J. (1987). Testing aspects of Carl Rogers's theory of creative environments in young adolescents. *Journal of Personality and Social Psychology, 52*, 851–856.

Harris, L., & Associates (1986). *American teens speak: Sex, myths, TV and birth control: The Planned Parenthood poll.* New York: Planned Parenthood Federation of America.

Harris, M. (1992). *Language experience and early language development: From input to uptake.* Hove, England: Erlbaum.

Harris, M. J., & Rosenthal, R. (1986). Four factors in the mediation of teacher expectancy effects. In R. S. Feldman (Ed.), *The social psychology of education. Current research and theory.* Cambridge, England: Cambridge University Press.

Harris, N. B. (1992). Sex, race, and the experiences of aggression. *Aggressive Behavior, 18*, 201–217.

Harris, P. L. (1989). *Children and emotion: The development of psychological understanding.* Oxford: Basil Blackwell.

Harris, P. L., Kavanaugh, R. D., & Meredith, M. C. (1994). Young children's comprehension of pretend episodes: The integration of successive actions. *Child Development, 65*, 16–30.

Harrison, L. F., & Williams, T. (1986). Television and cognitive development. In T. Williams (Ed.), *The impact of television: A natural experiment in three communities.* Orlando, FL: Academic.

Hart, B., & Risley, T. R. (1992). American parenting of language-learning children: Persisting differences in family-child interactions observed in natural home environments. *Developmental Psychology, 28*, 1096–1105.

Hart, C. H., DeWolf, D. M., Wozniak, P., & Burts, D. C. (1992). Maternal and paternal disciplinary styles: Relations with preschoolers' playground behavioral orientations and peer status. *Child Development, 63*, 879–892.

Hart, C. H., Ladd, G. W., & Burleson, B. R. (1990). Children's expectations of the outcomes of social strategies: Relations with socioeconomic status and maternal disciplinary styles. *Child Development, 61*, 127–137.

Hart, D., & Chmiel, S. (1992). Influence of defense mechanisms on moral judgment development: A longitudinal study. *Developmental Psychology, 28*, 722–730.

Hart, S. N. (1991). From property to person status: Historical perspective on children's rights. *American Psychologist, 46*, 53–59.

Hart, S. N., & Brassard, M. R. (1987). A major threat to children's mental health. Psychological maltreatment. *American Psychologist, 42*, 160–165.

Harter, S. (1982). The perceived competence scale for children. *Child Development, 53*, 87–97.

Harter, S. (1983). Developmental perspectives on the self-system. In P. H. Mussen (Ed.), *Handbook of child psychology. Vol. 4: Socialization, personality, and social development.* New York: Wiley.

Harter, S. (1986). Cognitive-developmental processes in the integration of concepts about emotions and the self. *Social Cognition, 4*, 119–151.

Harter, S. (1988). Developmental processes in the construction of the self. In T. D. Yawkey & J. E. Johnson (Eds.), *Integrative processes and socialization: Early to middle childhood.* Hillsdale, NJ: Erlbaum.

Harter, S. (1990). Issues in the assessment of the self-concept of children and adolescents. In A. M. LaGreca (Ed.), *Through the eyes of the child: Obtaining self-reports from children and adolescents.* Boston: Allyn & Bacon.

Harter, S., & Buddin, B. J. (1987). Children's understanding of the simultaneity of two emotions: A five-stage developmental acquisition sequence. *Developmental Psychology, 23*, 388–399.

Harter, S., & Monsour, A. (1992). Developmental analysis of conflict caused by opposing attributes in the adolescent self-portrait. *Developmental Psychology, 28*, 251–260.

Harter, S., & Pike, R. (1984). The pictorial scale of perceived competence and social acceptance for young children. *Child Development, 55*, 1969–1982.

Harter, S., & Whitesell, N. (1989). Developmental changes in children's understanding of simple, multiple, and blended emotion concepts. In C. Saarni & P. Harris (Eds.), *Children's understanding of emotion.* Cambridge, England: Cambridge University Press.

Hartshorne, H., & May, M. S. (1928–1930). *Studies in the nature of character. Vol. 1: Studies in deceit. Vol. 2: Studies in self control. Vol. 3: Studies in the organization of character.* New York: Macmillan.

Hartung, B., & Sweeney, K. (1991). Why adult children return home. *Social Science Journal, 28*, 467–480.

Hartup, W. W. (1974). Aggression in childhood: Developmental perspectives. *American Psychologist, 29*, 336–341. Contemporary perspectives. Hove, England: Erlbaum.

Hartup, W. W. (1983). Peer relations. In P. H. Mussen (Ed.), *Handbook of child psychology. Vol. 4: Socialization, personality, and social development.* New York: Wiley.

Hartup, W. W. (1989). Social relationships and their developmental significance. *American Psychologist, 44*, 120–126.

Hartup, W. W. (1992). Friendships and their developmental significance. In H. McGurk (Ed.), *Childhood social development: Contemporary perspectives.* Hove, England: Erlbaum.

Hartup, W. W., French, D. C., Laursen, B., Johnston, M. K., & Ogawa, J. R. (1993). Conflict and friendship relations in middle childhood: Behavior in a closed-field situation. *Child Development, 64*, 445–454.

Hartup, W. W., Laursen, B., Stewart, M. I., & Eastenson, A. (1988). Conflict and friendship relations of young children. *Child Development, 59*, 1590–1600.

Hashima, P. Y., & Amato, P. R. (1994). Poverty, social support, and parental behavior. *Child Development, 65*, 394–403.

Haskett, M. E., & Kistner, J. A. (1991). Social interactions and peer perceptions of young physically abused children. *Child Development, 62*, 979–990.

Haskins, R. (1989). Beyond metaphor: The efficacy of early childhood education. *American Psychologist, 44*, 274–282.

Hasselhorn, M. (1992). Task dependency and the role of category typicality and metamemory in the development of an organizational strategy. *Child Development, 63*, 202–214.

Hatcher, P. J., Hulme, C., & Ellis, A. W. (1994). Ameliorating early reading failure by integrating the teaching of reading and phonological skills: The phonological linkage hypothesis. *Child Development, 65*, 41–57.

Haugaard, J. J., & Reppucci, N. D. (1988). *The sexual abuse of children.* San Francisco: Jossey-Bass.

Haviland, J. M., & Lelwica, M. (1987). The induced affect response: 10-week-old infants' responses to three emotion expressions. *Developmental Psychology, 23*, 97–104.

Hawley, T. L., & Disney, E. R. (1992). Crack's children: The consequences of maternal cocaine abuse. *Social Policy Report, Society for Research in Child Development, 6*, 1–23.

Hay, D. F. (1984). Conflict in early childhood. In G. J. Whitehurst (Ed.), *Annals of child development* (Vol. 1). Greenwich, CT: JAI Press.

Hay, D. F. (1985). Learning to form relationships in infancy: Parallel attainments with parents and peers. *Developmental Review, 5*, 122–161.

Hay, D. F., Caplan, M., Castle, J., & Stimson, C. A. (1991). Does sharing become increasingly "rational" in the second year of life? *Developmental Psychology, 27*, 987–993.

Hay, D. F., Nash, A., & Pedersen, J. (1983). Interaction between six-month-old peers. *Child Development, 54*, 557–562.

Hazan, C., & Shaver, P. (1987). Romantic love conceptualized as an attachment process. *Journal of Personality and Social Psychology, 52*, 511–524.

Hearold, S. (1986). A synthesis of 1043 effects of television on social behavior. In G. Comstock (Ed.), *Public communications and behavior* (Vol. I) New York: Academic Press.

Heath, S. B. (1982). Questioning at home and at school: A comparative study. In G. Spindler (Ed.), *Doing the ethnography of schooling: Educational anthropology in action.* New York: Holt.

Heath, S. B. (1989). Oral and literate traditions among black Americans living in poverty. *American Psychologist, 44*, 367–373.

Hebb, D. O. (1980). *Essay on mind.* Hillsdale, NJ: Erlbaum.

Heinonen, O. P., Slone, D., & Shapiro, S. (1977). *Birth defects and drugs in pregnancy.* Littleton, MA: Publishing Sciences Group.

Held, R., & Hein, A. (1963). Movement-produced stimulation in the development of visually guided behavior. *Journal of Comparative and Physiological Psychology, 56*, 872–876.

Helms, J. E. (1992). Why is there no study of cultural equivalence in standardized cognitive-ability testing? *American Psychologist, 47*, 1083–1101.

Hendrick, B. (1994a, November 17). Sexual orientation linked to biology, brain study suggests. *Atlanta Constitution*, A1.

Hendrick, B. (1994b, June 7). Teen sexual activity increases, as does kids' use of condoms. *Atlanta Constitution*, A1, A6.

Henker, B., & Whalen, C. K. (1989). Hyperactivity and attention deficits. *American Psychologist, 44*, 216–223.

Hennessey, B. A., & Amabile, T. M. (1988). The conditions of creativity. In R. J. Sternberg (Ed.), *The nature of creativity. Contemporary psychological perspectives.* Cambridge, England: Cambridge University Press.

Herdt, G. H., & Davidson, J. (1988). The Sambia "turnim-man": Sociocultural and clinical aspects of gender formation in male pseudohermaphrodites with 5-alpha-reductase deficiency in Papua New Guinea. *Archives of Sexual Behavior, 17*, 33–56.

Herkowitz, J. (1978). Sex-role expectations and motor behavior of the young child. In M. V. Ridenour (Ed.), *Motor development: Issues and applications.* Princeton, NJ: Princeton Book Company.

Herrnstein, R. J., & Murray, C. (1994). *The bell curve: Intelligence and class structure in American life.* New York: Free Press.

Hertzog, C. (1989). Influences of cognitive slowing on age differences in intelligence. *Developmental Psychology, 25*, 636–651.

Herzberger, S. D., & Hall, J. A. (1993). Consequences of retaliatory aggression against siblings and peers: Urban minority children's expectations. *Child Development, 64*, 1773–1785.

Hess, R. D. (1970). Social class and ethnic influences upon socialization. In P. H. Mussen (Ed.), *Carmichael's manual of child psychology* (Vol. 2). New York: Wiley.

Hetherington, E. M. (1981). Children and divorce. In R. W. Henderson (Ed.), *Parent-child interaction: Theory, research, and prospects.* New York: Academic Press.

Hetherington, E. M. (1989). Coping with family transitions: Winners, losers, and survivors. *Child Development, 60,* 1–14.

Hetherington, E. M., & Camara, K. A. (1984). Families in transition: The processes of dissolution and reconstitution. In R. D. Parke (Ed.), *Review of child development research. Vol. 7: The family.* Chicago: University of Chicago Press.

Hetherington, E. M., Clingempeel, W. G., & Associates (1992). Coping with marital transitions. *Monographs of the Society for Research in Child Development, 57*(2–3, Serial No. 227).

Hetherington, E. M., Cox, M., & Cox, R. (1982). Effects of divorce on parents and children. In M. E. Lamb (Ed.), *Nontraditional families.* Hillsdale, NJ: Erlbaum.

Hetherington, E. M., & Frankie, G. (1967). Effect of parental dominance, warmth, and conflict on imitation in children. *Journal of Personality and Social Psychology, 6,* 119–125.

Hetherington, E. M., & Parke, R. D. (1975). *Child psychology: A contemporary viewpoint.* New York: McGraw-Hill.

Hetherington, E. M., Stanley-Hagan, M., & Anderson, E. R. (1989). Marital transitions: A child's perspective. *American Psychologist, 44,* 303–312.

Heyman, G. D., Dweck, C. S., & Cain, K. M. (1992). Young children's vulnerability to self-blame and helplessness: Relationship to beliefs about goodness. *Child Development, 63,* 401–415.

Higgins, E. T., & Parsons, J. E. (1983). Stages as subcultures: Social-cognitive development and the social life of the child. In E. T. Higgins, W. W. Hartup, & D. N. Ruble (Eds.), *Social cognition and social development: A sociocultural perspective.* New York: Cambridge University Press.

Higley, J. D., Hopkins, W. D., Thompson, W. W., Byrne, E. A., Hirsh, R. M., & Suomi, S. J. (1992). Peers as primary attachment sources in yearling rhesus monkeys. *Developmental Psychology, 28,* 1163–1171.

Hill, J. P. (1988). Adapting to menarche: Familial control and conflict. In M. R. Gunnar & W. A. Collins (Eds.), *Development during the transition to adolescence. Vol. 21: Minnesota Symposia on Child Psychology.* Hillsdale, NJ: Erlbaum.

Hill, J. P., & Lynch, M. E. (1983). The intensification of gender-related role expectations during early adolescence. In J. Brooks-Gunn & A. C. Petersen (Eds.), *Girls at puberty: Biological and psychosocial perspectives.* New York: Plenum.

Hill, P. T., Foster, G. E., & Gendler, T. (1990). *High schools with character: Alternatives to bureaucracy.* Santa Monica, CA: Rand Corporation.

Hill, S. D., & Tomlin, C. (1981). Self-recognition in retarded children. *Child Development, 53,* 1320–1329.

Hinde, R. A. (1983). Ethology and child development. In M. M. Haith & J. J. Campos (Eds.), *Handbook of child psychology* (Vol. 2), *Infancy and developmental psychobiology.* New York: Wiley.

Hinde, R. A. (1989). Ethological and relationships approaches. In R. Vasta (Ed.), *Annals of child development: Vol. 6. Theories of child development: Revised formulations and current issues.* Greenwich, CT: JAI Press.

Hindley, C. B., & Owen, C. F. (1978). The extent of individual changes in IQ for ages between 6 months and 17 years in a British longitudinal sample. *Journal of Child Psychology and Psychiatry, 19,* 329–350.

Hines, M., & Kaufman, F. R. (1994). Androgen and the development of human sex-typical behavior: Rough-and-tumble play and sex of preferred playmates in children with congenital adrenal hyperplasia. *Child Development, 65,* 1042–1053.

Hirsh-Pasek, K., Kemler Nelson, D. G., Jusczyk, P. W., Cassidy, K. W., Druss, B., & Kennedy, L. (1987). Clauses are perceptual units for young infants. *Cognition, 26,* 269–286.

Hobbes, T. (1904). *Leviathan.* Cambridge, England: Cambridge University Press. (Original work published 1651)

Hock, E., & DeMeis, D. K. (1990). Depression in mothers of infants: The role of maternal employment. *Developmental Psychology, 26,* 285–291.

Hock, E., DeMeis, D., & McBride, S. (1988). Maternal separation: Its role in the balance of employment and motherhood in mothers of infants. In A. E. Gottfried & A. W. Gottfried (Eds.), *Maternal employment and children's development: Longitudinal research.* New York: Plenum.

Hodges, J., & Tizard, B. (1989). IQ and behavioral adjustment of ex-institutional adolescents. *Journal of Child Psychology and Psychiatry, 30,* 53–75.

Hodnett, E. D., & Osborn, R. W. (1989). A randomized trial of the effects of monitrice support during labor: Mother's views two to four weeks postpartum. *Birth, 16,* 177–183.

Hoff-Ginsberg, E. (1986). Function and structure in maternal speech: Their relation to the child's development of syntax. *Developmental Psychology, 22,* 155–163.

Hoffman, L. W. (1989). Effects of maternal employment in the two-parent family. *American Psychologist, 44,* 283–292.

Hoffman, L. W. (1991). The influence of family environment on personality: Accounting for sibling differences. *Psychological Bulletin, 108,* 187–203.

Hoffman, M. L. (1970). Moral development. In P. H. Mussen (Ed.), *Carmichael's manual of child psychology* (Vol. 2). New York: Wiley.

Hoffman, M. L. (1975). Moral internalization, parental power, and the nature of parent-child interaction. *Developmental Psychology, 11,* 228–239.

Hoffman, M. L. (1981). Is altruism part of human nature? *Journal of Personality and Social Psychology, 40,* 121–137.

Hoffman, M. L. (1988). Moral development. In M. H. Bornstein & M. E. Lamb (Eds.), *Developmental Psychology: An advanced textbook* (2nd ed.). Hillsdale, NJ: Erlbaum.

Hoffman, M. L. (1993). Empathy, social cognition, and moral education. In A. Garrod (Ed.), *Approaches to moral development: New research and emerging themes.* New York: Teachers College Press.

Hoffner, C., & Badzinski, D. M. (1989). Children's integration of facial and situational cues to emotion. *Child Development, 60,* 411–422.

Hofsten, C. von. (1984). Developmental changes in the organization of prereaching movements. *Developmental Psychology, 20,* 378–388.

Hofsten, C. von, & Spelke, E. S. (1985). Object perception and object-directed reaching in infancy. *Journal of Experimental Psychology: General, 114,* 198–212.

Holden, G. W. (1988). Adults' thinking about a child rearing problem: Effects of experience, parental status, and gender. *Child Development, 59,* 1623–1632.

Holden, G. W., & Ritchie, K. L. (1991). Linking extreme marital discord, child rearing, and child behavior problems: Evidence from battered women. *Child Development, 62,* 311–327.

Holmeck, G. N., & Hill, J. P. (1991). Conflictive engagement, positive affect, and menarche in families with seventh-grade girls. *Child Development, 62,* 1030–1048.

Honzik, M. P. (1983). Measuring mental abilities in infancy. The value and limitations. In M. Lewis (Ed.), *Origins of intelligence. Infancy and early childhood* (2nd ed.). New York: Plenum.

Honzik, M. P., Macfarlane, J. W., & Allen, L. (1948). The stability of mental test performance between two and eighteen years. *Journal of Experimental Education, 17,* 309–324.

Hopkins, B. (1991). Facilitating early motor development: An intracultural study of West Indian mothers and their infants living in Britain. In J. K. Nugent, B. M. Lester, & T. B. Brazelton (Eds.), *The cultural context of infancy. Vol. 2: Multicultural and interdisciplinary approaches to parent-infant relations.* Norwood, NJ: Ablex.

Hopwood, N. J., Kelch, R. P., Hale, P. M., Mendes, T. M., Foster, C. M., & Beitins, I. Z. (1990). The onset of human puberty: Biological and environmental factors. In J. Bancroft & J. M. Reinisch (Eds.), *Adolescence and puberty.* New York: Oxford University Press.

Horn, J. L., & Catell, R. B. (1982). Whimsy and misunderstandings of G_f-G_c theory: A comment on Guilford. *Psychological Bulletin, 91,* 623–633.

Horn, J. L., & Hofer, S. M. (1992). Major abilities and development in the adult period. In R. J. Sternberg & C. A. Berg (Eds.), *Intellectual development.* New York: Cambridge University Press.

Horney, K. (1967). *Feminine psychology.* New York: Norton. (Original work published 1923–1937)

Hornik, R., & Gunnar, M. R. (1988). A descriptive analysis of social referencing. *Child Development, 59,* 626–634.

Horobin, K., & Acredolo, L. (1986). The role of attentiveness, mobility history, and separation of hiding sites on Stage IV behavior. *Journal of Experimental Child Psychology, 41,* 114–127.

Horowitz, F. D. (1992). John B. Watson's legacy: Learning and environment. *Developmental Psychology, 28,* 360–367.

House, B. J. (1982). Learning processes: Developmental trends. In J. Worell (Ed.), *Psychological development in the elementary years.* New York: Academic Press.

Howard, L., & Polich, J. (1985). P300 latency and memory span development. *Developmental Psychology, 21,* 283–289.

Howard-Pitney, B., LaFramboise, T. D., Basil, M., September, B., & Johnson, M. (1992). Psychological and social indicators of suicide ideation and suicide attempts in Zuni adolescents. *Journal of Consulting and Clinical Psychology, 60,* 473–476.

Howe, M. L., & Courage, M. L. (1993). On resolving the enigma of infantile amnesia. *Psychological Bulletin, 113,* 305–326.

Howe, N., & Ross, H. S. (1990). Socialization, perspective-taking, and the sibling relationship. *Developmental Psychology, 26,* 160–165.

Howes, C. (1988a). Peer interaction of young children. *Monographs of the Society for Research in Child Development, 53*(1, Serial No. 217).

Howes, C. (1988b). Relations between early child care and schooling. *Developmental Psychology, 24,* 53–57.

Howes, C. (1990). Can age of entry into child care and the quality of child care predict adjustment in kindergarten? *Developmental Psychology, 26,* 292–303.

Howes, C., Droege, K., & Matheson, C. C. (1994). Play and communicative processes within long-term and short-term friendship dyads. *Journal of Social and Personal Relationships, 11,* 401–410.

Howes, C., Hamilton, C. E., & Matheson, C. C. (1994). Children's relationships with peers: Differential associations with aspects of the parent-child relationship. *Child Development, 65,* 253–263.

Howes, C., & Matheson, C. C. (1992). Sequences in the development of competent play with peers: Social and social pretend play. *Developmental Psychology, 28,* 961–974.

Howes, C., Phillips, D. A., & Whitebook, M. (1992). Thresholds of quality: Implications for the social development of children in center-based child care. *Child Development, 63,* 449–460.

Howes, P., & Markman, H. J. (1989). Marital quality and child functioning: A longitudinal investigation. *Child Development, 60,* 1044–1051.

Howieson, N. (1981). A longitudinal study of creativity: 1965–1975. *Journal of Creative Behavior, 15,* 117–134.

Hsu, L. K. G. (1990). *Eating disorders.* New York: Guilford Press.

Hudson, J., & Nelson, K. (1983). Effects of script structure on children's story recall. *Developmental Psychology, 19,* 625–635.

Hudson, J. A. (1990). Constructive processing in children's event memory. *Developmental Psychology, 26,* 180–187.

Hudson, L. M., Forman, E. R., & Brion-Meisels, S. (1982). Role-taking as a predictor of prosocial behavior in cross-age tutors. *Child Development, 53,* 1320–1329.

Huesmann, L. R. (1986). Psychological processes promoting the relation between exposure to media violence and aggressive behavior by the viewer. *Journal of Social Issues, 42,* 125–139.

Huesmann, L. R., Eron, L. D., Lefkowitz, M. M., & Walder, L. O. (1984). Stability of aggression over time and generations. *Developmental Psychology, 20,* 1120–1134.

Huesmann, L. R., Lagerspitz, K., & Eron, L. D. (1984). Intervening variables in the TV violence-aggression relation: Evidence from two countries. *Developmental Psychology, 20,* 746–775.

Hughes, R., Jr., Tingle, B. A., & Sawin, D. B. (1981). Development of empathic understanding in children. *Child Development, 52,* 122–128.

Humphreys, A. P., & Smith, P. K. (1987). Rough and tumble, friendship, and dominance in school children: Evidence for continuity and change with age. *Child Development, 58,* 201–212.

Humphreys, L. G., Rich, S. A. & Davey, T. C. (1985). A Piagetian test of general intelligence. *Developmental Psychology, 21,* 872–877.

Hunter, J. E., & Hunter, R. F. (1984). Validity and utility of alternative predictors of job performance. *Psychological Bulletin, 96,* 72–98.

Hurley, J. R., & Hohn, R. L. (1971). Shifts in child-rearing attitudes linked with parenthood and occupation. *Developmental Psychology, 4,* 324–328.

Husted, A. (1993, October 15). Promising therapy offers hope to cystic fibrosis patients. *Atlanta Journal,* F4.

Huston, A. C. (1983). Sex-typing. In P. H. Mussen (Ed.), *Handbook of child psychology: Vol. 4. Socialization, personality, and social development.* New York: Wiley.

Huston, A. C., Donnerstein, E., Fairchild, H., Feshbach, N. D., Katz, P. A., Murray, J. P., Rubinstein, E. A., Wilcox, B. L., & Zuckerman, D. (1992). *Big world, small screen.* Lincoln, NB: University of Nebraska Press.

Huston, A. C., McLoyd, V. C., & Garcia-Coll, C. (1994). Children and poverty: Issues in contemporary research. *Child Development, 65,* 275–282.

Hutt, C. (1972). *Males and females.* Baltimore: Penguin Books.

Huttenlocher, J., Haight, W., Bryk, A., Seltzer, M., & Lyons, T. (1991). Early vocabulary growth: Relation to language input and gender. *Developmental Psychology, 27,* 236–248.

Hwang, C. P. (1986). Behavior of Swedish primary and secondary caretaking fathers in relation to mother's presence. *Developmental Psychology, 22,* 749–751.

Hyde, J. S. (1984). How large are sex differences in aggression? A developmental meta-analysis. *Developmental Psychology, 20,* 722–736.

Hyde, J. S., Fennema, E., & Lamon, S. J. (1990). Gender differences in mathematics performance: A meta-analysis. *Psychological Bulletin, 107,* 139–155.

Hyde, J. S., & Linn, M. C. (1988). Gender differences in verbal ability: A meta-analysis. *Psychological Bulletin, 104,* 53–69.

Hyde, J. S., & Plant, E. A. (1995). Magnitude of psychological gender differences: Another side to the story. *American Psychologist, 50,* 159–161.

Hymel, S. (1983). Preschool children's peer relations: Issues in sociometric assessment. *Merrill-Palmer Quarterly, 19,* 237–260.

Hymel, S., Bowker, A., & Woody, E. (1993). Aggressive versus withdrawn unpopular children: Variations in peer and self-perceptions in multiple domains. *Child Development, 64,* 879–896.

Hymel, S., Rubin, K. H., Rowden, L. & LeMare, L. (1990). Children's peer relationships: Longitudinal prediction of internalizing and externalizing problems from middle to late childhood. *Child Development, 61,* 2004–2021.

Hymes, J. L. (1990). *The year in review: A look at 1989.* Washington D.C.: National Association for the Education of Young Children.

Hyson, M. C., Hirsch-Pasek, K., & Rescorla, L. (1989). *Academic environments in early childhood: Challenge or pressure?* Summary report to the Spencer Foundation.

Iannotti, R. J. (1978). Effect of role-taking experiences on role-taking, empathy, altruism, and aggression. *Developmental Psychology, 14,* 119–124.

Imperato-McGinley, J., Peterson, R. E., Gautier, T., & Sturla, E. (1979). Androgynes and the evolution of male gender identity among male pseudohermaphrodites with 5a-reductase deficiency. *New England Journal of Medicine, 300,* 1233–1237.

Ingram, D. (1986). Phonological development: Production. In P. Fletcher & M. Garman (Eds.), *Language acquisition* (2nd ed.). Cambridge, England: Cambridge University Press.

Ingram, D. (1989). *First language acquisition: Method, description, and explanation.* Cambridge, England: Cambridge University Press.

Inhelder, B. (1966). Cognitive development and its contribution to the diagnosis of some phenomena of mental deficiency. *Merrill-Palmer Quarterly, 12,* 299–319.

Inhelder, B., & Piaget, J. (1958). *The growth of logical thinking from childhood to adolescence.* New York: Basic Books.

Intons-Peterson, M. J., & Reddel, M. (1984). What do people ask about a neonate? *Developmental Psychology, 20,* 358–359.

Irwin, R. R. (1991). Reconceptualizing the nature of dialectical postformal operational thinking: The effects of affectively mediated social experiences. In J. D. Sinnott & J. C. Cavanaugh (Eds.), *Bridging paradigms: Positive development in adulthood and cognitive aging.* New York: Praeger.

Isabella, R. A. (1993). Origins of attachment: Maternal interactive behavior across the first year. *Child Development, 29,* 605–621.

Isabella, R. A., & Belsky, J. (1991). Interactional synchrony and the origins of infant-mother attachment. *Child Development, 62,* 373–384.

Isberg, R. S., Hauser, S. T., Jacobson, A. M., Powers, S. I., Noam, G., Weiss-Perry, B., & Follansbee, D. (1989). Parental contexts of adolescent self-esteem: A developmental perspective. *Journal of Youth and Adolescence, 18,* 1–23.

Ismail, M. A. (1993). Maternal-fetal infections. In C. Lin, M. S. Verp, & R. E. Sabbagha (Eds.), *The high-risk fetus: Pathophysiology, diagnosis, management.* New York: Springer-Verlag.

Izard, C. E. (1982). *Measuring emotions in infants and children.* New York: Cambridge University Press.

Izard, C. E. (1993). Four systems for emotion activation: Cognitive and noncognitive processes. *Psychological Review, 100,* 68–90.

Izard, C. E., Haynes, O. M., Chisholm, G., & Baak, K. (1991). Emotional determinants of infant-mother attachment. *Child Development, 62,* 906–917.

Jacklin, C. N. (1989). Male and female: Issues of gender. *American Psychologist, 44,* 127–133.

Jacklin, C. N., & Maccoby, E. E. (1978). Social behavior at 33 months in same-sex and mixed-sex dyads. *Child Development, 49,* 557–569.

Jackson, S. (1965). The growth of logical thinking in normal and subnormal children. *British Journal of Educational Psychology, 35,* 255–258.

Jacobs, J. E., & Eccles, J. S. (1992). The impact of mothers' gender-role stereotypic beliefs on mothers' and children's ability perceptions. *Journal of Personality and Social Psychology, 63,* 932–944.

Jacobson, C. K., & Heaton, T. B. (1991). Voluntary childlessness among American men and women in the late 1980s. *Social Biology, 38,* 79–93.

Jacobson, J. L., Jacobson, S. W., Fein, G. G., Schwartz, P. M., & Dowler, J. K. (1984). Prenatal exposure to an environmental toxin: A test of the multiple effects model. *Developmental Psychology, 20,* 523–532.

Jacobson, J. L., Jacobson, S. W., & Humphrey, H. E. (1990). Effects of in utero exposure to poly chlorinated biphenyls and related contaminants on cognitive functioning in young children. *Journal of Pediatrics, 116,* 38–45.

Jacobson, J. L., Jacobson, S. W., Sokol, R. J., Martier, S. S., Ager, J. W., & Kaplan-Estrin, M. G. (1993). Teratogenic effects of alcohol on infant development. *Alcoholism: Clinical and Experimental Research, 17,* 174–183.

Jacobson, J. L., & Wille, D. E. (1986). The influence of attachment pattern on developmental changes in peer interaction from the toddler to the preschool period. *Child Development, 57,* 338–347.

Jacobson, S. W., & Frye, K. F. (1991). Effect of maternal support on attachment: Experimental evidence. *Child Development, 62,* 572–582.

Jacobvitz, D., & Sroufe, L. A. (1987). The early caregiver-child relationship and attention-deficit disorder with hyperactivity in kindergarten: A prospective study. *Child Development, 58,* 1496–1504.

Jahnke, H. C., & Blanchard-Fields, F. (1993). A test of two models of adolescent egocentrism. *Journal of Youth and Adolescence, 22,* 313–326.

James, W. (1890). *Principles of psychology* (2 vols.). New York: Holt.

Janowsky, J. S., & Finlay, B. L. (1986). The outcome of perinatal brain damage: The role of normal neuron loss and axon retraction. *Developmental Medicine and Child Neurology, 28,* 375–389.

Jenkins, E. C., Shapiro, L. R., & Brown, W. T. (1992). Prenatal diagnosis of the Fragile X syndrome. In A. Milunsky (Ed.), *Genetic disorders and the fetus: Diagnosis, prevention, and treatment.* Baltimore: Johns Hopkins University Press.

Jensen, A. R. (1969). How much can we boost IQ and scholastic achievement? *Harvard Educational Review, 39,* 1–123.

Jensen, A. R. (1977). Cumulative deficit in the IQ of blacks in the rural South. *Developmental Psychology, 13,* 184–191.

Jensen, A. R. (1980). *Bias in mental testing.* New York: Free Press.

Jensen, A. R. (1985). The nature of black-white difference on various psycho-metric tests: Spearman's hypothesis. *Behavioral and Brain Sciences, 8,* 193–263.

Johnsen, E. P. (1991). Searching for the social and cognitive outcomes of children's play: A selective second look. *Play and Culture, 4,* 201–213.

Johnson, C. J., Pick, H. L., Siegel, G. M., Cicciarelli, A. W., & Garber, S. R. (1981). Effects of interpersonal distance on children's vocal intensity. *Child Development, 52,* 721–723.

Johnson, D. W., Johnson, R. T., & Maruyama, G. (1983). Interdependence and interpersonal attraction among heterogeneous and homogeneous individuals: A theoretical formulation and a meta-analysis of the research. *Review of Educational Research, 53,* 5–54.

Johnson, H., & Smith, L. B. (1981). Children's inferential abilities in the context of reading to understand. *Child Development, 52,* 1216–1223.

Johnson, J., & Newport, E. (1989). Critical period effects in second language learning: The influence of maturational state on the acquisition of English as a second language. *Cognitive Psychology, 21,* 60–99.

Johnson, M. H., Dziurawiec, S., Ellis, H., & Morton, J. (1991). Newborns' preferential tracking of face-like stimuli and its subsequent decline. *Cognition, 40,* 1–19.

Johnson, W., Emde, R. N., Pannabecker, B., Stenberg, C., & Davis, M. (1982). Maternal perception of infant emotion from birth through 18 months. *Infant Behavior and Development, 5,* 313–322.

Johnston, J., & Ettema, J. S. (1982). *Positive images.* Newbury Park, CA: Sage.

Jones, D. S., Byers, R. H., Bush, T. J., Oxtoby, M. J., & Rogers, M. F. (1992). Epidemiology of transfusion-associated acquired immunodeficiency syndrome in children in the United States, 1981 through 1989. *Pediatrics, 89,* 123–127.

Jones, K. L., Smith, D. W., Ulleland, C. N., & Streissguth, A. P. (1973). Pattern of malformation in offspring of chronic alcoholic mothers. *Lancet, 1,* 1267–1271.

Jones, M. C. (1924). A laboratory study of fear: The case of Peter. *Pedagogical Seminary, 31,* 308–315.

Jones, M. C. (1965). Psychological correlates of somatic development. *Child Development, 36,* 899–911.

Jones, M. C., & Bayley, N. (1950). Physical maturing among boys as related to behavior. *Journal of Educational Psychology, 41,* 129–148.

Joos, S. K., Pollitt, E., Mueller, W. H., & Albright, D. L. (1983). The bacon chow study: Maternal nutritional supplementation and infant behavioral development. *Child Development, 54,* 669–676.

Jose, P. M. (1990). Just world reasoning in children's immanent justice arguments. *Child Development, 61,* 1024–1033.

Jusczyk, P. W., Cutler, A., & Redanz, N. J. (1993). Infants' preference for the predominant stress patterns of English words. *Child Development, 64,* 675–687.

Jussim, L., & Eccles, J. S. (1992). Teacher expectations. II: Construction and reflection of student achievement. *Journal of Personality and Social Psychology, 63,* 947–961.

Justice, E. M. (1985). Categorization as a preferred memory strategy: Developmental changes during elementary school. *Developmental Psychology, 21,* 1105–1110.

Kagan, J. (1972). Do infants think? *Scientific American, 226,* 74–82.

Kagan, J. (1976). Emergent themes in human development. *American Scientist, 64,* 186–196.

Kagan, J. (1984). *The nature of the child.* New York: Basic Books.

Kagan, J. (1989). The concept of behavioral inhibition to the unfamiliar. In J. S. Reznick (Ed.), *Perspectives on behavioral inhibition.* Chicago: University of Chicago Press.

Kagan, J. (1991). Continuity and discontinuity. In S. E. Brauth, W. S. Hall, & R. J. Dooling (Eds.), *Plasticity of development.* Cambridge, MA: Bradford/MIT Press.

Kagan, J., Kearsley, R. B., & Zelazo, P. R. (1978). *Infancy: Its place in human development.* Cambridge, MA: Harvard University Press.

Kagan, J., & Moss, H. A. (1962). *Birth to maturity.* New York: Wiley.

Kagan, J., Reznick, J. S., & Gibbons, J. (1989). Inhibited and uninhibited types of children. *Child Development, 60,* 838–845.

Kagan, J., Reznick, J. S., & Snidman, N. (1988). Biological bases of childhood shyness. *Science, 240,* 167–171.

Kahan, L. D., & Richards, D. D. (1986). The effects of context on referential communication strategies. *Child Development, 57,* 1130–1141.

Kahn, P. H., Jr. (1992). Children's obligatory and discretionary moral judgments. *Child Development, 63,* 416–430.

Kail, R. (1991). Processing time declines exponentially during childhood and adolescence. *Developmental Psychology, 27,* 259–266.

Kail, R. (1992). Processing speed, speech rate, and memory. *Developmental Psychology, 28,* 899–904.

Kail, R., & Bisanz, J. (1992). The information-processing perspective on cognitive development in childhood and adolescence. In R. J. Sternberg & C. A. Berg (Eds.), *Intellectual development.* New York: Cambridge University Press.

Kaitz, M., Meschulach-Sarfaty, O., Auerbach, J., & Eidelman, A. (1988). A reexamination of newborns' ability to imitate facial expressions. *Developmental Psychology, 24,* 3–7.

Kandel, D. (1973). Adolescent marijuana use: Role of parents and peers. *Science, 181,* 1067–1070.

Kanfer, F. H., Stifter, E., & Morris, S. J. (1981). Self-control and altruism: Delay of gratification for another. *Child Development, 52,* 674–682.

Kant, I. (1958). *Critique of pure reason.* New York: Modern Library. (Original work published 1781)

Kaplan, B. (1983). A trio of trials. In R. M. Lerner (Ed.), *Developmental psychology: Historical and philosophical perspectives.* Hillsdale, NJ: Erlbaum.

Kaplan, B. J. (1986). A psychobiological review of depression during pregnancy. *Psychology of Women Quarterly, 10,* 35–48.

Katcher, A. (1955). The discrimination of sex differences by young children. *Journal of Genetic Psychology, 87,* 131–143.

Katz, P. A. (1979). The development of female identity. *Sex Roles, 5,* 155–178.

Katz, P. A., & Walsh, P. V. (1991). Modification of children's gender-stereotyped behavior. *Child Development, 62,* 338–351.

Katz, V. L., Jenkins, T., Haley, L., & Bowes, W. A. (1991). Catecholamine levels in pregnant physicians and nurses: A pilot study of stress and pregnancy. *Obstetrics and Gynecology, 77,* 338–342.

Kaufman, A. S., Kamphaus, R. W., & Kaufman, N. L. (1985). New directions in intelligence testing: The Kaufman Assessment Battery for Children (K-ABC). In B. B. Wolman (Ed.), *Handbook of intelligence.* New York: Wiley.

Kaufman, A. S., & Kaufman, N. L. (1983). *Kaufman Assessment Battery for Children: Interpretive manual.* Circle Pines, MN: American Guidance Service.

Kaufman, J., & Zigler, E. (1989). The intergenerational transmission of child abuse. In D. Cicchetti & V. Carlson (Eds.), *Child maltreatment: Theory and research on the causes and consequences of child abuse and neglect.* New York: Cambridge University Press.

Kay, D. W. K. (1989). Genetics, Alzheimer's disease, and senile dementia. *British Journal of Psychiatry, 154,* 311–320.

Kaye, K., & Marcus, J. (1981). Infant imitation: The sensorimotor agenda. *Developmental Psychology, 17,* 258–265.

Kazdin, A. E. (1987). *Conduct disorders in childhood and adolescence.* Newbury Park, CA: Sage.

Kean, A. W. G. (1937). The history of the criminal liability of children. *Law Quarterly Review, 3,* 364–370.

Keane, S. P., Brown, K. P., & Crenshaw, T. M. (1990). Children's intention-cue detection as a function of maternal social behavior: Pathways to social rejection. *Developmental Psychology, 26,* 1004–1009.

Kearins, J. M. (1981). Visual-spatial memory in Australian aboriginal children of desert regions. *Cognitive Psychology, 13,* 434–460.

Keasey, C. B. (1971). Social participation as a factor in the moral development of preadolescents. *Developmental Psychology, 5,* 216–220.

Keating, D., & Clark, L. V. (1980). Development of physical and social reasoning in adolescence. *Developmental Psychology, 16,* 23–30.

Kee, D. W. (1986). Computer play. In A. W. Gottfried & C. C. Brown (Eds.), *Play interactions: The contribution of play materials and parental involvement to children's development.* Lexington, MA: Lexington Books.

Kee, D. W. (1994). Developmental differences in associative memory: Strategy use, mental effort, and knowledge-access interactions. In H. W. Reese (Ed.), *Advances in child development and behavior* (Vol. 25). New York: Academic Press.

Kee, D. W., & Bell, T. S. (1981). The development of organizational strategies in the storage and retrieval of categorical items in free-recall learning. *Child Development, 52,* 1163–1171.

Keith, J. (1985). Age in anthropological research. In R. H. Binstock & E. Shanus (Eds.), *Handbook of aging and the social sciences* (2nd ed.). New York: Van Nostrand Reinhold.

Keller, A., Ford, L. H., Jr., & Meachum, J. A. (1978). Dimensions of self-concept in preschool children. *Developmental Psychology, 14,* 483–489.

Keller, H., & Scholmerich, A. (1987). Infant vocalizations and parental reactions during the first four months of life. *Developmental Psychology, 23,* 62–67.

Kelley, M. L., Power, T. G., & Wimbush, D. D. (1992). Determinants of disciplinary practices in low-income Black mothers. *Child Development, 63,* 573–582.

Kelley-Buchanan, C. (1988). *Peace of mind during pregnancy: An A–Z guide to the substances that could affect your unborn baby.* New York: Facts on File Publications.

Kellman, P. J., & Spelke, E. S. (1983). Perception of partly occluded objects in infancy. *Cognitive Psychology, 15,* 483–524.

Kellman, P. J., Spelke, E. S., & Short, K. R. (1986). Infant perception of object unity from translatory motion in depth and vertical translation. *Child Development, 57,* 72–86.

Kempe, R. S., & Kempe, C. H. (1978). *Child abuse.* Cambridge, MA: Harvard University Press.

Kendall-Tackett, K. A., Williams, L. M., & Finkelhor, D. (1993). Impact of sexual abuse on children: A review and synthesis of recent empirical studies. *Psychological Bulletin, 113,* 164–180.

Kennedy, W. Z., van de Reit, V., White, J. E. (1963). A normative sample of intelligence and achievement of Negro elementary school children in the southeastern United States. *Monographs of the Society for Research in Child Development, 28*(6, Serial No. 90).

Kennell, J., Klaus, M., McGrath, S., Robertson, S., & Hinkley, C. (1991). Continuous emotional support during labor in a U.S. hospital. A randomized controlled trial. *Journal of the American Medical Association, 265,* 2197–2201.

Kennell, J. H., Voos, D. K., & Klaus, M. H. (1979). Parent-infant bonding. In J. D. Osofsky (Ed.), *Handbook of infant development.* New York: Wiley.

Keough, J., & Sugden, D. (1985). *Movement skill development.* New York: Macmillan.

Kermoian, R., & Campos, J. J. (1988). Locomotor experience: A facilitator of spatial cognitive development. *Child Development, 59,* 908–917.

Kerns, K. A. (1994). A longitudinal examination of links between mother-child attachment and children's friendships in early childhood. *Journal of Social and Personal Relationships, 11,* 379–381.

Kerns, K. A., & Berenbaum, S. A. (1991). Sex differences in spatial ability in children. *Behavior Genetics, 21,* 383–396.

Kerr, M., Lambert, W. W., Stattin, H., & Klackenberg-Larsson, I. (1994). Stability of inhibition in a Swedish longitudinal sample. *Child Development, 65,* 138–146.

Kerwin, C., Ponterotto, J. G., Jackson, B. L., & Harris, A. (1993). Racial identity in biracial children: A qualitative investigation. *Journal of Counseling Psychology, 40,* 221–231.

Kessen, W. (1965). *The child.* New York: Wiley.

Kessen, W. (1975). *Childhood in China.* New Haven, CT: Yale University Press.

Kessler, S. (1975). Psychiatric genetics. In D. A. Hamburg & K. Brodie (Eds.), *American handbook of psychiatry. Vol. 6: New psychiatric frontiers.* New York: Basic Books.

Kessner, D. M. (1973). *Infant death: An analysis by maternal risk and health care.* Washington, D.C.: National Academy of Sciences.

Kett, J. F. (1979). *Rites of passage. Adolescence in America, 1790 to the present.* New York: Basic Books.

Kimball, M. M. (1986). Television and sex-role attitudes. In T. Williams (Ed.), *The impact of television: A natural experiment in three communities.* Orlando, FL: Academic Press.

Kimura, D. (1992). Sex differences in the brain. *Scientific American, 267,* 119–125.

Kinney, D. A. (1993). From nerds to normals: The recovery of identity among adolescents from middle school to high school. *Sociology of Education, 66,* 21–40.

Kinsbourne, M. (1989). Mechanisms and development of hemisphere specialization in children. In C. R. Reynolds & E. Fletcher-Janzen (Eds.), *Handbook of clinical child neuropsychology.* New York: Plenum Press.

Kinsey, A. C., Pomeroy, W. B., & Martin, C. E. (1948). *Sexual behavior in the human male.* Philadelphia: Saunders.

Kisilevsky, B. S., & Muir, D. W. (1984). Neonatal habituation and dishabituation to tactile stimulation during sleep. *Developmental Psychology, 20,* 367–373.

Kitchner, K. S., Lynch, C. L., Fischer, K. W., & Wood, P. K. (1993). Developmental range of reflective judgment: The effect of contextual support and practice on developmental stage. *Developmental Psychology, 29,* 893–906.

Kitson, G. C., & Morgan, L. A. (1990). The multiple consequences of divorce: A decade review. *Journal of Marriage and the Family, 52,* 913–924.

Klahr, D. (1992). Information-processing approaches to cognitive development. In M. H. Bornstein & M. E. Lamb (Eds.), *Developmental psychology: An advanced textbook* (3rd ed.). Hillsdale, NJ: Erlbaum.

Klahr, D., & Robinson, M. (1981). Formal assessment of problem-solving and planning processes in preschool children. *Cognitive Psychology, 13,* 113–148.

Klaus, M. H., & Kennell, J. H. (1976). *Maternal-infant bonding.* St. Louis: C. V. Mosby.

Klaus, M. H., & Kennell, J. H. (1982). *Parent-infant bonding.* St. Louis: C. V. Mosby.

Klee, L. (1986). Home away from home: The alternative birth center. *Social Science and Medicine, 23,* 9–16.

Klesges, R. C., Marlott, J. M., Bosbee, P. F., & Weber, J. M. (1986). The effect of parental influences on children's food intake, physical activity, and relative weight. *International Journal of Eating Disorders, 5,* 335–346.

Klimes-Dougan, B., & Kistner, J. (1990). Physically abused preschoolers' responses to peers' distress. *Developmental Psychology, 26,* 599–602.

Kline, M., Tschann, J. M., Johnston, J. R., & Wallerstein, J. S. (1989). Children's adjustment to joint and sole physical custody families. *Developmental Psychology, 25,* 430–438.

Klineberg, O. (1963). Negro-white differences in intelligence test performance: A new look at an old problem. *American Psychologist, 18,* 198–203.

Klinnert, M. D., Emde, R. N., Butterfield, P., & Campos, J. J. (1986). Social referencing: The infant's use of emotional signals from a friendly adult with mother present. *Developmental Psychology, 22,* 427–432.

Knight, G. P., Bernal, M. E., Garza, C. A., Cota, M. K., & Ocampo, K. A. (1993). Family socialization and the ethnic identity of Mexican-American children. *Journal of Cross Cultural Psychology, 24,* 99–114.

Kobak, R. R., Cole, H. E., Ferenz-Gilles, R., Fleming, W. S., & Gamble, W. (1993). Attachment and emotional regulation during mother-teen problem solving. A control theory analysis. *Child Development, 64,* 231–245.

Kochanska, G. (1992). Children's interpersonal influence with mothers and peers. *Developmental Psychology, 28,* 491–499.

Kochanska, G. (1993). Toward a synthesis of parental socialization and child temperament in early development of conscience. *Child Development, 64,* 325–347.

Kochanska, G., De Vet, K., Goldman, M., Murray, K., & Putnam, S. P. (1994). Maternal reports of conscience development and temperament in young children. *Child Development, 65,* 852–868.

Koestner, R., Zuroff, D. C., & Powers, T. A. (1991). Family origins of adolescent self-criticism and its continuity into adulthood. *Journal of Abnormal Psychology, 100,* 191–197.

Kogan, N. (1983). Stylistic variation in childhood and adolescence: Creativity, metaphor, and cognitive styles. In J. H. Flavell & E. H. Markman (Eds.), *Handbook of child psychology: Vol. 3. Cognitive development* (4th ed.). New York: Wiley.

Kohlberg, L. (1963). The development of children's orientations toward a moral order. I: Sequence in the development of moral thought. *Vita Humana, 6,* 11–33.

Kohlberg, L. (1966). A cognitive-developmental analysis of children's sex-role concepts and attitudes. In E. E. Maccoby (Ed.), *The development of sex differences.* Stanford, CA: Stanford University Press.

Kohlberg, L. (1975, June). The cognitive-developmental approach to moral education. *Phi Delta Kappan,* 670–677.

Kohlberg, L. (1981). *Essays on moral development. Vol. 1: The philosophy of moral development.* San Francisco: Harper & Row.

Kohlberg, L. (1984). *Essays on moral development. Vol. 2: The psychology of moral development.* San Francisco: Harper & Row.

Kohlberg, L., Yaeger, J., & Hjertholm, E. (1968). Private speech: Four studies and a review of theories. *Child Development, 39,* 691–736.

Kohn, M. L. (1979). The effects of social class on parental values and practices. In D. Reiss & H. A. Hoffman (Eds.), *The American family: Dying or developing?* New York: Plenum.

Kolata, G. B. (1986). Obese children: A growing problem. *Science, 232,* 20–21.

Kolb, B., & Fantie, B. (1989). Development of the child's brain and behavior. In C. R. Reynolds & E. Fletcher-Janzen (Eds.), *Handbook of clinical child neuropsychology.* New York: Plenum Press.

Kopp, C. B. (1983). Risk factors in development. In M. M. Haith & J. J. Campos (Eds.), *Handbook of child psychology. Vol. 2: Infancy and developmental psychobiology.* New York: Wiley.

Kopp, C. B. (1987). The growth of self-regulation: Caregivers and children. In N. Eisenberg (Ed.), *Contemporary topics in developmental psychology.* New York: Wiley.

Kopp, C. B. (1989). Regulation of distress and negative emotions: A developmental view. *Developmental Psychology, 25,* 343–354.

Kopp, C. B., & Kahler, S. R. (1989). Risk in infancy. *American Psychologist, 44,* 224–230.

Kopp, C. B., & Krakow, J. B. (1982). *The child: Development in a social context.* Reading, MA: Addison-Wesley.

Korner, A. F. (1972). State as a variable, as obstacle and as mediator of stimulation in infant research. *Merrill Palmer Quarterly, 18,* 77–94.

Kortenhaus, C. M., & Demarest, J. (1993). Gender role stereotyping in children's literature: An update. *Sex Roles, 28,* 219–232.

Kraus, M. A., & Redman, E. S. (1986). Postpartum depression: An interactional view. *Journal of Marital and Family Therapy, 12,* 63–74.

Krauss, R. M., & Glucksberg, S. (1977). Social and nonsocial speech. *Scientific American, 236,* 100–105.

Kreutzer, M. A., Leonard, C., & Flavell, J. H. (1975). An interview study of children's knowledge about memory. *Monographs of the Society for Research in Child Development, 40*(1, Serial No. 159).

Kroger, J. (1988). A longitudinal study of ego identity status interview domains. *Journal of Adolescence, 11,* 49–64.

Kroll, J. (1977). The concept of childhood in the Middle Ages. *Journal of the History of the Behavioral Sciences, 13,* 384–393.

Kruger, A. C. (1992). The effect of peer and adult-child transductive discussions on moral reasoning. *Merrill-Palmer Quarterly, 38,* 191–211.

Kruger, A. C., & Tomasello, M. (1986). Transactive discussions with peers and adults. *Developmental Psychology, 22,* 681–685.

Krumhansl, C. L., & Jusczyk, P. W. (1990). Infants' perception of phrase structure in music. *Psychological Science, 1,* 70–73.

Kuchuk, A., Vibbert, M., & Bornstein, M. H. (1986). The perception of smiling and its experiential correlates in three-month-old infants. *Child Development, 57,* 1054–1061.

Kuczynski, L. (1983). Reasoning, prohibitions, and motivations for compliance. *Developmental Psychology, 19,* 126–134.

Kuczynski, L., & Kochanska, G. (1990). Development of children's noncompliance strategies from toddlerhood to age 5. *Developmental Psychology, 26,* 398–408.

Kuczynski, L., Zahn-Waxler, C., & Radke-Yarrow, M. (1987). Development and content of imitation in the second and third years of life: A socialization perspective. *Developmental Psychology, 23,* 276–282.

Kuebli, J., & Fivush, R. (1992). Gender differences in parent-child conversations about past emotions. *Sex Roles, 27,* 683–698.

Kuhl, P. K. (1991). Perception, cognition, and the ontogenetic and phylogenetic emergence of human speech. In S. E. Brauth, W. S. Hall, & R. J. Dooling (Eds.), *Plasticity of development.* Cambridge, MA: Bradford/MIT Press.

Kuhn, D. (1992). Cognitive development. In M. H. Bornstein & M. E. Lamb (Eds.), *Developmental psychology: An advanced textbook* (3rd ed.). Hillsdale, NJ: Erlbaum.

Kuhn, D., Kohlberg, L., Langer, J., & Haan, N. (1977). The development of formal operations in logical and moral judgment. *Genetic Psychology Monographs, 95,* 97–188.

Kuhn, D., Nash, S. C., & Brucken, L. (1978). Sex-role concepts of two- and three-year-olds. *Child Development, 49,* 445–451.

Kulik, J. A., & Kulik, C. C. (1992). Meta-analytic findings on grouping programs. *Gifted Child Quarterly, 36,* 73–77.

Kunkel, D., & Roberts, D. (1991). Young minds and marketplace value: Issues in children's advertising. *Journal of Social Issues, 47*(1), 57–72.

Kunzinger, E. L., III (1985). A short-term longitudinal study of memorial development during early grade school. *Developmental Psychology, 21,* 642–646.

Kupersmidt, J. B., & Coie, J. D. (1990). Preadolescent peer status, aggression, and school adjustment as predictors of externalizing problems in adolescence. *Child Development, 61,* 1350–1362.

Kurdek, L. A., Blisk, D., & Siesky, A. E., Jr. (1981). Correlates of children's long-term adjustment to their parents' divorce. *Developmental Psychology, 17,* 565–579.

Kurdek, L. A., & Fine, M. A. (1994). Family acceptance and family control as predictors of adjustment in young adolescents: Linear, curvilinear, or interactive effects? *Child Development, 65,* 1137–1146.

Kurdek, L. A., & Krile, D. (1982). A developmental analysis of the relation between peer acceptance and both interpersonal understanding and perceived social self-competence. *Child Development, 53,* 1485–1491.

Kurtines, W. M. (1986). Moral behavior as rule governed behavior: Person and situation effects on moral decision making. *Journal of Personality and Social Psychology, 50,* 784–791.

Kurtz, B. E. (1990). Cultural influences on children's cognitive and meta-cognitive development. In W. Schneider & F. E. Weinart (Eds.), *Interactions among aptitude, strategies, and knowledge in cognitive performance.* Hillsdale, NJ: Erlbaum.

La Barbera, J. D., Izard, C. E., Vietze, P., & Parisi, S. A. (1976). Four- and six-month-old infants' visual responses to joy, anger, and neutral expressions. *Child Development, 47,* 535–538.

Laboratory of Comparative Human Cognition (1983). Culture and cognitive development. In W. Kessen (Ed.), *Handbook of child psychology: Vol. 1: History, theory, and methods* (4th ed.). New York: Wiley.

Ladd, G. W. (1990). Having friends, keeping friends, making friends, and being liked by peers in the classroom: Predictors of children's early school adjustment. *Child Development, 61,* 1081–1100.

Ladd, G. W., & Golter, B. S. (1988). Parents' management of preschoolers' peer relations: Is it related to children's social competence? *Developmental Psychology, 24,* 109–117.

Ladd, G. W., & Hart, C. H. (1992). Creating informal play opportunities: Are parents' and preschoolers' initiations related to children's competence with peers? *Developmental Psychology, 28,* 1179–1187.

Ladd, G. W., Lange, G., & Stremmel, A. (1983). Personal and situational influences on children's helping behavior: Factors that mediate compliant helping. *Child Development, 54,* 488–501.

Ladd, G. W., & Price, J. M. (1987). Predicting children's social and school adjustment following the transition from preschool to kindergarten. *Child Development, 58,* 1168–1189.

Ladd, G. W., Price, J. M., & Hart, C. H. (1988). Predicting preschoolers' play status from their playground behavior. *Child Development, 59,* 986–992.

La Freniere, P., Strayer, F. F., & Gauthier, R. (1984). The emergence of same-sex affiliative preferences among preschool peers: A developmental ethological perspective. *Child Development, 55,* 1958–1965.

Lamaze, F. (1958). *Painless childbirth: Psychoprophylactic method.* London: Burke.

Lamb, M. E. (1975). Fathers: Forgotten contributors to child development. *Human Development, 18,* 245–266.

Lamb, M. E. (1981). *The role of the father in child development.* New York: Wiley.

Lamb, M. E., Easterbrooks, M. A., & Holden, G. W. (1980). Reinforcement and punishment among preschoolers: Characteristics, effects, and correlates. *Child Development, 51,* 1230–1236.

Lamb, M. E., & Elster, A. B. (1985). Adolescent mother-infant-father relationships. *Developmental Psychology, 21,* 768–773.

Lamb, M. E., Hwang, C., Bookstein, F. L., Broberg, A., Hult, G., & Frodi, M. (1988). Determinants of social competence in Swedish preschoolers. *Developmental Psychology, 24,* 58–70.

Lamb, M. E., & Oppenheim, D. (1989). Fatherhood and father-child relations. Five years of research. In S. H. Cath, A. Gurwitt, & L. Gunsberg (Eds.), *Fathers and their families.* Hillsdale, NJ: Erlbaum.

Lamb, M. E., Sternberg, K. J., & Prodromidis, M. (1992). Nonmaternal care and the security of infant-mother attachment: A reanalysis of the data. *Infant Behavior and Development, 15,* 71–83.

Lamborn, S. D., Mounts, N. S., Steinberg, L., & Dornbusch, S. M. (1991). Patterns of competence and adjustment among adolescents from authoritative, authoritarian, indulgent, and neglectful families. *Child Development, 62,* 1049–1065.

Lamborn, S. D., & Steinberg, L. (1993). Emotional autonomy redux: Revising Ryan and Lynch. *Child Development, 64,* 483–499.

Landau, S., Milich, S., & Lorch, E. P. (1992). Visual attention to and comprehension of television in attention-deficit hyperactivity disordered and normal boys. *Child Development, 63,* 928–937.

Langlois, J. H. (1986). From the eye of the beholder to behavioral reality: Development of social behaviors and social relations as a function of physical attractiveness. In C. P. Herman, M. P. Zanna, & E. T. Higgins (Eds.), *Physical appearance, stigma, and social behavior: The Ontario Symposium* (Vol. 3). Hillsdale, NJ: Erlbaum.

Langlois, J. H., & Downs, A. C. (1979). Peer relations as a function of physical attractiveness: The eye of the beholder or behavioral reality. *Child Development, 50,* 409–418.

Langlois, J. H., & Downs, A. C. (1980). Mothers, fathers, and peers as socialization agents of sex-typed play behaviors in young children. *Child Development, 51,* 1237–1247.

Langlois, J. H., Ritter, J. M., Roggman, L. A., & Vaughn, L. S. (1991). Facial diversity and infant preferences for attractive faces. *Developmental Psychology, 27,* 79–84.

Langlois, J. H., Roggman, L. A., Casey, R. J., Ritter, J. M., Reiser-Danner, L. A., & Jenkins, V. Y. (1987). Infant preferences for attractive faces: Rudiments of a stereotype? *Developmental Psychology, 23,* 363–369.

Langlois, J. H., Roggman, L. A., & Rieser-Danner, L. A. (1990). Infants' differential social responses to attractive and unattractive faces. *Developmental Psychology, 26,* 153–159.

Lanza, E. (1992). Can bilingual 2-year-olds code-switch? *Journal of Child Language, 19,* 633–658.

Laosa, L. M. (1981). Maternal behavior: Sociocultural diversity in modes of family interaction. In R. W. Henderson (Ed.), *Parent-child interaction: Theory, research, and prospects.* Orlando, FL: Academic Press.

Lapsley, D. K., Milstead, M., Quintana, S. M., Flannery, D., & Buss, R. R. (1986). Adolescent egocentrism and formal operations: Tests of a theoretical assumption. *Developmental Psychology, 22,* 800–807.

Larson, R., & Ham, M. (1993). Stress and "storm and stress" in early adolescence: The relationship of negative events with dysphoric affect. *Developmental Psychology, 29,* 130–140.

Laupa, M. (1991). Children's reasoning about three authority attributes: Adult status, knowledge, and social position. *Developmental Psychology, 27,* 321–329.

Lazar, I., & Darlington, R. (1982). Lasting effects of early education: A report from the Consortium for Longitudinal Studies. *Monographs of the Society for Research in Child Development, 47*(2–3, Serial No. 195).

Leboyer, F. (1975). *Birth without violence.* New York: Knopf.

Lee, V. E., Brooks-Gunn, J., & Schnur, E. (1988). Does Head Start work? A 1-year follow-up comparison of disadvantaged children attending Head Start, no preschool, and other preschool programs. *Developmental Psychology, 24,* 210–222.

Lee, V. E., Brooks-Gunn, J., Schnur, E., & Liaw, F. (1990). Are Head Start efforts sustained? A longitudinal follow-up comparison of disadvantaged children attending Head Start, no preschool, and other preschool programs. *Child Development, 61,* 495–507.

Lefkowitz, M. M. (1981). Smoking during pregnancy: Long-term effects on offspring. *Developmental Psychology, 17,* 192–194.

Lefkowitz, M. M., & Tesiny, E. P. (1984). Rejection and depression: Prospective and contemporaneous analyses. *Developmental Psychology, 20,* 776–785.

Leinbach, M. D., & Fagot, B. I. (1986). Acquisition of gender labeling: A test for toddlers. *Sex Roles, 15,* 655–666.

Leinbach, M. D., & Fagot, B. I. (1993). Categorical habituation to male and female faces: Gender schematic processing in infancy. *Infant Behavior and Development, 16,* 317–322.

LeMare, L. J., & Rubin, K. H. (1987). Perspective taking and peer interaction: Structural and developmental analyses. *Child Development, 58,* 306–315.

Lenneberg, E. H. (1967). *Biological foundations of language.* New York: Wiley.

Leon, M. (1984). Rules mothers and sons use to integrate intent and damage information in their moral judgments. *Child Development, 55,* 2106–2113.

Lepper, M. R. (1983). Social control processes and the internalization of social values. In E. T. Higgins, D. N. Ruble, & W. W. Hartup (Eds.), *Social cognition and social behavior: A developmental perspective.* San Francisco: Jossey-Bass.

Lepper, M. R. (1985). Microcomputers in education: Motivation and social issues. *American Psychologist, 40,* 1–18.

Lepper, M. R., Greene, D., & Nisbett, R. E. (1973). Undermining children's intrinsic interest with extrinsic reward: A test of the overjustification hypothesis. *Journal of Personality and Social Psychology, 28,* 129–137.

Lepper, M. R., & Gurtner, J. (1989). Children and computers: Approaching the twenty-first century. *American Psychologist, 44,* 170–178.

Lepper, M. R., & Hodell, M. (1988). Intrinsic motivation in the classroom. In C. Ames & R. Ames (Eds.), *Research on motivation in education* (Vol. 3). Orlando, FL: Academic Press.

Leppert, P. C., Namerow, P. B., & Barker, D. (1986). Pregnancy outcomes among adolescent and older women receiving comprehensive prenatal care. *Journal of Adolescent Health Care, 7,* 112–117.

Lerner, J. V. (1993). The influence of child temperamental characteristics on parent behaviors. In T. Luster & L. Okagaki (Eds.), *Parenting. An ecological perspective.* Hillsdale, NJ: Erlbaum.

Lerner, J. V., & Galambos, N. L. (1988). The influence of maternal employment across life: The New York Longitudinal Study. In A. E. Gottfried & A. W. Gottfried (Eds.), *Maternal employment and children's development: Longitudinal research.* New York: Plenum.

Lerner, J. V., Nitz, K., Talwar, R., & Lerner, R. M. (1989). On the functional significance of temperamental individuality: A developmental contextual view of the concept of goodness of fit. In G. A. Kohnstamm, J. E. Bates, & M. K. Rothbart (Eds.), *Temperament in childhood.* Chichester, England: John Wiley and Sons.

Lerner, R. M. (1991). Changing organism-context relations as the basic process of development: A developmental contextual perspective. *Developmental Psychology, 27,* 27–32.

Leroy, M. (1988). *Miscarriage.* London: Macdonald & Company.

Lester, B. M. (1984). A biosocial model of infant crying. In L. P. Lipsitt (Ed.), *Advances in infancy research.* Norwood, NJ: Ablex.

Lester, B. M., Corwin, M. J., Sepkoski, C., Seifer, R., Peucker, M., McLaughlin, S., & Golub, H. L. (1991). Neurobehavioral syndromes in cocaine-exposed newborn infants. *Child Development, 62,* 694–705.

Lester, B. M., & Dreher, M. (1989). Effects of marijuana use during pregnancy on newborn cry. *Child Development, 60,* 765–771.

Lester, B. M., Hoffman, J., & Brazelton, T. B. (1985). The rhythmic structure of mother-infant interactions in term and preterm infants. *Child Development, 56,* 15–27.

Lester, B. M., Kotelchuck, M., Spelke, E., Sellers, M. J., & Klein, R. E. (1974). Separation protest in Guatemalan infants: Cross-cultural and cognitive findings. *Developmental Psychology, 10,* 79–85.

Levin, I., & Druyan, S. (1993). When sociocognitive transaction among peers fails: The case of misconceptions in science. *Child Development, 64,* 1571–1591.

LeVine, R. A. (1974). Parental goals: A cross-cultural view. *Teachers College Record, 76,* 226–239.

LeVine, R. A., & LeVine, S. E. (1988). Parental strategies among the Gusii of Kenya. In R. A. LeVine, P. M. Miller, & M. M. West (Eds.), *Parental behavior in diverse societies.* San Francisco: Jossey-Bass.

Levinson, D. (1989). *Family violence in cross-cultural perspective.* Newbury Park, CA: Sage.

Levitt, M. J., Weber, R. A., Clark, M. C., & McDonnell, P. (1985). Reciprocity of exchange in toddler sharing behavior. *Developmental Psychology, 21,* 122–123.

Levy, G. D., & Carter, D. B. (1989). Gender schema, gender constancy, and gender-role knowledge: The roles of cognitive factors in preschoolers' gender-role stereotype attributions. *Developmental Psychology, 25,* 444–449.

Levy-Shiff, R., Goldschmidt, I., & Har-Even, D. (1991). Transition to parenthood in adoptive families. *Developmental Psychology, 27,* 131–140.

Levy-Shiff, R., & Israelashvili, R. (1988). Antecedents of fathering: Some further exploration. *Developmental Psychology, 24,* 434–440.

Lewin, L. M., Hops, H., Davis, B., & Dishion, T. J. (1993). Multimethod comparison of similarity in school adjustment of siblings and unrelated children. *Developmental Psychology, 24,* 963–969.

Lewin, M., & Tragos, L. M. (1987). Has the feminist movement influenced adolescent sex role attitudes? A reassessment after a quarter century. *Sex Roles, 16,* 125–135.

Lewin, R. (1975, September). Starved brains. *Psychology Today,* 29–33.

Lewis, M., Alessandri, S. M., & Sullivan, M. W. (1990). Violation of expectancy, loss of control, and anger expressions in young infants. *Developmental Psychology, 26,* 745–751.

Lewis, M., Alessandri, S. M., & Sullivan, M. W. (1992). Differences in shame and pride as a function of children's gender and task difficulty. *Child Development, 63,* 630–638.

Lewis, M., & Brooks-Gunn, J. (1979). *Social cognition and the acquisition of self.* New York: Plenum Press.

Lewis, M., & Rosenblum, M. A. (1975). *Friendship and peer relations.* New York: Wiley.

Lewis, M., Stanger, C., & Sullivan, M. W. (1989). Deception in 3-year-olds. *Developmental Psychology, 24,* 434–440.

Lewis, M., Sullivan, M. W., Stanger, C., & Weiss, M. (1989). Self-development and self-conscious emotions. *Child Development, 60,* 146–156.

Lewkowicz, D. J. (1988). Sensory dominance in infants. 1: Six-month-old infants' response to auditory-visual compounds. *Developmental Psychology, 24,* 155–171.

Lewontin, R. C. (1976). Race and intelligence. In N. J. Block & G. Dworkin (Eds.), *The IQ controversy.* New York: Pantheon.

Leyens, J. P., Parke, R. D., Camino, L., & Berkowitz, L. (1975). Effects of movie violence on aggression in a field setting as a function of group dominance and cohesion. *Journal of Personality and Social Psychology, 32,* 346–360.

Liben, L. S., & Signorella, M. L. (1993). Gender-schematic processing in children: The role of initial interrpretations of stimuli. *Developmental Psychology, 29,* 141–149.

Lickona, T. (1976). Research on Piaget's theory of moral development. In T. Lickona (Ed.), *Moral development and behavior.* New York: Holt, Rinehart & Winston.

Lieberman, P. (1984). *The biology and evolution of language.* Cambridge, MA: Harvard University Press.

Liebert, R. M., & Baron, R. A. (1972). Some immediate effects of televised violence on children's behavior. *Developmental Psychology, 6,* 469–475.

Liebert, R. M., & Sprafkin, J. (1988). *The early window: Effects of television on children and youth* (3rd ed.). New York: Pergamon Press.

Light, R. J. (1973). Abused and neglected children in America: A study of alternative policies. *Harvard Educational Review, 43,* 556–598.

Lillard, A. S. (1993). Pretend play skills and the child's theory of mind. *Child Development, 64,* 348–371.

Lin, C. (1989). High risk situations: The very low birthweight fetus. In M. I. Evans, J. C. Fletcher, A. O. Dixler, & J. D. Shulman (Eds.), *Fetal diagnosis and Therapy: Science, ethics, and the law.* Philadelphia: J. B. Lippincott.

Lin, C. (1993a). Breech presentation. In C. Lin, M. S. Verp, & R. E. Sabbagha (Eds.), *The high-risk fetus: Pathophysiology, diagnosis, management.* New York: Springer-Verlag.

Lin, C. (1993b). Fetal growth retardation. In C. Lin, M. S. Verp, & R. E. Sabbagha (Eds.), *The high-risk fetus: Pathophysiology, diagnosis, management.* New York: Springer-Verlag.

Lin, C., Verp, M. S., & Sabbagha, R. E. (1993). *The high-risk fetus: Pathophysiology, diagnosis, management.* New York: Springer-Verlag.

Lin, C. C., & Fu, V. R. (1990). A comparison of child-rearing practices among Chinese, immigrant Chinese, and Caucasian-American parents. *Child Development, 61,* 429–433.

Lindberg, M. A. (1980). Is knowledge base development a necessary and sufficient conditon for memory development? *Journal of Experimental Child Psychology, 30,* 401–410.

Lindell, S. G. (1988). Education for childbirth: A time for change. *Journal of Obstetrics, Gynecology, and Neonatal Nursing, 17,* 108–112.

Linn, M. C., de Benedictis, T., & Delucchi, K. (1982). Adolescent reasoning about advertisements: Preliminary investigations. *Child Development, 53,* 1599–1613.

Linn, M. C., & Petersen, A. C. (1985). Emergence and characterization of sex differences in spatial ability: A meta-analysis. *Child Development, 56,* 1479–1498.

Linney, J. A., & Seidman, E. (1989). The future of schooling. *American Psychologist, 44,* 336–340.

Lipsitt, L. P. (1979). Critical conditions in infancy: A psychological perspective. *American Psychologist, 34,* 973–980.

Lipsitt, L. P., & Kaye, H. (1964). Conditioned sucking in the human newborn. *Psychonomic Science, 1,* 29–30.

Littenberg, R., Tulkin, S., & Kagan, J. (1971). Cognitive components of separation anxiety. *Developmental Psychology, 4,* 387–388.

Little, A. H., Lipsitt, L. P., & Rovee-Collier, C. K. (1984). Classical conditioning and retention of the infant's eyelid response: Effects of age and interstimulus interval. *Journal of Experimental Child Psychology, 37,* 512–524.

Littschwager, J. C., & Markman, E. M. (1994). Sixteen- and 24-month-olds' use of mutual exclusivity as a default assumption in second-label learning. *Developmental Psychology, 30,* 955–968.

Livesley, W. J., & Bromley, D. B. (1973). *Person perception in childhood and adolescence.* London: Wiley.

Livson, N., & Peskin, H. (1980). Perspectives on adolescence from longitudinal research. In J. Adelson (Ed.), *Handbook of adolescent psychology.* New York: Wiley.

Lobel, T. E., & Menashri, J. (1993). Relations of conceptions of gender-role transgressions and gender constancy to gender-typed toy preferences. *Developmental Psychology, 29,* 150–155.

Locke, J. (1913). *Some thoughts concerning education.* Sections 38 and 40. London: Cambridge University Press. (Original work published 1690).

Locke, J. (1939). An essay concerning human understanding. In E. A. Burtt (Ed.), *The English philosophers from Bacon to Mill.* New York: Modern Library. (Original work published 1690)

Lockheed, M. E. (1986). Reshaping the social order: The case of gender segregation. *Sex Roles, 14,* 617–628.

Loeber, R. (1982). The stability of antisocial behavior: A review. *Child Development, 53,* 1431–1446.

Loehlin, J. C. (1985). Fitting heredity-environment models jointly to twin and adoption data from the California Psychological Inventory. *Behavior Genetics, 15,* 199–221.

Loehlin, J. C. (1992). *Individual Differences and Development Series. Vol. 2: Genes and environment in personality development.* Newbury Park, CA: Sage.

Loehlin, J. C., Lindzey, G., & Spuhler, J. N. (1975). *Race differences in intelligence.* New York: W. H. Freeman.

Loehlin, J. C., & Nichols, R. C. (1976). *Heredity, environment, and personality.* Austin: University of Texas Press.

Loewenstein, G., & Furstenberg, F. (1991). Is teenage sexual behavior rational? *Journal of Applied Social Psychology, 21,* 957–986.

London, P. (1970). The rescuers: Motivational hypotheses about Christians who saved Jews from the Nazis. In J. Macaulay & L. Berkowitz (Eds.), *Altruism and helping behavior.* Orlando, FL: Academic Press.

Long, N., & Forehand, R. (1987). The effects of parental divorce and marital conflict on children: An overview. *Journal of Developmental and Behavioral Pediatrics, 8,* 292–296.

Longstreth, L., Davis, B., Carter, L., Flint, D., Owen, J., Rickert, M., & Taylor, E. (1981). Separation of home intellectual environment and maternal IQ as determinants of child IQ. *Developmental Psychology, 17,* 532–541.

Lonner, W. J., Thorndike, R. M., Forbes, N. E., & Ashworth, C. (1985). The influence of television on measured cognitive abilities. A study with native Alaskan children. *Journal of Cross-Cultural Psychology, 16,* 355–380.

Lorber, J. (1986). Dismantling Noah's ark. *Sex Roles, 14,* 567–580.

Lorenz, K. Z. (1937). The companion in the bird's world. *Auk, 54,* 245–273.

Lorenz, K. Z. (1943). The innate forms of possible experience. *Zeitschrift fur Tierpsychologie, 5,* 233–409.

Lorenz, K. Z. (1966). *On aggression.* San Diego, CA: Harcourt Brace Jovanovich.

Loveland, K. K., & Olley, J. G. (1979). The effect of external reward on interest and quality of task performance in children of high or low intrinsic motivation. *Child Development, 50,* 1207–1210.

Lozoff, B. (1989). Nutrition and behavior. *American Psychologist, 44,* 231–236.

Ludemann, P. M. (1991). Generalized discrimination of positive facial expressions by seven- and ten-month-old infants. *Child Development, 62,* 55–67.

Lummis, M., & Stevenson, H. W. (1990). Gender differences in beliefs and achievement: A cross-cultural study. *Developmental Psychology, 26,* 254–263.

Luria, A. R. (1961). *The role of speech in the regulation of normal and abnormal behavior.* New York: Liveright.

Lustig, J. L., Wolchik, S. A., & Braver, S. L. (1992). Social support in chumships and adjustment in children of divorce. *American Journal of Community Psychology, 20,* 393–399.

Lynch, M. P., Eilers, R. E., Oller, D. K., & Urbano, R. C. (1990). Innateness, experience, and music perception. *Psychological Science, 1,* 272–276.

Lyon, T. D., & Flavell, J. H. (1993). Young children's understanding of forgetting over time. *Child Development, 64,* 789–800.

Lyons-Ruth, K., Alpern, L., & Repacholi, B. (1993). Disorganized infant attachment classification and maternal psychosocial problems as predictors of hostile-aggressive behavior in the preschool classroom. *Child Development, 64,* 572–585.

Lyons-Ruth, K., Connell, D. B., Grunebaum, H. U., & Botein, S. (1990). Infants at social risk: Maternal depression and family support services as mediators of infant development and security of attachment. *Child Development, 61,* 85–98.

Lytton, H. (1990). Child and parent effects in boys' conduct disorder: A reinterpretation. *Developmental Psychology, 26,* 683–697.

Lytton, H., & Romney, D. M. (1991). Parents' differential socialization of boys and girls: A meta-analysis. *Psychological Bulletin, 109,* 267–296.

Maccoby, E. E. (1967). Selective auditory attention in children. In L. P. Lipsitt & C. C. Spiker (Eds.), *Advances in child development and behavior.* Orlando, FL: Academic Press.

Maccoby, E. E. (1980). *Social development.* San Diego, CA: Harcourt Brace Jovanovich.

Maccoby, E. E. (1988). Gender as a social category. *Developmental Psychology, 24,* 755–765.

Maccoby, E. E. (1990). Gender and relationships: A developmental account. *American Psychologist, 45,* 513–520.

Maccoby, E. E. (1992). Family structure and children's adjustment: Is quality of parenting the major mediator? In E. M. Hetherington, W. G. Clingempeel, & Associates, Coping with marital transitions. *Monographs of the Society for Research in Child Development, 57*(2–3, Serial No. 227).

Maccoby, E. E., & Jacklin, C. N. (1974). *The psychology of sex differences.* Stanford, CA: Stanford University Press.

Maccoby, E. E., & Martin, J. A. (1983). Socialization in the context of the family: Parent-child interaction. In P. H. Mussen (Ed.), *Handbook of child psychology. Vol. 4: Socialization, personality, and social development.* New York: Wiley.

MacDonald, K. (1987). Parent-child physical play with rejected, neglected, and popular boys. *Developmental Psychology, 23,* 705–711.

MacDonald, K. (1992). Warmth as a developmental construct: An evolutionary analysis. *Child Development, 63,* 753–773.

MacFarlane, A. (1977). *The psychology of childbirth.* Cambridge, MA: Harvard University Press.

MacGregor, S. N., & Chasnoff, I. J. (1993). Substance abuse in pregnancy. In C. Lin, M. S. Verp, & R. E. Sabbagha (Eds.), *The high-risk fetus: Pathophysiology, diagnosis, management.* New York: Springer-Verlag.

Mac Iver, D., & Reuman, D. A. (1988, April). *Decision-making in the classroom and early adolescents' valuing of mathematics.* Paper presented at the annual meeting of the American Educational Research Association, New Orleans, LA.

MacKay-Soroka, S., Trehub, S. E., & Thorpe, L. A. (1987). Deaf children's referential messages to mother. *Child Development, 58,* 385–394.

MacKay-Soroka, S., Trehub, S. E., & Thorpe, L. A. (1988). Reception of mothers' referential messages by deaf and hearing children. *Developmental Psychology, 24,* 277–285.

MacKinnon-Lewis, C., Volling, B. L., Lamb, M. E., Dechman, K., Rabiner, D., & Curtner, M. E. (1994). A cross-contextual analysis of boys' social competence: From family to school. *Developmental Psychology, 30,* 325–333.

MacPhee, D., Ramey, C. T., & Yeates, K. O. (1984). Home environment and early cognitive development: Implications for intervention. In A. W. Gottfried (Ed.), *Home environment and early cognitive development. Longitudinal research.* Orlando, FL: Academic Press.

Madden, J., Levenstein, P., & Levenstein, S. (1976). Longitudinal IQ outcomes of the mother-child home program. *Child Development, 47,* 1015–1025.

Madden, N. A., & Slavin, R. E. (1983). Mainstreaming students with mild handicaps: Academic and social outcomes. *Review of Educational Research, 53,* 519–569.

Madison, L. S., Madison, J. K., & Adubato, S. A. (1986). Infant behavior and development in relation to fetal movement and habituation. *Child Development, 57,* 1475–1482.

Magenis, R. E., Overton, K. M., Chamberlin, J., Brady, T., & Lorrien, E. (1977). Parental origin of the extra chromosome in Down's syndrome. *Human Genetics, 37,* 7–16.

Mahler, M. S., Pine, F., & Bergman, A. (1975). *The psychological birth of the infant.* New York: Basic Books.

Main, M., & Cassidy, J. (1988). Categories of response to reunion with the parent at age 6: Predictable from infant attachment classifications and stable over a 1-month period. *Developmental Psychology, 24,* 415–426.

Main, M., & George, C. (1985). Responses of abused and disadvantaged toddlers to distress in agemates: A study in the day-care setting. *Developmental Psychology, 21,* 407–412.

Main, M., & Solomon, J. (1990). Procedures for identifying infants as disorganized/disoriented during the Ainsworth Strange Situation. In M. T. Greenberg, D. Cicchetti, & E. M. Cummings (Eds.), *Attachment in the preschool years: Theory, research, and intervention.* Chicago: University of Chicago Press.

Main, M., & Weston, D. R. (1981). The quality of the toddler's relationship to mother and to father: Related to conflict and the readiness to establish new relationships. *Child Development, 52,* 932–940.

Malatesta, C. Z., Culver, C., Tesman, J. R., & Shepard, B. (1989). The development of emotion expression during the first two years of life. *Monographs of the Society for Research in Child Development, 54*(1–2, Serial No. 219).

Malatesta, C. Z., Grigoryev, P., Lamb, C., Albin, M., & Culver, C. (1986). Emotional socialization and expressive development in preterm and full-term infants. *Child Development, 57,* 316–330.

Malatesta, C. Z., & Haviland, J. M. (1982). Learning display rules: The socialization of emotion expression in infancy. *Child Development, 53,* 991–1003.

Malina, R. M. (1990). Physical growth and performance during the transitional years (9–16). In R. Montemayer, G. R. Adams, & T. P. Gullotta (Eds.), *From childhood to adolescence: A transitional period?* Newbury Park, CA: Sage.

Malinosky-Rummell, R., & Hansen, D. J. (1993). Long-term consequences of childhood physical abuse. *Psychological Bulletin, 114,* 68–79.

Mallick, S. K., & McCandless, B. R. (1966). A study of the catharsis of aggression. *Journal of Personality and Social Psychology, 4,* 591–596.

Mangelsdorf, S. (1992). Developmental changes in infant-stranger interaction. *Infant Behavior and Development, 15,* 191–208.

Mangelsdorf, S., Gunnar, M., Kestenbaum, R., Lang, S., & Andreas, D. (1990). Infant proneness-to-distress temperament, maternal personality, and mother-infant attachment. Associations and goodness of fit. *Child Development, 61,* 820–831.

Mannuzza, S., Klein, R. G., Bessler, A., Malloy, P., & LaPadula, M. (1993). Adult outcome of hyperactive boys: Educational achievement, occupational rank, and psychiatric status. *Archives of General Psychiatry, 50,* 565–576.

Marcia, J. E. (1980). Identity in adolescence. In J. Adelson (Ed.), *Handbook of adolescent psychology.* New York: Wiley.

Marcus, D. E., & Overton, W. F. (1978). The development of cognitive gender constancy and sex-role preferences. *Child Development, 49,* 434–444.

Marcus, G. F. (1993). Negative evidence in language acquisition. *Cognition, 46,* 53–85.

Marcus, G. F., Pinker, S., Ullman, M., Hollander, M., Rosen, T. J., & Xu, F. (1992). Overregularization in language acquisition. *Monographs of the Society for Research in Child Development, 57*(4, Serial No. 228).

Marean, G. C., Werner, L. A., & Kuhl, P. K. (1992). Vowel categorization by very young infants. *Developmental Psychology, 28,* 396–405.

Marini, Z., & Case, R. (1994). The development of abstract reasoning about the physical and social world. *Child Development, 65,* 147–159.

Markstrom-Adams, C. (1992). A consideration of intervening factors in adolescent identity formation. In G. R. Adams, T. P. Gullotta, & R. Montemayer (Eds.), *Advances in adolescent development, Vol. 4: Adolescent identity formation.* Newbury Park, CA: Sage.

Markus, G. B., & Zajonc, R. B. (1977). Family configuration and intellectual development: A simulation. *Behavioral Science, 22,* 137–142.

Marsh, H. W. (1989). Age and sex effects in multiple dimensions of self-concept: Preadolescence to early adulthood. *Journal of Educational Psychology, 81,* 417–430.

Marshall, W. A. (1977). *Human growth and its disorders.* Orlando, FL: Academic Press.

Martin, C. L. (1989). Children's use of gender-related information in making social judgments. *Developmental Psychology, 25,* 80–88.

Martin, C. L. (1990). Attitudes and expectations about children with non-traditional gender roles. *Sex Roles, 22,* 151–165.

Martin, C. L., & Halverson, C. F., Jr. (1981). A schematic processing model of sex typing and stereotyping in children. *Child Development, 52,* 1119–1134.

Martin, C. L., & Halverson, C. F., Jr. (1983). The effects of sex-typing schemas on young children's memory. *Child Development, 54,* 563–574.

Martin, C. L., & Halverson, C. F., Jr. (1987). The roles of cognition in sex-roles and sex-typing. In D. B. Carter (Ed.), *Current conceptions of sex roles and sex-typing: Theory and research.* New York: Praeger.

Martin, C. L., & Little, J. K. (1990). The relation of gender understanding to children's sex-typed preferences and gender stereotypes. *Child Development, 61,* 1429–1439.

Martin, G. B., & Clark, R. D., III (1982). Distress crying in neonates: Species and peer specificity. *Developmental Psychology, 18,* 3–9.

Martin, N. G., & Jardine, R. (1986). Eysenck's contributions to behavior genetics. In S. Modgil & C. Modgil (Eds.), *Hans Eysenck: Consensus and controversy.* Philadelphia: Falmer.

Martorell, R. (1980). Interrelationships between diet, infectious disease, and nutritional status. In L. S. Green & F. E. Johnston (Eds.), *Social and biological predictors of nutritional status, physical growth, and neurological development.* New York: Academic Press.

Masataka, N. (1992). Early ontogeny of vocal behavior of Japanese infants in response to maternal speech. *Child Development, 63,* 1177–1185.

Mason, M. G., & Gibbs, J. C. (1993). Social perspective taking and moral judgment among college students. *Journal of Adolescent Research, 8,* 109–123.

Massad, C. M. (1981). Sex-role identity and adjustment during adolescence. *Child Development, 52,* 1290–1298.

Massey, C. M., & Gelman, R. (1988). Preschooler's ability to decide whether a photographed unfamiliar object can move itself. *Developmental Psychology, 24,* 307–317.

Masters, J. C., Ford, M. E., Arend, R., Grotevant, H. D., & Clark, L. V. (1979). Modeling and labeling as integrated determinants of children's sex-typed imitative behavior. *Child Development, 50,* 364–371.

Matejcek, Z., Dytrych, Z., & Schuller, V. (1979). The Prague study of children born from unwanted pregnancies. *International Journal of Mental Health, 7,* 63–74.

Matias, R., & Cohn, J. F. (1993). Are Max-specified infant facial expressions during face-to-face interaction consistent with differential emotions theory? *Developmental Psychology, 29,* 524–531.

Maticka-Tyndale, E. (1991). Modification of sexual activities in the era of AIDS: A trend analysis of adolescent sexual activities. *Youth and Society, 23,* 31–39.

Matthews, K. A., Batson, C. D., Horn, J., & Rosenman, R. H. (1981). "Principles in his nature which interest him in the fortune of others": The heritability of empathic concern for others. *Journal of Personality, 49,* 237–247.

Matula, K. E., Huston, T. L., Grotevant, H. D., & Zamutt, A. (1992). Identity and dating commitment among women and men in college. *Journal of Youth and Adolescence, 21,* 339–356.

Mayer, J. (1975). Obesity during childhood. In M. Winick (Ed.), *Childhood obesity.* New York: Wiley.

Mayer, R. E. (1985). Mathematical ability. In R. J. Sternberg (Ed.), *Human abilities: An information-processing approach.* New York: W. H. Freeman.

Mayes, L. C., & Zigler, E. (1992). An observational study of the affective concomitants of mastery in infants. *Journal of Psychology and Psychiatry, 4,* 659–667.

Maziade, M., Boudreault, M., Cote, R., & Thivierge, J. (1986). Influence of gentle birth delivery procedures and other perinatal circumstances on infant temperament: Developmental and social implications. *Journal of Pediatrics, 108,* 134–136.

McAdams, D. P. (1990). *The person: An introduction to personality psychology.* San Diego, CA: Harcourt Brace Jovanovich.

McCall, R. B. (1977). Challenges to a science of developmental psychology. *Child Development, 48,* 333–344.

McCall, R. B. (1983). A conceptual approach to early mental development. In M. Lewis (Ed.), *Origins of intelligence. Infancy and early childhood* (2nd ed.). New York: Plenum.

McCall, R. B., Applebaum, M. I., & Hogarty, P. S. (1973). Developmental changes in mental test performance. *Monographs of the Society for Research in Child Development, 38*(3, Serial No. 150).

McCall, R. B., & Carriger, M. S. (1993). A meta-analysis of infant habituation and recognition memory performance as predictors of later IQ. *Child Development, 64,* 57–79.

McCartney, K., Harris, M. J., & Bernieri, F. (1990). Growing up and growing apart: A developmental meta-analysis of twin studies. *Psychological Bulletin, 107,* 226–237.

McClelland, D. C., Atkinson, J. W., Clark, R. A., & Lowell, E. L. (1953). *The achievement motive.* East Norwalk, CT: Appleton-Century-Crofts.

McCormick, C., & Mauer, D. M. (1988). Unimanual hand preference in 6-month-olds: Consistency and relation to familial handedness. *Infant Behavior and Development, 11,* 21–29.

McDonald, R. L. (1968). The role of emotional factors in obstetric complications: A review. *Psychosomatic Medicine, 30,* 222–237.

McGhee, P. E. (1979). *Humor: Its origin and development.* San Francisco: W. H. Freeman.

McGhee, P. E., & Chapman, A. J. (1980). *Children's humour.* London: Wiley.

McGhee, P. E., & Frueh, T. (1980). Television viewing and the learning of sex-role stereotypes. *Sex Roles, 6,* 179–188.

McGhee-Bidlack, B. (1991). The development of noun definitions: A meta-linguistic analysis. *Journal of Child Language, 18,* 417–434.

McGraw, M. B. (1935). *Growth: A study of Johnny and Jimmy.* East Norwalk, CT: Appleton-Century-Crofts.

McGue, M., Bacon, S., & Lykken, D. T. (1993). Personality stability and change in early adulthood: A behavioral genetic analysis. *Developmental Psychology, 29,* 96–109.

McGuire, K. D., & Weisz, J. R. (1982). Social cognition and behavioral correlates of preadolescent chumship. *Child Development, 53,* 1478–1484.

McHale, S. M., & Gamble, W. C. (1989). Sibling relationships of children with disabled and nondisabled brothers and sisters. *Developmental Psychology, 25,* 421–429.

McKenna, J. (1986). An anthropological perspective on the Sudden Infant Death Syndrome (SIDS): The role of parental breathing cues and speech breathing adaptations. *Medical Anthropology, 10,* 90–92.

McKnight, C. C., Crosswhite, F. J., Dossey, J. A., Kifer, E., Swafford, J. O., Travers, K. J., & Cooney, T. J. (1987). *The underachieving curriculum: Assessing U.S. school mathematics from an international perspective.* Champaign, IL: Stipes.

McKusick, V. A. (1989). *Mendelian inheritance in man* (9th ed.). Baltimore: Johns Hopkins University Press.

McLoyd, V. C. (1979). The effects of extrinsic rewards of differential value on high and low intrinsic interest. *Child Development, 50,* 1010–1019.

McLoyd, V. C. (1989). Socialization and development in a changing economy: The effects of paternal job and income loss on children. *American Psychologist, 44,* 293–302.

McLoyd, V. C. (1990). The impact of economic hardship on Black families and children: Psychological distress, parenting, and socioemotional development. *Child Development, 61,* 311–346.

McLoyd, V. C., Jayaratne, T. E., Ceballo, R., & Borquez, J. (1994). Unemployment and work interruption among African-American single mothers: Effects on parenting and adolescent socioemotional functioning. *Child Development, 65,* 562–589.

McNeill, D. (1970). *The acquisition of language.* New York: Harper & Row.

Mead, G. H. (1934). *Mind, self, and society.* Chicago: University of Chicago Press.

Mead, M. (1935). *Sex and temperament in three primitive societies.* New York: William Morrow.

Mead, M., & Newton, N. (1967). Cultural patterning of perinatal behavior. In S. A. Richardson & A. F. Guttmacher (Eds.), *Childbearing: Its social and psychological aspects.* Baltimore: Williams & Wilkins.

Medrich, E. A., Rosen, J., Rubin, V., & Buckley, S. (1982). *The serious business of growing up.* Berkeley: University of California Press.

Meilman, P. W. (1979). Cross-sectional age changes in ego identity status during adolescence. *Developmental Psychology, 15,* 230–231.

Meltzoff, A. N. (1988a). Imitation of televised models by infants. *Child Development, 59,* 1221–1229.

Meltzoff, A. N. (1988b). Infant imitation after a 1-week delay: Long-term memory for novel acts and multiple stimuli. *Developmental Psychology, 24,* 470–476.

Meltzoff, A. N. (1988c). Infant imitation and memory: Nine-month-olds in immediate and deferred tests. *Child Development, 59,* 217–225.

Meltzoff, A. N., & Moore, M. K. (1983). Newborn infants imitate adult facial gestures. *Child Development, 54,* 702–709.

Meltzoff, A. N., & Moore, M. K. (1989). Imitation in newborn infants: Exploring the range of gestures initiated and the underlying mechanisms. *Developmental Psychology, 25,* 954–962.

Mervis, C. B., & Johnson, K. E. (1991). Acquisition of the plural morpheme: A case study. *Developmental Psychology, 27,* 222–235.

Meyer, D. R., & Garasky, S. (1993). Custodial fathers: Myths, realities, and child support policy. *Journal of Marriage and the Family, 55,* 73–89.

Meyer-Bahlburg, H. F. L., Ehrhardt, A. A., Rosen, L. R., Gruen, R. S., Veridiano, N. P., Vann, F. H., & Neuwalder, H. F. (1995). Prenatal estrogens and the development of homosexual orientation. *Developmental Psychology, 31,* 12–21.

Michel, G. F. (1981). Right-handedness: A consequence of infant supine head-orientation preference. *Science, 212,* 685–687.

Midgley, C., Feldlaufer, H., & Eccles, J. S. (1989). Student/teacher relations and attitudes toward mathematics before and after the transition to junior high school. *Child Development, 60,* 981–992.

Midlarsky, E., & Bryan, J. H. (1972). Affect expressions and children's imitative altruism. *Journal of Experimental Research in Personality, 6,* 195–203.

Millar, W. S., & Watson, J. S. (1979). The effect of delayed feedback on infant-learning reexamined. *Child Development, 50,* 747–751.

Miller, C. L. (1983). Developmental changes in male/female voice classification by infants. *Infant Behavior and Development, 6,* 313–330.

Miller, N., & Maruyama, G. (1976). Ordinal position and peer popularity. *Journal of Personality and Social Psychology, 33,* 123–131.

Miller, N. B., Cowan, P. A., Cowan, C. P., Hetherington, E. M., & Clingempeel, W. G. (1993). Externalizing in preschoolers and early adolescents: A cross-study replication of a family model. *Developmental Psychology, 29,* 3–18.

Miller, P. A., & Eisenberg, N. (1988). The relation of empathy to aggressive and externalizing/antisocial behavior. *Psychological Bulletin, 103,* 324–344.

Miller, P. H., & Aloise, P. A. (1989). Young children's understanding of the psychological causes of behavior: A review. *Child Development, 60,* 257–285.

Miller, P. H., & Harris, Y. R. (1988). Preschoolers' strategies of attention on a same-different task. *Developmental Psychology, 24,* 621–633.

Miller, P. H., & Seier, W. L. (1994). Strategy utilization deficiencies in children. In H. W. Reese (Ed.), *Advances in child development and behavior (Vol. 25).* New York: Academic Press.

Miller, P. H., Seier, W. L., Probert, J. S., & Aloise, P. A. (1991). Age differences in the capacity demands of a strategy among spontaneously strategic children. *Journal of Experimental Child Psychology, 52,* 149–165.

Miller, P. H., & Weiss, M. G. (1981). Children's attention allocation, understanding of attention, and performance on the incidental learning task. *Child Development, 52,* 1183–1190.

Miller, P. H., & Weiss, M. G. (1982). Children's and adults' knowledge about what variables affect selective attention. *Child Development, 53,* 543–549.

Miller, P. H., Woody-Ramsey, J., & Aloise, P. A. (1991). The role of strategy effortfulness in strategy effectiveness. *Developmental Psychology, 27,* 738–745.

Mills, R. S. L., & Rubin, K. H. (1990). Parental beliefs about problematic social behaviors in early childhood. *Child Development, 61,* 138–151.

Milstein, R. M. (1980). Responsiveness in newborn infants of overweight and normal weight parents. *Appetite, 1,* 65–74.

Milunsky, A. (1992). *Genetic disorders and the fetus: Diagnosis, prevention, and treatment* (3rd ed.). Baltimore: Johns Hopkins University Press.

Minton, H. L., & Schneider, F. W. (1980). *Differential psychology.* Pacific Grove: Brooks/Cole.

Minuchin, P. P., & Shapiro, E. K. (1983). The school as a context for social development. In P. H. Mussen (Ed.), *Handbook of child psychology. Vol. 4: Socialization, personality, and social development.* New York: Wiley.

Minuchin, S., Rosman, B. L., & Baker, L. (1978). *Psychomatic families: Anorexia nervosa in context.* Cambridge, MA: Harvard University Press.

Mischel, H. N., & Mischel, W. (1983). The development of children's knowledge of self-control strategies. *Child Development, 53,* 603–619.

Mischel, W. (1970). Sex-typing and socialization. In P. H. Mussen (Ed.), *Carmichael's manual of child psychology* (Vol. 2). New York: Wiley.

Mischel, W. (1974). Processes in the delay of gratification. In L. Berkowitz (Ed.), *Advances in experimental social psychology* (Vol. 7). New York: Academic.

Mischel, W. (1986). *Introduction to personality* (4th ed.). New York: Holt, Rinehart & Winston.

Mischel, W., & Baker, N. (1975). Cognitive appraisals and transformations in delay behavior. *Journal of Personality and Social Psychology, 31,* 254–261.

Mischel, W., & Ebbesen, E. B. (1970). Attention in delay of gratification. *Journal of Personality and Social Psychology, 16,* 329–337.

Mischel, W., & Patterson, C. J. (1976). Substantive and structural elements of effective plans for self-control. *Journal of Personality and Social Psychology, 34,* 942–950.

Mischel, W., Shoda, Y., & Peake, P. K. (1988). The nature of adolescent competencies predicted by preschool delay of gratification. *Journal of Personality and Social Psychology, 54,* 687–696.

Mitchell, D. E. (1988). The recovery from early monocular visual deprivation in kittens. In A. Yonas (Ed.), *Minnesota Symposia on Child Psychology. Vol. 20: Perceptual development in infancy.* Hillsdale, NJ: Erlbaum.

Mitchell, D. E., Freeman, R. D., Millodot, M., & Haegerstrom, G. (1973). Meridional amblyopia: Evidence for modification of the human visual system by early visual experience. *Vision Research, 13,* 535–558.

Mitchell, J. E., Baker, L. A., & Jacklin, C. N. (1989). Masculinity and femininity in twin children: Genetic and environmental factors. *Child Development, 60,* 1475–1485.

Mitchell, J. L. (1989). Drug abuse and AIDS in women and their affected offspring. *Journal of the National Medical Association, 81,* 841–842.

Miyawaki, K., Strange, W., Verbrugge, R., Liberman, A. M., Jenkins, J. J., & Fujimura, D. (1975). An effect of linguistic experience: The discrimination of [r] and [l] by native speakers of Japanese and English. *Perception and Psychophysics, 18,* 331–340.

Mize, J., & Ladd, G. W. (1990). A cognitive-social learning approach to social skill training with low-status preschool children. *Developmental Psychology, 26,* 388–397.

Moely, B. E., Hart, S. S., Leal, L., Santulli, K. A., Rao, N., Johnson, T., & Hamilton, L. B. (1992). The teacher's role in facilitating memory and study strategy development in the elementary school classroom. *Child Development, 63,* 653–672.

Moerk, E. L. (1989). The LAD was a lady and the tasks were ill-defined. *Developmental Review, 9,* 21–57.

Mohr, D. M. (1978). Development of attributes of personal identity. *Developmental Psychology, 14,* 427–428.

Molfese, D. L. (1977). Infant cerebral asymmetry. In S. J. Segalowitz & F. A. Gruber (Eds.), *Language development and neurological theory.* Orlando, FL: Academic Press.

Monass, J. A., & Engelhard, J. A., Jr. (1990). Home environment and the competitiveness of accomplished individuals in four talent fields. *Developmental Psychology, 26,* 264–268.

Money, J. (1965). Psychosexual differentiation. In J. Money (Ed.), *Sex research: New developments.* New York: Holt, Rinehart & Winston.

Money, J. (1985). Pediatric sexology and hermaphrodism. *Journal of Sex and Marital Therapy, 11,* 139–156.

Money, J. (1988). *Gay, straight, and in-between: The sexology of erotic orientation.* New York: Oxford University Press.

Money, J., & Ehrhardt, A. (1972). *Man and woman, boy and girl.* Baltimore: Johns Hopkins University Press.

Money, J., & Tucker, P. (1975). *Sexual signatures: On being a man or a woman.* Boston: Little, Brown.

Montemayor, R., & Eisen, M. (1977). The development of self-conceptions from childhood to adolescence. *Developmental Psychology, 13,* 314–319.

Montgomery, D. E. (1993). Young children's understanding of interpretive diversity between different-age listeners. *Developmental Psychology, 29,* 337–345.

Moog, H. (1976). *The musical experience of the preschool child.* London: Schott.

Moore, E. G. J. (1986). Family socialization and the IQ test performance of traditionally and transracially adopted black children. *Developmental Psychology, 22,* 317–326.

Moore, K. L. (1989). *Before we are born* (3rd ed.). Philadelphia: Saunders.

Morelli, G. A., Rogoff, B., Oppenheim, D., & Goldsmith, D. (1992). Cultural variation in infants' sleeping arrangements: Questions of independence. *Developmental Psychology, 28,* 604–613.

Morgan, G. A., & Ricciuti, H. N. (1969). Infants' responses to strangers during the first year. In B. M. Foss (Ed.), *Determinants of infant behavior* (Vol. 4). London: Methuen.

Morgan, M. (1982). Television and adolescents' sex-role stereotypes: A longitudinal study. *Journal of Personality and Social Psychology, 43,* 947–955.

Morison, P., & Masten, A. S. (1991). Peer reputation in middle childhood as a predictor of adaptation in adolescence: A seven-year follow-up. *Child Development, 62,* 991–1007.

Morrison, F. J. (1984). Reading disability: A problem in rule learning and word decoding. *Developmental Review, 4,* 36–47.

Morrison, F. J. (1991, April). *Making the cut: Early schooling and cognitive growth.* Paper presented at the biennial meeting of the Society for Research in Child Development, Seattle, WA.

Morrongiello, B. A., Fenwick, K. D., & Chance, G. (1990). Sound localization activity in very young infants: An observer-based testing procedure. *Developmental Psychology, 26,* 75–84.

Mueller, E., & Lucas, T. (1975). A developmental analysis of peer interactions among toddlers. In M. Lewis & L. Rosenblum (Eds.), *Friendship and peer relations.* New York: Wiley.

Muir, D. W. (1985). The development of infants' auditory spatial sensitivity. In S. E. Trehub & B. Schneider (Eds.), *Advances in the study of communication and affect. Vol. 10: Auditory development in infancy.* New York: Plenum.

Mullis, A. K., Mullis, R. L., & Normandin, D. (1992). Cross-sectional and longitudinal comparisons of adolescent self-esteem. *Adolescence, 27,* 51–61.

Mumford, M. D., & Gustafson, S. B. (1988). Creativity syndrome: Integration, application, and innovation. *Psychological Bulletin, 103,* 27–43.

Mundy, P., Sigman, M., Kasari, C., & Yirmiya, N. (1988). Nonverbal communication skills in Down syndrome children. *Child Development, 59,* 235–249.

Munro, G., & Adams, G. R. (1977). Ego-identity formation in college students and working youth. *Developmental Psychology, 13,* 523–524.

Munroe, R. H., Shimmin, H. S., & Munroe, R. L. (1984). Gender understanding and sex-role preferences in four cultures. *Developmental Psychology, 20,* 673–682.

Murphy, K., & Schneider, B. (1994). Coaching socially-rejected early adolescents regarding behaviors used by peers to infer liking: A dyad-specific intervention. *Journal of Early Adolescence, 14,* 82–94.

Murray, A. D., Dolby, R. M., Nation, R. L., & Thomas, D. B. (1981). Effects of epidural anesthesia on newborns and their mothers. *Child Development, 52,* 71–82.

Murray, L. (1992). The impact of postnatal depression on infant development. *Journal of Child Psychology and Psychiatry and Allied Disciplines, 33,* 543–561.

Mussen, P. H., & Rutherford, E. (1963). Parent-child relations and parental personality in relation to young children's sex-role preferences. *Child Development, 34,* 589–607.

Myers, B. J. (1982). Early intervention using Brazelton training with middle-class mothers and fathers of newborns. *Child Development, 53,* 462–471.

Myers, B. J. (1987). Mother-infant bonding as a critical period. In M. H. Bornstein (Ed.), *Sensitive periods in development: Interdisciplinary perspectives.* Hillsdale, NJ: Erlbaum.

Myers, N. A., Clifton, R. K., & Clarkson, M. G. (1987). When they were very young: Almost-threes remember two years ago. *Infant Behavior and Development, 10,* 123–132.

Myers, R. E. (1980). Reply to Drs. Kron and Brackbill. *American Journal of Obstetrics and Gynecology, 136,* 819–820.

Myers, R. E., & Myers, S. E. (1979). Use of sedative, analgesic, and anesthetic drugs during labor and delivery: Bane or boon? *American Journal of Obstetrics and Gynecology, 133,* 83–104.

Nadler, A. (1986). Help-seeking as a cultural phenomenon: Differences between city and kibbutz dwellers. *Journal of Personality and Social Psychology, 51,* 976–982.

Nadler, A. (1991). Help-seeking behavior: Psychological costs and instrumental benefits. In M. S. Clark (Ed.), *Prosocial behavior.* Newbury Park, CA: Sage.

Naeye, R. L. (1980). Sudden infant death syndrome. *Scientific American, 242*(4), 56–62.

Naeye, R. L., & Peters, E. C. (1984). Mental development of children whose mothers smoked during pregnancy. *Obstetrics and Gynecology, 64,* 601–607.

Naigles, L. (1990). Children use syntax to learn verb meanings. *Journal of Child Language, 17,* 357–374.

Naigles, L. G., & Kako, E. T. (1993). First contact in verb acquisition: Defining a role for syntax. *Child Development, 64,* 1665–1687.

Nanez, J. (1987). Perception of impending collision in 3- to 6-week-old infants. *Infant Behavior and Development, 11,* 447–463.

National Education Goals Panel (1992). *The National Education Goals Report, 1992.* Washington, D.C.: U.S. Department of Education.

Neimark, E. D. (1979). Current status of formal operations research. *Human Development, 22,* 60–67.

Neisser, U. (1980). The concept of intelligence. In R. J. Sternberg & D. K. Detterman (Eds.), *Human intelligence: Perspectives on its theory and measurement.* Norwood, NJ: Ablex.

Nelson, C. A. (1987). The recognition of facial expressions in the first two years of life: Mechanisms of development. *Child Development, 58,* 889–909.

Nelson, E. A., Grinder, R. E., & Biaggio, A. M. B. (1969). Relationships between behavioral, cognitive-developmental, and self-report measures of morality and personality. *Multivariate Behavioral Research, 4,* 483–500.

Nelson, E. A., Grinder, R. E., & Mutterer, M. L. (1969). Sources of variance in behavioral measures of honesty in temptation situations: Methodological analyses. *Developmental Psychology, 1,* 265–279.

Nelson, J., & Aboud, F. E. (1985). The resolution of social conflict among friends. *Child Development, 56,* 1009–1017.

Nelson, K. (1973). Structure and strategy in learning to talk. *Monographs of the Society for Research in Child Development, 38* (1-2, Serial No. 149).

Nelson, K. (1984). The transition from infant to child memory. In M. Moscovitch (Ed.), *Infant memory. Its relation to normal and pathological memory in humans and other animals.* New York: Plenum.

Nelson, K. (1986). *Event knowledge.* Hillsdale, NJ: Erlbaum.

Nelson, K. (1993). The psychological and social origins of autobiographical memory. *Psychological Science, 4,* 7–14.

Nelson, K., Hampson, J., & Shaw, L. K. (1993). Nouns in early lexicons: Evidence, explanations, and implications. *Journal of Child Language, 20,* 61–84.

Nelson, N. M., Enkin, M. W., Saigal, S., Bennet, K. J., Milner, R., & Sackett, D. L. (1980). A randomized clinical trial of the Leboyer approach to childbirth. *New England Journal of Medicine, 302,* 655–660.

Nelson, S. A. (1980). Factors influencing young children's use of motives and outcomes as moral criteria. *Child Development, 51,* 823–829.

Nelson-LeGall, S. A. (1985). Motive-outcome matching and outcome foreseeability: Effects on attribution of intentionality and moral judgments. *Developmental Psychology, 21,* 332–337.

Neuspiel, D. R., & Hamel, S. C. (1991). Cocaine and infant behavior. *Developmental and Behavioral Pediatrics, 12,* 55–64.

Newcomb, M. D., & Bentler, P. M. (1989). Substance use and abuse among children and teenagers. *American Psychologist, 44,* 242–248.

Newcombe, N., & Dubas, J. S. (1987). Individual differences in cognitive ability: Are they related to timing of puberty? In R. M. Lerner & T. T. Foch (Eds.), *Biological-psychosocial interactions in early adolescence: A life-span perspective.* Hillsdale, NJ: Erlbaum.

Newcombe, N., & Dubas, J. S. (1992). A longitudinal study of predictors of spatial ability in adolescent females. *Child Development, 63,* 37–46.

Newcombe, N., & Fox, N. A. (1994). Infantile amnesia: Through a glass darkly. *Child Development, 65,* 31–40.

Newell, A., & Simon, H. A. (1961). Computer simulation of human thinking. *Science, 134,* 2011–2017.

Newport, E. L. (1991). Contrasting conceptions of the critical period for language. In S. Carey & R. Gelman (Eds.), *The epigenesis of mind: Essays on biology and cognition.* Hillsdale, NJ: Erlbaum.

Newport, E. L., Gleitman, H., & Gleitman, L. R. (1977). Mother, I'd rather do it myself: Some effects and non-effects of maternal speech style. In C. E. Snow & C. A. Ferguson (Eds.), *Talking to children: Language input and acquisition.* Cambridge, England: Cambridge University Press.

Nicholls, J. G., & Miller, A. T. (1984). Reasoning about the ability of self and others: A developmental study. *Child Development, 55,* 1990–1999.

Ninio, A., & Rinott, N. (1988). Fathers' involvement in the care of their infants and their attributions of cognitive competence to infants. *Child Development, 59,* 652–663.

Noble, K. D., Robinson, N. M., & Gunderson, S. A. (1993). All rivers lead to the sea: A follow-up study of gifted young adults. *Roeper Review, 15,* 124–130.

Norman-Jackson, J. (1982). Family interactions, language development, and primary reading achievement of Black children in families of low income. *Child Development, 53,* 349–358.

Nottelmann, E. D. (1987). Competence and self-esteem during transition from childhood to adolescence. *Developmental Psychology, 23,* 441–450.

Nucci, L., & Turiel, E. (1993). God's word, religious rules, and their relation to Christian and Jewish children's concepts of morality. *Child Development, 64,* 1475–1491.

Nugent, J. K., Lester, B. M., & Brazelton, T. B. (1989). *Biology, culture, and development* (Vol. 1). Norwood, NJ: Ablex.

Nunner-Winkler, G., & Sodian, S. (1988). Children's understanding of moral emotions. *Child Development, 59,* 1323–1338.

Oakland, T., & Parmelee, R. (1985). Mental measurement of minority-group children. In B. B. Wolman (Ed.), *Handbook of intelligence. Theories, measurements, and applications.* New York: Wiley.

Oates, K. (1986). *Child abuse and neglect: What happens eventually.* New York: Brunner/Mazel.

Ochs, E. (1982). Talking to children in western Samoa. *Language in Society, 11,* 77–104.

O'Connor, B. P., & Nikolic, J. (1990). Identity development and formal operations as sources of adolescent egocentrism. *Journal of Youth and Adolescence, 19,* 149–158.

O'Connor, N., & Hermelin, B. (1991). Talents and preoccupations in idiot-savants. *Psychological Medicine, 21,* 959–964.

Odden, A. (1990). Class size and student achievement: Research-based policy alternatives. *Educational Evaluation and Policy Analysis, 12,* 213–227.

Oden, S., & Asher, S. R. (1977). Coaching children in social skills for friendship making. *Child Development, 48,* 495–506.

O'Donohue, W. T., & Elliott, A. N. (1992). Treatment of the sexually abused child: A review. *Journal of Clinical Child Psychology, 21,* 218–228.

Ogbu, J. U. (1981). Origins of human competence: A cultural-ethological perspective. *Child Development, 52,* 413–429.

Ogbu, J. U. (1988). Black education: A cultural-ecological perspective. In H. P. McAdoo (Ed.), *Black families.* Beverly Hills: Sage.

Ogbu, J. U. (1990). Cultural model, identity, and literacy. In J. W. Stigler, R. A. Shweder, & G. Herdt (Eds.), *Cultural psychology: Essays on comparative human development.* Cambridge, England: Cambridge University Press.

Ogletree, S. M., & Williams, S. W. (1990). Sex and sex-typing effects on computer attitudes and aptitude. *Sex Roles, 23,* 703–712.

O'Hara, M. W., Schlechte, J. A., Lewis, D. A., & Varner, M. W. (1991). Controlled prospective study of postpartum mood disorders: Psychological, environmental, and hormonal variables. *Journal of Abnormal Psychology, 100,* 63–73.

O'Heron, C. A., & Orlofsky, J. L. (1990). Stereotypic and nonstereotypic sex role trait and behavior orientations, gender identity, and psychological adjustment. *Journal of Personality and Social Psychology, 58,* 134–143.

Okagaki, L., & Sternberg, R. J. (1993). Parental beliefs and children's school performance. *Child Development, 64,* 36–56.

Oller, D. K., & Eilers, R. E. (1988). The role of audition in infant babbling. *Child Development, 59,* 441–449.

Olson, G. M., & Sherman, T. (1983). Attention, learning, and memory in infants. In P. H. Mussen (Ed.), *Handbook of child psychology* (Vol. 2). New York: Wiley.

Olthof, T., Ferguson, T. J., & Luiten, A. (1989). Personal responsibility and antecedents of anger and blame reactions in children. *Child Development, 60,* 1326–1336.

Olvera-Ezzell, N., Power, T. G., & Cousins, J. H. (1990). Maternal socialization of children's eating habits: Strategies used by obese Mexican-American mothers. *Child Development, 61,* 395–400.

Olweus, D. (1978). *Aggression in the schools: Bullies and whipping boys.* Washington, D.C.: Hemisphere.

Olweus, D. (1984). Aggressors and their victims: Bullying at school. In H. Frude & H. Gault (Eds.), *Disruptive behaviors in schools.* New York: Wiley.

Olweus, D., Mattsson, A., Schalling, D., & Low, H. (1980). Testosterone, aggression, physical and personality dimensions in normal adolescent males. *Psychosomatic Medicine, 42,* 253–269.

O'Mahoney, J. F. (1989). Development of thinking about things and people: Social and nonsocial cognition during adolescence. *Journal of Genetic Psychology, 150,* 217–224.

Oppenheim, D., Sagi, A., & Lamb, M. E. (1988). Infant-adult attachments on the kibbutz and their relation to socioemotional development 4 years later. *Developmental Psychology, 24,* 427–433.

O'Reilly, A. W., & Bornstein, M. H. (1993). Caregiver-child interaction in play. In M. H. Bornstein & A. W. O'Reilly (Eds.), *The role of play in the development of thought* (New Directions for Child Development, No. 59). San Francisco: Jossey-Bass.

Orlick, T. D. (1981). Positive socialization via cooperative games. *Developmental Psychology, 17,* 426–429.

Orlofsky, J. L. (1979). Parental antecedents of sex-role orientation in college men and women. *Sex Roles, 5,* 495–512.

Orlofsky, J. L., & O'Heron, C. A. (1987). Stereotypic and nonstereotypic sex role trait and behavior organizations: Implications for personal adjustment. *Journal of Personality and Social Psychology, 52,* 1034–1042.

Ornstein, P. A., Medlin, R. G., Stone, B. P., & Naus, M. J. (1985). Retrieving for rehearsal: An analysis of active rehearsal in children's memory. *Developmental Psychology, 21,* 633–641.

Ornstein, P. A., Naus, M. J., & Liberty, C. (1975). Rehearsal and organizational processes in children's memory. *Child Development, 46,* 818–830.

Oster, H., Hegley, D., & Nagel, L. (1992). Adult judgments and fine-grained analysis of infant facial expressions: Testing the validity of a priori coding formulas. *Developmental Psychology, 28,* 1115–1131.

Overton, W. F. (1984). World views and their influence on psychological theory and research: Kuhn-Lakotes-Lunden. In H. W. Reese (Ed.), *Advances in child development and behavior* (Vol. 18). New York: Academic.

Overton, W. F., Ward, S. L., Noveck, I. A., Black, J., & O'Brien, D. P. (1987). Form and content in the development of deductive reasoning. *Developmental Psychology, 23,* 22–30.

Oviatt, S. L. (1980). The emerging ability to comprehend language: An experimental approach. *Child Development, 51,* 97–106.

Paikoff, R. L., & Brooks-Gunn, J. (1991). Do parent-child relationships change during puberty? *Psychological Bulletin, 110,* 47–66.

Palkovitz, R. (1984). Parental attitudes and fathers' interactions with their 5-month-old infants. *Developmental Psychology, 20,* 1054–1060.

Palkovitz, R. (1985). Fathers' birth attendance, early contact, and extended contact with their newborns: A critical review. *Child Development, 56,* 392–406.

Pallak, S. R., Costomiris, S., Sroka, S., & Pittman, T. S. (1982). School experience, reward characteristics, and intrinsic motivation. *Child Development, 53,* 1382–1391.

Palmer, C. F. (1989). The discriminating nature of infants' exploratory actions. *Developmental Psychology, 25,* 885–893.

Palmer, E. L. (1984). Providing quality television for America's children. In J. P. Murray & G. Salomon (Eds.), *The future of children's television.* Boys Town, NE: Boys Town Center.

Papousek, H. (1967). Experimental studies of appetitional behavior in human newborns and infants. In H. W. Stevenson, E. H. Hess, & H. L. Rheingold (Eds.), *Early behavior: Comparative and developmental approaches.* New York: Wiley.

Paris, S. G. (1988). Models and metaphors of learning strategies. In C. E. Weinstein, E. T. Goetz, & P. A. Alexander (Eds.), *Learning and study strategies: Issues in assessment, instruction, and evaluation.* Orlando, FL: Academic Press.

Park, K. A., & Waters, E. (1989). Security of attachment and preschool friendships. *Child Development, 60,* 1076–1081.

Parke, R. D. (1972). Some effects of punishment on children's behavior. In W. W. Hartup (Ed.), *The young child* (Vol. 2). Washington, D.C.: National Association for the Education of Young Children.

Parke, R. D. (1977). Some effects of punishment on children's behavior—revisited. In E. M. Hetherington & R. D. Parke (Eds.), *Contemporary readings in child psychology.* New York: McGraw-Hill.

Parke, R. D. (1981). *Fathers.* Cambridge, MA: Harvard University Press.

Parke, R. D., & Lewis, N. G. (1981). The family in context: A multilevel interactional analysis of child abuse. In R. W. Henderson (Ed.), *Parent-child interaction: Theory, research, and prospects.* New York: Academic Press.

Parke, R. D., & Slaby, R. G. (1983). The development of aggression. In P. H. Mussen (Ed.), *Handbook of child psychology. Vol. 4: Socialization, personality, and social development.* New York: Wiley.

Parker, J. G., & Asher, S. R. (1987). Peer relations and later adjustment: Are low-accepted children "at risk"? *Psychological Bulletin, 102,* 357–389.

Parker, J. G., & Asher, S. R. (1993). Friendship and friendship quality in middle childhood: Links with peer group acceptance and feelings of loneliness and social dissatisfaction. *Developmental Psychology, 29,* 611–621.

Parkhurst, J. T., & Asher, S. R. (1992). Peer rejection in middle school: Subgroup differences in behavior, loneliness, and interpersonal concerns. *Developmental Psychology, 28,* 231–241.

Parsons, J. E., Adler, T. F., & Kaczala, C. M. (1982). Socialization of achievement attitudes and beliefs: Parental influences. *Child Development, 53,* 310–321.

Parsons, T. (1955). Family structure and the socialization of the child. In T. Parsons & R. F. Bales (Eds.), *Family socialization and interaction processes.* New York: Free Press.

Parten, M. (1932). Social participation among preschool children. *Journal of Abnormal and Social Psychology, 27,* 243–269.

Pascual-Leone, J. (1984). Attentional, dialectic, and mental effort: Toward an organismic theory of life stages. In M. L. Commons, F. A. Richards, & C. Armon (Eds.), *Beyond formal operations: Late adolescent and adult cognitive development.* New York: Praeger.

Pascual-Leone, J. (1988). Organismic processes for neo-Piagetian theories: A dialectical causal account of cognitive development. In A. Demetriou (Ed.), *The neo-Piagetian theories of cognitive development: Toward an integration.* North Holland: Elsevier.

Passingham, R. E. (1982). *The human primate.* Oxford: W. H. Freeman.

Passman, R. H., & Longeway, K. P. (1982). The role of vision in maternal attachment: Giving 2-year-olds a photograph of their mother during separation. *Developmental Psychology, 18,* 530–533.

Passman, R. H., & Weisberg, P. (1975). Mothers and blankets as agents for promoting play and exploration by young children in a novel environment: The effects of social and nonsocial attachment objects. *Developmental Psychology, 11,* 170–177.

Pataki, S. P., Shapiro, C., & Clark, M. S. (1994). Children's acquisition of appropriate norms for friendships and acquaintances. *Journal of Social and Personal Relationships, 11,* 427–442.

Patterson, C. J., Kupersmidt, J. B., & Vaden, N. A. (1990). Income level, gender, ethnicity, and household composition as predictors of children's school-based competence. *Child Development, 61,* 485–494.

Patterson, G. R. (1981). Mothers: The unacknowledged victims. *Monographs of the Society for Research in Child Development, 45*(5, Serial No. 186).

Patterson, G. R. (1982). *Coercive family processes.* Eugene, OR: Castilia Press.

Patterson, G. R., DeBaryshe, B. D., & Ramsey, E. (1989). A developmental perspective on antisocial behavior. *American Psychologist, 44,* 329–335.

Patterson, G. R., Littman, R. A., & Bricker, W. (1967). Assertive behavior in children: A step toward a theory of aggression. *Monographs of the Society for Research in Child Development, 32*(5, Serial No. 113).

Patterson, G. R., Reid, J. B., & Dishion, T. (1992). *Antisocial boys.* Eugene, OR: Castalia Publishing.

Patterson, G. R., & Stouthamer-Loeber, M. (1984). The correlation of family management practices and delinquency. *Child Development, 55,* 1299–1307.

Patterson, S. J., Sochting, I., & Marcia, L. E. (1992). The inner space and beyond: Women and identity. In G. R. Adams, T. P. Gullotta, & R. Montemayor (Eds.), *Advances in adolescent development. Vol. 4: Adolescent identity formation.* Newbury Park, CA: Sage.

Paul, J. P. (1993). Childhood cross-gender behavior and adult homosexuality: The resurgence of biological models of sexuality. *Journal of Homosexuality, 24,* 41–54.

Paulhus, D., & Shaffer, D. R. (1981). Sex differences in the impact of number of older and number of younger siblings on scholastic aptitude. *Social Psychology Quarterly, 44,* 363–368.

Pearlman, C. (1984). The effects of level of effectance motivation, IQ, and a penalty/reward contingency on the choice of problem difficulty. *Child Development, 55,* 2000–2016.

Pearson, J. L., Hunter, A. G., Ensminger, M. E., & Kellam, S. G. (1990). Black grandmothers in multigenerational households: Diversity in family structure and parenting involvement in the Woodlawn community. *Child Development, 61,* 434–442.

Pedlow, R., Sanson, A., Prior, M., & Oberklaid, F. (1993). Stability of maternally reported temperament from infancy to 8 years. *Developmental Psychology, 29,* 998–1007.

Pedro-Carroll, J. L., & Cowen, E. L. (1985). The children of divorce intervention program: An investigation of the efficacy of a school-based prevention program. *Journal of Consulting and Clinical Psychology, 53,* 603–611.

Peevers, B. H., & Secord, P. F. (1973). Developmental changes in attribution of descriptive concepts to persons. *Journal of Personality and Social Psychology, 27,* 120–128.

Pegg, J. E., Werker, J. F., & McLeod, P. J. (1992). Preference for infant-directed over adult-directed speech: Evidence from 7-week-old infants. *Infant Behavior and Development, 15,* 325–345.

Pelham, W. E., Jr., Carlson, C., Sams, S. E., Vallano, G., Dixon, M. J., & Hoza, B. (1993). Separate and combined effects of methylphenidate and behavior modification on boys with attention deficit-hyperactivity disorder in the classroom. *Journal of Consulting and Clinical Psychology, 61,* 506–515.

Pellegrini, D. S. (1985). Social cognition and competence in middle childhood. *Child Development, 56,* 253–264.

Penner, S. G. (1987). Parental responses to grammatical and ungrammatical child utterances. *Child Development, 58,* 376–384.

Pergament, E., & Fine, B. (1993). The current status of chorionic villus sampling. In R. G. Edwards (Ed.), *Preconception and preimplantation diagnosis of human genetic disease.* Cambridge, England: Cambridge University Press.

Perlmutter, M. (1986). A life-span view of memory. In P. B. Baltes, D. L. Featherman, & R. M. Lerner (Eds.), *Life-span development and behavior* (Vol. 7). Hillsdale, NJ: Erlbaum.

Perris, E. E., Myers, N. A., & Clifton, R. K. (1990). Long-term memory for a single infancy experience. *Child Development, 61,* 1796–1807.

Perry, D. G., Kusel, S. J., & Perry, L. C. (1988). Victims of peer aggression. *Developmental Psychology, 24,* 807–814.

Perry, D. G., & Parke, R. D. (1975). Punishment and alternative response training as determinants of response inhibition in children. *Genetic Psychology Monographs, 91,* 257–279.

Perry, D. G., & Perry, L. C. (1974). Denial of suffering in the victim as a stimulus to violence in aggressive boys. *Child Development, 45,* 55–62.

Perry, D. G., Perry, L. C., Bussey, K., English, D., & Arnold, G. (1980). Processes of attribution and children's self-punishment following misbehavior. *Child Development, 51,* 545–551.

Perry, D. G., Perry, L. C., & Rasmussen, P. (1986). Cognitive social learning mediators of aggression. *Child Development, 57,* 700–711.

Perry, D. G., Perry, L. C., & Weiss, R. J. (1989). Sex differences in the consequences that children anticipate for aggression. *Developmental Psychology, 25,* 312–319.

Perry, D. G., Williard, J. C., & Perry, L. C. (1990). Peers' perceptions of the consequences that victimized children provide aggressors. *Child Development, 61,* 1310–1325.

Peskin, J. (1992). Ruse and representations: On children's ability to conceal information. *Developmental Psychology, 28,* 84–89.

Peterson, A. C. (1988). Adolescent development. *Annual Review of Psychology, 39,* 583–607.

Peterson, G. H., Mehl, L. E., & Liederman, P. H. (1979). The role of some birth-related variables in father attachment. *American Journal of Orthopsychiatry, 49,* 330–338.

Peterson, L., Ewigman, B., & Kivlahan, C. (1993). Judgments regarding appropriate child supervision to prevent injury: The role of environmental risk and child age. *Child Development, 64,* 934–950.

Petitto, L. A., & Marentette, P. F. (1991). Babbling in the manual mode: Evidence for the ontogeny of language. *Science, 251,* 1493–1496.

Petretic, P. A., & Tweney, R. D. (1977). Does comprehension precede production? The development of children's responses to telegraphic sentences of varying grammatical adequacy. *Journal of Child Language, 4,* 201–209.

Pettersen, L., Yonas, A., & Fisch, R. O. (1980). The development of blinking in response to impending collision in preterm, full-term, and postterm infants. *Infant Behavior and Development, 3,* 155–165.

Pettit, G. S., & Bates, J. E. (1989). Family interaction patterns and children's behavior problems from infancy to 4 years. *Developmental Psychology, 25,* 413–420.

Pettit, G. S., Dodge, K. A., & Brown, M. M. (1988). Early family experience, social problem-solving patterns, and children's social competence. *Child Development, 59,* 107–120.

Phillips, D. (1984). The illusion of incompetence among academically competent children. *Child Development, 55,* 2000–2016.

Phillips, D. A., Voran, M., Kisker, E., Howes, C., & Whitebook, M. (1994). Child care for children in poverty: Opportunity or inequity? *Child Development, 65,* 472–492.

Phinney, J. S. (1989). Stages of ethnic identity development in minority group adolescents. *Journal of Early Adolescence, 9,* 34–49.

Phinney, J. S., & Rosenthal, D. A. (1992). Ethnic identity in adolescence: Process, context, and outcome. In G. R. Adams, T. P. Gullotta, & R. Montemayor (Eds.), *Advances in adolescent development. Vol. 4: Adolescent identity formation.* Newbury Park, CA: Sage.

Piacentini, J., & Hynd, G. (1988). Language after dominant hemispherectomy: Are plasticity of function and equipotentiality viable concepts? *Clinical Psychology Review, 8,* 595–609.

Piaget, J. (1926). *The language and thought of the child.* New York: Harcourt, Brace & World.

Piaget, J. (1950). *The psychology of intelligence.* San Diego, CA: Harcourt Brace Jovanovich.

Piaget, J. (1951). *Play, dreams, and imitation in childhood.* New York: Norton.

Piaget, J. (1952). *The origins of intelligence in children.* New York: International Universities Press.

Piaget, J. (1954). *The construction of reality in the child.* New York: Basic Books.

Piaget, J. (1960). *Psychology of intelligence.* Paterson, NJ: Littlefield, Adams.

Piaget, J. (1965). *The moral judgment of the child.* New York: Free Press. (Original work published 1932)

Piaget, J. (1970a, May). A conversation with Jean Piaget. *Psychology Today,* 25–32.

Piaget, J. (1970b). Piaget's theory. In P. H. Mussen (Ed.), *Carmichael's manual of child psychology* (Vol. 1). New York: Wiley.

Piaget, J. (1971). *Science of education and the psychology of the child.* New York: Viking Press.

Piaget, J. (1972). Intellectual evolution from adolescence to adulthood. *Human Development, 15,* 1–12.

Piaget, J. (1976). *To understand is to invent: The future of education.* New York: Penguin.

Piaget, J. (1977). The role of action in the development of thinking. In W. F. Overton & J. M. Gallagher (Eds.), *Knowledge and development* (Vol. 1). New York: Plenum.

Piaget, J., & Inhelder, B. (1969). *The psychology of the child.* New York: Basic Books.

Pickens, J. (1994). Perception of auditory-visual distance relations by 5-month-old infants. *Developmental Psychology, 30,* 537–544.

Pickens, J., & Field, T. (1993). Facial expressivity in infants of depressed mothers. *Developmental Psychology, 29,* 986–988.

Pillow, B. H. (1988). Young children's understanding of attentional limits. *Child Development, 59,* 31–46.

Pillow, B. H. (1989). Early understanding of perception as a source of knowledge. *Journal of Experimental Child Psychology, 47,* 116–129.

Pinker, S. (1991). Rules of language. *Science, 253,* 530–535.

Pinon, M., Huston, A. C., & Wright, J. C. (1989). Family ecology and child characteristics that predict young children's educational television viewing. *Child Development, 60,* 846–856.

Pinto, A., Folkers, E., & Sines, J. O. (1991). Dimensions of behavior and home environment in school-age children: India and the United States. *Journal of Cross-Cultural Psychology, 22,* 491–508.

Pipp, S., Easterbrooks, M. A., & Harmon, R. J. (1992). The relation between attachment and knowledge of self and mother in one-year-old infants to three-year-old infants. *Child Development, 63,* 738–750.

Planned Parenthood Federation of America (1976). *11 million teenagers: What can be done about the epidemic of adolescent pregnancies in the United States?* New York: Alan Guttmacher Institute.

Plomin, R. (1986). *Development, genetics, and psychology.* Hillsdale, NJ: Erlbaum.

Plomin, R. (1990). *Nature and nurture: An introduction to behavior genetics.* Pacific Grove, CA: Brooks/Cole.

Plomin, R., DeFries, J. C., & Loehlin, J. C. (1977). Genotype-environment interaction and correlation in the analysis of human behavior. *Psychological Bulletin, 84,* 309–322.

Plomin, R., DeFries, J. C., & McClearn, G. E. (1989). *Behavioral genetics: A primer* (2nd ed.). New York: W. H. Freeman.

Plomin, R., Reiss, D., Hetherington, E. M., & Howe, G. W. (1994). Nature and nurture: Genetic contributions to measures of the family environment. *Developmental Psychology, 30,* 32–43.

Plomin, R., & Rende, R. (1991). Human behavioral genetics. *Annual Review of Psychology, 42,* 161–190.

Pollitt, E. (1994). Poverty and child development: Relevance of research in developing countries to the United States. *Child Development, 65,* 283–295.

Pollitt, E., Gorman, K., & Metallinos-Katsaras, E. (1992). Long-term developmental consequences of intrauterine and postnatal growth retardation in rural Guatemala. In G. J. Suci & S. S. Robertson (Eds.), *Future directions in infant development research*. New York: Springer-Verlag.

Pomerleau, A., Bolduc, D., Malcuit, G., & Cossette, L. (1990). Pink or blue: Environmental gender stereotypes in the first two years of life. *Sex Roles, 22*, 359–367.

Porter, F. L., Porges, S. W., & Marshall, R. E. (1988). Newborn pain cries and vagal tone: Parallel changes in response to circumcision. *Child Development, 59*, 495–505.

Porter, R. H., Makin, J. W., Davis, L. B., & Christensen, K. M. (1992). Breast-fed infants respond to olfactory clues from their own mother and unfamiliar lactating females. *Infant Behavior and Development, 15*, 85–93.

Posner, J. K., & Vandell, D. L. (1994). Low-income children's after-school care: Are there beneficial effects of after-school programs? *Child Development, 65*, 440–456.

Poulin-Dubois, D., Serbin, L. A., Kenyon, B., & Derbyshire, A. (1994). Infants' intermodal knowledge about gender. *Developmental Psychology, 30*, 436–442.

Powell, G. J. (1985). Self-concepts among Afro-American students in racially isolated minority schools: Some regional differences. *Journal of the American Academy of Child Psychiatry, 24*, 142–149.

Powlishta, K. K., Serbin, L. A., Doyle, A., & White, D. R. (1994). Gender, ethnic, and body type biases: The generality of prejudice in childhood. *Developmental Psychology, 30*, 526–536.

Pratt, K. C. (1954). The neonate. In L. Carmichael (Ed.), *Manual of child psychology*. New York: Wiley.

Pratt, M. W., & Bates, K. R. (1982). Young editors: Preschoolers' evaluation and production of ambiguous messages. *Developmental Psychology, 18*, 30–42.

Pratt, M. W., Diessner, R., Hunsberger, B., Pancer, S. M., & Savoy, K. (1991). Four pathways in the analysis of adult development and aging: Comparing analyses of reasoning about personal-life dilemmas. *Psychology and Aging, 4*, 666–675.

Pratt, M. W., Golding, G., Hunter, W., & Norris, J. (1988). From inquiry to judgment: Age and sex differences in patterns of adult moral thinking and information-seeking. *International Journal of Aging and Human Development, 27*, 109–124.

Pressley, M., Cariglia-Bull, T., Deane, S., & Schneider, W. (1987). Short-term memory, verbal competence, and age as predictors of imagery instructional effectiveness. *Journal of Experimental Child Psychology, 43*, 194–211.

Pressley, M., & Levin, J. R. (1980). The development of mental imagery retrieval. *Child Development, 51*, 558–560.

Previc, F. H. (1991). A general theory concerning the prenatal origins of cerebral lateralization in humans. *Psychological Review, 98*, 299–334.

Pridjian, G., & Lin, C. (1993). Multifetal gestation. In C. Lin, M. S. Verp, & R. E. Sabbagha (Eds.), *The high-risk fetus: Pathophysiology, diagnosis, management*. New York: Springer-Verlag.

Priel, B., & deSchonen, S. (1986). Self-recognition: A study of a population without mirrors. *Journal of Experimental Child Psychology, 41*, 237–250.

Provence, S., & Lipton, R. C. (1962). *Infants in institutions*. New York: International Universities Press.

Public Health Service (1986). Premature mortality due to sudden infant death syndrome. *Mortality and Morbidity Weekly Report, 35*, 169–170.

Pueschel, S. M., & Goldstein, A. (1983). Genetic counseling. In J. L. Matson & J. A. Mulick (Eds.), *Handbook of mental retardation*. Oxford: Pergamon Press.

Pulkkinen, L. (1982). Self-control and continuity from childhood to adolescence. In P. B. Baltes & O. G. Brim, Jr. (Eds.), *Life-span development and behavior* (Vol. 4). Orlando, FL: Academic Press.

Putallaz, M., & Heflin, A. H. (1990). Parent-child interactions. In S. R. Asher & J. D. Coie (Eds.), *Peer rejection in childhood*. Cambridge, England: Cambridge University Press.

Quay, L. C. (1971). Language dialect, reinforcement, and the intelligence-test performance of Negro children. *Child Development, 42*, 5–15.

Quiggle, N. L., Garber, J., Panak, W. F., & Dodge, K. A. (1992). Social information processing in aggressive and depressed children. *Child Development, 63*, 1305–1320.

Quinn, R. A., Houts, A. C., & Graesser, A. C. (1994). Naturalistic conceptions of morality: A question-answering approach. *Journal of Personality, 62*, 260–267.

Rabiner, D. L., Keane, S. P., & MacKinnon-Lewis, C. (1993). Children's beliefs about familiar and unfamiliar peers in relation to their sociometric status. *Developmental Psychology, 29*, 236–243.

Rabiner, D. L., Lenhart, L., & Lochman, J. E. (1990). Automatic versus reflective social problem solving in relation to children's sociometric status. *Developmental Psychology, 26*, 1010–1016.

Radke-Yarrow, M., Cummings, E. M., Kuczynski, L., & Chapman, M. (1985). Patterns of attachment in two- and three-year-olds in normal families and families with parental depression. *Child Development, 56*, 884–893.

Radke-Yarrow, M., Zahn-Waxler, C., & Chapman, M. (1983). Children's prosocial dispositions and behavior. In P. H. Mussen (Ed.), *Handbook of child psychology. Vol. 4: Socialization, personality, and social development*. New York: Wiley.

Rakic, P. (1991). Plasticity of cortical development. In S. E. Brauth, W. S. Hall, & R. J. Dooling (Eds.), *Plasticity of development*. Cambridge, MA: Bradford/MIT Press.

Ramey, C. T. (1982). Commentary. In I. Lazar & R. Darlington, Lasting effects of early education: A report from the Consortium for Longitudinal Studies. *Monographs of the Society for Research in Child Development, 47*(2–3, Serial No. 195).

Ramey, C. T., & Ramey, S. L. (1992). Effective early intervention. *Mental Retardation, 30*, 337–345.

Reeder, K. (1981). How young children learn to do things with words. In P. S. Dale & D. Ingram (Eds.), *Child language—an international perspective*. Baltimore: University Park Press.

Reese, E., & Fivush, R. (1992). Parental styles of talking about the past. *Developmental Psychology, 29*, 596–606.

Reich, P. A. (1986). *Language development*. Englewood Cliffs, NJ: Prentice-Hall.

Reid, P. T., Tate, C. S., & Berman, P. W. (1989). Preschool children's self-presentations in situations with infants: Effects of sex and race. *Child Development, 60*, 710–714.

Reikehof, L. (1963). *Talk to the deaf*. Springfield, MO: Gospel Publishing House.

Reinisch, J. M., Sanders, S. A., Hill, C. A., & Ziemba-Davis, M. (1992). High-risk sexual behavior among heterosexual undergraduates at a midwestern university. *Family Planning Perspectives, 24*, 116.

Reissland, N. (1988). Neonatal imitation in the first hour of life: Observations in rural Nepal. *Developmental Psychology, 24*, 464–469.

Remley, A. (1988, October). The great parental value shift: From obedience to independence. *Psychology Today*, 56–59.

Resnick, S. M., Berenbaum, S. A., Gottesman, I. I., & Bouchard, T. J. (1986). Early hormonal influences on cognitive functioning in congenital adrenal hyperplasia. *Developmental Psychology, 22*, 191–198.

Rest, J. R. (1993). Research on moral judgment in college students. In A. Garrod (Ed.), *Approaches to moral development: New research and emerging themes*. New York: Teachers College Press.

Rest, J. R., & Thoma, S. J. (1985). Relation of moral judgment development to formal education. *Developmental Psychology, 21*, 709–714.

Revelle, G. L., Wellman, H. M., & Karabenick, J. D. (1985). Comprehension monitoring in preschool children. *Child Development, 56*, 654–663.

Reynolds, D. (1992). School effectiveness and school improvement: An updated review of the British literature. In D. Reynolds & P. Cuttance (Eds.), *School effectiveness: Research, policy, and practice*. London: Cassell.

Reznick, J. S., & Goldfield, B. A. (1992). Rapid change in lexical development in comprehension and production. *Developmental Psychology, 28*, 406–413.

Rheingold, H. L. (1982). Little children's participation in the work of adults, a nascent prosocial behavior. *Child Development, 53*, 114–125.

Rheingold, H. L., & Adams, J. L. (1980). The significance of speech to newborns. *Developmental Psychology, 16*, 397–403.

Rholes, W. S., Jones, M., & Wade, C. (1988). Children's understanding of personal disposition and its relationship to behavior. *Journal of Experimental Child Psychology, 45*, 1–17.

Rholes, W. S., & Ruble, D. N. (1984). Children's understanding of dispositional characteristics of others. *Child Development, 55*, 550–560.

Rholes, W. S., Simpson, J. A., & Blakely, B. S. (in press). Adult attachment styles and parents' relationships with their children. *Personal Relationships*.

Ribble, M. (1943). *The rights of infants*. New York: Columbia University Press.

Ricco, R. B. (1989). Operational thought and the acquisition of taxonomic relations involving figurative dissimilarity. *Developmental Psychology, 25*, 996–1003.

Rice, M. E., & Grusec, J. E. (1975). Saying and doing: Effects on observer performance. *Journal of Personality and Social Psychology, 32*, 584–593.

Rice, M. L. (1989). Children's language acquisition. *American Psychologist, 44*, 149–156.

Rice, M. L., Huston, A. C., Truglio, R., & Wright, J. (1990). Words from "Sesame Street": Learning vocabulary while viewing. *Developmental Psychology, 26*, 421–428.

Rice, M. L., & Woodsmall, L. (1988). Lessons from television: Children's word learning when viewing. *Child Development, 59*, 420–429.

Richards, F. A., & Commons, M. L. (1990). Post-formal cognitive-developmental theory and research: A review of its current status. In C. N. Alexander & E. J. Langer (Eds.), *Higher stages of human development: Perspectives on adult growth*. New York: Oxford University Press.

Richards, J. M., Jr., Holland, J. L., & Lutz, S. W. (1967). Prediction of student accomplishment in college. *Journal of Educational Psychology, 58*, 343–355.

Richards, M. H., Boxer, A. M., Petersen, A. C., & Albrecht, R. (1990). Relation of weight to body image in pubertal girls and boys from two communities. *Developmental Psychology, 26*, 313–321.

Richards, M. H., & Duckett, E. (1994). The relationship of maternal employment to early adolescent daily experience with and without parents. *Child Development, 65*, 225–236.

Richardson, J. G., & Simpson, C. H. (1982). Children, gender, and social structure: An analysis of the contents of letters to Santa Claus. *Child Development, 53*, 429–436.

Richardson, J. L., Dwyer, K., McGuigan, K., Hansen, W. B., Dent, C., Johnson, C., Sussman, S. Y., Brannon, B., & Flay, B. (1989). Substance use among eighth-grade students who take care of themselves after school. *Pediatrics, 84*, 556–560.

Richardson, T. M., & Benbow, C. P. (1990). Long-term effects of acceleration on the social-emotional adjustment of mathematically precocious youths. *Journal of Educational Psychology, 82*, 464–470.

Riese, M. L. (1990). Neonatal temperament in monozygotic and dizygotic twin pairs. *Child Development, 61*, 1230–1237.

Riesen, A. H. (1947). The development of visual perception in man and chimpanzee. *Science, 106*, 107–108.

Riesen, A. H. (1965). Effects of visual deprivation on perceptual function and the neural substrate. In J. de Ajuriaguerra (Ed.), *Dessaferentation experimental et clinique*. Geneva: Georg.

Riesen, A. H., Chow, K. L., Semmes, J., & Nissen, H. W. (1951). Chimpanzee vision after four conditions of light deprivation. *American Psychologist, 6,* 282.

Rieser, J., Yonas, A., & Wilkner, K. (1976). Radial localization of odors by human newborns. *Child Development, 47,* 856–859.

Rinkoff, R. F., & Corter, C. M. (1980). Effects of setting and maternal accessibility on the infant's response to brief separation. *Child Development, 51,* 603–606.

Rist, R. C. (1970). Student social class and teacher expectations: The self-fulfilling prophecy in ghetto education. *Harvard Educational Review, 40,* 411–451.

Ritter, J. M., Casey, R. J., & Langlois, J. H. (1991). Adults' responses to infants varying in appearance of age and attractiveness. *Child Development, 62,* 68–82.

Roberts, C. J., & Lowe, C. R. (1975). Where have all of the conceptions gone? *Lancet, 1,* 498–499.

Roberts, K. (1988). Retrieval of a basic-level category in prelinguistic infants. *Developmental Psychology, 24,* 21–27.

Roberts, L. R., Sarigiani, P. A., Petersen, A. C., & Newman, J. L. (1990). Gender differences in the relationship between achievement and self-image during early adolescence. *Journal of Early Adolescence, 10,* 159–175.

Robertson, T. S., & Rossiter, J. R. (1974). Children and commercial persuasion: An attribution theory analysis. *Journal of Consumer Research, 1,* 13–20.

Robinson, A., Bender, B. G., & Linden, M. G. (1992). Prenatal diagnosis of sex chromosome abnormalities. In A. Milunsky (Ed.), *Genetic disorders and the fetus: Diagnosis, prevention, and treatment.* Baltimore: Johns Hopkins University Press.

Robinson, C. C., & Morris, J. T. (1986). The gender-stereotyped nature of Christmas toys received by 36-, 48-, and 60-month-old children: A comparison between nonrequested vs. requested toys. *Sex Roles, 15,* 21–32.

Robinson, I., Ziss, K., Ganza, B., Katz, S., & Robinson, E. (1991). Twenty years of sexual revolution, 1965–1985: An upate. *Journal of Marriage and the Family, 53,* 216–220.

Robinson, J. L., Kagan, J., Reznick, J. S., & Corley, R. (1992). The heritability of inhibited and uninhibited behavior: A twin study. *Developmental Psychology, 28,* 1030–1037.

Robinson, N. M., & Janos, P. M. (1986). Psychological adjustment in a college-level program of marked academic acceleration. *Journal of Youth and Adolescence, 15,* 51–60.

Rochat, P. (1989). Object manipulation and exploration in 2- to 5-month-old infants. *Developmental Psychology, 25,* 871–884.

Roche, A. F. (1981). The adipocyte-number hypothesis. *Child Development, 52,* 31–43.

Rodgers, J. L., & Rowe, D. C. (1988). Influence of siblings on adolescent sexual behavior. *Developmental Psychology, 24,* 722–728.

Rodning, C., Beckwith, L., & Howard, J. (1991). Quality of attachment and home environments in children prenatally exposed to PCP and cocaine. *Development and Psychopathology, 3,* 351–366.

Roffwarg, H. P., Muzio, J. W., & Dement, W. C. (1966). Ontogenetic development of the human sleep-dream cycle. *Science, 152,* 604–619.

Roggman, L. A., Langlois, J. H., Hubbs-Tait, L., & Rieser-Danner, L. A. (1994). Infant day care, attachment, and the "file drawer problem." *Child Development, 65,* 1429–1443.

Rogoff, B. (1990). *Apprenticeship in thinking: Cognitive development in social context.* New York: Oxford University Press.

Rogoff, B., Mistry, J., Goncu, A., & Mosier, C. (1993). Guided participation in cultural activity by toddlers and caregivers. *Monographs of the Society for Research in Child Development, 58*(8, Serial No. 236).

Roland, M. G. M., Cole, T. J., & Whitehead, R. G. (1977). A quantitative study into the role of infection in determining nutritional status in Gambian village children. *British Journal of Nutrition, 37,* 441–450.

Roopnarine, J. L., Talukder, E., Jain, D., Joshi, P., & Srivastave, P. (1990). Characteristics of holding, patterns of play, and social behaviors between parents and infants in New Delhi, India. *Developmental Psychology, 26,* 667–673.

Rose, R. M., Bernstein, I. S., & Gordon, T. P. (1975). Consequences of social conflict on plasma testosterone levels in rhesus monkeys. *Psychosomatic Medicine, 37,* 50–61.

Rose, S. A. (1988). Shape recognition in infancy: Visual integration of sequential information. *Child Development, 59,* 1161–1176.

Rose, S. A. (1994). Relation between physical growth and information processing in infants born in India. *Child Development, 65,* 889–902.

Rose, S. A., Feldman, J. F., McCarton, C. M., & Wolfson, J. (1988). Information processing in seven-month-old infants as a function of risk status. *Child Development, 59,* 589–603.

Rose, S. A., Feldman, J. F., & Wallace, I. F. (1992). Infant information processing in relation to six-year cognitive outcomes. *Child Development, 63,* 1126–1141.

Rose, S. A., Feldman, J. F., Wallace, I. F., & McCarton, C. (1989). Infant visual attention: Relation to birth status and developmental outcome during the first 5 years. *Developmental Psychology, 25,* 560–576.

Rose, S. A., Feldman, J. F., Wallace, I. F., & McCarton, C. (1991). Information processing at 1 year: Relation to birth status and developmental outcome during the first 5 years. *Developmental Psychology, 27,* 723–737.

Rose, S. A., Gottfried, A. W., & Bridger, W. H. (1981). Cross-modal transfer in 6-month-old infants. *Developmental Psychology, 17,* 661–669.

Rosen, B. C., & D'Andrade, R. (1959). The psychosocial origins of achievement motivation. *Sociometry, 22,* 185–218.

Rosen, K. S., & Rothbaum, F. (1993). Quality of parental caregiving and security of attachment. *Developmental Psychology, 29,* 358–367.

Rosen, R., & Hall, E. (1984). *Sexuality.* New York: Random House.

Rosen, W. D., Adamson, L. B., & Bakeman, R. (1992). An experimental investigation of infant social referencing: Mothers' messages and gender differences. *Developmental Psychology, 28,* 1172–1178.

Rosenberg, M. (1979). *Conceiving the self.* New York: Basic Books.

Rosenblatt, P. C., & Cunningham, M. R. (1976). Sex differences in cross-cultural perspective. In B. Lloyd & J. Archer (Eds.), *Exploring sex differences.* London: Academic Press.

Rosenhan, D. L. (1970). The natural socialization of altruistic autonomy. In J. L. Macaulay & L. Berkowitz (Eds.), *Altruism and helping behavior.* New York: Academic Press.

Rosenholtz, S. J., & Simpson, C. (1984). The formation of ability conceptions: Developmental trend or social construction? *Review of Educational Research, 54,* 31–63.

Rosenstein, D., & Oster, H. (1988). Differential facial responses to four basic tastes in newborns. *Child Development, 59,* 1555–1568.

Rosenthal, D. A., & Feldman, S. S. (1992). The relationship between parenting behaviour and ethnic identity in Chinese-American and Chinese-Australian adolescents. *International Journal of Psychology, 27,* 19–31.

Rosenthal, M. K. (1982). Vocal dialogues in the neonatal period. *Developmental Psychology, 18,* 17–21.

Rosenthal, R., & Jacobson, L. (1968). *Pygmalion in the classroom.* New York: Holt, Rinehart & Winston.

Rosenwasser, S. M., Lingenfelter, M., & Harrington, A. F. (1989). Nontraditional gender role portrayals and children's gender role perceptions. *Journal of Applied Developmental Psychology, 10,* 97–105.

Rosenzweig, M. R. (1966). Environmental complexity, cerebral change, and behavior. *American Psychologist, 21,* 321–332.

Rosenzweig, M. R. (1984). Experience, memory, and the brain. *American Psychologist, 39,* 365–376.

Ross, H., Tesla, C., Kenyon, B., & Lollis, S. (1990). Maternal intervention in toddler peer conflict: The socialization of principles of justice. *Developmental Psychology, 26,* 994–1003.

Ross, H. S., & Lollis, S. P. (1987). Communication within infant social games. *Developmental Psychology, 23,* 241–248.

Ross, R. T., Begab, M. J., Dondis, E. H., Giampiccolo, J. S., Jr., & Meyers, C. E. (1985). *Lives of the mentally retarded. A forty-year follow-up study.* Stanford, CA: Stanford University Press.

Rothbart, M. K. (1971). Birth order and mother-child interaction in an achievement situation. *Journal of Personality and Social Psychology, 17,* 113–120.

Rothbart, M. K. (1981). Measurement of temperament in infancy. *Child Development, 52,* 569–578.

Rothberg, A. D., & Lits, B. (1991). Psychosocial support for maternal stress during pregnancy: Effect on birth weight. *American Journal of Obstetrics and Gynecology, 165,* 403–407.

Rousseau, J. J. (1955). *Emile.* New York: Dutton. (Original work published 1762)

Rovee-Collier, C. K. (1984). The ontogeny of learning and memory in human infancy. In R. Kail & N. E. Spear (Eds.), *Comparative perspectives on the development of memory.* Hillsdale, NJ: Erlbaum.

Rovee-Collier, C. K. (1987). Learning and memory in infancy. In J. D. Osofsky (Ed.), *Handbook of infant development* (2nd ed.). New York: Wiley.

Rovee-Collier, C. K., Schechter, A., Shyi, G. C., & Shields, P. J. (1992). Perceptual identification of contextual attributes and infant memory retrieval. *Developmental Psychology, 28,* 307–318.

Rowe, D. C. (1993). *The limits of family influence: Genes, experience, and behavior.* New York: Guilford.

Rowe, D. C., & Plomin, R. (1981). The importance off nonshared (E_1) environmental influences in behavioral development. *Developmental Psychology, 17,* 517–531.

Rowe, D. C., Rodgers, J. L., & Meseck-Bushey, S. (1992). Sibling delinquency and the family environment: Shared and unshared influences. *Child Development, 63,* 59–67.

Rubenstein, J. L., Heeren, T., Housman, D., Rubin, C., & Stechler, G. (1989). Suicidal behavior in normal adolescents: Risks and protective factors. *American Journal of Orthopsychiatry, 59,* 59–71.

Rubin, D. H., Krasilnikoff, P. A., Leventhal, J. M., Weile, B., & Berget, A. (1986). Effect of passive smoking on birth-weight. *Lancet, 2,* 415–417.

Rubin, K. H., Fein, G., & Vandenberg, B. (1983). Play. In P. H. Mussen (Ed.), *Handbook of child psychology. Vol. 4: Social development.* New York: Wiley.

Ruble, D. N. (1988). Sex-role development. In M. H. Bornstein & M. E. Lamb (Eds.), *Developmental psychology: An advanced textbook.* Hillsdale, NJ: Erlbaum.

Ruble, D. N., Balaban, T., & Cooper, J. (1981). Gender constancy and the effects of sex-typed televised toy commercials. *Child Development, 52,* 667–673.

Ruble, D. N., & Brooks-Gunn, J. (1982). The experience of menarche. *Child Development, 53,* 1557–1566.

Ruble, D. N., Eisenberg, R., & Higgins, E. T. (1994). Developmental changes in achievement evaluations: Motivational implications of self-other differences. *Child Development, 65,* 1095–1110.

Ruble, D. N., & Flett, G. L. (1988). Conflicting goals in self-evaluative information seeking: Developmental and ability level analyses. *Child Development, 59,* 97–106.

Ruble, T. L. (1983). Sex stereotypes: Issues of change in the 1970s. *Sex Roles, 9,* 397–402.

Rudolph, F. (1965). *Essays on early education in the republic.* Cambridge, MA: Harvard University Press.

Ruff, H. A., & Lawson, K. R. (1990). Development of sustained focused attention in young children during free play. *Developmental Psychology, 26,* 85–93.

Ruff, H. A., Lawson, K. R., Parrinello, R., & Weissberg, R. (1990). Long-term stability of individual differences in sustained attention in the early years. *Child Development, 61,* 60–75.

Ruffman, T. K., & Olson, D. R. (1989). Children's ascriptions of knowledge to others. *Developmental Psychology, 25,* 601–606.

Ruffman, T. K., Olson, D. R., Ash, T., & Keenan, T. (1993). The ABCs of deception: Do young children understand deception in the same way as adults? *Developmental Psychology, 29,* 74–87.

Runco, M. A. (1992). Children's divergent thinking and creative ideation. *Developmental Review, 12,* 233–264.

Rushton, J. P. (1980). *Altruism, socialization, and society.* Englewood Cliffs: NJ: Prentice Hall.

Rushton, J. P., Fulker, D. W., Neale, M. C., Nias, K. K. B., & Eysenck, H. J. (1986). Altruism and aggression. The heritability of individual differences. *Journal of Personality and Social Psychology, 50,* 1192–1198.

Russell, A., & Finnie, V. (1990). Preschool children's social status and maternal instructions to assist group entry. *Developmental Psychology, 26,* 600–611.

Russell, G. F. M., Szmukler, G. I., Dare, C., & Eisler, I. (1987). An evaluation of family therapy in anorexia nervosa and bulimia nervosa. *Archives of General Psychiatry, 44,* 1047–1056.

Rutter, D. R., & Durkin, K. (1987). Turn-taking in mother-infant interaction: An examination of vocalizations and gaze. *Developmental Psychology, 23,* 54–61.

Rutter, M. (1979). Protective factors in children's responses to stress and disadvantage. In M. W. Kent & J. E. Rolf (Eds.), *Primary prevention of psychopathology. Vol. 3: Social competence in children.* Hanover, NH: University Press of New England.

Rutter, M. (1981). *Maternal deprivation revisited* (2nd ed.). New York: Penguin Books.

Rutter, M. (1983). School effects on pupil progress: Research findings and policy implications. *Child Development, 54,* 1–29.

Rutter, M., Maughan, B., Mortimore, P., Ouston, J., & Smith, A. (1979). *Fifteen thousand hours: Secondary schools and their effects on children.* Cambridge, MA: Harvard University Press.

Ryan, R. M., & Lynch, J. H. (1989). Emotional autonomy versus detachment: Revisiting the vicissitudes of adolescence and young adulthood. *Child Development, 60,* 340–356.

Saarni, C. (1984). An observational study of children's attempts to monitor their expressive behavior. *Child Development, 55,* 1504–1513.

Saarni, C. (1989). Children's understanding of strategic control of emotional expression in social transactions. In C. Saarni & P. L. Harris (Eds.), *Children's understanding of emotion.* New York: Cambridge University Press.

Saarni, C. (1990). Emotional competence: How emotions and relationships become integrated. In R. A. Thompson (Ed.), Socioemotional development. *Nebraska Symposium on Motivation* (Vol. 36). Lincoln: University of Nebraska Press.

Saccuzzo, D. P., Johnson, N. E., & Russell, G. (1992). Verbal versus performance IQs for gifted African-American, Caucasion, Filipino, and Hispanic children. *Psychological Assessment, 4,* 239–244.

Sachs, J. (1985). Prelinguistic development. In J. Berko Gleason (Ed.), *The development of language.* Columbus, OH: Merrill.

Sacks, E. L. (1952). Intelligence scores as a function of experimentally established social relationships between child and examiner. *Journal of Abnormal and Social Psychology, 47,* 354–358.

Sagi, A., & Hoffman, M. L. (1976). Empathic distress in newborns. *Developmental Psychology, 12,* 175–176.

Sagi, A., van IJzendoorn, M. H., Aviezer, O., Donnell, F., & Mayseless, O. (1994). Sleeping out of home in a kibbutz communal arrangement: It makes a difference for mother-infant attachment. *Child Development, 65,* 992–1004.

Sagotsky, G., & Lepper, M. R. (1982). Generalization of changes in children's preferences for easy or difficult goals induced through peer modeling. *Child Development, 53,* 372–375.

Sagov, S. E., & Brodsky, A. (1984). The issue of safety. In S. E. Sagov, R. I. Feinbloom, P. Spindel, & A. Brodsky (Eds.), *Home birth: A practitioner's guide to birth outside the hospital.* Rockville, MD: Aspen.

Salapatek, P. (1975). Pattern perception in early infancy. In L. B. Cohen & P. Salapatek (Eds.), *Infant perception: From sensation to cognition.* New York: Academic Press.

Salthouse, T. A. (1993). Speed mediation of age differences in cognition. *Developmental Psychology, 29,* 722–738.

Saltz, E., Campbell, S., & Skotko, D. (1983). Verbal control of behavior: The effects of shouting. *Developmental Psychology, 19,* 461–464.

Salzinger, S., Feldman, R. S., Hammer, M., & Rosario, M. (1993). The effects of physical abuse on children's social relationships. *Child Development, 64,* 169–187.

Sameroff, A. J. (1983). Developmental systems: Contexts and evolution. In W. Kessen (Ed.), *Handbook of child psychology. Vol. 1: History, theory, and methods* (4th ed.). New York: Wiley.

Sameroff, A. J., & Chandler, M. J. (1975). Reproductive risk and the continuum of caretaking casualty. In F. D. Horowitz, M. Hetherington, S. Scarr-Salapatek, & G. Siegel (Eds.), *Review of child development research* (Vol.4). Chicago: University of Chicago Press.

Sameroff, A. J., Seifer, R., Baldwin, A., & Baldwin, C. (1993). Stability of intelligence from preschool to adolescence: The influence of social and family risk factors. *Child Development, 64,* 80–97.

Samuels, C. (1986). Bases for the infant's development of self-awareness. *Human Development, 29,* 36–48.

Sancilio, M. F. M., Plumert, J. M., & Hartup, W. W. (1989). Friendship and aggressiveness as determinants of conflict outcomes in middle childhood. *Developmental Psychology, 25,* 812–819.

Santrock, J. W. (1975). Moral structure: The interrelations of moral behavior, moral judgment, and moral affect. *Journal of Genetic Psychology, 127,* 201–213.

Santrock, J. W., & Sitterle, K. A. (1987). Parent-child relationships in stepmother families. In K. Pasley & M. Ihinger-Tallman (Eds.), *Remarriage and stepparenting: Current research and theory.* New York: Guilford Press.

Sattler, R. P. (1988). *Assessment of children's intelligence and special abilities* (3rd ed.). San Diego, CA: J. M. Sattler.

Savage-Rumbaugh, E. S., Murphy, J., Sevcik, R. A., Brakke, K. E., Williams, S. L., & Rumbaugh, D. M. (1993). Language comprehension in ape and child. *Monographs of the Society for Research in Child Development, 58*(3–4, Serial No. 233).

Savage-Rumbaugh, E. S., Rumbaugh, D. M., & Boysen, S. (1978). Symbolic communication between two chimpanzees (Pan troglodytes). *Science, 201,* 641–644.

Savin-Williams, R. C. (1995). An exploratory study of pubertal maturation timing and self-esteem among gay and bisexual male youths. *Developmental Psychology, 31,* 56–64.

Savin-Williams, R. C., & Demo, D. H. (1984). Developmental change and stability in adolescent self-concept. *Developmental Psychology, 20,* 1100–1110.

Savin-Williams, R. C., & Small, S. A. (1986). The timing of puberty and its relationship to adolescent and parent perceptions of family interactions. *Developmental Psychology, 32,* 342–347.

Saxe, G. B. (1988). The mathematics of child street vendors. *Child Development, 59,* 1415–1425.

Saxe, G. B. (1991). *Culture and cognitive development: Studies in mathematical understanding.* Hillsdale, NJ: Erlbaum.

Scafidi, F. A., Field, T. M., Schanberg, S. M., Bauer, C. R., Vega-Lahr, N., Garcia, R., Poirier, J., Nystrom, G., & Kuhn, C. M. (1986). Effects of tactile/kinesthetic stimulation on the clinical course and sleep/wake behavior pattern of preterm neonates. *Infant Behavior and Development, 9,* 91–105.

Scafidi, F. A., Field, T. M., Schanberg, S. M., Bauer, C. R., Vega-Lahr, N., Garcia, R., Poirer, J., Nystrom, G., & Kuhn, C. M. (1990). Massage stimulates growth in preterm infants: A replication. *Infant Behavior and Development, 13,* 167–188.

Scarborough, H. S. (1990). Very early language deficits in dyslexic children. *Child Development, 61,* 1728–1743.

Scarr, S. (1984). *Mother care/other care.* New York: Basic Books.

Scarr, S., & Eisenberg, M. (1993). Child care research: Issues, perspectives, and results. *Annual Review of Psychology, 44,* 613–644.

Scarr, S., & Kidd, K. K. (1983). Developmental behavior genetics. P. H. Mussen (Ed.), *Handbook of child psychology. Vol. 2: Infancy, and developmental psychobiology.* New York: Wiley.

Scarr, S., & McCartney, K. (1983). How people make their own environments: A theory of genotype→environment effects. *Child Development, 54,* 424–435.

Scarr, S., Pakstis, A. J., Katz, S. H., & Barker, W. (1977). The absence of a relationship between degree of white ancestry and intellectual skills within a black population. *Human Genetics, 39,* 69–86.

Scarr, S., Phillips, D., McCartney, K., & Abbott-Shim, M. (1993). Quality of child care as an aspect of family and child care policy in the United States. *Pediatrics, 91,* 182–188.

Scarr, S., Webber, P. L., Weinberg, R. A., & Wittig, M. A. (1981). Personality resemblance among adolescents and their parents in biologically related and adoptive families. *Journal of Personality and Social Psychology, 40,* 885–898.

Scarr, S., & Weinberg, R. A. (1976). IQ test performance of black children adopted by white families. *American Psychologist, 31,* 726–739.

Scarr, S., & Weinberg, R. A. (1978). The influence of family background on intellectual attainment. *American Sociological Review, 43,* 674–692.

Scarr, S., & Weinberg, R. A. (1983). The Minnesota adoption studies: Genetic differences and malleability. *Child Development, 54,* 260–267.

Schachter, F. F. (1981). Toddlers with employed mothers. *Child Development, 52,* 958–964.

Schaefer, M., Hatcher, R. P., & Barglow, P. D. (1980). Prematurity and infant stimulation: A review of research. *Child Psychiatry and Human Development, 10,* 199–212.

Schaffer, H. R. (1971). *The growth of sociability.* Baltimore: Penguin Books.

Schaffer, H. R. (1977). *Mothering.* Cambridge, MA: Harvard University Press.

Schaffer, H. R., & Emerson, P. E. (1964). The development of social attachments in infancy. *Monographs of the Society for Research in Child Development, 29*(3, Serial No. 94).

Schaie, K. W. (1965). A general model for the study of developmental problems. *Psychological Bulletin, 64,* 91–107.

Schaie, K. W. (1986). Beyond calendar definitions of age, time, and cohort: The general developmental model revisited. *Developmental Review, 6,* 252–277.

Schaie, K. W. (1990). Intellectual development in adulthood. In J. E. Birren & K. W. Schaie (Eds.), *The handbook of the psychology of aging* (3rd ed.). San Diego, CA: Academic.

Schaie, K. W., & Hertzog, C. (1986). Toward a comprehensive model of adult intellectual development: Contributions of the Seattle longitudinal study. In R. J. Sternberg (Ed.), *Advances in the psychology of human intelligence* (Vol. 3). Hillsdale, NJ: Erlbaum.

Schalock, R. L., Holl, C., Elliott, B., & Ross, I. (1992). A longitudinal follow-up of graduates from a rural special education program. *Learning Disability Quarterly, 15,* 29–38.

Schardein, J. L. (1985). *Chemically induced birth defects.* New York: Dekker.

Schieffelin, B. B. (1986). *How Kaluli children learn what to say, what to do, and how to feel.* New York: Cambridge University Press.

Schiff-Myers, N. (1988). Hearing children of deaf parents. In D. Bishop & K. Mogford (Eds.), *Language development in exceptional circumstances.* Edinburgh: Churchill Livingstone.

Schinke, S. P., Schilling, R. F., II, Barth, R. P., Gilchrist, L. D., & Maxwell, J. S. (1986). Stress-management intervention to prevent family violence. *Journal of Family Violence, 1,* 13–26.

Schliemann, A. D. (1992). Mathematical concepts in and out of school in Brazil: From developmental psychology to better teaching. *Newsletter of the International Society for the Study of Behavioral Development* (Serial No. 22, No. 2), 1–3.

Schneider, B. H. (1992). Didactic methods for enhancing children's peer relations: A quantitative review. *Clinical Psychology Review, 12,* 363–382.

Schneider, W., & Bjorklund, D. F. (1992). Expertise, aptitude, and strategic remembering. *Child Development, 63,* 461–471.

Schneider, W., Korkel, J., & Weinert, F. E. (1989). Domain-specific knowledge and memory performance: A comparison of high- and low-aptitude children. *Journal of Educational Psychology, 81,* 306–312.

Schneider, W., & Pressley, M. (1989). *Memory development between 2 and 20.* New York: Springer-Verlag.

Schneider-Rosen, K., & Wenz-Gross, M. (1990). Patterns of compliance from eighteen to thirty months of age. *Child Development, 61,* 104–112.

Schnoll, S. H. (1986). Pharmacologic basis of perinatal addiction. In I. J. Chasnoff (Ed.), *Drug use in pregnancy: Mother and child.* Boston: MTP Press Limited.

Schramm, W., Barnes, D., & Bakewell, J. (1987). Neonatal mortality in Missouri home births. *American Journal of Public Health, 77,* 930–935.

Schulman, J. D., & Black, S. H. (1993). Genetics of some common inherited diseases. In R. G. Edwards (Ed.), *Preconception and preimplantation diagnosis of human genetic disease.* Cambridge, England: Cambridge University Press.

Schuster, D. T. (1990). Fulfillment of potential, life satisfaction, and competence: Comparing four cohorts of gifted women at midlife. *Journal of Educational Psychology, 82,* 471–478.

Schwartz, D., Dodge, K. A., & Coie, J. D. (1993). The emergence of chronic peer victimization in boys' play groups. *Child Development, 64,* 1755–1772.

Scott, J. P. (1992). Aggression: Functions and control in social systems. *Aggressive Behavior, 18,* 1–20.

Scott, W. A., Scott, R., & McCabe, M. (1991). Family relationships and children's personality: A cross-cultural, cross-source comparison. *British Journal of Social Psychology, 30,* 1–20

Seabrook, C. (1987, March 23). Binge eating can be hazardous to your health. *Atlanta Journal,* 18.

Seabrook, C. (1994, July 9). Early fetal test can cause birth defects. *Atlanta Constitution,* D7.

Sears, R. R. (1963). Dependency motivation. In M. Jones (Ed.), *Nebraska Symposium on Motivation* (Vol. 11). Lincoln: University of Nebraska Press.

Sears, R. R., Maccoby, E. E., & Levin, H. (1957). *Patterns of child rearing.* New York: Harper & Row.

Sebald, H. (1986). Adolescents' shifting orientation toward parents and peers: A curvilinear trend over recent decades. *Journal of Marriage and the Family, 48,* 5–13.

Sedlak, A. J., & Kurtz, S. T. (1981). A review of children's use of causal inference principles. *Child Development, 52,* 759–784.

Seidman, E., Allen, L., Aber, J. L., Mitchell, C., & Feinman, J. (1994). The impact of school transitions in early adolescence on the self-system and perceived social context of poor urban youth. *Child Development, 65,* 507–522.

Seitz, V., & Apfel, N. H. (1994a). Effects of a school for pregnant students on the incidence of low-birthweight deliveries. *Child Development, 65,* 666–676.

Seitz, V., & Apfel, N. H. (1994b). Parent-focused intervention: Diffusion effects on siblings. *Child Development, 65,* 677–683.

Seitz, V., Rosenbaum, L. K., & Apfel, N. H. (1985). Effects of family support intervention: A ten-year follow-up. *Child Development, 56,* 376–391.

Seligman, J. (1990, October 1). Curing cystic fibrosis? Genes convert sick cells. *Newsweek,* 64.

Selman, R. L. (1971). The relation of role-taking to the development of moral judgment in children. *Child Development, 42,* 79–91.

Selman, R. L. (1976). Social-cognitive understanding: A guide to educational and clinical practice. In T. Lickona (Ed.), *Moral development and behavior: Theory, research, and social issues.* New York: Holt, Rinehart & Winston.

Selman, R. L. (1980). *The growth of interpersonal understanding.* Orlando, FL: Academic Press.

Selman, R. L., & Byrne, D. (1974). A structural developmental analysis of role-taking in middle childhood. *Child Development, 45,* 803–806.

Seltzer, J. A., & Bianchi, S. M. (1988). Children's contact with absent parents. *Journal of Marriage and the Family, 50,* 663–677.

Sena, R., & Smith, L. B. (1990). New evidence on the development of the word *Big. Child Development, 61,* 1034–1052.

Serbin, L. A., Powlishta, K. K., & Gulko, J. (1993). The development of sex typing in middle childhood. *Monographs of the Society for Research in Child Development, 58*(2, Serial No. 232).

Shaffer, D. R. (1973). *Children's responses to a hypothetical proposition.* Unpublished manuscript, Kent State University.

Shaffer, D. R. (1994a). Do naturalistic conceptions of morality provide any novel answers? *Journal of Personality, 62,* 263–268.

Shaffer, D. R. (1994b). *Social and personality development* (3rd ed.). Pacific Grove, CA: Brooks/Cole.

Shaffer, D. R., Pegalis, L. J., & Cornell, D. P. (1992). Gender and self-disclosure revisited: Personal and contextual variations in self-disclosure to same-sex acquaintants. *Journal of Social Psychology, 132,* 307–315.

Shannon, D. C., Kelly, D. H., Askelrod, S., & Kilborn, K. M. (1987). Increased respiratory frequency and variability in high risk babies who die of sudden infant death syndrome. *Pediatric Research, 22,* 158–162.

Shantz, C. U. (1983). Social cognition. In P. H. Mussen (Ed.), *Handbook of child psychology. Vol. 3: Cognitive development.* New York: Wiley.

Shantz, C. U. (1987). Conflicts between children. *Child Development, 58,* 283–305.

Shatz, M. (1983). Communication. In P. H. Mussen (Ed.), *Handbook of child psychology* (Vol. 3). New York: Wiley.

Shatz, M., & Gelman, R. (1973). The development of communication skills: Modifications in the speech of young children as a function of listener. *Monographs of the Society for Research in Child Development, 38* (5, Serial No. 152).

Shaw, D. S., Keenan, K., & Vondra, J. I. (1994). Developmental precursors of externalizing behavior: Ages 1 to 3. *Developmental Psychology, 30,* 355–364.

Shearer, L. (1994, April 2). U.Ga. symposium speaker raps "crack babies" research. *Athens Banner-Herald,* 1A, 10A.

Sheingold, K., & Tenney, Y. J. (1982). Memory for a salient childhood event. In U. Neisser (Ed.), *Memory observed: Remembering in natural contexts.* San Francisco: W. H. Freeman.

Sherif, M., Harvey, O. J., White, B. J., Hood, W. R., & Sherif, C. W. (1961). *Intergroup conflict and cooperation: The Robber's Cave experiment.* Norman: University of Oklahoma Press.

Sherman, M., & Key, C. B. (1932). The intelligence of isolated mountain children. *Child Development, 3,* 279–290.

Sherrod, K. B., O'Connor, S., Vietze, P. M., & Altemeier, W. A., III (1984). Child health and maltreatment. *Child Development, 55,* 1174–1183.

Shigetomi, C. C., Hartmann, D. P., & Gelfand, D. M. (1981). Sex differences in children's altruistic behavior and reputations for helpfulness. *Developmental Psychology, 17,* 434–437.

Shirley, M. M. (1933). *The first two years: A study of 25 babies. Vol. 1: Postural and locomotor development.* Minneapolis: University of Minnesota Press.

Shoda, Y., Mischel, W., & Peake, P. K. (1990). Predicting adolescent cognitive and self-regulatory competencies from preschool delay of gratification: Identifying diagnostic conditions. *Developmental Psychology, 26,* 978–986.

Shuey, A. (1966). *The testing of Negro intelligence.* New York: Social Science Press.

Shure, M. B. (1989). Interpersonal competence training. In W. Damon (Ed.), *Child development today and tomorrow.* San Francisco: Jossey-Bass.

Shure, M. B., & Spivack, G. (1978). *Problem-solving techniques in childrearing.* San Francisco: Jossey-Bass.

Shurkin, J. N. (1992). *Terman's kids. The groundbreaking study of how the gifted grow up.* Boston: Little, Brown.

Shweder, R. A., Mahapatra, M., & Miller, J. G. (1990). Culture and moral development. In J. W. Stigler, R. A. Shweder, & G. Herdt (Eds.) *Cultural psychology: Essays on comparative human development.* Cambridge, England: Cambridge University Press.

Siegal, M., & Cowen, J. (1984). Appraisals of intervention: The mother's versus the culprit's behavior as determinants of children's evaluations of discipline techniques. *Child Development, 55,* 1760–1766.

Siegler, R. S. (1976). Three aspects of cognitive development. *Cognitive Psychology, 8,* 481–520.

Siegler, R. S. (1981). Developmental sequences within and between concepts. *Monographs of the Society for Research in Child Development, 46* (2, Serial No. 189).

Siegler, R. S. (1983). Information-processing approaches to development. In P. H. Mussen (Ed.), *Handbook of child psychology. Vol. 1: History, theory, and methods.* New York: Wiley.

Siegler, R. S. (1988). Individual differences in strategy choices: Good students, not-so-good students, and perfectionists. *Child Development, 59,* 833–851.

Siegler, R. S. (1991). *Children's thinking* (2nd ed.). Englewood Cliffs, NJ: Prentice Hall.

Sigel, I. E., Roeper, A., & Hooper, F. H. (1968). A training procedure for the acquisition of Piaget's conservation of quantity: A pilot study and its replication. In I. E. Sigel & F. H. Hooper (Eds.), *Logical thinking in children: Research based on Piaget's theory.* New York: Holt, Rinehart & Winston.

Sigelman, C. K., Carr, M. B., & Begley, N. L. (1986) Developmental changes in the influence of sex-role stereotypes on person perception. *Child Study Journal, 16,* 191–205.

Sigelman, C. K., Miller, T. E., & Whitworth, L. A. (1986). The early development of stigmatizing reactions to physical differences. *Journal of Applied Developmental Psychology, 7,* 17–32.

Sigelman, C. K., & Shaffer, D. R. (1995). *Life-span human development* (2nd ed.), Pacific Grove, CA: Brooks/Cole.

Sigelman, C. K., & Waitzman, K. A. (1991). The development of distributive justice orientations: Contextual influences on children's resource allocations. *Child Development, 62,* 1367–1378.

Sigman, M., & Sena, R. (1993). Pretend play in high-risk and developmentally delayed children. In M. H. Bornstein & A. W. O'Reilly (Eds.), *The role of play in the development of thought* (New Directions for Child Development, No. 59). San Francisco: Jossey-Bass.

Signorella, M. L., & Jamison, W. (1986). Masculinity, femininity, androgyny, and cognitive performance: A meta-analysis. *Psychological Bulletin, 16,* 207–228.

Signorella, M. L., Jamison, W., & Krupa, M. H. (1989). Predicting spatial performance from gender stereotyping in activity preferences and in self-concept. *Developmental Psychology, 25,* 89–95.

Signorielli, N. (1991). *A sourcebook on children and television.* Westport, CT: Greenwood Press.

Signorielli, N., & Lears, M. (1992). Children, television, and conceptions about chores: Attitudes and behaviors. *Sex Roles, 27,* 157–170.

Silver, L. B. (1992). *Attention-deficit hyperactivity disorder: A clinical guide to diagnosis and treatment.* Washington, D.C.: American Psychiatric Press.

Simmons, R. G., & Blyth, G. A. (1987). *Moving into adolescence: The impact of pubertal change in school context.* New York: A. de Gruyter.

Simmons, R. G., Burgeson, R., Carlton-Ford, S., & Blyth, D. A. (1987). The impact of cumulative change in early adolescence. *Child Development, 58,* 1220–1234.

Simons, R. L., Beaman, J. Conger, R. D., & Chao, W. (1993). Stress, support, and antisocial behavior trait as determinants of emotional well-being and parenting practices among single mothers. *Journal of Marriage and the Family, 55,* 385–398.

Simons, R. L., Lorenz, F. O., Wu, C., & Conger, R. D. (1993). Social network and marital support as mediators and moderators of the impact of stress and depression on parental behavior. *Developmental Psychology, 29,* 368–381.

Simons, R. L., Whitbeck, L. B., Conger, R. D., & Wu, C. (1991). Intergenerational transmission of harsh parenting. *Developmental Psychology, 27,* 159–171.

Simpson, J. L. (1993). Genetic causes of spontaneous abortion. In C. Lin, M. S. Verp, & R. E. Sabbagha (Eds.), *The high-risk fetus: Pathophysiology, diagnosis, management.* New York: Springer-Verlag.

Simpson, J. R., Rholes, W. S., & Nelligan, J. S. (1992). Support seeking and support giving within couples in an anxiety-provoking situation: The role of attachment styles. *Journal of Personality and Social Psychology, 62,* 434–446.

Sinclair, A. H., Berta, P., Palmer, M. S., Hawkins, J. R., Griffiths, B. L., Smith, M. J., Foster, J. W., Frishauf, A. M., Lovell-Badge, R., & Goodfellow, P. N. (1990). A gene from the human sex-determining region encodes a protein with homology to a conserved DNA-binding motif. *Nature, 346,* 240–244.

Singer, D. G., & Singer, J. L. (1990). *The house of make-believe: Children's play and the developing imagination.* Cambridge, MA: Harvard University Press.

Singer, L., Farkas, K., & Kleigman, R. (1992). Childhood medical and behavioral consequences of maternal cocaine use. *Journal of Pediatric Psychology, 17,* 389–406.

Singer, L. M., Brodzinsky, D. M., Ramsay, D., Steir, M., & Waters, E. (1985). Mother-infant attachments in adoptive families. *Child Development, 56,* 1543–1551.

Skinner, B. F. (1953). *Science and human behavior.* New York: Macmillan.

Skinner, B. F. (1957). *Verbal behavior.* East Norwalk, CT: Appleton-Century-Crofts.

Skinner, B. F. (1971). *Beyond freedom and dignity.* New York: Knopf.

Skodak, M., & Skeels, H. M. (1949). A final follow-up study of children in adoptive homes. *Journal of Genetic Psychology, 75,* 85–125.

Skolnick, A. (1986). Early attachment and personal relationships across the life course. In P. B. Baltes, D. L. Featherman, & R. M. Lerner (Eds.), *Life-span development and behavior* (Vol. 7). Hillsdale, NJ: Erlbaum.

Skouteris, H., McKenzie, B. E., & Day, R. H. (1992). Integration of sequential information for shape perception by infants: A developmental study. *Child Development, 63,* 1164–1176.

Slaby, R. G., & Crowley, C. G. (1977). Modification of cooperation and aggression through teacher attention to children's speech. *Journal of Experimental Child Psychology, 23,* 442–458.

Slaby, R. G., & Frey, K. S. (1975). Development of gender constancy and selective attention to same-sex models. *Child Development, 46,* 849–856.

Slaby, R. G., & Guerra, N. G. (1988). Cognitive mediators of aggression in adolescent offenders. 1: Assessment. *Developmental Psychology, 24,* 580–588.

Slade, A. (1987). A longitudinal study of maternal involvement and symbolic play during the toddler period. *Child Development, 58,* 367–375.

Slater, A., Mattock, A., & Brown, E. (1990a). Size constancy at birth: Newborn infants' responses to retinal and real size. *Journal of Experimental Child Psychology, 49,* 314–322.

Slater, A., Morison, V., Somers, M., Mattock, A., Brown, E., & Taylor, D. (1990b). Newborn and older infants' perception of partly occluded objects. *Infant Behavior and Development, 13,* 33–49.

Slater, A., Morison, V., Town, C., & Rose, D. (1985). Movement perception and identity constancy in the new-born baby. *British Journal of Developmental Psychology, 3,* 211–220.

Slaughter-Defoe, D. T., Nakagawa, K., Takanishi, R., & Johnson, D. J. (1990). Toward cultural/ecological perspectives on schooling and achievement in African- and Asian-American children. *Child Development, 61,* 363–383.

Slavin, R. E. (1986). Cooperative learning: Engineering social psychology in the classroom. In R. S. Feldman (Ed.), *The social psychology of education: Current research and theory.* Cambridge, England: Cambridge University Press.

Slavin, R. E. (1987). Ability grouping and student achievement in elementary schools: A best evidence synthesis. *Review of Educational Research, 57,* 293–336.

Slavin, R. E. (1989). Class size and student achievement: Small effects of small classes. *Educational Psychologist, 24,* 99–110.

Slavin, R. E. (1991). Cooperative learning and group contingencies. *Journal of Behavioral Education, 1,* 105–115.

Sleek, S. (1994). Bilingualism enhances student growth. *Monitor of the American Psychological Association, 25*(4), 48–49.

Slobin, D. I. (1966). The acquisition of Russian as a native language. In F. Smith & G. A. Miller (Eds.), *The genesis of language: A psycholinguistic approach.* Cambridge, MA: MIT Press.

Slobin, D. I. (1979). *Psycholinguistics.* Glenview, IL: Scott, Foresman.

Slobin, D. I. (1985). Crosslinguistic evidence for the language making capacity. In D. I. Slobin (Ed.), *The crosslinguistic study of language acquisition. Vol. 2: Theoretical issues.* Hillsdale, NJ: Erlbaum.

Smetana, J. G. (1981). Preschool children's conceptions of moral and social rules. *Child Development, 52,* 1333–1336.

Smetana, J. G. (1985). Preschool children's conceptions of transgressions: Effects of varying moral and conventional domain-related attributes. *Developmental Psychology, 21,* 18–29.

Smetana, J. G., & Asquith, P. (1994). Adolescents' and parents' conceptions of parental authority and personal autonomy. *Child Development, 65,* 1147–1162.

Smetana, J. G., Schlagman, N., & Adams, P. W. (1993). Preschool children's judgments about hypothetical and actual transgressions. *Child Development, 64,* 202–214.

Smiley, P. A., & Dweck, C. S. (1994). Individual differences in achievement goals among young children. *Child Development, 65,* 1723–1743.

Smith, F. (1977). Making sense of reading—and of reading instruction. *Harvard Educational Review, 47,* 386–395.

Smith, K., & Crawford, S. (1986). Suicidal behavior among "normal" high school students. *Suicide and Life-Threatening Behavior, 16,* 313–325.

Smith, P. K., & Connolly, K. J. (1980). *The ecology of preschool behavior.* New York: Cambridge University Press.

Smith, P. K., & Daglish, L. (1977). Sex differences in parent and infant behavior in the home. *Child Development, 48,* 1250–1254.

Smith, S. (1942). Language and nonverbal test performance of racial groups in Honolulu before and after a 14-year interval. *Journal of General Psychology, 26,* 51–93.

Smith, T. W. (1990). Academic achievement and teaching younger siblings. *Social Psychology Quarterly, 53,* 352–363.

Smock, P. J. (1993). The economic costs of marital disruption for young women over the past two decades. *Demography, 30,* 353–371.

Smolak, L., & Levine, M. P. (1993). Separation-individuation difficulties and the distinction between bulimia nervosa and anorexia nervosa in college women. *International Journal of Eating Disorders, 14,* 33–41.

Smoll, F. L., & Schutz, R. W. (1990). Quantifying gender differences in physical performance: A developmental perspective. *Developmental Psychology, 26,* 360–369.

Snarey, J. R. (1985). Cross-cultural universality of social-moral development: A critical review of Kohlbergian research. *Psychological Bulletin, 97,* 202–232.

Snarey, J. R., & Keljo, K. (1991). In a gemeinschaft voice: The cross-cultural expansion of moral development theory. In W. M. Kurtines & J. L. Gewirtz (Eds.), *Handbook of moral behavior and development* (Vol. 1). Hillsdale, NJ: Erlbaum.

Snow, C. E., Arlman-Rupp, A., Hassing, Y., Jobse, J., Joosken, J., & Vorster, J. (1976). Mother's speech in three social classes. *Journal of Psycholinguistic Research, 5,* 1–20.

Snow, C. E., & Ferguson, C. A. (Eds.). (1977). *Talking to children.* Cambridge, England: Cambridge University Press.

Snow, C. W. (1989). *Infant development.* Englewood Cliffs, NJ: Prentice Hall.

Snow, M. E., Jacklin, C. N., & Maccoby, E. E. (1983). Sex-of-child differences in father-child interaction at one year of age. *Child Development, 54,* 227–232.

Society for Research in Child Development, Committee for Ethical Conduct in Child Development Research (1990, Winter). SRCD ethical standards for research with children. *SRCD Newsletter,* 5–7.

Sodian, B. (1988). Children's attribution of knowledge to the listener in a referential communication task. *Child Development, 59,* 378–385.

Sodian, B. (1990). Understanding verbal communication: Children's ability to deliberately manipulate ambiguity in referential messages. *Cognitive Development, 5,* 209–222.

Sodian, B., Taylor, C., Harris, P. L., & Perner, J. (1991). Early deception and the child's theory of mind: False trails and genuine markers. *Child Development, 62,* 468–483.

Sokolov, J. L. (1993). A local contingency analysis of the fine-tuning hypothesis. *Developmental Psychology, 29,* 1008–1023.

Somerville, S. C., Wellman, H. M., & Cultice, J. C. (1983). Young children's deliberate reminding. *Journal of Genetic Psychology, 143,* 87–96.

Sonnenschein, S. (1986a). Development of referential communication: Deciding that a message is uninformative. *Developmental Psychology, 22,* 164–168.

Sonnenschein, S. (1986b). Development of referential communication skills: How familiarity with a listener affects a speaker's production of redundant messages. *Developmental Psychology, 22,* 549–555.

Sonnenschein, S. (1988). The development of referential communication: Speaking to different listeners. *Child Development, 59,* 694–702.

Sontag, L. W. (1944). War and the fetal maternal relationship. *Marriage and Family Living, 6,* 1–5.

Sorensen, A. B., & Hallinan, M. T. (1986). Effects of ability grouping on growth in academic achievement. *American Educational Research Journal, 23,* 519–542.

Spaulding, D. A. (1873). Instinct with original observation in young animals. *MacMillans Magazine, 27,* 282–283.

Spearman, C. (1927). *The abilities of man.* New York: Macmillan.

Speicher, B. (1994). Family patterns of moral judgment during adolescence and early adulthood. *Developmental Psychology, 30,* 624–632.

Spelke, E. S., Hofsten, C. von, & Kestenbaum, R. (1989). Object perception in infancy: Interaction of spatial and kinetic information for object boundaries. *Developmental Psychology, 2,* 185–196.

Spence, J. T. (1993). Gender-related traits and gender ideology: Evidence for a multifactorial theory. *Journal of Personality and Social Psychology, 64,* 624–635.

Spence, J. T., & Helmreich, R. L. (1978). *Masculinity and femininity:* Their psychological dimensions, correlates, and antecedents. Austin: TX: University of Texas Press.

Spencer, M. B. (1988). Self-concept development. In D. T. Slaughter (Ed.), *Black children in poverty: Developmental perspectives.* San Francisco: Jossey-Bass.

Spencer, M. B., & Markstrom-Adams, C. (1990). Identity processes among racial and ethnic minority children in America. *Child Development, 61,* 290–310.

Spieker, S. J., & Bensley, L. (1994). Roles of living arrangements and grandmother social support in adolescent mothering and infant attachment. *Developmental Psychology, 30,* 102–111.

Spiker, D., Ferguson, J., & Brooks-Gunn, J. (1993). Enhancing maternal interactive behavior and child social competence in low birthweight, premature infants. *Child Development, 64,* 754–768.

Spitz, H. H., & Borland, M. D. (1971). Redundancy in line drawings of familiar objects: Effects of age and intelligence. *Cognitive Psychology, 2,* 196–205.

Spitz, R. A. (1945). Hospitalism: An inquiry into the genesis of psychiatric conditions in early childhood. In A. Freud (Ed.), *The psychoanalytic study of the child* (Vol. 1). New York: International Universities Press.

Spitz, R. A. (1965). *The first year of life: A psychoanalytic study of normal and deviant object relations.* New York: International Universities Press.

Spitze, G. (1988). Women's employment and family relations: A review. *Journal of Marriage and the Family, 50,* 595–618.

Sprigle, J. E., & Schaefer, L. (1985). Longitudinal evaluation of the effects of two compensatory preschool programs on fourth- through sixth-grade students. *Developmental Psychology, 21,* 702–708.

Sroufe, L. A. (1977). Wariness of strangers and the study of infant development. *Child Development, 48,* 1184–1199.

Sroufe, L. A. (1985). Attachment classification from the perspective of infant-caregiver relationships and infant temperament. *Child Development, 56,* 1–14.

Sroufe, L. A., Bennett, C., Englund, M., Urban, J., & Shulman, S. (1993). The significance of gender boundaries in preadolescence: Contemporary correlates and antecedents of boundary violation and maintenance. *Child Development, 64,* 455–466.

Sroufe, L. A., Egeland, B., & Kreutzer, T. (1990). The fate of early experience following developmental change: Longitudinal approaches to individual adaptation in childhood. *Child Development, 61,* 1363–1373.

Sroufe, L. A., Fox, N. E., & Pancake, V. R. (1983). Attachment and dependency in developmental perspective. *Child Development, 54,* 1615–1627.

Sroufe, L. A., Waters, E., & Matas, L. (1974). Contextual determinants of infant affectional response. In M. Lewis & L. A. Rosenblum (Eds.), *The origins of fear.* New York: Wiley.

Staats, A. (1975). *Social behaviorism.* Homewood, IL: Dorsey Press.

Staffieri, J. R. (1967). A study of social stereotype of body image in children. *Journal of Personality and Social Psychology, 7,* 101–104.

Starr, R. H., Jr. (1979). Child abuse. *American Psychologist, 34,* 872–878.

Stattin, H., & Magnusson, D. (1990). *Paths through life. Vol. 2: Pubertal maturation in female development.* Hillsdale, NJ: Erlbaum.

Steele, B. F., & Pollack, C. B. (1974). A psychiatric study of parents who abuse infants and small children. In R. E. Helfer & C. H. Kempe (Eds.), *The battered child.* Chicago: University of Chicago Press.

Stein, Z. A., & Susser, M. W. (1976). Prenatal nutrition and mental competence. In J. D. Lloyd-Still (Ed.), *Malnutrition and intellectual development.* Littleton, MA: Publishing Sciences Group.

Stein, Z. A., Susser, M. W., Saenger, G., & Marolla, F. (1975). *Famine and human development: The Dutch hunger winter of 1944–1945.* New York: Oxford University Press.

Steinberg, L. (1981). Tranformations in family relations at puberty. *Developmental Psychology, 17,* 833–840.

Steinberg, L. (1984). The varieties and effects of work during adolescence. In M. E. Lamb, A. L. Brown, & B. Rogoff (Eds.), *Advances in developmental psychology* (Vol. 3). Hillsdale, NJ: Erlbaum.

Steinberg, L. (1985). *Adolescence.* New York: Knopf.

Steinberg, L. (1986). Latchkey children and suspectibility to peer pressure: An ecological analysis. *Developmental Psychology, 22,* 433–439.

Steinberg, L. (1987). Single parents, stepparents, and the susceptibility of adolescents to antisocial peer pressure. *Child Development, 58,* 269–275.

Steinberg, L. (1988). Reciprocal relation between parent-child distance and puberbal maturation. *Developmental Psychology, 24,* 122–128.

Steinberg, L., & Dornbusch, S. M. (1991). Negative correlates of part-time employment during adolescence: Replication and elaboration. *Developmental Psychology, 27,* 304–313.

Steinberg, L., Dornbusch, S. M., & Brown, B. B. (1992). Ethnic differences in adolescent achievement: An ecological perspective. *American Psychologist, 47,* 723–729.

Steinberg, L., Elmen, J. D., & Mounts, N. S. (1989). Authoritative parenting, psychosocial maturity, and academic success among adolescents. *Child Development, 60,* 1424–1436.

Steinberg, L., Fegley, S., & Dornbusch, S. M. (1993). Negative impact of part-time work on adolescent adjustment: Evidence from a longitudinal study. *Developmental Psychology, 29,* 171–180.

Steinberg, L., Lamborn, S. D., Darling, N., Mounts, N. S., & Dornbusch, S. M. (1994). Over-time changes in adjustment and competence among adolescents from authoritative, authoritarian, indulgent, and neglectful families. *Child Development, 65,* 754–770.

Steinberg, L., Mounts, N. S., Lamborn, S., & Dornbusch, S. M. (1991). Authoritative parenting and adolescent adjustment across various ecological niches. *Journal of Research on Adolescence, 1,* 19–36.

Steinberg, L., & Silverberg, S. B. (1986). The vicissitudes of autonomy in early adolescence. *Child Development, 57,* 841–851.

Steinberg, L. D. (1981). Transformations in family relations at puberty. *Developmental Psychology, 17,* 833–840.

Steiner, J. E. (1979). Human facial expressions in response to taste and smell stimulation. In H. W. Reese & L. P. Lipsitt (Eds.), *Advances in child development and behavior* (Vol. 13). Orlando, FL: Academic Press.

Stephan, W. G. (1978). School desegregation: An evaluation of the predictions made in *Brown v. Board of Education. Psychological Bulletin, 85,* 217–238.

Stern, D. (1977). *The first relationship: Infant and mother.* Cambridge, MA: Harvard University Press.

Stern, D., Spieker, S., & MacKain, K. (1982). Intonational contours as signals in maternal speech to prelinguistic infants. *Developmental Psychology, 18,* 727–735.

Sternberg, K. J., Lamb, M. E., Greenbaum, C., Cicchetti, D., Dawud, S., Cortes, R. M., Krispin, O., & Lorey, F. (1993). Effects of domestic violence on children's behavior problems and depression. *Developmental Psychology, 29,* 44–52.

Sternberg, R. J. (1984). The Kaufman Assessment Battery for Children: An information-processing analysis and critique. *Journal of Special Education, 18,* 267–279.

Sternberg, R. J. (1985). *Beyond IQ. A triarchic theory of human intelligence.* Cambridge, England: Cambridge University Press.

Sternberg, R. J. (1991). Theory-based testing of intellectual abilities: Rationale for the triarchic abilities test. In H. A. H. Rowe (Ed.), *Intelligence: Reconceptualization and measurement.* Hillsdale, NJ: Erlbaum.

Stevenson, H. W., Chen, C., & Lee, S. (1993). Mathematics achievement of Chinese, Japanese, and American children: Ten years later. *Science, 259,* 53–58.

Stevenson, H. W., Chen, C., & Uttal, D. H. (1990). Beliefs and achievement: A study of black, white, and Hispanic children. *Child Development, 61,* 508–523.

Stevenson, H. W., & Lee, S. Y. (1990). Contexts of achievement: A study of American, Chinese, and Japanese children. *Monographs of the Society for Research in Child Development, 55*(1–2, Serial No. 221).

Stevenson, H. W., Lee, S. Y., & Stigler, J. W. (1986). Mathematics achievement of Chinese, Japanese, and American children. *Science, 231,* 693–699.

Stevenson, H. W., Stigler, J. W., Lee, S. Y., Lucker, G. W., Litamura, S., & Hsu, C. (1985). Cognitive performance and academic achievement of Japanese, Chinese, and American children. *Child Development, 56,* 718–734.

Stevenson, M. R., & Black, K. N. (1988). Paternal absence and sex-role development: A meta-analysis. *Child Development, 59,* 793–814.

Stewart, R. B. (1983). Sibling attachment relationships: Child-infant interactions in the strange situation. *Developmental Psychology, 19,* 192–199.

Stewart, R. B., & Marvin, R. S. (1984). Sibling relations: The role of conceptual perspective-taking in the ontogeny of sibling caregiving. *Child Development, 55,* 1322–1332.

Stewart, R. B., Mobley, L. A., Van Tuyl, S. S., & Salvador, M. A. (1987). The firstborn's adjustment to the birth of a sibling: A longitudinal assessment. *Child Development, 58,* 341–355.

Stigler, J. W., Lee, S. Y., & Stevenson, H. W. (1987). Mathematics classrooms in Japan, Taiwan, and the United States. *Child Development, 58,* 1272–1285.

Stipek, D., Gralinski, H., & Kopp, C. (1990). Self-concept development in the toddler years. *Developmental Psychology, 26,* 972–977.

Stipek, D., & Mac Iver, D. (1989). Developmental change in children's assessment of intellectual competence. *Child Development, 60,* 521–538.

Stipek, D. J., Recchia, S., & McClintic, S. (1992). Self-evaluation in young children. *Monographs of the Society for Research in Child Development, 57*(1, Serial No. 226).

Stipek, D. J., Roberts, T. A., & Sanborn, M. E. (1984). Preschool-age children's performance expectations for themselves and another child as a function of the incentive value of success and the salience of past performance. *Child Development, 55,* 1983–1989.

St. John, N. H. (1975). *School desegregation: Outcomes for children.* New York: Wiley.

Stoddart, T., & Turiel, E. (1985). Children's concepts of cross-gender activities. *Child Development, 56,* 1241–1252.

Stone, R. (1992). Can a father's exposure lead to illness in his children? *Science, 258,* 31.

Stott, D. H., & Latchford, S. A. (1976). Prenatal antecedents of child health, development, and behavior: An epidemiological report of incidence and association. *Journal of the American Academy of Child Psychiatry, 15,* 161–191.

St. Peters, M., Fitch, M., Huston, A. C., Wright, J. C., & Eakins, D. J. (1991). Television and families: What do young children watch with their parents? *Child Development, 62,* 1409–1423.

Strauss, S., & Levin, J. (1981). Comment on Siegler's "Developmental sequences within and between concepts." *Monographs of the Society for Research in Child Development, 46*(2, Serial No. 189).

Strayer, J. (1993). Children's concordant emotions and cognitions in response to observed emotions. *Child Development, 64,* 188–201.

Streissguth, A. P., Barr, H. M., Sampson, P. D., Darby, B. L., & Martin, D. C. (1989). IQ at age 4 in relation to maternal alcohol use and smoking during pregnancy. *Developmental Psychology, 25,* 3–11.

Streissguth, A. P., Bookstein, F. L., Sampson, P. D., & Barr, H. M. (1993). *The enduring effects of prenatal alcohol exposure on child development.* Ann Arbor, MI: University of Michigan Press.

Streitmatter, J. (1993). Gender differences in identity development: An examination of longitudinal data. *Adolescence, 28,* 55–66.

Streri, A., & Pecheux, M. (1986). Vision-to-touch and touch-to-vision transfer of form in 5-month-old infants. *British Journal of Developmental Psychology, 4,* 161–167.

Streri, A., & Spelke, E. S. (1988). Haptic perception of objects in infancy. *Cognitive Psychology, 20,* 1–23.

Strigini, P., Sanone, R., Carobbi, S., & Pierluigi, M. (1990). Radiation and Down's syndrome. *Nature, 347,* 717.

Stryker, M. P., Sherk, H., Leventhal, A. G., & Hirsch, V. H. B. (1978). Physiological consequences for the cat's visual cortex of effectively restricting early visual experience with oriented contours. *Journal of Neurophysiology, 41,* 896–909.

Stuckey, M. R., McGhee, P. E., & Bell, N. J. (1982). Parent-child interaction: The influence of maternal employment. *Developmental Psychology, 18,* 635–644.

Stumphauzer, J. S. (1972). Increased delay of gratification in young inmates through imitation of high-delay peer models. *Journal of Personality and Social Psychology, 21,* 10–17.

Stunkard, A. J., Harris, J. R., Pedersen, N., & McClearn, G. E. (1990). The body-mass index of twins who have been reared apart. *New England Journal of Medicine, 322,* 1483–1487.

Subotnik, R. F., Karp, D. E., & Morgan, E. R. (1989). High IQ children at midlife: An investigation into the generalizability of Terman's genetic studies of genius. *Roeper Review, 11,* 139–144.

Sudhalter, V., & Braine, M. D. S. (1985). How does comprehension of passives develop? A comparison of actional and experiential verbs. *Journal of Child Language, 12,* 455–470.

Sue, S., & Okazaki, S. (1990). Asian-American educational achievements: A phenomenon in search of explanation. *American Psychologist, 45,* 913–920.

Sullivan, H. S. (1953). *The interpersonal theory of psychiatry.* New York: Norton.

Sullivan, M. W., Lewis, M., & Alessandri, S. M. (1992). Cross-age stability in emotional expressions during learning and extinction. *Developmental Psychology, 28,* 58–63.

Suomi, S. J., & Harlow, H. F. (1978). Early experience and social development in rhesus monkeys. In M. E. Lamb (Ed.), *Social and personality development.* New York: Holt, Rinehart & Winston.

Super, C. M. (1981). Cross-cultural research on infancy. In H. C. Triandis & A. Heron (Eds.), *Handbook of cross-cultural psychology. Vol. 4: Developmental psychology.* London: Allyn & Bacon.

Super, C. M., Herrera, M. G., & Mora, J. O. (1990). Long-term effects of food supplementation and psychosocial intervention on the physical growth of Columbian infants at risk of malnutrition. *Child Development, 61,* 29–49.

Surber, C. F. (1982). Separable effects of motives, consequences, and presentation order on children's moral judgments. *Developmental Psychology, 18,* 257–266.

Tamis-LeMonda, C. S., & Bornstein, M. H. (1989). Habituation and maternal encouragement of attention as predictors of toddler language, play, and representational competence. *Child Development, 60,* 738–751.

Tan, L. E. (1985). Laterality and motor skills in 4-year-olds. *Child Development, 56,* 119–124.

Tanner, J. M. (1978). *Education and physical growth* (2nd ed.). London: Hodder and Stroughton.

Tanner, J. M. (1981). Growth and maturation during adolescence. *Nutrition Review, 39,* 43–55.

Tanner, J. M. (1990). *Fetus into man: Physical growth from conception to maturity.* Cambridge, MA: Harvard University Press.

Tannock, R., Schachar, R. J., & Logan, G. D. (1993). Does methylphenidate induce overfocusing in hyperactive children? *Journal of Clinical Child Psychology, 22,* 28–41.

Tarquinio, N., Zelazo, P. R., & Weiss, M. J. (1990). Recovery of neonatal head turning to decreased sound pressure level. *Developmental Psychology, 26,* 752–758.

Task Force on Pediatric AIDS (1989). Pediatric AIDS and human immunodeficiency virus infection. *American Psychologist, 44,* 258–264.

Taylor, A. R., Asher, S. R., & Williams, G. A. (1987). The social adaptation of mainstreamed mildly retarded children. *Child Development, 58,* 1321–1334.

Taylor, M., & Gelman, S. A. (1988). Adjectives and nouns: Children's strategies for learning new words. *Child Development, 59,* 411–419.

Taylor, M., & Gelman, S. A. (1989). Incorporating new words into the lexicon: Preliminary evidence for language hierarchies in two-year-old children. *Child Development, 60,* 625–636.

Taylor, R. D., Casten, R., & Flickinger, S. M. (1993). Influence of kinship social support on the parenting experiences and psychosocial adjustment of African-American adolescents. *Developmental Psychology, 29,* 382–388.

Taylor, R. E., & Richards, S. B. (1991). Patterns of intellectual differences of black, Hispanic, and white children. *Psychology in the Schools, 28,* 5–9.

Teegartin, C. (1994, July 25). Never-marrieds soar among single parents. *Atlanta Constitution,* A1, A7.

Teeven, R. C., & McGhee, P. E. (1972). Childhood development of fear of failure motivation. *Journal of Personality and Social Psychology, 21,* 345–348.

Terman, L. M. (1954). The discovery and encouragement of exceptional talent. *American Psychologist, 9,* 221–238.

Terman, L. M., & Oden, M. H. (1959). *The gifted group at mid-life.* Stanford, CA: Stanford University Press.

Terrace, H. S. (1979, November). How Nim Chimpsky changed my mind. *Psychology Today,* 65–76.

Terrace, H. S., Petitto, L. A., Sanders, R. J., & Bever, T. G. (1980). On the grammatical capacity of apes. In K. E. Nelson (Ed.), *Children's language.* New York: Gardner Press.

Terry, R., & Coie, J. D. (1991). A comparison of methods for defining sociometric status among children. *Developmental Psychology, 27,* 867–880.

Teti, D. M., & Ablard, K. E. (1989). Security of attachment and infant-sibling relationships: A laboratory study. *Child Development, 60,* 1519–1528.

Teti, D. M., & Gelfand, D. M. (1991). Behavioral competence among mothers of infants in the first year: The mediational role of maternal self-efficacy. *Child Develoment, 62,* 918–929.

Tharp, R. G. (1989). Psychocultural variables and constants: Effects on teaching and learning in schools. *American Psychologist, 44,* 349–359.

Tharp, R. G., & Gallimore, R. (1988). *Rousing minds to life: Teaching, learning, and schooling in social context.* Cambridge, England: Cambridge University Press.

Thelen, E. (1984). Learning to walk: Ecological demands and phylogenetic constraints. In L. P. Lipsitt & C. Rovee-Collier (Eds.), *Advances in infancy research* (Vol. 3). Norwood, NJ: Ablex.

Thelen, E. (1986). Treadmill-elicited stepping in seven-month-old infants. *Child Development, 57,* 1498–1506.

Thelen, E. (1989). The (re)discovery of motor development: Learning new things from an old field. *Developmental Psychology, 25,* 946–949.

Thelen, E. (1995). Motor development: A new synthesis. *American Psychologist, 50,* 79–95.

Thelen, E., Corbetta, D., Kamm, K., Spencer, J. P., Schneider, K., & Zernicke, R. F. (1993). The transition to reaching: Mapping intention and intrinsic dynamics. *Child Development, 64,* 1058–1098.

Thelen, E., & Fisher, D. M. (1982). Newborn stepping: An explanation for a disappearing reflex. *Developmental Psychology, 18,* 760–775.

Thoma, S. J., Rest, J. R., & Davison, M. L. (1991). Describing and testing a moderator of the moral judgment and action relationship. *Journal of Personality and Social Psychology, 61,* 659–669.

Thoman, E. B. (1990). Sleeping and waking states in infants: A functional perspective. *Neuroscience and Behavioral Review, 14,* 93–107.

Thoman, E. B., & Ingersoll, E. W. (1993). Learning in premature infants. *Developmental Psychology, 28,* 692–700.

Thoman, E. B., & Whitney, M. P. (1989). Sleep states of infants monitored in the home: Individual differences, developmental trends, and origins of diurnal cyclicity. *Infant Behavior and Development, 12,* 59–75.

Thomas, A., & Chess, S. (1977). *Temperament and development.* New York: Brunner/Mazel.

Thomas, A., & Chess, S. (1986). The New York longitudinal study: From infancy to early adult life. In R. Plomin & J. Dunn (Eds.), *The study of temperament: Changes, continuities, and challenges.* Hillsdale, NJ: Erlbaum.

Thomas, A., Chess, S., & Birch, H. G. (1970). The origin of personality. *Scientific American, 223,* 102–109.

Thomas, A., Chess, S., & Korn, S. (1982). The reality of difficult temperament. *Merrill-Palmer Quarterly, 28,* 1–20.

Thomas, D., Campos, J. J., Shucard, D. W., Ramsay, D. S., & Shucard, J. (1981). Semantic comprehension in infancy: A signal detection approach. *Child Development, 52,* 798–803.

Thomas, J. R., & French, K. E. (1985). Gender differences across age in motor performance: A meta-analysis. *Psychological Bulletin, 98,* 260–282.

Thomas, M. H., Horton, R. W., Lippincott, E. C., & Drabman, R. S. (1977). Desensitization to portrayals of real-life aggression as a function of exposure to television violence. *Journal of Personality and Social Psychology, 35,* 450–458.

Thompson, J. R., & Chapman, R. S. (1977). Who is "Daddy" revisited? The status of two-year-olds' overextended words in use and comprehension. *Journal of Child Language, 4,* 359–375.

Thompson, L. A., Fagan, J. F., & Fulker, D. W. (1991). Longitudinal prediction of specific cognitive abilities from infant novelty preference. *Child Development, 62,* 530–538.

Thompson, R. A. (1990). Vulnerability in research: A developmental perspective on research risk. *Child Development, 61,* 1–16.

Thompson, R. A. (1994). Emotion regulation: A theme in search of definition. In N. A. Fox (Ed.), *The development of emotion regulation: Biological and behavioral considerations. Monographs of the Society for Research in Child Development, 59*(2–3, Serial No. 240).

Thompson, R. A., Cicchetti, D., Lamb, M. E., & Malkin, C. (1985). Emotional responses of Down's syndrome and normal infants in the strange situation: The organization of affective behavior in infants. *Developmental Psychology, 21,* 828–841.

Thompson, R. A., Lamb, M. E., & Estes, D. (1982). Stability of infant-mother attachment and its relationship to changing life circumstances in an unselected middle-class sample. *Child Development, 53,* 144–148.

Thompson, S. K. (1975). Gender labels and early sex-role development. *Child Development, 46,* 339–347.

Thornburg, H. D. (1986). Adolescent delinquency and families. In G. K. Leigh & G. W. Peterson (Eds.), *Adolescents in families.* Cincinnati: South-Western.

Thorndike, R. L., Hagen, E. P., & Sattler, J. M. (1986). *The Stanford-Binet Intelligence Scale* (4th ed.). Chicago: Riverside Publishing.

Thorne, B. (1993). *Gender play. Girls and boys in school.* New Brunswick, NJ: Rutgers University Press.

Thurstone, L. L. (1938). *Primary mental abilities.* Chicago: University of Chicago Press.

Thurstone, L. L., & Thurstone, T. G. (1941). Factorial studies of intelligence. *Psychometric Monographs,* No. 2.

Tietjen, A. M. (1986). Prosocial reasoning among children and adults in a Papua New Guinea society. *Developmental Psychology, 22,* 861–868.

Tietjen, A. M., & Walker, L. J. (1985). Moral reasoning and leadership among men in a Papua New Guinea society. *Developmental Psychology, 21,* 982–992.

Tinsley, B. J. (1992). Multiple influences on the acquisition and socialization of children's health attitudes and behavior: An integrative review. *Child Development, 63,* 1043–1069.

Tisak, M. S., & Tisak, J. (1990). Children's conceptions of parental authority, friendship, and sibling relations. *Merrill-Palmer Quarterly, 36,* 347–368.

Tizard, B. (1977). *Adoption: A second chance.* London: Open Books.

Tomasello, M., & Barton, M. (1994). Learning words in nonostensive contexts. *Developmental Psychology, 30,* 639–650.

Tomasello, M., & Farrar, M. J. (1986). Joint attention and early language. *Child Development, 57,* 1454–1463.

Tomasello, M., Savage-Rumbaugh, S., & Kruger, A. C. (1993). Imitative learning of actions on objects by children, chimpanzees, and enculturated chimpanzees. *Child Development, 64,* 1688–1705.

Tomlinson-Keasey, C., Eisert, D. C., Kahle, L. R., Hardy-Brown, K., & Keasey, B. (1979). The structure of concrete-operational thought. *Child Development, 50,* 1153–1163.

Tomlinson-Keasey, C., & Keasey, C. B. (1974). The mediating role of cognitive development in moral judgment. *Child Development, 45,* 291–298.

Tomlinson-Keasey, C., & Little, T. D. (1990). Predicting educational attainment, occupational achievement, intellectual skill, and personal adjustment among gifted men and women. *Journal of Educational Psychology, 82,* 442–455.

Toner, I. J. (1981). Role involvement and delay maintenance behavior in pre-school children. *Journal of Genetic Psychology, 138,* 245–251.

Toner, I. J., Moore, L. P., & Ashley, P. K. (1978). The effect of serving as a model of self-control on subsequent resistance to deviation in children. *Journal of Experimental Child Psychology, 26,* 85–91.

Toner, I. J., Moore, L. P., & Emmons, B. A. (1980). The effect of being labeled on subsequent self-control in children. *Child Development, 51,* 618–621.

Toner, I. J., Parke, R. D., & Yussen, S. R. (1978). The effect of observation of model behavior on the establishment and stability of resistance to deviation in children. *Journal of Genetic Psychology, 132,* 283–290.

Toner, I. J., & Potts, R. (1981). Effect of modeled rationales on moral behavior, moral choice, and level of moral judgment in children. *Journal of Psychology, 107,* 153–162.

Toner, M. (1991, Feb. 18). Worries mount as studies link birth defects to fathers' job perils. *Atlanta Journal,* A9.

Torrance, E. P. (1975). Creativity research in education: Still alive. In I. A. Taylor & J. W. Getzels (Eds.), *Perspectives in creativity.* Chicago: Aldine-Atherton.

Torrance, E. P. (1988). The nature of creativity as manifest in its testing. In R. J. Sternberg (Ed.), *The nature of creativity: Contemporary psychological perspectives.* Cambridge, England: Cambridge University Press.

Trabasso, T. (1975). Representation, memory, and reasoning: How do we make transitive inferences? In A. D. Pick (Ed.), *Minnesota symposia on child psychology* (Vol. 9). Minneapolis: University of Minnesota Press.

Trachtenberg, S., & Viken, R. J. (1994). Aggressive boys in the classroom: Biased attributions or shared perceptions. *Child Development, 65,* 829–835.

Trehub, S. E. (1985). Auditory pattern perception in infancy. In S. E. Trehub & B. Schneider (Eds.), *Advances in the study of communication and affect. Vol. 10: Auditory development in infancy.* New York: Plenum.

Trehub, S. E., Schneider, B. A., Thorpe, L. A., & Judge, P. (1991). Observational measures of auditory sensitivity in early infancy. *Developmental Psychology, 27,* 40–49.

Trickett, P. K., Aber, J. L., Carlson, V., & Cicchetti, D. (1991). Relationship of socioeconomic status to the etiology and developmental sequelae of physical child abuse. *Developmental Psychology, 27,* 148–158.

Trickett, P. K., & Putnam, F. W. (1993). Impact of child sexual abuse on females: Toward a developmental, psychobiological integration. *Psychological Science, 4,* 81–87.

Trickett, P. K., & Susman, E. J. (1988). Parental perceptions of child-rearing practices in physically abusive and nonabusive families. *Developmental Psychology, 24,* 270–276.

Tronick, E. Z. (1989). Emotions and emotional communications in infants. *American Psychologist, 44,* 112–119.

Tronick, E. Z., Morelli, G. A., & Ivey, P. K. (1992). The Efe forager infant and toddler's pattern of social relationships: Multiple and simultaneous. *Developmental Psychology, 28,* 568–577.

Tronick, E. Z., Thomas, R. B., & Daltabuit, M. (1994). The Quechua manta pouch: A caregiving practice for buffering the Peruvian infant against the multiple stressors of high altitude. *Child Development, 65,* 1005–1013.

Tryon, R. C. (1940). Genetic differences in maze learning in rats. *Yearbook of the National Society for Studies in Education, 39,* 111–119.

Tudge, J. R. H. (1992). Processes and consequences of peer collaboration: A Vygotskian analysis. *Child Development, 63,* 1364–1379.

Tulkin, S. R., & Konner, M. J. (1973). Alternative conceptions of intellectual functioning. *Human Development, 16,* 33–52.

Turiel, E. (1983). *The development of social knowledge: Morality and convention.* Cambridge, England: Cambridge University Press.

Turkheimer, E. (1991). Individual and group differences in adoption studies of IQ. *Psychological Bulletin, 110,* 392–405.

Turnbull, C. M. (1972). *The mountain people.* New York: Simon & Schuster.

Turner, C. W., & Goldsmith, D. (1976). Effects of toy guns and airplanes on children's antisocial free play behavior. *Journal of Experimental Child Psychology, 21,* 303–315.

Tyack, D., & Ingram, D. (1977). Children's production and comprehension of questions. *Journal of Child Language, 4,* 211–224.

Tyson, P., & Tyson, R. L. (1990). *Psychoanalytic theories of development: An integration.* New Haven, CT: Yale University Press.

Udry, J. R. (1990). Hormonal and social determinants of adolescent sexual initiation. In J. Bancroft & J. M. Reinisch (Eds.), *Adolescence and puberty.* New York: Oxford University Press.

Underwood, B., & Moore, B. (1982). Perspective-taking and altruism. *Psychological Bulletin, 91,* 143–173.

Underwood, M. K., Coie, J. D., & Herbsman, C. R. (1992). Display rules for anger and aggression in school-age children. *Child Development, 63,* 366–380.

Uniform Crime Reports for the United States, 1989. Federal Bureau of Investigation. Washington, D.C.: U.S. Government Printing Office.

University of Georgia Fact Book (1994). Athens, GA: University of Georgia Press.

Urberg, K. A. (1979). Sex-role conceptualization in adolescents and adults. *Developmental Psychology, 15,* 90–92.

U.S. Bureau of the Census (1989). *Statistical abstract of the United States, 1989* (109th ed.) Washington, D.C.: U.S. Government Printing Office.

U.S. Bureau of the Census (1990). *Statistical abstract of the United States: 1990* (110th ed.). Washington, D.C.: U.S. Government Printing Office.

U.S. Bureau of the Census (1992a). Current population reports, series P-60, No. 181. *Poverty in the United States, 1991.* Washington, D.C.: U.S. Government Printing Office.

U.S. Bureau of the Census (1992b). *Statistical Abstract of the United States: 1992* (112th ed.). Washington, D.C.: U.S. Government Printing Office.

U.S. Bureau of the Census (1993). *Statistical abstract of the United States: 1993* (113th ed.). Washington, D.C.: U.S. Government Printing Office.

U.S. Department of Health, Education and Welfare (1979). *Smoking and health: A report to the Surgeon General* (DHEW Pub. No. PHS 79–50066). Washington, D.C.: U.S. Government Printing Office.

U.S. Department of Justice (1992). *Crime in the United States.* Washington, D.C.: U.S. Government Printing Office.

Usher, J. A., & Neisser, U. (1993). Childhood amnesia and the beginnings of memory for four early life events. *Journal of Experimental Psychology: General, 122,* 155–165.

Vaillant, G. E. (1983). Childhood environment and maturity of defense mechanisms. In D. Magnusson & V. L. Allen (Eds.), *Human development: An interactional perspective.* New York: Academic Press.

Valdez-Menchaca, M. C., & Whitehurst, G. J. (1992). Accelerating language development through picture book reading: A systematic extension to Mexican day care. *Developmental Psychology, 28,* 1106–1114.

Valenzuela, M. (1990). Attachment in chronically underweight young children. *Child Development, 61,* 1984–1996.

Vandell, D. L., & Corasantini, M. A. (1988). The relation between third graders' after-school care and social, academic, and emotional functioning. *Child Development, 59,* 868–875.

Vandell, D. L., & Corasantini, M. A. (1990). Variations in early child care: Do they predict subsequent social, emotional, and cognitive differences? *Early Childhood Research Quarterly, 5,* 555–572.

Vandell, D. L., Henderson, V. K., & Wilson, K. S. (1988). A longitudinal study of children with day-care experiences of varying quality. *Child Development, 59,* 1286–1292.

Vandell, D. L., & Ramanan, J. (1991). Children of the National Longitudinal Survey of Youth: Choices in after-school care and child development. *Developmental Psychology, 27,* 637–643.

Vandell, D. L., & Ramanan, J. (1992). Effects of early and recent maternal employment on children from low-income families. *Child Development, 63,* 938–949.

Vandell, D. L., & Wilson, K. S. (1987). Infants' interactions with mother, sibling, and peer: Contrasts and relations between interaction systems. *Child Development, 58,* 176–186.

Vandell, D. L., Wilson, K. S., & Buchanan, N. R. (1980). Peer interaction in the first year of life: An examination of its structure, content, and sensitivity to toys. *Child Development, 51,* 481–488.

van den Boom, D. C. (1994). Influence of attachment and mothering on attachment and exploration: An experimental manipulation of sensitive responsiveness among lower-class mothers with irritable infants. *Child Development, 65,* 1457–1477.

van den Broek, P. (1989). Causal reasoning and inference making in judging the importance of story statements. *Child Development, 60,* 286–297.

van Doorninck, W. J., Caldwell, B. M., Wright, C., & Frankenberg, W. K. (1981). The relationship between twelve-month home stimulation and school achievement. *Child Development, 52,* 1080–1083.

van IJzendoorn, M. H. (1992). Intergenerational transmission of parenting: A review of studies in nonclinical populations. *Developmental Review, 12,* 76–99.

van IJzendoorn, M. H., Goldberg, S., Kroonenberg, P. M., & Frenkel, O. J. (1992). The relative effects of maternal and child problems on the quality of attachment: A meta-analysis of attachment in clinical samples. *Child Development, 63,* 840–858.

van IJzendoorn, M. H., & Kroonenberg, P. M. (1988). Cross-cultural patterns of attachment: A meta-analysis of the Strange Situation. *Child Development, 59,* 147–156.

Van Tuinen, I., & Wolfe, S. M. (1993). *Unnecessary cesarean sections: Halfing a national epidemic.* Washington, D.C.: Public Citizens Health Research Group.

Varnhagen, C. K., Morrison, F. J., & Everall, R. (1994). Age and schooling effects in story recall and story production. *Developmental Psychology, 30,* 969–979.

Vasudev, J., & Hummel, R. C. (1987). Moral stage sequence and principled reasoning in an Indian sample. *Human Development, 30,* 105–118.

Vaughn, B. E., Bradley, C. F., Joffe, L. S., Seifer, R., & Barglow, P. (1987). Maternal characteristics measured prenatally are predictive of ratings of temperamental "difficulty" on the Carey Infant Temperament Questionnaire. *Developmental Psychology, 23,* 152–161.

Vaughn, B. E., Kopp, C. B., & Krakow, J. B. (1984). The emergence and consolidation of self-control from eighteen to thirty months of age: Normative trends and individual differences. *Child Development, 55,* 990–1004.

Vaughn, B. E., Lefever, G. B., Seifer, R., & Barglow, P. (1989). Attachment behavior, attachment security, and temperament during infancy. *Child Development, 60,* 728–737.

Vaughn, B. E., Stevenson-Hinde, J., Waters, E., Kotsaftis, A., Lefever, G. B., Shouldice, A., Trudel, M., & Belsky, J. (1992). Attachment security and temperament in infancy and early childhood: Some conceptual clarification. *Developmental Psychology, 28,* 463–473.

Vaughn, V. C., McKay, J. R., & Behrman, R. E. (1984). *Nelson textbook of pediatrics* (12th ed.). Philadelphia: W. B. Saunders.

Vellutino, F. (1991). Introduction to three studies on reading acquisition: Convergent findings on theoretical foundations of code-oriented versus whole language approaches to reading instruction. *Journal of Educational Psychology, 83,* 437–443.

Verp, M. S. (1993a). Environmental causes of pregnancy loss and malformations. In C. Lin, M. S. Verp, & R. E. Sabbagha (Eds.), *The high-risk fetus: Pathophysiology, diagnosis, management.* New York: Springer-Verlag.

Verp, M. S. (1993b). Genetic counseling and screening. In C. Lin, M. S. Verp, & R. E. Sabbagha (Eds.), *The high-risk fetus: Pathophysiology, diagnosis, management.* New York: Springer-Verlag.

Verp, M. S., Simpson, J. L., & Ober, C. (1993). Prenatal diagnosis of genetic disorders. In C. Lin, M. S. Verp, & R. E. Sabbagha (Eds.), *The high-risk fetus: Pathophysiology, diagnosis, management.* New York: Springer-Verlag.

Vinter, A. (1986). The role of movement in eliciting early imitations. *Child Development, 57,* 66–71.

Vlietstra, A. G. (1982). Children's responses to task instructions: Age changes and training effects. *Child Development, 53,* 534–532.

Vobejda, B. (1991, September 15). The future deferred. Longer road from adolescence to adulthood often leads back through parents' home. *The Washington Post,* A1, A29.

Volling, B. L., & Belsky, J. (1992). The contribution of mother-child and father-child relationships to the quality of sibling interaction. A longitudinal study. *Child Development, 63,* 1209–1222.

Vondra, J., & Belsky, J. (1993). Developmental origins of parenting: Personality and relationship factors. In T. Luster & L. Okagaki (Eds.), *Parenting: An ecological perspective.* Hillsdale, NJ: Erlbaum.

Von Wright, M. R. (1989). Body image satisfaction in adolescent boys and girls: A longitudinal study. *Journal of Youth and Adolescence, 18,* 71–83.

Vorhees, C. V., & Mollnow, E. (1987). Behavioral teratogenesis: Long-term influences on behavior from early exposure to environmental agents. In J. D. Osofsky (Ed.), *Handbook of infant development* (2nd ed.). New York: Wiley.

Vuchinich, S., Bank, L., & Patterson, G. R. (1992). Parenting, peers, and the stability of antisocial behavior in preadolescent boys. *Developmental Psychology, 28,* 510–521.

Vuchinich, S., Hetherington, E. M., Vuchinich, R. A., & Clingempeel, W. G. (1991). Parent-child interaction and gender differences in early adolescents' adaptation to stepfamilies. *Developmental Psychology, 27,* 618–626.

Vurpillot, E. (1968). The development of scanning strategies and their relation to visual differentiation. *Journal of Experimental Child Psychology, 6,* 632–650.

Vygotsky, L. S. (1962). *Thought and language.* Cambridge, MA: MIT Press. (Original work published 1934)

Vygotsky, L. S. (1978). *Mind in society: The development of higher mental processes* (M. Cole, V. John-Steiner, S. Scribner, & E. Souberman, Eds.). Cambridge, MA: Harvard University Press. (Original work published 1930, 1933, 1935)

Wachs, T. D. (1992). *The nature of nurture.* Newbury Park, CA: Sage.

Waddington, C. H. (1966). *Principles of development and differentiation.* New York: Macmillan.

Wagner, R. K., Torgesen, J. K., & Rashotte, C. A. (1994). Development of reading-related phonological processing abilities: New evidence of bidirectional causality from a latent variable longitudinal study. *Developmental Psychology, 30,* 73–87.

Wainryb, C. (1993). The application of moral judgments to other cultures: Relativism and universality. *Child Development, 64,* 924–933.

Walden, T. A., & Baxter, A. (1989). The effect of context and age on social referencing. *Child Development, 60,* 1511–1518.

Walk, R. D. (1981). *Perceptual development.* Pacific Grove, CA: Brooks/Cole.

Walker, D., Greenwood, C., Hart, B., & Carta, J. (1994). Prediction of school outcomes based on early language production and socioeconomic factors. *Child Development, 65,* 606–621.

Walker, L. J. (1980). Cognitive and perspective-taking prerequisites for moral development. *Child Development, 51,* 131–139.

Walker, L. J. (1989). A longitudinal study of moral development. *Child Development, 60,* 157–166.

Walker, L. J. (1991). Sex differences in moral reasoning. In W. M. Kurtines & J. L. Gewirtz (Eds.), *Handbook of moral behavior and development* (Vol. 2). Hillsdale, NJ: Erlbaum.

Walker, L. J., & Taylor, J. H. (1991a). Family interactions and the development of moral reasoning. *Child Development, 62,* 264–283.

Walker, L. J., & Taylor, J. H. (1991b). Stage transitions in moral reasoning: A longitudinal study of developmental processes. *Developmental Psychology, 27,* 330–337.

Walker-Andrews, A. S., & Lennon, E. M. (1985). Auditory-visual perception of changing distance by human infants. *Child Development, 56,* 544–548.

Wallach, M. A. (1985). Creativity testing and giftedness. In F. D. Horowitz & M. O'Brien (Eds.), *The gifted and talented. Developmental perspectives.* Washington, D.C.: American Psychological Association.

Wallach, M. A., & Kogan, N. (1965). *Thinking in young children.* New York: Holt, Rinehart & Winston.

Wallerstein, J. S. (1987). Children of divorce: Report from a ten-year follow-up of early latency-age children. *American Journal of Orthopsychiatry, 57,* 119–211.

Wallerstein, J. S., & Blakeslee, S. (1989). *Second chances: Men, women, and children a decade after divorce.* New York: Ticknor and Fields.

Wallerstein, J. S., & Corbin, S. B. (1989). Daughters of divorce: Report from a ten-year follow-up. *American Journal of Orthopsychiatry, 59,* 593–604.

Wallerstein, J. S., & Kelly, J. B. (1980). *Surviving the breakup: How children and parents cope with divorce.* New York: Basic Books.

Walters, R. H., & Brown, M. (1963). Studies of reinforcement of aggression: Transfer of responses to an interpersonal situation. *Child Development, 34,* 562–571.

Ward, S. L., & Overton, W. F. (1990). Semantic familiarity, relevance, and the development of deductive reasoning. *Developmental Psychology, 26,* 488–493.

Warren-Leubecker, A., & Bohannon, J. N., III (1989). Pragmatics: Language in social contexts. In J. Berko Gleason (Ed.), *The development of language* (2nd ed.). Columbus, OH: Merrill.

Warren-Leubecker, A., & Carter, B. W. (1988). Reading and growth in metalinguistic awareness: Relations to socioeconomic status and reading readiness skills. *Child Development, 59,* 728–742.

Wartner, U. G., Grossmann, K., Fremmer-Bombik, E., & Suess, G. (1994). Attachment patterns at age six in south Germany: Predictability from infancy and implications for preschool behavior. *Child Development, 65,* 1014–1027.

Waterman, A. S. (1982). Identity development from adolescence to adulthood: An extension of theory and a review of research. *Developmental Psychology, 18,* 341–358.

Waterman, A. S. (1992). Identity as an aspect of optimal psychological functioning. In G. R. Adams, T. P. Gullotta, & R. Montemayor (Eds.), *Advances in adolescent development. Vol. 4: Adolescent identity formation.* Newbury Park, CA: Sage.

Waterman, A. S., & Archer, S. L. (1990). A life-span perspective on identity formation: Developments in form, function, and process. In P. B. Baltes, D. L. Featterman, & R. M. Lerner (Eds.), *Life-span development and behavior: Vol. 10.* Hillsdale, NJ: Erlbaum.

Waters, E., Vaughn, B. E., & Egeland, B. R. (1980). Individual differences in mother-infant attachment relationships at age one: Antecedents in neonatal behavior in an urban, economically disadvantaged sample. *Child Development, 51,* 208–216.

Waters, E., Wippman, J., & Sroufe, L. A. (1979). Attachment, positive affect, and competence in the peer group: Two studies in construct validation. *Child Development, 50,* 821–829.

Watson, J. B. (1913). Psychology as the behaviorist views it. *Psychological Review, 20,* 158–177.

Watson, J. B. (1925). *Behaviorism.* New York: Norton.

Watson, J. B. (1928). *Psychological care of infant and child.* New York: Norton.

Watson, J. B., & Raynor, R. (1920). Conditioned emotional reactions. *Journal of Experimental Psychology, 3,* 1–14.

Watson, J. S., Hayes, L. A., Vietze, P., & Becker, J. (1979). Discriminative infant smiling to orientations of talking faces of mother and stranger. *Journal of Experimental Child Psychology, 28,* 92–99.

Watson, J. S., & Ramey, C. T. (1972). Reactions to response-contingent stimulation in early infancy. *Merrill-Palmer Quarterly, 18,* 219–228.

Waxman, S. R., & Hatch, T. (1992). Beyond the basics: Preschool children label objects flexibly at multiple hierarchical levels. *Journal of Child Language, 19,* 153–166.

Waxman, S. R., & Senghas, A. (1992). Relations among word meanings in early lexical development. *Developmental Psychology, 28,* 862–873.

Weaver, K. F. (1985). Stones, bones, and early man: The search for our ancestors. *National Geographic, 168,* 561–623.

Wechsler, D. (1989). *Manual for the Wechsler Preschool and Primary Scale of Intelligence—Revised.* New York: Psychological Corporation.

Wechsler, D. (1991). *Manual, WISC-III: Wechsler Intelligence Scale for Children—Third Edition.* San Antonio, TX: Psychological Corporation.

Weinberg, R. A. (1989). Intelligence and IQ: Landmark issues and great debates. *American Psychologist, 44,* 98–104.

Weinberg, R. A., Scarr, S., & Waldman, I. D. (1992). The Minnesota transracial adoption study: A follow-up of IQ test performance at adolescence. *Intelligence, 16,* 117–135.

Weiner, B. (1974). *Achievement and attribution theory.* Morristown, NJ: General Learning Press.

Weiner, B. (1986). *An attributional theory of motivation and emotion.* New York: Springer-Verlag.

Weinraub, M., Clemens, L. P., Sockloff, A., Ethridge, T., Gracely, E., & Myers, B. (1984). The development of sex-role stereotypes in the third year: Relationships to gender labeling, gender identity, sex-typed toy preferences, and family characteristics. *Child Development, 55,* 1493–1503.

Weinraub, M., & Lewis, M. (1977). The determinants of children's responses to separation. *Monographs of the Society for Research in Child Development, 42*(4, Serial No. 172).

Weinstein, C. S. (1991). The classroom as a social context for learning. *Annual Review of Psychology, 42,* 493–525.

Weinstein, R. S., Marshall, H. H., Sharp, L., & Botkin, M. (1987). Pygmalion and the student: Age and classroom differences in children's awareness of teacher expectations. *Child Development, 58,* 1079–1093.

Weisner, T. S., & Gallimore, R. (1977). My brother's keeper: Child and sibling caretaking. *Current Anthropology, 18,* 169–190.

Weisner, T. S., & Wilson-Mitchell, J. E. (1990). Nonconventional family lifestyles and sex typing in six-year-olds. *Child Development, 61,* 1915–1933.

Weiss, B., Dodge, K. A., Bates, J. E., & Pettit, G. S. (1992). Some consequences of early harsh discipline: Child aggression and a maladaptive social information processing style. *Child Development, 63,* 1321–1335.

Wellman, H. M. (1985). *Children's searching: The development of search skill and spatial representation.* Hillsdale, NJ: Erlbaum.

Wellman, H. M., Collins, J., & Glieberman, J. (1981). Understanding the combination of memory variables: Developing conceptions of memory limitations. *Child Development, 52,* 1313–1317.

Wellman, H. M., & Gelman, S. A. (1992). Cognitive development: Foundational theories of core domains. *Annual Review of Psychology, 43,* 337–375.

Wellman, H. M., & Lempers, J. D. (1977). The naturalistic communicative abilities of two-year-olds. *Child Development, 48,* 1052–1057.

Wellman, H. M., & Woolley, J. (1990). From simple desires to ordinary beliefs: The early development of everyday psychology. *Cognition, 35,* 245–275.

Wells, L. E. (1989). Self-enhancement through delinquency: A conditional test of self-derogation theory. *Journal of Research in Crime and Delinquency, 26,* 226–252.

Werker, J. F., & Tees, R. C. (1992). The organization and reorganization of human speech perception. *Annual Review of Neuroscience, 15,* 377–402.

Werner, E. E., & Smith, R. S. (1982). *Vulnerable but invincible: A longitudinal study of resilient children and youth.* New York: McGraw-Hill.

Werner, E. E., & Smith, R. S. (1992). *Overcoming the odds. High risk children from birth to adulthood.* Ithaca, NY: Cornell University Press.

Wertsch, J. V., & Tulviste, P. (1992). L. S. Vygotsky and contemporary developmental psychology. *Developmental Psychology, 28,* 548–557.

Whalen, C. K., & Henker, B. (1991). Therapies for hyperactive children: Comparisons, combinations, and compromises. *Journal of Consulting and Clinical Psychology, 59,* 126–137.

Whaley, K. L., & Rubenstein, T. S. (1994). How toddlers "do" friendship: A descriptive analysis of naturally occurring friendships in a group child care setting. *Journal of Social and Personal Relationships, 11,* 383–400.

Wheeler, L. R. (1932). The intelligence of East Tennessee children. *Journal of Educational Psychology, 23,* 351–370.

Wheeler, L. R. (1942). A comparative study of the intelligence of East Tennessee mountain children. *Journal of Educational Psychology, 33,* 321–334.

Whiffen, V. E. (1992). Is postpartum depression a distinct diagnosis? *Clinical Psychology Review, 12,* 485–508.

Whipp, B. J., & Ward, S. A. (1992). Will women soon outrun men? *Nature, 355,* 25.

Whitbourne, S. K. (1986). *The me I know: A study of adult identity.* New York: Springer-Verlag.

White, A. S. (1994, August 31). Nation's report card: Better marks but deficiencies still apparent. *Fresno Bee,* A1, A7.

White, K. J., & Kistner, J. (1992). The influence of teacher feedback on young children's peer preferences and perceptions. *Developmental Psychology, 28,* 933–940.

White, R. W. (1959). Motivation reconsidered: The concept of competence. *Psychological Review, 66,* 297–333.

White, S. H. (1992). G. Stanley Hall: From philosophy to developmental psychology. *Developmental Psychology, 28,* 25–34.

Whitehurst, G. J., Falco, F. L., Lonigan, C. J., Fischel, J. E., DeBaryshe, B. D., Valdez-Menchaca, M. C., & Caulfield, M. (1988). Accelerating language development through picture book reading. *Child Development, 59,* 552–559.

Whitehurst, G. J., & Valdez-Menchaca, M. C. (1988). What is the role of reinforcement in early language acquisition? *Child Development, 59,* 430–440.

Whitehurst, G. J., & Vasta, R. (1975). Is language acquired through imitation? *Journal of Psycholinguistic Research, 4,* 37–59.

Whiting, B. B., & Edwards, C. P. (1988). *Children of different worlds: The formation of social behavior.* Cambridge, MA: Harvard University Press.

Whiting, B. B., & Whiting, J. W. M. (1975). *Children of six cultures.* Cambridge, MA: Harvard University Press.

Whitley, B. E., Jr. (1983). Sex-role orientation and self-esteem: A critical meta-analytic review. *Journal of Personality and Social Psychology, 44,* 765–778.

Whitney, E. N., & Hamilton, E. N. (1987). *Understanding nutrition.* St. Paul, MN: West.

Widdowson, E. M. (1951). Mental contentment and physical growth. *Lancet, 1,* 1316–1318.

Wideman, M. V., & Singer, J. E. (1984). The role of psychological mechanisms in preparation for childbirth. *American Psychologist, 39,* 1357–1371.

Widmayer, S., & Field, T. (1980). Effects of Brazelton demonstrations on early interactions of preterm infants and their teen-age mothers. *Infant Behavior and Development, 3,* 79–89.

Wielandt, H., & Boldsen, J. (1989). Age at first intercourse. *Journal of Biosocial Science, 21,* 169–177.

Wiesenfeld, A., Malatesta, C., & DeLoach, L. (1981). Differential parental response to familiar and unfamiliar infant distress signals. *Infant Behavior and Development, 4,* 281–285.

Wigfield, A., Eccles, J. S., Mac Iver, D., Reuman, D. A., & Midgley, C. (1991). Transitions during early adolescence: Changes in children's domain-specific self-perceptions and general self-esteem across the transition to junior high school. *Developmental Psychology, 27,* 552–565.

Wiggam, A. E. (1923). *The new decalogue of science.* Indianapolis: Bobbs-Merrill.

Wiggins, S., Whyte, P., Huggins, M., Adam, S., Theilman, J., Block, M., Sheps, S. B., Schechter, M. T., & Hayden, M. R. (1992). The psychological consequences of predictive testing for Huntington's disease. *New England Journal of Medicine, 327,* 1410–1405.

Wilens, T. E., & Biederman, J. (1992). The stimulants. *Psychiatric Clinics of North America, 15,* 191–222.

Wilkinson, R. T., & Allison, S. (1989). Age and simple reaction time: Decade differences for 5,325 subjects. *Journal of Gerontology: Psychological Sciences, 44,* P29–P35.

Wilks, J. (1986). The relative importance of parents and friends in adolescent decision making. *Journal of Youth and Adolescence, 15,* 323–334.

Willems, E. P., & Alexander, J. L. (1982). The naturalistic perspective in research. In B. B. Wolman (Ed.), *Handbook of developmental psychology.* Englewood Cliffs, NJ: Prentice Hall.

Williams, C., & Bybee, J. (1994). What do children feel guilty about? Developmental and gender differences. *Developmental Psychology, 30,* 617–623.

Williams, E., & Radin, N. (1993). Parental involvement, maternal employment, and adolescents' academic achievement: An 11-year follow-up. *American Journal of Orthopsychiatry, 63,* 306–312.

Williams, J. E., Bennett, S. M., & Best, D. L. (1975). Awareness and expression of sex stereotypes in young children. *Developmental Psychology, 11,* 635–642.

Williams, J. E., & Best, D. L. (1990). *Measuring sex stereotypes: A multination study* (rev. ed.). Newbury Park, CA: Sage.

Wilson, A. L., & Neidich, G. (1991). Infant mortality and public policy. *Social Policy Report of the Society for Research in Child Development, 5*(2).

Wilson, E. O. (1975). *Sociobiology: The new synthesis.* Cambridge, MA: Harvard University Press.

Wilson, M. N. (1986). The black extended family: An analytical consideration. *Developmental Psychology, 22,* 246–258.

Wilson, M. N. (1989). Child development in the context of the black extended family. *American Psychologist, 44,* 380–385.

Wilson, R. S. (1976). Concordance in physical growth for monozygotic and dizygotic twins. *Annals of Human Biology, 3,* 1–10.

Wilson, R. S. (1978). Synchronies in mental development: An epigenetic perspective. *Science, 202,* 939–948.

Wilson, R. S. (1983). The Louisville twin study: Developmental synchronies in behavior. *Child Development, 54,* 298–316.

Wilson, R. S. (1985). Risk and resilience in early mental development. *Developmental Psychology, 21,* 795–805.

Wilson, R. S., & Matheny, A. P., Jr. (1986). Behavior genetics research in infant temperament: The Louisville twin study. In R. Plomin & J. Dunn (Eds.), *The study of temperament: Changes, continuities, and challenges.* Hillsdale, NJ: Erlbaum.

Winick, M. (1976). *Malnutrition and brain development.* New York: Oxford University Press.

Winterbottom, M. (1958). The relation of need for achievement to learning experiences in independence and mastery. In J. Atkinson (Ed.), *Motives in fantasy, action, and society.* Princeton, NJ: Van Nostrand.

Wintre, M. G., Polivy, J., & Murray, M. A. (1990). Self-predictions of emotional response patterns: Age, sex, and situational determinants. *Child Development, 61,* 1124–1133.

Wishart, J. G., & Bower, T. G. R. (1985). A longitudinal study of the development of the object concept. *British Journal of Developmental Psychology, 3,* 243–258.

Witelson, S. F. (1977). Developmental dyslexia: Two right hemispheres and none left. *Science, 195,* 309–311.

Witelson, S. F. (1987). Neurobiological aspects of language in children. *Child Development, 58,* 653–688.

Witkin, H. A. (1967). A cognitive style approach to cross-cultural research. *International Journal of Psychology, 2,* 233–250.

Witkin, H. A., & Berry, J. W. (1975). Psychological differentiation in cross-cultural perspective. *Journal of Cross-Cultural Psychology, 6,* 4–87.

Witkin, H. A., & Goodenough, D. R. (1981). *Cognitive style: Essence and origin.* New York: International Universities Press.

Witkin, H. A., Goodenough, D. R., & Oltman, P. K. (1979). Psychological differentiation: Current status. *Journal of Personality and Social Psychology, 37,* 1127–1145.

Wolf, M., & Dickinson, D. (1985). From oral to written language: Transitions in the school years. In J. Berko Gleason (Ed.), *The development of language.* Westerville, OH: Merrill.

Wolfe, D. A., Edwards, B., Manion, I., & Koverola, C. (1988). Early intervention for parents at risk of child abuse and neglect: A preliminary investigation. *Journal of Consulting and Clinical Psychology, 56,* 40–47.

Wolff, M., Rutten, P., & Bayer, A. F., III (1992). *Where we stand: Can America make it in the race for health, wealth, and happiness?* New York: Bantam Books.

Wolff, P. H. (1966). The causes, controls, and organization of behavior in the neonate. *Psychological Issues, 5*(1, Whole No. 17).

Wolff, P. H. (1969). The natural history of crying and other vocalizations in early infancy. In B. M. Foss (Ed.), *Determinants of infant behavior* (Vol. 4). London: Methuen.

Wolff, P. H., Michel, G. F., Ovrut, M., & Drake, C. (1990). Rate and timing precision of motor coordination in developmental dyslexia. *Developmental Psychology, 26,* 349–359.

Wolfner, G. D., & Gelles, R. J. (1993). A profile of violence toward children: A national study. *Child Abuse and Neglect, 17,* 197–212.

Woodward, A. L., Markman, E. M., & Fitzsimmons, C. M. (1994). Rapid word learning in 13- and 18-month-olds. *Developmental Psychology, 30,* 553–566.

Worobey, J. (1985). A review of Brazelton-based interventions to enhance parent-infant interaction. *Journal of Reproductive and Infant Psychology, 3,* 64–73.

Worobey, J., & Brazelton, T. B. (1986). Experimenting with the family in the newborn period: A commentary. *Child Development, 57,* 1298–1300.

Wright, J. C., & Huston, A. C. (1983). A matter of form: Potentials of television for young viewers. *American Psychologist, 38,* 835–843.

Wrightsman, L. S., & Sanford, F. H. (1975). *Psychology: A scientific study of human behavior.* Pacific Grove, CA: Brooks/Cole.

Wyatt, G. E., Guthrie, D., & Notgrass, C. M. (1992). Differential effects of women's child sexual abuse and subsequent sexual revictimization. *Journal of Consulting and Clinical Psychology, 60,* 167–173.

Yalisove, D. (1978). The effect of riddle structure on children's comprehension of riddles. *Developmental Psychology, 14,* 173–180.

Yarrow, L. J., MacTurk, R. H., Vietze, P. M., McCarthy, M. E., Klein, R. P., & McQuiston, S. (1984). Developmental course of parental stimulation and its relationship to mastery motivation during infancy. *Developmental Psychology, 20,* 492–503.

Yarrow, M. R., Scott, P. M., & Waxler, C. Z. (1973). Learning concern for others. *Developmental Psychology, 8,* 240–260.

Yazigi, R. A., Odem, R. R., & Polakoski, K. L. (1991). Demonstration of specific binding of cocaine to human spermatoza. *Journal of the American Medical Association, 266,* 1956–1959.

Yeates, K. O., MacPhee, D., Campbell, F. A., & Ramey, C. T. (1983). Maternal IQ and home environment as determinants of early childhood intellectual competence: A developmental analysis. *Developmental Psychology, 19,* 731–739.

Yeates, K. O., & Selman, R. L. (1989). Social competence in the schools: Toward an integrative developmental model for intervention. *Developmental Review, 9,* 64–100.

Yendovitskaya, T. V. (1971). Development of attention. In A. V. Zaporozhets & D. B. Elkonin (Eds.), *The psychology of preschool children.* Cambridge, MA: MIT Press.

Yonas, A. (1981). Infants' responses to optical information for collision. In R. N. Aslin, J. R. Alberts, and M. R. Petersen (Eds.), *Development of perception: Psychobiological perspectives. Vol. 2: The visual system.* New York: Academic Press.

Yonas, A., Arterberry, M., & Granrud, C. E. (1987). Space perception in infancy. In R. A. Vasta (Ed.) *Annals of child development.* Greenwich, CT: JAI Press.

Yonas, A., Cleaves, W., & Pettersen, L. (1978). Development of sensitivity to pictorial depth. *Science, 200,* 77–79.

Young, W. C., Goy, R. W., & Phoenix, C. H. (1964). Hormones and sexual behavior. *Science, 143,* 212–218.

Youngblade, L. M., & Belsky, J. (1992). Parent-child antecedents of 5-year-olds' close friendships: A longitudinal analysis. *Developmental Psychology, 28,* 700–713.

Younger, A. J., & Daniels, T. M. (1992). Children's reasons for nominating their peers as withdrawn: Passive withdrawal versus active isolation. *Developmental Psychology, 28,* 955–960.

Younger, B. (1990). Infants' detection of correlations among feature categories. *Child Development, 61,* 614–620.

Younger, B. (1993). Understanding category members as "the same sort of thing": Explicit categorization in ten-month infants. *Child Development, 64,* 309–320.

Youniss, J., & Smollar, J. (1985). *Adolescent relations with mothers, fathers, and friends.* Chicago: University of Chicago Press.

Zahavi, S., & Asher, S. R. (1978). The effect of verbal instructions on preschool children's aggressive behavior. *Journal of School Psychology, 16,* 146–153.

Zahn-Waxler, C., Radke-Yarrow, M., & King, R. A. (1979). Child rearing and children's prosocial initiations toward victims of distress. *Child Development, 50,* 319–330.

Zahn-Waxler, C., Radke-Yarrow, M., Wagner, E., & Chapman, M. (1992). Development of concern for others. *Developmental Psychology, 28,* 126–136.

Zahn-Waxler, C., Robinson, J. L., & Emde, R. N. (1992). The development of empathy in twins. *Developmental Psychology, 28,* 1038–1047.

Zajonc, R. B. (1975, August). Birth order and intelligence: Dumber by the dozen. *Psychology Today,* 39–43.

Zajonc, R. B., & Markus, G. B. (1975). Birth order and intellectual development. *Psychological Review, 82,* 74–88.

Zani, B. (1991). Male and female patterns in the discovery of sexuality during adolescence. *Journal of Adolescence, 14,* 163–178.

Zaporozhets, A. V. (1965). The development of perception in the preschool child. *Monographs of the Society for Research in Child Development, 30*(2, Serial No. 100).

Zarbatany, L., Hartmann, D. P., Gelfand, D. M., & Vinciguerra, P. (1985). Gender differences in altruistic reputation: Are they artifactual? *Developmental Psychology, 21,* 97–101.

Zaslow, M. (1980). Relationships among peers in kibbutz toddler groups. *Child Psychiatry and Human Development, 10,* 178–189.

Zaslow, M. J. (1989). Sex differences in children's response to parental divorce. 2: Samples of variables, ages, and sources. *American Journal of Orthopsychiatry, 59,* 118–141.

Zebrowitz, L. A., & Montepare, J. M. (1992). Impressions of babyfaced individuals across the life span. *Developmental Psychology, 28,* 1143–1152.

Zelazo, N. A., Zelazo, P. R., Cohen, K. M., & Zelazo, P. D. (1993). Specificity of practice effects in elementary neuromotor patterns. *Developmental Psychology, 29,* 686–691.

Zelazo, P. R., Zelazo, N. A., & Kolb, S. (1972). "Walking" in the newborn. *Science, 176,* 314–315.

Zerbe, K. J. (1993). *The body betrayed: Women, eating disorders, and treatment.* Washington, D.C.: American Psychiatric Press.

Zern, D. S. (1984). Relationships among selected child-rearing variables in a cross-cultural sample of 110 societies. *Developmental Psychology, 20,* 683–690.

Zeskind, P. S. (1980). Adult responses to the cries of low and high risk infants. *Infant Behavior and Development, 3,* 167–177.

Zeskind, P. S., Klein, L., & Marshall, T. R. (1992). Adults' perceptions of experimental modifications of durations of pauses and expiratory sounds in infant crying. *Developmental Psychology, 28,* 1153–1162.

Zeskind, P. S., & Ramey, C. T. (1981). Preventing intellectual and interactional sequelae of fetal malnutrition: A longitudinal, transactional, and synergistic approach to development. *Child Development, 52,* 213–218.

Zeskind, P. S., Sale, J., Maio, M. L., Huntington, L., & Weiseman, J. R. (1985). Adult perceptions of pain and hunger cries: A synchrony of arousal. *Child Development, 56,* 549–554.

Zigler, E. F. (1987). Formal schooling for four-year-olds? No. *American Psychologist, 42,* 254–260.

Zigler, E. F., Abelson, W. D., Trickett, P. K., & Seitz, V. (1982). Is an intervention program necessary to improve economically disadvantaged children's IQ scores? *Child Development, 53,* 340–348.

Zigler, E. F., & Finn-Stevenson, M. (1992). Applied developmental psychology. In M. H. Bornstein & M. E. Lamb (Eds.), *Developmental psychology: An advanced textbook* (3rd ed.). Hillsdale, NJ: Erlbaum.

Zigler, E. F., & Finn-Stevenson, M. F. (1993). *Children in a changing world: Developmental and social issues.* Pacific Grove, CA: Brooks/Cole.

Zigler, E. F., & Gilman, E. (1993). Day care in America: What is needed? *Pediatrics, 91,* 175–178.

Zigler, E. F., & Hodapp, R. M. (1991). Behavioral functioning in individuals with mental retardation. *Annual Review of Psychology, 42,* 29–50.

Zigler, E. F., & Seitz, V. (1982). Social policy and intelligence. In R. Sternberg (Ed.), *Handbook of human intelligence.* Cambridge, England: Cambridge University Press.

Zigler, E. F., & Styfco, S. J. (1994). Head Start: Criticisms in a constructive context. *American Psychologist, 49,* 127–132.

Zimiles, H., & Lee, V. E. (1991). Adolescent family structure and educational progress. *Developmental Psychology, 27,* 314–320.

Zuckerman, B., Frank, D. A., Hingson, R., Amaro, H., Levenson, S. M., Kayne, H., Parker, S., Vinci, R., Aboagye, K., Fried, L., Cabral, H., Timperi, R., & Bauchner, H. (1989). Effects of maternal marijuana and cocaine use on fetal growth. *New England Journal of Medicine, 320,* 762–768.

Zupan, B. A., Hammen, C., & Jaenicke, C. (1987). The effects of current mood and prior depressive history on self-schematic processing in children. *Journal of Experimental Child Psychology, 43,* 149–158.

Name Index

Subject Index

Environmental hypothesis, of group differences in IQ, 362–366
Environmental influences (see also Cultural influences; Family influences; Parenting):
on caregiver-to-infant attachments, 433–434
on child abuse, 632–633
on creativity, 371–372
ecological perspective on, 59–60
on emotional development, 424–426
on infantile anxieties, 441–443
on intellectual performance, 102, 103, 104, 346, 350, 353–358
on language development, 378, 379–383, 388–390, 399
learning theory perspective on, 54–58
on mental illness, 110
on moral reasoning, 581–582
on neural development, 170, 171
on parenting, 612–615
on perceptual development, 234–239
on perinatal development, 142–154
on personality, 107–109
on prenatal development, 126–141
on physical growth, 191–197
on sex typing, 504, 505, 509, 512, 517, 523–526
on sexuality, 536–538, 539
on temperament, 105–106
Epistemology, defined, 60
Equilibration, and cognitive development, 244, 247, 248
Eros, defined, 46
Estrogen, and physical development, 190–191
Eskimo society, 11
Ethnic influences, see Cultural influences; Race
Ethological theory:
of attachment, 438–439
compared to behavioral genetics, 98
evaluation of, 68–69
philosophical assumptions of, 71
principles of, 65–67
of separation/stranger anxieties, 440, 442
Ethology, defined, 65
Evocative genotype/environment correlations, 112, 113, 115
Evoked potentials, 206–207
Evolutionary theory, 65–69 (see also Ethological theory)
Executive control processes, defined, 305
Exosystem, defined, 61
Expansions, and language development, 381–382
Experimental control, defined, 23
Experimental design, 22–23, 24, 33
Expiatory punishment, 571
Expressive role, defined, 505
Extended families, 603–604
Extinction, defined, 286
Extrafamilial influences (see also Peers; Schools; Teachers; Television):
defined, 642
on children and adolescents, 642–686
Extrinsic reinforcement:
of altruism, 566
and task performance, 292
Eye-blink reflex, 160, 161

Facial attractiveness:
and infants' looking preferences, 216
and parent-to-infant attachments, 429–430
and peer acceptance, 676

Facial perception, 211–212, 215–216
Factor analysis, defined, 334
Failure to thrive, 195–197
Falsifiability, 41
Families (see also Family influences; Parenting; Siblings):
abuse within, 630–637
changing character of, 605–606
and childrearing patterns, 606–615
configuration of, and child development, 357–358, 617–622
cross-cultural studies of, 601–602, 604, 610, 612–614, 621–622, 633
defined, 602
divorce and, 622–625, 626
functions of, 600–602
reconstituted, 625, 627–628
as social systems, 553–554, 555, 602–605
Family influences (see also Parenting; Siblings):
on achievement, 476–477, 658–659
on aggression/delinquency, 552–556
on altruism, 560, 567–568
on attachment, 433–434, 458–459
on attention deficits, 310
on cognitive development, 277, 317
on creativity, 371–372
on eating disorders, 186, 194, 195
on emotional development, 424, 425, 427
on friendships, 682
on identity formation, 485–486
on intellectual performance, 346, 350, 354–358, 363–365
on language development, 380–383, 392, 401
on low-birth-weight babies, 149, 150
on moral development, 573, 575, 589–592
on peer acceptance, 673–674, 684–685
on perceptual development, 238
on self-esteem, 471–473
on self-regulation/self-control, 488, 492
on sex typing, 504, 512, 517, 523, 524–526
on sexuality, 535–536, 537, 538, 539
Family social systems, 553–554, 555, 602–605
Family studies:
of aggression, 550
of creativity, 370–371
defined, 98
of intelligence, 100–101, 103–104, 352, 363–365
of mental illness, 109–110
of personality, 106–107
of physical development, 189–190, 194
of sex typing, 521
of sexual orientation, 99–100, 538
of temperament, 104–105
Farming and pastoral societies, 238, 601–602
Fast-mapping, 394–395
Fathers:
as attachment objects, 449
effects on birth outcomes, 143
as contributors to congenital defects, 92, 140
as playmates, 435
reactions to newborns, 144, 449
as secure base, 449
and sex typing, 524–525
and sexual orientation, 538
stepchildren's reactions to, 625

Felt responsibility hypothesis (of altruism), 563–564
Feminine sex-typed individuals, 531–532
Fetal alcohol effects (FAE), 136
Fetal alcohol syndrome (FAS), 135–136
Fetus:
defined, 123
period of the, 119, 123–126
Field dependence/independence, 238–239
Field experiment, 24, 33
Fixation, and personality development, 49
Fluid intelligence, 336
Follicle stimulating hormone (FSH), 190, 191
"Forbidden toy" paradigm, defined, 587
Forceps delivery, 147
Foreclosure status, of identity formation, 483
Formal-operational stage:
defined, 267
and egocentrism, 269–270
and higher stages, 272
and hypothetical-deductive reasoning, 267–269
and hypothetical propositions, 63, 267, 268
incidence of, 271
and moral reasoning, 580
schooling and, 271
and social cognition, 495
social implications of, 269–270
Formats, defined, 392
Form perception:
in childhood, 230–232, 233
environmental influences on, 234–235, 238
in infancy, 211–217
Foundation for the Improvement of Television, 644
Fragile-X syndrome, 89, 94
Fraternal twins, see Dizygotic twins, Freedom riders, 567
Friend(ship)s:
and adjustment to parents' divorce, 624
and altruism, 678, 680
attachment quality and, 682
children's conceptions of, 497–498, 678
and conflict resolution, 682
handicapped children and, 661
interactions between, 678, 680
parenting, and quality of, 682
as preparation for intimate love, 682
as providers of security/support, 681–682
and role-taking skills, 499
vs. siblings as social partners, 619, 667
and social competencies, 681
stability of, 498, 680

g, defined, 335
Gametes, production of, 80–81, 124
Gebusi society, 551
Gender consistency, stage of:
cognitive development and, 528
defined, 527
and sex typing, 527–528, 530, 531
Gender, determination of, 83, 504
Gender identity:
defined, 513
development of, 513, 527–528, 530, 531
Gender intensification, 515
Gender reassignment, 522, 523
Gender schemas, defined, 529
Gender schema theory, of sex typing, 528–530, 531

Gender segregation:
in peer groups, 668, 678
in playmate selection, 516–517
Gender stability, stage of, 527
Gene/environment correlations, 110–116
Generativity vs. stagnation, 52
Gene replacement therapy, 97
Genes, defined, 78
Genetic abnormalities:
detection of, 94–96
examples of, 93
treatment of, 96–97
Genetic counseling, 94–96
Genetic dominance, 84–87
Genetic expression, patterns of, 84–88
Genetic hypothesis:
of group differences in IQ, 361–362
of home environment effects, 356–357
Genetic influences, see Hereditary influences; Heritability
Genital herpes, and prenatal development, 132
Genital stage, of psychosexual development, 50
Genotype:
defined, 78
relation to phenotype, 84–88, 110–116
Gentle birthing, 145
Germinal period, of prenatal development, 119, 120
Gestures, and language development, 392–393, 397, 400, 401
Giftedness (see also Creativity):
defined, 370
and health and happiness, 348–350
Glia, 169
Gonorrhea, and prenatal development, 132
"Good boy"/"good girl" stage, of moral reasoning, 577
Goodness of fit:
model of parenting, 106
of parenting, and attachment quality, 448
of schools, and scholastic achievement, 656–658
Grammatical morphemes:
defined, 402
development of, 402–404
errors in usage, 404, 408–409
Graduate Record Examination (GRE), 344
Grandparents:
as caregivers in extended families, 604
involvement with grandchildren in reconstituted familes, 627
Grasping reflex, 160, 161, 162, 178
Growth, see Physical development
Growth hormone (GH):
defined, 190
and physical development, 190–191, 196
Growth spurt, see Adolescent growth spurt
Gusii society, 424

Habit, defined, 54
Habituation:
defined, 206, 285
developmental trends, 285
as a predictor of intellectual performance, 286, 345–346
Habituation method, 206
Hallucinogenic drugs, and prenatal development, 137, 139
Hawaiian culture, 656
Head Start, 332, 366, 367, 368, 370
Hearing, see Audition, development of
Hemophilia, 87, 93, 94, 95, 97

Jamaican society, 176
Japanese society, 662–664
Joint physical custody, and child development, 626

Kaluli society, 382
Karotype, defined, 83
Kaufman Assessment Battery for Children (K-ABC), 344, 361
Kenyan society, 565
Kewpie-doll effect, 429–430
Kinship, defined, 98
Klinefelter's syndrome, 90, 91, 92, 96
Knowledge base, and recall memory, 320–321
Kohlberg's theory:
  of moral development, 575–585
  of sex-role development, 527–528, 530, 531
Kwashiorkor, defined, 192
Kwoma society, 537

Labor, stages of, 142
Language:
  components of, 376–378
  defined, 376
  properties of, 376
Language acquisition device (LAD):
  defined, 383
  and language development, 383–387, 388, 389
Language development (see also Communication skills):
  biological influences on, 378, 383–388, 389
  in chimpanzees, 385
  cognitive development and, 254–255, 278–279, 388, 390, 405
  in deaf children, 382–383, 391, 401
  and emotional development, 424–425, 427
  environmental influences on, 378, 379–383, 388–390, 391, 399
  holophrastic period of, 394–398
  interactionist theory of, 388, 390, 401
  learning theories of, 379–383
  in mentally retarded children, 385
  in middle childhood and adolescence, 408–412
  nativist theory of, 383–388, 401
  prelinguistic period of, 390–394
  during the preschool period, 402–408
  and self-control, 488–489
  telegraphic period of, 398–402
  television and, 379, 648
Language-making capacity (LMC):
  defined, 383
  and language development, 383–387, 388, 389
Latchkey children, see Self-care children
Latency period, of psychosexual development:
  defined, 50, 536
  and sexual behavior, 536
Learned helplessness:
  defined, 291
  development of, 291, 480–481
  goal-based model of, 482
  in institutionalized infants, 454
  prevention of, 482
  remediation of, 481
  teacher's influence on, 480
Learned helplessness orientation, to achievement tasks, 480–481, 482
Learning:
  as a cognitive process, 302–303
  defined, 5, 284

as a developmental process, 5, 302
development of, 285–301
of fears and prejudices, 55, 287–288
as reciprocal determinism, 57–58
theories of, 54–60, 285–301
varieties of, 285–301
Learning goals, defined, 482
Learning/performance distinction, 298
Learning Potential Assessment Device, 344
Learning theory:
  of attachment, 436–437
  Bandura's social-cognitive approach, 56–58, 297–299
  evaluation of, 58, 60, 302–303
  of language development, 378, 379–383
  of moral development, 585–589
  operant-learning approach, 55–56, 288–293
  philosophical assumptions of, 70, 71, 302–303
  of sex-role development, 525–527, 530, 531
  Watson's behavioristic approach, 54–55
Lepcha society, 551
Level I abilities, 362
Level II abilities, 362
Levels of processing model, of information processing, 305–306
Lexical contrast constraint, 396
Libido, defined, 48
Linguistic universals, 378, 384, 388
Locus of control, 478
Longitudinal design, 28–29, 33
Long-term memory (LTM):
  defined, 304
  development of, 313
  retrieval of information from, 293–294, 310–311, 312, 318
Looking chamber, 205, 206
Looking-glass self:
  in chimpanzees, 465
  defined, 463
  and self-esteem, 470
Love withdrawal:
  children's view of, 592
  defined, 589
  and moral development, 590
Low birth weight:
  causes of, 148
  immediate complications, 149
  and infant mortality, 125–126
  long-term complications, 150
  mother's emotional stress and, 127–128
Luteinizing hormone (LH), 190, 191

Macrosystem, defined, 61
Mad cry, 165
Mainstreaming, 661
Malnutrition:
  and intellectual development, 129, 192–193
  and physical development, 191–194
  and prenatal development, 128–129
Manic depression, 109
Marasmus, defined, 192
Marital quality:
  and caregiver-to-infant attachment, 433–434
  and child abuse, 632
  and child's adjustment, 625
  child's effect on, 603
  and parent/infant interactions, 433
Masculine sex-typed individuals, 531, 532
Mastery motivation, see Effectance motivation

Mastery orientation, to achievement tasks:
  defined, 480
  development of, 480–481
Maternal age:
  and chromosomal abnormalities of offspring, 91–92
  and children's cognitive performance, 540
  and prenatal complications, 126–127
Maternal deprivation hypothesis, 453–454
Maternal employment:
  and children's aggression, 628
  and children's cognitive competencies, 628
  and children's gender stereotyping, 534, 628
  and children's social/emotional development, 456–459, 628
  incidence of, 456, 605
  and parenting styles, 628–629
Maternity blues, see Postpartum depression
Maturation:
  and cognitive development, 62, 248, 253, 275, 314
  defined, 5
  and IQ, 336
  and language development, 378, 384, 386, 388–389, 391
  and peer acceptance, 676
  and perceptual development, 204, 216–217, 221, 234–235
  and physical development, 167–184
Mature strategy use, defined, 316
Mean-World beliefs, 644
Mechanistic model (or world view), 70
Mediation deficiency, defined, 316
Meiosis, defined, 81
Memory:
  cultural influences on, 317–318
  defined, 309
  development of, 309–322
  knowledge base and, 320–321
  metamemory and, 319–320
  and object permanence, 253
  and problem solving, 314
  varieties of, 305, 310, 311
Memory span, defined, 313
Menarche:
  defined, 183
  girls' reactions to, 185
  secular trends in, 183–184
Mental age (MA), 333, 341–342
Mental illness:
  environmental influences on, 110
  hereditary influences on, 109, 110
Mental retardation:
  defined, 350
  Down syndrome and, 91
  fragile-X syndrome and, 89
  and language development, 385
  and life outcomes, 350–351
  phenylketonuria and, 93, 96
  sex chromosome abnormalities and, 90
Mesoderm, 121
Mesosystem, defined, 61
Metacognition:
  computers and, 649
  defined, 318
  schooling and, 320, 327, 651
Metalinguistic awareness:
  defined, 409
  development of, 409–410, 413
Metamemory:
  defined, 319
  development of, 319
  relation to recall memory, 319–320
Mexican society, 565, 566

Microsystem, defined, 61
Middle schools, and achievement, 657
Mind/computer analogy, 303
Minority stereotyping:
  by preschool children, 466
  by teachers, 659–660
  television and, 645
Mister Rogers' Neighborhood, 646, 647
Mitosis, defined, 80
Monozygotic (MZ) twins, defined, 82
Moral affect:
  defined, 568
  discipline and, 590
  punishment and, 588
  relation to moral behavior, 569, 570, 585, 586–587
Moral behavior:
  cognitive rationales and, 588
  consistency of, 586–587
  discipline and, 590
  moral affect and, 569, 570, 585, 586–587
  moral reasoning and, 584–585, 586–587
  observational learning of, 589
  peer influences on, 684–685
  punishment and, 587–588
  reinforcement and, 587
  self-concept training and, 588–589
Morality (see also Moral affect; Moral behavior; Moral reasoning):
  consistency of, 586–587
  defined, 568
  development of, 569–593
Morality of care, 584
Morality of contract, individual rights, and democratically accepted law, stage of, 578
Morality of individual principles of conscience, stage of, 578–579
Morality of justice, 584
Moral realism, see Heteronomous morality
Moral reasoning:
  cognitive development and, 570, 572, 577, 580
  cultural influences on, 582, 583
  defined, 568
  development of, 570–585
  discipline and, 590
  measurement of, 571, 575–576
  and moral behavior, 584–585, 586, 587
  parental influences on, 573, 575
  peer influences on, 572–573, 581
  schooling and, 581–582
  sex differences, 583–584
  stages of, 571–572, 576–579
Moral relativism, see Autonomous morality
Moral rules, 574–575
Moral self-concept training, 588–589
Moratorium status, of identity formation, 483
Moro reflex, 161
Morphemes, defined, 377
Morphological knowledge, 409
Motherese, 381, 382
"Mother-only" monkeys, 668
Motion hypothesis, of perceptual development, 235, 236
Motivational hypothesis, for group differences in IQ, 361
Motor development:
  in adolescence, 180–182
  in childhood, 179–180
  cultural influences on, 176
  in infancy, 174–175, 177–178
  maturation and, 174–175
  motivation and, 177
  and perceptual development, 221, 226
  practice and, 175–176

Information-processing view of, 296–297, 588
intensity of, and effectiveness, 295, 588
and moral behavior, 587–588
vs. reinforcement, 290
and sex-typing, 526
timing of, and effectiveness, 295, 588
varieties of, 290, 291
verbal rationales for, and effectiveness, 295, 296–297, 588
warmth of punitive agent, and effectiveness, 295, 588
Punishment and obedience stage, of moral reasoning, 576–577
Pupillary reflex, 161, 207
Pygmalion effect, 660

Quasi experiment, *see* Natural experiment
Questionnaire:
defined, 13
as a research instrument, 13, 16, 20

Race:
and aggression, 551
differences in IQ, 359–366
differences in parenting, 364, 658–659
differences in scholastic achievement, 477, 658
and identity formation, 487
and infant soothability, 166
and motor development, 176
and peer group influences, 658–659
and self-concept, 465
stereotyping of, on television, 645
teacher's reactions to, 659–660
Radiation:
and mutations, 92
and prenatal development, 137–138, 141
Radical behaviorism, 55–56, 302 (*see also* Operant learning theory)
Random assignment, defined, 23
Range of reaction principle, 111
Rate of maturation:
heritability of, 190
individual differences in, 183, 184
and peer acceptance, 187–188, 676
and personality development, 187–189
Raven Progressive Matrices Test, 360–361
Reaction time, defined, 180
Reading:
cerebral lateralization and, 173
metalinguistic awareness and, 410
perceptual development and, 232, 233
television and, 648
Recall memory:
defined, 305
development of, 309–321
Recasts, and language development, 381–382
Receptive language, defined, 394
Receptive vocabulary, 409
Recessive allele, defined, 84
Reciprocal determinism:
defined, 57
of discipline administered, 591–592
in family social systems, 602–605
Reciprocal punishment, 572
Recognition memory, defined, 305
Reconstituted families:
children's adjustment to, 625, 627
defined, 605
and delinquent behavior, 627–628
incidence of, 606, 622
parenting within, 625, 627
parents' adjustment to, 625, 627

Referential communication skills:
defined, 408
development of, 408, 410–412
Reflexes:
adaptive significance of, 160, 161
as contributors to attachment, 430, 438–439
defined, 160
and intellectual development, 247, 248
and neonatal assessment, 158, 162
and sudden infant death syndrome (SIDS), 164
Regression, and personality development, 49
Regulatory genes, 84
Rehearsal:
defined, 315
development of, 315–316
Reinforcer, defined, 55, 288
Reinforcement:
and achievement motivation, 476–477
and aggression, 554, 555
and altruism, 566
and attachments, 436–437
defined, 55, 288
informational value of, 290–292
and language development, 379–381, 388
and moral development, 587
and observational learning, 298
peers as agents of, 682–683
vs. punishment, 290, 291
schedules of, 290
and sex typing, 525–526, 527, 531
in social-skills training, 679
timing of, and effectiveness, 290
Rejected children:
behavioral characteristics of, 675–676, 677
defined, 675
long-term implications for, 675–676
treatment of, 679–680
Reliability, defined, 15
REM (rapid eye movement) sleep, 163
Repression:
defined, 48
and personality development, 49
Research designs:
comparative, 31
correlational, 20–22, 33
cross-cultural, 31–32
cross-sectional, 26–28, 33
experimental, 22–23, 24, 33
longitudinal, 29–29, 33
quasi-experimental, 23–25, 33
sequential, 29–31, 33
Research ethics, 34–36
Research methods:
in achievement research, 474, 475
in attachment research, 444, 445
in behavioral genetics research, 98–102
in cognitive development research, 243, 260, 263, 313, 322–324
in developmental psychology, 14–34
in emotional development research, 422
in ethological research, 65
in moral development research, 570–571, 575–576, 587
in peer acceptance research, 674–675
in perceptual development research, 205–207, 220, 234, 238
practical benefits of studying, 36–38
in prosocial moral reasoning research, 561
in self/social cognition research, 464–465, 467, 470, 489–490, 495–496

Respiratory distress syndrome, 149
Resistant attachment:
cultural influences on, 445
defined, 444
development of, 446, 447
underlying working models of, 450, 451
Retaliatory aggression, defined, 546
Reticular formation, 171, 228
Retrieval processes, 293–294, 311, 318, 404
Reversibility, 246, 260, 262, 263
RH disease, 133
Role taking:
and adolescent egocentrism, 270
and aggression, 546
and altruism, 561, 563, 568
cognitive development and, 497
defined, 495
friends as contributors to, 499, 682
and impressions of friendships, 497–498
measurement of, 495–496
and moral reasoning, 573–580
and peer acceptance, 498, 676
peers as contributors to, 499
and sex typing, 518
social experience and, 498–500
in social-skills training, 679
stages of, 496
Roman society, 9
Rooting reflex, 160, 161, 162
Rouge test, 464–465, 560
Rubella, and prenatal development, 130–131
Rule assessment approach, to problem-solving research:
defined, 322
educational implications of, 325, 327
limitations of, 325–326
principles of, 322–325

s, defined, 335
Sambia society, 523
Samoan society, 382
Scheme:
defined, 61, 244
development of, 61–62, 247–248
varieties of, 245–246
Schizophrenia, defined, 109
Scholastic achievement (*see also* Schools; Teachers):
ability tracking and, 654
achievement expectancies and, 478–479
achievement motivation and, 475
attention deficits and, 310
child abuse and, 634
class size and, 653–654
compensatory education and, 367–369
computers and, 649
cross-cultural comparisons, 662–665
divorce and, 623
in effective and ineffective schools, 652–653
ethnic differences in, 658–660
home environment and, 476
IQ and, 347
learned helplessness and, 480–481
locus of control and, 478
mainstreaming and, 661
maternal age and, 540
maternal employment and, 628
monetary resources and, 653
parenting and, 476–477, 658–659, 663, 664
part-time employment and, 616
and peer acceptance, 7, 676, 679
peer influences on, 477, 658–659
preschool attendance and, 652, 673
school desegregation and, 661

self-control and, 492
and self-esteem, 470
sibling influences on, 620
teachers and, 659–661
television and, 642, 643
Scholastic Aptitude Test (SAT), 344, 492
Schools (*see also* Teachers):
and cognitive development, 266, 267, 316, 327, 651
cross-national comparisons, 662–665
desegregation of, 661
education of handicapped pupils, 661
effectiveness of, 652–658
functions of, 651
and identity formation, 476
and minority student achievement, 658–661
and moral reasoning, 581
for preschool children, 652
and prosocial moral reasoning, 566
Scientific method, 14–15
Scripts, and memory development, 311
Secondary (or complex) emotions, 423–424
Secondary circular reactions:
defined, 249
and development of self-concept, 464
Secondary reinforcer, defined, 436
Second trimester, of prenatal development, 124–125
Secular trend, defined, 184
Secure attachment:
defined, 444
development of, 446, 447
long-term correlates of, 448, 450
underlying working models of, 450, 451
Secure base:
defined, 435
and separation/stranger anxieties, 441, 442
Selective attention:
defined, 229
development of, 229–230, 308–309
to same-sex models, 526, 527, 528, 531
Selective breeding, 98, 104
Self (*see also*, Self-concept; Self-esteem):
defined, 463
destruction of, 472
development of, 464–473
Self-actualization goal, of parenting, 601, 602
Self-assertion, 488
Self-care (or latchkey) children, 629–630
Self-concept:
in adolescence, 468–469
cognitive development and, 464, 465, 469
defined, 464
during grade school, 468
during infancy, 464–466
during the preschool period, 466–468
theory of mind and, 466–467
timing of puberty and, 187–189
Self-concept training:
and altruism, 564–565
and delay of gratification, 491–492
and moral behavior, 588–589
Self-conscious emotions, *see* Secondary (or complex) emotions
Self-control (*see also* Delay of gratification; Inhibitory controls):
in adolescence, 490–491
defined, 486

Credits

These pages constitute an extension of the copyright page. We have made every effort to trace the ownership of all copyrighted material and to secure permission from copyright holders. In the event of any question arising as to the use of any material, we will be pleased to make the necessary correction in future printings.

PHOTOGRAPHS

Chapter 1
1: © 1994 PhotoDisc, Inc. 3: © 1994 PhotoDisc, Inc. 5: © The Bettmann Archives. 10: © W.P. Wilstach Collection Philadelphia Museum of Art. 11: © The Image Works. 13: © The Bettmann Archive. 18: © Mary Kate Denny/Photo Edit. 19: © Ann Clark. 29: © The Bettmann Archive. 29: © David Young-Wolff/Photo Edit. 32: © Jeffrey Aaronson/Network Aspen. 36: © Pedrick/The Image Works.

Chapter 2
40: © 1994 PhotoDisc, Inc. 47: © Bettmann News photos. 50: © Bachmann/The Image Works. 51: © UPI/Bettmann. 54: © The Bettmann Archive. 56: © Archives of the History of American Psychology, University of Akron. 57: © Courtesy of Albert Bandura. 61: © Archives of the History of American Psychology, University of Akron. 62: © Anna Kaufman Moon/Stock Boston. 66: © Bob Daemmrich/Stock Boston.

Chapter 3
74: © 1994 PhotoDisc, Inc. 77: © Candy Cameron 1989. 79: © Francis Leroy/Photo Researchers, Inc. 82: © Ann Clark. 82: © Ann Clark. 83a: © Biophoto Assoc./Photo Researchers, Inc. 83b: © Biophoto Assoc./Photo Researchers, Inc. 87: © Science Source/Photo Researchers, Inc. 91: © Jose Carrillo/Stock Boston. 107: © James L Shaffer/Shaffer Photography. 114: © Robert Burroughs.

Chapter 4
118: © 1994 PhotoDisc, Inc. 120: © Andy Walker/Midland Fertility Services/Photo Researchers, Inc. 123 a: © John Giannicchi. 123 b: © Dr. Landrum B. Shettles. 125: © Dr. Landrum B. Shettles. 129: © Joseph Nettis/Stock Boston. 135. © Stern/Heggemann from Black Star. 136: © George Steinmetz. 145: © Blair Seitz. 153: © Anthro Photo File.

Chapter 5
157: © 1994 PhotoDisc, Inc. 159: © Suzanne Arms/The Image Works. 162a: © Charles Gupton/Stock Boston. 162b: © Charles Gupton/Stock Boston. 162c: © Charles Gupton/Stock Boston. 166: © Eastcott/Momatiuk/The Image Works. 176: © E. Crews/The Image Works. 178: © B. Plotkin/The Image Works. 179: © John Eastcott/VVA Momatiuk/The Image Works. 180: © Peter Vandermark/Stock Boston. 185: © Bob Dammrich/Stock Boston. 187: © Tony Freeman/Photo Edit. 192: © Photo Researchers Inc.

Chapter 6
200: © John Coletti/Stock Boston. 203: © 1994 PhotoDisc, Inc. 206: © David Linton from *Scientific American*. 209: © Stacy Pick/Stock Boston. 221: © Enrico Ferorelli. 225: © Bruce Plotkin/The Image Works. 227a: © Courtesy of Lorraine Bahrick-From *Intermodal Learning in Infancy: Learning on the Basis...* 227b: © Courtesy of Lorraine Bahrick-From *Intermodal Learning in Infancy: Learning on the Basis...* 233: © Mary Kate Denny/Photo Edit.

Chapter 7
244: © 1994 PhotoDisc, Inc. 245: © Gabor Demjen/Stock Boston. 250: © Myrleen Ferguson/Photo Edit. 252: © Jean Claude Le Jeune/Stock Boston. 257: © Jeff Greenberg/Photo Edit. 259a: © Courtesy of Rheta de Vries. 259b: © Courtesy of Rheta de Vries. 267: © Tony Freeman/Photo Edit. 270: © W. Hill/The Image Works. 276: © Archives of the History of American Psychology, University of Akron. 278: © Elizabeth Crews/The Image Works. 279: © Elizabeth Crews/The Image Works.

Chapter 8
283: © 1994 PhotoDisc, Inc. 285: © Cathy Waterson/Gail Meese Photography. 288: © D. Greco/The Image Works. 293: © Courtesy of Carolyn Rovee-Collier, Rutgers University. 295: © Ann Clark. 300: © A.N. Meltzoff, A.K. Moore, University of Washington. 300: © Ann Clark. 309: © B. Bachmann/The Image Works. 317: © David Young-Wolff/Photo Edit. 326: © David Wells/The Image Works.

Chapter 9
331: © Laura Dwight/Photo Edit. 333: © The Bettman Archive. 338: © Cameramann/The Image Works. 348: © Ann Clark. 357: © Chris Marona/Photo Researchers, Inc. 357: © Alan S. Weiner/Gamma Liaison. 368: © Tony Freeman/Photo Edit. 371: © Alan Carey/The Image Works. 372: © Paul Conklin/Gail Meese Photography.

Chapter 10
375: © 1994 PhotoDisc, Inc. 377: © Sue Klemens/Stock Boston. 383: © The Bettmann Archive. 385a: © Courtesy of Sue Savage-Rumbaugh. 385b: © Courtesy of Sue Savage-Rumbaugh. 385c: © Courtesy of Sue Savage-Rumbaugh. 385d: © Courtesy of Sue Savage-Rumbaugh. 393: © David M. Grossman/Photo Researchers, Inc. 394: © Dorothy Littell Greco/Stock Boston. 405: © Ann Clark. 407: © Ann Clark. 410: © Joseph Nettis/Stock Boston. 414: © Ann Clark.

Chapter 11
418: © 1994 PhotoDisc, Inc. 421: © 1994 PhotoDisc, Inc. 423a: © Courtesy of Carroll E. Izard, University of Delaware. 423b: © Courtesy of Carroll E. Izard, University of Delaware. 423c: © Courtesy of Carroll E. Izard, University of Delaware. 423d: © Courtesy of Carroll E. Izard, University of Delaware. 423e: © Courtesy of Carroll E. Izard, University of Delaware. 423f: © Courtesy of Carroll E. Izard, University of Delaware. 425: © Elizabeth Crew/Elizabeth Crew Photography. 429: © Ann Clark. 431: © Laura Dwight/Photo Edit. 435: © Robert Brenner/Photo Edit. 437: © Harlow Primate Laboratory, University of Wisconsin. 439: © Lauren Goodsmith/The Image Works. 441: © Steve Grand/Photo Researchers, Inc. 453: © H. Bradner/The Image Works. 454: © Zev Radovan/Photo Edit. 457: © Paul Conklin/Photo Edit.

Chapter 12
462: © 1994 PhotoDisc, Inc. 465: © Gail Meese/Gail Meese Photography. 467: © Jeffery W. Myers/Photo Network. 474: © Miro Vinoniv/Stock Boston. 475: © Robert Reichert/Liaison International. 477: © Tony Freeman/Photo Edit. 487: © Tom Prettyman/Photo Edit. 491: © Chad Elders/Photo Network. 499: © Paul S. Conklin/Photo Edit.

Chapter 13
503: © 1994 PhotoDisc, Inc. 504: © Frank Pedrick/The Image Works. 509: © Elizabeth Zuckerman/Photo Edit. 514: © J. Kramer/The Image Works. 514: © Lawrence Migdale/Photo Researchers, Inc.. 521: © E. Crews/The Image Works. 525: © David Young-Wolff/Photo Edit. 534: © Ann Clark. 536: © Kim Robbie/Stock Market. 540: © Eastcott-Momatiuk/The Image Works.

Chapter 14
543: © 1994 PhotoDisc, Inc. 545: © Elizabeth Crews. 546: © Catherine Ursillo/Photo Researchers, Inc. 549: © Dennis Budd Gray/Stock Boston. 553: © Dan Habib/Impact Visuals. 560: © Mary Kate Denny/Photo Edit. 563: © David Young-Wolff/Photo Edit. 567: © Bob Daemmrich/Stock Boston. 569: © Ann Clark. 581: © Bob Daemmrich/Stock Boston. 587: © Mary Kate Denny/Photo Edit.

Chapter 15
597: © Bill Bachman/Photo Edit. 599: © 1994 PhotoDisc, Inc. 601: © Gianni Tortoli/Photo Researchers. 604: © David Young-Wolff/Photo Edit. 609: © Brooks Dodge/Photo Network. 615: © Michael Newman/Photo Edit. 620: © Dennis MacDonald/Photo Edit. 624: © Michael Newman/Photo Edit. 630: © Gail Meese/Gail Meese Photography. 632: © Lionel Delevingne/Stock Boston.

Chapter 16
641: © 1994 PhotoDisc, Inc. 645: © Dan Habib/Impact Visuals. 647: © Big Bird © Jim Henson Productions, Inc. 649: © Bob Daemmrich/Stock Boston. 657: © Bob Daemmrich/The Image Works. 659: © W. Hill, Jr./The Image Works. 662: © Paul Conklin/Photo Edit. 664: © Fujifotos/The Image Works. 667: © George Disario/The Stock Market. 669: © Harlow Primate Laboratory, University of Wisconsin. 670: © Laura Dwight/Peter Arnold. 681: © Fredrik D. Bodin/Stock Boston. 686: © Gail Meese/Gail Meese Photography.

TABLES AND FIGURES

Chapter 1

24: Figure in Box 1-2 adapted from "Effects of Movie Violence on Aggression in a Field Setting as a Function of Group Dominance and Cohesion," by J. P. Leyens, R. D. Parke, L. Camino, & L. Berkowitz, 1975, *Journal of Personality and Social Psychology, 32,* pp. 346–360. Copyright © 1975 by the American Psychological Association. Adapted by permission. **27:** Figure 1-2 adapted from "Age and Verbalization in Observational Learning," by B. Coates & W. W. Hartup, 1969, *Developmental Psychology, 1,* pp. 556–562. Copyright © 1969 by the American Psychological Association. Adapted by permission.

Chapter 2

57: Figure 2-3 adapted from "The Self System in Reciprocal Determinism," by Albert Bandura, 1978, *American Psychologist, 33,* p. 335. Copyright © 1978 by the American Psychological Association. Adapted by permission. **59:** Figure in Box 2-3 based on *The Ecology of Human Development,* by U. Bronfenbrenner, 1979, Cambridge, MA: Harvard University Press.

Chapter 3

96: Figure 3-10 adapted from *Before We Are Born,* 4th ed., by K. L. Moore, & T. V. N. Persaud, 1993, p. 89, Philadelphia: Saunders. Adapted by permission of the author and publisher. **99:** Figure 3-11 from *Behaviorial Genetics: A Primer,* by R. Plomin, J. C. DeFries, & G. E. McClearn, 1989. Copyright © W. H. Freeman and Company. Reprinted by permission. **101:** Table 3-4 based on "Familial Studies of Intelligence: A Review," by T. J. Bouchard, Jr., and M. McGue, 1981, *Science, 212,* pp. 1055–1059; and *An Approach to Understanding Linkages between Parent-Infant and Spouse Relationships,* 1985, paper presented at the biennial meeting of the Society for Research in Child Development, New Orleans. **104:** Figure 3-12 from "The Louisville Twin Study: Developmental Synchronies in Behavior," by R. S. Wilson, 1983, *Child Development, 54,* pp. 298–316. Copyright © 1983 by the Society for Research in Child Development, Inc. **111:** Figure 3-13 adapted from "Heritability of Personality: A Demonstration," by I. Gottesman, 1963, *Psychological Monographs, 11* (Whole No. 572). American Psychological Association.

Chapter 4

124: Figure 4-5 adapted from *Before We Are Born,* 4th ed., by K. L. Moore & T. V. N. Persaud, 1993, Philadelphia: Saunders. Adapted by permission of the author and publisher. **125:** Data for Table 4-1 from "High Risk Situations: The Very Low Birthweight Fetus," by C. Lin, 1989, in M. I. Evans et al. (Eds.), *Fetal Diagnosis and Therapy: Science, Ethics, and the Law,* Philadelphia: Lippincott. **127:** Figure 4-6 from *Infant Death: An Analysis by Maternal Risk and Health Care,* by D. Kessner, 1973, p. 100. Copyright © 1973 by the National Academy of Sciences, Washington, D. C. **131:** Figure 4-7 adapted from *Before We Are Born,* 4th ed., by K. L. Moore & T. V. N. Persaud, 1993, p. 130, Philadelphia: Saunders. Adapted by permission of the author and publisher. **151:** Figure 4-11 adapted from "Risk and Resilience in Early Mental Development," by R. S. Wilson, 1985, *Developmental Psychology, 21,* pp. 795–805. Copyright © 1985 by the American Psychological Association. Adapted by permission.

Chapter 5

163: Data for Table 5-2 from "The Causes, Controls, and Organization of Behavior in the Neonate," by P. H. Wolff, 1966, *Psychological Issues, 5* (1, Whole No. 17). **164:** Figure in Box 5-2 adapted from "Sudden Infant Death Syndrome," by R. L. Naeye, 1980, *Scientific American, 242,* pp. 56–62. Copyright © 1980 by Scientific American, Inc. All rights reserved. **175:** Table 5-3 adapted from "The Denver Developmental Screening Test," by W. K. Frankenberg & J. B. Dodds, 1967, *Journal of Pediatrics, 71,* pp. 181 191. Copyright © 1967 C. V. Mosby Company. Reprinted by permission. **181:** Figure 5-5 from *Science and Medicine of Exercise and Sport,* 2nd ed., by Warren K. Johnson & Elsworth R. Buskirk, 1974. Copyright © 1974 by Warren K. Johnson & Ellsworth R. Buskirk. Reprinted by permission of HarperCollins Publishers, Inc. **184:** Figure 5-6 reprinted by permission of the publishers from *Foetus into Man: Physical Growth from Conception to Maturity,* 2nd ed.,1990, by J. M. Tanner, p. 158, Cambridge, MA: Harvard University Press. Copyright © 1978, 1989 by J. M. Tanner. **193:** Figure 5-7 reprinted by permission of the publishers from *Foetus into Man: Physical Growth from Conception to Maturity,* 2nd ed., 1990, by J. M. Tanner, p. 158, Cambridge, MA: Harvard University Press. Copyright © 1978, 1989 by J. M. Tanner. **195:** Figure 5-8 adapted from "Long-Term Effects of Family-Based Treatment of Childhood Obesity," by L. H. Epstein, R. R. Wing, R. Koeske, & A. Valoski, 1987, *Journal of Consulting and Clinical Psychology, 55,* pp. 91–95. **196:** Figure 5-9 from "Deprivation Dwarfism," by L. I. Gardner, 1972, *Scientific American, 227,* pp. 76–82. Copyright © 1972 by Scientific American, Inc. All rights reserved.

Chapter 6

205: Figure 6-1 adapted from "'Perceptual Set' in Young Children," by H. W. Reese, 1963, *Child Development, 34,* pp. 151–159. Adapted by permission. **212:** Figure 6-3 adapted from "The Origin of Form Perception," by R. L. Fantz, May 1961, *Scientific American, 204,* p. 72 (top). Copyright © 1961 by Scientific American, Inc. All rights reserved. Adapted by permission. **213:** Figure 6-4 adapted from "Infant Visual Perception," by M. S. Banks, in collaboration with P. Salapatek, 1983, in M. M. Haith & J. J. Campos (Eds.), *Handbook of Child Psychology, Vol. 2: Infancy and Developmental Psychobiology,* New York: Wiley. Figure 6-5 adapted from "Pattern Perception in Infancy," by P. Salapatek, 1975, in L. B. Cohen and P. Salapatek (Eds.), *Infant Cognition: From Sensation to Perception.* Copyright © 1975 by Academic Press, Inc. Adapted by permission. **214:** Figure 6-6 adapted from "Perception of Partly Occluded Objects in Infancy," by P. J. Kellman & E. S. Spelke, 1983, *Cognitive Psychology, 15,* pp. 483–524. Copyright © 1983 by Academic Press. Adapted by permission. **215:** Figure 6-7 adapted from "Development of Visual Organization: The Perception of Subjective Contours," by B. I. Bertenthal, J. J. Campos, & M. M. Haith, 1980, *Child Development, 51,* pp. 1077–1080. Copyright © 1980 by the Society for Research in Child Development, Inc. Adapted by permission. Figure 6-8 from "Infant Sensitivity to Figural Coherence in Biomechanical Motions," by B. I. Bertenthal, D. R. Proffitt, & J. E. Cutting, 1984, *Journal of Experimental Child Psychology, 37,* pp. 213–230. Copyright © 1984 by Academic Press. Reprinted by permission. **216:** Figure 6-9 adapted from "A Critical Test of Infant Pattern Preference Models," by J. L. Dannemiller & B. R. Stephens, 1988, *Child Development, 59,* pp. 210–216. Copyright © 1988 by the Society for Research in Child Development, Inc. **220:** Figure 6-10 adapted with permission from "Development of Sensitivity to Pictorial Depth," by A. Yonas, W. Cleaves, & L. Pettersen, 1978, *Science, 200,* pp. 77–79. Copyright © 1978 by the American Association for the Advancement of Science. **221:** Figure 6-11 from "Infants' Perceptions of Pictorially Specified Interposition," by C. E. Grunrud & A. Yonas, 1984, *Journal of Experimental Child Psychology, 377,* pp. 500–511. Copyright © 1984 by Academic Press. Reprinted by permission. **223:** Figure 6-13 from "Influence of Contingent Auditory Stimulation upon Non-Nutritional Suckle," by E. C. Butterfield & G. N. Siperstein, 1972, in J. F. Bosma (Ed.), *Third Symposium on Oral Sensation and Perception: The Mouth of the Infant.* Copyright © by Charles C. Thomas Publisher, Springfield, Ill. Reprinted by permission. **229:** Figure 6-14 based on "The Development of Scanning Strategies and Their Relation to Visual Differentiation," by E. Vurpillot, 1968, *Journal of Experimental Child Psychology, 6,* pp. 632–650. **230:** Figure 6-15 adapted from "Selective Auditory Attention in Children," by E. E. Maccoby, 1967, in L. P. Lippsitt and C. C. Spiker (Eds.), *Advances in Child Development and Behavior,* p. 177. Copyright © 1967 by Academic Press. Adapted by permission. **231:** Figure 6-16 from "Perception of Overlapping and Embedded Figures by Children of Different Ages," by L. Ghent, 1956, *American Journal of Psychology, 69,* pp. 575–587. Copyright © 1956 by the Board of Trustees of the University of Illinois. Reprinted by permission of the University of Illinois Press. Figure 6-17 adapted with permission of the author and publisher from "Factors Affecting the Visual Recognition of Incomplete Objects: A Comparative Investigation of Children and Adults," by E. S. Gollin, 1962, *Perceptual and Motor Skills, 15,* pp. 583–590. Copyright © Southern Universities Press, 1962. **232:** Figure 6-18 adapted from "A Developmental Study of the Discrimination of Letter-Like Forms," by E. J. Gibson, J. J. Gibson, A. D. Pick, & H. A. Osser, 1962, *Journal of Comparative and Physiological Psychology, 55,* pp. 897–906. **235:** Figure 6-19 adapted from "Movement-Produced Stimulation in the Development of Visually Guided Behavior," by R. Held & A. Hein, 1963, *Journal of Comparative and Physiological Psychology, 56,* pp. 872–876. **237:** Figure 6-20 adapted from "Locomotor Status and the Development of Spatial Search Skills," by D. L. Bai & B. I. Bertenthal, 1992, *Child Development, 63,* pp. 215–226. Copyright © 1992 by the Society for Research in Child Development, Inc.

Chapter 7

253: Figure in Box 7-1 based on "Object Permanence in 3½- and 4½-month-old Infants," by R. Baillargen, 1987, *Developmental Psychology, 23,* pp. 655–664. Copyright © 1987 by the American Psychological Association. **256:** Figure 7-1 from "Retrieval of Basic-Level Category in Prelinguistic Infants," by K. Roberts, 1988, *Developmental Psychology, 24,* p. 23. Copyright © 1988 by the American Psychological Association. Reprinted by permission. **271:** Figure 7-6 adapted from "Individual Differences in College Students' Performance on Formal Operations Tasks," by R. De Lisi & J. Staudt, 1980, *Journal of Applied Developmental Psychology, 1,* pp. 163–174. Reprinted with the permission of Ablex Publishing Company.

Chapter 8

298: Figure 8-5 adapted from "Influence of Models' Reinforcement Contingencies on the Acquisition of Imitative Responses," by A. Bandura, 1965, *Journal of Personality and Social Psychology, 1,* pp. 589–595. Copyright © 1965 by the American Psychological Association. Adapted by permission. **304:** Figure 8-6 adapted from "Human Memory: A Proposed System and Its Control Processes," by R. C. Atkinson & R. M. Shiffrin, 1968, in K. W. Spence & J. T. Spence (Eds.), *The Psychology of Learning and Motivation: Advances in Research and Theory (Vol.2).* Copyright © 1968 by Academic Press, Inc. Adapted by permission. **312:** Figure in Box 8-4 from "Childhood Amnesia and the Beginnings of Memory for Four Early Life Events," by J. A. Usher & U. Neisser, 1993, *Journal of Experimental Psychology: General, 122,* pp. 155–165. Copyright © 1993 by the American Psychological Association. **315:** Figure 8-8 adapted from *Intellectual Development: Birth to Adulthood,* by R. Case, 1985, Orlando, FL: Academic Press. **321:** Figure 8-10 from "Knowledge Structures and Memory Development," by M. H. T. Chi, 1978, in R. S. Siegle (Ed.), *Children's Thinking: What Develops?* Copyright © 1978 by Lawrence Erlbaum Associates, Inc. Reprinted by permission. **323:** Table 8-3 adapted from "Developmental Sequences Within and Between Concepts," by R. S. Siegler, 1981, *Monographs of the Society for Research in Child Development, 46* (serial No. 189). Copyright © 1981 by the Society for Research in Child Development, Inc. Adapted by permission.

Chapter 9

336: Figure 9-2 adapted from a table in *The Nature of Human Intelligence*, by J. P. Guilford, 1967. Copyright © 1967 by McGraw-Hill, Inc. Adapted by permission. **340:** Table 9-1 adapted from *Frames of Mind: The Theory of Multiple Intelligences*, by Howard Gardner, 1983. Copyright © 1983 by Howard Gardner. Reprinted by permission of BasicBooks, a division of HarperCollins Publishers, Inc. **343:** Figure 9-4 adapted from *Assessment of Children's Intelligence and Special Abilities*, 2nd ed., by J. M. Sattler, p. 16. Copyright © by J. M. Sattler. Adapted by permission. **347:** Table 9-3 adapted from "The Stability of Mental Test Performance Between Two and Eighteen Years," by M. P. Honzik, J. W. MacFarlane, & L. Allen, 1948, *Journal of Experimental Education, 17,* pp. 309–324. **349:** Table 9-4 adapted from "Army General Classification Test Scores for Civilian Populations," by T. W. Harrell & M. S. Harrell, 1945, *Educational and Psychological Measurement, 5,* pp. 229–239. **351:** Table in Box 9-1 adapted from *Lives of the Mentally Retarded: A Forty-Year Follow-up,* by R. T. Ross, M. J. Begab, E. H. Dondis, J. S. Giampicolo, Jr., & C. E. Meyers. Copyright © 1985 by Stanford University Press. Adapted by permission. **354:** Data and descriptions for Table 9-5 compiled from "Stability of Intelligence from Preschool to Adolescence: The Influence of Social and Family Risk Factors," by A. J. Sameroff, R. Seifer, A. Baldwin, & C. Baldwin, 1993, *Child Development, 64,* pp. 80–97. **355:** Table 9-6 adapted from the *Manual for the HOME Observation for Measurement of the Environment,* by B. M. Caldwell & R. H. Bradley, 1984, University of Arkansas. Copyright © 1984. Adapted by permission. **358:** Figure 9-5 adapted from "Birth Order and Intellectual Development," by R. B. Zajonc & G. B. Marcus, 1975, *Psychological Review, 82,* pp. 74–88. Copyright © 1975 by the American Psychological Association. Reprinted by permission. **360:** Table 9-7 adapted from the "Chitling Test," by A. Dove, *Newsweek,* July 15, 1968. **363:** Figure in Box 9-2 adapted from *Psychology,* 3rd ed., by Henry Gleitman, p. 699, with the permission of W. W. Norton & Company, Inc. Copyright © 1991, 1986, 1981 by W. W. Norton. **369:** Figure 9-8 from "The Carolina Abecedarian Project," by F. A. Campbell & C. T. Ramey, 1991, in M. Burchinal (Chair), *Early Experience and Children's Competencies: New Findings from Four Longitudinal Studies.* Symposium presented at the biennial meeting of the Society for Research in Child Development, Seattle, WA. **378:** Figure 9-9 adapted from Figure 2 in *Modes of Thinking in Young Children,* by Michael A. Wallach & Nathan Kogan, p. 34. Copyright © 1965 by Holt, Rinehart and Winston, Inc. Adapted by permission.

Chapter 10

386: Figure 10-2 adapted from "Critical Period Effects in Second Language Learning: The Influence of Maturational State on the Acquisition of English as a Second Language," by J. S. Johnson & E. L. Newport, 1989, *Cognitive Psychology, 21,* pp. 60–99. Copyright © 1989 by Academic Press. Reprinted by permission. **395:** Table 10-1 adapted from "Structure and Strategy in Learning to Talk," by K. Nelson, 1973, *Monographs of the Society for Research in Child Development, 38* (Whole No. 149). Copyright © 1973 by the Society for Research in Child Development, Inc. Adapted by permission. **399:** Table 10-3 adapted from *Psycholinguistics,* 2nd ed., by Dan Isaac Slobin, 1979, pp. 86–87. Copyright © 1979, 1974, 1971 by Scott, Foresman and Company. Adapted by permission of HarperCollins Publishers, Inc. **400:** Table 10-4 based on data from *A First Language: The Early Stages,* by Roger Brown, p. 173, Cambridge, Mass: Harvard University Press. Copyright © 1973 by the President and Fellows of Harvard College. **401:** Figure in Box 10-3 from *Talk to the Deaf,* by Lottie Reikehof, 1963, Springfield, MO: Gospel Publishing House. Reprinted by permission. **403:** Table 10-5 adapted from *The Acquisition of Language: The Study of Developmental Linguistics,* by D. McNeill, 1970. Harper & Row Publishers. Copyright © 1970 HarperCollins, Inc. Table 10-6 adapted from *Psychology and Language: An Introduction to Psycholinguistics,* by Herbert H. Clark & Eve V. Clark, p. 345. Copyright © 1977 by Harcourt Brace Jovanovich, Inc. Reprinted by permission of the publisher. **404:** Figure 10-4 from "The Child's Learning of English Morphology," by J. Berko, 1958, *Word, 14,* pp. 150–177. **406:** Figure 10-5 adapted from "New Evidence on the Development of the Word Big," by R. Sena & L. B. Smith, 1990, *Child Development, 61,* pp. 1034–1052. Copyright © 1990 by the Society for Research in Child Development, Inc. Adapted by permission. **411:** Table 10-7 adapted from "Social and Non-Social Speech," by R. M. Krauss & S. Glucksberg, February, 1977, *Scientific American, 236,* p. 104. Copyright © 1977 by Scientific American, Inc. All rights reserved. Adapted by permission.

Chapter 11

426: Figure 11-2 adapted from "An Observational Study of Children's Attempts to Monitor Their Expressive Behavior," by C. Saarni, 1984, *Child Development, 55,* pp. 1504–1513. Copyright © 1984 by the Society for Research in Child Development, Inc. Adapted by permission. **430:** Figure 11-3 adapted from "The Innate Forms of Possible Experience," by K. Z. Lorenz, 1943, *Zeitschrift für Tierpsychologie, 5,* pp. 233–409. **435:** Figure 11-4 from "The Development of Social Attachments in Infancy," by H. R. Schaffer & P. E. Emerson, 1964, *Monographs of the Society for Research in Child Development, 29* (3, Serial No. 94). **445:** Table 11-1 from *Patterns of Attachment: A Psychological Study of the Strange Situation,* by M. D. S. Ainsworth, M. C. Blehar, E. Waters, & S. Wall. Copyright © 1978 by Lawrence Erlbaum Associates, Inc. Reprinted by permission. **449:** Table in Box 11-3 adapted from "The Quality of the Toddler's Relationship to Mother and Father: Related to Conflict Behavior and the Readiness to Establish New Relationships," by M. Main & D. R. Weston, 1981, *Child Development, 52,* pp. 932–940. Copyright © 1981 by the Society for Research in Child Development, Inc. Adapted by permission. **451:** Figure 11-6 adapted from "Attachment Styles among Young Adults: A Test of a Four-Category Model," by K. Bartholomew & L. M. Horowitz, 1991, *Journal of Personality and Social Psychology, 61,* pp. 226–244. Copyright © 1991 by the American Psychological Association. **458:** Table 11-3 adapted from *Looking at Children,* by D. F. Bjorkland & B. R. Bjorkland, pp. 354–355. Copyright © 1992 by Brooks/Cole Publishing Co.

Chapter 12

469: Figure 12-1 adapted from "Developmental Analysis of Conflict Caused by Opposing Attributes in the Adolescent Self-Portrait," by S. Harter & A. Monsour, 1992, *Developmental Psychology, 28,* pp. 251–260. Copyright © 1992 by the American Psychological Association. **470:** Figure 12-2 from "Developmental Processes in the Construction of the Self," by S. Harter, 1988, in T. D. Yawkey & J. E. Johnson (Eds.), *Integrative Processes and Socialization: Early to Middle Childhood,* p. 63, Hillsdale, NJ: Erlbaum. Copyright © 1988 by Erlbaum. Reprinted by permission. **472:** Data for figure in Box 12-1 from National Center for Health Statistics, reported in U. S. Bureau of the Census (1992) Statistical Abstract of the United States, 1992 (112th ed.), p. 90 (1989 data), Washington, D. C.: U. S. Government Printing Office. **476:** Table 12-1 adapted from "The Relationship Between Twelve-Month Home Stimulation and School Achievement," by W. J. van Doorninck, B. M. Caldwell, C. Wright, & W. K. Frankenburg, 1981, *Child Development, 52,* pp. 1080–1083. Copyright © 1981 by the Society for Research in Child Development, Inc. **484:** Figure 12-5 from "Cross-Sectional Age Changes in Ego Identity Status During Adolescence," by P. W. Meilman, 1979, *Developmental Psychology, 15,* pp. 230–231. Copyright © 1979 by the American Psychological Association. Reprinted by permission.

489: Figure 12-6 adapted from "The Emergence and Consolidation of Self-Control from Eighteen to Thirty Months of Age: Normative Trends and Individual Differences" by B. E. Vaughn, C. B. Kopp, & J. B. Krakow, 1984, *Child Development, 55,* pp. 990–1004. Copyright © 1984 by the Society for Research in Child Development, Inc. **490:** Figure 12-7 from "Verbal Control of Behavior: The Effects of Shouting," by E. Saltz, S. Campbell, & D. Skotko, 1983, *Developmental Psychology, 19,* pp. 461–464. Copyright © 1983 by the American Psychological Association. Reprinted by permission. **494:** Figure 12-8 from "The Development of Person Perception in Childhood and Adolescence: From Behavioral Comparisons to Psychological Constructs to Psychological Comparisons," by C. Barenboim, 1981, *Child Development, 52,* pp. 129–144. Copyright © 1981 by the Society for Research in Child Development, Inc. Reprinted by permission. **496:** Table 12-3 adapted from "Social Cognitive Understanding: A Guide to Educational and Clinical Experience," by R. L. Selman, 1976, in T. Lickona (Ed.), *Moral Development and Behavior: Theory, Research, and Social Issues.* Copyright © 1976 by Holt, Rinehart & Winston. Adapted by permission.

Chapter 13

506: Table 13-1 adapted from "A Cross-Cultural Survey of Some Sex Differences in Socialization," by H. Barry III, M. K. Bacon, and I. L. Child, 1957, *Journal of Abnormal and Social Psychology, 55,* pp. 327–332. **508:** Figure 13-1 from "Emergence and Characteristics of Sex Differences in Spatial Ability: A Meta-Analysis," by M. C. Linn & A. C. Petersen, 1985. *Child Development, 56,* pp. 1479–1498. Copyright © 1985 by the Society for Research in Child Development, Inc. Reprinted by permission. Figure 13-2 adapted from "Gender Differences in Mathematics Performance: A Meta-Analysis," by J. S. Hyde, E. Fennema, & S. J. Lamon, 1990, *Psychological Bulletin, 107,* pp. 139–155. Copyright © 1990 by the American Psychological Association. Adapted by permission. **510:** Table 13-2 adapted from *The Psychology of Sex Differences,* by Eleanor E. Maccoby & Carol N. Jacklin. Copyright © 1974 by Stanford University Press. Reprinted by permission of the Board of Trustees for the Leland Stanford Junior University. **516:** Figure 13-3 adapted from "Children's Concepts of Cross-Gender Activities," by T. Stoddart & E. Turiel, 1985, *Child Development, 59,* pp. 793–814. Copyright © 1985 by the Society for Research in Child Development, Inc. **517:** Figure 13-4 adapted from "Social Behavior at 33 Months in Same-Sex and Mixed-Sex Dyads," by C. N. Jacklin & E. E. Maccoby, 1978, *Child Development, 49,* pp. 557–569. Copyright © 1978 by the Society for Research in Child Development, Inc. Table 13-3 adapted from "Children, Gender and Social Structure: An Analysis of the Contents of Letters to Santa Claus," by J. G. Richardson & C. H. Simpson, 1982, *Child Development, 53,* pp. 429–436. Copyright © 1982 by the Society for Research in Child Development, Inc. Adapted by permission. **520:** Figure 13-5 from *Man and Woman, Boy and Girl,* by J. Money & A. Ehrhardt, 1972. Copyright © 1972 by John Hopkins University Press. Reprinted by permission. **529:** Figure 13-6 adapted from "The Roles of Cognition in Sex Roles and Sex-Typing," by C. L. Martin & C. S. Halverson, Jr., 1987, in D. B. Carter (Ed.), *Current Conceptions of Sex Roles and Sex Typing: Theory and Research.* Copyright © 1987 by Praeger Publishing. **532:** Table 13-5 adapted from "Assessing Sex-Typing and Androgyny in Children: The Children's Sex-Role Inventory," by J. P. Boldizar, 1991, *Developmental Psychology, 27,* pp. 505–515. Copyright © 1991 by the American Psychological Association. Adapted by permission.

Chapter 14

551: Figure 14-2 from "Stability of Aggression Over Time and Generations," by L. R. Huesmann, L. D. Eron, M. M. Lefkowitz, & L. O. Walder, 1984, *Developmental Psychology, 20*, p. 1125. Copyright © by the American Psychological Association. Reprinted by permission. 552: Figure 14-3 adapted from *Where We Stand: Can America Make It in the Race for Health, Wealth, and Happiness?* by Michael Wolff & The World Research Team. Copyright © 1992 by Michael Wolff & Company, Inc. Used by permission of Bantam Books, a division of Bantam Doubleday Dell Publishing Group, Inc. 556: Figure 14-4 adapted from "A Developmental Perspective on Antisocial Behavior," by G. R. Patterson, B. D. DeBaryshe, & E. Ramsey, 1989, *American Psychologist, 44*, pp. 329–335. Copyright © 1989 by the American Psychological Association. Adapted by permission. 562: Table 14-1 adapted from "Prosocial Development: A Longitudinal Study," by N. Eisenberg, R. Lennon, & K. Roth, 1983, *Developmental Psychology, 19*, pp. 846–855. Copyright © 1983 by the American Psychological Association. Adapted by permission. 565: Table 14-2 based on data from *Children of Six Cultures*, by B. B. Whiting & J. W. M. Whiting. Cambridge, MA: Harvard University Press. Copyright © 1975 by the President and Fellows of Harvard College. 573: Figure 14-6 adapted from "Factors Influencing Young Children's Use of Motives and Outcomes as Moral Criteria," by S. A. Nelson, 1980, *Child Development, 51*, pp. 823–829. Copyright © 1980 by the Society for Research in Child Development, Inc. 574: Figure 14-7 adapted from "Factors Influencing Young Children's Use of Motives and Outcomes as Moral Criteria," by S. A. Nelson, 1980, *Child Development, 51*, pp. 823–829. Copyright © 1980 by the Society for Research in Child Development, Inc. 580: Figure 14-8 adapted from "A Longitudinal Study of Moral Judgment," by A. Colby, L. Kohlberg, J. Gibbs, & M. Lieberman, 1983, *Monographs of the Society for Research in Child Development, 48* (Nos. 1-2, Serial No. 200). Copyright © 1983 by the Society for Research in Child Development, Inc. 583: Figure in Box 14-3 adapted from "Culture and Moral Development," by R. Shweder, M. Mahapatra, & J. G. Miller, 1987, in Jerome Kagan & Sharon Lamb (Eds.), *The Emergence of Morality in Young Children*, Chicago and London: University of Chicago Press. Copyright © 1987 University of Chicago Press. 590: Table 14-3 adapted from "Contributions of Parents and Peers to Children's Moral Socialization," by G. H. Brody & D. R. Shaffer, 1982, *Developmental Review, 2*, pp. 31–75. Copyright © 1982 Academic Press, Inc. Adapted by permission.

Chapter 15

603: Figure 15-1 from "Early Human Experience: A Family Perspective," by J. Belsky, 1981, *Developmental Psychology, 17*, pp. 3–23. Copyright © 1981 by the American Psychological Association. Reprinted by permission. 606: Figure 15-2 based on census data from "Never Marrieds Soar Among Single Parents," C. Teegarten, 1994, *Atlanta Constitution*, July 25, pp. A1, A7. 608: Figure 15-3 based on data from "Socialization in the Context of the Family: Parent-Child Interaction," by E. E. Maccoby & J. A. Martin, 1983, in E. M. Hetherington (Ed.; P. H. Mussen, General Ed.), *Handbook of Child Psychology. Vol. 4: Socialization, Personality, and Social Development* (4th ed.), New York: John Wiley and Sons. 611: Table 15-1 from *Socialization Determinants of Personal Agency*, by D. Baumrind, March 1977. Paper presented at the biennial meeting of the Society for Research in Child Development, New Orleans. Excerpted by permission. 613: Figure 15-4 adapted from "A Family Process Model of Economic Hardship and Adjustment of Early Adolescent Boys," by R. D. Conger, K. J. Conger, G. H. Elder, Jr., F. O. Lorenz, R. L. Simons, & L. B. Whitbeck, 1992, *Child Development, 63*, pp. 526–541. Copyright © 1992 by the Society for research in Child Development, Inc. Adapted by permission. 616: Figure in Box 15-1 adapted from "Negative Correlates of Part-Time Employment During Adolescence: Replication and Elaboration," by L. Steinberg & S. M. Dornbusch, 1991, *Developmental Psychology, 27*, pp. 304–313. Copyright © 1991 by the American Psychological Association. Adapted by permission. 625: Figure 15-5 from "Relation of Parental Transitions to Boys' Adjustment Problems: I. A Linear Hypothesis. II. Mothers at Risk for Transition and Unskilled Parenting," by D. M. Capaldi & G. R. Patterson, 1991, *Developmental Psychology, 27*, pp. 489–504. Copyright © 1991 by the American Psychological Association. 637: Figure 15-6 adapted from "Responses of Abused and Disadvantaged Toddlers to Distress in Agemates: A Study in the Day-Care Setting," by M. Main & C. George, 1985, *Developmental Psychology, 21*, pp. 407–412. Copyright © 1985 by the American Psychological Association. Adapted by permission.

Chapter 16

642: Figure 16-1 from *The Early Window: Effects of Television on Children and Youth*, 3rd ed., by Robert M. Liebert & Joyce Sprafkin, 1988. Copyright © 1988. Reprinted by permission of Allyn & Bacon. 644: Figure 16-2 adapted from "Psychological Processes Promoting the Relation Between Exposure to Media Violence and Aggressive Behavior by the Viewer," by L. R. Huesmann, 1986, *Journal of Social Issues, 42*, pp. 125–139. Copyright © 1986 by Journal of Social Issues. Adapted by permission. 647: Figure 16-3 from *The Early Window: Effects of Television on Children and Youth*, 3rd ed., by Robert M. Liebert & Joyce Sprafkin, 1988. Copyright © 1988. Reprinted by permission of Allyn & Bacon. 653: Figure 16-4 reprinted from *Fifteen Thousand Hours: Secondary Schools and Their Effects on Children*, by Michael Rutter, Barbara Maughan, Peter Mortimore, & Janet Ouston, 1979, p. 86, Cambridge, MA: Harvard University Press. Copyright © 1979 by Michael Rutter, Barbara Maughan, Peter Mortimore, & Janet Ouston. Reprinted by permission. 656: Figure 16-6 adapted from *Rousing Minds to Life: Teaching, Learning, and Schooling in Social Context*, by R. G. Tharp & R. Gallimore, 1988, p. 116, Cambridge, England: Cambridge University Press. Adapted with the permission of Cambridge University Press. 663: Figure 16-7 based on data from "Homework: A Cross-Cultural Examination," by C. Chen & H. W. Stevenson, 1989, *Child Development, 60*, pp. 551–561; and "Contexts of Achievement: A Study of American, Chinese, and Japanese Children," *Monographs of the Society for Research in Child Development, 55* (1-2, Serial No. 221). 667: Figure 16-8 adapted from "Age Segregation in Children's Social Interactions," by S. Ellis, B. Rogoff, & C. C. Cromer, 1981, *Developmental Psychology, 17*, pp. 399–407. Copyright © 1981 by the American Psychological Association. Adapted by permission. 671: Table 16-1 adapted from "Sequences in the Development of Competent Play with Peers: Social and Social Pretend Play," by C. Howes & C. C. Matheson, 1992, *Developmental Psychology, 28*, pp. 961–974. Copyright © 1992 the American Psychological Association. Adapted by permission. 675: Figure 16-9 based on "Parents' Management for Preschoolers' Peer Relations: Is It Related to Children's Social Competence?" by G. W. Ladd & B. S. Golter, 1988, *Developmental Psychology, 24*, pp. 109–117. Copyright © 1988 by the American Psychological Association. 684: Figure 16-10 adapted from "Developmental Changes in Conformity to Peers and Parents," by T. J. Berndt, 1979, *Developmental Psychology, 15*, pp. 608–616. Copyright © 1979 by the American Psychological Association. Adapted by permission.

TO THE OWNER OF THIS BOOK:

We hope that you have found *Developmental Psychology*, 4th Edition, useful. So that this book can be improved in a future edition, would you take the time to complete this sheet and return it? Thank you.

School and address: _____

Department: _____

Instructor's name: _____

1. What I like most about this book is: _____

_____

_____

2. What I like least about this book is: _____

_____

_____

3. My general reaction to this book is: _____

_____

4. The name of the course in which I used this book is: _____

_____

5. Were all of the chapters of the book assigned for you to read? _____

   If not, which ones weren't? _____

 6. In the space below, or on a separate sheet of paper, please write specific suggestions for improving this book and anything else you'd care to share about your experience in using the book.

_____

_____

_____

_____

_____

Optional:

Your name: _____ Date: _____

May Brooks/Cole quote you, either in promotion for *Developmental Psychology,
4th Edition,* or in future publishing ventures?

Yes: _____ No: _____

Sincerely,

David R. Shaffer

- -

FOLD HERE

NO POSTAGE
NECESSARY
IF MAILED
IN THE
UNITED STATES

BUSINESS REPLY MAIL

FIRST CLASS   PERMIT NO. 358   PACIFIC GROVE, CA

POSTAGE WILL BE PAID BY ADDRESSEE

ATT: *David R. Shaffer* _____

**Brooks/Cole Publishing Company
511 Forest Lodge Road
Pacific Grove, California 93950-9968**

- -

FOLD HERE